Heresies of the High Middle Ages

NUMBER LXXXI OF THE
RECORDS OF CIVILIZATION
SOURCES AND STUDIES

Heresies of the
High Middle Ages

SELECTED SOURCES
TRANSLATED AND ANNOTATED

by WALTER L. WAKEFIELD

and AUSTIN P. EVANS

COLUMBIA UNIVERSITY PRESS

NEW YORK AND LONDON 1969

Walter L. Wakefield is Professor of History
at the State University College in Potsdam,
New York. The late Austin P. Evans was
Professor of History at Columbia University.

Preface

This volume is the outcome of a larger project begun by the late Austin P. Evans more than two decades ago. He intended to publish translations of numerous documents which would illustrate the nature of the popular heresies of the Middle Ages, the social context in which they appeared, and the attempts to suppress them. To this end, he worked for a time with the late Professor Anna M. Campbell and, after her retirement, invited me into collaboration. Progress was slow and intermittent because of professional and personal difficulties. At the time of Professor Evans's death in 1962 most of the documents included in the present volume had been selected and were in the process of being translated, but much less had been done with translations which were to illuminate the social background of the heresies and the operations of the Inquisition. It therefore seemed more practical to offer a volume less ambitious than originally planned, yet one which might be of service to those interested in this aspect of medieval history.

No substantial collection of sources for the study of medieval heresies has been brought together in English translation since Samuel R. Maitland in 1832 published his *Facts and Documents Illustrative of the History, Doctrine and Rites of the Ancient Albigenses and Waldenses.* A small collection for the use of students is found in *The Pre-Reformation Period* (Vol. III, No. 6, of *Translations and Reprints*, published by the University of Pennsylvania [1897]); several pieces are included in Ray C. Petry, *A History of Christianity: Readings in the History of the Early and Medieval Church* (Englewood Cliffs, N.J., 1962). Although a few of the documents in the present volume appear in full or in part in those collections or are to be found in translations of the works of their respective authors, it seemed best in most cases to prepare our own translations, for the sake of uniformity in style.

Relying in several instances on texts already prepared by Professor Campbell, Professor Evans and I worked in the closest harmony and cooperation. The result was an English text in which, apart from the pieces which were added after his death, our respective contributions could not be differentiated, though because of his long experience he had assumed the task of general editorial supervision. Had he lived, Professor Evans would have written an Introduction quite different in form and content from the one I have supplied, for he intended to make it an extended essay incorporating translated excerpts from further sources which would reveal the socioeconomic setting of heresy. Although I have altered the basic plan of our work, to remark that in the course of our collaboration I learned a great deal from him about making a book would be only to repeat what contributors to the Records of Civilization have said of him as an editor; beyond that I had always the benefit of his learning and the pleasure of his gentle, never-failing friendship.

A large number of scholars and publishers gave us permission to translate from works which they produced. Acknowledgment is expressed in connection with the translations of these items. Special gratitude is owed to Professor Charles C. Mierow and to Miss Marjorie Chibnall for the use of excerpts from translations which they have published. The late Miss Marion Sherwood carefully read and improved the translation of the Catharist ritual from the Provençal. Miss Joan Ferrante did a skillful rendering of the Provençal text of the two items comprised in Number 60.

Over the years a great many persons patiently answered our questions, gave advice, helped us to obtain materials. Professor Evans would have wished to acknowledge the help of his friend and colleague the late Professor Dino Bigongiari, with whom he discussed many problems, great and small. Professor Yosef Yerushalmi gave me the benefit of his competence in the subject of the Inquisition and the Jews. Professor Martin Grabmann sent us material which was at the time unobtainable in this country. Professor Morton S. Enslin answered questions most kindly, as did the staff of the Italian Information Center, especially Miss Lucia Pallavicini. In the circumstances under which most of this volume was prepared, far from library source collections, the cooperation of many libraries was essential, as was the help of the library staff of the State University College at Potsdam, notably Mrs. Marion Hess.

The extent to which any student of medieval heresy is indebted to the work of great scholars in this field—Father Antoine Dondaine, O.P.; Ilarino da Milano, O.F.M. Cap.; Herbert Grundmann; Arno Borst; and

Mlle Christine Thouzellier, to name only a few—will be obvious from a glance at the notes in this volume. Professors Jeffrey B. Russell and Walter R. Weitzmann read parts of the manuscript; Professor William T. H. Jackson, the general editor of the Records of Civilization, read it all. Their suggestions were invariably most helpful. I was fortunate in that Mrs. Michelle Kamhi of Columbia University Press was the editor of this volume. Her skill and patience saved me from numerous pitfalls. Any flaws which exist are my responsibility alone.

A grant from the New York State University Research Foundation, and financial assistance made available by the late Dr. Frederick W. Crumb of the State University College at Potsdam, helped to defray the costs of materials and the preparation of the typescript, which Mrs. Margaret P. Yolton expertly typed and retyped.

Mrs. Evans and my wife bore with Professor Evans and me constantly, encouraged and helped us, and listened patiently to the tales of tribulations which beset what must have seemed to them—as it did at times to us—a work never to be finished.

W. L.W.

Potsdam, N.Y.
December 1, 1968

Contents

Introduction

A Historical Sketch of the Medieval Popular Heresies

This volume presents translations of documents relating to the popular heresies in Western Europe in the eleventh, twelfth, and thirteenth centuries. Neither this Introduction nor the translations which follow constitute a complete history of medieval heresy or heretical sects. But since some readers perhaps are approaching the subject in detail for the first time, it seems advisable in introductory comment to speak of the general characteristics of the heretical movements and to trace their history briefly, wherever possible calling attention to the thickets of scholarly controversy which lie along the path.[1] Mention must also be made of the nature of the available source materials from which these translations were selected and some of the problems encountered in studying them.

CHARACTERISTICS OF THE POPULAR HERESIES

First, we must examine the meaning of the word "heresy" in the Middle Ages and attempt to define more specifically the term "popular heresies." Medieval Christianity comprised a body of faith drawn from the Scriptures, discussed and defined by the Church Fathers, the popes, and the ecclesiastical councils, and taught by the clergy. The criterion of orthodoxy in the West was the teaching of the Roman see,[2] which the good Christian would accept as a whole, although as late as the eleventh century considerable variations in practice and belief did not raise serious questions about the fundamental unity of the Western Church. But the experience of every Christian generation had corroborated Paul's warning: "There must also be heresies."[3] Disavowal of, or dissent from, the truth preserved by the Church meant damnation; outside the Church there was no salvation, for Paul had also commanded: "A man that is a heretic, after the first and second admonition, avoid"; and "Anathema to those who preach false doctrine."[4] Heresy was treason to God, the worst of offenses against Christian society, a challenge to every duly constituted authority. It was a deadly contamination, making necessary constant vigilance against infection, and the Fathers had agreed that to deal with it was the duty of the whole hierarchy, aided by the secular arm as circumstances required.[5]

Theologically, heresy was defined in the Middle Ages as doctrinal error held stubbornly in defiance of authority. Gratian, for example, quoted the Fathers, especially St. Jerome and St. Augustine, to the effect that heresy was the persistent rejection of part or all of orthodox doctrine after correction had been offered.[6] For Aquinas heresy was the denial of matters of faith which had been defined by the Church.[7] The authors of medieval polemics against heretics did little more than paraphrase the Fathers in defining heresy, repeating the emphasis on individual choice: "The Greek word *hereses* is rendered *secte* in Latin. In them each chooses and pursues what to him seems right."[8] Or, "He is a heretic who, while keeping the outward appearance of Christian religion, devises or follows false opinion, either contemptuously or in contumacy or from a desire for human approval, earthly reward, or worldly pleasures."[9] From such definitions, controversialists, canonists, and theologians could proceed to discuss matters raised by the existence of heresy: description of it and refutation, methods by which heresy could be corrected or suppressed, the permissibility of punishments, and the respective roles of the Church and the secular authority.

The situation, especially in the early years of our period, was such, however, that it was not always easy to determine clearly at a given moment what was or was not heresy. Examining the popular movements that were labeled heretical, particularly those before the middle of the twelfth century, one sees a certain imprecision about them in the minds of contemporaries. Churchmen had read of the heresies of the early Church and sometimes knew more of them than they could readily learn about contemporary sects; an initial reaction to dissent in their own time often was to see the past revived in the present and to attribute to suspect groups of their own day the errors they found discussed in the polemics of the Fathers.[10] Popes issuing warnings or exhortations or answering appeals were usually content to speak in generalities.[11] Bishops reviewing cases under their jurisdiction found it necessary to consult with each other or to seek more learned advice, and even then would be somewhat uncertain about the degree of offense.[12] There were clergy who had neither the knowledge, the ability, nor the will to instruct their communicants soundly enough to permit them to distinguish error from approved doctrine.[13] Hence, there was a looseness in the use of the word "heresy" that did not entirely disappear even when the great scholastics had done their work and when definitions in matters of faith were more readily available.

In common usage, moreover, "heresy" could denote more than erroneous theology,[14] and many tensions in medieval life gave rise to controversies in which charges of heresy were loosely made. The usurpation of ecclesiastical prerogatives by secular powers, or too ambitious an exercise of papal or episcopal authority, made for situations like the investiture controversy, in which the cry of heresy was raised by both sides. A glance at the index of Lea's *History of the Inquisition* under the entry "Heresy" will show the variety of individuals, beliefs, sects, and actions which were condemned as heretical by one authority or another. Men could speak of "heresy" when they meant schism, resistance within the Church to papal administration, political opposition to the hierarchy from secular powers, advocacy of religious toleration, sorcery, or intellectual arrogance; in most cases they could make a show of theological justification for using the term, even if the Church did not always officially accept these enlargements of meaning.

In this study of the popular heresies we may ignore most of the misuses of the term, or uses barely justified. We may also exclude the doctrinal deviations that sprang from learned discussions among intellectuals, arising in and usually confined to the schools and the universities.[15] However important or provocative the speculations of such men as Berengar, Gilbert de la Porrée, or Abelard, the resultant controversy directly affected relatively few persons and the appeal was to the mind, not to the heart.

Lea observed that the really dangerous sectarian movements were those which aroused the emotions.[16] There is more to popular heresies than excited passions, of course, but it is significant that they aroused the fervor of the laity, who became active participants and were moved to give evidence of their spiritual convictions in their daily lives. The reception of heresy may partly be explained by the extent to which the teaching of the dissenters encouraged the expression of religious ideals simply and in daily life, that is, without the assumption of clerical or monastic status. Many men and women who were stirred by the deepening piety of the eleventh century and after must have found inadequate opportunity as laymen within the Church to express their religious aspirations, and were tempted to find spiritual satisfaction outside it. Thus, to a certain extent, the popular heresies give the appearance of religions for the laity,[17] but we must beware of overstatement. The desire for a pure Church and for greater morality in human life also revitalized medieval monasticism, as it had the eleventh-century papacy. Reformist ideas were first explicitly formulated in clerical circles; they then spilled over into lay society, where they were welcomed and extended.[18]

Unquestionably the motivation of the popular heresies was religious,[19] but this did not reduce their importance on the social scene. They were part of the general spiritual revival which may be dimly seen to have begun as early as the eighth century and which reached its height in the twelfth and thirteenth centuries. Their rise paralleled the expressions of vitality in such diverse forms as the crusades, expanding commerce, new social forms in countryside and town, movement toward the new horizons glimpsed on earth or in men's minds. It would be better to say that all of these phenomena were interwoven. Investigation of the social and economic context in which the heresies appeared has not produced satisfactory explanations of their origins in material terms alone,[20] yet religion had everywhere an impact on daily life, and similarly the social base influenced the expression of religious aspirations. Certain religious ideas, for example, were especially attractive to groups affected by the partial transformation of a feudal-agrarian society to an urban-commercial one. The Church was responding to the needs of this changing society with new institutions: expansion of its pastoral and educational services, new monastic orders, and refinements of dogma, all of which reflected its perception of spiritual needs. Yet these did not satisfy all men, and patterns of belief and behavior more radical than those sponsored by the Church appeared. Some of them were clearly intended to be religious reforms, entirely Christian in character, looking backward, or forward, to what was deemed to be a purer Church; beside these, however, appeared other movements which seemed to orthodox eyes to abandon the fundamental bases of Christian society.

When we speak of the popular heresies, which challenged the authority and sometimes, it seemed, the existence of the Roman Church, we must be content with a definition in general terms: The reference should be to religious doctrines which influenced numbers of people in all ranks of society to act in patterns outside contemporary orthodox Christian observance and to reject interpretation of doctrine by any authority but their own. The popular heresies were widely varied in their expression. At the beginning of our period they appeared in isolated communities; in the twelfth century, magnetic leaders aroused the enthusiasm of crowds by their preaching, while others worked quietly at organizing and formulating ideologies. Thus sects formed.[21] Their members might share certain viewpoints with other groups, without diminishing the bitter disagreement about other propositions over which they quarreled as bitterly with each other as they did with the Roman Church. Some common characteristics were advocacy of a return to the apostolic practice of preaching and poverty, and the intent to free the Christian people and Church from enslavement to worldly ambition and wealth. There was protest against concentration of authority in the hierarchy, against any disciplinary power in matters of faith, against abuse of the sacraments. The sacramental system itself was challenged. All sects thought of themselves as the true Christians and they usually emphasized chastity, preaching, and communal life; required moral purity as a qualification for one who administered the sacraments; and deemphasized the role of any intermediary between God and man. Even the Cathars, the most extreme of all sects in opposition to the Roman Church, and by it regarded as the greatest enemy in the twelfth and thirteenth centuries, insisted that only they were true followers of Christ and successors to the apostles; and it is probable that they won their first following in the West by their demonstration of piety and rigorous morality, which appealed so strongly to religious sentiments of the era, rather than because of their dualistic theology.

No one can say how many people were involved in the medieval popular heresies. There were few areas of Europe in which heresy was not reported during the Middle Ages. The Rhineland, the Low Countries, the valleys of the Seine and the Marne, the Midi of France, and northern Italy are the areas most frequently mentioned as affected in the eleventh and twelfth centuries. After about A.D. 1150 the influence of heretics as against that of the Catholic clergy grew to be predominant in parts of Languedoc and in some cities of northern Italy. Contemporary estimates of their numbers are vague.[22] Relatively few malcontents or nonconformists can sometimes provoke a great stir among men who take issues as seriously as religion was regarded in that period, yet the situation did seem grave enough early in the thirteenth century to persuade popes to call for a crusade against heretics and to create a new legal tribunal to pursue them vigorously.

Nearly every discussion of the medieval sects attempts some schematic classification of them. Nineteenth-century historians were apt to see two major movements. One was the heresy of the Cathars, which was presumably a continuation of the long history of religious dualism and a successor of the ancient Manichaean heresy. It was based on the concept of a fundamental conflict between principles or gods of good and evil, and between spirit and matter, their respective domains—a premise which led to the complete rejection of the Roman Church as a creature and servant of the devil, the prince of this world. The other movement was thought to comprise those heresies whose participants believed that the existing Church had lost its authority because it had fallen away from Christian ideals, or was unnecessary, or had been displaced by the revelation of a new order.[23] In the broadest sense, this twofold classification—dualists with ancient Eastern antecedents, and reformers arising within the Western Church—has some validity, but it is oversimplified. Not only are the Eastern origins of the Cathars disputed, but this group shared the puritanical views of most of the reforming sects, and some of their practices. Thus, more elaborate classifications have been suggested in which, in addition to the "Neo-Manichaean" or "Neo-Gnostic" heresy, distinctions are made between sects which were evangelistic and emphasized asceticism or poverty; those which were excessively penitential in their practice; those which were in rebellion against some aspect of the hierarchy, discipline, or services of the Church; and those which had Judaistic aspects.[24]

THE PROBLEM OF ORIGINS

To explain the emergence of heresy as an important element in European society in the eleventh and twelfth centuries, historians have suggested a variety of reasons, most of which would have astonished or amused men of that day, who had no doubt at all that heresy was a product of the devil's wiles, a recurrence of the ancient wickedness which had vexed the early Church. Something of that attitude has persisted into more recent times in the minds of those who see the origin of heresy in human pride, fallibility, and ignorance,[25] but other theories may be more fully documented. Many historians have concluded that heresy arose as a protest against defects in the medieval Church and against corruption among its clergy.[26] Others have thought it to be a protest against material conditions of life; some have worked it into theories of class struggle.[27] Heresy has been explained as part of the general intellectual revival of the Middle Ages[28] and in half a dozen other ways.

The major tendency in recent studies has been to see the popular heresies as an integral part of the development of medieval Christian life and to explain their appearance as a result of the increased and deepened piety which lies behind so many other events of the time. The revolutionary reform program sponsored by the papacy in the eleventh century, the vigor and energy of the crusades, the rush to new monastic orders, the enthusiasm for church-building, the cult of relics, and the flowering of religious art and architecture flowed from this pious ebullience. Piety produced heretics as well as saints. Closer aquaintance with the Gospels stimulated in receptive minds a desire for morality and behavior closer to that of apostolic times. Acceptance of the monastic ideals of asceticism, personal poverty, and chastity as the highest Christian code led to criticism of prevailing ecclesiastical standards. In the Hildebrandine reform program, simony and clerical marriage and incontinence were excoriated by the supreme Christian authority. Small wonder, then, when the incapacity of many of the clergy to give spiritual guidance either by teaching or example was apparent and when to sensitive consciences they seemed unfit to mediate between God and man, that anticlericalism, criticism of the functioning of the clergy, should appear. This sometimes developed into antisacerdotalism, something more serious, which denies the powers of the clergy and encourages the repudiation of other institutions of the Church.

The majority of historians today would no doubt agree that the increased piety and spirit of reform operating entirely within the Church had a great deal in common with the piety and moral fervor which led men out of the Church and into heresy.[29] That attitude would not have entered the minds of most orthodox men of the Middle Ages. Heretics, to them, were dangerously different, and the terms applied to them emphasized their personal wickedness. Heresiarchs and their followers, common report said, were antichrists, magicians, loathsome creatures; gossip and rumor put at their door all kinds of nasty practices, such as child murder, indiscriminate sexuality, even worship of the devil.

That last charge, no doubt encouraged by folk tales and spread by the scurrilous talk that often surrounds nonconformists, was promoted by misinterpretation of the doctrines of the Cathars. Other revivalist and reforming sects, for all their opposition to the Church and clergy, accepted the fundamental Christian dogmas: God as Creator of all, Christ as his Son become truly man; the Trinity; the doctrine of the last days. Not so the Cathars. Once they could be clearly seen, in the later twelfth century (their origins are still in dispute), they appeared to deny orthodox doctrines completely. They divorced God the Father from this world, which belonged to the god of evil, author of all that is visible. Human souls they held to be angels, imprisoned after falling from their celestial estate through sin. The Trinity was denied; Christ was an emissary from, but not the Son of, God; only in appearance, not in actuality, did he become man. The Roman Church was not holy but the devil's instrument. Salvation could come only to "good Christians" by the baptism Christ taught to the apostles, a baptism in the Spirit, not in water.

It is this dualistic creed which raises the disputed question of Catharist origins. To explain the rise of reforming sects no one seeks reasons outside the conditions of their time in Western Europe. Attempts to give the Waldenses an apostolic foundation, for example, have been abandoned,[30] and the Donatist element in many medieval sects is not traced back to the great heresy of the fourth century.[31] But the dualists' explanation for the origin of good and evil and for the conflict between spirit and matter is older than Christianity; it existed side by side with the orthodox Church for centuries and influenced Christian theologians even as they fought it. After the sixth century, there were few traces of dualism in Western Europe until it reappeared, perhaps in the eleventh century, certainly in the twelfth. Sects which held dualistic tenets, however, had been found repeatedly during the Christian era in Asia Minor, Greece, and the Balkans; one of them, the heresy of the Bogomils, was spreading vigorously in the eleventh century. Does this mean that dualism, which in the Cathars constituted the basis for the most feared of medieval heresies, did not spring from native roots but was an importation from the East?

Contemporary observers had no hesitation in identifying medieval dualistic sects with ancient heresy. Today there are historians who argue that those sects were indeed created by missionaries from the Balkans and thus were inheritors of the ancient tradition; but other scholars disagree and explain dualistic tendencies in Western heresy, at least in the eleventh and early twelfth centuries, as a product of contemporary Western conditions. No one on either side of the argument insists on one explanation to the complete exclusion of the other. Those who argue for the ancient lineage admit that the revival of piety in the West created conditions which made the acceptance of dualism easier; those who see dualism as intrinsic in Western religious development allow for some modifying influences from Eastern sects. But the differences of opinion about where the emphases should fall are sharp. Thus, a brief review of the chief expressions of religious dualism in the Christian era may provide a basis for assessing these historical theories, and will serve to introduce the names of the older heresies so often encountered in medieval sources. What occupies the next few pages is the merest sketch of the dualist sects that are often brought into the discussions of the origins of the Cathars.

The Dualist Tradition

In its most explicit form, religious dualism gives an answer to the question: "If God is good, whence comes evil?"[32] Surely, whatever is eternal and spiritual in the universe and in man is the work of a divine creator. But can evil—that which is temporal and material—derive from the same source? Fully developed, dualism replies that there must be two creative forces operating in two irreconcilably opposed realms of existence. Man then is seen as one of the battlegrounds where the forces of good and evil clash.

Elements of dualism are present in some degree in most of the "religions of salvation" originating in the millennium preceding Christ. To single out only some of its manifestations: It appears in the teachings of Zoroaster (d. *ca.* 531 B.C.) in Persia; it found a place in Greek religion, especially in the Orphic sects, and was reinforced by the philosophical dualism of Pythagoras and Plato; and in the Hellenistic world when Christianity emerged, dualistic ideas developed from Greek and oriental sources had already begun to influence Judaism.[33]

Within Christianity there were elements which might encourage a kind of dualistic attitude. The teachings of Jesus, especially as interpreted by Paul, speak of God's grace affecting a world which is not by nature evil but above which we may be lifted up; by love we may transcend the world. There is a kingdom of God and a kingdom of this world; there is the love of God and there is affection for things of this earth. Paul spoke also of the law in contrast to grace, of bondage to Satan and freedom of the spirit. This world is not evil by nature, but man may renounce it for higher things, put away the false and know the true, enter the kingdom of God. As Christianity developed, the tendency to emphasize the contrast of spirit and matter may have been stimulated by preoccupation with the "forces of darkness" that besiege the soul and by the desire to emphasize spirituality through mortification of the flesh. Moreover, the influence of Neo-Platonism, the last of the great schools of Greek philosophy, reinforced that contrast. For the Neo-Platonist, God was a transcendent, indefinable One, apart from the world. From the One a hierarchy of emanations flow down to the individual soul, which longs to return to union with the divine. In the thought of Plotinus (d. A.D. 270), matter is more illusory than it is evil, but it confines the soul, and the powers of darkness work to thwart the soul's escape from the flesh and the world. Through Augustine and other Christian thinkers Neo-Platonism profoundly influenced Christian philosophy over succeeding centuries and its influence may have paved the way for more radical dualistic concepts. To note this should not obscure the fact that the main body of Christian orthodox thought rejected any dualism which would deny God as creator of all or negate the humanity of Jesus.[34]

But there were, in the early centuries of Christianity, groups which called themselves Christian, most of them sharing philosophical-religious theories known as Gnosticism, in which open and explicit dualism was very much in evidence. Gnosticism seems to have derived from many sources—Persian, Jewish, Greek, and Egyptian—and was exhibited in an extraordinary variety of sects. What these sects had in common was to take away from God the responsibility for a wicked world where the souls of men are temporarily incarcerated in human bodies, from which they are promised release and salvation through *gnosis*, secret knowledge.[35] Gnostics accepted Christ as the bearer of knowledge and interpreted him in their own terms, formulating a "Christian dualism" which early churchmen, after some hesitation, renounced and strenuously fought. For most Gnostics, God was the First Principle, beneath whom many lesser, semidivine, eternal beings (eons) were arrayed in a perfect spiritual creation (the pleroma). Among the eons, about whose nature Gnostic sects disagreed, transgression of some kind led to a fall from perfection, which in turn gave rise to a subordinate creator (the Demiurge). He it was who formed the world, which like its maker is imperfect and antagonistic to the supreme, remote, and perfect Divine Being. But somehow elements of divinity were encased in the material world as souls of men. It became God's purpose to release them from the worldly prison by revealed knowledge of himself. Jesus, who was variously interpreted as an eon, as part of God, or as an emanation from him, brought the revelation to man, but in his mission he never assumed a human body or shared characteristics of this world except in appearance. Gnostics generally envisaged mankind as sharing the divine element in unequal amounts and thus as being divided into classes. Those who were called Perfect or Elect were considered relatively near to redemption through possession of wisdom. Among the remainder of mankind, those who became "believers" might eventually achieve salvation; for others there was no hope of eternal life because they entirely lacked the divine knowledge.

Many Gnostic teachers who claimed *gnosis* directly from God or by secret tradition from the apostles had no more than a temporary influence; some, however, did create communities or sects which perpetuated their doctrines on the fringes of Christianity or completely outside it. Of the great variety of Gnostic groups, two may be chosen to illustrate the relationships between them and Christianity.

In the middle of the second century, in Asia Minor and at Rome, Marcion taught that the universe was composed of a visible world, created by the Demiurge, the Jehovah of the Old Testament, in opposition to the world of the true God. Jesus was a manifestation of the Father, who came to teach a gospel of love and mercy standing in irreconcilable opposition to the stern justice of the Old Testament. For his scriptures Marcion used only ten epistles of Paul and part of the Gospel of Luke, edited to remove traces of Judaism. He accepted the distinction between the Elect, the believers, and those who were without hope of redemption. Initiates in his communities had to practice the sternest asceticism, but believers could postpone baptism and withdrawal from the world until the moment of death.[36] Marcion's doctrines were thought to be a serious danger in the second century, and their memory lingered for a long time.[37] But the archetype of dualist heresy in Christian eyes soon came to be another offshoot of Gnosticism, which also incorporated Zoroastrian, Buddhist, and Christian ideas. This was Manichaeism.

Mani (d. *ca.* 276), teaching in the Sassanid kingdom of Persia, founded a church organization which spread rapidly in the next three centuries. He postulated two realms of being, Light and Darkness, each under its own lord. The visible world was called into existence in the course of a vast struggle in which Evil attacked Good and was with difficulty repulsed, but not before the Lord of Darkness had seized particles of Light and imprisoned them in the bodies of Adam and Eve, whom he created. Jesus was one of the divine Messengers sent to Adam and his descendants with God's message of redemption for the Light imprisoned in them. He devised a process by which Light was distilled from souls by the influence of the moon and the sun and was drawn back to its own kingdom. This would continue until all of it had been restored and the two realms were again entirely separate. Like Marcion, Mani divided his followers into the Elect, filled with Light, who lived in strict poverty and celibacy, wandering and preaching, and hearers, or laity, bound by somewhat less rigid rules requiring fasting and confession and forbidding any kind of killing, fraud, or lies. By metempsychosis a hearer could hope for future rebirth as an Elect.[38]

Manichaeism spread rapidly and widely throughout Asia and the Roman Empire, flourishing in the Empire until the sixth century, and leaving traces in the East until the tenth century, despite condemnation and persecution by Christians, Persians, and Moslems. The horror and alarm it aroused among orthodox Christians was so great, the publicity given to it by the powerful refutations of St. Augustine (who in his youth had been a Manichaean) was so widespread, that afterward whenever a churchman was confronted by heresy the epithet likely to spring to his lips first was "Manichaean."[39]

Dualism did not disappear with the waning of active Marcionite and Manichaean communities, but we will pass over the numerous minor groups within and outside the Gnostic movement in the second and third centuries and will comment only briefly on the major sects which revived or continued dualist concepts.

In the fourth century the Messalians, who inhabited regions around Edessa and in Armenia, expressed essentially Gnostic ideas in a form which emphasized evangelical practices. For them, Satan was a son of the First Principle. He rebelled in pride and after his fall created the material world in which men are confined. Release comes when, through constant prayer, the believer replaces the demonic spirit in his body with the Holy Spirit.[40] At the other extreme of the Roman Empire, in Spain, also in the fourth century, Priscillian (d. 385) combined the ideals of monastic asceticism with astrological lore and certain dualistic ideas which are not clearly known but which may owe something to Gnostic influence. Priscillian was put to death as a magician by the Roman emperor. His doctrines were not formally condemned by the Church until the sixth century, after which they seem to have left little trace except in books.[41]

The Paulicians[42] of the seventh century (there are other lesser dualist groups, chiefly in Asia Minor,[43] which we do not mention) might detain us longer if our knowledge of their doctrines were not so cloudy and disputed. The sect apparently originated in Armenia in the sixth century and spread into the eastern Byzantine Empire in about A.D. 640. Its followers formed a group of warriors in the borderland between the Byzantine Empire and the Arabs, harassing the Empire and in turn attacked by it, until they were repressed and scattered late in the ninth century. Thereafter, some of them were transferred to the Balkans, where their existence as a sect of some notoriety and influence was reported as late as the twelfth century. In Armenia they lingered even longer. Western crusaders probably picked up the name "Paulician" as the equivalent of "heretic" from Byzantine usage, and their version of the word, "Publican," became a common epithet for heretics in the twelfth century in the West.[44]

The history of the Paulicians is clearer than their doctrines, which "must remain largely a matter of conjecture."[45] Among various, sometimes conflicting, reports are these: that they believed in two independent principles or deities, that they considered Christ to be a man adopted by God and filled with the Holy Spirit, and that they rejected the Old and some of the New Testament, repudiated Christian sacraments, and practiced a vigorous iconoclasm. There are, in fact, two major groups of sources, Greek and Armenian, which present rather different views of the Paulicians. The Greek writers represent them as dualists, teaching a docetic interpretation of Christ (that his body was celestial substance); the Armenian sources depict them as adoptionists, who accepted the unity of God, attributed all creation to him, and denied the divinity of Christ. Both groups of sources emphasize the iconoclasm of the sect.[46]

The greatest of the Balkan heresies and the one which was to have the most influence on the heresies of medieval Europe was that of the Bogomils, which made its appearance in Bulgaria in the tenth century.[47] South Slavs, who moved into Bulgaria in the sixth century as tillers of the soil, had been followed by Bulgar conquerors; this created a society of peasants and aristocrats in which Slavonic language and culture prevailed, while a once-free peasantry was subjected to a regime of oppression. The Bulgar aristocracy, Slavicized by the tenth century, also copied Byzantine manners. Bulgaria became a land of uneasy internal stresses and was frequently at war with the Byzantine Empire. In the second half of the tenth century, Kievan Russia was drawn into these conflicts, and half of Bulgaria was conquered by the Empire.[48]

In matters of religion there were also many complexities in Bulgaria. The original paganism of the Slav peasantry had been diluted by Roman and Eastern Orthodox missionaries. Although the Bulgarian ruler became a convert to the Orthodox Church in 864 or 865, his brief flirtation with the Roman papacy thereafter added to controversies surviving from earlier missionary competition. As the official Bulgarian church fell deeper into the Byzantine pattern of Christianity, its hold on the peasantry weakened, while the reluctance of Byzantine patriarchs to allow Bulgarian religious autonomy promoted a kind of religious nationalism in return.[49] This and the worsening conditions of life no doubt abetted the proliferation of monasteries in the mid-tenth century. Moreover, there were Jews, Syrians, and Armenians in Bulgaria as a result of colonization by the Byzantine emperors, and among the Armenians were Paulician heretics. The Messalian sect was also reported to exist, together with the Manichaeans,[50] although the latter term was not much more than a generic name for heretics by that time.[51] In short, Bulgaria in the tenth century seems to have displayed every influence which has been alleged as a direct or contributory cause of heresy.

It was in the second quarter of the tenth century that a priest named Bogomil, meaning "beloved of God," or "worthy of God's pity," or "one who entreats God,"[52] began to preach in Macedonia.[53] In reaction against turmoil, misery, and oppression, Bogomil taught a life of penitence, prayer, wandering, and simple worship, in order to escape a world which was evil by nature. His message is known only from the words of indignant opponents, especially a priest named Cosmas (fl. *ca.* 972);[54] but there is no doubt that Bogomil attributed the wickedness of the visible world to its creator, the devil, who was the rebellious elder son of God. Bogomil's dualism, then, was not "absolute"—that is, it did not stem from a concept of two independent principles and creations— but was "moderate," or "mitigated," in that the evil creator was regarded as inferior to God.

In Bogomil belief, the lord of this world was the author of the Old Testament and the Mosaic Law. God sent his younger son, Christ,[55] on a divine mission to redeem the souls of men, but except in appearance he never became man, and he worked no real miracles. The Virgin Mary deserves no reverence as his mother. Only the New Testament, espe- cially the Gospels, could be credited as the word of God. The sacraments were rejected, as was all the customary ritual of the Church: feast days, icons, veneration of the Cross or of the saints, the liturgy, ecclesiastical vestments. The only Bogomil prayer was the Lord's Prayer, frequently repeated. Their ethical teaching demanded a renunciation of the world to avoid contamination from evil. Meat and wine were forbidden, and marriage was discouraged to avoid propagation of the devil's work. The existing hierarchy of the Church had no authority over them, and even obedience to civil rulers was disparaged. The Bogomils were beginning to divide themselves into two classes—the Perfect, who lived according to the strictest asceticism, and the believers, who were not bound to this rigorous discipline—but it is not assured that in the early years they regarded themselves as a separate church.[56]

Some of Bogomil's teaching (the doctrine of the two sons of God, the use only of the Lord's Prayer, and theories about how the soul was introduced into Adam's body) seems to have been original, while other elements in it might have been adopted from the Messalians or Pauli- cians;[57] the question is debatable. The ethical content of Bogomilism conceivably could have arisen spontaneously from concentration on the New Testament and from the fervent desire to achieve apostolic purity and simplicity.[58]

Catastrophic wars in the last quarter of the tenth century, and the final conquest of Bulgaria by the Empire in 1018, no doubt gave impetus to the Bogomil instinct to withdraw from the world, but at the same time the Byzantine victory facilitated the spread of the heresy to other parts of the Empire, especially to Constantinople. Under the influence of Byzantine theological speculation, Bogomilism was transformed from an ethical teaching, tinged with dualism, and appealing especially to the peasantry, into a doctrinal and speculative philosophy with a coherent system, one which was readily acceptable to the upper classes in Constantinople. The growth of Bogomilism there caused alarm and resulted in vigorous persecution about 1110 and again after 1143, which weakened the sect in the city but spread it into Asia Minor and westward and northward into Dalmatia and Bosnia.[59] During these years, the Bogomils developed religious communities or "churches" with a well-developed ritual. There was now a clear distinction between the Perfect and the believers. The former achieved their status by baptism of the Holy Spirit, effected when those who were already baptized placed their hands on the believer while the Gospel of John was held over his head, thus making him a member of the true Church.[60] To buttress and illustrate their original doctrines the Bogomils also made wide use of apocryphal literature.[61]

Of equal importance was schism within the sect. At some point, probably in the eleventh century, and perhaps as a result of Byzantine theological speculation, the moderate, or mitigated, dualism of the early Bogomils, teaching one God, Father and Creator of all, but allotting to the devil as a fallen being a subordinate role as maker of what was visible and evil, was challenged by an absolute or radical dualism, in which the principles of good and evil were held to be coequal, coeternal, each a creator omnipotent within his own realm. Scholars do not agree whether this absolute dualism developed within Bogomilism or was adopted from earlier sects. It has, indeed, been suggested that moderate dualism is a Christian heresy but that absolute dualism is another religion entirely. Yet both schools of thought adopted the same manner of life and a similar organization of their sects. Those who gave the evil principle equal status with the good formed the Church or "order" of Dragovitsa—the name apparently comes from a region in Thrace— while the Bogomils who still held to moderate dualism called themselves the Church of Bulgaria.[62] Both groups sent out offshoots into Serbia, Bosnia, and Dalmatia, and ultimately sent missionaries to Western Europe.[63]

Such missionary activity continued, and in the second Bulgarian empire, after 1218, the Bogomils prospered. In Bosnia, where they were commonly called Patarines, Bogomilism became a state religion, with doctrines comparable to the moderate dualism of the Bulgarian order. In the fourteenth century some decline in its vitality under the attacks of Roman Catholic missionaries was already evident. Then in Bosnia, as earlier in Bulgaria, conquest by the Turks brought about the end of Bogomilism as a major cult.[64]

The chief reason for reviewing the earlier dualist sects, as has been said, is that many historians argue or assume that ancient dualism passed successively from Manichaean and Gnostic origins through other groups over the centuries to become eventually the Catharism of the Middle Ages; hence the use of the term "Neo-Manichaean" for the medieval sect.[65] A recent statement by Steven Runciman argues for a "tradition" of dualism stemming from the Gnostics and the Manichaeans in two streams, one through the Paulicians, another through the Messalians, which join again in the Bogomils of the Balkans and thus continue to the Patarines of Bosnia and the Cathars of Europe. Other historians differ in their interpretation of how dualism was transmitted, so that among those who insist on deriving Cathar doctrines from the doctrines of earlier sects there is no consensus in identifying the line of descent. The basic reason for insisting that connections do exist is the similarity of later sects to earlier ones, despite an intervening span of many years.[66] Yet rather important differences are discernible between the Manichaeans and other Gnostics, between Gnostics and Messalians, Paulicians, and Bogomils. A more serious difficulty is that for none of the sects that have been discussed is an uninterrupted line of succession demonstrable from concrete historical evidence. These sects apparently did not form a continuous chain over a thousand years. Similar characteristics may suggest, but cannot prove, direct historical relationships when there are gaps of one or more centuries between the sects which are compared. In books and in the memories of men who hated and feared it, a heresy might have a longer life than its real existence, thereby creating misleading testimony about its survival.

Dmitri Obolensky admits that the way in which Manichaean doctrines were transmitted in the Near East between the third and seventh centuries cannot be precisely determined, although he insists on the probability that they were passed down until they "found a new and powerful expression in Paulicianism."[67] Yet Nina Garsoian categorically denies that the available evidence permits a conclusion that the Paulicians

were exponents of Manichaean ideas.[68] Hans Söderberg thinks it unlikely that there was contact between Messalians and Bogomils and
argues for a Gnostic tradition outside of the sects usually named.[69] Even
the nature of the relationship between Paulicians and Bogomils in the
Balkans is not explained with precision. Other difficulties are raised by
historians who can see little essential similarity between ancient Manichaeism and medieval Catharism.[70] The theory that after the sixth
century the embers of Manichaeism smoldered in Africa and the western
Mediterranean lands until they were fanned into flame again in the
twelfth century is also afflicted by lack of historical evidence,[71] as is the
explanation that Priscillianism survived to inspire Catharism.[72] With the
present state of the evidence, then, many hypotheses are possible, but
none is entirely satisfactory.

For the proposition that the Bogomils of Bulgaria and Constantinople
were closely connected with the Cathars of Western Europe, the evidence is more convincing, although details are in dispute. In a thoughtful
review, Henri Puech[73] canvassed the various theories of Bogomil-
Paulician-Cathar relationships, showing their diversities.[74] What Puech
regards as demonstrable beyond doubt is that the Bogomils did have a
decisive influence on the Cathars, for although some of the latter's traits
could have come from non-Bogomil sources or have been independently
developed, there are others (selective acceptance of books of the Bible
and apocryphal works; explanation of the devil's role; customs of
fasting, prayer, and baptism) which are too close to Bogomilism to be
thought coincidental.[75] But when did Bogomilism make its impact on
the West? Whether it came before the middle of the twelfth century
—Puech thinks not[76]—is a question which will be examined presently
in these pages.

Is it not possible that the kind of dualism which is inherent in
Christian thought could have been re-emphasized in Western Europe in
the Middle Ages, quite independently of outside influences? None of the
historians who have asserted the transmission of a dualist tradition over
the centuries has ignored the consideration that under different circumstances, expressions of dualism will differ and the sects embodying them
will have their own individuality. Emile G. Leonard, whom Puech
quotes, has some pertinent observations. Some solutions of religious
problems, he remarks, may be spontaneously reinvented at different
times. The innovators may then assume a place in a movement of which

they were not originally a part, thus acquiring a fictitious genealogy; Leonard believes that in this way Western heretics acquired Manichaean doctrines at the hands of a Bogomil missionary in the twelfth century.[77] Arno Borst made a related point, that dualism "is not the product of a historic tradition but of a rebellion against the world." It appears, he wrote, when there is a conflict of spiritual or political forces which shakes minds out of their equanimity. "The nature of dualism changes according to the circumstances of time and place," and sects arise from various causes. Only after the religious experiences develop into dogma does the tradition become important.[78] Borst applies this judgment to the Bogomil-Cathar relationship, finding that the later sect had close affinities with the earlier, from which it took its belief in dualism. "But Bogomils and Cathars are not identical. . . . Dogmas, scriptures, missionaries may have come from the East, but from the beginning of our millennium heresy in the West follows its own laws."[79]

In a recent work Jeffrey Russell argues that Western conditions alone, after the eighth century, explain the origins of Western heresy.[80] Norman Cantor, in a general survey of medieval religious experience, suggests that it was quite possible for a dualist theology to develop out of Neo-Platonist philosophy and that Catharism may be the result of a combination of antisacerdotalism with Neo-Platonism.[81]

Thus, it is possible to conceive of an independently developed kind of dualism, native to the West, inherent in the antithesis between spirit and matter, God and mammon, which the Christian tradition has always sheltered, and which appeals to minds sensitive to the discrepancy between what is and what ought to be. In the view of this writer, in fact, whatever dualism existed in the medieval heresies before the twelfth century was of just such an indigenous nature, and although foreign influences—like those from the Bogomils—might have made a limited impression by suggesting ideas or practices, neither were they the basic cause of heretical dissent nor, in the eleventh century, did they fundamentally affect its expression. Then, in the efflorescence of piety in the twelfth century, ideas carried westward from the Balkans by missionaries, merchants, or crusaders returning home gave definition and formal structure to some of the already existing dissenting groups and produced the Catharist heresy, strongly influenced but not created by the importations from the East.

THE RISE OF MEDIEVAL SECTS

Early Appearances of Heresy in the West

Religious disaffection and charges of heresy were by no means un-known in medieval Europe before the eleventh century, especially after St. Boniface began his apostolate. It is probable that some of the influences which would produce the great heresies of the High Middle Ages were already at work.[82] But it is only for the late tenth century and more clearly for the eleventh that the sources offer enough detail to be of profit in a volume of translations. At that time there appeared at widely scattered places in Western Europe groups of persons who put themselves in opposition to some of the dogmas or practices of the Church and devoted themselves to a way of life which religious or secular authority found damnable. Heresy was detected at Ravenna about A.D. 970, in the diocese of Châlons-sur-Marne in France about the year 1000, thereafter in Aquitaine, then among the scholars at Orléans in 1022, among workers or peasants in Arras about 1025, again in Italy, at Monforte near Milan, about 1028. About two decades later heretics were found again in Châlons and in Goslar, Germany. There were also imprecise statements about their appearance in Italy at large, in Spain, and in the domains of the French king.[83]

Whether there were links among the groups of dissenters is a moot question. There were reports of persons who carried heresy northward from Italy as far as Arras, or from one place to another in France. Merchants and pilgrims as well as missionaries are supposed to have been the agents who disseminated the doctrines. About the social status of those who were involved in the various sects generalizations are hazardous. In one place or another all levels of society were rep-resented.[84]

What gave rise to the charges of heresy against these persons were varying combinations of ascetic practices, anticlerical attitudes, and rejection of the services and authority of the clergy.[85] Most frequent are reports that the sectaries rejected the institution of marriage and put an undue stress on virginity and chastity, and that they abstained from certain foods, especially meat. Refusal to venerate the Cross is several times mentioned. The traditional form of baptism was abandoned by some, in favor of a ceremony of imposition of hands; and sometimes the other sacraments were spurned. The authority of the Old Testament was disputed. The heretics were variously charged with denying the Trinity, refusing veneration of saints, rejecting all the hierarchy, institutions, and liturgy of the Church, denying the need for church buildings, and refusing to pay tithes.

The sense of alarm among clergy and princes was shared by lesser folk and was no doubt sharpened for all by the stories which rumor supplied of secret assemblies, demon-worship, magic, and lewd behavior. Reaction by the authorities varied. Their tendency to speak of "Manichaeans" or "Arians" is probably best explained by the notoriety of those ancient sects.[86] The bishops took the lead in attempting to discover the character of the offenders. When the counsel and correction offered to the accused was rejected, the clergy left the disposition of the recalcitrants to the secular arm.[87] Indeed, kings on occasion took the lead in the prosecution. Men like Bishop Wazo of Liège and his biographer, both of whom spoke out for toleration, were rare.

On the surface, the records of the eleventh century reveal a desire to practice a simple Christianity, stripped of some of its traditional institutions and sacramental practices, basing itself on the Gospels, and emphasizing puritanical standards for personal behavior. Behind it may lie the dualism which contrasts spiritual needs with desires of the flesh, Gospel ideals with actual practice. But is that all? Does not the influence of Bogomilism on the origins of eleventh century dissent also appear? The question has been debated by Father Antoine Dondaine, O.P., one of the foremost historians of medieval heresy, and Professor Raffaello Morghen, historian of medieval Christianity. In his *Medioevo cristiano*, published in 1951,[88] the latter restated conclusions expressed some years before: that the heretical movements of the early eleventh century were primarily moral in character, growing out of the nascent religious sentiments which would also support the great movement of reform within the Church. The sources of heretical ideas, he insisted, were to be found in aspirations to a pure and simple faith, inspired by the Scriptures among humble elements of society. There could be no question of Manichaean origins, for there was no evidence of the transmission of Mani's teaching over the centuries; Manichaean dualism had been cosmological and metaphysical; the dualism of the eleventh century was anthropological and ethical. The heretics were not theologians, but simple people condemning a worldly priesthood out of zeal for a purer evangelistic Christian life.

Morghen's thesis was challenged by Dondaine, whose own views had altered over the years since 1939, when he had doubted the supposed filiation from Manichaeism, questioning the amount of Manichaean teaching found among the Cathars, and suggesting that Gnostic influences might have been more important.[89] In 1950, he was more certain that Catharism came from the Balkans but was not willing to admit that it existed in Western Europe in the eleventh century, only that there may have been some Bogomil penetration.[90] In 1952, however, in an article criticizing Morghen's *Medioevo cristiano*, Dondaine categorically asserted that Bogomil missionary activity was responsible for the earliest appearances of heresy in the West.[91] He maintained that comparison of the eleventh-century Western heresies with Bogomil doctrine described in the treatise of Cosmas[92] showed such close similarities as to prove that the apparently isolated heresies of the eleventh century were linked together by a common origin in Bogomilism. Catharism did adapt itself to Western conditions thereafter, Dondaine wrote, but the contemporaries who called the eleventh-century heretics "Manichaeans" were right. The Cathars were the heirs of the Bogomils, who were the heirs of the Manichaeans.

After some replies from Professor Morghen, reaffirming and expanding his point of view, had been published,[93] Henri Puech intervened in the dialogue in 1956, with the discussion of Bogomil-Cathar relationships to which we have already referred.[94] He could not accept Dondaine's proofs of Bogomil impact in the eleventh century and he agreed with Morghen that ascetic and spiritual impulses account for the kind of dualism then displayed. But, Puech concluded, Bogomilism did eventually have a real effect on Western dualism, so much so that Catharism can be said to have existed only after Bogomil influence had given organization and theology to unorthodox ideas already in existence. That occurred about the middle of the twelfth century.[95] Probably the last word has not been said in this amiable scholarly discussion, but until further documentary evidence can be produced from Balkan or European research, continued dispute would not be very profitable. At the moment, however, it seems difficult to find fault with Puech's conclusions.

Whatever the inspiration of the heretics in the earlier years of the eleventh century, it apparently ceased to produce marked results, for evidence of popular heresy disappears from the sources for the next fifty years. The epithet "heretic" was hurled back and forth in the scholars' controversy over the theories of Berengar of Tours on the Eucharist, and was used by both sides in the great struggle over the papal program of reform in the days of Gregory VII, but there were no reports of the kind of heresies noticed earlier. However, two incidents which show the tendency to see heresy in reforming movements may be mentioned. In an attempt to reform the Church in Milan, the papacy found allies in a group of citizens who rebelled against the feudal-hierarchical domination of the archbishop. Their primary program was to require clerical celibacy and to put an end to simony.[96] Landulf the Elder, the chronicler of these events in Milan, attempted to link the followers of the Pataria (the reform party) with the heretics of Monforte, but, in view of the support given to the former by the pope, the accusation carries little weight.[97] Again, in Cambrai in 1076 a man named Ramihrdus, who was apprehended by the bishop as a heretic, seems to have been guilty of no more than enthusiastically sponsoring the proposals of the papal reform, for inquiries could find no fault in him about the articles of faith. But when Ramihrdus accused the bishop and clergy of simony, in their eyes he stood guilty of heresy.[98]

Various reasons have been advanced for the silence of the sources about heresy in the second half of the eleventh century. There is the suggestion that the success of oppressive measures forced heresy to move underground and to adopt tactics of unobtrusive propaganda.[99] Or it may be that the great events of the conflict between Church and state, followed by the crusades, diverted attention from the small, isolated groups of dissidents.[100] More persuasive is the explanation of Arno Borst, that heretics disappear from the sources because heretical dissent waned sharply, because the emphasis that the heretics had put on personal purity and asceticism, on spiritual as opposed to material values, was absorbed in and more powerfully expressed by the Cluny-Gorze movement of monastic renovation and the Gregorian reform. Attitudes that had been called heretical in earlier years would have ceased to prompt criticism because the same motives and aims were taken over by other movements in Christian society.[101]

Wandering Preachers and the Apostolic Life in the Twelfth Century

From the beginning of the twelfth century, heresy moved forward on the European scene. The narrative of occurrences in the following pages

is keyed to the documents which have been translated in this volume and
follows the sequence in which they are arranged. Ideally, heresy should
be discussed within the full context of medieval life. Here we attempt
only to recount various incidents in the rise of heresy and to note aspects
of the contemporary reaction to it. For full interpretation the reader
must refer to general histories of the period or to special studies of the
sects in their contemporary settings.[102]

Between 1100 and 1120 heretical movements swirled around dominant personalities, chief among them Tanchelm in the Low Countries;[103]
Henry, so called of Lausanne, active first at Le Mans and then in regions
to the south;[104] and Peter of Bruys, in the area near the mouth of the
Rhone, where he and Henry joined forces briefly.[105] Near Soissons and
Trier sects appeared,[106] then vanished, at least from the sources. By the
fifth decade of the century, of the earlier leaders only Henry was still
alive to become the unfortunate object of the attention of St. Bernard,
but by that time the eccentric Eudo was troubling Brittany,[107] Arnold
of Brescia moved through dramatic events in Rome,[108] and warnings of
danger were heard from Cologne, Périgueux, and Liège.[109] The last
three places were scenes of very significant events; there the sect of the
Cathars first appeared, its organization and dogma then taking form.

Certain characteristics of the heresies of this half-century—leaving
the Cathars aside for the moment—are salient. Individuals played a
central role. The leaders often were clerics, monks, or canons. Laymen,
too, were leaders in their own right, or grouped themselves about the
heresiarchs as lieutenants and disciples. The followers were no longer
isolated and localized groups but made up a popular movement over
wide areas. There is little evidence to show that they drew apart in
distinctive communities or sects at this time. Interrelationships of dogma
among the heresiarchs are not obvious, for it was less theology than
religious practice that was in question, yet it is quite clear that the state
of mind of these dissident preachers and their hearers was much the
same everywhere. They were unanimous in denying that the existing
Church met their demands for religious life and leadership. The need
for church buildings and consecrated cemeteries was brought in question;
tithes were refused; and Peter of Bruys was notorious for denouncing
veneration of the Cross. Tanchelm and Henry are said to have declared
that only their followers were true Christians. The efficacy of the sacraments, the heretics insisted, depended on the worth of the ministrant,

and almost without exception the various groups held that the function of the clergy of their day was invalidated by moral unworthiness— Arnold of Brescia's slashing attacks on the hierarchy and clergy were the most extreme examples of this view. Peter of Bruys and the heretics near Trier explicitly denied transubstantiation. Virtually all rejected infant baptism. Henry taught that there was no need to confess to priests. On marriage there was not so much unanimity, however. The group near Soissons was said to reject it entirely. Henry encouraged his adherents at Le Mans to marry, but neither then nor later did he regard marriage as sacramental. Heretics at Cologne approved of marriage only between virgins. Prayers and the efficacy of works for the dead, several reports indicate, were denied; the heretics of Cologne taught that there was no purgatory.

The elements common to all of these diverse leaders and followers were the radical and far-reaching conclusions that they drew from two basic assumptions: that the apostolic life is the truly Christian life, and that the duty of men and women to practice it and to preach repentance is fundamental.[110] The heresies of the twelfth century were stimulated by the renovation of religious ideas produced by the reform program in the Church in the preceding century, and especially by the appeal to the example of the apostles. Precepts of the Gospels and the narrative of the early Church in the Acts of the Apostles have repeatedly been a rejuvenating and disturbing force in Christianity, never more potently than in the Middle Ages; one need only mention three saints from three centuries—Peter Damiani, Bernard of Clairvaux, and Francis of Assisi. In a great many ordinary men and women the New Testament awoke comparable ardor. Church reformers had focused pious sentiments on the imitation of the apostles by lives in which penitence outwardly expressed the inward search for grace, communal association fostered brotherly love, and poverty exalted the spiritual over the material. To penitence, brotherhood, and poverty, add the necessity of preaching in order to reach all men with the renewed gospel. This was the *vita apostolica*, a key element in the transformation of twelfth-century religious orders, in the rise of associations of lay brothers, in the renewal of asceticism, in puritanism and religious enthusiasm. It brought forward new advocates of itinerant evangelism. It also led to new heresies.

The apostolic impulse is discernible in the heresies of the early eleventh century but its impact on those of the twelfth century is far better attested. The anticlericalism which accompanied it, ironically enough owes something to the eleventh-century papal reform program. In its more radical phase, the Gregorian reform had revived the Donatist assertion that only a truly moral clergy could effectively mediate between God and man. Gregory VII withdrew from the stand that the life of the ministrant can affect the sacrament, but not before a great many people had heard the message that bad priests were to be avoided. Now, in the outburst of enthusiasm for the apostolic life, pious opinion required of the clergy something approaching the rigor and asceticism of the monastery, and when this was not in evidence, it often turned against them. At their most extreme, critics of an immoral clergy declared that ordination could give no power that was not nullified by impure life. In the place of an ineffective clergy and invalid sacraments, heretical leaders offered their own example and precepts; and the evidence they gave, in deed as well as word, of their devotion to the apostolic ideal had potent attraction.

The Rise of the Cathars

The first solid evidence of a "new heresy"—as it was called by an observer—one that was to outdo all others in challenging the orthodox Church, comes from Cologne in 1143.[111] There, side by side with the reformers who have already been mentioned, but easily distinguished from them, were found persons who claimed, because they followed the apostolic tradition, to constitute the only true church. They were, in their own words, "apostles, Christ's poor," owning nothing, laboring only for daily sustenance, divorced from the world by their perseverance in prayer and fasting. They abhorred marriage, spurned milk and foods born of coition, replaced the Catholic sacraments with their own rites of blessing bread at meals and baptism by the imposition of hands. Their church, they said, was world-wide, having persisted in Greece and other lands from the days of the apostles. In Cologne they were led by a bishop and his assistant and when examined by the clergy were defended by their own theologians. The report of the discussion contains no mention of dualism, but there need be no hesitation in identifying them as Cathars,[112] although contemporaries did not yet know the name.[113]

Evidence of the existence of similar groups was not long in coming. At Liège, a group of heretics said to have come from France, rejected the sacraments and claimed to be the only true church.[114] About the same time, from Périgueux came a shrill warning about "apostolics" who fasted and prayed constantly and added to the Lord's Prayer a doxology not found in the Vulgate version of Matthew, but common in Greek and Slavonic Bibles. Popular report, moreover, made wonder-workers of the heretics.[115] Clear-cut statements that dualism was taught by the heretics of Liège and Périgueux is lacking, but most of the evidence points to the conclusion that they were Cathars.

How had the new heresy reached the Rhineland and been so widely dispersed elsewhere? One suggested answer is that the persecution of Bogomils in Constantinople in 1143[116] accelerated a dispersion already stimulated by their missionary spirit. More than a century later, an inquisitor would recount how heresy spread from Bulgaria to Constantinople, thence to Bosnia, and soon afterward, by the medium of returning crusaders, to France.[117] Christine Thouzellier has reconstructed a sequence of events from that narrative and other evidence. She supposes Bogomil influence to have been felt in the eleventh century and to have manifested itself again at Soissons (1114), Montwimers (before 1145), and Liège (1135, 1143). Perhaps the first crusaders had made contact with heretics in the East and carried back some of their ideas. At any rate, Bogomil influence had produced a church of mitigated dualists in Cologne by 1143. The prosecutions of that year did not exterminate them, and Germans returning in 1149 from the Second Crusade reinvigorated the heresy and precipitated a crisis of dogma, for they had made contact in Constantinople with the absolute-dualist doctrines of the Dragovitsan order. The latter won out in the Rhineland and Germany within twenty years. Meanwhile, other returning crusaders had also carried the modified dualism of the Bulgarian Bogomils into northern France and created a center there, with its own bishop, from which missionaries pushed southward into Aquitaine and Italy. The result, Mlle Thouzellier concludes, was that this new influence from the Balkans canalized various movements, gave existing groups greater doctrinal unity, and provided heretical nuclei in southern France and northern Italy from which the Cathars would grow rapidly.[118]

Whatever the cosmological or metaphysical doctrines that were being purveyed in these middle years of the century, they seem to have been less important in the popular reception of the new heresy than the humility, poverty, abstinence, and prayer which the Cathars practiced. Most Catholic sources of this period, in fact, are silent on the question

of dualism, apart from the use of the epithet "Manichaean." It may be
that the missionaries and heresiarchs were careful not to reveal their full
doctrine until the reliability of converts was thoroughly established,[119]
or that the bishops who examined prisoners were put off by evasive
answers and did not press their questions hard enough. Among the
people who heard the Cathars preach and who were attracted to their
company, surely the heretics' great appeal was to the now fully awak-
ened sentiments of piety. The ground had been prepared by the wandering preachers and the radical reformers; now upon it strode the Cathars.
None were humbler; none were more assiduous in prayer, more constant
under persecution; none made more insistent claims to be "good
men";[120] and it was on those terms that they were received by many of
the common people.

As for the orthodox reaction, the procedure for dealing with alleged
heretics was not yet regularized. Suspects were interrogated by bishops
or abbots with attendant clergy, or sometimes by a specially convened
council.[121] Doubt about appropriate penalties often affected the deliberations, and in most cases when the accused died, it was as a result of
mob action.[122] What was more evident was the sense of alarm among
churchmen and the impulse to publicize the dangers by letters and
sermons. To the region of Toulouse, which was already becoming
notorious for heresy, the first special preaching mission was led by St.
Bernard,[123] in an attempt to win back disaffected people by persuasion,
an attempt which the Church would repeat later without notable
success.

THE SPREAD OF HERESY

The six decades after 1150 were the great age of growth of medieval
heresy. All the currents already in motion ran faster and deeper, some
converging, some finding new channels. Motives of ecclesiastical reform,
evangelism, personal piety, and poverty were restated; a scathing attack
on the hierarchy continued in the vein of Arnold of Brescia, while other
critics rejected the clergy as vigorously on other grounds. In the bur-
geoning towns, groups such as the Humiliati came together to express
their piety in simple lives of labor and preaching. Other nonconformists
spoke of returning to the rigid law and observances of the Old Testament. Apocalyptic teachings were heard and with some pantheistic
additions were popularized by a little group in the vicinity of Paris.

Many sects of which only the names or briefest mention survive sprang up. And everywhere the Cathars spread, meeting savage repression in the North, but winning so much support in southern France that they threatened to replace the Church in the loyalties of nobles and townsmen. They had almost as much influence in the cities of northern Italy. This survey will touch on the development of heretical sects in this period in three geographical areas: Italy, southern France, and northern Europe. If such a scheme occasionally requires some repetition, it has also the merit of pointing up differences among heretical movements. Heresies spread throughout Europe but not even the greatest of them was homogeneous or monolithic, for in different areas varying emphases, different tenets and forms of organization came into being. The metaphor which might be used to describe this phenomenon is not of a river confined to one great channel but of a delta, where a dozen channels diverge.

Reform Movements and Catharism in Italy

In so far as social unrest could encourage dissenting religious opinions, the Lombard and Tuscan towns were well prepared for heretical propaganda. Opposition to the German emperor, papal-imperial strife and the ensuing schism of the papacy, internal party divisions along these lines or based on economic or class interests, and the desire for municipal independence revived the tradition of the Pataria and raised the perennial questions of ecclesiastical morality and reform.[124]

In the decade after 1170 the harvest of heresies ripened in Italy. No doubt the conflict between the vested interests of the clergy and the economic ambitions of the townsmen of Piacenza did its part to embitter Hugo Speroni, a jurist of that city, toward the clergy. The ideas he formulated grew out of his concept of predestination, in which salvation was the lot only of those who, by the foreordination of God, possessed an inner holiness, a state attainable by no act of their own. In consequence Speroni denied the validity of sacraments and all other visible acts of piety. He rejected the priesthood, because he insisted that priests were bound by sin, that they defiled rather than sanctified whatever they touched. How much of a following Speroni collected in Piacenza and how long they survived as a sect is not known. Speronists yet were condemned in 1184, and were still important enough to be denounced by a Catholic writer in Piacenza in 1235. The name continued to occur regularly in official pronouncements for the remainder of the century.[125]

The Humiliati constituted a sect that grew out of the reactions of pious consciences to conditions of economic change in Italian towns. In 1179—the date is most probable but not absolutely verified—Alexander III received an appeal from some communities of urban laborers, who asked his approval of their honest and humble customs. Without giving up family life, they wished to live as a community, wearing plain garb as a mark of their piety, putting an absolute ban on lies, oaths, and litigation, and spreading the Gospel among themselves and to others by preaching. The pope applauded all these propositions, except that of preaching. This he forbade, and when the prohibition was ignored, the Humiliati were excommunicated as heretics in 1184. Some of them made common cause with the Waldenses, who were then beginning their missionary work in Italy. Later, Innocent III was able to recall others to the Church by allowing them to continue their chosen way of life under clerical supervision.[126]

The sect of "Lombards," which Arnold of Brescia is said to have organized before his death, seems not to have continued under that name. By 1184 a group called the Arnoldists, after their supposed originator, was restating the teaching of the rebellious reformer. They held that prelates and priests were entirely unworthy to represent the Church of Jesus Christ, to administer the sacraments, or to impose ecclesiastical discipline. For them the test of the true Christian was profession of the poverty of the apostles, and they considered that laymen in that state had full right to preach the Gospel. They did not concern themselves with doctrinal or philosophical speculations; anti-sacerdotalism was the paramount theme. Condemned in 1184 with the Speronists and Humiliati, and like the latter making common cause with the Waldenses, the Arnoldists continued to be mentioned as a separate sect in edicts and bulls of condemnation long afterward.[127]

Somewhat of an anomaly were the Passagians, whose time and place of origin are only imprecisely known. An insistence on observing all the laws of the Old Testament, including circumcision, was joined in this sect to a rejection of the divinity of Christ and to a denial of the Trinity. Most of the sacramental services of the Church they regarded as human inventions which deserved no respect.[128]

The existence in Italy of various sects which cherished some single heretical idea was attested by the Franciscan inquisitor Stephen of

Bourbon on the evidence of a Waldensian he had interrogated. There were the "Tortolani," who took the Eucharist only from their own Perfect leader once a year; the "Rebaptizati," who performed a new baptism for adults; the "Communiati," who practiced community of goods; and the "Josephini" (named with no statement of their doctrines).[129] Most of these can probably be classed among the reformers, but the greatest expression of the motives of evangelism and reform in Italy came through the growth there of the Waldenses, or Poor of Lyons.

To postpone for the moment the story of the origin of the Poor of Lyons, it may be noted that members of the sect made a first impression in Italy in 1179 or soon thereafter. Insisting on the right of laymen to preach, emphasizing holy poverty, reading the Gospel in the vernacular, and criticizing the Catholic clergy, they drew into their ranks many of the Arnoldists and the Humiliati. The last-named, however, were dedicated to communal lives of labor, while the Poor of Lyons were committed entirely to poverty and itinerant preaching. This difference, combined with disagreements that arose about organization and about the propriety of accepting the sacraments from the orthodox clergy, culminated in schism in 1205 and the Italian Waldenses broke away from the Poor of Lyons, adopting the name "Poor Lombards." Further dissension over the consecration of the Eucharist in turn split the Poor Lombards and gave occasion for some of them to return to the Church.[130] Before that, as the Poor of Lyons had done from the beginning, the Poor Lombards were attacking the Cathars vigorously while defending their own way of life as superior to that permitted by the orthodox Church.

Even before the sects which have just been mentioned had made their appearance, the heresy of the Cathars, soon to be heresy par excellence to orthodox contemporaries, had been quietly established in Italy.[131] It was probably between 1150 and 1160 and probably from the Cathar community in northern France that missionaries first came to make converts among people of humble station in Lombardy and Tuscany and set them to preaching to and converting others. Their numbers grew so rapidly that soon the Cathars were being blamed for a chief share in the perennial political and ecclesiastical troubles of the Italian cities. Meanwhile, among themselves, disputes over doctrine revealed the influence of missionaries from the Bogomil churches in Constantinople and Bulgaria. The first Cathars in Italy accepted the modified dualism then prevalent to the north. But in the decade 1160-1170, emissaries from Constantinople made contact with them, preaching the doctrines of absolute dualism, and producing problems of dogma which were accentuated by the importance placed on baptism by imposition of hands. By this act, which soon came to be called the *consolamentum* in the West, the soul was cleansed of sin, but only if the ministrants themselves were sinless. Moreover, used to confirm bishops and their assistants in office, the consolamentum passed on the tradition of the church or "order." [132] Thus serious crises of conscience could arise if there were uncertainty either about the personal purity of the participants or the legitimacy of the doctrinal tradition of the church which they represented.

A mission from Constantinople, about 1165, won over most Italian Cathars to absolute dualism, as was to be the case presently in southern France. But further problems arose in Italy when Bulgarian mitigated-dualist missionaries came in their turn. Conflicting opinions about the validity of the consolamentum, abetted no doubt by personal ambitions and regional rivalries, had by about 1190 splintered the Italian Cathars into six churches, to which was added another, composed of migrants from France. [133] There were, however, no clear geographical lines dividing the churches or bishoprics. These all quarreled with each other, and in the thirteenth century doctrinal questions further divided the two most important groups. It was at about the time of the first schisms that Italian Cathars, visiting various Balkan areas to validate their consecration through a new consolamentum, brought back some apocryphal books used by the Bogomils which became popular also in the West. [134]

While disagreement divided the Cathars into rival factions, Catholic authorities began to display alarm about the heresy in Italy. A chronicler of much later date wrote that as early as 1163, the Emperor Frederick Barbarossa had noticed large numbers of heretics in Milan. [135] Between 1167 and 1176, Archbishop Galdinus preached against the Cathars there, [136] as did the bishops of Orvieto and Florence in their own dioceses. [137] Soon the kind of information which allowed Catholics to understand the nature of the heresy more clearly and which increased their horror and indignation at it began to become available. One of the first examples of this was the confession of a convert from Catharism named Bonacursus, in Milan. Other hands soon added to his statement various materials gleaned from the Scriptures which could be used to refute the teachings of the Cathars, then rounded this out with similar compilations to be used against the Passagians and Arnoldists.[138] The inner complexities of the Cathar churches, however, did not become clear to observers for some time, and more than half a century later inquisitors were still attempting to explain them.[139]

Until 1184, action to check or repress heresy in Italy was the affair of bishops in the areas affected. The Third Lateran Council of 1179, which discussed heresy, had its eyes focused on southern France,[140] but heretics of Italy got their full share of attention from the papal see when Lucius III and the Emperor Frederick Barbarossa meeting at Verona in 1184 jointly condemned and proscribed the sects of Cathars, Patarines, Humiliati, Poor of Lyons, Passagians, Josephini, and Arnoldists. The papal bull *Ad abolendam* also prescribed penalties for heretical clerics and laymen and established a procedure of systematic inquisition by bishops.[141] Succeeding popes followed this with pronouncements about heresy in specific areas, Rimini, Ferrara, Modena, and Prato, among others.[142]

It was Innocent III (1198-1216) who pressed papal action to wider limits. From the moment he came to the Chair of Peter, Innocent dispatched a stream of letters about heresy to archbishops, bishops, secular rulers, and municipal governments, and sent legates to work on the spot. He saw the basic necessity, reform of the Church, as the first requirement; he urged, cajoled, and threatened, in attempts to correct unsavory situations. Italy was not the scene of preaching missions against heresy or of a crusade, which was, as we shall see, visited upon southern France; but all the other papal programs were pressed there. In the cities specific measures were ordered; legates worked at recruiting the cooperation of secular governments, and drew up statutes against heresy to be enforced by them. At the papal court, converts who returned to the Church from the Humiliati and the Waldensian societies were greeted with warmth and favor. In 1215, the Fourth Lateran Council summed up and reaffirmed the pontifical legislation already in existence. In its first canon, the council provided a statement of doctrine based on traditional professions of faith, but amended to take account of present heresies. The third canon specified procedures against heretics and their accomplices and reproduced, among other provisions, the *Ad abolendam* of Lucius III. Several other canons touched on the matter of heresy in various ways. Although the council's attention was fixed primarily on the situation in southern France, the legislation was equally pertinent to Italy where, by the time of Innocent's death, the Church was mobilizing its forces against heresy and lacked only the papal inquisition, for which the precedents were already being established.[143]

Waldenses and Cathars in Southern France

In southern France, more particularly in the domain nominally ruled by the counts of Toulouse—which soon would come to be called Languedoc, land of the southern dialect—heresy put down its firmest roots in the twelfth century. Religious dissent had been chronic there since the eleventh century. The Church, by admission of its own members, was often wanting, for although the Gregorian reform and the revitalizing effect of the Cistercian movement had been felt, a vital element, support of the established Church by the nobility, did not exist. Spokesmen for the Cathars found a ready hearing, as did the itinerant preachers of the Poor of Lyons. Both sects prospered, even while quarreling with each other, until the situation became so notorious as to prompt intervention, sponsored by the papacy and supported by the Capetian king, who had claim to feudal overlordship of the affected regions.[144] The two sects will be discussed separately below; this should not obscure the fact that they existed side by side—although not in amity—and ultimately were the joint object of repressive measures.

The only heresy of the Middle Ages that has survived as an organized church in modern times is that which began with the preaching of Waldes of Lyons.[145] Sometime about 1170, Waldes, a merchant of that city, underwent a religious experience most appropriately likened to that which affected Francis of Assisi a little later, one that led him to rid himself of his wealth and his family and to appear in the streets with urgent appeals to his fellow citizens to repent.[146] Disciples gathered, and the reformer sought papal approval for their preaching and the practice of holy poverty. As with the Humiliati, the pope approved the piety but not the preaching. Returning to Lyons, Waldes was required to prove his orthodoxy by a profession of faith, to which he added the statement of his intent to live by the rule of the Gospels in poverty and obedience to authority. When despite the archbishop's prohibition he continued to preach, the Poor of Lyons, as they now called themselves, were expelled from the city, and in 1184 they were included among the sects excommunicated by Lucius III. The Poor of Lyons spread southward, where the legacy of Peter of Bruys and Henry was theirs to collect. Within a decade or so they were disclaiming any obedience to the Roman clergy, arguing that any worthy layman could preach and perform the sacraments, and challenging the judicial powers of secular authority. At the same time, they stoutly attacked their more numerous contemporaries, the Cathars, so that churchmen who were well enough informed carefully distinguished between the two sects and regarded the Poor of Lyons as the lesser evil.

It has already been noted that in Italy, the Poor of Lyons had picked up adherents from existing groups inclined to antisacerdotalism and to the concept of a church purified by poverty. After the break between the Poor of Lyons and the Poor Lombards in 1205, the latter's influence crossed the Alps into southern Germany and the Rhine valley. Attempts to reunite these groups were to be made, but without success.[147]

The names applied to the Cathars in Europe varied from place to place. Of the names based on the regions or towns in which the heretics were established, none became more widely known than "Albigenses,"[148] derived from the town of Albi, in or near which probably the first Cathar bishopric in southern France was established.[149] The heretics were by no means confined to that area, and it was actually in and around Toulouse that the Catholic clergy were first aroused to resist them. A conference between prelates and heretics at Lombers in 1165 revealed the inability of the orthodox hierarchy to take effective measures. How little the heretics were perturbed appears from their convening shortly afterward at Saint-Félix-de-Caraman, a village outside Toulouse, to discuss doctrinal and organizational affairs. There Nicheta, the emissary of absolute dualists in Constantinople who had already left his stamp on the Italian Cathars, won over to absolute dualism the representatives from northern France and Languedoc. At this heretical council also new bishoprics were created, to supplement those already established in northern France and at Albi.[150] The Albigenses thus acquired an administrative structure and doctrinal unity unknown among the Cathars in Italy, although modified dualism was not left without its partisans among them.

Heresy and politics were intermingled in Languedoc even more closely than in the Italian cities, because so many of the nobility were either receptive to the doctrines or eager to see local prelates lose secular influence and power. Aware that his territories were notorious for heresy, Count Raymond V of Toulouse found it expedient to demonstrate his orthodox sentiments. At his instigation, in 1178 a mission of prelates, reminiscent of St. Bernard's visit in 1145, came to Toulouse to investigate and to preach. Their chief accomplishment was to successfully prosecute a wealthy merchant who was reputed to be a heresiarch (although there is, in fact, no documentary evidence that he was a Cathar). They also encountered two spokesmen for the heretics, who defended themselves as entirely orthodox until they were shouted down by members of the audience, who accused them of teaching the doctrine of two gods and of utterly repudiating the Church.[151]

No doubt this experience influenced the legislation adopted by the Third Lateran Council in 1179, but neither that nor an abortive crusade in 1181 was effective in checking the spread of heresy.[152] Cathars were welcomed in the courts of nobles, moved unmolested in the streets, debated with Catholic bishops and Waldensian spokesmen. The Catholic clergy was too indolent, too infected with heretical views in some cases, and too much hampered by public opinion, which favored the heretics, to be able to counteract their influence. However, some sporadic activities by churchmen began to produce valuable information about the heresies and when this was published abroad, it intensified the concern of the Church. By the year 1200 the main lines of Catharist and Waldensian teaching and the extent of their defection from the Church were known, but the question of what to do about it still remained.

It was during the pontificate of Innocent III that real countermeasures to heresy were first devised for Languedoc. Through papal legates, the pontiff first sought to reform the Church in Languedoc from the top down and to persuade the nobility to cooperate against the heretics.[153] In 1204, he sponsored a campaign of counterpropaganda through the preaching of Cistercian monks, which was given vigorous assistance in 1206 when Diego, bishop of Osma, and his companion, Dominic, joined the legates in Languedoc.[154] Out of the preaching campaign of 1206-1208 were born preaching orders, first the short-lived Poor Catholics, then the more prominent and permanent Order of Preachers, founded by Dominic.

In 1207, a conference of Catholics and heretics at Pamiers induced some Waldenses, notably Durand of Huesca, to return to the Church. Durand and a few companions then persuaded Innocent III to allow them to form a society in which they would continue certain pious practices current among the Waldenses but profess full orthodoxy in doctrine, be obedient to the papacy, and dedicate themselves to unremitting preaching against heresy. Under the name of Poor Catholics,[155] they were active for several decades, and during their brief life they produced some very important pieces of antiheretical literature.[156] A companion group recruited primarily from among the Lombard Poor also appeared but was equally short-lived.

Far more important were the mendicant friars which succeeded these first preaching societies. The Dominican and Franciscan orders[157] are outside the limits of this survey; however, it must be noted that the purpose "to root out the corruption of heresy, to drive out vice, to teach the creed and inculcate in men sound morals," expressed when the Dominicans were being formed,[158] was important to both orders, which were effective agents against heresy not only because of their preaching and because they furnished inquisitors for the new tribunal of the Inquisition, but even more because they helped to satisfy within the Church the insistent popular pressure for piety and morality in daily life.

Legatine missions which carried out papal policies against heresy have been briefly referred to. We must also pass quickly over the history of the Albigensian Crusade. Innocent III had broached the plan of using force against heretics and their protectors in earlier years, but in 1208 the murder of a papal legate, a crime laid at the door of Count Raymond VI of Toulouse, hardened Innocent's resolution. A summons to northern nobles brought a crusading army into Languedoc in 1209. Twenty years later, after intermittent warfare, although Languedoc was not crushed, the power of the counts of Toulouse had been much reduced, numbers of the lesser southern nobility had been killed or disinherited, and the intervention of the French king had shown the folly of further armed conflict. The ravages on the brilliant culture of the south were severe, but heresy was by no means extirpated.[159] Some of the nobility continued, as best they could, to shelter heretics; the devotion of a large proportion of the populace to the Catharist Perfect had not been seriously weakened; thus new methods had to be devised for continuing the struggle against infidelity. The chief of them was the papal Inquisition.

Heresy in Northern Europe

As has been said, Cathars had been found in Cologne in 1143. It may be surmised that from there the heresy spread into Flanders, at the same time that it was pushing into Aquitaine and Italy from some center in northern France; but neither the Cathars nor any of the other popular heresies of the twelfth century won wide support in northern Europe (which, for our purposes, we take to be the area north of a line drawn along the valley of the Loire east to the Rhine, and including the Rhineland, Flanders, France, and England). Not that this region was free of heresy, but the prosecution which was pushed more vigorously in the north than elsewhere seems to have kept the sects subdued and relatively isolated. The records are less precise about doctrines than those available for Languedoc or Italy; there are no confessions of converts, and we hear more of punishments than of beliefs. Dualist ideas were present, but in most cases it is impossible to be specific about the exact character of the heresy reported.

The first mention of heretics in this period forthrightly calls them Manichaeans. The first canon of the Council of Rheims (1157)[160] makes clear the exasperation the prelates felt: Slippery Manichaeans, they declared, hide among the innocent folk, especially among weavers who move from place to place and change their names. Although they condemn marriage, they are accompanied by wicked women. The council prescribed severe penalties, imprisonment or worse, for the heresiarchs; followers were to have their faces branded and be exiled.[161]

In 1163, a small group of heretics was apprehended at Cologne. When they refused to recant after interrogation, they were handed over to the secular officials to be burned. Writing after the event, Eckbert, a monk of Schönau who claimed experience in debate with heretics, described their errors in thirteen sermons which constitute a polemical tract.[162] He calls the heretics "Cathars," or "Piphles," or "weavers," and declares that they rejected marriage and infant baptism or any baptism in water, spurned the Eucharist, and denied purgatory. They refused to eat meat. Christ, they said, had only seemed to assume flesh, and the souls of men were apostate angels. Not all the heretics known to Eckbert were of one mind; he mentions the followers of one Hartuvinus, who approved the marriage of virgins,[163] a tenet reminiscent of the reformers described by Eberwin. Eckbert's insistence on seeing in the heretics of Cologne the Manichaeans of St. Augustine's day may have colored his description.

It was in the decade of the sixties that the Rhineland and Flanders constituted a center from which heresy radiated. In 1162 a group of townsmen of Flanders were prosecuted as Manichaeans or Publicans by the archbishop of Rheims. They unsuccessfully offered him a large bribe for release, then appealed to the pope, with unknown results.[164] A cleric, Jonas, was at about this time convicted of the heresy of the Cathars but seems to have gone free,[165] being more fortunate in that than another man, Robert, who was burned at Arras in 1172 after being convicted by the ordeal of hot iron.[166] From Flanders or the Rhineland, between 1160 and 1166, a group of thirty or so heretics made their way to England, where they were detected and savagely punished by the king for rejecting the sacraments.[167] In 1167, a group at Vézelay suffered a like fate for the same offense.[168]

Wherever heretics were detected in following years prosecution continued, but few details of their belief are preserved in the reports. The old stories of devil-worship and lewd assemblies were revived, and tales of magical prowess derived from the powers of darkness are a commonplace in the reports.[169] Heresy was chronic in the diocese of Auxerre as the thirteenth century began. Bishop Hugh attacked it there, and, when the Albigensian Crusade began, a number of prosecutions elsewhere were in progress.[170] From time to time papal assistance or advice was asked for, but usually the local authorities acted vigorously and ruthlessly in prosecution. Not until the very end of the century were the Waldenses noticed, however. Then, in Metz, some of them who had come from Montpellier, treated the bishop disrespectfully—but without immediate reprisal—and probably attracted a group of sympathizers by their encouragement of Bible-reading in the vernacular.[171]

Prompt and effective action was taken in response to a new kind of heresy discovered in Paris in 1210. For some years, the prophecies and apocalyptic teachings of Joachim of Flora, in Calabria, had been taken up here and there. Especially popular was his doctrine of three ages or dispensations in history: those of the Father, of Christ, and of the Holy Spirit. The third of these was generally thought to be about to begin in the thirteenth century, after which the perfect glory of the Spirit would bring the world to a new kind of perfection.[172] The Amalricians, followers of Amalric of Bena (d. *ca.* 1206), a master of arts at the University of Paris, combined Joachim's ideas with pantheism in a sect whose devotees declared themselves to be so imbued with the Holy

Spirit that no act of theirs could be sin, nor for them were any sacraments necessary. This heresy was exposed by an "undercover agent" and the sect, which had begun to attract some followers in adjacent dioceses, was promptly broken up by the execution or imprisonment of its leaders.[173] The apocalyptical and pantheistic elements in it, however, were to recur repeatedly in the next three centuries, especially among the Brethren of the Free Spirit.[174]

Sects of the Later Middle Ages

In the first three or four decades of the thirteenth century the great medieval heresies of the Cathars and Waldenses had reached their peak. Crusaders cruelly ravaged Languedoc, but the hold of heresy on the people was not easily broken and its proponents were still capable of effective propaganda,[175] although they moved less openly than before. It was not until the number of the Perfect was reduced by a combination of military action and judicial procedures, and the persistent pursuit by the Inquisition made life difficult for their sympathizers, that Catharism began to wane seriously.[176] In retrospect one can see that by the third quarter of the century, the Albigenses were clearly doomed.[177] In Italian cities the political situation gave Catharism greater security, and it retained its vitality there for decades after it was dying out elsewhere.[178] This meant that heretics could travel between Languedoc and Italy, protected and guided by sympathizers, to find shelter with their co-religionists for a time.[179]

The Waldenses expanded during the first half of the century, across the Pyrenees from southern France and from Italy and Germany eastward toward Bohemia.[180] They were the target of inquisitorial attention equally with the Cathars but were perhaps less easily recognized or better able to work quietly in humble levels of society and so to escape notice. At any rate, they survived over ensuing centuries and in 1532 made common cause with Protestantism.[181] Of other sects, little can be said with certainty. The names of the Passagians, Humiliati, Arnoldists, Amalricians, and others still appeared in edicts of condemnation, but it is likely that these sects lost effective existence, absorbed by other movements, or dwindling to obscurity.

Although some of the earlier sects waned or completely disappeared in the thirteenth century, the fundamental causes of heresy were still present and continued to find outlets in religious activities beyond the

limits of orthodoxy. Communities of religious men, and more frequently of women, called Beghards and Beguines, were forming in
Europe in the mid-thirteenth century whose aim was to live in chastity
and by labor under proper ecclesiastical guidance, yet heterodox notions
could find a home among them and they were sometimes harassed by
suspicious prelates.[182] Apocalyptic preaching and the inspiration of a
"free spirit" repeatedly animated individuals and groups.[183] Apostolic
poverty became an issue which split the Franciscan order early in the
fourteenth century. Some of the radical faction, the Spirituals, were
burned as heretics, but they left behind lay followers who tried to
perpetuate their teachings.[184] In short, in the fourteenth and fifteenth
centuries doctrinal criticism, spiritual discontent, and extravagant or
unorthodox expressions of piety would continue to appear, in old and
new forms.[185]

After about 1250, however, in the literature on heresy, the most
important theme is not the rise of heresies but their suppression, which
reflects the increased scope of efforts by Church and state. The papacy
had recruited the cooperation of monarchs, with the result that legislation by Louis VIII of France, James I of Aragon, and the Emperor
Frederick II was added to that by popes and councils and the statutes
urged on the cities by papal legates.[186] By 1250, the papal inquisition
had regularized and expanded its procedures of search, examination,
and condemnation.[187] Now the testimony of witnesses, which was carefully recorded and indexed, began to provide abundant information
about heretical ideas and customs.[188] To promote more efficient oper-
ation, inquisitors compiled manuals of procedure and model interrogatories,[189] and summarized what they had learned about heretical
doctrines for the benefit of their colleagues.[190] Tracts of this sort drew
some of their information about the heresies from earlier polemical
works but are often valuable sources in their own right.[191] The translations of orthodox sources in this volume end with one such inquisitorial manual of the early fourteenth century.

ORGANIZATION AND DOCTRINE OF THE MEDIEVAL SECTS

The Cathars

A great many names were used by orthodox Christianity to designate
the dualist heretics of the twelfth and thirteenth centuries. The name

"Cathars" came into use after 1163,[192] but the heretics themselves, from their earliest appearance, preferred to be called "Christians" or "Good Men," a name restricted of course to the Perfect, who were also called the "Elect" or "Consoled."[193] The earlier designations of heretics as "Arians" or "Manichaeans" continued to be used by Catholic writers, on the assumption that the Cathars were direct descendants of the early sects.[194] Some authors attempted to establish a genealogy of heresy, in which many individuals and sects of the past were named.[195] One thirteenth-century controversialist also calls the Cathars "Marcionites."[196]

As the Cathars multiplied, spread, and divided, and as knowledge of them increased, these generic names yielded to others without being entirely replaced. In northern Europe the name "Publicans," an adaptation of "Paulicians," of whose heresy crusaders had heard in the East,[197] was popular. "Patarine" was also used in the twelfth century in northern Europe but not as commonly as it was in Italy.[198] In France, the name "Bulgars" (in the vernacular "Bougres") showed an awareness of the connection with the Balkans.[199] But by the early thirteenth century "Albigenses" had become by far the most common name.

In Italy, "Patarines" and "Cathars" were used interchangeably after 1179, perhaps showing a recollection of the eleventh-century Milanese reform movement. The appearance of factions among the Cathars also produced special names for each of the resulting churches, names which might be derived from Balkan affiliations, from the name of a bishop, or the place in which a bishopric was established.[200] The mitigated dualists who sent their bishop to Bulgaria for confirmation were called "Bulgars," but this name soon was supplemented by "Garatenses," which derived from the name of a first bishop and persisted among the heretics themselves. By the middle of the thirteenth century, Catholic writers were more commonly calling them "Concorezzenses," after an Italian town not far from Milan.[201] Their vigorous rivals, absolute dualists, occasionally were called "Drugunthians" (a derivative of "Dragovitsa," the seat of Balkan absolute dualism), but more commonly were known as "the sect of Desenzano" (an Italian village) or "Albanenses," the name which they preferred. The last may be derived from either a person or a village.[202] A third group, holding somewhat of a middle position doctrinally, were first called "Slavs" or "Sclavini" from their connection with Bosnian Bogomils, or "Caloianni" after their first bishop. These names were superseded in the thirteenth century by

"Bagnolenses," adapted from the name of a village.[203]

Three other groups of Italian Cathars which came into existence as a result of the twelfth-century doctrinal disputes had names based on the regions where they were established: the sect of the March of Treviso or of Vicenza; that of Tuscany or Florence; that of the Spoletan Valley.[204] Finally, French immigrants were known in Italy as "those of France," or "Francigene."[205]

Cathars regarded themselves as the true Church of God, which over the centuries had preserved the teachings of Christ and the baptism that he had given to the disciples. The Church was in the lives of its members; nothing man-made of wood or stone had a part. True Christians obeyed the "law of life," guarding themselves from all the impurities Christ had warned against, and shunning other persons who refused to believe. Like Christ's, their lot in the world was persecution and martyrdom. As a church, then, the Cathars set themselves in forthright opposition to the Roman Catholic organization, which, being of this world, in their eyes represented the prince of this world, the devil.[206]

Christ had granted to his Church the power to forgive sins through prayer and baptism in the ceremony by which one entered the company of true Christians, a baptism in the Holy Spirit. It could be received only by those who had faith, and thus was denied, generally but not invariably, to children. Baptism, called the consolamentum, brought forgiveness of the great sin which the soul had incurred in its fall from heaven, and a return of the guiding spirit which had then been lost; no other work had that efficacy. To baptize in water was to use the material of the very world from which the soul must be freed. The rite of the consolamentum was a simple one, having, in fact, considerable likeness to baptism in the early Church.[207] How it survived or was re-created is not now known, although the Cathars surely obtained its chief features from the Bogomils. First the initiate underwent a time of testing and instruction, enduring the ascetic discipline which would be required of him after baptism, and being instructed in the doctrines which he would teach and defend to the death. When ready, he was presented in a two-part ceremony to the Perfect, those who had already been baptized. At his first appearance, the believer received the right and power to say the Lord's Prayer with proper understanding.[208] The actual consolamentum might be deferred for a time, but normally it followed immediately. In that ceremony, after a discourse from the ministrant, the postulant requested baptism and promised to maintain it unsullied, after which the Perfect laid their hands upon him while the ministrant held the Gospels over his head, repeated certain ceremonial invocations, and read seventeen verses from the first chapter of the Gospel of John.[209]

The man or woman thus made perfect, thereafter undertook a life of severest austerity, in which any indulgence of the flesh was forbidden and even sinful thoughts were to be eschewed. Any physical contact between men and women was forbidden. Dietary discipline forbade the use of meat, milk, eggs, or cheese at any time. On certain days each week and for three forty-day periods each year even stricter fasting was required.[210] Perfected Cathars thus constituted a picked group who pursued a life unendurable by ordinary men and women; hence baptism was usually postponed by believers until the approach of death, when the consolamentum could be conferred in an abbreviated ritual. If the invalid subsequently recovered, a period of probation and a second consolamentum might be required. In their earlier days, the perfected Cathars donned a black robe at baptism; when persecution made distinctive garb dangerous, this was replaced by a thread or a cord worn next to the skin by the heretic.[211] The practice of *endura*, suicide by starvation after receiving the consolamentum, in order to prevent recontamination of the soul, has often been commented on. It seems, however, to have been a relatively late development and probably has been more emphasized than is warranted by actual Catharist practice.[212]

Although in theory the consolamentum made one perfect, it might be repeated. In the early days of the Cathars, those who shifted allegiance from one group to another were "reconsoled." Officials were confirmed by imposition of hands. Also, those who sinned after baptism had to be reconsoled after suitable penitential fasting.[213] And finally, since the purity of the ministrant was of overriding importance, the consolamentum might require repetition if doubt arose as to the qualifications of the one who first imposed it. At least, that is what Catholic sources tell us; in the sources which survive, the heretics say nothing on this matter.

Cathar ecclesiastical organization was not complicated, but we risk confusion if we understand the terms "church" and "bishop" in the sense that they are used in orthodox terminology. After about 1167, the dualists of Languedoc were for the most part absolute-dualist in doctrine; the continued presence of some mitigated dualists did not create the internal controversies known in Italy. In Languedoc administration was by bishops, whose administrative areas followed the lines of Catholic dioceses, so that one spoke of the Albigensian church, or the church of Toulouse, or that of Carcassonne. In Italy, the distinction between churches was also between the orders of dualism but no geographic lines of episcopal authority were fixed. The various groups intermingled, although one might have preponderance in a certain area and the seat of the bishop might be in a particular town or village.

Each community elected a bishop, who had primacy among his equals, the other Perfect. Also elected were an "elder son" and a "younger son" (the Latin terms are *maior* and *minor* and have nothing to do with age). They would succeed to the bishop's office when he died or was deposed for some cause. Schism within a sect could of course upset that orderly succession. The bishop and the sons combined spiritual and administrative leadership but in no exclusive sense, for all Cathars had the power to give the consolamentum and were under an obligation to preach and teach. The most numerous officials were the deacons, who were charged with the conduct of hospices for the Perfect, where shelter was offered to travelers of the faith and where believers underwent the period of prebaptismal probation. The deacons also exercised pastoral care over the believers of their town or region and presided over the monthly confessional service; and among their number, no doubt, were found the "wise ones" especially qualified to defend their faith and debate with opponents.[214]

People among whom the Perfect moved and who accepted their teaching as true doctrine attached themselves to the Perfect as "believers." Living fully in the world, the believers supported the Perfect with gifts, sheltered them, guided them from place to place, protected them from persecution when they could,[215] and attended their various religious ceremonies. When it became dangerous for the heretics to congregate in public, their meetings might take place in any sort of gathering place.[216] Believers were welcome at the daily worship services and at the monthly confession of venial sins by the Perfect; they might also witness the consolamentum of one who was being initiated as a Perfect, whether he intended to devote his life to that vocation or, as was much more common, was being baptized only on his deathbed. These occasions were concluded with a kiss of peace among all participants and onlookers.[217] Believers frequently shared in the ceremony of breaking bread at meals.[218] Whenever a believer encountered a Perfect they exchanged a ritual greeting, the *melioramentum*, in which the believer, bowing deeply and repeatedly, asked for a blessing and for a prayer that he might end his life in the sect. The Perfect responded with a short prayer. (The same salutation was exchanged between Perfect, except that they prayed to remain in God's service.) Catholic observers, somewhat misinterpreting the nature of this exchange, called it "adoration."[219] In effect, the melioramentum was an engagement by the believer to seek baptism before he died. By mid-thirteenth century this promise was called the *covenensa* or *convenentia*[220] and had a formal nature, allowing the believer to be consoled even if he had lost the power of speech.

There is no doubt at all that the life of the perfected Cathars was one of most rigorous asceticism. Their worst enemies admitted that this was true, even while they insisted that it was a hypocritical surface morality adopted to cloak their secret vices. But because the consolamentum cleansed one of sin and because it was normally postponed to the last hours of life, it has been asserted that Cathar believers, in expectation of final forgiveness by the one act, would disregard ordinary rules of morality. Contemporary polemicists represented the Perfect as regretting that they had not tasted more of worldly pleasures before their baptism, and modern authors have concluded that acceptance of Cathar teaching threatened to break the moral bonds of society by promoting indifference to spiritual truth and freedom from any constraint on appetites of the flesh.[221] Yet it is not easy to reconcile the moral and ethical teaching of the Cathars[222] and their reproach of the luxury and laxity of the Catholic clergy with the assertion that they condoned gross immorality among their followers. Certainly, intensity of belief and observance of moral laws would have varied among the followers of the Cathars, as among all men. It seems reasonable to suppose that some would have been guilty of improper behavior. But, if we are right in thinking that much of the appeal of the Catharist teachers came from the demonstration of their own personal piety, it seems equally reasonable to suppose that there would have been incentives for their believers to follow their example as far as they were able. Furthermore, in assessing the charges of immorality among Catharist believers, one must recall that the moral code taught by the Church was more strict than the ordinary practice in feudal society, for example in the matter of relationships between the sexes, and it is possible that what was not at all uncommon in everyday life was used as an example of depravity when observed among the followers of the heretics.[223]

The doctrines of thirteenth-century Catharism were much the same in the various splinter groups, but there were some crucial differences, the most important being that between mitigated (or "modified" or "monarchian") and absolute dualism.[224] The former, as has been said, was the original teaching in Western Europe, as it probably had been among the Bogomils. For these Cathars, there was a single God, Father of all, Creator of a spiritual universe. But one of his creatures, or his son Lucifer, rebelled in heaven through pride and was cast out. With God's permission, Lucifer in his exile divided the then undifferentiated elements and from them constructed the visible world. Therein he placed the bodies of the first man and woman, imprisoning in Adam an angel of the good God. The souls of humans were either spirits derived from the first prisoner, spirits born of spirit as flesh is of flesh, or souls which had already been created and were introduced into new human bodies as the bodies were produced. God wished to save his fallen angels, and through Christ provided the message of salvation: Accept baptism, reject the wicked world, do penance until the death of the body and the final release of the spirit. Those who did not attain purification in one life might pass, by metempsychosis, from body to body, even through animals. At the final judgment day, the good would be separated from the evil.

Since all the visible world was considered the devil's work, the mitigated dualists rejected the Old Testament as the record of his deeds. They disagreed, however, on how to interpret the prophets who had foretold the coming of Christ and seemed to speak the will of the good God. John the Baptist was regarded as an agent of the devil, a view which was being modified in the mid-thirteenth century toward acceptance of him as a good man.

The absolute dualists, on the other hand, began with the premise that there were two principles or gods, one good and one evil, each of whom created his own universe in which he was all-powerful but was nonetheless subject to some interference from the adversary. The son of the evil principle—Lucifer—secretly made his way into the heaven of the good God, where he rose to be a steward over angels and seduced some of them from their divine allegiance. A battle ensued in heaven in which Lucifer and his allies were expelled. Here enters the doctrine of a triple composition of angels: The angelic creatures had body, soul, and spirit. After the Fall the bodies remained like dry bones in heaven, the souls became the prisoners of the devil on earth, while the spirits which had been their guides and preceptors lost contact with them. Christ came to save the fallen angelic souls imprisoned in human bodies, but the events of his life, death, and resurrection took place in another world, superior to this earth, which is hell. Some Cathars held that Christ had never appeared here except spiritually in the body of Paul. Souls might pass from one material body to another, until through the consolamentum they were forgiven the great sin of rebellion in heaven and brought again under the guidance of their heavenly spirits, after which they would wait in a "land of the living" for the time to rejoin the highest heaven. Then good and evil creations would again stand separate. Since this was foreordained, the concept of a final day of judgment had no foundation. The absolute dualists also agreed that the God of the Old Testament was the evil principle, but were willing to accept a considerable part of the book, especially the prophets.

Teachings about Christ differed not only between the absolute and mitigated schools of dualism but also from group to group within the latter. For absolute dualists, Christ was an angel who came into the world through the body of another angel, Mary. He never put on real human flesh nor had real contact with the evil material creation. For some mitigated dualists, Christ, Mary, and John the Evangelist were all angels. Others admitted that Mary was a woman and that Christ had taken real human flesh from her. Still others said that he put on a body which was human in appearance but composed of a substance different from that of men.[225]

Within each school of dualism there were varying interpretations of other dogmas, and early in the thirteenth century some Catharist theologians caused further dissension within Italian groups. Among the Concorezzenses, who were mitigated dualists, Desiderius, an elder son, taught for a time certain doctrines which approached orthodox Christianity: for example, that Christ really performed miracles and had a truly human body in which he actually died and rose again.[226] Among the Albanenses, absolute dualists, John of Lugio, also an elder son, developed his own interpretation of the absolute opposition of the good and evil principles and their realms, which were eternal. Creation, then, could mean only a change in the mode of existence, as from good to better. In the creatures of the good God there could be no free will because all things existed within his knowledge and could not be otherwise. John accepted the whole Bible as a true record of events which took place in a higher world created by the good God.[227] An important treatise, *The Book of the Two Principles* (translated in No. 59), preserves the defense of John of Lugio's system and his attacks on other Catharist groups.

In many ways, however, especially in the appearance they presented to the world, all Cathars agreed. They were united in rejecting the orthodox sacraments as worthless, the institutions of the Church as unsound, and its authority as without foundation. All followed the same ascetic regimen. They eschewed oaths and denied the right of the secular power to punish them. The devil was considered the prince of this world, and all its natural phenomena were his work. All Cathars used the same form of the consolamentum and repeated the Lord's Prayer with additions uncommon in Roman Catholic usage.

How are the Cathars to be interpreted? It is not unusual today to find Catharism characterized as a "sick" religion, promoting individual and collective suicide out of a profound pessimism. Yet in the surviving Catharist literature one searches in vain for expressions more morbid than the expectation of suffering in the world, as Christ had suffered. It has been said that success for the Cathars would have meant the dissolution of morality among men, would have spread anarchy and destroyed Western civilization. On the other hand, a group of modern partisans see in the Cathars a profound spirituality, and regard the world as poorer for their passing out of it. Was Catharism a rebellion against Roman Christianity or was it an alien religion? Contemporary descriptions so emphasize the rejection of the Church that they may obscure the positive elements of a faith capable of inspiring many martyrs.

If we could observe the Catharist Perfect through the eyes of a layman of their time, unversed in the niceties of dogma, we might be impressed by their appearance as zealous followers of Christ: the Gospels were their guide for conduct; their celibacy and their austerities were those of the monastic ideal; their criticism of the orthodox clergy was hardly more severe than that characteristic of other puritans and reformers; their disdain for the material world was rivaled by that of anchorites whose sanctity was revered by the Church. To this extent the Cathars were formed by the Western world of the Middle Ages.

Yet in fully developed Catharist dogma there are elements strange to the main currents of Western religious development, because the influence of Bogomilist cosmology in the mid-twelfth century led the Cathars beyond the essentially Christian asceticism of the earlier period to a total rejection of this world. And to reject the world entirely was to abandon the hope of transforming human life in this world, which is the basis of Christian evangelism. The extreme dualist doctrine was never adequately fused with the apostolic ideal. To the extent that these two elements—metaphysical rejection of the world and popular yearning to seek spiritual values in the world—remained unreconciled, Catharism as a system was weakened. Lacking a hierarchical unity, the Cathars never succeeded in harmonizing theology and cosmology with the popular piety out of which their movement grew. They were the products and the victims of the age-old desire to pursue a spiritual life in a world which places great difficulties in the way. In pursuit of purity they went beyond reform to rejection, refusing any compromise between spirit and flesh, good and evil, heavenly perfection and an imperfect world.[228]

The Waldenses

In the sources of the thirteenth century, a number of names for the followers of Waldes of Lyons are found. They liked to refer to themselves as the "Poor in Spirit." The Italians, who broke away from the French group in 1205, were known as "Poor Lombards" or "Runcarii," after their leader, John of Ronco; they called their French coreligionists "companions of Waldes," "ultramontanes," and "Waldenses." From the orginal name, "Poor of Lyons," were derived the shorter forms, "Lyonists," and "Leonists." In both groups, in allusion to the habit of wearing special sandals, terms such as "Sandal-wearers" were applied to their preachers, who also became known as the "Perfect."

After the Poor of Lyons were expelled from their native city and their movement expanded into Italy, Spain, and Germany, problems of organization led to disputes between the Waldenses in northern Italy and those in France which culminated in schism in 1205.[229] These factions developed other differences in dogma and practice, which they sought to reconcile at a conference held in 1218. They were able to come to agreement about the election of leaders within the groups, baptism in water, the question of dissolving a marriage when one of the partners wished to take up the ascetic life of a preacher, and the right of the Lombards to continue their tutelage of communities of pious laborers. But the reverence of the French party for Waldes, who had died at some time after 1205, was too excessive for the Lombards, and the Poor of Lyons advocated greater leniency toward the qualifications of a priest than the Lombards would accept.[230] The attempt at unity failed, and each group retained its individuality thereafter, although both remained faithful in principle to the fundamentals of poverty and preaching established by Waldes.[231]

For all groups of Waldenses in the early thirteenth century, the apostolic life was all-important. Apostolicism led them to reject the authority of the Roman hierarchy as ill-founded and unnecessary. The Roman Church, they declared, had strayed from the true path when Pope Sylvester I accepted the Donation of Constantine.[232] The Poor of Lyons were more willing to accept the ministry of Catholic priests of good life than were the Lombards. In the early years of the thirteenth century, both the Poor Lombards and the Poor of Lyons held that only an ordained priest could consecrate the Eucharist, baptize, or hear confessions. After 1218, this restriction was gradually amended, more rapidly among the Poor of Lyons, and in the second half of the century it was admitted that any good man or woman could consecrate the Eucharist. This was done once a year, on Holy Thursday, when, in the presence of an assemblage of the faithful, the priest consecrated the bread and wine by multiple repetitions of the Lord's Prayer and the sign of the Cross.[233]

Over the years, the sandal-shod preachers assumed the status of priests among the Waldenses. The Lombards allowed them a kind of penitential power called "giving good advice"; other Waldenses permitted only a prayer that God would forgive the sinner. The Poor of Lyons were more extreme in their dislike of marriage, the Lombards more insistent that the separation of married couples be permitted only with the full consent of both persons. The Poor Lombards were more tolerant of the possession of property in their earlier years than were the Poor of Lyons, but in the course of the thirteenth century they moved back again to the affirmation, established by Waldes and preserved by the Poor of Lyons, that the sandal-wearer must live in apostolic poverty.[234]

All Waldenses agreed that men and women of holy life who lived in poverty could preach with full authority. Oaths and lies were forbidden and it was believed to be a sin to kill anyone, even in executing a penalty prescribed by lawful authority.[235] Toward the middle of the thirteenth century unorthodox ideas about the creation of bodies and about the souls of men appeared in France, according to one inquisitor, who said that "almost all" the Poor of Lyons believed that God had formed men in bodies of clay and breathed life into them. The soul was thus considered to be the Holy Spirit and part of God. Any good man shares in divinity and may be called the son of God, and in his life are repeated the incarnation, birth, martyrdom, and resurrection of Christ. The concept of the Trinity was modified accordingly: The Father is he who inspires good, the Son is whoever is converted to good, the Holy Spirit is the agency of conversion.[236] It is not assured, however, that these beliefs were, in fact, widely accepted.

At all times, the Waldenses continued to emphasize the reading of the Scriptures and preaching. Even simple laymen learned whole books of the Bible by heart. Bibles in the vernacular and collections of excerpts from the writings of the Church Fathers had been used from the first, and sometimes schools were established for training preachers.[237]

Waldensian communities also underwent changes in administrative organization during the thirteenth century. After Waldes's death, all communities chose officials to handle their affairs. In 1218, the Poor Lombards had twelve officials elected for life, while the Poor of Lyons chose two annually.[238] By the early fourteenth century, the Poor of Lyons were choosing one elected head, elected for life, who presided over all affairs, while delegates from various localities met every year to discuss matters of common concern. The communities who elected these officials probably consisted only of those who had chosen to follow the apostolic life in every respect, for a formal distinction had emerged between the preachers, now called Perfect, and their adherents, known as "believers" or "friends," who accepted baptism from the Perfect and heard their instruction, but lived in the world and were free to marry and to own property.

The Perfect were ordained by the imposition of the hands of their fellows after a period of probation and instruction, during which they took the vows of poverty, chastity, and obedience. There were three elective orders among the Perfect: bishops, priests, and deacons. The first two could preach, hear confessions, and celebrate the Eucharist, but the deacons, acting as their assistants, did not have sacramental powers. The Perfect usually lived in houses of two or three men and two or three women together, following a routine of prayer, religious instruction, and visitation of the hostels where aged members of the sect were cared for. They also traveled about to preach to believers in their villages and to hear their confessions. These functions were their whole concern, for they were supported entirely by the contributions of the faithful.[239] Thus, by the fourteenth century the Waldenses had developed from an informal society of preachers dedicated to poverty into an ecclesiastical organization which continued to emphasize the original ideals but restricted preaching to a special group.

It may seem that the Waldenses adopted some things from other heretical sects. It is indeed likely that the Poor of Lyons in their early years were influenced by the anticlerical ideas disseminated in southern France by Peter of Bruys and Henry. It may be that pantheistic doctrines, such as those accepted by the Amalricians, came to have some influence among the Waldenses of northern Europe, and among the Poor Lombards the doctrine of generation of souls from souls was probably Catharist in origin. For the most part, resemblances between the Waldenses and the Cathars fall in the area of ritual, such as the emphasis on the Lord's Prayer, and these similarities may be ascribed to coincidence rather than imitation. The Waldensian practice when they ordained their Perfect, for example, may have been as much inspired by the orthodox ceremonies for ordaining priests as by the consolamentum,[240] or it might have come from very close attention to the Gospels and the Acts of the Apostles.

The question arises, Were the Waldenses pre-Reformation Protestants, as some Protestant and Catholic scholars have asserted in the past? It is difficult to support this, for Waldes had far more in common with Francis of Assisi than with Luther or Calvin. The circumstances of the twelfth century were not those of the sixteenth; the initial impetus of apostolicism and poverty was thoroughly medieval, and the Waldenses did not until the fifteenth century completely sever their ties with the Roman Church, despite the fierce criticism which they launched against it for the departure of its hierarchy from the apostolic tradition.

Other Sects

About other sects of the time fewer details are available than for the Waldenses and the Cathars. The Passagians and the other "Judaizers," who stressed observance of the Old Testament Law, must have had a priesthood, but nothing is known of their formal organization. The Amalricians of Paris—whose doctrines sprang, as has been said, from a mixture of pantheism and the Joachimite theory of the three ages of the world—declared that God was everywhere in all creation; furthermore, they held that the Father had been incarnate in Abraham, the Son in Christ through Mary, and now, as the third age began, the Holy Spirit was incarnate in themselves. The perfect freedom with which they were thus endowed meant repudiation of all formal religious institutions and law. No hierarchy was needed. One of the group was known as a "prophet" and apparently was their chief spokesman, although any of the company might experience visions which would be recounted in their private meetings. At least one Catholic priest taught some of their ideas to his parishioners.[241]

New sects which came into being at the end of the thirteenth century and in the early years of the fourteenth put great stress on preaching and poverty as the foundation of holy life, but did not forego settled community existence. The "pseudo-Apostles," led by Gerard Segarelli and Dolcino of Novara, taught that holy poverty was the only perfect state, one in which all human restraints on religious expressions were lifted. The Roman Church had no authority over them, for theirs was the power that Christ had given to Peter, and in them was the only true Church. Repentance and poverty as a way of life made churches, monasteries, and legal institutions unnecessary. In the ceremony to become an apostle the initiate, after suitable instruction, shed all clothing, as a token of his renunciation of property; donned semimonastic garb, as a symbol of his new profession; and then, under oath to live in complete poverty, was free to preach anywhere and everywhere.[242]

The ideal of poverty, which had become a point of controversy within the Franciscan order at the beginning of the fourteenth century, inspired the sect of Beguins[243] in southern France. Men and women who were attracted by the teaching of the Spiritual Franciscans formed associations dedicated to upholding the original rule of Francis as the first law of life, accepting the dictum of the Spirituals that truly holy life forbids the possession of property in any form, individually or collectively. For them

St. Francis was the perfect Christian, and Brother Peter John Olivi (d. 1298) of the Spiritual faction was a prophet who had received God's revelation of things to come. From him the Beguins accepted the Joachimite doctrine of the three ages. The world, they believed, was now approaching the seventh and last subdivision of the second age, in which a cataclysm would herald the coming of the Antichrist, whose servant the Roman Church had plainly shown itself to be, in the eyes of the Beguins, by condemning the advocates of complete poverty within the Franciscan order. Soon would dawn the third age, that of the Holy Spirit. The Beguins referred to themselves as "Brethren of Penitence," wore simple, drab clothing, and lived quietly in their own homes or in "houses of poverty," where men and women conducted services of prayer and the reading of devotional works in the vernacular. In Italy, groups of somewhat similar character were called "Little Brothers" (*Fraticelli*), a term very loosely used and apparently applied to many rebellious anticlerical dissenters in the turbulent fourteenth century.[244]

Such were some aspects of heretical sects of the thirteenth and early fourteenth centuries. The remainder of this Introduction will be devoted to a survey of the source materials from which the translations were chosen.

Sources for the History of the Heresies

The historian of medieval heresy must utilize several kinds of sources, of varying quality. Annals and chronicles, letters, biographies, sermons, and more-or-less conventional types of other records have information to offer, as do the enactments of councils, papal letters, and documents produced by the Inquisition. Of greatest value and meriting most attention here is the literature directly inspired by heresy—that is, the works produced by the heretics themselves and the writings of those who sought to controvert heresy.

ORTHODOX LITERATURE

Annals, Chronicles, and Histories

For the eleventh and early twelfth centuries, monastic or episcopal annals and the chronicles provide a considerable part of the information about incidents of heresy, but, generally speaking, even the best of these is of limited value.[1] Information came rather haphazardly to most compilers of these historical records, and nearby events might be ignored, while news which had traveled some distance was recorded.[2] When connected with an important event, however, such as the actions of a monarch or the session of a church council, heresy might draw widespread attention.[3] The quality of historical writing improved rapidly in the twelfth century, and erudite and well-informed observers like John of Salisbury, who left a revealing portrait of Arnold of Brescia,[4] were capable of discussing men and events with insight and clarity; it may be thought regrettable that John and his contemporary, the great historian Otto of Freising, did not add to their interest in speculative and philosophical issues a greater concern with the popular heretical sects.[5] There is historical writing of good quality on the Albigensian Crusade, as in the chronicle of Peter of Vaux-de-Cernay.[6] Yet on the whole, if there were only such narrative sources to depend on, a map could be made of outbreaks of heresy and a record could be compiled of attempts to suppress it, but knowledge of heretical doctrines would be scant.

In connection with the historical narratives, mention may be made here of compilers of anecdotes such as Walter Map, Caesarius of Heisterbach, and Stephen of Bourbon. Map wrote to entertain court circles; Caesarius and Stephen collected stories to instruct monks and preachers; but all knew how to tell a story well. They were alert for tales they could use, but, like the annalist and chroniclers, they relished the unusual, so that in their pages are found comments which may be taken to reveal something of the "folk attitudes" toward heresy.[7]

Autobiography and Biography

Perhaps the most noteworthy autobiography of the Middle Ages, that of Guibert of Nogent, contains the recital of his encounter with heretics and reveals the preconceptions about heresy in the mind of an intelligent, well-educated man.[8] Hagiographers, on the other hand, being primarily concerned with evidence of the sanctity of their subjects, seldom recorded material of any great value to us, as may be illustrated by the short account taken from a typical life of a saint of twelfth-century Italy.[9] More revealing is another passage, drawn from the biography of Bernard of Clairvaux by his one-time secretary Geoffrey of Auxerre;[10] but, in general, biographical works do not contain much that is useful for our purpose.[11]

Letters

Letters, being relatively abundant, constitute a valuable group of sources about heresy, especially in the twelfth and thirteenth centuries. As evidence they must be used with no less care than any other document, but letters so often recount personal experience that they convey a sense of life and participation in the events of which they speak. Churchmen wrote to seek advice from colleagues or to give it; they reported to superiors or sought to warn fellow Christians about heresy.[12] By letters, Bernard of Clairvaux harried Arnold of Brescia throughout Europe and urged secular powers to assist the Church.[13] Some polemical tracts also took the form of letters.[14]

The voluminous papal correspondence has been drawn on less for this volume than might be expected because popes often referred to heresy without being explicit about the doctrines involved,[15] although their letters are indispensable for knowledge of affairs which fall outside our immediate concern: elucidation of official policies toward heresy, decisions on individual cases, definition of inquisitorial powers, and the like. For certain times and places, as in Italian cities of the late twelfth century, letters of the popes constitute the chief evidence that heresy was a problem.[16]

A unique document is the letter reporting a conference which sought to heal the schism between two factions in the Waldensian movement, one of the few documents to have survived from a Waldensian milieu of the thirteenth century.[17]

Sermons

Although forceful methods, ranging from formal investigation and judicial condemnation to lynching, were used against heretics from the earliest years, there was also a persistent desire to protect the faithful by proper instruction in religion and, if possible, to convert those who were in error. Preaching was the chosen method for both. Preaching against heresy was advocated and practiced ever more widely in the twelfth century,[18] and in the early thirteenth century special missions preached in the areas most affected,[19] their example inducing converts to continue the same work.[20] Celebrated individuals in the mendicant orders, such as the Dominican Peter of Verona and the Franciscan "hammer of heretics," Anthony of Padua, were acclaimed by their biographers for their public sermons against heresy, although their miracles rather than their choice of words are usually given credit for their successes.[21]

Not many of the actual sermons have survived:[22] We know one homily of Ralph the Ardent from the second half of the twelfth century[23] and three sermons in the series on the Canticles, written somewhat earlier by Bernard of Clairvaux.[24] Philip of Grève, chancellor of Paris (1218-1236), several times spoke of heresy.[25]. Otherwise, the sermon collections do not disclose much that is pertinent to our present purpose. Nor have the texts of the argumentative discourses—as much sermons as debates—which resulted from the occasional confrontations of Catholic and heretical spokesmen, survived. Delivered under conditions which militated against their being recorded, they have left only traces in the narratives about the Cistercian preaching mission in Languedoc[26] or the early days of the mendicant orders, or in the lists of biblical texts sometimes gathered in a summa against heresy.[27]

Conciliar and Synodal Records

Synods and regional and general councils of the Church dealt with heresy from the first years of the eleventh century. At first treated as a local phenomenon, by the twelfth century heresy was recognized as a problem of larger scale, and in the ecumenical councils of 1179 and 1215 the fundamental policies of the Church were stated. Of conciliar enactments in general, it may be said that they are important in showing the awareness of heresy and for tracing the evolution of ecclesiastical policy, but the canons seldom illuminate the nature of the heretical doctrines. Only a phrase or two may be devoted to the points at issue or the areas of danger;[28] often only names of sects are preserved in lists which became stereotyped in the thirteenth century.[29] There were exceptions under special circumstances: The conversion of heretics in a synod at Arras in 1025, a debate between heretics and Catholics at Lombers in 1165, the profession of faith of Waldes at Lyons about 1180, and a condemnation of the Amalricians at Paris in 1210 are included in this volume.[30]

Inquisitorial Records

Much of the record of the transactions of the Inquisition has been lost; of what survives, only a part has been put in print. Two valuable guides to the manuscript materials were produced by Charles Molinier.[31] Depositions and sentences from the years 1244 to 1267 were published by Monsignor Célestin Douais;[32] the documents from a special investigation at Albi at the end of the thirteenth century were published by Georgene W. Davis.[33] Philip van Limborch published the sentences of Bernard Gui,[34] and J. J. I. von Döllinger made copious but careless extracts from many inquisitorial records.[35] The printed and manuscript sources have been drawn on by historians of heresy and the Inquisition in works too numerous to list,[36] but they have been little utilized for the translations in this volume.

Polemical Treatises

By the middle of the twelfth century, alarm at the prevalence of heresy stimulated the desire for effective counteraction. A fundamental problem was lack of detailed knowledge of the adversaries, a difficulty

that became more acute with the spread of dualist sects and the proliferation of the various ascetic and reforming groups after mid-century. At
the same time, the development of orthodox popular preaching as a
defense against the incursions heretics were making among the people
required the education of preachers in the nature of heresy and the
terms in which it might be rebutted. Such instruction was provided by
polemical treatises, which appeared in increasing numbers. Later, in the
operations of the Inquisition, the need to identify heretics and the necessity of having a basis on which to construct suitable interrogatories
added to the incentives of controversialist writers. There came into
being a literature specifically devoted to heresy, made up of *summae
contra haereticos*, treatises describing doctrinal errors and offering arguments against them. That they were useful to contemporaries is obvious,
and today they furnish the most substantial body of information available for the study of medieval heresy.

The polemical literature falls into three fairly distinct groupings.
Some tracts are "full-scale" in that they not only describe heresy and
the arguments of its partisans—a few are elaborate analyses of heretical
mythology, theology, and methods of biblical exegesis—but also provide
refutation of these arguments and give major attention to explaining the
scriptural and philosophical basis of orthodox doctrine.[37] Others are
composed only of materials useful for the defense of orthodox doctrines,
and neglect the description of heresy or heretical arguments; at their
simplest, these are no more than lists of biblical texts assembled under
appropriate headings for the use of preachers who wished to encourage
the faithful and forewarn them against heretical ideas.[38] A third type
includes tracts which describe heresy without attempting a rebuttal.
Some of these are manifestoes with alarmist overtones; others are careful
accounts giving descriptions which would have been of considerable
utility to episcopal officials and inquisitors. Several were, in fact, written
by inquisitors.

In content and style the polemical literature reflects how knowledge
of heresy was acquired and disseminated among the literate. Some
pieces, in the form of debates, show the influence of face-to-face disputation, which at first occurred freely in public or took place during
interrogations of suspects—events which became far less frequent as
prosecution grew more intense and the Inquisition adopted the rule that
no disputation with heretics under examination was desirable. Some

authors acquired information from the writings of heretics themselves. Confessions of converts and systematic interrogation of prisoners produced data in increasing amounts in the thirteenth century.

Not all the authors of the polemics were churchmen; some laymen were eager to wield the pen in defense of the faith. Nor was the controversy only two-sided. Discoveries of recent years have emphasized the controversies between the Waldenses and the Cathars. That the two sects were inveterate enemies has long been known,[39] as has also the career of Durand of Huesca, who left the Waldenses to return to the Church and thereafter undertook to combat all heresy. But hitherto unnoticed polemical works written by Durand against the Cathars have recently been discovered, and the attribution of a long-known tract to his companion, Ermengaud of Béziers, has been confirmed. Thus there is disclosed a "school" of controversialists, Waldenses who became Poor Catholics, and who, before and after their reconciliation, were active in debate with the Cathars.[40] Their polemical techniques differed little from those of other contemporaries.

More than half of the tracts which survive were written between 1200 and 1250. About a third of the total number attacked only the Cathars; nearly twice as many deal with both Cathars and Waldenses. In about half a dozen of them other heresies are mentioned; one or two sects, in fact, are known to us only from these sources.

The popularity and usefulness of the polemical treatises in their own day may be roughly reckoned from the number of manuscripts of them which have survived. Most are known today in two to four copies; but for one of them there are twenty-eight manuscripts, for another thirty-two, and there are more than fifty exemplars of another.[41] But how valid is the evidence that this literature provides? How much can be accepted of the descriptions of heresies in these avowedly hostile sources? Scholars have not been in agreement on the question.[42] That substantially the same statement about a sect may be found in several different treatises has led some historians to conclude that the treatises corroborate each other and that the evidence is reliable[43] but other investigators have argued that the orthodox view of the heretics was stereotyped.[44] Some of the similarities appear because one author borrowed from another, or both worked from a common source.[45] Many of the polemics, too, neglect the diversity within Catharism and other sects, although we know from a variety of sources that none of the important popular heresies conformed to a single mold, that none had a unity or rigidity of doctrine such as a centralized organization might have encouraged. The Catholic controversialists, it has been argued, oversimplified the doctrines of their opponents, attributing to them a system that was not actually there.[46] It has been stated that the testimony of polemicists is corroborated by that elicited from witnesses by inquisitors; yet it may be replied that the interrogations themselves could have been based on misconceptions derived from the polemical literature. A further problem arises from the attitude of Catholic writers, who treated heresy only as negation of Christian orthodoxy, although surely none of the great heresies drew its strength from denial alone.[47] Thus is posed a problem of historical criticism. Even the recent discoveries of heretical writings allow the evidence of hostile witnesses to be tested against the words of the heretics themselves for only a few of the points at issue. But it seems possible to use at least some of the polemics with moderate assurance. Those ought to be considered most reliable which are devoted primarily to description, which are least strident in denunciation, and of whose authors enough is known to establish their personal qualifications and their exposure to the subject.[48]

To select for translation a few items from the many that are available was a problem. The aims were to provide the fullest information about heresy and to illustrate the variety of the polemical works. To meet the first objective, documents which emphasize description rather than argument were given preference. Some repetition of information was inevitable. To show variety, relatively short excerpts were taken from a number of polemics. In addition, since relatively few of this valuable category of sources could be drawn on, a list of polemical tracts is provided in the Appendix.

THE LITERATURE OF THE HERETICS

The works which the heretics of the Middle Ages wrote, read, or discussed have been harshly handled by time and men. Destruction of heretical literature by implacable and victorious opponents was a natural consequence of the spirit in which religious controversies were waged, and although book-burning has seldom been able to eradicate a literature completely, scholars supposed until quite recently that most of the writings of heretics had disappeared with the triumph of the Church.

The question, How much heretical literature was there in the Middle Ages? may be asked, but without hope of a definitive answer. One can reasonably say that a great deal more was written than has survived. But since search has recovered some of what once was presumed lost, we may hope that still more will be found and identified.

Although there is evidence that at least a limited number of documents were produced by heretics in the eleventh and twelfth centuries, no literary remains of the popular heresies before the end of the twelfth century are known today, with the exception of the apocryphal works imported from the Bogomils at about that time and used by the Cathars.[49] What we do have are indefinite references to some written works. The teaching of the heretic Henry may have been written down by a disciple, as it was by an opponent.[50] Eudo of Brittany is said to have had some "little writings" which were produced at his trial in 1148.[51] Hugo Speroni, as was to be expected of a man of education, recorded his convictions in a book which has disappeared.[52] Heretics at Toulouse in 1178 produced a written statement of their faith, to prove its orthodoxy,[53] and the spokesmen for the Poor of Lyons showed the pope at the Third Lateran Council a book containing the Psalms, a gloss on them, and several books of the Old and New Testaments.[54] Mlle Thouzellier believes that Durand of Huesca wrote his *Liber Antiheresis* attacking the Cathars and extolling the teaching of Waldes at least as early as the last decade of the twelfth century.[55] Such is the evidence of heretical literature before 1200. For later years there is much more.

The Waldenses and Minor Sects

The Waldenses—at least, before the late fourteenth century—were less prolific in religious writing than the Cathars, perhaps because of their insistence on propaganda by word of mouth and by example and because they labored among the humbler folk.[56] Their emphasis on Bible reading is reflected in some surviving manuscripts of vernacular translations of the Scriptures,[57] and we hear of their using the Gospels, the Psalter, Gregory the Great's *Moralia* on Job,[58] and excerpts from patristic literature which they called "sentences"; in the fourteenth century they had compilations of their articles of faith.[59] Perhaps some documents relative to their internal affairs were circulated, for Moneta of Cremona knew the theories of a Poor Lombard on the controversial question of Waldes's right to leadership.[60] These views caused such a stir that it seems likely they had been spread in written form, although it is possible that Moneta knew them from the letter which the Poor Lombards wrote to their German colleagues. Otherwise, apart from Waldes's profession of faith, which was not entirely original with him, and the works of controversy against the Cathars by Waldenses or ex-Waldenses, already referred to, it is only from later centuries that any considerable body of Waldensian literature has been preserved.[61]

As for other sects, the short-lived group of Amalricians at Paris in the first decade of the thirteenth century was undoubtedly literate. But the only reference to writings other than those of Amalric of Bena, now lost, is in the decree condemning the group, which requires all persons to surrender to the bishop theological works in the vernacular—copies of the Creed, the Lord's Prayer, and lives of the saints—under pain of being condemned as heretics for possessing them.[62] A century later it was said that the Beguins had a considerable number of vernacular works discussing their particular doctrines, and Peter John Olivi, of course, was a prolific writer.[63]

The Cathars

The Cathars of the thirteenth century, without neglecting preaching, lived with books, for they attracted members from the social classes apt to be literate.[64] There are references to their own schools[65] as well as to their practice of sending qualified persons to study at the great universities.[66] They knew and used apocrypha from the remote or recent past, they studied the Scriptures and preached from them, they explained and defended their doctrines in writing. These general facts have long been known from statements of their adversaries. It is only since 1939 that their literary activity can be evaluated from their own writings, although what relation the Catharist works which have now been discovered bear to the total that once existed is still a question for scholars to debate.[67] On the present evidence we may attempt to classify their written works tentatively into certain types and to sketch the general characteristics of these types.

Bibles. Latin and vernacular copies of the Gospels and Epistles, the Psalter, and other portions of the Holy Scriptures were in common use. There is no longer any question of the version; it was based on the Vulgate tradition rather than derived, as sometimes has been suggested, from some Eastern version or a pre-Jerome translation.[68] Vernacular translations were desirable for religious instruction of the believers and were circulated among them in southern France; we may assume the same of Lombardy and elsewhere.[69] In retrospect, one can see that the attempt by the Church to ban vernacular translations of the Scriptures in order to prevent the Cathars and Waldenses from making use of them was an attempt to dam a torrent with twigs.[70]

In this connection the prayers of the Cathars may be mentioned. The Lord's Prayer was always said in Latin, as was the Gospel of John in the ritual of the consolamentum; but the Lord's Prayer might be glossed, and other prayers recited, in the vernacular.[71]

Apocryphal Works. The Cathars' use of *The Vision of Isaiah* and *The Secret Supper* in their "Bogomil editions" is commented on in more detail in the introductions to these pieces, Number 56. These borrowed works, which reached the West probably not before the very end of the twelfth century, were used to confirm or illustrate Catharist teaching, rather than as a source of dogma. That the Cathars also drew on other legendary and apocryphal writings has been suggested but not demonstrated.[72] Luke, bishop of Tuy, remarks on the activities of a heretic named Arnold, from Gascony or Languedoc, a very skilled copyist, who was in the habit of counterfeiting the works of the Fathers by introducing heretical propositions therein, to the discomfiture of the clergy and faithful in the kingdom of Leon.[73] Can there be a reference here to copies of apocryphal works?

Creeds and Professions of Faith. Statements of faith which at first glance seemed to be unobjectionably orthodox were sometimes prepared, perhaps to deceive prosecutors, or as the first steps in religious propaganda among the people. Heretics appeared before a mission in Toulouse in 1178 with such a credo, its content perhaps analogous to the first chapter of the "Manichaean" treatise which will be referred to in the next paragraph. Some general circulation of such documents is hinted at elsewhere: In the early fourteenth century, the heretic James Autier possessed an exposition in Latin of creation by God, in which one who read it found nothing contrary to the orthodox faith;[74] and Peter Autier promised to send to a believer a book in which he would find "good words" to tell him of the right beliefs.[75]

Discussions of Doctrine. Treatises for use in instruction or as polemics are known through certain references to them and from two which have survived: A "Manichaean" treatise of about 1220, written in Lan-

guedoc, and *The Book of the Two Principles,* written in Lombardy in
the middle years of the thirteenth century (translated in Nos. 58 and 59,
respectively). The first of these is no less important because it has been
preserved only in part—Durand of Huesca copied extracts from it into
his treatise of refutation and designated it as a Manichaean work. It is
devoted to an exposition of absolute dualism, with adroit use of the Bible
to convey its message and support its contentions. *The Book of the Two
Principles,* if not written by John of Lugio himself, was produced within
the circle of his followers among the Albanenses after 1230.[76] Although
rather harsh judgments of its quality have been made,[77] this remains
our chief monument of Catharist theology. Comparison of the concepts
in these two works and of their use of the Scriptures reveals a community of ideas among the Albigenses of southern France and some of
the Albanenses of Italy.

Of more restricted scope, but most revealing of the Cathars' view of
themselves and their church, are the discourses to initiates preserved in
the rituals which they used (see No. 57) and another little treatise, *A
Vindication of the Church of God* (No. 60, part A). This treatise and
one of the rituals were written in Provençal dialects; the other ritual is
in Latin. The point of view expressed in the rituals is exactly reproduced
in *A Vindication of the Church of God:* the Cathars saw themselves as
true Christians, their morality as that of Christ and the apostles. Still
another document in Provençal, in the form of a commentary on the
Lord's Prayer, reveals a mystical, Neo-Gnostic concept of the means of
salvation (No. 60, part B). It has in common with other pieces of
Catharist authorship the acceptance of absolute dualism, a reference to
The Vision of Isaiah, and the use of some phrases important to the
Cathars (e.g., "people of God"), but neither the time nor place of its
origin can be suggested with any assurance.

Works of Unknown Character. There are a number of references to
heretical works which give very little clue to their contents. On occasion
the heretics of southern France, like their Cistercian opponents, summarized the arguments made in open debates in little written compen-
diums for consideration by judges of these theological jousts.[78] A layman
of Piacenza, Salvo Burci, wrote a reply to a heretical work which was
circulating in that city under the title *Stella.*[79] Peter Gallus, a heretical
bishop of Lombardy, is presumed to have written a treatise known to
the inquisitor Peter of Verona and to Albert the Great.[80] Luke of Tuy

refers to a heretical *Perpendiculum scientiarum* which presented the scriptural basis for their faith.[81] Moneta of Cremona among his other sources had before him the writings of two heretics whom he named. One, Tetricus, was a proponent of absolute dualism; his treatise was of some length, for Moneta identifies a passage as appearing in the eleventh chapter of one of its divisions. All we know of its content through Moneta is that Tetricus discussed the antiquity of the angelic creation, the identification of fallen angels as souls of men (which, he held, were never created *de novo* by God), and the proper method (taking the literal sense) of interpreting the prophecies of the Old Testament.[82] The other heresiarch was Desiderius, leader of a schism among the Concorezzenses, mitigated dualists of Lombardy.[83] An Albigensian teacher claimed to have many works describing the role of Lucifer in the struggle between good and evil,[84] and there was some trade in the writings of the heretics.[85] And as our last bit of evidence we may refer to the tantalizing story told by Stephen of Bourbon about Robert, dauphin of Auvergne, marquis of Montferrand (d. 1234). Robert was a poet and for forty years had collected books of all the heretical sects. To friars who investigated this interest of his, he explained that he sought out the heretical books so that by reading them his own loyalty to the Church would be encouraged and he might learn how to refute their errors. His contempt for heresy, he declared, was shown by the fact that he kept the volumes in a box in his chamber, so that they would be under his feet in his most private moments. But discretion overcame curiosity, and Robert had all the offensive works burned.[86]

One more category of sources must be mentioned. It has been alleged that Catharist thought is expressed in some of the poems of the troubadours, in the medieval versions of the Arthurian cycle, and especially in the legends of the quest for the Holy Grail. The search for traces of Catharism in such literature has been pressed with enthusiasm but has not produced convincing results.[87]

A Note on the Translations

The documents translated in this volume come from the eleventh, twelfth, and thirteenth centuries, with the following exceptions: Two apocryphal works borrowed by the Cathars from the Bogomils (No. 56) were composed before A.D. 1000; Bernard Gui's manual for inquisitors (No. 55) dates from 1323-1324; and the date of a Provençal commentary on the Lord's Prayer (No. 60, part B) is conjectural.

These were the criteria for our choice of materials for translation: All known major works of heretical authorship were to be included.[1] In selections from other sources, the objectives were to illustrate as many aspects of heretical doctrines as possible and, at the risk of redundancy, to show the diversities within the major heretical movements; to indicate something of the origin of the available sources in time and place, thereby to show when and where the heresies attracted attention; and to give examples of the kind of literature produced in the religious controversy. To the last stated aim, however, there is an important exception: sources which pertain primarily to the repression of heresy, as far as these can be differentiated from others, were seldom drawn on. Of course, the report of heresy is often a report of action against it, but omitted here are the records of ecclesiastical or secular legislation, documents dealing primarily with the establishment or operations of the Inquisition, and narratives of the crusades against the Albigenses, the Stedingers, or the Fraticelli.

The translations are arranged generally in chronological order, although the date of several pieces is difficult to fix accurately. We have placed narrative passages according to the year of the event's occurrence and descriptive or polemical works according to the date of composition, with some exceptions, as for Nos. 24 and 33. The documents are arranged in four general divisions. In the first are the earliest substantial

descriptions of heresy from the late tenth century to about the middle
of the twelfth. Then follow others carrying the story to the end of the
pontificate of Innocent III (1216), a time when heresies were still expanding but the Church was mustering its forces strongly against them.
Here the profusion of materials suggested three subdivisions of sources,.
relating to Italy, southern France, and northern Europe, respectively.
A third group contains works produced from about 1216 to 1324. All
of the pieces so far mentioned were written by orthodox authors, with
the exception of a letter (No. 46) which originated among the Waldenses. Last among the translations come works written by the Cathars,.
together with two apocrypha they received from the Bogomils.

In putting the texts into English, we considered fidelity to the original
to be of first importance, sometimes, perhaps, at the expense of the
readability which a freer rendering would allow. For biblical quotations,.
the language of the Douay-Rheims translation (Challoner's revision) of
the Vulgate is used, with these exceptions: For personal and place
names, the more familiar forms from the Authorized Version are used;
for general vocabulary, American orthography is used to correspond to
the style of the rest of the text; and on occasion the archaic terms or
expressions of the Douay translation are replaced with the more familiar
terms from the Authorized Version, attention being called to such sub-
stitutions in the notes. "Holy Spirit" is used throughout in place of the
"Holy Ghost" of the Douay-Rheims. The words of the source are
followed when they differ from the Vulgate, but the difference is mentioned in the notes only when it is extreme or significant to the meaning
of the passage. In general, modern English equivalents for medieval
personal and place names are used, except where such usage would be
unfamiliar and confusing.

The introduction and notes to each translated piece seek to place the
document in its historical context, identify persons and places mentioned
in the piece, offer some discussion of any unusual terminology, and
refer to the scholarly investigations which have made this work possible.
Scarcely one of the sources has escaped being the subject of dispute in
some particular. It may be the duty of the translator to call attention
to such differences of learned opinion without becoming involved in
them. It is not one that we have always been able to carry out.

Early Appearances of the Heresies in Western Europe

1. Early Traces of Heresy in France, Italy, and Spain

Two narratives of popular heresy recounted by Ralph the Bald (*Radulphus Glaber*) are given here in the order in which Ralph presents them, although the second probably antedates the first by some two decades. As far as can be discerned from the scanty evidence, the motivation and aims of the central figures—the peasant of Châlons and the scholar of Ravenna—were very different, and the significance of their views, particularly those of the former, is open to various interpretations, chiefly on the question of Bogomil influence.[1] Yet both of these episodes show currents running in the West: the first, ascetic piety; the second, enthusiasm for learning. It was the first of these motives which became more evident and important in other instances of heresy in the following half-century.

Ralph the Bald wrote his history presumably during some two decades in the second quarter of the eleventh century, dedicating it to Odilo, abbot of Cluny—one of the several monastic communities of which Ralph was a member at one time or another. Both the facts of Ralph's life and the credibility of his narrative have been the subject of scholarly dispute. He certainly shared with contemporaries a belief in miracles, signs, and wonders, and looked forward to the imminent end of the world, but intelligence and a lively curiosity are also displayed in his work, with an interest in drawing meaning from the events which are recounted. Although Ralph's knowledge of heresy was vague and fragmentary, there seems to be no good reason to question the honesty of his references to it.

The best discussion of the incidents described here is in Ilarino da Milano, "Le eresie popolari," in *Studi Gregoriani*, II, 46-49. See also Russell, *Dissent and Reform*, pp. 110-13. The Introduction to Prou's edition of Ralph the Bald's history assembles most of what is known of Ralph, but one may also consult Paul Rousset, "Raoul Glaber, interprète de la pensée commune au XIe siècle," *Revue d'histoire de l'église de France*, XXXVI (1950), 5-24.

The two selections which follow are translated, by permission of Editions A. and J. Picard, from *Raoul Glaber: Les cinq livres de ses histoires* II.xi,xii, ed. by Maurice Prou (Collection de textes pour servir à l'étude et à l'enseignement de l'histoire, I [Paris, 1866]), pp. 49-50.

A. LEUTARD AND THE BEES

circa 1000

About the end of the year 1000 there appeared in Gaul, in a village called Vertus, in the district of Châlons, a peasant named Leutard.[2] As the outcome of the matter proved, he could well be regarded as an emissary of Satan. His stubborn insanity began like this: He was once laboring alone in a field and had just about finished a piece of work when, wearied by his exertions, he fell asleep and it seemed to him that a great swarm of bees entered his body through his privates. These same bees, as they made their way out through his mouth with a loud noise, tormented him by their stings; and after he had been greatly vexed in this fashion for some time, they seemed to speak to him, bidding him to do things impossible to men.[3]

At length, he arose exhausted and went home. He sent away his wife as though he effected the separation by command of the Gospel; then going forth, he entered the church as if to pray, seized and broke to bits the cross and image of the Savior. Those who watched this trembled with fear, thinking him to be mad, as he was; and since rustics are prone to fall into error, he persuaded them that these things were done by a miraculous revelation from God.

But he indulged too much in empty words, devoid of utility or truth, and in his desire to appear learned, he taught the opposite of a master of learning, for he said it was altogether needless and foolish to give tithes. And just as other heresies cloak themselves with the Holy Scriptures which they contradict, so that they may practice more wily deception, he too declared that the prophets had set forth some useful things and some not to be believed. In a short time, his fame, as if it were that of a sane and religious person, drew to him no small part of the common people.

But the most erudite Gebuin [4]—the elderly bishop in whose diocese the man lived—on learning of this, commanded that the man be brought before him. When the bishop had questioned Leutard about those things which, according to report, he had said and done, the man began to conceal the poison of his wickedness, wishing that he had not presumed to take on himself the interpretation of the Holy Scriptures. But the very wise bishop, hearing unseemly things—nay, rather what was indeed base and damnable—made it clear that the lunatic had become a heretic; he recalled the partly deluded people from insanity and reinstated them more firmly in the Catholic faith.[5] But Leutard, realizing that he had been completely overcome and deprived of the adulation of the people, threw himself to his death in a well.

B. VILGARD AT RAVENNA, AND OTHER DISTURBANCES

circa 970

At that time [6] also, mischief not unlike the above appeared at Ravenna. A certain man named Vilgard occupied himself with more eagerness than constancy in literary studies, for it was always the Italian habit to pursue these to the neglect of the other arts. Then one night when, puffed up with pride in the knowledge of his art, he had begun to reveal himself to be more stupid than wise, demons in the likeness of the poets Vergil, Horace, and Juvenal appeared to him, pretending thanks for the loving study which he devoted to the contents of their books and for serving as their happy herald to posterity. They promised him, moreover, that he would soon share their renown. Corrupted by these devilish deceptions, he began pompously to teach many things contrary to holy faith and made the assertion that the words of the poets deserved belief in all instances. But he was at last discovered to be a heretic [7] and was condemned by Peter, archbishop of that city.[8]

Many others holding this noxious doctrine were discovered throughout Italy, and they too died by sword and pyre.[9] Indeed, at this same period some went forth from the island of Sardinia—which usually teems with this sort of folk—to infect the people of Spain, but they were exterminated [10] by the Catholics. This accords with the prophecy of the apostle John, in which he said that Satan would be released when a thousand years had passed.[11] Of this we shall treat more fully in a third book.

2. *"Manichaeans" in Aquitaine*

The brief notices translated here and in Number 3, part A, were written by Adémar of Chabannes (998-1034). Like many other writers of succeeding generations, he assumed a direct filiation from the Manichaeans of the third and fourth centuries to the heretics of his own day and his use of that name may have arisen from a comparison of contemporary sects with the picture of Manichaeans drawn by St. Augustine. Adémar, born a member of the lesser nobility of the Limousin in west-central France, was placed at an early age in the monastery of St. Cybard in Angoulême, where he devoted himself to copying manuscripts and writing history. His most important work, the chronicle from which this excerpt comes, is a history of France to the year 1028. Much of it is merely a compilation from earlier sources, but the latter part of the third book is his own and an important narrative source for the history of France, especially of Aquitaine, in the later tenth century and the first quarter of the eleventh. Although he was an intelligent and well-informed observer, Adémar seems to have had only hearsay knowledge of the heretical movements to which he occasionally refers. On the incident reported here, see Ilarino da Milano, "Le eresie popolari," in *Studi Gregoriani*, II, 51-52. For what little is known of Adémar's life and a characterization of his work, consult the Introduction by Chavanon to the edition of the chronicle and Thompson, *A History of Historical Writing*, I, 229-30.

The following is translated, by permission of Editions A. and J. Picard, from Adémar of Chabannes *Chronique* III.xlix, ed. by Jules Chavanon (Collection de textes pour servir à l'étude et à l'enseignement de l'histoire, XX [Paris, 1897]), p. 173.

circa 1018

A little later, Manichaeans [1] appeared throughout Aquitaine leading the people astray. They denied baptism and the Cross and every sound doctrine. They abstained from food and seemed like monks; they pretended chastity, but among themselves they practiced every debauchery. They were ambassadors of Antichrist and caused many to turn away from the faith.[2]

3. Heresy at Orléans

An incident at Orléans in 1022 provides us with the first circumstantial description of a popular heresy in the Middle Ages. Certain aspects of the heretical group involved have drawn much comment: the participation of nobles as well as clergy and scholars, the belief in Docetic doctrine, the repudiation of the material world, and an emphasis on inner spirituality—all of which raise the question of possible Bogomil influence. We also encounter here the earliest charges of devil-worship as a concomitant of heresy. Of the dozen accounts of the incident which have survived, two are translated below. One is by Adémar of Chabannes, whose work has already been drawn upon; the second and more elaborate narrative was written by Paul, a monk of the Benedictine monastery of Saint-Peter-in-the-Valley, situated outside the walls of Chartres. When Paul, at the bidding of his abbot, began to compile a chartulary of his monastery,[1] he inserted among the documents mention of events in Chartres and nearby regions. He wrote apparently some fifty years after the incident at Orléans, but he had known Aréfast, one of its principals, as a monk at Saint-Peter and, it may be presumed, had obtained some of the information from him.

The heresy at Orléans is discussed in Ilarino da Milano, "Le eresie popolari," in *Studi Gregoriani*, II, 52-60; Russell, *Dissent and Reform*, pp. 27-35 and 276, n. 24; and Borst, pp. 74-76. All that is known of the life of Paul, the monk of Saint-Peter-in-the-Valley, is found in the introduction to the published chartulary, pp. cclxvii-cclxxv.

Part A is translated, by permission of Editions A. and J. Picard, from Adémar of Chabannes *Chronique* iii.lix, ed. by Jules Chavanon (Collection de textes pour servir à l'étude et à l'enseignement de l'histoire, XX [Paris, 1897]), pp. 184-85. Part B is translated from *Vetus Aganon* vi.iii, ed. by Benjamin-Edmé-Charles Guérard, in *Cartulaire de l'abbaye de Saint-Père de Chartres* (Collection des cartulaires de France, Vol. I; in Collection de documents inédits sur l'histoire de France, ser. I: Histoire politique [Paris, 1840]), I, 109-15.

A.   A REPORT BY ADÉMAR OF CHABANNES

1022

At that time ten of the canons of the Church of the Holy Cross at Orléans who appeared to be more religious than others were proved to be Manichaeans. When they would not return to the faith, King Robert [2] commanded that they be first deposed from priestly rank, then cast out of the Church, and finally consumed by fire. For they were deceived by a certain rustic from Périgord [3] who claimed that he performed miracles and who carried about with him the ashes of dead children, by which he soon made a Manichaean of anyone to whom he could give them. They adored the devil, who appeared to them first as an Ethiopian, then as an angel of light, and who daily brought them much money. In obedience to his works, in private they completely rejected Christ and secretly practiced abominations and crimes of which it is shameful even to speak,[4] while publicly they pretended to be true Christians.

No less were Manichaeans discovered and destroyed at Toulouse; and in various parts of the West, messengers of Antichrist arose, disguised themselves with care, and led astray whatever men and women they could. Also, a certain cantor of the canons of Orléans, named Theodatus, had given every appearance of piety but, as trustworthy persons declared, had died in that heresy three years before. When this was proved, his body was dug up from the cemetery by command of Bishop Odalric [5] and was thrown out into a waste place.

The ten [6] persons mentioned above were sentenced to the flames, among them Lisoius,[7] whom the king had greatly loved for the sanctity which he believed to be in him. Unconcerned, they showed no fear of the fire, predicted that they would emerge unscathed from the flames, and laughed as they were bound on the pyre.[8] They were promptly reduced to ashes, so completely that not a trace of their bones was found.

B. THE NARRATIVE OF PAUL, A MONK OF CHARTRES

1022

Furthermore, I consider it worth recording how this afore-mentioned Aréfast,[9] by divine aid and by the keenness of his own healthy wit, not only detected but entirely suppressed in the city of Orléans the heretical depravity which at that time was secretly spreading and pouring the poison of wicked error throughout the Gallic lands.

He was of the lineage of the dukes of Normandy, a man refined in speech, wise in counsel, blessed with good habits, and therefore very well known for his services as emissary, not only to the king of the French but also among the great nobles. It is told that he had in his household at that time a certain cleric named Heribert, who for the purposes of study had decided to go to the city of Orléans. But, in fact, while busily seeking authors of truth, he strayed down a blind path into a pit of flagrant heresy. For in the same city at that season two clerics, Stephen and Lisoius,[10] were in popular repute distinguished above all others in wisdom, eminent in holiness and piety, bountiful in charity. The aforesaid cleric sought them out and after a brief interval, now become a docile disciple by the sweetness of the holy word, he was made drunken by them with deadly draughts of evil. Ensnared in madness and devilish error, lacking all knowledge of theology, he believed himself to have ascended the peak of wisdom. Returning to his homeland, he sought by gradual and subtle suggestion to draw his master (whom he cherished with singular affection) with him into the path of error, alleging that the city of Orléans shone more than other cities with the light of wisdom and the luster of holiness. His master, lending an intelligent ear, perceived by the man's words that he had strayed from the path of righteousness. He quickly informed Duke Richard [11] of the situation, asked that the latter disclose to King Robert by letter the pest then lurking in his kingdom, before it could spread, and requested that the king not refuse needful assistance to this same Aréfast in driving it out.

And so, the king, thunderstruck by the unexpected disclosure, ordered the man speedily to proceed to Orléans with his cleric, promising his every aid in this affair. When Aréfast began to journey in compliance with the king's order, he passed through Chartres for the purpose of consulting the venerable prelate Fulbert[12] in regard to the matter; but it chanced that Fulbert was absent, for he had gone to Rome to pray. So [Aréfast] disclosed the reason for the journey to a certain wise cleric named Evrard, sacristan of the church at Chartres, and entreated the boon of his advice: how ought he to conduct himself in discussion, by what arms could he fortify himself against the multitudinous wiles of devilish deceit? Evrard, well versed in wise counsel, instructed him to go piously to church every day, the first thing in the morning, to seek the aid of the Almighty, to devote himself to prayer, and to fortify himself with the Most Holy Communion of the body and blood of Christ. Then, protected by the sign of the Holy Cross, he should confidently proceed to listen to the heretical depravity. He should contradict nothing that he would hear from them but, in his assumed role of a disciple, should silently store up all things in his breast.

So, when Aréfast came to Orléans thus instructed, daily strengthened by Holy Communion and prayer for aid, attending their instruction in the guise of an ignorant disciple, he was at last admitted within the house of errors. When first they taught him by stories from Holy Writ and by certain analogies and when they observed him attending with submissive ear like a perfect disciple, they explained to him, among other analogies, one of the forest tree:

"You are to be treated by us," they said, "like a tree of the forest which, when transplanted into a garden, is amply supplied with water until it is well rooted in the soil. It is then pruned of thorns and superfluous branches so that, after it is cut off near the ground with a hoe, it may be grafted with a better cutting, which later will bear sweet fruit. So you, in like manner, being transferred from the evil world into our holy companionship, will be well supplied with the water of wisdom until you are instructed and are strong enough to be shorn of the thorns of evil by the sword of the Word of God, and when we have driven absurd teachings from the shelter of your heart, you can receive with purity of mind our teaching, bestowed by the Holy Spirit."

Now, he always gave thanks to God for every word which they uttered to him, whence they were sure that he was converted to their error. And then the reckless men disclosed the dregs of their wickedness, hitherto buried under the words of Holy Writ: they said that Christ was not born of the Virgin, nor did He suffer for men, nor was He truly laid in the tomb, nor did He arise from the dead; and they added that in baptism there was no cleansing of sins, nor was there a sacrament in the consecration by a priest of the body and blood of Christ. They held for naught the invocation of holy martyrs and confessors. When these abandoned and utterly wretched men had vomited forth these and other detestable things from their stinking breasts, Aréfast is said to have spoken to them as follows: "If in these points which you have enumerated there can, as you say, be none of the hoped-for salvation of men, I beseech you urgently to show me in what things one may trust, lest my soul, being thrown into doubt, fall quickly into the catastrophe of desperation."

"Without doubt, Brother," they replied, "you have thus far been immersed with the ignorant in the Charybdis of false belief; now, indeed, raised on the peak of total truth, you have begun to open the eyes of a sound mind to the light of true faith. We throw open to you the gateway of salvation, by which—to wit, by the imposition of our hands—if you enter you will be cleansed from the stain of all sin and you will be filled by the gift of the Holy Spirit, who will teach you without reserve the profundity and divine excellence of all the Scriptures. Then, nourished by heavenly fare, refreshed by inward fullness, often will you see with us angelic visions, in which, sustained by their consolation, you can visit whatsoever places you wish without delay or difficulty. And nothing shall you want, since the God of all, in Whom are the treasuries of wisdom and riches, will never cease to be your companion."

Meanwhile, the king and Queen Constance had come to Orléans with a company of bishops, in accordance with a request from Aréfast. The day after their arrival, at the suggestion of the man himself, royal officers dragged that most wicked group, all together, from the house where they had gathered, and they were brought to the Church of the Holy Cross into the presence of the king and an assemblage of bishops and clergy. But before we come to the encounter, I shall take pains to reveal to the uninformed something about that food which they called celestial, and by what art it was confected.

They gathered, indeed, on certain nights in a designated house, everyone carrying a light in his hands, and like merry-makers they chanted the names of demons until suddenly they saw descend among them a demon in the likeness of some sort of little beast. As soon as the apparition was visible to everyone, all the lights were forthwith extinguished and each, with the least possible delay, seized the woman who first came to hand, to abuse her, without thought of sin. Whether it were mother, sister, or nun whom they embraced, they deemed it an act of sanctity and piety to lie with her. When a child was born of this most filthy union, on the eighth day thereafter a great fire was lighted and the child was purified by fire in the manner of the old pagans, and so was cremated. Its ashes were collected and preserved with as great veneration as Christian reverence is wont to guard the body of Christ, being given to the sick as a viaticum at the moment of their departing this world. Indeed, such power of devilish fraud was in these ashes that whoever had been imbued with the aforesaid heresy and had partaken of no matter how small a portion of them was scarcely ever afterward able to direct the course of his thought from this heresy to the path of truth.[13] Let it suffice to have said a little on this subject, so that worshipers of Christ may guard themselves against this wicked work and not busy themselves to imitate it by forming sects.

However, since I seem to have digressed, the discussion should be brought back to the point where I left it. The barbarity of the infidels will be recounted in brief fashion, lest a more prolix recital of the controversy induce disgust in the fastidious reader.

Now when, as has been related, these persons were taken before the king and the convocation of bishops, Aréfast first addressed the king, saying, "My Lord King, I am a knight, the man of Richard, your most faithful duke of Normandy, and without cause am I held in bonds and chains before you." To him the king replied thus: "State quickly the reason for your presence here, so that when it is revealed you may be kept in bonds as guilty, or, innocent and released from the chains, you may be discharged." To this the man made answer, "Having heard of the wisdom and piety of those who with me stand captive before you, I chose to come to this city so that thereafter I might return home, made better by the example of their good works and doctrine. This, indeed, is the reason why I chose to leave my homeland and why I sought this city. Now let the prelates present with you consider and judge if I am held in any way guilty in this act."

The bishops thereupon said, "If you will explain to us the nature of the wisdom and piety which you learned from them, we can easily reach a decision." To which the man replied, "Let Your Royal Majesty and Your Authority order these men to disclose to you the things which they taught me, to the end that when you have heard them, they may be judged worthy of praise or consigned to oblivion as unworthy."

When the king and bishops ordered these persons to reply and to make clear the pattern of their faith, the enemies of all truth, some of whom spoke for the others, had no intention of entering upon the filthiness of their heresy by any avenue, but, like the serpent which the more easily eludes the grasp the more tightly it is held in the hands, the more they in their slipperiness were hemmed in by the word of truth, so much the more did they seem to get away.

Then Aréfast, seeing how they would gain time and how, behind a shield of words, they would hasten to obscure the error of their faith, turned to them and said: "I thought to have in you masters of truth, not of error, when you consistently preached to me that teaching as health-giving. I witnessed your instruction, and you promised me that you would never deny it to avoid punishment, not even in peril of death. Now indeed, I see that in fear of death, forgetful of the faith which you held forth, you wish to disassociate yourselves from that teaching, and you think little of sending me, an untrained disciple, into peril of death. Now the royal command ought to be carried out and it is fitting to obey the authority of prelates such as these, to the end that if any of these things which I have learned from you are contrary to Christian piety, I, cognizant of the judgment of these men, shall know which are to be followed and which are to be rejected. Now, certainly you taught me that no forgiveness of sins is acquired in baptism, that Christ was not born of the Virgin, that He did not suffer for men, nor was He truly buried, nor did He rise again from the dead, nor can the bread and wine which on the altar in the hands of priests, by action of the Holy Spirit, seems to be made a sacrament actually be changed into the body and blood of Christ."

When Aréfast had pronounced these charges in a loud voice, Guarin, bishop of Beauvais, asked Stephen and Lisoius, who seemed to be the leaders in this error, if their thoughts had this bent and if they believed the things which were enunciated by Aréfast. These men, for whom an abode in hell with the devil was already waiting, declared the enumerated articles to be true, that these were their doctrines and thus steadfastly they believed. When the bishop said to them that he preferred a

Christ who was born of the Virgin—as was possible—and who suffered in His humanity for our salvation, so that on the third day, death defeated, He might arise in His divinity and might teach us that we, cleansed of sin, shall rise again, they replied with the tongues of vipers, "We were not there and we cannot believe that to be true." At this the bishop questioned them as follows: "Do you or do you not believe in parents of the flesh?" When they affirmed that they did, the bishop replied, "If you believe that before you existed you were begotten by your parents, why do you refuse to believe in God generated of God, without a mother, before time began, and at the appointed time born of the Virgin by the overshadowing of the Holy Spirit?" But they said, "What nature denies is always out of harmony with the Creator." Then the bishop answered, "Do you not believe that before anything was made through nature God the Father created everything from nothing through the Son?" To which these exiles from the faith said, "You may spin stories in that way to those who have earthly wisdom and believe the fictions of carnal men, scribbled on animal skins. To us, however, who have the law written upon the heart by the Holy Spirit (and we recognize nothing but what we have learned from God, Creator of all), in vain you spin out superfluities and things inconsistent with the Divinity. Therefore, make an end to words and do whatever you wish with us. For we shall see our King, reigning in heaven, Who will raise us in heavenly joys to everlasting triumphs at His right hand." [14]

After all had striven in manifold ways from the first to the ninth hour of the day to recall them from their error and they, harder than iron, paid not the least attention, they were ordered each to be garbed in the sacred dress of his order; and forthwith each was deposed from his particular office by the bishops. At the king's order, Queen Constance stationed herself before the doors of the church, lest the people should slay them within it. Thus were they expelled from the bosom of Holy Church. And as they were being led out, the queen, with a staff which she held in her hand, struck out the eye of Stephen, who formerly was her own confessor.[15]

Thereafter, when they had been taken out beyond the walls of the city to a little hut where a great fire was kindled, they were burned, except for one cleric and one nun; and with them were burned the evil ashes of which we spoke earlier. The cleric and the nun, by divine will, recovered their senses.[16]

4. The Conversion of Heretics by
the Bishop of Arras-Cambrai

When Bishop Gerard I (1013-1048) of Arras-Cambrai [1] discovered and seized some alleged heretics in his diocese, he convened at Arras the synod which is described in the following passage. Subsequently he sent a copy of the proceedings to a fellow bishop, designated only by the initial *R* in the covering letter, in which Gerard comments that certain suspects whom "R." had previously interrogated and released had, indeed, been heretics, and they, emboldened by their escape, had extended their activities to the vicinity of Arras. Detected there, they had resisted all efforts to obtain confessions but some of their followers had revealed their doctrines in part.[2] The originals of both the report of the synod and the letter are lost, but not before they had been published by Luc d'Achéry in 1677;[3] all subsequent editions are based on his work. We have followed Fredericq in omitting part of the text but have summarized the omitted portion. For discussions of the episode, see Ilarino da Milano, "Le eresie popolari," in *Studi Gregoriani*, II, 60-67; Edouard de Moreau, *Histoire de l'église en Belgique*, II, 410-14; and Russell, *Dissent and Reform*, pp. 22-27; as well as the studies cited here in the notes.

The translation is from *Acta synodi Atrebatensi a Gerardo Cameracensi et Atrebatensi episcopo celebrata anno 1025*, in Paul Fredericq, *Corpus documentorum inquisitionis haereticae pravitatis Neerlandicae* (5 vols., Ghent, 1899-1902), I, 2-5, by permission of the publisher, Martinus Nijhoff.

1025

In the year of our Lord 1025,[4] the eighth indiction, while Gerard presided over the church of Cambrai and that of the city of Arras, it came about that after Christmas and Epiphany had been observed with solemn ceremony in the see of Cambrai, in accordance with the custom annually followed he was to stay for several days in the see of Arras. There, while he was performing ecclesiastical ceremonies appropriate to the time, he was informed that certain men had come to that locality from Italy. These men were introducing new heretical doctrines, by which they were endeavoring to overturn teaching supported by evangelical and apostolic authority; they set forth a certain way of righteousness and asserted that men were purified by it alone and that there was no other sacrament in the Church whereby they could be saved.

On hearing these things, the lord bishop commanded that the men be sought out and brought before him when found. They secretly prepared for flight when they learned the reason for the search, but were thwarted by the magistrates and dragged into the bishop's presence. Since he was then very busy in finishing other matters, for the moment he put only a few questions about their faith and, perceiving that they were in the grip of certain errors of perverse doctrine, ordered that they be held in custody until the third day. And for the following day he imposed a fast on clerics and monks in the hope that divine grace might grant the prisoners recovery of understanding of the Catholic faith.

Then on the third day, which was a Sunday, the bishop in full regalia, together with his archdeacons bearing crosses and the Gospels and surrounded by a great throng of all the clergy and people, proceeded to the Church of the Blessed Mary to hold a synod. After the antiphon *Resurget Deus* (let God arise) had been sung, they completed the whole of the psalm.[5] Then the bishop seated himself in consistory with abbots, monks, archdeacons, and others on either side, ranked according to ecclesiastical office, and the men were brought from confinement and stood before them.

To open the discussion, the bishop made some general remarks about them to the people; then, turning to them, he asked, "Just what is your teaching, law, and religious observance, and who is the originator of your doctrine?" They replied that they were the followers of one Gundulf, an Italian,[6] by whom they had been instructed in the precepts of the Gospels and of the apostles; they accepted no scripture other than this but to this they held in word and act.

It had, in fact, come to the bishop's attention that they utterly abhorred the mystery of baptism, rejected the sacrament of the body and blood of Christ, denied that penance was of any use to those who lapsed into sin after baptism, held the Church as naught, despised lawful marriage, saw no gift of special power in holy confessors, and thought that no one but the apostles and martyrs should be venerated.

The bishop questioned them about tenets of this sort. "How," he asked, "can your belief in evangelical and apostolic precepts be reconciled with your contrary preaching? For the text of the Gospel says that when Nicodemus, prince of the Jews, avowed that through signs and miracles he believed Jesus to have come from God, the Lord forthwith replied that no one could merit the kingdom of heaven by this gift of confession alone unless he 'be born again of water and the Holy Spirit.'[7] And, indeed, you must either fully accept the mystery of regeneration [8] or deny the words of the Gospel, since it is undisputed that Jesus spoke these words."

To these remarks they replied as follows: "Anyone who chooses to examine carefully our law and doctrine, which we have learned from our master, sees it to be contrary neither to evangelical principles nor to apostolic sanctions. For it is of this sort: to abandon the world, to restrain our flesh from carnal longings, to earn our bread by the labor of our hands, to wish harm to none, to show loving-kindness to all who are gripped by zeal for our way of life. Therefore, if this way of righteousness (*justitia*) be observed, there is no need of baptism; if it be transgressed, baptism does not avail for salvation. This is the whole of our justification to which the practice of baptism can add nothing more, for within its bounds are included every evangelical and apostolic precept. Moreover, if anyone says that any sacrament inheres in baptism, he is rebutted on three counts: first, because of the evil life of the ministrants it can offer no salutary cleansing to those who are to be baptized; second, because whatever sins are disavowed at the font are repeated in later life; third, because the will of another, the faith of another, the confession of another obviously can never affect the child who has no wish or desire to cooperate, who is ignorant of faith and heedless of his safety and advantage, and within whom there can be no plea for regeneration, no confession of faith."

[At this point, the record gives the bishop's discourse on various errors.[9] Perhaps the errors of which he spoke had been discovered by earlier interrogation. There is some discrepancy between what the accused had so far admitted in open examination and the greater range of matters on which the bishop touched, as there is also between the content of his discourse and the subsequent abjuration by the group. The bishop spoke of: (1) denial of baptism of water but use of a custom of washing each other's feet, (2) rejection of the Eucharist, (3) denial that a church is the house of God, (4) denial of the altar and the use of incense, (5) objection to bells (*signis*) in churches, (6) scorn of ordination, (7) deprecating burial in holy ground because priests insisted on it only for their own gain, (8) denial of the efficacy of penance, (9) opposition to prayers for the dead, (10) objections to marriage, (11) finding no validity in confession, (12) objection to psalmody in church services, (13) jeering at veneration of the Cross, (14) spurning images of Christ on the Cross or of the saints because they were only the work of human hands, (15) opposing the hierarchy, (16) holding a false notion of justification. To all of these points the bishop addressed his rebuttal.]

In truth, at such words from the lord bishop those who shortly before seemed to themselves to be invincible in argument and incapable of restraint by any manner of speech, stood as though stunned by the gravity of the [bishop's] discourse and the manifest power of God, and as if they had never learned any argument which could be employed in refutation. Silenced, their sole response to all points was the avowal that the sum of Christian salvation now seemed to them to consist only in the explanation which the bishop had just given. To them the bishop made rejoinder: "If you believe these things are so, put aside the perfidy of so much unbelief and with us condemn and anathematize this heresy, together with its authors unless they return to their senses."

Then the bishop and all who were there—abbots, archdeacons, and all the clergy together—with the approval of the people began thus: "This heresy and all who profess it, which today has been found to have conspired against the true and catholic Church—to wit, which holds that baptism will not avail toward washing away the stain of original sin, or of sins actually committed; which professes that sins can never be remitted through penance; which considers God's Holy Church, the most sacred altar, and the sacrament of the Lord's body and blood to be nothing more than that which the eyes of the flesh behold, and looks upon the latter as a dirty transaction for gain; and which shuns legitimate marriages—this we condemn and anathematize together with all who profess it." [The remainder of this passage is a statement of the orthodox belief on each of the points just enumerated.]

Since those who a little while before were in the grip of heretical infidelity could not well understand what was being said in Latin, through an interpreter they heard in the vernacular the sentence of excommunication and made the profession of holy faith, after which, by a similar oath, they confessed openly that they both abjured what had been condemned and believed what was believed by the faithful. Then to confirm the avowal of their faith, each of them made a certain mark in the form of a cross in this fashion ✠, so that if they held to this faith this sign might be presented for them at the Last Judgment for their salvation, but if they should violate it, it would bring about their confusion.

And so, all united in returning thanks to God and, after they had been given the boon of benediction by the lord bishop, returned happily to their own homes.

5. Heretics at Monforte

A heretical group at Monforte, a fortified village south of Turin,[1] is the subject of the following account.[2] Of its author, Landulf, little is known, and there is no agreement among scholars about the credibility of his chronicle. He was a member of the clergy in Milan, active during the latter half of the eleventh century, when that city and province were torn by party strife, and he belonged to the group who opposed both the imperial pretensions of Henry IV (1056-1105) and the reform program of Pope Gregory VII (1073-1087). In his Introduction (pp. iii-viii) the editor of Landulf's history summarizes the points of view of various scholars over the past two centuries and concludes that Landulf was a man of his time and mirrored in his work the tempestuous character of life about him.

Various dates ranging from 1028 to 1040 have been suggested for this occurrence. We follow Ilarino da Milano, "Le eresie popolari," in *Studi Gregoriani*, II, 68-74, the best discussion of the heresy. See also Russell, *Dissent and Reform*, pp. 35-38; and C. Violante, *La società milanese nell'età precomunale*, pp. 176-86. There is a brief biography of Landulf by O. Kurth, *Landulf der Aeltere von Mailand*; and an Italian translation of his chronicle, with an introduction on the author and his work by A. Visconti, *La Cronica milanese di Landolfo Seniore* (Milan, 1928).

The account which follows is translated, by permission of Nicola Zanichelli Editore, from *Landulphi senioris Mediolanensis historiae libri quatuor* II.27, ed. by Alessandro Cutolo, in L. A. Muratori, *Rerum italicarum scriptores*, new ed. (Bologna, 1900), Vol. IV, pt. 2, pp. 67-69.

circa 1028

At this time, when Bishop Aribert [3] had visited nearly all the suffragans of the cities of the Blessed Ambrose, for the sake of whom he had traversed Italy,[4] exhorting them to all good works, he came at length to Turin, accompanied by a large number of devoted clerics and a troop of brave knights. When he had established himself there for several days, preaching to the bishop and clergy of the city and the people of the whole town [5] with prophetic and apostolic admonitions, as was fitting in so great a man, he heard of a strange heresy which had recently taken root in the citadel [6] above the place called Monforte.[7]

Now when Aribert had heard of this, he ordered that one of the heretics from the stronghold be brought before him so that he might obtain more precise knowledge of the matter. The man [Gerard], having been brought into his presence, stood with eager countenance ready to answer all questions, his mind fully prepared for suffering, happy if he were to end his life in the severest torture. Then Aribert, on seeing the fellow to be imbued with so much fixity of purpose, began to question him earnestly and in due order about the life, customs, and faith of these people. So, after permission was given to him and silence was enjoined, Gerard arose, saying: "To God Omnipotent—the Father, the Son, and the Holy Spirit—I give boundless thanks that you take the pains to examine me so carefully. And may He who knew you from the beginning in the loins of Adam grant that you live unto Him and die unto Him and be glorified, reigning with Him forever and ever. I will lay bare to you my life and the faith of my brethren in the same spirit in which you inquire into them. We esteem virginity above all else, although we have wives. He who is virgin keeps his virginity, but he who has lost it, after receiving permission from our elder (*nostro maiori*), may observe perpetual chastity. No one knows his wife carnally, but carefully treats her as his mother or sister. We never eat meats. We fast continually and pour forth prayers unceasingly; our leaders [8] pray always, day and night, in turn, that no hour may pass without prayer. We hold all our possessions in common with all men. None of us ends his life without torments, that we may thus avoid eternal torments. We believe in and confess the Father, the Son, and the Holy Spirit. We believe truly that we are bound and loosed by those who have the power of binding and loosing. We hold to both the Old and the New Testament and to the holy canons, and we read them daily."

When Gerard had said these and other things with extreme cleverness, to some persons they seemed to be great and terrible. Notwithstanding, Bishop Aribert, recognizing his astuteness and evil genius from certain phrases he had uttered, commanded him to make clear exactly what he and his associates believed, more particularly what they believed about the Father, the Son, and the Holy Spirit, and ordered him to explain each point separately.

On hearing this, Gerard gladly began: "What I called the Father, He is God eternal, who made all things from the beginning and in whom all things have their being. What I called the Son, He is the soul of man beloved of God. What I called the Holy Spirit, He is the comprehension of divine truths by which all things are separately governed."

To these statements Aribert answered, "My friend, what do you say of our Lord Jesus Christ, who was born of the Virgin Mary—the Word of the Father?" He replied, "He whom you call Jesus Christ is the soul of man, in the flesh born of the Virgin Mary, that is, born of Sacred

Scripture. The Holy Spirit is the devout comprehension of the Sacred Scriptures." [9] Aribert: "Why do you take wives except to beget offspring, whence stems the human race?" He replied, "If the whole human race should agree not to experience corruption, the human race would be begotten like bees without coition.'" [10] Aribert: "In whom is absolution of our sins—in the pope, in a bishop, or in any priest?" He replied, "We do not have that Roman pontiff, but another, who daily visits our brothers, scattered throughout the world, and when he brings God to us, pardon of our sins is granted, with the greatest piety." Aribert: "How does your life end in torments?" He replied, "If we expire through torments inflicted upon us by the wicked, we rejoice; but if nature at any time brings us near death, the one nearest us kills us in some way before we yield up our soul."

When Aribert with ears intent had heard all these things, silently marveling, while others too shook their heads in wonder, he inquired of Gerard whether he believed in the Catholic faith which the Roman Church holds and whether he believed that He is truly the Son of God, who was born of the Virgin Mary according to the flesh, and that it is the true body and the true blood which a Catholic priest, though a sinner, sanctifies through the word of God. He replied, "There is no other pontiff beside our Pontiff, though he is without tonsure of the head or any sacred mystery." [11]

This hearing made it clear that the truth of the matter was in accord with their reputation. Aribert sent a very large body of knights to Monforte and seized all whom he could find there, among them the countess of that stronghold, as being infected with this heresy. When he had brought them to Milan and had with the help of his priests labored for many days, greatly desiring to restore her to the Catholic faith, he was grievously troubled by the fear that the folk of this part of Italy might be contaminated by heresy. But those most wicked persons, who had come into Italy from some unknown part of the world, daily, albeit secretly, like good priests were implanting false principles wrenched from Holy Scripture in the countryfolk who had gathered in the city to see them. When the leading citizens of the city had learned of this, they caused a huge pyre to be lit and the Cross of the Lord to be set up nearby. Then, over the protests of Aribert, they had all these persons brought out, and offered them the following choice: if they abandoned all perfidy and chose to adore the Cross and to confess the faith which the whole world holds, they would be saved; if not, they would be thrown alive into the flames and burned. What happened was that some came to the Cross of the Lord, confessed the true Catholic faith, and thus were saved; many, however, covering their faces with their hands, leaped into the flames and, dying piteously, were reduced to pitiable ashes.

6. Heretics at Châlons-sur-Marne and Bishop Wazo

The passage translated here is of interest because of the affirmation of "Manichaean" doctrines among heretics in the diocese of Châlons, even more because of the strong argument offered by Bishop Wazo of Liège (1042-1048) against the execution of heretics. Wazo, who was highly regarded by his contemporaries and whose advice was sought on occasion by Emperor Henry III, was an advocate of the independence of the Church from secular control as well as of toleration in matters of faith.[1] His statement about tolerance was made in response to a letter from Roger II, bishop of Châlons-sur-Marne (1043-1062), and the date therefore falls between 1043 and 1048—probably closer to the latter year. The presumed author of that portion of the *Gesta episcoporum Leodiensium* in which it is preserved was Anselm, canon and later dean of the cathedral at Liège, who took up the story of the bishops of Liège in the mid-seventh century, where Heriger, abbot of Lobbes (d. 1007), had left it. Anselm's continuation has considerable value for the history of his own time. Brief biographical notices on Heriger and Anselm will be found in *Histoire littéraire de la France*, VII, 194-208, 472-76. For discussion of this episode, see Ilarino da Milano, "Le eresie popolari," in *Studi Gregoriani*, II, 74-76; and Russell, *Dissent and Reform*, pp. 38-40. The latter also describes other versions of the *Gesta* (p. 278, n. 36).

The following is translated, by permission of the publisher, Anton Hiersemann, and the Monumenta Germaniae Historica, from *Herigeri et Anselmi Gesta episcoporum Leodiensium* II.62-64, ed. by Rudolp Koepke, in *Monumenta Germaniae historica, Scriptores*, VIII, 226-28.

1043-1048

Moreover, apostolic sublimity deemed our bishop [Wazo] worthy of frequent correspondence, which he was wont to receive most reverently and to answer humbly, if it happened that a question was put to him therein. Various bishops, too, appealed to their distinguished colleague by letter, in which they drew upon his wisdom in various matters. No one of them, provided his questions bore upon some useful subject, was refused a careful reply to his inquiries. The bishop of Châlons, among them, felt the need to consult His Holiness because of a danger to the souls entrusted to his care, a danger which he outlined in his letter as follows: In a certain region of his diocese there were some countryfolk who eagerly followed the evil teachings of Manichaeans and frequented their secret conventicles, in which they engaged in I know not what filthy acts, shameful to mention, in a certain religious rite. And they lyingly asserted that the Holy Spirit is given by a sacrilegious imposition of hands; to buttress their faith in this error, they most falsely proclaimed Him to have been sent by God only in their heresiarch Mani, as though Mani were none other than the Holy Spirit. By this they fell into that blasphemy which, according to the Voice of Truth, can be forgiven neither here nor in the hereafter.[2]

These people, it was said, constrained whomever they could to join their number. They abhorred marriage and not only avoided the eating of meat but also considered it wicked to kill any animal at all, assuming as justification for their error the command of God against killing in the Old Law. If it happened that any ignorant, tongue-tied persons were enrolled among the partisans of this error, it was stoutly asserted that at once they became more eloquent than even the most learned Catholics, so that it almost seemed as if the really true eloquence of the wise could be overcome by their garrulity.[3] The bishop also added that he personally was more grieved over the daily seduction of others than by the damnation of these persons.

The troubled bishop asked the advice of the sure repository of wisdom as to the best procedure to adopt in dealing with such persons: whether or not the sword of earthly authority should be directed against them lest, were they not exterminated,[4] the whole lump be corrupted by a little leaven. In reply, our bishop writes, among other things:

"In regard to those of whom you wrote, their error is indeed evident, brought into the open by the holy fathers of old and confuted by their brilliant discussion. For, to pass over the most insensate blasphemies with which they deceive themselves in respect of the Holy Spirit, your Esteemed Self may perceive how they go out of their way to entangle themselves with numerous incongruities, by misinterpreting the commandment of the Lord which in the Old Law says, 'Thou shalt not kill.'[5] Unless they realize that therein only homicide was forbidden, they would find forbidden to them in like manner the use of those things which they think it lawful to eat, such as grain, vegetables, and wine. These things, as is their nature, have grown from seeds consigned to the earth in their own kind of life, and, unless destroyed in their prime, they could not serve the needs of mankind. Even if we make no mention of worldly authors, the Psalmist is witness to this fact when he says: 'And he destroyed their vineyards with hail.'[6] So too the Apostle: 'Senseless man, that which thou sowest is not quickened, except it die first.'[7] And Truth himself says, 'Unless the grain of wheat falling into the ground die, itself remaineth alone.'[8] It stands to reason, therefore, that of necessity they acknowledge that what manifestly can be killed by accident has had life. Therefore, let them choose what they will: either let them believe the Catholic interpretation, that only in respect of man was it written, 'Thou shalt not kill,' and with us lawfully avail themselves of the abundance of beasts for slaughter; or, if they insist on denying themselves this, we, by the very terms of their own error, will deny to them the use of bread, vegetables, and other things of this sort, because these things, did they not suffer death after their own fashion, could nowise be adapted to support human fallacies.

"Although Christian piety despises these tenets and although it condemns the sacrilege of the Arian heresy,[9] nevertheless, in emulation of our Savior, who, mild and humble of heart, did not come to wrangle or contend but rather to suffer abuse, shameful treatment, blows, and finally death on the Cross, we are commanded for a time to bear with such things in some measure. For, as the Blessed Gregory says, no Abel will maintain his innocence whom the malice of a Cain has not harassed, nor will the grape dissolve into the savor of the wine unless it is crushed by the heel.[10] Moreover, to be prepared for doing what the merciful and compassionate Lord, who does not judge sinners straightway but waits patiently for repentance, desires to be done about such persons, let us hearken to what He deemed fitting to teach His disciples—nay, rather us—when in His Gospel He expounded the parable of the field of wheat and the cockle. He said: 'The man that soweth the good seed in his field is the Son of Man. And the good seed are the children of the kingdom. And the field is the world. And the man, the enemy, that sowed the cockle is the devil. And the cockle are the children of the wicked one. But the harvest is the end of the world. And the reapers are the angels.'[11] What, moreover, but the role of preachers is signified by the servants who wish to gather up the cockle when it first appears? Do not preachers, as they seek to separate good from evil in Holy Church, attempt as it were to root out the cockle from the good seed of the field? But with notable discretion that Goodman of the house restrains their reckless zeal, saying: 'Do not so; lest perhaps gathering up the cockle you root up the wheat also together with it. Suffer both to grow until the harvest, and in the time of the harvest I will say to the reapers: Gather up first the cockle and bind it into bundles to burn, but the wheat gather ye into my barn.'¹² What does the Lord reveal by these words but His patience, which He wishes His preachers to display to their erring fellow men, particularly since it may be possible for those who today are cockle, tomorrow to be converted and be wheat?

"The fervor of spiritual zeal burning in your breast for souls deceived by devilish fraud shows that you surely are numbered among these servants. Out of this zeal you strive with the hoe of judicial decision to rid the grainfield of cockle, that the good be not corrupted by evil. But lest you do this hastily, lest it be done before its time, the holy text is rather to be obeyed, so that although we think we are practicing righteousness by punishing transgressors, whose impiety is veiled under semblance of strict life, we do no disservice to Him, who desires not the death of sinners nor rejoices in the damnation of the dying, but rather knows how to bring sinners back to repentance through His patience and long-suffering. Therefore, heeding the words of the Maker, let the decision of the arena wait; let us not seek to remove from this life by the sword of secular authority those whom God himself, Creator and Redeemer, wishes to spare, as He has revealed, to the end that they may turn again to His will from the snares of the devil in which they were entrapped. Thus, because it is indubitably proper for us to reserve such persons to the last harvest of that Goodman of the house, for whatever He may command His harvesters to do about them, so also, for our part, it behooves us to await the harvesters in fear and trembling. For perchance that harvest may disclose to be wheat some of those who grow as cockle in the field of this world, and it is possible for omnipotent God to make those whom we now consider to be enemies of the way of the Lord superior even to us in that heavenly home. Certainly we read that Saul, raging more than all the others, assisted at the stoning of the blessed first martyr, Stephen, and the martyr apostle now rejoices to recognize as a superior apostle the one who once was his persecutor.

"Moreover, we must meanwhile bear in mind that we who are called bishops do not receive at ordination the sword which belongs to the secular power and for that reason we are enjoined by God our Father not to do unto death but rather to quicken unto life. There is, however, another point about the aforesaid schismatics which should be carefully heeded, one of which you are not at all unmindful. They and those associating with them should be deprived of Catholic communion. Let it be officially and publicly announced to all others, so that, heeding the warning of the prophet, they may leave their midst and eschew their most unclean sect, for 'He that toucheth pitch shall be defiled with it.' " [13]

So very earnestly did the man of God, after the example of the Blessed Martin, strive to impress these ideas that in a measure he curbed the habitual headstrong madness of the French, who yearned to shed blood. For he had heard that they identified heretics by pallor alone, as if it were certain fact that those who have a pale complexion are heretics.[14] Thus, through error coupled with cruelty, many truly Catholic persons had been killed in the past.

This being the situation and because nothing of like reasonableness can be advanced in rebuttal of such clear reasoning supported by Gospel decree, let them to whom it is unknown see how reprehensible [15] was the deed when certain partisans of a comparable sect had been seized at Goslar. After much discussion of their vagaries and a proper excommunication for obstinacy in error, they were also sentenced to be hanged.[16] When we carefully investigated the course of this examination, we could learn no other reason for their condemnation than that they refused to obey some one of the bishops when he ordered them to kill a chicken. For I can truly say, and I will not keep silent, that if it had happened in his time, our Wazo would have agreed not at all with this verdict, after the example of the Blessed Martin, who, in order to intercede for Priscillianists condemned by edict of the depraved Emperor Maximin on advice of the priests who basely flattered him, preferred to incur a slur on his most excellent virtue than to be unsolicitous even for heretics who were soon to die.[17] We say these things not because we seek to defend the error of heretics, but to show that we do not approve of that which is nowhere sanctioned in the Sacred Laws.

The Development of Heresy
from the Late Eleventh to
the Mid-Twelfth Century

7. Ramihrdus: Heretic or Reformer?

Throughout most of the second half of the twelfth century, the years of papal reform and of the First Crusade, the sources are devoid of references to heretical movements akin to those of earlier years.[1]

One episode throws light on the notion of what constituted heresy in the minds of some contemporaries affected by the policies of Gregory VII and raises also the question of the relationship of religious dissent to the changing patterns of a society being altered by economic and political growth. In Cambrai, a newly elected bishop had accepted investiture from the emperor and, in consequence, was denied papal consecration, pending an investigation.[2] At the same time, civic protest against the temporal power of the bishop—one of the first of the communal uprisings—had embittered and complicated the situation. Our sources give no positive evidence of a link between what was here called heresy and the social tumult; but that the Gregorian reform program was involved is strongly suggested by the pope's action in ordering an investigation when it was reported that a man who denounced simony and clerical immorality had been burned as a heretic. On the situation in Cambrai, see Alfred Cauchie, *La Querelle des investitures dans les diocèses de Liège et de Cambrai, I: Les réformes grégoriennes et les agitations réactionnaires (1075-1092)*, pp. vii-xcii, 1-12;[3] W. Reinecke, *Geschichte der Stadt Cambrai bis zur Erteilung der "Lex Godefridi," 1227*, pp. 106 ff.; and Moreau, *Histoire de l'église en Belgique*, II, 74-76, 124, 26, 411. There are brief discussions of the religious implications in Ilarino da Milano, "Le eresie popolari," in *Studi Gregoriani*, II, 80-82; and Russell, *Dissent and Reform*, pp. 43-44.

The translation is from an anonymous chronicle presumably written in 1133, the third book of which is devoted to a life of Bishop Gerard: *Chronicon S. Andreae Castri-Cameracesii* III.3, ed. by L. C. Bethmann, in *Monumenta Germaniae historica, Scriptores*, VII, 540; by permission of the publisher, Anton Hiersemann, and the Monumenta Germaniae Historica.

1076 or 1077

It happened after this [4] that the bishop stopped at the village of Lambres,[5] which was then under his jurisdiction, and remained there for a short time. It was reported to him by some informants that a man named Ramihrdus, living in the adjacent village of Schere,[6] was laying down doctrine not consonant with the faith and by his teaching had already gathered around him many disciples and a very numerous group of both sexes who were in agreement with him. The man was promptly summoned for inquiry into his life and teaching. The bishop heard his reply to the charges, then ordered him brought to his court at Cambrai, where fuller inquiry might be made into these matters.

And so, on the designated day, the man was led before the abbots and learned clergy who had been convened and was questioned about the Catholic faith, but in all things he avowed the precepts of the true faith. When he was directed by the bishop to partake of the sacrament of the Lord's Supper to confirm this, he refused, asserting that he would take it from none of the abbots or priests, not even from the bishop himself, because they were all deeply involved in the crime of simony or other greedy practice. All were enraged by these words and declared that he should be considered a heresiarch; there the matter was left.

However, some of the bishop's attendants and a number of other persons took the man away and thrust him into a hut. Putting a torch to the hut, they burned him, unresisting, fearless, and (so it is said) prostrate in prayer. Such was the end of this man who had done and taught many things.[7] But many of his adherents collected some of his bones and ashes for themselves. In some towns, numerous members of this group persist even today, among whom are to be counted those who practice the craft of weaving.[8]

8. The Heresy of Tanchelm

The career of Tanchelm (or Tanchelin) in the Low Countries was described only by his enemies, especially the clergy of Utrecht, whose attitude colors all other accounts by contemporaries. Their portrait of him as an unprincipled and debauched demagogue, making extreme claims to sanctity and arousing the masses to violent rejection of the Church, was occasionally softened in some of its details by modern scholars and finally has been challenged in every point by recent interpretations. As a result of revisionist studies, Tanchelm is now presented as probably a monk and priest, one of the wandering preachers whose activities were so prominent in the early twelfth century; his theme, the furthering of the Gregorian reforms. Tanchelm's activities included a trip to Rome about 1112-1113 in connection with a proposed transfer of jurisdiction over certain areas from the diocese of Utrecht, the see of which was then vacant, to the bishop of Thérouanne.[1] This was a move in the struggle between Louis VI of France and the German emperor, Henry V, with some significance also for the strife between the emperor and the pope. Count Robert II of Flanders (1093-1111), who was a vassal and supporter of Louis VI, initiated it to weaken the clergy of Utrecht, who were partisans of the emperor against France and against the papacy. The proposed transfer was rejected by Paschal II. On his return to Flanders, Tanchelm again took up his preaching and was accused of heresy. The wrath of the clergy of Utrecht at the attempt to interfere with their diocese accounts for the vitriolic and probably untruthful accusations of personal immorality hurled at Tanchelm in their letter which is translated here, which has, moreover, such close parallels with the tale of a "prophet" and his following told by Gregory of Tours five centuries earlier that it seems undoubtedly to have been influenced by that old story.[2]

Of the many studies of Tanchelm and his heresy written from various points of view may be cited H. Q. Janssen, "Tanchelijn," *Annales de l'Académie royale d'archéologie de Belgique*, 2d ser., III (1867) 347-450; L. J. M. Philippen, "De Hl. Norbertus en de strijd tegen Tanchelmisme te Antwerpen," *Bijdragen tot de Geschiedenis*, XXV (1934), 251-88; and Norman Cohn, *The Pursuit of the Millennium*, pp. 35-38. The recent critical investigations which have revised the interpretation of Tanchelm are those of De Smet, Mohr, and Russell (see nn. 1 and 2).

Many of the sources are gathered in Fredericq, *Corpus*, I, 15-18, 22-29. The letter by the clergy of Utrecht, however, is translated here (part A), by permission of the publisher, Weidmannsche Verlags Buchhandlung, from a critical edition which differs slightly from the text in Fredericq. It is "Traiectenses Fridericum I archiepiscopum Coloniensem hortantus, quod ceperit Tanchelmum haereticum eiusque socios, Manassen et Everwacherum, ne eos dimittat," No. 168 in the *Codex Udalrici*, ed by P. Jaffé, in *Monumenta Bambergensis*, pp. 296-300. Part B is translated, by permission of the publisher, Anton Hiersemann, and the Monumenta Germaniae Historica, from *Sigiberti Gemblacensis chronographia: Continuatio Praemonstratensis*, ed. by L. C. Bethmann, in *Monumenta Germaniae historica, Scriptores*, VI, 449.

A. AN ACCUSATION BY THE CANONS OF UTRECHT

1112-1114

To their lord and venerable father, Frederick, archbishop [1100-1131] of the holy church of Cologne, from the humble church of Utrecht, out of true affection the most devout prayers with protestations of due obedience.

We give thanks to Your Holiness, most venerable Father, that out of paternal pity you have grieved for our affliction and have checked the career and onslaught of our Antichrist, who disturbs and blasphemes the Church of Christ; who opened his mouth against heaven and against the sacraments of the Church and dared to revive a heresy once silenced by the decrees of the Holy Fathers. For, puffed up by the spirit of pride, which is the root of every heresy and apostasy, he declared that the pope was naught, archbishops naught, bishops naught, priests and clerics naught. He shook the pillars of the Church of God to their foundations; he even dared to split the rock of our faith, that is Christ, holding that the Church consisted only of himself and his followers; like the Donatist heretics, who argued that the Church existed only in Africa, he sought to limit the Church—that Church which Christ desired and received from the Father, "Gentiles for his inheritance and the utmost parts of the earth for his possessions" [3]—to Tanchelmites alone.

Now, indeed, Holy Father, give ear to our cries of distress and be alert to the precursor of Antichrist who now traces the very path, in exactly the course that the Antichrist will follow. First in the coastal provinces he injected the venom of his wickedness into an untutored people of weak faith. Gradually he began to spread his errors by way of matrons and harlots whose intimacies, confidential conversation, and private couch he was most willing to enjoy. Through them he also entangled the husbands in the snares of his iniquity. Afterwards he no longer preached in hidden places and in bedrooms but upon the rooftops and delivered his sermons in the open fields to a multitude thronging about him on all sides. He put on the pomp of a monarch going out to harangue the people, attended by a retinue who bore banner and sword before him as though he went forth to speak amidst royal trappings. On his words the deluded people hung as if he were an angel of God. But he, being in fact the angel of Satan, proclaimed that the churches of God were to be reckoned as houses of ill repute, that the function of priests at the Lord's table was worthless, fit rather to be called pollution than sacrament, that the efficacy of the sacraments depends on the merits and sanctity of the ministers. But hear the words of St. Augustine: "The Lord Christ sent His betrayer, whom He called the devil—one who, before betraying the Lord, could not even keep faith about the Lord's purse— with the other apostles to preach the Kingdom of Heaven, in order to prove that the gifts of God come to those who receive them with faith, even though he through whom they receive them be such as Judas." [4] And again Augustine: "If, in administering the sacraments, the merits of the giver and recipient are to be considered, let it be the merit of God giving and of my conscience receiving; for these two things, His goodness and my faith, are not in doubt to me. Why do you interpose yourself, of whom I can know nothing certain? Permit me to say, 'I trust in God.' For if I trust in you, how am I assured that you have done nothing wrong this night?" [5]

In ranting about these and like matters, that man [Tanchelm] warned the people against partaking of the sacrament of the body and blood of the Lord and also forbade paying tithes to the ministers of the Church. To this he easily persuaded those who were already willing, for he preached only those things which he knew would please, either by their novelty or by the predisposition of the people.

He attained great successes in iniquity and then went so far in his wickedness that the wretched man even proclaimed himself God; for he declared that if Christ is God because He had received the Holy Spirit, he himself was no less God in exactly the same way,[6] inasmuch as he had received the fullness of the Holy Spirit. He carried this nonsense so far in his impertinence and some people so worshiped divinity in him that he could distribute his bath water to those most foolish persons, to be drunk as a blessing, as a sacrament that would most sacredly and efficaciously conduce to health of body and salvation of soul.

At the same time, also, when casting about for a new device in his search for novelty, he ordered a certain statue of St. Mary (how the mind is appalled at the mere mention!) carried into the midst of the throng. Then he stretched out his hand to that of the statue and by the symbolism of that gesture he betrothed St. Mary to himself, sacrilegiously reciting the pledge and all those solemn words of betrothal as is the common custom. "Behold," he said, "dearly beloved, I have betrothed the Virgin Mary to myself. Do you furnish the betrothal feast and the expenses of the marriage." He produced two chests, placing one at the right, the other at the left hand of the statue. "Let men put their offerings in this one, women in that. I shall then see in which sex burns the greater love for me and my betrothed." And lo! the utterly insane people eagerly rushed forward with gifts and offerings. The women cast in earrings and necklaces and thus, with outrageous sacrilege, he collected an enormous sum of money.[7]

Now, there is also a certain blacksmith, Manasses by name, who is reported to have been arrested by you along with that wicked man. He, in imitation of his utterly evil master, had founded a certain brotherhood, such as that commonly called a guild, in which he enrolled twelve men to represent the twelve apostles and one lone woman to represent the Blessed Mary. She, so they say, was taken by each of these twelve in turn to confirm their brotherhood; to the outrage of the Most Holy Virgin, she had carnal intercourse with each one in the vilest shame.

Also, a certain priest, Everwacher by name, apostatized from the priestly office and went over to the teaching of this abominable man. He followed him to Rome, where he sought to have the maritime regions —that is, a fourth part of our diocese—transferred by authority of the lord pope to the episcopate of Thérouanne of the kingdom of France. This man, too, we have rejoiced to hear, has been arrested by Your Holiness. The same priest, a thoroughgoing supporter of Tanchelm, has usurped the tithes belonging to the brethren of the Church of St. Peter and by force of arms has ejected their priest from the altar and the church.

Boundless, our lord, are the crimes of those men. Most of them we have omitted for the sake of the brevity required in a letter. Be it enough to have said in brief that divine matters are so contemptuously treated that the holier a church is in reputation, the more despicable do all hold it to be.

Inasmuch, Holy Father, as divine mercy, unable to tolerate further dangers to its Church, has given these men into your hands, we beg you, we implore you in the Lord, not to let them slip from your grasp. If they do, we declare to you and unhesitatingly bear witness that there will result further irreparable damage to our Church, and the ruin of souls beyond number as well. Our lord, our Church will certainly suffer the gravest misfortune if it should happen by any chance that they escape, for their speech, in the words of the Apostle, "spreadeth like a cancer," [8] and by its blandishment brings the souls of the simple to ruin. . . . [The letter concludes with a plea for action and a quotation from St. Augustine to show the desirability of calling on secular princes to intervene.]

B. TANCHELM'S INFLUENCE AND HIS DEATH

circa 1115

The citizens of the town [Antwerp] under the influence of a certain heretic, Tanchelm (or Tandem), had gradually broken with faith and morals, because he, with remarkable subtlety (notwithstanding his status as a layman, he was more clever of speech than many eloquent clerics), taught that the lower grades of holy orders and the episcopal and priestly ranks were of no value, and he denied that partaking of the body and blood of Christ would be of any use for the salvation of the communicants.[9] He went around clothed in rich and gilded garments, his curled locks bound with ribbons. With persuasive words and ostentatious feasts he won the allegiance of followers, to the number of some three thousand armed men, whom he employed to vent his murderous rage on those who opposed him.[10] His followers believed in and reverenced him to such a degree that they drank the water in which he had bathed and carried it off as a sacred relic. He was so incontinent and beastly that he violated girls in the presence of their mothers and wives in the sight of their husbands, asserting that this was a spiritual act.

At length, after much wickedness and many murders, he was put to rest by a blow on the head, delivered by a priest while they were in a boat.[11] But even after his death his evil teachings could not easily be rooted out. Therefore, through the good offices of the bishop, a church with a considerable endowment was given by the clergy of that place to be administered by Norbert,[12] in the hope that by his salutary teaching the heresy might be eradicated from their midst. And so it happened. For, by his preaching alone, men and women were stung with remorse; they brought out again the Lord's body, which for ten years and more had lain in chests and crannies, and through his teaching they gradually returned to holy faith.

9. *"Manichaeans" near Soissons*

The nature of the heresy which Guibert of Nogent describes in this passage is not made entirely clear, despite the vividness of the author's report, and although Guibert had no doubt of its Manichaean character. It seems surely to have been anticlerical, and there is an intimation of that desire to imitate the apostolic life which is elsewhere so much in evidence. The episode also reveals again the stories of immorality associated with heresy and shows a rude folk justice being exercised when clerical authorities were uncertain how to proceed. The date is fixed by a reference at the end of the passage to a synod which was held at Beauvais in 1114. The question of heresy was there put over to another synod, to be held at Soissons in January of the following year, but by then the question had been settled, as Guibert relates, by direct action.

Guibert was a scion of the lesser nobility of the region of Beauvais. Early in life he became a monk and settled down to a serious study of biblical and patristic literature. He became abbot of Nogent in 1104. Among his numerous writings, the *Autobiography* is of importance, partially because of its novelty in the early twelfth century, but also for the picture it presents of the intellectual, religious, and social life of northeastern France at the time. Guibert had little use for Jews (on religious rather than ethnic grounds), he looked with jaundiced eye on the attempts of commoners to establish communes in the towns, especially Laon, and he cordially disliked the heretics and those who protected them, notably John, count of Soissons. The passage translated here is not always easy of interpretation, for Guibert's writing is "involved, pretentious, 'full of rare and unusual terms,' " [1] but an attempt has been made to render it into English that can be understood. For the background of the life and work of Guilbert, Bourgin's introduction to his edition of the autobiography is excellent. A study by Bernard Monod, *Le Moine Guibert et son temps (1053-1124)*, emphasizes Guibert's contribution to the cultural history of his time. The *Autobiography* has been translated by C. C. Swinton Bland.

This episode is translated, by permission of Editions A. and J. Picard, from *Guibert de Nogent: Histoire de sa vie (1053-1124)* III.xvii, ed. by Georges Bourgin (Collection de textes pour servir à l'étude et à l'enseignement de l'histoire, XI [Paris, 1907]), pp. 212-15.

circa 1114

But since we are speaking of heretics, on whom this detestable man [2] doted, there was a country fellow, Clement by name, who lived with his brother Evrard at Bucy,[3] a manor near Soissons. Clement was commonly recognized as one of the leaders of his heresy. That vile count used to assert of him that he acknowledged no man to be wiser. The heresy, however, is not one that frankly defends its teaching, but, after being condemned, spreads in secret by word of mouth.

The gist of it is reported to be this: They avow that the dispensation[4] of the Son of the Virgin is only an illusion. They hold the baptism of children not yet at the age of understanding to be worthless, no matter who the sponsors; they call their own [baptism], which is performed by I know not what long-winded circumlocutions, the Word of God. They so abhor the mystery performed at our altar that they call the mouths of all priests the mouth of hell. And if now and then they partake with others of our sacrament, as a cloak for their heresy, they regard it as a meal and they eat nothing else all day. They make no distinction between consecrated cemeteries and other land. They condemn marriage and the begetting of offspring through intercourse. And surely, wherever they are scattered throughout the Latin world, you may see men living with women but not under the name of husband and wife, and in such fashion that man does not dwell with woman, male with female, but men are known to lie with men, women with women; for among them it is unlawful for men to approach women. They reject foods of all sorts which are the product of coition.

They hold meetings in cellars and secret places, the sexes mingling freely. When (*qui*) candles have been lighted, in the sight of all, light women with bare buttocks (it is said) offer themselves to a certain one lying behind them. Directly the candles are extinguished, they all cry out together "Chaos!" and each one lies with her who first comes to hand.[5]

Now if it so happens that a woman has there been gotten with child, as soon as the offspring is delivered, it is brought back to the same place. A great fire is lit, and the child is thrown from hand to hand through the flames by those sitting around the fire until it is dead. It is then reduced to ashes; from the ashes bread is made, of which a morsel is given to each as a sacrament. Once that has been eaten, it is very rarely that one is brought back to his senses from that heresy.

If you will reread the various accounts of heresies by Augustine,[6] you will find that this resembles none more than that of the Manichaeans. Though this heresy had its origin in former times among learned persons, its dregs sank down to the countryfolk, who, boasting that they hold to the way of life of the apostles, choose to read only their Acts.

The two men named above were, therefore, compelled to stand examination by the most distinguished lord bishop of Soissons, Lisiard.[7] When the bishop charged them with holding meetings outside the church and with being heretics by common report among their neighbors, Clement replied: "Have you not read the Gospel, my lord, where it is written, 'Blessed are the heretics (*beati eritis*)' "?[8]—for, because he was illiterate, he thought that *eritis* meant heretics. He also thought that heretics were so called as being "inheritors" (*hereditarii*), no doubt of God. But when they were questioned as to what they believed, they replied in a most Christian fashion; they did not, however, deny the meetings. Now, because it is the nature of such persons to deny, while secretly seducing the hearts of dullards, they were sentenced to the ordeal of exorcised water.

The bishop had asked me, while this was in preparation to find out their beliefs in private; and when I raised with them the question of infant baptism, they said, "He that believeth and is baptized shall be saved."[9] Since I saw how much iniquity among them lay hidden behind fair words, I asked their views about those who are baptized in the faith of others. Their reply was: "For God's sake, pray do not ask us to probe so deeply"; and likewise, to each separate subject mentioned, "We believe everything that you say." Then, calling to mind that verse on which the Priscillianists once agreed: "Swear, truly or falsely, but betray not the secret,"[10] I said to the bishop: "Let them be taken to the ordeal which has been prepared, because the witnesses who heard them teaching these things are not present here." For there was a certain matron whom Clement had deluded within the year, and there was also a deacon who had heard other evil matters from the tongue of the aforesaid individual.

And so the bishop celebrated Mass, and from his hand they received the consecrated elements in these words, "Let the body and blood of the Lord try you today." When this was done, the most devout bishop and the archdeacon Peter, a man of very sound faith who had scorned the promises which they made to avoid being subjected to the ordeal, proceeded to the water. With many tears, the bishop chanted the litany, then performed the exorcism. Then the men took oath that they had never believed or taught anything contrary to our faith. Clement, when cast into the vat, floated on top like a stick, at which sight the whole church was carried away with boundless joy. The report of this event had brought together a great throng of both sexes, such as none of those present recalled having seen. The other man, confessing his error but still impenitent, was held in bonds with his convicted brother. Two others, who were very obviously heretics, had come to the spectacle from the village of Dormans [11] and they likewise were held.

Meanwhile, we proceeded to the Council of Beauvais to consult the bishops about what should be done in this case. But during that time, the faithful people, fearing clerical leniency, rushed to the prison, seized the men, and having laid a fire under them, burnt them all together outside the city. The people of God were righteously wrathful against them, lest their cancer be spread.[12]

10. *Heresy in Ivoy, near Trier*

The group of heretics discovered in the diocese of Trier has been linked with Tanchelm because of their disdain of the sacraments,[1] and for the same reason they have been called followers of Berengar of Tours.[2] There is, in fact, too little specific information in the charges against them to guarantee that either of these suggestions has merit, but there is illustrated here the problem of proving and punishing heresy. The incident has been variously dated from 1112 to 1122, the later date being more likely.[3]

The passage translated is taken, by permission of the publisher, Anton Hiersemann, and the Monumenta Germaniae Historica, from *Gesta Treverorum: Additamentum et continuatio prima* 20, ed. by Georg Waitz, in *Monumenta Germaniae historica, Scriptores*, VIII, 193.

1122 (?)

There is yet another memorable act of his [4] which I happened to witness and must mention. At that time in Ivoy,[5] which lies within the diocese of Trier, there were heretics who denied that the substance of the bread and wine which priests bless on the altar is really changed into the body and blood of Christ. They also said that the sacrament of baptism of infants has no efficacy for salvation, and they professed many other errors of various kinds which I think it wrong to hand down to posterity. Four of them were brought before Bishop Bruno; two were priests, two others laymen. One of the priests was called Frederick, the other had two names, Dominic William; one of the laymen was named Durand, the other Amalric.

While the bishop was engaged in questioning them and instructing them in the principles of Christian teaching, Amalric escaped. But Durand confessed voluntarily that he had, indeed, hitherto been among those who practiced this wickedness but henceforth desired no part in it; and he confirmed his words by oath upon relics of the saints which were placed before him.

But one of the priests, Frederick, when summoned to a hearing, not only did not deny but even asserted the truth of his belief, declaring that he acted honestly and correctly. To him Bishop Bruno replied: "You, who should have been a teacher of the faithful, ought to have preached sound doctrine to all and to have curbed your infidel babbling. It is clearer than day to all believers that you lied, since the Blessed Augustine says: 'Though it is not meet that Christ be actually torn by the teeth, Christ himself desired that in the mystery of the Mass this bread and this wine become His very body and blood through the consecration of the Holy Spirit, to be mystically offered every day for the life of the world. Just as true flesh was engendered from the Virgin through the Holy Spirit without carnal intercourse, so through the same Holy Spirit the very body of Christ may be mystically consecrated from the substance of the bread and wine.' Also, in his letter "Concerning the Catholic Faith," the Blessed Augustine says: 'Hold most firmly and doubt not that the sacrament of faith and penitence, which is holy baptism, suffices for the salvation of infants, who can neither believe of their own volition nor do penance for the original sin which they bear, so long as their age is not such as to be capable of reason.' " [6]

After these and other appropriate passages of the same import had been brought to the attention of all, and when, although he had been soundly castigated by the assembled faithful, jointly and severally, and had been urged to return to Christian truth, he [Frederick] refused to yield, but chose rather in stubbornness of mind to stand fast in infidelity, sentence was loudly approved by all in the words of the Lord: "And if he will not hear the church, let him be to thee as the heathen and the publican";[7] and they added, "Let him be degraded, and condemned!" As this was happening and all were jostling together, the man seized the chance to flee, hid himself amidst the assembled crowd, and thus escaped. Then, when he had been sought without success, to put it briefly, he was condemned in accordance with the penalties of the canons that he who will not come to a hearing when summoned shall suffer the same penalty in absence.[8]

The other one—that is, he who was called by two names to conceal the infamy of this wickedness—was questioned as to whether he too was a propagator of the aforesaid heresy. He testified that he had never professed it nor did he wish to. His accusers, on the contrary, affirmed and testified that they had once happened unexpectedly upon conventicles of the same heretics and had seen him worshiping with them. In fear lest he should lose the honor of the priesthood if he were convicted, he replied that to clear himself of this suspicion he would willingly accept the verdict of a most searching test.

Everyone welcomed this declaration and he was directed to celebrate Mass and to chant the Sacred Canon, which is called the *Secreta* or *Actio*,[9] in full voice just as the other parts, so that one who had presumed to disparage the mystery of the precious body and blood of

Christ might be tested by its virtue. Therefore, when the Mass was underway and the moment came for him to receive the sacrament, the bishop uttered words of solemn warning in this wise: "If with impious mouth you have dared to babble that this life-giving sacrament of our salvation which you hold in your hands is not truly the body and blood of Christ, thus questioning its power, I utterly forbid you to dare to receive it. If, however, this is not the fact, but you declare your orthodoxy, you may receive it." And he received it.

But I should not fail to record how this sacrament of redemption entered his mouth to his own damnation. For while he was under the stress of the investigation, with contrite heart he humbly implored penance for his guilt from Almightly God, promising to keep himself from future sins, and he obtained release from his present troubles. But then, on his return home, he did not scruple to break his promises and with greater pertinacity than before he encouraged the heresy which he had foresworn, forgetting that since God is a just judge, strong and forbearing, the more patiently He endures the sins of transgressors, the more severely He punishes them. Thus it befell that the man rushed from vice to vice, as has been written: "He that is filthy, let him be filthy still." [10] Seduced by the spirit of fornication, he was taken in adultery not long afterward and suffered a death befitting his iniquity.

11. Henry of Le Mans

This item and Numbers 12-14 bear upon the activities of two men who gravely troubled the Church and whose influence far outlived them. They are Henry, so-called of Le Mans or of Lausanne,[1] and Peter of Bruys. The present piece deals with Henry in the first appearance of his career, which was to last some thirty years. At Le Mans, his welcome or, at least, the acceptance of him by the clergy as an eccentric but highly popular preacher soon turned to fear and hatred as his preaching stirred an anticlerical uproar among the people. He is called a heretic, but beyond its anticlericalism the nature of his teaching is not made clear. After Bishop Hildebert succeeded in expelling him from the city, Henry traveled southward, continuing to preach, and seems also to have moved into an openly heretical position in respect of some sacraments and of the Church's authority. It was probably he who was the target of the Council of Toulouse (1119), the third canon of which excommunicates as heretics those who attacked the sacraments of the Eucharist and baptism, disparaged the validity of priestly orders, and held errors about the conditions of legitimate matrimony.[2] As the chronicler of

Le Mans then recounts, Henry was eventually seized; after being examined before the Council of Pisa in 1135, the heretic renounced his errors and was ordered to a monastery. But not long afterward he was again at large, the danger of his activities seeming ever greater to contemporary orthodox eyes.

The widest disagreement long prevailed among scholars on details of the life and doctrines of Henry, as of Peter of Bruys, with whom Henry joined forces at some time before 1133 (see No. 13). But in recent years new studies have clarified the record and even increased the estimate of the importance of these men in the story of twelfth-century heresy. It has been shown that Henry, for example, was no exponent of dualism, although his influence exacerbated the antagonism to the Church from which the Cathars would eventually profit. More significant, perhaps, was his influence on the Waldenses of the later part of the century, who were to absorb some of his teachings.[3]

Three of the many studies on Henry may be cited: Johannes Wilhelm von Walter, *Die ersten Wanderprediger Frankreichs: Studien zur Geschichte des Mönchtums, Neue Folge,* pp. 130-40; Raoul Manselli, "Il monaco Enrico e la sua eresia," *Bullettino dell'Istituto storico italiano per il medio evo e Archivio Muratoriano,* LXV (1953), 1-63; and the same author's *Studi sulle eresie,* pp. 1-67.

Two excerpts are translated here from a narrative of the deeds of the bishops of Le Mans which was compiled by a number of authors from the ninth to the thirteenth century. The author of the portion from which these were taken was apparently a contemporary of Bishop Hildebert of Le Mans (1096-1125), the prelate who had to deal with Henry.[4]

Parts A and B are both translated, by permission of the Société historique de la province du Mans, from *Actus pontificum Cenomannis in urbe degentium,* ed. by G. Busson and A. Ledru (Archives historiques du Maine, II [Le Mans, 1901]), pp. 407-15 and 437-38, respectively.

A. HENRY AT LE MANS

circa 1115

About the same time, in nearby districts there appeared a certain charlatan whose personal conduct, evil habits, and detestable doctrine testified that he deserved flogging and the punishments of a murderer. He hid the madness of a ravening wolf under sheep's clothing; the driving power in his countenance and glance was like that of the cruel sea. Hair cropped, beard untrimmed, tall of stature, quick of pace, he glided along the ground barefoot as winter raged; easy of address, awe-inspiring in voice, young in years, scornful of ornate dress; his unconventional way of life was on the surface unlike that of ordinary folk—shelter in the houses of burghers, a night's lodging as a transient, a meal, a bed in a garret (not at all in keeping with the prophet Daniel but in accord with that verse which reads, "For death is come up through our windows").[5] What more can be said? For everywhere he gained an increasing reputation for astonishing holiness and wisdom; not by merit, but by deceit; not by truth, but by appearance; not in character nor habits nor piety, but by mere hearsay. Matrons and adolescent boys (for he enjoyed the pandering of both sexes), attending him at different times, avowed openly their aberrations and increased them, caressed his feet, his buttocks, his groin, with tender hands. Completely carried away by this fellow's wantonness and by the enormity of adultery, they publicly proclaimed that they had never touched a man of such strength, such humanity, such power. By his speech even a heart of stone could be moved to repentance; monks, anchorites, and all the cloistered clergy could well imitate his piety and celibate life. Indeed, they declared, the Lord God had bestowed upon him the ancient and veritable blessing and spirit of the prophets, through which, by only scanning their faces, he might know and declare the sins of mortal men which they hid from others.

When rumors of this sort floated into our district, the people, applauding their own destruction with their peculiar fickleness, daily and every day longed to be beguiled by his discourse, longed for his advent, by which they might the more quickly become intimates and participants in his heresy. For it often happens that those things are the more welcome to the masses which are the worse for them. Indeed, the cycle of the days brought still more! The man, determined on the infection of our fellow-citizens with his venemous breath, in imitation of the Savior dispatched before him to the bishop two of his disciples, like him in life and character. When they entered the outskirts of our city on Ash Wednesday, the whole population, eager for the wickedness offered them, received them as angels of the Lord of all. As teachers do, they carried staves, to the tips of which a standard like a cross, made of iron, was fastened; in outward appearance and in speech they put on the appearance of penitents. The pontiff [Hildebert], a man of the greatest piety, little suspecting the deceits of a Trojan horse, received them courteously and in good faith and turned upon them a gracious and friendly countenance. Although he had undertaken to go to Rome, he instructed his archdeacons, among other things, to grant to the pseudohermit Henry (for that was the heretic's name), peaceful entry and license to preach to the people.

Henry entered within the city walls, and the populace, as usual, applauded novelty, as we have said, and were more interested in an unknown character than in one of proven worth. How strange! They thought his virtues exceeded his reputation, and, as usual, gossip had made full use of its frequent repetition and inflated it still further. Some of the clergy, led astray in his schism by quarrels and private donations, encouraged the rabble by their ranting and prepared a platform from which that demagogue might harangue the crowds of people who hung on his lips. Furthermore, when he addressed the people, these clerics sat weeping at his feet as he roared pronouncements like an oracle. It was as if legions of demons were all making their noise in one blast through his mouth. Nevertheless, he was remarkably fluent. When his speech entered the ears of the mob, it stuck in their minds. Like a potent poison, it penetrated to the inner organs, vented an inexorable hatred on life. Ever more eagerly it changes its form and renews its attacks. By this heresy the people were so charged with hatred for the clergy that they threatened their servants with torture and sought to allow no one to sell anything to them or to buy from them. Indeed, they treated them like heathen and publicans. Furthermore, they had resolved not only to tear down their dwellings and pillage their goods, but to stone them or hang them from the gibbet as well [and would have done so] had not the count [6] and his vassals learned of the wickedness of these people and prevented their abominable attempts by force rather than by argument, for beasts hearken not to reason.

Some of the clergy who lived in the city, namely Hugh Bird, William Drinknowater, and Pagan Aldric,[7] approached Henry one day, intending to debate with him, and were violently assaulted and abusively tumbled and fouled with mud and filth in the gutters and barely escaped from the attack of the furious crowd with their lives; indeed, once they were out of immediate danger their retreat seemed like flight. Surrounded by the mob, they would never have escaped the peril, had not the protection of the count and his vassals permitted them to reach shelter. For, as we said, the lord of the city opposed the folly of those people and was resolved never to abandon the defense of the clergy.

The clergy did not dare to speak to the charlatan personally so they sent a letter by one of the canons, couched in the following terms:

"In peace and respect our Church received you and your companions, who came in sheep's clothing but who inwardly devised the wiles of ravening wolves. It likewise displayed toward you the promise and performance of brotherly love, believing that you would honestly admonish the people for the salvation of their souls and would faithfully sow the seed of the word of God in their hearts. But you took upon yourself to give in return the very opposite of what you should—wrath for peace, disgrace for honor, hatred for love, a curse for a blessing—and to disturb the Church of God by your knavery. You have sown discord between clergy and people, and by treachery ten times repeated you have moved the mass of unruly people with swords and cudgels against Mother Church. You have proffered us the kiss of Judas; you have, as a public insult, called us and the whole clergy heretics. Above all—and what is worse—you have banefully and perfidiously uttered much that is contrary to the Catholic faith, which a faithful Christian trembles to recapitulate. Therefore, by the authority of the high and indivisible Trinity, of the whole orthodox Church, of Mary, Holy Mother of God, of St. Peter, prince of the apostles, and of his vicar, our reverend father, Pope Paschal,[8] and of our bishop, Hildebert, we altogether forbid you and the companions who so wickedly and damnably associate themselves with your error to preach further in the entire diocese of Le Mans, privately or publicly; nor shall you dare to disseminate the absurdities of your wicked doctrines. If, however, you assert yourself against such authority and open wide your jaws again to spew out poison, we, buttressed by this authority and its prerogative, excommunicate you and all your accomplices, supporters, and assistants; and He, whose divinity you unceasingly oppose, shall cause you to be delivered to eternal malediction on the day of stern judgment."

The fellow, however, refused to accept the letter, so William Muscha read it aloud, phrase by phrase, in his presence. To William the bystanders threatened bodily injury, for it seemed to them that he had publicly and rudely put Henry to shame. The latter, at each phrase of the letter, shook his head and kept repeating, "You lie." Surely, if the count's steward, under whose protection William had undertaken the mission, had not been there, William would never have returned to Mother Church alive.

After these events, Henry nonetheless held sacrilegious meetings even at Saint-Germain and Saint-Vincent,[9] where he proclaimed a new doctrine: that women who had lived unchastely should, all unclothed, burn their garments, together with their hair, in the sight of everyone; that no one in the future should receive gold, silver, property, or betrothal gifts with his wife, nor should she bring him a dowry, but the naked should marry the nude, the ailing the sick, the pauper the destitute. Nor was he concerned whether the chaste or the unchaste married.

While they behaved as the charlatan suggested, the fellow admired the beautiful features of individual women, how one surpassed the other in whiteness, while another was more attractive for plumpness of body. The whole behavior and mood of the people hung upon his dictate. What a shower of gold and silver he might have reveled in, had he wished, but he restrained his avarice for fear of being thought too greedy. In reality, while keeping much for himself, he did devote a little to replacing the clothing which, as we have recorded, had been burned. Also, at his behest many young men took in marriage women of the streets, for whom Henry bought clothing worth four shillings (*solidi*), scarcely sufficient to cover their nakedness.

But the Just Judge destroyed the works of the heretic and revealed to others what sort of tree this was: one which bears leaves but no fruit, which monopolizes the ground and chokes out everything that sprouts nearby, one which cannot endure until the rainy season, but withers and dies in summer. For after a short lapse of time, the young men who had taken wives according to his wicked advice ran away to other parts, driven thereto either by hunger or by the debauchery of the women, and left their wives totally destitute of support. And so the men took other women to themselves in adultery; the women, though their husbands were still alive, sought illicit union with other men. Although they were many, no man or woman of those who entered into matrimony at this man's urging ever displayed faithfulness or respect to wife or husband. Nor could any other woman who by oath renounced fornication and the pleasures of dress restrain herself, but within a matter of days, as her misdeeds increased, she would lapse into worse habits.

As this publican[10] was constantly engaged in such acts and many others like them, he learned of the return of the bishop, who, as we have already indicated, had set out for Rome. He withdrew to the village of Saint-Calais and lived there and in places nearby. He was far from abandoning his career; on the contrary, he steadily introduced worse innovations. For on the most sacred day of Pentecost, when faithful children, indeed, are wont devoutly to attend divine service, this lowest of men attached to himself a certain very young cleric (by whose report

so much of the sensuality of the man was later exposed)[11] and set out
stealthily and in the solitary quiet of the night for the house of a certain
knight and there lay wantonly in bed with the matron of the house until
midday. Thus, neither out of holy fear or for shame before men would
he moderate his lewdness, until he had displayed the enormity of his
villainy to people near and far.

While these things were going on, the bishop already mentioned approached the outskirts of the city, accompanied by a great and mighty
throng of his clergy. When with fatherly kindness he bestowed the blessing of the living God by word and sign upon the people, they were stirred
in animosity of thought and speech to disparagement of the Creator.
Spurning his sign of the Cross and the episcopal blessing, they cried out,
"We want no knowledge of your ways! We don't want your blessing!
Bless filth! Consecrate filth! We have a father, we have a pontiff, we
have an advocate who surpasses you in authority; he exceeds you in
probity and knowledge. The wicked clergy, your clergy, oppose him.
They gainsay his teaching. They despise and reject him as guilty of
sacrilege, fearing that by prophetic insight he would expose their crimes.
They condemned his heresy and incontinence behind the prerogative of a
letter, but all these things shall fall back at once upon the heads of those
who have presumed by unimaginably overweening audacity to forbid to
the holy man of God the word of heavenly preaching."

The bishop had compassion on their error and stupidity and patiently
bore the insults which they heaped upon him, praying without cease to
the God of Majesty that He would restrain popular delusion compounded
with pride, lest they succeed in creating a schism in His Church. But in
accordance with the words of the Psalmist pleading for the salvation of
transgressors, "Fill their faces with shame and they shall seek thy name,
O Lord," [12] the same Lord God allowed the major part of the city's
suburbs to be burned by a sudden conflagration, that by the loss of
worldly goods at least, they might abandon their evil way of life and call
upon the sacred name, the name of the living God. Indeed, the pontiff
(echoing the words of the prophet, "O how great is the multitude of thy
sweetness, O Lord, which thou hast hidden for them that fear thee") [13]
a few days later sought out the seducer and put a stop to his irreverence
by divine authority. For when they met in parley the bishop inquired on
the basis of what special fitness the man had chosen his vocation. He was
mute, not understanding what "vocation" meant. The bishop tried again,

inquiring what office the man exercised. "I am a deacon," said he. Then said the bishop, "Tell me, now, did you go to Mass today?" "No." "Then let us sing the morning hymns unto God." But when they began to do so, Henry acknowledged that he did not know the order of service for the day. Still the bishop, wishing to disclose to the full the fellow's lack of knowledge, began to sing the customary hymns to the Mother of God. Of these the man knew neither the words nor the sequence. And so, covered with shame, he acknowledged his life, his way of preaching, his presumption. In reality he was a camp-follower, completely untaught, and wholly given over to sensuality, yet he had gained notoriety by haranguing the people and throwing dice.[14] Of such is it written: "True glory takes root and grows; all shams quickly pass away and wither like flowers, nor can anything which is based on pretense be long lasting." [15]

So the bishop, because he recognized the shallowness and irreverence of Henry, by apostolic authority ordered him to tarry no longer in his diocese but to make his way elsewhere and spare our people. Indeed, the man was overcome by the pontiff's persistence and fled secretly, and (if the report be valid) disturbed other regions [16] in the same fashion and spread infection by his poisonous breath. I have recorded these facts about Henry and recounted the deeds of Hildebert for the convenience and instruction of posterity, that care may be taken lest the Church of Christ be disturbed at some other time by a delusion of this sort.

Thereafter, the same Hildebert arranged in various ways, by persuasion and humility in equal parts, to calm the madness of the people whom Henry had so seditiously incited against the clergy. Henry had so won them over to himself that even now it is scarcely possible to destroy his memory and to drive affection for him from their hearts.

B. HENRY BEFORE THE COUNCIL OF PISA

circa 1135

At this time the pseudohermit of whom we wrote in a previous passage began anew to spread the poison of his heresy in far-off lands and to lay waste the Church of God by the blackness of his villainy. Lending his ear solely to the narratives and writings of the prophets, he propounded a perverted dogma which a faithful Christian ought neither recapitulate nor hear. But by the pity of God, who always "hath had regard to the prayer of the humble and hath not despised their petition," [17] that fellow Henry was seized by the archbishop of Arles [18] and brought before Lord Pope Innocent [19] in a council at Pisa.[20] There he was again convicted and by common consent named as a heretic; at the council's close he was delivered into confinement.[21] Later, when he had been given leave to go to another province, he took up a new sect, a new course, a new path of transgression.[22] This region he has kept so constantly in turmoil that Christians hardly visit the churches; rather they condemn the holy service. They refuse offerings to the priests, first fruits, tithes, visitation of the sick, and the usual reverences.[23] But now we must pass over such things and hasten on to other matters.

12. A Monk's Description of the Errors of Henry

A tract against the errors of Henry gives the clearest description we have of the doctrines he professed. The author depicts himself as having sought out the heretic for discussion, after which he recorded Henry's assertions and his own lengthier rebuttals to be sent to some unnamed prelate. The date was probably 1133-1135.[1] There are two versions of the tract. One, discovered by Mario Esposito in 1940 in a manuscript of Nice (MS 3 [R.18], fols. 136-43), gives the name of the author as William.[2] Raoul Manselli, in 1953, identified and published another version, from Paris (B. N. MS Lat. 3371, fols. 1r-4r). It is earlier in date, more detailed, and was probably the basis for the Nice copy, although it has no statement of authorship.[3] From Manselli's edition of the Paris manuscript are translated here the statements attributed to Henry. The arguments of the Catholic are omitted, because they do not advance our knowledge of Henry's heresy. We add, as Manselli did, one passage which appears only in the Nice manuscript, and have throughout noted other differences between the two versions, using photographs of the Nice manuscript for this purpose.

The significance of the work is not limited to its revelation of Henry's teaching. Some three quarters of a century later, when followers of Waldes of Lyons were engaging in controversy with the Cathars, William's work was taken over almost completely into a polemical tract attributed to Durand of Huesca, a Waldensian who was most active in that debate.[4]

The translation comes from the text in Raoul Manselli, "Il monaco Enrico e la sua eresia," *Bullettino dell'Istituto storico italiano per il medio evo e Archivio Muratoriano,* LXV (1953), 44-63, *passim*; by permission of that journal.

circa 1133-1135

After parting from Your Worthy Presence, I came to a place where

I had a bitter controversy with the heresiarch Henry. I have taken pains to describe to Your Prudence the course of the argument, so that if the beast, by any chance, comes into your vicinity you may be forewarned that by many arguments and proofs he bas been clearly shown to be a heretic and you may firmly keep him away from the limits of your church.[5]

Thereupon, I addressed the fellow in these words: "I ask you who propose such wicked tenets, so hurtful to our faith: In obedience to whom do you preach? Who commissioned you to this function? What Scriptures do you accept?" And he [replied]: "To answer your question about obedience: I confess that I obey God rather than man, for obedience is owed to God rather than to men.[6] To answer your question about my mission: He sent me who said, 'Go, teach ye all nations.'[7] He who imposed the duty was the same as He who said, 'Thou shalt love thy neighbor as thyself.'[8] Furthermore, I accept the Scriptures of the New Testament, by which I verify and corroborate the aforesaid statements. But in case you seek to draw arguments against me from Jerome, Augustine, and other doctors of the Church, I admit giving their words due regard but not as vital to salvation" [pp. 44-45]. . . .[9]

Concerning Children Who Die before the Age of Understanding. You [Henry] argue that children attain salvation if they die before the age of understanding and by this you destroy the doctrine of original sin; thus you fall into the Pelagian heresy.[10] For you say: "It is a wicked thing to condemn a man for another person's sin, in accordance with the text, 'The soul that sinneth, the same shall die,'[11] and likewise, 'The son shall not bear the iniquity of the father. Everyone shall bear his own burden' " [p. 47]. . . .[12]

That Baptism Should Not Be Given with Chrism and Oil.[13] Now we pass on to another point. You say: "There is no Gospel command to baptize with chrism and oil" [p. 51]. . . .

That the Body of Christ Cannot Be Consecrated by Unworthy Ministers.[14] Now we come to a third article. "The body of Christ," so you say, "cannot be consecrated by an unworthy minister." In this I see your wickedness explicitly, for you wish to make this a means of weakening the basis of a great sacrament and of depriving the Church of that by which the body of man is strengthened and the spirit sustained. For you say: "Mass may be sung and Christ's body consecrated, provided anyone can be found worthy to do so"; thus enjoining us to discover an imaginary person who never can be found, because no one is without sin, not even a day-old child. "For all have sinned and do need the glory of God."[15] You ask the impossible, seeking to shatter the ordinances of our faith. You, together with the Arians [16] and other heretics, never cease to rend the robe of Christ [p. 53]. . . .

Merely the Agreement of the Persons Concerned Constitutes a Marriage. Give attention, if you can, and let us go on to the sacrament of matrimony, on which you are in error. "Merely the agreement of the persons concerned, without any rite or ecclesiastical ceremony, constitutes a marriage," you say, "and what is so contracted cannot be dissolved save on grounds of fornication." In this your error is disgraceful [p. 55]. . . .[17]

Priests of the Present Day Do Not Have the Power to Bind or Loose. But since you do not know what things constitute, or are impediments to, or dissolve marriages, I forbear to discuss them with you. Let us now turn to the subject of priests and prelates of the Church, against whom you rave. "Priests of today," you represent, "have not the power to bind or loose, for they are stripped of this power by having criminally sinned" [p. 56]. . . .

There is No Gospel Command to Go to a Priest for Penance. Now let us pass on to another point, which concerns penance. You say: "There is no Gospel command to go to a priest for penance, for the apostle James says, 'Confess your sins one to another,' [18] and so on. He did not say, 'Confess to priests,' but 'Confess one to another'" [p. 58]. . . .

Bishops and Priests Ought Not to Have Wealth or Benefices.[19] Now you say: "Bishops and priests ought not to have benefices or wealth." In this you do not abate your frenzy against priests [p. 60]. . . .

On the Ring, the Miter, and the Pastoral Staff [p. 61. The heretic is not quoted in this passage but is represented as opposing the use of these appurtenances of the episcopal office.]

That Churches of Wood or Stone Should Not Be Constructed. Of churches, which you have discussed in your first chapter,[20] you say that they ought not to be built of wood or stone. . . . Yet you seek to subvert and trouble the house of God and its beauty, and the whole condition of the Church [p. 61]. . . . What follows—"No good work helps the dead, for as soon as men die they either are utterly damned or are saved"— is openly heretical [p. 62]. . . .[21]

13. The Teachings of Peter of Bruys

About the year 1112, Peter of Bruys began a career of preaching in defiance
of the Church in the Alpine foothills east of the Rhone.[1] Like his contemporary Henry, he railed at the Roman clergy for their worldly life, insisting
on the spiritual character of the true Church to the exclusion of its material
attributes. To orthodox observers, the two men seemed much alike. Indeed,
shortly before Peter of Bruys died, he and Henry came into some kind of
alliance. Although Henry was called the heir to Peter's iniquities, he was
more than a mere disciple, however, for on some points they disagreed.
Peter of Bruys was murdered, not long after 1131, by certain of the faithful
who were outraged at his sacrilegious treatment of the Cross, the veneration
of which he despised.

One of the great abbots of Cluny, Peter the Venerable (1152-1156), wrote
the only detailed account we now have of the teaching of Peter of Bruys.[2]
The abbot was one of the reformers of his order, a man of wide-ranging
interests and travels, whose letters constitute an excellent source for the
history of his life and times. Between 1131 and 1133 he wrote a letter
which was, in effect, a tractate in refutation of the doctrines of the heretic.
It was not made public, however, until after Peter of Bruys's death when,
in 1133 or 1134, the abbot added as a preface to it another shorter letter,
summarizing the career and tenets of the heretic. We translate only this
second and prefatory letter.[3]

On Peter of Bruys, one may consult particularly Manselli, *Studi sulle
eresie*, chaps. I, II; and J. C. Reagan, "Did the Petrobrusians Teach Salvation by Faith Alone?" *Journal of Religion*, VII (1927), 81-91. A recent
biography of Peter the Venerable is Jean Leclercq's *Pierre le Vénérable*;
there is also a brief biography of Peter in English in Herbert Thurston and
Donald Attwater, eds., *Butler's Lives of the Saints*, rev. ed., IV, 640-41.

The following piece is translated from *Petri Venerabilis . . . Epistola sive
tractatus adversus petrobrusianos haereticos: Praefatio*, in Migne, *Patrologia
latina*, CLXXXIX, 719-24.

1133-1134

To the lords and fathers, ministers of the Church of God, the archbishops of Arles and Embrun, the bishops of Die and Gap,[4] Brother
Peter, the lowly abbot of Cluny, offers greeting and obedience.

Recently I wrote a letter to Your Reverence,[5] opposing the heresies of
Peter of Bruys, but a large quantity of important business kept my mind
from composing and my pen from writing; so I have put off sending it
until this moment. Now, at last, I send it to Your Discretion, so that
through you it may come to the attention of the heretics against whom it
is written and also to the attention of Catholics, to whom, perchance, it

may be of use. I send it to you because in the lands administered by you or in adjacent areas this foolish and impious heresy, a serious pestilence, has slain many people and infected more; but the grace of God has helped and spurred on your efforts, and it has now moved a little apart from your localities. However, as I have heard, it has shifted to a place not very far from you. When driven out of your region of Septimania [6] by your energetic action, it made its lair in the province of *Novempopulana*, which is commonly called Gascony, and in nearby areas. Therein, at one moment it cowers in terror, at the next sallies forth when it has mustered boldness; it deceives those whom it can, corrupts those whom it can, and administers its lethal poison to people in various places. It is therefore up to you, to whom especially by reason of office and of exceptional knowledge pertains the care of the Church of God and on whom the Church rests on sturdy pillars; it is your affair, I say, to root out the heresy by preaching and even, if it shall prove necessary, by force of arms of the laity from those places in which the heresy rejoices at having found its hiding places. But since it is right that Christian charity should put the greater effort on converting heretics than on driving them out, let authority be cited to them, let reason also be added, so that they may be compelled to yield—to authority if they choose to remain Christians, to reason if they choose to remain men.

Perhaps it will be of advantage to them for this purpose if they choose to pay heed to the letter which I wrote to you in refutation of their errors; and if they are willing to put aside contentiousness and obstinacy after they have read it carefully, even though they have erred egregiously, they may return to their senses from the stupidity of such error. But if they have been "delivered up to a reprobate sense" [7] and choose to be foolish rather than wise, to perish rather than to be saved, to die rather than to live, perhaps the reading of this letter will satisfy the inner questionings of some Catholics and either heal their minds of listlessness of faith, not apparent to men, or fortify them against those whose tongue the prophet called "a sharp sword." [8] This reason, which I list in last place, was to me the more important one for writing, so that, even though this letter be spurned by the heretics, it still may be of some utility to the Church of God. For the Church, as Your Wisdom knows, has throughout past ages been wont always so to proceed that she has never passed over in silence any of the numerous and varied heresies which have repeatedly striven to taint her purity, but has, for her own security and for the continual instruction of all, purged the blasphemies of all heretics by appeal to holy authorities and also by reason. This I— although one of the least members of the body of Christ, that is, of his Church—have ventured to do in writing these things, so that what I have written may be of use to the heretics, if that be possible. Catholics into whose hands it may fall may be made more wary of reprehensible teaching and the like.

And because the first seeds of erroneous doctrine, sown and nurtured by Peter of Bruys for nearly twenty years, have produced five principal poisonous plants, I have directed my discussion, in so far as I could, against these especially, so that thought and word may occupy themselves the more fully with those things in which the greater injury to faith shows the more serious danger to lie. Thus, since the tract itself is rather prolix, nor is, perhaps, a prolonged period for reading available to you who are occupied with the affairs of several churches, I here briefly resume those propositions and set forth the errors with which the long letter deals more fully.

The first proposition of the heretics denies that infants presented before the age of understanding can be saved through the baptism of Christ and that another's faith can be of advantage to those who cannot exercise their own, since, according to the heretics, not another's faith but one's own brings salvation through baptism. For the Lord said, "He that believeth and is baptized shall be saved; but he that believeth not shall be condemned." [9]

The second proposition holds that construction of temples or churches ought not to be undertaken; moreover, if built, they should be torn down. Nor are holy places necessary to Christians for prayer, since God hears as well when invoked in a tavern as in a church, in a market place as in a temple, before an altar or in a stable, and He hearkens to those who are worthy.

The third proposition prescribes that holy crosses be broken and burned, because that shape or contrivance, on which Christ was so bitterly tortured and so cruelly killed, is not worthy of adoration or veneration or prayer of any kind; but, in revenge for His torments and death, they should be disgraced with every dishonor, hacked to pieces by swords, burned by fire.

The fourth proposition not only denies the verity of the body and blood of the Lord, daily and continually presented through the sacrament in the Church, but declares that it is nothing at all, and that it ought not be offered to God.

The fifth proposition scorns the sacrificial offerings, prayers, charities, and the rest of the good works done by the faithful who live, on behalf of the faithful who are dead; and it affirms that they can in no way be of service to the dead.

I have answered these five propositions to the extent that God allows me in that letter which I am sending to Your Sanctity. And I have much concerned myself with whatever ways the impiety of the faithless may be either converted or confounded and the confident belief of the just may be encouraged.

Now, after the destruction of Peter of Bruys, whom the zeal of the faithful at Saint-Gilles punished by burning in the flames from the wood of the Lord's Cross which he had set afire, after this impious man had assuredly made the transit from fire to fire, from brief passing flame to eternal flame, the heir of his iniquity, Henry, has altered but indeed not improved his diabolical teaching with I know not what other matters and has put out not five but many propositions, as I have seen inscribed in a volume which is said to have been written down from his very words.[10] Against this, one's mind is kindled to act in turn and to set holy phrases over against demoniacal words. However, since full assurance has not yet been given me that this truly represents his thought or teaching, I have deferred a response until the time when I shall have undoubted certainty about the things which are there set forth. But if I may in the future reach assurance, through the evidence of your thorough investigation, I shall put forth what effort I can to see that the cup of death, offered by the most miserable of men to their peers in misery, which is drained of one part shall, by renewed refutations, be wholly emptied of its remaining dregs. Meanwhile, please make known the letter, drawn up for the convenience of readers and by you transmitted to those to whom it shall seem appropriate in time and place. It may succeed, as I have said, in correcting some of the heretics against whom it is written, or in making Catholics, for whom it is written, more cautious in these and like matters. If anyone wants to copy it, let him not fail to set this shorter letter as a preface, for in this the occasion for and the content of the larger tract are briefly indicated.

14. Bernard of Clairvaux against Henry

The career of Bernard of Clairvaux is too well known to need review here. His pre-eminence in the religious life of the twelfth century made him a natural champion of orthodoxy against every kind of attack. It may be recalled that he was the leader in the fight against the theological teaching of Abelard which culminated in the latter's condemnation at Sens in 1140. Subsequently, he harried Abelard's disciple, Arnold of Brescia, out of France (see No. 19) and in 1148 he was to press an unsuccessful proposal for the condemnation of Gilbert de la Porrée at the Council of Rheims. In the two translations presented here we see him joining in the attack on the popular heresies. The first is a letter addressed to Alphonse Jordan, count of Toulouse (1112-1148), announcing Bernard's participation in a mission to Toulouse to combat the influence of the heretic Henry; the second is from a biography of Bernard by his secretary, Geoffrey of Auxerre, describing that visit. Before coming to Clairvaux, Geoffrey had been a student of Abelard; later he became, successively, abbot of Clairvaux (1162), of Fosseneuve (1170), and of Hautecombe (1176), and was to be present at an important moment in the history of Waldes and the Poor of Lyons (see No. 32). Among his numerous works are Books III and IV of the _Magna vita_ or _Vita prima_ of St. Bernard, from which the excerpt in part B is taken.

An excellent biography of St. Bernard, although not of special value for the study of the heresies, is Watkin Williams, _Saint Bernard of Clairvaux_. The older biography by Elphège Vacandard, _Vie de Saint Bernard, abbé de Clairvaux_, contains a better treatment of the abbot's efforts against the popular heresies.[1] On the life and works of Geoffrey of Auxerre, consult Jean Leclercq, "Les Ecrits de Geoffroy d'Auxerre," _Revue bénédictine_, LXII (1952), 274-91; and the _Histoire littéraire de la France_, XIV, 430-51.

Part A below is translated from _Sancti Bernardi . . . epistolae_ 241, in Migne, _Patrologia latina_, CLXXXII, 434-36. Part B is translated from _Sancti Bernardi . . . vita et res gestae libris septem comprehensae: Liber tertius auctore Gaufrido monacho_ . . . VI.16,17, in Migne, _Patrologia latina_, CLXXXV, 312-13.

A. BERNARD'S DENUNCIATION OF HENRY

_1145_

1. I have learned and realize fully how great are the evils which the heretic Henry has committed and is still committing daily against the churches of God. A ravening wolf in sheep's clothing is abroad in your land, but as the Lord has shown, we know him by his fruits.[2] The churches are without congregations, congregations are without priests, priests are without proper reverence, and, finally, Christians are without Christ. Churches are looked upon as synagogues; it is denied that God's sanctu-

ary is holy; sacraments are not deemed sacred; solemn feast days are stultified. Men die in their sins. Souls everywhere are snatched away to the dread tribunal, alas, unreconciled by penance, unfortified by Holy Communion. So long as the grace of baptism is denied them, the life of Christ is barred to the children of Christians, nor are they allowed to draw near to salvation, although the Savior tenderly calls them, saying, "Suffer the little children to come to me." [3] Is it from innocents alone, then, that God, who has saved both men and beasts as He has multiplied His mercies, withholds that same overflowing mercy? Why, I ask, why does this man begrudge to children the child Savior who was born to them? This is diabolical jealousy! Because of it, death has entered the world.[4] Or does the man assume that children need no savior because they are children? If that is so, then for naught did the mighty Lord become a little child, not to mention that He was scourged, was spat upon, was crucified, and finally died.

2. That man is not from God who thus acts and speaks in contradiction of God. O woe! that he is nonetheless listened to by many and has a following who believe him. O unhappiest of people! In them, at the voice of one heretic, have grown silent all the voices of prophets and apostles that had rung out in one spirit of truth to call together the Church in the faith of Christ out of all nations. Thus have holy oracles deceived! Thus are deceived the eyes and minds of all who perceive the fulfillment of the prophecy whereof they read! That truth so assuredly obvious to all, this man alone, with amazing and truly Jewish blindness, either sees not, or hates to see fulfilled. And at the same time he has swayed a silly and foolish people, by I know not what devilish wiles, not to believe their own eyes in a matter so obvious. The fathers were deceived and the children go astray! The whole world goes to perdition, even after Christ's blood was shed, and it is only those whom he is deceiving who [according to him] have won the full riches of God's mercies and have attained the fullness of His grace.[5]

And now for this reason, although enfeebled in body, I am undertaking a hurried journey to those places where that singular wild beast feeds,[6] since there is no one to offer him resistance or to afford protection from him. Indeed, because for evil deeds like these he has been forced to flee from all parts of France, he has found only those lands open to him. There boldly he revels in all his fury among the flock of Christ under your rule. Be yourself the judge, illustrious prince, whether this befits your honor. Yet it is not strange that the wily serpent has deceived you, for he does, indeed, have the appearance of piety though he has entirely rejected its excellence.

3. But hear now the sort of person he is! He is an apostate who cast off his religious habit—for he was a monk—and returned to the filth of the flesh and of the world, like a dog to its vomit.[7] Moreover, because of his shameful conduct, not being able to endure life among his relatives and acquaintances, or rather, not being permitted to do so on account of the enormity of his offense, he girded his loins and journeyed aimlessly about, having become a wanderer [8] and fugitive on the face of the earth. When he had begun to beg, he put a price on the Gospel, for he was educated, and, offering the Word of God for sale at retail, he preached in order to eat. If he were able to wheedle anything beyond his daily needs from the simpler folk or from some one of the married women, he basely squandered it at dice or used it for purposes more foul. Often, indeed, after a day of applause from the people the distinguished preacher was found that night with harlots and sometimes even with married women! Ask, if you please, noble Sir, under what circumstances he left the city of Lausanne, or Le Mans, or Poitiers, or Bordeaux! And nowhere is a way of return open to him, for everywhere he has left behind him foul footprints. Did you hope for good fruit from such a tree? Since he came to the land where he now is, he has made of it a stench throughout the whole earth, because, according to the word of the Lord, an evil tree cannot bring forth good fruit.[9]

4. This, as I have said, is the reason for my visit. Nor do I now come of myself alone but I am equally drawn by the summons of and by compassion for the Church. Perchance that thorn and its evil seeds can be rooted out of the field of the Lord while they are still small, not by my hand, for I am nothing, but by that of the holy bishops in whose company I am, with the help of your own strong right hand. Chief among these is the venerable bishop of Ostia, sent by the Apostolic See for this purpose. He is a man "who has done great things in Israel," [10] and through him has Almighty God given victory to His Church in many instances. It is incumbent upon you, illustrious Sir, to receive him and his associates [11] with honor and to exert yourself, in accordance with the power vouchsafed you from on high, so that this great labor of these great men, which is undertaken especially for your own salvation and the salvation of your people, be not in vain.

B. BERNARD'S MISSION TO TOULOUSE

1145

In the neighborhood of Toulouse a certain Henry, once a monk, later a base apostate of very wicked life and destructive teaching, had caught the fickle attention of the people of that region with winning words and, as the Apostle foretold of certain men, "speaking lies in hypocrisy" [12] he trafficked with them in false words. He was, moreover, an open enemy of the Church, irreverently disparaging the sacraments as well as the ministers of the Church. He had already progressed immoderately in this wickedness. For the venerable father, when he wrote about him to the prince of Toulouse, says, among other things: "Now everywhere were found churches without congregations, congregations without priests, priests without proper reverence. The life of Christ was barred to the children of Christians so long as the grace of baptism was denied them. Prayers and offerings for the dead were ridiculed as were the invocation of saints, pilgrimages by the faithful, the building of temples, holidays on holy days, the anointing with the chrism; and, in a word, all the institutions of the Church were scorned."

Because of the great need, the holy man undertook the journey to which he had already often been urged by the church of that region; he was at last persuaded, as well as accompanied, by the very reverend Alberic, bishop of Ostia and legate of the Apostolic See. Then, when he arrived, he was received by the people of the land with incredible devotion, as if an angel from heaven had descended into their midst. He could not tarry with them, because no one could restrain the crowds of people who pressed upon him, so great was the multitude day and night who approached him to ask his blessing and implore his help.

He did, however, preach in the city of Toulouse for several days and in other places more often frequented and more seriously infected by that miserable heretic. He instructed many simple folk in the faith, called back the wandering, restored those who had been subverted. And by his authority he bore down upon and overwhelmed the subverters and the obstinate so that they dared not resist or even appear.[13] As for the rest, although that heretic went into hiding, nevertheless his ways were so obstructed and his paths so hedged that he was hardly safe anywhere afterward and he was finally captured and handed over in chains to the bishop.[14] On this journey, God was also glorified in his

servant by a great many miraculous works; the hearts of some he recalled from impious errors, the bodies of others he healed of various ailments.

15. An Appeal to Bernard of Clairvaux and a Sermon in Reply

For the sake of grouping together all the items which dealt specifically
with the heretic Henry, we have violated chronological order slightly by
deferring to this point a letter written by Eberwin, prior of the Premonstratensian abbey of Steinfeld, in 1143 or 1144, and a sermon of the abbot
of Clairvaux which in some measure answered a request made by Eberwin.
Eberwin wrote to describe events which had recently occurred in Cologne
and to solicit Bernard's comments.[1] He announced the presence of "new
heretics," who constituted two different groups. In one of these we may
clearly perceive the sect of the Cathars, for Eberwin enumerates all the
essentials of their doctrine and practice, except that there is no explicit
reference to dualism. He mentions their claim to the true apostolic tradition;
their alleged link with Eastern groups; [2] their rejection of this material world,
and the ascetic practices thus entailed; their emphasis on the Lord's Prayer
and the blessing of bread; the status of their perfected heretics (here called
"the Elect"), which was acquired by the imposition of hands; and the fact
that the sect had a bishop.[3] We shall not pause over these characteristics at
this point; all will be repeatedly encountered in greater detail in later pieces.[4]
The second group in Cologne was clearly distinct from, and often in dispute
with, the first-named. Their scorn for the existing Church and its priesthood,
because of its deviation from the apostolic tradition, and their rejection of
infant baptism and of the doctrine of purgatory were widely shared among
protesting groups in the first half of the twelfth century and were to be even
more strenuously asserted in later movements.[5]

   It seems most probable that the sermons on the problem of heresy, which
Bernard composed for his series on the Song of Songs, were also written in
1144, just prior to his trip to Languedoc.[6] Not restricted to the two instances
from Cologne and southern France which were at that time pressed upon
Bernard's attention, the sermons speak generally of heretics, whose great
faults are secrecy, deception, and the scandal of their improper relationships
with women; the danger is to those, who are, like themselves, ignorant and
ill-informed. Of specific doctrines, Bernard singles out those concerning
marriage, baptism, purgatory, prayers for the dead, and the invocation of
saints.[7]

   On the episode at Cologne and Bernard's sermons, see the works cited
in the introduction to Number 14, and also Manselli, *Studi sulle eresie*,
chap. V. A new critical edition of the works of Bernard is in the process
of preparation under the auspices of the Cistercian order; the sermons on

the Song of Songs comprise the first two volumes.[8] There are a number of translations of his letters, sermons, and separate treatises. Especially useful for our purposes were the translation made from the work of Jean Mabillon: *Life and Works of Saint Bernard, Abbot of Clairvaux*, trans. by Samuel J. Eales,[9] and that of the sermons by a priest of Mt. Melleray [Ailbe J. Luddy], *Saint Bernard's Sermons on the Canticle of Canticles*.[10] On Eberwin of Steinfeld, consult B. Heurtebize, "Eberwin de Helfenstein," *Dictionnaire de théologie catholique*, IV, 1986-87.[11]

Part A is translated from *Sancti Bernardi . . . epistolae*, Ep. 472 (*Everwini Steinfeldensis praepositi ad S. Bernardum*), in Migne, *Patrologia latina*, CLXXXII, 676-80. Part B is translated by permission of the publisher, Edizioni Cisterciensi, from *Sancti Bernardi Sermones super Cantica canticorum*, Sermon 65, ed. by Jean Leclercq, C. H. Talbot, and H. M. Rochais (*Sancti Bernardi Opera*, I-II [2 vols., Rome, 1957-1958]), II, 172-77.

A. AN APPEAL FROM EBERWIN OF STEINFELD
AGAINST HERETICS AT COLOGNE

1143-1144

To his reverend Lord and Father, Bernard, abbot of Clairvaux, Eberwin, humble servant of the abbey of Steinfeld, sends wishes that he may be made strong in the Lord and may strengthen the Church of Christ.

1. "I will rejoice at thy words, as one that hath found great spoil." [12] It is your wont in everything you say and write to publish to us "the memory of the abundance of [God's] sweetness," [13] especially in the song of the love of the Bridegroom and the Bride,[14] which is of Christ and the Church, so that we can truthfully say to the Bridegroom, "Thou hast kept the good wine until now." [15] He has made you our cupbearer of this, the wine so precious: may you not pause in giving us to drink, may you not hesitate. You will not be able to empty the waterpots.[16] Nor, Holy Father, may your infirmity excuse you, for in the discharge of that duty piety will do more than the exercise of physical strength. Neither may you plead that you are busy. I know of nothing that should take precedence over this task, so vital to the common good.

From the waterpots,[17] Most Holy Father, how much you have already given us to drink! Enough has been poured out of the first to give wisdom and strength against the teaching and attack of the scribes and Pharisees; from the second, against the arguments and vexations of the pagans; from the third, against the subtle deceptions of heretics; from the fourth, against false Christians; from the fifth, against the heretics who shall appear toward the end of the world, of whom, speaking through the Apostle [Paul], "the Spirit manifestly saith that in the last times some shall depart from the faith, giving heed to spirits of error and doctrines of devils, speaking lies in hypocrisy, forbidding to marry, [enjoining] to abstain from meats, which God hath created to be received with thanksgiving."[18] From the sixth waterpot shall the faithful be filled to satiety, strengthening them against him who shall undoubtedly be revealed amid this departure from the faith, to wit, that son of sin, the man of perdition,[19] "who opposeth and is lifted up above all that is called God or that is worshiped, whose coming is according to the working of Satan, in all power, and signs, and lying wonders, and in all seduction of iniquity."[20] After this a seventh waterpot will be unneeded, when "the children of men shall be inebriated with the plenty of the house of God and the torrent of His pleasure."[21]

O good Father, you have already given enough to drink from the fourth waterpot[22] to correct us, to edify us, to perfect us in measure as we are starting toward, progressing to, or coming near to perfection. To the end of time your teaching will afford strong defense against the indifference and perversity of false brethren.

It is now time for you to draw from the fifth waterpot and publicly stand forth against the new heretics who everywhere in almost all churches boil up from the pit of hell as though already their prince were about to be loosed and the day of the Lord were at hand.[23] And that passage in the bridal song of Christ and the Church, of which you, Father, have told me you are about to treat, to wit, "Catch us the little foxes that destroy the vines,"[24] is applicable to this mystery and has brought you naturally to the fifth waterpot. Therefore, Father, I beg you to analyze all the articles of the heresy of those people which have come to your notice, set against them the arguments and authoritative texts of our faith, and thus destroy them.

2. Here in the neighborhood of Cologne, there have recently been discovered certain heretics, of whom some have returned to the Church after performing the requisite penance. Two, however—a man who was called their bishop and his assistant—held their ground against us in an assembly of clergy and laymen, in the presence of the lord archbishop himself and some great nobles, defending their heresy with the words of Christ and the Apostle [Paul]. But when they had realized that they could not prove their points, they asked for a day to be set on which

they might present from among their associates men learned in their faith, promising that they would be reconciled to the Church if they should find their teachers unable to offer satisfactory response; otherwise, they would rather die than be swayed from their beliefs. This being agreed upon, they were reasoned with for three days but would not recant. Whereupon, against our will, they were seized by the people, who were moved by rather too great zeal, and thrown into the fire and burned. What is more marvelous, they met and bore the agony of the fire not only with patience but even with joy. At this point, Holy Father, were I with you, I should like you to explain whence comes to those limbs of the devil constancy such as is scarcely to be found even in men most devoted to the faith of Christ.

3. This is the heresy of those people. They say that theirs alone is the Church, inasmuch as only they follow in the footsteps of Christ. They continue to be the true imitators of the apostolic life, seeking not those things which are of the world, possessing no house, or lands, or anything of their own, even as Christ had no property nor allowed His disciples the right of possession.

"You, however," they say to us, "add house to house, field to field, and seek the things that are of this world. You do this to the point that they who are considered the most perfect among you, such as monks and canons regular, although owning nothing of their own and holding everything in common, nevertheless possess all these things."

Of themselves they say: "We, the poor of Christ, who have no fixed abode and flee from city to city like sheep amidst wolves, are persecuted as were the apostles and the martyrs, despite the fact that we lead a most strict and holy life, persevering day and night in fasts and abstinence, in prayers, and in labor from which we seek only the necessities of life. We undergo this because we are not of this world. But you, lovers of the world, have peace with it because you are of the world. False apostles, who pollute the word of Christ, who seek after their own interest, have led you and your fathers astray from the true path. We and our fathers, of apostolic descent, have continued in the grace of Christ and shall so remain until the end of time. To distinguish between us and you Christ said, 'By their fruits you shall know them.' [25] Our fruits consist in following the footsteps of Christ."

In their diet they forbid every kind of milk and what is made therefrom and whatever is born of coition. In this respect they differ from us, in their way of life. In regard to their sacraments they observe much secrecy. However, they have openly confessed to us that at their daily meals, after the manner of Christ and the apostles, by the Lord's Prayer they consecrate their food and drink, thus changing it into the body and blood of Christ so as therefrom to nourish themselves as the members and body of Christ. We, they say, do not hold to the truth in the sacraments but to a sort of shadow, a tradition of men.

They have openly confessed, also, that besides [baptism in] water, they baptize and have been baptized in fire and the Spirit, adducing that testimony of John the Baptist, who, while baptizing in water, said of Christ, "He shall baptize you in the Holy Spirit and fire"; [26] and in another place, "I baptize with water; but there hath stood one in the midst of you, whom you know not," [27] as though he were to add: "He will baptize you with another baptism beyond that with water." That such baptism should be performed by the imposition of hands they have sought to show by the testimony of Luke in the Acts of the Apostles, who, in describing the baptism which Paul received from Ananias at Christ's command, made no mention of water but only of the imposition of hands.[28] Whatever else they find about the imposition of hands, both in the Acts of the Apostles and in the Epistles of Paul, they read as applying to this baptism. Anyone among them who is thus baptized they refer to as "Elect," and say that he has the power to baptize others who shall be found worthy, and to consecrate the body and blood of Christ at his table. By the imposition of hands one is first received from the ranks of those they call "auditors" into the number of the "believers"; thus he gains permission to be present at their prayers until they deem him sufficiently tested to be made an "Elect." They give no credence to our baptism. They condemn marriage, but I could not learn from them the reason, either because they dared not reveal it or, more probably, because they did not know.

4. There are also certain other heretics in our land, differing completely from those described. By their mutual discord and contention both have been discovered to us. These latter deny that the miracle of the body of Christ takes place upon the altar, because no priests of the Church are validly ordained. For, they say, the apostolic office has been corrupted through involvement in secular business and, by failure to wage God's warfare as did Peter; he who sits in the Chair of Peter has lost the power to ordain which was bestowed upon Peter. And because the

Apostolic See does not have this power, the archbishops and bishops,[29] who lead worldly lives within the Church, cannot receive from that see the power to ordain anyone. They presume to derive this from the words of Christ: "The scribes and the Pharisees have sitten on the chair of Moses. All things therefore whatsoever they shall say to you, observe and do," [30] as if to such prelates were given only the power to command and teach, and nothing more.

Thus they render void the priesthood of the Church and condemn its sacraments, save baptism alone, and this [they approve] only for adults, who, they say, are baptized by Christ, no matter who may actually administer the sacrament. They do not [31] believe in infant baptism because of[32] the text of the Gospel, "He that believeth and is baptized shall be saved." [33] All marriage they call fornication except that contracted between virgins, male and female, basing this belief on the words with which the Lord answered the Pharisees, "What therefore God hath joined together, let no man put asunder," as though God had joined only such [i.e. virgins] in likeness to the union of the first of mankind. They also base their belief on His reply to the same persons, who raised objections to Him about a bill of divorce commanded by Moses: "From the beginning it was not so," and also on the words which follow in the same passage, "He that shall marry her that is put away committeth adultery"; [34] and on the words of the Apostle, "Marriage [is] honorable in all and the bed undefiled." [35]

5. They put no reliance on the intercession of saints. Fasts and other self-castigations which are performed for sins, they add, are not required of the righteous nor even of sinners, because on whatever day the sinner shall have lamented his sins, all are forgiven. Observances of the Church, other than those which Christ and the apostles who succeeded him established, they call mere superstitions. They do not admit that there is purgatorial fire after death, but teach that souls go immediately unto eternal rest or punishment at the moment of leaving the body, pursuant to the words of Solomon, "If the tree fall to the south or to the north, in what place soever it shall fall there shall it be." [36] And thus they nullify the prayers and offerings of the faithful for the dead.

6. Holy Father, we solicit your watchful concern over these manifold evils, and urge that you direct the point of your shaft against the wild beasts. Answer us not that "the tower of David" to which we fly for refuge has been sufficiently "built with bulwarks; a thousand bucklers

hang upon it, all the armor of valiant men." [37] For we are inexperienced
and inept; we would, therefore, Father, that by your zeal this armor be
assembled in one place, where it may be the more readily available for
our use against these monsters so numerous, and may be the more effective in resisting them.

You should also know, my Lord, that those who have returned to the
Church have told us that these heretics have a very large number of adherents scattered widely throughout the world, among whom are many
of our clergy and monks. Indeed, those who were burned told us during
their defense that this heresy has lain concealed from the time of the
martyrs even to our own day, and has persisted thus in Greece and
certain other lands. They are those heretics who call themselves apostles
and who have their own pope.[38] There are others who do not accept our
pope, nor do they acknowledge another in his place. These apostolics [39]
of Satan have among them women vowed to continence (so they say):
widows, virgins, and their wives, some among the Elect, some among the
believers. In this they claim to be following the example of the apostles,
to whom was granted the right of taking women around with them.

Farewell in the Lord.

B. A SERMON BY BERNARD OF CLAIRVAUX AGAINST HERESY

1144

1. I have already preached you two sermons on one verse; [40] I am
preparing to deliver a third if, indeed, it will not bore you to hear it. And
I believe it necessary. For, in truth, what concerns our own domestic
vine—and by this I refer to you—has, I think, been covered well enough
in the two previous sermons to guard that vine against the wiles of three
kinds of foxes: flatterers, slanderers, and certain seductive spirits who
are skilled and practiced in presenting evil under the guise of good.

But I have not adequately treated the vine of the Lord, by which I
mean that vine which has filled the earth and of which we, too, are a
part—a far-spreading vine planted by the hand of the Lord, purchased
with His blood, watered by His word, propagated by His grace, made
fruitful by His spirit. The result of taking the more care of our own vine
is that I have been of less use to the common one. Now, however, the
great number of those who demolish it, the fewness of its defenders, the
difficulty of defense move me in its behalf.

Concealment causes the difficulty. Although the Church from the beginning has always had her foxes, they were all soon discovered and taken; the heretic fought openly (for he was a heretic chiefly for the reason that he desired to conquer openly) and was overcome. And so these foxes were easily caught. For what mattered it if a heretic should remain in the darkness of his obstinacy after the truth had been made clearly manifest and, as an outcast in bonds, should wither away alone? The fox was, indeed, known to have been taken, its impiety condemned, and the impious one itself driven forth, assuredly now to drag out an existence as a fearful example, bearing no fruit, a sterile thing. Thenceforth, in the words of the prophet, such a one would have "dry breasts and a sterile womb," [41] because error publicly refuted does not sprout again, and manifest falsehood does not germinate.

2. What shall we do to catch those most malicious foxes, they who would rather injure than conquer and who do not even wish to disclose themselves, but prefer to slink about in the shadows? For all previous heretics the constant desire was to win notoriety through a display of unusual knowledge. This heresy only, more malignant and crafty than any other, feeds upon others' hurt, unmindful of its own renown. Warned, I believe, by the examples of the early heresies (which, when uncovered, could not escape, but were quickly seized), with a new sort of craftiness it has been careful to work its "mystery of iniquity," [42] doing this the more freely as it is the more furtive. Finally, its members are reported to have arranged for themselves secret hiding places; "they are resolute in wickedness": [43] "Swear, truly or falsely, but betray not the secret." [44] They say, to be sure, that they do not otherwise consent, under any circumstances, to take an oath, because of that precept of the Gospel, "Swear not at all, neither by heaven nor by the earth," [45] and so on. "O foolish and slow of heart," [46] clearly filled with the spirit of the Pharisees, "who strain out a gnat, and swallow a camel"! [47] Is it unlawful to swear, but lawful to swear falsely? Is it permissible in the one case alone and not in the other? From what passage of the Gospel, pray, do you draw this exception, you who, by your false boast, pass over not a single iota? It is evident that you are both superstitiously careful about an oath and shamefully ready with perjury. O perversity! What was given as cautionary advice, namely, not to swear, these people observe as obstinately as if it were a commandment; what was ordained as unchangeable law, namely, not to swear falsely, they dispense with by their

own choice, as if it were a matter of no importance. They say, "No, but we may not reveal our mystery," as if it were not "the glory of God to reveal the speech." [48] Do they envy the glory of God? I believe, rather, that, conscious of the shameful nature of their mystery, they blush to make it known. For they are reported to engage secretly in abominable and obscene practices, just as the hinder parts of foxes have an evil odor.

3. But I pass over what they would deny. Let them make answer to proven facts. Can it be that, in accordance with the Gospel precept, they would avoid giving that which is holy to dogs, or pearls to swine? [49] But this is to confess openly that they, who regard all who are of the Church as dogs and swine, are not of the Church. Now, they think their secret, whatever it be, is to be withheld from all, without exception, who do not belong to their sect. Moreover, in addition to this conviction, they will not answer questions for fear of exposure, a thing which they assuredly seek by every means to avoid. But they will not avoid it! Give me a plain answer, my fine fellow, you who are more wise than behooves you [50] and foolish beyond utterance: This mystery which you hide, is it of God or is it not? If it is, why do you not make it known to His glory? For "the glory of God is to reveal the speech." If [the mystery] is not [of God], why do you put faith in that which is not of God, unless because you are a heretic? Therefore, let them [*sic*] either disclose God's secret, to the glory of God, or deny that the mystery is of God and admit that they are heretics. Or at least let them confess that they are open enemies of the glory of God, since they are unwilling to reveal that which they know would be to His glory. The truth of the Scripture stands without doubt, "It is the glory of kings to conceal the word, the glory of God to reveal the speech." [51] Are you unwilling to reveal it? Then you are unwilling to glorify God.

But perhaps you do not accept this book [i.e. Proverbs (?)]. Be it so. However, of the Gospel alone they profess to be the sole zealous followers. Let them, then, reply to this passage from the Gospel where it says, "That which I tell you in the dark, speak ye in the light, and that which you hear in the ear, preach ye upon the housetops." [52] Silence is no longer permissible. Is that to be kept always secret which God commands to be made known? Is your gospel always to remain hidden? I suspect yours is not Paul's, for he affirms that his is not hidden; he says, "And if our gospel be also hid, it is hid to them that are lost." [53] Reflect whether he is speaking of you, among whom the Gospel is found to be hidden. What is clearer than that you will perish? Or do you, by chance, not accept Paul either? I have heard this about some persons. [54] For you do not all agree among yourselves about everything, even though you are one in disagreeing with us.

4. But in any case, if I am not mistaken, you all do accept without distinction, as having equal authority with the Gospel itself, all the words, writings, and traditions of those who were bodily present with the Savior. Did they keep their Gospel hidden? Did they remain silent about the weaknesses of the flesh in Christ (*Deum*), the dread facts of His death, the ignominy of the Cross? Of a truth, "their sound hath gone forth into all the earth." [55] Where is the apostolic model and life of which you boast? They cry aloud, you whisper. They preach in public, you in a corner. They "fly as the clouds," [56] you lurk in your homes, in darkness, and in cellars. What do you show in yourselves like unto them? Is it that you do not, indeed, take women about with you on your journeys, but live with them at home? Going about together is not as much open to suspicion as is living together. But who would suspect anything evil of those who raised the dead? Do you likewise, and I will believe in man and woman sleeping together! Otherwise, you are boldly usurping for yourselves the prerogative of those whose sanctity you have not. To be always with a woman and not to know her carnally, is not this more than to raise the dead? The lesser of these you cannot do, so why shall I believe that you are capable of the greater? Daily you sit beside a maiden at the table, your bed is next to hers in the chamber, your eyes meet hers in conversation, your hands touch hers in work—and do you wish to be thought continent? [57] Perhaps you are, but I doubt it. To me you are a scandal. Remove the cause of scandal; you may thereby prove that you are a true follower of the Gospel, as you boast. Does not he who has been a cause of offense to one member of the Church cast blame upon that Gospel? You are a cause of offense to the whole Church. You are a fox destroying the vine. Help me, comrades, to take it! Or rather, do you take it for us, O holy angels! It is exceedingly crafty. "It is covered with its iniquity and its wickedness." [58] Assuredly, anything so small and cunning may easily deceive human eyes. Will this be true also of yours? It is to you [holy angels], therefore, as companions of the Bridegroom, that the words are addressed: "Take us the foxes, the little foxes." [59] Therefore, do what you are commanded; take for us this crafty little fox which till now we have pursued but, alas, in vain! Instruct and

advise us how to detect the deception. For to do this is to have taken the fox, because he does more harm by far as a pretended Catholic than a real heretic. But a man cannot know what may be in the mind of another unless he, perchance, has to this end been either enlightened by the spirit of God or inspired by the solicitude of angels. What sign will you vouchsafe us whereby this most wicked heresy, skilled in falsehood not only of speech but of life, may be exposed?

5. Recent damage to the vine, in truth, shows that the fox has been at work, but I know not by what deceptive trick that most cunning animal so covers his tracks that it is by no means easy for men to discover the points of his entry or departure. Though the mischief is clear enough, its perpetrator remains invisible, so artfully does he conceal, in those things which remain in view, every trace of himself.

Finally, if you question the heretic about his faith, nothing is more Christian; if about his daily converse, nothing more blameless; and what he says he proves by actions. As witness to his faith you may see the man go often to church, show respect to priests, offer his gift, make confession, partake of the sacraments. What could be more orthodox? As regards his life and conduct, he cheats no one, pushes ahead of no one, does violence to no one. Moreover, his cheeks are pale with fasting; he does not eat the bread of idleness; he labors with his hands and thus makes his living.

Where is the fox now? We had it; how did it escape from our hands? How did it disappear so suddenly? Let us pursue. Let us search it out; by its fruits we shall know it.[60] And certainly, the destruction of the vines is evidence of the fox. Women are leaving their husbands, men are putting aside their wives, and they all flock to those heretics! Clerics and priests, the youthful and the adult among them, are leaving their congregations and churches and are often found in the company of weavers of both sexes. Is that not serious damage? Is not this the work of foxes?

6. But perhaps these aberrations are not so clearly displayed by all of them; and if they were, there is no way of proving the fact. How can we catch them? Let us consider again their association and living together with women, for there is no one of them who does not follow this manner of life. I question any of them at random:

"Ho, you, good man! Who is this woman and what is her relationship to you? Is she your wife?"

"No," he says, "for that is not consistent with my vow."

"Your daughter, then?"

"No."

"What then? Is she not your sister or niece, or at least connected with you by some degree of consanguinity or marriage?"

"Absolutely none."

"How, then, do you manage to guard your continence? Surely, this sort of thing is not permitted you. If you do not happen to know it, the Church forbids men and women who have taken a vow of chastity to live together.[61] If you do not wish to offend the Church, send the woman away. Otherwise, from this one sin others, though not at present manifest, will undoubtedly be considered probable."

7. "But," he says, "can you show me in what text of the Gospel this is forbidden?"

"You have appealed to the Gospel? To the Gospel you shall go! If you obey the Gospel, you will not cause scandal, for the Gospel plainly forbids the causing of scandal. Yet you do so by not putting that woman away, in accordance with the law of the Church. You had been under suspicion and now you will be openly adjudged both a despiser of the Gospel and an enemy of the Church."

What is your judgment, brethren? If he has been headstrong in not obeying the Gospel or in not yielding to the Church, how can there be any uncertainty? Does it not seem clear to you that guile has been revealed and the fox caught? If he does not put away the woman, he does not remove the scandal; and if he does not remove the scandal when he is able to do so, he is to be held a transgressor of the Gospel. What is the Church to do but cast off one who is unwilling to cast off scandal, if she is not to be, like him, disobedient? For she is commanded by that passage in the Gospel not to spare her eye, her hand, or her foot, if it be an occasion of scandal, but to pluck it out, cut it off, cast it from her.[62] "If," He says, "he will not hear the Church, let him be to thee as the heathen and publican." [63]

8. Have we accomplished anything? I think that we have. We have taken the fox, since we have discovered the fraud. The false Catholics who lay hid have been unmasked as the real plunderers of the vine of the earth. For while you [as a false Catholic] "didst take sweetmeats together with me" (I speak of the body and blood of Christ), while "in the house of God we walked with consent,"[64] there was room for persuasion, nay, opportunity for seduction, in harmony with that passage in the

Book of Wisdom, "The dissembler with his mouth deceiveth his friend." [65] But now I shall easily avoid "a man that is a heretic, after the first and second admonition, knowing that he that is such a one is subverted," [66] as Paul wisely remarks. And I shall take due care to be on my guard that he be not my subverter also.

Hence, it is no small matter that, to quote the Book of Wisdom, "the unjust be caught in their own snares," [67] especially those wicked ones who have chosen to use snares instead of arms. For such have then lost completely the means of attack and defense. In reality, they are a base and rustic folk, unlettered and entirely devoid of fighting qualities; indeed, they are foxes and very small ones. Nor are those subjects on which they are reported to hold wrong opinions capable of real defense; they are not even subtle or persuasive, except to the minds of country women and ignorant people, such, certainly, as are all those whom I have till now found to be of this sect.

For I do not recall having heard anything new or strange in all their mouthings, numerous as they are, but that which is worn by use and long agitated by the heretics of old, and which has been well threshed and winnowed by our theologians. Yet, what those absurdities are should be told and I shall recount them: partly those things which they have unguardedly confessed to Catholics who questioned them; partly those things which they have betrayed from time to time when disputing among themselves; partly, also, those things which some of them have revealed on returning to the Church. Not that I shall reply to them all, for that is not necessary, but only that they may become fully known. For this, another sermon will be necessary.

To the praise and glory of the name of the Bridegroom of the Church, our Lord Jesus Christ, who is God over all, blessed forever. Amen.

16. A Warning from Périgueux

Catharist tenets and practices seem to be revealed in this letter, but without any reference to dualism. No other source tells us anything of the situation to which Heribert refers, and even its date is uncertain.[1] It has been suggested on no very sure ground that Heribert was a Cistercian monk who later became archbishop of Torres in Sardinia.[2]

The letter is translated from *Heriberti monachi epistola de haereticis Petragoricis*, in Migne, *Patrologia latina*, CLXXXI, 1721-22.

circa 1147

I, Heribert, a monk, wish to announce to all Christians how warily they should deal with the pseudoprophets who are endeavoring to subvert Christianity, for numerous heretics who say that they follow the apostolic life have appeared in the neighborhood of Périgueux. They eat no meat, drink no wine beyond a measure every third day. They make a hundred genuflections daily,[3] and will not handle money. A most corrupt and secret aspect of their cult is that they do not say the doxology but instead of "Glory be to the Father" say "For Thine is the kingdom, and Thou shalt rule over all creation, forever and ever. Amen." [4] They say that charity is a useless act because no one should possess the property from which alms can be given. They consider the Mass worthless and assert that the sacrament should be understood as only a morsel of bread. If one of them chants the Mass as a tactic of deception, he does not repeat the Canon [5] or partake of the sacrament, but throws the Host down beside or behind the altar or thrusts it into the missal. They do not adore the Cross or the likeness of the Lord, but restrain those who would adore them, for example, by declaring before the likeness of the Lord, "How pitiful are those who adore Thee," repeating the psalm "The idols of the Gentiles," [6] and so on. Very many persons have already gone over to this deception, not only some who abandoned their noble status, but also the clergy—priests, monks, and nuns. No one is such a rustic that, if he but ally himself with them, he may not become in the space of eight days so wise a scholar that he can be overcome neither in discussion nor in citation. There is no way to confine them, for, when they are captured, no chains will hold them, because the devil himself sets them free. Thus, perversely, they desire and seek out persons to torture or execute them. They perform many prodigies: Wherever they have been bound with iron shackles and placed in a wine tun turned bottom side up, with the strongest guard posted, they were not to be found on the morrow until they again disclosed themselves of their own free will; a wine cask which has recently been emptied is found full in the morning. They also perform many other wonders. Their leader is called Pons.[7]

17. An Appeal from Liège to the Pope

The date given to this letter depends on the identification of the pope who is addressed by the initial *L*. For undisclosed reasons, Martène and Durand, the first editors of the manuscript (which is now lost), chose the date 1144, and thus identified the pope as Lucius II (1144-1145). Fredericq, who reprints the letter in his *Corpus* (I, 31-33), accepted the identification as Lucius II and dated the letter at 1145;[1] but Jeffrey Russell, after re-examining the evidence, dissented, arguing that the letter was written to Leo IX (1048-1054).[2] There is independent evidence of the existence of heresy in the vicinity of Liège in both the eleventh and twelfth centuries, but the similarity between the errors attributed to the heretics in this letter and those in the description by Eberwin of Steinfeld (No. 15, part A) seems good reason for choosing the date 1145.[3]

The letter is translated from *Epistola ecclesiae Leodiensis ad Lucum papam II*, in Edmond Martène and Ursin Durand, *Veterum scriptorum et monumentorum historicum, dogmaticarum, moralium amplissima collectio* (9 vols., Paris, 1724-1733), I, 776-78.

1145

To our very reverend lord and father, L., by the grace of God supreme pontiff, the church of Liège sends devout prayers and the obedience of due subjection in Christ.

As we believe and as history itself proves, Divine Providence has placed the Roman see at the head of the universal Church, by its watchful care to secure protection for its members and to provide a refuge for those to whom growing conflict threatens destruction. For this reason we report to Your Paternity, as one entrusted with the responsibility for all churches, the newly discovered snares of ancient enemies, so that by your unremitting care may be rendered unavailing the efforts of those who, under appearance of religion, lead the minds of simple folk astray. Then Holy Church may again grow strong in the soundness of the one faith, which, we find, has in many places been weakened.

From Montwimers,[4] which is the name of a village in France, a certain heresy appears to have overflowed various regions of the land, a heresy so varied and manifold that it seems impossible to characterize it under one single name. Some of its devotees have been found among us, were convicted, and have confessed. A turbulent crowd seized them and thought to consign them to the flames, but we, by God's mercy, with some difficulty snatched nearly all of them from instant death, because we hoped for better things of them. He whom we have thought it wise to refer to Your Paternity with his request for absolution is one of their number.

This heresy comprises different ranks among its adherents: It has auditors, who are being initiated into error, and believers, who have already been led astray; it has its Christians, its priests, and its other prelates, just as we have. Its blasphemies are abominable: It denies that sins are remitted in baptism; it holds the sacrament of the body and blood of Christ to be useless; it asserts that nothing is bestowed by the imposition of the episcopal hand; it believes that no one receives the Holy Spirit except by merit of previous good works; it condemns marriage; it preaches that only in itself does the Catholic Church exist; it adjudges every oath a crime. But those who are followers of this wickedness feign to join in celebration of our sacraments in order to veil their own iniquity.

Until recently this Amery was one of their auditors. For this reason we have sent him to you, that in accordance with your decision he may make amends to God and to His Holy Church, and that he may fulfill the solemn promise made to the blessed apostles when he was in danger of his life. For he vowed, as he says, that if by their merits and their prayers he might escape, he would make devout pilgrimage to their shrines to give thanks for his safekeeping. The other participants in this error we have distributed among religious houses to await whatever action you may take for their correction.

Furthermore, we make known to Your Charity that, according to what we have learned from those whom we apprehended, all the communities of the Gallic realm and of our own have been infected to a great degree with the poison of this error. Therefore, may Your Fatherly Sagacity be vigilant against the further and more dangerous spread of this poison. Let it be burned forthwith with the cautery of salutary diligence, that it may disappear. Farewell.

18. Eudo of Brittany

The career of the heretic who is known as Eudo or Eon *de Stella*[1] covered a period of about three years. Attacks on churches and monasteries in Brittany by bands of his followers were recorded in 1145, along with reports of sinister and sacrilegious behavior.[2] In 1148, their instigator, Eudo, with some of his lieutenants, was brought as a prisoner before the general council sitting at Rheims during Lent, where his bizarre claims to divinity aroused amusement; the council remanded him to protective custody but sent some of his obstinate followers to the stake. The incident caught the attention of monastic chroniclers, in whose pages are found more than a dozen notices of Eudo's fate.[3] Behind the fantasies which he cherished or which rumor put to his account there are hints of an aspiration toward preaching and the penitential life,[4] but there is too little evidence for any solid conclusion about a relationship with contemporary apostolic and reforming movements, or with the dualist sects which were infiltrating northern Europe. Some historians at that time and later dismissed Eudo as a lunatic.[5]

Two of the numerous contemporary references are translated here. The first is from the anonymous continuation of the world history of Sigibert of Gembloux, which was written at Gembloux and covers the years 1136-1148. Its comments are typical of the shorter entries about Eudo in the chronicles. The second, the most circumstantial of the surviving descriptions of Eudo, is an excerpt from William of Newburgh's history of the kings of England. The author, ranked among the best of twelfth-century historians, wrote his history between 1199 and his death in 1201.[6] Even though written so many years after the event, his account is of interest because he had talked with some of the surviving followers of Eudo and because his report of magical happenings illustrates a not uncommon concept of heresy as the devil's work. There is an English translation by Joseph Stevenson, *The History of William of Newburgh*.

Part A is translated from *Sigiberti Gemblacensis chronographia: Continuatio Gemblacensis*, ed. by L. C. Bethmann in *Monumenta Germaniae historica, Scriptores*, VI, 389-90, by permission of the publisher Anton Hiersemann Verlag and the Monumenta Germaniae Historica. Part B is translated by permission of Her Majesty's Stationery Office and the Kraus Reprint Corporation from William of Newburgh's *Historia rerum anglicarum* I.xiii, ed. by Richard Howlett, in *Chronicles of the Reigns of Stephen, Henry II and Richard I* (Rolls Series, LXXXII [4 vols., London, 1884-1889]), I, 60-64.

A.   A DESCRIPTION OF EUDO BY AN ANONYMOUS CHRONICLER

1146

The heresy of the Eonists spread among the Bretons.[7] Their leader was a certain man of evil disposition named Eon.[8] Although he was uneducated and scarcely knew even the letters of the alphabet, he discoursed and preached from Holy Writ with a filthy mouth. Although not in holy orders, with impious boldness he disgracefully celebrated Mass, to the error and destruction of the corrupted people; he even ordained bishops and archbishops from his following; and he committed many other wicked violations of divine law. At last, filled with a diabolic spirit, he exploded into madness so great as to announce—and demand belief therein—that he was the son of God and that it was he in whose name the priests customarily end the general Collect in church when they say,

"Through Him (*per eundem*) our Lord." Yet it is well to draw the veil of silence over such base and abominable things as those heretics who are called Eonists—that is, the followers of Eon—do in secret, lest they inspire dread or even breed error in light-minded listeners.

1148

Pope Eugene assembled a general council at Rheims. . . .[9] To this council the above-mentioned heretic, Eon, was brought by a certain Catholic bishop of Brittany,[10] to appear before the pope. In a public hearing he was forthwith examined upon his wicked heresy and declared guilty. He did, indeed, escape with life and limb but, by papal command and despite the protest of the bishop who had brought him, was placed in confinement, where he died within a short time.[11]

B. A DESCRIPTION OF EUDO BY WILLIAM OF NEWBURGH

1148

About the same time, the Roman pope, Eugene, elevated to the headship of the Apostolic See because of the strictness of his monastic life, came to France to promote Church discipline and held a general council at Rheims. While he was sitting therein with a full attendance of bishops and nobles, there was brought before him a certain pernicious individual, who, filled with a diabolic spirit, had led astray so many persons by his cunning trickery that, relying on the number of his followers, he roved throughout various localities, arousing terror and destroying churches and monasteries in particular. Finally, after he had raged long and widely, wisdom overcame evil; he was captured by the archbishop of Rheims [12] and produced at the holy council. Eudo, he was called, with the surname *de Stella*; born a Breton,[13] an unlettered and ignorant man, so deranged by the delusions of demons that, because his name was pronounced "Eon" in the French tongue, he believed that the phrase recited in ecclesiastical exorcism, "Through Him (*eum*) who shall come to judge the quick and the dead, and the world through fire," referred to himself. So utterly stupid was he as not to know the difference between "Eum" and "Eon"; but even more, with amazing blindness, he thought that he was the ruler and judge of the quick and the dead. He was so adept in devilish tricks for entrapping the souls of simple persons that he gathered about himself a deluded throng like flies entangled in spiders' webs, all of them devotedly accepting him as their lord of lords. Sometimes, indeed, he betook himself throughout various regions with astonishing speed; at other times he tarried with all his followers in wild and inaccessible places, and thence, at the devil's urging, burst out unexpectedly, destroying churches and monasteries particularly.

There gathered around him many of his friends and kinfolk (for he was not of ignoble birth), either in order to correct him by a family effort or to ascertain circumspectly how affairs were with him. There seemed to be, moreover, a remarkable luster about him, a royal sumptuousness and arrogance; those who attended him, free from care and labor, expensively garbed, feasting ostentatiously, seemed to live in the greatest joyousness, so much so that many who came to attack him were beguiled, not by his true aspect but by his illusion of splendor. These deceptive appearances were produced by demons, by whom that wretched throng was nourished in the wilderness, not with real and substantial sustenance but rather by ethereal foods. For, as we heard later from some persons who had been of his company and who after his capture wandered the world over as though doing penance, there were ready for them as often as they liked, bread, meat, fish, and every sumptuous food. The truth that these were not solid foods but were ethereal—invisibly supplied by spirits of the air to ensnare rather than to nourish souls—is made clear by the fact that, at the least belch, weakness would replace any repletion from such foods and thereupon such hunger would ensue that they were constrained on the spot to seek the same food again. Whoever happened upon them by chance and took but the least taste of their food was mentally affected as he shared the diabolic repast, and forthwith joined this most filthy throng; [14] and whoever received anything of any sort from them was not free from danger. At length, it is reported that a certain knight, a relative of this wicked fellow, came to him and warned him plainly to forswear that wicked sect and return to his own people by communion in the Christian sacrament.[15] Slyly keeping the man in suspense, Eon showed him a lavish display of marvels of many kinds, so as to captivate him by the seductive charm of the things he saw. "You are our kinsman," he said. "Take whatever and as much as you wish of our possessions." But this prudent man withdrew to take his leave, because he had cast his warning to the wind. His squire, however, seeing a falcon of remarkable beauty, coveted it, to his own destruction. He asked for and received it and, rejoicing, followed his lord as he then departed. The latter said to him, "Cast away at once that thing you are carrying, for it is not the bird it seems to be but a demon in disguise." Presently the truth of his words became evident. For after the silly fellow refused to heed the advice, he first complained of that falcon's clutching his fist too tightly with its talons; soon it lifted him by the hand into the air, and he was not seen again thereafter.

Indeed, this evildoer through the devil's influence so raged about, it is reported, that armed force was frequently sent out by the magnates to seek for him and hunt him down, but in vain; he was sought for but not found. Finally, however, he lost the assistance of demons when they were no longer suffered to rage through him, for they can do no more than is permitted them by higher powers in the righteous judgment of God. He was captured by the archbishop of Rheims with little trouble. The stupid folk in his retinue were dispersed but those disciples who were more closely attached to him and were his collaborators were seized with him.

Now, when he stood before the council and was asked by the supreme pontiff who he was, he replied, "I am Eon, who shall come to judge the quick and the dead, and the world through fire." Moreover, he had a staff of unusual design, it being forked at its upper end. Asked what the staff meant to him, he said, "This is a matter of sublime mystery. For so long as it looks to heaven with its two prongs, as now you see it, God has two parts of the world and the third part he yields to me. On the other hand, if I turn these two topmost points of the staff downward toward earth and raise the lower end, which is single, to point toward heaven, keeping two thirds of the world for myself, I relinquish only the third portion to God." At this the council laughed and mocked the man so deeply given up to a reprobate sense.[16]

However, after it was ordered by conciliar decree that he be held in close custody lest his pestilence again spread, he lived on for only a short time. His disciples, indeed—on whom he had bestowed great names, calling one Wisdom, another Knowledge, another Judgment,[17] and the others after the same fashion—being escorted first to the tribunal and then to the flames, chose rather to die than to reform their lives,[18] because they would accept sound doctrine by no argument, but most obstinately prided themselves on their false names, so much so that he who was called Judgment, with misplaced confidence threatened with a vengeful penalty those who held him. I have learned from one venerable person who was present when this happened that he heard the man called Judgment repeatedly exclaim as he was led out to the punishment, "Earth, open thyself up!" as if the earth ought to gape at his command to swallow his enemies, like Dathan and Abiron.[19] How great was the power of error once it fixed itself in the heart!

19. Arnold of Brescia

Among the twelfth-century advocates of religious reform who, intent on purifying the Church, leveled their attacks on its worldly commitments and wealth, none was more extreme than Arnold of Brescia. It was less his theological doctrines than the violence of his advocacy of the apostolic ideal which entitles him to a place among the promoters of heresy. If applied from top to bottom in the Church, as he proposed, Arnold's program would have made a social as well as an ecclesiastical revolution.

The two pieces which follow give the essentials of his career. As for his influence, no other source names the "heretical sect of the Lombards" mentioned by John of Salisbury, but before the end of the century a sect called "Arnoldists" existed in northern Italy. They denied the validity of sacraments administered by unworthy priests, refused to admit the coercive or judicial power of the Church, insisted on the right of lay preaching, and advocated poverty as the essential condition of a true priesthood. That they were directly the product of Arnold's teaching is probable but not assured.[1]

Part A below is from the work of John of Salisbury (b. 1115-1120), who was one of the great literary figures of the twelfth century. After nearly twelve years of study at Paris and Chartres, he took service in the papal court under Eugene III; then, perhaps in 1153 or 1154, he became secretary to Archbishop Theobald of Canterbury and thereafter, as friend and adviser, shared the exile of Thomas Becket and witnessed his martyrdom. The last four years before his death in 1180 John spent as bishop of Chartres. His *Historia pontificalis* was written not later than 1164. John's remarks about Arnold may not rest on firsthand observation, but they do afford a most valuable appreciation of him by a well-informed contemporary.[2] Miss Marjorie Chibnall has translated the *Historia pontificalis* under the title *John of Salisbury's Memoirs of the Papal Court* (London, 1956); the excerpt given below is taken from that translation (chap. XXXI, pp. 62-65) by permission of the publishers, Thomas Nelson and Sons, Ltd.

The account in part B comes from the work of Otto of Freising, who was born about 1110, studied at Paris, entered the Cistercian order, and from 1137 to his death in 1158 was bishop of Freising. A member of the ruling house of Germany (he was uncle to the Emperor Frederick I), Otto was at once churchman, scholar, and man of affairs. He was also one of the ablest historians of the twelfth century. The excerpts which we publish here are from his biography of the emperor, of which Otto had completed only the first two books, covering events to the year 1156, when death overtook him.[3]

We are indebted to Professor Charles C. Mierow for permission to print portions of his translation, *The Deeds of Frederick Barbarossa by Otto of Freising and His Continuator, Rahewin* i.xxviii (xxvii), ii. xxviii, translated with the collaboration of Richard Emery (Records of Civilization, XLIX [New York, 1953]), pp. 61, 142-44.

In reprinting these translations, we have retained many of the translators' notes, designated by [C] and [M], respectively; on occasion we have added further comment of our own.

A. JOHN OF SALISBURY'S ESTIMATE OF ARNOLD

1149

Negotiations for peace were proceeding between the pope and the Romans,[4] and numerous legations sped to and fro between the two parties. But there were many obstacles in the way of peace, the greatest of all being the refusal of the Romans to expel Arnold of Brescia,[5] who was said to have bound himself by oath to uphold the honour of the city and the Roman republic. The Romans in their turn promised him aid and counsel against all men, and explicitly against the lord pope; for the Roman church had excommunicated him and ordered him to be shunned as a heretic. This man was a priest by office, a canon regular by profession, and one who had mortified his flesh with fasting and coarse raiment: of keen intelligence, persevering in his study of the scriptures, eloquent in speech, and a vehement preacher against the vanities of the world. Nevertheless he was reputed to be factious and a leader of schism, who wherever he lived prevented the citizens from being at peace with the clergy. He had been abbot of Brescia, and when the bishop was absent on a short visit to Rome had so swayed the minds of the citizens that they would scarcely open their gates to the bishop on his return. For this he was deposed by Pope Innocent and expelled from Italy; crossing the Alps into France he became a disciple of Peter Abailard, and together with Master Hyacinth,[6] who is now a cardinal, zealously fostered his cause against the abbot of Clairvaux. After Master Peter had set out for Cluny,[7] he remained at Paris on the Mont Sainte Geneviève, expounding the scriptures to scholars at the church of St. Hilary where Peter had been lodged. But he had no listeners except poor students who publicly begged their bread from door to door to support themselves and their master. He said things that were entirely consistent with the law accepted by Christian people, but not at

all with the life they led. To the bishops he was merciless on account of
their avarice and filthy lucre; most of all because of stains on their
personal lives, and their striving to build the church of God in blood.
He denounced the abbot,[8] whose name is renowned above all others
for his many virtues, as a seeker after vainglory, envious of all who won
distinction in learning or religion unless they were his own disciples. In
consequence the abbot prevailed on the most Christian king to expel
him from the Frankish kingdom; from there he returned to Italy after
Pope Innocent's death and, after promising reparation and obedience to
the Roman church, was received at Viterbo by Pope Eugenius.[9] Penance
was imposed on him, which he claimed to have performed in fasts, vigils
and prayers in the holy places of the city; and again he took a solemn
oath to show obedience. Whilst dwelling in Rome under pretext of
penance he won the city to his side, and preaching all the more freely
because the lord pope was occupied in Gaul he built up a faction known
as the heretical sect of the Lombards.[10] He had disciples who imitated
his austerities and won favour with the populace through outward
decency and austerity of life, but found their chief supporters among
pious women. He himself was frequently heard on the Capitol and in
public gatherings. He had already publicly denounced the cardinals,
saying that their college, by its pride, avarice, hypocrisy and manifold
shame was not the church of God, but a place of business [11] and a den
of thieves,[12] which took the place of the scribes and Pharisees amongst
Christian peoples. The pope himself was not what he professed to be—
an apostolic man and shepherd of souls—but a man of blood who maintained his authority by fire and sword,[13] a tormentor of churches and
oppressor of the innocent, who did nothing in the world save gratify his
lust and empty other men's coffers to fill his own. He was, he said, so
far from apostolic that he imitated neither the life nor the doctrine of the
apostles, wherefore neither obedience nor reverence was due to him:
and in any case no man could be admitted who wished to impose a yoke
of servitude on Rome, the seat of Empire, fountain of liberty and mistress
of the world.

A. ARNOLD'S INFLUENCE IN ROME AND HIS DEATH
AS DESCRIBED BY OTTO OF FREISING

1147

During these days,[14] a certain Arnold, who wore a religious garb but was by no means faithful to it, as was evident from his teaching, entered the city of Rome. Because of his hatred for the honors paid to the Church, and seeking to restore the dignity of the senate and the equestrian order to their ancient status, he aroused almost the entire City, and especially the populace, against his pope.

1155

Now on his way to the City the king encamped near Viterbo. Thither came the Roman pope, Hadrian,[15] with his cardinals, and was received with the honor due to his office. He was given a deferential hearing as he uttered bitter complaints against his people. For the aforesaid people, since their endeavor to reinstate the order of senators, in their rash daring did not shrink from inflicting many outrages on their popes. There was this additional aggravation of their seditious conduct, that a certain Arnold of Brescia, of whom mention has been made above, under guise of religion and—to use the words of the Gospel [16]—acting as a wolf in sheep's clothing, entered the City, inflamed to violence the minds of the simple people by his exceedingly destructive doctrines, and induced— nay, rather, seduced [17]—a countless throng to espouse that cause.

That Arnold, a native of Italy from the city of Brescia, a cleric ordained only as a lector of the church there, had once had Peter Abelard as his teacher. He was a man not indeed dull of intellect, yet abounding rather in profusion of words than in the weight of his ideas; a lover of originality and eager for novelty. The minds of such men are inclined to devise heresies and the tumult of schisms. Returning from his studies in France to Italy, he assumed the religious habit that he might deceive the more, assailing all things, carping at everything, sparing no one—a disparager of the clergy and of bishops, a persecutor of monks, a flatterer only of the laity. For he used to say that neither clerics that owned property, nor bishops that had regalia, nor monks with possessions could in any wise be saved. All these things belong to the prince, and should be bestowed of his beneficence for the use of the laity only. Besides this, he is said to have held unreasonable views with regard to the sacrament of the altar and infant baptism. While he was keeping the church of Brescia in uproar in these and other ways, which it would take too long to enumerate, and was maliciously defaming ecclesiastical personalities to the laity of that land, who have itching ears as regards the clergy, he was accused by the bishop and pious men of that city at the great council held at Rome under Innocent.[18] Therefore the Roman pontiff decided that silence should be imposed upon the man, that his pernicious teaching might not spread to more people. And thus it was done.

So that man, fleeing from Italy, betook himself to the lands beyond the Alps,[19] and there assuming the role of teacher in Zurich, a town of Swabia, he sowed his pernicious doctrine for some time. But when he learned of the death of Innocent he entered the City, near the beginning of the pontificate of Eugenius. As he found it aroused to rebellion against its pope, he incited it all the more to revolt, not following the counsel of the wise man who says of a situation of this kind: "Heap not wood upon his fire." [20] He set forth the examples of the ancient Romans, who by virtue of the ripened judgment of the senate and the disciplined integrity of the valiant spirit of youth made the whole world their own. Wherefore he advocated that the Capitol should be rebuilt, the senatorial dignity restored, and the equestrian order reinstituted. Nothing in the administration of the City was the concern of the Roman pontiff; the ecclesiastical courts should be enough for him. Moreover, the menace of this baneful doctrine began to grow so strong that not only were the houses and splendid palaces of Roman nobles and cardinals being destroyed, but even the reverend persons of some of the cardinals were shamefully treated by the infuriated populace, and several were wounded.[21] Although he incessantly and irreverently perpetrated these things and others like them for many days (that is, from the death of Celestine[22] until this time) and despised the judgment of the pastors, justly and canonically pronounced against him, as though in his opinion they were void of all authority, at last he fell into the hands of certain men and was taken captive within the limits of Tuscany. He was held for trial by the prince and finally was brought to the pyre by the prefect of the City.[23] After his corpse had been reduced to ashes in the fire, it was scattered on the Tiber, lest his body be held in veneration by the mad populace.

The Spread of Heresy in Italy
1160-1216

20. Civil Unrest as a Background for Heresy

We use this excerpt from the life of St. Galdinus, archbishop of Milan
(1166-1176), to illustrate the lack of precision about heresy in the conventional narrative sources for Italy in the twelfth century. Yet heresy was rife
there, especially in the rapid spread of Catharism after 1160, and Milan
was no exception.[1] In the struggle of the Holy Roman Emperor, Frederick
I, to assert control in Lombardy, and the subsequent conflict of the emperor
with Pope Alexander III (1159-1181), Milan suffered severely. When it was
captured and sacked by imperial forces in 1162, the archbishop went into
exile with his clergy, including Galdinus, a member of the famous Della
Scala family. In 1165 Galdinus was made a cardinal and in 1166, still in
exile, became archbishop of Milan. In the following year, he returned to his
see to begin a notable career in rebuilding the city and reconstituting the
clergy of his province. He died in 1176. For a brief reference to St. Galdinus
in English, see Thurston and Attwater, eds., *Butler's Lives of the Saints*,
rev. ed., II, 122-23.

This piece is translated from *Vita sancti Galdini*, in *Acta sanctorum*,
April 18, II, 591.

circa 1176

In due time he [Archbishop Galdinus] consecrated nearly all his suffragans and with the help of God the city and his church were finally
restored to their original condition. The heresy of the Cathars [2] began to
spread in the city and was the cause of growing dissension and schism.
It grew so much under pressure of sin that many persons publicly
preached it and other errors with reckless audacity and the souls of
many simple folk were caught in the snares of the devil's deceit. Then
the holy man set himself to combat that deadly plague. By many discourses and much preaching he recalled the people from that foolish and
vicious error and, by instructing them in the fundamentals of the Catholic
faith in so far as he was able, he advanced his cause by both word and
example.

21. The Letter of Master Vacarius against the Errors of Hugo Speroni

The Speronists [1] comprised a minor sect which apparently never spread far from its place of origin in Piacenza. Their founder, Hugo Speroni, had studied civil law, probably about 1145, at Bologna, where his friend Vacarius shared his lodgings. Vacarius went on to a distinguished career as one of the first professors of Roman law in England; Speroni became a consul in Piacenza. As such, he was active in litigation over family and communal claims against the monastery of St. Julia in the matter of harbor and bridge revenues. How much this controversy may have influenced the bent of his thought is conjectural, but by about 1177 Speroni was committed to a position of hostility to the Church and its ministry. He denied the validity of the priesthood, which he regarded as indelibly stained by sin. He denied, too, the need of the sacraments of baptism, the Eucharist, or confession, because justification depended not on them but on an inner purity. Nor was salvation earned by good works, for the inner holiness which justified man was the gift of God to those whom He predestined to receive it and was not augmented by the externals of piety. In this respect Speroni has been interpreted as a twelfth-century forerunner of Luther and Calvin.[2]

To his old friend Vacarius, Hugo Speroni sent a copy of a work expounding his views. Vacarius replied in a friendly tone but with an extensive refutation of the errors he had discovered in Speroni's tract. The only manuscript of this reply bears the title *Liber contra multiplices et varios errores* [book against many and various errors]. In the Prologue to that reply, which is translated here, Vacarius enumerates the major points of Speroni's teaching and refutes each one briefly and firmly but without rancor. All that is known of Speroni, together with an edition of Vacarius's work, is presented in the intensive study by Ilarino da Milano which precedes his edition of the treatise.

The translation is from Ilarino da Milano, *L'Eresia di Ugo Speroni nella confutazione del Maestro Vacario: Testo inedito del secolo XII con studio storico e dottrinale* (Studi e Testi, CXV [Vatican City, 1945]), pp. 475-81, by kind permission of the editor and of the Biblioteca Vaticana.

1177-1185

Here begins the Prologue of the *Book against Many and Various Errors*. To Hugo Speroni, once his companion and friend, Vacarius, called Master, sends good wishes, to him personally and for the opportune betterment of us both.

[A] I would not have you think that I have forgotten the brotherly affection of companionship and intimacy which was so strong between us in school—so strong, indeed, that when we shared the same lodgings it pleased you to take my advice in your affairs. Therefore, not merely the motive of brotherliness but of that friendship to which I referred more particularly moves me to sympathy with you in your tribulations. The graver these are, the more earnestly they weigh upon me and arouse me to compassion for you who are beset by many woes. For, as I have learned from your letter and from talking with other persons, you have disturbed the Church of God not a little, to the hazard of your soul's salvation. You publish many injurious things against the Church in a certain book which my nephew Leonard delivered to me in your name. I have read and reread it, again and again. Although some excellent passages are to be found therein, on re-examination I discovered more which, however worthy and valid they may be, are nevertheless corrupted and rendered worthless by the addition of certain untruths, particularly in that they are equivocally phrased and directed to a wicked conclusion.

[B] On the priests of the Old Law: In the first place, citing the prophets, you point out many and various defects of the priests of the Old Law, failings by which they were cut off from God; and likewise, indeed, much more, are our priests estranged, so that, citing Dionysius the Areopagite,[3] you deem them by the rule there stated not to be priests. To prove this, you have taken pains to collect all the recorded texts. Yet these do not pertain to the priestly office itself but to the worthiness of the priests' lives; that is, they do not lose the power of the office but the grace of God, and it is thus that they are cut off from God by such faults. The sum of your proposition in other succeeding articles is the same and the argument in refutation is the same; that is, that although they may be unclean, thieves and robbers, nevertheless, they remain priests, unless, for due cause, they are lawfully removed from office.

[C] You labor to prove by the Apostle that only the pure may be purified;[4] but I will show presently that you do not understand the Apostle. Now what is the meaning of "purify" but to remove the uncleanliness which makes one impure? For as every impurity makes one unclean before God, as it does in the sight of men, so also everyone who is unclean among men is unclean before God, even, indeed, all who are predestined to eternal life. Moreover, those who are murderers, adulterers, fornicators, or are stained by any vice are surely unclean before God. When even the angels themselves were held to be unclean in His sight,[5] and when even such as these were purified, it is not, as you think, that the pure are purified, but rather that the unclean are cleansed of their impurities.

Furthermore, you say that just as one who is polluted in body—for example, by excrement—fouls whoever touches him to cleanse him, so the one who is polluted in soul does not purify but stains whomever he may touch in purification. But this does not hold together very well. Intangible defilements, such as [are incurred in] murders and thefts, are not transferred from one soul to another as easily as bodily filth is passed from one body to another. Indeed, you go astray by the fact that you quote: "Whatsoever a person toucheth who is unclean, he maketh it unclean";[6] also, "If one that is unclean by occasion of a soul shall touch bread or pottage or shall consecrate anything, the whole shall be defiled."[7] But this is to be understood only in regard to the one polluted, who touches or consecrates anything; namely, it is only in relation to himself that what he touches or consecrates is regarded as though it were intrinsically unclean.

It will not, however, be held to be unclean or defiled either intrinsically or in so far as it affects other persons. Thus, the Lord himself said that He was profaned by the priests, declaring, "I was profaned in the midst of them."[8]

By reason of this error of yours, you render a large part of your book worthless and full of falsity, although many things which are good in themselves may be found intermingled therein.

[D] On the baptism of children: You put together a captious and slanderous attack upon infant baptism by following, without much insight, the verbal formulas and noting in them a defect of misrepresentation where none exists.

The words which are repeated by the priest and by the one who holds the child are not used in baptizing for the purpose of stating that of which they are a sign, but in order to make manifest that which is accomplished in baptism, which is, reception into the faith of Christ. The reason for baptizing is, indeed, clearly set forth by these words so that it may be better known by everyone, lest at some time it might in some way be called into doubt; for peril to the soul is incurred if a child is baptized for some reason other than this.

This you do not accept because you ignore original sin, washed away by baptism, and the cause thereof, which the Lord voiced in respect of those who were circumcised, when He said: "The child who shall not be circumcised, that soul shall be taken away from his people"; and He added the reason therefor: "Because he hath broken my covenant." [9] For in Adam all have broken the covenant not to eat of the apple which the Lord made with Adam in Eden. Therefore, just as carnal circumcision was once performed out of necessity, so now is the ablution of water, lest the soul of the child be taken away from his people.

[E] Of the body of Christ: With much vanity and deceptiveness you are in error about the body and blood of Christ. For you pretend that some persons in the Church explain that Christ is sacrificed on the altar, mangled and chewed, suffers, and mystically dies, even though it is certain that "Christ died once," and that "death shall have no more dominion over Him," [10] so that He cannot suffer, be broken or bruised with the teeth.

If you ask how His flesh can be eaten, one thing I know, that it is not mangled by the teeth in a carnal sense. For the manner and mode of eating to which allusion here is made is entirely unique, not natural and common; yet human reason may fail even to account for a natural manner of eating. Lo, from five loaves, five thousand people were well fed.[11] Is it not silly and foolish to ask how this may have been done? Therefore, although the whole Church believes, in reliance on the words of the Lord which the Apostle also followed,[12] that the flesh and blood of Christ are taken into the mouth, you alone gainsay it with numerous untruths and with sophistical and vexatious scoffing, as will be more fully apparent later.

[F] In error also, you say that the Lord Jesus enjoined His disciples to share a meal in His memory.

When He . . .[13] shared only bread with them all and, after the meal, gave them one cup, He commanded that all drink from it and that they do this in commemoration of Him; as for the meal itself, He gave them no instruction. Nor did the Apostle give any to the Corinthians, but he did reprove them because the manner of their eating, when they came into the church to eat, was not that of sharing the Lord's Supper. For the Lord's Supper will have so much love that the Lord will give His body to be eaten; but their supper was of such impiety that, glutting themselves to drunkenness, they, to their own perdition, gave nothing to the brethren who were impoverished and hungry.[14] For that reason they could not worthily come to the body of the Lord. What is consecrated today in the Mass by a priest in the Church is not the Lord's Supper nor does it symbolize it; it is rather that which the Lord taught His disciples, which is to do for others in memory of Him what He himself did for them, blessing and giving to them the bread and the chalice of benediction, saying, "Take, eat and drink of this, all of you; this is my body and my blood," [15] and so on.

The Mass is the most holy and well-considered office established in the Church of God, comprising, according to the most pious teaching of the Apostle, "supplications, prayers, intercessions, and thanksgivings," [16] to the mutual salvation of the living and the dead. The sacrifice of the Lord's body and blood which is celebrated at the end of the Mass occurs for him who participates therein. Nor is the ministry of an unworthy priest who may by chance minister in the Mass an impediment in respect of other persons, although he may, in himself, be unworthy, for the Apostle speaks in this wise: "Neither he that planteth is anything, nor he that watereth, but God alone who giveth the increase," [17] that is, the effect itself.

Nor is it an obstacle, as you think, that thus it may seem that God had fellowship with the unclean. Never! Because wicked men minister daily before God, may one say that He is the companion of the wicked? Even the most impious Judas ministered especially to Him, but from this he formed no fellowship with Him.

[G] Also that argument of yours, in which you assert that God has forbidden that a sinner expound His statutes because of the fact that He said to the sinner, "Why dost thou declare my justices?" [18] is worthless.

Indeed, He demanded this of him so that the latter would know that, as far as concerned himself, he labored in vain in expounding the statutes, for he would obtain no reward. This is not true of the effect on other persons, among whom it is difficult to know and recognize who are sinners and who are not. For even if one may know them to be sinners or Pharisees, one should observe the good things which they say.[19] Moreover, it is ridiculous to adopt your conjecture by which we must ask who are sinners and who are not so that we do not hearken to them if they be sinners.

You, however, go further in the declaration that he is not a Christian who is not a son of God; that is, who has not, in your words, the law of God written on his heart. For, by your assertion, even if one has been baptized and is indubitably clean, purified, and sanctified, one may not be a Christian except as one is a saint.

But were they not Christians to whom the Apostle wrote the words: "I hear that when you are come together in the church there is schism among you"? [20] And again, "One is hungry, another is drunk." [21] Could ever sanctity own such vices as schism, as impious drunkenness? Such certainly are the enemies of love and sanctity, yet these people met together in the faith of Christ in the church, that is, in a house of prayer. Indeed, the Apostle considered them to be Christian, for he said: "Do I praise you?" [22] and later, "He that eateth and drinketh unworthily, eateth and drinketh judgment to himself, not discerning the body of Christ. Therefore there are many infirm and weak among you, and many asleep." [23] He numbered them among the Christians, although they were poor and weak. Therefore not all Christians are saints.

[H] Hugo's opinion: You also think that because it is said, "All the Law is fulfilled in one word," [24] that by this phrase the Apostle explained that no burden but the love of Christ—that is, without works—is imposed on us by law.

The Apostle obviously denies this in the words, "If any man will not work, neither let him eat." [25] For the liberty which is given to us by the law of Jesus Christ does not free us from subjection to the Law and its works nor from subjection to the works of love.

Likewise, in much ignorance and unwisdom you protest against us because out of love we observe Sundays [and also] [26] saints' days. In religious celebrations such as these we ought to abstain day and night from lowly labor of our hands, in accordance with the teaching of the prophetic Scriptures,[27] so that we may spend all of such periods, as the Apostle says, in "psalms, and hymns, and spiritual canticles," [28] and prayers to the honor of God.

[I] Surely, although you are in no small way at fault in the errors already enumerated, you obviously go much too far when you say that we are enjoined to preach the word of God, to baptize in water, to praise God, and to undertake similar activities, yet, if these be undertaken, they justify not, nor avail for salvation. But in a preceding passage on another topic you show by the words of the Lord—which are that thou shalt not kill, thou shalt not commit adultery [29]—that these commandments, if observed, do avail for eternal life; yet it is a far better thing to do good than to refrain from evil.

Nay, rather, it is most absurd to suppose that the Apostle, who subjected himself to so many labors, so many wrongs, so many wants, in preaching to convert the nations, deserved no reward for the labor of such preaching. For the Apostle himself says in the letter to the Corinthians: "I have planted, Apollo watered, but God gave the increase. And every man shall receive his own reward, according to his own labor." [30]

Moreover, what reply was made to the man in Horace who boasted that he had not committed murder? When he said vauntingly, "I have not killed a man," the answer to him was, "You shall not then feed the carrion crows on the cross," [31] as if this were reward enough. Therefore if this man deserves eternal life because he sins not, how much more will that one who preaches, who prays, who does good works, receive reward in proportion to his labor, through that justice which justifies those who labor thus, giving to each according to his own desserts.

[L] In conclusion, I must not pass over this point which touches on the matter of circumspection, namely, that the ill-advised definitions in which your work abounds plunge those who accept them into the various errors found in the work itself, as will appear later. For although it is particularly laid down that "in law definitions are hazardous," [32] yet they are not without danger also in other subjects, and consequently it is necessary to proceed cautiously when propounding something in general terms or in making definitions. Since you have paid no heed to this, I find many harmful matters embedded in your book, to all of which . . .[33] I have replied carefully to these; what should be said in answer to others which might be censurable can be readily comprehended.

22. The Origins of the Humiliati

The impulse toward the expression of piety by lives of simple poverty and evangelism conceived to be in imitation of the apostles was an increasingly potent stimulus of religious diversity in the second half of the twelfth century. Sometimes groups with such aims broke away from or were thrust out of the Church, but occasionally they were able later to find a way of return, especially when Innocent III (1198-1216) strove to conserve this religious impulse for the Church. The most sweeping of such movements—we are speaking of those which antedated the great mendicant orders of the thirteenth century—was embodied by the Waldenses, but even before their influence had reached Italy comparable developments were appearing there. The Humiliati, described in this short passage, perhaps reacting against the developing commercialism of the time, expressed their pious aspirations in a commitment to personal poverty, communal life, and evangelism within their own class of workers. Their defiance of restrictions on preaching led to their excommunication in 1184. Some fifteen years later, Innocent III drew some of the Humiliati back to the Church, approving an organization in three orders: Laymen living with their families, laymen and women in semimonastic communities of workers, and a clerical order including the religious and priests. Those who remained apart from the Church seem to have been absorbed by the Waldenses and to have played a part in the internal dissensions of that group (see No. 45, parts B and C; and No. 46).

There is a considerable literature on the Humiliati, which expresses various interpretations of their character and significance; for example, Zanoni, *Gli Umiliati*, and Girolamo Tiraboschi, *Vetera humiliatorum monumenta*, each of which prints various sources. Convenient short accounts are Stefano, *Riformatori ed eretici*, pp. 125-84; Félix Vernet, "Humiliés," *Dictionnaire de théologie catholique*, VII, 313-21; Ilarino da Milano, *L'Eresia di Ugo Speroni*, pp. 455-57; and in English, Davison, *Forerunners of St. Francis*, chap. V.

The excerpt here translated is from the chronicle of an anonymous canon of Premontré who wrote in Laon. For the later years of the twelfth century and the first part of the thirteenth it is regarded as generally trustworthy. The translation is from *Chronicon universale anonymi Laudunensis*, ed. by Georg Waitz, in *Monumenta Germaniae historica, Scriptores*, XXVI, 449-50, by permission of Anton Hiersemann Verlag and the Monumenta Germaniae Historica.

circa 1178-1184

At that time there were certain inhabitants of Lombard towns who lived at home with their families, chose a peculiar form of religious life, refrained from lies, oaths, and law suits, were satisfied with plain clothing, and presented themselves as upholding the Catholic faith. They approached the pope [1] and besought him to confirm their way of life. This the pope granted them, provided that they did all things humbly and decently, but he expressly forbade them to hold private meetings or to presume to preach in public. But spurning the apostolic command, they became disobedient, for which they suffered excommunication.[2] They called themselves Humiliati, because they did not use colored cloth for clothing but restricted themselves to plain dress.

23. The Heresy of the Cathars in Lombardy

During the two decades after the middle of the twelfth century, the heresy of the Cathars was making substantial gains; but, as far as the sources now known to us disclose, it was not until the Cathars were already well entrenched in northern Italy that detailed written evidence of their doctrines began to be made available to their orthodox contemporaries. The treatise here translated was not the first to describe them,[1] but the historical events it recounts began soon after mid-century and for that reason we place it here. Of the author we know no more than that he was a Lombard, perhaps from Milan, and so well informed about Catharist groups and leaders that he himself may have been a member of the sect at one time.[2] His work falls into three divisions: (1) a narrative of the growth and proliferation of Italian dualist sects; (2) a description of the tenets of several of their "churches" about the beginning of the thirteenth century; and (3) a short list of the heretical hierarchy at the time of writing. In this form the treatise escaped the notice of later historians of heresy until recently, although the first, or narrative, portion had been published separately by Nicholas Vignier in 1601 from a manuscript now lost. Polemical writers of the thirteenth century also made excerpts from the second part and in later centuries, when their various works were edited, the relationships and ultimate source of these borrowed passages created a puzzle for scholars.[3] Not until 1949 did Father Antoine Dondaine find the treatise in its complete form in manuscript, establish its authenticity, and edit it.

The *De heresi catharorum*[4] is one of the three most important sources for the history of Catharism in Italy. It and the treatise on heresy by Anselm of Alessandria, translated in Nos. 24 and 54, narrate events arising in the second half of the twelfth century from the extension of Bogomil influence to Italy. A third *summa*, that of Rainerius Sacconi (No. 51), is the major source for the situation of the Italian Cathars after they had split into competing churches,[5] producing persistent divisions and a new nomenclature of heresy.[6] The first comprehensive study of the Italian churches and their hierarchy was in Dondaine, "La Hiérarchie cathare, II-III," *Archivum fratrum praedicatorum*, XX (1950), 278-305. Borst (pp. 231-39) gives a catalogue of sects and their hierarchy which extends and amends that of Dondaine.[7]

The following translation is made from Antoine Dondaine, "La Hiérarchie cathare en Italie, I: Le 'De heresi catharorum in Lombardia,'" *Archivum fratrum praedicatorum*, XIX (1949), 306-12, by permission of Father Dondaine and the Istituto storico domenicano di S. Sabina. We retain in brackets the numbers and titles for subdivisions which were supplied by Dondaine.

1150-1200 (written circa 1200-1214)

[1. *How the Schism Began.*] In the early days, when the heresy of the Cathars began to increase in Lombardy, they first had a certain bishop named Mark,[9] under whose rule all the Lombard, Tuscan, and Trevisan [heretics] were governed. Mark was consecrated in the sect of Bulgaria.[10] Then there came to Lombardy from Constantinople a man called Papa

Nicheta,[11] who began to declaim against the Bulgarian consecration which Mark had received. This raised doubts in the minds of Bishop Mark and his followers; he gave up the Bulgarian consecration and accepted, at the hands of Nicheta himself,[12] that of Drugunthia,[13] and in this sect of Drugunthia he and all his associates remained for some time. Somewhat later, a man named Petracius [14] came with companions from across the sea and brought news about one Simon,[15] a bishop of Drugunthia, from whom stemmed the consecration received from Nicheta. Petracius said that Simon had been discovered in a room with a woman and had committed other acts contrary to doctrine. Now, by the time Petracius appeared, Mark had already died and another person, named John Judeus,[16] who had been ordained as a bishop by Mark, had succeeded him. Some persons were thrown into doubt by the testimony of Petracius about the consecration derived from Simon; some were not. On this account a quarrel arose among them and thereby they divided into two groups. It came to such a pass, moreover, that one group adhered to John Judeus, the other chose as bishop Peter of Florence.[17] In this situation the two parties remained for several years.

Some of the wiser heads among them, grieved by this schism and hoping to restore them to unity, hit on the plan to have delegates chosen from both parties, and these they dispatched in a group to a certain bishop north of the Alps, with the agreement that they would submit without demur to the opinion of the bishop, however he should decide on the question of the schism among them.[18] Now, the bishop, once he had heard and carefully considered the arguments of both parties, handed down this verdict: These two bishops of Lombardy and their followers should meet together; lots should be cast between the two bishops, John Judeus and Peter of Florence, respectively; to whichever one of them on whom the lot of the episcopate should fall, the other would submit; and the whole body of followers, now divided into two groups, should obey him. And the bishop, thus chosen by lot, should go to Bulgaria to receive consecration as bishop; and when he returned home again after receiving the Bulgarian consecration, their whole community should be reconsoled by the imposition of hands. When they had received this decision the delegates came back to Lombardy and made it public. After a period was fixed within which the judgment should be acted upon and the lots cast, Peter of Florence, bishop of one group, refused to carry out the decision and cast lots. Thereupon, he was deposed from the office of bishop by his followers and thus, pursuant to the decision, he ceded legal claim to all episcopal authority to John Judeus, who was willing to carry it out. But some of the other party, opposed to John Judeus, refused out of ill will to submit to him.

Meanwhile, some wiser ones had approached John Judeus and had prayerfully besought him in all humility to resign the episcopal office because he was disliked by so many, asserting that from this withdrawal could come peace and concord among them. They added that they would then choose one from his group to represent him, and one from the other party would be chosen in place of Peter of Florence, who had refused to carry out the decision. Lots would be cast by the two persons selected, as had been proposed in the verdict; a bishop would be chosen by that lot and he would exercise episcopal authority over the whole community without any reservation.[19] John was persuaded by these pleas, realizing that he could not preside in peace and tranquillity, and, hopeful of restoring the sundered group to unity, submitted to their recommendation and divested himself of what power he had. The report of this was spread widely.

Thus it was that within the period which they had already set, they assembled in a place called Mosio [20] and there decided on the following procedure: One party would choose a man from the other group, whomsoever they wished, and vice versa. Thus it transpired that from the party of John Judeus a man named Garattus [21] was selected by the other group, and from the opposing party of Peter of Florence, one by the name of John *de Judice*.[22] The whole body agreed to follow without demur the one of these two whom the lots decided to be bishop. In this way, Garattus was chosen bishop by lot, and forthwith all were there brought to concord. They set a certain period of time for selecting associates and gathering funds for the journey of Garattus to Bulgaria to be consoled and receive episcopal consecration and, after his return, for the group to be reconsoled in fulfillment of the verdict of the ultramontane bishop.

But within the period agreed on, Garattus was accused on the testimony of two witnesses of being guilty of relations with a woman, for which reason he was deemed unworthy of the episcopal office by a great many of them, and therefore they did not hold themselves bound by the pledge of obedience which they had made to him. Whence the group, once divided in two, was now split up into six parts. For, within the period mentioned above, in which they had promised to provide associates and expenses for this Garattus to go to Bulgaria, some from Desenzano [23] established a congregation and chose a man named John the Good [24] as their bishop and sent him across the sea to Drugunthia, there to be ordained bishop. This is now the party of Amizo. [25] Also, some from Mantua, with their followers, chose as their bishop a man named Caloiannes, [26] who, being sent to Sclavonia [27] after his consecration, filled the episcopate for them. In the same fashion another man, named Nicola, [28] chosen by a congregation at Vicenza and sent to Sclavonia to be consecrated, was received as their bishop on his return. Similarly in Tuscany two bishops were ordained. [29] And so Garattus, although all were by their promise supposed to obey him, was abandoned by those we have named. He forbade their usurpation of the leadership of the group in this way but they rejected his order and did not give up their undertaking.

After all these bishops had been consecrated, as has been recounted, some of the Milanese, who did not concur in the decisions and actions of the others, sought to have Garattus for bishop as they had promised. But Garattus, well aware that he had been abandoned by the majority, would not consent. He suggested that John Judeus, who, in humility and to bring unity out of schism, had given up the episcopate, was more worthy of this office. Since John Judeus was reluctant to accept it, this group again sent delegates across the mountains to confer on the matter with the bishop who had first given judgment. At the news of the schism, the bishop greatly deplored what had been done and sent word to John Judeus to go to Bulgaria to carry out what had been propounded in the verdict, so that he might be prelate in Lombardy over all who were willing to submit. This he did. After John's death, another man, named Joseph, [30] took his place, and when Joseph died, Garattus succeeded him. Now, Garattus and his followers argued that the aforesaid bishops with their followers were bound by the former promise made to him, unless he released them from it, and he declared that they had accepted episcopal ordination against God's will and against right reason. On this account he refused to join in the ritual of bestowing the prayer or in the performance of reverences [31] with any of these bishops except Caloiannes, whom he had recently absolved and with whom he had made peace. In this fashion, as we have related, the whole body of Cathars—that is to say, heretics and evildoers, adulterers of the teaching of Christ—once living in unity was first split in two and then again into six parts.[32]

[2a] *This Is the Belief of One Group of the Heretics.*—Marchisius of Sojano,[33] bishop of those of Desenzano, and Amizo, his elder son, prelates of one party of the Cathars, having their consecration in the sect of Drugunthia, believe and preach that there are two gods or lords without beginning and without end, one good, the other wholly evil. And they say that each created angels: the good God good angels and the evil one evil ones, and that the good God is almighty in the heavenly home, the evil one rules in all this worldly structure.[34] They say that Lucifer is the son of the god of darkness, inasmuch as it is said in the Gospel of John: "You are of your father the devil," and following that, "For he is a liar, and his father the devil," [35] that is, Lucifer in their explanation is the liar. They say that this Lucifer ascended from his kingdom here into the heaven above, conformably to that written by the prophet Isaiah, "I will ascend into heaven," [36] and so on. There he transfigured himself into an angel of light. Since the angels regarded him with admiration for his appearance and interceded with the Lord on his behalf, he was received [into heaven and there was appointed a steward of the angels]; [37] whence it is said in the Gospel of Luke, "There was a certain rich man who had a steward." [38] In the office of steward, he led the angels astray. Then, they say, was waged a great battle in heaven, "and that dragon was cast out, that old serpent," [39] together with the seduced angels, according to the text of the Apocalypse: "And his tail drew the third part of the stars of heaven." [40] Those angels had a triple composition: body, soul, and spirit. And they say that the slain bodies, which are called "dry bones" in Ezechiel,[41] remained in heaven; the spirits also remained there. The souls, however, were seized by Lucifer and were put into bodies in this world. They say that Christ, the Son of God, came to save only these souls, according to the text: "The Son of man came not to destroy souls, but to save"; [42] and again, in the Gospel of Matthew, "I was not sent but to the sheep that are lost of the house of Israel"; [43] and again, further on, "The Son of man is come to save that which was lost." [44] And He led back the hundredth sheep which had strayed. Of the afore-mentioned battle they repeat this psalm, "O God, the heathens are come." [45] They declare that there are still in heaven the garments, the crowns, and the places which they lost, and that they ought to receive them again, of which the Apostle [says], "As to the rest, there is laid up for me a crown of justice which the Lord, the just judge, will

render to me in that day." [46] They assert that judgment is already rendered because of the text, "The prince of this world is already judged." [47] They explain that human bodies are in part animated by those evil spirits whom the devil created and in part by those souls [48] that fell. Those souls do penance in these bodies and, if not saved in one body, a soul goes into another body and does penance. When penance is accomplished, the bodies and spirits which remained in heaven shall be recovered, according to that text from the Apostle: "And may the God of peace himself sanctify you in all things, that your whole spirit and soul and body, may be preserved blameless in the coming of our Lord Jesus Christ." [49]

[2b] *This Is the Opinion or Belief of Another Group of Heretics.*—Caloiannes, bishop of a party of heretics consecrated in the sect of Sclavonia, and Garattus, bishop of another group of the adulterers of the teaching of Christ, which draws its consecration from the sect of Bulgaria,[50] believe in and preach one only good God, almighty, without beginning, who created angels and the four elements. They assert that Lucifer and his accomplices sinned in heaven, but some among them are uncertain as to how their sin arose. Some, indeed, hold—but it is a secret— that there was a certain evil spirit having four faces: one of a man, the second of a bird, the third of a fish, and the fourth of a beast. It had no beginning and remained in this chaos,[51] having no power of creation. They say that Lucifer, while yet he was good, came down and, beholding the spectacle of this evil spirit, was filled with wonder, and was led astray by the conversation and the prompting of this evil spirit. He returned to heaven and there seduced others. They were cast out of heaven but did not lose the natural attributes which they possessed. These heretics assert that Lucifer and the other evil spirit wished to separate the elements, but could not. Thereupon, they begged from God a good angel as assistant, and thus with God"s acquiescence, with the aid of this good angel, and by his strength and wisdom, they separated the elements. And, they say, Lucifer is the God who, in Genesis, is said to have created heaven and earth and to have accomplished this work in six days. They explain that Lucifer fashioned the body of Adam from the clay of the earth and into that body by force pressed the good angel, in accord with the text in the Gospel: "Laying hold of him, he throttled him, saying: Pay what thou owest." [52] And for him Lucifer made Eve, in order to cause him to sin through her. And they say that eating of the

forbidden tree was fornication. According to some of them, just as flesh comes from flesh, so spirit is born of spirit, following the verse of the Gospel: "That which is born of the flesh, is flesh; and that which is born of the Spirit, is spirit." [53] There is a certain controversy among them on this point. Certain others of their number, rejecting this opinion, say that all the spirits destined to be saved were created at one time and were infused little by little into human bodies by the will of God. However, those who say that spirit is born of spirit affirm that all this world is peopled by those wicked spirits, including both those who are to be damned and those who are to be saved. The ones, indeed, who say that all the spirits destined for salvation were created simultaneously assert that those spirits who fell were not destined for salvation at the time of their embodiment, and so they pass from body to body. This will continue, even to the end of the world; and at the world's judgment the good and the evil will be numbered. The good will resume their own places; the evil will have everlasting punishment. On this point they are somewhat at odds, for some of them agree that a part of those that fell are to be saved: those who sinned not of their own accord but, as it were, under compulsion. Those who sinned deliberately are to be damned. They assert that other spirits have been created by Almighty God to fill the places of those not destined for salvation.

The common belief of all Cathars is that all things recounted in Genesis—namely, about the flood, the deliverance of Noah, God's speaking to Abraham, the destruction of Sodom and Gomorrah—were done by the devil, who there is called god. And likewise this very god led the people out of Egypt, and gave them the Law in the desert, and led them into the Promised Land. And he sent prophets to them through whose prophecies he caused the blood of animals to be offered unto him, so that he might be honored as god. And if sometimes these prophets foretold something about Christ by the power of the Holy Spirit, they prophesied all unknowingly, as if forced thereto. They avow that Almighty God did all these things, not through himself, but through the devil as His minister. In this way, they say, with reference to what the devil performed by the wisdom and power accorded to him in creation by God, he caused all these things, with the purpose of ruling over them without limit, with God's permission. God permitted it for another purpose, that He might draw out of this world through penance the fruit of those destined to be saved.

The Sclavini believe that in the time of grace the Son of God (who is Jesus Christ), John the Evangelist, and Mary were three angels appearing in the flesh. They say that Christ did not really put on flesh, nor did He eat or drink, nor was He crucified, dead, or buried; that everything He did as man was only semblance, not actuality, and but seemed to be real.

Some of the heretics of Bulgaria believe that Mary was a true woman and that the Son of God took on true human flesh from her, truly ate, and was crucified in the flesh, but did not ascend in this flesh, for He put it off at His ascension. Of John the Baptist, they say that he was sent by the devil with the baptism of water to hinder the preaching of Christ. When he pointed at Christ with his finger or preached anything about Him, it was not of his own doing but that of the Holy Spirit, speaking through him as through a tube, as though he were under compulsion, not knowing what he said, just as Caiphas prophesied all unknowingly.[54] Few, indeed, of the Cathars disagree with this opinion; even the Bulgars believe it. All reject matrimony and deny the resurrection of these visible bodies. All say that the baptism of water never brought salvation, even the baptism which the apostles performed in water.

[3. *These Are Their Prelates.*] The bishop Garattus, ordained in Bulgaria, resides at Concorezzo;[55] his elder son is Nazarius[56] and his younger son, Gerald of Brescia.[57] Caloiannes is bishop of Mantua; he has his ordination from Sclavonia. His elder son was Orto of Bagnolo,[58] but he is now a bishop; his younger son was Aldricus *de Gilinguellis*, from Milan. Marchisius of Sojano is a bishop of the Drugunthian sect; his elder son is Amizo. Nicola of Vicenza is a bishop of the Sclavonian sect; his elder son is Peter Gallus,[59] his younger son is named Prandus.

24. The Origins of the Cathars in Italy

About a century after the appearance of the Cathars in Lombardy a Dominican inquisitor wrote an account of their origins. Although several of the same individuals and some of the events described in Number 23 appear, the narrative is different enough in detail to show its independence of that earlier work. It formed part of various notes jotted down by an inquisitor in a collection of materials useful to his office: descriptions of the beliefs and practices of Cathars and Waldenses, remarks on the schism within each group and on the consolamentum and other Catharist practices, formularies of procedure, and a list of the heretical hierarchy of his day. Here we translate only the first item, on the history of the Cathars, although several other excerpts will appear in a later place (No. 54). The author of this treatise on heresy is designated only by the initial *A.* in the one known manuscript, but his obvious role as an inquisitor made fuller identification possible. He was Anselm of Alessandria, who was active in the business of the Holy Office as early as 1256 in Genoa and was named inquisitor for the province of Milan and the March of Genoa in January of 1267. His name appears in other documents as late as 1279, after which nothing more is known of him. From internal evidence, the first elements of the treatise can be dated between 1260 and 1270, perhaps, to be more precise, in 1266-1267; others notes were added over about a decade.¹ All that is known of the author is discussed by Dondaine in connection with the edition from which we made the translation.²

The following is translated from Antoine Dondaine, "La Hiérarchie cathare en Italie, II: Le 'Tractatus de hereticis' d'Anselme d'Alexandrie, O.P.; III: Catalogue de la hiérarchie cathare d'Italie," *Archivum fratrum praedicatorum*, XX (1950), 308-10, by permission of Father Dondaine and the Istituto storico domenicano di S. Sabina.

1150-1200 (written circa 1266-1267)

[1] *The Foundation and Earliest Beginning of Heresies.*—It should be remarked that there was in Persia an individual named Mani,³ who first began to ask himself: If there is a god, whence do evils arise? And if there is no god, whence comes good? As a result, he postulated two principles. He taught in the regions of Drugunthia, Bulgaria, and Philadelphia,⁴ and heresy increased there so much that men set up three bishops, one of Drugunthia, another of Bulgaria, and another of Philadelphia. Presently, Greeks from Constantinople, who are neighbors to Bulgaria at a distance of about three days' travel, went as merchants to the latter country; and, on return to their homeland, as their numbers grew, they set up there a bishop who is called bishop of the Greeks. Then Frenchmen went to Constantinople, intending to conquer the land,⁵ and discovered this sect; increasing in number, they established a bishop who is called bishop of the Latins. Thereafter, certain persons from Sclavonia, that is, from the area called Bosnia, went as merchants to Constantinople. On return to their own land, they preached and, having increased in number, established a bishop who is called the bishop of Sclavonia or of Bosnia. Later on, the French who had gone to Constantinople returned to their homeland and preached and, as their numbers grew, set up a bishop of France. Because the French were originally led astray in Constantinople by Bulgars, throughout France

these persons are called Bulgarian heretics. Also, people of Provence who are neighbors of those of France, hearing the teaching of the French and led astray by them, grew so numerous that they set up four bishops, namely, bishops of Carcassonne, of Albi, of Toulouse, and of Agen.

After a considerable period of time, there came a certain notary from France to Lombardy, in fact, to Milanese territory in the vicinity of Concorezzo. He fell in with a man named Mark, a native of a place called Cologno,[6] and led him astray. This man Mark talked to two of his friends, namely, John Judeus and Joseph. Note that Mark was a gravedigger; John, a weaver; and Joseph, a smith. One of these men made his way to Milan, to the Porta Orientale or Porta Conrencia [7] and there found a friend of his named Aldricus of Bando,[8] and led him astray. All these deluded persons took counsel with the aforesaid notary, who sent them to Roccavione [9]—that is a place near Cuneo—where dwelt Cathars who had come from France to settle. The bishop of the heretics was not there, being at Naples. Thither they went and sought him out, staying in that city for a year.[10] Thereafter, having received the imposition of the hand, Mark was made a deacon. The aforesaid bishop sent him back to his native place near Concorezzo, where Mark himself began to preach. As a result of his preaching in Lombardy, then in the March of Treviso, and later in Tuscany, the number of heretics greatly increased.

Somewhat later there arrived a certain individual named Papa Nicheta, who was bishop of the heretics in Constantinople. He said, "There are so many of you that you ought to have a bishop." Accordingly, they chose the aforesaid Mark as bishop, and all the aforesaid Lombard, Tuscan, and Trevisan heretics acknowledged his authority. Papa Nicheta himself confirmed him. After some time, Mark heard a report that Papa Nicheta had brought his life to a bad end. Consequently, Mark proposed to travel across the sea to obtain episcopal ordination from the bishop of Bulgaria. When he reached Calabria, he encountered a certain Cathar deacon named Hillary,[11] who told him that the voyage across the sea was impossible, so he turned back. He had reached the territory called Argentea [12] when he was captured and thrust into prison. Afflicted by mortal illness, he sent word to Lombardy to John Judeus and the other Cathars to elect a bishop, because he was gravely ill. All the Cathars of Lombardy together chose John Judeus of Concorezzo. John Judeus went to Argentea and had himself confirmed as bishop by the aforesaid

Mark, then he returned to Lombardy. A few days later Mark was released from confinement but, on arriving in Lombardy, died before reaching John Judeus. All the Cathars in Lombardy, John Judeus as well as the others, had been thrown into doubt because Papa Nicheta had come to an evil end, for from him derived the office of Bishop Mark who had confirmed the aforesaid John. A certain Nicholas of the March of Treviso, who himself wished to be bishop, realized this. He sought to stir up a controversy by saying to the Cathars: "What do you think about Lord Mark? Do you think he came to a good end or not?" All would reply, "Yes, we think he came to a good end." The man would then rejoin, "John Judeus says that Lord Mark came to an evil end, and for that reason he wants to cross the sea to be reconsoled." Thus, a fivefold division appeared among the heretics, corresponding to the five localities they inhabited. Those of Concorezzo kept John Judeus as bishop. Those of Desenzano, which is located in the diocese of Brescia, chose a man named Philip [13] as bishop. He became involved a little later with two Cathar women and so, abandoning the Cathars, returned to secular life with both women. Philip is reported to have been of the opinion that no man or woman can commit sin from the waist down; in this he had many followers.[14] The people of Mantua chose an individual named Caloiannes and when he died, a short time after his election, they chose Orto of Bagnolo,[15] from which fact they are called Bagnolenses. Those of the March of Treviso chose the aforesaid Nicholas, who had sowed the dissension among them. The Florentines elected one Peter of Florence, who was bishop there and throughout Tuscany.[16]

25. Bonacursus: A Description of the Catharist Heresy

A statement (*manifestatio*) exposing the teaching of Italian Cathars was, perhaps, one result of the efforts of St. Galdinus against heresy in Milan (see No. 20). At some time between 1176 and 1190, Bonacursus, a convert from the Cathars, revealed the doctrines of their heresy in a confession made in Milan. His statement became the nucleus from which a tract against heresy grew. To his confession other materials were soon added, probably by other hands: lists of biblical citations thought pertinent for use in refutation of various dualist tenets; a brief statement of the beliefs of another sect, the Passagians (see No. 26), with appropriate texts for their rebuttal; and an argument against the heresy of the Arnoldists.[1] These accumulated materials constitute the tract in the form published by Migne; other versions of its component parts also exist. We translate only Bonacursus's confession of the beliefs of the Cathars.

The treatise is studied by Ilarino da Milano in "La 'Manifestatio heresis catarorum,' " *Aevum* XII (1938), 281-333.[2] The portion revealing the tenets of the Cathars is the particular subject of investigation by Raoul Manselli, "Per la storia dell'eresia," *Bullettino dell'Istituto storico italiano per il medio evo e Archivio Muratoriano*, LXVII (1955), 189-211. Manselli studied and printed from a manuscript of the Bibliothèque nationale (lat. 14927) a version of the confession somewhat different from that found in Migne. He believed the Paris text to represent the original confession, which was later reworked for polemical purposes into the version we translate. We have noted the most important variants between the two.

The following piece is translated from Migne, *Patrologia latina*, CCIV, 775-77, where it is given the title *Vita haereticorum*. The treatise is more commonly referred to as *Manifestatio haeresis catharorum quam fecit Bonacursus*.

1176-1190

An Exposure of the Heresy of the Cathars, Made before the People of Milan by Bonacursus, Who Formerly Was One of Their Masters

In the name of our Lord Jesus Christ.

Our Lord Jesus Christ, who always and everywhere protects and guides His Church and confirms and preserves the Catholic faith, desiring in His holy mercy to make public and expose the error of those who are called Cathars, compassionately illumined a certain teacher [3] among them, Bonacursus by name, by the grace of His Holy Spirit and restored him by grace to the bosom of Holy Mother Church, for which we give boundless praise to God and all the saints. Their heresy is, indeed, not only terrifying but is, truly, too frightful and execrable to speak of or hear about.[4] For some of them say that God created all the elements, others say that the devil created these elements; but their common opinion is that the devil divided the elements. They state also that the same devil made Adam from dust of the earth and with very great force imprisoned in him a certain angel of light, of whom they think it was said in the Gospel, "A certain man went down from Jerusalem to Jericho,"[5] and so on. They say that the devil made Eve, with whom he lay, and from this union Cain was born. On discovering this, Adam came to know Eve and she bore Abel, whom Cain killed; and of the latter's blood, they declare dogs are born, and are, for that reason, so faithful to men.[6] The union of Adam and Eve was, in their words, the forbidden fruit. They put forward another error, which is that all things that have been made—in the air, in the sea, and on the earth, such as men and animate and inanimate things—were made by the devil.[7] From the daughters of Eve and demons were born giants,[8] who learned from the demons, their fathers, that the devil had created all things. Hence, the devil, sorrowing at their knowledge thereof, said, "It repenteth me that I have made man";[9] and Noah, because he had not that knowledge, was delivered from the flood and was told by the devil, as they say, to "Go into the ark."[10] They say that Enoch was translated[11] by the same devil.

Again, they assert that whatever things were done or said by Abraham, Isaac, or Jacob were said and done by a demon. They also aver that it was the devil who appeared to Moses in the bush and spoke to him. Moreover, the miracles performed by Moses in Pharaoh's presence, the fact that the children of Israel passed through the Red Sea and were led into the Promised Land, God's speaking to Moses,[12] and the Law which God gave to him—all these, they say and believe were the work of this same devil, their master. In regard to the utterances of the holy prophets, they affirm that some of the prophecies were disclosed by the Spirit of God, others by a wicked spirit; hence the Apostle: "Prove all things; hold fast that which is good."[13] They condemn David for adultery and murder; they say Elijah was carried off in a chariot by the devil.[14] They assert that the angel sent to Zacharias by God was an angel of the devil. They also condemn John [the Baptist] himself, than whom none is greater, according to the word of the Lord. Why? Because the Lord says in the Gospel, "He that is the lesser in the kingdom of God is greater than he,"[15] and because he [John] doubted Christ by saying: "Art thou he that art to come, or look we for another?"[16] Mary, the mother of our Lord, they believe to have been born of woman alone, not of man.[17] Of Christ, they declare that He did not have a living body,[18] that He did not eat, drink, or do anything else as men do, but that it only seemed that he did. They say that the thief on the left hand is in hell.[19] They do not believe that the body of Christ rose again or was taken into heaven, nor in the resurrection of the flesh, nor that Christ descended into hell. They do not think the Son equal to the Father, for He said, "The Father is greater than I."[20] They say that the Cross is the sign of the beast of which one reads in the Apocalypse and is an abomination in a holy place.[21] They assert that the Blessed Sylvester [22] was the Antichrist of whom one reads in the Epistle: "The son of perdition," is he "who is lifted up above all that is called God."[23] From that day, they say, the Church was lost. They believe that in matrimony no one can attain salvation.

They condemn all the doctors—that is, they damn Ambrose, Gregory, Augustine, Jerome and the others all together. If anyone shall have eaten meat, eggs, or cheese, or anything of an animal nature, [they believe] he consumed damnation for himself. They think that the Holy Spirit can in no way be received in the baptism of water,[24] nor do they believe that any visible substance can by any means be changed into the body of Christ. They believe, also, that anyone who takes an oath will be damned, and they think that no one can be saved except by a certain imposition of hands which they call baptism and the renewal of the Holy Spirit. They hold that the devil himself is the sun, Eve the moon; and each month, they say, they commit adultery, like a man with some harlot.[25] All the stars they believe to be demons. Finally, they say that no one can attain salvation outside of their sect. Lo, such is the heresy of the Cathars, from which God keep all Catholics. Amen.[26]

26. *The Heresy of the Passagians*

The Passagians,[1] a minor sect of the late twelfth century, were distinguished particularly by their insistence on observing strictly the legal precepts of the Old Testament, including the practice of circumcision,[2] although in common with various other heretics they also rejected orthodox views on the divinity of Christ and on the Trinity and spurned some of the sacraments and other institutions of the Church.[3] There is no mention in the sources of a distinctive church organization or hierarchy among them. The earliest reference to the sect occurs in a papal condemnation of 1184; the name appears thereafter, as late as 1291, in the stereotyped lists of sects which were under official condemnation, but this in itself is not reliable evidence of actual survival.[4] Polemics written after the middle of the thirteenth century do not discuss them, nor is the sect referred to in the inquisitorial literature. It has been suggested that the Passagians were found only in Lombardy.[5]

The most important source for the doctrines of the Passagians is the summa of unknown authorship and date from which excerpts are here translated.[6] It has been ascribed on inconclusive evidence to Prevostin of Cremona, chancellor at Paris from 1206 to 1210, who is said to have preached against and converted heretics.[7] The date of writing is presumed to fall between 1184 and 1210, most probably at the very end of the twelfth century.[8] The tract, in ten known manuscripts,[9] is devoted primarily to refutation of the doctrines of the Cathars and the Passagians, greater space being given to the latter; but certain unnamed heretics are spoken of briefly in the concluding chapters.[10]

Because this is the first example of the systematic scholastic polemic[11] presented in these translations, a word about its organization and style may be pertinent. The author's usual practice is to state in successive chapters the tenets of the heretics and the arguments, primarily based on scriptural texts, which they advance to uphold them. Normally, each of these quotations is at once reinterpreted by the author to prove the weakness of the heretical position.[12] Within each chapter, also, a separate portion expounds the Catholic view on the point in question, with its own scriptural or rational support. In this fashion, the first four chapters deal with the Cathars; the remainder are devoted primarily to the Passagians, but in several cases where their tenets parallel Catharist beliefs, separate portions of a chapter are given to each sect and, as we have said, certain other heretics are brought briefly into the discussion.

We have selected for translation those portions of six chapters which present the Passagians' statements about the nature of Christ, the need to observe the Old Testament and Mosaic Law, circumcision, the Sabbath, the prohibition of certain foods, and the invalidity of the institutions and practices of the Roman Church, but we have omitted all of the Catholic responses. The complex editorial problem of establishing a text from manuscripts often widely at variance led Garvin and Corbett, the editors, to print considerable portions of their edition in parallel columns.[13] Of these, we have chosen to follow the recension which incorporates the version of the treatise found in Vatican Latin manuscript 4304, which is one of the earliest in date and, in the opinion of George Lacombe, has the better textual tradition.

A meticulous description of the manuscripts and a summary of the contents of the summa are given in the Introduction to the edition of Garvin and Corbett. Discussions of the author and of the heresy by Lacombe and Molinier have already been cited; to them may be added a chapter which associates the Passagians with other "Judaizing" religious movements in Italy, in Louis I. Newman, *Jewish Influence on Christian Reform Movements*, pp. 240-302; an article by Paul Alphandéry, "Sur les Passagiens," *Revue des études juives*, LXXXII (1926), 353-61; and most recently, Raoul Manselli's "I Passagini," *Bullettino dell'Istituto storico italiano per il medio evo e Archivio Muratoriano*, LXXV (1963), 189-210, which interprets the Passagians as a short-lived Christian heresy motivated by aspirations to purity and sanctity of life.

The following translation is made from *The* Summa contra haereticos *Ascribed to Praepositinus of Cremona*, ed. by Joseph N. Garvin and James A. Corbett (Publications in Mediaeval Studies, XV [Notre Dame, 1958]), pp. 75-164, by permission of the editors and the Publications in Mediaeval

Studies of the University of Notre Dame. Those chapter numbers and titles which were supplied by Garvin and Corbett are in brackets.

circa 1200

A SUMMA AGAINST HERETICS

[*Chapter V: On the Passagians, Who Say That Christ Is a Created Being*]

Having discussed the sect of the Cathars, we have now to consider the sect of the Passagians. They say that Christ is the first and a pure created being and that the Old Testament is to be observed in the matter of feasts, circumcision, choice of foods, and in almost all other respects, with the exception of sacrifices.

They attempt the proof of the first point, that Christ is a pure created being, in this way:

1. Isaiah, representing the Father as speaking of Christ, says, "I am the Lord that make all things, that raise up the word of my servant and perform the counsel of my messengers." [15] Note that here Christ is called a servant. He, who in Isaiah's time had but one nature, was with regard to it spoken of as a servant. Therefore, in that respect He was less than the Father, and thus His existence had a beginning. By that fact, He was a created being. . . .

2. Also, Isaiah, representing the Father as speaking of Christ, "Behold my servant, I will uphold him, my elect whom I have chosen." [16]. . .

3. Also, in the same book: "Drop down dew, ye heavens, from above and let the clouds rain the just; let the earth be opened and bud forth a savior. I the Lord have created him." [17]. . .

4. Also, Solomon, in Proverbs, speaking in the character of Wisdom, says: "The Lord created me in the beginning of his ways"; and in another version, "The Lord created me the beginning of his ways," or following another reading, "the beginning of his works." [18]

5. Also, in Ecclesiasticus, "Wisdom hath been created before all things." [19] The words refer to the Son of God; therefore He is a created being. Also, in the same book, "From the beginning and before the world was I created." [20]. . .

6. Also, we find in the Gospel of Matthew: "When evening was come, the lord of the vineyard called his steward" [21]—meaning that the Father called the Son. And so we learn that the Son is a steward for the Father.

From this the heretic concludes: Therefore He is not of the same substance as the Father nor of the same rank. . . .

7. Also, in the Gospel of Matthew, "All power is given to me in heaven and in earth." [22] Therefore, this power was bestowed, not innate. . . .

8. Also, in Mark, "But of that day or hour no man knoweth, neither the angels in heaven nor the Son, but only the Father." [23]. . .

9. Also, in the Gospel of John, "If you did believe in Moses, you would perhaps believe me also." [24] Lo, He uses words of uncertainty; hence, He was in doubt and so He did not know all things. . . .

10. Also, in the Gospel of Matthew, "Father, let this chalice pass from me." [25] Christ here was making a request for something; therefore for something which He either did or did not desire. If it was for something that He did not want, why did He ask? If it was something that He wished for, then it was something He either could or could not bring about. If it was something that He could not bring about, then He was not omnipotent; if it was something that He could bring to pass, why did He seek it of someone else?. . .

11. Also, in the Gospel of John, the Jews said to Jesus: " 'For a good work we stone thee not, but for blasphemy, and because that thou, being a man, makest thyself God.' Jesus answered, 'Is it not written in your law, *I said you are gods*?' If he called them gods to whom the word of God was spoken, and the Scripture cannot be broken, do you say of Him whom the Father hath sanctified and sent into the world, 'He has blasphemed, because he said, *I am the son of God*?'" [26] Note that here He seems to reveal in what sense He might call himself God, citing the text of the Psalmist, "I have said, 'You are gods,' " [27] wherein they are called gods only by adoption. Hence, He was God by adoption, not by nature. . . .

12. Also, in the same Gospel, "And the glory which Thou hast given me I have given to them, that they themselves may be one even as we also are one." [28] Note that here is to be seen the significance of His earlier statement, "I and the Father are one"; [29] one, namely, by love and not by essence, for He says of the apostles, "that they themselves may be one," and so on. . . .

13. Also, in the same Gospel, the Son says, "The Father is greater than I." [30] So, therefore, the Son is less than the Father; therefore, the Son is not equal to Him. . . .

14. Also, in the first Epistle to the Corinthians, "And when all things shall be subdued unto Him, then the Son also himself shall be subject unto Him that put all things under Him, that God may be all in all."[31] Note that here it is said that the Son shall be subject to the Father; so, therefore, He is lesser than the Father. . . .

15. Also, in Isaiah, "I the Lord, this is my name; I will not give my glory to another." [32] But His glory is that He himself is omnipotent God. Therefore, He will not give it to another, hence, not to the Son. Therefore, the Son is not God omnipotent. . . .

16. Also, in Ecclesiasticus, it is said of Christ, "He that could have transgressed and hath not transgressed,"[33] and so on. Therefore, He could commit mortal sin; hence, He could be damned. Therefore, He is not omnipotent God. . . .

17. Also, in the Apocalypse, John says: "To the seven churches which are in Asia: Grace be unto you and peace from Him that is and that was and that is to come, and from the seven spirits which are before his throne, and from Jesus Christ, who is the faithful witness, the first begotten of the dead and the prince of the kings of the earth."[34] Note that in that salutation first is set down, "From Him that is and that was and that is to come," and then follows, "And from the seven spirits which are before his throne," and at the end it has, "And from Jesus Christ," and so on. From that it appears that Jesus Christ is below and of lesser rank than the seven spirits, for which reason He is not omnipotent God. . . .

18. Also, the Son is from the Father, therefore He comes after the Father. An example: Heat is from fire; therefore it follows after fire.

Also, the Son is God, the Father is God; the Son is not the Father nor is the reverse true. Therefore, there are several gods. . . .

[Chapter VI: That the Old Testament Is To Be Observed to the Letter]

To the foregoing the heretics also add that the Old Testament is to be observed to the letter. First they propose to us certain things in respect of the Law, deriving therefrom some particular points dealing with circumcision, the Sabbath, and the choice of foods, also various other matters which we will discuss in the proper place.

They attempt to prove that the Old Testament is to be observed:

1a. By the authority of the Lord speaking in Matthew, "Do not think that I am come to destroy the Law or the prophets. I am not come to destroy but to fulfill." [35] Note that He who was Lord of the Law does not destroy the Law but fulfills it. For this reason we ought to observe the Law.

1b. Also, in the same Gospel, "For amen, I say unto you, till heaven and earth pass one jot or one tittle shall not pass of the Law, till all be fulfilled." [36] "Jot" means the least of the commandments, "tittle" means the least part of the least commandment. For this reason, it seems that the least commandment and the least part of a commandment are to be observed "till heaven and earth pass." Therefore, all the precepts of the Law are to be kept until the Day of Judgment. . . .

2. Also, in the same Gospel of Matthew, "He therefore that shall break one of these least commandments and shall so teach men shall be called the least in the kingdom of heaven." [37] So, therefore, the least precepts of the Law are to be observed; much more, therefore, the greater. And thereafter, "But he that shall do and teach, he shall be called great in the kingdom of heaven." [38] So, therefore, the least precepts of the Law are to be observed. . . .

3. Also, in the same Gospel, "Unless your justice abound more than that of the scribes and Pharisees, you shall not enter into the kingdom of heaven." [39] But the justice of the scribes and Pharisees was in keeping the Law. Therefore, "Unless your justice abound more,"—meaning, in the acceptance of the Gospel—"you shall not enter into the kingdom of heaven." By this it appears that each Testament is to be observed. . . .

4. Also, in the same Gospel, the Lord says to the leper whom He had cleansed, "Go, show thyself to the priests and offer the gift which Moses commanded in the Law for a testimony unto them." [40] Note how the Lord ordered that the sacred usages be observed. Much more, therefore, are we bound to keep the major parts of the Law. Therefore, all things that the Law includes are to be observed. . . .

5. Also, in the same Gospel: "The scribes and the Pharisees have sitten on the chair of Moses. All things, therefore, whatsoever they shall say to you do," but those things which they do, "do ye not." [41] But they spoke of nothing but that which was included in the Law, word for word. Therefore, all things comprised in the Law are to be observed to the letter. . . .

6. Also, in the same Gospel, "All things, therefore, whatsoever that you would that men should do to you, do you also to them. For these are the Law and the prophets." [42] But whatsoever things are included in

this commandment are to be kept and nothing rejected.[43] For this reason, whatsoever things are included in the Law and the prophets are to be observed. . . .

7. Also, in the same Gospel, a certain man skilled in law came to the Lord Jesus and said to Him, "Master, which is the great commandment of the Law?" And He answered: "Thou shalt love the Lord thy God with thy whole heart and with thy whole mind and with thy whole soul. This is the greatest and the first commandment. And the second is like unto this: and thy neighbor as thyself. On these two commandments dependeth the whole Law and the prophets." [44] Therefore, all things that are contained in the Law and the prophets are bound up with the love of God and of one's neighbor. But nothing that is bound up with the love of God and one's neighbor is to be rejected. For this reason all things that are included in the Law are to be observed. . . .

8. Also, the Apostle in the Epistle to the Romans: "Do we destroy the Law through faith? God forbid! But we establish the Law." [45] Note that the Apostle says that the Law is not destroyed through faith, that is, through the Gospel; therefore, it is to be kept. Furthermore, he says, "But we establish the Law." If the Apostle establishes it, it is to be observed. . . .

9. Also, in the same Epistle: "The Law indeed is holy, and the commandment holy and just and good";[46] and thereafter, "The Law is spiritual." [47] Here is a statement that the Law is holy and spiritual. For that reason, it is to be observed. . . .

10. Also James, "And whosoever shall keep the whole Law but offend in one point is become guilty of all." [48] Note here the statement that if anyone shall observe the whole Law and offend in one point, he becomes guilty of all. Therefore, nothing of the Law is to be rejected. For this reason, all things which are included in the Law are to be kept. . . .

[*Chapter VII: Circumcision Is To Be Accepted Literally*]

Having considered and discussed the Law in general, we must now examine some particular points relating to matters of the Law; first, circumcision, which they seek to uphold in this way.

1. In Genesis the Lord says to Abraham: "I am, and my covenant is with thee. Thou shalt keep my covenant and thy seed after thee in their generations. This is my covenant which you shall observe. All the male

kind of you shall be circumcised. And you shall circumcise the flesh of your foreskin. And my covenant shall be in your flesh for a perpetual covenant. The male, whose flesh of his foreskin shall not be circumcised, that soul shall be destroyed out of his people because he hath broken my covenant." [49] From these words the heretic concludes that actual circumcision is needful for salvation, and is to be observed forever. . . .

2. Also, Ezechiel says, "No stranger uncircumcised in heart and uncircumcised in flesh shall enter into my sanctuary, saith the Lord." [50] And thus it appears manifest that each of these circumcisions is to be observed. . . .

3. Also, circumcision was given before the Law was given, that is, to Abraham, and was observed and confirmed in the time of the Law, and in the time of Christ was confirmed and accepted by Christ. Therefore, if it was kept and fulfilled by Christ and if in His time He did not annul it, then it is still to be observed. . . .

4. Also, the Lord says in the Gospel of John, "If a man receive circumcision on the Sabbath day that the law of Moses may not be broken, are you angry at me because I have healed the whole man on the Sabbath day?" [51] So, therefore, it seems that at that time circumcision itself purified and healed a man in part. Therefore, it must have done so for either the soul or the body; not the body, therefore the soul.[52] Therefore, it cleansed the soul either from personal sin or from original sin; but not personal sin, since a child is not guilty of personal sin, therefore from original sin. Now, it had this very effect before the advent of Christ, therefore, since circumcision was not annulled by Christ, it is still to be accepted. . . .

5. Also, the Apostle says in the Epistle to the Romans, "Circumcision profiteth indeed, if thou keep the Law." [53] Therefore, the Law is to be kept. . . .

6. Also, they may argue against us: The Apostle says in the Epistle to the Galatians, "When they had seen that to me was committed the gospel of the uncircumcision, as to Peter was that of the circumcision." [54] Note that he says the gospel of the circumcision was committed to Peter. Therefore, Peter preached the circumcision. For that reason circumcision is to be accepted. . . .

7. Also, they argue against us thus: The Apostle says in the Epistle to the Romans that it was said, "that Christ Jesus was minister of the circumcision for the truth of God, to confirm the promises of the

Father." [55] Note that here he says that Christ was minister of the circumcision and accepted it. For that reason, we also ought to accept it. . . .

[*Chapter VIII: The Sabbath Is To Be Kept to the Letter*]

To the foregoing, the aforesaid heretics add the keeping of the Sabbath, which they attempt to support in this way.

1. In Genesis it is said, "And God blessed the seventh day and sanctified it, because in it he had rested from all his work which he created and made." [56] Of this text, a commentator [57] says: " 'And sanctified it'—meaning that He wished it to be holy and solemn. For it is believed that prior to the Law the Sabbath was ever observed by certain peoples, whose observance the Lord calls sanctified, saying, 'Remember that thou keep holy the Sabbath day. Thou shalt do no work on it.' " [58]

2. And in a subsequent place, "You shall kindle no fire in any of your habitations on the Sabbath day." [59]

3. And elsewhere: "Everyone that shall do any work on this day shall die. Let the children of Israel, therefore, keep the Sabbath and celebrate it in their generations, for it is an everlasting covenant between me and the children of Israel and a perpetual sign." [60]

5. And in Deuteronomy: "Six days shalt thou labor and shalt do all thy works. The seventh is the day of the Sabbath, that is, the rest of the Lord. Thou shalt not do any work therein, thou, nor thy son, nor thy daughter, nor thy manservant, nor thy maidservant, nor thy ox, nor thy ass, nor any of thy beasts, nor the stranger that is with thee, that thy manservant and thy maidservant may rest, even as thyself." [61]

6. Also, Jeremiah: "Carry no burdens on the Sabbath day and bring them not in by the gates of Jerusalem. And do not bring burdens out of your houses on the Sabbath day, neither do ye any work." [62] From all these words they conclude that the Sabbath was observed before the Law, was commanded in the Law, and is to be kept forever after the Law. . . .

[*Chapter X: On Observances in Respect of Foods*]

We come at this point to observances in respect of foods, on which they oppose us in this way.

1. The Lord in Genesis says to Noah and his sons, "Even as the green herbs have I delivered all living things to you, saving that flesh with blood you shall not eat" [63] (meaning an animal which has been

strangled). For this reason, it is not permissible to eat blood or strangled flesh. Also, in Leviticus, "You shall not eat the blood of any flesh at all." [64] Likewise, in the Acts of the Apostles, the apostles wrote to converted Gentiles, "It seemed good to the Holy Spirit and to us to lay no further burden upon you than these necessary things: that you abstain from things sacrificed to idols, from blood, things strangled, and fornication." [65]

2. Also, in Leviticus, "If anyone sin," [66] and so on. Of this verse a commentator [67] says: "It reads 'anyone,' not adding, 'of the people of the earth.' For it refers to sins from which it is also needful for Gentiles to avoid, that is, offerings to idols, strangled flesh, and fornication."

3. Also, in the same book, "When there had been an ulcer in the flesh and the skin, and it has been healed, and in the place of the ulcer there appeareth a white scar, or somewhat red." [68] Of this verse a commentator says: " 'In flesh and skin' (meaning in man or in the soul) 'when there has been an ulcer' (meaning sin) 'and it has been healed' (meaning through repentance) 'and in the place of the ulcer' (meaning by act or counsel) 'a white scar' (meaning sinful pursuits) 'appeareth' (meaning plainly in violation of the Law) 'or somewhat red' (meaning corrupting the Gospel, as by eating blood sacrificed to idols or suffocated flesh, for each is a denial of Christ, from whom come the Law and the Gospel)." Note that from these two Testaments, the Old and the New, it is obviously to be concluded that one may eat neither of what is sacrificed to idols nor of strangled blood.

[*Chapter XI: On Ecclesiastical Institutions*]

Now we come to ecclesiastical institutions which the heretics seek to annul entirely, calling them superfluous. They argue against them as a whole in this way.

1. In Exodus it is said: "And this shall everyone give that passeth at the numbering, half a sicle according to the standard of the temple. The rich man shall not add to half a sicle and the poor man shall diminish nothing." [69] Of this passage a commentator says: " 'And this shall everyone give that passeth at the numbering' (which is recorded in heaven, meaning everyone who is to be saved) 'half a sicle' (which is ten oboli, namely, observance of the decalogue together with the faith of Christ) 'according to the standard of the temple' (meaning not at his own pleasure but pursuant to what is determined in the Law or by a priest).

'The rich man shall not add to a half' (meaning that one who is perfect is not required to add 'to half a sicle').'' Therefore, he is not bound to observe anything but the decalogue and the faith of Christ; that is, those things which are prescribed in the Law and the Gospel. For this reason, we are not bound to observe ecclesiastical regulations, which are human institutions. . . .

2. Also, it is said in Leviticus, "And Nadab, moreover, and Abihu, the sons of Aaron, taking their censers, put fire therein, and incense on it, offering before the Lord strange fire which was not commanded them. And fire coming out from the Lord destroyed them and they died.'' [70] Of this passage, a commentator remarks: "They offer a 'strange fire' who, spurning the traditions of God, yearn for strange doctrines and introduce the rule of a human institution.'' But ecclesiastical institutions are rules of human institution. For this reason, they should be destroyed and, like Nadab and Abihu, deserve to perish, because they introduce "a strange fire.''

3. Also, in Leviticus, "Do not any unjust thing in judgment, in rule, in weight, and in measure. Let the balance be just for you and the weights equal.'' [71] Of this passage, a commentator says: " 'Just balance'— let us keep the law of Holy Scripture sacred and just, adding thereto nothing of our own nor taking away anything from it.'' But every ecclesiastical institution is something "of our own'' and should not, therefore, be put forward for observance.

4. Also, in Deuteronomy, "You shall not add to the word that I speak, neither shall you take away from it.'' [72]. . .

5. Also, in the same book, "What I command thee, that only do thou; neither add anything or diminish.'' [73] We are, therefore, bound to do nothing but what the Lord commanded. But man, not God, decreed ecclesiastical institutions, and for that reason no one is bound to their observance.

6. Also, in Isaiah, "And in vain do they worship me, teaching precepts and doctrines of men.'' [74] But ecclesiastical institutions are doctrines and precepts of men. Therefore, they who teach and learn them worship God in vain; such are not, then, to be taught or learned, and thus are not to be observed. . . .

7. Also, in the same book, "Get thee up upon a high mountain, thou that bringest good tidings to Zion,'' [75] Of this passage a commentator remarks: " 'Upon a high mountain,' and so on, means Christ, so that

you may proclaim nothing but what you have from Him." But not every ecclesiastical institution is from Christ. For that reason, not every one is to be proclaimed or observed. Or: If every one of them is from Christ, every one is to be observed.

8. Also, in Osee, "The princes of Judah are become as they that take up the bound"—or, in another version, "move the bound"—"I will pour out my wrath upon them like water." [76] On this passage, a commentator remarks, " 'Taking up' or 'moving the bound' are those who preach other things than that which they received from the apostles. . . .

9. Also, in Jonas, "They that are vain observe vanities, forsake their own mercy." [77] Of this passage, a commentator says: "The Jews, while observing the traditions of men, forsook the commandments of God who was always merciful unto them." By the same token, men of our day, while observing the institutions of the Church, which are traditions of men, put aside the commandments of God. . . .

10. Also, in the one hundred-and-third psalm, "Over them the birds," [78] and so on. Augustine comments on this passage: [79] " 'Over them,' that is, those things which have been spoken, namely, the springs in the vales—or, to use the other words, 'over them,' the hills [80]—'the birds of the air' (meaning spiritual men) 'shall dwell'; not in their own hearts but 'in the hills,' that is, in the authority of the prophets and apostles. And lest you suppose that the birds [spiritual men] follow their own authority, he adds 'that from the midst of the rocks shall they give forth their voices,' [81] which means, not by their own authority but by that of the Lord's words, with which Christ makes the rocks resound." Therefore, prelates of the churches should never proclaim anything but the words of the Lord or that which can be derived from the words of the Lord. Therefore, since the ecclesiastical institutions in greater part are neither the words of the Lord nor can they be proved by nor derived from them, it obvious that they are useless and superfluous. . . .

11. Also, in Proverbs, "Every word of God is fire tried; he is a buckler to them that hope in him. Add not anything to his words lest thou be reproved and found a liar." [82]. . .

12. Also, in Matthew, "I am not come to destroy the Law but to fulfill." [83] Note that Christ came. He completed the Law adequately in deed and word, adding what was lacking in the Law. Therefore, no further things were to be added and, in light of this, it appears that all additional ecclesiastical institutions are unnecessary. . . .

13. Also, in the Epistle to the Romans, "For I dare not to speak of

any of those things which Christ worketh not by me for the obedience of the Gentiles, by word and deed, by the virtue of signs and wonders in the power of the Holy Spirit." [84] Note that the Apostle here says that he dare not speak or proclaim or lay upon others that which he did not have from Christ; much less may any bishop or prince, however great. Hence, it appears that ecclesiastical institutions, which for the most part are not the words of Christ and cannot be derived from Christ's words, are useless and superfluous. . . .

14. Also, to the Galatians, "If any one preach to you a gospel besides that which you have received, let him be anathema." [85]. . .

15. Also, in the Apocalypse, "If any man shall add to these things, God shall add unto him the plagues written in this book." [86]. . .

27. An Account of the Hospitality of Heretics by Yves of Narbonne

The following piece is excerpted from a letter written by one Yves of Narbonne and included by Matthew Paris in his history of England. The greater part of this letter is devoted to a description of the terrible ravages of the Mongols (whom Matthew Paris calls Tartars or Tatars) in their invasion of central Europe in 1241, that being, no doubt, the reason why Matthew copied it, for he was much interested in information about the Mongols, as well as fond of reproducing documents in his text. We have not translated those remarks but only the opening paragraphs of the letter, in which the writer refers back to his earlier adventures. Yves addresses himself to Gerald of Mallemort, archbishop of Bordeaux (1227-1261), one of whose clerics he had been until, about 1214, he fled from threatened prosecution for heresy and found refuge in Italy. The date is fixed by reference to the activities of Robert of Curson, papal legate and preacher of the crusade, who was in southern France late in 1213 and for some months in 1214,[1] and presided at a council at Bordeaux in June of that year. Questions can be raised about the validity of the letter. If it is genuine, it was written many years after the events described. Furthermore, although Matthew Paris has often been highly praised as a historian, the most recent study judges that, while he was an assiduous compiler of contemporary events, he was neither critical about the materials he used nor above altering the text of documents to suit his own purposes. However, Yves's narrative is cited by several scholars as valid evidence.[2] We translate it because it is one of the few documents which purport to give a first-person account of close association with heretics and because it illustrates the undoubted ease of movement among heretical communities in northern Italy.

For the portion of his *Chronica majora* [greater chronicle] which covers the period from Creation to 1236, Matthew Paris was dependent on earlier writings; thereafter until 1259, the date of his death, the work is his own. (The continuation after 1259 was the work of William Rishanger.) The most recent study of the author is Richard Vaughan's *Matthew Paris*. The *Chronica majora* was translated in part by J. A. Giles as *Matthew Paris's English History from the Year 1235 to 1273*.

The following passage is translated from *Matthaei Parisiensis Chronica majora*, ed. by H. R. Luard (Rolls Series, LVII [7 vols., London, 1872-1883]), IV, 270-72, by permission of Her Majesty's Stationery Office and the Kraus Reprint Corporation.

1214 (written circa 1241)

To Gerald, by grace of God, archbishop of Bordeaux, Yves, so-called of Narbonne and once the lowliest of his clerics, sends greeting. . . .

I was once, as you know, charged by my rivals with heretical depravity before Master Robert of Curson, at that time legate of the Roman Curia. Because I was ashamed, not from a troubled conscience but at the baseness of the charge, I refused to stand trial and by that very fact was the more suspect. Therefore, with the threats of that man of authority in my ears, I fled from the face of the pursuer and thereafter was driven to wander through many lands. I laid my complaint before the Patarines [3] who inhabit the city of Como: how on account of their beliefs (which, as God is my witness, I had never learned or accepted), I became an exile from the judgments hurled against me. They were pleased to hear this and considered me fortunate to be persecuted for the sake of righteousness. I dwelt there among them for three months, sumptuously and delightfully, and kept silence, as every day I listened to the many errors, or rather horrors, which they propounded against the apostolic faith. By kindness, they put me under obligation to promise that henceforth I would try to convince any Christians with whom I fell into serious conversation that no one could gain salvation in the faith of Peter, and that I would consistently teach this doctrine. And when I had given my word for this, they began to disclose their secrets, revealing that they sent to Paris capable students from nearly all Lombard and from some Tuscan cities. There some studied logic, others theology, with the aim of strengthening their own error and overthrowing the Catholic faith. To the same purpose they also sent numerous merchants to the fairs, where they might pervert wealthy laymen who shared their table, or their hosts, with whom they had the opportunity for talk on intimate terms. Thus they engaged in manifold pursuits, at one moment enriching themselves with others' money, at the next, in equal degree, collecting a treasure of souls for Antichrist.

When I begged leave from these degenerate brethren, they sent me to enjoy the hospitality of their fellows in faith in Milan. I traveled through all the cities of Lombardy situated in the Po valley, living always among the Patarines; always, when I left, receiving from them an introduction to others.[4] At last I reached the famous town of Gemona in Friuli, where I drank the superb Patarine wine, ate raisins,[5] cherries, and other delicious food, and deceived the deceivers by professing to be a Patarine. But, as God is my witness, I remained a Christian in faith if not in perfect deed. After three days in Gemona, I traveled on in the company of a lay brother, with leave from my hosts but under the curse of one of their bishops, Peter Gallus by name, to whom I was an object of suspicion. I heard later that he was deposed for fornication.[6] We reached the canals of Aquileia and, journeying thence, found lodging among the brethren in a town called Friesach.

The next morning the lay brother left me, and alone I crossed Carinthia to reach a town in Austria called Neustadt [7] in German, which means "New City." There I was welcomed by some members of a new religious group called Beguins.[8] For several years I found shelter in the nearby city of Vienna and in neighboring places, and there combined, alas, good behavior with bad, for by the devil's urging I lived incontinently and did harm to my soul; but meanwhile I recalled many persons from the above-mentioned heresy.

Roused to wrath by these and many other sins which made their appearance in the Christian community, God has become a hostile destroyer and a terrible avenger. . . . [The remainder of the letter describes in lurid fashion the atrocities of the Tatars.]

Heresy in Southern France
1155-1216

28. A Debate between Catholics and Heretics

The spread of heresy in Languedoc met no consistently effective resistance during the second half of the twelfth century. The Church was everywhere in low esteem, its authority discredited by the sorry character of certain of its ministers. The teaching of the Cathars made an appeal to some elements in every class and locality; their proselytizing was tacitly permitted when it was not actively abetted by nobles of the countryside and burghers of the towns. Attempts by local ecclesiastics to curb Catharist influence little availed, as the following account shows. In the early summer of 1165,[1] the bishop of Albi, accompanied by some notable representatives of Church and lay authority in the region, interrogated and debated with spokesmen for an alleged heretical sect at Lombers, a walled village overlooked by a feudal stronghold, some ten miles south of Albi. The nobles of Lombers, even though (or perhaps because) they held from the bishop of Albi, were sympathetic protectors of the accused; thus the bishop may have hoped to prove the fact of heresy and thus bring into play the ban on dealings of any kind between Christians and heretics which had been enacted by the Council of Tours in 1163.[2] There seems to be little doubt of the Catharist influence on the alleged heretics, although their tenets are also reminiscent of the teaching of Peter of Bruys and Henry, and the question of dualism was not explicitly evoked. The procedure followed at Lombers—confrontation of heretics and their accusers in open debate before judges—became not unusual in southern France in the following years.[3] The episode at Lombers is included here primarily because it illustrates the growth of heresy in the region and the increasing boldness of the heretics.[4]

For the situation of the Church and of heresy at that time in Languedoc, see Louis de Lacger, "L'Albigeois pendant la crise de l'albigéisme," *Revue d'histoire ecclésiastique*, XXIX (1933), 272-315, 586-633, 849-904 (the Lombers episode is discussed on pp. 281-82); Guiraud, *Histoire de l'inquisition*, Vol. I, chaps. IX-XII; and Luchaire, *Innocent III et la croisade des albigeois*, pp. 1-46.

The text translated here is from *Acta concilii Lumbariensis*, in *Recueil des historiens des Gaules et de la France*, ed. by Martin Bouquet *et al.* (24 vols., Paris, 1738-1904), XIV, 431-34. It also appears in Mansi, *Concilia*, XXII, 157-68, where it is expanded by inclusion of the numerous scriptural texts cited by the adversaries.[5]

1165

In the year of the Lord 1165, this definitive judgment was rendered in an affair involving controversy, accusation, and attack upon the Catholic faith which certain persons, who chose to be called Good Men[6] and who had the support of the knights of Lombers,[7] wished to overthrow. This judgment was rendered through Bishop William of Albi,[8] by assessors chosen and assigned by each of the two sides, who examined the matter and assisted the aforementioned bishop—to wit, Bishop Gaucelin of Lodève, Abbot [Rigaud] of Castres, Abbot [Peter] of Ardorel, Abbot [Gausbert] of Candeil, and Arnold Beben—in the presence of good men, both clergy and laity, namely, the Lord Archbishop Pons of Narbonne; Bishop Aldebert of Nîmes; Bishop Gerard of Toulouse; Bishop William of Agde; Abbot Raymond of Saint-Pons; Abbot Peter of Cendras; [Vidal], abbot of Fontfroide; [Henry], abbot of Gaillac; [Maurin], provost of Toulouse; [William], provost of Albi; the archdeacons of Narbonne and Albi: [Guy], prior of Saint-Mary of Montpellier; B[ernard], prior of Goudargues; Master Blanc and Hugh *de Vereiras*; and, of the laity, Viscount [Raymond] Trencavel of Béziers; [Constance], wife of Count Raymond of Toulouse; Viscount Sicard of Lautrec; Isarn of Dourgne; and many other persons, almost the whole population of Albi and of Lombers, together with people of other towns.

In the first instance, the bishop of Lodève, commanded thereto by the bishop of Albi and his assessors, asked those who chose to be called Good Men whether they accepted the law of Moses, the Prophets, the Psalms, the Old Testament, and the doctors of the New Testament. Before the whole assemblage they replied that they did not accept the law of Moses, nor the Prophets, nor the Psalms, nor the Old Testament, but only the Gospels, the Epistles of Paul, the seven canonical Epistles, the Acts of the Apostles, and the Apocalypse.

Second, he asked about their faith, as they themselves were wont to expound it. In reply, they said they would not speak to that point unless forced to do so.

Third, he asked them about the baptism of children, and whether they were saved by baptism. They answered that they would not discuss this but that they would answer questions on the Gospels and the Epistles.

Fourth, he questioned them about the body and blood of the Lord:

where they were consecrated, by whom, who partook thereof, and if the consecration was more efficaciously or better done by a good man than by an evil one. They replied that those who partook worthily were saved; those who did so unworthily took unto themselves damnation. And they said that the consecration was effected by any good man, cleric or laymen as well; and they would answer nothing further, because they ought not to be forced to answer questions about their faith.

Fifth, he asked them about marriage and if husband and wife who were carnally united could be saved. They were not willing to reply except to say only that man and woman were joined together to avoid lewdness and fornication, as St. Paul said in his Epistle.[9]

Sixth, he questioned them about repentance: whether repentance at the moment of death led to salvation; whether warriors who were mortally wounded would be saved if they repented at the last moment; if each person ought to confess his sins to the priests and ministers of the Church or to any layman at all, or to those of whom St. James says, "Confess your sins one to another."[10] They said in reply that for the sick it was sufficient to confess to whomever they chose. They were unwilling, however, to reply to the question about warriors, since St. James speaks only of the sick.

He also asked them if contrition of the heart and confession by the mouth alone were enough, or if one must make atonement after penance was imposed, by fasts, flagellations, and almsgiving, lamenting their sins if they were capable of doing so. They answered, saying that James said no more than that they should confess and so be saved; they did not seek to be better than the apostle and add anything of their own, as bishops do.

They also made many unsolicited statements. They affirmed that they should not swear any kind of oath, as Jesus said in the Gospel and James in his Epistle.[11] They said also that Paul stated in his Epistle what kind of bishops and priests were to be ordained in the churches,[12] and that if the men ordained were not such as Paul had specified, they were not bishops and priests but ravening wolves, hypocrites, and seducers, lovers of salutations in the marketplace, of the chief seats and the higher places at table, desirous of being called rabbis and masters, contrary to the command of Christ, wearers of albs and gleaming raiment, displaying bejeweled gold rings on their fingers, which their Master Jesus did not command; and they poured forth many other reproaches. Therefore, because these were not bishops or priests, except such priests as those who had betrayed Jesus, they owed them no obedience, for they were wicked, not good teachers, but hired servants.

In rebuttal of these assertions, many New Testament texts were quoted by Lord Pons, archbishop of Narbonne, and Bishop Aldebert of Nîmes, and Abbot Peter of Cendras, and the abbot of Fontfroide. When the allegations and the New Testament authorities from both sides had been heard—for those persons would accept no decision except on the basis of the New Testament—the bishop of Lodève, calling for silence from all, pronounced the following definitive sentence on the basis of law and of the New Testament, by command of the bishop of Albi and the advisers named above, in the presence of all those aforenamed:

"I, Gaucelin, bishop of Lodève, by command of the bishop of Albi and his assessors, do adjudge those who call themselves Good Men to be heretics. I condemn the sect of Oliver[13] and his companions, and those who adhere to the sect of the heretics of Lombers, wherever they may be. This judgment we find on the basis of the texts of the New Testament, to wit, the Gospels, the Epistles, the Psalms [*sic*], the Acts of the Apostles, and the Apocalypse."

The heretics retorted that the bishop who delivered the sentence was a heretic, not they; that he was their enemy; that he was a ravening wolf, a hypocrite, an enemy to God; and that he had not delivered a proper judgment. They were not willing to answer questions about their faith because they were on their guard against him, as the Lord enjoined on them in the Gospel, "Beware of false prophets who come to you in the clothing of sheep but inwardly they are ravening wolves."[14] This man was their deceitful persecutor, and they were prepared to prove by the Gospel and the Epistles that he was no good shepherd, neither he nor the other bishops and priests, but rather they were hirelings.

The bishop replied that the judgment found against them was based on law. He was prepared to uphold it in the court of the Catholic pope, Lord Alexander,[15] or in the court of Louis, king of France,[16] or in the court of Raymond, count of Toulouse,[17] or in that of his wife, who was present, or in the court of Trencavel,[18] who was present; that it was properly adjudged; and that they were manifestly heretics and notorious for heresy. And he promised that he himself would charge them with heresy in any Catholic court and would submit himself to the decision of a trial.

When, indeed, they saw that they were overcome and confounded, they turned to the whole people and said: "Listen, good people, to our faith which we will declare. We do this now, moreover, out of love for you and for your sake." The aforesaid bishop replied, "You do not say that you will speak for the sake of the Lord but for the sake of the people." They went on:

"We believe in one God, living and true, triune and one, the Father, the Son, and the Holy Spirit. The Son of God took on flesh, was baptized in the Jordan, fasted in the wilderness, preached our salvation, suffered, died, and was buried, descended into hell, arose on the third day, and ascended into heaven. On Pentecost, he sent the Spirit, the Paraclete, unto his disciples, and he shall come on the Day of Judgment to judge the quick, the dead, and all who will rise again. We acknowledge also that what we believe in our hearts we ought to confess with our mouths. We believe that no one shall be saved who does not partake of the body of Christ, and that it is not consecrated except in the Church and also unless by a priest, whether he be good or bad, nor is consecration more effectively done by a good man than by an evil one. We believe also that one is saved only by baptism and that children are saved by baptism. We also believe that husband and wife may be saved, even though they know each other carnally, and that everyone should accept penance by mouth and in heart, and be baptized by a priest in a church. And if there be anything further in the Church that can be shown from the Gospels and the Epistles, that we will accept and confess."

The aforesaid bishop also demanded of them if they would take an oath to uphold and believe this faith, and whether or not there was anything further on which they held and preached wrongful opinions which they should confess. In reply, they declared that they would take no oath of any kind because that would be done contrary to the Gospel and the Epistles. Then passages from the New Testament were quoted against them by the aforesaid Catholics.

Having heard the citations from both parties, the aforesaid bishop rose and pronounced judgment in these words:

"I, Gaucelin, bishop of Lodève, at the bidding and by the mandate of the bishop of Albi and his assessors, adjudge and pronounce sentence that these heretics hold wrong opinions in the matter of oath-taking.

They ought to take oath if they wish to be reasonable, and an oath should be taken when the faith is in question. Because they are notorious and defamed for heresy, they ought to prove their innocence and, coming again into the unity of the Church, they ought to affirm their faith by taking an oath in the form which the Church adopts and accepts, lest weak persons who are in the Church be misled and lest one sick sheep infect the whole flock.[19] Nor does this contradict the Gospel and the Pauline Epistles. For the words of the Gospel—'Let your speech be yea, yea; no, no;' 'Swear not, neither by heaven nor by the earth'[20]—do not prohibit swearing in God's name but only in the name of creatures."

Seeing that they were overcome on this point, they said that the bishop of Albi had made an agreement with them that they would not be required to take an oath. This the bishop of Albi himself denied.

Then the bishop of Albi arose, saying: "I confirm and approve the sentence which Bishop Gaucelin of Lodève here promulgated at my command. I warn the knights of Lombers no longer to support those persons, by reason of the solemn promise that they made in my hands."

[The document concludes with statements approving the sentence, by each of the Catholic participants and observers listed in the first paragraph.]

29. Action against Heresy in Toulouse

Before the last decade of the twelfth century, the energy if not the initiative for most attempts to restrain or repress heretics in Languedoc came from outside that area. One such in 1178, while it had small result in Toulouse itself, was important for the precedents it established and for the wide publicity that it gained. In 1176, Raymond V, count of Toulouse (1148-1194), found it expedient to appeal for aid against heretics within his own lands. He had been involved in large political events for more than a decade but rather less than successfully. He contended for possession of Provence with Alphonse II, king of Aragon (1162-1196), but lost it by 1176, and Aragonese pressure against the western borders of the county of Toulouse continued unremittingly. His ally, Frederick Barbarossa, was about to yield in the struggle with Pope Alexander III. His neighbors in Aquitaine were a chronic threat, and the count had lost control of his chief city to its consuls. While he was by no means powerless, the course of wisdom for Raymond V was to re-establish his credit in the Christian world by action to defend the faith against the heresy for which Toulouse was becoming notorious.[1] In 1178, therefore, he appealed to the Cistercian order for services such as St. Bernard had rendered in Toulouse in 1145 (see No. 15), supplementing this with an entreaty for assistance of a more forceful kind from the monarchs of France and England, to each of whom he had done homage.[2] The appeals did not fall on deaf ears. Louis VII and Henry II discussed the situation in 1177 and pondered their personal intervention. The abbot of Clairvaux, Henry of Marcy, urgently demanded of Alexander III that the papal legate in France be empowered to act. The pope yielded to Henry's importunacy, but the two kings ultimately decided only to dispatch a mission in their name. Thus in 1178 a joint legatine and royal commission arrived in Toulouse, empowered to preach, to investigate, to condemn, and to use force as necessary against heretics; it was, in the opinion of Henri Maisonneuve, a "real inquisitorial tribunal," which operated for three months in the city. The heretics they pursued were called Arians, perhaps because St. Bernard's terminology of 1145 was still in the minds of the reporters; but the doctrines with which they were charged (and which they denied) were Catharist.

Both the legate, Peter of Pavia, who was cardinal-priest of San Crisogono, and Henry of Marcy, abbot of Clairvaux, wrote letters for general circulation, describing their experiences in Toulouse and its vicinity.[3] These formed the basis for an entry in the *Gesta Henrici*,[4] an English chronicle of the reign of Henry II, which in turn was adopted and slightly revised by Roger of Hoveden, with copies of the legate's and abbot's letters appended, as in the *Gesta Henrici*. Roger's narrative is thus by no means independent, but it does summarize the events of 1178 at convenient length without sacrifice of essentials. Roger of Hoveden was one of the clerks of Henry II. He apparently retired from royal service on the death of the king. His chronicle is dependent on earlier sources for events to 1192, independent and valuable thereafter to 1201, in which year the author probably died. However, even the portion which relies on the anonymous *Gesta Henrici* does not follow it slavishly. On Roger of Hoveden, see Stubbs's introduction to his edition (I, 13 ff.); and *Dictionary of National Biography*, IX, 1322-23. There is an English translation of the chronicle by Henry T. Riley, *The Annals of Roger de Hoveden* (2 vols., London, 1853).

An excellent account of the situation in Toulouse and of the events of 1178 appears in Theloe, *Die Ketzerverfolgungen*, pp. 74-87. Shorter treatments will be found in Maisonneuve, pp. 129-35, and Lea, *History of the Inquisition*, I, 121-23. Devic and Vaissete, *Histoire de Languedoc*, VI, 77-86, with the notes in VII, 11-14, is still basic.

The narrative translated here is from *Chronica magistri Rogeri de Houedene*, ed. by William Stubbs (Rolls Series, LI [4 vols., London, 1868-1871]), II, 150-55, by permission of Her Majesty's Stationery Office and the Kraus Reprint Corporation.

1178

Meanwhile, the Arian heresy, which, as we have already said, had been condemned in the province of Toulouse,[5] had again revived. When this came to the attention of the king of France and the king of England, they were aroused by zeal for the Christian faith to a determination to go there personally in order to drive entirely out of their lands those aforesaid heretics. But with the passage of a little time, it seemed to them that more effective than for themselves to hasten there in person would be to send wise men to convert those heretics to the Christian faith by preaching and teaching. For they were reminded of the saying: "It is enough to command vengeance. The dread of your name will accomplish more than your sword. Your presence diminishes your fame." [6]

Therefore, they dispatched thither Peter, cardinal-priest of San Crisogono, the legate from the Apostolic See;[7] the archbishops of Bourges and Narbonne;[8] Reginald and John, bishops of Bath and Poitiers respectively;[9] Henry, abbot of Clairvaux;[10] and many other churchmen, with instructions to convert those heretics to the Christian faith by their preaching or to prove them, on solid grounds, to be heretics and drive them from the bounds of Holy Mother Church and from the company of the faithful. "Who when they were come, prayed for them that they might receive the Holy Spirit, for he was not as yet come upon any of them." [11] Furthermore, these kings chose Raymond, count of Toulouse; the viscount of Turenne, Raymond of Castelnau;[12] and other mighty men, and commanded them to attend the cardinal and his companions in the faith of Christ, and to banish those heretics from their lands by the force of their power.

Now, when the cardinal and the other Catholic men had entered the city of Toulouse, they found there a certain rich man,[13] who possessed two mansions (*castella*), one within the city, the other outside the city walls.[14] Before their arrival, he had admitted that he was a sectary of heretical depravity, but now, swayed by fear and wishing to conceal that detestable sect, he pretended to be the most Christian of men. When this was disclosed to him,[15] the cardinal ordered to appear before him the wealthy man in question, who, when he came to confess his faith, was found to impugn all the articles of the Christian faith. And consequently he was adjudged a manifest heretic by the cardinal and the bishops with him, and was condemned.[16] Their verdict was that his property would be confiscated; his towers which were rich and very beautiful, should be demolished. When the man found himself condemned and his goods confiscated, he approached the cardinal and the bishops, his associates, prostrating himself at their feet to beg for forgiveness. Penance was imposed upon him: Naked, he was flogged through the squares and streets of the city; thereafter he took oath that he would journey to Jerusalem and remain there in service to God for a period of three years. If he returned home after three years, his possessions would be restored to him,[17] on condition that his towers be razed in testimony of heretical depravity, and that he would pay five hundred pounds of silver to his lord, the count of Toulouse. Upon accomplishment of these things, many heretics, fearing that they might be treated in similar fashion, came to the cardinal and his associates to confess their error in secret and, seeking pardon, they were treated with mercy.

Among other things, it came to their attention that certain false brethren, namely Raymond and Bernard Raymond,[18] and some other heresiarchs, transforming themselves into angels of light,[19] although they were minions of Satan, and preaching matters contrary to the Christian faith, had by their false teaching deceived the souls of many persons, whom they drew with themselves to hell. On being summoned to come before the cardinal and his associates to confess their faith, they replied that they would appear before them if they had safe-conduct to come and to return.[20] Once this safe-conduct to come and depart was granted, they presented themselves before the cardinal and the bishops, the counts, barons, clergy, and attendant people, and brought with them a certain document in which they had written the articles of their faith. After they had read it through very carefully there seemed to be some suspect statements therein which might conceal the heresy the men had preached unless they were explained in greater detail. But when one of them, speaking in Latin, sought to expound those written statements, he could scarcely put two words together, for he was totally ignorant of the Latin language. Thereupon, it was necessary for the cardinal and the bishops to make a concession to them and to use the vernacular because of their ignorance. To an examination on the articles of the Christian faith, the men answered on all points as soundly and prudently as though they were thoroughly Christian. But when the count of Toulouse and others who had previously heard them preaching things contrary to the Christian faith heard this, they were struck with astonishment and were kindled with zeal for the Christian faith. Rising to their feet, they proved to the very faces of the men that they had manifestly lied. They asserted that they had heard from some of them that there were two gods, one good, the other evil; the good had created only invisible things, those which could not be altered or corrupted; the evil one had formed the heavens, the earth, men, and other visible things. Others affirmed that they had heard in their preaching that the body of Christ was not consecrated by the ministry of an unworthy priest or of one who was trammeled by any crime. Moreover, other persons declared that they had heard them say in their preaching that a man and wife could not be saved if each rendered the other their marital due. Others also said that they had heard from them that baptism was of no benefit to children and declared that they had uttered many other blasphemies against God and Holy Church and the Catholic faith, of which, because of their detestable enormity, it is better to be silent than to speak.

But these heretics retorted to those charges with a declaration that false witness was brought against them. Publicly, before the cardinal and the bishops and all those who were present, they stated, confessed, and resolutely declared that there is one God most high, who had created all things visible and invisible. They utterly denied that there were two principles. They also confessed that a priest, whether good or wicked, righteous or unrighteous, even if he were known indubitably to be an adulterer or a criminal of some other sort, could consecrate the body and blood of Christ, and that by the ministry of such a priest and the virtue of the holy words which were spoken by the Lord, the bread and wine were truly transubstantiated into the body and blood of Christ. Also, they asserted, children or adults baptized in our baptism are saved and no one can be saved without this baptism, denying absolutely that they used any other baptism, or the imposition of the hand which was charged against them. No less did they affirm that man or woman united in marriage, even if each rendered the other their marital due, could be saved—being absolved by the blessing of blameless matrimony, if no other sin stands in the way—and they are never damned for that reason. Furthermore, they declared that archbishops, bishops, priests, monks, canons, hermits, Templars, and Hospitalers may attain salvation. They said it was worthy and just to enter churches founded to the honor of God and of the saints and, showing honor and reverence to their priests and other ministers, one should give them the first fruits and tithes, and undertake devoutly and faithfully all parochial duties. They declared in praiseworthy fashion, among other things, that alms should be given to churches as well as to the poor or to any beggar. All these things, they insisted, they understood with right understanding, although previously they had been accused of denying them.

The cardinal and the bishops ordered the men to take an oath that they believed in their hearts what their lips had confessed. But verily, like men of twisted mind and warped purpose, they were still unwilling to abandon their heresy, in which the superficial meaning of any authority seemed to delight their gross and dull minds. They took as pretext the words of the verse in which, as one reads in the Gospel, the Lord said, "Swear not at all; let your communication be yea, yea; nay, nay,"[21] asserting that they must not be sworn, even though the Lord himself, one often reads, took oath, as is written: "The Lord hath sworn and he will not repent";[22] "By my own self have I sworn, saith the Lord";[23] and the Apostle, "An oath is the end of all controversy."[24] Furthermore, like lunatics not understanding the Scriptures, they fell into the trap from which they had hidden. For although they held the oath in abhorrence as an execrable thing forbidden by the Lord, they are convicted of taking an oath in the very text of their confession, for they had said, "In truth, as God exists, we believe in this way and we say that this is our faith." They were not aware that to adduce verity and the word of God in witness of a true statement is, without any doubt at all, to swear, as that which we read of the Apostle, when he said, "For we say unto you in the word of the Lord";[25] and elsewhere, "God is my witness,"[26] and other similar passages verify. These can easily be found by persons who have read and understood Holy Writ.

Since the Church is not wont to deny the bosom of pity to those who return, when these men had been convicted by numerous competent witnesses and many more were still coming forward to give evidence against them, they [the legate and bishops] exhorted them most carefully to put aside all the depravity of heresy and return to the verity of faith. And since the men had been excommunicated by the lord pope, by the cardinal, by the archbishops of Bourges and Narbonne, and by the bishop of Toulouse for their perverse preaching and sect, they were urged to accept reconciliation according to the usage of the Church. They were turned aside as a crooked bow[27] and were hardened in an incorrigible attitude and refused to do so. The cardinal and bishops, in the presence of the whole people, together with the bishop of Poitiers and the other religious men who were present with them in all things, after lighting candles, denounced them as excommunicate and damned them, together with their sponsor the devil, and they commanded the faithful of Christ carefully to shun the aforesaid Bernard and Raymond and their accomplices as excommunicates and men given over to Satan. If in the future the men should preach to them anything but that which had been confessed in their hearing, they should reject the preaching as false and contrary to the Catholic and apostolic faith, and they should drive them far from their lands as heretics and forerunners of Antichrist.

Moreover, the count of Toulouse and the other eminent men of this province attested by taking oath before all the people that from then on, neither on petition or for bribes, would they shelter heretics.[28]

30. The Origins of the Waldensian Heresy

The origin of the Poor of Lyons, or Waldenses,[1] their break with the Church on the issue of the right of laymen to preach, and their lapse into heresy in this and other matters are recounted here and in Numbers 31-38. These documents together tell the story of Waldes,[2] a merchant of Lyons, his conversion to the apostolic ideal, and the first years of the religious movement he inspired, which was to be the most enduring of the medieval heresies. Until his insistent evangelism overrode the papal and archiepiscopal prohibitions on preaching, Waldes appears in every respect as a forerunner of Francis of Assisi; willingness to obey authority was the fundamental difference between them.[3]

There is an extensive literature on the Waldenses and related groups, although of their origins there are not many detailed accounts in English. We may cite Davison, *Forerunners of St. Francis*; and Bernard Marthaler, "Forerunners of the Franciscans," *Franciscan Studies*, new ser., XVIII (1958), 133-42. Dondaine cast new light on Waldes with his "Aux Origines du Valdéisme," *Archivum fratrum praedicatorum*, XVI (1946), 191-235; and Christine Thouzellier has recently restudied the movement in *Catharisme et Valdéisme*, pp. 16-18, 24-36, and *passim*.[4]

Two excerpts from the *Chronicon universale anonymi Laudunensis*, ed. by Georg Waitz, in *Monumenta Germaniae historica, Scriptores*, XXVI, 447, 449, are translated here by permission of Anton Hiersemann Verlag and the Monumenta Germaniae Historica.

1173

In the course of the same year (that is, 1173) of our Lord's incarnation, there was at Lyons in Gaul[5] a certain citizen named Waldes, who had amassed a great fortune through the wicked practice of lending at interest. One Sunday he had been attracted by the crowd gathered around a minstrel and had been touched by the latter's words. Wishing to talk to him more fully, he took him to his home, for the minstrel was at a place in his narrative in which Alexis had come peacefully to a happy end in his father's house.[6]

On the following morning, the said citizen hastened to the school of theology to seek counsel for his soul's welfare and, when he had been instructed in the many ways of attaining to God, asked the master which was the most sure and perfect way of all. The master replied to him in the words of the Lord: "If thou wilt be perfect, go sell what thou hast,"[7] and so on. Waldes came to his wife and offered her the choice of keeping for herself all his property in either movable goods or real estate, that is, in lands, waters, woods, meadows, houses, rents, vineyards, mills, and ovens. Though greatly saddened by the necessity, she chose the real estate. From his movable goods, he made restitution to those from whom he had profited unjustly; another considerable portion of his wealth he bestowed upon his two small daughters, whom without their mother's knowledge he confided to the order of Fontevrault; but the greatest part he disbursed for the needs of the poor.

Now, a very severe famine was then raging throughout all Gaul and Germany. Wherefore Waldes, the citizen mentioned above, on three days a week from Pentecost to St. Peter in Chains[8] gave bountifully of bread, vegetables, and meat to all who came to him. On the feast of the Assumption of the Blessed Virgin,[9] as he was in the streets distributing an appreciable sum of money among the poor, he cried out, "No man can serve two masters, God and mammon."[10] Then all the citizens hurried to him, supposing that he had lost his senses, but he climbed to a commanding spot and adressed them thus: "My friends and fellow townsmen! Indeed, I am not, as you think, insane, but I have taken vengeance on my enemies who held me in bondage to them, so that I was always more anxious about money than about God and served the creature more than the Creator. I know that a great many find fault with me for having done this publicly. But I did it for myself and also for you: for myself, so that they who may henceforth see me in possession of money may think I am mad; in part also for you, so that you may learn to fix your hope in God and to trust not in riches."

As he was leaving the church on the following day, he asked a certain citizen, one of his former associates, to give him food for the love of

God. The latter took him to his home and said, "As long as I live I will give you the necessities of life." His wife, on learning of this incident, was no little saddened. Like one beside herself, she rushed into the presence of the archbishop of the city[11] to complain that her husband had begged his bread from another rather than from her. This situation moved all who were present to tears, including the archbishop himself. At the archbishop's bidding, the citizen brought his guest [Waldes] with him into his presence, whereupon the woman, clinging to her husband's garments, cried, "Is it not better, O my husband, that I, rather than strangers, should atone for my sins through alms to you?" And from that time forth, by command of the archbishop, he was not permitted in that city to take food with others than his wife.

1177

Waldes, the citizen of Lyons whom we have already mentioned, having taken a vow to the God of heaven henceforth and throughout his life never to possess either gold or silver or to take thought for the morrow,[12] began to gather associates in his way of life. They followed his example in giving their all to the poor and became devotees of voluntary poverty. Little by little, both publicly and privately, they began to declaim against their own sins and those of others.

31. The Waldenses at the Third Lateran Council

The first of these two items is another excerpt from the anonymous chronicle of Laon. The second item is by the Englishman Walter Map, who encountered the Waldenses at Rome. Born about 1140, Map served as an itinerant justice for Henry II after 1162, and before 1186 he had risen to the post of chancellor of the bishop of Lincoln. He died between 1208 and 1210. In his own day Map had a reputation as a wit and raconteur; his *De nugis curialium* [courtier's trifles], a collection of legends, anecdotes, gossip, and personal observations, was probably written in bits and snatches between 1182 and 1192. It has previously been translated into English by Montague R. James, as *Walter Map's "De nugis curialium,"* and also by Frederick Tupper and Marbury B. Ogle, as *Master Walter Map's Book* De nugis curialium.

Part A is translated from *Chronicon universale anonymi Laudunensis,* ed. by Georg Waitz, in *Monumenta Germaniae historica, Scriptores,* XXVI, 449, by permission of Anton Hiersemann Verlag and the Monumenta Ger-

maniae Historica. Part B is translated from Walter Map *De nugis curialium*
i.xxxi, ed. by Montague R. James (Anecdota oxoniensia ... medieval and
modern series, XIV [Oxford, 1914]), pp. 60-62, by permission of the Clarendon Press.

A. A REPORT IN THE CHRONICLE OF LAON
1179
   The [Lateran] Council was summoned by Pope Alexander III....
This council condemned heresy and all protectors and defenders of
heretics.[1] The pope embraced Waldes,[2] approving his vow of voluntary
poverty but forbidding preaching by either himself or his followers
unless welcomed by the local priests.[3] This injunction they observed for
a short time; then, from the day they became disobedient, they were the
cause of scandal to many and disaster to themselves.

B. WALTER MAP'S ACCOUNT OF THE WALDENSES
1179
   At the Roman council held under Pope Alexander III, I saw simple
and illiterate men called Waldenses, after their leader, Waldes, who was
a citizen of Lyons on the Rhone. They presented to the lord pope a
book written in French which contained the text and a gloss of the
Psalms and many of the books of both Testaments. They most urgently
requested him to authorize them to preach because they saw themselves
as experienced persons, although they were nothing more than dabblers.
It is the way of birds who see not the fine snares or the nets to suppose
that everywhere there is free passage. Do not men who engage in
sophistical discourse all their lives, who can trap and only with difficulty
be trapped, who are probers of the most profound depths, do not they,
for fear of giving offense, speak with reverence all the thoughts which
they reveal about God, whose state is so exalted that no praises or
powers of prayer can mount thereto except as mercy may draw them?
In every letter of the sacred page, so many precepts fly on wings of
virtue, such riches of wisdom are accumulated, that anyone to whom
God has granted the means[4] may draw from its fullness. Shall pearls,
then, be cast before swine?[5] Shall the Word be given to the ignorant,
whom we know to be incapable of receiving it, much less of giving in
their turn what they have received? Away with this, erase it! Let the
precious ointment on the head run down upon the beard, and thence
down to the skirt of the garment.[6] Let waters be drawn from the

fountain,[7] not from puddles in the streets.

I, the least among the many thousands who were summoned, was scoffing at the Waldenses [and expressing surprise] that there should be any consultation or delay in deciding their request, when I was summoned by a certain great prelate to whom the supreme pontiff had entrusted the charge of confessions. A target for shafts,[8] I took my seat. When many lawyers and men of learning had assembled, two Waldenses who seemed the leaders of their group were brought before me to argue about the faith, not for love of seeking the truth but hoping that when I had been refuted my mouth might be stopped like one speaking wicked things.[9] I confess that I sat in fear lest in punishment for my sins the gift of speech might be denied me before so great a gathering. The bishop commanded me, who was preparing to answer,[10] to test my skill against them. First, then, knowing that the lips of an ass which eats thistles find lettuce unworthy of them,[11] I put very easy questions of which no one could be ignorant. "Do you believe in God the Father?" They replied, "We do." "And in the Son?" They answered, "We do." "And in the Holy Spirit?" They answered, "We do." I went on, "And in the mother of Christ?" They again, "We do." They were answered with derisive laughter from everyone present and withdrew in confusion;[12] deservedly, for, like Phaëthon, who did not even know the names of his horses,[13] they who were taught by none sought to become teachers.

They have no fixed habitations. They go about two by two, barefoot, clad in woolen garments, owning nothing, holding all things common like the apostles,[14] naked, following a naked Christ. They are making their first moves now in the humblest manner because they cannot launch an attack. If we admit them, we shall be driven out.

32. A Profession of Faith by Waldes of Lyons

Henry of Marcy, newly appointed cardinal and legate to France, came to Lyons in March, 1180, or 1181, to preside over a diocesan council summoned by Archbishop Guichard.[1] Henry, as abbot of Clairvaux, had taken a leading part in a mission against the Cathars of Toulouse in 1178 (see No. 29). Also present at the council was Geoffrey of Auxerre, abbot of Hautecombe, who had accompanied St. Bernard on an earlier mission to Toulouse, in 1145 (see No. 14). Archbishop Guichard had assisted in the condemnation of heretics at Vézelay in 1167 (see No. 41). Before these dignitaries and other clergy, Waldes of Lyons presented himself to declare his orthodoxy and affirm his staunch allegiance to the Church. This was made necessary, we are told by Geoffrey of Auxerre, because Waldes and his companions had been guilty of sacrilegious presumption in assuming the office of preaching, in pretending to lives of poverty, and in living without the labor of their own hands while they spoke in derogation of the clergy.[2] The profession of faith made by Waldes on that occasion is, in fact, orthodox in every way. It ends with a reaffirmation of his devotion to the life of poverty but says no word about preaching.[3]

At first glance, the profession of faith of Waldes seems to be an explicit, point-by-point repudiation of the contemporary teaching of the Cathars as we know it from other sources. Such may have been Waldes's intent, but the credo was not originally drafted for use at Lyons and its basic elements have a history long antedating the appearance of the Cathars. The essentials of the profession of faith appear as early as the beginning of the sixth century in an interrogatory forming part of the procedure for ordination of bishops in the Gallican rite;[4] they persisted thereafter in formularies connected with episcopal ordination.[5] One very well known use of the profession was in the ordination of Gerbert of Aurillac, later Pope Sylvester II (999-1003), as archbishop of Rheims in 991.[6] Although Gerbert has been exculpated from the suspicions of heresy which some historians raised against him because of the phrasing of his profession of faith,[7] his statement does have a tenuous link with contemporary heresies. Andrew of Fleury describes the outbreak of heresy at Orléans in 1022 in his biography of Gaucelin, abbot of Fleury and archbishop of Bourges (d. 1029), and to that recital appends a profession of faith to which Gaucelin subscribed at the time. Except for the last sentence it is identical with the statement of Gerbert.[8]

But when in 1180 or 1181 this traditional text was presented to Waldes, certain additions were made which reflect the concern of the prelates over contemporary heresies. They included a declaration of belief in one God, creator of all things visible and invisible, a statement that John the Baptist was a holy and righteous man, and an affirmation that the hardships which Christ endured in His human body were real, as was His passion. These indubitably were inserted so that Waldes might repudiate the teaching of the Cathars on these points. Other additions affirmed the validity of the sacraments at the hands of sinful priests, approved the baptism of infants and the sacrament of confirmation, declared belief in the real sacrifice of the Eucharist, and approved both ecclesiastical orders and the utility of good works for the dead. Errors on these matters were charged to the Cathars but they were equally emphasized by other sects, notably the followers of Henry of Lausanne and Peter of Bruys (see Nos. 12 and 13). Thus, taking into account the character and experience of the dignitaries at the Council of Lyons and the agitation which Waldes and his group had already aroused in the city, it is most probable that the reformer was required to submit this statement of his faith not only because of his own activities but also because of the prelates' recollection of earlier movements of protest and their apprehension about the Cathars. But, as has already been said, Waldes's oath was to be only an interlude in the development of hostility between the Poor of Lyons and the Church. Within a short time a new archbishop would expel them from the city and they would pass over into outright heresy.

In the translation which follows, we have italicized those portions of Waldes's profession which are additions to the formula as it was used by Gerbert at the end of the tenth century. The basic study of this episode is the article by Dondaine from which we translate. The profession of Waldes is printed and collated with later ones which were modeled on it [9] in Gonnet, *Enchiridion fontium Valdensium*, I, 32-36. An English translation also appears in Petry, *History of Christianity*, pp. 350-52.

Our translation is from Antoine Dondaine, "Aux Origines du Valdéisme: Une profession de foi de Valdès," *Archivum fratrum praedicatorum*, XVI (1946), 231-32, by permission of the Istituto storico domenicano di S. Sabina.

1180 or 1181

In the name of the Father, and of the Son, and of the Holy Spirit, and of the Most Blessed Mary, ever virgin.

Let it be known to all the faithful that I, Waldes, and all my brethren, with the Holy Gospels placed before us, believe *in heart, perceive through faith, confess in speech,* and in unequivocal words affirm that the Father, the Son, and the Holy Spirit are *three persons, one God,* the whole Trinity of Godhead coessential, consubstantial, coeternal, and co-omnipotent; and that each Person of the Trinity is fully God, all three persons one God, *as is contained in the creeds, the Apostles' Creed, the Nicene Creed, and the Athanasian Creed. We believe in heart and confess in words that the Father, the Son, and the Holy Spirit, the one God to whom we testify is creator, maker, governor, and, in due time and place, disposer of all things visible and invisible, all things of the heavens, in the air, and in the waters, and upon the earth.* We believe that the author of the New and Old Testaments, *that is, of the Law of Moses and of the prophets and of the apostles,* is one and the same God *who, existing in the Trinity as we have said, created all things; John the Baptist, holy and righteous, was sent by Him and was filled with the Holy Spirit in his mother's womb.* We believe *in heart and confess in words* that the incarnation of divinity came to pass, not in the Father or in the Holy Spirit, but only in the Son, so that He who in divinity was the Son of God the Father, true God from the Father, was true man from His mother, having true flesh from the womb of His mother and a rational human soul, of both natures at one and the same time; that is, He was both God and man, one Person, one Son, one Christ, one God with the Father and the Holy Spirit, ruler and author of all, *born of the Virgin Mary by true birth of the flesh. We believe in heart and confess in words that He ate, drank, slept, and rested when weary from travel*; He suffered with true passion of His flesh, died in a true death of His body, rose again with true resurrection of His flesh and true restoration of His soul; *in that flesh He afterward ate and drank, ascended into heaven, sits at the right hand of the Father, and* in it shall come to judge the quick and the dead. We believe in one Church, Catholic, *holy, apostolic, and immaculate*, outside of which no one can be saved. *We do not in any way reject the sacraments which are celebrated in it with the aid of the inestimable and invisible power of the Holy Spirit, even though they be ministered by a sinful priest, as long as the Church accepts him; nor do we disparage the ecclesiastical offices or the blessings celebrated by such a one, but with devout mind we embrace them as if performed by the most righteous. We approve, therefore, of the baptism of infants, for we confess and believe that they are saved if they shall die after baptism before they commit sin.* We believe, indeed, that in baptism all sins are remitted as well that original inherited sin as those which are committed voluntarily. *We hold that confirmation performed by a bishop, that is, by the imposition of hands, is holy and worthy of reverent acceptance. We firmly believe and absolutely affirm that the Eucharist, that is, the bread and wine after consecration, is the body and blood of Jesus Christ and in this nothing more is accomplished by a good priest, nothing less by an evil one.* We acknowledge that God grants forgiveness to sinners truly penitent in heart, *who confess in words and do works of satisfaction in accordance with the Scriptures,* and most willingly will we consort with them. *We venerate the anointing of the sick with consecrated oil.* We do not deny that carnal marriage may be contracted, *as the Apostle says; we utterly forbid that those united in lawful fashion may separate*; also, we do not condemn a second marriage. *We humbly praise and faithfully venerate the ecclesiastical orders, that is, the episcopate and the priesthood and the others of higher and lower degree, and all that is in good order appointed to be read and sung as holy in the Church.* We believe that the devil was made evil not by nature but by his will. We put no reproach at all upon the eating of meat. We believe in *heart and confess in words* the resurrection of this flesh which we bear and no other. We firmly believe and affirm that judgment is still to come and that each person will receive either reward or punishment for those things committed in this flesh. *We do not doubt that alms, and the Mass, and other good works can be of benefit to the faithful who have died. And since, according to James the Apostle, "faith without works is dead,"*[10] *we have renounced the world; whatever we had we have given to the poor, as the Lord advised, and we have resolved to be poor in such fashion that we shall take no thought for the morrow, nor shall we accept gold or silver, or anything of that sort from anyone beyond food and clothing sufficient for the day. Our resolve is to follow the precepts of the Gospel as commands. We wholeheartedly confess and believe that persons remaining in the world, owning their own goods, giving alms and doing other good works out of their own, and observing the commandments of the Lord, may be saved.*

Wherefore, we earnestly assure Your Grace that if any shall chance to come to your vicinity, declaring that they come from us but having not this faith, you may know with certainty that they come not from us.[11]

33. Stephen of Bourbon on the Early Waldenses

The comments of Stephen of Bourbon on the origin of the Poor of Lyons are of particular value—even though he wrote more than half a century after the events of which he speaks—because of the firsthand testimony he had from those who had known Waldes. After studying at Paris, Stephen entered the Dominican convent at Lyons in 1223 and some nine years later became an inquisitor, active chiefly in the valley of the Saône and the Rhone. About 1249 he retired to a cloister, and before his death in 1261 he compiled a treatise intended primarily for the use of preachers, *De septem donis Spiritus Sancti* [on the seven gifts of the Holy Spirit]. At a later place (No. 52) we will present his observations on Waldensian doctrines as they had developed by the mid-thirteenth century; here appears only his recollection of what he had heard about the origin of the sect. On Stephen see pages ii-xx of the Introduction to the edition of his work.

The following passage is translated from *Stephani de Borbone tractatus de diversis materiis praedicabilis* IV.vii.342, ed. by Albert Lecoy de la Marche, as *Anecdotes historiques, légendes et apologues tirées du recueil inédit d'Etienne de Bourbon, dominicain du XIIIᵉ siècle* (Société de l'histoire de France, Publications, CLXXXV [Paris, 1887]), pp. 290-92.

1173-1184 (written after 1249)

Now, the Waldenses are so named from the founder of this heresy, who was named Waldes. They are also called the Poor of Lyons because it was in that city that they entered upon their life of poverty. They also refer to themselves as the Poor in Spirit because of what the Lord said, "Blessed are the poor in spirit."[1] Verily, they are poor in spirit—in spiritual blessings and in the Holy Spirit.

The sect began in this way, according to what I have heard from several persons who observed its earliest members and from a certain priest, named Bernard Ydros, in the city of Lyons, who was himself quite respected and well-to-do and a friend of our brethren [the Dominicans]. When he was a young man and a scribe, he was employed by Waldes to write in the vernacular the first books possessed by those people, while a certain grammarian, Stephen of Anse by name—whom I often encountered—translated and dictated them to him. Stephen, a prebendary of the cathedral of Lyons, subsequently came to a sudden death by falling from the upper story of a house which he was building.

There was in that city a rich man named Waldes, who was not well educated, but on hearing the Gospels was anxious to learn more precisely what was in them. He made a contract with these priests, the one to translate them into the vernacular and the other to write them down at his dictation. This they did, not only for many books of the Bible but also for many passages from the Fathers, grouped by topics, which are called Sentences. When this citizen had pored over these texts and learned them by heart, he resolved to devote himself to evangelical perfection, just as the apostles had pursued it. Selling all his possessions, in contempt of the world he broadcast his money to the poor and presumptuously arrogated to himself the office of the apostles. Preaching in the streets and the broad ways[2] the Gospels and those things that he had learned by heart, he drew to himself many men and women that they might do the same, and he strengthened them in the Gospel. He also sent out persons even of the basest occupations to preach in the nearby villages. Men and women alike, stupid and uneducated, they wandered through the villages, entered homes, preached in the squares and even in the churches, and induced others to do likewise.

Now, when they had spread error and scandal everywhere as a result of their rashness and ignorance, they were summoned before the archbishop of Lyons, whose name was John,[3] and were forbidden by him to concern themselves with expounding the Scriptures or with preaching. They, in turn, fell back on the reply made by the apostles. Their leader, assuming the role of Peter, replied with his words to the chief priests: "We ought to obey God, rather than men"[4]—the God who had commanded the apostles to "Preach the gospel to every creature."[5] He asserted this as though the Lord had said to them what He said to the apostles; the latter, however, did not presume to preach until they had been clothed with power from on high, until they had been illuminated by the best and fullest knowledge, and had received the gift of tongues. But these persons, that is to say, Waldes and his fellows, fell first into disobedience by their presumption and their usurpation of the apostolic office, then into contumacy, and finally under the sentence of excommunication. After they were driven out of these parts and were summoned to the council which was held in Rome before the Lateran Council, they remained obdurate and were finally judged to be schismatics.[6] Thereafter, since they mingled in Provence and Lombardy with other heretics whose errors they imbibed and propagated, they have been adjudged by the Church most hostile, infectious, and dangerous heretics, who wander everywhere, assuming the appearance but not the reality of holiness and sincerity.[7] The more dangerous the more they lie hidden from sight, they conceal themselves under various disguises and occupations. Once there was captured a leader of their sect who carried with him the trappings of various crafts by which he could transform himself like Proteus. If he were sought in one disguise and realized the fact, he would change to another. Sometimes he wore the garb and marks of a pilgrim, at others he bore the staff and irons of a penitent,[8] at still other times he pretended to be a cobbler or a barber or a harvester, and so on. Others do the same. This sect began about the year of our Lord 1170, in the episcopacy of John, called "of the Fair Hands," archbishop of Lyons.

34. A Debate between Catholics and Waldenses

Some of the Poor of Lyons moved southward after their expulsion from that city and within a few years were preaching in the vicinity of Narbonne, undeterred by their condemnation at a synod convened, probably shortly before 1190, by Bernard Gaucelin, archbishop of Narbonne (1181-1191).

When they continued to preach, the procedure used at Lombers in 1165 was revived. Spokesmen for the Church and for the heretics came together for discussion and debate in or near Narbonne in about 1190.[1] What was said furnished most of the material for a treatise by Bernard of Fontcaude. Bernard had, in 1172, become head of a Premonstratensian abbey which was the successor to an Augustinian community at Fontcaude, north of Narbonne. Little more is known of him than can be gathered from this work, written sometime after the death of Pope Lucius III in 1185, and from the appearance of his name on a few other documents. He seems to have died by 1193. The tract he wrote falls into three main divisions: the error of the Waldensian refusal to obey prelates (chaps. I-III); the arguments for and against their preaching (chaps. IV-VIII); and various other points of doctrine challenged by heretics, among whom are to be recognized sects other than the Waldenses (chaps. IX-XII). We translate here only the Prologue and the headings of the various chapters.

A recent study of Bernard's work is Libert Verrees, "Le Traité de l'abbé Bernard de Fontcaude contre les Vaudois et les Ariens," *Analecta Praemonstratensia*, XXXI (1955), 5-35; and it has been analyzed in Thouzellier, *Catharisme et valdéisme*, pp. 50-57. There is a partial, rather free translation into English in Comba, *History of the Waldenses*, pp. 47 ff. The chapter headings and certain statements of heretical belief from the treatise are also printed in Gonnet, *Enchiridion*, I, 64-90.

The translation which follows is made from *Bernardi abbatis Fontis callidi, ordinis praemonstratensis, Adversus Waldensium sectam liber*, in Migne, *Patrologia latina*, CCIV, 793-95, 795-840, *passim*.

circa 1190

A TREATISE AGAINST THE WALDENSES[2]

Prologue

1. At the time when Lord Lucius[3] of glorious memory presided over the Holy Roman Church, new heretics suddenly raised their head who, choosing by chance a name with a forecast of the future, were called Waldenses, a name surely derived from "dense vale" (*valle densa*), inasmuch as they were enveloped in the deep, dense darkness of error. Although condemned by the aforesaid highest pontiff, they spewed the poison of their unbelief far and wide with rash impudence.

2. Because of this, Lord Bernard, archbishop of Narbonne, renowned for piety and integrity before God, an ardent lover of God's law, set himself as a strong wall against them and, therefore, convening many clerics and laymen, monks and secular clergy, he summoned them to judgment. What more is there to say? After the case was considered with the greatest care, they were condemned.

3. Nevertheless, they dared thereafter to sow the seed of their wickedness privately and publicly. And so again, although it was more than was required, they were invited to a discussion with certain persons, both clerics and laymen. So that the argument would not drag on too long, a certain priest, Raymond of Deventer,[4] a man, indeed, devout and God-fearing, noble by birth, nobler in conduct, was chosen by both parties as a judge.

4. So when the day set for the debate arrived and both parties assembled, together with many other clerics and laymen, they [the Waldenses] were called to account by the true Catholics for certain matters on which their views were erroneous. As they replied to each charge, the argument was pursued at length, now by one side, now by the other, and many biblical texts were advanced by each party. When he had heard the statements of both sides, the afore-mentioned judge rendered a definitive verdict in writing and pronounced the Waldenses heretics on the points of which they had been accused.

5. In the present little tract we describe the texts and arguments by which they defended their stand and the reply to them by us Catholics, with the scriptural texts by which the Catholic faith was defended; and we add certain other passages against other heresies. All this we have done particularly to instruct or encourage some of the clergy, who, either because they are burdened by inexperience or for want of books, become an offense and a scandal to the faithful under their charge by their failure to stand against the enemies of the truth; for they neither confirm [their parishioners] in the Catholic faith nor refresh them with the nourishment of the Holy Scriptures, wherefore they languish like starvelings on the journey through this world, deprived of spiritual powers and unable to find their way again to the homeland, that is, to paradise. This, indeed, is the real cause of the greater evil we have described: that the ravening wolves, to wit, the demon-heretics and tyrants, are not being driven out of the folds of Christ's sheep either by the word of preaching or by the rod of discipline or strictness.

6. Wherefore, may it please [such clerics] to accept from our humble self the little gift of this tract. Let them commit the texts of the Holy Fathers to memory, so that by God's mercy they may have invincible weapons against the masters of darkness, against the spinners of lies, against the worshipers of perverse dogmas who are the demon-heretics, to the end that, guided by the grace of God, they may win triumph over

them and may be worthy to receive from the Highest Shepherd "a never-fading crown of glory"[5] for the governance and instruction of those under their charge.

Chapter I: This opposes their statement that no obedience is owed to the supreme pontiff or to other prelates. . . .

Chapter II: This treats of the authority of prelates: that deference and obedience are owed to them. . . .

Chapter III: Against those who disparage the holders of the cure of souls. . . .

Chapter IV: Refutes the proposition that all persons, even laymen, may preach: What they may say in this regard and what we may say against them. . . .

Chapter V: That it is not permissible for them to minister the word of God to the faithful. . . .

Chapter VI: An answer to the argument in which they say with the Apostle, "We ought to obey God rather than men";[6] also there are some other matters. . . .

Chapter VII: In this are described the persons whom they chiefly seduce, and whom they do not. . . .

Chapter VIII: Against the assertion that women may preach. . . .

Chapter IX: Against their statement that alms, fasting, the ceremony of the Mass, or other prayers of the living are of no profit to the faithful who have died. . . .[7]

Chapter X: Against those who deny that there is purgatorial fire and who say that souls released from the flesh go directly to heaven or hell. . . .[8]

Chapter XI: Against those persons who say that before the Last Judgment those souls of the dead go neither to heaven nor to hell but remain in other places of refuge. . . .[9]

Chapter XII: Against those who refuse to pray in a church and who declare that a church does not deserve that name. Here it is proved that a church is properly so named, that one should pray therein, and that it should be regarded with the greatest veneration. Here also is the answer to a particular argument of those heretics, in which, relying on the words of the Blessed Stephen, they say that "the Most High dwelleth not in houses made by hands,"[10] and therefore not in a church. . . .[11]

35. *Alan of Lille: A Scholar's Attack on Heretics*

As the twelfth century drew to a close, Languedoc was the scene of religious ferment and discord.[1] The Cathars attracted sympathetic attention and adherents from every rank of society; the Poor of Lyons were increasing in number as they tapped the same wells of reformist and evangelistic piety from which predecessors such as Henry of Le Mans and his adherents had drawn. Catholic spokesmen slowly began to do what they might to curb both groups of dissidents and, in the very last years of the century, moves were undertaken in a papal program which was to lead first to a campaign of evangelization to win back the disaffected and then to crusade and repression to wipe out the adamant enemies of the faith.

A literary monument of the religious controversy at the end of the twelfth century is the work of Alan of Lille. Poet, philosopher, theologian, teacher, one of the leading literary and academic figures of his day, he won such admiring epithets as "the Great" and "the Universal Doctor" from contemporaries. Yet precise knowledge of his life is lacking. He was born in Lille, perhaps in 1128, studied perhaps at Chartres, taught at Paris. Legend has him disputing against heretics at Rome before the pope, and it has been suggested that he was a member of a preaching mission against the Cathars, but when and where is not known. He entered the Cistercian order and for some time taught at Montpellier. His poems, *De planctu naturae* (*ca.* 1160-1170) and *Anticlaudianus* (1183-1184), were very popular;[2] so too his theological writings, and not least among the latter, to judge from the number of surviving manuscripts,[3] his four-part treatise in defense of the Christian faith against heretics (Cathars),[4] Waldenses, Jews, and infidels. Alan died in 1203.[5]

The *De fide catholica* (or, as it is usually entitled in the manuscripts, *Quadripartita editio contra hereticos, Waldenses, Judeos, et paganos*) was written after 1179 and before 1202, probably in the last decade of the century.[6] Only the first two of its four books are in point here. The style and organization throughout is "scholastic": First, there is a methodical presentation of the heretical position with its scriptural basis and supporting rational arguments. These are then examined, reinterpreted, and rebutted. Last, the soundness of orthodox doctrine is demonstrated. Alan's knowledge about Cathars and Waldenses may have been partly based on personal encounters, but there is no hint of that in his writing. His approach is primarily academic; his interest chiefly in their theology, although this does not bar the use on occasion of vigorous invective against their practices. His display of scriptural erudition is impressive; even more interesting is his development of logical and philosophical arguments, with citations from classical authors as well as from the Church Fathers.[7]

The most recent biography of Alan is Guy Raynaud de Lage's *Alain de Lille, poète du XIIᵉ siècle*. There is no adequate edition of the *De fide catholica*; that from which we translate is the only one which brings all four books together. From it are excerpted the introductory first chapter and three others which present certain Catharist tenets, together with one, heavily laden with diatribe, on the Waldenses.

The following translation comes from *Alani de Insulis De fide catholica contra haereticos sui temporis* i.i,iii,ix; ii.i, in Migne, *Patrologia latina*, CCX, 307-9, 316, 377-80.

1190-1202

Book I

Chapter I: A Comparison of Pagans and Christians in Physical and Spiritual Activity

As we read in the books of the ancients that the chiefs and princes of the pagans, pursuing human fame, nobly slew monsters of various sorts, as Hercules slew Antaeus, Theseus the Minotaur, Jason the fire-breathing bull, Meleager the enormous boar, Coroebus the Stygian monster, Perseus the sea-monster, even so we read that noble princes of Holy Church with spiritual weapons overcame the monsters of various heresies and heretics. But just as Antaeus became more powerful by recovering strength from the earth, and the hydra, on loss of its heads, became more endowed therewith, so also when old former heresies were rooted out, they sprouted anew. Yet there is a great difference here: The strength of Antaeus came to its end, the hydra was totally destroyed; but among moderns there are not those who are able to resist renewed heresies, to uproot those which sprout anew. Yet I, least among the sons of Jesse chosen from later generations, will strive to kill Goliath with his own sword and put to death the Egyptian who taunts the Hebrews.

Chapter II: The Heretics, Relying on Certain Texts, Say There Are Two Principles of Things

The heretics of our time say that there are two principles of things, the principle of light and the principle of darkness.

The principle of light, they say, is God, from whom are spiritual things, to wit, souls and angels. The principle of darkness, Lucifer, is he from whom are temporal things. They seek, moreover, to prove this by texts and rational arguments. By texts thus: "A good tree cannot bring forth evil fruit, neither can an evil tree bring forth good fruit."[8] Therefore, since God is the highest good, evils are not from Him; but since evils exist, and not from God himself, they come, therefore, from something other than God. Therefore, since God is the principle of good, there is another, the principle of evil.

Also, at the beginning of Genesis, one reads that "darkness was upon the face of the deep."[9] Thus the world had its beginning in darkness. Therefore, the creator of the world was the principle of darkness, and the founder of the world, who initiated its creation from darkness, was evil.

Also, Christ says in the Gospel, "The prince of this world cometh and in me he hath not anything."[10] There He gives Lucifer rather than himself the name of prince of the world, so Lucifer, not Christ, was founder of the world. Elsewhere is the saying, "No man can serve two masters," that is, "God and mammon."[11] There Christ refers to himself and to the devil as masters (*domini*). Now Christ is called lord (*dominus*) only by reason of creation; therefore the devil is called lord also for reason of creation. Also, He says, "You are of your father the devil."[12]

Also, the Apostle: "It is no more I that do it but what dwelleth in me" (that is, in my flesh)—"sin."[13] If sin dwells in the flesh and is of the flesh, and if the flesh cannot exist without sin, the flesh is evil, and thus not from God. I feel "another law in my members, fighting against the law of my mind and captivating me in the law of sin, that is, in my members."[14] Now if the law of the flesh is the law of sin and death, the flesh is perceived to be evil and consequently not from God. Also, the Apostle says: "The flesh fights against the spirit and the spirit against the flesh."[15] If the flesh is always in opposition to the intellect,[16] the flesh is evil and from evil.

Chapter III: The Heretics, Relying on Certain Rational Arguments, Say That There Are Two Principles of Things

The heretics confirm their opinion also by these rational arguments. If God made these visible things, either He could make them incorruptible or not. If He could not, He was weak; if He could do so and refused, He was malevolent. Also, if a cause is immutable, its effect will be immutable. But it is established that corporeal things are subject to change. Therefore, their cause is mutable. Also, since many things in the world occur by chance, they do not appear to be done by divine command. Also, since the flesh of man is given generation in and by sin, it seems not to be from the principle of good. Also, there are certain creatures, such as serpents, flies, and spiders, which yield nothing useful but produce manifold damage. Therefore, since they are destined for evil, not for good, they are from evil, not from good. . . .

Chapter IX: The Contention of Certain Heretics Who Say That There Are No Souls in Human Bodies Other than the Apostate Angels Who Fell from Heaven

Moreover, certain of the aforesaid heretics, seeking aid for their ignorance, deny that souls are created every day and infused into bodies. They declare that alone the apostate angels who fell from heaven are infused into human bodies by God's permission, to the end that they may be able to do penance therein. They also say of these that one spirit may be infused successively into eight bodies, so that if penance is not completed in one, it may be done in another. Furthermore, they say that the spirit of man is nothing other than an apostate angel and that there are no spirits in heaven because all that were in heaven fell with Lucifer. This these persons seek to prove by the text, "I was not sent but to the sheep that are lost of the house of Israel."[17] They mean by "the house of Israel" the assembly of angels who were created in heaven so that they might behold God, but who fell away through sin. They also quote another text, "No man hath ascended into heaven, but he that descended from heaven, the Son of man, who is in heaven."[18] . . .

Book II: Against the Waldenses
Chapter I: It Is Demonstrated from Texts and by Rational Arguments That No One Should Preach Unless He Is Sent by a Prelate His Superior

There are certain heretics who pretend that they are righteous, although they are wolves in sheep's clothing. In the Gospel the Lord said of them, "Beware of false prophets who come to you in the clothing of sheep, but inwardly they are ravening wolves."[19] They are called Waldenses after their heresiarch, who was named Waldes. He, by the prompting of his own spirit, not sent by God, invented a new sect in that, without authority from a prelate, without divine inspiration, without knowledge, without learning, he presumed to preach; a philosopher without thought, a prophet without vision, an apostle without a mission, a teacher without a tutor.[20] His disciples, or rather deceivers,[21] seduce the simple folk in various regions of the world, divert them from rather than convert them to the truth. They dare to preach to fill their bellies rather than their minds and, because they do not wish to work with their own hands to obtain food, they make the evil choice of living without employment, preaching falsities so that they may buy food, since Paul says, "He who does not labor, neither let him eat."[22] In the first place, these persons proceed against divine authority and against the proclamation of Holy Writ because they preach, being sent neither by a superior nor by God; for they neither prove that they are sent by God in their works nor confirm it by miracles. A mission from God is both proved by good works and confirmed by miracles. Also, we do not read that any holy person preached unless he was sent. For Christ was sent by the Father and came to preach only at God's good pleasure. This is shown likewise by the prophets and the apostles and those whom they delegated. We read that John was sent by God.[23] And the Lord said to Jeremiah, "Before I formed thee in the bowels of thy mother, I knew thee and before thou camest forth out of the womb I sanctified thee and made thee a prophet unto the nations."[24] Amos says that he was sent by God when he was a shepherd.[25] And the Holy Spirit is presented in Malachi, speaking thus to the Father about John, "Behold, I send my angel before your face."[26] Isaiah also, we read, was sent by God.[27] Why enumerate every single instance? We read that all the prophets of the Old Testament were sent by God. Likewise, Christ's disciples are called apostles as though, beyond others, they were sent; in like manner those whom they delegated were sent. By the fact that Christ sent the apostles and others to preach is signified that lesser persons in the Church of God ought not to preach unless they are sent by superiors. Since orders in the Church of God are assigned by superior officials, so also the function of preaching, because it is the most important in the Church. Just as no one should be promoted to the priesthood except in the way that Aaron was, that is, no one should take it upon himself, so no one ought to undertake the functions of a preacher on his own authority. Hence Korah and his associates, as we read in Numbers,[28] perished by fire because he usurped another's function. We read also in the fourth book of Kings that Uzziah the king was afflicted with leprosy because he took upon himself the function of making sacrifices.[29] Similarly, spiritual leprosy, meaning mortal sin, afflicts him who usurps for himself the office of preaching. For the Apostle says to the Romans, "How shall they preach unless they be sent?"[30]—for they are not true apostles unless they are sent. Also, in the second Epistle to the Corinthians he reproves pseudopreachers.[31] He himself was indeed sent by his superior, that is, by Christ, for he also says to the Romans, speaking of Christ, "By whom we have received grace and apostleship."[32] Also, how will unlettered persons preach who do not understand the Scriptures? Will not their preaching result rather in the ruin of many than in their resurrection? Again, how may they be literate who have never learned their letters? Now we see that persons, such as many Cistercians, holier than they and who know the Holy Scriptures, do not preach, indubitably because they were not sent. If it is a dangerous thing for wise and holy men to preach, it is most dangerous for the uneducated who do not know what should be preached; to whom, how, when, and where[33] there should be preaching. These persons resist the Apostle in that they have women with them and have them preach in the gatherings of the faithful, although the Apostle says in the first Epistle to the Corinthians: "Let women keep silence in the churches, for it is not permitted them to speak, but to be subject, as also the law saith. But if they would learn anything, let them ask their husbands at home."[34] Also, the Apostle in the first Epistle to Timothy, "Let the woman learn in silence, with all subjection. But I suffer not a woman to teach nor to use authority over the man."[35] The Apostle also speaks of these heretics in the second Epistle to Timothy: "Know also this, that in the last days shall come dangerous times. Men shall be lovers of themselves, covetus, haughty, proud, blasphemers, disobedient to parents, ungrateful, wicked, without affection, without peace, slanderers, incontinent, unmerciful, without kindness, traitors, stubborn, puffed up, and lovers of pleasures more than of God, having an appearance indeed of godliness, but denying the power thereof. Now these avoid. For of these sort are they who creep into houses and lead captive silly women laden with sins, who are led away with divers desires, ever learning, and never attaining to the knowledge of the truth."[36] All of these words fit the Waldenses especially, who are haughty; slanderers of the prelates of the Church; proud, in boasting of their own works; blasphemers of God through heresy; disobedient to their real and their spiritual parents, because they deny obedience to their prelates; wicked, because they slay their own and others' souls with perverse doctrines; without affection for anyone; without peace, disturbing others; slanderers, because they impute faults to others; incontinent, moreover, for in their assemblies they indulge in gluttony and devote themselves to excesses, as those who have ceased to consort with them testify; unmerciful in raising accusations; without kindness, because they seek to subvert others; traitors, because they reveal the secrets of others; puffed up, swollen in heart, shameless and insolent in unhallowed worship; having an appearance, indeed of godliness, but denying the power thereof, because they falsely put on an external piety, yet within are ravening wolves; blind men who understand not what they speak nor what they do; lovers of pleasures, putting carnal delights before the spiritual. These are they who creep into the houses of widows and lead them astray. They are the ones who ever labor in their schools at learning more, but never attain knowledge of the truth.[37]

36. The Reconciliation of a Group of Waldenses to the Church

Three documents grouped here illustrate the complexities of the situation in the early thirteenth century, when Waldenses, Cathars, and Catholics were engaged in controversy and small parties from the first-named came back to the Church, with the intention of continuing under its aegis the attack on the Cathars in which they were already engaged. Their conversion was a result of the Cistercian preaching mission in Languedoc after 1204, which Bishop Diego of Osma and Dominic of Caleruega, his companion, had joined in 1206.[1] In a public debate at Pamiers in August, 1207, Bishop Diego and his colleagues overcame the arguments of Waldensian spokesmen, of whom some, according to the chronicler William of Puylaurens, "approached the Apostolic See and received penance. I have heard that they were given permission to live under a rule. Durand of Huesca was foremost (*prior*) among them. He wrote certain works against the heretics.[2] These persons lived thus, indeed, in one part of Catalonia for several years but thereafter, little by little, they disappeared." [3]

Durand of Huesca and four companions had, indeed, gone to the papal see to make their submission. In December, 1208, Innocent III accepted from them a profession of faith derived directly from that made by Waldes in Lyons (No. 32), now amended so that it not only incorporated the traditional doctrine of the Church but repudiated the errors commonly charged against the Waldenses. To it was joined the proposal for a new religious society to be called the Poor Catholics, also inspired by Waldes's words but going beyond them. Under papal guidance, the Poor Catholics planned three levels of action against heresy—disputation with heretics, religious education of their own members, and preaching to the people at large— while retaining certain Waldensian characteristics which did not conflict with the standards of the Church.[4] The approval of Innocent III was announced in a letter of December 18, 1208 (see part A).

Durand and his friends set to work promptly. By April, 1209, they had made some recruits in Milan, and Durand informed the pope that one hundred more potential converts were at hand.[5] They came from the ranks of the Poor Lombards, Italian Waldenses who had broken away from the Poor of Lyons in 1205.[6] Now, after further internal dissension, some of them wished to return to the Church.[7] The action in the case of these hundred converts is not known, but in 1210, under the leadership of one Bernard Prim,[8] some former Poor Lombards were received into the Church, as the Poor Catholics had been, and took as their new name "the Reconciled Poor." [9] But at the same time complaints were reaching the pope that the behavior of the Poor Catholics raised doubts about the sincerity of their conversion. The letter in which Innocent ordered Durand to correct the situation shows the nature of these suspicions; it is translated as part B, below. Furthermore, a new profession of faith was drafted in 1210. It included specific disavowal of the charges that were being made against the Poor Catholics: that they, like the Waldenses denied the right of secular justice to impose the death penalty and that they did not show proper deference to the Catholic clergy.[10]

For some years the Poor Catholics had a certain measure of success. In 1212, for example, a group of penitents in the diocese of Elne put themselves under the spiritual guidance of the Poor Catholics, with the intention of founding a hospice for the sick, poor, and homeless; the fate of the venture is not known.[11] But the origins of the society continued to arouse suspicion, the secular clergy clearly resented them, and despite the support of Innocent III, they led a precarious existence.[12] By 1247 they had been forbidden to preach in Narbonne, and soon after the middle of the century both they and the Reconciled Poor (who probably preceded them in this) had been merged with or put under the control of other religious orders.[13]

The confusion created by papal approval of these preaching societies of former heretics, at the very moment when the two great mendicant orders founded by St. Francis and St. Dominic were taking shape, is illustrated by the third document, translated as part C. The author of the chronicle from which it comes was Burchard, provost of the Premonstratensian monastery of Ursberg in Germany from 1215 until his death, probably in 1231. Much of his work, a continuation of a history of the world by Ekkehard of Aura (d. 1125), is borrowed from others, but the excerpt we translate here was based on Burchard's personal experience. Burchard made two trips to Rome, in 1198 and 1210. We do not know which one involved his encounter with the groups he calls the Poor of Lyons and the Humiliati, for he did not record his experience until 1229 or 1230, and it is possible that he confused and combined his recollections of both trips.[14]

On the Poor Catholics, see Johann B. Pierron, *Die katholischen Armen*, and, with special reference to their polemical activity and the career of

Durand of Huesca, Thouzellier, *Catharisme et Valdéisme*.

In part A of the following, the additions to the earlier profession made by Waldes are italicized. The translations in parts A and B are from *Innocenti III romani pontificis Regestorum sive epistolarum libri XV* xi.196, and xii.69, in Migne, *Patrologia latina*, CCXV, 1510-13, and CCXVI, 75-77. Part C is translated from *Die Chronik des Propstes Burchard von Ursberg*, ed. by Oswald Holder-Egger and Bernard von Simson (Scriptores rerum Germanicarum in usum scholarum [Hanover and Leipzig, 1916]), pp. 107-8, by permission of Hansche Buchhandlung and the Monumenta Germaniae Historica.

A. THE ESTABLISHMENT OF THE SOCIETY OF POOR CATHOLICS

December 18, 1208

To the archbishop and suffragans of the Church of Tarragona.[15]

In imitation of Him who is the God, not of discord but of peace, who desires that all men shall be saved and come to the knowledge of truth, we received with fatherly kindness our beloved sons Durand of Huesca and his companions when they came to the Apostolic See and we have acquired full understanding of the matters which they charged themselves to explain to us on their own behalf as well as for their brethren. We know, therefore, from the things which they said to us about the articles of faith and the sacraments of the Church when they were carefully examined, that they are versed in the orthodox faith and that they build upon Catholic truth. Moreover, for greater assurance, bringing forth the Gospels and placing the text of their confession thereon, we received this oath from them:

"I (it begins), Durand of Huesca, in your consecrated hands, Most High Pontiff, Lord Innocent, invoke God as my soul's witness that I absolutely and truly believe what is contained in this document in all things, and I will never believe the contrary; but I will resist with all my might those who do believe contrary to this. To you, truly, as successor to the Blessed Apostle Peter, to archbishops, bishops, and other prelates in whose dioceses or parishes I may dwell, I tender obedience and reverence, as deserved as it is devout."

The text of the confession follows:

"Let it be known to all the faithful that I, Durand of Huesca, and J., and E., and B.,[16] and all our brethren, believe in heart, perceive through faith, confess in speech, and in unequivocal words affirm that the

Father, the Son, and the Holy Spirit are three persons, one God, the whole Trinity, the same in essence and substance, coeternal and omnipotent, and that each person of the Trinity is fully God, as is expressed in the creeds, the Apostle's Creed, the Nicene Creed, and the Athanasian Creed. We believe in heart and confess in words that the Father, the Son, and the Holy Spirit of whom we testify, is creator, maker, governor, and disposer of all things, corporeal and spiritual, visible and invisible. We believe that the author of the New and Old Testaments is one and the same God who, existing in the Trinity, as we have said, created everything out of nothing. We believe that John the Baptist, holy and righteous, was sent by Him and was filled with the Holy Spirit in his mother's womb.

We believe in heart and confess in words that the incarnation of divinity came to pass not in the Father or in the Holy Spirit but only in the Son, so that He who in divinity was the Son of God the Father, true God from the Father, was in humanity the son of man, true man from his mother, having true flesh from the womb of his mother and a rational human soul, of both natures at one and the same time, that is, God and man, one person, one son, one Christ, one God with the Father and the Holy Spirit, author and ruler of all. Born of the Virgin Mary by true birth of the flesh, He ate and drank, slept and rested when wearied by travel, suffered with true suffering of His flesh, died in a true death of His body, and rose again with true resurrection of His flesh and true restoration of His soul *to the body*;[17] in that flesh He afterward ate and drank, ascended into heaven, sits at the right hand of the Father, and in it shall come to judge the quick and the dead.

We believe in heart and confess by mouth that there is one Church, *not that of heretics*, but holy, *Roman*, catholic, and apostolic, outside of which, we believe, no one can be saved. We do not in any way reject the sacraments which are celebrated in it with the aid of the inestimable and invisible power of the Holy Spirit, even though they be ministered by a sinful priest, as long as the Church accepts him. Nor do we disparage the ecclesiastical offices or benedictions celebrated by such a one, but with devout mind we embrace them as if performed by the most righteous; *for the wickedness of a bishop or of a priest has no harmful effect upon the baptism of children, nor on the celebration of the Eucharist, nor on the performance of other ecclesiastical offices for those in their charge.* We approve, therefore, of the baptism of infants, whom we confess and believe to be saved if they shall die after baptism before they commit sin. We believe that in baptism all sins are remitted, that original inherited sin as well as those which are committed by one's own will. We hold that confirmation performed by a bishop, that is, by the imposition of hands, is holy and worthy of reverent acceptance. We firmly and indisputably with pure heart believe and affirm in unequivocal, faithful words that the sacrifice, that is, the bread and wine, is, after consecration, the true body and true blood of our Lord Jesus Christ; in this, we believe, nothing more is accomplished by a good priest, nothing less by an evil one, *for it is effected not by the merit of the consecrant but by the word of the Creator and in the power of the Holy Spirit. Hence, we firmly believe and confess that no one, however worthy, religious, holy, and prudent he may be, can or ought to consecrate the Eucharist or perform the sacrifice of the altar unless he is a priest regularly ordained by a visible and tangible bishop. To this office there are, we believe, three things necessary: a certain person, the priest himself, duly established in that office by a bishop, as we have already said; those solemn words which are set forth by the Holy Fathers in the Canon; and the faithful purpose of him who offers them. And consequently, we firmly believe and confess that whosoever believes and expresses himself as qualified to perform the sacrament of the Eucharist without the preceding episcopal ordination, as we have said, is a heretic, a participant and partner in the damnation of Korah and his accomplices, and ought to be cut off from the whole Holy Roman Church.*

We believe that forgiveness is granted by God to truly penitent sinners and most willingly will we consort with them. We venerate the anointing of the sick with consecrated oil. We do not deny that carnal marriage may be contracted as the Apostle says; we utterly forbid that those united in lawful fashion shall separate. *We believe and confess that a man united with his wife may be saved* and we do not even condemn a second *or later* marriage. We put no reproach at all upon the eating of meat.

We believe preaching to be necessary and most praiseworthy but we believe it is to be exercised by the authority or license of the highest pontiff or by permission of prelates. In all places, indeed, where manifest heretics abide, where they forsake and blaspheme God and the faith of the Holy Roman Church, we believe that we should confound them by disputation and exhortation in all ways according to God, as adversaries of Christ and the Church, and with bold countenance oppose them with the word of the Lord, even unto death. We humbly praise and faithfully venerate the ecclesiastical orders and all that is appointed to be read or sung as holy in the Holy Roman Church. We believe that the devil was made evil not by nature but by his will. We believe in heart and confess in words the resurrection of this flesh which we bear and no other. We firmly believe and affirm that the judgment by Jesus Christ is still to come, and that each person will receive either punishment or reward for those things committed in this flesh which we bear. *We believe that alms, the Mass, and other good works can benefit the faithful who have died.* We believe and confess that persons remaining in the world and owning their own goods, giving alms and doing other good works out of their own, and observing the commandments of the Lord may be saved. *We believe that by the Lord's command clerics ought to receive tithes, first fruits, and oblations."*

Verily, since not only true faith but good performance is requisite for salvation, for even as it is impossible to please God without faith, so faith without works is dead,[18] we have caused a record to be made in these pages of the proposal for their way of life, the content of which follows.

"To the honor of God and His Catholic Church and for the salvation of our souls, we have resolved to believe in heart and confess in words the Catholic faith, whole and inviolate in its entirety, maintaining ourselves under the direction and governance of the Roman pontiff. We have renounced the world; whatever we may come to have we shall bestow upon the poor according to the Lord's commandment. We have resolved to be poor in such fashion that we shall take no thought for the morrow, nor shall we accept gold or silver, or anything of that sort from anyone, beyond food and clothing sufficient for the day. Our resolve is to follow the precepts of the Gospel as commands,[19] devoting ourselves to prayer according to the seven canonical hours, saying the Lord's Prayer fifteen times, followed by the Apostle's Creed, the Miserere, and other prayers. Inasmuch as most of us are clerics and almost all are educated, we are resolved to devote ourselves to study, exhortation, teaching, and disputation against all sects of error. Disputations, however, are to be conducted by the more learned brethren, proved in the Catholic faith and instructed in the law of the Lord, so that enemies of the Catholic and apostolic faith are confounded,

Through especially worthy persons, well versed in the law of the Lord and in the sentences of the Fathers, we propose to set forth the word of the Lord in our schools to our brethren and friends. With license from and due veneration for prelates, the qualified brethren, learned in the sacred page, who may be powerful in sound doctrine, will reprove sinful folk and by every means draw them to the faith and into the bosom of the Holy Roman Church. We are resolved that we will inviolably preserve unbroken virginity and chastity and will observe two Lents and the fasts instituted each year in accordance with ecclesiastical rule. We have elected to wear the modest religious garb to which we are accustomed, the shoes being cut away at the top and shaped in a special and distinct style, so that we will openly and clearly be recognized as separated in body as in heart from the Poor of Lyons,[20] now and forever more, unless they become reconciled to Catholic unity. We will receive the Church's sacraments from bishops and priests in whose dioceses and parishes we reside, to whom we shall proffer due obedience and reverence. If, indeed, any laymen express a desire to accept our guidance, we shall take care that apart from those qualified to exhort and to dispute against heretics, they shall abide together religiously and in due order, disposing their affairs in justice and mercy, subsisting by the work of their hands, giving the tithes, first fruits, and oblations due to the Church."

We, therefore, having taken counsel with our brethren, order by apostolic letter that if you shall receive a similar vow from other brothers, you shall reconcile them to ecclesiastical unity by an oath like this, and you shall make it known by proclamation and in other ways that they are truly Catholic and rightly faithful, keeping them under God free from all scandal and infamy; and you shall mercifully aid them with testimonial letters and other assistance, for the sake of God.

Given at the Lateran, December 18, 1208, in the eleventh year of our pontificate.

B. COMPLAINTS AGAINST THE POOR CATHOLICS

July 5, 1209

To Durand of Huesca and his brethren, who were restored to ecclesiastical unity.

We have received a serious charge against you from our brethren, the archbishop of Narbonne and the bishops of Béziers, Uzès, Nîmes, and Carcassonne, to the effect that you, presuming more than is proper on the favor of our good will, grow quite insolent toward them; likewise, that before their eyes you brought some Waldenses, heretics who were not yet restored to ecclesiastical unity, into a church, with the result that they were present with you at the consecration of the body of the Lord and you acted together with them in all things. They charge that you keep in your company certain monks who have left their monasteries and others who have abandoned their vocation. They allege that you have in no way at all changed the garb denoting that superstition which formerly caused scandal among Catholics. Furthermore, on account of your doctrinal instruction, which you deliver to your brethren and friends in your schools, many have been drawn away from the Church, not seeking to hear divine offices or sacerdotal preaching therein. Indeed, even the clergy among your associates, who are organized in sacred orders, do not attend the divine office according to canonical regulations. And, above all, some of you assert that no secular authority can, without mortal sin, impose a judgment of blood.

Now, when we heard this, we were touched to the heart with sorrow, fearing no little that what we had designed for good should turn to harm. Therefore, lest the most recent error make the earlier one worse, we have directed that your zeal be solicited and admonished, prescribing by apostolic letter that you recall the divine law according to which one who has been expelled from the town for the disease of leprosy be not readmitted except by decision of a priest.[21] Do you carefully shun those persons who, for the disease of heretical depravity, are cut off from the bosom of the Church until they may be recalled to her by decision of pontifical authority, lest you bring evangelical and apostolic judgment into contempt by acting otherwise. . . .[22] Although those who act by the spirit of God are not under the Law,[23] for where the spirit of God is, there is liberty,[24] do not allow into your company apostates whom men hold to be unworthy, who lightly withdraw from their way of life. Do not keep those whom you have admitted but return them to their prelates so that they may remain in that vocation to which they were called. . . . And because the kingdom of God is not in outer garb but within,[25] take care to still the scandal which grows more serious because of the former garb which you still keep. Alter this habit as you promised us to do, changing it in such a way that you show yourselves also set apart from heretics in outer raiment as you are within. . . . Being un-

willing to destroy the work of God for the sake of footwear, be mindful
of what the same apostle [Paul] said: "For if because of thy meat thy
brother be grieved, thou walkest not now according to charity. Destroy
not him with thy meat, for whom Christ died."[26] ... Therefore, we
admonish, we advise, we exhort those of you who have not yet adopted
this fashion or those who shall be associated with you in the future not
to bind themselves to the custom of wearing sandals open at the top
nor to wear such footgear, so that thus scandal may entirely disappear.
Wisely warn your friends and brothers who come together to hear your
words, effectively persuade them to attend churches often and to hear
the word of God therein, especially on the appointed days, so that they
do not show contempt for the holy temple or the priestly office, both of
which the faithful should venerate with pious devotion.... Let not,
therefore, your clerics refuse to celebrate the daily and nocturnal hours
in the churches according to canonical practice, lest they, indeed, come
to be violaters of the clerical order. This, which is an error, let no one
of you presume to assert: that the secular power cannot carry out
judgment of blood without mortal sin, for the law, not the judge, puts
to death so long as one acts to impose punishment, not in hatred, not
rashly, but with counsel.... That you may properly and without suspicion
wield against heretics the spiritual sword which is the word of God, we
desire and command that you join yourselves to other Catholic preachers
in the office of preaching against the foxes of any kind who seek to
destroy the vines of the Lord....[27] So let preachers already proved in
sound doctrine be joined to you who were recently converted from
error to truth, so that they with you and you with them, wholly free
from suspicion, may sow the word of God while humbly rendering
obedience and reverence to archbishops, bishops, and other prelates.
Thus you may erect the structure of good works upon the foundation
of humility, imitating the teaching of Him who said of himself, "Learn
of me, because I am meek and humble of heart."[28]

Given at Viterbo, July 5, 1209, in the twelfth year [of our pontifi-
cate].[29]

C. WALDENSES, HUMILIATI, AND FRIARS MINOR

1210-1216

At this time, as the world was growing old, there arose in the Church,
whose youth is renewed like the eagle's,[30] two religious orders which

were also confirmed by the Apostolic See, to wit, the Friars Minor and the Preachers. The reason for this approval may have been the persistence of two sects which had previously appeared in Italy and which called themselves, respectively, the Humiliati[31] and the Poor of Lyons. A former pope, Lucius [III], listed these among heretics, chiefly because unsound doctrines and practices were observed among them and because, in secret sermons which they usually delivered in hidden places, they heaped scorn on the Church of God and the priesthood. We saw at the time several of those who were called the Poor of Lyons, with a certain one of their leaders named Bernard, I believe, at the Apostolic See. They were seeking to have their sect confirmed and endowed with privileges by the pope. Indeed, they traveled about through villages and towns, insisting that they followed the apostolic life, desiring neither possessions nor fixed abode. But the lord pope accused them of certain unsound practices in their way of life, to wit, that they cut away the tops of their shoes and so walked about as if barefooted; moreover, although they wore hoods after the manner of a religious order, they trimmed their hair only in the fashion of laymen. This also seemed reprehensible in respect of them, that men and women traveled the roads together, often lodged together in the same house, and, it was said, sometimes slept together in the same bed. All this they claimed to have received from the apostles.

But, in their stead, the lord pope did authorize certain others who were becoming known under the name of "the Lesser Poor" (*Pauperes minores*). These rejected the unsound and scandalous practices described above, but traveled completely barefoot both summer and winter and accepted neither money nor anything else except food for the day or sometimes a needed garment which someone might give them of his own volition, for they asked nothing of anyone. But subsequently, after reflecting that not infrequently a name for too much humility induces boastfulness and that in the name of poverty (since many bore it deceitfully) they were the more vainly boasting in the eyes of the Lord, this group chose to be called Friars Minor (*minores fratres*) rather than Lesser Poor, and to render obedience to the Apostolic See in all things.[32]

The others, that is to say, the Preachers, are considered to be successors to the Humiliati. Now the Humiliati, although they had no authorization or permission from prelates, thrust their sickle into the harvest of others,[33] preached to the people and often busied themselves with ordering their lives, hearing confessions, and disparaging the ministry of the priesthood. Out of a desire to rectify this situation, the lord pope established and confirmed the Order of Preachers. The former, who were indeed simple and unlearned folk, worked with their hands while preaching, and received their support from those who believed in them. The Preachers, on the other hand, put great emphasis upon study and reading of Holy Writ, worked only at copying books and most attentively hearing them expounded by their masters, so that they might be prepared to go forth with bow and arrows and "all the armor of valiant men"[34] to stand in defense of Holy Mother Church— "to go up against the enemy" and to place themselves as a "wall for the house of Israel."[35] While they strengthen the faith, they train and develop virtues and good habits, teach and extol the laws of the Church, reprove and correct the sins and depravities of men. Nevertheless, they are obedient in all things to the Apostolic See, from which they derive especial authority.

37. An Exposure of the Albigensian and Waldensian Heresies

The statement here translated enumerates the tenets of the Albigenses much as the manifesto of Bonacursus (No. 25) had done for the Italian Cathars, but this has more details and also includes some comments on the Waldenses. The sole manuscript in which it is found also contains a copy of the *Contra haereticos* of Ermengaud of Béziers, companion of Durand of Huesca [1]—a fact which, combined with the assertion, in the text, of the author's familiarity with Waldenses, led the editor to suggest that Ermengaud might have written this manifesto. Furthermore, it is not unlikely that it was one of the sources used by Peter of Vaux-de-Cernay, writing about 1213 (see No. 38). As to the date, Dondaine contented himself with the suggestion that this statement was perhaps as old as that of Bonacursus.[2] However, because of the author's concluding remarks on the need to use force against the heretics, we tentatively suggest a date nearer the beginning of the Albigensian Crusade.

On the situation in Languedoc at the beginning of the thirteenth century, in addition to the works cited in the introduction to Number 28, see these articles by Yves Dossat: "Cathares et Vaudois à la veille de la croisade albigeoise," *Revue historique et littéraire de Languedoc*, II (1945), 390-97, and III (1946), 70-83; "Le Clergé méridional à la veille de la croisade albigeoise," *Revue historique et littéraire de Languedoc*, I (1944), 263-78; "Le Comté de Toulouse et la féodalité languedocienne à la veille de la croisade albigeoise," *Revue de Tarn*, IX (1943), 75-90; "La Société méridionale à la veille de la croisade albigeoise," *Revue historique et littéraire de Languedoc*, I (1944), 66-87. See also Delaruelle, "Le Catharisme en Languedoc," *Annales du Midi*, LXXII (1960), 149-67.

The translation is made from the text printed in Antoine Dondaine, "Durand de Huesca et la polémique anti-cathare," *Archivum fratrum praedicatorum*, XXIX (1959), 268-71, by permission of the Istituto storico domenicano di S. Sabina.

1208-1213

The group of heretics inhabiting our region, that is to say, the dioceses of Narbonne, Béziers, Carcassonne, Toulouse, Albi, Rodez, Cahors, Agen, and Périgueux, believe and have the effrontery to say that there are two gods, that is, a good God and a strange god, using the text of Jeremiah: "As you have forsaken me," He said, "and served a strange god in your own land, so you shall serve strangers in a land not your own." [3] The present world and all that is visible therein, they declare, were created and made by the malign god, for they show by whatever arguments they can command that these are evil. Of the world they say that it is "wholly seated in wickedness," [4] and that "a good tree cannot bring forth evil fruit, neither can an evil tree bring forth good fruit." [5] They hold that all good things came from the good God and from the evil one all evil things. The Mosaic law, they say, was imparted by the evil god, for they cite from the words of the Apostle, "The Law is one of sin and death" and "worketh wrath." [6] They declare that when Christ gave the bread to His disciples, He told them, "Take ye and eat," and, touching Himself with His hand, said, "This is my body"; [7] wherefore they do not believe that anyone consecrates the Host. They speak slightingly of marriage of the flesh because Christ said, "Whoever shall look on a woman," [8] and so on. They reject baptism of children performed with actual water because children do not have faith, for which they cite the Gospel, "He that believeth not shall be condemned." [9] They do not believe in the resurrection of the bodies of this world, for Paul said, "Flesh and blood cannot possess the kingdom of God." [10] Whatever is ritually observed in the Church Universal they call vain and absurd, for they hold that doctrine to be a thing of men and without basis, whereby one worships God in vain.

In their secret meetings their elders recount that the wicked god first fashioned his creatures and at the beginning of his act of creation, made four beings, two male and two female, a lion and a bee-eater, [11] an eagle and a spirit. The good God took from him the spirit and the eagle and with them He produced the things which He made.[12] After a long time, the malign god, enraged by his spoliation, sent a certain son of his, whom they call Melchizedek, Seir, or Lucifer,[13] with a great and splendid host of men and women to the court of the good God, to find whether guile might not avenge his father for his own. And on beholding him, distinguished in beauty and intelligence, the good God appointed him prince, priest, and steward over His own people, and through him gave a testament[14] to the people of Israel. In the absence of the Lord, he beguiled the people into disbelief of the truth, promising them that much more, better, and delightful things than those which they had in their own land would be given them in his.[15] They yielded to his blandishments, spurning their God and the testament given them. He bore away some of them and scattered them throughout his realms. The more noble, a designation which these people took to themselves, he sent into this world, which they call the last lake, the farthest earth, and the deepest hell. He sent the souls, so they say, leaving the bodies prostrate in the desert, abandoned by the spirits, for, as John says in the Apocalypse, "The great dragon, that old serpent, devil and Satan, struck with his tail the third part of the stars and dashed them to earth."[16] Such, they say, are "the sheep which are lost of the house of Israel,"[17] to whom Christ was sent, as He himself says in the Gospel: "The Son of man is come to seek and to save that which was lost";[18] and also, "The Son of man came not to destroy souls but to save."[19] That Seir, as they assert, was the father of the lawgiver, for which they cite in the Law: "The Lord came from Sinai, and from Seir he was born to us";[20] and in Ezechiel, "Son of man, set thy face against Mount Seir, and prophesy concerning it, and say to it: Behold, Mount Seir, and I will make thee desolate and waste. I will destroy thy cities and thou shalt be desolate; and thou shalt know that I am the Lord, because thou hast been an everlasting enemy and hast shut up the children of Israel in the hands of the sword."[21] Also, they say that the malign god exists without beginning or end, and rules as many and as extensive lands, heavens, people, and creatures as the good God. The present world, they say, will never pass away or be depopulated.[22] They have the daring to assert that the Blessed Mary, mother of Christ, was not of this world. For they say in their secret meetings that Christ, in whom they hope for salvation, was not in this world except in a spiritual sense within the body of Paul, citing Paul himself: "Do you seek a proof of Christ that speaketh in me?"[23] For they say that Paul, "sold under sin,"[24] brought the Scriptures into this world and was held prisoner, that he might reveal the ministry of Christ.

For they believe that Christ was born in the "land of the living,"[25] of Joseph and Mary, whom they say were Adam and Eve; there He suffered and rose again; thence He ascended to His Father; there He did and said all that was recorded of Him in the New Testament. With this testament, and with His disciples, His father and mother, He passed through seven realms, and thence freed His people. In that land of the living, they believe, there are cities and outside them castles, villages and woodlands, meadows, pastures, sweet water and salt, beasts of the forest and domestic animals, dogs and birds for the hunt, gold and silver, utensils of various kinds, and furniture. They also say that everyone shall have his wife there and sometimes a mistress. They shall eat and drink, play and sleep, and do all things just as they do in the world of the present. And all will be, as they say, well pleasing to God when "the saints shall rejoice in glory; they shall be joyful in their beds," and when they shall have "two-edged swords in their hands to execute vengeance upon the nations," and when the children of Zion shall praise his name in choir and with the timbrel, for "this glory will be to all his saints."[26] For God himself, they say, has two wives, Collam and Colibam,[27] and from them He engendered sons and daughters, as do humans. On the basis of this belief, some of them hold there is no sin in man and woman kissing and embracing each other, or even lying together for intercourse, nor can one sin in doing so for payment.

They also believe that when the soul leaves the human body, it passes to another body, either of a human or of a beast, unless the person shall have died while under their instruction. If, however, he shall have died while continuing steadfast among them, they say that the soul goes to a new earth, prepared by God for all the souls that are to be saved, where it finds clothing, that is, the body prepared for it by its own father and mother. There all await the general resurrection which they shall experience, so they say, in the land of the living, with all their inheritance which they shall recover by force of arms. For they say that until then they shall possess that land of the malign spirit and shall make use of the clothing of the sheep, and shall eat the good things of the earth, and shall not depart thence until all Israel is saved. Also they teach in their secret meetings that Mary Magdalen was the wife of Christ. She was the Samaritan woman to whom He said, "Call thy husband."[28] She was the woman taken in adultery, whom Christ set free lest the Jews stone her, and she was with Him in three places, in the temple, at the well, and in the garden.[29] After the Resurrection, He appeared first to her. They say that John the Baptist is one of the chief malign spirits.

And thus they are diverse and cut off from other men by faith and practice; so also among themselves they adopt various heresies and each one strives with all his might to find something novel and unheard of. He will be accounted the wisest who can invent the greatest novelty. There is, moreover, a certain heresy which recently has sprung up among them, for some of them believe that there is only one god,[30] whom they say had two sons, Christ and the prince of this world, for which they cite the Gospel, "A certain man had two sons."[31] They believe that both sons committed sins but that Christ, with all His people, is now reconciled with the Father.[32] And they say that the Last Judgment has already been pronounced: The sheep and the wise virgins have received the kingdom with the Bridegroom; the goats and the foolish virgins have been cast out into the present darkness to be punished. They also say that whatever happens to anyone, good fortune or bad, comes by judgment or destiny; a good man prospers no more than a bad one, but in the reconciliation of the Son, all shall be reconciled.

There are, moreover, other heretics, who are called "the Lyonists," from Lyons; "the Waldenses," from Waldes; "the Poor," because they say they take no thought for the morrow; "the Sandal-shod," because they wear perforated footgear.[33] From Catalonia to the sea at Narbonne and thence to the sea at Bordeaux, these persons publicly confess the Catholic faith by mouth but not in heart, yet in their secret meetings, with which I am in fact very familiar, they say that they alone, as disciples of Christ, have the right to baptize. Whence they baptize the children of their believers and of those who shelter them whenever they can. Out of this practive, the sect of Rebaptizers arose from them.[34] They also believe and say that one sins criminally in inflicting or approving the infliction of bodily punishment on malefactors; so also does one who takes an oath. They say in addition that if anyone intending to offer an oblation to a priest or before an altar should meet a pauper, he ought rather to give it to the poor man, for such an act is more blessed than to make offering. Revisiting a cemetery, asperging with exorcised water, employing incense, saying Mass for the dead avail naught, so they say. They also believe—and it is shameful to recount it—that the Roman Church gives them no more of a spiritual viaticum than may any man or woman of their number, lacking ecclesiastical garb or without tonsure; and such have the right to consecrate the Host. They say further, that no one can be perfect and thus no one can be saved unless he die completely a pauper and—let me confess the truth—they trouble and attack the Church of God more than other heretics. And it seems to me that neither those persons nor the others can be wholly extirpated except by the secular arm.[35]

38. A Description of Cathars and Waldenses by Peter of Vaux-de-Cernay

The following account was written by a young Cistercian monk of the abbey of Vaux-de-Cernay, some twenty-five miles southwest of Paris. His uncle, Guy, had been abbot of the monastery since 1184; when Guy joined the Albigensian crusaders in Languedoc in 1212 he took Peter with him. There, during the following six years, Peter spent a considerable portion of his time following the army of Simon of Montfort, and there he wrote the history of the crusade up to the death of Simon in 1218. The work appears to have been written in parts; the first of these, from which the following excerpt is taken, was probably composed in 1213. The author had robust prejudices, which, coupled with his enthusiasm for the miraculous, might lead the reader to question the authenticity of the work. He did have good sources of information, however; in many of the events of which he writes he was himself a participant, and where his facts can be checked by other accounts he displays a high degree of accuracy. His biases are so evident and forthright that they may be readily discounted by the reader. The piece here translated shows an excellent grasp of the tenets of the Cathars, despite the fact that Peter seems to have been a young man—possibly scarcely more than twenty years of age—when he wrote. As we mentioned earlier, it has been suggested that Peter drew on "An Exposure of the Heresies of the Albigenses and Waldenses" (translated in No. 37); there are indeed similarities between the two accounts, but also considerable differences. Peter's narrative ends abruptly, shortly after the death of Simon of Montfort, and nothing further is known of the author.

The *Hystoria albigensis* has been several times edited, translated into French, and commented upon, but the edition by Guébin and Lyon supersedes all previous ones, and the best discussion of the author and his work appears therein (III, i-cvii). To that edition we are indebted for several of our notes. A French translation was published by Guébin and Henri Maisonneuve under the title *Histoire albigeoise* (Paris, 1951).

Our translation is from *Petri Vallium Sarnaii monachi Hystoria albigensis* I.5-19, ed. by Pascal Guébin and Ernest Lyon (3 vols., Paris, 1926-1939), I, 5-20. The work was published by the Librairie Honoré Champion.

circa 1213

   Part I: Concerning the Heretics

   ... [5] *In the Name of Our Lord Jesus Christ, and to His Glory and Honor, Here Begins the History of the Albigenses.*[1]—In the province of Narbonne, where once the faith had flourished, the enemy of the faith began to oversow cockle.[2] The people became fatuous; by profaning the sacraments of Christ, who is the savor and wisdom of God, they were rendered foolish; turning aside from true reverence (*theosebia*), they wandered hither and yon through the pathless waste of error, "where there was no passing, and out of the way."[3]

   [6] Two Cistercian monks, Brother Peter of Castelnau and Brother Ralph,[4] burning with zeal for the faith, were by the supreme pontiff commissioned as legates to fight against the pestilence of infidelity. Casting off all sloth and performing with great diligence the mission entrusted to them, they boldly entered and assailed the city of Toulouse, which was the principal source of the baleful poison that was infecting the people and was thus turning them from the knowledge of Christ, from His true splendor, from His divine radiance.[5] "The root of bitterness, springing up to hinder,"[6] had so deeply embedded itself in the hearts of men that it could be eradicated only with great difficulty. The people of Toulouse had been urged frequently and earnestly to abjure heresy and expel the heretics. Urged they had been by apostolic men, but not at all persuaded;[7] with such tenacity, indeed, had those who had abandoned life clung to death, weakened and poisoned by base cleverness, sensual, earthly, devilish, having no part in that "wisdom that is from above, easy to be persuaded, consenting to the good."[8]

   [7] Finally, those "two olive trees," those "two candlesticks" shining before the Lord,[9] struck slavish terror in the servile, threatened them with the loss of their property, forcefully assured them of the wrath of kings and princes, and thus persuaded them to abjure heresy and expel the heretics. They ceased to sin, not from love of virtue, but rather, as

the poet says, from fear of punishment.[10] This they made abundantly clear; for immediately they committed perjury and suffered a return to their wretched condition, and secreted heretics who, under cover of darkness, preached in their assemblies. Alas, how difficult it is to break with old habit!

[8] This Toulouse, totally sunk in deceit,[11] is said from the very day of its founding rarely or never to have been free from the abominable pestilence of this heretical depravity, the poison of superstitious infidelity being handed down from fathers to sons over the generations. For this reason, and in punishment for such wickedness, she is said justly to have suffered a long time ago the hand of the avenger and the destruction of her people to the point that the plow had extended the open fields to the very center of the city. Indeed, one of their most renowned kings, named Alaric, I believe, who was then ruling in the city, suffered the ultimate disgrace of hanging from a gibbet before the gates.[12]

[9] Fouled by the dregs of that ancient slime, the brood of Toulouse, a "generation of vipers,"[13] could not, even in our day, be torn from the root of its perversity; nay rather, on every occasion it permits the return of heretical nature and natural heresy, "driven out by the pitchfork" of condign vengeance,[14] and thirsts to follow in the footsteps of its fathers and spurns a breach with the past. "Just as one bunch of grapes takes on its sickly color from the aspect of its neighbor, and in the fields the scab of one sheep or the mange of one pig destroys an entire herd,"[15] so, influenced by the proximity of Toulouse, neighboring towns and villages in which heresiarchs had put down their roots were wonderfully and woefully infected by this spreading disease as the sprouts of its infidelity multiplied. The nobles of the Provençal land[16] had nearly all become defenders and receivers[17] of heretics; they warmly cherished and protected them against God and the Church.

[10] *Concerning the Sects of Heretics.*—Since this seems an appropriate place, I think it worthwhile to describe with clarity and brevity the heresies and sects of heretics. It should first be understood that the heretics postulated[18] two creators, to wit, one of the invisible world, whom they called the benign God, and one of the visible world, or the malign god. They ascribed the New Testament to the benign God, the Old Testament to the malign one; the latter book they wholly rejected, except for a few passages which have found their way into the

New Testament and which on this account they esteemed worthy of acceptance. They claimed that the author of the Old Testament was a liar in that he said to our first ancestors, "In what day soever thou shalt eat of the tree of knowledge of good and evil thou shalt die the death";[19] but they did not die as he had said, after eating of it (although in reality they were subject to the pitiable limitations of death immediately upon eating the forbidden fruit). They also called him a murderer because he burned the people of Sodom and Gomorrah and destroyed the world in the flood, and also because he overwhelmed Pharaoh and the Egyptians in the Red Sea. They held that all the patriarchs of the Old Testament were damned, and declared that St. John the Baptist was one of the greatest devils.

[11] The heretics even affirmed in their secret assemblies that the Christ who was born in terrestrial and visible Bethlehem and crucified in Jerusalem was evil, and that Mary Magdalen was his concubine and the very woman taken in adultery of whom we read in the Gospel;[20] for the good Christ, they said, never ate nor drank nor took on real flesh, and was never of this world, except in a spiritual sense in the body of Paul. That is why we said "born in terrestrial and visible Bethlehem," because the heretics professed to believe that there is another new and invisible land, in which, according to certain of them, the good Christ was born and was crucified. The heretics also taught that the good God had two wives, Oolla and Ooliba [*sic*], upon whom He begat sons and daughters. There were other heretics, who said that there is but one Creator, who had two sons, Christ and the devil. And these also said that all created beings were originally good, but that by the vials of which we read in the Apocalypse all things were corrupted.[21]

[12] All of these, limbs of Antichrist, the first born of Satan, "wicked seed, ungracious children," "speaking lies in hypocrisy," "seducing the hearts of the innocent,"[22] corrupted almost the whole province of Narbonne with the poison of their perfidy. They called the Roman Church a "den of thieves" and that harlot of whom we read in Apocalypse.[23] They held as naught the sacraments of the Church to the point of teaching publicly that the water of holy baptism differs not at all from water of a river; that the consecrated bread of the most holy body of Christ is no different from ordinary bread; instilling into the ears of simple folk the blasphemy that the body of Christ, even were it as great as the Alps, would long since have been completely consumed by

communicants who partook of it;[24] that confirmation, extreme unction, and confession are trifling and silly matters; and that holy matrimony is nothing else than harlotry, nor can anyone fathering sons and daughters in that state achieve salvation. They denied the resurrection of the body; they concocted certain unheard-of fables, averring that our souls are those of angelic spirits who were thrown out of heaven because of the apostasy of pride and who left their glorified bodies in the ether. These souls, after successive indwellings in any seven terrestrial bodies whatsoever, return again to those bodies which they had left, as though they had thus completed their penance.

[13] Now, it must be understood that certain of the heretics were called the Perfect or the Good Men; the others were called the believers of heretics. Those who were called Perfect wore a black mantle; they falsely claimed that they kept themselves chaste; they wholly refused to eat meat, eggs, or cheese; they sought to give the impression of never telling a lie, when they lied constantly, especially concerning God; and they held that one should never for any reason take an oath. Those were called believers of heretics who, while living in the world, did not strive to attain the life of the perfected, but hoped nonetheless to achieve salvation in their faith; they differed, indeed, in their manner of life, but in faith (or, rather, in infidelity) they were at one. Those who were called believers were absorbed in usuries, robberies, murders, sins of the flesh, perjuries, and all sorts of perversities. They felt, in truth, more secure and unbridled in their sinning because they believed that they would be saved, without restitution of ill-gotten gains, without confession and penance, so long as they were able in the last throes of death to repeat the Lord's Prayer and receive the imposition of hands by their officials.

[14] For they had among the perfected heretics a hierarchy whom they called "deacons" and "bishops,"[25] without the imposition of whose hands just prior to death no one of the believers thought he could attain salvation. Indeed, if the officials imposed their hands upon anyone about to die, however profligate he might be, so long as he was able to repeat the Lord's Prayer they believed him to be saved, and, as they commonly said, "consoled," so that, with no reparation, without further good works, his soul would immediately fly up to heaven.

[15] Here, I am minded to recount an absurdity which, I am told, occurred in connection with the above. A certain believer of heretics,

in the last throes of death, received the consolamentum[26] through the imposition of hands by his master but was unable to repeat the Lord's Prayer. And thus he died. The one who consoled him was at a loss to know what to say about him; he appeared to be saved through the imposition of hands but likewise to be damned through his failure to repeat the Lord's Prayer. What further? The heretics took counsel with a certain heretical knight, Bertrand of Saissac,[27] about the decision that should be made in the case. The knight gave his counsel and reply as follows: "In the case of this man, I should support him and declare him to be saved. It is my judgment that all others, unless at the last moment they have repeated the Lord's Prayer, are damned."

[16] And here is another absurdity: A certain believer of heretics at death bequeathed to them three hundred sous and bade his son to remit that sum to the heretics. But when, upon the father's death, the heretics asked the son for this legacy, he said to them: "Tell me first, if you please, how it is with my father now." They replied: "You may be sure that he is saved and is already gathered with the spirits above." To which the son smilingly rejoined: "Thanks be to God and to you! Of a surety, since my father is already in glory his soul has no further need of alms; and I know you to be so kindly that you would not now recall my father from glory. Be assured, therefore, that you will receive no money from me."

[17] Nor do I think the remark of certain heretics that no one can sin from the waist down should be passed over in silence.[28] They called the placing of images in churches idolatry; insisted that church bells are trumpets of devils; averred that one sins no more grievously in sleeping with mother or sister than with anyone else; and, among the most extreme heretical follies, they affirmed that if any one of the perfected should commit mortal sin (for example, by eating the very smallest morsel of meat, cheese, egg, or any other food forbidden to them), all those consoled by him lose the Holy Spirit and must be reconsoled; and they even said that those already saved fall from heaven because of the sin of the one who consoled them.

[18] Besides these, there were other heretics, called Waldenses from a certain Waldes, a citizen of Lyons. These were bad enough, but in comparison with the other heretics they were much less wicked. Indeed, on many matters they were in agreement with us, on others they differed. But to pass over many points of their unbelief, their error con-

sisted chiefly in four things: to wit, in the wearing of sandals after the fashion of the apostles; in their refusal, under any circumstances, to swear an oath; [their refusal] to take life; and in their claim that any one of them in case of necessity, so long as he is a sandal-wearer (*haberet sandalia*) may perform the sacrament of the Eucharist, even though he may not have been ordained by a bishop. This brief survey of the heretical sects seems to us sufficient.

[19] *The Method of Conversion, or Rather Perversion, of the Heretics.*—When one yields himself to the heretics, the one who receives him addresses him as follows: "My friend, if you wish to become one of us you must renounce all belief in the tenets of the Roman Church." He replies: "I renounce it." "Receive, then, the Spirit from the good men"; and he breathes in his mouth seven times.[29] Again, he says to him: "Do you renounce that cross which at baptism the priest made with oil and chrism on your breast, shoulders, and head?" He replies: "I renounce it." "Do you believe that that water effects your salvation?" He replies: "I do not believe that." "Do you renounce the veil which at baptism the priest places upon your head?" He replies: "I renounce it." Thus he receives the baptism of the heretics and rejects the baptism of the Church. Then all place their hands upon his head, kiss him, and clothe him in a black mantle. From that hour he is as one of them.

Heretical Movements in Northern Europe, 1155-1216

39. An Incident at Cologne in 1163

Two decades after Eberwin had appealed to St. Bernard for counsel about heretics in Cologne (No. 16), another discovery of heretical activity alarmed the city. The group now detected was small; perhaps these heretics had persisted quietly in the Rhineland over the two decades, or they may have been refugees from the prosecutions then being mounted in Flanders.[1] Once discovered, they faced formidable accusers. In addition to the usual array of the city's clergy, Eckbert, a monk of nearby Schönau who claimed previous experience with heretics, may have been called into the investigation; he subsequently wrote an antiheretical tract in the form of thirteen sermons.[2] The saintly Hildegard of Bingen also wrote and preached against the heresy.[2] In Eckbert's work and in the chronicles are the earliest uses of the sect name "Cathar." The doctrines were probably those of mitigated dualism, but it is not easy to tell from Eckbert's diatribes because he places so much reliance on St. Augustine's description of the ancient Manichaeans.[3] He does make it clear, however, that all heretics of the time were not in perfect agreement.[4]

Several of the entries in the chronicles about this episode are reprinted in Fredericq, *Corpus*, I, 40-44, and there are brief notices in Lea, *History of the Inquisition*, I, 112-13, and Theloe, *Die Ketzerverfolgungen*, pp. 57-58; see also Thouzellier, "Hérésie et croisade," *Revue d'histoire ecclésiastique*, XLIX (1954), 862-65.

More than half a century later, the burning at Cologne was recalled by Caesarius of Heisterbach, who, characteristically, was able to make an interesting story out of it without being explicit about the heretics' errors. Caesarius (*ca.* 1170-*ca.* 1240) was a monk of the Cistercian community at Heisterbach, near Bonn. As master of the novices, charged with their instruction in theology, he produced for their enlightenment his best-known work, the *Dialogus miraculorum*, a mine of information on many aspects of contemporary life, even though Caesarius was often a vague reporter of historical events, with a taste for tales of the marvelous. The work has been translated into English by Henry von Essen Scott and C. C. Swinton Bland, as *The Dialogue on Miracles*.

The present translation is made from *Caesarii Heisterbacensis dialogus miraculorum* v.xix, ed. by Joseph Strange (2 vols., Cologne, 1851), I, 298-99.

August 5, 1163

About this time, several heretics were apprehended at Cologne, under Archbishop Rainald,[5] and after they were examined and convicted by learned men, they were condemned by secular authority. After sentence had been imposed and when they were about to be dragged away to the pyre, one of them, Arnold by name, whom the others acknowledged as their master,[6] asked (as persons who were present tell it) to be given bread and a bowl of water. The more prudent persons dissuaded the ones who wished to comply with his request, saying that by the devil's help something might be done with these to bring scandal and ruin on the weak.

NOVICE: I wonder what he wanted to do with the bread and water.

MONK: I suppose, from the words of another heretic, who was seized and burned by the king of Spain three years ago, he wanted to perform a sacrilegious communion with them which might be a viaticum to eternal damnation for his companions. For a Spanish abbot of our order, who had joined the bishops and prelates of the Church in condemning the errors of this heretic, when he visited us while on his travels, quoted the man as saying that any countryman could make the body of Christ out of his own bread at his own table.[7] This cursed fellow was a blacksmith.

NOVICE: What was done with the heretics at Cologne?

MONK: They were taken outside the town, near the cemetery of the Jews, and all cast into the fire together. And as many stood to watch and listen while they fiercely burned, Arnold, putting his hand on the heads of his disciples who were already aflame, said, "Be firm in your faith, for today you shall be with Lawrence"[8]—although theirs was quite unlike the faith of Lawrence. Now there was among them a girl, comely but a heretic. She was led away from the fire, thanks to the pity of some persons who promised that they either would see her married or, if it suited her better, would place her in a nunnery. She had apparently agreed to this. But after the heretics were dead, she said to those holding her, "Tell me, where lies that seducer?" And when they pointed out to her the master, Arnold, wrenching herself from their grasp, she covered her face with her robe and threw herself upon the body of the dead man, with him descending into hell to burn forever.[9]

40. The Fate of Heretics in England

This episode is the most important occurrence of heresy in England in the twelfth century of which we have record.[1] The heretics came from abroad, from Flanders or the Rhineland, and while no report of their doctrines is explicit enough to assure us that they were Cathars, this is not unlikely. In the chief source, William of Newburgh's history, their arrival is placed about 1161, but a somewhat later date is more probable, for they apparently were not condemned at Oxford until 1165 or 1166 and it is difficult to reconcile a sojourn of even four years with the author's statements that they lived only a little while in England and that they were unable to escape suspicion because of their foreign origin.[2] Other accounts of the incident in English chronicles give no help in the dating.

On William of Newburgh, see the introduction to Number 18. The best recent treatment of the incident is in Russèll, *Dissent and Reform*, pp. 224-27, with discussion of the date on p. 309, n. 79.

Our translation is from *Willelmi Parvi, canonici de Novoburgo, historia rerum anglicarum* I.xiii, ed. by Richard Howlett, in *Chronicles of the Reigns of Stephen, Henry II, and Richard I* (Rolls Series, LXXXII [4 vols., London, 1884-1889]), I, 131-34. The same passage has appeared in an excellent English translation by David C. Douglas and George W. Greenaway, in *English Historical Documents*, II, 329-30.

1161-1166

In those days there came to England certain erring folk of the sect commonly thought to be called Publicans.[3] These seem to have originated in Gascony under an unknown founder, and they spread the poison of their infidelity in a great many regions; for in the broad lands of France, Spain, Italy, and Germany so many are said to be infected with this pestilence that, as the Psalmist of old complained, they seem to have multiplied beyond number.[4] For everywhere, when prelates of the Church and princes of the provinces act too leniently toward them, the wicked foxes come forth from their holes and, under an appearance of piety, seduce the simple folk, grievously and openly laying waste the vineyard of the Lord of hosts.[5] However, when the zeal of the faithful is kindled against them by the fire of God, they hide away in their dens and are less harmful, but still they cease not to do harm by spreading their secret poison. Countryfolk, uneducated and sluggish of mind, once they are poisoned by a draught of this virus, stubbornly resist all discipline; whence it very rarely chances that any of them, when they are discovered and dragged from their hiding places, are converted to piety. Truly, England has always been free of this and other heretical pestilences, even though so many heresies have spread in other parts of the world. Indeed, when this island was called Britain from its inhabitants, the Britons, it sent forth to the East Pelagius,[6] who subsequently became a heresiarch, and in the course of time it gave admittance to his error, to destroy which the Gallican church with pious foresight twice sent the Most Blessed Germanus.[7] But when, after the Britons were driven out, the nation of Angles took possession of this island and it came to be called England instead of Britain, no poison of this heresy ever bubbled up from it, nor, until the time of Henry II, did any such come from abroad to be propagated and extended here. And then, indeed, by God's help such resistance was offered to the pestilence which crept in that in the future it must fear to invade this island.

There were some thirty or more men and women who came here in the guise of peaceable persons—hiding their error, the more readily to spread the pestilence—under the leadership of one Gerard,[8] whom they all looked up to as teacher and guide. For he alone had a smattering of learning; the others were entirely uneducated and stupid, uncouth and loutish, Germans by birth and speech.[9] After living a little while in England, they added to their company only one poor woman, who was deceived by their poisonous whisperings and, so it is said, was entranced by certain sorceries. They could not lie hidden for long, but after careful investigation by certain persons because of their foreign origin, they were arrested, confined, and held in public custody. Being unwilling to release or punish them without examination, the king ordered an episcopal synod to meet at Oxford. There, when the heretics had been solemnly charged in the matter of their faith, they declared (he who seemed to be educated undertaking the cause of all and speaking for all) that they were Christians and that they venerated apostolic teaching. When they were questioned systematically upon the articles of holy faith, they answered correctly enough on the nature of the Celestial Physician, but as to the remedies by which He deigns to heal human infirmities—that is, the divine sacraments—they gave wrong replies. They scorned holy baptism, the Eucharist, and matrimony, and with wicked rashness they disparaged the Catholic unity which these divine aids instill. When they were challenged by divine texts drawn from the Holy Scriptures, they answered that they believed what they had been taught and were unwilling to argue about their faith. Being warned that they should repent and be united to the body of the Church, they rejected all wholesome advice. They laughed at threats uttered in all piety against them in the hope that through fear they might be brought to their senses, and misapplied the word of the Lord, "Blessed are they that suffer persecution for justice's sake, for theirs is the kingdom of heaven."[10] Thereupon, the bishops, taking precautions lest the heretical poison should spread more widely, publicly denounced them as heretics and handed them over to His Catholic Highness for corporal punishment. He commanded that the brand of heretical infamy be burned on their brows, that they be flogged in the presence of the people, and that they be driven out of the city. And he strictly enjoined anyone from presuming to give them shelter or offer them any comfort. When the sentence had been declared, they were led away, rejoicing in their just punishment, their master leading them jauntily and chanting, "Blessed are ye when men shall revile you."[11] To such an extent did the deceiver abuse the minds of those he had seduced! But the woman whom they had led astray in England abandoned them out of fear of punishment and, by confessing her error, obtained reconciliation. Then the detestable group were branded on the brows, and suffered a just severity—as a mark of his primacy he who was their leader receiving a double brand on brow and chin. Stripped of their clothing to the waist and publicly flogged with resounding blows, they were driven out of the city, and perished miserably in the bitter cold, for it was winter and no one offered them the slightest pity. This pious harshness not only purged the kingdom of England of that pestilence which crept in at this time but, by striking the heretics with terror, prevented it from ever again intruding.[12]

41. *"Publicans" at Vézelay*

Heresy occurred at Vézelay in 1167 in the midst of civic tumult and a monastery's contest against episcopal and secular interference. Evidence about the nature of the heresy is inconclusive; in some ways the errors are reminiscent of the teaching of Henry and Peter of Bruys, but they may reflect Catharist doctrine. The author of the history from which this account is taken was Hugh of Poitiers, who spent his adult life in the monastery of Ste. Madeleine in Vézelay, where he began to write a history of the monastery in 1156 at the bidding of Abbot Pons.[1] The work was divided into four books, the first a chartulary of the monastery; the other three a history of the period from 1140 to 1167. The second book emphasizes the quarrel between the abbots of Ste. Madeleine and the bishops of Autun, who were disputing the abbot's claims to immunity from their control. The third and fourth recount the struggles of the abbots against the enchroachments of the counts of Nevers—which drew to an end only in 1166—as well as their conflicts with the townsmen of Vézelay, who in 1152 revolted against the abbot as their temporal lord.[2] It was during these conflicts that Hugh wrote his history, the last entry in which is the story of the heresy, appended to the narrative, seemingly apropos of nothing that went before. The history has been preserved only in mutilated condition. Hugh wrote from his own experience; probably he was among the group who examined the heretics, although this is not stated in his own words. For a brief discussion of the author and his work, see *Histoire littéraire de la France*, XII, 688-75. There is only passing reference to the incident at Vézelay in the literature on heresy; see Havet, "L'Hérésie et le bras séculier," *Bibliothèque de l'école des chartes*, XLI (1880), 510-12; and Theloe, *Die Ketzerverfolgungen*, pp. 43-46.

The only complete edition of Hugh's *Historia Vizeliacensis monasterii* is that of Luc d'Achéry, which was republished in *Recueil des historiens des Gaules et de la France*, ed. by Bouquet *et al.* (24 vols., Paris, 1738-1904), XII, 317-44; the portion translated here is found on pp. 343-44. D'Achéry's edition was also republished in Migne, *Patrologia latina*, CXCIV, 1561-1682.

1167

At this time, certain heretics who are called *Deonarii* or Publicans[3] were arrested at Vézelay. Brought up for examination, they sought to conceal the utterly loathsome tenets of their heresy by evasion and circumlocutions. So the abbot ordered them placed in solitary confinement until their guilt could be established by bishops and other distinguished persons who were being called together.[4] They were held for some sixty days or more, and were frequently brought before the gathering and questioned—now with threats and again with soft words— about the Catholic faith. At length, after the vain expenditure of much effort, with the advice and assistance of the archbishops of Lyons[5] and Narbonne,[6] the bishop of Nevers,[7] several abbots, and many other learned men, they were adjudged guilty of the charge that, while paying lip service to the unity of the Divine Essence, they rejected absolutely all the holy sacraments of the Universal Church: specifically, the baptism of children, the Eucharist, the seal of the life-giving Cross, sprinkling with holy water, the building of churches, good works in tithes and offerings, the marital relations of husband and wife, the monastic life, and all the functions of clergy and priests. As the celebration of Easter began, two of them, realizing that they were very near to being condemned to a fiery death, pretended that their belief was that of the

Universal Church and, for peace with the Church, they would seek purgation by the ordeal of water.

Therefore, during the solemn Easter procession they were brought before a great throng which filled the whole cloister, where were present Guichard, archbishop of Lyons; Bernard, bishop of Nevers; and Master Walter, bishop of Laon;[8] together with Abbot William of Vézelay. They were questioned on each tenet of the faith, and declared that they held absolutely the beliefs of the Universal Church. To questions about the abominable mystery of their error, they replied that they knew no more than the aforesaid denial of the sacraments of the Church. When asked if they would prove by ordeal of water that they believed what they professed and knew nothing more of the mystery of error, they answered that they would willingly undertake to do so, without further judgment. At this, the entire congregation exclaimed with one voice, "Thanks be to God!" The abbot, addressing the whole assemblage, asked, "Brethren, what is your advice for dealing with those who still remain obdurate?" and all answered, "Let them be burned! Let them be burned!"

On the following day, the two men, who gave the appearance of having recanted, were conducted to the judgment by ordeal of water. In everyone's opinon, one of them was acquitted by the water (nevertheless, there were some who thought it a dubious decision). On the other hand, the second man, when plunged into the water, was declared guilty by nearly unanimous acclaim. Remanded to confinement, since opinion was not unanimous even among the clergy, he again underwent the ordeal of water, at his own request, and was a second time immersed, but the water scarcely received him at all. Thus twice condemned, he was sentenced by all to the fire. But the abbot came to his assistance and ordered instead that he be banished after a public flogging. Others of the accused, however, to the number of seven, were given to the flames and were burned in the vale of Ecouan.[9]

42. From Heresy to Witchcraft

Magic and sorcery, like other manifestations of superstition, are not confined to one age; their roots lie in the early history of man, and their expression is conditioned by the times. The Middle Ages inherited a substantial residue of pagan magic, which was transmuted and modified under Christian influence; pagan deities, for example, were often numbered among the demons, whose existence not even the Church doubted. To speak only in the general terms to which we are limited here, magic and sorcery were regarded in the Middle Ages, as in all times, as means of controlling the environment, including one's fellow men. Spirits might be invoked to bring rain or drought, wind or burning heat, disease or fatal accident, to men, animals, or plants. With demonic aid, the future might be foretold. Occult forces could even be summoned in aid of good causes.

The Church and its priesthood might use its power to avert harm from malign spirits, but it frowned on the use of magic to enlist the aid of the spirit world.[1] Penitential books contain many references to penances prescribed for those who sought to control occult powers; the canon entitled *Episcopi*, of uncertain date but current by the late ninth century, set forth what was for long the guiding principle of ecclesiastical authority in disciplining those who practiced or believed in sorcery or magic: If they persisted, the local bishop should excommunicate them and expel them from his diocese.[2]

Yet belief in the interference of the spirit world in human affairs could not be easily eradicated. Innumerable stories of demonic activity, and learned explanations of how spirits were permitted to operate within the providence of God, attest that magic and sorcery were given wide credence at every level of society. Though the Church censured the belief in man's ability to invoke demons, such belief was not initially considered heresy. Only slowly did the Church come to emphasize the danger that communing with demons might involve veneration of them, which is heresy.

There have already appeared in these pages accounts of nocturnal gatherings in which the devil was worshiped, and of magical powers—manifested in levitation, appearance and disappearance at will, and illusory banquets— which heretics exercised with demonic assistance.[3] The two narratives translated here throw light on the relationship between magic, witchcraft, and heresy in popular opinion in the last quarter of the twelfth century. Yet not until the middle of the thirteenth century did the Church adopt the position that all dabbling with occult powers involved demon-worship; and even so, official prosecution of witchcraft did not begin in earnest until some time thereafter. To trace the ensuing developments would take us beyond the limits of this volume, but some of the antecedents of the witchcraft epidemic of early modern times may be indicated here.

In the second quarter of the thirteenth century, certain inquisitors sought to bring within their purview cases in which individuals were thought to have entered into pacts with the devil, pacts whereby they were granted special powers in this world, at the cost of their souls. Between 1231 and 1233, for example, Conrad of Marburg, commissioned by Gregory IX to act against heresy in Germany, revealed to the pope testimony about a cult of demon-worship and was urged most emphatically to press his investigations and to root out the evil.[4] Yet in 1258 and 1260 Pope Alexander IV, in reply to questions from inquisitors about the scope of their authority and the proper procedure to be followed, counseled them that they confine their activities to searching out and punishing heretics, that they take cognizance of divination and sorcery only when manifest heresy was involved. Through that loophole some cases of witchcraft did find their way into the courts of the Inquisition from the end of the thirteenth century on, but it was not until 1484 that Pope Innocent VIII fully reversed the rule laid down by Alexander IV; inquisitors were then instructed to prosecute ruthlessly those who invoked the devil.[5] The great furor about witchcraft followed in the sixteenth and seventeenth centuries.[6]

Part A of the following translations is taken from the chronicle of Ralph, abbot of the Cistercian monastery of Coggeshall (1207-1218). The date of the episode he recounts must lie between the consecration of William of Champagne as archbishop of Rheims (1176) and the death of Louis VII of France (1180). Ralph's work is his own from the last quarter of the twelfth century, a period for which he had good sources of information, especially on events in France. The excerpt here is translated from *Radulphi de Coggeshall Chronicon anglicanum*, ed. by Joseph Stevenson (Rolls Series, LXVI [London, 1875]), pp. 121-25, by permission of Her Majesty's Stationery Office and the Kraus Reprint Corporation. Part of this passage has already appeared in translation in G.G. Coulton's *Life in the Middle Ages,* I, 29-32, and in his *Inquisition and Liberty*, pp. 35-38.

Part B is translated from the work of Walter Map, from which Number 31, part B, was also drawn. Since this incident cannot be precisely dated, we have entered it under the year in which Walter Map began to compile his work. The text is from *De nugis curialium* I.xxx, ed. by Montague R. James (Anecdota oxoniensa . . ., medieval and modern series, XIV [Oxford, 1914]), pp. 57-59, by permission of the Clarendon Press.

A. A MARVELOUS INCIDENT AT RHEIMS

1176-1180

In the time of Louis, king of France, who fathered King Philip, while the error of certain heretics, who are called Publicans in the vernacular, was spreading through several of the provinces of France, a marvelous thing happened in the city of Rheims in connection with an old woman infected with that plague. For one day when Lord William,[7] archbishop of that city and King Philip's uncle, was taking a canter with his clergy outside the city, one of his clerks, Master Gervais of Tilbury by name,[8] noticed a girl walking alone in a vineyard. Urged by the curiosity of hot-blooded youth, he turned aside to her, as we later heard from his own lips when he was a canon. He greeted her and attentively inquired whose daughter she was and what she was doing there alone, and then, after admiring her beauty for a while, he at length in courtly fashion made her a proposal of wanton love. She was much abashed, and with eyes cast down, she answered him with simple gesture and a certain gravity of speech: "Good youth, the Lord does not desire me ever to be your friend or the friend of any man, for if ever I forsook my virginity and my body had once been defiled, I should most assuredly fall under eternal damnation without hope of recall."

As he heard this, Master Gervais at once realized that she was one of that most impious sect of Publicans, who at that time were everywhere being sought out and destroyed, especially by Philip, count of Flanders, who was harassing them pitilessly with righteous cruelty.[9] Some of them, indeed, had come to England and were seized at Oxford, where by command of King Henry II they were shamefully branded on their foreheads with a red-hot key.[10] While the aforesaid clerk was arguing with the girl to demonstrate the error of such an answer, the archbishop approached with his retinue and, learning the cause of the argument, ordered the girl seized and brought with him to the city. When he addressed her in the presence of his clergy and advanced many scriptural passages and reasonable arguments to confute her error, she replied that she had not yet been well enough taught to demonstrate the falsity of such statements but she admitted that she had a mistress in the city who, by her arguments, would very easily refute everyone's objections. So, when the girl had disclosed the woman's name and abode, she was immediately sought out, found, and haled before the archbishop by his officials. When she was assailed from all sides by the archbishop himself and the clergy with many questions and with texts of the Holy Scriptures which might destroy such error, by perverse interpretation she so altered all the texts advanced that it became obvious to everyone that the spirit of all error spoke through her mouth. Indeed, to the texts and narratives of both the Old and New Testaments which they put to her, she answered as easily, as much by memory, as though she had mastered a knowledge of all the Scriptures and had been well trained in this kind of response, mixing the false with the true and mocking the true interpretation of our faith with a kind of perverted insight. Therefore, because it was impossible to recall the obstinate minds of both these persons from the error of their ways by threat or persuasion, or by any arguments or scriptural texts, they were placed in prison until the following day.

On the morrow they were recalled to the archiepiscopal court, before the archbishop and all the clergy, and in the presence of the nobility were again confronted with many reasons for renouncing their error publicly. But since they yielded not at all to salutary admonitions but persisted stubbornly in error once adopted, it was unanimously decreed that they be delivered to the flames. When the fire had been lighted in the city and the officials were about to drag them to the punishment decreed, that mistress of vile error exclaimed, "O foolish and unjust judges, do you think now to burn me in your flames? I fear not your judgment, nor do I tremble at the waiting fire!" With these words, she suddenly pulled a ball of thread from her heaving bosom and threw it out of a large window, but keeping the end of the thread in her hands; then in a loud voice, audible to all, she said "Catch!" At the word, she was lifted from the earth before everyone's eyes and followed the ball out the window in rapid flight, sustained, we believe, by the ministry of the evil spirits who once caught Simon Magus up into the air.[11] What became of that wicked woman, or whither she was transported, the onlookers could in no wise discover. But the girl had not yet become so deeply involved in the madness of that sect; and, since she still was present, yet could be recalled from the stubborn course upon which she had embarked neither by the inducement of reason nor by the promise of riches, she was burned. She caused a great deal of astonishment to many, for she emitted no sigh, not a tear, no groan, but endured all the agony of the conflagration steadfastly and eagerly, like a martyr of Christ. But for how different a cause from the Christian religion, for which they of the past were slaughtered by pagans! People of this wicked sect choose to die rather than be converted from error; but they have nothing in common with the constancy and steadfastness of martyrs for Christ, since it is piety which brings contempt for death to the latter, to the former it is hardness of heart.

These heretics allege that children should not be baptized until they reach the age of understanding; they add that prayers should not be offered for the dead, nor intercession asked of the saints. They condemn marriages; they preach virginity as a cover for their lasciviousness. They abhor milk and anything made thereof and all food which is the product of coition. They do not believe that purgatorial fire awaits one after death but that once the soul is released it goes immediately to rest or to damnation. They accept no scriptures as holy except the Gospels and the canonical letters. They are countryfolk and so cannot be over-come by rational argument, corrected by scriptural texts, or swayed by persuasions. They choose rather to die than to be converted from this most impious sect. Those who have delved into their secrets declare also that these persons do not believe that God administers human affairs or exercises any direction or control over earthly creatures. Instead, an apostate angel, whom they call Luzabel,[12] presides over all the material creation, and all things on earth are done by his will. The body is shaped by the devil, the soul is created by God and infused into the body; whence it comes about that a persistent struggle is always being waged between body and soul. Some also say that in their subterranean haunts they perform execrable sacrifices to their Lucifer at stated times and that there they enact certain sacrilegious infamies.

B.   A VICTORY OF FAITH OVER "HERETICAL MAGIC"

circa 1182

Another old heresy[13] has recently spread beyond measure, arising from those who forsook the Lord when He spoke about eating His flesh and drinking His blood, declaring "this saying is hard" and turning back.[14] They are called Publicans or Patarines.[15] Everywhere among Christians they have lain hidden since the time of the Lord's Passion, straying in error.[16] At first they had special houses in the villages where they lived, and all of them, whencesoever they came, recognized their houses by the smoke, as the saying goes.[17] They do not accept the Gospel of John;[18] in the matter of the body and blood of Christ, the blessed bread, they laugh at us. Men and women live together, but no sons or daughters are born of that intimacy.

Many, however, have recovered their senses and have returned to the faith. These have told how, about the first watch of the night, when gates, doors, and windows have been closed, the groups sit waiting in silence in their respective synagogues,[19] and a black cat of marvelous size climbs down a rope which hangs in their midst. On seeing it, they put out the lights. They do not sing hymns or repeat them distinctly, but hum through clenched teeth and pantingly feel their way toward the place where they saw their lord. When thay have found him they kiss him, each the more humbly as he is the more inflamed with frenzy— some the feet, more under the tail, most the private parts. And, as if drawing license for lasciviousness from the place of foulness, each seizes the man or woman next to him and they commingle as long as each is able to prolong the wantonness. The masters also say, and teach the novices, that it is perfect charity to do or suffer what brother or sister may have desired or sought, namely, to soothe one another when burning with passion; and from submitting they are called Patarines.[20]

Only sixteen have as yet come to England, and they disappeared after they had been branded and beaten with rods by order of King Henry II.[21] They are not known in Normandy or Brittany; in Anjou there are many, but in Aquitaine and Burgundy their number is great beyond all bounds.

Their compatriots say also that they snare their table guests by means of one of their dishes and so make like themselves those whom they dare not approach with the secret preachments they commonly use. For instance, there occurred an incident about which Lord William, archbishop of Rheims, brother to the queen of France, told me and confirmed by many witnesses.[22] It seems that a certain noble prince of the region of Vienne, in fear of this detestable rapine, always carried with him some consecrated salt in a pouch, not knowing whose house he was going to enter and fearing the wiles of the enemy everywhere; this salt he put on all foods, even at his own table. By chance, news was brought to him that two knights had subverted his nephew, the lord of many people and towns, so he forthwith went to his nephew's home. While they were eating together in their usual fashion the nephew, unaware of what was at hand, had his uncle served a dish consisting of a whole red mullet, which appeared "fair to the eyes" and "good to eat."[23] But the nobleman put the salt on it and the fish suddenly disappeared, leaving on the dish what looked like pellets of rabbit's dung. The knight and those who were with him were horrified. He pointed out the miracle to his nephew and most devoutly urged repentance upon him; and with floods of tears he expounded to him the multitude of the Lord's mercies, and how all the efforts of demons were overcome by faith alone, as had just been displayed before his eyes.[24]

The nephew took the admonition with bad grace and retired to his private apartment. Thereupon the prince, grieving that he had been deceived, carried away with him in chains the knights who had misled his nephew; in the presence of a large throng he shut them, firmly bound to a post, in a hut, and setting fire to it, he burned the whole building. But the fire did not touch the men at all nor was even the slightest burn found on their clothing. At this a tumult of the people arose against the prince, for they declared, "We have sinned against most righteous men, against the faith confirmed by true miracles."[25]

The prince, in no wise doubting or questioning his Christian faith because of so strange an event, soothed the wrath and outcries of the mob with flatteries and affirmed the faith with kindly words. He took counsel with the archbishop of Vienne,[26] who shut the knights, bound as before, in a larger house and, making a circuit of its whole exterior, sprinkled it with holy water to counteract the magic. He then had fire brought, but by no blowing or feeding could it be made to ignite the house or to burn anything whatever.

At this the people of the city felt their faith to be under attack, and so railed at the archbishop that many broke out openly with foolish shouts against him; and had not fear of their lord prince prevented, they would have thrown the archbishop himself into the flames and liberated the innocent men. They did, however, tear down the doors, and rushed into the house. But when they came to the post, they found that the bones and flesh of the men had become charcoal and glowing ashes; they saw that the bonds were unharmed, the post untouched, and that the most righteous fire had punished only those who had sinned. Thus the good Lord turned the hearts of the wayward to repentance and blasphemies to praise.

43. The Spread of Heresy in Northern Europe

Between 1180 and 1215, incidents of heresy were reported in Arras, Auxerre, Besançon, La Charité-sur-Loire, Metz, Nevers, Rouen, Soissons, and Troyes.[1] Most of the information comes from chronicles, where the reports are brief and not very informative except as to the fate of the accused. The accounts translated here were chosen as typical. They serve to illustrate the sparsity of detail in these sources as well as the spread of heresy—or, perhaps, the increasing alertness of orthodox contemporaries to heresy.

Both passages in part A are from one of the continuators of the chronicle of Sigibert of Gembloux, *Sigiberti Gemblacensis chronographia: Continuatio Acquinctina,* ed. by L. C. Bethmann, in *Monumenta Germaniae historica, Scriptores,* VI, 421, translated by permission of Anton Hiersemann Verlag and the Monumenta Germaniae Historica. Part B comes from *Caesarii Heisterbacensis dialogus miraculorum* v.xx, ed. b. Joseph Strange (2 vols., Cologne, 1851), I, 299-300.

A. HERETICS IN ARRAS

1182

Four heretics seized in the city of Arras were imprisoned by Frumald, the bishop of that city.[2] One of them, named Adam, was an educated man; another, called Ralph, was a most eloquent layman; the names of their followers are unknown to us. The bishop, who was suffering severely from palsy, reserved the case for the archbishop.

1183

As soon as the Christmas season was past, William, archbishop of Rheims,[3] and Philip, count of Flanders [1168-1191], met in the city to discuss their private affairs. There, the deceits of numerous heresies in the count's domain were exposed by a certain woman. These heretics were not organized under the leadership of any heresiarch. Some give them the name of Manichaeans, others Catafrigians,[4] others Arians; but Pope Alexander [III] calls them Patarines.[5] Whatever they may be, they were convicted as the filthiest heretics out of their own mouths. Many were accused before the archbishop and the count: nobles and commoners, clerics and knights, countryfolk, maids, widows, and married women. The official verdict was established by the archbishop and the count: that the prisoners be delivered to the stake, their property to be confiscated by the bishop and the prince.[6] Now shone forth the excellence of confession. For, as is reliably attested by those who were in attendance, many persons who previously deserved punishment for heresy escaped with their lives by the compassionate grace of God through the ordeal of the hot iron and trial by water. In the town of Ypres, twelve men were submitted to the ordeal of the hot iron, but by this virtue of confession, all were delivered safely.

B. WALDENSES IN METZ

circa 1199-1200

Some years ago, in the time of Bishop Bertrand,[7] a very learned man, the Waldensian heresy appeared in Metz in the following way. On a certain feast day, while preaching to the people in the cathedral, he saw standing in the crowd two men, ministers of the devil, and he called out: "I see the devil's messengers among you," and, pointing to them, "Behold, there stand persons who in my presence were condemned for heresy at Montpellier and banished."[8] The men answered the bishop boldly, for they were accompanied by a scholar who barked at him like a dog, heaping insults upon him. Then they left the church with a

throng gathered about them and preached their errors to the people.
When one of the clergy challenged them: "Masters, did not the Apostle
say, 'How shall they preach unless they be sent'?[9] We ask who sent you
here to preach," they replied to him, "The Spirit." Now the bishop
could not use force against them, since some important citizens encouraged them out of hatred toward him, for he had exhumed from the
atrium of the church the body of a certain usurer, a relative of theirs.
Truly the men were sent by the spirit of error, and through their mouths
the Waldensian heresy, so called after one of the sect, was sown in this
city and has not since been entirely extinguished.[10]

44. The Amalricians

Among the narratives of popular heresies, we include here two documents
in which may be seen the origin and fate of a heretical group born, like
that at Orléans in 1022, in the intellectual climate of the schools. The heresy
was just beginning to spread to a wider audience when is was discovered.

Amalric of Bena lectured on the arts, especially logic, at Paris during the
last half of the twelfth century, and ultimately ventured into theology. After
his death he was condemned as a heretic, but there is still much uncertainty
about the cause of that judgment. It is probable that Amalric based his
teaching on the work of the ninth-century scholar, John Scotus Erigena, but
links between his ideas and Gnosticism or the contemporary apocalyptic
views of Joachim of Flora or the doctrines of the Beguins have been suggested by various investigators, as has the possible influence of Aristotelian
works which, with their Arabic commentaries, were reaching the West at
that time. Amalric died in 1206. A few years later a sect of heretics bearing
his name was discovered in Paris and in neighboring dioceses, professing
doctrines in which the strongest elements were apocalyptic prophecy and
pantheism. Although the Amalricians were ruthlessly dealt with at the time,
doctrines comparable to theirs reappeared in later years, among the Brethren
of the Free Spirit and in other movements.[1]

A recent sketch of the Amalricians in English is in Norman Cohn's *Pursuit
of the Millennium*, pp. 156-61. The best treatment of their doctrines accom-
panies Clemens Bäumker's edition of *Contra Amaurianos*, a thirteenth-
century tract against them, in his *Ein anonymer, wahrscheinlich dem Garnerius von Rochefort zugehöriger Traktat aus dem Anfang des XIII Jahrhunderts*.[2]

Part A of the following is translated from *Caesarii Heisterbacensis dialogus miraculorum* v.xxii, ed. by Joseph Strange (2 vols., Cologne, 1851),
I, 304-7. Part B is from *Chartularium universitatis Parisiensis*, ed. by Heinrich Denifle and Emile Chatelain (4 vols., Paris, 1889-1897), I, 71-72, by
permission of Librairie Delalain.

A. THE CONDEMNATION OF AMALRICIANS AT PARIS

1210

At the same time that the heresies of the Albigenses came to light, in the city of Paris, wherein is a font of all knowledge and a well of Holy Scripture, the blandishments of the devil instilled perverse understanding into the minds of certain learned men. These are their names:[3] Master William of Poitiers, a subdeacon who lectured in the arts at Paris and had studied theology for three years; Bernard, a subdeacon; William the Goldsmith, their "prophet"; Stephen, a priest of Vieux-Corbeil; Stephen, a priest of La Celle-Saint-Cloud; John, a priest of Orsigny— except Bernard, these were all students of theology—Dudo, private secretary of the priest Master Amalric, and one who had studied theology for some ten years; Elinand, an acolyte; Odo, a deacon; Master Guarin, who had come to Paris to study in the arts and, as a priest, had studied theology there under Master Stephen, archbishop of Canterbury;[4] Ulrich, a priest of Lorris, a sexagenarian who had studied theology for a long time; Peter of Saint-Cloud, a priest sixty years of age, who also had studied theology; and Stephen, a deacon of Vieux-Corbeil. At the devil's instigation, these men had devised many great heresies and had already diffused them in numerous places.

NOVICE: What were the categories in which men so advanced in learning and age could have erred?

MONK: They said that in the bread on the altar the body of Christ was present in exactly the same way as in other bread or in any other thing, and that God spoke in the same way through Ovid as He did through Augustine. They denied the resurrection of bodies and said that there was no paradise or hell; one who possessed the knowledge of God, as did they, had paradise within himself, but one who was in mortal sin had hell within himself, like a decayed tooth in his mouth. They said that to erect altars to the saints and to use incense before sacred images was idolatry. They made mock of persons who kissed the bones of martyrs. They dared to utter their worst blasphemy against the Holy Spirit from whom comes all purity and holiness. If anyone was "in the Spirit," they said, even if he were to commit fornication or to be fouled by any other filthiness, there would be no sin in him, because that Spirit, who is God, being entirely distinct from the body, cannot sin. Man, who is nothing, cannot sin so long as that Spirit, who is God, is within him, for He "worketh all in all."[5] Whence they avowed that each one of them was Christ and the Holy Spirit. In them was fulfilled the statement of the Gospel: "There shall arise false Christs and false prophets,"[6] and so on. These wretches also had arguments of absolutely no validity wherewith they sought to buttress their error.

Their infidelity was discovered in this way. William the Goldsmith, whom we have mentioned, approached Master Ralph of Namur,[7] saying that he had been sent by the Lord, and to him he propounded the following points of unbelief: the Father has worked under certain forms in the Old Testament, to wit, those of the Law; the Son likewise has worked under certain forms, such as the Eucharist, baptism, and the other sacraments. Just as the forms of the Law fell away with the first coming of Christ, so now all the forms in which the Son has worked will fall, and the sacraments will come to an end, because the person of the Holy Spirit will clearly reveal himself in those in whom he is incarnated. He will speak chiefly through seven men, of whom William himself was one. William also prophesied that within five years these four plagues would occur: first, one upon the people, who will be destroyed by famine; the second will be the sword, by which the nobles will kill each other; in the third, the earth will open and swallow up the townspeople; and in the fourth, fire will come down upon the prelates of the Church, who are members of Antichrist. For, he said, the pope was Antichrist, Rome was Babylon; the pope himself reigns upon Mount Olivet, that is, in the grossness of power. But thirteen years have gone by and not one of the things has happened which that false prophet predicted would happen within five years.

Also, in order to curry favor with King Philip of France,[8] William added this further prophecy: To the king of the French will all kingdoms be made subject and to his son,[9] who will live in the age of the Holy Spirit and will not die.[10] To the king of the French, twelve loaves shall be given, which are the knowledge and power of the Scriptures.

Upon hearing this, Master Ralph inquired if the man had any associates to whom these revelations had been made. When he replied, "I have many," naming the men listed above, the worthy man realized the imminent danger to the Church and that he alone was not capable of investigating their wickedness and obtaining their conviction. He adopted a kind of subterfuge in saying that a revelation from the Holy Spirit had come to him in regard to a certain priest, who might preach their doctrines with him.

In order to keep his reputation unblemished, Master Ralph reported the whole affair to the abbot of Saint-Victor,[11] to Master Robert, and to Brother Thomas. With them, he went to the bishop of Paris,[12] and to three masters who taught theology there—the dean of Salzburg, Master Robert of Curson,[13] and Master Stephen—to disclose all these things to them. Very much alarmed, these men instructed Ralph and the other priest for the remission of their sins to pretend to join the fellowship until they had heard all their teaching and had searched out all the tenets of their unbelief. In fulfillment of this task, Master Ralph and his companion priest traveled for three months with those heretics throughout the dioceses of Paris, Langres, Troyes, and the province of Sens and discovered many, indeed, of their sect.[14] In order to persuade the heretics to trust him completely, Master Ralph would sometimes, with uplifted face, pretend that his soul was wafted to heaven. Afterward, in their private meetings, he would recount some of the things he said he had seen and would vow to preach their faith publicly, day in and day out.

At length he returned to the bishop to report on what he had seen and learned, and on hearing this the bishop sent out for those persons throughout his diocese, for, with the exception of Bernard, they lived outside the city. Once they were in the bishop's custody, neighboring bishops and the masters of theology were assembled to examine them. The statements mentioned above were read to them and, in the presence of all, some of the persons defended them; others among them, however, would have preferred to withdraw and realized that they were guilty, but they stood fast with the former in the same perverse obstinacy and would not retract.[15] After the hearing had disclosed such perversity, they were taken out to Les Champeaux by the advice of the bishops and theologians, to be degraded in the presence of all the clergy and people, and when the king returned—for he was absent at the time—they were burned.[16] Stubborn of will, they answered no questions, nor in them could any indication of repentance be discerned at the very moment of death. While they were being led to the torment, such a storm arose as to leave no doubt that the atmosphere was troubled by the beings who had fixed such error in the men who were about to die.

That very night the man who had been the chief figure among them knocked at the door of a certain recluse and confessed his error, too late. He declared that he was a chief tenant of hell and was doomed to eternal flames.

Four of those who were examined were not burned, namely, Master Guarin, the priest Ulrich, and the deacon Stephen—who were sentenced to life imprisonment—and Peter, who before he was arrested had in fright become a monk.[17] The body of Master Amalric, who was the leader in the aforesaid depravity, was exhumed from the cemetery and buried in a field. At the same time, it was ordered at Paris that no one should teach from the books on natural philosophy for three years.[18] The writings of Master David and the theological works in the French language[19] were banned forever and burned. And so, by God's grace, the heresy was mowed down just as it was springing up.

B. THE ERRORS OF THE AMALRICIANS

In this manner they, who are creatures, detract from the Creator:

Sacred authority declares: "The works of the Trinity are indivisible." They, on the contrary, say, "The Father worked from the beginning without the Son and the Holy Spirit, even to the incarnation of the Son."

Again authority: "The Son alone was incarnate." They, on the contrary, "The Father was incarnate in Abraham, the Son in Mary, the Holy Spirit is daily made incarnate in us."

Again authority: "Everything under the sun is vanity."[20] They, on the contrary, "All things are one, for whatever is, is God." Whence one of them, a man named Bernard, had the boldness to declare that he could not be consumed on the pyre or hurt by other torment, whatever it might be, since what was in him he called God.

Then: "God was endowed with visible means through which He could be perceived by creatures and could be corrupted by extrinsic accidents." And so, led astray by this error, they sought to declare that the body of Christ lay concealed in the visible accidents of the bread before the pronouncement of the words, although authority says the opposite. "The Word affects the element and the sacrament comes to exist." This they have explained as follows: "That which was there earlier is, by the utterance of the words, shown to underlie the visible forms."

Also: "The Son became incarnate, that is, was brought into visible form." Nor are they willing to recognize that that Man was God any more than one of themselves.

Also, they say that the Holy Spirit, incarnate in them, revealed all things to them, and this revelation was no other than the resurrection of the dead; whence they declare that they themselves are now risen from the dead. In their hearts they deny a place to faith and hope, asserting the falsehood that they are moved by knowledge alone.

Also, confident of merits, deprecating grace, they uttered the lie that if they should unite in carnal intercourse with women of their own status, the children would not be in need of the benefits of baptism.

Also: "The Son has worked up to now, but the Holy Spirit begins to work from now on, even to the end of the world."

Four priests, two deacons, and three subdeacons were proved to have wholly adopted this doctrine. They were degraded on November 14 at the Church of St. Honoré and, on the twentieth of that same month, they departed this world in unhappy martyrdom. On account of these facts, we have forbidden certain books, even to those whom we know to be learned.

Heresy in the Thirteenth and Early Fourteenth Centuries, 1216-1325

45. The Varieties of Heresy

The following excerpts from a chronicle and two polemical tracts, all written at about the same time, show the diversity of currents in thirteenth-century heresy. From a German chronicle comes comment on various groups reported at Trier in 1231. Tenets of the Waldenses, Cathars, and other sects may be recognized, and the rumor of nocturnal assemblies for devil-worship is repeated, all prefaced by a narrative of the reckless and unrestrained conduct of heresy hunters in Germany at that time. Of the two treatises written in Italy from which excerpts are taken, one author was a layman, the other a Dominican friar. Each regarded the Cathars as the greatest enemy of the orthodox Church but also commented, although in somewhat less detail, on other contemporary sects: among them, Speronists, Passagians, and Waldenses. The layman, Salvo Burci, also delighted in pointing out the antagonisms between the several branches of the Cathars. The testimony of both authors is particularly valuable for the history of the Waldenses in providing information on the events of 1205 and the following years, when the Italian branch of the Waldensian movement broke away. The quarrel had arisen, perhaps, from questions of administration and organization, but soon was exacerbated by growing differences in doctrine.

Part A below is an account taken from one of the continuations of the deeds of the Trier archbishops, from which the report on heresy at Ivoy (our No. 10) also came. In part B are translated excerpts from the polemic written in 1235 by Salvo Burci, a noble layman of Piacenza, against the heretics who, emboldened by the turbulent political struggles there, plagued his native city. In 1204 the bishop and the clergy had been driven into three years of exile by the citizens' violent protests against ecclesiastical authority, and in ensuing years the clergy were drawn into the chronic struggle between aristocratic and popular political parties. In 1230 heretics were executed in the city, and in 1233 a special mission headed by the famous Dominican preacher Roland of Cremona (who then bore the title of inquisitor) was sent there by Gregory IX, only to be greeted at its first public appearance by a deadly barrage of stones from the crowd. After a pontifical investigation the blame was officially placed on heretics. Two years after this incident Salvo Burci produced his book. No more is known of the author than is told of him by the anonymous composer of the Prologue to the treatise, who made a careful record of authorship and date of writing, and commented that Salvo Burci was not overskilled in letters. The author's style, indeed, is vigorous, abrupt, and forceful rather than polished, but he had a good command of the Scriptures, on which his refutation of heretical errors rests. His familiarity with the heresies which he attacks so heatedly is indisputable, and he wrote, we are told, particularly to answer a certain heretical book, *Stella* [the star]; this was the reason for entitling his own work *Supra Stella* [the higher star]. Presumably other documents were also before him.[1] Only part of the text of the *Supra Stella* has been edited. Döllinger published excerpts taken at random from the sole extant manuscript.[2] Ilarino da Milano studied the treatise and edited selected portions describing heretical tenets and practices: "Il 'Liber supra Stella' del piacentino Salvo Burci contra i Catari e altre correnti ereticali," *Aevum*, XVI (1942), 272-319; XVII (1943), 90-146; XIX (1945), 218-341. This translation is made from the text in the last installment of his article, and on his study are also based the preceding comments.

Though there is less certainty about the authorship of the *Summa contra hereticos* from which part C comes, the document is as informative as the *Supra Stella*. There are persuasive arguments in favor of Peter of Verona as author. Peter was born at the beginning of the thirteenth century of a family involved in heresy, but he forsook that heritage to become a Dominican friar. He was an active preacher for two decades before being chosen as prior of the convents at Asti, Piacenza, and Como, successively, between the years 1248 and 1251. In 1251 he was also appointed by Innocent IV as inquisitor in Como and Milan. Peter had previously had close contact with religious affairs in Milan—tradition produced stories of his ardent and belligerent attacks on heresy there, although careful historical investigation has not lent much support to these tales. His brief career as inquisitor was cut short by assassination at the hands of some Catharist sympathizers on April 6, 1252. Eleven months later (March 9, 1253) he was canonized as St. Peter Martyr. His career has been studied by Antoine Dondaine, in "Saint Pierre Martyr," *Archivum fratrum praedicatorum*, XXIII (1953), 66-162; and there is a brief biography of him in Thurston and Attwater, eds., *Butler's Lives of the Saints*, rev. ed., II, 186-87.

The summa attributed to Peter was written in 1235 or within two or three years thereafter. It is a voluminous work—incomplete as now known in the manuscripts and perhaps never finished by the author—in which is revealed a considerable knowledge of the Cathars and other sects as well, knowledge acquired through both personal experience and written sources. The refutation of heretical errors is developed in a rational argument, supplemented by extensive citation from the Scriptures and from writers such as St. Augustine and Aristotle. The only extended discussion of the summa is by Thomas Käppeli in "Une Somme contre les hérétiques de S. Pierre Martyr?" *Archivum fratrum praedicatorum*, XVII (1947), 295-355, where also are printed various passages exposing the heretical tenets. Portions describing five sects other than the Cathars are translated here.

Part A is translated from *Gesta Treverorum: Continuatio quarta*, ed. by Georg Waitz, in *Monumenta Germaniae historica, Scriptores*, XXIV, 400-2, by permission of Anton Hiersemann Verlag and the Monumenta Germaniae Historica. Part B is translated from the previously cited article of Ilarino da Milano, pp. 307-8, 309, 316-17, 327, 328, 336-37, by permission of the Università cattolica del S. Cuore; and part C comes from the article by Käppeli, pp. 331-35, by permission of the Istituto storico domenicano di S. Sabina.

A. HERETICAL SECTS IN TRIER

1231

In the year of our Lord 1231 began a persecution of heretics throughout the whole of Germany, and over a period of three years many were burned. The guiding genius of this persecution was Master Conrad of Marburg;[3] his agents were a certain Conrad, surnamed Tors, and John, who had lost an eye and a hand. Both of these were said to have been converted heretics.[4] It is this Master Conrad who, renowned for active preaching, especially in behalf of the crusades, had built up a great following among the people; who interfered in the visitation of clergy and nuns and sought to constrain them to strict observance and continence; and who, supported by apostolic authority and endowed with firmness of purpose, became so bold that he feared no one—not even a king or a bishop, who rated no higher with him than a poor layman. Throughout various cities the Preaching Friars [Dominicans] cooperated with him and with his afore-mentioned lieutenants; so great was the zeal of all that from no one, even though merely under suspicion, would any excuse or counterplea be accepted, no exception or testimony be admitted, no opportunity for defense be afforded, nor even a recess for deliberation be allowed. Forthwith, he must confess himself guilty and have his head shaved as a sign of penance, or deny his crime and be burned.

Furthermore, one who has thus been shaved must make known his associates, otherwise he again risks the penalty of death by burning. Whence it is thought that some innocents have been burned, for many, because of love of earthly existence or out of affection for their heirs, confessed themselves to have been what they were not and, constrained to make accusation, brought charges of which they were ignorant against those to whom they wished ill. Indeed, it was finally discovered that heretics instigated some of their number to permit themselves to be shaved in penance and thus to accuse Catholics and the innocent. Of such three were taken at Mainz; thereafter there was no one so pure of conscience as not to fear meeting a calamity of this sort. For no one dared, I will not say to intercede for the accused, but even to make the mildest observation in their behalf, for he would immediately be considered a defender of heretics. And, indeed, in accordance with the decision pronounced by the lord pope,[5] he [Conrad] proceeded against defenders and receivers of heretics exactly as against heretics themselves. Furthermore, if anyone had once abjured this impiety and was reported to have relapsed, he was apprehended and without any reconsideration was burned.

Nor was the diocese of Trier free from this infection.[6] For in the city of Trier itself three groups of heretics were uncovered. There was burned a certain Leuchard, who was reputed to have been of a most saintly life, but who bewailed with dreadful laments the unjust banishment from heaven of Lucifer, whom she wished again restored to heaven.[7] Nor was it surprising that such occurrences happened in other cities, since in Rome itself, according to a letter from the pope,[8] not a few had been thus infected. There were a large number in this sect. Many of them were versed in the Holy Scriptures, which they had in German translation. Some, indeed, performed a second baptism; some did not believe in the sacrament of the Lord's body; some held that the body of the Lord could not be consecrated by evil priests; some said that the body of the Lord could be consecrated with salver and chalice in any place whatsoever, equally well by a man or a woman, whether ordained or not; some judged confirmation and extreme unction to be superfluous; some scorned the supreme pontiff, the clergy, and the monastic life; some denied the value of prayers of the Church for the souls of the dead; some took their own mothers in marriage, making amends for the consanguinity that existed by the payment of eighteen pence; some kissed a pallid man or even a cat, and performed still worse acts; some, believing all days to be the same, refused to keep holidays or fasts, and thus worked on feast days and ate meat on Good Friday. Let this suffice as a catalogue of their errors, not that we have listed them all but only noted the most outstanding.

At that time the archbishop of Trier convened a synod in which he publicly announced that the heretics in his diocese had a bishop, to whom they had given his own name, Theodoric, and that others did the same elsewhere after the bishops of other places; and he also announced that they shared in common a pope,[9] whom they called Gregory after the bishop of the Church Universal, so that, should they be questioned about the faith, they could say that they had the same faith as did Pope Gregory and bishop so-and-so (giving the name of the bishop), naming our bishop and meaning theirs.[10]

Three heretics were cited before this synod, of whom two were released and one burned.[11]

B. SALVO BURCI ON DISSENT AMONG HERETICS
1235

THE HIGHER STAR

Here begins the Prologue to the book against all heretics, entitled *The Higher Star*, which was composed and prepared by a certain nobleman, Salvo Burci, of the city of Piacenza.

In the name of Christ, amen. Sunday, May 6, 1235, eighth indiction, in the house of Monachus of Cario.[12]

Although the date on which this book entitled *The Higher Star* was composed is recorded here, that is, when its preparation was first undertaken, let no one be surprised to encounter the same in subsequent pages. We have entered the date here for no reason other than to allow one the more readily to know the time when it was begun.

Inasmuch as many have undertaken to set forth in order narratives of the things which, we believe, have been fully discussed in this book,[13] we must warn the copyist and the reader of the need for careful attention to its words, for we know that herein are many matters difficult to understand, many things that lie hidden between the lines. By poring over these, the assiduous reader will find the heretics and their errors exposed and refuted, with the result that he will not be deluded by any of their wiles. Not without reason do we entitle the book *The Higher Star*, for as a star guides the course of seafarers and leads them to harbor, so this book charts the course of true faith and guides toward the haven of salvation. Moreover, it is entitled *The Higher Star* to distinguish it from a certain heretical work which has already been given the title *The Star*, a name derived from the star called Wormwood in the Apocalypse.[14] The name *The Higher Star* is well chosen. For this one, rising, proclaims one God, creator of all, above all; the other, assuredly declining toward the pit of error, babbles nonsense about two opposing gods. This one teaches truth, that one falsehood. This book was produced by the efforts of a certain layman, noble but not skilled in letters, a native of Piacenza, Salvo by name, moreover an emissary of the Savior, Jesus Christ. Surely it was meet for the Savior and Salvo to be associated in this book.

Separate chapters are marked off herein as far as possible. As far as possible, I say, because in places there is a lack of order or systematic arrangement, and quite often a topic is treated in a chapter devoted to some other subject. This occurred, however, because the cunning of the heretics made it necessary. For since they avoid the path of truth instead of searching for it, they shift from one subject to several others and from several to one; as a result, a reply to each point is needful. . . .

Here begins the book against all heretics, entitled *The Higher Star.* . . .

Against the Cathars who are called Albanenses and the Concorezzenses, who disagree sharply so that each damns the other to the death, the Albanenses maintaining against the Concorezzenses that they themselves are the Church of God, that the Concorezzenses were once associated with them, having broken away from us; the Concorezzenses in turn making a counteraccusation of like nature.

It is well known that Albanenses and Concorezzenses have met together many times and have often taken counsel together to discuss how they might agree on one faith, both Albanenses and Concorezzenses seeking—for the sake of the believers of both sects, among whom a sense of scandal was being aroused by what was preached—to find a compromise in their teaching. In this hope of bringing themselves back to a common faith, they spent heavily on many different journeys, traveling now here, now there, on the face of the earth. And some say [the same is true] of the Cathars called Caloianni and also the Francigene,[15] who, in general, do not share the beliefs of the Albanenses or the Concorezzenses. But although they could not come to an agreement, they made the attempt and sought, to the limit of their ability, to have both sects combine in a common faith, admitting that their Church suffered from the scandal of their disunity, as a consequence of which many of their believers have come back to the Roman Church. Although, as we have said, they met together many times, they achieved no harmony. For each sought mastery for their group, but violent quarrels persisted within both parties, and every individual is sorely affected by the great discord. Whence it is obvious that they are not the Church of God, for here is what one finds in the Bible: "Every kingdom divided against itself shall be brought to desolation."[16] It is, therefore, clear that they are the church of the devil. For originally they were members of the Roman Church by baptism, nor can they deny that. But the Holy Mother Roman Church was the first Church, wherefore it is indubitably the Church of God. We have recounted something of how the heretics met together in the past. . . .

Chapter IX: On the Poor among the Heretics

O Poor Leonists and Poor Lombards and you Speronists![17] You can plainly see that those who are called Cathars have been convicted of heresy by the arguments of this book and out of the New Testament, for they hold depraved views on matrimony and very many other matters. And although you may not be in such profound heresy as the heretics who are called Cathars, heretics you are, nonetheless. For you are cut off from the Holy Roman Church, from which you received baptism and confirmation, those two sacraments by which man becomes Christian and receives the Holy Spirit. For that reason, then, we propose to say certain things against you. . . .[18]

For it is an evident fact that the Cathars were once part of the Roman Church and in that faith received baptism and confirmation and the other sacraments, and in it they remained for a time. But they left it. And against that Church they make ever more blasphemous statements which arise from their fatuous discernment—whatever occurs to them— declaring the Church to be a harlot, a den of serpents, a beast. And you stupid people say the same things. Now notice that the Apostle said "some,"[19] by which word he gives us to understand that those who have broken away are few, or virtually nothing by comparison with those who remain. Give even more heed to the fact that the Cathars are not to be termed "some" in comparison with you, but, on the contrary, you are almost nonexistent when compared to them, they being much more numerous throughout the world than you are. And the Cathars are virtually nothing in comparison with those among whom they once were numbered, that is, the members of the Roman Church. Therefore, you can perceive that you are not the Church of God and hence your labor is in vain. Also, recall your belief that the congregation and the

Church of the Old Testament was God-given, because He led them out of Egypt, and gave them the Law, and was with them, and led them through the desert. In this respect your belief is correct. . . .[20]

Sunday, May 6, 1235, the eighth indiction, in the house of Monachus of Cario. It is evident that the Church of God existed from the apostles to this day and shall exist from now until the end, and that in the Church of God there must be bishops, priests, deacons, provosts, and so on. Waldes (*Valdexius*), who came from Lyons, was your leader, but before Waldes you had no head but the Roman Church; this was about sixty years ago. Many of those men who were his disciples are still alive, and Waldes himself was a member of the Roman Church. How, then, can you believe that the Church did not exist before the time of Waldes? You are stupid! Speroni was the head of the Speronists and that was about fifty years ago. The Poor Lombards broke off from the Poor of Lyons and that occurred about thirty years ago. John of Ronco[21] who was one of their elders, took the lead. He was an ignorant man, without education. Therefore, you can realize that you are stupid and your labor is in vain. . . .[22]

Also, pay good attention to the date recorded above. Why? Because, if you were wise, you would see very well how new you are. That was the reason for setting down the date, so that you might recognize your novelty. Waldes the Leonist, and Hugo Speroni, and John of Ronco, these three were the first heads of your congregations, but in the case of John of Ronco this was thirty years ago, of Hugo Speroni, indeed, about fifty, and of Waldes, about sixty years ago. Therefore, you can recognize your stupidity. So hold your tongues, and speak no more against the Holy Roman Church. . . .

O heretics, well may you be in terror of those things a Catholic says! The Concorezzenses, who are called Cathars, believe in a God who is good. The Albanenses, who are called Cathars, hold that he is evil. There can be no greater difference. The Poor Leonists and the Poor Lombards are set apart from each other. These four sects are as different, each from the other, as fire from water, and one damns the other to the death. Each among them calls himself a disciple of Christ, and if any of them die, they are called Christian martyrs. Therefore, you can see how great is your dread. Why? Suppose one to be saved; then the others are damned. Great ought to be your fear. . . .

O Poor Lombards! You were once members of the Roman Church. Because that Church did not satisfy you, you joined the Poor Leonists and with them you were under the governance of Waldes,[23] staying for some time under his rule. Afterward, you chose another leader and gave offense to Waldes and the Poor Leonists. He was John of Ronco and I knew him. And for several years you taught just what the Poor Leonists were teaching, asserting that you had no quarrel with them, but now there is the greatest discord between you two. Also, you say that flesh is born of flesh and spirit of spirit,[24] and yet you assert that a husband, against his will, may be separated from his wife, or wife from husband.[25] You say that you are authorized to do this by the text of Matthew: "And everyone that hath left house, or brethren, or sisters, or father, or mother, or wife, or children, or lands for my name's sake, shall receive a hundredfold, and shall possess life everlasting."[26] . . .

O Albanenses, O Concorezzenses, O Bagnolenses! There are and ought to be seven sacraments in the Church of God, without which it is not nor can it be the Church of God. One is baptism in actual water, which has been defended in this book. The second is confirmation; the third, the breaking of bread; the fourth, unction with oil; the fifth, the instructions by one's prelate as to penance; the sixth, ordination of priests and bishops; the seventh, lawful matrimony. Of these seven, you have but two, which are the imposition of hands[27] and the breaking of bread. But you, particularly you Albanenses, do not lay much emphasis upon the breaking of bread, because the actual bread which you break is not made better or worse thereby, nor is he who receives and eats that bread the better or worse for it. Now I ask: Why do you do this, especially you Albanenses? Perhaps the Albanenses and heretics will say in reply: "The Lord Jesus Christ at the Last Supper took bread and broke it and gave to his disciples, saying, 'Take ye and eat. This is my body,' "[28] and so on. He said, "Do this for a commemoration of me."[29] I answer: If the bread which He took was created by the devil or by the evil god, it is inconceivable that He ever would have broken it and given it to His disciples, and He would not have blessed it. You stupid people declare and affirm that it was made and created by the evil god or by the devil. Yet you perform the ceremony of breaking bread. O heretics! How well even dullards may see that you are the worst of heretics!

O Albanenses, O Concorezzenses, O Bagnolenses! One finds in the New Testament that there ought to be bishops, priests, deacons, and provosts in the Church of God. This terminology is used in the Church of God. Your terms include "bishops"; "elder sons"; "younger sons";

and "deacons."[30] Let us suppose that the terms "elder son" and "younger son" do not prove you are in error. Where is the name of priest? The title "priest," which is wanting among you, is found in many passages of the New Testament. Therefore, it does not seem that you are of the Church of God.

O Albanenses, O Concorezzenses, O Bagnolenses! It does not appear that you repent of your sins, past, present, or future, either with inward or with visible tears, with prayer or without it. You seem not to know divine love—which is the very worst of torments. In the Church of God, one sees that when men sin, they feel contrition for their sins. Thus, when Peter sinned and denied Christ under oath, it is recorded that he "wept bitterly" for his sin.[31] Note the word "bitterly"; that means with the utmost sorrow. Yet this you do not do. Why? Because you do not know the perfect divine love, you mourn not. Also, in the Gospel: "Blessed are they that mourn,"[32] meaning that they who sincerely repent of their sins shall be blessed. Take heed of the Magdalen, who was a great harlot. When Jesus took food in the house of Simon, she washed His feet with tears and wiped them with the hairs of her head.[33] O miserable ones! It appears, indeed, that she sincerely repented of her sins, for He sent the mercy of God into her heart and mind. And no one may call it a spiritual mourning. Why? Because Simon was not a spiritual being but a carnal man; therefore, he did not perceive spiritual things but actually observed the Magdalen's behavior, because he said, "This man, if he were a prophet, would not suffer her to approach him, for she is a harlot."[34] Therefore, you have it plainly stated that the Magdalen literally did these things. O you sneaks! You deal most slightingly with human bodies after death. You lay them secretly in pits here and there, as best you can. This was not done with Christ's body, which was composed of the four elements. You may say it was a spiritual body, but take note to the contrary, that it was buried according to the Jewish rite. Hence you may clearly apprehend that it was a material body, for the Jews were not spiritual beings, but flesh and blood, and they performed burials in the earthly sense, as with the body of Christ. . . .

C. FIVE MINOR SECTS IN ITALY

1235-1238

[*Book II*]

. . . 23. We have already discussed in the preceding book the errors in which only the Patarines or Cathars are found to go astray. Now in this second book we shall speak of the particular damages done by five other heresies, which are those of the Predestinarians, the Circumcisers, the Speronists, the Poor Leonists, and the Rebaptizers.

Because the Predestinarians, among all other heretics, are second only to the Patarines in the seriousness of their deviation, we will start with a discussion of them next in sequence to the section on the latter. Here we seek first to know why they are called Predestinarians, how many kinds of Predestinarians there are, on what articles of faith they err, and what the origin of their errors was; thereafter we will disprove their ravings following the method adopted above.

Now, they are called Predestinarians because they say that all things happen just as preordained or predestined—not because they themselves are predestined to life but are rather, I fear, for the most part set down to death. There are, moreover, four types of Predestinarians. For there are some who say that all good things are preordained by the good God, all evil things whatsoever by the devil. This error they took from Simon Magus[35] and the Manichaeans, who, it is recorded, had spread this wickedness. But others in their folly say that all things here below, even the soul itself while it is clothed with flesh, are controlled by the motion and course of the stars and other superior bodies; also, they add that the world is eternal, that Adam was not the first man. They seem to have gotten this error chiefly from the words of Aristotle, as will become clear from their assertions in a subsequent passage.[36] Some of these persons, indeed, say that God sometimes alters the sort of effect that should proceed from the nature of superior bodies. A third type of Predestinarian consists of those who assert that all things, good and evil, are preordained by the good principle, that is, by God. The fourth group consists of those who blasphemously say that neither angels nor the souls of men have existence after this life has come to an end. The Sadducees were the first authors of this stupidity;[37] it was later amended by a certain individual named Arabs,[38] who, with his followers, spread the dogma that the soul's existence ended with that of the flesh. And another individual named Zeno, and his disciples, further added that a short interval after the flesh is destroyed so also will be the soul.[39] These Predestinarians, who may properly be called "the hopeless ones,"[40] say that all things from eternity follow this course and that at the end of a year which they call the Great Year—which they say comprises thirty thousand or fifteen thousand ordinary years—they will be restored. A multitude of these hopeless ones are found in the city of Sodom.[41]

It was incumbent upon us first to consider the beliefs of the Predestinarians which are accepted by the Patarines, thus bringing together all that is peculiar to them; our refutation will be made by solid reasoning as well as the Holy Scriptures.

24. *Of the Particular Errors of the Circumcisers,*[42] *Who Seem to Err More Seriously than Other Heretics.*—Let us now examine the particular errors of the Circumcisers, who seem to err more seriously than other heretics known to us, with the exception of the Patarines and the Predestinarians. For they assert that circumcision and the sacraments of the Old Law must be observed to the letter equally with the sacraments of the New Law.

25. *On the Errors of the Speronists, of Which There Are Three Particularly Their Own.*—We come now to the errors of the Speronists, of which there are three particularly their own. The first is that all men bear the sin of Adam only in the flesh, not in the soul. The second is that before the advent of Christ, good men ascended into glory. And they share with the Patarines, moreover, an error about the sacrament of the Eucharist, a matter which we discussed in Book I. They also share the common errors which we shall presently discuss in Book III.[43] These heretics derive from a former judge of Piacenza who was named Speroni, hence they are called Speronists, and they came into existence at the very same time as the Poor Leonists, although they are their opposite in manner of life, for the Leonists exist on alms, without property, and unmarried. These persons, on the contrary, own property and marry. We will refute their three particular errors from Holy Scripture.

26. *On the Poor Leonists, Whose Particular Errors Are Four.*— What follows concerns the Poor Leonists, whose particular errors are four, namely, that it is permissible for any good man to minister and perform the sacraments, that no one who owns property or who labors in worldly affairs can be saved, nor can one who fulfills the carnal obligations of matrimony. They fell into this fourth error in recent times. For some sixty years this heresy has been spreading; it had its rise with Waldes in the city of Lyons on the Rhone, whence these persons are called Lyonists or Leonists. These Poor Leonists originated within the

Roman Church but subsequently were led by pride into contumacy and, being excommunicated, lapsed into many errors and later on split into two groups. The aforesaid Waldes was made the heresiarch of one; John of Roncarola (*Runcharola*), who was a native of Piacenza, of the other. The former are called the Ultramontane Poor, the latter the Lombards. A schism has arisen between them, the Ultramontanes believing that there are many good men in the Roman Church and that an evil priest or prelate fulfills his office, which the Lombards deny. The Lombards subsequently split into two groups at a certain council which convened in the region of Milan. This schism arose over an incident involving a large goblet of wine which was knocked over by a fowl. The aforesaid John had consecrated the wine in his own fashion after women of the sect had trodden it out under their very feet. At the sight, some of them indignantly cried out that no one could consecrate the body and blood of Christ unless he were a priest ordained by the Roman Church. These persons were called "those of the meadow," but their party has entirely disappeared.[44]

However, some of these Poor Leonists, drawn from among the Ultramontanes and the Lombards as well, were converted to the Catholic Church at the same time as Bernard Prim.[45] They were called the Reconciled Poor. Later on, on the advice of the supreme pontiff, they entered orders of our Church. Some of them continue piously to this day in our order, others are asleep in the Lord.

There are also other errors common to the aforesaid heretics, which we will take up below in Book III, where the discussion centers on the Roman Church, the oath, civil power, and the like. In the present section we will rebut their particular errors, which are the first three we listed above; the fourth, on matrimony, has already been refuted in Book I. . . .

27. *On the Rebaptizers, Whose Particular Error Is to Baptize a Second Time.*—We come now to the Rebaptizers, whose particular error is to baptize a second time. Their heresy arose at the same time as that of the Leonists. . . .[46] Note that these Rebaptizers also have other errors peculiar to themselves, which are that during his whole lifetime a man need fast for no more than one Lent, and others of a similar sort which I have not bothered to include here. There were several other heresies which appeared at the same time as those just described,

namely, the *Arnaldones*, the *Corrucani*, the *Milui*, the *Levantes*, the *Cappelleti*, and the like. Since they have been wholly rooted out in our own time, I have not bothered to waste paper on them.[47]

46. Dissent between the Poor Lombards and the Poor of Lyons

The origins of the schism which in 1205 divided the Italian Waldenses from their French comrades are known only from the comments of orthodox writers (see No. 45, parts B and C), but to the Waldenses themselves we owe a report of an attempt to heal that breach. The conference described here took place in 1218; the letter which we translate was probably written soon thereafter [1] but has been deferred to this place so that these translations may carry the story in proper sequence. The Italian faction, the Poor Lombards—they refer to themselves as the Poor, the Poor in Spirit, and the Italian Brethren—wrote to some Waldenses in Germany to describe a conference between themselves and the Poor of Lyons, whom they call the Ultramontanes, the comrades of Waldes, and the Waldenses.[2] Since there is no mention of John of Ronco, it may be presumed that he was dead; in 1218 leadership of the Poor Lombards was vested in the twelve persons who prepared this letter in the name of their "society" or "brotherhood." Waldes, too, had died before 1218, and the French group entrusted its common affairs to two persons, elected annually.[3]

The initiative toward healing the schism had come from the Italians, and preliminary negotiations had posed the problems which were to be resolved at a conference: These involved differing views on the terms of office for officials; on the relationship between the brethren and the lay communities of workers, which were of long standing in Italy [4] although they had been denounced by Waldes; on the efficacy of baptism in water, the causes for which married persons might separate, and the question of disciplining individuals of either group whose opinions offended members of the other; and on the Lombards' insistence that they be allowed to disagree about the scriptural sanction for certain practices, without fear of coercion.[5] A compromise solution to these questions had already been attempted by written exchange of views before six negotiators from each side met in the vicinity of Bergamo in May, 1218, for further discussion. They were able to reach final agreement on the problems so far enumerated. But then two further issues appeared and the differences on them proved irreconcilable. Were Waldes and his companion Vivetus in paradise? That they were was for the Poor of Lyons an article of belief, but the Lombards felt able to accept the doctrine only conditionally. More important was the disagreement over the sacrament of the Eucharist. For the Ultramontanes the moral character of the priest had no effect on the transformation of bread and wine into the body and blood of Christ. But the Lombards, though admitting that they had once believed otherwise, held that the celebrant himself must be worthy. Over these two questions arguments in speech and writing were exchanged until the conference broke up in disagreement. The Italian community then sent their account of the event to their German friends.

This letter, first edited by Preger, has been several times reprinted. Müller re-examined the manuscripts and suggested emendations of Preger's text in his *Die Waldenser* (pp. 22-23). Giovanni Gonnet, reprinting the letter in his *Enchiridion fontium Valdensium* (pp. 169-83), annotates it with the corrections proposed by Müller and the variants found in an edition in Döllinger, *Beiträge zur Sektengeschichte des Mittelalters*, II, 42-52, and adds a short bibliography (p. 183). It is translated here from Wilhelm Preger, "Beiträge zur Geschichte der Waldesier im Mittelalter," *Abhandlungen der historischen Classe der königlich bayerischen Akademie der Wissenschaften*, XIII (Munich, 1877), 234-41.

1218

To the honor of the Father, of the Son, and of the Holy Spirit, amen. [1] Otto *de Ramezello*, by grace of God, confrater of the Poor in Spirit,[6] J[ohn] *de Sarnago*, Thaddeus, Marinus, G. *de Papia*, L. *de Leganio*, G. *de Moltasio*, J. *de Mutina*, J[ohn] Franceschus, Jordan *de Dogno*, Bononius, and Thomas[7] send wishes for health in true wholesomeness and for the steadfastness of eternal love to our beloved brothers and sisters, our friends of both sexes who live in piety beyond the Alps.[8]

[2] It behooves the keen and prudent mind to abandon that which is hurtful, flee that which is transitory, pursue that which is pure, and grasp that which is firm. "We give thanks to our God in every remembrance of you, always in our prayers making supplication for you all with joy for your communication in the Gospel of Christ from the first day until now, being confident of this very thing, that He who hath begun a good work in you will perfect it unto the day of Christ Jesus. As it is meet for us to think this for you all, for that we have you in our hearts, and in the defence and confirmation of the Gospel you are all partakers of our joy. For God is our witness how we long after you in the bowels of Jesus Christ. And this we pray, that your charity may more and more abound in all knowledge and in all understanding, that you may show forth better things, that you may be sincere and without offense unto the day of Christ, filled with the fruit of justice, through Jesus Christ, unto the glory and praise of God."[9]

[3] Brothers, we wish you to know of the result we were able to

achieve some time ago, in the month of May, 1218, near Bergamo, in the dispute which for long has existed between us and the chosen ultramontane comrades of Waldes, after each party had exchanged a number of inquiries with the other.

[4] Now, at first we had raised one particular question about leadership, of which this is the substance: "We ask you, ultramontane brothers, first of all about something which we have heard Waldes said, to wit, that he did not desire to have anyone chosen as the head of the ultramontane brothers or of the Italian brothers during his lifetime or after his death. Do you or do you not wish to abide by this rule without taking from or adding to it?" To this they made answer by presenting a certain spurious document, forged by a certain Brother Massarius[10] in the city of Verona. In this document appear the words: "And as a community to choose provosts and rectors." They added what we take to be a straightforward affirmation, without obscurity: that our community and theirs, gathered together—so it was stated—into one single community, may jointly choose either provosts for life or rectors for a set term, in the light of what may seem more expedient to the community or may produce the greater harmony. This, as stated, was the Ultramontane reply on the question of leadership.

[5] They then replied to our question about the ministerial order, the substance of which is this: "In the second place, we ask what your sentiments are and what position you wish to take on ordination, or on the ministerial order." Just as before, they gave a reply that was put forth in the afore-mentioned false document: "And as a community thus to choose ministers, either for life or for a set term, to oversee the affairs of recent converts or of friends who continue their life in the world, in the light of what may seem more expedient to the community or may produce the greater harmony." This, as we have said, was the Ultramontane reply on the question of the ministry.

[6] Then we had raised a question regarding an association of working people, of which the following is the substance: "Thirdly, we inquire about something which Waldes is reported to have said, that although in all things else there might be harmony and concord between him and the Italian brothers, they could have no peace with him unless they severed the relationship with the associations of working people which prevailed at that time in Italy, so that there would no longer be any connection of one with the other. Do you or do you not wish to abide

by this statement without taking from or adding to it?" The reply of the Ultramontanes to this inquiry was read, among other things, from that same oft-mentioned deceptive tract. "If any person wishing to continue to live by worldly toil, seeks guidance from the Poor, let guidance be given him according to God and His law, whether the person wishes to live alone or join with other persons."

[7] As we have said, the ultramontane comrades of Waldes gave the foregoing written answers to the questions stated above. They added certain other comments on the question of an association of working people, to which we sent the following reply: "We seek wholly to excise all the blemishes which the ultramontane brothers have specifically mentioned to us Italians and likewise any others, if any there be, in the matter of an association of working people, with this stipulation: We humbly urge upon them the concession that the said laboring folk, by the common counsel and concord of each society, may continue to exist to the honor of God." Thus we were mutually agreed on these three major issues over which there had once been dissension; and if we might come to be of the same mind on all other matters, no dispute at all—this we have heard from them and they from us—would remain between us and them, provided, however, that they would ratify their words by deeds and give effect to that which one reads in the con-cluding passage of a certain affidavit which they handed to us and which they have promised. We seek from them the three things de-scribed above[11] and desire to act straightforwardly and without ob-scurity toward them according to God and His law, putting aside all quarrel and controversy.

[8] Furthermore, we gave this answer to a particular inquiry of theirs about baptism: "We declare that no one who rejects the actual baptism of water can be saved; indeed, we do not believe that unbaptized children can be saved. We pray that they accept and acknowledge this belief."

[9] Replying to another particular question of theirs, on matrimony, we said: "We believe that no one ought to put asunder persons joined in legitimate marriage, except by reason of fornication, or with the assent of each party;[12] we beseech our ultramontane brothers to accept and acknowledge this belief."

[10] On the other hand, to the inquiry of the Ultramontanes about the affair of Brother Thomas, or of any other brother, we replied: "Our

wish is that, if the ultramontane brothers bring charges against Brother Thomas or any other of our companions, Thomas himself and the others should present and receive explanation according to God and His law. Let the Ultramontanes be prepared to allow him this, on their own behalf and on behalf of any other of their comrades. Brother Thomas requests and prays for the same."[13]

On these matters, the reply of the Ultramontanes was:

[11] "With reference to our questions about baptism, we assert our belief that no one can be saved unless he shall have actually been baptized in water.

[12] "In regard to legitimate marriage, we say that it may not be dissolved without the consent of each party, unless a rightful motive shall arise, of which the community shall be the judge.

[13] "In regard to the statement about Thomas and John Francigenas,[14] or any other person, that he may be separated from the society for particular reasons, we say that they may justify themselves to our society according to God and His law, and our society may act toward them and accept explanation from them according to God and His law."

Such, as stated, was the substance of the answers of the ultramontane comrades of Waldes on the subjects of baptism and matrimony, and in regard to Thomas or any other of our comrades at odds with their congregation, or any of them at odds with ours for particular reasons. Therefore, in these matters we were in mutual agreement on the basis of the aforesaid profession of each party, just as we have described it in regard to the preceding subjects, that is, as we have already remarked, if their statements are put into effect.

[14] In regard to a particular inquiry of ours, the substance of which is this: "We raise a question about any particular custom or belief of yours, one which you cannot prove by Holy Scripture that the Church of Christ has held or ought to hold, whether or not you wish to abide by it and force us to adopt the same?" Should their reply be sincere— and its substance is this: "We say that we do not take this position nor do we wish to use coercion against them"—if, we repeat, this response of theirs (we mean of the ultramontane comrades of Waldes) should be sincere, we believe no doubt at all remains that we and they now have a basis for solid peace and sound agreement between us.

[15] However, whether or not their reply was sincere the discreet reader and auditor may by the help of God determine from the follow-

ing account. For when still another of their questions was presented in regard to Waldes and Vivetus,[15] now deceased, we answered: "Waldes and Vivetus may have attained salvation, if before their death they made amends before God for all their sins and offenses." This response the aforesaid Ultramontanes flatly rejected. There were six of them, whose names were Peter *de Relana* and Berengar *de Aquaviva* (these two at that time were charged with conduct of affairs for the year, in accordance with their custom), G. *de Cerviano*,[16] G. Turantus, Optandus *de Bonate*, and Julian. They, as they informed us, were by common counsel of their society meeting with an equal number of our brothers, whose names are John *de Sarnago*, Thaddeus, Thomas, Manfred, John Franceschus, and Jordan *de Dogno*, to seek harmony with us. One of their number, Peter *de Relana*, stood up in the presence of their brothers and ours as we have named them and among other things made the bald assertion: "We hold that Waldes is in paradise." And he went on to say that if we refused to make the same declaration about Waldes that they did, never could they come to agreement with us.

[16] This is one of the two matters in which disagreement still persists between us and the comrades of Waldes. The other is the question of breaking bread, or the sacrament, about which, as we have been informed, there are three different views among the Ultramontanes.

One of these beliefs, as some of the comrades of Waldes state it, is this: that the substance of the bread and wine are transformed into the body and blood of Christ solely through the utterance of the words of God. They explained: "We attribute this power not to man but to the words of God." Against these persons we must raise the objection that if the substance of the bread and wine is changed into the body and blood of Christ solely through the utterance of God's words, then, according to their statement, anyone, Jew or Gentile, who pronounces the words of God over the bread and wine may consecrate the body and blood of Christ. This is a wicked thing to say, for it can never be proved by any valid text or argument. To the attempt made by some to corroborate that opinion by adducing the text of the Apostle, "For it is sanctified by the word of God and prayer,"[17] we reply that the Apostle does not support their mistake but rather destroys and refutes it, for in the text cited the Apostle spoke of foodstuffs, not of the sacrament, and not only stipulated "by the word of God" but also added "by prayer." Whether or not their prayer is of any value for consecration will presently be made plain in the following remarks, God willing.

[17] The second statement of some of the comrades of Waldes on the subject of breaking bread is this: "No one can perform baptism who is not worthy to consecrate the body of Christ." It seems necessary to protest to them that, in accordance with their statement, they must perforce admit either that the body of Christ may be consecrated not only by laymen and evildoers but also by women, even harlots, or that no one may ever have valid baptism from such persons. Each of these statements, the one that the body of Christ may be consecrated by laymen, that is, by unordained persons, and the other, that no one can be baptized by such persons, is quite in contradiction to the profession of those who,[18] as we have already said, forgathered by common counsel of the whole Waldensian society to seek harmony with us. And, indeed, when we pressed them with questions about the breaking of bread, they admitted that this sacrament can be performed only by a priest, not by a woman or a layman.

[18] They also said that no one, whether good or evil, except He who is God and man, that is, Christ, could change the substance of the actual bread and wine into the body and blood of Christ. To this extent we and they were of one mind in this third matter regarding this sacrament.

[19] But we disagree with them on the point which they added, that the prayer of an adulterer or evildoer may be hearkened to and accepted by the Lord in this sacrament, for this strays from the path of truth. Now, Truth says in Matthew: "You are the salt of the earth; but if the salt lose its savor, wherewith shall it be salted? It is good for nothing any more but to be cast out and to be trodden on by men."[19] And in Luke, He says: "Salt is good; but if the salt shall lose its savor, wherewith shall it be seasoned? It is neither profitable for the land nor for the dunghill, but shall be cast out. He that hath ears to hear, let him hear."[20] And in John, the blind man who was given sight says: "Now we know that God doth not hear sinners, but if a man be a server of God and doth His will, him He heareth."[21] Also, Truth says in the same Gospel: "As the branch cannot bear fruit of itself unless it abide in the vine, so neither can you unless you abide in me"; and a little later, "He that abideth in me and I in him, the same beareth much fruit, for without me you can do nothing."[22] And again, "If you abide in me, and my words abide in you, you shall ask whatever you will and it shall be done unto you."[23] Hence one can infer the exact opposite of this: If you do not

abide in me and my words do not abide in you, none of the things that you shall ask shall be done unto you. Here, too, the Apostle says: "Bear not the yoke with unbelievers. For what participation hath justice with injustice? Or what fellowship hath light with darkness? And what concord hath Christ with Belial? Or what part hath the faithful with the unbeliever? And what agreement hath the temple of God with idols?"[24] And again: "All things are clean to the clean, but to them that are defiled and to unbelievers nothing is clean; but both their mind and their conscience are defiled. They profess that they know God, but in their works they deny him, being abominable, and incredulous, and to every good work reprobate."[25]

[20] Also, it appears everywhere in the following that the Lord does not accept the ministry of the wicked and hearkens not to their prayer; for, indeed, one reads. . . . [At this point the letter quotes more than thirty scriptural passages, all but two from the Old Testament. They bear on the qualifications of priests and of those who may serve God. The editor did not transcribe these quotations but listed only the chapter and verse for each.]

[21] We find not only these verses in the Scriptures but much more evidence as well in Holy Writ which teaches us to destroy the aforesaid statement of the Waldenses. Now, if one wishes to protest that "The old things are passed away, behold, all things are made new,"[26] let him hear also what Paul calls to the attention of the Hebrews: "For if the word spoken by angels became steadfast,"[27] and so on, to which theme he recurs again in the same book.[28] And, as the same Apostle further testifies, because "Now we know that what things soever the Law speaketh it speaketh to them that are in the Law,"[29] and "What things soever were written were written for our learning,"[30]

[22] we utterly reject the statement of belief about the breaking of bread which the Waldenses produced, written in these words: "On the question which was put to us about the breaking of bread, we believe as follows: that the bread and wine become the body and blood of God after benediction by a priest ordained in the Roman Church, whether righteous or unrighteous, so long as the congregation of the baptized upholds him in his office, if he shall take the bread and wine and bless it in commemoration of the body and blood of God. On the question posed about one who is secretly a sinner, we believe that when such a one shall have blessed the bread and wine, it becomes the body and

blood of Jesus Christ after the benediction." We say that this is the Waldenses' profession, to which they hold despite so much sacred testimony to the contrary. And we take care in this letter to present to your discretion the profession, corroborated by the texts already enumerated, which we made orally in their presence and handed to them in written form.

[23] "This is the reply of the Italians in the matter of the breaking of bread, or the sacrament. We say that no one, whether good or evil, but He who is God and man can transform the substance of the visible bread and wine into the body and blood of Christ. Whence, if a minister —we mean a minister ordained in the order of the priesthood of Christ—shall undertake to consecrate it and God shall hearken to his prayer, we believe that the substance of the bread and wine is, after the benediction, the body and blood of Christ, yet never is this due to the ministrant himself or done through the ministrant.[31] We now explain what we mean by these words. By 'yet never,' we mean to say that if God shall not hearken to him, what is more clear, more evident, than that it is in God's authority, not man's, whether the prayer of a minister is to be heard by the Lord? Nor is it 'due to the ministrant himself,' that is, in the case of a reprobate minister, even if he shall presume to partake of it; nor is it 'done through the ministrant,' that is, through such a person's prayer, if he should seek to transmit it to anyone else. Moreover, we believe that if anyone shall present himself as worthy to partake of this sacrament, he obtains what he desires from the Lord, but not by way of the prayer or from the blessing of an unworthy or reprobate minister; that is, he accepts the body of the Lord for his own salvation according to his desire, to which the scriptural texts which speak of the righteous testify: 'Thy desire shall be satisfied with good things';[32] and again, 'He will do the will of them that fear him, and He will hear their prayer and save them';[33] and again, 'The Lord hath heard the desire of the poor; Thy ear hath heard the preparation of their heart.'[34] Nor does it disturb us when some persons cite in rebuttal the case of the betrayer Judas, for it is not credible that he partook of the same as did the other apostles, yet it was one body to them, as Paul is witness when he says, 'For we being many, are one bread, one body, all that partake of one bread and of one chalice.'[35] Other like criticism may be answered in the same fashion."

[24] We believe that what should be thought of their ministry, as far

as pertains to the sacrament, is made quite clear to you in the foregoing. But because the disbelief of certain persons, of whom we understand the Apostle to speak,[36] seeks to bring against us teachers who have nothing to impart, let them listen to teachers who foresaw their ignorance:

Cyprian: "It is manifest that the Eucharist can never be consecrated among persons in whom there is no hope and faith is not true, where all things are done by falsehood. Like monkeys, who without being men counterfeit human aspect, the heretic lays claim to the authority and truth of the Catholic Church. Although not in the Church of God, he gives blessings; although cursed by God, he promises life; although dead, he calls on God; although a blasphemer, he exercises priesthood; sacrilegious, he constructs a wicked altar. To it he brings all things. How evil it is that the devil's priest should dare to perform the Eucharist of Christ, for no offering can be made holy where the Holy Spirit is not, nor will the Lord grant good unto anyone because of the intercessions and prayers of someone who himself does dishonor to the Lord."[37]

Jerome on Zephaniah: "Priests who celebrate the Eucharist and unworthily consecrate His blood act in impiety against the law of Christ when they suppose that words, not life, consecrate the Eucharist for the worshiper, and that only the customary prayer is necessary, not the worthiness of the priesthood, of which it is said that 'the priest in whom there is any blemish whatsoever shall not approach to offer sacrifices to the Lord.'"[38] And the same on Haggai: "Although holy seem the offerings, yet because they are touched by 'one that is unclean by occasion of a soul,' all are defiled."[39]

Gregory: "They who sell or buy holy offices cannot be priests, whence it is written: 'Damnation to him who gives, damnation to him who receives.'" This is the heresy of simony. How, therefore, if they are anathema and are not holy, can they make others holy, and when they are not in the body of Christ, how can they consecrate or partake of Christ's body? How can he give a blessing who is accursed? And the same author: "Whoever pays money to be ordained so that he may receive advancement, is by that act a heretic."[40]

From a letter of Pope Innocent: "Let them hear this, they who, like heretical thorns piercing the whole body of Holy Church on every side, bring death when they say, 'I do not listen to the simoniac but to the words of benediction which come from his mouth.' O pitiful ones, more miserable than all other men, who dare to utter such wickedness with sacrilegious tongue! Why do they not attend the words of Solomon? 'He that turneth away his ears from hearing the Law, his prayer shall be an abomination.' And the Lord, proclaiming through Malachi that the benediction of evil priests is to be reckoned a malediction, says: 'I will curse your blessings.'"[41]

Let this be enough on this subject.

[25] To anyone who bases an argument against us on our former profession or credulity about this sacrament, we make this brief answer: "When I was a child, I spoke as a child, I understood as a child, I thought as a child; but when I became a man, I put away the things of a child."[42] Nor do we believe that any of the brethren, servants of the Lord, who lived in piety unto their death, are damned because of this credulity. If anyone assails us, saying: "Why, therefore, do you not confess yourselves still to believe the like?" we answer that it is because we cannot believe what is contrary to the truth now made manifest from the Scriptures nor, even though the Waldenses seek to coerce us in this regard, will we assent to this profession, "for one must obey God rather than men."[43] Not for an hour did Paul, as he himself testifies, yield by subjection to those who wished to bring him under servitude of the Law.[44] Nor, after the explanation of the story of the vision and the conversion of Cornelius, did the faithful of the circumcision adduce in contradiction to the Blessed Peter the fact that neither Peter nor the other apostles in times past had believed Gentiles could be admitted uncircumcised to the faith; and the Blessed Stephen, the first martyr after the passion of the Lord, who had been of like mind, was saved.[45] Nor among the brethren did these things arouse controversy, but they said, glorifying God, "God then hath also to the Gentiles given repentance unto life."[46]

[26] We have accounted it worthwhile to touch cursorily on the controversy with the Waldenses and on their inapposite arguments described above, leaving to your discretion many of the things needful to refute them, and to dispatch these to you by our most beloved Ugolus and Algossus,[47] by whom will be explained that old and spurious usage, and the truth which deserves the praise of those who have ear to hear.

Whence, dearly beloved, in conclusion we earnestly solicit your thoughtful care—not unmindful of the following precepts: "Thy word is a lamp to my feet and a light to my paths";[48] and, "The commandment of the Lord is lightsome, enlightening the eyes";[49] and "He that believeth in me, as the Scripture saith, 'Out of his belly shall flow rivers of living water'"[50]—that you may work to serve Jesus in yourselves and your hearers, according to your strength and age and grace and wisdom, vouchsafed to you by Him who, three and one, rules over all forever and ever.

Our society greets you. Pray for us. "The grace of our Lord Jesus Christ and the charity of God and the communication of the Holy Spirit be always with you all. Amen."[51]

47. A Debate between a Catholic and a Patarine

The literary device adopted by the author of this piece was derived, no doubt, from those actual disputations which were not uncommon in southern France before the Albigensian Crusade and for perhaps half a century thereafter in northern Italy.[1] The author of this summa cast in the form of a debate was probably Italian, but we know no more of him than his name, George, and that he was a layman.[2] His adversary defends views characteristic of the Bagnolenses, whose members, about the year 1250, were found particularly in Mantua, Brescia, and Bergamo, with a few in the region of Milan and in the Romagna.[3] To judge from the survival of some twenty-eight manuscripts, this treatise had a wide circulation. The copies fall into two families, differentiated by the inclusion in some of them of a chapter on the Eucharist. Also a short passage on predestination is appended to the one manuscript from which the treatise was printed, and appears in the printed edition. These additions characterize what has been called a "French" version of the original "Italian" text. Probably the copyist who introduced them to the tract borrowed the additions from the work of Moneta of Cremona (see No. 50), with the intention of providing material on the Eucharist and predestination for the preachers and controversialists for whom he wrote.[4]

The most complete study of the treatise is that of Ilarino da Milano, "Fr. Gregorio, O.P., vescovo di Fano, e la 'Disputatio inter catholicum et paterinum hereticum,'" *Aevum*, XIV (1940), 85-140. From the text printed by Martène and Durand, we translate the Prologue, which reveals the author's zeal for controversy, and the first chapter, which presents the adversaries' discussion of a fundamental tenet of dualism. In a few instances we have adopted the readings given by Ilarino da Milano, who, in the work just cited (pp. 125-27), edited the Prologue from other manuscripts. Our translation is from [George] *Disputatio inter catholicum et paterinum hereticum*, in Edmond Martène and Ursin Durand, *Thesaurus novum anecdotorum* (5 vols., Paris, 1717), V, 1705-11.

1240-1250 (?)

[Prologue]

As the world moves toward decline and dangerous times impend, wherein many persons departing from the faith[5] have to their own destruction formed sects and have assembled followers with itching ears,[6] every faithful person, in so far as God divides to him the measure of faith,[7] ought to rise up against those heretics who are called Patarines and who are in error, not alone on one article of faith but in all. For they say that Christ was a phantasm, not a man, and thus, they believe, was not in reality baptized, nor truly tempted, suffered not, nor was buried, neither rose again, nor ascended into heaven. They hold wicked ideas about the Trinity of Persons, declaring that after the Last Judgment the three will become one person, paying no heed to the text of James, "With Whom there is no change, nor shadow of alteration."[8] They also postulate two creators; they set forth two eternal principles, two gods, one of visible things, the other of the invisible. What more? They corrupt the faith in all ways. I, however, not that I may call myself a wall for the house of the Lord,[9] but standing upon the walls of Jerusalem, that is, upon the Gospel and the apostolic texts, hurl the things that you will read in the following pages as living stones against the afore-mentioned heretics. Let those who are more powerful than I attack them hand to hand with stronger weapons. I have not believed that I could excuse myself before the Heavenly Ruler if I did not resist His enemies at least to the extent of my abilities.

The Argument Opens.—That through this little book a way may be illumined whereby to oppose the Patarines, we present our material in the form of a debate between a heretic and a Catholic. . . .[10]

Chapter I: Concerning the Creation of Visible Things

Arise, O God, and judge Thy cause!

The Catholic Speaks.[11]—In the Gospel of John it is written: "All things were made by Him";[12] and subsequently, "The world was made by Him, and His own knew Him not."[13] And Paul to the Ephesians, chapter 3: "Who created all things";[14] and in the same book, the second chapter, "We are His workmanship, created in Christ Jesus."[15] Hebrews, chapter 3, "He that created all things is God."[16] Romans, chapter 11: "O the depth of the riches of the wisdom and of the knowl-

edge of God";[17] and again in the same book, "And of Him, and by
Him, and in Him are all things."[18] Timothy, chapter 4: "Forbidding to
marry, to abstain from meats, which God hath created to be received
with thanksgiving by the faithful."[19] Apocalypse, chapter 10: "And he
swore by Him that liveth forever and ever, Who created heaven and all
the things which are therein, and the earth and all the things which are
in it, and the sea and the things that are therein."[20] Acts, chapter 4:
"Lord, thou art he that didst make heaven and earth, the sea, and all
things that are in them";[21] and chapter 17, "God, who made this world
and all things therein; He, being the Lord of heaven and earth, dwelleth
not in temples made with hands."[22] It therefore appears from these
citations that the one God is creator of all things.

The Patarine Replies.—I admit that God created all things. This
means all good things, but He did not make the evil, vain, perishable,
and visible things; a lesser creator, Lucifer, made them, whence the
words of John, "Without Him was made nothing."[23] Moreover, [we
must] interpret the phrase, "The world was made by Him,"[24] as meaning worldly souls, namely, our own. But our bodies and all other visible
things[25] were made by a lesser creator, the devil. Yet God also created
"the heavens," which are our heavenly souls; "the earth," which means
the earthbound souls of believers; "the sea," which means our souls,
abounding with the water of doctrine; and "all things which are therein,"
which means our whole faith which is in these aforesaid souls. All these
things God created.

Rebuttal of the Foregoing Response.—Most wicked Manichaean,
how do you explain, "His own received him not"? In what way were
they His who received him not? By grace they were not His; therefore,
they were His by creation, for no other explanation can be found. As
for your statement that all good things were made by God and that
visible, perishable things were made by the devil, hearken to Paul
contradicting you in the Epistle to the Colossians, chapter 1, where he
says of Christ: "Who is the image of the invisible God, the first-born
of every creature, for in him were all things created in heaven and on
earth, visible and invisible."[26] Also, Hebrews, chapter 1: "And Thou in
the beginning, O Lord, didst found the earth, and the works of thy
hands are the heavens."[27] If you wish to use the interpretation you
suggested, in which you explain "earth" as meaning the souls of believers, "heaven" the perfect souls of the Patarines, hearken to what

follows: "They shall perish."[28] Therefore, the souls of the Patarines shall perish.

Also, Peter in the third chapter of the second Epistle, "But the heavens and the earth which are now, by the same word are kept in store."[29] If you interpret this to mean the visible heavens, then God created visible things; if you interpret it to mean the souls of Patarines, listen to what follows: "Reserved unto fire against the Day of Judgment and perdition of the ungodly men."[30] Therefore, the souls of the Patarines shall perish in fire with ungodly men.

Also, in the first Epistle to the Corinthians, chapter 11: "For as the man is of the woman, so also is the man by the woman, but all things of God."[31] Therefore, the birth of the first men and of their descendants is from God, not from the devil as you lyingly say. If, however, you interpret "man" to mean Christ, "woman" to mean the Church, then the Apostle would have lied, for this man, Christ, is not by woman, the Church; on the contrary the Church is and ought to be by Him and from Him.

The Arguments of the Patarines That There Are Two Gods and That the Devil, Not God, Created This World.[32]—The Gospel of John, chapter 8, "You are of your father the devil."[33] Ephesians, chapter 2, "We were by nature children of wrath."[34] Romans, chapter 9, "Vessels of wrath, fitted for destruction."[35] The Gospel of John, chapter 14, "The prince of this world cometh."[36] Matthew, chapter 4: "[The devil] showed him all the kingdoms of the world," saying, "All these will I give thee, if falling down thou wilt adore me."[37] And the first Epistle of John, the last chapter, "The world is seated in wickedness."[38] Therefore, the devil is the father of men and they are his vessels, and so he is the prince of the world; therefore, he is god and prince of the world.

The Reply of the Catholic.—I willingly admit the first propositions of this argument, to wit, that the devil is the father and prince of this world, that is, of worldly men and of worldly pleasures; they are his children who imitate him in evil. This you have done: You say, "Therefore, he is creator and god." Zebedee was the father of John and James; therefore, he was god and creator—this is false.

Here is another example: "The kings of the Gentiles lord it over them."[39] Therefore, the kings are their creators and gods—which is false. Moreover, when the devil promised Christ all the kingdoms of the world, he lied, as is his wont, for he knew not that he was speaking to the King of Kings.

The Reply of the Patarine.—The Apostle says in II Corinthians, chapter 4, "In whom the god of this world hath blinded the minds of unbelievers."[40] Therefore, the god of this world is he who blinds minds, that is, the devil.

The Reply of the Catholic.—Interpret it thus: God, the Heavenly Father, blinded, that is, He allowed to be blinded, the minds of unbelievers of this world, as the Apostle says to the Romans, chapter 9: "God hath mercy on whom he will, and whom he will, he hardeneth,"[41] that is, He permits to be hardened. Or it can be interpreted as meaning a god of this world, that is, of this world's wickedness—namely, the devil. He is not god, a creator, but a tempter, for he lures men to wickedness, as the same Apostle says to the Philippians, chapter 3: "Whose god is their belly,"[42] those whom the belly tempts. Just as the belly is called god, not because it created or made anything but only because it tempts, so also is the devil the god of the world, that is, of worldly wickedness.

The Reply of the Patarine.—In the Gospel of John, chapter 1, he says, "That which was made in Him was life."[43] But bodies die, therefore they were not "made"; therefore Christ did not make bodies.

The Reply of the Catholic.—O stupid one! The passage does not read "That which was made by Him (*ab ipso*) was life," as you understand it, for both life and death were made by Him. He "killeth and maketh alive";[44] He commits men to hell and draws them forth again. Therefore, the words "That which was made in him," were used because in Him was effected the prophecy, the nativity, circumcision, baptism, fasting, suffering, crucifixion, and resurrection. And all this that was made in Him was life, for through His suffering we live and experience the other things which we have enumerated. That we give the proper interpretation is evident, also, from what follows, "And the life was the light of men,"[45] for here he [John] refers to another life, rather than to Him.

The Patarine on the Same Subject.—"No man can serve two masters."[46] This is in the sixth chapter of Matthew. Since there are, indeed, "gods many and lords many,"[47] it is not without reason, therefore, that we say there are two gods.

The Reply of the Catholic.—The Gospel does not say two gods but two masters. Indeed, the devil himself is a so-called god, one in name but not in reality, as the Apostle himself interprets to the Corinthians that very text which you have advanced against us, where he adds: "For although there be that are called gods, either in heaven or on earth; yet to us there is but one God, the Father, of whom are all things, and we unto Him, and one Lord Jesus Christ, by whom are all things, and we by Him."[48] Let us recast the argument now: Let us declare that the Gospel texts and the words of the Apostle say that one may be called god but not be God; on the other hand, there is only one God the Father. And one may be called lord of those who serve him, as do you, but nothing is created by him. There is, on the other hand, one Christ only, through whom are all things.

The Argument of the Patarine on the Same Subject.—Why do you say in the rite of baptism, "We renounce Satan"? Why is it recounted in the Gospel that the Lord cast seven devils out of Mary Magdalen,[49] unless the devil is in those who are to be baptized and in all evil things? Therefore, he created them.

The Reply of the Catholic.—Truly the devil is in many things, as he is in you, not, however, as a creator but as a thief, an intruder, a robber, just as the Lord says in the Gospel, "And ought not this daughter of Abraham whom Satan hath bound,"[50] and so on. As a thief, an intruder, a robber, Satan bound her, but Abraham, not he, was the father.

The Reply of the Patarine.—"Vanity of vanities and all is vanity";[51] again, "All things are vanity, every man living."[52] And [II] Corinthians, chapter 4, "The things which are seen are temporal; the things which are not seen are eternal."[53] Therefore, because the things which are visible are vain, they were not created by God, who is eternal; because they are evil, they were not created by the good God.

Reply of the Catholic.—There is nothing vain and nothing evil in that which was created by God; on the contrary, all things are good in that which was created by Him. By nature, all things are good in themselves, but they are disfigured and corrupted by vice. This, also, is an example of your argument: She is a virgin; therefore she is not among corrupted things.

The Patarine.—John on the Passion: "My kingdom is not of this world."[54] Therefore Christ is not king of this world.

The Catholic.—Jesus did not say that His kingdom was not over this world but that it was not of this world, that is, from the world, for the world did not give Him this power. Therefore His kingdom is truly not from this world but from the Father. The kingdom of earthly beings is of the world, for it is from the world, that is, from men, that rulers have this power.

The Argument against the Patarine.—Ephesians, chapter 3, "In the beginning, for this cause I bow my knees to the Father of our Lord Jesus Christ, of whom all,"[55] and so on. Timothy, chapter 1: "To the king of ages";[56] also, Hebrews, chapter 1, "Whom He hath appointed heir of all things, by Whom also He made the world."[57] Also, Hebrews, chapter 11, "By faith we understand that the world was framed by the word of God."[58] Also, Romans, chapter 9: "Hath not the potter power over the same lump of clay, to make one vessel unto dishonor and another unto honor?"[59] The furnace tests the potter's vase, as Scripture affirms, and the temptation of tribulation tests chaste men. Also, Jude, chapter 1, "Denying the only sovereign Ruler and Lord,"[60] who is Christ. Just before these words he called those who denied Christ "ungodly men."[61] So both worlds were created by God, not, as you say, one by God, the other by the devil. There is one potter, who is God, Who makes vessels unto honor, that is, those who are good, and vessels unto dishonor, that is, those who are evil. And he who denies that Christ alone is Lord is ungodly.

The Manichaean in Rebuttal.—Man was born of sin, therefore not of God.

The Catholic Replies.—Man is not born of sin, but we are conceived in sin, as a pearl is not of the mud, but in the mud. No substance is born of sin, but death is; as James says, "Sin, when it is completed, begetteth death."[62]

The Patarine.—We must believe that the tree which was in the midst of Paradise is the womb of woman, of which is said, "Of the tree of the knowledge of good and evil, thou shalt not eat,"[63] meaning, seek not fornication with woman. But the serpent, which is the devil, first ate of the tree, for he fornicated with Eve, whereof Cain was born. Eve thereafter offered and gave it to her man for she subsequently committed adultery with Adam, from which were born Abel and Seth. "And the sons of God," that is, demons, "seeing the daughters of men, that they were fair, took to themselves wives of all which they chose."[64]

The Catholic Replies.—O most abominable heretics! This is what you teach to simple folk, taking your pretext for this doctrine from Genesis, but we will prove from Genesis itself that your interpretation is false. For it is said there that God "planted a Paradise of pleasure from the beginning."[65] But He did not make woman until the sixth day, after man, for He made her from his rib. Therefore, Paradise was made previously, and man was formed therein before woman. So, therefore, woman is not Paradise, nor is the tree in the midst of Paradise her womb, as you allege. Also, one reads there that man was driven out of Paradise, but obviously he was not driven away from woman. Therefore woman is not Paradise. Moreover, you offer an evil interpretation when you say that demons took the daughters of men, for demons do not have virile powers or flesh. But this is the interpretation: "The sons of God," that is, those who descended from Seth, who was good and was sent by God to replace Abel, "seeing the daughters of men," that is, women who descended from Cain, who came from iniquity by imitation —and so on for the other points which follow.

48. Subjects and Texts for Preaching against Heresy

Lists of scriptural texts appropriate for the refutation of heretical tenets form one of the types of antiheretical literature from the thirteenth century. Although they hardly deserve the name of *summae*, which they bear, they illustrate well the nonviolent aspect of the religious struggle; apparently they were compiled for the use of preachers, either for warning the faithful against wrongful teaching or for engaging in face-to-face debates with heretics.[1] The experience of the preaching missions in Languedoc in the first decade of the century and the subsequent increase in public preaching by the friars and companion orders such as the Poor Catholics may well have inspired such lists.

We have no basis for dating the compilations which have survived, other than certain similarities between them and more elaborate polemical works of the second quarter of the thirteenth century. Presumably the need for these aids for preachers would have decreased appreciably as the Inquisition evolved.

The structure of these skeletal tracts in simple. Each chapter heading states a point of doctrine or practice which was denied by heretics; if the statement were phrased on the negative it would represent a heretical tenet. Under each heading are listed scriptural texts which support the point in question; they are cited by book and chapter, and only a few words of the verse are given. Occasionally the compiler adds further words of comment, explanation, or argument. Thus the value for our purposes is chiefly in the revelation of the range of subjects on which a defender of the faith had to be prepared to speak. Only the more elaborate of the full-scale polemical treatises treat of so many particulars.

The few compilations of this sort that are known raise certain questions which may be stated here, if not answered. There are marked similarities between these lists of subjects and texts and more fully developed polemics. For example, no less than a dozen of the chapters in the two works presented here display very close affinities—in the choice of biblical texts, in the order in which they are presented, and occasionally in the comment which is added to them—to passages in the summa of James Capelli (No. 49);[2] to a somewhat lesser extent the same is true of certain other chapters and the *Summa contra haereticos* attributed to Prevostin of Cremona (No 26). How did these similarities arise? Did one author borrow from another? Or was there a common source—if so, of what sort? Such questions are not, perhaps, of first importance but are of interest in assessing the technique of the polemicists and evaluating the quality of their work.

Monsignor Célestin Douais published the compilations which we translate here. He had found in one manuscript an incomplete tract which broke off in the middle of the thirteenth chapter, in another manuscript a tract very like it but beginning only with the eleventh chapter. Although Douais published these as separate items, numbered I and II, they are, as he suspected might be the case, two exemplars of the same work. This is proved by Manuscript 894 of the University Library of Leipzig, where we have found the tract in its entirety (fols. 74v-77v). Douais also published, as his Number III, another compilation of texts defending the sacraments, which was found in the same manuscript as his Number II. This also appears in the Leipzig manuscript (fols. 77v-79r). Still another item was added by Douais as Number IV. It differs from the others only in having more comment by the compiler in explanation of the scriptural verses to advance the argument.[3]

From Douais's editions of his Numbers I, II, and III we translate only the chapter titles, except that, to show the format, we give the first ten citations in the first chapter of the first tract in full. The reading of the printed text has been amended in a few instances on the basis of the Leipzig manuscript.

The translation is made from Célestin Douais, *La Somme des autorités à l'usage des prédicateurs méridionaux au XIIIe siècle* (Paris, 1896), pp. 34-66.

circa 1225-1250

I. A SUMMA AGAINST MANICHAEAN HERETICS

Here begins a summa against Manichaean heretics, dealing with the articles of faith and the sacraments of the Church.

> [I] In the first chapter it is proved that the Father, the Son, and the Holy Spirit are one substance and one God.
>
> Matt. 1:[23:] His name shall be called Immanuel.
>
> The same book, 8:[2:] Behold a leper came and adored him, saying.

In the same chapter, [v. 26:] Then rising up he commanded.

The same book, 9:[4:] And Jesus seeing their thoughts.

The same book, 28:[19:] Going therefore, teach ye all nations.

Luke 8:[46:] For I know that virtue is gone out from me.

The same book, 10:[18:] I saw Satan like lightning, falling.

John 1:[1 and 14:] In the beginning was the word. . . . We saw His glory.

In the same chapter, [v. 18:] No man hath seen God at any time.

The same book, 3:[16:] God so loved the world. . . .

[II] In the second chapter it is proved that God, who is triune in person and one in essence, is the creator of all things visible and invisible. . . .

[III] In the third chapter it is proved that the omnipotent God is not only creator but maker. . . .

[IV] In the fourth chapter it is proved that the omnipotent God formed the nature of Adam and Eve and other bodies. . . .

[V] In the fifth chapter it is proved that Abel was a good man and just, and that he was pleasing to God. . . .

[VI] In the sixth chapter it is proved that Enoch was a good man and just, and that he was pleasing to God. . . .

[VII] In the seventh chapter it is proved that in the days of Noah the omnipotent God brought about a flood upon the earth and that Noah was a good man. . . .

[VIII] In the eighth chapter it is proved that the good God appeared to Abraham and spoke to him. . . .

[IX] In the ninth chapter it is proved that they were good angels whom Abraham received with hospitality. . . .

[X] In the tenth chapter it is proved that the omnipotent God gave the covenant of circumcision to Abraham. . . .

[XI] That the omnipotent God is He who spoke to Isaac. . . .[4]

[XII] That the omnipotent God destroyed Sodom and Gomorrah, Adama, Seboim, and Segor. . . .

[XIII] That the omnipotent and good [God] led the people [of Israel] out of Egypt; on Mount Sinai He gave the Law to His servant Moses. . . .

[XIV] That the prophets were holy and just and prophesied by the inspiration of the Holy Spirit. . . .

[xv]   That David⁵ was holy and just. . . .

[xvi]   That the prophet Elijah was holy and just. . . .

[xvii]   That John the Baptist was holy and just. . . .

[xviii] That Christ in His divinity⁶ was the Son of God. . . .

[xix]   That God infuses new souls into new bodies. . . .

[xx]   That there is a soul, not an angel, in the body. . . .

[xxi]   That the soul of man is immortal. . . .

[xxii]   That Christ came to save the souls of men. . . .

[xxiii] That demons⁷ are absolutely damned. . . .

[xxiv]   That angelic spirits remained in heaven after the fall of Lucifer. . . .

[xxv]   That the Most Blessed Mary was a woman. . . .

[xxvi]   That the Blessed Mary had a father and a mother. . . .

[xxvii] That Christ in his humanity was the son of the Blessed Mary. . . .

[xxviii] That Christ took on true flesh from the Virgin. . . .⁸

[xxix]   That Christ truly had the attributes of humanity. . . .

[xxx]   That Christ had a true soul. . . .⁹

[xxxi]   That Christ descended into hell. . . .

[xxxii] That He truly had the attributes of a soul. . . .

[xxxiii] That Christ died in His humanity. . . .

[xxxiv] That Christ rose again from the dead. . . .

[xxxv]   That Christ ascended into heaven. . . .

[xxxvi] That Christ shall come to judge the quick and the dead. . . .

[xxxvii] That there shall be a true resurrection of bodies, glorification of the saints, and eternal damnation of the wicked. . . .

III. A COMPILATION OF TEXTS ON THE SACRAMENTS OF THE CHURCH

Here begins a compilation of texts on the sacraments of the Church against the Manichaean heretics. . . .

[i]   Proof that before His passion Christ, at the Last Supper, gave to His disciples His body, which the Church daily consecrates on the altar. . . .

[ii]   That the Church may without sin possess property. . . .

[iii]   That the institutions of the Church are not to be nullified. . . .¹⁰

[iv]   That forgiveness comes in the baptism of water. . . .

[v]   That everyone must be baptized and that baptism has good

effect before the age of discretion. . . .[11]

[VI]   That children are sinful and stand in need of atonement. . . .

[VII] That children attain salvation through the faith of their sponsors. . . .

[VIII] That baptism is of good effect without the imposition of hands. . . .

[IX]   That contrition is effective toward remission of sins. . . .

[X]   That confession is effective toward remission of sins. . . .

[XI]   That penance is effective toward remission of sins. . . .

[XII] That penance may be repeated. . . .

[XIII] That men in a state of carnal matrimony may attain salvation. . . .

[XIV] That the apostles ordained deacons, priests, and bishops. . . .

[XV]   That a material place may be called a church, the house of God, and a house of prayer. . . .

[XVI] That prayers ought to be said for the living and the dead and that extreme unction is doubly of value. . . .

[XVII] That Christ ate of the paschal lamb with His disciples. . . .[12]

[XVIII] That a man may make use of all foods unless he is restrained by a vow. . . .[13]

[XIX] That in case of necessity a man may swear to the truth without mortal sin. . . .

[XX]   Against the Passagians and the Circumcisers, that the Old Testament is not to be observed to the letter. . . .[14]

[XXI] Against the same sects, that the Sabbath is not to be kept to the letter. . . .[15]

[XXII] That circumcision is not to be accepted literally. . . .

[XXIII] That punishments are not equal nor are rewards and sins equal. . . .

[XXIV] That there is true resurrection of bodies and glorification of saints. . . .

Here ends the abridged summa against the Manichaean and Patarine heretics and against the Passagians, the Circumcisers, and many other heretics who attempt to overthrow the truth, "whose judgment now of a long time lingereth not, and their perdition slumbereth not."[16] From such damnation may He who sits at the right hand of Majesty, above the nine orders of angels in the heavens, preserve His own. Amen.

49. James Capelli on the Cathars

Ascribed to James Capelli, a Franciscan friar, the summa from which excerpts are here translated is of particular interest because of the author's care to do justice to his adversaries. In denying popular rumors about them and in giving them credit for fervent, although mistaken, zeal, he displays scruples rarely encountered in other authors of polemical tracts.

Only one of the manuscripts of the treatise bears an indication of James Capelli's authorship; the others are anonymous. James was the lector of the Franciscan convent in Milan about the middle of the thirteenth century and the author also of a series of Lenten sermons and of a devotional work, *Stimulus amoris*, inspired by the thought and example of St. Bonaventure.[1]

Not only is the summa somewhat unusual for its mildness of tone, but it presents a puzzle in the matter of its relationship to contemporary works. In chapters devoted to descriptions of the heretics and their beliefs, there are many passages closely similar to portions of the much longer treatise of Moneta of Cremona (see No. 50) although Moneta omits all the observations which give the present work its tone of moderation. Furthermore, in many other chapters in which orthodox beliefs are defended by the presentation of their scriptural basis, the biblical texts cited are those found, often in the same order, and on occasion with the same exposition of their application to the argument, in some of the compilations for the use of preachers from which we drew Number 48. From an analysis of these similarities it may be surmised that our author borrowed from these compilations, or from works very like them, and that his words in turn formed one of the numerous sources used by Moneta of Cremona.[2]

The summa was first described by Charles Molinier after a manuscript of Milan which bears James Capelli's name.[3] Shortly thereafter, Döllinger printed some excerpt from an anonymous tract in a manuscript of Cesena,[4] the whole text of which was later published by Bazzocchi. It remained for Ilarino da Milano ("La 'Summa contra haereticos' di Giacomo Capelli, O.F.M., e un suo 'Quaresimale' inedito [secolo XIII]," *Collectanea franciscana*, X [1940], 66-82) to show that the same treatise appeared in all these works.[5] Molinier and Ilarino da Milano agree that the treatise was probably written between 1240 and 1260.[6] In view of its probable relationship with the work of Moneta, who wrote about 1241 (see No. 50), we suggest that it was prepared about 1240.

The translation is made from Dino Bazzocchi, *La Eresia catara: Saggio storico filosofico con in appendice* Disputationes nonnullae adversus haereticos, *codice inedito de secolo XIII della biblioteca Malatestiana di Cesena* (Essay and appendix published separately, Bologna, 1919, 1920), Appendix, pp. cxxxvi-cxxxix, cxlix-cl, clvii-clviii, and clxxxvi-clxxxvii, by permission of the publisher, Licinio Capelli. The Bazzocchi edition is marred by certain errors of transcription and by misprints. We have, therefore, collated it with the Cesena manuscript for this translation, but do not enumerate all the corrections of the printed text which resulted; only those are noted which markedly affect the translation.

circa 1240

Heretical Opinions about the Baptism of Water.—Our Lord Jesus Christ, after glorious ascension into heaven and elevation to the right hand of the Father of mankind, sent the promised Spirit Paraclete to His disciples, Who by inspiration would recall to their minds all that He had said when He dwelt among them. Supported by His teaching and authority, they spread the preaching of the Gospel abroad through all the earth by the aid of the Lord, confirming the word by subsequent miracles. Those who were converted by their preaching were baptized with the healing and health-giving laver of rebirth, so that through the baptism of water believers might reap the reward of salvation, in accord with the text, "He that believeth and is baptized shall be saved."[8] But the persistent babbling of the heretics impugns this reverend sacrament with poisonous phrases. For they say that the baptism of water does nothing toward man's salvation, since neither is remission of sins a consequence of baptism nor does the grace of the Holy Spirit accompany it.

On the Customs of Heretics.—They have a sacrament of imposition of hands, which they call the baptism of the Holy Spirit, without which, they think, no one can be saved. Their bishop performs this imposition of hands or, if the bishop is not present, the two sons of the bishop have the power to perform it. Now, they ordain two officers holding ranks below the bishop, whom they call the sons of the Church. They are something like visitors.[9] These two travel about to the localities and towns where they have conventicles, visit their brethren, and by their instruction confirm them in the way of life of the sect, correcting whatever requires amendment. Indeed, if they find any persons who are less than circumspect, they expend much effort to steal them away from the unity of the Catholic faith and to gulp them into the belly of their error by baneful bites of blasphemy.

Furthermore, they have other officials, whom they call deacons, each of whom is established in a single town, presiding over the men and women of their sect and governing them at his discretion.[10] The deacons maintain a hospice for their own members, in which brethren who come from other places receive the boon of hospitality, cheerfully providing for the latter's necessities with careful attention, for they are strongly linked to each other by a bond of affection. The deacons in like manner have the power to perform the imposition of hands if the bishop and the above-mentioned two sons are not present. They do not have other prelates. In truth, this power is granted also to subordinate persons if emergency so requires.

They perform the ceremony of this sacrament, after a large number of brothers and sisters have assembled, by calling into their midst the man or woman who, after one year's probation, is to receive it. There, one of the aforesaid officials or some other person especially qualified by age or wisdom utters[11] a long prayer. He instructs[12] the believer in the tenets he must accept and the customs he must observe among them, tells him to retain no hope of salvation in the faith of the Roman Church or in its sacraments, and warns him of the need to bear all misfortune with constancy and steadfastness for the preservation of his faith and doctrine. Thereafter, when the question of whether he wishes to comply is posed, the believer answers that he will cheerfully accept all the things proposed and will not cease to do so throughout his whole life, disdaining all adversity. And so the senior prelate holds the text of the Gospels over his head and all the brethren gathered there come forward, each to put his right hand on the believer's head or shoulder. Then the prelate who holds the Book speaks these words, "In the name of the Father, and of the Son, and of the Holy Spirit"; and after repeating the Lord's Prayer seven times, he proceeds to read the Gospel of John which is chanted in church at Christmas, which is, "In the beginning was the Word,"[13] and so on.

With the performance of these rites they believe that all sins are forgiven the initiate and that the grace of the Holy Spirit is infused in him, for they hold that without such imposition of hands no one can be saved. If, indeed, any one of them chances to fall into mortal sin,[14] they do not think that he can in any way attain forgiveness without the repetition of this sacrament. For this reason, it is very often repeated among them. In particular, they administer this imposition of hands to believers in their sect who are ill, out of which has stemmed the popular rumor that they kill them by strangulation, so that they may be martyrs or confessors.[15] From personal knowledge we affirm this to be untrue and we urge that no one believe that they commit so shameful an act. For we know that they suppose their behavior to be virtuous[16] and they do many things that are in the nature of good works; in frequent prayer, in vigils, in sparsity of food and clothing, and—let me acknowledge the truth—in austerity of abstinence they surpass all other religious, so that truly in them are fulfilled the words of the Apostle: "For such false apostles are deceitful workmen, transforming themselves into the apostles of Christ. And no wonder, for Satan himself transformeth himself into an angel of light. Therefore it is no great thing if his ministers be transformed as the ministers of justice." "For I bear them witness that they have a zeal of God, but not according to knowledge. For they, not knowing the justice of God and seeking to establish their own, have not submitted themselves to the justice of God." [17]

But under this cloak of good works, in fact, they steal away the hearts of the foolish through sweet words [18] and blessings and by magnifying the wickedness and the bad customs of the clergy they make them pretexts for blaspheming the Church of God before men and for destroying the Catholic faith. Thus they cause many to share their error. . . .

Concerning the Sacrament of the Lord's Body Which Is Performed at the Altar. [19]—Now that we have refuted the opinions of the heretics about the sacrament of baptism, we come to a discussion of the sacrament of the Eucharist and will call attention to what they say about it. It is established that those whom the wickedness of perfidy [20] sets apart from the unity of the faithful it also keeps from communion in the sacraments of the Church, that those who sin through their bodily parts waste away in starvation, being cut off from the abundance of the body and blood of the Lord. For they deny that the bread and wine consecrated on the altar by a priest are changed or transubstantiated into the body of Christ. They think it impossible that the substance of bread and wine can, through the ministry of any man, be changed by transubstantiation into flesh and blood, for this they cannot comprehend in terms of human reason. And so, they are unwilling to believe, nay more, they ridicule those who do. For how [21] could they believe any substance be changed into the flesh and blood of the body of Jesus Christ who, as we said above, mendaciously assert that He had not a true body but its phantasm only? They recount, however, that the bread which Christ blessed and broke at the Last Supper was his body only in token, not by change; wherefore they explain the words "This is my body" [22] as meaning "This signifies my body," in the same way that the words "And the rock was Christ" [23] denoted not the actuality but the token. But, indeed, since the words were spoken to the disciples, "Do this whenso-ever you shall eat for a commemoration of me,"[24] for that reason they have a similar custom, for they believe themselves to be successors to the apostles. At all times[25] that they eat or drink, once all the foodstuffs are on the table and everyone standing around it, the oldest among them takes and breaks bread, giving thanks and saying the Lord's Prayer, and distributes to each one a small portion[26] to be eaten. There are various views about this custom among them. Some of them say that the purpose of the act is to ward off contamination from partaking of food, for they believe foods to be evil by having origin from the earth. As we said previously, they believe the devil divided the elements and gave fertility to the earth so that it might bear fruit. Certain others, however, say that this is done only in commemoration of the death of Christ, although they do not believe that He really died, and they do in imitation just what He had done. . . .[27]

The Protests of the Heretics That in Matrimony No One Can Be Saved.[28]—Having discussed the sacrament of the Eucharist, we turn to the subject of matrimony. Now matrimony is the legitimate union of man and woman who seek an inseparable community of life under faith and worship of one God. Against this the ferocious rabies of the heretics foams out false phrases full of idle superstition. They babble that no one can ever be saved in matrimony. Indeed, these most stupid of people, seeking the purity of virginity and chastity, say that all carnal coition is shameful, base, and odious, and thus damnable. Although spiritually they are prostituted and they pollute the word of God, they are, however,[29] most chaste of body. For men and women observing the vow and way of life of this sect are in no way soiled by the corruption of debauchery. Whence, if any one of them, man or woman, happens to be fouled by fornication, if convicted by two or three witnesses, he forthwith either is ejected from their group or, if he repents, is recon-soled by the imposition of their hands, and a heavy penitential burden is placed upon him as amends for sin.[30] Actually, the rumor of the forni-cation which is said to prevail among them is most false. For it is true that once a month, either by day or by night, in order to avoid gossip by the people, men and women meet together, not, as some lyingly say, for purposes of fornication, but so that they may hear preaching and make confession to their presiding official, as though from his prayers pardon for their sins would ensue. They are wrongfully wounded in popular rumor by many malicious charges of blasphemy from those who say that they commit many shameful and horrid acts of which they are innocent. And, therefore, they vaunt themselves to be disciples of Christ, who said, "If they have persecuted me, they will also persecute you";[31] and "You shall be hated by all men for my name's sake."[32] And, indeed, they believe fulfilled in them the text, "Blessed are ye when they shall revile you and reproach you and speak all that is evil against you untruly for my sake."[33] Furthermore, they gather each month as though to receive the fruit of penitence, since it is written in the Apocalypse, "And on both sides of the river was the tree of life, bearing twelve fruits, yielding its fruits every month."[34] This, by false interpretation, they expound as applying to their conventicles.[35] They are all bound by their superstitious and false religion, as we said, to the vow of continence. Hence, the devil having suggested to them that they condemn marriages, they call all other persons sensuous and lewd, and thus they are cast out from the chaste body of the Church and lose the reward of their continence. . . .

The Heretics Declare That One Must Abstain from Meat, Eggs, and Cheese.[36]—Because no truth adheres to the pernicious traditions of the heretics, they flavor them in consequence with a certain seasoning of simulated virtue so that the underlying poison is less perceptible through the pleasing sweetness of the honey. They put on a certain show of piety but, exercising the rapacity of wolves in sheep's clothing, they have not the virtue of sanctity. For, puffed up by awareness of their flesh to the piety and humility of angels, they seek to convince others of what they know not. Yet anyone who regards himself as religious and restrains not his tongue, but turns his heart astray, possesses a hollow sanctity. Surely their religion is shown to be false when with unbridled tongue they utter poisonous words out of a pestilential heart. Bound by superstition, they insist dogmatically that all meat, eggs, fowl, or cheese are to be eschewed and that no man nourished by these foods can attain salvation. Now, in order to spread false doctrine under a veil of good works, they abstain from these foods at all times and, abstaining also in repeated fasts from wine, they crucify the flesh, as the Apostle says, with vices and concupiscenses.[37] For they are cunning serpents, hucksters adulterating wine, so that, with a show of simplicity, they proffer to unwary hearers a draught of death. And what is most dangerous, by such blindness of the mind are they stricken that, raging like lunatics, they are not aware that they are afflicted with the malady of error. . . .

50. Moneta of Cremona: Excerpts from a Summa against the Cathars

In range of subjects discussed and prolixity of argument on each topic, the peak of Catholic polemical effort against the Cathars was the summa of Moneta of Cremona, a Dominican friar who wrote the work about 1241 [1] and from it gained fame in his own day. The summa is divided into five books. The first is primarily concerned with the arguments of the absolute dualists and the Catholic replies on the subjects of God and the devil, creation, angels and men, prophecies, and miracles. The second book goes over some of the same subjects again, defending the faith against the attacks of the mitigated dualists. Books III and IV carry on the argument against both groups of heretics for their errors on Christ, John the Baptist, the Virgin, the Holy Spirit, the sacraments, and doctrine concerning the end of the world. The last book defends the Roman Church in its structure and practice, and for its teaching on the subjects of oaths, secular justice, usury, and free will. Throughout, the Cathars are the heretics with whom Moneta is chiefly concerned; the Waldenses receive attention only briefly in the fifth book.

For each subject of discussion Moneta methodically analyzes the heretical statements, discusses each of their arguments, whether based on scriptural or rational grounds, and then passes on to the equally detailed demonstration of the correctness of orthodox belief. The treatise commands respect, even awe, at the multiplicity of its arguments, objections, responses, and solutions. As for the soundness of its evidence about the heretics, it has been uniformly cited by historians of heresy as a most reliable exposé of Catharist doctrine, primarily because Moneta asserts (p. 2) that he presents no argument that he has not heard from the lips of heretics or gathered from their writings. He cites by name Tetricus,[2] an absolute dualist, and Desiderius,[3] a member of the sect of Concorezzo, and refers also to certain unidentified heretical works.[4] There is also reason to believe that he exploited the work of orthodox predecessors for his descriptions of heresy, just as others presumably borrowed from him.[5]

Moneta was a professor at the University of Bologna when he joined the Dominican order in 1218 or 1219 but we have few additional details of his life. He may have been an inquisitor. The date of his death, perhaps 1250, is not definitely known.[6] The only edition of his summa is that of Ricchini,[7] in the Introduction to which (pp. vii-ix) the editor discusses Moneta's career. The basic biographical materials are in J. Quetif and J. Echard, *Scriptores ordinis praedicatorum* (2 vols., Paris, 1719-1721), I, 122-23. Brief résumés of Moneta's life and work will be found in Borst, 17-19, and in the articles on him in the *Dictionnaire de théologie catholique*, X, 2211-15 (by M. Gorce), and the *Catholic Encyclopedia*, X, 479.

To choose passages which faithfully reflect the information presented by the summa and its laborious, methodical progress through point after point of argument is not easy. The excerpts translated here were selected primarily for their revelation of heretical tenets, but also with the secondary aim of showing how the argument from scriptural authority was handled. The first passage is a statement of heretical beliefs—both absolute and mitigated dualism are summarized—which Moneta placed as an introduction to his work. The second gives part of the heretical argument and Catholic reply on the question of free will. The third is another statement of the teaching of mitigated dualists, with illustrations of how they interpreted certain New Testament parables to bolster it. The fourth is an excerpt from a long discussion of the Roman Church; only Moneta's opening statement and the arguments which he attributes to the heretics are translated.

The translation is from *Monetae Cremonensis adversus Catharos et Valdenses libri quinque* I (*Descriptio fidei haereticorum*); I.v.1; II.i.1-2; v.1, *passim*, ed. by Thomas A. Ricchini (Rome, 1743), pp. 2-6, 63-65, 109-12, and 389-97 *passim*.

1241-1244

   Book I

   Preface: A Description of Heretical Belief

   What Heretics May Believe, or Rather, Concoct; First, Those Who Postulate Two Principles.—So that what follows may be clearer, before we deal with each particular article in itself, let us describe the erroneous beliefs of both parties of Cathars (for there are two major groups of them) and explain how they may agree or disagree.

   Some of them assert that there are two principles, without beginning or end. One they say is the Father of Christ and of all the Just, the God of Light; the other they believe to be him of whom Christ said in John 14:30, "The prince of this world cometh." Him they believe to be the god blinding the minds of unbelievers,[8] the god of darkness.

   These persons believe that the latter created these four elements which we can see, namely, earth, water, air, and fire, and all things which are in this earth, this water, or this air, and that likewise he created these visible heavens and all their embellishments, the sun, the moon, and the stars.

   They also believe him to be the God of whom Moses spoke in the first chapter of Genesis (1:1): "In the beginning God created heaven and earth," and so on. And those things which are recounted in the Pentateuch, in the books of Joshua, Judges, Ruth, Kings, and the Paralipomenon they believe were said and done by him. With the exception of the sixteen prophets, the Psalms, and the five books of Solomon, they think that all the books of the Old Testament came from him—although some of them, indeed, do accept Job and the whole of Esdras, as they do the aforesaid prophets and the five books mentioned.

These persons believe that these visible and transitory things are of the evil one by creation. On the other hand, they believe that God, the Father of Christ and of the Just, is the creator only of everlasting and eternal things. They believe that He created another four elements of His own, and all things which are formed thereof, and His own heavens, and that He embellished them with a sun other than that which we see, and another moon and other stars.

They also say and believe that this holy and true God had His own heavenly people composed of three constituents: body, soul, and spirit. The soul dwelt within the body, but the spirit, which is custodian and governor of the soul, was not within the body; each soul created by the good God had its own spirit as custodian.

They also believe that the devil, who is called Satan, being envious of the All Highest, warily ascended into the heavens of the holy God and there by his deceitful discourse led astray the souls just referred to, and drew them to this earth and murky clime; and they believe him to be the unjust steward spoken of by the Lord in Luke 16:8, "The Lord commended the unjust steward."

They also say and teach that this devil, puffed up by the deception which he had practiced in heaven, presumed to ascend into heaven with his cohorts and there joined battle with the archangel Michael and was defeated and driven out. They think that the verse Apocalypse 12:7, "And there was a great battle in heaven. Michael and his angels fought with the dragon, and the dragon fought with his angels," is to be interpreted with reference to this battle. This they take literally.

They believe also that when Satan was expelled from heaven by Michael, he shut up the souls referred to above into these bodies as in a prison, and daily he imprisons them.

Also, they speak of these souls as the third part of the stars of heaven mentioned in Apocalypse 12:4, "The dragon drew the third part of the stars of heaven," in consequence of the fact that they are a third part of the people who, in their opinion, were created by the holy God—since they assert, as we have already mentioned, that each being of the heavenly court is made up of the three components aforesaid.

Moreover, these persons believe and say that these souls were cast out by the Father of the Just for their sin of conspiring with the devil in heaven; and they believe that it was to redeem these souls that the Lord Jesus came from heaven to earth.

They also believe that since the advent of Christ these heavenly souls, which we call demons, do penance in the bodies in this life, as well for the sin they committed in heaven as for other sins committed in the present world. The souls undertake this penance, these persons declare, when they first accept their faith and receive from them the imposition of the hand [*sic*]. They say this imposition of hands is the baptism of the Holy Spirit, not the baptism of water, and they believe that by the imposition of the hand each of the heavenly souls receives its own spirit, the one which in heaven it had for its governance and protection. At the end, moreover, that is, on the Last Day, when all have accomplished their penance they shall return together to heaven and recover the bodies which were abandoned in the land of the heavenly court. As to this they cite the text of Matthew 24:28, "Wheresoever the body shall be, there shall the eagles also be gathered together." This recovery of the bodies of those who ascend to the heavenly home they declare to be the resurrection of the dead which is so often mentioned in the Scriptures.

These persons do not believe that either the Son or the Holy Spirit is God by nature, but that each is only a creature of Almighty God.

They also believe that the Father is greater than the Son and is different from Him and from the Holy Spirit in substance, and the Son is greater than the Holy Spirit and different in substance.

These persons differentiate between soul and spirit. They also make a distinction between the Holy Spirit (*spiritum sanctum*), the Spirit Paraclete (*spiritum paraclitum*), and the Perfect Spirit (*spiritum principalem*).[9] They call each spirit which, in their view, God the Father gave to those [heavenly] souls as custodian a holy spirit; they call those spirits holy, meaning steadfast, because they remained steadfast and had been neither deceived nor seduced by the devil. The Paraclete they call the consoling spirit, which also they receive through the reception of consolation in Christ; and they assert that there are many Paracletes created by God. The Perfect Spirit they say is the Holy Spirit. To Him they believe they refer in the words which they use in prayer: "We adore the Father and the Son and the Holy Spirit."[10] Moreover, they call Him greater than all other holy spirits and therefore designate Him as Perfect. They declare that He is of such ineffable beauty that, in Peter's words, the angels desire to look upon Him.[11]

They also believe that to no one was the Holy Spirit given before Christ's resurrection. This other Cathars accept; indeed, with the possible exception of some among those who postulate two principles, He is not believed to have been sent before Pentecost. Of this more will be said later.

They also believe that the Blessed Virgin Mary was a heavenly being who had not a human, but a heavenly body, not of this transitory creation. She had a soul, and a spirit appointed for the protection of the soul.

They also say and believe that Christ came down into the womb of Mary, sent by the Father in His soul, body, and spirit, and He drew nothing more from the Virgin than that which He bore into her. They declare that in His time He came forth and was born of the body of Mary, taking nothing from her. On this account they think that the words in John 2:4 spoken by Christ, "Woman, what is that to me and to thee?" as they perversely interpret them, were meant to mean: I have nothing from you. They also believe that He made no use of actual food nor did He feel real hunger or thirst.

They believe also that Christ suffered in this heavenly body and died, yet without sorrow, when the soul, and the spirit also, left the body, as found in John 19:30: "And bowing his head, he gave up the ghost." And after three days, they say, that soul and spirit returned to the body in the sepulcher and thus He rose from the dead. In that very body, they believe, He appeared to the disciples for forty days and was seen by them, and they say that this body was palpable and visible to men only by the power and the wish of God. They say also that in this body He ascended into heaven on the fortieth day and sits in great triumph at the right hand of God, because He conquered the devil, who had power over death; because of this victory, they say, the Father gave Him all power in heaven and earth. But whether He shall come to judgment in that same flesh is in question, for some of them believe that judgment is already delivered.

These persons do not believe that Christ performed any physical miracle, although, according to the words of the Scriptures, He appeared to do so. Therefore, they give a spiritual interpretation to the gift of sight to the blind and the raising of Lazarus; spiritually also were the sick healed.

These persons deny the resurrection of all bodies, assuming that the resurrection is of the spiritual bodies of which we have already spoken.

They deny, also, all the sacraments of the Roman Church, namely, baptism, confirmation, the body of the Lord, the sacrament of penance as we have it, matrimony, and extreme unction. They deny that the hardships of the present life or the infirmities of the bodies of this life are from God, the Father of the Just. They do not believe it permissible to make use of meat, eggs, or cheese or to swear or kill for any reason. They also attack the use of images in the Church and the adoration of the Cross.

These persons deny free will and suppose that the people of God are ancient (*antiquus*),[12] for they do not believe that the holy God creates new spirits and souls.

They also believe that the prophets prophesied in another world before the formation of this one and that the prophecies are to be interpreted in their literal sense.

The opinions of those who assume that there are two principles have been surveyed in part; they will be further expounded when we deal with individual articles of faith. Now we must examine in part the opinions of those who assert that there is one Creator. For these persons agree in some things with the others and in some they disagree. They differ in declaring that there is one Creator, while the others say that there are two, for they suppose that there is a prince of the world whom the Scriptures call the devil and Satan, who, after the creation of primal matter by God, divided that matter into four elements. From these he fashioned the external forms of things as we see them. This subject we will put aside for a moment, since it will be more fully discussed in the first portion of the second part of this work.

However, they believe that the prince of the world is called the god of this world, concurring in this with the others, although they do not believe him to be god by nature but, on the contrary, a creature of the highest God, Father of the Just. In this they differ from the others. These persons also agree with those who were discussed above in the belief that the Old Testament is from the devil. In respect of the prophets they differ in saying that sometimes the prophets spoke by their own spirit, sometimes by a wicked spirit, sometimes by the power of the Holy Spirit. Hence, they accept them only as they see fit. The group first mentioned [the absolute dualists], indeed, accepts them entirely and calls them good; these others believe that the prophets were evil, although they did speak some good words about Christ. The last-mentioned persons deny all the sacraments of the Church, just as the others do, and they suppose the imposition of hands to be the baptism of the Holy Spirit; in this they agree with the others. They deny also the resurrection of these bodies just as do the others, differing from them, however, in that the others conceive, as we have said, of a resurrection of the heavenly bodies; these persons speak of spiritual bodies, meaning inward men. They firmly believe that God the Father is greater than the Son, and the Son greater than the Holy Spirit; in this they are no different from the others, although they do disagree in believing the Son and likewise the Holy Spirit to be God by nature, which the first group denies.

These persons believe, just as the first group does, that Christ brought his human nature from heaven but that he put it on in the womb of the Virgin Mary. They disagree among themselves, however, in that some of them believe that His body was physically constituted from the body of the Virgin; some among them do not accept this.

These persons accept free will, which the first group denies. Some of them also suppose—and in this they differ from the first-mentioned group—that spirits or new souls are not created by God, but they say that the soul springs from soul, just as flesh from flesh. They also accept the physical miracles performed by Christ and His disciples, which the first group denies. They assert that this propagation of souls is propagation of the angelic seed, that is, of the soul of Adam, who, they say, was a heavenly angel. He came down to this world and was forcibly enclosed in an earthly body by the devil, as will be set forth in the second part of this work.

These persons, like the first-mentioned, forbid the eating of meat, eggs, and cheese, deny secular justice and the oath. They attack the Church on the matter of images and the Cross, as do the others. . . .

Chapter V: On Free Will: How the Heretics Attempt to Destroy the Concept

Now comes the fifth chapter, which treats of free will, the existence of which in the "people of God"[13] these heretics deny. This chapter, however, is divided into two parts: In the first are recorded their reasons for the denial; in the second are arguments against them.

1. *The Basis for the Denial of Free Will.*—First let us examine their

motives for this denial. One reason is that if the people of God had a will free to choose both good and evil, good and evil would have the same source and nature. Hence, it would not be necessary to suppose there are two gods, of whom one would be the principle of all good, the other the principle of all evil.

A second reason is that God did not have free will. He had no flexibility for good and for evil. How, then, would the people of God acquire free will? In this argument they are seen to signify that God cannot grant free will, capable of turning to both good and evil, because He himself has it not.

But the solution of this argument is revealed by a parallel case. Now, the people of God has its being from someone else, created by God. But whence did they acquire this created condition if God cannot bestow that which He does not have? Furthermore, God is unchangeable, yet His creatures change: Psalm 101:27-28, "Thou shalt change them and they shall be changed, but thou art always the self same." [14]

A third reason is that they do not understand how evil can come from good. But the solution to this is proposed in the first chapter under the topic dealing with one principle.

A fourth reason is that the Apostle says in Romans 9:16, "Not of him that willeth nor of him that runneth, but of God that showeth mercy." Also in I Corinthians 3:7, "Neither he that planteth is anything, nor he that watereth, but God that giveth the increase." Philippians 1:6, "He who hath begun a good work in you will perfect it unto the day of Christ Jesus"; also, Philippians 2:13, "For it is God who worketh in you, both to will and to accomplish according to his good will."

Of the first text, we say that it is to be interpreted in this way: "Not of him that willeth nor of him that runneth" ("not of him alone" must be added) means that good will does not arise from the one who desires, nor does the motion, that is, the effort, come only from him who runs. It comes from him and from the God "that showeth mercy." For were it not right for man to desire or to do good, why should God command him to desire good and to do it? Why should He reprove him if he did not do good or desire it—saying through David in Psalm 35:4, "He would not understand that he might do well"? [15]

Another interpretation is also possible: "Not of him that willeth, nor of him that runneth" ("does salvation come" must be added). Salvation comes, as Origen says, not by one's desire, motion, or exertion alone. Do you seek to understand this? David says in Psalm 126:1, "Unless the Lord keep the city, he watcheth in vain that keepeth it."[16] Therefore, both the Lord and men keep watch, but men in vain without God; John 15:5, "Without me you can do nothing"; also, I Corinthians 3:9, "For we are God's coadjutors." Also, in I Corinthians 15:10, when the Apostle said, "I have labored more abundantly than all they," he added at once, "yet not I, but the grace of God with me," as though he would say: I am not alone, but I am with grace, nor is the grace of God alone, but it is with me.

If, however, you wish to assert that salvation in no way comes from human will or activity, why, then, does the Apostle say in Philippians 2:12, "With fear and trembling work out your salvation"? But lest they think that they might do so alone, he continued [v. 13], "For it is God who worketh in you, both to will and to accomplish according to his good will," that is, He helps you to work to this end. Thus it appears that the fourth authority is of no advantage to the heretics.

Similarly, there is no advantage for them in the words, "Who hath begun [a good work] in you," and so on. For He, who in the beginning assisted them in working toward good, will aid them in achieving it. Furthermore, the Apostle wishes to point out by his words "who hath begun" that God is the primary cause of all good; hence all good ought to be attributed to Him and not to others. Similarly, He is shown to be, by reason of His goodness, the first cause of all such things and the source of all good; hence, Philippians 2:13, "For it is God," and so on.

Furthermore, why should He sternly warn the negligent to work out their own salvation if it were not in their power to seek it and work toward it? Hebrews 2:2 [-3], "For if the word spoken by angels became steadfast, and every transgression and disobedience received a just recompense of reward, how shall we escape if we neglect so great salvation?"

In regard to the words "Neither he that planteth [is anything]" and so on, I ask how this can stand. Were they [Paul and Apollo] not men, and good men? Therefore, each of them was "something."

If you say: "Neither he that planteth," means that he is not "anything-which-acts" (*aliquid faciens*), the counterargument is this: Did he not say there [I Cor. 3:6], "I have planted, Apollo watered"? Therefore, may you agree with me that the Apostle's meaning was that neither he

himself, nor Apollo, nor any other person, however holy, gives goodness (which he calls "increase," that is, something in addition), because
God adds it to the nature of man. For first is man born, and thus he
accepts existence in good. It was for this reason that the Lord said to
Nicodemus in John 3:7, "You must be born again."

Heretical argument: On the same point, they cite the text of Romans
7:15, "For I do not that good which I will; but the evil which I hate,
that I do." Therefore, man, who is part of the good creation, does evil,
but is reluctant. Therefore, he does not have a will free to do evil.

I answer: By the same reasoning, I prove that he does not have will
free to do good, for the Apostle speaks thus, "For I do not that good
which I will."

Furthermore, the Apostle there adds in verse 17[-18], "Now then it
is no more I that do it, but sin that dwelleth in me. For I know that,"
and so on. Here speaks the inward man, who is part of the good creation, saying that he himself does not commit that evil, therefore, it is
not to be charged against him by God; but rather against that which
commits it, meaning the sin which dwells in him.

Furthermore, to whom was that commandment, "Thou shalt not
covet" [Exod. 20:17] given? Was it to the inward man? Certainly! But
why, if the inward man was unable to covet? Yet it was not given to
the outward man. Why not? Because [you say] he is part of the evil
creation. Therefore it was not given to anyone, but this is false. Therefore it was given at least to the inward man; therefore he has a will free
to covet. Nor did the Apostle say, I cannot desire this which I do; but
said, I do desire it; for he coveted according to the law of the flesh,
which is in the members of man. Yet he did not covet according to the
law of the mind; hence he says in the same chapter [Rom. 7], verse 25:
"I myself, with the mind serve the law of God, but with the flesh the
law of sin." The words are those of a righteous man who was in Christ
Jesus, whence he concludes, in Romans 8:1, "There is now therefore
no condemnation to them that are in Christ Jesus, who walk not according to the flesh."

Note, moreover, that although he did not desire evil, he did it, to wit,
the evil of covetousness. Yet he did have the ability to desire it, because
the Apostle says in Romans 6:12, "Let not sin therefore reign in your
mortal body, so as to obey the lusts thereof." He would in no wise have
said this to the inward man, unless the heart had the free ability to covet;

otherwise, why would David say in Psalms 61:11, "Trust not in iniquity," [17] and so on?

Heretical argument: To the same point, they cite the text of James 3:11, "Doth a fountain send forth out of the same hole sweet and bitter water?"

To that I make answer in this way. To what are you referring as an actual fountain? How can you cite this testimony of James against free will, when he says not a word about free will? If you call God himself, the Father of the Just, the fountain, you do not have any argument in that against free will. If you say it means "a fountain of free will," where is your authority that a fountain may be called free will?

Furthermore, granting the point, I say: "The fountain"—that is, free will—"from the same hole"—meaning the mouth—"sends forth sweet and bitter water"—that is, benediction and malediction. But as James says in the same epistle, verse 10, "These things [blessing and cursing] ought not to be so. . . .

> *Book II*
> *Chapter I: The Bases on Which the Heretics Who Assert That There Is One Creator Build; These Bases Are Destroyed; Also, on the Erroneous Opinions of Those Who Postulate a Single Principle, and How They Seek to Support Them*

Throughout this chapter let us inquire whether these visible and transitory things were formed and differentiated according to their external forms by one holy God. Although attacking all Cathars, we direct this chapter particularly against those who, declaring there is only one God, assert that He created all heavenly things, that is, all angels, and all things terrestrial. But with this truth the heretics mix a leaven of heretical depravity by saying that God brought the four elements of the world, that is, the matter thereof, into existence from nothing. This the other Cathars do not admit. The persons discussed here, however, say that the devil divided this undifferentiated matter into the four elements, and shaped the forms of things from these four elements, and differentiated them by their particular, specific, and varying characteristics. Therefore, God gave material beginning to these forms; for this reason they also say that God is the Creator of all things which are visible. They do not, however, except in an obscure way, call Him the maker of these things. The devil, however, in their view, gave to these things their specific forms. Thus they designate him exclusively the maker of visible things because he worked with some [pre-existent] material; for this reason, they say, he was called prince of the world by Christ. They do not concede that he is a creator, because they assert that to create means to make something from nothing.

They say also that the devil is Lucifer, created by God; he was good, but because of his arrogance before his creator he was cast out of heaven with many angels who took his part. This we do not deny.

They also assert that sin had its origin from the devil through free will, which is our belief. However, as they describe it, this is the way that sin had its origin from him: First Satan came to behold that which was created by God, and yearned to reign there. This cupidity was the root of all evils, something, they say, which the Apostle declared in I Timothy 6:10. Subsequently, he returned and seduced the stars of heaven, meaning many of the angels; of them, in the view of these persons, the Apostle spoke in I Corinthians 15:41, "One is the glory of the sun, another the glory of the moon, and another the glory of the stars." For they say that the sun, the moon, and the stars are demons, adding that the sun and the moon commit adultery once each month because one reads in astronomical works of the conjunction of sun and moon. They say also that moisture from that conjunction is sprinkled through the air and on earth, because they lose clarity. They hold that those[18] are to attain salvation who have been generated from angelic seed, that is, from Adam, for they believe and say that the spirit of Adam was an angel. From this spirit was all humankind propagated on the face of the earth. This they believe the Apostle stated in Acts 17:26, "And he made of one all mankind to dwell upon the whole face of the earth." This has been accomplished.

They also believe that just as flesh by coition is born of flesh so is spirit procreated from spirit. For they say that the spirit of Adam, which was a heavenly angel, came by God's command to see how Lucifer had divided the elements and had made from them the external forms of things before there was man on earth. Lucifer seized the angel and shut him in a fleshly body as in a prison, saying to him: "Pay what thou owest," meaning, Subject yourself to human flesh. But Adam, fallling down, besought him, saying, "Have patience with me,"[19] meaning, Release me and shut me not up in a body of clay. Satan, however, refused to release him but shut him into the body of clay until he should pay the whole debt, that is, lust, and should complete the sin of the flesh with Eve.

1. *On the Parable of the Servant Who Was Unwillingly to Pity His Fellow Servant.*—They seek to adapt to this myth that parable found in Matthew 18:23 [-28], where is said: "The kingdom of heaven is likened to a king who would take an account of his servants," meaning the angels. "And when he had begun to take the account, one was brought to him"—that is, Satan—"that owed him ten thousand talents"—that is, who had done numerous irreparable offenses against him. "And as he had not wherewith to pay it, his lord commanded that he should be sold and his wife and children and all that he had and payment to be made." To his wife they give the name "Wisdom"; his children they call the other angels subject to him and cleaving to him; "all that he had," they say, meant his natural good characteristics. "But that servant falling down, besought him, saying, 'Have patience with me and I will pay thee all.' And the lord of that servant let him go and forgave him the debt." For he did not take away from him his wisdom, nor those who were subject unto him, nor all his natural good characteristics, because he said, "I will pay thee." This is interpreted in this way: If you will have patience with me, if you will permit me to do so, I will make so many men that you will be able to restore from among them the full number of your angels which I stole from you. And so he "let him go," that is, he gave him leave for six days to make what he wished from the first-created matter. "But when that servant was gone out," he [Satan] performed all that is recounted in Genesis up to the moment of making man, in whom when made, he subjected the unwilling spirit, Adam, to human flesh, as we have said. This, in their opinion, is what Paul meant in Romans 8:20, "For the creature was made subject to vanity, not willingly."

Whence, they also expound as pertaining to Adam that parable of the Lord in Luke 10:30 [-35], "A certain man went down from Jerusalem to Jericho," referring to Adam's spirit because it descended from the heavenly Jerusalem to the world. "And fell among robbers"—that is, among malign spirits—"who also stripped him" of the light which he had. They also say that the sun, the moon, and the stars stole that light from him, citing for this, "and having wounded him went away, leaving him half dead." They say the wounds are sins. Of his being left half dead they have a triple interpretation: either that his carnal life was comparable to death, or that he might yet be restored, or that they did not take away from him his faith, although they precipitated him into other sins. "And it chanced that a certain priest went down the same way and seeing him, passed by. In like manner also a Levite, when he was near the place and saw him, passed by." The priest means Melchizedek and the Levite Aaron, who, going down "the same way," that is, in the same sins, could not help him. "But a Samaritan"—meaning Christ, making the journey from heaven to earth out of His mercy— "came near him"—that is, assumed flesh—"bound up his wounds"— that is, had compassion on his concupiscence and forgave him his sins —"pouring in oil and wine"—which means penance and the Holy Spirit. "And setting him upon his own beast"—that is, saving him through His own body—"brought him to an inn"—meaning the Church—"and took care of him. And the next day"—that is, after His resurrection— "he took out two pence"—which means the Gospel and the gift of the Holy Spirit—"and gave to the host"—that is, to the leaders of the Church—"and said, 'Take care of him'"—meaning, "Feed my sheep."[20] "And whatsoever thou shalt spend over and above, I, at my return, will repay thee." Paul spent more than was needed because he preached and lived by the labor of his hands, although Christ had said, "The workman is worthy of his hire,"[21] meaning his food. "And at my return" —namely, at the Day of Judgment—"I will pay it to you," and to everyone according to his works.[22]

These persons say that Satan was the unjust steward who is described in Luke 16:1 [-9], "There was a certain rich man who had a steward," that is, the steward is he who is now prince of the world and at that time was a prince of angels. "And the same was accused unto him, that he had wasted his goods," meaning that he had not governed himself and others according to God's will. "And he called him and said to him: 'How is it that I hear this of thee? Give an account of thy stewardship, for now thou canst be steward no longer,'" that is, no longer may you have dominion over the angels. "And the steward said within himself, 'What shall I do, because my lord taketh away from me the stewardship? To dig I am not able, to beg I am ashamed. I know what I will do, that when I shall be removed from the stewardship they may receive me into their houses.' Therefore calling together every one of his lord's debtors"—meaning the angels—"he said to one of them,

'How much dost thou owe my lord?' But he said, 'A hundred barrels of oil,'" meaning a hundred prayers. "And he said to him, 'Take thy bill and sit down quickly and write fifty,'" as though he meant to say: The Lord has imposed too great a burden on thee. "Then he said to another, 'And how much dost thou owe?' who said, 'A hundred quarters of wheat,'" that is, a hundred prayers. "He said to him, 'Take thy bill, and write eighty,'" And thus, so the heretics say, Satan, by reducing their labor, fraudulently drew them to consort with him. Hence they followed him in plunging down from the heavens, for "they are the children of this world"—namely, of the malign spirit—"and evil men," children of the devil, who are wiser in evil and in transitory things than the children of light, that is, the children of God. "Therefore, make unto you friends"—you faithful Christians, meaning the Cathars—"of the mammon of iniquity,"[23] that is, of the transitory riches of this world.

These persons also say that the spirit of Adam was the younger son of whom one reads in Luke 15:11, "A certain man had two sons." They were the aforesaid prince and the spirit of Adam.[24] Now we have re-counted what they think about Satan and about Adam.

2. *On Adam's Sin: What the Heretics Think It Was.*—Now we must discuss the nature of Adam's sin, as they see it. For better understanding of this, one must know that, according to them, Satan shut another angel into the body of a woman made from Adam's side while he slept. With her Adam sinned. Adam's sin, they declare, was fornication, for they say that the serpent[25] came to the woman and corrupted her with his tail; and from that coition was Cain born, they say, seeking to prove it by the statement in I John 3:12 that Cain "was of the wicked one."

They also say that the woman, having become accustomed to the sin of the flesh, went to Adam and showed him how he might lie with her, and persuaded him, and at Eve's urging Adam in fact committed the act; and this, they declare, is the eating of the tree of the knowledge of good and evil, which, they believe, was designated in veiled words by Moses as the forbidden fruit. Hence, they also think that because of this, man and woman always cover those shameful parts. That this was the reason they cannot prove. (It was done, not because they had sinned with these members but because they were rebels against their superior, the true God; their baser part, the flesh, rebelled against its superior, the spirit. Hence, the Apostle says to the Romans, "I consent to the Law that it is good."[26]) They believe that Abel was born from this copulation of Adam with Eve, and that in this way flesh from flesh and soul from soul are propagated as the work of Satan.

These persons believe, moreover, that Satan caused the flood and that he spoke to Abraham.[27]

Also, they believe that when Satan desired to destroy the whole human race, the holy God preserved Noah with his wife, and his sons with their wives, as seed for mankind, and preserved male and female of all living creatures and fowls of the air in their kind for the same reason.

Also they believe that it was Satan, not God himself, who spoke to Isaac and Jacob and gave the circumcision of the flesh to Abraham and his seed.

They also believe that Satan destroyed Sodom and Gomorrah and other cities.

They believe also that Satan gave the Law to Moses and led the people of the Jews through the desert from Egypt into the land of Canaan, and drowned Pharaoh and his army in the Red Sea. All the other events of which we read in the Old Testament, they declare, were done by him.

Also, just as they believe Moses to have been the minister of the devil and mediator between him and the children of Israel, so they believe the prophets were Satan's messengers. If sometimes they said anything good in reference to Christ, they spoke because forced to do so by the Holy Spirit; this they also believe was true of Moses when he spoke of Christ.

They also believe that no one could attain salvation by his acts before the advent of Christ unless, after Christ, he again assumed flesh in which he might receive penance and the sacrament of baptism, which they believe to be nothing other than the imposition of hands. Whence, they believe that those who are spoken of in Matthew 27:52, "Many bodies of the saints that had slept arose," having received the imposition of hands, again did penance. Of them they believe the Apostle also spoke when he said of Christ in I Corinthians 15:6, "Then he was seen by more than five hundred brethren."

Also, they believe that Christ is lesser than the Father in Godhood, and the Holy Spirit lesser than Christ.

They also believe—with the exception of some of whom we shall speak later[28]—that Christ did not put on true flesh of the flesh of Adam.

They also deny all the sacraments of the Church, the resurrection of the flesh, and the exercise of temporal authority. They say that an oath is forbidden under any circumstances. This is their faith, a very false one, as, with the aid of the grace of God, will appear in separate articles below. . . .

Book V
Chapter I: What Constitutes the Catholic Church?

With regard to the first chapter, we should be aware that as the Scriptures attest, the Church appears in this world in two forms: One is the church of the saints, referred to in Psalm 149:1, "Sing ye to the Lord a new canticle: Let his praise be in the church of the saints." The second is the church of the malignant, of which, as we read, the Holy Spirit spoke through David in Psalm 25:5, "I have hated the assembly of the malignant."[29] Like a tree and its root, Holy Church has its root in faith; hence Romans 1:17, "The just man liveth by faith." Faith is the foundation of the spiritual edifice; hence it is said in Hebrews 11:1, "Faith is the substance of things to be hoped for, the evidence of things that appear not," and for that reason in I Corinthians 3:11, "Other foundation no man can lay but that which is laid, which is Christ Jesus," that is, the foundation is His faith, by which Christ lives in the hearts of the faithful, as is said in Ephesians 3:17.

The heretic, however, is wont to ask: What constitutes the Church of God?

To this the answer is that the heretic first should have asked: What is the essence of the Church (*quid sit ecclesia*)? In resolving that question, I say that the Church is the congregation of the faithful. Moreover, no matter what its enemies may pretend, the Church is the one which is called Roman. The evidence for this fact comes from examination of its faith, that faith from which it originates. Faith precedes good works, hence consideration of faith precedes consideration of works. For, as the essence of the Church originates from faith, as we have already remarked, and from faith the Church comes unto works in harmony with faith, so also the first recognition of the Church is by faith, through which it is primarily identified and distinguished from the church of the malignant; hence, Galatians 3:7, "Know ye therefore that they who are of faith, the same are the children of Abraham"; John 1:12, "He gave them power to be made the sons of God, to them that believe in His name." Faith, therefore, makes the sons of God. It cleanses their hearts: Acts 15:9, "Purifying their hearts by faith." It produces justice, that is, just works; hence, in Hebrews 11:33 it is said of some that through faith they wrought justice. It gives life, leading on to the glory of eternal happiness; hence, John 3:16, "For God so loved the world as to give his only begotten Son, that whosoever believeth in him may not perish but have life everlasting." In us, faith produces purity, justice, and glory: purity by which we are restored; justice by which we are led onward; glory to which we are guided. We are restored from impassable places to the way; we are led onward from strength to strength; we are guided, moreover, from exile to our homeland.

Again, the Blessed Peter points out the need to examine faith, in the third chapter of his first epistle, verse 15, "Being ready always to satisfy everyone that asketh you a reason of that hope which is in you." But because faith without works is not sufficient for salvation, another test of the Church must be by works, for in the second place it is known by works. Since the faith of the Roman Church is attested by the Law and the prophets, as appears in each article which we have discussed in the preceding four books, while your faith, O Cathar, not only finds no witness among them but contradicts them, it is obvious that the Roman Church, which has faith and good works, two things in which the Church abides, is the Church of God.

The heretic makes an objection, saying: As we find in Matthew 7:17-18, a tree is known by its fruits. The fruit of the Roman Church is evil; therefore the Roman Church is evil. . . .[30]

Also, the heretic objects, saying: Since the fruit of the Roman faith is evil, its faith is evil. . . .

The heretic in opposition objects: Ten parts or more of the Roman Church are evil; therefore it ought to be called the church of the devil rather than of God. . . .

Also [the heretic says]: The faith of the Roman Church is dead; hence, so also is the Roman Church. For from dead faith there is no life. But if the Roman Church is dead, while the Church of God is life, it is not the Church of God. . . .

Also, the heretic bases an objection on a wicked prelate or some other wicked Christian, accusing him by quoting James 2:18, "But some man will say, 'Thou hast faith, and I have works; show me thy faith without works and I will show thee by works, my faith.'" . . .

Also, the heretic again seeks to prove that the Roman Church is not the Church of God because of its many usages which are not recorded in the Gospel or any other book of the New Testament, nor is there proof that they were practiced in the primitive Church. . . .

Again, to defame the Church the heretic quotes Matthew 23:4 about the Pharisees and scribes among the Jews, "For they bind heavy and insupportable burdens and lay them on men's shoulders, but with a finger of their own they will not move them." Such, they say, are the priests of the Roman Church. . . .

They also cite against the Church the words of the Lord to the scribes and Pharisees, Matthew 23:13, "But woe to you scribes and Pharisees, hypocrites! because you shut the kingdom of heaven against men; for you yourselves do not enter in, and those that are going in you suffer not to enter." Now they say that we are like them because we do not enter the kingdom of heaven, that is, we do not enter the Church of God through faith, nor do we allow those who wish to enter to do so. . . . This they say because we do not join their congregation, which they call the kingdom of heaven. . . .

They also base an objection on the Lord's words to the scribes and Pharisees in Matthew 23:29-33, "Woe to you scribes and Pharisees, hypocrites! that build the sepulchers of the prophets and adorn the monuments of the just and say, 'If we had been in the days of our fathers, we would not have been partakers with them in the blood of the prophets.' Wherefore you are witnesses against yourselves, that you are the sons of them that killed the prophets. Fill ye up then the measure of your fathers. You serpents, generation of vipers, how will you flee from the judgment of hell?" Christ's intent was to say that as they were the children of murderers in the natural sense, to which they bore witness, so also were they their children in imitating them. For the fathers killed the prophets, and these, who built and adorned the sepulchers, reproving the evil deeds of the fathers, filled up the measure of the fathers because they put Lord Jesus and His apostles to death. In saying to them, "Fill up," and so on, He did not bid them do so but predicted that which would be done, since He said: "You will fill up," using the imperative for the indicative mood. The heretics say that the priests of the Roman Church, whom they call modern Pharisees, fired by the same wrath, plot the same kind of murders. They say that the Pharisees among the Jews, whom they call the fathers of our priests, killed the apostles, persecuted the primitive church of the saints; our priests build and adorn the sepulchers of the slain and construct altars over them. But also fired by the same wrath, they fill up the measure of the Pharisees by murders and by persecuting the church of the heretics. . . .

Also, the heretic says that the Roman Church talks about good but does it not. If it does any good thing, its purpose is that the eyes of men may behold it. Hence, it decorates the front and sides of the altar, but not the back, which is not exposed to men's eyes. It says long prayers, so as to lay hold of the goods of widows, and that it may collect tithes and the first fruits of oil and beasts from a prince. Of all these things Christ harshly accused the scribes and Pharisees in Matthew, chapter 23.

Also, the heretic says: If the head be good, how astonishing that it has such evil members. . . .

Also, the heretic says: The Church should suffer persecution in this world, not practice it on others. But the Roman Church persecutes others, while itself remaining free from persecution. . . .

Also, the heretic objects: The Church of Christ, threatened by persecution, was often hungry and thirsty, was naked and buffeted, and made weak; it worked with its hands, not seeking the wealth of others, gladly giving of its own to Christ's poor, so that there was no one in want in their midst. It was cursed and it blessed; hence I Corinthians 4:11, "Even unto this hour we both hunger and thirst, and are naked and are buffeted," and so on. The Roman Church is not in this condition. For the Roman Church is rich in great possessions, in luxuries; it is garbed in purple and linen, and it has splendid feasts every day. It is untroubled and is established in this world, works not with its hands; but being itself wanton and idle, devours the labors of others. It is blessed by others and it curses. . . .

Also, they say: The Church of Christ was scorned and blasphemed by the world; on the other hand, the world honors the Roman Church. . . .

Also, they say that the Church of Christ first gave instruction before it would baptize anyone, as is found in Matthew 28:19, "Going therefore, teach ye all nations, baptizing them," and so on. The Roman Church baptizes before it teaches, as is obvious in the case of infants. Furthermore, Christ and His disciples are never known to have baptized anyone who lacked faith and the ability to reason. But the Roman Church does so. . . .

Also, they attempt to prove that the Roman Church is not the Church of God by the example of the widow to whom there is reference in I Timothy 5:9, "Let a widow be chosen of no less than threescore years of age," and so on. The Church of God should choose such a woman, but the Roman Church does not. . . .[31]

Also, the heretic says: The Church of God did not kill or swear. The Roman Church does so. . . .

Also, the heretic says that the children of the Roman Church rob and steal, contrary to God's command. . . .

Also, they object that many there are in the Roman Church who are in want, half dead from hunger, thirst, and cold, on whom the wealthy members of the Roman Church have no pity, but allow them to weep, to be afflicted by these sufferings. In what way does the love of God abide in such persons? Not at all, as also is said in I John 3:17, "He that hath the substance of this world," and so on. Yet if the love of God does not abide in them, how can they be the Church of God?

Also, the heretic objects that the Roman Church has multiplied and spread throughout the world, but the Church of God, on the contrary, is few in number: Matthew 7:14, "Strait is the way that leads to life. . . ."

Also, the heretic objects, saying: The Church of Christ is called a heresy by the priests and their leaders, as appears in Acts 24:14, where Paul says to Felix, the governor, "But this I confess to thee, that according to the way which they call a heresy so do I serve the Father and my God," and so on. . . .

Also, everywhere Paul was contradicted, as described in Acts, chapter 28. But the Roman Church is called holy and Catholic by men of this world, and is treated with favor everywhere in the world.

Also, the heretic objects, saying: Orders such as the Augustinian and Benedictine orders were not present in the Church of Christ. They exist in the Roman Church. . . .

Also, in the Church of God there were only bishops, sons, priests or elders, and deacons. There were no archbishops, primates, cardinals; no archeacons, acolytes, exorcists, readers, doorkeepers; no precentors or sacristans.

Also the heretics object: There is only one mode of salvation, since there is only one way of salvation, according to Christ, who said in John 14:6, "I am the way and the truth and the life. No man cometh

to the Father but by me." Yet the way of the Roman Church is multi-
fold, for there is one way for monks, another for canons regular, another for other clerics. There is one for the Friars Preachers and another
for the Friars Minor. Therefore, the Roman Church is not the way of
salvation. . . .

They say also that no one may be saved but in Christ's teaching,
which the Apostle transmitted. . . .

Also, they seek in another way to prove that the Roman Church is
not the Church of God, because it blesses the *carroccio*³² prepared for
unjust combat, that is, for battles against brothers and neighbors, and
so urges men to fight unjustly.

If we reply to them, to the contrary, that some battles against
neighbors and brothers are just, they retort: When several cities fight
against each other, surely the cause of one of them is not just. Why,
then, does the prelate bless the *carroccio* of this faction? . . .

The heretic also objects that the Roman Church is not the Church of
God because it is placed before others and set over them, although the
Church of God ought, by the testimony of Peter [I, 2:13], be subject
to every creature. . . .

1. *What Constitutes the Church? How the Heretics Prove That the
Roman Church Is Not the Church of God.*—In execration of the Roman
Church also, the heretic cites the text of Apocalypse 17:3, where John
says that he saw "a woman sitting upon a scarlet-colored beast, full of
the names of blasphemy"; and, to sum it up briefly, the Cathars, and
the Leonists as well, believe that all or almost all of what is found in
the Apocalypse, chapters 17, 18, and in the first part of chapter 19 to
the words of verse 3, "And her smoke ascended forever and ever," was
recorded against the Roman Church. For they interpret "the beast" and
"the woman" as references to the Roman Church. The beast, we read,
was scarlet; likewise, we find in verse 4 that the woman was clothed
with "scarlet and purple, and gilt with gold, and precious stones and
pearls, having a golden cup in her hand." These words are applicable
to the lord pope, who is the head of the Roman Church. The woman
"drunk with the blood of the saints" (verse 6) is referred to in the same
connection. This symbol they attach to the Roman Church because it
orders their death, for they believe that they are saints. At the end of
the chapter [verse 18] one reads, "And the woman which thou sawest
is the great city which has kingdom over the kings of the earth" [Apoc.

17:18]. They seek to prove their point from the fact that that woman is called Babylon at the end of chapter 16[:19], and in Apocalypse 18:2, "Babylon the great is fallen, is fallen," and because Peter, at the end of his [first] epistle, 5:13, says, "The church that is in Babylon, elected together with you," that is, in Rome. . . .

51. The Summa of Rainerius Sacconi

Rainerius Sacconi, onetime heretic become Dominican friar and inquisitor, wrote the most widely circulated tract on the Cathars and Waldenses of the thirteenth century.[1] He was a native of Piacenza, that city so torn by civic and religious strife, but after many years in heresy—"formerly a heresiarch" he says of himself—he was converted, about the year 1245, by the influence of Peter of Verona, and entered the Dominican order. The careers of these two men then ran together for several years. In 1252 Rainerius was also a target of the plot which took Peter's life,[2] but he escaped. He later sat with the commission investigating the miracles attributed to his martyred associate and, as inquisitor, took part in the proceedings against the assassins. From 1254 to 1259 he was inquisitor for Lombardy. The last record of him is in a papal letter of July, 1262.

In 1250, Rainerius wrote his *Summa de Catharis et Pauperibus de Lugduno* [summa on the Cathars and the Poor of Lyons]. Its great historical value in details of Catharist churches and sects and in the catalogue of their beliefs [3] is qualified only by a certain terseness and by the obvious antipathy of the convert for his former coreligionists. As Father Dondaine remarks, without Rainerius's description of the doctrinal system of John of Lugio, our understanding of an important heretical work, the *Liber de duobus principiis* (see No. 59), would be much more difficult.

The translation is of the summa as printed by Antoine Dondaine, in his preface to *Un Traité néo-manichéen du XIIIe siècle: Le* Liber du duobus principiis, *suivi d'un fragment de rituel cathare* (Rome, 1939), pp. 64-78,[4] by permission of the Istituto storico domenicano di S. Sabina. For our comments on the author we have relied heavily on the sketch of his career in that same work.[5]

1250

THE SUMMA OF BROTHER RAINERIUS OF THE ORDER OF PREACHERS ON THE CATHARS AND THE POOR OF LYONS

In the name of our Lord Jesus Christ.

Although at one time sects of heretics were numerous, by the grace of Jesus Christ they have been almost completely destroyed; yet, two in particular are now found, one of which is called the Cathars or Patarines, the other the Leonists or Poor of Lyons. Their beliefs are set forth in the pages which follow.

[1] *On the Various Sects of the Cathars.*—Now it should be noted at the outset that the foremost sect, to wit, the Cathars, is divided into three parts or principal groups, the first of which is called the Albanenses, the second the Concorezzenses, the third the Bagnolenses; all these are in Lombardy. Other Cathars, whether in Tuscany or in the March [of Treviso] or in Provence, do not differ in beliefs from the Cathars just named or from some part of them. For all the Cathars have general beliefs in which they agree and particular ones in which they differ. We shall discuss all of these and first those which they hold in common.

[2] *On the General Beliefs of the Cathars.*—The general beliefs of all Cathars are as follows: That the devil made this world and everything in it. Also, that all the sacraments of the Church, namely, baptism of actual water and the other sacraments, are of no avail for salvation and that they are not the true sacraments of Christ and His Church but are deceptive and diabolical and belong to the church of the wicked. How many sacraments, which ones, and of what sort the aforesaid heretics do have is recounted below. Also, a belief common to all Cathars is that carnal matrimony has always been a mortal sin and that in the future life one incurs no heavier a penalty for adultery or incest than for legitimate marriage, nor indeed among them should anyone be more severely punished on this account. Also, all Cathars deny the future resurrection of the body. Also, they believe that to eat meat, eggs, or cheese, even in pressing need, is a mortal sin; this for the reason that they are begotten by coition. Also, that taking an oath is in no case permissible; this, consequently, is a mortal sin. Also, that secular authorities commit mortal sin in punishing malefactors or heretics. Also, that no one can attain salvation except in their sect. Also, that all children, even the baptized, will endure no lighter punishment in eternity than will thieves and murderers.[6] On this point the Albanenses seem to disagree somewhat, as will be explained below. Also, they all deny purgatory.

[3] *On the Sacraments of the Cathars.*—The Cathars, indeed, like apes who try to imitate the acts of man, have four sacraments, though

false and vain, unlawful and sacrilegious. They are the imposition of the hand, blessing of bread, penance, and consecration,[7] which will be treated in this sequence.

[4] *On the Imposition of the Hand.*—The imposition of the hand is called by them the consolamentum, spiritual baptism, or baptism of the Holy Spirit. According to them, without it mortal sin is not forgiven, nor is the Holy Spirit imparted to anyone; both of these occur only when the rite is performed by them. But the Albanenses differ a little from the others in this; for they say that in this rite the hand accomplishes nothing (since according to them it was itself created by the devil, as will be explained below), but only the Lord's Prayer, which those who impose the hand repeat at the time.[8] All the other Cathars, however, say that both, that is, the imposition of the hand and the Lord's Prayer, are necessary and requisite for the rite. It is also the common belief of all Cathars that no remission of sins is accomplished by that imposition of the hand if those who impose the hand are in any mortal sin at the time. This imposition of the hand is performed by at least two persons, and not only by their prelates but by those under them, even, in case of need, by Cathar women.

[5] *On the Breaking of Bread.*—The blessing of bread by the Cathars is a certain bread-breaking which they perform daily at the morning and evening meal. This breaking of bread is done thus: When the Cathars, men and women, have come to the table, they remain standing while they say the Lord's Prayer. Meanwhile, one who has precedence in length of membership or rank[9] holds a loaf, or several if necessary for the group which happens to be present, and with the words, "May the grace of our Lord Jesus Christ be always with us all," he breaks the loaf or loaves and distributes the bread to all those at the table, not only to Cathars but also to their believers, to thieves, adulterers, and murderers. The Albanenses, however, say that the actual bread is not blessed nor can it receive any blessing, since according to them the bread itself is the creation of the devil. In this they differ from all the others, who say that the bread is truly blessed. Nevertheless, none of them believes that the bread is changed into the body of Christ.

[6] *On the False Penance of the Cathars.*—The next point of discussion is the nature of the penance of the Cathars. The penance of the Cathars is altogether false and vain, deceptive and poisonous, as is shown below. For in true penance three things are requisite: contrition

of heart, confession of the lips, and satisfaction by works. But I, Brother Rainerius, formerly a heresiarch but now by the grace of God a priest in the Order of Preachers, although unworthy, say positively and testify before God, who knows that I do not lie, that not one of these three appears among the Cathars or in their penance. For the poison of error which they have sucked from the mouth of the old serpent does not let them feel any sorrow for their sins. This error is fourfold, namely, that eternal glory is not lessened for any penitent by any sin, that the punishment of hell is not increased thereby for the impenitent, that for no one is purgatorial fire reserved, and that guilt and penalty are blotted out by God through the imposition of the hand. Judas the traitor will be punished no more severely than a child one day old, but all will be equal in glory as well as in punishment. This they believe, except the Albanenses, who say that each one will be restored to his former status, although not by his own merits, and that in each kingdom, whether of God or of the devil, some are greater than others.

And I add this further statement, that many of them who have been infected by the errors set forth above often grieve when they recall that they did not indulge their passions more frequently in the days when they had not yet professed the heresy of the Cathars. Moreover, this is why many believers, both men and women, no more fear to give themselves to sister or brother, daughter or son, niece or nephew, relation by blood or marriage, than to their own wife or husband. But from acts of this kind some of them are perhaps restrained by horror or by a natural human feeling of shame.

That they do not feel contrition for sins committed before the profession of their heresy is clearly proved by the fact that they make restitution to no man for usury, theft, or rapine; on the contrary they keep the gain for themselves, or rather they leave it to their children or relatives who are still of the world. They say that usury is no sin.

Furthermore, I say positively that during the seventeen years when I was in intimate converse with them, I did not see any one of them pray secretly, apart from the others, or show himself contrite for his sins, or weep, or beat his breast and say, "Be gracious, O Lord, to me, a sinner," or anything of this sort, which might be a sign of contrition. Never do they implore the aid or intervention of angels, or of the Blessed Virgin Mary, or of the saints, nor fortify themselves by the sign of the Cross.

[7] *On the Confession of the Cathars.*—Now to be considered is the

confession of the Cathars: what it is and how constituted, when they make it, and to whom they confess. Their confession is made in this manner: "I am here before God and before you to make confession and to take upon myself the guilt for all my sins which in any way are in me and to obtain pardon from God and from you all." The confession is made publicly and in the presence of all who have met together, where oftentimes there are a hundred or more Cathars, men and women, and their believers. Every one of them makes the confession quoted when he receives the imposition of the hand described above, reciting it primarily to their prelate, who holds the Gospels or the whole New Testament before his breast. After absolution has been granted, the prelate places the Book, and the other Cathars who are present put their right hand upon the convert's head; then they begin their prayers.

When, moreover, any one of them, after he has received the imposition of the hand, commits a sin of the flesh or any other which is a mortal sin according to their belief, he need confess that sin only and no others and may again receive the imposition of the hand, privately, from his prelate and at least one associate.[10]

Also, confession of venial sins is made in this manner: One says in a loud voice, speaking for all who are bowed to the ground before the prelate, who holds the Book before his breast, "We come before God and before you to confess our sins, for we have sinned much in word and in deed, in our purposes and in thoughts," and more of this sort. Whence it is clearly apparent that all the Cathars die in their sins without confession. In this fashion they confess once a month if they can conveniently do so.

The next question is whether the Cathars do works in satisfaction of the sins which they committed before they professed heresy. To this I say no, although this may perchance seem strange to the undiscerning. For they do pray often and they fast and they always abstain from meat, eggs, and cheese, all of which seem to be in the nature of acts to amend for their sins; and of them they often boast vaingloriously. But there is among them a threefold error which prevents the said works from being reparations. The first is that guilt and punishment are totally wiped out by their imposition of the hand and by prayer, or by prayer alone according to the Albanenses, as was stated above. The second is that God inflicts on no one purgatorial punishment, the existence of which they totally deny, or temporal punishment, which they think is inflicted by the devil in this life. Here also we must say that from the time they become Cathars the works referred to are not required of them for penance or for the remission of sins.[11] The third is that everyone is bound of necessity to perform these works as if they were the commands of God. For instance, a boy ten years old who had never committed any mortal sin at all before he became a Cathar is in the same class as an old man who had never ceased from sinning. For no Cathar among them would be punished any more severely if he drank poison from a desire to commit suicide than if, on a physician's advice, he ate a fowl to avoid death or for some other imperative reason; nor, in their view, would he be punished more severely in the hereafter. They speak in the same way about matrimony, as has already been explained above.

Also, they do little or no almsgiving, none to outsiders, except to avoid scandal among their neighbors and to be held in esteem by them, and little to their own needy. The reason for this is threefold. The first is that they do not thereby expect greater glory in the hereafter or forgiveness of their sins. The second is that almost all of them are very avaricious and grasping. This is why the poor among them, who in time of persecution do not have the necessities of life or anything with which to repay those who harbor them for goods or houses destroyed on their account, can hardly find anyone who is then willing to receive them; but wealthy Cathars can find many. Wherefore every one of them accumulates wealth if he can and saves it.

Furthermore, the question of their prayer should not be overlooked; the times at which they think it must be said, most particularly when they partake of food and drink. Since many of them when ill have sometimes asked those who nursed them not to put any food or drink into their mouths if the invalids could not at least say the Lord's Prayer, it is quite evident that many of them thus commit suicide.

So, from what has been said above, it is abundantly clear that the Cathars perform no penance, especially since they do not feel contrition for their sins or confess them or do works in satisfaction of them (although they do greatly afflict themselves), and that for their errors they will be heavily punished throughout eternity.

Now we have to deal with the fourth and last sacrament of the Cathars, namely, consecration. First, how many offices they have; second, their names; third, the function of each office; fourth and fifth, by whom and how they are constituted; and last is added the number and location of the churches of the Cathars.

[8] *On the Offices of the Cathars and Their Duties.*—The offices of the Cathars are four. He who has been established in the first and highest office is called bishop; in the second, the elder son; in the third, the younger son; and in the fourth and last, the deacon. The others among them, who are without office, are called Christian men and women.

[9] *On the Functions of the Bishops.*—It is the duty of the bishop always to take the first place in everything they do, namely, in the imposition of the hand, the breaking of bread, and beginning the prayer. In the absence of the bishop, the elder son presides, and in the absence of the bishop and the elder son, the younger son does so.

Moreover, these two sons, together or separately, go about visiting all the Cathar men and women who are in the bishop's charge, and all persons owe them obedience. Likewise, the deacons preside and perform all functions, each among his charges, in the absence of the bishop and the sons. It is to be noted that the bishops and the sons have particular deacons in their own particular cities, especially where Cathars abide.

[10] *On the Duty of the Deacons.*—It is also the function of the deacons to hear from those in their charge the confession of venial sins, which is made once a month, as mentioned above, and to give them absolution by enjoining on them a three-day fast or one hundred genuflections. This is called the Service, or, in other words, to impose (*caregare*) the Service.

[11] *How the Bishop Is Ordained.*—The offices just described are conferred by the bishop and also, with the bishop's consent, by the sons. The ordination of a bishop once usually took place in this fashion: When a bishop died, the younger son ordained the elder son as bishop, the latter thereupon ordained the younger son as elder son. Then a younger son was elected by all the prelates and those in their charge who were gathered at the place set for the election, and he was ordained as younger son by the bishop. The ordination of the younger son has not been changed among them. But that described above for the bishop has been changed by all the Cathars dwelling on this side of the sea,[12] who say that by the former ordination the son would appear to install the father, which seems rather unnatural. Consequently, it is now done

in a different way, namely, the bishop before his death consecrates the elder son as bishop. Upon the death of either one of these, the younger son is made elder son and bishop on the same day. Thus almost every church of the Cathars has two bishops. Hence, John of Lugio, who is one of those so consecrated, always describes himself in his letters, "John, by grace of God elder son and ordained bishop," etc. Nevertheless, both ordinations are manifestly reprehensible, for a carnal son never appoints his parent and nowhere do we read that one and the same church had two bishops at the same time, just as one woman does not legally have two husbands.

[12] *The Method of Ordination.*—All the offices described above are conferred by the imposition of the hand, and that grace of conferring the offices listed and of bestowing the Holy Spirit is assigned to their bishop alone, or to any one of them who has precedence and who officiates by holding the New Testament over the head of the one on whom the hand is imposed.

[13] *A Notable Uncertainty among Them.*—Hence, all Cathars labor under very great doubt and danger of soul. To specify, if their prelate, especially their bishop, may secretly have committed some mortal sin —and many such persons have been found among them in the past— all those upon whom he has imposed his hand have been misled and perish if they die in that state. In order to avoid this peril all the churches of the Cathars, excepting only one or two, have allowed the consolamentum for the second, or even for the third time, that is, the imposition of the hand, which is their baptism, as described above. These facts are a matter of common report among them.

[14] *These Are the Churches of the Cathars.*—There are in all sixteen Cathar churches but, reader, do not blame me for calling them churches, rather blame them, since this is how they refer to themselves: The church of the Albanenses or of Desenzano,[13] the church of Concorezzo, the church of the Bagnolenses or of Bagnolo, the church of Vicenza or of the March [of Treviso], the church of Florence, the church of the Spoletan Valley, the church of France, the Toulousan church, the church of Carcassonne, the Albigensian church, the church of Sclavonia, the church of the Latins of Constantinople, the church of the Greeks of the same place, the church of Philadelphia in Romania, the church of Bulgaria, the church of Drugunthia. All sprang from the last two named.

[15] *The Places Where They Are Located.*—The first group, namely, the Albanenses dwell in Verona and several cities of Lombardy and number about five hundred of both sexes. Those of Concorezzo are scattered throughout almost all of Lombardy, and there are fifteen hundred or more of both sexes. The Bagnolenses are at Mantua, Brescia, Bergamo, and in the region of Milan (but in very small numbers), and in Romagna; there are about two hundred of them. The church of the March [of Treviso] persists at Vicenza[14] but has no members at Verona; there are about one hundred of them. Those of Tuscany and of the Spoletan Valley number not quite a hundred. The church of France is in Verona and Lombardy, about one hundred and fifty strong. The Toulousan church, the Albigensian, and that of Carcassonne, together with some who were formerly of the church of Agen, which has been almost totally destroyed, number nearly two hundred. The church of the Latins in Constantinople comprises less than fifty people. Likewise, the church of Sclavonia, that of Philadelphia, and those of the Greeks, of Bulgaria, and of Drugunthia, number altogether something under five hundred. O reader, you can safely say that in the whole world there are not as many as four thousand Cathars of both sexes,[15] and the computation given here has been made many times in the past among them.

[16] *On Beliefs Peculiar to the Albanenses.*—An account has been given in the preceding of the beliefs and sacraments common to the Cathars and also of their ministers. It remains now to describe the ideas peculiar to each group, beginning with the church of the Albanenses, which is also called by the name of Desenzano, because they err in more ways than the others.

First, then, it is important to note that these Albanenses are divided into two groups with contrary and different opinions. The head of one group is Belesmanza of Verona,[16] their bishop, whom most of the older and a few of the younger persons of that sect follow. The leader of the other group is John of Lugio of Bergamo,[17] their elder son and ordained bishop. He is followed, in distinction from the first group, by the younger men and a few of the older ones; this group is somewhat larger than the first.

[17] *On the Beliefs of Belesmanza.*—The first group maintains the old beliefs, which all the Cathars and Albanenses used to hold in the period of approximately A.D. 1200 to 1230. Thus, their peculiar beliefs,

besides the common ones set forth above, are these:

That there are from eternity two principles, to wit, of good and of evil.

Also, that the Trinity, namely, the Father, the Son, and the Holy Spirit, is not one God, but that the Father is greater than the Son and than the Holy Spirit.

Also, that each principle, or each God, created his own angels and his own world, and that this world and all which is in it was created, made, and formed by the evil deity.

Also, that the devil with his angels ascended into heaven and there, after doing battle with the archangel Michael and the angels of the good God, carried off a third part of the creatures created by God. These he implants daily in human bodies and in those of lower animals, and also transfers them from one body to another until such time as all shall be brought back to heaven. According to these heretics, these beings created by God are called "the people of God," "souls," "the sheep of Israel," and also by many other names.

Also, that the Son of God did not acquire human nature in reality but only its semblance from the Blessed Virgin, who, they say, was an angel. Neither did He really eat, drink, or suffer, nor was He really dead and buried, nor was His resurrection real, but all these things were in appearance only, as one reads of Him in Luke, "being (as it was supposed) the son of Joseph."[18] They teach the same about all the miracles which Christ performed.

Also, that Abraham, Isaac, Jacob, Moses, and all the fathers of old, and John the Baptist, were enemies of God and ministers of the devil.

Also, that the devil was the author of all of the Old Testament except these books: Job, the Psalms, the books of Solomon, of Jesus the son of Sirach, of Isaiah, Jeremiah, Ezechiel, Daniel, and of the twelve prophets. Some of these, they say, were written in heaven, to wit, those which were written before the destruction of Jerusalem, which, they say, was the heavenly land.

Also, that the world will never come to an end.

Also, that the "future" judgment has already been made and will not be made again.

Also, that hell and eternal fire or eternal punishment are in this world only and nowhere else.

In general, all the Albanenses in the time we have stated held the beliefs described above, except those who were less well informed, to whom special points were not revealed.

[18] *On Beliefs Peculiar to John of Lugio.*—Next to be described here are the beliefs of the John of Lugio mentioned above and his followers. It should first be noted that John still holds some of the beliefs mentioned above, some of them he has completely changed for the worse, and some other errors he has devised for himself, as appears below.

[19] *On the Two Principles.*—This John of Lugio, an Albanensian, asserts that there are from eternity two principles, or gods, or lords, namely, one of good and the other of evil, but in rather a different fashion from the earlier ideas, as will soon be apparent. He completely spurns the Trinity and its unity in God as held in the Catholic faith.

[20] *The Names He Gives to the Evil Principle.*—The first principle of evil, he maintains, is called by many names in the Holy Scriptures. It is called malice, iniquity, cupidity, impiety, sin, pride, death, hell, calumny, vanity, injustice, perdition, confusion, corruption, and fornication. And he also says that all the evils named are gods or goddesses, that they have their being from the malice which, he asserts, is a first cause, and that this first cause is signified from time to time by the vices named.[19]

Moreover, he says that the evil principle is denoted by "the tongue," which St. James characterizes as "an unquiet evil, full of deadly poisons";[20] likewise by "day," whereof the Lord says in the Gospel, "Sufficient for the day is the evil thereof."[21] It is also referred to in that phrase of the Apostle in his second epistle to the Corinthians, "*It is*, and *It is not*."[22] It is called also Mount Seir, concerning which it is said in Ezechiel, "Because thou hast been an everlasting enemy of the Lord."[23] It is also said to be the belly, whereof the Apostle says, "Whose God is their belly."[24]

He says further that the idols of the nations of which one reads throughout the entire Old Testament are really evil gods, that is, malign spirits, and that the Gentiles made images of them the better to worship them. But why say more? It disgusts me to record the many fabulous things which this John has written about the above-mentioned evils and idols in an attempt to buttress his errors.

[21] *On the Beliefs of John of Lugio about Creation and What Creation Is, According to Him.*[25]—What this John believes about the

creator of all things visible and invisible remains to be told. First, what creation is; second, whether created things were made or created from nothing; third, whether creatures of the good God were created absolutely good and pure, without any evil; fourth, whether anyone ever had freedom of will.

According to him, to create is to make something from some pre-existent matter, and it is always so considered, never to make from nothing. And he distinguishes a threefold creation: First, from good to better; according to this distinction, Christ was created or made by the Father, whence Isaiah, "I the Lord have created Him,"[26] and, the Apostle says, "made a high priest forever."[27] Secondly, to change from evil to good is called "to create," in accord with the word of the Apostle, "For we are his workmanship, created in Christ Jesus,"[28] and the sentence in Genesis, "In the beginning, God created heaven and earth,"[29] which John explains thus: "In the beginning," that is, in the Son who says: "[I am] the beginning, who also speak unto you."[30] And John explicitly says that at that time God the Father created heaven and earth, not from nothing but from something to something good, as with those of whom the Apostle says, "Created in Christ Jesus in good works."[31] Thirdly, creating also refers to making bad into worse. In support of this he adduces that passage in The Code [of Justinian] under the title *De haereticis et Manichaeis:* "All heresies forbidden by divine laws and imperial constitutions," and so on, as far as "to create ministers because they are not."[32] And so, he says, all creatures exist from eternity, good creatures with the good God and evil with the evil god; that creators do not precede creatures in eternity except causally; and that creatures are from God from eternity, like the splendor or rays of the sun which does not precede its rays in time, but only as cause or by nature.

Also, he thinks that the good God has another world wherein are people and animals and everything else comparable to the visible and corruptible creatures here; marriages and fornications and adulteries take place there, from which children are born. And what is even more base, there the people of the good God, against His command, have taken foreign women to wife, that is, daughters of a strange god or of evil gods, and from such shameful and forbidden intercourse have been born giants[33] and many other beings at various times.

[22] *Whether the Good God Created His Creatures Free of Evil.*— The next point is whether the good God created His creatures pure,

without any evil. In this connection it is necessary to pass over many blasphemies uttered by this John, such as that God is not omnipotent. He says, however, that God wills and can do all good as far as lies in Him and in His creatures, who of necessity render him obedience, but that this will and power of God are hindered by His enemy.

Also, that each of these gods has been active against the other from eternity and that the evil cause, that is, the evil god, has from eternity attacked the true God and His Son and all His works. In support of these points he cites many authorities, such as that speech of the Lord to Satan in Job, "Thou hast moved me against Job, that I should afflict him without cause";[34] and again, Job to God, "Thou art changed to be cruel toward me."[35]

Also, he says that he who is chief in evil is more powerful than the creatures who are subjects of the highest God of good; whence, he concludes from these premises that the good God could not make His creatures perfect even though He wished to. And this befell Him and His creatures because of the opposition of the evil god, who from eternity has forced into them his own impulse (*actum*) or a certain malice, from which evil they have the capability of sinning. In support of this he cites that passage in Ecclesiasticus, "He that could have transgressed, and hath not transgressed, and could do evil things, and hath not done them,"[36] the whole of which he simply explains as referring to Christ; and that passage from Job, "In his angels he found wickedness,"[37] and again, "The stars are not pure,"[38] and so on; and the passage in the beginning of Genesis, "Now the serpent was more subtle than any of the beasts of the earth which the Lord God had made."[39] From this he draws the inference: Therefore all the beasts of the field are endowed with cunning, but the serpent more than all the others, and therefore through him has deceitfulness come about. In addition to the foregoing, he also makes another assertion on his own authority, to wit, that there is nothing which has free will, not even God most high, since even He could not carry out His own will because of the opposition of His enemy.

Also, he says that every creature of the good God received the capacity for action under influence of error. He calls error the greatest god of evil. Christ is an exception. In Him that capacity for sinning or the power of transgression was so suppressed by the highest good that it failed of its effect—which was marvelous and extraordinary, even for

Christ. Wherefore, He is greatly to be praised, as says Ecclesiasticus, "Who is He, and we will praise Him?"[40] and so on. All other creatures of the good God became blameworthy. In support of this he cites the word of the Apostle, "For the creature was made subject to vanity, not willingly,"[41] and so on; and again, "We know that every creature groaneth,"[42] and so on.

Also, he says that when God inflicts punishments for sins upon His creatures, He does evil and does not comport Himself as God but rather serves His adversary.

Also, he says that when God declares, "I am God and there is no other,"[43] and again, "See that I alone am God,"[44] and the like, repetitiously, then He is influenced by His adversary, for the true God speaks but once and, as Job says, does not repeat Himself.[45]

Also, he says that God, by the power of His own knowledge, does not have foreknowledge of anything evil, since it does not emanate from Him, but sometimes He does have foreknowledge of it through His adversary.

Also, he believes that the true God brought about the Flood, destroyed Pentapolis, and overthrew Jerusalem, because of the sins of His creatures; and, to summarize, the true God, provoked by His adversary, brought upon His people Israel all the afore-mentioned evils which they suffered in Judea or in the Promised Land because of the sins which they had committed. So this John says; he also believes that all the events mentioned took place in a certain other world, belonging to the true God.

Also, he believes that the souls who are of God are transferred from body to body and that in the end all will be freed from punishment and guilt.

Also, this John accepts the whole Bible, but thinks that it was written in another world, and that there Adam and Eve were formed.

Also, he believes that Noah, Abraham, Isaac, Jacob, and the other patriarchs, and Moses, Joshua, and all the prophets, and the Blessed John the Baptist were pleasing to God and that they were men in another world.

Also, that Christ was born according to the flesh of the fathers of old, just named, and that He really assumed flesh from the Blessed Virgin and really suffered, was crucified, dead, and buried, and rose again on the third day, but he thinks that all these things took place in another, higher world, not in this one.

Also, that in the aforesaid world, the whole human race incurred death because of sin to which it yielded, sin which this John calls the principle and cause of all evil, as we have repeatedly remarked. And after their bodies were buried in that world, their souls necessarily descended into hell, that is, into this world, and to this hell Christ came down to help them.

Also, he believes that in the upper world will come the resurrection of the dead, namely, that each soul belonging to God will receive its own body.

Also, that in that same world the true God gave the law of Moses to the people we have described. There, also, priests offered sacrifices and burnt offerings for the sins of the people, as their offering is commanded in the Law.

Also, in that same place Christ literally wrought true miracles in raising the dead, giving sight to the blind, and feeding five thousand men, not counting the women and children, from five barley loaves and two fishes.

Why say more? Whatever in the whole Bible is stated to have been in this world he changes to have actually taken place in that other world.

[23] *How John of Lugio Wrote a Book about His Errors.*—Indeed, the oft-mentioned heresiarch John of Lugio fabricated the blasphemies and errors described above and many others which would take too long and be too disgusting for me to recount. From them he compiled a large volume of ten quires, a copy of which I have.[46] I have read it all and from it have extracted the errors cited above. It is also to be noted especially that this John and his associates do not dare to reveal to their believers the errors described,[47] lest their own believers desert them on account of these novel errors and because of the schism existing among the Albanensian Cathars, of which they are the cause. The Albanensian Cathars censure the Concorezzenses and are in turn censured by the latter.

[24] *The Following Concerns the Particular Errors of the Church of the Cathars of Concorezzo.*—These people rightly believe in one Principle only, but many of them err in respect of the Trinity and unity.

Also, they confess that God created the angels and the four elements from nothing; but they err in believing that the devil, with God's permission, made all visible things, or this world.

Also, they believe that the devil formed the body of the first man and into it infused an angel who had already sinned slightly.

Also, that all souls exist by propagation from that angel.

Also, they reject the whole of the Old Testament, thinking that the devil was its author, except for those phrases which were carried over into the New Testament by Christ and the apostles, such as, "Behold a virgin shall be with child,"[48] and the like.

Also, they all reject Moses, and many of them are doubtful about Abraham, Isaac, and Jacob, and the other patriarchs, and also especially the prophets. And many of them only recently came to believe correctly about the Blessed John the Baptist, whom they all formerly condemned.

Also, they say that Christ did not take on a human soul, but almost all believe that He did assume flesh from the Blessed Virgin.

[25] *The Errors of Nazarius, Their Bishop.*—Nazarius, a former bishop of theirs and a very old man, said before me and many others that the Blessed Virgin was an angel and that Christ did not assume human nature but an angelic one, or a celestial body. And he said he got this error from the bishop and elder son of the church of Bulgaria almost sixty years ago.

Moreover, it should be noted that all the Cathars who profess that Christ assumed a true human body deny that that body was glorified and is to be glorified. They say that Christ on the day of His ascension laid it aside in the shining sky and will resume it again on the Day of Judgment, and after the judgment it will be resolved into pre-existent matter like a putrid corpse.

Also, they say that the soul of the Blessed Virgin Mary and those of the apostles and of all the saints are not yet in glory, nor will they be until the Day of Judgment, but they are in that ether, in the same place as the body of Jesus Christ.

[26] *On the Bagnolensian Cathars.*—The next matter for discussion is the beliefs of the church of Bagnolo.

These people agree with the aforesaid Cathars of Concorezzo in almost all the beliefs described above, except for this: They say that souls were created by God before the foundation of the world and that they sinned even then.

Also, they believe, along with the aforesaid Nazarius, that the Blessed Virgin was an angel and that Christ did not assume human nature from her, nor did He undergo any real suffering in death, but that He assumed a celestial body.

[27] *On the Toulousan Cathars, the Albigenses, and Those of Carcassonne.*—Lastly, it is to be noted that the Cathars of the Toulousan church, and those of Albi and Carcassonne, maintain the errors of Belesmanza and the old Albanenses, as do almost all the churches of Cathars beyond the seas which I have named.

No church of Cathars, in truth, agrees on all points with the church of Concorezzo. The church of France (*Franciae*) agrees with that of Bagnolo. Those of the March of Treviso, indeed, and of Tuscany, and of the valley of Spoleto agree in more points with the said Bagnolenses than with the Albanenses, but little by little they are being drawn to the Albanenses.

Also, all the churches of the Cathars recognize each other, although they may have differing and contrary opinions, except the Albanenses and the Concorezzenses, who censure each other, as mentioned above. If any Cathar, of either sex, refuses to admit the particular errors described, or at least those held in common, then one may indisputably say of him that he utters lies in hypocrisy, which is a characteristic of the Cathars—witness thereto is the Apostle, who so clearly prophesied about them[49]—unless perhaps that person be someone simple or a novice among them, for to many such they do not reveal their secrets.

[28] *On the Heresy of the Leonists, or the Poor of Lyons.*—Enough has now been said about the heresy of the Cathars. Our next subject is the heresy of the Leonists, or Poor of Lyons. However, this heresy is divided into two parts, the first called the Ultramontane Poor, the second the Poor of Lombardy. The latter are descended from the former. The first, namely, the Ultramontane Poor, say that in the New Testament every oath is forbidden as a mortal sin. And they say the same about secular justice, to wit, that kings, princes, and potentates are not permitted to punish malefactors.

Also, they affirm that a simple layman can consecrate the body of the Lord. I believe, also, ‧‧‧ as to women they say the same thing, since they have not denied it b ‧ me.

Also, that the Roman ‧ ‧u ch is not the Church of Jesus Christ.

[29] *On the Poor of Lombardy.*—The Poor of Lombardy agree with the first group as regards the oath and secular justice. About the body of the Lord, indeed, their beliefs are even worse than those of the others:

They say that any man without mortal sin is allowed to consecrate it.

Also, they say that the Roman Church is the church of the wicked, the beast and the harlot which are described in the Apocalypse; consequently, they say that it is no sin to eat meat during Lent and on Fridays, despite the precepts of the Church, provided it be done without scandal to others.

Also, [they say] that the Church of Christ subsisted in the bishops and other prelates down to the time of the Blessed Sylvester,[50] and in him it fell away until they themselves restored it. Nevertheless, they assert that there were always some who feared God and were saved.

Also, they say that infants are saved without baptism.[51]

The foregoing work has been faithfully compiled by the said Brother Rainerius, in the year of our Lord 1250. Thanks be to God!

52. Waldenses in the Thirteenth Century

We have already presented the narrative of the origin of the Poor of Lyons told by Stephen of Bourbon (No. 33). Here we translate his remarks on the sect as he knew it from his experience as an inquisitor between 1232 and 1249.

The translation is from *Stephani de Borbone tractatus de diversis materiis praedicabilibus* iv.vii.343, ed. by Albert Lecoy de la Marche, as *Anecdotes historiques, légendes et apologues tirées du recueil inédit d'Etienne de Bourbon, dominicain du XIIIᵉ siècle* (Société de l'histoire de France, Publications, CLXXXV [Paris, 1887]), pp. 292-99.

1249-1261

Now these are the errors by which the Waldenses are poisoned and corrupted; their beliefs are abhorrent not merely in respect of a single article of faith or of one sacrament but in all, directly and indirectly, as I have come to know through much questioning and from confessions under oath, written verbatim from the lips of the Perfect[1] as well as of their believers, and also from witnesses testifying against them. They believe that every lie is a mortal sin and an oath is the same. However, I have heard some of them say that under fear of death it is permissible for those who are not perfected to lie and to take oaths. They themselves do lie and commit perjury, nor do they think it a sin, since they excuse and disguise their lies by wiles and sophistries.

Also, the fundamental point of their error—nay rather, the negation of all faith—is their assertion, which I have found in the confessions of nearly all the Perfect and others, that the soul of the first man was a part of the divine substance, the very spirit of God or a partaker of His essence. When I was preaching in the town of Valence twenty-five years ago, before I knew much about their activities and before the office of inquisitor had been entrusted to me, a certain Catholic told me that he had heard teachers expounding this text, "The Lord God formed man of the slime of the earth and breathed into his face,"[2] as follows: God made and shaped one human figure of soft clay, as do children, and placed it in the sun to dry. When it had dried, where the heat of the sun had made little cracks there were veins for the blood. Finally, by blowing on its face He infused His spirit into it, and thus was man made with a living soul; and in the same way, the man said, God made other souls. Nearly all of them agree that the soul of every good man is in very truth the Holy Spirit, who is God, and that a good man, so long as he remains good, has no soul other than the Holy Spirit, or God. When one sins, the Holy Spirit departs and the devil enters in, just as we read that he entered into the heart of Judas, whom the Lord declared to be a devil.[3] This they confirm from the Gospel, in which God says: "It is not you that speak, but the Spirit of your Father that speaketh in you";[4] and again in Matthew, "For that which is conceived in her is of the Holy Spirit and is begotten."[5] And these wretched creatures, who have not the Spirit, do not understand that the Holy Spirit spoke through the saints by inspiration and guidance, as is stated in John,[6] nor do they realize that Christ was not conceived by a male act, but that conception was effected by the Holy Spirit; nor are they aware of how numberless and obvious are the abuses, abominations, and follies which follow from their assumption. For if the soul of man were the Holy Spirit, it would be omnipotent, all-knowing, eternal, inviolable, and immutable, so that it could act neither for better nor for worse; it could not be damned, nor could it desire or do wicked things. He who does not recognize that this is the utmost folly is lacking in sense.

Also, they state—and this, perhaps, follows from their first proposition—that there is no purgatorial punishment other than in the present life. For the dead, neither the good offices of the Church nor anything done in their behalf has any effect.

Also, they say that all good men are priests and that any good man has as much power to absolve sins as we believe the pope to possess. Moreover—to expose the true nature of their belief—they hold that God alone can absolve from sins, but they also say that all good men can effect this, since God, who dwells in them, and through whom they are able to bind and loose all things, works only through them to this end. They scorn the absolutions and excommunications of the Church, since, as they say, only God can excommunicate.

Also, one of their leading teachers and missionaries drew for me the following distinction. There are, he said, some persons who are ordained neither by God nor by men, for example, wicked laymen; there are others, such as our wicked priests, ordained by men but not by God; and there are others, ordained by God but not by men, such as good laymen who keep God's commandments, who have the power to bind and loose, to consecrate and ordain, if they use the words of God specified for this. But, as he said in reference to the last-named persons, some make a distinction between sexes and say that only members of the male sex can be ordained; others make no such distinction, for they say that a woman, if she is a good woman, can fulfill the priestly office. (I have seen one heretical woman who was burned, who believed that she could, and who sought to perform it atop a box prepared like an altar.)[7] He also said that there are other persons ordained by both God and men if, as priests ordained by men, they also keep God's commandments, for God will not hearken to sinners.

Also, they say that evil men, who live in sin, cannot bind and loose, bestow indulgences or remissions on sinners, or ordain, or do anything such that God approves or that is done to the end that it may please God, but only do that which is pleasing in the eyes of men. They deride papal indulgences and absolutions and the keys of the Church, calling the dedication and consecration of churches and altars a feast of stones.

Also, they say that all ground is equally consecrated and blessed by God. They hold Christian cemeteries and churches in contempt.

Also, they say that all judges commit a sin in pronouncing the death penalty, and they regard as murderers and damned souls those who preach war against the Saracens and the Albigenses or other men, except for war against the "infernal" Saracens and Albigenses, whom they call devils.[8]

Also, they say that it suffices for salvation to confess only to God and not to man, and that good works are not necessary to salvation. But no matter how great and numerous the sins he may have committed, when any sinner repents and then dies, he ascends at once to heaven.

Also, the spirit of man, in so far as he is a good man, when he dies, is one with the spirit of God and is God himself; whence many of them, resting upon their first proposition, will agree, I think, that there is no spirit in heaven but the spirit of God, who is himself God, and that there is in heaven no soul except God. And when one asks them if the souls of Peter and Paul and other saints are in heaven, they avow that there is no soul in heaven but God, none which is not God. This some of them believe.

Also, they say that our clerics and priests who possess wealth and worldly goods are sons of the devil and of damnation, and that one who gives them tithes or oblations commits a sin, for they say that to do this is like adding fat to lard.

Also, those who offer candles to the saints for lighting the churches they find worthy of derision.

Also, they scorn the chants of the Church and the holy offices, affirming that those who sing their invocations to Him seem to deride God, as though He could not understand unless one sings to Him or beseeches Him in song.

Also, they say that there is no sanctity except that of a good man or woman.

Also, they assert that the Roman Church is the harlot of Babylon of whom one reads in the Apocalypse.[9]

Also, they say that those who observe saints' days are a laughing-stock and that those who work on these days commit no sin, except perhaps in giving scandal to men. Also, they say that those who disregard the rules for fasting and who eat meat on any day whatsoever commit no sin, except perhaps for the scandal arising therefrom. But in private it is permissible to eat on any day, so they say, and wherever there will be no scandal to men.

Also, they deny entirely the necessity of obedience to the Roman Church.

Also, they assert that God alone is to be adored with every kind of adoration and that persons who adore the Cross or that which we say and believe to be the body of Christ, or the other saints of God or their images, commit sin.

Also, on the basis of their first proposition, many of them hold—as

I have heard in the confessions of a large number of their leading members—that any good man is the son of God, just as Christ is. And in the same way, they say of Him that He had no other soul but God, or the Holy Spirit, who is God; this they also affirm of other good men. And when they say that they believe in the incarnation, nativity, suffering, and resurrection of Christ, they are saying that they believe the true conception of Christ, His nativity, suffering, resurrection, and ascension to be when a good man is conceived, born, or resurrected by penance, or ascends to heaven when he suffers martyrdom; this is the true passion of Christ. Likewise, when they state that they believe in baptism, penance, and so on for all the other sacraments, they are saying that the true sacraments are consummated when, and only when, a good man, in a state of grace, performs them. Then there is true baptism, true confirmation, the true Eucharist (since then is the body of Christ made), then is ordination, then are marriage and extreme unction, performed in Him. By means of this very spirituality, many of them negate our faith in rites and sacraments. Those who seem to be somewhat less wrong in their thinking do err in saying that the body of Christ can be made or consecrated by any good man who says the words prescribed for this ceremony, although he may not have been ordained by man.

Also, they say that in carnal marriage the wife may leave her husband without his consent, and the same with the husband, to adopt their fellowship or the practice of continence.

Also, this is the Trinity which, or in which, they believe: That, as the Father is He who turns someone to good, the one who is converted is the Son; He through whom or in whom one is converted is the Holy Spirit. This is what they mean when they say they believe in the Father, the Son, and the Holy Spirit, and in Christ, conceived, born, who suffered, and so on, as comprised in the creed, which they know very well how to repeat in the vernacular. The reasons for their falling into these abominations, I think, were arrogance, hatred of the clergy, and decay of the faith; because they had lost the foundation they fell into the labyrinth and the pit of evils. However, an educated man, if he is imbued with the spirit of God, can quickly disprove all this by reason and by Scripture.

Furthermore, they quarrel among themselves about these errors, depending upon the degree to which they have been indoctrinated. I have heard a daughter arguing with her mother, both of whom were infected with the same error and were very well versed in its tenets. Because of the uncompromising character of their error, to which they tenaciously clung, they were burned together. I have put down these matters here, thinking it good that the brethren, defenders of the faith, be not ignorant of them.

53. *Tenets of the Italian Cathars*

It was probably a Franciscan friar interested in preaching against heresy who copied into a few folios of his manuscript Bible various materials about heresy intended for his own use. Later, another owner of the Bible added to these a prologue, emphasizing the necessity of combating heresy, and gave to the whole the title *Brevis summula contra herrores notatos hereticorum.*[1] This composite treatise was once regarded as a valuable source for the study of heresy,[2] but it is less highly thought of today, because none of the component parts seems to have been the original work of the compiler. He copied first a description of the tenets of absolute dualists, perhaps drawing on a document Moneta of Cremona had also used or perhaps adapting Moneta's own words,[3] to which he appended an inferior copy of the *De heresi catharorum in Lombardia* (see No. 23) without its historical narrative.[4] Then he went on to enumerate the beliefs of the Albanenses (here misnamed Albigenses)[5] and, after a brief paragraph on the Bagnolenses, to give a catalogue of the beliefs of the three major Italian groups of Cathars,[6] together with some chapters of refutation of their errors.[7] Similarities of phrasing in the statement of beliefs, the catalogue, and the refutation show that they were all composed by the same author.[8] The compilation as a whole is difficult to date, but it may well have been put together within a decade after 1250.[9]

We translate here the prologue, which, as has been said, was the final touch, but we pass over the portions enumerated above as (1) and (2) to translate the statement on the Albanenses and Bagnolenses and the catalogue of heretical beliefs. We also omit the concluding chapters of refutation.

The *Brevis summula* has been printed by both Douais and Molinier; Molinier, however, omitted the statement of beliefs of the Albanenses and the chapters of refutation which conclude the tract. In one case we have ventured to supply from another closely related source a passage which Douais found almost illegible and Molinier omitted. The editions are Célestin Douais, *La Somme des autorités à l'usage des prédicateurs méridionaux au XIIIe siècle* (Paris, 1896) from pp. 114-15 and 125-33 of which passages are translated; and Charles Molinier, "Un Texte de Muratori concernant les sectes cathares: Sa provenance réelle et sa valeur," *Annales du Midi*, XXII (1910), 212-16.

1250-1260 (?)

A BRIEF TREATISE AGAINST THE DISTINCTIVE
ERRORS OF HERETICS

In the name of our Lord Jesus Christ, amen. In praise of the Blessed
Virgin and of all the saints and of the Holy Roman Church. Here
begins a brief treatise against the distinctive errors of heretics.

[*Prologue*]

Inasmuch as the Holy Spirit spoke through Solomon in the Canticles,
to the prelates and custodians of the vines of the Lord, that is, the
Church, "Catch us the little foxes that destroy the vines,"[10] to catch
and silence the foxes—meaning the heretical depravities which lay waste
the Church—we will, with the inspiration[11] and aid of the same Holy
Spirit, first expose the errors and fatuities of heretics, in so far as we
have been able to discover them, for, as Leo[12] says, "Evil is not avoided
unless known." Thereafter in this little work, we add certain texts of
the New Testament for the refutation of the chief points of their heresy
and for giving credence to and extolling the faith of the Holy Catholic
Church, which we call Roman. We buttress it by the opinions of the
saints, so that those who are therein shall steadfastly remain, and those
who have left it through the deceptions of heretics shall be brought
back.[13] For this is the Catholic faith and unless every faithful one shall
steadfastly believe in it he cannot be saved. It is what was signified by
the ship of which Paul speaks in the twenty-seventh chapter of Acts,
"Except these stay in the ship, you cannot be saved."[14] Likewise, it is
signified by the ark of Noah, in which were saved those who were
therein, while others perished, and so in faith the faithful shall be saved;
and this the apostle Peter intimates in the second epistle, chapter 3.[15]
Also, it is signified by Simon's ship, which Jesus entered, as says Luke,
chapter 5.[16] And since James says, "He who causeth a sinner to be
converted from the error of his way shall save his soul from death,"[17]
it is quite apparent that all heretics are in the death of sin and incline
toward eternal death. Also, St. Augustine, in *De fide catholica*, says,
"Hold most firmly and doubt not that every heretic or schismatic is to
share with the devil and his angels the flames of eternal fire unless
before the end of his life he shall have been brought into and renewed
in the Catholic Church."[18] Also, in the same work a little later, "Neither

baptism nor charity, however profuse, nor death undergone for the name of Christ can profit any man for salvation who does not hold fast to the unity of the Catholic Church."[19] Also, in the *Extravagantes, De haereticis,* the decretal says, "The dubious in faith is an unbeliever, nor is any trust to be placed in him who knows not the true faith."[20] Also, Pope Leo says in the same place, "He who does not, when he can, recall others from error shows that he himself errs."[21] Accordingly, dearly beloved, so that you may rejoice in your own and many others' salvation, by the example of good works, by devout prayers, by pious admonitions, and by the testimony of holy authorities, according as the Holy Spirit shall deem it worthy to endow you, do you deem it worthy to recall both those of doubtful faith and those actually in error and inducing others to err, to the praise and glory of our Lord Jesus Christ, who with the Father and the Holy Spirit lives and reigns, one God, world without end. Amen.

[*Beliefs of the Albanenses*]

Also the Albanenses.[22]—These likewise wickedly pervert Holy Writ to their evil error and thus they sin.

Also, it is the heresy of the Albigenses which says that Lucifer was the son of the evil god and that he ascended into heaven and found the wife of the celestial king without her husband, that is, God.[23] There he went so far as to lie with her. As she at first defended herself, Lucifer said to her that if he should beget a son he would make him god in his kingdom, and have him worshiped as a god. And so she yielded to him. They cite that verse of the Apocalypse, "The kingdom of this world is become our Lord's,"[24] and so on. And they say that thus Christ was born and thus He brought His flesh down from heaven and this is their great secret. They seek also to maintain that He was not true man but an angel incarnate, that He was not the son of the Blessed Mary and so did not take on flesh from her, and that He did not eat or drink in the flesh,[25] did not suffer in the flesh, and in His body did not die. They say that all these and like acts which He performed He did in appearance only, not in fact. And likewise they say that He did not rise again and was not dead; so, when they confess that Christ had true flesh and did such things as these, they are saying that all these things occurred only in outward appearance. They also say that He did not ascend in human flesh but in that which He had brought from heaven. They say that He did not suffer our afflictions, such as hunger, cold, and the like. They allege also that He is not greater than all others, nor equal to the Father; and they say He is not God.

Of the Blessed Virgin, they say that she was not a woman, but an angel sent from heaven.

They assert also that John the Baptist was another evil angel, sent by the devil to hinder the preaching of Christ by his baptism, and they contend that the baptism of water is worthless and of no efficacy; they explain away the fact that it is recorded in Holy Writ that the apostles baptized in water by saying, "in water, that is, in doctrine." Thus, they say, the Spirit is never given in the baptism of water; the Spirit is not given except by the imposition of hands, and baptism is administered by the imposition of hands. They also say that no one can be saved unless he has the imposition of hands from them. The Holy Spirit and the Spirit Paraclete, they say, are not the same, and they say that the blessed spirits are those which are given to men, namely, the Perfect Spirit, the spirit of clemency, the spirit of fear, and many others, all of which, they assert, are different in essence.

They say also that man can give the Holy Spirit.

They say also that under no circumstances can man be saved by faith alone.

They say also that the Lord will not condemn for all eternity.

They say also that not everyone can be saved, because of the words, "I was not sent but to the sheep,"[26] and so forth.

They say also that before the coming of Christ there were no good men. They say that the prophecies and the law of Moses came not from the good God, yet when it happens to suit their purpose they cite the prophets. Of them, they say that they spoke to men only out of their diabolical spirit, and when it was by their own spirit or by that of the devil, then they spoke wickedness; but when it was by the spirit of God, they spoke good things, sometimes being compelled thereto.[27] Sometimes they revealed what they remembered of the things they saw in heaven.

Also, they say that not one of the patriarchs of the Old Testament is saved; that none are to be saved except the fallen angels, and these they believe to be none other than the sheep of which the Lord said in the Gospel, "I was not sent but to the sheep,"[28] and so forth.

Also, that. . . .[29]

They say that the good God is not the creator of all things, in regard either to substance or to its fashioning; that things mutable are not from God; that not He but the devil created those bodies. Whence, they say, the devil has power over created things. They say that the good God did not and does not make anything of a perishable nature. Thus, they say, bodies must perish; and, moreover, they say that all things are not subject to one God.

They say also that the Lord does not infuse or create new souls, that souls do not go directly to rest or punishment after death, and that there will be[30] equal reward in the heavenly home. For this reason they declare that they will have as much glory as Christ or anyone else.

They say that there will be no resurrection of bodies and that Christ did not descend into hell.

They say also that [the New Testament was] given and prepared [by the good God][31] and that the Old Testament is not from the good God but from the evil one, who included some excellent precepts the better to deceive. He caused sacrifice of animals and offerings of blood to himself, so that he might be thought to be God. They assert that Moses was wicked and also that it was the evil god who led the people out of Egypt and killed the Egyptians.

They say that there is no salvation through the Law.

They say also that God the Father did not speak to the fathers of old.

They say that the good God did not prescribe circumcision.

They say that Adam was not formed by God but that whatsoever things are recorded in Genesis were performed by Lucifer.

They say that the good God does not give life to and kill bodies; He only gives life, He does not kill. The evil one, however, kills. One is wicked who judges and grants no grace at all; hence they wish to say that the torment of punishment is not the work of God. And so, they also say, no one should impose a penalty for evil deeds, that the death penalty must not be used as a punishment, and that such an action is nothing other than the work of the devil and is a sin.

They say that sin is a substance in itself, and a spirit which suggests wicked work to men. Then this work is called sin, since it is committed by that spirit which is so named. They say that man cannot do penance after sin, because they believe that no sin can be committed other than that which has been committed in heaven. Hence, they say, that souls will not be condemned, for they do not believe in hell, because one does not find in Genesis that the god who, in their view, created this world, namely Lucifer, made one during the six days. They say that there is no purgatorial fire and no purgatory.

Now, they say that the world always existed because they believe that Lucifer and his father always existed—this is according to one theory—wherefore they say that there were always souls and bodies here in the realm of their lord. Others among them, moreover, say that there is no hell or paradise but only the lower realm, comprising "heaven and earth," as described in Genesis, and the higher realm, which is that of the good God. Therefore, in declaring that no soul will be saved other than the spirits who fell, who they think will all be saved, they assert that the other souls created by the devil, the evil god, will be condemned, not for eternity but temporally, for a period as long as the world endures. This condemnation, they think, is here in the darkness of this world, that is, to sustain hunger, cold, weariness, and the like. In this, they do not think that they are repudiating the statements made above to the effect that souls will not be condemned and that they always existed here in the realm of their lord, which cannot persist, for it is their explanation that souls will not be condemned, that is, by a second condemnation, because they are already damned. Thus they deny that future day when, it is said, souls will be condemned, because it has already passed.

They say that original sin was not incurred by Adam, and that it is naught. Some sinners, they say, are born in personal sin.

They say also that both good persons and wicked ones are not part of the Church of God; that the Church of God cannot institute customs beyond those established by the apostles; that it should possess nothing except property in common; that it ought not to have the extensive possessions it holds; and that it should not perform burial services in the way it does. They declare that sinful priests cannot perform their functions or confer any benefit; also, that the evil life of a prelate harms both the communicant and the sacrament.

They say that no sinful man can be a priest or a deacon in the Church of God; and they insist that the Church cannot excommunicate.

They say that there is no sacrament in the Eucharist.

They say that a church edifice is not a good thing nor should prayers be said therein; that the Church ought not to prosecute evildoers; and that priests cannot and should not govern the people.

They say that anointing with oil is useless; that there should be no prayer or chants other than the Lord's Prayer; that no person ought to be worshiped; that tithes[32] should be given only to good men; that no man should be excommunicated; that it is not permissible to put anyone to death; that marriage is evil because of the procreation of children; that a man need not restore ill-gotten gains;[33] that usury is not forbidden; and that one ought not to take an oath.

They say also that it is a sin to eat meat; that sin does not arise from free will;[34] that "neighbor" is not to be interpreted as meaning every man;[35] that according to the Old Testament an enemy is not to be loved; that no sinful man can be a bishop; that heads ought not to be tonsured; that "the inward man" does not mean the soul;[36] that justice should be deferred for the purpose of converting men to believers. In opposition to the heretics, who say there is no right of justice, believers, indeed, say that justice can be served by the death penalty.[37]

They say also that the good God does not become wrathful or disturbed.

They state that all those things of which one reads in the New Testament were good. Those things which were recorded in the Old Testament, such as references to Moses, David, and others, and to the lineage of Christ—that He was descended from David—and other things as well, occurred in another place. They cite the words of Ecclesiasticus, "All things are double, one against another,"[38] good and evil. Accordingly, they believe in a good Father and an evil one, a good Son and an evil one, a good Holy Spirit and an evil one, and so on for other things.

The heretics who are called the sect of Bagnolo believe and preach all the above with this exception:[39] They say that the good God creates new spirits and souls and introduces them into new bodies, and they believe that some of these new spirits are to be saved. Of those that fell, they believe that some are damned. And so they say that all will be present at the judgment when the world is judged. Then the newly created good spirits will take the place of the evil ones who fell; and so, they say, some of the new spirits and some of the old are to be saved.

The items, summarily stated, which we are about to set down contain almost all the errors of three sects, which are the Albanenses, the sect of Bagnolo, and the sect of Concorezzo. On some of these they disagree and on some they are all in accord. We will mark them all briefly with A, B, or C. By A, we will indicate the sect of the Albanenses; by B, that of Bagnolo; by C, that of Concorezzo. Where these three letters appear, the three sects are in agreement on that point; where two letters, two only agree; where there is only one letter, only one sect holds this tenet.

[*A Catalogue of Heretical Tenets*]
Here are summarily noted the errors of three sects of heretics: By A, the Albanenses; by B, those of Bagnolo; by C, those of Concorezzo.[40]

That [there are] two principles, one wholly good, the other wholly evil (A, B).
That the good God did not create these corporeal bodies (A, B).
That the good God is not the creator of all things (A, B, C).
That all things are not subject to one God only (A, B).
That Christ is not greater than all others (A, B, C).
That [God] will not condemn for all eternity (A, B).
That God neither infuses nor creates new souls (A).
That men do not go directly to hell or to rest (A, B, C).
That Christ did not suffer our afflictions (A, B, C).
That [God] does not make nor has He made anything of a perishable nature (A, B, C).
That Christ brought flesh from heaven (A, B).
That Christ is not God (A, B, C).
That Christ is not the son of the Blessed Mary (A, B).
That Christ did not take on flesh from the Blessed Mary (A, B).
That the Blessed Mary was not a woman (A, B).
That Christ was not true man (A, B).
That He did not eat in the bodily sense (A, B).
That He did not suffer in the flesh (A, B).
That He did not die (A, B).
That He did not ascend in the flesh (C).
That He did not truly rise again, because He was not dead (A, B).
That He did not rise again in the flesh (C).
That He did not descend into hell (A, B, C).
That the Holy Spirit is not given in the baptism of water (A, B, C).
That John the Baptist was evil (A, B, and some of C).
That he was not a man in the corporeal sense (A, B, and some of C).
That there is no resurrection of bodies (A, B, C).
That children cannot be saved (A, B, C).
That the law of Moses is not good nor are the prophecies (A, B, C).

That the patriarchs of the Old Testament are not saved (A, B, C).

That the Old Testament is not from the good God (A, B, C).

That Moses was evil (A, B, C).

That there was no salvation through the law of Moses nor is there any (A, B, C).

That the good God did not lead the people out of Egypt (A, B, C).

That God the Father did not speak to the patriarchs of old (A, B, C).

That the good God did not prescribe circumcision (A, B, C).

That Adam was not from God (A, B, C).

That before the advent of Christ there were no good men (A, B, C).

That Christ is not equal to the Father (A, B).

That those things which are visible are not from God. Those of Concorezzo, however, say that they were created by God in that He made the four elements, and out of these Lucifer shaped all creatures whatsoever of their kind, just as they now are. But the others say that neither in substance, shape, or form did God make anything which is visible to us. If sometimes they admit that He made visible things they are speaking of those things which are visible to angels.

That according to the Old Testament[41] an enemy is not to be loved (A, B, C).

That the angels who fell are the sheep spoken of in the Gospel (A and part of those of B[42]).

That the baptism of water is nothing and of no efficacy (A, B, C).

That the Holy Spirit is not given without the imposition of hands (A, B, C).

That there are not both good and wicked persons in the Church of God (A, B, C).

That priests and deacons, if sinful, ought not to be in the Church of God (A, B, C).

That the evil life of a prelate harms both the communicant and the sacrament (A, B, C).

That priests ought not to govern the people (A, B, C).

That evil priests cannot perform their function or confer any good thing (A, B, C).

That the Church of God ought not and cannot own anything except as property in common (A, B, C).

That there should not be subdeacons or acolytes in the Church (A, B, C).

That the Church cannot institute customs (A, B, C).

That no sinful person can be a bishop (A, B, C).

That a church edifice is not a good thing nor should one pray there
   (A, B, C).

That [the Church] ought not to prosecute evildoers (A, B, C).

That the Church cannot excommunicate (A, B, C).

That the Church ought not to perform burial services in the way it does
   (A, B, C).

That anointing with oil is worthless (A, B, C).

That the sacrament of the altar is worthless (A, B, C).

That alms should be given only to the good (A, B, C).

That there should be no prayers or chants except the Lord's Prayer
   (A, B, C).

That sin does not arise from free will (A, B, C).

That there is no original sin (A, B, C).

That a man cannot do penance after sin (A, B, C).[43]

That no sin can be committed except that which was committed in
   heaven (A, B).

That the work of the devil is nothing other[44] than sin (A, B, C). All
   differ somewhat in explaining this point.

That there is no purgatorial fire (A, B).

That there is no hell (A, B).

That the good God gives life and does not kill (A, B, C).

That the evil god gives life to and kills bodies[45] (A, B, C).

That the God who grants grace does not impose punishment through
   either good or wicked persons (A, B, C).

That the god who punishes does not grant grace (A, B, C).

That the torment of punishment is not the work of the good God
   (A, B, C).

That souls are not damned (A, B, C).

That the world always has existed and always will exist (A, B).

That under no circumstances can a man be saved by faith alone
   (A, B, C).

That a man cannot be saved [through the faith of his] father and mother
   (A, B, C).

That one need not go to confession (A, B, C).

That judgment has already been rendered (A, B,[46] C).

That matrimony is evil (A, B, C).

That not everyone can be saved (A, B).

That it is a sin to eat meat (A, B, C).

That "neighbor" does not mean every man (A, B, C).
That no one should be excommunicate (A, B, C).
That usury is not forbidden (A, B, C).
That a man need not restore ill-gotten gains (A, B, C).
That one ought not to take an oath (A, B, C).
That it is not permissible for anyone to kill (A, B, C).
That punishments ought not to be inflicted (A, B, C).
That justice ought not to be rendered by man (A, B, C).
That justice should be deferred for the purpose of conversion (A, B, C).
That the devil has power over created things (A, B, C).
That rewards are equal in the heavenly home (A, B, C).
That man can give the Holy Spirit (A, B, C).
That the Holy Spirit and the Spirit Paraclete are not the same (A, B, C).
That the inner man is not the soul (A, B, C).
That heads ought not to be tonsured (A, B, C).

54. An Inquisitor's Notebook, by Anselm of Alessandria

A narrative of the origin of the Cathars, written by Anselm of Alessandria, a Dominican inquisitor in Italy, has already been presented (No. 24). The remainder of Anselm's treatise comprises materials jotted down in 1266 and following years to supplement the information in the summa of Rainerius Sacconi, who had been Anselm's superior in the Inquisition in 1256 and whose treatise was in his possession.[1] Of these items, all but four are translated here.[2] Much of what Anselm recorded was based on his personal experience—or consisted of copies of materials he found useful in his office—and is valuable for its illuminating detail.

The translation is from Antoine Dondaine, "La Hiérarchie cathare en Italie, II: Le 'Tractatus de hereticis' d'Anselme d'Alexandrie, O.P.; III: Catalogue de la hiérarchie cathare d'Italie," *Archivum fratrum praedicatorum*, XX (1950), 310-24, by permission of the Istituto storico domenicano di S. Sabina.

1266-1276

[A TREATISE ON HERETICS]

... [2] *A Note on the Four Bishops of the Cathars in Lombardy.*— It should be noted that the Cathars have four bishops in Lombardy. Those of Concorezzo have Master [Hubert] Mandennus,[3] but the first of their particular bishops was John Judeus and after him Garattus, on

whose account they are called Garatenses. After him they had Nazarius
for about forty years; after him, Gerard *de Cambiate*[4] and then Mandennus, whom they now have as bishop. The Albanenses first had
Philip, then Belesmanza for perhaps forty years, then John of Luzano,[5]
and after him Bonaventure of Verona,[6] whom they now have as bishop.
Those of Bagnolo first had Caloiannes, after whom they are called the
Caloianni; then Orto of Bagnolo, on whose account they are called
Bagnolenses; later Andrew;[7] and then Hamundus of Casalolto,[8] whom
they now have as bishop. Those who are said to be from France have
as bishop, I believe, Viventius of Verona.[9]

[3] *How Those of Concorezzo Have Been Divided.*—Also, it is to be
noted that those of Concorezzo have divided into "ancients" and
"moderns." For some of them hold to the old beliefs with Nazarius,
their old bishop; some of them, on the other hand, accept new beliefs
with Desiderius, a former elder son of this sect.[10] So their bishop and
elder son disagree,[11] for Nazarius and his adherents did not believe that
Christ truly ate material food, that He actually died, or truly rose again.
Also, they did not believe that Christ performed any real miracle affecting the bodies of men. Desiderius and his followers, on the contrary,
believed that He truly performed real miracles. Also, all the Cathars
agree on the tenet that Christ did not descend into hell. Also, the belief
of Nazarius and his followers is that one and the same spirit was in John
the Baptist as had been in Elijah and that this was an evil spirit, a devil.
Also, Nazarius possesses a certain document which he calls *The Secret*.[12]
Desiderius and his followers do not accept this *Secret*, but believe it to
be evil. Also, Nazarius says that Christ did not have a soul but godhead
rather than a soul. However, Desiderius and the very few who agree
with him on this point believe that he had a soul. Also, Nazarius believes
that Christ was not God, one with the Father, while Desiderius believes
that Christ is truly God and the same in essence as the Father. Also,
Nazarius says that Christ brought His body down from heaven, entered
into the Virgin through her ear and emerged from her ear and in His
ascension bore that same body. Desiderius, however, says He truly had
a body of the stuff of Adam and that the Blessed Virgin truly had a
body of the stuff of Adam and was truly a woman. He says that in that
body Christ really died and truly rose again, but when He ascended
into heaven He put it into a terrestrial paradise where the Blessed
Virgin is, who, according to him, never died. There, he believes, lives

John the Evangelist, and there are all the souls of the righteous dead. This he confirms by the verse, "Wheresoever the body shall be,"[13] and so on. He declares that they will remain there even to the Day of Judgment. In judgment, Christ will again put on that body and in it shall judge all the good and the evil. Then He will put it off and it will return to primordial matter, just as will the bodies of dumb animals. Also, all the Concorezzenses believe that the prophets spoke sometimes by their own inspiration, sometimes when inspired by the Holy Spirit, and sometimes when inspired by an evil spirit. All say that these sixteen prophets were good men but that whensoever they spoke by the evil spirit the devil always provided them with that which they should say. But anent the assertion that they sometimes spoke by divine inspiration, they say that God had a certain indwelling in the prophets so that sometimes they might speak to God's purpose, as in that verse, "Behold a virgin,"[14] and others which are found in the New Testament. However, the prince of the world, the devil, did not know of this. Also, take note that all the Concorezzenses despise David and reject his words, except those which are repeated in the New Testament. Also, all the Concorezzenses believe that these sixteen prophets and all the other persons of the Old Testament who were saved arose again in the death of Christ and are they of whom it is said, "Many bodies of the saints arose."[15] They received the imposition of hands from Christ, they say. Also, note that Nazarius believes that from Adam's crown the devil made the sun, that is, from one part of it, and from another he made the moon; from the crown of Eve he made the moon and the stars and the five stars which are not in the firmament. From another part [of Eve's crown] he believes that the devil made the throne where Satan sits in the starry heaven and from which he rules over all the world below, with the exception of good souls. And he believes that all the other stars were made from stones. Desiderius accepts none of these things. Nazarius also says that the sun and the moon are animate beings, that they fornicate every month, and he asserts that dew and honey come from the lewdness of the sun and the moon; hence his refusal to eat honey.[16] Also, note that Nazarius and his followers, together with those of Bagnolo and the Albanenses, interpret all the texts about matrimony in a spiritual sense[17] and believe that these were precepts laid down for those who are members of the Church. But Desiderius and his followers interpret them as referring to carnal matrimony and as precepts applying to those who are members of the Church by faith but not by profession; that is, these precepts are for their believers. Also, note that a certain Albanensian teacher named Lanfranc *de Vaure*,[18] says (and this is a tenet of the Albanenses) that not all the sheep, or the souls who came down or fell from heaven, are confined in bodies but that some are cleansed in the fiery ether, bodiless. They will bear a greater punishment than those who are embodied but will be the sooner saved; they are the ones of whom it is said in the Gospel, "And other sheep I have that are not of [this fold],"[19] and so on.

Also, one may demand of all Concorezzenses whether God made the body of Adam and whether He formed Eve from a rib, or if He himself shaped your hand or your body in reality and by direct act, without an intermediary. Should the reply be in the affirmative, one asks whether God the Father did this by His own fiat or whether the devil ever received from God any power or ministry by which he could do this, and so on. The Cathar will not be able to hide his error. Also, note that a Cathar of Concorezzo, when he wishes to conceal his error, says that God made Eve from a rib and shaped and formed your hand, but he interprets this as "in potentiality"; he means that in reality it is done by the devil. However, by "in potentiality" he means either that the power the devil possessed he had as a natural consequence of his primary creation by God, or that, on the occasion when the devil, in their view, said to God, "Have patience with me,"[20] and so on, God gave the devil the power to form all things.

[4] *On the Belief of the Bagnolenses.*—The belief of the Bagnolenses is threefold, for some of them agree with those of Concorezzo, others uphold the beliefs of the Albanenses, and some follow a middle course. The last-mentioned believe in one Principle. They talk about "creation" and "formation" as do the Concorezzenses, but of the angels who sinned in heaven they say that some sinned by voluntarily yielding to the serpent. These shall never return or be saved and there are no demons but these. Some angels they hold to have been forcibly abducted by the serpent and they alone among those who sinned will be saved. The spirits of Adam and Eve were among the number of those who were forcibly abducted. They say that from the spirits of Adam and Eve other spirits are derived to repair and restore the loss of those evil spirits who sinned voluntarily and that they, that is, the spirits of Adam and Eve, existed in bodies made by the devil. This propagation of spirit from spirit is as natural as that of flesh from flesh and plant from

plant, but is done by the devil's contriving. Also, these Bagnolenses, just like the Concorezzenses, believe that all [future] punishments are equal, so too are the rewards of the good. They do not believe that Christ was true man or that he had a real body, but believe that He brought one from heaven. Nor do they believe that He actually suffered or really died or endured any tribulation, or rose again, for they say that these things only seemed to happen. Also, they believe that Christ is inferior to the Father and that it is the devil who produces rain, snow, thunder, storms, and the violence of the wind. This is a traditional and general opinion of all Cathars. Also, no Cathar fasts on the vigils of any saint, of the apostles, or of the Blessed Virgin. Rather, he says that the harlot, the Roman Church, established vigils, doing so for profit. They observe neither the feast day of any saint nor the Lord's day, nor do they respect days of rest, except to avoid scandal.

[5] *On the Imposition of Hands among the Cathars.*—In regard to the imposition of hands among all the Cathars—that which they call baptism, or the consolamentum—one should note that it is always performed by several persons, with the exception that in extreme urgency it may be accomplished adequately by one alone, even a single Cathar woman. The Concorezzenses say that nothing is accomplished in the imposition of the hand unless one touches the recipient on the head, the shoulder, or elsewhere. Whence, they also believe that even if a Cathar should thrust his arm and hand through an aperture, seeking to bestow the consolamentum on some sick person lying on a bed from which he cannot rise, even though the Cathar should place his hand as close to the invalid as the nose is to the mouth, it is of no avail unless he actually touches him. But the Albanenses think they perform the consolamentum satisfactorily without contact if touch is impossible in the circumstances, even though they may be as far away from the recipient as the voice will carry. Thus they confer the consolamentum adequately even when separated by the walls of a house or a city, or by a river. Therefore great care is necessary when we detain any suspects, lest Cathars come near those who are ill, or even come close to the buildings in which they are being held.

Note this.[21] First, he on whom the hand is to be imposed makes three genuflections before the prelate, saying: "Bless, bless, bless [us]. Good Christians, pray that God will lead me to a good end and keep me from an evil death. I beg you through God's mercy, do unto me that good which the Lord has done to you." The prelate replies, "May the Lord bless you." Three times he says this; then he adds, "We will gladly do unto you that good which the Lord has done to us in so far as the Lord shall give us grace." Then he explains to him that which he must observe. If the communicant says that he is ready in all things, the prelate holds out to him a book, the New Testament or the Gospels, which he accepts and holds to his breast, but closed. Then the prelate says, "You have now received the Testament in which is recorded the divine law. Never, for all time, may it leave your heart." The answer is, "Pray God to give me the grace to observe it, for I desire to observe it always." Then he hands the Testament back to the prelate and makes three genuflections, saying, "Let us adore the Father, the Son, and the Holy Spirit. Before Holy Church and good Christians I confess to you all the sins committed by me since my birth. Do you pray the Lord to pardon me. May you, too, do so, in so far as you have the power from the Lord and from Holy Church." Then he rises and the prelate says, "May He who has power in heaven and on earth absolve you of all your sins, as do we in so far as we have the power from God and from Holy Church." Then the prelate places the Testament on the initiate's head and places a hand on his shoulder, as do all the professed Cathars. The prelate then says, "Lord God, grant indulgence to Thy servant for all his sins and receive him into Thy righteousness." The prelate repeats the Lord's Prayer aloud seven times. The others do the same, he likewise on whom the hand was laid. After this, the prelate says three times, "Let us adore the Father, the Son, and the Holy Spirit." The others respond, "He is worthy and just." The prelate says the Lord's Prayer; the others do likewise, as before. Then the prelate says, "Let us adore the Father, the Son, and the Holy Spirit," and the others respond, "He is worthy and just." The prelate then recites the Gospel, "In the beginning was the Word,"[22] or the Gospel of Matthew, "Take up my yoke."[23] When the Gospel is finished, the prelate says, "May the grace of our Lord Jesus Christ be always with you all." They respond, "Amen." The prelate says, "Bless, have mercy upon us." They reply, "May the Father, the Son, and the Holy Spirit grant indulgence for all our sins." All the others say to the prelate, "Bless, have mercy upon us," as before. Then he takes the Testament away from the head of the initiate, who is now numbered among the Cathars. They say to him, "From now on you are one of us and you live in the world in precisely the situation of a sheep among wolves." Forthwith, they perform the Double.[24]

[6] *On the Ordering of Penance among the Cathars.*—Four variations are to be noted among all the Cathars in the assignment of penances. Now, for an openly committed mortal sin, their prelate imposes three successive days of "withdrawal" (*ad trapassandum*), as they call it, that is, he who has sinned eats or drinks nothing at all for these three days; the prelate thereafter imposes on him three forty-day fasts on bread and water. Note that all Cathars observe three forty-day fasts [each year], but he upon whom the aforesaid penance for mortal sin is imposed must arrange that his fasts do not coincide with the others which they universally observe. He loses forever all his priority (*prioratum*) among them nor may he ever perform the imposition of the hand except in an emergency.[25] The second variation: If he mortally sins in secret, he may be reconsoled and at that point be given twenty-seven days of withdrawal, that is, days on which he does not eat or drink, but they do not run consecutively. He does not lose his priority but does forfeit his office (*prelacionem*). He may never perform the imposition of the hand except in an emergency. The third variation is that if anyone yearns and overwhelmingly desires to do something which is a mortal sin in their eyes, but does not do so, seven days of withdrawal, but not consecutive, are imposed on him. It is left to his discretion whether he will be reconsoled or not; however, he loses his office, but not his priority. The fourth variation pertains to daily sins, which they confess, one speaking for all, just as is recounted in the summa of Brother Rainerius. Three days on bread and water are enjoined on them. They call these "the days of the Service."

[7] *On Fasts by the Cathars.*—The common practice of fasting among them is that each Cathar, whatever his sect, fasts three days a week, that is, on Monday, Wednesday, and Friday. They tell people that they fast on bread and water but that is not true, because they abstain only from wine, oil, fish, and shellfish, yet eat all other things which they are wont to eat on other days. Also, all Cathars in general observe three forty-day fasts.[26] One begins when we begin Lent and lasts until Easter. The second, they begin on the first Monday after Pentecost, and it lasts to the feast of St. Peter.[27] The third they begin on the first Monday after the feast of St. Martin;[28] it lasts until Christmas. In the first fast, they observe two weeks—the first and the last—which they call strict (*strictas*)—the reason for calling these strict is that they

do not venture to drink wine or eat vegetables or oil; it should also be noted that in these three fasts they do not eat fish or shellfish except in serious illness. In the other two fasts they observe only one strict week in each period, which is the first one.

[8a] *On the Times for Meals [and for Prayer].*[29]—When the cook has prepared the food, he goes to the elder[30] and says, "Tell me if it is acceptable unto God and to you." The elder answers, "May God inform you if it is acceptable to Him." Making a deep genuflection,[31] the cook says, "Bless [us]." The elder says, "May the Lord bless you." The cook does the same a second time, saying the same words; the elder replies, "May the Lord bless you." A third time the cook says with a genuflection, "Bless, have mercy upon us," if he is a professed heretic but if he is only a believer he says, "Bless us. Good Christians, pray the Lord that He may lead me to a good end and deliver me from an evil death." He continues, "The meal is ready. You may go to the table when it is acceptable to God and yourself." The elder answers, "May God reward you well." The elder thereupon calls the other Cathars, saying, "Let us make another [melioramentum]."[32] Forthwith, he begins to pray in these words, "Bless, have mercy upon us." All the others respond, "May the Father, the Son, and the Holy Spirit indulge us and have mercy on all our sins." Then he says three times, "Let us adore the Father, the Son, and the Holy Spirit." The first time he says it aloud, the second time silently, the third time aloud. All the Cathars reply, "He is worthy and just." Then all say the Lord's Prayer thirteen times and, on completing a fourteenth Lord's Prayer, the elder says, in just the way that he said before, "Let us adore the Father, the Son, and the Holy Spirit." All the others respond, "He is worthy and just." Next, all say the Lord's Prayer once and, this being completed, the elder says the Lord's Prayer three more times [and afterward], "Let us adore the Father, the Son, and the Holy Spirit." The others respond as before. The elder says, "The grace of our Lord Jesus Christ be always with us all." All respond, "Amen." Thereupon, the elder says, "Bless, have mercy upon us," and they reply, "May the Father, the Son, and the Holy Spirit," as before. In this manner they pray fifteen times between daybreak and nightfall.

[8b] *How They Comport Themselves at Meals.*—When all are now seated at the table, on which are placed at least bread and wine—or water, according to the season—all rise. The elder takes a loaf and cutting it but not sharing it out says, "Bless, have mercy upon us." All

respond as before, and as before all say the Lord's Prayer. This done, the elder says, "Let us adore the Father, the Son, and the Holy Spirit." They answer as before. He says, "May the grace of our Lord," as before, and they reply, "Amen." Then the elder says, "Bless, have mercy [upon us]" as before. Then he gives some of this bread to all persons, believers and others. If there is more bread than is needed, it does not matter at all if it be fed to pigs.

[9] *How They Comport Themselves on Going to Someone's House.*— When any Cathar or a believer of any sect enters a strange house of any Cathars, especially if he does not know who are the Cathars among those he encounters there, he says, "*Bessea trona!* Can we do something for our betterment?"[33] Or he may say, "Is there a crooked stick here?"[34] Then, if there is anyone there who is not of their belief and of whom they are suspicious, the elder answers, "Be seated." By this the newcomer understands that there is someone there whom they fear. If, however, there is no one there to be feared, the elder answers, "Do as you wish." The newcomer responds, "Tell me if it is acceptable to God and to you." The elder replies, "May God inform us if it is acceptable to Him." Then the newcomer bows and makes a deep reverence. He says, "Bless [us]." A second time he bows and says, "Bless, have mercy upon us," if he is a professed Cathar, but if he is only a believer, he says: "Bless, have mercy upon us. Good Christians, pray to God that He may bring me to a good end and deliver me from an evil death." If the man is a perfected heretic, the other responds, "May God bless us and keep us in His service," but to a believer he says, "May the Lord bring you to a good end and preserve you[35] from an evil death." Then he rises and gives him the *caron*, that is, a sort of embrace, putting his head once on the left and once on the right. This they call the *caron*.[36]

[10] *On the Differences between the Lombard and the Ultramontane Waldenses.*—A difference between the ultramontane Waldenses and the Lombards is this: The Ultramontane says that any man, whether good or bad, even though he is not a priest, can say Mass and perform the other sacraments. The Lombard says that he cannot unless he is in a state of grace. Also, the Lombard is in error about the sacrament, nor does he perform baptism properly. Also, the Lombard works. Also, they all, Lombards as well as Ultramontanes, scorn the regulations of the Church. Whence they believe marriage between relatives to be legitimate, since they find it banned only in the regulations of the

Church. . . .[37] The Ultramontanes do not genuflect to the Cross or to the altar, adducing this verse, "The idols of the Gentiles [are] silver and gold,"[38] and so on. The Lombards act the same way. Also, they believe that every good man is a priest and is the Church. Not so the Lombards, who say that unless two are gathered together, the Church is not there. Also, the Ultramontanes condemn the Lombards and are condemned in return. Also, the Ultramontane neither works for himself nor for wages from others, nor does he practice a trade or profession. He is a sandal-wearer and adopts a "tonsured" style of footgear,[39] or shoes cut away at the top. He does not store up money but his companion does so for him; nor does he keep food from one day for the next. He carries only one cloak. Women follow the same practice except that they do not wear the sandal-like footgear. But the Lombards also include sandal-wearers. Also, the Ultramontanes say that the pope can no more indulge one [for sin] than another man; also that the Roman Church is not the Church of God but a harlot. The Lombard believes the same. Also, [the Ultramontane says] that the pope does not fill the office of Peter on earth. The Lombard says the same. The first-named accept the baptism and anointing done by the Roman Church; however, they do not accept the laws of the Church nor do they keep the fasts established by the Roman Church nor do they regard it as a sin to break them. The Lombard believes the same. Also, their [the Ultramontanes'] women preach. Also, they put no belief in the indulgences which the Roman Church grants. Also, they make the sign of the Cross properly upon themselves and upon all the things they eat; the Lombard does not, but only passes his hand over them. The former give credence to the doctors of the Church in so far as the words favor their interests. They say that St. Sylvester was corrupted when he accepted worldly wealth.[40] Also, William the Albigensian[41] is their bishop. The question of labor was the cause of the division among them, also the Lombards' assertion that evil priests cannot perform the Mass. Also, John the Good, of Ronco,[42] was the leader of the Lombards at the time they separated themselves from the Ultramontanes and the Ultramontanes excommunicated the Lombards. The end.

I, Brother A., inscribed this.[43] I learned it from two women who for a long time adhered to the Waldenses and were of the ultramontane party. After they had been converted they did their penance in the prison at Alba. . . .[44]

[12] *Learned from Another Person [about the Lombards].*—The things that follow I have learned from one Louis of the sect of the Lombards, who was apprehended at Genoa and converted. He said that Andrew of Gruara[45] is a bishop of the Lombards, who do not number more than one hundred of both sexes. According to him, they believe that no evil priest can celebrate the Mass, yet they think that such a one can indeed baptize and give good advice. Now, what we call imposing penance they refer to as giving good advice. Also, he said that he did not believe, as do those of Lyons, that a sinful priest can give extreme unction. Also, the Lombards confirm their priests and bishop by the imposition of hands. Also, they accept none of the orders of the Church but create orders among themselves. Also, the sandal-wearers among them, whom they call priests, carry only one cloak and either go about barefooted or wear shoes or sandals cut away at the top. They do not possess money or handle it, but some other person does this for them. However, the others, who are not priests, do handle and possess it. They do not buy vineyards or houses. It is to be noted that for the most part they live two or three or more together; but if need be, one may live alone. Also, their sandal-wearer does not work for pay but is cared for by others. Women are not ordained, but they preach; however, they cannot impose penance. Also, they say that no one but God can have mercy on sins and that man or priest only gives advice. They make no ordinance or laws. Like the others [the Ultramontanes], they do not believe in purgatory, the oath, or the right of justice. He does not know what their belief is about the doctors of the Church. They believe that only a priest ordained by them can celebrate the Mass; a woman cannot. Just like the others, they see no worth at all in pilgrimages. Also, they believe that the voyage across the sea[46] is evil. They believe not at all in the indulgences of the Church nor its laws, just as is true of the others. They believe that one who owns worldly goods can be saved.

[13] *The* Secret *of Concorezzo.*—"I, John, your brother and partner in tribulation," and so on. I have another copy of this *Secret,* so this much suffices here: "This is the *Secret* of the heretics of Concorezzo, full of errors."[47] And also of bad Latin. These men brought heresy to Lombardy from Naples: Mark, John Judeus, Joseph, and Aldricus—in about the year 1174. . . .[48]

[15a] *On the Similarities between the Poor of Lyons and the Lombards.*[49]—The Poor of Lyons agree on this point in opposition to the

Church, that Pope Sylvester and the martyr Lawrence are not saints. Also, that the Roman Church pursuing the course it does is not the Church of Christ but a wicked church. Also, that there is no purgatory. Also, that man gains nothing by visiting the sepulchers of the saints, by adoring the Cross, by building churches, or by prayer, masses performed, or alms given for the dead. Also, that there is no salvation for those who take an oath in any way. Also, that it is not permissible to inflict corporal punishment on malefactors. Also, that it is no sin to eat meat, eggs, or cheese on any day of the year, except perhaps for the scandal [it causes], nor, likewise, is there any sin if a man should take to wife a relative or even his sister. Also, they believe that from the Blessed Clement down to Master Waldes, without exception, there was no successor to the blessed apostle Peter nor to Linus or Clement[50] who had the power to bind and to loose. Also, they believe that Pope Sylvester was, by the devil's prompting, the first builder of the Roman Church.

[15b] *On the Lombards.*—The Poor Lombards believe that an evil priest cannot consecrate the body of Christ, nor will God do so at his prayers. Also, they believe that souls are produced by propagation (*ex traduce*). Also, that children baptized by priests of the Roman Church do not attain salvation.

[15c] *On the Poor of Lyons: How They Consecrate the Mass Once a Year.*—The aforesaid Poor of Lyons consecrate the Mass only once a year, namely, on Holy Thursday. On that day, just at nightfall, he who is chief among them, if he is a priest, assembles all his following of both sexes and has a bench or a stool made ready before them on which they put a clean cloth, and thereupon they put a good goblet of good, pure wine and an unleavened loaf. Then he who is presiding says to the participants: "Let us ask our Lord out of his mercy to forgive our sins and offenses and that He may out of his mercy grant those things for which we worthily strive. That He may bring these things to pass, let us repeat the Lord's Prayer seven times, to the honor of God and the Holy Trinity." Whereupon they all kneel and repeat the Lord's Prayer seven times. Then they rise. Then he who is performing the consecration makes the sign of the Cross over the bread and the goblet of wine; and, breaking the bread, he gives to each of the participants his portion and thereafter he gives all to drink of the cup. They remain standing throughout, and thus ends their sacrament. And they firmly believe and main-

tain that this is the body and blood of our Lord Jesus Christ. If anything is left of the Host, they keep it until Easter and then consume it all. If, however, some others should ask for it, they might well give it to them. Through all the rest of the year they give their sick only consecrated bread and wine. In this fashion all the Poor of both sects held to the same rite of consecration, that which was just described, prior to the schism which occurred among them. . . .[51]

[19] *On the Ministers of the Albanenses and the Concorezzenses:*[52]— Bishop of the sect of Albanenses, Bonaventure of Verona; he is dead. Elder son, Bertholus of Verona; he is now a convert. Younger son, Henry of Arezzo; he is now bishop. Deacon of Bergamo, Lanfranc of Brescia. Deacon of *Seprio*, Ventura of Bergamo. Deacon of Pavia. Deacon of Brescia, Peter of Pavia; he was burned at Cremona. Deacon of Alessandria, Octo Balistorius. Deacon of Cremona, John Vulnerus. Deacon of Piacenza, Lauterius. Deacon of Verona, Albertinus of Reggio. Bishop of the Concorezzenses, Hubert Manderius. Elder son, Peter of *Limadi*. Younger son, Lanfranc of Brescia. Deacon of Lodi, Odonus of Piacenza. Deacon of Piacenza, Gerald of Cremona. Deacon of Cremona, Bonderus of Cremona. Deacon of Alessandria, Peter Pastor of Alessandria. Deacon of Brescia, Laurence *de Gradi*.

55. *Bernard Gui's Description of Heresies*

Bernard Gui was a Dominican friar and one of the most notable officials in the history of the medieval Inquisition, which he served for nearly a quarter of a century. He was born in the Limousin in 1261 or 1262, probably of the lesser nobility, but little is known of his early life. He took the Dominican habit in 1279 and made his solemn profession a year later; there followed years of study—first in logic, then in theology—which ended at Montpellier in 1290. For the next seventeen years he served as prior successively in several Dominican convents in southern France until, on January 16, 1307, he was commissioned as an inquisitor by Pope Clement V, with headquarters in the diocese of Toulouse. There he remained, except for a few diplomatic missions for the papacy to Italy and northern France, until 1324. On August 26, 1323, he was appointed bishop of Tuy by Pope John XXII, but seems never to have taken up residence at Tuy. He was transferred to the see of Lodève on July 20, 1324, and died at Lodève on December 31, 1331.

Bernard Gui was not only a devoted and able administrator, he was also a prolific writer, producing a mass of material on a variety of subjects, particularly in the fields of history and theology. His written work is characterized by directness and fidelity to detail rather than by great philosophical grasp or felicity of expression. His style is usually clear and understandable, although at times succinct to the point of obscurity.[1] Of his works, those which are of special interest to us are two dealing with the Inquisition. One of these, which requires only brief mention here, is a collection of the sentences declared by Gui over a period of seventeen years in eighteen "sermons" or autos-da-fé.[2] It was published under the title *Liber sententiarum inquisitionis Tholosanae ab anno Christi MCCCVII ad annum MCCCXXIII*, forming the second part of Limborch's *Historia inquisitionis*. (The manuscript from which Limborch worked has disappeared.) During his years as inquisitor Gui sentenced 930 individuals to what he and members of the local clergy associated with him in the proceedings considered appropriate penalties; the collected sentences, forming a quarto volume of 394 pages, summarize the cases and indicate the basis for the judgments pronounced against the accused.[3]

More immediate to our purpose is the work in which Bernard Gui summed up his experience as an inquisitor for his fellows. Entitled *Practica inquisitionis heretice pravitatis* [the conduct of the inquisition of heretical depravity], it was composed at intervals toward the end of his career and probably was finished in 1323-1324.[4] There are five parts. The first three are made up of formulas appropriate to the conduct of the Inquisition: forms for sentencing those before the court, for the amelioration of penalties, and for sentences delivered at the "sermon" and certain other times. These are based on notarial records of action in Bernard Gui's court or on the sentences reproduced in the *Liber sententiarum*.[5] The fourth part is a collection of papal bulls, canons of councils, and other acts fixing the extent and limitations of inquisitorial powers. It is based on an earlier, anonymous Italian tractate of similar import, written about 1280-1292,[6] but Bernard Gui worked it over and made additions to such an extent that the product is substantially his own.[7]

The fifth and most important part of the *Practica* comprises principally a review of the tenets of those heretics whom Gui considered important in his day: Cathars, Waldenses, "pseudo-Apostles," [8] Beguins, Jews, and sorcerers or invokers of demons. Certain formulas to be employed in the cases of those who abjured heresy are also included. The descriptions of the heresies are based to a considerable extent on earlier works, to which Gui made additions out of his own experience. For the statement on the Cathars he utilized the confession of a famous Languedocian heretic of his own day, Peter Autier, and perhaps some polemical works of the thirteenth century.[9] The chapter on the Waldenses exploited several sources, two of which deserve particular notice. One is the account of the origins of the sect given by Stephen of Bourbon (No. 33). Even more, Gui relied on the *De inquisitione hereticorum* attributed to the Franciscan David of Augsburg.[10] He made some changes, a few of which unfortunately obscure the sense of what he copied, but he also added observations of his own.[11] For the description of the pseudo-Apostles, Gui drew on a treatise which he also made the basis of a longer, separate exposition (the treatise, of Italian origin, is dated May 1, 1316).[12] In contrast to Bernard Gui's first three chapters, his fourth, on the Beguins, is derived from his own investigations, interrogations, and perusal of documents. The last two chapters, on Jews and sorcerers, are in part adaptations of earlier interrogatories and, in respect of the Jews, in part based on information from a witness questioned by Gui himself.[13] Thus, the *Practica* is a combination of information drawn from the work of others —no rarity among the treatises on heresy— and from personal experience. The organization of the fifth part reflects the author's preoccupation with the orderly processes of the Inquisition. We may well echo Father Dondaine's judgment that the *Practica*, by its scope, the number and selection of its documents, and the authority of its author, holds first place among the inquisitorial manuals from the first century of the Inquisition.[14] Even if other works surpass its description of heresies in precision and detail, it affords us an excellent overview of heresies, through the eyes of an eminently qualified observer, at the end of the period we are concerned with here.

On Bernard Gui and his work, in addition to the essay of Antoine Thomas already cited (n. 1), one may consult Leopold Delisle, "Notice sur les manuscrits de Bernard Gui," *Notices et extraits de manuscrits de la Bibliothèque nationale*, Vol. XXVII, part II (1879), pp. 169-455; and the Introduction to the edition from which we translate. The *Practica* has been edited as a complete work by Célestin Douais (Paris, 1886). We have, however, used the edition by Guillaume Mollat of the fifth part only of the *Practica*.[15] It is Bernard Gui, *Manuel de l'inquisiteur*, ed. with a French translation by Guillaume Mollat (Les Classiques de l'histoire de France au moyen âge, VIII, IX [Paris, 1926-1927]).[16] The translation is made by permission of the copyright holder, Belles-lettres.

1323-1324

THE CONDUCT OF THE INQUISITION OF HERETICAL DEPRAVITY

Part V: On the Method, Practice, and Procedure Used in Seeking Out and Interrogating Heretics, Their Believers, and Accomplices

[*Preface*]

Here follows the fifth and last part of the treatise, wherein are discussed the method, practice, and procedure used in searching out and interrogating heretics, their believers, and accomplices. It includes the separate frauds, devices, and wiles whereby they conceal themselves, each the more subtly to escape from the interrogations aimed especially at him. Among them are included the Manichaeans; and the Waldenses, or Poor of Lyons; as well as certain pseudo-Apostles, who falsely claim to be the apostles of Christ although they are rather apostles of Antichrist. There are also included a considerable number of others of a certain pestiferous sect which emerged in recent times, who, in simulation rather than assimilation of the poverty of evangelical perfection, call themselves the Poor of Christ, saying that theirs is the third order or third rule of St. Francis and who, in the vernacular, are commonly called Beguins and Beguines. It also includes others, who, after having been converted from the perfidy of the Jews to the faith of Christ, return to the vomit of Judaism. Lastly are given the methods of attack upon the pestilence or the pestilential error of sorcerers, diviners, invokers of demons, and others of that kind. Various special forms for abjuring heresy during the course of a hearing are also set forth.[1]

General Advice and Remarks.—This is the procedure when anyone is to be heard or examined, whether he has come in person of his own free will, has been cited, or has been summoned as suspect, noted, defamed, or accused of the crime of heresy, of showing favor or hospitality to heretics, or of anything else which falls within the cognizance of the Inquisition of heretical depravity or has any connection with it.[2] In the first place, after he has been quietly and unostentatiously summoned and warned by the inquisitor or the inquisitor's deputy, have him swear upon the Holy Gospels of God to tell the whole truth and nothing but the truth in regard to the matter of heresy and whatever touches thereupon or is connected in any way with the office of the Inquisition. He is to do this both in respect of himself as a principal and also as a witness in the case of other persons, living or dead.[3]

Once the oath has been taken and registered, let the witness be urgently exhorted to tell the truth, of his own accord, in the matter of heresy, so far as he knows, has known, or has heard of it. If, however, he requests time or opportunity for deliberation in order to give a more carefully considered response, that may be granted him if it seems expedient to the inquisitor, especially if he seems to be seeking it in good faith, not guilefully. Otherwise, he is required to answer about himself without delay.

Thereupon, the date of the hearing may be entered by a notary, thus: "In such a year, on such date, one N., from such town or village, of such diocese, who came of his own free will, or was cited or summoned, was formally placed in judgment before the religious person N.—inquisitor of heretical depravity, deputed by the Apostolic See to the kingdom of France—having taken oath upon the Holy Gospels of God to speak the whole truth and nothing but the truth about the fact or the crime of heresy and everything pertaining thereto, both in respect of himself as a principal and also as a witness in the case of other persons, living or dead, has said and confessed," etc.

It should be noted further that if anyone should argue openly and obviously against the faith, adducing the arguments and the authorities upon which heretics are wont to rely, such a person may easily be proved guilty of heresy by loyal, learned sons of the Church, for one is presumed to be a heretic from the very fact of striving to defend error. But because modern heretics endeavor and seek covertly to disguise their errors rather than openly to confess them, even men versed in the Scriptures cannot prove their guilt, because they manage to escape by verbal trickery and carefully contrived subtleties. The result of this is that men of learning are rather thrown into confusion by them, and those heretics, glorying therein, are further encouraged by observing how they thus elude learned men, slipping cleverly out of their hands by the sly cunning and tortuous ambiguity of their replies.

For it is exceedingly difficult to catch heretics when they themselves do not frankly avow error but conceal it, or when sure and sufficient evidence against them is not at hand. Under such circumstances, serious problems beset the investigator from every side. For, on the one hand, his conscience torments him if an individual is punished who has neither confessed nor been proved guilty; on the other, it causes even more anguish to the mind of the inquisitor, familiar through much experience with the falsity, cunning, and malice of such persons, if by their wily astuteness they escape punishment, to the detriment of the faith, since thereby they are strengthened, multiplied, and rendered more crafty. Another consideration, too, is that the faithful laity see occasion for scandal in the fact that the proceedings of the Inquisition, once started against someone, are abandoned, as it were, in confusion, and they are to some extent weakened in the faith by observing that learned men are thus mocked by low and uncouth persons. For they believe that we have at our command in support of the faith arguments so clear and obvious that no one may oppose us in these matters without our knowing at once how to overcome him, in such wise that even laymen may clearly perceive just what these reasons are. Hence, in such a situation, it is not expedient to dispute in matters of the faith against such astute heretics in the presence of laymen.

Furthermore, a point worthy of attention is that just as no one medicine is for all diseases, but rather different and specific medicines exist for particular diseases, so neither is the same method of questioning, investigation, and examination to be employed for all heretics of the various sects, but for each, whether there be one or many, a particular and suitable method ought to be utilized. So the inquisitor, like a prudent physician of souls, will proceed cautiously in regard to the persons whom he questions or concerning whom he makes inquiry. He will weigh their quality, condition, standing, health, and local circumstances, and will act with caution on the matters upon which there is to be inquiry and examination. He should not impose or force all the following interrogatories upon everyone without distinction and in the same order; nor, in the case of some, should he be satisfied with these questions and only these. But with the bridle of discretion let him so harness the wiles of heretical persons that, with the help of God and the skill of a midwife, he may draw the writhing serpent from the sink and abyss of errors.

In these matters, no single and infallible pattern can be set, for, if that were done, the children of darkness might anticipate too far in advance the sole customary method and might too easily avoid or guard against it as a trap. Therefore, the wise inquisitor should be careful to set his course by the replies of the witnesses, the sworn statements of accusers, the counsel of men taught by experience, the shrewdness of his own natural intelligence, and the following questions or interrogatories, as God shall direct.

We shall append in order in the following pages material of use in giving some sort of idea as to how examinations may be conducted against five sects—the Manichaeans; the Waldenses, or Poor of Lyons; the pseudo-Apostles; those who are called in the vernacular Beguins; Jews who have been converted to the faith of Christ and have returned to the vomit of Judaism—and also against sorcerers, diviners, and invokers of demons, whose noxious influence is exceedingly harmful to the purity of the faith. A general outline of the error of each sect will be given first, followed by an outline of the plan and method of conducting the examination, as will appear on the following pages.

[*Chapter I: Manichaeans of the Present Time*]

[1] *Concerning the Errors of the Manichaeans of the Present Time.*—
The sect and heresy of the Manichaeans and the supporters of its aber-
ration declare and confess that there are two gods and two lords, to wit,
a beneficent God and an evil one. They assert that the creation of
everything visible and corporeal was wrought, not by God the Heavenly
Father, whom they term the beneficent God, but by the devil, or Satan,
the wicked God—for him they call the evil god, the god of this age, and
the prince of this world. Thus, they postulate two creators, namely, God
and the devil; and two creations, that is, one invisible and incorporeal,
the other visible and corporeal.

Also, they pretend that there are two churches: The beneficent one,
they say, is their sect, which they declare to be the Church of Jesus
Christ. But the other they call the evil church; this they hold to be the
Roman Church, which they shamelessly refer to as the mother of
fornication, the great Babylon, the harlot and cathedral of the devil, and
the synagogue of Satan. They despise and distort all its offices, its
orders, its ordinations, and its statutes. They call all who hold its faith
heretics and sinners, and they declare as dogma that no one can be
saved in the faith of the Roman Church.

Also, all the sacraments of the Roman Church of our Lord Jesus
Christ—the Eucharist or sacrament of the altar, baptism which makes
use of actual water, confirmation, ordination, extreme unction, penance,
and marriage of man and woman—each and every one they declare
empty and vain. And, like monkeys, they devise in imitation certain
others which seem almost like them. In place of baptism by water, they
concoct another baptism, a spiritual one, which they call the consolamentum of the Holy Spirit, whenever they admit anyone, in health or
in sickness, into their sect and order by the imposition of hands, in
accordance with their abominable rite. In place of the consecrated bread
of the Eucharist, the body of Christ, they concoct a certain bread which
they call "blessed bread" or "bread of holy prayer." This they hold in
their hands at the beginning of their meal; and, following their ritual,
they bless, break, and distribute it to those present and to their believers. As for the sacrament of penance, they say that true penance
consists in entering and remaining faithful to their sect and order. They

say that all sins have been forgiven those who enter their sect and order, whether in sickness or in health; that such persons have been absolved from all their sins without any atonement whatsoever and even without making restitution, should they possess another's property, so long as they remain true to their sect and order. They claim that they have the identical and equivalent power over these matters that Peter, Paul, and the other apostles of the Lord possessed. Confession of sins made to priests of the Roman Church they hold to be utterly without value for salvation, and they say that neither the pope nor anyone else connected with the Roman Church has the power to absolve anyone from his sins. Instead of the sacrament of carnal marriage between man and woman, they pretend that there is a spiritual marriage between the soul and God, namely, when the perfected or consoled heretics themselves receive anyone into their sect or order.

Also, they deny the incarnation of the Lord Jesus Christ through Mary, ever virgin, declaring that He did not have a true human body or true human flesh such as other men have because of their human substance, that He did not really suffer and die on the Cross, nor really rise from the dead, nor really ascend into heaven in human body and flesh, but that all these things happened only figuratively. Also, they deny that the Blessed Virgin Mary was the true mother of our Lord Jesus Christ or was a carnal woman, but say that their sect and order is the Virgin Mary, that is, the true, chaste, and virginal repentance which gives birth to sons of God on the occasion of their reception into this very sect and order. Also, they deny that there will be a resurrection of human bodies, imagining in its stead certain spiritual bodies and a sort of inner man. They say that the future resurrection is to be understood in terms of these two concepts.

They hold, believe, and teach the afore-mentioned errors and very many others which necessarily proceed therefrom. Nevertheless, because of misleading expressions and terms, to inexperienced persons and to laymen they seem at first sight to profess the true faith, for they say that they believe in God the Father, the Son, and the Holy Spirit, the creator of all; that they believe in the Holy Roman Church, in the Lord Jesus Christ, in the Blessed Virgin Mary, in the incarnation, passion, resurrection, and ascension of the same Lord Jesus Christ, in holy baptism, in true penance, in the true body of Christ, and in the sacrament of matrimony. Yet, when the truth is more attentively tested, sought for, and searched out, it appears that they utter all the foregoing in duplicity and falsehood, in accordance with their ideas as set forth and explained above, in order thus to deceive simple persons and even highly educated men if they happen to be inexperienced. They teach and expound to their believers all the errors mentioned above and, once they have been discovered and cannot hide, they openly defend, affirm, and profess them before inquisitors. Thenceforth, what is needful is to exhort them to conversion and, in every possible way, to show them their error, using the services of specially trained and diligent men.

Inquisitors, in normal practice, detain such perfected heretics for a rather long time for a number of reasons, first, in order more frequently to urge them to conversion, for their conversion is especially helpful. The conversion of Manichaean heretics is usually genuine and seldom feigned; when they are converted, they tell everything, reveal the truth, and betray their confederates, whence results a great harvest. Also, as long as such perfected heretics are held, their believers and accomplices more readily confess and expose themselves and others, fearing to be betrayed by the heretics if the latter are converted. However, after their conversion has been repeatedly urged and invited, if the heretics are unwilling to return to the faith and seem to be obdurate, sentence is pronounced against them and they are abandoned to the secular arm and tribunal.

[2] *Concerning the Way of Life and the Practices of These Manichaeans.*—It is expedient, also, to touch on some facts in regard to the way of life, the customs, and the behavior of these heretics, since thereby they are more easily recognized and apprehended.

In the first place, it should be known that under no circumstances do they take an oath.

Also, they observe annually three forty-day fasts, namely, from the feast of St. Brice [November 13] until Christmas, from Shrove Sunday until Easter, and from the feast of Pentecost until the feasts of the apostles Peter and Paul [June 29]. The first and last week of each period they call "strict," for then they fast on bread and water, whereas, during the other weeks, they fast on bread and water for three days only. All the rest of the year they fast on bread and water three days each week, unless they are traveling or are ill. Also, they never eat meats or even touch them, or cheese, eggs, or anything which is born of the flesh by generation or coition.[4]

Also, under no circumstances will they kill any animal or any winged creature, for they say and believe that there are in brute animals and even in birds those spirits which leave the bodies of men (if they have not been received into their sect and order through the imposition of hands according to their custom), and that these spirits pass from one body to another.

Also, they touch no woman.

Also, at the beginning of the month, when they are gathered together with their believers or by themselves, they bless a loaf or a piece of bread. Holding it in their hands, with a towel or some white cloth hanging from their necks, they say the Lord's Prayer and break the bread into small pieces. This bread they call "bread of holy prayer," and "broken bread"; their believers call it "blessed bread" or "consecrated bread" (*panem signatum*). They partake of it as communion at the beginning of a meal; they give and distribute it to their believers.

Also, they teach their believers to show them reverence in a ceremony which they call the melioramentum, although we call it adoration. The believer bends the knees and, with hands clasped, bows low before the heretics over some bench or down to the ground. He bows three times, each time saying as he rises, "Bless us," and finally concluding, "Good Christians, give us God's blessing and yours. Pray the Lord for us that God may keep us from an evil death and bring us to a good end or into the hands of faithful Christians." The heretic replies: "From God and from us you have it (that is, the benediction); and may God bless you and save your soul from an evil death, and bring you to a good end." By "evil death," the heretics mean dying in the faith of the Roman Church, while by "a good end" and by "the hands of faithful Christians," they mean being received at the end of one's life into their own sect and order, according to their practice; this they hold to be a good end. However, they say that the reverence described above is made not to themselves but to the Holy Spirit, who, they say, is in them and by Whom they have been received into the sect and order which they claim is theirs.

Also, they teach their believers to make with them a pact, which they call "the agreement" (*la covenensa*), to the effect that the believers desire to be taken into the heretics' sect and order at the end of their life. Once that pact is sealed, the heretics may accept them during an illness, even though they should have lost the power of speech or their memory should have failed.[5]

[3] *Concerning the Method of Heretication or the Reception of the Sick into This Sect or Order.*—The following is the method of admitting persons to their sect or order during an illness or near the end of life of the suppliant. The heretic asks the individual who is to be received, if [the invalid] can speak, if he or she wishes to become a good Christian man or woman and wishes to receive holy baptism. Upon receiving an affirmative answer, accompanied by the request, "Bless us," the heretic, with his hand over the head of the sick person (but not touching her if it be a woman) and holding the Book, repeats the Gospel, "In the beginning was the Word," as far as "the Word was made flesh and dwelt among us."[6] At the conclusion of the reading, the invalid repeats the Lord's Prayer, if he can; if not, one of those present says it for him. Thereafter, the sick man, if able, bows his head over clasped hands and says three times, "Bless us," while all the others present adore the heretic in the fashion described above. On the spot, or in a place apart, the heretic makes many prostrations, obeisances, and genuflections to the ground, repeating the Lord's Prayer several times while bowing and rising.

[4] *Concerning Their Method of Religious Instruction.*—It would take long to treat in detail of the methods by which these Manichaean heretics preach and propound their doctrines to their believers, but it is well to present some of them briefly here.

In the first place, they usually say of themselves that they are good Christians who do not swear or lie or speak evil of anyone; that they kill neither man nor beast nor anything which has the breath of life; and that they hold the faith of the Lord Jesus Christ and His Gospel, as Christ and the apostles taught it. They say that they occupy the place of the apostles and that it is because of the foregoing facts that the members of the Roman Church, to wit, the prelates, the secular and regular clergy, and especially the inquisitors of heretics, persecute them and call them heretics, just as the Pharisees persecuted Christ and His apostles, although they are really good men and good Christians.

Also, they discuss with laymen at every opportunity the wicked life of clerics and prelates of the Roman Church. They give examples and speak at length about their pride, cupidity, avarice, their uncleanliness of life, and whatever other evils they know. In this connection, they cite the texts of the Gospels and the Epistles, as they interpret and understand them, against the state of prelates, clergy, and members of religious orders, whom they refer to as Pharisees and false prophets, those who "say, and do not."[7]

One by one, they tear down and disparage all the sacraments of the Church, especially the sacrament of the Eucharist, saying that the body of Christ is not therein, for were it large as the greatest mountain, Christians would already have eaten all of it. Also, they say, the Host comes from straw and passes through the tails of stallions and mares (referring to the flour's being passed through the sieve); also, that it goes into the latrine of the stomach and is ejected through the basest part of the body, which could not happen, they insist, if God were present.

Also, in the matter of baptism, [they say] that the water is a material substance and corruptible, and therefore is part of the work and creation of the evil God and cannot hallow the soul, but the clergy sell that water out of avarice, just as they sell land for the burial of the dead and oil for the sick when they anoint them, and just as they make a profit from the confession of sins to the priests. Also, they claim that confessions made to priests of the Roman Church are of no value, for, inasmuch as the priests are sinners, they cannot bind and loose and, being themselves unclean, they cannot cleanse another person.

Also, they say that the Cross of Christ deserves no adoration or veneration because, according to them, no one adores or venerates the gallows on which his father or some relative or friend has been hanged. Also, they say that those who adore the Cross should, with equal right, adore all thorns and all lances, for just as in Christ's passion the Cross was for His body, so were the thorns for His head and the soldier's lance for His side. Many other offensive teachings do they set forth on the subject of the sacraments of the Church.

Also, they read the Gospels and the Epistles in the vernacular, interpreting and expounding them in their own favor and against the existing establishments of the Roman Church. It would take too long to deal with these points individually here, but one may read them at greater length in their books, which they have filled and defiled with that material, and may hear them fully in the confessions of their believers after conversion.[8]

[5] *The Following Are Suggested Questions to Be Put to Believers of the Sect of the Manichaeans.*—In the first place, let the one under examination be asked whether he has anywhere seen or known a heretic

or heretics, knowing or believing them to be such or to have that name or reputation; where he saw them; how often; with whom; and when.

Also, [ask] whether he had any familiar association with them; when; how; and who was responsible for it; also, whether he received any heretical person or persons in his home; who they were; who brought them there; how long they stayed; who visited them there and escorted them thence; and where they went; also, whether he heard their preaching; and what they said and taught; also, whether he adored them or saw them adored by others, or saw reverences made to them in the heretical fashion; and about the practice of adoration; also, whether he ate of their blessed bread; and about the method of blessing the said bread; also, whether he made a pact or covenant with them to the effect that he wished to be received into their sect and order at the point of death.

Also, [ask] whether he saluted them or saw them saluted by others in the heretical fashion, which is to place a hand upon each of the heretic's cheeks, bending one's head, and turning it toward each cheek, and saying thrice, "Your blessing," a mode of salutation which the believers who [are to become] perfected observe upon the arrival or departure of heretics.

Also, [ask] whether he was present at a heretication of any person and about the method of heretication; the names of the heretic or heretics; the persons there present; the place in the house where the invalid lay; the time and hour; whether the hereticated person bequeathed anything to the heretics—what, how much, and who paid the legacy; whether adoration was performed there to the said heretic; whether the hereticated person died of that illness and where he was buried; and who brought there and escorted thence the heretic or heretics; also, whether he believed that the hereticated person could be saved in the faith of the heretics.

Also, [ask] what he heard said or taught by the heretics against the faith and sacraments of the Roman Church; what he heard them saying about the sacrament of the Eucharist; about baptism, matrimony, confession of sins to priests, adoration or veneration of the Holy Cross; and similarly for other errors enumerated above; also, whether he believed that heretics were good men and truthful; that they had and kept a good faith, a good sect, and good doctrine; that the heretics themselves and their believers could be saved in their faith and sect; also, how long he has shared in or persisted in the said belief; also, when he first began to accept this belief; also, whether he still believes it; also, when and why he abandoned it.

Also, [ask] whether he has ever on any other occasion been summoned or cited before any inquisitor; when and why; whether on any other occasion he has confessed in the matter of heresy; whether he has abjured heresy before any inquisitor; whether he was restored to the communion of the Church or absolved; also, whether since that time he has in any way been involved in the matter of heresy; which heresy; and in what way, as listed above; also, whether he knows any person or persons who are believers in or sympathizers with the activity of heretics, or are their harborers; also, whether he has ever accompanied a heretic or heretics from place to place or has had their books in his possession; also, whether his relatives were believers or were sympathizers with the activities of heretics or had been penanced for complicity in heresy.

This is the general line of questioning for the sect under consideration, from which special questions often may be developed through the diligence and alertness of the inquisitor.

[6] *A Few Words of Advice and Suggestion.*—In regard to the foregoing items, one should note well and be advised that, although such elaborate questions may be posed—sometimes together with others, in view of the diversity of persons and actions—to draw and worm out the truth more completely, it is not expedient that all interrogations be formally recorded but only those which more clearly touch the core or essence of the matter and seem designed the better to elicit the truth. For, if so great a number of questions are posed in any one deposition, another deposition which comprises fewer may seem too brief. Also, with such a multiplicity of written questions in the course of the hearing, agreement in the testimony of witnesses can hardly be achieved, a contingency to be borne in mind and avoided.

[Chapter II: Concerning the Sect of the Waldenses]
[1] *The Following Deals with the Sect of the Waldenses, First, with Its Origins and the Time at Which It Began.*—The sect and heresy of the Waldenses or Poor of Lyons began about the year of our Lord 1170. Its moving spirit and founder was a certain citizen of Lyons named Waldes, or Waldens, from whom his followers received their name. He

was a rich man who, having given up all his property, resolved to devote himself to poverty and to evangelical perfection, just as the apostles had done. He had procured for himself translations of the Gospels and some other books of the Bible in vernacular French, also some texts from St. Augustine, St. Jerome, St. Ambrose, and St. Gregory, arranged topically, which he and his adherents called "sentences." On frequently reading these over among themselves, although very seldom understanding them aright, they were carried away by their emotions and, although they had but little learning, they usurped the function of the apostles by daring to preach "in the streets and the broad ways."[1]

This man Waldes, or Waldens, won over to a like presumption many people of both sexes, made men and women his accomplices, and sent them out to preach as his disciples. They, men and women alike, although they were stupid and uneducated, wandered through villages, entered homes, preached in the squares and even in churches, the men especially, and spread many errors everywhere. Moreover, when they were summoned by the archbishop of Lyons, John of the Fair Hands, and by him forbidden such audacity, they were not at all willing to obey, alleging as excuse for their madness that "we ought to obey God rather than men,"[2] Who had commanded His apostles to "preach the gospel to every creature."[3] By virtue of a false profession of poverty and a feigned appearance of sanctity, they arrogated to themselves what had been said to the apostles. Boldly declaring that they were imitators and successors of these apostles, they cast aspersions upon prelates and clergy for abundant wealth and lives of luxury.

Thus, through presumptuously usurping the office of preaching, they became teachers of error. After they had been warned to desist, they rendered themselves disobedient and contumacious, for which they were excommunicated and driven from that city and their native land. Finally, indeed, because they remained obdurate, they were pronounced schismatics at a certain council which was held at Rome before the Lateran Council, and were then condemned as heretics. And so, as they had grown in number on the earth, they scattered throughout that province and neighboring areas and into the region of Lombardy. Separated and cut off from the Church, when they mingled with other heretics and imbibed their errors, they combined with their own fantasies the errors and heresies of heretics of earlier days.[4]

[2] *Concerning the Three Names Commonly Used for These Waldenses.*—The sect of the Waldenses, Poor of Lyons, or "Sandal-Shod"[5] was so called or named from a certain man, Waldes, or Waldens, the moving spirit and first founder of this sect; they were also called Poor of Lyons, from the place where the sect began and had its origin; and they were called the Sandal-Shod because, from the very beginning of the sect, perfected Waldenses wore a device shaped roughly like a shield, on the upper part of their sandals, by this sign being distinguishable from their associates and believers.

The errors of this sect are subjoined in the following pages in order to make possible a more discreet inquest and examination on the basis of advance information.

[3] *Concerning the Errors of the Waldenses of Recent Times, for in the Past They Had Many Others.*—Now, the principal heresy of the aforesaid Waldenses was and still continues to be contempt of ecclesiastical authority. Then, having been excommunicated for this and given over to Satan, they were plunged by him into countless errors, and they combined with their own fantasies the errors of heretics of an earlier day.

The foolish followers and impious teachers of this sect hold and teach that they are not subject to our lord pope, the Roman pontiff, or to other prelates of the Roman Church, for they declare that the Roman Church persecutes and censures them unjustly and unduly. Also, they declare positively that they cannot be excommunicated by the said Roman pontiff and prelates, to none of whom ought obedience be given should he enjoin or command the members and teachers of this sect to desert and abjure it—this despite the fact that it has been condemned as heretical by the Roman Church.

Also, they hold and teach that every oath, in or out of court, without exception or qualification, has been forbidden by God as unlawful and sinful. Here they apply the words of the Holy Gospel and of St. James the apostle[6] about not swearing, although with an interpretation as extravagant as it is erroneous. For, in fact, as a matter of law and duty an oath may be taken to establish truth in court, according to the sound teaching of the saints, of the doctors of the Church, of the tradition of the same Holy Catholic Church, and also in consonance with the following decree of the Church, announced some time ago against the said error: "If any among them are unwilling to take an oath because, out of damnable superstition, they reject the religious obligation of the oath, they are by that very fact to be considered heretics."[7]

It should be noted, however, that these Waldenses relax the prohibition on oaths by permitting any of their number to swear in order to avoid or prevent his own or another's death, and also to keep from betraying his associates or revealing the secrets of his sect. For they say that the unforgivable crime and sin against the Holy Spirit is to betray any perfected member of their sect.

Also, out of the same font of error, the aforesaid sect and heresy declares that any judicial process is forbidden by God and is, consequently, a sin and that it is contrary to God's command for any judge, in any case or for any reason, to sentence a man to corporal punishment involving bloodshed, or to death. They seize on the words of the Holy Gospels—"Judge not that ye be not judged"; "Thou shalt not kill";[8] and other similar passages—without the proper explanation essential to their interpretation. This they do without understanding the sense or accepting the signification or explanation which the Holy Roman Church wisely perceives and transmits to the faithful in accordance with the teaching of the Fathers, the doctors, and the canonical decrees.

Also, as it strays from the way and the right path, this sect does not accept or consider valid, but despises, rejects, and damns the canonical decrees, the decretals of the supreme pontiffs, the rules concerning observance of fasts and holy days, and the precepts of the Fathers.

Also, in a more pernicious error in respect of the sacrament of penance and the keys of the Church, these sectaries say, hold, and teach that, just as the apostles had it from Christ, they have from God alone and from no other the power to hear confessions from men and women who wish to confess to them, to give absolution, and to impose penance. And they do hear the confessions of such persons, they do give absolution and impose penance, although they are not priests or clerics ordained by any bishop of the Roman Church but are laymen and nothing more. They do not claim to have any such power from the Roman Church, but rather disclaim it; and, in truth, they have it neither from God nor from his Church, because they are outside the Church and have been cut off by the Church itself, beyond whose portals there is no true penance or salvation.

Also, this sect and heresy ridicules the indulgences which are published and granted by prelates of the Church, asserting that they are of no value whatever.

In regard to the sacrament of the Eucharist they err, saying, not publicly but in private among themselves, that if the priest who celebrates or consecrates the Mass is a sinner, the bread and wine do not change into the body and blood of Christ in the sacrament of the altar; and in their view anyone is a sinner who is not a member of their sect. Also, they say that any righteous person, even though he be a layman and not a cleric ordained by a Catholic bishop, can perform the consecration of the body and blood of Christ, provided only that he be a member of their sect. This they apply even to women, with the same proviso that they belong to their sect. Thus they teach that every holy person is a priest.[9]

[4] *Concerning Their Method or Ritual for the Celebration of Mass.*— The following is their usual method or ritual for celebrating Mass. They consecrate or celebrate it only once a year, on Holy Thursday. On that day, just at nightfall, he who is chief among them, even though he is not a cleric ordained by a Catholic bishop, assembles all his following of both sexes. He has a suitable bench or chest made ready before them with a clean cloth spread upon it. Next, they place thereon a goblet, full of good, pure wine, and an ashcake, an unleavened cake, or a loaf of unleavened bread. Then he who is presiding says to the participants: "Let us ask our Lord in His mercy to forgive our sins and our short-comings and in His mercy to grant those things for which we worthily strive. And that He may bring these things to pass, let us repeat the Lord's Prayer seven times, to the honor of God and the Holy Trinity." Whereupon, they all kneel, repeat the Lord's Prayer seven times, and then rise.

Then he who is performing the consecration makes the sign of the Cross over the bread and the goblet of wine and, breaking the bread, gives to each of the participants his portion. Thereafter, he gives all to drink of the cup. They remain standing during the whole ceremony. Thus ends their sacrifice. They firmly believe and maintain that this is the body and blood of our Lord Jesus Christ. If anything is left of the Host, they keep it until Easter and then consume it all. Through all the rest of the year, too, they give their sick only consecrated bread and wine. In this fashion all the Poor of Lyons, or Waldenses, observed the same rite of consecration prior to the schism which occurred among them, that is, before they split into the Poor called the Lombards and the Poor on this side of the Alps.

Also, these Waldenses deny that there is a purgatory for souls after this life and, in consequence, declare that prayers, alms, celebration of masses, and other pious services done by the faithful on behalf of the dead are of no avail.

Also, they censure and condemn prelates and the secular and regular clergy of the Roman Church, speaking disparagingly of their office. They hold them to be the blind who lead the blind, who neither preserve Gospel truth nor practice apostolic poverty. In a bitter lie, they aver that the Roman Church is a house of falsehood. Also, comparing apostolic life and perfection with their own and considering their merits to be on an equal level, they vaunt themselves vainly, saying they are successors to the apostles, boasting that they maintain and observe evangelical and apostolic poverty.

Also, they assert that there are three orders in their church, which are deacon, priest, and bishop, whose particular powers stem only from themselves, not from the Roman Church.[10] Nay more, they do not think that the holy orders of the Roman Church come from God but say they are the result of human tradition. So, they use the deceptive trick of professing their belief in the existence of the holy orders of episcopate, priesthood, and diaconate in the Holy Church, meaning, however, their own.

Also, they say there are no real miracles performed in the Church by the merits and prayers of the saints, for none of the saints ever performed miracles. Also, they say and affirm in private that the saints in heaven hearken not to the prayers of the faithful nor do they heed the acts of veneration whereby we on earth honor them. They say that the saints do not pray for us and so it is useless for us to seek their help. Hence, they scorn the festivals which we celebrate in veneration of the saints and the other acts by which we venerate and honor them, and on feast days they labor, when they can do so with safety.

These three tenets they do not reveal indiscriminately to their believers but keep within the circle of the perfected of the sect: namely, disbelief in the miracles of the saints; refusal to seek their help; and nonobservance of holy days, except for Sunday and the days of the Blessed Virgin Mary (but some add those of the apostles and the evangelists).

In their conventicles, however, they do impart secretly to their believers these and not a few other erroneous and unsound teachings which necessarily follow from them. Also, they preach to their believers from the Gospels, the Epistles, and from other Holy Scriptures, which they corrupt as they expound them, like masters of error who do not know how to be disciples of truth, notwithstanding the fact that preaching is wholly forbidden to laymen.

One should be aware, also, that this sect has preserved and observed many other errors from former days and is said still to cling to them secretly in some localities. Among these are the celebration of Mass on Holy Thursday, as we have said above; the detestable intercourse of any man with any woman, which is indiscriminately practiced in darkness; the apparition of a cat and sprinkling with the tail; and various other practices which are discussed in more detail in little tracts dealing with the subject.[11]

[5] *Concerning the Waldensian Way of Life.*—The customs and the way of life of the Waldenses should also be touched on briefly to aid somewhat in singling them out and recognizing them.

In the first place, one should know that the Waldenses have and install one superior over themselves, whom they call their "majoral,"[12] one whom all are bound to obey, just as all Catholics are under the obligation of obedience to our lord pope.

Also, the Waldenses commonly eat and drink the ordinary foods. Also, those who can and who so desire, fast on Monday and Wednesday, but while fasting, they eat meat. Also, they fast on Friday and during Lent, at which times they abstain from meat in order to avoid shocking others, for they say it is not a sin to eat meat on any day, inasmuch as Christ did not forbid eating meat or command abstinence therefrom.

Also, after they are accepted into that society, which they call "the brotherhood," and have promised to obey their superior and to observe evangelical poverty, they must preserve chastity and possess nothing of their own, but must sell all that they have, put the proceeds in a common fund, and live on alms given to them by their believers and sympathizers. He who is chief among them distributes and dispenses to each one according to his need.

Also, the Waldenses praise continence to their believers, yet they admit that burning passion must be satisfied, however base the means. Citing the words of the Apostle, "It is better to marry than to be burnt,"[13] they declare that it is better to satisfy passion by any means, however shameful, than to be tempted within the heart. This, however, they keep very secret, lest they fall into disrepute with their believers.

Also, they take collections among their believers and friends and turn that which has been given and collected over to their superior.

Also, every year they hold or celebrate one or two chapters-general in some important community, as secretly as possible, gathering, as if they were merchants, in a house leased long before by one or more of their believers. In those chapters, the chief (*major*) of them all arranges and disposes of the business involving priests and deacons and those who are to be sent out among their believers and friends in various regions and districts to hear confessions and collect alms. He is also informed and given an accounting of the collections and expenditures.

Also, they do not work with their hands after they have become perfected, nor do they undertake any task for money, unless perhaps as a stratagem in an emergency, to avoid being detected or seized.

Also, they commonly refer to themselves as "brothers," and say that they are the Poor of Christ, or the Poor of Lyons.

Also, in order to protect themselves, they sometimes push themselves into feigned familiarity with members of religious orders and the clergy, lavish favors or gifts upon them, or adopt a fawning or servile attitude toward them, thus to acquire for themselves and theirs a freer opportunity to remain undiscovered, to live, and to injure souls. Also, they attend churches and sermons, in all outward ways comport themselves in a religious and seemly manner, and strive to use a vocabulary that seems unctuous and discreet.

Also, they pray very often during the day and warn and instruct their believers to imitate and accompany them. Now, their manner of prayer is this: Kneeling on the ground, they bend forward over and support themselves upon some bench or other object of the kind; on bended knees, bowed down to earth, they hold their position in silence long enough to repeat the Lord's Prayer thirty or forty times, or occasionally more. They do this regularly every day when they are among their believers and those who consort with them in heresy, but excluding outsiders: before and after the noon meal; before and after dinner; at night when they propose to retire, before getting into bed; also in the morning after arising; and at certain other times during the day, both morning and afternoon.

Also, at those times they say no other prayer, nor do they teach or have any other than the Lord's Prayer. They have no use for the salutation to the Blessed Mary, the Hail Mary, or for the Apostles' Creed, "I believe in God," because, they say, these were provided and composed by the Roman Church, not by Christ, However, they do recite and teach seven articles of faith on divinity, seven on humanity, the ten commandments of the Decalogue, and seven works of mercy, which they have arranged and composed in fixed form in a sort of compendium. In this they have exceedingly great pride and show themselves instantly ready to answer for their faith. They can, then, be trapped in this way: "Recite to me the Creed, that is, 'I believe in God,' as the Catholic Church has it, inasmuch as all the articles of faith are included therein." To this, they reply, "I do not know it, for no one has taught it to me in that form."

Also, before seating themselves at table, they bless it, saying: "Bless us, O Lord, have mercy upon us. O Christ, have mercy upon us. O Lord, have mercy upon us, Thou our Father."[14] Then the one longest among them says in the vernacular, "May God, who for his disciples blessed the five barley loaves and two fishes in the desert,[15] bless this table, what is upon it, and what shall be placed thereon." Then he makes the sign of the Cross, saying, "In the name of the Father, of the Son, and of the Holy Spirit. Amen."

Also, when they rise from the table after the midday meal or after dinner, they give thanks thus: The one longest among them repeats in the vernacular the words from the Apocalypse: "Benediction and glory and wisdom and thanksgiving, honor and power and strength to our God forever and ever."[16] Then he adds: "May God render good reward and return to all those who do good unto us and bless us"; and, "May God, who has given us food for our bodies, give us also food for our souls"; and "May God be with us always and we with Him." The others respond, "Amen." Also, when they ask the blessing upon the meal and when they return thanks, they usually clasp their hands and raise them to heaven.

Also, after the noon meal, once they have given thanks and prayed as above, they preach, teach, or deliver their exhortations about their doctrine to those present, if they are in a safe place where they are not apprehensive about outsiders or servants who might not be in sympathy with them. But more often they do their preaching at night, after dinner.

For then, with their believers assembled after returning from work, they can discourse in greater secrecy, more securely and more freely. Now and then, at the conclusion of the preaching, they all kneel in the position for prayer described above, sometimes putting out the light, if there is one, in order, it is said, to avoid being observed or detected by strangers or outsiders not in sympathy with them.

Also, they tell and instruct their believers not to betray them in any way to chaplains, clerics, members of religious orders, or inquisitors for, if disclosed, they would be seized because—so they tell their believers—inquisitors and others in the Roman Church persecute them unjustly for serving God and observing His commandments, for pursuing evangelical poverty and perfection as did Christ and the apostles. They say, too, that they know the truth and God's way better than do chaplains, clerics, or members of religious orders of the Roman Church, who, out of ignorance of the truth, persecute them. They also say that they flee before the persecutions of their adversaries because Christ in the Gospel told His apostles and disciples to flee from city to city when persecuted for the name of God.[17]

[6] *Concerning the Waldensian Manner of Teaching.*—Some information should also briefly be given here about the manner of teaching or preaching of these Waldensian heretics.

There are two ranks within their sect. There are, first, the Perfect, they who are called Waldenses in the proper sense of the word.[18] After passing through a period of instruction, they have been received into their order according to its rite, to learn how to teach others. They say they have nothing of their own, no houses, property, or fixed abodes. Moreover, if once they had wives, they give them up on being received into the order. They claim to be successors to the apostles and are teachers and confessors for the others. They go about the country visiting their disciples and confirming them in error. Their disciples and believers minister to their necessities. When they have come to any place, word of their arrival is put about and many gather at their lodging place to hear and see them. People send whatever they have in the way of food and drink; they listen to the preaching in conventicles, held chiefly at night while other folk sleep or rest.

At the outset, however, the Perfect do not at once reveal the secrets of their error. At first their discourse describes what disciples of Christ should be like, based on the words of the Gospel and of the apostles, saying that those only may be successors of the apostles who imitate and uphold their way of life. From this, they argue and conclude that the pope, bishops, prelates, and clerics, who own the riches of this world and do not imitate the sanctity of the apostles, are not true pastors and governors of the Church of God but are rapacious and devouring wolves; that to such Christ does not deem it fitting to entrust the Church, His spouse, and that, therefore, they should not be obeyed. They say also that an unclean person cannot cleanse another, nor he who is bound loose another, nor can a criminal soothe a judge's wrath against another criminal, nor can one who is headed for destruction serve as another's guide to heaven. Thus do they disparage the clergy and prelates to render them detestable, lest they be believed or obeyed.

So, among the first things which the Waldenses ordinarily tell and teach their believers are some precepts which seem good and moral, such as to practice virtues and good works, to avoid and flee from vices —this in order to gain a more receptive audience for other subjects and to secure a hold over their auditors. They say that one must not lie, since, according to the Scriptures, everyone who does so kills his soul.[19] Also, that one should not do unto another that which he does not wish done to himself; that one must keep God's commandments.[20] Also, that no one should swear in any case, since God has forbidden every oath, saying in the Gospel: "Swear not at all, neither by heaven, for it is the throne of God, nor by the earth, for it is his footstool, nor by any other creature, for man cannot make one hair white or black. But let your speech be, 'Yea, yea; no, no'; and that which is over and above these, is of evil."[21] These words they deeply impress upon their believers and admit of no interpretation of them. Also, they say and teach that to swear is a mortal sin, always and under any circumstances whatsoever; and if one of their believers is compelled by any secular or ecclesiastical authority to take an oath in court, the oath-taker must afterward confess it and receive penance as for a sin.

Also, in order to give their words greater weight among their listeners when they preach from the Gospels, the Epistles, and the *exempla* and sentences of the saints, they say by way of proof, "That is found in the Gospel, or in the Epistle of St. Peter, or of St. Paul, or of St. James"; or they cite a given saint or a given doctor. Moreover, they commonly possess the Gospels and the Epistles in the vernacular and in Latin as well, for some of them understand it. Some know how to read; at times they read from a book what they recite or preach. Sometimes they use no book, particularly in the case of those who cannot read but have learned the words by heart.[22] Also, they preach in the homes of their believers, as was mentioned above, but at other times while traveling, or out in the open.

Also, they tell and teach their believers that true penance and purgatory for sin come only in this life, not in another. And so they instruct and teach their believers to confess their sins to them. They hear their confessions and absolve those who make them, imposing penance upon them. This usually consists of fasts on Fridays and repetitions of the Lord's Prayer. They have, they say, the same sort of power from God as had the holy apostles.

Also, according to them, souls, upon leaving bodies, pass immediately either into paradise, if they are to be saved, or into hell, if they are to be damned, and there is no other abode for souls after this life but heaven or hell. Also, they say that prayers for the dead help them not at all, inasmuch as they who are in paradise do not need them, while for those in hell there is no release.

Also, when they hear confessions they instruct the penitents that when they make their confession to priests, they are not to tell or disclose in any way that they have confessed to Waldenses.

[7] *Concerning the Artifices and Deceptions in Which They Take Refuge When Examined.*—It should be noted, moreover, that it is very difficult to examine and question Waldenses and to get the truth from them about their errors. This is due to the tricks and double meanings of the words they use in their testimony, behind which they hide in order to prevent being entrapped. Therefore, some facts should here be set forth briefly to show their wiles and their deceptive use of words.

In the first place, then, their course of action is something like this: When one of them has been seized and is brought up for examination, he comes as if without a qualm, as if conscious of no wrongdoing on his part, and as if he felt entirely safe. When asked if he knows why he has been arrested, he replies quite calmly and with a smile, "Sir, I should be glad to learn the reason from you." When he is questioned about the faith which he holds and believes, he replies, "I believe all that a good Christian should believe." Pressed as to what he means by "a good Christian," he answers, "One who believes as the Holy Church teaches us to believe and hold." When asked what he calls the Holy Church, he replies, "Sir, what you say and believe to be the Holy Church." If he is told, "I believe the Holy Church to be the Roman Church, over which presides our lord pope and other prelates subordinate to him," then he responds, "That I do believe," meaning that he believes that I believe this.

When asked about the articles of faith which he accepts, such as the incarnation of Christ and His resurrection and ascension, he answers with alacrity, saying, "I firmly believe." Asked if he believes that the bread and wine in the Mass are, at the words of the priest and by divine power, transubstantiated into the body and blood of Christ, he replies, "In truth, should I not believe it?" If, however, the examiner says to him, "I do not ask you if you should believe but if you do believe," he answers, "I believe anything you and the other good doctors command me to believe." He is told, "Those good doctors whom you are willing to believe are members of your sect; if I agree with them, you believe me and them, but otherwise you do not." He then responds, "You yourself I willingly believe, if you teach me something which is good for me." He is told: "You consider it good for you if I instruct you as your other masters do. But answer simply whether you believe the body of the Lord Jesus Christ to be on the altar." To this he replies promptly, "I believe," meaning that a body is there and that all bodies belong to the Lord Jesus Christ. Then, being questioned more closely as to whether he believes the body there to be that of the Lord, that which was born of the Virgin, that which hung on the Cross, arose from the dead, and ascended into heaven, he responds, "And you, sir, do you so believe?" I tell him, "I believe it unreservedly," and he answers, "And I believe likewise," meaning that he believes that I so believe.

When he is asked to reply explicitly and directly about these tricks and many others of the same sort, he responds: "If you wish to interpret everything I say otherwise than sensibly and simply, then I do not know how I may answer you. I am a simple man, without learning; pray do not trap me in my words." He is told, "If you are a simple man, answer and act simply without a screen of words." To this he replies, "Willingly."

Thereupon, he is asked, "Will you, then, swear that you have never learned anything contrary to the faith which we say and believe to be true?" Somewhat perturbed, he replies, "If I must swear, I will do so willingly." He is told, "It is not a question of whether you must, but of whether you are willing to swear." He answers, "If you command me to swear, I will swear." I say to him: "I do not compel you to swear, for since you believe an oath to be unlawful, you would like to cast the blame back upon me for having forced you to swear. But if you will swear, I will hear you." To this he replies, "But why, then, shall I swear, if you do not command it?" He is told, "To remove the suspicion which exists about you, that you are reputed to be a Waldensian heretic, one who believes and maintains that every oath is unlawful and a sin." His reply to this is, "What must I say when I swear?" He is told, "Take the form of oath which you know." He answers, "Master, I do not know how, unless you instruct me." Thereupon, I say to him: "Well, if I were going to swear, raising my hand and touching the most Holy Gospels of God, I should say, 'I swear by these Holy Gospels of God that I have never heard or believed anything contrary to the true faith, which the Roman Church believes and upholds.'" Then, trembling, acting as if he cannot pronounce the words, he will falter repeatedly in saying them, so that either he or someone else will interrupt and interpose some words, with the result that a straightforward form of oath is not taken but rather a certain jumble of words, which is not juratory, but which gives others the impression that he has taken an oath. Even if he has repeated those words correctly throughout, he mentally means to twist them deceitfully, to avoid using them as an oath, and so deceive those present into thinking that he has sworn. For he either changes the form of the oath into the form of a prayer, thus: "So help me God and these Holy Gospels, I am not a heretic. I have neither done nor said thus and so," or else he only mumbles the words of the oath, with no intention of being sworn. But when he is asked whether he has taken oath, he answers, "Did you not hear me swear?"

Now, when they are hard pressed by the interrogation, they either ponder carefully how by shrewdness to avoid a direct reply to questions in which they fear a trap, or they answer to something other than the main point. Or they say that they are simple people and do not know how to answer wisely. Then too, when they see that those present are inclined to sympathize with them as simple people who are being mistreated and in whom no evil is found, they gain confidence, pretend to weep, appear miserable, and fawn upon their examiners in an effort to turn them aside from their investigation, saying: "Master, if I have done wrong in anything, I will willingly undergo penance. Only help me to be cleared of that infamy of which I am guiltless and with which I have been impugned out of ill will."

But if anyone agrees to take the oath without reservation, then he should be told: "If you are taking the oath now in order to be released, understand that one oath does not satisfy me, or two, or ten, or a hundred, but as many and taken as often as I may require. For I know that in your sect you have dispensations and arrangements for a certain number of oaths when necessity requires, by which you may win liberty for yourself or others. But I intend to demand oaths without number. Furthermore, if I shall find witnesses against you to the contrary, your oaths will have brought you no benefit. Then you will have stained your conscience by swearing against it, and yet you will not have escaped [sentence of death]."[23]

I have, moreover, seen some in such anguish as to confess their errors as a way out of their difficulties.[24] Some I have seen at such times confess openly that if swearing once, or a given number of times and no more, would not help them to escape, then they would refuse to swear at all, making the assertion that every oath was unlawful and a sin. When any one of them was asked why he had been willing to swear if he considered it unlawful, he replied, "I wished by so doing to free myself from death and to save my life and afterward to undergo penance for the sin."

[8] *Concerning the Sophistries and Ambiguities of Their Statements.*— It is to be noted that the heretics, being unable to vindicate themselves against the truth of the faith by force, by arguments, or by authorities, in consequence immediately fall back upon verbal sophisms, ambiguities, and evasions to avoid being entrapped in their errors. The use of ambiguous replies is one plain sign by which heretics can be recognized. One kind of deception which they use is equivocation. For instance, when asked if they believe in the sacraments of baptism, the Eucharist, penance, matrimony, ordination, and extreme unction, they reply that they do indeed believe, but what they mean by all this is either good will in the heart or an inner penance. Likewise, they may take "the true body of Christ" to mean His mystical body, the Church, or the body of any good man, which they say belongs to Christ, as do other bodies also. So, when asked whether they believe in the body of Christ, they reply ambiguously or with a double meaning.

Also, they have another sort of equivocation. When asked, "Do you believe that Christ was born, suffered, rose from the dead, and so forth?" they reply, "Truly and firmly." By this, they understand and mean, "That is to say, I have a true and firm belief in such of these doctrines as are held by my sect."

Also, there is another way of employing sophistry by including a condition. For example, when asked, "Do you believe this or that?" they reply, "If it please God, I truly believe this or that," feeling assured that it does not please God for them so to believe.

Also, another method is to meet question with question, in order to blunt one spike on another.

Also, another method is to get the answer from the questioner in one way or another, as when asked, "Do you believe that any oath may be taken, or that a sentence involving bloodshed may be imposed without sin?" the heretic responds, "And how do you and others believe?" At the reply, "We so believe," he answers, "And I truly believe it," meaning that he is sure that we so believe and declare, not that he believes that which was demanded of him.

Also, another method of dodging is to display surprise. Upon being asked if he believes so and so, the suspect replies in surprise, as if indignant, "What else should I believe? Is not this what I ought to believe?"

Also, another variety of their sophistries is a retort which confuses the issue. For instance, when one is asked if he believes that everyone who takes oath commits a sin by so doing, he replies, "He who speaks the truth does not sin," or he gives the answer, "He who swears does not sin in telling the truth." Yet he does believe that one sins by taking an oath, although not by speaking the truth.

Also, another method is transferral, or shifting the reply from what has been asked to something else.

Also, a question which is put to the accused by the questioner, he shifts to others, bringing them into the discussion.

Also, another device is self-vindication; as when an individual is asked about his faith, he excuses himself by saying, "I am a simple and unlearned man. I am ignorant in these matters, these subtleties. You could easily trip me up and lead me into error."

They have a great number of other methods of deception, which one learns better from practice than from theory.

It should also be noted that heretics sometimes pretend to be simpletons or madmen, as did David in the presence of Achish.[25] When they disclose their errors, they introduce irrelevant, ridiculous, and seemingly idiotic statements, doing so to cover up their lies and to make whatever they say appear to be laughable. I have often seen examples of this.[26]

By resorting in their replies to the enumerated tricks and many others, which it would be too tedious and distasteful to write out—and they invent new ones daily—it is their design either so to shield themselves that they may escape as innocent and blameless, or to weary their inquisitors until they cease to pursue them, or to bring the inquisitor into ill repute among laymen for seeming to molest simple folk without cause and for appearing to seek an excuse for ruining them by overzealous examination. Hence, in the following pages are briefly set forth suggestions for a method of examining and questioning those of the Waldensian sect and heresy who are converted and confess.

[9] *Special Questions for Persons of the Waldensian Sect.*—First, let him who confesses membership in the Waldensian sect be asked whether he has ever seen or heard any person or persons of the sect, affiliation, or "brotherhood" of those whom we call Waldenses, or Poor of Lyons (although among themselves they use the name of "the Brethren" or "the Poor of Christ").

Also, [ask] where, when, with whom he saw them and who they were; also, whether he ever heard their preaching, teaching, admonitions, or discourse; also, what instruction he heard from them and about their teaching; also, what he heard them say about an oath, whether it is a sin always and under all circumstances.

Also, [ask] about purgatory for souls after death or after this life; also, about prayers for the dead; also, about indulgences granted or proclaimed by the pope or prelates of the Roman Church (albeit they do not speak indiscriminately and explicitly about these last three points in the presence of the simpler sort among their believers, but do so only before those who are more advanced and perfected in their secrets).

Also, [ask] whether he ate at the same table with them or saw them eating the noon meal or at dinner; also, about the manner of blessing the meal and returning thanks after the meal; also, whether he saw them pray before the noon meal or after, before dinner or after, how they prayed, how they stood at prayer; also, whether he himself prayed or saw others praying with them, who, where, when, and what they said in prayer; also, whether he ever confessed his sins to any one or more

Waldenses and to whom; also, whether he received absolution and penance for his sins from these persons, what the penance was, whether he performed it, and what the method of absolution was; also, whether he heard them say or did he know or believe that these persons were not priests ordained by some bishop of the Roman Church.

Also, [ask] whether he believed at that time or has ever believed that the confession of sins which he made to them and the absolution and penance he received from them were of as much value to him toward the saving of his soul as would have been confession to his own local priest—ordained by a bishop of the Roman Church—and absolution and penance received from him. Now, if he replies in the negative, the question should be vigorously pressed as to why he confessed to one whom he knew not to be a priest, unless he was convinced that it would be of value to him. Nor should easy credence be given to a person making such a statement.

Also, [ask] whether he confessed his sins once a year to his own priest, during Lent or before Easter, and at that time confessed, among other things, that he had seen Waldenses, heard their teaching, and to them had confessed his sins. If he replies that he did not, let him be questioned as to why he did not make this confession.[27]

Also, ask whether he took Communion once a year at Easter. For the Waldenses do not receive the sacrament, nor do their believers, except to dissemble, having no faith in the sacrifice performed by the priests of the Roman Church; although they keep that fact most secret, except among the Perfect [and] their believers.[28]

Also, [ask] whether he believed that Waldenses, or those who call themselves the Poor of Christ, taking the appellation "Brothers," were good men, just and holy; whether they had and upheld a good faith and a good sect, wherein they and those who believed like them could be saved; whether he did so despite the fact that he had heard and knew that they were not in agreement with the faith of adherents of the Roman Church, and that the latter prosecuted them; also, how long he remained of that belief; who induced him to believe thus; when he withdrew from the aforesaid belief, and why; also, whether he gave anything to Waldenses or received anything from them or knew of such an act in the case of other persons; also, whether he escorted them from place to place and whom he thus escorted; also, whether he knows any person or persons who shelter or believe in them.

Also, [ask] whether he has at any other time been cited, summoned, or haled before any inquisitor on a charge having to do with the Waldenses; whether he confessed, was absolved, received penance, and before the court abjured the heresy and sect of the Waldenses; and similar questions of the same nature.

[*Chapter III: Concerning the Sect of the Pseudo-Apostles*]

[1] *The Following Treats of the Sect of the Pseudo-Apostles, Who Call Themselves the Apostles of Christ.*[1]—The apostate and heretical sect of the "Apostles" originated about the year of our Lord 1260. It was founded by a certain Gerard Segarelli of Parma, who was finally condemned as a heresiarch by judgment of the Church in the same city and was burned. Succeeding him as teacher and leader was one Dolcino of Novara, bastard son of a priest, who attracted a large number of followers to his faction. He was finally captured, together with one Margarita, his consort in heresy and crime. Both were, by judgment of the Church, condemned as heretics and burned, as is described in more detail in a treatise devoted especially to this subject.[2]

[2] *The Form of Initiation into That Sect and Order.*—The form of initiation by which these pseudo-Apostles are admitted into that sect and order is reported in the testimony of some of their number during trial to be this: He who is to be received into or is to profess that order is first instructed by one or several persons of the same sect or order about their conduct, their way of life, and the perfection of that life which they call apostolic. Subsequently, in some church, before some altar, or even in some public place in the presence of members of that sect and order, and even of nonmembers, he divests himself of all his garments, in token of abnegation, and renounces all his property to symbolize the perfection of evangelical poverty; in his heart he vows to God henceforth to live in evangelical poverty. And from then on he may not accept money, possess or carry it, but must live on the charity offered him by others out of their own free will and accord, saving nothing for the morrow.

Also, he promises to obey no mortal man, but only God. Henceforth, he considers himself to be in a condition of apostolic and evangelical poverty and perfection, subject to God alone and to no man, as the apostles were subject to no one but Christ.

[3] *The Following Deals with the Errors of This Sect.*—The incon-

stant adherents of the aforesaid apostolic, or rather apostate and heretical, sect at first taught their doctrines in stealth—and now they teach even more covertly and stealthily, to whom, when, and where they may —that all the authority once conferred upon the Roman Church by our Lord Jesus Christ has become utterly void and has ceased to exist because of the wickedness of prelates; also, that the Roman Church, which popes, cardinals, prelates, secular and monastic clergy control, is not the Church of God but a church rejected and fruitless; also, that the Roman Church is that Babylon, the great harlot, of which John writes in the Apocalypse[3] and which has forsaken the faith of Christ; also, that all the spiritual power which, from the beginning, Christ gave to the Church has been transferred to the sect of those who call themselves the Apostles or the Order of Apostles. This sect or order they regard as a spiritual congregation sent by God and chosen for these last days.

Also, [they teach] that they who call themselves Apostles of Christ, they and none other, have the power which the blessed apostle Peter received from God; also, that the Gerard Segarelli of Parma referred to above was the moving spirit and founder of this sect; also, that in his epistles Dolcino of Novara wrote of the aforesaid Gerard[4] that he was an offshoot of God, springing from the root of faith, through whom God began to lead His Church back to the perfection, life, condition, and poverty of the primitive Church, the condition in which Christ committed the Church to the blessed apostle Peter.

Also, they say that only those who are called Apostles of the aforesaid sect or congregation are the Church of God. They have that state of perfection in which the first apostles of Christ lived. And they declare themselves not bound to obey any man, the supreme pontiff or any other, inasmuch as their rule, which they claim came directly from Christ, is one of freedom and of a most perfect life.

Also, [they declare] that neither the pope nor any other man may order them to abandon that condition or a life of such perfection; also, that neither the pope nor anyone else can excommunicate them; also, that anyone of whatever rank or order, be he of the monastic or the secular clergy, may lawfully and at his pleasure transfer to their life, condition, or order; that a man without his wife's consent, or a wife without her husband's, may give up the matrimonial state to enter their order. No prelate of the Roman Church can sever the bonds of matrimony, but they have this power.

Also, [they hold] that no one of their way of life, condition, or order may lawfully change to another order or rule without mortal sin, nor can he yield himself in obedience to any man at all, for to do so would be to fall from the most perfect life to one less perfect; also, that no man can be saved or enter into the kingdom of heaven unless he is of their condition or order, for hereafter, according to them, no one who is not included in that condition or order can be saved; also, that all who persecute them commit sin and are in a state of damnation and perdition.

Also, [they say] that no pope of the Roman Church can absolve anyone, unless he be as holy as was the blessed apostle Peter, living in complete poverty, without property of his own, and in humility, not engaging in wars or molesting anyone, but permitting everyone to live as he likes; also, that all the prelates of the Roman Church, the greater as well as the less important, from the time of St. Sylvester (for since that time they have fallen away from the mode of life of the first saints) are liars and seducers, with the exception of Brother Peter of Murrone, who took the name of Pope Celestine;[5] also, that all monastic orders and all the hierarchy of priests, deacons, subdeacons, and prelates are an offense to the Catholic faith; also, that laymen should not be and are not bound to give tithes to any priest or prelate of the Roman Church who does not observe a state of perfection and poverty like that of the first apostles; likewise, they say that no tithes should be given to any but to those who are called the Apostles, who are the poor of Christ.

Also, [they believe] that any man and woman may lie naked together in one and the same bed and lawfully touch each other in every part, and may, without sin, caress each other. It is no sin for them to engage in carnal intercourse with each other to put an end to temptation, if the man is carnally stimulated. Also, that to lie with a woman and to engage in carnal intercourse with her is a greater deed than to bring the dead back to life. However, they do not disclose the two tenets just mentioned indiscriminately to all, but only discuss them with one another and with their warmer adherents.

Also, [they teach] that to live without taking a vow is a more perfect life than to live under a vow; also, that it is no better to worship God in a consecrated church than in a shed for horses and swine, and that Christ may be worshiped in groves as well as or better than in churches; also, that no one should ever take an oath for any reason or under any circumstances except in the matter of the articles of faith and God's commandments. Everything else may be kept secret. And, however often men may swear to tell the truth before prelates and inquisitors, they are not bound to answer concerning another person or to reveal their doctrine or errors, nor are they obligated to defend the latter in words, but they are always to keep them in their hearts. However, in the event that they are forced to swear, through fear of death, then they are to take the oath verbally, in words alone, but with the mental reservation that they are bound to tell the truth in nothing but what is contained in so many words in the articles of faith or in God's commandments. If they are questioned about other things, they may tell lies without sin. In order to escape the power of the inquisitor they may deny the truth about their sect with their tongues, provided they keep it in their hearts. In their replies they should color the truth, deny it, gloss it over in any way they can devise. However, in the event that it becomes impossible to avoid death, they are openly to profess and to defend their doctrine in every way and under all circumstances, to die patiently and un-flinchingly in their faith, revealing nothing at all about their associates or believers.

The errors listed above and certain others necessarily connected with them they hold and teach as dogma to their believers in secret but not openly. Nor do they reveal them all at once, but gradually: now one point, now another, now a number of them, as seems appropriate. Usu-ally with some show of goodness or piety to make their words the more credible, they open their exhortations to the laity with whatever can be said which will carry conviction about the evil life of prelates and of the secular and regular clergy. They claim that prelates and the secular and regular clergy persecute them, out of hatred, for speaking and teaching the truth.

[4] *Concerning the Method of Proselytizing Publicly Employed by the Pseudo-Apostles.*—This is their usual method of proselytizing and indoctrinating at the outset, especially in their public appearances. They make certain remarks which, on the surface, seem praiseworthy, in order to draw the attention of their audience and win them over. Hence,

they say, "Watch and pray, for this is good for the soul"; also, they recite the Lord's Prayer, the Hail Mary, and the Creed. Also, as they pass through villages, sometimes in the squares, or wherever they find listeners, they chant, "Do penance, for the kingdom of heaven is at hand,"[6] and the words to the apostles, "Behold I send you as sheep in the midst of wolves";[7] also, "Let not your heart be troubled, nor let it be afraid."[8] Also, they chant the *Salve regina* and some other hymns to attract listeners. They adopt the outward marks of devotion to God, all of which, at first glance, seem good and pious to their auditors. They particularly seek to appear before men as outwardly penitent and as leading a perfect life.

They eat in public, in the streets at some table placed there for them, on food brought to them at the time. On rising from the table, they do not pick up or take with them the remainder of the bread, wine, or other things proffered to them there, but leave it where it is. This is to show that they are the perfect poor of Christ, having, so to speak, no thought of the morrow, no home or dwelling. Thus it is that they beg their bread.

[5] *Concerning the Procedure for Questioning and Examining the Pseudo-Apostles.*—One should be aware that it is very difficult to examine these people and get a valid indictment against them. The chief reason is that however often they may have taken oath before the court to tell the truth, they nevertheless refuse to reveal their sect openly or to confess their errors publicly or to respond directly to questions; but covertly and with many verbal subterfuges they dodge the issue and take refuge in lies, so that skill and diligence on the part of the questioner are necessary in dealing with them. Therefore, a method of questioning and examining them, such as will be presented here, one which is from the beginning directed at their cunning, may be very helpful to investigators in accomplishing their exposure.

After the persons summoned to the court have sworn on the Holy Gospels of God to speak the whole truth and nothing but the truth on the subject of heresy in general and, in particular, on what pertains to those who falsely take the name Apostles or claim to hold to their life, sect, and practice, and also in regard to anything else on which they may be questioned before the court, then let the following general questions be put to them, to be followed later by special ones.

[6] *General Questions for the Pseudo-Apostles.*—First, then, let them

be questioned about their native land and their relatives, to get information as to the country and people from which they came;[9] why and when
they left their homeland and came to these parts; with whom and how
long they dwelt in foreign lands; in what villages they stopped and with
whom they there had dealings.

Also, [ask] whether they have ever heard Gerard Segarelli of Parma
and Dolcino of Novara in Lombardy mentioned; whether they have
seen one or both of them or have talked with them; what they believe
and feel about them, their life, sect, and doctrine; whether they consider
them to have been good men and to have maintained a good sect and
to have taught a good doctrine; also, whether they have heard any
reference to the said Gerard as the original founder of the sect in question or to the said Dolcino as his follower; also, whether they have ever
seen any person or persons belonging to the sect of the men just mentioned, the one which is called Apostles or the Order of Apostles; who
they were; whether they have had any dealings or association with such
men and, if so, with whom.

Also, [ask] about the garb they wear and its cut (which resembles
the habit of some religious order); when and where they assumed such
garb; to what order they belong; whether they profess any rule; whether
the order they uphold and the habit they wear have been approved by
the Roman Church; whether they know any others who belong to such
an order and wear such garb; also, whether they have urged or persuaded any other person or persons to adopt and wear such a habit, to
adopt a similar practice and way of life, and to do other like things;
whom, how many, and how; also, about the method and procedure of
reception into the said order and the manner of assuming the habit.

Also, [inquire] about the doctrine they teach and the method of
teaching in the ceremonies one sees commonly performed, spoken, and
sung by them before the people in public squares; how they came by
these practices; who taught them; why they engage in them, inasmuch
as these things were not authorized for use by the Roman Church or by
prelates of the Church. For by these practices they mark themselves as
singular, differing in life, mode of living, and custom from the common
conduct of the faithful, whether members of religious orders or others;
also, [ask] how long since they began to engage in such practices.

Also, [ask] whether during the past year they confessed their sins to
any priest; if so, to whom; whether they partook of Communion or

received the body of Christ at Easter and, if so, where. For they themselves preach that one must do penance; and for true penance, after
contrition of heart, is required oral confession of sin, made to a priest
ordained by a bishop of the Roman Church and no other. Inasmuch as
all the faithful are bound to confess their sins to their own priest once
a year and to partake of Communion at Easter, there would seem to be
a special obligation to do so laid upon those who outwardly claim and
parade such perfection of life.

Therefore, by using the general questions given above, and others
similar to them which will suggest themselves as cause and occasion
arise, it will be possible therefrom and from the replies of the heretics
to catch the latter in their double-talk and inconsistencies. This will be
particularly true if they confront a vigilant, shrewd, and zealous interrogator, for they will be unable to give reasoned replies to the inquiry.

[7] *Special Questions for the Examination of Pseudo-Apostles.*—
After this, let them also be questioned and examined in detail about
some of the errors of the sect in question. First, let them be tested on
the subject of the Roman Church, over which the Roman pope has
universal rule, with lord cardinals, archbishops, bishops, prelates,
clerics, and monks under him, all of whom reject, prosecute, and censure
the sect of those who are called the Order of Apostles: whether the
suspects believe the Roman Church to be good and holy; whether they
believe that it is the Church of God, having that power to bind and to
loose and to excommunicate which Christ gave and transmitted to the
blessed apostle Peter;[10] whether they believe that any other sect or
congregation outside the Roman Church has that power. Also, whether
they believe and hold themselves subject to the Roman pontiff in such
manner that they are bound to obey him and can be excommunicated
by him and by other prelates of the Roman Church, even though they
may have made a vow to God alone and not to man.

Also, [inquire] whether they believe that it is lawful for them to
swear to tell the truth about the aforesaid sect or order before prelates,
or inquisitors of heretical depravity; whether they believe that after
they have taken oath they are bound to tell the truth about each and
every matter on which they are questioned and examined; whether they
consider it lawful for them to hide their sect and their errors in matters
where they diverge and differ from the Roman Church; whether they

may deny the truth before the court, and under such circumstances be free to lie without sin, with the aim of slipping out of the grasp of the prelates or inquisitors who are conducting the examination of them.

[8] *Some Precautionary Advice or Information about the Pseudo-Apostles.*—It may happen that before the court some of the sect refuse to confess any of the errors listed above, or others of like nature, and obstinately persist in denying them. Since they diverge from the commonly approved life and manners of the faithful, however, they are seriously suspect: [11] because of the custom and way of life of their sect, which they are seen openly to hold; because of the costume, curious and distinctive in some respects, which they wear as though it were a habit peculiar to some monastic order (albeit they are not of any religious order approved by the Church; nay, rather they are disapproved, and the wearing of unauthorized garb suggestive of any religious order is forbidden and prohibited, lest one who is not a monk should from his habit appear to be one); because of the character of the doctrine which they hold and observe, which was handed down to them by Gerard and Dolcino and their followers, who call themselves Apostles; because of their private gatherings and conventicles, at which they have frequently been surprised in secret meetings; and finally because of the fact that a considerable number from that sect and order have been clearly discovered by judicial examination to be heretics and have been condemned and burned. [12] Therefore such individuals as are seriously suspect should be kept in prison until they have confessed the truth.

Take care, however, not to keep several of them together in one prison; but hold each one separately, so that they are unable to talk to each other; thus the truth is better wrested from them. For, as has already been said, in a group they strengthen their obstinacy against confessing the truth. I have seen and had experience with one who, after being held in prison and examined frequently for almost two years, was still quibbling with the truth and would not confess. Finally, he spoke out and revealed it, repented, and was imprisoned as a penitent heretic to perform his penance. [13]

[*Chapter IV: Concerning the Sect of the Beguins*]
[1] *The Following Deals with the Sect of Those Who Are Commonly Called Beguins or Beguines.*—The sect of Beguins, who call themselves

the Poor Brethren and who say that they keep and profess the third rule of St. Francis, appeared in recent times in the provinces of Provence and Narbonne, and in certain parts of the province of Toulouse, which has from early times been included in the province of Narbonne.[1] They began to be recognized and exposed in their erroneous opinions in the year of our Lord 1315, or a little before or after that time, although many persons earlier had commonly thought them to be suspect. Thereafter, year by year, in the provinces of Narbonne and Toulouse and in Catalonia, many were seized, held, and their errors unmasked. Many of both sexes were found to be heretics, were so adjudged, and were burned, from the year of our Lord 1317 onward,[2] particularly in Narbonne, in Béziers, in the diocese of Agde, in Lovède, around Lunel in the diocese of Maguelonne, in Carcassonne, and in Toulouse, where three foreigners[3] were involved.

[2] *Concerning the Errors or Erroneous Opinions of the Beguins of Recent Times: Their Origin.*—Now Beguins (for by this name are commonly called those who refer to themselves as the Poor Brethren of Penitence of the third order of St. Francis and who wear a garb of coarse brown or greyish brown woolen cloth, with or without a cape) of both sexes in recent times were discovered in the year of our Lord 1317, and year by year thereafter, in various places in the province of Narbonne and in some parts of the province of Toulouse, and they confessed before the court to having and clinging to many errors and wrong opinions. They set themselves up against the Roman Church and the Apostolic See, against the primacy of that see, and against the apostolic power of the lord pope and of the prelates of the Roman Church.

By lawful inquisition and through the depositions and confessions of a number of them, recorded before the court, as well as through declarations by many of them, in and for which they have chosen to die by burning rather than to recant as is canonically required, the source of their errors and pernicious opinions has been discovered. They have culled these, at least in part, from the books and pamphlets of Brother Peter John Olivi,[4] who was born at Sérignan, near Béziers—that is to say, from his commentary on the Apocalypse,[5] which they have both in Latin and in vernacular translation, and also from some treatises which the Beguins say and believe that he wrote: one dealing with poverty, another with mendicancy, and a third with dispensations. [They took them] also from certain other writings they attribute to him, all of which they have in vernacular translations. They read, believe in, and treat these as veritable Scriptures.

They say and believe that this Brother Peter John received his knowledge by revelation from God, especially in his commentary or exposition on the Apocalypse. In part, they also assembled the errors and opinions mentioned from the teaching attributed to the same Brother Peter John, teaching or instruction which they say he gave to his associates and to Beguins of his day. They recite to one another these maxims and sayings of his, handed down from the first devotees to their successors, and pass them on to one another in turn, and regard them as veritable and genuine documents. In part, too, these Beguins of both sexes were taught many things by the associates and followers of the aforesaid Brother Peter John. Some things the Beguins themselves have added, like a people blinded, led astray by their own imagination, made masters of error by ceasing to be disciples of truth. In the works mentioned above or in some other writings of the associates and followers of the aforesaid Brother Peter John many other passages are found, said or written in general terms; these the Beguins apply to themselves and expound in accordance with their own wicked concepts. They accept and explain them in support of their own position and against those whom they call their persecutors. Thus they fall from one error into many others, going from bad to worse.

Indeed, it should be known that when the above-mentioned commentary on the Apocalypse was carefully examined by eight masters of theology at Avignon in the year of our Lord 1319, they found numerous articles which they judged heretical and many others which contained intolerable falsity or error, unfounded opinions, or unreliable predictions of future events. The masters drew up this judgment concerning the foregoing in legal form and attested it as a public record with their seals;[6] one who has seen it, read it through, and held it in his hands testifies to its truth.

Furthermore, one should observe and note that among these Beguins some are found who know, uphold, and believe in many or all of the errors described below; they have become, as it were, steeped and hardened in them. There are others who are able to discuss only a few of them and yet are sometimes found to be more stubborn in their convictions and beliefs than their equally misguided fellows. Then, there is a third sort, who have heard or remembered only a little and who yield to right reason and sane counsel. Some there are, to be sure, who obstinately persist and will not retract, who elect rather to die than to abjure, for by so doing they claim to defend evangelical truth, the life of Christ, and evangelical and apostolic poverty. Yet one also finds some among them reluctant to be involved in errors or wrong opinions and who are on their guard against them.

[3] *The Following Deals with Their Manner and Way of Life.*—The Beguins live in villages and small towns, where some of them live together in little dwellings which, in the phraseology they affect, they call "houses of poverty." Both the occupants and those who dwell in their own private homes quite frequently gather together in these houses with associates and friends of the Beguins on feast days and Sundays. There they read or listen to the reading in the vernacular from the above-mentioned pamphlets or tracts, out of which they imbide poison, although certain other things are also read there—the commandments, the articles of faith, legends of the saints, and a summa on vices and virtues.[7] Thus the school of the devil, with its appearance of good, seems, in monkey fashion, to imitate the school of Christ in some ways. But in Holy Church the commandments of God and the articles of faith must be preached and expounded publicly, and not secretly, by rectors and pastors of the Church—not by simple laymen, but by doctors and preachers of the word of God.

It should also be noted that there are some among them who beg publicly from door to door, for they claim to have embraced evangelical poverty. There are others who do not beg publicly but do perform some manual labor, thus earning money and leading a life of poverty. Furthermore, some of the more simple among them, of both sexes, do not clearly grasp the articles and errors described below but are in a state of ignorance. Yet among them are those who generally have a firm conviction of the injustice and unwarranted character of the condemnations of Beguins which have occurred since the year of our Lord 1318 by judgment of prelates and inquisitors of heretical depravity in several localities in the province of Narbonne (namely, in Narbonne, Capestang, and Béziers, in the vicinity of Lodève, in the diocese of Agde, and around Lunel in the diocese of Maguelonne), in Marseilles, and in Catalonia. They revere as just and good those persons who were condemned as heretics.

[4] *Outward Signs by Which They May Also Be Recognized.*—It

should also be noted that, in keeping with the remark of Augustine in his *Contra Faustum*, Book XIX: "Men cannot be held together in any bond of religon, whether true or false, unless they are bound by some common performance of visible signs or sacraments,"[8] these Beguins have certain patterns of overt behavior, in speech and other actions, by which one may distinguish them from other people.

Their method of address or of returning a salutation is this: As they approach or enter a house, or meet on a journey or on the street, they say, "Blessed be Jesus Christ," or "Blessed be the name of Jesus Christ." Also, at prayer, in church or elsewhere, they sit bending over, head covered, usually turning their face toward an opposite wall or some such spot, or toward the ground; rarely are they seen to kneel with clasped hands like other men. Also, at the midday meal, after the food has been blessed, those who know it repeat the *Gloria in excelsis Deo* on their knees, while the others listen. At the evening meal, also, those who know it recite the *Salve regina*.

[5] *The Following Deals with the Erroneous, Schismatic, Presumptuous, or False Beliefs of the Said Beguins and Their Followers.*—In the first place, those who are commonly called Beguins (although they themselves say they are the Poor Brethren of Penitence of the third order of St. Francis) say and affirm that they believe and maintain that the Lord Jesus Christ, while He was man, and His apostles also, owned nothing personally or even in common, for they were the perfect poor in this world. They say that this is perfect evangelical poverty, which is to own nothing personally or in common. Also, they say that to own anything in common detracts from the perfection of evangelical poverty; also, that the apostles could not have owned anything personally or in common without sin or without diminishing their perfection. Also, they declare it heretical to believe and assert anything contrary to the foregoing.[9]

Also, they say that the rule of St. Francis is the very life of Jesus Christ as Christ observed it in this world and which He handed on to His apostles, charging them to observe it. Also, that which St. Francis transmitted to the brethren of his order in his rule, relative to evangelical poverty, requires that those who profess this rule may own nothing personally or in common beyond "poor usage" (*usus pauper*), that which is necessary to life, while always tasting the destitution of poverty and having nothing superfluous.[10]

Also, they say that the Blessed Francis was, after Christ and His mother (and, some add, after the apostles), the chief and foremost observer of the evangelical life and rule, and its restorer in that sixth era of the Church in which they say we now are.[11] Also, they hold that this said rule of St. Francis is the Gospel of Christ or is one and the same with the Gospel of Christ. Also, they say that those who impugn or in any respect contradict the rule of St. Francis, which they call the Gospel, impugn and contradict the Gospel of Christ and in consequence err and become heretics if they persist in their error.

Also, just as they say that since neither the pope nor any other can change anything in the Gospel of Christ, neither add to nor take from it, so no one can change anything in the aforesaid rule of St. Francis, neither add to nor subtract from it as far as concerns the vows and evangelical counsels or precepts contained therein. Also, and in consequence, they say that the pope cannot annul the evangelical rule of St. Francis, or change it, or remove from amongst the other orders the order of St. Francis which they call the evangelical order. They also make the same claim in every respect regarding the third order of St. Francis and his third rule.

Also, they say that no pope, nor even a general council, can annul or decree anything contrary to any one of the acts which have been confirmed, decreed, or prescribed by a previous pope or a preceding general council. Hence, they commonly maintain that the two rules of St. Francis mentioned above (some of them even include any of the other rules, confirmed by Roman pontiffs), cannot be annulled by any succeeding pope or even by a general council.

Also, they say that if the pope should alter any part of the rule of St. Francis, should add or suppress anything, above all in respect of the vow of poverty, or if he should annul the said rule, he would thereby be acting against the Gospel of Christ. They contend that no Friar Minor or any other person would be obliged to obey him in such an event, no matter how often he should command it, not even under pain of excommunication for disobedience, because such excommunication would be unjust and would bind no one.

Also, they claim that the pope cannot grant dispensation to anyone from vows made under the rule of St. Francis, to wit, those of chastity, poverty, and obedience. Also, that he cannot give dispensation to any one from a vow of poverty made to God, even should that vow have been simple and not solemn,[12] because a person who has taken a vow of poverty is irrevocably bound to it. An individual receiving such a dispensation would fall from a greater and higher degree of virtue and perfection to a lesser and lower one; and the power of the pope, in their opinion, serves only constructive, not destructive ends.

Also, they say that the pope cannot issue a constitution or a decretal granting a dispensation or giving to Friars Minor the right to keep grain and wine in common granaries or cellars for use or necessary provision at a future time, because this would be contrary to the evangelical rule of St. Francis and, in consequence, to the Gospel of Christ. Also, they say that our Lord Pope John XXII acted against the Gospel of Christ when he issued a certain constitution beginning *Quorundam*,[13] wherein he grants Friars Minor permission or dispensation to gather grain and wine in granaries and cellars for future use, at the discretion of the prelates of their order. And they say that by this he fell into heresy, and that, so long as he persists in this, he has lost the power to bind or loose, as well as other pontifical powers; prelates installed by him since he issued the said constitution have no ecclesiastical jurisdiction or power. They say, also, that all prelates and others who agreed or who knowingly shall agree with the lord pope in the issuance of the said constitution have for this reason become heretics, if stubbornly they persist therein, and they have lost all ecclesiastical power or jurisdiction. Also, they say that the Friars Minor who were responsible for the issuance of the said constitution, or those who consent to it and accept it and take advantage of it, have become heretics by so doing.

Also, they say that the pope cannot, under God, permit any Friar Minor, even by papal license, to transfer to another religious brotherhood or order in which the Friar Minor himself as well as the other brethren of the same order may possess wealth in common. For, they say, this would be to fall from a greater and higher condition of perfection or virtue to a lesser and lower one, which would be to pull down, not to build up, while the power of the pope was given only for constructive, not for destructive use. Also, they say that if any Friar Minor should ever go over to another religious brotherhood or order, he is bound, notwithstanding any papal permission, always to observe the vow of poverty taken by him earlier under the rule of St. Francis. Thus, he can never own anything personally or in common, beyond bare necessity.

Also, they say that if any Friar Minor is made a bishop, a cardinal, or even pope, he is always bound to keep the vow of poverty taken earlier under the rule of St. Francis. The intent is that he shall give his full attention to the administration and care of spiritual matters, but all temporal affairs are to be directed and managed by suitable deputies.

Also, they say that the pope has no right to grant a dispensation affecting the size or cost of the habits of the Friars Minor in such a way as to sanction any superfluity in violation of the rule of St. Francis. Friars Minor should not obey him in this or in anything else which runs counter to the perfection of the rule of St. Francis.

Also, they say that there is no more perfect state in the Church of God than that of the order of Friars Minor who have vowed and promised evangelical poverty. The status of prelates does not attain its perfection, except in the case of those who are chosen from that order, wherein they have promised evangelical poverty and have bound themselves to observe it forever. They attain the same perfection if they keep their earlier vow.

Also, they say that those four Friars Minor who, in the year of our Lord 1318, were condemned as heretics in Marseilles by an inquisitor of heretical depravity who was also a Friar Minor, were unjustly condemned for defending the truth of the evangelical rule. For, they say, those men wished to observe and hold to the purity, truth, and poverty of the rule of St. Francis and were unwilling to consent to the relaxation of that rule or to accept a dispensation which the above-mentioned lord pope issued concerning these matters, or to obey him and others in this respect. For this reason, they say, those men were not heretics but Catholics, glorious martyrs whose prayers and good offices with God they entreat. Also, many of them declare their conviction that these four men have no less merit in God's eyes than the martyr saints, Lawrence and Vincent. Also, some of them say that in those four Friars Minor, Christ was again crucified spiritually, as on four arms of the Cross, and that in them the poverty of Christ and His life were condemned. Also, they say that if the lord pope ordered, or if he consented, then or now, to the condemnation of the four friars as heretics by an inquisitor, he himself is by this fact a heretic, the greatest of all, because as head of the Church his duty is to defend evangelical perfection. Consequently, they say, he lost the papal power. They do not accept him as pope. They hold that no obedience at all is owed him by the faithful, and from that moment on, the papal office has been vacant.

Also, they say that [unjustly treated] were all those persons commonly called Beguins (but who refer to themselves as Poor Brethren of Penitence of the third order of St. Francis) who, during the past three years—that is, since the year of our Lord 1318—have been condemned as heretics by judgment of prelates and inquisitors of heretical depravity in the province of Narbonne (namely, in Narbonne, Capestang, and Béziers, in the vicinity of Lodève, in the diocese of Agde, and around Lunel in the diocese of Maguelonne). These condemned persons believed that the four Friars Minor just mentioned were blessed martyrs, with whom they shared the same beliefs, tenets, and sentiments about evangelical poverty and the power of the pope—that is, that he lost it and that he became a heretic, as did by their actions the prelates and inquisitors who persecuted the said friars. They believed that the teaching of Brother Peter John Olivi was altogether true and catholic and that the carnal church, that is, the Roman Church, was the great harlot of Babylon, destined to be destroyed and cast down, as was in times past the synagogue of the Jews at the beginning of the primitive Church. Such Beguins, I say, although they believed and defended all these things, were, from the viewpoint of their fellow Beguins, unjustly condemned for defending the truth; they were not heretics but Catholics and their fellows say that in the eyes of God they are glorious martyrs.

Also, they say that the Church of God will in time recognize as holy martyrs these four Friars Minor and those Beguins who were condemned as heretics, and that a solemn festival will be proclaimed for them in the Church, as for the great martyrs. Also, they say that the prelates and inquisitors who judged and condemned them as heretics, together with all those who knowingly consented or do now consent to their condemnation, have by this act become heretics, if they persist. In consequence these persons have lost the ecclesiastical power to bind and loose and to administer the sacraments of the Church; and faithful Christians owe them no obedience.

Also, they say that none, not one, of those who fell into heresy according to their account as just given, are the Church or are part of the Church of God or are numbered among the faithful. They are outside the Church of God if they persist in their attitude. Also, not in but outside the Church of God are all those who are reluctant to or who refuse to believe those tenets upheld by those four Friars Minor and by the Beguins who were condemned as heretics. All those who do not believe that the men condemned as heretics were glorious martyrs, all such, they say, are no part of the Church of God but are outside it.

Also, they say that all those persons who hold and believe in the matters aforesaid in the fashion of the Beguins, the Poor Brethren of the third order, are the Church of God and live within the Church of God. With them are included others of the faithful who are not part of the third order—be they secular or regular clergy, or laymen—who believe and hold in these matters as do the Beguins themselves.

Also, many Beguins of both sexes, together with their believers, secretly gathered up to preserve as relics the charred bones of the persons who were burned after their condemnation as heretics. And out of devotion and reverence they kiss and venerate them as one does in the veneration of other saints. This was discovered and attested by inquisition and in the confessions and depositions received by the court from certain Beguins who had such objects with them and who had seen and known others who had them or once possessed them. I myself, while conducting inquiries about such relics among them, have seen and touched them, finding visible proof of their existence.[14]

Also, some of the Beguins have recorded in writing the names of those condemned persons, with the days and months when, as they claim, they suffered martyrdom, just as the Church of God is accustomed to do in the case of saints and true martyrs. They have included their names in their calendars and invoke them in their litanies.

Also, they say that the pope cannot grant anyone a dispensation from the vow of virginity or chastity, even though that vow may have been simple and not a solemn one, no matter how great a benefit to the community might ensue from such a dispensation—such as the reestablishment of peace in some province or kingdom, or the conversion of a people to the faith of Christ—because the person receiving the dispensation would fall from a greater and higher degree of perfection to a lesser one. Also in this respect, they add that even if all women had died except one who had vowed to God virginity and chastity, and even though the human race would fail unless she should marry, the pope could not grant her dispensation, nor would she be bound to obey him if he should order her to marry. Moreover, if she did obey, she would commit mortal sin. If her refusal brought excommunication by the pope, the excommunication would be unjust and not binding. If the refusal cost her life, she would be a martyr. Also, some of them further assert that if a person who had taken a vow of chastity should marry, even with papal dispensation, the marriage would not be genuine or legitimate and the children born from it would be not legitimate but adulterine.

Also, they say that prelates and members of religious orders who wear unnecessary and costly apparel act contrary to the perfection of the Gospel, against the precepts of Christ, and in obedience to the command of Antichrist. They, and with them members of the clergy of pompous mien, are of the family of Antichrist.

Also, they say that they, the Beguins, or the Poor of the third order, are not required to take oath before prelates and inquisitors in regard to anything but the faith and the articles of faith, even though they have been brought to answer charges before them concerning the sect and heresy of the Beguins. Also, they add that prelates and inquisitors should question them about nothing other than the articles of faith, the commandments, and the sacraments. If questioned about other things, they have no obligation to answer, because, they say, they are laymen and simple folk. As a matter of fact, they are astute, shrewd, and crafty.

Also, they say that they are not obliged to take oath or to expose or reveal under oath their believers, accomplices, or associates, for this, they assert, would run counter to love of one's neighbor and would tend to injure him. Also, they say that if they are excommunicated for their refusal, when ordered, to swear simply and to speak the absolute truth before the court, beyond the subject of the articles of faith, the commandments, or the sacraments, or because they refuse to testify against others and refuse to expose their associates, such excommunication is unjust and does not bind them, and in their hearts they consider it of no moment.

Also, they say that the pope cannot, under God, prevent Beguins from begging their livelihood, even by sentence of excommunication, on the grounds that they might be able to work and earn a suitable living by their trade and that they do not labor in the Gospel, since it is not fitting for them to teach or preach. For they say that their perfection would thereby be lessened, and so they are not bound to obey the pope in this nor would such a sentence bind them. Should they be condemned to death for this, they say they would be glorious martyrs.

Also, they say and affirm that all the teachings and writings of Brother Peter John Olivi of the order of Friars Minor are true and catholic. They believe and declare that they were revealed to him by the Lord and that the said Brother Peter John himself disclosed this to his familiars during his lifetime. Also, they commonly refer to Brother Peter John as a holy father who has not been canonized. Also, he is, they say, so great a doctor that there has been none greater since the apostles and evangelists. Some add that there has been none so great in sanctity and teaching. Also, some of them say that there has been no doctor in the Church of God, with the exception of St. Paul and the said Brother Peter John, whose opinions have not in some point been refuted by the Church.[15] But the whole doctrine of St. Paul and of Brother Peter John must be kept in its entirety by the Church, diminished by not a single letter.

Also, some of them say that Brother Peter John held and spoke the truth in saying and affirming that Christ was still alive when He hung on the Cross after His side was pierced by the lance and when he declared the truth to be that Christ's soul was still in His body but, since He was totally exhausted, He appeared to the onlookers to be dead. John the Evangelist, therefore, said He was dead at the time because He seemed to be dead.[16] The evangelist Matthew, however, wrote that Christ was living, as in truth He was. The Church expunged this from the Gospel of Matthew lest it seem to contradict the Gospel of John.

Also, they say and explain that the said Brother Peter John was in spirit that angel of whom it is written in the tenth chapter of the Apocalypse that his "face was as the sun,"[17] and that he had a book open in his hand. For, they declare, to him alone of all the learned doctors was made plain the truth of Christ and the understanding of the book of the Apocalypse. It is thus that they understand and explain what he wrote on the above-mentioned passage of the Apocalypse in his commentary, which they have in vernacular translation.

Also, they say that the writings and teachings of the aforesaid Brother Peter John are more necessary to the Church of God for this last day than any other writings of any doctors or saints whatsoever, apart from those of the apostles and evangelists. For, they claim, he discloses more plainly and intelligibly than the others the malice of Antichrist and his disciples, namely, the Pharisees, who are, in their opinion, the prelates, monks, and friars of the present day.

Also, they say that if God had not provided for His Church through the said Brother Peter John or some other like him, the whole world would be blind and heretical.

Also, they say that those who do not accept the teachings and writings of Brother Peter John are blind in that they do not feel or see the truth of Christ. Those who reject and condemn his doctrine are heretics.[18]

Also, they say that Brother Peter John is a lamp and a light sent by God into the world, and those who do not see that light walk in darkness.

Also, they say that if the pope should condem the teaching or writings of Brother Peter John, he would in this be a heretic, for he would be condemning the life and teaching of Christ.

Also, they say that if the pope should condem the said teaching and writings, they would not consider them condemned. If he should excommunicate them on this account, they would not hold themselves to be excommunicate; nor would they obey him or give up the books in question.

Also, these Beguins have the books of Brother Peter John in translation from the Latin into the vernacular, made by some of his followers. These include the commentary on the Apocalypse, a short treatise on poverty, another rather brief one on mendicancy, another on the seven evil spirits, and certain other pieces. To them all they attach the name of Brother Peter John, ascribing them to him whether he wrote them himself or some other person compiled them out of his teaching and its tradition, for they have the same flavor and agree in dogma. They read these books in the vernacular to themselves, their associates and friends, in their assemblies and their little dwellings, which they call "houses of poverty," in the phraseology which they affect. From the pernicious teachings of these works they derive instruction for themselves and, when they can, for others.[19]

Also, thus informed, or rather deformed, by the doctrine which they draw from the commentary on the Apocalypse by the said Peter John, they say that the carnal Church, by which they mean the Roman Church (not merely Rome herself, but the whole area of the Roman jurisdiction), is that Babylon, the great harlot, of which John speaks in the Apocalypse.[20] Of her they set forth and explain the evils one reads about in that book, to wit, that she is drunk with the blood of the martyrs of Jesus Christ—the blood, they explain, of those four Friars Minor who were condemned and burned at Marseilles as heretics, the blood of the Beguins of the third order who in years past were condemned as heretics in the province of Narbonne, as we have recounted more fully above. These, they assert, were martyrs of Jesus Christ.

Also, they contend that the Church herself has given to drink of the wine of her fornication to all the rulers of the earth, the kings and princes of Christendom, and the great prelates who put on the pomp of the world.

Also, they distinguish as it were two churches: the carnal Church, which is the Roman Church, with its reprobate multitude, and the spiritual Church, composed of people whom they call spiritual and evangelical, who follow the life of Christ and the apostles. The latter, they claim, is their Church. But some of them say there is only one, the one they call carnal—the great harlot in so far as it touches the reprobate, but spiritual and virginal, without stain or blemish, in respect of the elect, whom they call the evangelicals, meaning themselves, who claim to observe evangelical poverty, defend it, and suffer for it.

Also, they teach that the carnal Church, which is the Roman Church, will be destroyed before the preaching of the Antichrist, by wars waged against it by Frederick, the reigning king of Sicily, and his allies, called the ten kings, who are prefigured by the ten horns of the beast described in the Apocalypse. They put about some other tales on this subject, as false as they are foolish, having to do with the struggle between King Frederick and the king of France and King Robert [of Naples].[21]

Also, they teach that at the end of the sixth era of the Church, the era in which they say we now are, which began with St. Francis, the carnal Church, Babylon, the great harlot, shall be rejected by Christ, just as the synagogue of the Jews was rejected for crucifying Christ. For the carnal Church crucifies and persecutes the life of Christ in those brethren whom they call the Poor and the Spirituals of the order of St. Francis. They are speaking here of both the first and the third order, with reference to their persecution as described above, which took place in the provinces of Provence and Narbonne.

Also, they teach that, just as Christ chose from the synagogue of the Jews, after it had been rejected, a few poor men through whom the primitive Church of Christ was founded in the first era of the Church, so, after the rejection and destruction of the carnal Church of Rome in the sixth or present era, there will remain a few chosen men, spiritual, poor, and evangelical. The majority of these, they say, will be drawn from both the orders of St. Francis, the first and the third, and through them will be founded the spiritual Church, which will be humble and good, in the seventh and last era of the Church, which begins with the death of Antichrist.

Also, they teach that all religious brotherhoods or orders will be destroyed by the persecution of Antichrist, except the order of St. Francis. This they divide into three groups: One is the general body of the order; the second consists of those in Italy who are called Fraticelli;[22] the third is composed of both the brethren whom they call the Spirituals, who preserve the spiritual purity of the rule of St. Francis, and the brethren of the third order who adhere to their teachings.[23] The first two groups will be destroyed, they say, but the third will remain, enduring until the end of the world, for this, they say, was God's promise to St. Francis.

Also, some of them teach that upon those men, the spiritual and evangelical elect through whom the spiritual Holy Church will be founded in the seventh and last era, the Holy Spirit will be poured out in abundance greater than, or at least equal to, its outpouring upon the apostles, Christ's disciples, on the day of Pentecost in the primitive Church. They say that it will descend upon them like a fiery flame of a furnace and, as they anticipate, not only will their souls be filled with the Holy Spirit, but also will they feel its dwelling within their bodies.

Also, they teach that the Antichrist is dual; that is, there is one who is spiritual or mystical, and another, the real, greater Antichrist. The first prepares the way for the second. They say, too, that the first Antichrist is that pope[24] under whom will occur and, in their opinion, is now occurring the persecution and condemnation of their sect.

Also, they fix the time within which the greater Antichrist will come, begin to preach, and run his course. This Antichrist, they say, has already been born and will run his course, according to some of them, in the year of our Lord 1325. Others say it will be in the year 1330; while still others put it later, in the year 1335.

Also, they teach that those Spirituals whom they call evangelical (concerning whom we have written above), in whom and through whom the Church will be established, will preach to the twelve tribes of Israel after the death of Antichrist and will convert twelve thousand of each tribe. All these assembled together will number one hundred and forty-four thousand. This will be the army marked by the angel bearing the sign of the living God. The angel, they explain, will be the Blessed Francis, who bore the stigmata of the wounds of Christ. Forthwith, this army, so marked, will fight with Antichrist and will be slain by him before the advent of Elijah and Enoch.[25]

Also, drawing further upon their imaginations, they teach that the destruction of the carnal Church will occur amid mighty wars and great destruction of Christian peoples. Large numbers of men will fall in the war they wage in defense of the carnal Church.[26] Then, when almost all the men are dead, the surviving Christian women will embrace trees out of love and longing for men. On this subject they tell a number of other fabulous tales, which they read in the vernacular translation of the above-mentioned commentary.

Also, they say that after the destruction of the carnal Church, Saracens will come to seize the Christians' land. They will invade this region of the kingdom of France, that is, Narbonne. They will abuse Christian women, taking many of them captive to misuse them. This, they claim, was revealed by God to Brother Peter John in Narbonne.

Also, they say that at the time of the persecutions, which are the work of Antichrist, and of the aforesaid wars, carnal Christians will be so afflicted that in despair they will cry that if Christ were God He would not permit Christians to suffer so many and such great evils. In their despair they will renounce their faith and die. But God will hide the aforesaid spiritual elect, lest they be found by Antichrist and his minions. Then the Church will be reduced to the same number of persons as founded the primitive Church; scarcely twelve shall survive. In them the Church will be established and upon them the Holy Spirit will be poured in equal or greater abundance than He came upon the apostles in the primitive Church, as is recounted above.

Also, they say that after the death of Antichrist, the said Spirituals will convert the whole world to the faith of Christ and the whole world will be good and merciful, so that there will be no malice or sin in the people of that era, with the possible exception of venial sin in some. Everything will be for use in common and there will be no one to offend another or tempt him to sin, for great love will there be among them. There will then be one flock and one shepherd. This state and condition of men will last, some of them think, for a hundred years. Then, as love wanes, malice will creep in little by little and gradually spread so far that Christ will be forced by the excesses of wickedness, as it were, to come to the universal judgment of all.

Also, they violently and shamefully inveigh against our lord the pope, vicar of Jesus Christ. Like madmen and schismatics, they call him the mystical Antichrist, the precursor who prepares the way for the greater

Antichrist. Also, they call him a rapacious wolf whom the faithful should avoid; a prophet, one-eyed or blind; Caiaphas, the high priest who condemned Christ; or Herod, who mocked Christ and made sport of Him. He, they say, condemns the life of Christ and mocks Him in His poor. Also, they liken him to the "boar out of the wood," and the "singular wild beast,"[27] tearing down and destroying the walls or strongholds of the Church of God so that therein may enter dogs and swine, which is to say, the men who tear and trample the perfection of the evangelical life. They aver that he has done more evil in the Church than all the heretics who preceded him, because in the day of heretics the Church held her position, but now in his time she seems not to be the Church of God but the synagogue of the devil. They say that in his time the carnal Church will be destroyed. He himself with two cardinals will flee into hiding, where he will die of woe and grief.

These are the mad and heretical teachings of the pernicious sect of the Beguins. All these and many others, which it would take too long to describe in detail, we have heard from their own mouths while we were conducting investigations among them and against them. Much of this we have read and noted in their pamphlets; it is to be found in more detail and at greater length in their depositions before the court and in the judicial proceedings connected therewith. But to bring the material more readily to hand, a compendious statement has here been presented. The first inquisition was undertaken against these Beguins in the province of Narbonne, during the year of our Lord 1318, and in the years following in Narbonne,[28] and at Pamiers in the province of Toulouse in the year of our Lord 1321,[29] and thereafter as occasion arose.

[6] *The Following Deals with the Method of Examining and Questioning These Beguins.*—Now it should be carefully noted that among these Beguins some have studied and know more, others less, about the erroneous articles and errors listed above, in proportion to the extent of their instruction and training in them. For in such matters it is their custom always to proceed step by step from bad to worse, disclosing everything not at once but by degrees. Consequently, in conducting an investigation the skillful inquisitor will be able to put questions on all errors or on one or some few only, passing over the others as may seem expedient and as the character and condition of the persons to be examined and the nature of the inquisitorial office may require. Hence, the questions below have been drawn up for use according to the nature

of the errors in which the individuals concerned are found to be wanting or to go astray. Of course, not all the questions are necessarily to be put to each and every one, but those which, in the judgment of the investigator, seem suitable, to the end that the form and direction of interrogation of different persons about different matters may be readily adapted to the peculiar characteristics of each. Indeed, by questions deftly put and by the answers returned, truth is more accurately and easily discovered, guile is thwarted more quickly, in those who do not reply clearly and to the point but cast about for shelter in words and opportunities for evasion, in order to avoid replying to the questions. All of this is learned more fully by experience.

[7] *Special Questions for the Present-Day Beguins.*[30]—First, let the person under examination be asked when, where, and by what minister of what order he was received into the order and to whom he made profession; also, whether at the time of his reception he was examined on his faith by the bishop of the place or someone acting for him, since the Lord Pope John XXII has decreed and ordained that examination or reception of any other kind is not valid but altogether null and void. Also, [ask] where and with whom he has lived since then; also, if the person under examination has been not a Beguin but a great believer and friend of Beguins, suspected of their errors, let him be asked when he began to believe them and to be intimately conversant with them.

Also, let the person under examination be asked whether he has heard any persons teaching and affirming that Christ and His apostles possessed nothing, either personally or in common; also, whether he has heard it said that to hold or believe the contrary makes one a heretic; also, whether he has heard it taught that to own anything in common diminishes the perfection of evangelical poverty; also, whether he has heard it said or taught, and whether he himself believed or now believes, that the rule of St. Francis is one and the same with the Gospel of Christ or is the Gospel of Christ; also, whether he believed or now believes that just as the pope cannot change anything in the Gospel, can neither add to nor subtract from it, he cannot change anything in the rule of St. Francis, can neither add to nor subtract therefrom, in respect of the vows, evangelical counsels, or precepts contained in that rule.

Also, [inquire] whether he believed or now believes, or has heard it taught, that the pope cannot suppress the order of Friars Minor founded under the first rule, nor even their third order, removing either or both of them from the community of the others, as has sometimes happened with some other religious communities; also, whether he has heard it taught, whether he has believed or now believes, that the pope cannot issue a constitution or decretal granting the Friars Minor dispensation or concession which permits them to accumulate grain and wine in a common store for their use and provision at a future time, at the discretion of prelates of their order.

Also, [ask] if he has heard it said, has believed or now believes, that by issuing a certain constitution, beginning *Quorundam*, wherein he is said to have granted the Friars Minor a dispensation or concession to possess grain and wine in common under the circumstances given above, our Lord Pope John XXII acted contrary to evangelical poverty or against the Gospel of Christ. Also, [ask] whether he has heard it taught, has believed or now believes, that no Friar Minor should obey the same lord pope in the matter of the above dispensation or of any other change made in the rule, even if the pope himself should command in virtue of obedience and under pain of excommunication that all friars should accept and observe the change.

Also, [inquire] whether he has heard it said, has believed or now believes, that our Lord Pope John XXII, by issuing the said constitution or dispensation, became a heretic and lost the papal power to bind and loose; also, whether he has heard it said, has believed or now believes, that the pope cannot grant permission to any Friar Minor to transfer to another religious brotherhood or order where he might own property in common like other brothers of that order, but that one is forever bound to keep the vow of poverty taken under the rule of St. Francis and so, in consequence, can never own anything personally or in common; also, whether he has heard it said, has believed or now believes, that a Friar Minor who becomes bishop or cardinal is bound always to observe the vow of poverty which he took under the rule of St. Francis.

Also, [ask] whether he has heard, has believed or now believes, that the pope cannot grant dispensation from the vow of chastity or virginity to any person under any circumstance, even though that vow may have been simple and not a solemn one, and no matter how great the good to the community which might follow from such a dispensation; and whether he believes that if an individual should marry under papal dispensation the marriage would not be valid or legal.

Also, [inquire] whether he has heard it said, has believed or now believes, that the pope cannot grant dispensation to anyone from the simple vow of poverty.

Also, [ask] whether he has heard or known that some Friars Minor were condemned as heretics at Marseilles by an inquisitor of heretical depravity from the same order; whether he has heard or known exactly what the reasons were for their condemnation; also, whether he has believed or now believes that they were and are Catholics and holy martyrs; whether he has known or heard of any other persons who so regarded them. Also, [ask] whether he has heard it said or has believed that the ones who condemned them as heretics acted unjustly, thereby becoming heretics themselves as well as persecutors of evangelical poverty; also, if he has heard it said, has believed or now believes, that the pope became a heretic and lost his papal power by consenting to the condemnation of those four Friars Minor as heretics at Marseilles.

Also, [inquire] whether he has heard or known that some Beguins or Beguines, who call themselves the Poor of the third order of St. Francis, were condemned in recent years by judgment of prelates and inquisitors of heretical depravity in the province of Narbonne or elsewhere; also, in what places or villages of the province such condemnation took place; also, how many Beguins and Beguines he has heard mentioned by name as persons condemned as heretics; also, whether he heard or knew the grounds on which they were condemned; also, if he believed or now believes that the said Beguins who were condemned as heretics were and are Catholics and holy martyrs, suffering death to defend the truth; whether he knows or has heard of any persons who believe, think, or say that the condemned heretics were holy martyrs or that they have attained salvation; also, whether he believed or now believes that those who condemned them as heretics themselves became heretics by so doing.

Also, [inquire] whether he has had in his possessions any bones, ashes, or any other objects belonging to the aforesaid persons who had been condemned or burned, which he keeps as relics out of devotion and reverence for their persons; also, from whom he got those relics, what he did with them, and whether he kissed them; also, whether he knows of any other persons who have had or kept any such bones or ashes as relics.

Also, [ask] if he believed or now believes that our lord pope became a heretic and lost the papal power by consenting to the condemnation of the aforesaid Beguins as heretics; also, whether he believed or now believes that these Beguins who were condemned as heretics and others who believed as they did are the Church of God or are of the Church of God, while those who condemned them or consented to their condemnation are outside the Church of God; also, whether he has known or heard that some persons have noted and recorded the dates of death of those condemned persons in calendars, or specifically mentioned them in litanies in the way that the deaths of other saints are recorded in litanies, and that their names are invoked in the litanies and their good offices besought.

Also, [ask] whether he has heard among the Beguins the teaching that prelates, members of religious orders, or clerics, who have superfluous and costly clothing, are acting contrary to the Gospel of Christ and in accord with the command of Antichrist, or that they are of the family of Antichrist, or that the poverty of Christ is reflected with peculiar luster in the rags and patches of the poor Beguins; also, whether he has heard men teach among the Beguins that the Church of God and the faith of Christ have survived in modern times only in the tiny company of poor Beguins of the third order and in the few other people who persecute neither them nor the evangelical rule of poverty.

Also, [ask] whether he has heard it said that for the Beguins themselves the greater perfection lies in a life of begging or mendicancy, rather than in labor or the work of their hands, and that the pope cannot forbid them this. Nor may he enforce by excommunication a ban on public begging, when they may be able without begging to live decently by their own labor, on the ground that they do not labor in preaching the Gospel, nor is it fitting that they should preach.

Also, in regard to the teaching or writing of Brother Peter John Olivi of the order of Friars Minor, [ask] whether it has been read to him in the vernacular or whether he himself has read it, alone or to others; where, how often, to whom; also, what books or parts of books of this same Brother John he has heard or read: Was it from the commentary on the Apocalypse, from the treatise on poverty, from that on mendicancy, or from the author's other works? Also, [ask] whether he thinks or believes the writing and teaching of Brother Peter John to be true and Catholic.

Also, [inquire] whether he has heard Beguins or some of them say that the writing and teaching of Brother Peter John is more necessary to the Church of God than that of any other doctor or saint whatever, except the apostles and evangelists, or that the man himself was the greatest doctor in the Church of God after the apostles and evangelists; also, whether he has heard it said or explained among the Beguins that Brother Peter John was, in a spiritual sense, that angel of whom it is written in the Apocalypse that his face was like the sun and that he had a book open in his hand because, as the Beguins say, the truth of Christ was particularly clear to him, as was the understanding of the book of the Apocalypse, as shown in his commentary.

Also, [ask] whether he has heard it said among the Beguins that the pope cannot condemn the teaching or writings of Brother Peter John, for the reason which they give, that they were revelations to him from God, and if the pope condemned them he would condemn the life of Christ; also, that the Beguins themselves would not respect this condemnation or rejection, nor would they obey the pope in this, and they did not think that they could on this account be excommunicated by him; also, what the person under investigation believes or has believed, among the items given above, about the teaching or writings of the said Brother Peter John.

Also, [ask] what he has heard the Beguins repeat on the subject of the prophecy and teaching of Brother Peter John during his lifetime about the condition of the Roman Church and other matters; also, what he has read or heard read in the aforesaid commentary as far as he can recall the reading or hearing of it.

Also, [ask] whether he has read or heard anyone read from the same commentary that there are seven eras of the Church and that at the end of the sixth era, which the commentary declares began with St. Francis and his rule, the era of the Roman Church must come to an end, just as that of the synagogue of the Jews ended at the coming of Christ; also, whether at the beginning of the seventh era, which they believe will commence with the death of Antichrist, another new Church must be founded to succeed the first Church, since the first, carnal Church, which is the Roman Church, will have been rejected and condemned.

Also, [ask] whether he has heard it put forth and explained in the same commentary that the Roman Church is that Babylon, the great harlot, described in the Apocalypse, that she is the city of the devil, and that at the end she is to be condemned and rejected as was the synagogue of the Jews; also, whether he has heard anyone read or explain that the primacy of the carnal Church, that is, the Church of Rome, will be transferred to a new Jerusalem, by which they mean that there will be a certain new Church of the future at the end of the sixth and beginning of the seventh era; also, whether he has heard anyone read and explain that the sixth era, the one beginning with the day and rule of St. Francis, will more perfectly observe the evangelical rule of poverty and the virtue of patience than any other era of times past.

Also, [ask] whether he has heard it explained that the rule of St. Francis is truly and essentially that evangelical life which Christ himself observed and imposed upon His apostles, and that the pope has no authority over it; also, whether he has heard it stated that the rule of St. Francis has been wickedly attacked and condemned by the Church of the carnal and the proud, as Christ was condemned by the synagogue of the Jews.

Also, [ask] whether he has heard it stated or explained in the said commentary that the Blessed Francis was, after Christ and His mother, the chief observer of the evangelical life and rule; also, that he was, under Christ, the first and principal founder, initiator, and exemplar of the sixth era of the Church and of the evangelical rule; also, that the constitution or rule of St. Francis would, in imitation of Christ, be crucified toward the end of the sixth era; also, that then the Blessed Francis would arise bodily in glory, with the result that just as in his life and in the stigmata of the Cross he came singularly to resemble Christ, so will he become like unto Him in bodily resurrection.

Also, [ask] whether he has heard anyone explain that the persecution or punishment now being inflicted upon those who remain tenaciously true to the aforesaid sect of the Beguins is like another crucifixion of the life of Christ and another piercing of His hands, His feet, and His side.

Also, [ask] whether he has heard them tell of a wild boar, a mystical Antichrist, like Caiaphas the high priest condemning Christ or like Herod mocking Christ; also, of a wild boar, a great Antichrist, comparable to Nero and Simon Magus.

Also, [ask] whether he has heard the explanation that the evangelical condition is that of those poor men who, in their view, are persecuted and punished by the Roman Church because they refuse obedience to the apostolic power and rebel against the interpretations of and statements about the rule of St. Francis issued by the Apostolic See.

Also, [ask] whether he has heard the statement that in the thirteenth century after the passion and resurrection of Christ, the Saracens and other infidels will be converted at the cost of much martyrdom among the Friars Minor; also, that in the thirteenth century after the birth of Christ, St. Francis and his evangelical order appeared; also, that in the thirteenth century after the death and ascension of Christ that evangelical order will be exalted on the Cross and its glory will take dominion over the whole earth.

Also, [ask whether he has heard it taught] that at the time of the attack and condemnation launched against the evangelical life and rule —which, in their opinion, is to occur under the mystical Antichrist, who is, they say, the pope, and which will be consummated under the great Antichrist—Christ will descend in spirit, together with His servant Francis and the evangelical band of his disciples, against all the errors and evils of the world. Also, that just as the whole world first received the Gospel through the apostolic order, so the whole world will be taught and converted through the evangelical order of St. Francis, between the time of the mystical Antichrist and that of the great Antichrist. Also, [ask whether he has heard it said that] by the beast "coming up out of the earth," referred to in the Apocalypse, is meant the pseudopope with his pseudoprophets, who will not directly of themselves effect the bodily destruction of men, just as the beast "coming up out of the bottomless pit" is the symbol of the worldly laymen who will slay the saints, by whom the Beguins mean themselves; also, that the sixth head of the dragon mentioned in the Apocalypse signifies the mystical Antichrist, the pope, while the seventh head represents the great Antichrist, meaning the royal monarch; also, whether he has heard the Beguins say or teach anything about the era of the Antichrist and the year of his advent.[31]

Also, [ask] what he has heard them say about the many other attacks on the situation of the Roman Church and her prelates, her monks and clerics, and about the many rash predictions of the future with which the said commentary is filled.

[8] *Advice and Recommendations for Countering the Cunning and Malice of Those Who, When Summoned, Are Unwilling to Confess the Truth before the Court.*—Since many of the Beguins (who call

themselves Poor Brethren of Penitence of the third order of St. Francis) wish to conceal and disguise their errors and erroneous opinions by sly cunning, they refuse to confess and, throughout the whole course of the inquiry, refuse the oath to tell the truth about themselves and their associates, living and dead, even though it is customarily and legally required of one called before the court. Some of them, to be sure, may take the oath but are nonetheless not at all willing to swear simply and absolutely. They insist upon expressing protest, conditions, and reservations, to the effect that they do not mean to swear simply or bind themselves by oath to say anything which they believe offensive to God or injurious or detrimental to a neighbor.

They assert, further, their belief that it offends God when the Roman Church, through its prelates and inquisitors, persecutes, reproaches, and condemns the Beguins and their sect. For their argument is that they observe and uphold the life of Christ and of evangelical poverty, at least in the fashion in which they conceive and expound it, as indicated above both in the articles of their faith and in the process of their interrogation. Also, they think it an offense against God, they say, to abjure those articles which we inquisitors and prelates adjudge to be erroneous or to contain error and heresy, but which they, on the contrary, say are not erroneous and contain no heresy but are in accord with evangelical truth. Thus they call good evil, and evil good, and turn light into darkness, darkness into light.

Also, they declare their belief that it would redound to the detriment and injury of their neighbors if they should expose or reveal their associates and believers, because they believe the latter would suffer persecution by inquisitors as a result and would be mistreated. Herein, like a people blinded, they do not see that, in the first place, God is not offended when error is disclosed and truth discovered and when anyone is turned from the devious path of error to be brought back into the straight path of truth, forsaking and abjuring his error. Again, in the second place, it does not redound to the detriment of one's neighbors but works to their good when sinners are led back to the path and light of truth, when they are no more corrupted and do not, by their pestilential contagion, destroy multitudes and, like blind leaders, drag them into the ditch.[32]

Therefore, in dealing with and opposing the malice and cunning of such persons, take care in the investigation by all means to force from them an oath quite simply and absolutely to tell the whole truth and nothing but the truth, with no condition or reservation, about themselves and any of their associates and also about their believers, fautors, receivers, and defenders. They are to use words in the sense intended by the investigator, without any ruse or artifice, whether confessing about themselves or others, whether replying to questions or making affirmations or denials, throughout the whole course of the inquiry. If they do not, they will by that very fact be guilty of perjury and incur the penalty therefor.

Consequently, one should be on guard against accepting from them an oath taken under some condition, reservation, or with the protest referred to above. On the other hand, one should explain and make clear to them that it is not an offense against God, nor is God offended, as they believe and state, when a judge seeks the truth in order to discover error and heresy. In this matter, the determinant is not their false notion but the judgment of the interrogator.

Also, when those persons who have been infected by any errors or implicated in them are discovered, it is not a betrayal of a neighbor or a cause of wrong or injury to him, as they say, but it works for his good and for the salvation of his soul. For this is done for the sake of correcting them, converting them from their errors to the way of truth, and reforming them. Thus they are prevented from becoming more corrupt themselves and from infecting and corrupting others by their errors.

But if persons under examination shall obstinately refuse to swear without the aforesaid condition and reservation—that is, in the event that persons enjoined by the court do not swear definitely to speak the whole truth and nothing else—let a written sentence of excommunication be pronounced against him who, when thus enjoined to take the oath, shall refuse. This is to be done unless he takes a definite oath immediately or at least by the hour or date which the presiding judge may, in his leniency and moderation, have peremptorily[33] designated. For, if one has been ordered to take a definite and simple oath, he may lawfully be compelled to do so at once, without delay. The sentence of excommunication, once decided, drawn up, and pronounced, will be attached in writing to the record of the case.

Now, if a person incurs sentence of excommunication and endures it pertinaciously for several days without yielding, let him again be summoned to court and asked whether he considers himself to be ex-communicated and bound by the aforesaid sentence. If he replies that he does not consider himself excommunicated and bound by the sentence, then by that very fact it will be evident that he is one who despises the keys of the Church. That is one article of error and heresy; anyone who obstinately persists therein is to be judged a heretic. Both the question and the answer on this point shall be made part of the record, and further action shall be taken against such a person according to law, the canonical warning and peremptory urging to retreat from the aforesaid error and heresy and abjure it. Otherwise, from that time on he will be adjudged a heretic and condemned, and as such will be abandoned to the judgment of the secular court.

Take note, also, that in order to prove the wickedness of such a person, so that his error may be quite clear, and to justify the proceedings against him, another new sentence of excommunication may be issued against him in writing, as against one who is contumacious in a matter of the faith. The justification here is his obstinate refusal to take a simple and definite oath to answer about matters pertaining to the faith and to abjure manifest error and heresy, wherein he obviously appears no less to be practicing evasion than he who, cited in other circumstances, contumaciously absents himself. Let the accused be notified that sentence is passed, and let the communication be put in writing. If such a one, who has been excommunicated for a matter of the faith, shall with stubborn mind endure the sentence of excommunication for more than a year, then he should be and may lawfully be condemned as a heretic.

Moreover, one should bear in mind that witnesses may be heard in the case against such an individual, if there be any against him, or even, in order to elicit the truth, he may be constrained in various ways: limited in food, held in prison, or chained; or he may even be put to the question [34] on the recommendation of qualified persons, as the nature of the case and the status of the individual involved may require. . . .[35]

[11] *Advice against a Ruse or Trick of Certain Persons Who Wish to Reply Not Clearly and Lucidly but Obscurely and Ambiguously.*— In order to veil the truth, to shield and conceal their associates, and to keep their error and baseness from being discovered, there are some Beguins, as wicked as they are crafty, who make their replies to inter-

rogation so ambiguous, so obscure, in such general terms, and with such confusion, that one cannot deduce the plain truth from their answers. Thus, when one inquires about their belief on a certain article or articles set forth, they respond in every instance, "I believe in this matter just what and in just the way that the Holy Church of God believes." They otherwise refuse to declare themselves explicitly or to give a different answer, no matter how often they are enjoined to do so.

In this event, in order to brush aside the deceit which they use, or rather abuse, in the words "Church of God," they should be diligently and searchingly questioned and examined as to what they mean by the Church of God, what the Church of God may be in their opinion. For they say "Church of God" misleadingly, as appears in the articles of their errors.[36] They say that they themselves and their associates and believers, are the Church of God or part of the Church of God. But they consider persons who hold beliefs contrary to theirs and who persecute them not to be the Church of God or any part of it.

On this account, the inquisitor must use diligence and ingenuity. These persons can and should, by sentence of excommunication as described in the preceding section, be forced or coerced into clear replies and into making explicit definition of what they mean by their generalized, equivocal, or confused responses.

[12] *Concerning a Little Book on the Passing of Brother Peter John Olivi, Which Beguin Men and Women Revere and Repeatedly Read or Hear Read in Their Meetings.*—In passing, we should note here that the Beguins, men and women, read or have read to them repeatedly in their meetings and hear with pleasure a very small volume which they have, entitled *Transitum sancti Patris* [the passing of the holy father].[37] Therein one finds inscribed:

"In the name of our Lord Jesus Christ, blessed without end. In the year of the Incarnation 1298,[38] on Wednesday, the fourteenth of March, at the sixth hour, in the city of Narbonne, there passed from this world the most holy father and most distinguished doctor Brother Peter John Olivi, in the fiftieth year of his life, the thirty-eighth of his membership in the order of Friars Minor. He was born in the village of Sérignan, which lies a thousand paces (*per miliare*) from the sea, in the diocese of Béziers. His most holy body rests in sanctity in the center of the choir in the church of the Friars Minor in Narbonne.

"Far better I deem it in holy silence to marvel at the growing perfection of his conversion and to venerate the most glorious end of his life as a friar than to expose them to the abuses and yappings of snarling dogs. I believe, however, that I must not pass over one thing. This venerable father, at the moment of his passing, after he had received extreme unction, in the presence of the Friars Minor of the convent at Narbonne declared that he had received all his knowledge by revelation from God and that at Paris, in the cathedral at the third hour, our Lord Jesus Christ had suddenly illumined him."

Such is the content of that little volume which the Beguin men and women read with great devotion or hear read in their meetings, out of reverence for him. They believe it to be entirely true. But his body was exhumed, carried away, and hidden in the year of our Lord 1318. There is much doubt as to where it may be, and different tales are told by different people about it.[39]

[*Chapter V: Concerning the Perfidy of the Jews*]
[1] *The Following Concerns the Perfidy of the Jews against the Christian Faith.*—Perfidious Jews secretly attempt, whenever and wherever possible, to pervert Christians and to attract them to Jewish perfidy. They do this particularly in the case of persons who once were Jews but have been converted and have accepted the baptism and faith of Christ, especially those in whom they have a personal interest or who are related to them by marriage or blood.

Against Christians who have converted or reverted to the cult of the Jews, if they have confessed the fact the decision has been made to proceed as against heretics, even though they who reverted had received baptism as infants or through fear of death—provided that they were not absolutely and definitely coerced.[1] Against the fautors, shelterers, or protectors of such persons, the procedure is the same as for the fautors, shelterers, and protectors of heretics.[2]

[2] *Concerning the Procedure or Ritual Which the Jews Follow in Re-Judaizing Converts.*[3]—This is the rite or procedure of the Jews for re-Judaizing baptized converts who return to the vomit of Judaism. He who is to be re-Judaized is questioned or examined by one of the Jews present as to whether he wishes to accept *tymla*[4]—the Hebrew term for taking a bath, either by washing or by bathing in running water—in

order to become a Jew. He replies "Yes," whereupon the presiding Jew says to him *Baaltussuna*,[5] which means "You return from the state of sin."

After this, the convert is completely undressed and sometimes is bathed in warm water. Then the Jews rub him very vigorously with sand over the whole body, but especially on the forehead, breast, and hands—on the very places, that is, which were anointed by the holy chrism in baptism. Then afterward all the nails of his hands and feet are filed to the quick.

Also, they shave his head and then place him in the water of a flowing stream and have him immerse his head in the water three times; after that immersion they pray thus, "Blessed be God, God the ruler of ages, who hath bidden us to be sanctified in that water, that bath" (which in Hebrew is called *tymla*).

After this act, he is brought out of the water and clothed in a new shirt and new breeches; all the Jews present kiss him; and he receives a name, usually that which he had prior to baptism.

Also, he who has thus been re-Judaized is required to confess the law of Moses, promising to keep and observe it, to live henceforth in accordance with it; also that he will renounce the Christian baptism and faith, and henceforth will not hold to nor heed it. Thus he promises to observe the Law and to abjure the baptism and faith of Christ.

Then, finally, they give him a certificate or testimonial document addressed to all other Jews, so that they will accept him, have confidence in him, and treat him well. Thenceforth, he lives and conducts himself as a Jew and attends the assembly or synagogue of the Jews.

[3] *Special Questions for Use with Jews and the Re-Judaized.*[6]—In the first place, let the Jew who is to be examined be asked his name and surname; also, where he was born and where he has lived; also, about his parents; whether they were and still are Jews; their names, and where they live; also, whether he has brothers and sisters; their names and surnames; where they live; whether any of them have been baptized; when and where; also, whether he himself is a Jew or a baptized Christian.

Also, [ask] which law is the better; under which does he wish to live and die; also, whether Jews are bound to keep an oath sworn on the law of Moses, by the word of God and the scroll of the Law; also, by what penalty are the perjured punished.

Also, [ask] whether he has a wife and children; how many of the latter; also, whether his wife and children were baptized; also, whether he himself has been baptized; when and where; who stood godfather for him at the sacred font; what name was given him in baptism; also, whether others were baptized with him; who their godfathers were;[7] what names were given them; also, whether they have reverted to Judaism; when and where; whether they have wives; also, when he himself was re-Judaized; where; by whom; who was re-Judaized with him; who were present; also, about the method and rite of being re-Judaized.

Also, [ask] how many years he remained or stayed firm in Christianity and in his baptismal faith; whether during that time he ever confessed his sins sacramentally to any priest; whether he partook of Communion as other Christians do; also, if at that time he believed in the faith of Christ and the sacraments of the Church.

Also, [ask] whether he married a Christian; also, whether he had children by her and whether they were baptized; also, whether he has learned the Lord's Prayer, the Hail Mary, and the Apostles' Creed.

Also, [ask] who induced him to revert to Judaism; also, whether he himself has induced any Christians to be Judaized or any convert to be re-Judaized; also, whether he knows any Judaizing or Judaized Christian, any baptized apostate, or any re-Judaized person; where [they live]; also, whether he has the certificate of his re-Judaization.

Also, [ask] in what manner the Jews pray against Gentiles (*goyim*) and against the clergy of the Roman Church.

Also, [ask] how the Jews circumcise Christian boys in a manner different from their own. Here it should be noted that Jews circumcise their own boys in one way and Christians, whether boys or adults, in another. For in circumcising Christian adults or children, they cut their foreskin only halfway around, not full circle as they do to their Jewish boys.[8]

Also, they give a certificate of their Judaization to Christians when they become Jews, which must always be carried with them; otherwise, Jews will not drink or eat with them. It must contain the name of each of the masters who revoked their christening.

[4] *Concerning the Intolerable Blasphemy of the Jews against Christ, His Faith, and the Christian People.*—It should be noted, moreover, that among the prayers which Jews repeat, teach, and have in written

form there is, among others, the following (translated from the Hebrew): "Blessed be Thou, O God, our Lord, king eternal, who hast not made me a Christian or a Gentile."[9] Also: "Let there be no hope for the lost, the converts to the Christian faith, for any heretics or unbelievers, for accusers or hypocrites, that is, any traitors. Let the moment come, that is, the moment in which they are destroyed. Let all the enemies of Thy people Israel be swiftly slain. Let the kingdom of iniquity be suddenly frenzied, be smashed and scattered, so that in our time it topples suddenly and swiftly, and falls ever lower. Blessed be Thou, O God, who crushest Thine enemies and bringest low the wicked."[10]

All these utterances are in Hebrew, and throughout they refer by circumlocution to the dominion of the Christian people, whom they regard as heretics, unbelievers, their enemies and persecutors.

Also, in another of their prayers, they say: "Over us let God be exalted above all to magnify the first creator, who made us not as the peoples of the world, or the Gentiles, and cast not our lot with them, nor our destiny with all the congregations of the peoples who, bowing down before vanity of vanities, worship a god powerless to give help or salvation. Wherefore we trust in Thee, O God, our Lord, to conquer swiftly and speedily in the beauty of Thy strength, to overthrow, to cast out the graven things, that is, the images which earthly Christians adore in honor of Christ. Let the idols be destroyed—and they will be destroyed—to make ready the world for the reign of the Almighty. Let all the sons of flesh call upon Thy name as they turn again to Thee; let all the wicked ones of earth call upon Thee and let those who live upon the earth or in the world to come know Thee. To Thee let every knee be bent and let all tongues unite in Thy presence and before Thy face, our God. Let them bow and fall prostrate, let them give glory to Thy name most dear. Do Thou bring all of them again under the yoke of Thy kingdom and speedily reign over them in eternal dominion, for Thine is the kingdom forever and ever. Thou shalt reign in glory as is recorded in Thy law: 'God shall reign eternally, forever and ever.'"[11] The preceding was taken from the Hebrew.

Note, moreover, that in the foregoing words the Jews mean to invoke harm to Christians. Although they do not expressly use the word "Christians" but employ circumlocution, nonetheless they very clearly refer to and have the Christian people in mind.

Note carefully, too, that the imprecations and curses mentioned above which the Jews utter against the Christian people, are contained in a certain book which the Jews of France call *maazor*,[12] which means a collection of prayers, and the Jews of Provence call *typhilloth*, meaning a book of prayers.

Also, in the prayer which they recite three times a day are many curses and imprecations against Christians and against the Roman faith, which they call a kingdom of wickedness doomed to destruction. And they pray that God will destroy it and all Christians. Although they do not explicitly use the word Christians, all the terms imply that meaning and they themselves understand and mean it so, as, for example, in the word *minim*, which signifies heretics.

Also, during the Day of Atonement, in September, they use a special prayer which they say against all their enemies, calling it *cematha*,[13] which means anathema or separation or curse. In that prayer, by circumlocution they call Christ a false son of a harlot, and the Blessed Virgin Mary a woman addicted to wantonness and excess, which is an abominable thing to say or even to think. They revile them both and the Roman faith and all who share it or believe in it.

Also, there is a certain book by an author named Solomon[14] which they entitle "Gloss on the Text of the Law." All Jews put special confidence and faith in it and are particularly guided by its statements. In numerous passages of that book occur the false, erroneous, and abusive words, ideas, and opinions of the condemned Talmud.[15] The Jews observe, cherish, and teach these glosses, even though they have been condemned equally with the Talmud and are expressly directed against Christ, who, they say, was not the Christ in any way nor the Messiah promised in the Law.

Also, that book gives the name of heretics and infidels to all those who follow and keep the way and faith of Jesus Christ; that prayer, referred to above, which the Jews recite three times daily, was composed with them in mind.

Also, a certain book, which the Jews call "Glosses of Moses of Egypt," [16] to which its author gave the title "Explanation and Restoration of the Law," contains objectionable and false statements from the Talmud; it also contains many errors and blasphemies against the Christian faith, especially in naming as heretics (in Hebrew *minim*) all those who follow the way and faith of Christ. Also, that book declares that Jesus Christ sinned against God and the Law, that He sinned worse

than Mohammed, and that Jesus caused the greater part of the world
to put its trust in the error of worshiping a God other than the one God,
and of destroying the Law which God gave. There are many other
blasphemies against Christ in this book.

Also, in another book called by the Jews "The Gloss of David the
Spaniard,"[17] which is a gloss on the Psalms, are found many attacks on
Christ, on Christians, and on those who embrace the Christian faith.

[*Chapter VI: Concerning Sorcerers, Diviners, and Those Who Invoke Demons*]

[1] *The Following Concerns Sorcerers, Diviners, and Those Who
Invoke Demons.*—In numerous and various aspects the deadly contagion
and error of sorceries, divination, and invocation of demons occurs in
divers countries and regions in association with various concoctions and
false contrivances of the vanity of superstitious men, who turn their
attention to spirits of evil and the teachings of demons.[1]

[2] *Questions for Sorcerers, Diviners, and Those Who Invoke
Demons.*—The sorcerer, diviner, or one who invokes demons, who is
subjected to examination should be asked about the kind and number
of sorceries, divinations, and invocations he knows and from whom he
learned them.[2]

Also, when one probes deeply into details, one must evaluate the
quality and status of persons, for the same interrogatory may not be
used in one and the same way for all; men are questioned in one
fashion and women in another. Questions may be formulated on the
following topics:

What they know or have learned or have done in respect of children
or infants on whom a spell has been cast or from whom a spell is to be
lifted; also, lost or damned souls; also, thieves subject to imprisonment;
also, peace or discord between husbands and wives; also, enabling the
barren to conceive.

Also, [ask about] substances they give to be eaten—hair, claws, and
other things; also, the situation of souls of the dead; also, forecasts of
future events; also, the fairy women, whom they call the "good folk,"
and who, they say, roam about at night; also, making incantations or
conjuring with incantations using fruits, herbs, girdles (*corrigia*), and
other materials.

Also, [ask] whom he taught to make incantations or to conjure by using incantations, and from whom he learned or heard such incantations and spells.

Also, [ask about] curing diseases by conjurations or incantations; also, the method of gathering herbs, in a kneeling position, with face to the east, while repeating the Lord's Prayer; also, prescribing pilgrimages, masses, offerings of candles, and almsgiving; also, the method for the discovery of thefts or the disclosure of secrets.

Also, one should inquire particularly as to what they know about any sort of superstitious, irreverent, or wrongful treatment of the sacraments of the Church, particularly the sacrament of the body of Christ; also, the use of divine worship and holy places;[3] also, about the Host which is saved, or the chrism or holy oil stolen from a church.

Also, [ask about] wax or other images which have been baptized; how they are baptized, and its results.[4]

Also, [ask] about the images of lead which sorcerers make, the method of fabrication and the use.

Also, [ask] from whom he learned or heard such practices; also, how long it has been since he began to employ such; also, what persons and how many have come to him seeking advice, particularly within the year; also, whether he has ever before been forbidden to engage in such practices, and by whom; whether he abjured them and promised never to do or make use of such things; also, whether after abjuration and promise he relapsed; also, whether he believed in the truth of what he taught others; also, what goods, gifts, or payments he received and retained for such practices.

Catharist Literature of the
Thirteenth and Fourteenth Centuries

56. Bogomil Literature Adopted by the Cathars

Two works which the Cathars of Western Europe took over from the
Bogomils are presented here as the first of a group of translations of Catharist
literature. *The Vision of Isaiah* (part A), is an apocryphal work of great
antiquity, probably composed about the end of the first century under
Gnostic influence. Before A.D 300 it had been joined to two other independently written items, *The Martyrdom of Isaiah* and *The Testament of
Hezekiah*: the first, by a Jew or a Jewish Christian; the second, Christian in
origin with traces of Gnosticism. The composite treatise circulated under
the title, *The Ascension of Isaiah*.[1] *The Vision of Isaiah*, which formed its
second half, may also have had an independent tradition; at any rate, it was
found as a separate work among Bogomils in the twelfth century.[2] About
the beginning of the thirteenth century it had reached Western Europe in
Latin translation.[3] Durand of Huesca mentions it in a polemic against the
Albigenses in 1222 or 1223,[4] as do James Capelli and Moneta of Cremona
about 1240.[5] The story of Isaiah's vision was still being repeated by Albigensian heresiarchs in the fourteenth century. To show the persistence of the
story, one of the later versions is translated here as an addendum to the
translation of *The Vision* itself.

The Vision of Isaiah recounts that the spirit of the prophet was conducted
by an angelic guide through the air of this world up through the firmament,
where forces of Satan and of God were locked in battle; then up through
seven heavens, where angels, their glory increasing with each heaven, sang
praises to God. In the seventh heaven Isaiah saw not only angels but the
righteous dead, who alone were able to behold the ineffable glory of the
Father. There he heard the Father command His Son to descend to the earth
and into hell to judge the rulers and angels or the world. Isaiah saw the
Son on earth, saw Him seized and hung on the tree by the prince of this
world, saw Him descend to hell to lay it waste—this part of the vision was
omitted in the Bogomil version—and then, having despoiled the prince of
death, arise on the third day. When Isaiah had beheld the ascent of the Son
of God again to heaven, he was told that what he had beheld no other eyes
of flesh might see and that, when the time came, he and other righteous men
would also receive their robes, thrones, and crowns of glory with God. It is
easy to see why absolute dualists among the Cathars were attracted by the

story, for it depicts a world in darkness and discord under Satan's rule, and a struggle on the earth and in its atmosphere between satanic and divine power. God the Father is superior to the Son and to the Holy Spirit. In His earthly sojourn, the Son never becomes truly man, and the souls of the righteous but not their carnal bodies are promised celestial reward in the last days.

Both the composite *Ascension of Isaiah* and *The Vision* as a separate work have received much scholarly attention. *The Ascension* was translated into English by the Rev. R. H. Charles,[7] who published the Latin, Greek, and Ethiopic texts in the same volume. *The Vision* has also been translated into French by René Nelli *(Cahiers d'études cathares, XXXIII* [1958], 23-38), who utilized an earlier translation by Tisserant.

Another Bogomil tract, *The Secret Supper* (part B), is also known as *Interrogatio Johannis* [the questions of John], because it presents Jesus as responding to John's inquiries. The tract has come down to us only in a Latin text. It was originally written in either Slavonic or Greek, and some of its doctrine is probably drawn from earlier apocrypha, but there is no doubt of its Bogomil character.[8] It reached Italy toward the end of the twelfth century in the hands of Nazarius, bishop of the sect of Concorezzo.[9] For him and his followers it afforded justification of many of their teachings, although a dissident faction, led by Desiderius, about 1230 defied Nazarius and repudiated the authority of *The Secret Supper*.[10] Its influence may also be seen among the Bagnolenses of Lombardy and some of the Albigenses of Languedoc.

The Secret Supper depicts John the Evangelist at a Last Supper with Christ in heaven, where he questions the Lord about the origin of the world and man, the rule of Satan, Christ's mission, and human salvation. Christ reveals that Satan, once second only to God and Christ in the powers of heaven, rebelled and won the allegiance of certain angels of the first five heavens. For this he and one third of the angels were cast out. In the firmament to which he was exiled, Satan found no peace until God allowed him seven days in which to build. In that time Satan made a universe consisting of the earth, a throne, the sun, the moon, the natural phenomena of this earth, its inhabitants, and his own angels. In man and woman he imprisoned fallen angels from heaven; in Paradise he hid as a serpent to seduce Eve, who taught Adam to lust. Enoch and Moses were his servants. When Christ was sent to earth through the ear of an angel, Mary, Satan sent John the Baptist with the spirit of Elijah to resist Him. But the Last Judgment will result in Christ casting out evil and releasing His elect from their imprisonment, so that in heaven they may receive imperishable raiment, crowns, and thrones.

Two versions of *The Secret Supper* exist. One is found in Manuscript 1137 of the National Library of Vienna; the other derives from a manuscript once in the possession of the Inquisition at Carcassonne. Although the Carcassonne manuscript has since been destroyed, its text was published in the seventeenth century,[11] and a copy was also preserved in the *Collection Doat* in Paris.[12] The considerable differences between the versions of Vienna and Carcassonne allow the surmise that each is rather far removed from the original text; perhaps they suffered modifications as they were used for preaching or teaching. Each version has been several times edited.[13] We follow the work of Reitzenstein.[14] There is a French translation of both the Vienna and the Carcassonne version by René Nelli.[15]

For *The Secret Supper*, as for *The Vision of Isaiah*, the date prefixed to our translation is that at which the tract probably reached Western Europe.

The Vision of Isaiah is translated from the Latin text in R. H. Charles, *The Ascension of Isaiah, Translated from the Ethiopic Version, Which Together with the New Greek Fragment, the Latin Versions and the Latin Translation of the Slavonic, Is Here Published in Full* (London, 1900), pp. 98-139, by permission of A. and C. Black, Ltd. Part B is translated from Richard Reitzenstein, *Die Vorgeschichte der christlichen Taufe* (Leipzig and Berlin, 1929), pp. 297-311, by permission of B. G. Teubner Verlaggesellschaft.

A. THE VISION OF ISAIAH

before 1222

Chapter I[1]

(1) The vision which Isaiah, the son of Amos, saw[2] in the twentieth year of the reign of Hezekiah, king of Judah: Isaiah the prophet, son of Amos, came to Hezekiah in Jerusalem; (2) and after he had come in, he sat down upon the king's couch. (3) And all the princes of Israel and the counselors of the king and the eunuchs stood before him. (3-4) And the prophets and the sons of prophets came from the villages and the fields and the mountains to salute him, when they learned that Isaiah had come from Gilgal, (5) and to anounce to him those things that were to come.[3] (6) Then he was speaking words of truth; the Holy Spirit came upon him and all saw and heard the words of the Holy Spirit. (7) The king summoned the prophets, and all entered together, as many as were found there. Now there were the aged Micah and Ananiah, Joel, and as many of them as were found there, on his right hand and on the left. (8) However, when they heard the voice of the Holy Spirit they fell to their knees and sang to the Highest God, who rests among the holy ones. (9) Who bestowed such power of words in the world. (10) Now, as he was speaking in the Holy Spirit in the hearing of all, he fell silent, and thereupon they saw one[4] standing before him. (11) His [Isaiah's] eyes were open, yet his mouth was closed, (12) but the inspiration of

the Spirit was with him.[5] (14) And they did not think that Isaiah had been exalted,[6] but the prophets recognized that it was a revelation. (15) The vision which he saw was not of this world but of what is hidden from all flesh. (16) And when he ceased to behold the vision, he returned to himself and recounted the vision to Hezekiah and his son Nason,

Chapter II

(1) and to Micah and the other prophets, saying, (2) "When I prophesied what you heard, which you witnessed,[7] I saw an angel, glorious not with the glory of the angels whom I have always seen, but having a particularly great glory and a light which I cannot describe. (3) Taking me by the hand he led me on high, and I said, 'Who are you, and what is your name, and why are you lifting me up like a bird?'—for the ability to speak to him was given me. (4) Then in answer he said to me, 'When I shall bear you on high I will show you the vision which is the purpose for which I have been sent; then you will know who I am, but my name you do not know, (5) because you wish to return again to your body. And when I raise you on high hereafter you will see.' (6) And I rejoiced because he answered me softly. (7) And he said to me, 'You have rejoiced because I replied gently to you, and you will see one greater than I am wishing to speak to thee; one gentler and wiser, (8) better and sweeter; for to this end was I sent, to explain all things to thee.' (9) And we ascended, he and I, upon the firmament, and there I saw the great battle of Satan and his might opposing the loyal followers (*honorantiae*) of God, and one surpassed the other in envy. (10) For just as it is on earth, so also is it in the firmament, because replicas of what are in the firmament are on earth. (11) And I said to the angel, 'What is this war and envy and struggle?' (12) And in reply he said to me, 'This is the devil's war and he will not rest until He whom you wish to see comes to slay him with the spirit of His virtue. (13) Thereafter, he raised me into that which is above the firmament, which is the first heaven. (14) And I saw in the midst thereof a throne on which an angel was seated in great glory, and angels sat at his right and his left. (15) Those on the right had a special glory, and they sang with one voice; and those who were on the left sang after them[8] but their song was not like that of the ones on the right. (16) And I questioned the angel who conducted me: 'To whom is this song raised?' (17) And in reply he said

to me, 'To the great glory of God, who is above the seventh heaven, and to His beloved Son, from whom I was sent to thee.' (18) And again he raised me up, into the second heaven; its height was the same as that of the first heaven above earth. (19) And I saw there, just as in the first heaven, angels on the right and on the left. (20) And the glory of these angels and their song were superior to those of the first heaven. (21) And I fell on my face to adore him,[9] and the angel who guided me said to me, 'Adore not the angel nor the throne of this heaven. This is the reason why I was sent to guide you; adore Him only of whom I will tell you, and in like fashion adore Him who is (22) above all angels, above thrones, and above the garments and crowns which you shall see hereafter.' (23) And I rejoiced with exceeding great joy, for such is the consummation for those who know the Most High and Eternal and His beloved Son, because they ascend to Them as by the angel of the Holy Spirit.[10] (24) And he raised me above the third heaven and in like manner I saw a small throne[11] and angels on the right and the left. The memory of this world, however, was given no name there.[12] (25) But the glory of my spirit was undergoing a transformation as I ascended into heaven[13] and I said, 'Nothing of that world is given a name here.' (26) And in reply the angel said to me, 'Nothing is given a name on account of its weakness and nothing is hidden of the things which are done there.' (27) And they sang a song and glorified him who was enthroned, and this angel was greater than the second angel.[14] (28) And again he raised me, unto the fourth heaven. The height from the third to the fourth heaven was greater.[15] (29) And I saw a throne and angels on the right hand and on the left.[16] (31) But the glory of him who was enthroned was greater than that of the angels on the right hand and their glory likewise surpassed the glory of those who were below. (32) And I ascended into the fifth heaven, (33) and there I saw innumerable angels (34) and their glory,[17] (36) and their song was more glorious than that of the fourth heaven. (37) And I marveled, beholding such a multitude of angels arrayed in the ranks of their diverse goodnesses; each, having his own glory, glorified Him who is on high (Whose name is not revealed to all flesh), because He gave so much glory to the angels who are above each heaven. But in reply the angel said to me, 'Why are you astonished that they are not all of one appearance? You have not yet seen the insuperable virtues and the thousands and thousands of thousands of angels.'

Chapter III

(1) "And thereafter he raised me into the air of the sixth heaven and I saw there a great glory which I had not seen in the fifth heaven. (2) And I beheld angels[18] in great glory. (3) And the deeds of the virtues were honorable and pre-eminent; their song was holy and wonderful. (4) And I said to the angel who guided me, 'What is it that I see, my lord?' (5) And he said to me, 'I am not your lord but your counselor.'[19] (7) And he spoke to me about the sixth heaven.[20] Herein are neither throne nor angels on the left,[21] but they receive their direction from the virtue of the seventh heaven, where dwells the mighty[22] Son of God. (8) And all the heavens and His angels hearken to Him, and I have been sent to bring you hither, so that you may see this glory (9) and the Lord of all the heavens and His angels and virtues.[23] (11) Therefore, I say to you, Isaiah, no one who desires to return to the flesh of that world has seen what you see nor is able to see what you have seen; (12) because it is your lot in the Lord to come here.' (13) And I magnified the Lord[24] in song because thus I go into His lot. (14) And he [the angel] said to me, 'When you shall have returned here through the will of the Father, then you will receive your garment, and then you will be equal to the angels who are in the seventh[25] heaven.' (16) And he led me into the sixth heaven, and neither thrones nor angels on the right and the left were there, but all had one appearance and identical song. (17) And it was given me to sing with them; and the angel who was with me and I, myself, were even as their glory, and their glory was one.[26] (18) And they glorified the Father of all and His beloved Son and the Holy Spirit; all with one voice (19) they sang, but not with a voice such as that of the fifth heaven, (20) but with a different voice. And there was a great light there. (21) And when I was in the sixth heaven I thought the light of the fifth heaven to be as darkness. (22) I rejoiced greatly and sang to Him who gave such joy to those who received His mercy. (23) And I begged the angel who guided me nevermore to return into that carnal world. (24) Moreover, I say unto you[27] that here is much darkness. (25) But the angel who guided me said to me, 'Since you rejoice in this light, how much more will you rejoice and exult when you see the light of the seventh heaven, in which sits the Heavenly Father with His only begotten Son; (26) where lie the vestments[28] and the thrones and the crowns of the righteous. (27) And as to your plea not to return into your flesh, the time is not yet fulfilled for

your coming here.' (28) And I sorrowed greatly at hearing these words.

Chapter IV

(1) "And he raised me up into the air of the seventh heaven and I heard a voice saying to me, 'Why do you who desire to live in the flesh come here?' And I was very much afraid and trembled. (2) Again, I heard another voice saying, 'Forbid him not to come in, since he is worthy of the glory of God, for here is his robe. (3) And I questioned the angel who was with me, 'Who is he who forbids me, and who is he who bids me come up?' (4) And he said to me, 'The one who forbids is he, the angel who is above the angels singing in the sixth heaven; (5) and He who commands is the Son of God, and His name you may not hear until you have departed from the flesh.' (6) When we ascended into the seventh heaven I saw there an astounding and indescribable light and innumerable angels. (7) And I saw certain of the righteous[29] (9) who, stripped of fleshly robes, were in heavenly robes and standing in great glory. (10) But they sat not on their thrones; moreover, their crowns of glory were not upon them. (11) And I questioned the angel, saying, 'Why have they received robes, and why have they not received thrones and crowns of glory?' (12-13) And he said to me, 'Now they receive them not, until the Son first brings here those thrones and crowns, when He shall be in your likeness.'[30] (14) And the prince of that world will stretch forth his hand upon the Son of God and will kill Him and hang Him on a tree, and he will kill Him not knowing who He is. (15) And He will descend into hell and will lay it waste, with all the phantoms of hell. (16) And He will seize the prince of death and despoil him, and crush all his powers, and will rise again on the third day; (17) having with him certain of the righteous. And He will send His preachers into the whole world, and will ascend into heaven. (18) Then these will receive their thrones and crowns.'[31] (19) And after [he said] these words, I said to him, 'In regard to that which I asked you in the first heaven, (20) show me, for this you promised.'[32] (21) And as I was addressing him, there was among those standing about us one angel, more glorious than he who conducted me and than all the angels. (22) And he showed me a book, and opening it, gave it to me; and I saw writing which was not like that of this world. And I read it, and lo, there were the deeds of Jerusalem recorded there, and the works of all men were there, among whom also was I. (23) I saw in truth that nothing

which was done in the world was hidden in the seventh heaven. And I questioned the angel, 'Who is this who is pre-eminent over all the angels in his glory?' And in reply to me he said, 'He is the great angel, Michael, who prays constantly for humanity and humility.'[33] (24) I saw many robes and thrones and crowns lying there. (25) And I said to the angel, 'For whom are these robes and crowns and thrones reserved?' (26) And he said to me, 'Many of that world lost these crowns, who are believers in the world of Him of whom I have spoken[34] to you.' (27) And, turning about, I saw the Lord in great glory and I was most sorely afraid. (28) And all the righteous approached Him and adored Him singing with one voice and [my] voice was like unto theirs. (29) And Michael, approaching Him, adored and together with him all the angels adored and sang. (30) And I was again transfigured and was like the angels. (31) Then the angel who conducted me said to me 'Adore Him and sing.' And I adored Him and sang. (32) And the angel who conducted me said to me, 'He is the Lord of all the glories which you have seen.' (33) And I saw another most glorious one, like unto Him in all things, and the righteous approached Him and adored Him and sang, and I sang[35] with them and I was not transfigured into their aspect.[36] (34) And the angels came with them and adored Him, and I adored Him and sang. (35) And again, I saw the other in great glory. And while walking, I questioned the angel, 'Who is He?' And he said to me, 'Adore Him, for he is the angel of the Holy Spirit, who speaks in you and in all the righteous.' (37) And after that, another indescribable and ineffable glory was revealed which I could not behold with the opened eyes of my spirit, nor could the angel who conducted me nor all the angels whom I saw adoring the Lord. (38) But I saw the righteous only in great glory beholding [His] glory. (39) And my Lord approached first and then the angel of the Holy Spirit (*angelus spiritualis*). (40) And they adored Him and the two[37] sang together. (41) Then all the righteous adored Him, (42) and with them Michael and all the angels adored and sang.

Chapter V

(1) "Thereafter I heard a voice there and the song which I heard in the six heavens[38] rose up and was heard in the seventh heaven. (2) And all glorified Him whose glory I could not behold.[39] (5) And the song of all six heavens was not only heard but seen. (6) And the angel said to me, 'He is the One Living Eternal, living in the highest eternity and

resting among the holy ones; we cannot endure to name or see Him who is praised by the Holy Spirit in the mouths of the holy [and] righteous. (7) And after that, I heard the voice of the Eternal saying to the Lord [His] Son:[40] (8) 'Go forth and descend from all the heavens and be in the world, and go even to the angel who is in hell; (9) transfiguring thyself into their form.[41] (11) And neither the angels nor the princes of that world shall know thee. (12) And thou shalt judge the prince of that world and his angels, and the rulers of the world, (13) because they have denied me and said, "We are and without us there is no one." (14) Thereafter, thou shalt not transfigure thyself as thou ascendest through the heavens in great glory, and thou wilt sit at my right hand. (15) Then the princes and the virtues and all the angels and all the principalities[42] of the heavens and of earth and of the lower regions will adore thee.' (16) And I heard the Great Glory commanding my Lord. (17) And then the Lord went out from the seventh heaven and descended into the sixth heaven. (18) And the angel who guided me said to me, 'Understand and see the manner of His transfiguration and descent.' (19) When the angels saw Him, they praised and glorified Him, for He was not transfigured into their image,[43] and I sang with them. (20) When He had descended into the fifth heaven, there at once He was transfigured into the form of those angels and they did not sing to Him or adore Him, for He was of a form like theirs. (21) And He descended into the fourth heaven and appeared to them in their form. (22) And they did not sing to Him for He was of a form like theirs. (23) Moreover, He came into the third heaven,[44] (25-28) and into the second and the first, transfiguring Himself in each of them. Consequently, they did not sing to Him or adore Him, for He appeared to them in [a form] like theirs. And He showed them a sign (*characterem*).[45] (29) Moreover, He descended into the firmament and there gave the signs (*signa*), and His form was like unto theirs, and they did not glorify Him and they did not sing to Him. (30) And He descended to the angels who were in this air as though He were one of them. (31) And He gave them no sign, nor did they sing to Him.[46]

Chapter VI

(1) "And after these things, the angel said to me, 'Know, Isaiah, son of Amos, this is why I was sent by God to show you all things. For no one before you has seen nor can anyone after you see what you have

seen and heard.' And I saw one like the Son of Man dwelling with men and in the world.[47] (19) And they did not recognize Him.[48] (23) And I saw Him ascending into the firmament and He was not transfigured into [their] form. And all the angels who were above the firmament were struck with fear at the sight and, adoring, (24) they said, 'How didst Thou descend[49] into our midst, Lord, and we did not recognize the King of Glory?' (25) And He ascended into the first heaven more gloriously and did not transfigure Himself. Then all the angels (26) adored and sang, saying, 'How didst Thou pass through our midst, Lord, and we did not see or adore Thee?' (27-30) Thus He ascended into the second heaven and into the third and into the fourth and into the fifth and into the sixth, (31) even to all the heavens, and His glories increased.[50] (32) When He ascended into the seventh heaven, all the righteous sang to him, and all the angels and virtues whom I could not see. (33) I saw a wonderful angel sit at His left hand, (34) who said to me, 'This suffices you, Isaiah, for you have seen what no other son of the flesh has seen, which eyes cannot see nor ears hear, nor can it rise in the heart of man, how much God has prepared for all who love Him.'[51] (35) And he said to me, 'Return in your robe until the time of your days shall be fulfilled and then you shall come here.'" (36) Having seen these things, Isaiah spoke to those standing about him; and, hearing these wonders, all sang and glorified the Lord, who gave such grace to men. And he said to Hezekiah the king, (37) "The consummation of this world (38) and works will be fulfilled in the last generations." (39) And he forbade them to proclaim these words to the children of Israel or to give them to any man to be recorded. (40) But how many things will be understood by the king and by the utterances in the prophets![52] And thus be you also in the Holy Spirit, so that you may receive your robes and thrones and crowns of glory placed in the heavens. He ceased then to speak and went out from King Hezekiah.[53]

The Vision of Isaiah AS RETOLD IN THE FOURTEENTH CENTURY

The following is part of the testimony of a witness before the Inquisition at Pamiers, 1321, published by J. J. I. von Döllinger, *Beiträge zur Sektengeschichte des Mittelalters* (2 vols., Munich, 1890), II, 166-67, from Vatican Latin manuscript 4030.

[The witness testified that a heretic had told him:] Once there was a good man of their sect who was in a quandary as to whether he held the right faith, and he besought God the Father to show him whether he held to a good faith and a right way, and also to show him His glory. And one day, while he was praying for this, an angel appeared to him and told him that he had come for the purpose of showing him the glory of the Holy Father and whether he held to the good faith and the right way. And he caused the man aforesaid to climb upon his shoulder and, carrying him, came to the first heaven after the turbulence of this world. And there he set him down. And the man saw the lord of the aforesaid world and heaven and, approaching him, sought to adore him, but was forbidden by the angel, who said he must not adore him because this was not his Father. Thereupon the angel, taking that good man on his shoulder, carried him to the second world and the second heaven, and there set him down. And the man, seeing the lord of the second world standing in greater glory than did the lord of the first, wished to adore him but was forbidden by the angel. And in the same way the man was carried by the angel through all the other heavens up to the seventh heaven, and he sought to adore the lords of the heavens and worlds, who were of the greater glory the higher they were, but was forbidden by the angel to adore them. Then, he was carried into the seventh heaven and beheld the Lord of that heaven; the angel told him that this was the Holy Father and that he should adore Him; and approaching the Father, the man adored Him. And the Holy Father questioned the man about whence he came. He answered: "From the land of tribulations." And as the man beheld in heaven great brilliance, many angels, beautiful groves and singing birds, and saw that joy without sadness was there, that neither hunger nor thirst existed there, nor cold nor heat, but most moderate temperatures, he said to the Holy Father that it would be pleasing to remain with Him thenceforth. But the Holy Father replied that he could not remain there at that time, since flesh born of corruption could not stay there, but it behooved him to descend to the land of tribulation and to preach that faith which he knew, since that was His faith. And the man requested the Father to let him stay with Him for a little while, which He conceded to him. And after a time, the angel told the man to climb upon his shoulder, since the hour had come to descend. And the man answered that he had not yet been with the Father [as long as] from the first to the third hour, but the angel told him that, on the contrary, he had been there thirty-two years, and this he found to be true when he was on earth. And having climbed upon the angel's shoulder and descended through all the heavens, he came to this earth. And afterward he preached what he had seen. And thus, the heretic said, their faith and sect were confirmed.[54]

B. THE SECRET SUPPER
circa 1190

In the name of the Father, of the Son, and of the Holy Spirit, amen.

The questions of John, the apostle and evangelist, at a secret supper[1] in the kingdom of heaven, about the governance of this world, about its ruler, and about Adam:

I, John, partner in tribulation so that I might be a partner in the kingdom of God,[2] leaning on the breast of Jesus Christ our Lord at the supper, said to Him; "Lord, who shall betray Thee?" And the Lord said unto me: "He that shall have dipped his hand in the dish, into him shall Satan enter. He shall betray me."[3]

I said, "Lord, before Satan fell, in what splendor did he attend the Father?" He said: "Among the virtues[4] of heaven and at the throne of the Father invisible; he was regulator of all things and sat with my Father.[5] He [Satan] it was who presided over the virtues of the heavens and those who attended on the Father. His power descended from the heavens even unto hell, and arose even unto the throne of the Father invisible. He had wardship of those splendors which were above all the heavens. And he pondered, wishing to place his throne upon the clouds and to 'be like the Most High.'[6] When he had come down to lower air, he descried an angel seated upon the air,[7] to whom he said, 'Open to me the portals of the air'; these the angels opened for him. And passing down, he descried an angel who guarded the waters,[8] to whom he said, 'Open to me the portals of the waters'; the angel opened them to him. And descending further, he found the whole earth covered with water; walking beneath this, he came upon two fish, lying upon the waters. These, indeed, were yoked together,[9] and they bore up the whole earth at the bidding of the Father invisible. And passing down further still, he found great clouds holding the massed waters of the sea. And descending lower, he found his hell, which is the Gehenna of fire; but thereafter he was unable to go further down, because of the flame of the fire which was raging.

"Then Satan retraced his path, filling himself with evil plots. He ascended to the angel who was over the air and to the angel who was over the waters, and unto them said: 'All things are mine. If you hearken to me, I will place my throne over the clouds and I will be like the Most High.[10] I will bear the waters up above this firmament and I will gather the other waters into wide seas.[11] After that there shall not be water upon the face of the whole earth, and I shall reign with you forever and ever.'[12] Thus he spoke to the angels. He ascended to the very heavens, even unto the third heaven, subverting the angels of the Father invisible, and saying to each of them, 'How much dost thou owe thy lord?' The first answered, 'A hundred barrels of oil.' He said to him, 'Take the bill and sit down and write fifty.' And he said to another, 'Now you, how much dost thou owe thy lord?' Who said, 'A hundred quarters of wheat.' To him he said, 'Take thy bill and sit down quickly and write eighty.'[13] To the other heavens he ascended with like speech; he ascended even unto the fifth heaven, seducing the angels of the Father invisible.

"And a voice came from the throne of the Father, saying: 'What dost thou, O thou devoid of hope, subverting the angels of the Father? Contriver of sin, do quickly what thou hast planned.'[14] Then the Father bade his angels, 'Take from all the angels who hearkened to him the garments, the thrones, and the crowns';[15] and these angels took the vestments, the thrones, and the crowns from all the angels who hearkened to him."

And once again I, John, questioned the Lord, saying, "When Satan fell, in what place did he dwell?" In answer He said to me: "Because of his self-exaltation, my Father decreed his transformation,[16] withdrawing from him the light of His glory. The face of Satan was like an iron glowing from the fire, and the whole aspect of his countenance was like that of a man. . . .[17] And he had seven tails with which he drew away the third part of the angels of God.[18] He was cast out from before the throne of God and from the stewardship of heaven. Falling down from heaven, Satan could find no peace in this firmament, nor could those who were with him. And he besought the Father, saying: 'I have sinned. Have patience with me, and I will pay thee all.'[19] The Lord was moved with pity for him and gave him peace to do what he would until the seventh day.[20]

"Then Satan took his seat above the firmament and gave command to the angel who was over the air and the angel who was over the waters, so that they raised two thirds of the waters high into the air. Of the remaining third they formed wide seas. The division of the waters was by command of the Father invisible. Again Satan bade the angel who was over the waters, 'Take a stand upon the two fish.' And the angel raised the earth upward with his head, and dry land appeared and was. . . .[21] When he took a crown from the angel who was over the air, from half of it he made himself a throne;[22] and when he took a crown from the angel who was over the waters, from half he made the light of the moon and from half the light of day. From precious stones he made fire, and from fire he made all the host of heaven and the stars,[23] and from them he made angels, his ministering spirits, according to the plan of the Governor Most High. He also made thunder, rain, hail, and snow, and over these he set his ministering angels.

"He commanded the earth to bring forth all living things[24]—animals, trees, and herbs. The sea he commanded to bring forth fish; and the air, birds of the heavens. And he pondered on making man to serve him; he took clay of the earth and made man like unto himself.[25] And he then bade an angel of the second heaven to enter the body of clay. Of this body he took a part and made another body in the form of a woman[26] and bade an angel of the first heaven[27] to enter into it. And the angels grieved deeply that they thus had a mortal form imposed upon them and that they now existed in different forms. And Satan bade them to perform the works of the flesh in their bodies of clay, but they did not know how to commit sin. The originator of sin accomplished his purpose by his seduction, in this way: He planted a paradise[28] and set men therein and bade them not to eat of its fruits. The devil entered Paradise and planted a bed of reeds in the midst of Paradise; of his spittle he made a serpent and bade him remain in the reeds. Thus the devil concealed the knowledge of his deceit so that they would not perceive his treachery. He went in to them saying, 'Eat of all the fruit in Paradise, but of the fruit of good and evil[29] eat not.' Thereafter the wicked devil, entering into the evil serpent, deceived the angel who was in the form of a woman and poured out upon her head a longing for sin,[30] and Eve's desire was like a glowing oven. Forthwith, the devil in the form of the serpent came out of the reeds and sated his lust on her[31] with the serpent's tail. That is why [the offspring] are called not sons of God[32] but sons of the devil and sons of the serpent,[33] fulfilling the diabolic desires of their father even unto the end of the world. After this, the devil poured out his longing upon the head of the angel who was in Adam; and [both angels] were affected by a lust for debauchery, together begetting children of the devil and of the serpent, until the consummation of the world."

[4] After that I, John, questioned the Lord, saying, "Why do men say that Adam and Eve were made by God and placed in Paradise to keep His commandments, and that for transgression of the Father's commandment they were delivered up unto death?" The Lord said unto me: "Hear, John, most beloved. Men are foolish who speak thus, for my Father did not, in transgression (*in praevaricatione*) [34] of His own law, shape bodies of clay, but by the Holy Spirit made [only] all the virtues of heaven. These, however, for their sins and by their fall are found possessing bodies of clay and are delivered up to death."

[5] And still I, John, questioned the Lord, saying, "Lord, how did man have spiritual origin in a carnal body?" And the Lord said to me: "By their fall spirits of heaven entered the female body of clay and took on flesh from the lusts of the flesh and took on [spirit at the same time]. . . .[35] Spirit is born of spirit and flesh of flesh;[36] and thus the reign of Satan ceases not in this world." [37]

[6] And I questioned the Lord, saying, "For how long will Satan have dominion in this world over the essences of men?" And the Lord replied, "My Father will permit him to reign seven days, that is, seven ages."

[7] Again I, John, questioned the Lord in this wise, "What will be the nature of this period [of seven ages]?" And He said to me: "From the time when the devil fell from the glory of the Father and desired his own glory, he took his seat among the clouds and sent forth his ministers, a searing fire, and . . .[38] in the land from Adam to Enoch. And he sent his minister to Enoch and translated him above the firmament and displayed to him his divine nature. He then commanded that he be given quill and ink. Seating himself, Enoch wrote seventy-six[39] books; these the devil bade him to take to earth. Enoch took the books and turned them over to his sons, and he taught them how to observe the form and place of sacrificial rites. This they did in such wise as to 'shut the kingdom of heaven against men.'[40] And he [the devil] said to them, 'See you that I am god and there is no other god beside me.'[41] Wherefore my Father sent me to this world to make manifest His name[42] to men, that they might recognize the devil and his wickedness. But when Satan

learned that I had come down to this world, he sent his angel to take three pieces of wood. These he gave to the prophet Moses for my crucifixion. This wood they have kept for me until the present.[43] And he revealed to Moses his divinity and bade him give laws to the children of Israel and lead them on dry ground through the midst of the sea.[44]

"When my Father thought to send me to this earth, He sent before me His angel, she who is called Mary, my mother, that she might receive me through the Holy Spirit. And when I descended, I entered and came forth through her ear. Now Satan, the prince of this world, knew that I was come to seek and 'to save that which was lost'; [45] and he sent his angel, the prophet Elijah, who baptized in water and was called John the Baptist.[46] Now, Elijah asked the prince of this world how he might recognize me.[47] And the devil said to him, 'Upon Whom thou shalt see the Holy Spirit descending as a dove, and remaining upon Him, He it is that baptizeth in the Holy Spirit and with fire.' John asked this because he did not know me, but the one who sent him to baptize in water, he revealed me. John himself gave testimony: 'I baptize in water unto penance, but He baptizes you with the Holy Spirit unto the remission of sins. He it is who is able to destroy and to save.' "

[8] And again I, John, questioned the Lord, "Can man be saved through the baptism [of John?" He replied:] [48] "Without my baptism, with which I baptize unto the remission of sins, I affirm that no one can receive salvation in God. For I am the bread of life that came down from the seventh heaven, wherefore whoso eats my flesh and drinks my blood, these shall be called the children of God." [49]

[9] I inquired of the Lord, "What is the meaning of your 'flesh' and your 'blood'?" To me the Lord answered: "Before the devil had fallen with all the angelic host of the Father, the angels in their prayers glorified my Father by repeating this prayer, 'Our Father who art in heaven.' This chant ascended to the throne of the Father; but the angels from the time of their fall could no longer glorify God in this prayer."

[10] And again I asked the Lord, "How is it that the whole world received the baptism of John, but Thine is not accepted by all?" The Lord replied to me: "That is because their works are evil and they come not to the light. The followers of John marry and are given in marriage, whereas my disciples marry not at all but remain as the angels of God in the heavenly kingdom." [50]

[11] Then I said to Him, "If it is a sin to have knowledge of women, is it then unwise to marry ?" And the Lord replied: "All men take not this word, but they to whom it is given. For there are eunuchs who were born so from their mother's womb; and there are eunuchs who were made so by men; and there are eunuchs who have made themselves eunuchs for the kingdom of heaven."[51]

[12] Afterward, I questioned the Lord about the Day of Judgment, "What shall be the sign of Thy coming?"[52] In reply He said: "When the number of the just shall equal the number of those crowned [angels] who fell.[53] Then shall Satan, raging mightily, be 'loosed out of his prison.'[54] He shall war upon the just, who shall cry out to the Lord their God; forthwith the Lord God shall command the archangel to sound his trumpet, and the voice of the archangel shall go forth from the heavens and be heard even unto the nether regions. Then 'the sun shall be darkened and the moon shall not give her light, and the stars shall fall from heaven.'[55] And there shall be loosed from their foundations the four great winds;[56] the earth, the sea, the mountains, and the hills shall tremble together. Then shall be revealed the sign of the Son, and all tribes of earth shall mourn.[57] Immediately the heaven shall tremble and be darkened, the sun shall shine until the ninth hour.[58] Then shall the Son of man be shown forth in his glory, and all the saints and angels with Him; they shall place their seats above the clouds. And He shall sit upon the seat of His glory, with the twelve apostles upon their twelve seats of glory.[59] The books shall be opened, and all the peoples of the earth shall be judged.[60] Then shall the faith be proclaimed. Then shall the Son of man send forth His angels. They shall gather His elect from the heights even to the uttermost limits of the heavens and shall bring them, gathered into their fold, to me above the clouds, into the air.[61] Then shall the Son of God send forth the evil demons and expel them in His wrath, together with all peoples (*linguas*) who believed in him [Satan] . . .[62] who said, 'Let us eat, drink, and lay hold on the things of this world';[63] and let us see what manner of aid they shall have from those things. Forthwith all peoples shall stand in fear before the judgment [throne]. The two books shall be opened and they shall lay bare all peoples with their teaching; they shall glorify the just for their sufferings joined with good works. Glory and boundless honor shall be the reward of those who have cherished the angelic life; while the portion of the servants of iniquity shall be wrath, fury, distress,

and displeasure. And the Son of man shall separate His just from the company of sinners and shall say to them, 'Come, ye blessed of my Father, possess you the kingdom prepared for you from the foundation of the world'; [64] while to the sinful He shall say, 'Depart from me, you cursed, into everlasting fire, which was prepared for the devil and his angels.' [65] Others shall witness the final division and 'the wicked shall be turned into hell.' [66] By the indulgence of my Father the unbelieving spirits shall at length withdraw from prison; 'they shall hear my voice, and there shall be one fold and one shepherd.' [67]

"Then, by permission of my Father, gloomy darkness shall spread over the lower regions of the earth and a hell of fire shall burn all the land from its lowest depths even unto the air of the firmament.[68] And the Lord shall be [supreme] [69] in the firmament even unto the nether regions of the earth. Should a man of thirty years pick up a stone and let it drop, it would scarcely strike the bottom within the space of three years, so great is the depth of the pool of fire wherein dwell the sinners.[70] Then Satan shall be bound and all his host, and he shall be cast into the pool of fire.[71] The Son of God, with his elect, shall walk above the firmament; and He shall shut up the devil, binding him with unbreakable bonds, with sinners weeping, wailing, and crying out 'Swallow us up, O land, hide us within thyself.'[72] Then shall the just shine as the sun in the kingdom of their Father. And Jesus shall lead them before the throne of the Father invisible and shall say to the Father, 'Behold, I and my children, whom God hath given me.[73] Just Father, the world hath not known Thee, but I have known Thee in truth because Thou hast sent me.' [74] And then the Father will reply to His Son, saying, 'My beloved Son, sit on my right hand, until I make thy enemies thy footstool [75]—thy enemies, who have denied me and said, "We are gods, and there is no other god beside us"; [76] who killed your prophets and persecuted your just. You shall persecute them in the exterior darkness; there shall be weeping and gnashing of teeth.' [77]

"And then the Son of God shall sit on the right hand of his Father, and the Father shall command His angels that they minister unto them [the just]; and He shall place them in the choir of angels and clothe them in imperishable raiment; and He shall give them crowns never fading and seats unmoving. And God shall be in their midst. 'They shall no more hunger nor thirst; neither shall the sun fall on them, nor any heat. And God shall wipe away all tears from their eyes.' [78] And [the Son] shall reign with his Holy Father, and his reign shall endure forevermore."

This is the *Secret* of the heretics of Concorrezzo, brought from Bulgaria by Nazarius, their bishop. It is full of errors.[79]

57. The Catharist Rituals

It has been disclosed repeatedly in the preceding documents that the act of central importance in the religious life of the Cathars was the consolamentum,[1] a spiritual baptism received on admission to the Church of Christ. When perfected Cathars imposed their hands on the body of the initiate while the Gospel was held over his head, their prayers were believed to win him forgiveness for the sin committed at the fall from heaven, as well as for his transgressions in this earthly life. Released from the power of the evil god, his soul would regain its guiding spirit and would find the way of return to its heavenly home.[2] It was not easy to attain this consecrated state nor to follow the way of life required during the remaining bodily existence on earth. Like a catechumen of the early Church—Catharist practices reflect the ancient usage[3]—a believer had to undergo a period of probation, normally at least a year, during which he was instructed in the faith and disciplined in a life of rigorous asceticism. When the postulant was judged ready, the right and obligation of saying the Lord's Prayer was conveyed to him in a short ceremony, in which he was instructed in the tradition of prayer as it was declared to have descended from the apostles. This preliminary rite brought him to the Church;[4] he might then proceed, either at once or after further probation, to the consolamentum, which would effect the complete spiritual transformation. Thereafter, the Christian[5] renounced the material world and accepted a strict moral and ethical code. His life was to be spent in imitation of the apostles. He was to return good for evil in every circumstance and suffer without retaliation the persecution which must be endured by every true follower of Christ. To kill, to lie, to take an oath was to commit mortal sin.[6] Sexual relationships which would reproduce the bodies of this world were forbidden. Meat, eggs, and cheese, as products of coition, must not be used. Obeying these injunctions, the Cathar was assured that on the death of his body his soul would be released from its material prison and would find salvation.

In addition to the important ceremonies described above, other occasions for personal prayer and public worship marked the daily life of the Cathars. Summary descriptions of all these religious practices are plentiful in orthodox sources, but the two documents translated here give the rituals as used in the thirteenth century. One was written in Latin and is judged to have been composed in the second quarter of the thirteenth century in Italy. The writer had before him, and on occasion followed closely, a document written in Provençal, which influenced his Latin style. Later, some other hand interpolated a special interpretation of the phrase "supersubstantial bread." [7] The other ritual was written in Provençal in a manuscript of the Bible in that language, perhaps as late as 1280, but this ritual may well represent early Catharist practice more closely than does the Latin version. It adds to the two major ceremonies the formulas for the monthly confession called the Service and for the baptism of an invalid, together with certain rules of conduct. Between the Latin and Provençal texts there are minor differences in the phrasing of invocations, the sequence of actions, and the titles given to the presiding officials. Other, more significant differences are that in the Latin version the believer is instructed not to scorn his earlier baptism in the Roman faith, even though it was insufficient for salvation—no hint of this instruction appears in the Provençal text [8]—and he promises more emphatically to live in obedience to the Church.

A preliminary sketch of the ceremonies described in the rituals and a word about the choice of English equivalents for the terms used in the Latin and the Provençal version is given here by way of introduction.

At the beginning of the ritual in Provençal is found a group of invocations and blessings, together with the Lord's Prayer and the opening of the Gospel of John (1:1-17), all written in Latin. This may be only a catalogue of the formal phrases which are many times repeated, always in Latin, during the religious ceremonies described in the following parts of the ritual. Some authors, however, have seen in this passage the form for a service of worship, to which they give the name of Benediction or Catharist Mass. [9] Neither phrase is appropriate, for more than blessings are included and the whole is in no way comparable to the orthodox Mass. We, therefore, while not insisting that this passage actually constitutes a separate ceremony, refer to it here as "phrases for worship."

The Service (*lo servisi*), described only in the Provençal ritual, was a monthly gathering for confession by the Perfect. [10] Catholic sources usually refer to it as the *apparellamentum*. The word "Service" (*servitium*) is applied in the Latin ritual to acts at the close of the more important ceremonies and designates a short sequence of confession and prayer, [11] the equivalent of the Double, described below.

The ministrants of the Prayer and the consolamentum have different titles in the two documents. In the Provençal, the minister is called "the elder" (*l'ancia*) and is assisted by "one of the Good Men," that is, by another perfected Cathar. In the Latin ritual, the presiding Cathar is the *ordinatus*, [12] which we render in English as "prior"; and his assistant has the title of "elder" (*ancianus*). The sponsor who presented the postulant, and who probably was the Perfect in charge of the hospice where the believer spent his probationary term, is also called an elder in the Provençal text. Any Cathar who had not been disqualified by sin was able to minister the consolamentum to a believer (at least two persons acting together were normally required), but it was primarily a function of the bishop, his sons, or the deacons. In their absence, the ministry fell to those who had been professed heretics for the longest period of time.[13]

The melioramentum was the common form of greeting by believers to the Perfect at any time and, with certain changes of phrasing, was the manner in which one Cathar greeted another.[14] It finds a place in the rituals (it is called *fasso so miloirer* or *milhoirer* in the Provençal text; the actions are described but no name is given to them in the Latin) as the formal salutation and leave-taking at the beginning and the end of the ceremonies. The melioramentum consisted of saying three times, "Bless us; have mercy upon us," accompanying each request with a prostration or genuflection, and following these with a plea that good be done to the believer.

"Let us adore the Father, the Son, and the Holy Spirit," was a phrase repeated almost as frequently as "Bless us; have mercy upon us"; it was said several times before and after the Lord's Prayer and at numerous other moments. Sometimes it is indicated in the rituals only by the first word (*adoremus*).

The Pardon was a formal exchange in which the presiding officials and the congregation asked forgiveness of their sins. They did so at the start of the ceremonies and at their conclusion. Just before receiving the consolamentum, the believer also participated in the Pardon. The Latin text uses the word *perdonum*; the Provençal the words *las parcias*. Both rituals prescribe much the same sequence of words and actions: the phrase "Bless us, etc." thrice repeated by the congregation or the believer with genuflections, followed by "May the Father, the Son, and the Holy Spirit forgive us (me) all our (my) sins. Let it be done unto us according to Thy word." The reply of the ministrant was to repeat the request for forgiveness from God.

The Grace (*la gratia* in Provençal, *gratia* in Latin) was the familiar invocation: "May the grace of our Lord Jesus Christ be with you all."

The Act of Peace (*far patz* in Provençal, *ire ad pacem* in Latin) was performed at the end of the ceremony. Male heretics saluted each other with an embrace and a kiss on each cheek; women kissed the Gospel and each other, sometimes the shoulder or elbow of a man. Believers also shared in these acts.[15]

Special terms designate multiple repetitions of the Lord's Prayer. The Six (*sezena*) of the Provençal ritual entailed six repetitions of the Lord's Prayer, as is shown by comparison with the Latin text. The Double (*dobla, dupla*), which concluded major ceremonies, consisted of sixteen repetitions of the Prayer, accompanied by genuflections. The Double was also performed in private prayer and at the end of the day, though on occasion the Single (*sembla*) could take its place.[16]

The Latin version of the ritual, edited by Dondaine, is analyzed at some length by him and compared with the Provençal text.[17] Borst also discusses its authorship, style, and content.[18] The Provençal version was published with a parallel French translation, by Léon Clédat. Both the Latin and Provençal versions were translated into French by René Nelli (*Ecritures cathares*, pp. 228-52, 211-27, respectively). There is an abridged English translation of

the ritual of the consolamentum and of the discourse to the initiate, in Oldenbourg, *Massacre at Montségur,* Appendices A and B. A short excerpt in
English will also be found in Petry, *History of Christianity,* pp. 348-49.

In part A, the ritual is translated from the Latin text in Antoine Dondaine,
Un Traité néo-manichéen du XIIIe siècle: Le Liber de duobus principiis,
suivi d'un fragment de rituel cathare (Rome, 1939), pp. 151-65, by permission of the Istituto storico domenicano di S. Sabina. The translation of the
Provençal text in part B is from Léon Clédat, *Le Nouveau Testament traduit
au XIIIe siècle en langue provençale, suivi d'un rituel cathare* (Paris, 1887),
pp. ix-xxvi (printed text and French translation), 470-82 (photograph of the
original manuscript), by permission of the Bibliothèque de la Faculté des
lettres et sciences humaines de l'Université de Lyon.

A. THE RITUAL TRANSLATED FROM THE LATIN TEXT

circa 1240-1250
[The Ministration of the Holy Prayer]

[The ministrant is addressing the initiate: " 'The meek] shall increase
their joy in the Lord, and the poor men shall rejoice in the Holy One of
Israel. For he that did prevail hath failed, the scorner is consumed, and
they are all cut off that watched for iniquity, that made men sin by
word and supplanted him that reproved them in the gate.' " [1]

On Compassion for the People.[2]—"Thus, by virtue of these and
many other proofs, is the understanding given that the Holy Father
desires to have compassion on His people and to receive them into His
peace and concord through the advent of His Son, Jesus Christ. This,
then, is the reason why you are here in the presence of the disciples of
Jesus Christ, where spiritually dwell the Father, the Son, and the Holy
Spirit, as was previously disclosed: that you may become worthy to
receive this Holy Prayer which the Lord Jesus Christ gave to His disciples, so that your supplications and prayers may be heard by our
Most Holy Father, as David says, 'Let my prayer be directed as incense in Thy sight.' " [3]

On Receiving the Holy Prayer.—"Thus, you should know how you
ought to receive this Holy Prayer, that is, 'Our Father.' [4] The Prayer
indeed is brief but it includes a great deal. He who should recite 'Our
Father,' then must honor Him with good works. The Son is called 'love
of the Father'; hence, he who desires to be a son by inheritance keeps
himself absolutely from evil deeds.

"The phrase 'Our Father' is an invocation, as though one were saying:

O Father of those only who are to achieve salvation.

" 'Who art in heaven,' that is, who dwells in the saints or in the heavenly powers. And, indeed, for that reason one says 'Our Father who art in heaven' to distinguish Him from the father of the devil, who is a liar and the father of the evil ones, namely, those who are utterly deprived of the mercy of salvation. And thus we say 'Our Father.'

" 'Hallowed be Thy name.' By the 'name' of God is meant the law of Christ, as if one were to say: May Thy law be confirmed in Thy people.

" 'Thy kingdom come.' By the 'kingdom' of God is meant Christ, just as Christ says in the Gospel, 'For lo, the kingdom of God is within you.' [5] Or, by the 'kingdom' of God is meant the people of God who are to achieve salvation, as if one were to say: Lord, lead Thy people out of the land of the enemy. Thus, the prophet Joel says: 'Between the porch and the altar the priests, the Lord's ministers, shall weep and shall say, "Spare, O Lord, spare Thy people and give not Thy inheritance to reproach, that the heathen should rule over them. Why should they say among the nations: Where is their God?" ' [6] And for that reason, Christians daily pray to their most benevolent God for the salvation of the people of God.

" 'Thy will be done on earth as it is in heaven'; as though one were saying: So let Thy will be done in this people who cling to an earthly nature as it is done in the higher kingdom or in Christ, who says, 'I came not to do my own will but the will of him that sent me, the Father.' [7]

" 'Our supersubstantial bread.' [8] By 'supersubstantial bread' is meant the law of Christ which was laid upon the whole people. Isaiah, we believe, says of this bread: 'And in that day seven women shall take hold of one man, saying, "We will eat our own bread, and wear our own apparel, only let us be called by thy name." ' [9] And David says: 'I am smitten as grass and my heart is withered because I forgot to eat my bread.' [10] And in the Book of Wisdom it is written: 'Thou didst feed Thy people with the food of angels and gavest them bread from heaven prepared without labor, having in it all that is delicious and the sweetness of every taste. For Thy sustenance showed Thy sweetness to Thy children and, serving every man's will, it was turned to what every man liked.' [11] And through Isaiah the Lord says: 'Deal thy bread to the hungry, and bring the needy and the harborless into thy house; when

thou shalt see one naked, cover him, and despise not thy own flesh.' [12]
Of this bread, we believe, Jeremiah says in Lamentations, 'The little
ones have asked for bread and there was none to break it unto them.' [13]
And Christ says to the Jews in the Gospel of John: 'Amen, amen, I say
to you, Moses gave you not bread from heaven, but my Father giveth
you the true bread from heaven. For the bread of God is that which
cometh down from heaven and giveth life to the world.' [14] And again,
'I am the bread of life'—that is, I have the commandments of life. 'He
that cometh to me shall not hunger, and he that believeth in me shall
never thirst.' [15] And again: 'Amen, amen, I say unto you, he that believeth in me hath everlasting life. I am the bread of life. This is the
bread which cometh down from heaven, that if any man eat of it, he
may not die. I am the living bread which came down from heaven. If
any man eat of this bread'—that is, if any man shall keep my commandments—'he shall live forever; and the bread that I will give to
him is my flesh, for the life of the world'—that is, of the people. 'The
Jews therefore strove among themselves, saying, "How can this man give
us his flesh to eat" '—as if one were to say: It was a question among
the Jewish people just how Christ could give them His commandments
to be kept, for they did not know the divinity of the Son of God. 'Then
Jesus said to them, "Amen, amen, I say unto you; except you eat the
flesh of the Son of man" '—that is, unless you keep the commandments of the Son of God—' "and drink his blood" '—that is, unless you
accept the spiritual intent of the New Testament—' "you shall not have
life in you. He that eateth my flesh and drinketh my blood hath everlasting life, and I will raise him up in the Last Day. For my flesh is
meat indeed, and my blood is drink indeed." ' [16] Elsewhere Christ says:
'My meat is to do the will of my Father who sent me, that I may perfect
his work'; [17] and again, 'He that eateth my flesh and drinketh my blood,
abideth in me, and I in him.' [18] Truly, therefore, false priests eat not
the flesh of our Lord Jesus Christ nor drink His blood, because they
abide not in the Lord Jesus. Accordingly, the Blessed John says in his
first Epistle: 'But he that keepeth His word, in him in very deed the
charity of God is perfected, and by this we know that we are in Him.
He that saith he abideth in Him ought himself also to walk, even as
He walked.' [19]

"Of this bread, we believe, is it written in the Gospel of the Blessed
Matthew: 'And whilst they were at supper, Jesus took bread' [20]—that is,

the spiritual commandments of the Law and the prophets—'and blessed'—that is, He praised and confirmed them—'and broke'—that is, He expounded them spiritually—'and gave to his disciples'—that is, He instructed them to keep them spiritually—'and said, "Take ye" '—that is, keep them—' "and eat" '—that is, preach to others. (Hence, it was said to the Blessed John the Evangelist, 'Take the book, and eat it up,' and so forth; 'and he [the angel] said to me, "Thou must prophesy again to many nations, and peoples, and tongues, and kings." ') [21] 'This is my body'—here He says of the bread, 'This is my body'; earlier He said, 'And the bread that I will give is my flesh, for the life of the world.' [22] He said, as we believe, 'This is my body' (or my flesh) in reference to the commandments of the Law and the prophets interpreted in a spiritual sense, as though He were saying: There am I, there dwell I. Therefore, the Apostle in the first Epistle to the Corinthians says: 'The chalice of benediction which we bless, is it not the communion of the blood of Christ? And the bread which we break, is it not the partaking of the body of the Lord? For we, being many, are one bread, one body, all that partake of one bread' [23] and of one chalice, that is, of one spiritual meaning of the Law, the prophets, and the New Testament. And again: 'For I have received of the Lord that which also I delivered unto you, that the Lord Jesus, the same night in which he was betrayed, took bread and, giving thanks, broke, and said, "Take ye, and eat; this is my body, which shall be delivered for you" '—as though He were saying: These spiritual commandments of the Old Testament are my body, which for you is given unto the people. " 'This do for the commemoration of me." In like manner also the chalice, after He had supped, saying, "This chalice is the new testament in my blood. This do ye, as often as you shall drink, for the commemoration of me." ' [24] Herein is the understanding of 'supersubstantial bread.'

"Then follows, 'Give us this day'—that is, in this time of grace, or while we are in this temporal life, give us Thy power, that we may be worthy to fulfill the law of Thy Son, Jesus Christ.

" 'And forgive us our debts'—that is, charge not against us, who seek to observe the commandments of Thy Son, our sins of commission or omission.

" 'As we forgive our debtors'—that is, as we forgive them that persecute and do evil unto us.

" 'And lead us not into temptation'—that is, permit us not, after we undertake to keep Thy law, to be led further into temptation. For, truly, there is a carnal temptation and a diabolical temptation. The diabolical is that which proceeds from the heart and the prompting of the devil, for example, sin, evil thoughts, hatred, and the like. The carnal is that which springs from human nature, such as hunger, thirst, cold, and the like; these we cannot avoid. Whence the Apostle says, in the first Epistle to the Corinthians: 'Let no temptation take hold on you but such as is human. And God is faithful, who will not suffer you to be tempted above that which you are able, but will make also with temptation issue, that you may be able to bear it.' [25]

" 'But deliver us from evil,' that is, from the devil, who is the tempter of the faithful, and from his works.

" 'For Thine is the kingdom.' This phrase is said to be in the Greek and Hebrew texts,[26] as though one were saying: For this is the reason why Thou mayest do unto us that for which we pray, for we are Thy people.

" 'And the power,' as though one were saying: Thou hast the power to bring us to salvation.

" 'And the glory'—that is, praise and honor is Thine, if this Thou do unto Thy people.

" 'Forever,' that is, over divinely created beings.[27]

" 'Amen,' that is, without fail.

"Now, you must understand, if you would receive this prayer, that it is needful for you to repent of all your sins and to forgive all men, for in the Gospel Christ says, 'But if you will not forgive men their sins, neither will your Father forgive your offenses.' [28] Also, it behooves you to resolve in your heart that, if God grants you the grace to receive it, you will keep this holy prayer throughout your whole lifetime, according to the usage of the Church of God, in obedience and chastity,[29] and in all other good virtues which God shall deign to grant unto you. Wherefore we pray the good Lord, who granted unto the disciples of Jesus Christ the power to receive this prayer with steadfastness, that He grant unto you the strength to receive it with steadfastness to His honor and your salvation. Have mercy upon us."

Then let the prior (*ordinatus*) take the Book [30] from the hands of the believer and say, "John" (if he is so named), "is it your will to receive this holy prayer as it has been expounded and to keep it throughout your whole lifetime, in chastity, truth, and humility, and in all other good virtues which God may deign to grant unto you?"

And let the believer answer: "Yes, it is. Pray to the Holy Father that He grant His strength unto me."

And let the prior say, "May God grant you the grace to receive it to His honor and your salvation."

On the Ministry of the Church.—Then let the prior say to the believer, "Say the Prayer with me, word for word, and say the Pardon (*perdonum*) as this man says it." And let the believer repeat the words of him who stands beside the prior.[31] Then let the prior begin the Pardon. Thereafter, let him say the Prayer as is the custom. When the Prayer and Grace are finished, let the believer say with an obeisance before the prior, "Bless us; have mercy upon us. Amen. Let it be done unto us, Lord, according to Thy word."

And let the prior say, "May the Father, the Son, and the Holy Spirit forgive all your sins."

And let the believer then rise. Let the prior say: "From God and from us, from the Church and its holy order,[32] and from its holy commandments and disciples, may you have the power to say this prayer at your food and drink, by day and night, alone and in company, as is the custom of the Church of Jesus Christ; and you must never eat or drink without this prayer. If you are in default in this, something which you will announce to the prior of the Church as soon as you can, you shall bear that penance which he chooses to lay upon you. May the true Lord God give you the grace to keep this, to His honor and your salvation."

Then let the believer make three obeisances, saying: "Bless us, bless us, bless us; have mercy upon us. May the Lord God render you rich reward for this good thing which you have done unto me for the love of God."

Then if the believer is not to be consoled, it is in order to undertake the Service and to proceed to the Peace.[33]

[*The Ministration of the Consolamentum*]

If the believer is to receive the consolamentum immediately after he has received the Prayer, then this believer should approach, accompanied by the one who is the elder (*ancianus*) of his house. They should make three obeisances before the prior and pray for the good [34] of this believer. This done, the prior and the Christian men and women should say seven prayers to God, asking that the prior be heard; and when this has been done, let the prior say: "Brothers and sisters, if I have said or done anything against God and my salvation, pray to the Lord God for me, that He have mercy upon me."

And let the elder who stands beside the prior say, "May the Holy Father, just, true, and merciful, Who in heaven and on earth hath the power to forgive sins, forgive you and have mercy on all your sins in this world, and in the future may He have pity on you."

Then let the prior say, "Amen. Let it be done unto us, Lord, according to Thy word."

Then let all the Christian men and women make three obeisances, saying: "Bless us, bless us, bless us; have mercy upon us. If we have said or done anything against God and our salvation, pray to the God of mercy that He have pity on us. Bless us; have mercy upon us."

And let the prior answer: "[May] the Holy Father, just, true, and merciful," and so on, just as was said earlier.

On Accepting the Book.—When this has been done, let the prior arrange a table before himself. Then let the believer approach the prior and take the Book from the hands of the prior with three obeisances, as he did at the [ministration of the] Prayer, as set forth above.

Then let the prior say: "John, is it your will to receive the spiritual baptism of Jesus Christ and pardon for your sins, through the supplications of good Christians, together with the imposition of hands, and to keep this throughout your whole lifetime in chastity and in humility, and in all other exemplary virtues which God may deign to grant unto you?"

And let the believer answer: "Yes, it is. Pray God to grant His strength unto me."

Let the prior say: "May God grant you the grace to receive it to His honor and to your salvation."

On the Sermon by the Prior.—Then let the prior begin to preach in this way, if he so chooses:

"O John, you must understand that now, for a second time, you come before God, Christ, and the Holy Spirit as you come before the Church of God, as was disclosed previously through the Scriptures, and you must understand that you are in the presence of the Church of God to receive pardon for your sins, through the supplications of good Christians, together with the imposition of hands. This is called the spiritual baptism of Jesus Christ and the baptism of the Holy Spirit as John the Baptist says, 'I indeed baptize you in water unto penance, but He that shall come after me is mightier than I, Whose shoes I am not worthy to bear; He shall baptize you in the Holy Spirit and fire' [35]— that is, He will wash and cleanse you in spiritual understanding and good works. By this baptism is meant the spiritual rebirth of which Christ said to Nicodemus, 'Unless a man be born again of water and the Holy Spirit, he cannot enter into the kingdom of God.' [36] Baptism means a laving or 'superbaptism.' [37] Now, one must understand that Christ did not come to wash the filth of the flesh, but to cleanse the filth of God's souls that have been soiled by contact with evil spirits. Thus, God said to the people of Israel through the prophet Baruch: 'Hear, O Israel, the commandments of life; give ear, that thou mayest learn wisdom. How happeneth it, O Israel, that thou art in thy enemies' land? Thou art grown old in a strange country, thou art defiled with the dead, thou art counted with them that go down into hell! Thou hast forgotten the fountain of life and of wisdom, for if thou hadst walked in the way of God, thou hadst surely dwelt in peace forever.' [38] And David says: 'O God, the heathens are come into Thy inheritance; they have defiled Thy holy temple; they have made Jerusalem as a place to keep fruit.' [39] And in this way have the people of God been defiled by contact with evil spirits. Whence it has pleased the Most Holy Father to wash His people of the filth of sins through the baptism of His Son, Jesus Christ, as the Blessed Apostle says to the Ephesians: 'Husbands, love your wives, as Christ also loved the church and delivered Himself up for it, that He might sanctify it, cleansing it by the laver of water in the word of life, that He might present it to Himself a glorious church, not having spot or wrinkle, or any such thing, but that it should be holy, and without blemish.' [40]

"And so, through the advent of our Lord Jesus Christ, by the power of the Most Holy Father, the disciples of Jesus Christ were cleansed of the filth of their sins by His spiritual baptism. They received strength and authority from the Lord Jesus Christ, as He had received it from his Most Holy Father, so that they too might cleanse other sinners through His baptism. Thus, in the Gospel of the Blessed John one finds the words of Jesus Christ to His disciples after His resurrection: ' "As the Father hath sent me, I also send you." When he had said this, he breathed on them, and he said to them, "Receive ye the Holy Spirit.

Whose sins you shall forgive, they are forgiven them, and whose sins you shall retain, they are retained." ' [41] And in the Gospel of the Blessed Matthew, He says to His disciples: 'Amen, I say to you, whatsoever you shall bind upon earth, shall be bound also in heaven, and whatsoever you shall loose upon earth, shall be loosed also in heaven. Again I say to you, that if two of you shall consent upon earth concerning anything whatsoever they shall ask, it shall be done to them by my Father who is in heaven.' [42] And again: ' "Who do men say that the Son of man is?" But they said, "Some John the Baptist, and some Elijah, and others Jeremiah or one of the prophets." Jesus saith to them, "But who do you say that I am?" Simon Peter answered and said, "Thou art Christ, the Son of the living God." And Jesus answering, said to him, "Blessed art thou, Simon Bar-Jona, because flesh and blood hath not revealed it to thee, but my Father who is in heaven. And I say to thee, that thou art Peter, and upon this rock I will build my church, and the gates of hell shall not prevail against it. And I will give to thee the keys of the kingdom of heaven" '—to you on behalf of all. "And whatsoever thou shalt bind upon earth, it shall be bound also in heaven; and whatsoever thou shalt loose on earth, it shall be loosed also in heaven." ' [43] And again, He says to His disciples: 'Go ye into the whole world and preach the gospel to every creature. He that believeth and is baptized shall be saved; but he that believeth not shall be condemned. And these signs shall follow them that believe: In my name they shall cast out devils; they shall speak with new tongues; they shall take up serpents; and if they shall drink any deadly thing, it shall not hurt them; they shall lay their hands upon the sick, and they shall recover.' [44] And again: 'The eleven disciples went into Galilee, unto the mountain where Jesus had appointed them. And seeing Him, they adored; but some doubted. And Jesus, coming, spoke to them, saying, "All power is given to me in heaven and in earth. Going therefore, teach ye all nations, baptizing them in the name of the Father, and of the Son, and of the Holy Spirit, teaching them to observe all things whatsoever I have commanded you; and behold, I am with you all days, even to the consummation of the world." ' ' [45]

"No wise man believes that the Church of Jesus Christ performs this baptism by imposition of hands without manifest proof from Scripture nor imagines that the Church of God performs this consecration out of the presumption and human intuition of its members or by unknown and unseen inspiration of spirits. No, the disciples of Jesus Christ actually went forth and stood with the Lord Jesus Christ, and they received from Him the authority to baptize and to forgive sins. So today do true Christians, who, as heirs of the disciples, in due order received from the Church of God the power actually to perform this baptism of the imposition of hands and to forgive sins. For it is plainly found in the New Testament Scriptures that after His ascension the disciples of Jesus Christ actually employed this ministry of the imposition of hands, as is clearly discussed in the Scriptures. In the Acts of the Apostles, it is written: 'Now when the apostles, who were in Jerusalem, had heard that Samaria had received the word of God, they sent unto them Peter and John, who, when they were come, prayed for them, that they might receive the Holy Spirit; for He was not as yet come upon any of them, but they were only baptized in the name of the Lord Jesus. Then they laid their hands upon them, and they received the Holy Spirit.' [46] And again: 'And it came to pass while Apollos was at Corinth, that Paul, having passed through the upper coasts, came to Ephesus, and found certain disciples. And he said to them, "Have ye received the Holy Spirit since ye believed?" But they said to him, "We have not so much as heard whether there be a Holy Spirit." And he said, "In what then were you baptized?" Who said, "In John's baptism." Then Paul said, "John baptized the people with the baptism of penance, saying that they should believe in Him who was to come after him, that is to say, in Jesus." Having heard these things, they were baptized in the name of the Lord Jesus. And when Paul had imposed his hands on them, the Holy Spirit came upon them and they spoke with tongues and prophesied. And all the men were about twelve.' [47] And in the same book, Christ says to Ananias, 'Arise, and go into the street that is called Strait, and seek in the house of Judas one named Saul of Tarsus. For behold he prayeth. (And he saw a man named Ananias coming in, and putting hands upon him, that he might receive his sight),' and so forth. 'And Ananias went his way, and entered into the house. And laying his hands upon him, he said, "Brother Saul, the Lord Jesus hath sent me, He that appeared to thee in the way as thou camest, that thou mayest receive thy sight and be filled with the Holy Spirit." And immediately there fell from his eyes as it were scales and he received his sight, and rising up, he was baptized. And when he had taken meat, he was strengthened.' [48] And again: 'And it happened that the father of

Publius lay sick of a fever and of a bloody flux; to whom Paul entered in, and when he had prayed and laid his hands on him, he healed him.' [49] And to Timothy, the Apostle says, 'For which cause I admonish thee that thou stir up the grace of God which is in thee by the imposition of my hands'; [50] and again, 'Impose not hands lightly upon any man, neither be partaker of other men's sins.' [51] And to the Hebrews, the same Apostle speaks 'of the doctrine of baptisms and imposition of hands.' [52]

"And of this baptism the Blessed Peter, we believe, says in the first Epistle: 'In the days of Noah, when the ark was a building, wherein a few, that is, eight souls, were saved by water. Whereunto baptism being of the like form now saveth you also, not the putting away of the filth of the flesh but the examination of a good conscience toward God by the resurrection of Jesus Christ.' [53] But this ought to be pondered to some extent, because those who were saved in Noah's ark, according to the story in the Old Testament, had not really been saved, as it seems, because it is found that Noah, with his sons, wives, and the living things, went out from the ark of his God and planted a vineyard, drank wine, and was made drunk, fell down, and showed his shame. He cursed his son, Canaan, saying, 'Cursed be Canaan; a servant of servants he shall be unto his brethren' [54]—he who was one of those saved from the ark. It is also found in the Old Testament that those who went out from that ark and their descendants committed many and most shameful misdeeds, and afterward they endured great want and severe hardships, with the result that they killed each other. Therefore, we believe that the Blessed Peter spoke not of that Noah of the Old Testament nor of that ark, but spoke of the ark of the testament which the Lord made for the salvation of His people of which the Apostle says to the Hebrews: 'By faith Noah, having received an answer concerning those things which as yet were not seen, moved with fear, framed the ark for the saving of his house; by the which he condemned the world and was instituted heir of the justice which is by faith.' [55] And Jesus the son of Sirach says: 'Noah was found perfect and in the time of wrath he was made a reconciliation. Therefore was there a remnant left to the earth when the flood came. The covenants of the world were made with him, that all flesh should no more be destroyed with the flood.' [56] And of this Noah the Blessed Peter spoke in the second Epistle, we believe: 'And spared not the original world, but preserved Noah, the eighth person, the preacher of justice, bringing in the flood upon the world of the ungodly.' [57] What is here expressed is that the Holy Father granted the Law and the Old Testament unto His people. All those who entered into that ark—that is to say, all who have kept to that testament—have been saved. And so, too, will be saved all who enter into the ark of the New Testament and remain therein.

With regard to this, well could the Blessed Peter say, 'Whereunto baptism being of the like form now saveth you,' [58] as though he were saying: Just as those had been saved through that dispensation *(ordinamentum)*, even so through the baptism of Jesus Christ, Christians are saved by a like form. With this agrees what the prophet David says, 'For God is our [king] before ages; he hath wrought salvation in the midst of the earth.' [59] And Jeremiah says, 'The harvest is past, the summer is ended, and we are not saved.' [60] And of Christ the Apostle says to the Hebrews: 'For it became Him for whom are all things and by whom are all things, who had brought many children into glory, to perfect the author of their salvation by His passion.' [61] And [the Blessed Peter says]: 'Not the putting away of the filth of the flesh saves us, but the examination of a good conscience toward God,' [62] as though he were saying: Without this baptism we cannot be saved through the works of the Church, that is, without the examination of a good conscience which is made toward God by the ministers of Christ. So the Apostle says, in the first Epistle to the Corinthians: 'And I show unto you yet a more excellent way. If I speak with the tongues of men and of angels, and have not charity, I am become as sounding brass or a tinkling cymbal. And if I should have prophecy and should know all mysteries and all knowledge, and if I should have all faith so that I could remove mountains, and have not charity, I am nothing. And if I should distribute all my goods to feed the poor, and if I should deliver my body to be burned, and have not charity, it profiteth me nothing.' [63] This means [that nothing avails] without this baptism of the spirit of charity. True Christians, then, taught by the primitive Church, actually perform this ministry of the imposition of hands without which, we believe, no one can be saved."

On Reception of the Spiritual Baptism.—"Accordingly, you must understand that this is the reason for your presence here before the Church of Jesus Christ: It is the occasion of your receiving this holy baptism of the imposition of hands and receiving pardon for your sins by the examination of a good conscience which is made toward God by good Christians. Therefore, you should know that even as you are in the temporal sense in the presence of the Church of God, where spiritually dwell the Father, the Son, and the Holy Spirit, so spiritually you should be with your soul in the presence of God, of Christ, and of the Holy Spirit, prepared to receive this holy consecration of Jesus Christ. And even as you took into your hands the Book, in which are written the commandments, the precepts, and the admonitions of Christ, so, spiritually, you must admit the law of Christ into the works of your soul, to keep it throughout your whole lifetime, as is written: 'Thou shalt love the Lord thy God with thy whole heart and with thy whole soul and with all thy strength, and with all thy mind, and thy neighbor as thyself.' [64]

"Consequently, you must understand how necessary it is that you love God in truth, in kindliness, in humility, in mercy, in chastity, and in other exemplary virtues, since it is written: 'Chastity makes a man near to God; in like manner, however, corruption draws him away'; and again, 'Chastity and virginity bringeth near to the angels.' [65] And Solomon says, 'Incorruption bringeth near to God.' [66]

"Also, you must understand how necessary it is that you be faithful and lawful in things of the world [67] and in things of the spirit, for if you have not been faithful in worldly things we do not believe that you can be faithful in things spiritual, nor do we believe that you can attain salvation, for the Apostle says, 'Nor thieves shall possess the kingdom of God.' [68] Then, too, you must make this commitment and promise to God: that you will never commit murder, adultery, or theft, open or secret, nor will you, of your own will, on any occasion, not even in matters of life and death, take an oath. For David says, 'I will pay my vows to the Lord before all his people. Precious in the sight of the Lord is the death of his saints.' [69] Moreover, you will make this commitment to God: that you will never, knowingly or of your own will, eat cheese, milk, the flesh of birds, of creeping things, or of animals, prohibited by the Church of God.

"Also, through the righteousness of Christ, it behooves you to endure hunger, thirst, dissension, persecution, and death; all these will you endure for the love of God and for your salvation.

"Also [you must promise] that you will, to the best of your ability, be obedient to God and to the Church, at the will of God and his Church, and that you will never put aside this gift [of spiritual baptism]—if the Lord shall grant unto you the grace to receive it—because of anything that may befall you, for the Apostle says to the Hebrews, 'We are not the children of withdrawing unto perdition, but of faith to the saving of the soul.' [70] And again, in his second Epistle to Timothy, he says, 'No man being a soldier to God entangleth himself with secular businesses, that he may please Him to whom he hath engaged himself.' [71] And in the Gospel of Luke [Christ] says, 'No man putting his hand to the plough and looking back is fit for the kingdom of God.' [72] And Jesus the son of Sirach says: 'He that washeth himself after touching the dead, if he toucheth him again, what doth his washing avail? So a man that fasteth for his sins and doth the same again, what doth his humbling himself profit him? Who will hear his prayer?' [73] And the Blessed Peter says in his second Epistle: 'For if, flying from the pollutions of the world through the knowledge of our Lord and Savior Jesus Christ, they be again entangled in them and overcome, their latter state is become unto them worse than their former. For it had been better for them not to have known the way of justice than, after they have known it, to turn back from that holy commandment which was delivered to them. For that of the true proverb has happened to them: The dog is returned to his vomit, and the sow that was washed to her wallowing in the mire.' [74]

"From this you must understand that if you shall receive this gift of God, it behooves you to hold it in purity of heart and mind throughout your whole lifetime.

"Also, let no one conclude that through this baptism, which you receive in understanding, you disdain the other baptism—either Christian observance or any good thing which you have done or said up to the present moment; on the other hand, you must understand that it is fitting for you to receive this holy consecration of Christ as a supplement to that which was insufficient for your salvation.[75]

"Now may the true Lord God grant you grace to receive this good, to His honor and your salvation. Have mercy upon us."

On the Ceremony of the Consolamentum.—Then let the prior take the Book from the hands of the believer and say: "John" (if he be so named), "is it your will to receive this holy baptism of Jesus Christ as it has been explained and to hold it in purity of heart and mind throughout your whole lifetime and not to fail in it for any reason?"

And let John answer: "Yes, it is. Pray to the good Lord for me, to give me His grace."

And let the prior say, "May the true Lord God grant you the grace to receive this gift, to His honor and to your good."

Then let the believer stand, make an obeisance before the prior, and let him repeat the words of the elder who stands beside the prior, saying: "I come to God, to you, to the Church, and to your holy order to receive pardon and mercy for all my sins which were committed or given effect in me at any time up to this moment. Pray to God for me that He forgive me. Bless us; have mercy upon us."

Then let the prior answer: "From God, from us, from the Church, from its holy order, and from its holy commandments and disciples, may you receive pardon and mercy for all the sins committed or given effect in you at any time up to this moment. May the Lord God of mercy forgive you and lead you to eternal life."

And let the believer say, "Amen. Let it be done unto us, Lord, according to Thy word."

Then let the believer, rising, place his hands on the table which stands before the prior, and let the prior hold the Book upon the believer's head, and let all the other consecrated persons and Christians who are present place their right hands upon him. And let the prior say, "In the name of the Father, and of the Son, and of the Holy Spirit."

And let him who is beside the prior say "Amen," and let all the others repeat it aloud.

Then let the prior say: "Bless us; have mercy upon us. Let it be done unto us, Lord, according to Thy word. May the Father, the Son, and the Holy Spirit forgive you and have mercy on all your sins. Let us adore the Father, the Son, and the Holy Spirit. Let us adore the Father, the Son, and the Holy Spirit. Let us adore the Father, the Son, and the Holy Spirit. Holy Father, just, true, and merciful, forgive Thy servant, receive him into Thy righteousness. 'Our Father who art in heaven, hallowed be Thy name,' " and so on. Let him repeat the Lord's Prayer five times aloud and then "Let us adore," thrice. And afterward, let him say the Lord's Prayer once and then "Let us adore the Father, the Son, and the Holy Spirit" thrice. And then, "In the beginning was the Word," [76] and so on. When the Gospel has been read, let him thrice say "Let us adore the Father, the Son, and the Holy Spirit" and then one prayer. Then let him say "Let us adore" thrice and proceed to the Grace.[77]

And let the Christian kiss the Book and thereafter make three obeisances, saying: "Bless us, bless us, bless us; have mercy upon us. May God render you rich reward for this good thing which you have done unto me for the love of God."

Then let the consecrated persons, the Christian men and women, receive the Service, as is the usage of the Church.

Let all good Christians pray to God on behalf of him who wrote these instructions. Amen. Thanks be to God.

B. THE RITUAL TRANSLATED FROM THE PROVENÇAL TEXT

circa 1250-1280

[Phrases for Worship] [1]

Bless us; have mercy upon us. Amen. Let it be done unto us according to Thy word. May the Father, the Son, and the Holy Spirit forgive all your sins. Let us adore the Father, the Son, and the Holy Spirit. (*Three times.*)

Our Father, who art in heaven, hallowed be Thy name. Thy kingdom come, Thy will be done, on earth as it is in heaven. Give us this day our supersubstantial bread; and forgive us our debts, as we forgive our debtors; and lead us not into temptation. But deliver us from evil.[2] For Thine is the kingdom and the power and the glory, forever and ever. Amen.[3]

Let us adore the Father, the Son, and the Holy Spirit. (*Three times.*) May the grace of our Lord Jesus Christ be with you all. Bless us; have mercy upon us. Let it be done unto us according to Thy word. May the Father, the Son, and the Holy Spirit forgive you all your sins.

"In the beginning was the Word, and the Word was with God, and the Word was God. The same was in the beginning with God. All things were made by Him, and without Him was made nothing. What was made in Him was life, and the life was the light of men. And the light shineth in darkness, and the darkness did not comprehend it. There was a man sent from God, whose name was John. This man came for a witness, to give testimony of the light, that all men might believe through him. He was not the light, but was to give testimony of the light. That was the true light, which enlighteneth every man that cometh into this world. He was in the world, and the world was made by Him, and the world knew Him not. He came unto His own, and His own received him not. But as many as received Him, He gave them power to be made the sons of God, to them that believe in His name; who are born not of blood nor of the will of the flesh nor of the will of man, but of God. And the Word was made flesh and dwelt among us; and we saw His glory, the glory as it were of the only begotten of the Father, full of grace and truth. John beareth witness of Him, and crieth out, saying, "This was He of whom I spoke. He that shall come after me is preferred before me, because He was before me. And of His fullness we all have received, and grace for grace. For the law was given by Moses; grace and truth came by Jesus Christ." [4]

[The Service]

We have come before God and before you and before the order of the Holy Church to receive the Service, pardon and penance for all our sins which we have committed in speech or thought, or effected from our birth to this moment. We ask mercy of God and of you, that you pray for us to the Holy Father of mercy to pardon us.

Let us adore God and acknowledge all our sins and our many grave offenses toward the Father, the Son, and the honored Holy Spirit, the honored Holy Gospels, and the honored holy apostles; by prayer and faith and by the salvation of all righteous, glorious Christians, and of blessed ancestors at rest, and of brothers here present, and we do so before Thee, Holy Lord, in order that Thou may forgive us for all wherein we have sinned. *Bless us; have mercy upon us.*[5]

For many are our sins wherein we offend every day, night and day, in word, in deed, and by thought, voluntarily and involuntarily, and more by our will which evil spirits arouse in us, in the flesh in which we are clothed. *Bless us; have mercy upon us.*

But, whereas the holy word of God teaches us, in the same way that the holy apostles and our spiritual brothers declare unto us, that we should put aside every desire of the flesh and every impurity, and that we should do the will of God by accomplishing perfect good, yet we, lax servants, not only do not the will of God as is fitting but more often we fulfill the desires of the flesh and the concerns of the world, thus doing harm to our souls. *Bless us; have mercy upon us.*

We go among worldly people, we mingle, talk, and eat with them, and thus we sin in many things so that we harm our brothers and our souls. *Bless us; have mercy upon us.*

With our tongues we fall into idle words, into vain conversations, into laughter, into mockeries and malicious acts, into detraction of brothers and sisters whom we are unworthy to judge, nor are we worthy to condemn their offenses. Among Christians we are sinners. *Bless us; have mercy upon us.*

The Service which we have received we have not kept as we should, neither the fast nor the Prayer. We have transgressed our days, we have betrayed our hours.[6] While we are at holy prayer our minds turn away to carnal desires, to worldly concerns, wherefore in that hour we scarcely know what thing we offer to the Father of the Just. *Bless us; have mercy upon us.*

O thou Holy and Good Lord, we confess to Thee all those things which have befallen us, in our senses and in our thought, and all the multitude of our sins we place on the mercy of God and on the Holy Prayer and on the Holy Gospel, for many are our sins. *Bless us; have mercy upon us.*

O Lord, judge and condemn the imperfections of the flesh. Have no pity on the flesh, born of corruption, but show mercy to the spirit which is imprisoned. Direct for us the days, the hours, and the obeisances,[7] the fasts, the prayers, and the preachings, as is the custom of Good Christians, that we be not judged or condemned among felons at the Day of Judgment. *Bless us; have mercy upon us.*

[The Ministration of the Prayer]

If a believer is in abstinence and if the Christians are agreed to administer the Prayer to him, let them wash their hands, and the believers likewise, if there be any. Then let one of the Good Men, he who stands next to the elder (*ancia*), make three obeisances to the elder. Then let him prepare a table, making three obeisances thereafter. And let him put a cloth on the table and make three more obeisances. And let him put the Book on the cloth. Then let him say, *Bless us; have mercy upon us.* And let the believer make his melioramentum and take the Book from the hand of the elder. And the elder should exhort him and preach to him with suitable scriptural verses. And if the believer is named Peter, let him speak to him thus:

"Peter, you must understand that when you are before the Church of

God you are in the presence of the Father, the Son, and the Holy Spirit. For the Church signifies a gathering together, and where there are true Christians, there are the Father, the Son, and the Holy Spirit, as the divine Scriptures attest. For Christ has said in the Gospel of St. Matthew: 'Where there are two or three gathered together in my name, there am I in the midst of them'; [8] and in the Gospel of St. John, He says, 'If anyone love me, he will keep my word, and my Father will love him, and we will come to him and will make our abode with him.' [9] And St. Paul says in the second Epistle to the Corinthians: 'You are the temple of the living God; as God saith through Isaiah, "I will dwell in them, and walk among them, and I will be their God, and they shall be my people." Wherefore, "Go out from among them, and be ye separate," saith the Lord, "and touch not the unclean thing; and I will receive you, and I will be a Father to you, and you shall be my sons and daughters, saith the Lord Almighty."' [10] And in another place, he [Paul] says, 'Do you seek a proof of Christ that speaketh in me?' [11] And in the first Epistle to Timothy, he says: 'These things I write to thee, hoping that I shall come to thee shortly but, if I tarry long, that thou mayest know how thou oughtest to behave thyself in the house of God, which is the church of the living God, the pillar and ground of the truth.' [12] And the same Apostle says to the Hebrews, 'But Christ is as the Son in his own house, which house are we.' [13]

"Let the Spirit of God be with the faithful of Jesus Christ. Christ so declares in the Gospel of St. John: 'If you love me, keep my commandments. And I will ask the Father, and He shall give you another Paraclete, that He may abide with you forever, the spirit of truth, whom the world cannot receive, because it seeth Him not nor knoweth Him; but you shall know Him, because He shall abide with you and shall be in you. I will not leave you orphans; I will come to you.' [14] And in the Gospel of St. Matthew, He says, 'Behold, I am with you all days, even to the consummation of the world.' [15] And St. Paul says in the first Epistle to the Corinthians: 'Know you not that you are the temple of God and that the Spirit of God dwelleth in you? But if any man violate the temple of God, him shall God destroy. For the temple of God is holy, which you are.' [16] So also Christ explains in the Gospel of St. Matthew, 'For it is not you that speak, but the Spirit of your Father that speaketh in you.' [17] And St. John in his Epistle says, 'In this we know that we abide in Him and He in us, because He hath given us of his spirit.' [18] And St. Paul says to the Galatians, 'Because you are sons of God, God hath sent the Spirit of His Son into your hearts crying, "Aba! Father!" ' [19]

"Thus it must be understood that the presentation which you make before the sons of Jesus Christ confirms the faith and preaching of the Church of God as Holy Scriptures give us to understand it. For the people of God departed in former times from their Lord God. They departed from the counsel and will of their Holy Father, as a result of the deception of evil spirits and submission to them. For these and many other reasons, is understanding given that the Holy Father desires to have compassion on His people and to receive them into His peace and concord through the advent of His Son, Jesus Christ.

"Hence, this is the occasion of your presence here before the disciples of Jesus Christ,[20] where spiritually dwell the Father, the Son, and the Holy Spirit, as was previously disclosed: that you may receive this holy prayer which the Lord Jesus Christ gave unto His disciples, so that your supplications and your prayers may be heard by our Holy Father. This is the reason why you must understand, if you would receive this holy prayer, that it is needful for you to repent of all your sins and to forgive all men. For our Lord Jesus Christ says, 'If you will not forgive men their sins, neither will your Father forgive your offenses.' [21]

"Furthermore, it behooves you to resolve in your heart that, if God grants you the grace to receive it, you will keep this holy prayer throughout your whole lifetime, according to the usage of the Church of God, in chastity, in truth, and in all the other good virtues which God shall deign to grant unto you. Wherefore we pray the good Lord, Who granted unto the disciples of Jesus Christ the power to receive this holy prayer with steadfastness, that He grant unto you also the grace to receive it with steadfastness, to His honor and your salvation. *Have* you must do penance therefor."

And let the believer say: "I receive it from God, from you, and from

And then let the elder say: "This holy prayer we deliver unto you, that you may receive it from God, from us, and from the Church, and that you may have the power to say it throughout your whole lifetime, by day and by night, alone and in company, and that you may never eat or drink without first saying this prayer. And if you should fail therein, you must do penance therefor.'"

And let the believer say: 'I receive it from God, from you, and from the Church." Then let him make his melioramentum and give thanks. And then let the Christians complete a Double with obeisances, and let the believer do the same.

[*The Ministration of the Consolamentum*]

If he is to receive the consolamentum forthwith, let him perform his melioramentum and take the Book from the hand of the elder. And let the elder exhort him and preach to him with suitable scriptural verses and in such words as are proper for the consolamentum. Let him speak thus:

"Peter, you wish to receive the spiritual baptism by which the Holy Spirit is given in the Church of God, together with the Holy Prayer and the imposition of hands by Good Men. Of this baptism our Lord Jesus Christ says in the Gospel of St. Matthew to His disciples: 'Going therefore, teach ye all nations, baptizing them in the name of the Father, and of the Son, and of the Holy Spirit, teaching them to observe all things whatsoever I have commanded you; and behold, I am with you all days, even to the consummation of the world.' [22] And in the Gospel of St. Mark, He says: 'Go ye into the whole world and preach the gospel to every creature. He that believeth and is baptized shall be saved; but he that believeth not shall be condemned.' [23] And in the Gospel of St. John, He says to Nicodemus: 'Amen, amen, I say to thee, unless a man be born again of water and the Holy Spirit, he cannot enter into the kingdom of God.' [24] And John the Baptist spoke of this baptism when he said, 'I baptize with water but He that shall come after me is mightier than I, the latchet of whose shoe I am not worthy to loose. He shall baptize you in the Holy Spirit and fire.' [25] And Jesus says in the Acts of the Apostles, 'For John indeed baptized with water, but you shall be baptized with the Holy Spirit.' [26]

"This holy baptism with the imposition of hands was instituted by Jesus Christ, according to that which St. Luke recounts, and He says that His friends shall perform it, as St. Mark relates, 'They shall lay their hands upon the sick and they shall recover.' [27] Ananias administered this baptism to St. Paul when the latter was converted and afterward Paul and Barnabas administered it in many places. And St. Peter and St. John administered it to the Samaritans, as St. Luke tells in the Acts of the Apostles: 'Now when the apostles, who were in Jerusalem, had heard that Samaria had received the word of God, they sent unto them Peter and John, who, when they were come, prayed for them, that they might receive the Holy Spirit. For He was not as yet come upon any of them. Then they laid their hands upon them and they received the Holy Spirit.' [28] This holy baptism, by which the Holy Spirit is given, the Church of God has preserved from the apostles until this time and it has passed from Good Men to Good Men until the present moment, and it will continue to do so until the end of the world.

"And you must understand that power is given to the Church of God to bind and to loose, to pardon sins and to retain them, as Christ says in the Gospel of St. John: ' "As the Father hath sent me, I also send you." When he had said this, he breathed on them, and he said to them, "Receive ye the Holy Spirit. Whose sins you shall forgive, they are forgiven them; and whose sins you shall retain, they are retained." ' [29] And in the Gospel of St. Matthew, He says to Simon Peter: 'And I say to thee, that thou art Peter, and upon this rock I will build my church, and the gates of hell shall not prevail against it. And I will give to thee the keys of the kingdom of heaven, and whatsoever thou shalt bind upon earth, it shall be bound also in heaven; and whatsoever thou shalt loose on earth, it shall be loosed also in heaven.' [30]And 'Again I say to you, that if two of you shall consent upon earth concerning anything whatsoever they shall ask, it shall be done to them by my Father who is in heaven. For where there are two or three gathered together in my name, there am I in the midst of them.' [31] And in another place He says, 'Heal the sick, raise the dead, cleanse the lepers, cast out devils.' [32] And in the Gospel of St. John, He says, 'He that believeth in me, the works that I do he also shall do.' [33] And in the Gospel of St. Mark, He says: 'These signs shall follow them that believe: In my name they shall cast out devils; they shall speak with new tongues; they shall take up serpents; and if they shall drink any deadly thing, it shall not hurt them; they shall lay their hands upon the sick, and they shall recover.' [34] And in the Gospel of St. Luke, He says, 'Behold, I have given you power to tread upon serpents and scorpions and upon all the power of the enemy; and nothing shall hurt you.' [35]

"And if you have the will to receive this strength and power, you must keep all the commandments of Christ and of the New Testament to the utmost of your ability. Know that He has commanded that a man should not commit adultery, or kill, or lie; should swear no oath, nor pilfer or steal; he should not do to others that which he would not wish done to himself; he should forgive one who does evil to him and love his enemies; he should bless and pray for those who persecute and calumniate him; and if anyone strike him on one cheek, he should offer the other to him also; if anyone take away his coat (*la gonela*), he should let go unto him also his cloak; he should judge not nor condemn.[36] And with these are many other commandments which are laid down for His Church by the Lord.

"And likewise, you must hate this world and its works and the things which are of this world. For St. John says in his Epistle: 'Dearly beloved, love not the world, nor the things which are in the world. If any man love the world, the charity of the Father is not in him. For all that is in the world is the concupiscence of the flesh, and the concupiscence of the eyes, and the pride of life, which is not of the Father, but is of the world. And the world passeth away, and the concupiscence thereof; but he that doth the will of God abideth forever.' [37] And Christ says to the nations: 'The world cannot hate you, but me it hateth because I give testimony of it, that the works thereof are evil.'[38] And in the book of Solomon is it written, 'I have seen all the things which are done under the sun; and they are all vanities and torments of the spirit.' [39] And Jude the brother of James, says for our instruction in his Epistle, 'Hating also the spotted garment which is carnal.' [40] Heeding these scriptural verses and many others, you must keep the commandments of God and hate this world. And if you do well to the end, we have hope that your soul will have eternal life."

And let the believer say: "I have this will. Pray God for me to give me His strength."

Then let one of the Good Men make his melioramentum with the believer before the elder and say: "*Have mercy upon us.* Good Christians, we pray you for the love of God to grant this good which God has given you unto this our friend."

Then let the believer make his melioramentum and say: "*Have mercy upon us.* For all the sins which I have done, in word, thought, or deed, I ask forgiveness from God, from the Church, and from you all."

Let the Christians say: "May they be forgiven you by God, by us, and by the Church; we pray God to forgive you."

And then let them give him the consolamentum. Let the elder take the Book and place it on the believer's head, and the other Good Men place each his right hand on him. Then let them say the Pardon[41] and the *Let us adore* [42] thrice, and then, *Holy Father, receive Thy servant in Thy righteousness and bestow Thy grace and Thy Holy Spirit upon him.*

Then let them pray to God with the Prayer and let him who conducts the service say the Six [43] in a low voice. When the Six is finished, let him say *Let us adore* thrice, the Prayer once in full voice, and then the Gospel. When the Gospel has been read, let them say *Let us adore* thrice, the Grace, and the Pardon. Then they should perform the Act of Peace [44] with each other and with the Book. If there be believers present, let them perform the Act of Peace also. Let women believers, if there are any present, perform the Act of Peace with the Book and with each other. And then let them pray to God with a Double,[45] with obeisances. And thus they will have administered [the consolamentum].[46]

[Rules of Conduct for Various Occasions]

The office of leading a Double or of saying the Prayer should not be confided to a layman.

If Christians go into a dangerous place, let them pray to God using the Grace. And if one of them travels on horseback, let him say a Double. He should say the Prayer when embarking in a boat, when entering a town, or when crossing a stream by a plank or a dangerous bridge. When Christians encounter a man with whom they must have speech while they are praying to God, if they have [said] eight prayers, these can be counted as a Single; [47] if they have finished sixteen, they can be accounted the Double. If they find some personal belonging along the road, let them not touch it unless they know that they can return it. If they see that persons to whom the object may be returned have passed that way ahead of them, let them take it to return it if they can. If this is not possible, they should put it back in the place where it was found. If they happen upon an animal or a bird in a trap, let them not trouble themselves about it. And if a Christian wants to drink during the day, he should have prayed to God twice or more after eating. And if Christians drink after the evening Double, let them perform another Double. And if there are any believers present, they should stand while the Christians say the Prayer before drinking. And if a Christian man prays to God with Christian women, let him always lead in the Prayer. And if there is with the Christian women a believer to whom the Prayer has been administered, let him go apart and say it by himself.

[*The Ministration of the Consolamentum to the Sick*]

If Christians to whom the ministry of the Church is entrusted receive a message from a believer who is sick, they should visit him and inquire privately how he has borne himself toward the Church since he received the faith; whether he is in any way in debt to the Church or has done it any injury. If he owes it any debt and can pay, he should do so. If he is unwilling to do this, let him not be received. For if one prays to God on behalf of a lawbreaker or a dishonest man, the prayer can be of no avail. But he should not be turned away if he is unable to pay.

And the Christians should explain the abstinence and usages of the Church and ask whether, provided he is received, he is willing to observe them. This he should not promise unless he has the firmest intention of doing so. For St. John says that the portion of liars shall be in a pool of fire and brimstone.[48] And if he says that he feels himself strong enough to endure all that abstinence, and if the Christians are agreed to receive him, they shall impose abstinence on him as follows: They shall ask him if he intends to refrain from lies and oaths and from transgressing the other prohibitions of God, [if he] intends to hold to the usages of the Church and the commandments of God and to keep his body and his goods—all that he now has and all that he may acquire —at the disposal of God, of the Church, and at the service of Christian men and women, from this time on and forever, to the utmost of his ability. And if he says "Yes," let them reply: "We impose this abstinence upon you so that you may receive it from God, from us, and from the Church, and so that you may observe it as long as you live. For if you observe it well, together with your other obligations, we have hope that your soul will have life." And he should say, "I receive it from God, from you, and from the Church."

Then they should ask him if he wishes to receive the Prayer. If he says "Yes," let them clothe him in shirt and breeches, if this is possible, and let them have him sit up, if he can raise his hands.[49] And let them put a tablecloth or other cloth on the bed in front of him, and put the Book thereon, saying *Bless us* once, and *Let us adore the Father, the Son, and the Holy Spirit* three times. And he should take the Book from the hand of the elder. And then, if the sick man is able to endure it, he who is conducting the administration should exhort him and preach to him with suitable scriptural texts. Then he should ask him, in regard to his covenant (*de la covenesa*) with them, whether his heart is fixed on holding to it and keeping it, as he has agreed. And if the answer is "Yes," let them have him confirm it. Then they should minister the Prayer unto him and he should heed it carefully. And then let the elder say to him: "This is the Prayer which Jesus Christ brought into this world, Who taught it to the Good Men. You must never eat or drink anything without first repeating this prayer. And if you should do so through negligence, you must undergo penance therefor." He should reply, "I receive it from God, from you, and from the Church." And then let them give him the greeting used for women.[50] And then they should pray to God in a Double with obeisances, and again put the Book before him. And he should say thrice *Let us adore the Father, the Son, and the Holy Spirit.*

Then let him take the Book from the hand of the elder, who should exhort him with scriptural texts and words such as are proper for the consolamentum. And then the elder should ask if he has it in his heart to keep and honor the covenant as he has agreed, and let them have him confirm it.

Then the elder should take up the Book, and the sick man should bow his head and say: "*Have mercy on us.* For all my sins of word or thought or deed I ask pardon from God, from the Church, and from you all." And the Christians should answer, "May you have pardon from God, from us, and from the Church; and we pray to God to pardon you." And then let them console him by placing their hands and the Book on his head, saying: *Bless us; have mercy upon us. Amen. Let it be done to us according to Thy word. May the Father, the Son, and the Holy Spirit have mercy on you for all your sins. Let us adore the Father, the Son, and the Holy Spirit* (saying this last three times). And then *Holy Father, receive Thy servant in Thy justice and send Thy grace and Thy Holy Spirit upon him;* or, if it is a woman, they should say *Holy Father, receive Thy handmaiden in Thy justice and send Thy grace and Thy Holy Spirit upon her.* And then let them pray to God with the Prayer and say the Six in a low voice, and, when the Six is finished, they should say three times *Let us adore the Father, the Son, and the Holy Spirit,* and the Prayer once in full voice, and then the Gospel. When the Gospel has been read, they should say three times *Let us adore the Father, the Son, and the Holy Spirit,* and the Prayer once in full voice. And then let them give him the greeting used for a man.[51] And then they should perform the Act of Peace among themselves and with the Book. And if there are believers, men or women, present, let them perform the Act of Peace. And then the Christians should ask for salvation and grant it.

And if the sick person dies, leaving them anything, or if he should give them anything, they must not keep it for themselves or take possession of it, but should put it at the disposal of the order. However, if the sick person lives, the Christians should present him to the order and pray that he receive the consolamentum again as soon as he can.[52] And let him do as he wishes.

58. A "Manichaean" Treatise

We translate here portions of a treatise by an Albigensian heretic. Though the rest of the treatise is lost, these portions survived because Durand of Huesca, the founder of the Poor Catholics and an enemy of the Cathars, copied them into his *Liber contra manicheos* [1] in order to refute the errors they contained. What part of the heretical work these nineteen excerpts comprised cannot be estimated.[2] The heretic, who gave no name to his sect, expressed the views of the Albigenses in the dioceses of Albi, Toulouse, and Carcassonne, according to Durand of Huesca,[3] who had no doubt that the author and his fellows were modern devotees of ancient errors; "Manichaeans, that is, modern Cathars," he calls them,[4] and labels the work before him a Manichaean treatise.[5] Some of the qualities of the anonymous heretic appear from his work: He had considerable biblical learning as well as skill in controversy on religious themes,[6] and he presents himself as spokesman for a group.[7] The names of two persons who might have written the treatise have been suggested.[8] One possibility is William, the canon of Nevers who fled in 1201 from the threat of prosecution as a heretic and became a spokesman, under the name of Theodoric,[9] for the Albigenses. Or the author might have been Bartholomew of Carcassonne, who in 1223 was accused by a papal legate in Languedoc of being the agent of a heretical "pope" seated in the Balkans.[10] Since the *Liber contra manicheos* was composed about 1222-1223, the heretical work from which it quotes probably was written about 1218-1222.[11]

The Catharist treatise was composed not as a polemic but as a statement of faith, adroitly supported by scriptural quotations,[12] which was perhaps intended to gain converts.[13] Its tenets are those of absolute dualism; on the whole, they accord with the beliefs of the Albanenses of Italy at that time.[14] More than casual reading is needed, however, to discern the particular heretical tenets which the author believes are implicit in the passages he selects from the Scriptures.[15] The major theme is the existence of two creations, good and evil, coeternal and entirely separate. The present material and visible world and its creatures are in no way the work of God the Father, but are the domain of Satan, who is the essence of sin; here angelic beings are imprisoned as a result of an invasion of heaven. To save the lost souls, Christ, the Son of God, became incarnate, not in this world but in a celestial realm of his own, to which God's people will be drawn when they are freed from the power of the enemy.[16]

The first chapter is, surprisingly, a profession of monotheism,[17] but this is subsequently qualified: God is Father and Creator of all, but "all" means what is spiritual and invisible. The word "all" must be understood to convey different meanings at different times: It may refer to the work of the good God, or to all that is evil and the work of Satan (chap. XII). Similarly, the word "nothing" reveals the difference between the two creations. The creation of Satan is nothing, nonbeing, for it is entirely without charity, which is the essence of good (chap. XIII).[18]

The truth, unperceived by some persons, the author states in chapter II, is that in addition to this wicked present world with its vain and corruptible creatures there is another world, eternal, invisible, incorruptible. Inhabitants of the present world walk in sin, unaware of God's wisdom (chap. III). They are enemies of God, steeped in their lusts, and cannot be the kingdom of Christ, who himself so testified. What is wicked cannot be the creation of God, and what is not of God is not of Christ (chap. IV). In contrast to the wicked world, Christ's kingdom is an everlasting one, established on the throne of David in the home of Jacob. Flesh and blood have no part therein, nor do sinners. It was granted by God to Christ, his son and high priest and inheritor (chap. V). The good creation comprises "a new heaven and a new earth," in which are found the holy Jerusalem, the tree of life and the river of life, and the angelic court of the Father (chap. VI). In God's creation, those things which are of Christ, into which he came, include his mother and the people of God. There only, not in this evil creation, did he become incarnate (chap. VII).

But into God's creation and among the people of God the devil came like an enemy to sow weeds in the field (chap. VIII). We are not told explicitly what occurred, but are probably justified in assuming that behind these words lies the story of the Satanic invasion of heaven and the carrying off of the angels.[19] Thus, in the wicked world, amidst its original inhabitants born of sin and flesh, are now found "the children of the kingdom." At this point the author declares that the children of evil, like the Pharisees whom Christ rebuked, are evil in body and also evil in heart, from which flow their vices. But he speaks also of the spirit, which he says cannot be identified with the inward parts of man. Is not this a reference to the heretical concept of the threefold angelic existence—body, soul, and spirit—of which only the spirit did not come under Satan's power, while body and soul are imprisoned in this wicked world?

However this may be, the present world is a place of darkness and misery (chap. VI). Its days are evil, as the Psalmist, caught in the misery of these days, declares (chap. IX). Its works, which are of darkness and sin, coming from the devil, are vain and corruptible and must pass away (chap. X).

In sharp contrast is the greater and more perfect creation of God, in which are the tabernacle of Christ and the angelic hierarchies. Because it is invisible, it must be apprehended by its works and by faith; its essence and form are spiritual (chaps. II, XIV). The earth in this good creation was given to Christ by God the Father and only in that "land of the living," rich in sapphires and gold, is the inheritance of the meek; only there may be seen the good things of God (chap. XV).

Concurrent with this description of the two realms runs the proof that this present world cannot in any way be part of God's creation. We are commanded in the Gospel not to love the world. This world is material and visible; it is lustful (chap. XIV). It is the strange land in which kings and princes conspire against Christ and thus prove that they are not of God. In its abysses lie Ashur (the devil) and the multitudes of his warriors, who had once spread their terror in the land of the living—here seems to be a reference to Satan's invasition of heaven and his repulse (chap. XVI).

The promise of redemption has been made to those who are good, who are imprisoned in evil and implore the Lord for salvation (chaps. IX, XV). God's creatures will be brought out of the countries of their exile to their own land, the new earth which God gave to Christ (chap. XVI). The means of salvation is Christ, who became incarnate and suffered in the superior realm in order to draw all unto himself. The fate of the present heavens is to disappear in heat and fire on the Day of Judgment,[20] when the day of the Lord will suddenly appear. The "new heavens," however, are said in the Scriptures to have perished or been lost, to grow old and change. It appears that these words refer to the "sheep that are lost of the house of Israel," to whom Christ was sent. They grow old among enemies, but on being regained will be changed into incorruptibility by the right hand of the Most High (chap. XVII). Then the lost sheep, the children of Jerusalem, will be gathered together, and to them, in the joy of their salvation will be restored the crowns of justice which they had lost by their sin (chap. XIX).

After first publishing Durand of Huesca's excerpts from the heretical work, with an exhaustive commentary, Mlle Thouzellier also edited separately Durand's *Liber contra manicheos*, under the title *Une Somme anti-cathare*. Some further details on the beliefs of the Albigenses are given therein. The Cathar treatise has also been translated into French by Jean Duvernoy, in *Cahiers d'études cathares*, 2d ser., XIII (1962), 22-54.

Our translation is made from Christine Thouzellier, *Un Traité cathare inédit du début du XIIIᵉ siècle, d'après le* Liber contra manicheos *de Durand de Huesca* (Bibliothèque de la Revue d'histoire ecclésiastique, XXXVII [Louvain, 1961], pp. 87-113, by permission of Mlle Thouzellier and the publisher, the Bibliothèque de l'Université de Louvain.

1218-1222

A "MANICHAEAN" TREATISE

I. On the Beginning of the Manichaean Treatise [21]

Since certain persons wrongfully reproach us for our beliefs in respect of divine works and creatures, we will confess in words and equally in heart what we do believe in these matters, so that those who in ignorance assail us may, when they are informed, more clearly recognize the truth.

At the outset, then, we absolutely acknowledge the true and highest God, Father Almighty, by whom, as we read and believe, were made "heaven and earth, the sea, and all things that are in them,"[22] a fact which the testimony of the prophets confirms and the words of the New Testament set forth more fully. For God himself speaks through His prophet Isaiah: "I am the first and I am the last. My hand also hath founded the earth and my right hand hath measured the heavens";[23] and again, "Behold, I create a new heaven and a new earth."[24] And the angel in the Apocalypse: "Fear the Lord and give him honor, because the hour of his judgment is come; and adore ye Him that made heaven and earth, the sea and all things that are in them."[25] And again, the four and twenty elders: "Thou art worthy, O Lord, to receive glory and honor and power, because Thou hast created all things, and for Thy will they were and have been created."[26]

Also Paul and Barnabas in the Acts: "Ye men, why do ye these things? We also are mortals, men like unto you, preaching to you to be converted from these vain things to the living and the true God, who made the heaven and the earth, the sea and all things that are in them."[27] Likewise, the other apostles in the same book: "Lord, thou art He that didst make heaven and earth, the sea, and all things that are in them";[28] also Paul in the same book, "God, who made the world and all things therein, He, being Lord of heaven and earth, dwelleth not in temples made with hands."[29] And David: "Blessed be you of the Lord, Who made heaven and earth."[30] And in the Apocalypse: "And to the angel of the church of Laodicea write: These things saith the Amen, the faithful and true witness, who is the beginning of the creation of God."[31]

Therefore, from these words of testimony and very many more, we believe that Almighty God made as well as created[32] the heaven, the earth, the sea, the world, and all things which are in them. And so on. . . .[33]

II. On the Beginning of Their Disclosure and Interpretation

Now, since there are many persons who pay little heed to the other world (*seculo*)[34] and to other created things beyond those visible in this wicked world, which are vain and corruptible, which as surely as they come from nothing shall return to nothing, we say that in truth there exists another world and other, incorruptible and eternal created things and in them rest our faith and hope.[35] For the substance of those things is faith, as the Apostle says to the Hebrews: "Faith is the substance of things to be hoped for, the evidence of things that appear not." [36] And so on. . . .

III. On the Two Worlds (Seculis)

The Son of God also spoke of the two worlds when He said: "The children of this world marry and are given in marriage, but they that shall be accounted worthy of that world and of the resurrection from the dead shall neither be married nor take wives." [37] Of the course of this world, the Apostle says to the Galatians: "Grace be to you, and peace from God the Father and from our own Lord Jesus Christ, who gave himself for our sins, that he might deliver us from this present wicked world";[38] and to the Ephesians, "And you, when you were dead in your offenses and sins, wherein in time past you walked according to the course of this world." [39] And elsewhere, to the Romans: "And be not conformed to this world"; [40] and in another place, in the first Epistle to the Corinthians: "We speak wisdom among the perfect, yet not the wisdom of this world, neither of the princes of this world that come to naught; but we speak the wisdom of God, which none of the princes of this world knew." [41] And so on. . . .

IV. On the Two Worlds (Mundis)

Of the present wicked world, wholly seated in wickedness,[42] James says in his Epistle: "Adulterers, know you not that the friendship of this world is the enemy of God? Whoever, therefore, will be a friend of this world becometh an enemy of God." [43] And Paul: "For the fashion of this world passeth away." [44] And John: "Love not the world, nor the things which are in the world. For all that is in the world is the concupiscence of the flesh," [45] and so on. And Christ: "The prince of this world cometh"; [46] and again, "My kingdom is not of this world"; [47] and in another place, "I pray not for the world"; [48] and elsewhere, "Father, the world hath not known Thee." [49] Again, He says of His own: "They are not of the world, as also I am not of the world"; [50] also, "In the world you shall have distress"; [51] again, "If you had been of the world, the world would love its own"; [52] again, "The world hath hated them." [53] And John [says]:

"Wonder not if the world hate you"; [54] and elsewhere, "Therefore the world knoweth not us, because it knew not Him." [55]

If the whole world is seated in wickedness, and if neither it nor the things which are in it are to be loved, then one cannot believe them to be Christ's possessions, since they are not of the Father; and if they are not of the Father, they are not of Christ. He himself said to the Father, "All my things are thine and thine are mine." [56] Also, if the kingdom of Christ is not of this world, and He does not pray for it, and if the things which are His are not of the world, but rather the world hates them and in it they have distress, and if the world persecutes and strives against them and Christ, then one cannot believe that the world is His, for it knows Him not nor understands Him.

Now, since we know the world to be evil, we will proceed to discuss to the best of our ability, its ages, days and works, its men, the prince and ruling powers, and something of its food and drink. And so on. . . .

V. On the Two Kingdoms

We believe that in that world (*ibi*) is the kingdom of which Christ said, "My kingdom is not of this world," [57] and so on, as we have remarked in the preceding chapter. In truth, Daniel says of His power and His kingdom, "His power is an everlasting power that shall not be taken away; and His kingdom a kingdom that shall not be destroyed." [58] And the angel [announced] to Mary: "Of His kingdom there shall be no end. The Lord God shall give unto Him the throne of David his father, and He shall reign in the house of Jacob forever." [59] And David: "Thy kingdom is a kingdom of all ages." [60] Paul, discussing the resurrection, says: "Now this I say, brethren, that flesh and blood cannot possess the kingdom of God"; [61] and elsewhere, "For know you this, that no fornicator or unclean or covetous person (which is a serving of idols) hath inheritance in the kingdom of Christ and of God." [62] Wherefore, we say that if the present kingdom, whose king we know to be iniquitous, were the kingdom of Christ and of God, never would it have such inhabitants nor would it be destroyed.

Of the other world and its making, in truth, John says in the Apocalypse, "The kingdom of this world is become our God's and His Christ's." [63] Lo, these "voices" [64] and the "world" and the "kingdom" were in heaven. But over against this kingdom, which is celestial, is found another kingdom, that of Satan, of which Christ said, "If Satan

cast out Satan, he is divided against himself; how then shall his kingdom stand?" [65] And those who are children of this kingdom "shall be
cast out into the exterior darkness. There shall be weeping and gnashing
of teeth." [66] And so on. . . .

VI. On the New Heaven and the New Earth

In that world, we believe, there are a new heaven and a new earth, of
which the Lord says to His people in Isaiah: "For as the new heavens
and the new earth which I will make to stand before me, saith the Lord,
so shall your seed stand and your name." [67] And in his Epistle, Peter
says, "We look for new heavens and a new earth, according to His
promises, in which justice dwelleth." [68] And John in the Apocalypse: "I
saw a new heaven and a new earth." [69] Therein are the sun and the moon
of which Isaiah spoke: "Thy sun shall go down no more and thy moon
shall not decrease." [70] And in the Book of Wisdom: "The sun of understanding hath not risen upon us." [71] Therein is the city of which John
speaks in the Apocalypse: "I, John, say the holy city, the new Jerusalem"; [72] of it he said, "The city itself pure gold, like to pure glass." [73] Of
it, also, the Apostle said, "But that Jerusalem which is above is free,
which is our mother." [74] Therein is the tree of life, of which John says
in the Apocalypse, "To him that overcometh, I will give to eat of the tree
of life, which is in the Paradise of my God." [75] Therein is "the river of the
water of life," of which John says in the Apocalypse: "And the angel
showed me a river of water of life, clear as crystal, proceeding from the
throne of God and of the Lamb. In the midst of the street thereof, and on
both sides of the river, was the tree of life, bearing twelve fruits, yielding its fruits every month." [76] Therein is the holy and angelic court of the
Father, of which Daniel speaks: "Thousands of thousands ministered to
him, and ten thousand times a hundred thousand stood before him." [77]

Of the works and the creatures which are there the Apostle says that
"eye hath not seen, nor ear heard, neither hath it entered into the heart
of man, what things God hath prepared for them that love Him." [78] And
so on. . . .

VII. On the Possessions into Which the Word of the Father Came

Many persons insist that this present world is the possession of which
John says, "He came into His own." [79] But John's words in his Epistle—
"Love not the world," [80] and elsewhere, "The whole world is seated in
wickedness" [81]—contradict their assertion. We prove by authentic evi-

dence that "His own" means His mother and the people of God. For the Virgin herself declares that she is His by saying to the angel, "Behold the handmaid of the Lord; be it done to me according to Thy word." [82] And so on. . . .

VIII.   On Sowing the Field; That is, On the Cockle and the Wheat

The devil engendered the children of this world, who are born of the flesh of sin, who are born of blood and of the will of the flesh and of the pleasure of men.[83] Thus, Christ says, "The kingdom of heaven is likened to a man that sowed good seed in his field," [84] and so on. This analogy He explained by saying: "He that soweth the good seed is the Son of man. And the field, indeed, is the world. And the good seed are the children of the kingdom. And the cockle are the children of the wicked one. And the enemy that sowed them is the devil." [85]

But false interpreters declare this field, which the Lord said was His, to be the present world, a statement which seems false to us. For in the world of which the Lord spoke the good were found first, and thereafter the evil. But in the present world, the evil ones were first present, and thereafter the good. And John says in his Epistle, "In this the children of God are manifest, and the children of the devil." [86] Wherein? In that some are good and others are evil. Moreover, the Lord says to the Pharisees in the Gospel: "Now you Pharisees make clean the outside of the cup and of the dish, but your inside is full of rapine and iniquity. Ye fools and blind men, did not He that made that which is without make also that which is within?" [87]

Now we believe that one and the same maker made that which is within and that which is without; but less capable interpreters, indeed, bluster that the words refer alike to the spirit and the flesh, declaring that the spirit is "that which is within," the flesh is "that which is without." And so they say that the Lord attested that He who made the flesh made the spirit also. But it cannot be admitted that Christ spoke thus of the spirit to the Pharisees, who cleansed neither the spirit within nor that which is without. They who adorn the body, cleansing the exterior, cleanse that which is "the outside of the cup and of the dish." They cleanse not "that which is within" who do not purify the heart from filth, of which the Lord says, "From the heart come forth evil thoughts, murders, adulteries, fornications, thefts, false testimonies, blasphemies. These are the things that defile a man." [88] And so on. . . .

IX. On the Good Days and the Evil Ones

We also call the days of this present world evil, in accordance with
the thought of Paul: "See, brethren," he said, "how you walk circumspectly, not as unwise, but as wise, redeeming the time, because the days
are evil"; [89] and again, "that you may be able to resist in the evil day." [90]
And in the Gospel: "Sufficient unto the day is the evil thereof." [91] The
Psalmist says of them, "My days have declined like a shadow." [92] And
Job: "My days have passed more swiftly than the web is cut by the
weaver, and are consumed without any hope." [93] He, who was set
amidst the miseries of the present days, sighed, "Who will grant me that I
might be according to the months past, according to the days in which
God kept me?" [94] Of those days Peter says: "Who will love life and see
good days"; [95] and elsewhere, "One day with the Lord is as a thousand
years, and a thousand years as one day." [96] And so on. . . .

X. On Good Works and Evil Ones

That the works of the world are indeed evil, Christ himself declared
when He said: "The world hateth me because I give testimony of it, that
the works thereof are evil"; [97] and again, "This is the judgment: because
the light is come into the world and men loved darkness rather than
light, for their works were evil. For everyone that doth evil hateth the
light and cometh not to the light" [98]—that is, cometh not to Christ, Who
is the true light—"that his works may not be reproved." [99] And again:
"Whosoever committeth sin is the servant of sin," [100] that is, of the devil,
who is called sin,[101] as the text has it in the Epistle of John: "He that committeth sin is of the devil, for the devil sinned from the beginning"; but
"for this purpose the Son of God appeared, that he might destroy the
works of the devil." [102] Of those works it is written in the Book of Wisdom, "Every work that is corruptible shall fail in the end, and the worker
thereof shall go with it." [103] And the Apostle: "The spirit that now
worketh on the children of unbelief"; [104] and elsewhere, "For such are
deceitful workmen." [105] And Ecclesiastes: "I have seen all things that
are done under the sun and behold, all is vanity and vexation of the
spirit"; [106] and again, "All things are subject to vanity. And all things go
to one place; of earth they were made and into earth they return together." [107]

But of good and eternal works in the Book of Wisdom we read this:
"All the works of the Lord are exceeding good"; [108] and again, "Thou

lovest, O Lord, all things that are, and hatest none of the things which
Thou hast made, for Thou didst not appoint or make anything hating
it"; [109] and again, "He hath made all things good in their time"; [110] and
again, "I have learned that all the works which God hath made continue forever"; [111] and again, "Every excellent work shall be justified,
and the worker thereof shall be honored therein." [112] And the Apostle:
"It is God who worketh in you." [113] And so on. . . .

XI. On Twofold Creation

Now because "creation" is sometimes taken in the sense of a work [114]
let us say something of the good creation and the evil one. About the
evil creation the Apostle spoke thus: "Christ, being come an high priest
of the good things to come, entered by a greater and more perfect tabernacle, not made with hands, that is, not of this creation." [115] And if it is
not of this creation, that is, the present one, then this present creation is
evil and has not the tabernacle which Christ entered, since the tabernacle
which Christ entered must be believed to be good, being of the good
creation. For the Apostle testifies that God, not man, constructed it.

Also, in the Book of Wisdom, with reference to the evil creation it is
said: "Their wives are foolish and their children wicked. Their offspring is
cursed." [116] Christ, indeed, is witness that the heaven and the earth of
the present creation shall pass,[117] that is, shall wholly disappear with all
that is in them, just as the Blessed Apostle Peter says: "For the scoffers
are ignorant that the heavens were before and the earth out of water, and
through water, consisting by the word of God, whereby the world that
then was, being overflowed with water, perished. But the heavens and the
earth which are now, by the same word are kept in store, reserved unto
fire against the Day of Judgment and perdition of the ungodly men," and
so on to the words, "the elements shall be melted with the heat of fire." [118]
Of this earth itself the Apostle says, "But that which bringeth forth thorns
and briers is reprobate, and very near a curse, whose end is to be
burnt." [119] Indeed, it is written in the Book of Wisdom, of the sun which
is in this heaven, "What is brighter than the sun; yet it shall be
eclipsed." [120] And so on. . . .

XII. On [the Word] "All"

But since many persons do not know what the Holy Scriptures mean
by the term "all," we will state that, for the most part, "all" bespeaks
only the good and spiritual things, but sometimes only evil things and

sin.[121] We believe that to the good and to the spiritual refer the words of the Apostle: "Because in Him it hath well pleased the Father that all fullness of the Godhead corporeally should dwell, and through Him all things be reconciled, making peace through the blood of His cross, both as to the things that are in heaven and the things that are on earth." [122]

One cannot believe, however, that all things which are on this earth will be reconciled through Christ in himself, for almost all things here are seen to exist in the greatest discord. Likewise, the Lord applied the term "all" only to the good and spiritual when he said, "And I, if I be lifted up from the earth will draw all things unto myself." [123] For Christ, lifted up from the earth, did not draw unto himself all things which are in this world, in which for the most part are things unclean and absolutely to be shunned or avoided. And He says elsewhere, "All things are delivered to me by my Father." [124] And John in the Gospel: "All things were made by Him, and without Him was made nothing." Indeed, because he said this of what is spiritual and good, John subsequently added: "What was made in Him, was life." [125]

In like manner "all" may be used to refer to evil things and sin, according to the words of the Apostle: "I have suffered the loss of all things and count them but as dung, that I may gain Christ." [126] And Solomon: "Vanity of vanities, and all is vanity"; [127] and again, "I have seen all things that are done under the sun and behold, all is vanity and vexation of spirit"; [128] and again, "All things are subject to vanity. And all things go to one place." [129] Therefore, it may be proved in this way that "all" in the Holy Scriptures is used sometimes to mean eternal things, sometimes temporal things, and on that account the word "all" must be taken in a double sense, in accordance with the text of Wisdom: "All things are double, one against another." [130] And so on. . . .

XIII. On This Word "Nothing"

The Apostle, indeed, explains that what is in the world, that is, of the world, truly should be called "nothing" when he says: "We know that an idol is nothing in the world"; [131] and again, "If I should have prophecy and should know all mysteries, and if I should have all faith so that I could remove mountains, and have not charity, I am nothing." [132] Whence it appears that if the Apostle were nothing without charity, all that is without charity is nothing. Hence, Isaiah also says, "All nations are before Him as if they had no being at all and are counted to Him as nothing and vanity." [133] And the Psalmist: "Thou shalt bring all nations to nothing"; [134] and elsewhere, "In his sight the malignant is brought to nothing." [135] And in Ezechiel it is said to the king of Tyre: "Thou art brought to nothing, and thou shalt never be any more." [136] And Isaiah: "Behold, you are of nothing and your work of that which hath no being; he that hath chosen you is an abomination." [137] And John in the Gospel: "Without Him was made nothing." [138]

If all the evil spirits and evil men and all things that are visible in this world are nothing because they are without charity, therefore they were made without God. Therefore God did not make them, since "without Him was made nothing," and as the Apostle testifies, "If I have not charity, I am nothing." [139]

XIV. On the Good Creation

Of the good creation the Apostle says to the Hebrews, "He that created all things is God." [140] And Solomon: "He that liveth forever created all things together." [141] Also the Apostle to the Colossians: "For in Him were all things created in heaven and on earth, visible and invisible, whether thrones, or dominations, or princes, or powers; all things were created by Him and in Him. And He is before all and by Him all things consist," [142] and so on. There is no doubt at all that this was said of spiritual beings, since the Apostle says "whether thrones," and so on.[143]

But that these may be called both visible and invisible appears from the words of the Apostle himself when he says, "For the invisible things of Him from the creation of the world are clearly seen, being understood by the things that are made, His eternal power also, and divinity." [144] And in the Gospel: "All things were made by Him, and without Him was made nothing." [145] Because John said this with reference to the spiritual and good, he added later: "What was made in Him, was life." [146] Further, Paul says of the good creatures, "For every creature of God is good." [147] If every creature of God is good, and the world, as some persons say, is God's creation, with all that are therein, what reason is there that they should not be loved? For John forbids loving them. If the world ought not to be loved, and if those that are therein ought not to be loved, then it cannot be admitted that they are of God, for everything which is of God is good and therefore to be loved. Is not the present world visible? What else does "world" mean but the heavens, the earth, the air, the sea,

and all things therein? And is not all that is in the world the concupiscence of the flesh and the concupiscence of the eyes? [148] What does the
eye lust after but what it may see? What can be seen but the visible?

O senseless men of learning, who hath bewitched you [149] into incom-
prehension of these things? O full of all guile and of all deceit, children
of the devil, enemies of the cross of Christ and of all justice,[150] why do
you not cease to resist the truth? O blind leaders of the blind,[151] what can
be plainer in Holy Scriptures? But why do I labor longer to reprove you
heretics? Have I not heard that Christ came in judgment so that seeing,
you see not, and hearing, you do not perceive? [152] I have assuredly heard
this and hence I despair of your conversion. And so on. . . .

XV. On the New Earth

But though you are thus blinded and concluded under sin,[153] let those
who do have ears to hear [154] listen to what the Spirit may say of the good
creatures, which certainly are of God, for He says in the Psalms, "The
Lord hath established the world which shall not be moved." [155] Of this
world the Apostle says to the Hebrews that God did not make it subject
to angels but to Christ His Son, "whom He hath appointed heir of all
things, by whom also He made the world."[156] Of the earth in this world
the same Apostle speaks in affirmation of the prophecy of the psalmist
David: "Thou, in the beginning, O Lord, didst found the earth." [157] It
was in that earth that the same prophet, seated in this land of woes and
darkness, hoped to see the good things of the Lord, saying, "I believe to
see the good things of the Lord in the land of the living," [158] thus revealing that the good things of the Lord cannot be fully seen except in the
land of the living. And the same says elsewhere: "I cried to Thee, O
Lord. I said, Thou art my hope, my portion in the land of the living"; [159]
and again, "Thy good spirit shall lead me into the right land"; [160] and
again, "The earth is the Lord's and the fullness thereof; the world and all
that dwell therein." [161]

Now these words do not seem to have been used with reference to the
earth, of which David himself, personifying the people of Israel, says,
"How shall we sing the song of the Lord in a strange land?" [162] nor to a
world in which dwell more evil ones than good, where stand the kings
of the earth and the princes met together "against the Lord and his
Christ," [163] as David prophesied. It is obvious, therefore, that the kings,
princes, Pharisees, and all who meet together against the Lord and His

Christ cannot be His, since Christ himself says: "He that is not with me is against me"; [164] and also, "Therefore you hear them not, because you are not of God." [165] If they were not of God, they did not inhabit God's world. But did not the Jews who heard not the word of the Lord inhabit this world? Assuredly they did.

This world, then, is not the one of which the prophet spoke, nor does this world and the plenitude thereof seem to be of the Lord, because in it reigns sin, rather than good. But on the contrary, it seems to be of the devil. But of that land of which David asserted that it is of the Lord, Christ himself says, "Blessed are the meek, for they shall possess the land"; [166] and of it Job said, "The stones of it are the place of sapphires and the clods of it are gold." [167] And so on. . . .

XVI. *On the Same, That Is, the New Earth*

And in Ezechiel the Lord says: "For I will take you from among the Gentiles and will gather you together out of all the countries, and will bring you into your own land," [168] of which Job says, "The stones of it are the place of sapphires and the clods of it are gold." [169] And in Ezechiel: "Ashur is there and all his multitude.[170] Their graves are round about him, all of them slain and that fell by the sword, whose graves are set in the lowest parts of the pit; and his multitude lay round about his grave, all of them slain and fallen by the sword; they that heretofore spread terror in the land of the living. There is Elam and all his multitude round about his grave, all of them slain and fallen by the sword; they that went down uncircumcised to the lowest parts of the earth, that caused their terror in the land of the living." [171]

"There is Mosoch and Thubal, and all their multitude. Their graves are round about him, all of them uncircumcised and slain and fallen by the sword, though they spread their terror in the land of the living. And now they shall sleep [172] with the brave and with them that fell uncircumcised, that went down to hell with their weapons and laid their swords under their heads; and their iniquities were in their bones, because they were the terror of the mighty in the land of the living." [173] And a little later: "There are all the princes of the north and all the hunters who were brought down with the slain, fearing and confounded in their strength, who sleep uncircumcised with them that are slain by the sword and have borne their shame with them that go down into the pit. Pharaoh saw them, and he was comforted concerning all his multitude which was slain by the sword: Pharaoh and all his army, saith the Lord God, because he spread his terror in the land of the living." [174] And again, "As you have forsaken me and served a strange god in your own land, so shall you serve strange gods in a land that is not your own." [175]

Lo, there is a strange god! Lo, there is our land and a land not ours! Of the former the Lord says in the same book, "So will I visit my sheep and will deliver them out of all the places where they have been scattered in the cloudy and dark day. And I will bring them out from the peoples, and will gather them out of the countries, and I will bring them to their own land." [176] Of this land the Lord says in Isaiah: "The earth is my footstool"; [177] and again, "I made the earth and I created man upon it"; [178] and elsewhere, "For behold, I create a new earth," [179] whereof elsewhere in Isaiah it is written, "Let the earth be opened and bud forth a savior." [180] And the Lord says through the prophet Jeremiah, "I made the earth and the men and the beasts that are upon all the face of the earth, and I have given it to whom it seemed good in my eyes." [181] And so on. . . .

XVII. On the New Heavens

Now that we have uttered ample testimony about the good earth which the Lord established in the beginning, we will bring forward valid and plentiful evidence of the heavens in which justice dwells and which God deems worthy for His throne, just as He has prepared it for us. The Father himself says, "Heaven is my throne." [182] And the Son in His prayer: "Our Father who art in heaven." [183] And again, the Father in Isaiah: "As the new heavens and the new earth, which I will make to stand before me, so shall your name stand." [184] And Peter in the Epistle: "We look for new heavens and a new earth, in which justice dwelleth." [185] And the Lord through the prophet: "My hand stretched forth the heavens and I have commanded all their host"; [186] and again in the same book, "Behold, I create new heavens"; [187] and in the same book again, "Hear, O ye heavens, and give ear, O earth." [188] And David says to the Lord, "The heavens are the work of Thy hands." [189]

But since there are many persons who in blindness of heart assert that these things were said of the present heavens, because the prophet added, "They shall perish," [190] we, who speak from the good treasury of our heart,[191] will affirm with greater truth and credibility the better and wholly imperishable heavens. For Peter says of the present heavens: "The heavens and the earth which are now, by the same word are kept in store, reserved unto fire against the Day of Judgment and perdition of the ungodly men"; [192] and a little later, "The day of the Lord shall come as a thief, in which the heavens shall pass away with great violence, and the elements shall be melted with the heat of fire, and the earth and the works which are in it shall be burnt up. Seeing then that all these things are to be dissolved, what manner of people ought you to be in holy conversation and godliness, looking for and hasting unto the coming of the day of the Lord, by which the heavens, being on fire, shall be dissolved, and the elements shall melt with the burning heat." [193] Of these very heavens the Lord also says through His prophet, "The heavens shall vanish like smoke." [194] And Christ says of the present creation, "Every plant which my heavenly Father hath not planted shall be rooted up." [195] If every plant which the Father did not plant shall be rooted up, then that which the Father did plant cannot be rooted up.

And so it is not credible that these things were said of the heavens which are the work of the hands of God, since all the works of God remain forever. Now David says of the heavens which are the work of the hands of God, that they shall perish; later he says that they shall grow old, and then that they shall be changed.[196] This is not to be interpreted as a reference to the present heavens, of which, in the foregoing, God and Peter spoke. For the present heavens shall pass away after great violence and, being on fire, shall be dissolved and vanish like smoke, and it is not to be believed that they shall grow old or, growing old, shall be changed. But the heavens which perish [197] are those of which the Lord says in Isaiah, "Hear, O ye heavens, and give ear, O earth." [198] Those heavens have ears for hearing, for unless they could hear, the Lord would not say to them "Hear!" Saying of them that they perish the Apostle tells the Corinthians in the first Epistle: "And were destroyed (*perierunt*) by the destroyer"; [199] and the Lord in Ezechiel, "I will seek that which was lost (*quod perierat*)." [200] And the Lord, while seeking, said," The Son of man is come to seek and to save that which was lost." [201] And elsewhere to the disciples: "Go ye not into the way of the Gentiles, and into the city of the Samaritans enter ye not. But go ye rather to the lost sheep of the house of Israel." [202] And again, "I was not sent but to the sheep that are lost of the house of Israel." [203] Of these which are regained, it is written in the psalm: "The heavens show forth the glory of God"; [204] and in the same book, "The heaven of heavens is the Lord's"; and again, "Praise the Lord, ye heaven of heavens." [205]

Moreover, Jeremiah says that those very things which perish shall have grown old: "O Israel, how art thou grown old in a strange country." [206] And David, personifying all Israel: "I have grown old," he said, "amongst all my enemies." [207] That in truth they shall be changed the Apostle says to the Corinthians: "We shall all indeed rise again, but we shall not all be changed"; [208] and again, "The dead shall rise again incorruptible, and we shall be changed." [209] And this change is "the change of the right hand of the Most High." [210] And so on. . . .

XVIII. On the Sheep of the House of Israel

Now Christ says: "I was not sent but to the sheep that are lost of the house of Israel"; [211] and to the apostles, "Go ye rather to the lost sheep of the house of Israel." [212] And in Ezechiel: "Behold, I myself will seek my sheep and will deliver them out of all the places where they have been scattered"; [213] and again, "I will seek that which was lost." [214] And while searching, He said: "The Son of man is come to seek and to save that which was lost"; [215] and elsewhere, "The Son of man came not to destroy souls but to save." [216] And again, to Jerusalem: "How often would I have gathered together thy children, as the hen doth gather her chickens under her wings, and thou wouldst not." [217] Also in Ezechiel, "I will gather you together out of all the countries." [218] And so on. . . .

XIX. On This Word "Restore"

"There is laid up for me," [the Apostle] said, " a crown of justice which the Lord, the just judge, will render to me in that day, and not only to me but to them also that love His coming." [219] And the word of the Psalmist: "Restore unto me the joy of thy salvation." [220] And the word of Jeremiah, "The crown is fallen from our head; woe to us, because we have sinned," [221] and others like these. . . .

. . . And since we have made a considerable digression in these two chapters [222] from those things which were written in the compilation of the Cathars, now, aided by the grace of the Holy Spirit, we turn again the pen of controversy [223] to those things which have been omitted.

Here ends the first book. There are twenty-one chapters in it, and there are as many in the next.

59. The Book of the Two Principles

The seven pieces comprising the treatise translated here constitute the most considerable body of Catharist literature that has come to light. They were written just before the middle of the thirteenth century by an Italian Cathar, whose intent was to affirm certain principles peculiar to the Albanenses. Six of the component parts are concerned with the problem posed by the existence of evil among the creatures of a God who is pure goodness: How could those angels who were created good have been turned to evil? The seventh part of the treatise is a compilation of scriptural verses emphasizing that the true followers of Christ must inevitably be persecuted.

The author accounts for the existence of evil amidst good by asserting that there is an absolute duality of gods, creators, and creations—an absolute opposition of good to evil—and by denying the existence of free will among the creatures of good. On those who fail to recognize these "truths" he turns his polemic, principally against the sect of Garatenses, who held to modified dualism, but also against Catholics. Zeal and conviction are more characteristic of his argument than clarity and precision. The treatise as a whole lacks unity; there are numerous repetitions and redundancies and some contradictory passages; the language in places is obscure, perhaps betraying the author's failure to comprehend fully some of the doctrines he attacks or defends. In organization and content the treatise compares poorly with the work of orthodox theologians or the better of the contemporary writers against heresy.[1] But with all of these qualifications, *The Book of the Two Principles* must be considered a work of first importance to us. It is one of the few Catharist works to have survived, and it presents specific tenets, as embraced and justified by an eager partisan of the Albanensian faction.

Who was the author? Nowhere does he give a direct clue to his identity, except for the statement that he was one of the "true Christians" called Albanenses (IV, 6; V, 1). It is most probable that he wrote in the decade 1240-1250 somewhere in the vicinity of Lake Garda (between Brescia and Verona), in the area which was the homeland of John of Lugio,[2] who it will be recalled was the leader, about 1230, of a dissenting faction among the Albanenses (see No. 51, §§ 19-23), and whose doctrines are certainly the basis for some portions of this work. Accordingly, Antoine Dondaine, who edited the treatise, tentatively suggests that John of Lugio was the author—an identification which has been accepted without reservation by some scholars but has been denied by others.[3] Whoever he was, the author did not prepare the manuscript which now preserves his work. Paleographical evidence reveals that two copyists were involved. One of them transcribed the first three pieces; the second scribe copied the remainder of the tract, corrected the work of the first in some places, and also wrote into the manuscript the text of the ritual for the consolamentum in Latin (No. 57, part A). The copyists worked after 1254 or 1258, perhaps as late as 1280, in the region where the work was composed. In the fourteenth century the manuscript fell into orthodox hands, and passed into a monastic library; by the eighteenth century it was the property of the Dominican convent of San Marco in Florence. Later transferred to the Biblioteca nazionale of that city, it was discovered there by Dondaine and published in 1939.[4]

Despite the author's anonymity, some of the influences shaping his thought are discernible. He was thoroughly familiar with the Bible in the Vulgate text, although with which of the manuscript families current in the Middle Ages has not been determined. The doctrines of John of Lugio so underlie the discussion that both René Nelli, who translated the treatise into French, and Dondaine insist that the particular themes can be understood only in the context of that heresiarch's teaching.[5] A few phrases reminiscent of the Catharist ritual in Latin may indicate the author's familiarity with the version we know. Presumably, he had also read works produced by his adversaries the Garatenses. There is reason to suppose that he was familiar, too, with the arguments based on scriptural texts which Catholic polemicists were wont to use. Included in the treatise are a citation from Roman law; one from a pseudo-Aristotelian work, the *Liber de causis*; others which are thought to be from Aristotle; and phrases which may derive from the eleventh-century Jewish philosopher Ibn Gabirol. Among the author's opponents, one whom he treats respectfully is a certain Master William. This may have been William of Auvergne, bishop of Paris (d. 1249). It has been persuasively argued that the author picked up his acquaintance with these various sources at second hand, through some orthodox treatise against heresy.[6]

The author wrote for the benefit of those "who are hampered in rightly understanding the truth" (I, 1) and, in part, "for the instruction of beginners," who are taking their first steps toward its comprehension (IV, 1). He explains the position held by those who are "true Christians" and "wise," whom he equates with members of the sect of Albanenses (IV, 6, 7). His adversaries are primarily the sect of the Garatenses—more commonly referred to by contemporaries as the sect of Concorezzo, whose rivalry with the Albanenses was a constant factor in the history of the Italian Cathars— and against them he directs part V. His other opponents he identifies only by epithets: They are the "unlearned" (*indocti:* I, 8); the "unenlightened" (*imperiti:* I, 18); and theirs is the "belief of the ignorant" (*fidem ignavorum:* IV, 11). On occasion the author seems to distinguish more than one group in his remarks (IV, 10; V, 2). We may assume that he had in view not only Cathars who did not share his doctrines but also Catholics, for sometimes he represents his opponents as citing the Old Testament profusely;[7] moreover, some of their arguments are found also in Catholic polemical sources.

The order of the component parts of *The Book of the Two Principles* in the manuscript may not be the actual order of their composition, for the argument occasionally fails of logical sequence and the titles of the divisions are not always exactly descriptive of the contents. In his Introduction (p. 15) Dondaine sees the work as composed of three major parts which are more closely related to each other than they are to three relatively minor pieces which follow them. His outline of its organization is the following (the numbers in parentheses are those used for the divisions made in this translation):

A. On the Two Principles
   1. On Free Will (I)
   2. On Creation (II)
   3. On the Terms of Universality (III)
B. A Compend for the Instruction of Beginners (IV)
C. Against the Garatenses
   1. A First Rebuttal (V, 1-3)
   2. A Declaration to the Faithful (V, 4-5)
   3. A Further Argument (V, 6)
D. On Will (VI, 1)
E. More on This Concept (*De sententia*) (VI, 2)
F. On Persecutions (VII)

Arno Borst, who has studied the work with equal care, proposes a different outline: [8]

A. A Compend for the Instruction of Beginners (IV)
B. On Creation and on the Terms of Universality (II, III)
C. On Free Will (I, 7ff. [I, 1-6, would no doubt be regarded as introductory])
D. On Will (VI)
E. Against the Garatenses (IV)
F. On Persecutions (VII)

Our translation follows the order of the parts in the manuscript and in the edition by Dondaine.

For an understanding of the treatise, the reader might profit from the comments of Rainerius Sacconi (No. 51) on the beliefs of John of Lugio, particularly in respect of his concept of another world between God's perfect heaven and this earth created by the devil.[9] It may also be of some use here to sketch briefly the author's line of argument in each part of the work.

I. *On Free Will.*—Opponents of the true concept of two principles declare that there is but one God, who is pure goodness, omniscient, and omnipotent (§§ 1-6). But a difficulty arises from their tenet because we know that His angelic creatures fell into sin. Since God's knowledge encompasses all that was, is, and shall be, He would have known before the event that His angels would sin; and because of His knowledge, their sin would have been inevitable, for in God knowledge and will are synonymous.[10] Therefore, we must conclude that there is a cause of evil other than the good God (§§ 7-8). Various arguments of the opponents who try to prove that the angels sinned of choice, not by necessity, are refuted (§§ 9-11). That we may carry out God's will in serving Him in His creation proves that He is afflicted by an enemy (§§ 12-13), although that service does not arise from our will but from His (§ 14). The absolute opposition of good to evil must be emphasized. It is axiomatic that no power can exist equally capable of good and evil at the same time; if it did, the angels having it could not avoid doing evil, for which God would have the ultimate responsibility—a wicked thought! (§§ 15-16). If an evil cause did not exist, no evil result would be produced (§ 17). If the angels had free will by God's creation, and He knew that they would sin, their sin was inevitable and thus attributable to God (§ 18). Master William's argument that, since God could not make His angels as perfect as Himself, they must covet His perfection, is rejected (§ 19).

II. *On Creation.*—To support the conclusion that there must be two creator-gods, the evidence of the Scriptures is adduced. Opponents of the truth insist on the omnipotence and eternity of God, the sole creator (§§ 1-3). They do not perceive the true meaning of "create" and "make." In no sense does "creation" mean to bring something out of nothing, for all matter exists for all time with its creator. Properly understood, "creation" embraces three modes of change: (a) that which is already good is changed for the better; thus Christ and other angels were "created" by God as ministers to those who had sinned; (b) "to create" may mean that those who have fallen under the domination of evil may be changed, "created" again to good, and redeemed by the illumination afforded them by Christ; and (c) it may mean that the good God allows His enemy for a time to afflict His people in order to achieve His own purposes. Each of these concepts is well attested by scriptural authority, but in no sense is God to be thought the source of any evil which exists (§§ 4-12).

III. *On the Terms of Universality.*—The threefold aspect of creation is confirmed by an examination of the concept of universals. Terms signifying universality in the Bible must be properly interpreted. One who has wisdom will perceive that such words as "all" and "every" are not all-embracing (§§ 1-3). Sometimes they refer to all that is good (§ 3), sometimes to all that is evil (§ 4), sometimes to all that was once good but fell under the power of evil and will be redeemed (§§ 5-7). The conclusion is reiterated: "All" that is evil cannot be the same as "all" that is good, nor can it arise from the same source; therefore two separate principles and sources must be postulated.

IV. *A Compend.*—In regard to creation, the terms "heaven" and "earth" used in the Scriptures refer to the intelligent creatures of the good God, the spiritual creation. The good God is not the creator of the base and tangible elements of this world; another creator is responsible for them (§ 1). God is almighty, but not in the sense that He can create evil (§ 2); what He does not desire He cannot do (§ 3). He is omnipotent over all good things (§ 4), but there must be another creator from whom all evils flow, who in no way derives from the good God (§§ 5-7). The evil one is eternal, as are his works. This the Scriptures prove (§§ 8-10). To him belongs all the wickedness reported in the Old Testament: adultery, theft, murder, the persecution of Christ, falsehoods, broken promises (§§ 11-17).

V. *Against the Garatenses.*—The Garatenses believe that there is one God, creator of all, but that an evil lord, God's creature, made this world. They cannot support this by divine testimony, for believing that the evil lord was the author of the Old Testament, how can they cite its evidence? Or if they cite it, how can they avoid its plain testimony that the evil one was a creator (§§ 1-2)? If they believe that a good God created all things, why do they spurn the meat, eggs, and cheese of His creation and why do they avoid matrimony (§ 3)? The Garatenses are challenged to debate the issues (§§ 4-5). Another question is posed: How can they uphold the belief in creation as the work of a good God and still deny His responsibility for the evil they discern in this world (§ 6)?

VI. *On Will.*—This returns to the themes enunciated in the first part, "On Free Will." How can free will be justified in the case of those who never have done, do not, and never will do good? If God did not know that angels would become demons, He was not omniscient; if He did know their fate, they could not avoid it, for His knowledge extends to all that of necessity occurs (§ 1). Furthermore, those who believe in free will and believe that new souls are daily being created fall into sad error. How many there would be who would be unable, because they were infants or were hampered by bodily infirmities, to do good and to merit salvation! Hence the concept of free will is untenable (§ 2).

VII. *On Persecutions.*[11]—Christ is the shepherd who sought to recover the lost sheep. He suffered for their sake but His suffering did not come from the good God. Instead, this wickedness was endured by the good God in order to accomplish His purpose, the redemption of His people. As Christ and the prophets suffered from the evil one's domination, so must all true Christians suffer, returning good for evil, for all who will live in Christ must first endure persecution.[12]

In our translation we have taken advantage of the detailed commentary in Borst, *Die Katharer,* pp. 284-318. We have also profited by consulting the French translation by René Nelli, *Ecritures cathares,* pp. 83-201. Our translation is from Antoine Dondaine, *Un Traité néo-manichéen du XIIIe siècle: Le* Liber de duobus principiis, *suivi d'un fragment de rituel cathare* (Rome, 1939), pp. 81-147, by permission of the Istituto storico domenicano di S. Sabina.

1240-1250 (?)

THE BOOK OF THE TWO PRINCIPLES

[*1. On Free Will*]

[1] *Here Begins the Book of the Two Principles.*—Since many persons are hampered in rightly understanding the truth, to enlighten them, to stimulate those who do have right understanding, and also for the

delight of my soul, I have made it my purpose to explain our true faith by evidence from the Holy Scriptures and with eminently suitable arguments, invoking thereto the aid of the Father, of the Son, and of the Holy Spirit.

[2] *On the Two Principles.*—To the honor of the Most Holy Father,[1] I wish to begin my discussion concerning the two principles by refuting the belief in one Principle, however much this may contradict well-nigh all religious persons. We may commence as follows: Either there is only one First Principle, or there is more than one.[2] If, indeed, there were one and not more, as the unenlightened say, then, of necessity, He would be either good or evil. But surely not evil, since then only evil would proceed from Him and not good, as Christ says in the Gospel of the Blessed Matthew: "And the evil tree bringeth forth evil fruit. A good tree cannot bring forth evil fruit, neither can an evil tree bring forth good fruit."[3] And the Blessed James says in his Epistle: "Doth a fountain send forth out of the same hole sweet and bitter water? Can the fig tree, my brethren, bear grapes; or the vine, figs? So neither can the salt water yield sweet."[4]

[3] *On the Goodness of God.*—Now, our opponents[5] are clear in their assertion that God is good, holy, just, wise, and true; that He is also called pure goodness and is above all praise, as they seek to prove by the following citations[6] and many others of like nature. For Jesus the son of Sirach says: "Glorify the Lord as much as ever you can, for He will yet far exceed, and His magnificence is wonderful. Blessing the Lord, exalt Him as much as you can, for He is above all praise."[7] And David says: "Great is the Lord, and greatly to be praised; and of His greatness there is no end";[8] and again, "Great is our Lord, and great is his power; and of His wisdom there is no number."[9] And Paul says to the Romans: "O the depth of the riches of the wisdom and of the knowledge of God! How incomprehensible are His judgments and how unsearchable His ways,"[10] and so on. And in the *Liber de causis* is written, "The first cause is far greater than can be described."[11]

[4] *That God Knows All Things from Eternity.*—Whence they stoutly affirm that God knows all things from eternity because of the greatness of His wisdom; that all the past, the present, and the future are always before Him and He knows all things before they come to pass, as says Susanna in the Book of Daniel, "O eternal God, who knowest hidden things, who knowest all things before they come to pass."[12] And Jesus,

son of Sirach, says, "For all things were known to the Lord God before they were created; so also after they were perfected He beholdeth all things." [13] And the Apostle writes to the Hebrews, "Neither is there any creature invisible in His sight, but all things are naked and open to His eyes." [14]

[5] *On the Goodness, Holiness, and Justice of God.*—It is clearly demonstrated, moreover, that our Lord God is good, holy, and just, as is said above. For David says: "How good is God to Israel, to them that are of a right heart"; [15] and again, "The Lord is faithful in all His words and holy in all His works"; [16] and again, "The Lord is sweet and righteous; therefore He will give a law to sinners in the way"; [17] and again, "God is a just judge, strong and patient; is He angry every day?" [18] And in the Book of Wisdom it is written, "For so much then as thou art just, Thou orderest all things justly." [19]

[6] *On the Omnipotence of God.*—For the Lord is called omnipotent, as our opponents avow, and He can do whatsoever pleases Him; nor can anyone resist Him,[20] or say, "Why dost Thou so?" As Ecclesiastes says: "For He will do all that pleaseth Him and His word is full of power; neither can any man say to Him: 'Why dost Thou so?' " [21] And David says, "But our God in heaven; He hath done all things whatsoever He would." [22] And in the Apocalypse is written: "Saith the Lord God, who is, and who was, and who is to come, the Almighty.[23] And again, "Great and wonderful are Thy works, O Lord God Almighty! Just and true are Thy ways, O King of Ages! Who shall not fear Thee, O Lord, and magnify Thy name? For Thou only art holy." [24]

[7] *On the First Proposition, against My Opponents.*—At this point I take issue with the thesis (*sententiam*) of those who assert that there is only one First Principle. For I say: Assume that God—who is good, just, holy, wise, righteous, "faithful in all His words, and holy in all His works," [25] who is almighty and knows all things before they come to pass, as I have shown above—created and arrayed His angels as He chose from the beginning through Himself alone and without any apparent extraneous compulsion from anyone; and assume, further, that He knew the fate of all His angels before they came into being, because within His providence existed all the causes for which those angels must be found wanting in the future and must remain for all time things of evil and demons in His sight, as nearly all our opponents say: then, without doubt, it follows ineluctably that those angels could never remain good,

holy, or humble with their Lord, in whose power of necessity all things occurred from eternity, except to the extent to which God himself had knowledge from the beginning. For one who knows fully all things that shall come to pass is powerless, in so far as he is self-consistent, to do anything except that which he himself has known from eternity that he shall do. This I prove.

[8] *On Impossibility.*—For I say that just as it is impossible for that which is past not to be in the past, so it is impossible for that which is in the future not to be in the future. This is especially true in God, who from the beginning understood and knew that which would come to pass, so that existence as something still to come was possible for an event before it occurred. It was without doubt necessary that the future itself should exist wholly in Him, because He would know and understand from eternity all the causes which are required for bringing the future to fruition. And it is the more true since, if there is only one First Principle, God himself is the sole cause of all causes; and above all if it is a fact, as the opponents of truth assert, that God does whatever pleases himself and His might is not affected by anyone.

I say further: If God understood all things from the beginning and knew that His angels would in the future become demons, because of the character which He himself gave them from the beginning (because all the causes which would make those angels become demons in the future arose entirely within His providence and it did not please God to make them otherwise than He did), it of necessity follows that the aforesaid angels could never in any way have avoided becoming demons. And this is particularly true because it is impossible that anything which God knows to be future may be in any way changed so that it does not come to pass in the future—above all, in Him who from eternity knows the future completely, as we have just seen explained.

How, then, can the unlearned say that the aforesaid angels could remain good, holy, and humble with their Lord for all time, since it was from eternity utterly impossible in God? They are therefore by the most valid reasoning forced to confess that, in accordance with their thesis, God knowingly and in full awareness created and made His angels of such imperfection from the beginning that they could in no way escape evil. And so God himself, of whom the words good, holy, just, wise, and righteous were used above, who is above all praise, as was previously declared, was the whole cause and origin of all evil—which is obviously to be denied. For this reason we are required to acknowledge two principles. One is good. The other is evil, the source and cause of the imperfection of the angels and also of all evil.[26]

[9] *A Reply to the Foregoing.*—But perchance someone will say: The wisdom and providence which God himself had from the beginning, induced in His own creatures no unavoidable necessity to do good or to do evil. For this, perhaps, they might offer an illustration thus: If a certain man in a mansion should see another man walking of his own free will along a way,[27] one might perchance say that it is not the wisdom nor the foresight of him in the mansion which makes the other man walk along the way, even though the former is fully cognizant of and sees the way the other is going.

So with God. Although He knew fully and foresaw from eternity the fate of all His angels, His wisdom and providence did not make His angels become demons, but they became demons and things of evil by their own will, because they did not wish to remain holy and humble before their Lord, but wickedly puffed themselves up in pride against Him.

[10] *Rejection of the Preceding Illustration.*—One must in truth reject this very misleading illustration. Since God in himself was—in the view of our opponents—from the beginning wholly the cause of all His angels, they indubitably derived exclusively and essentially from Him, in a way that was pleasing to Him, the character, the formation or creation,[28] which God himself gave them. And, according to these persons, that which the angels were, they were through Him wholly, in all their the causes which made it inevitable for them to become demons in the characteristics, nor did they derive anything at all from any other than Him alone, nor did it please their God to create or make the angels otherwise from the beginning. For these persons believe that had He so wished, He could most easily have made them otherwise. And so it seems clear that God did not seek to make His angels perfect from the beginning, but knowingly and in full awareness endowed them with all future. This was, of necessity, within the power of God, in whom all things occur inevitably from eternity. Whence, the assertion that the wisdom or providence of God did not cause His angels to become things of evil and demons is not valid in the same sense as is the statement that the foresight of the man in the mansion did not cause the other man to walk along the way. Above all, this is true because he who walked along

the way is not the creature of him who is in the mansion, nor does he have his being or even his strength from him. But if one had his strength from the other and all the causes whatsoever which were necessary for completion of that journey—just as the aforesaid angels, according to the belief of our opponents, had them from their God—it would be untrue to say that the foresight of the man in the mansion did not make the other man walk along the way, for it is clear that the latter would walk only because of the former, as is most plainly explained above with reference to God. And so no man can rationally condemn those angels when, owing to the character which they had from their Lord, they could do no other than they did. In the same way that an Ethiopian cannot change his skin or a leopard his spots,²⁹ because of the nature which they have from their maker, so the angels, if we accept the belief of our opponents, could in no way avoid evil, because of the character which their God gave to them from the beginning. This is a most wicked belief.

But now our opponents may, if they can, eagerly try another way of escape. For they plainly say: Had He wished it, God might well from the beginning have made His angels of such perfection that they would have been quite unable to sin or to do evil, and this on three counts, which are: that He is almighty, that He knows all things from eternity, and that His omnipotence is not qualified by anyone. But God was not willing to make them of such perfection; and they advance this reason: If God had from the beginning made His angels of such perfection that they could commit no sin or evil of any kind but inevitably must obey their Lord, the Lord himself would have given them no thanks for their obedience or service. For thus God could say to them: I give you no thanks for your service, since you cannot act otherwise. Perhaps our opponents might offer an illustration of this point: If a certain lord had a servant "who knew the will of his lord" ³⁰ in all things and could do nothing at all except follow it, this lord they say, would give no thanks at all to his servant for his service, because the latter would be unable to act otherwise.

[11] *On the Free Will of the Angels.*—And thus, they say, God created His angels of such nature from the beginning that they could at their pleasure do good or evil; and they call this "free will" (*liberum arbitrium*) or, according to some of them, "choice" (*arbitrium*), to wit, a certain free strength or power by which he to whom it is given is equally capable of good or evil. And so they insist that God in reason

and justice could allot glory or punishment to the angels; that is to say, they might receive punishment because they were able to do good and did not. Thus God could reasonably say to them: "Come, ye blessed of my Father, possess you the kingdom prepared for you from the foundation of the world; for I was hungry and you gave me to eat, I was thirsty and you gave me to drink," [31] and so on. This is as if He were to say: You were able to refrain from giving but because you gave, therefore do you in reason and justice possess the kingdom prepared for you from the foundation of the world. Then, on the other hand, the Lord himself could reasonably say to sinners: "Depart from me, you cursed, into everlasting fire which was prepared for the devil and his angels; for I was hungry and you gave me not to eat, I was thirsty and you gave me not to drink," [32] and so on. This is as if He were to say: You were able to give and did not; therefore, by reason and justice will you go to the fire eternal. For, they say, if they had no power at all to give Him to eat or drink, by what reason could the Lord himself have said to them, "for I was hungry and you gave me not to eat, I was thirsty and you gave me not to drink," and so on? Therefore, they affirm, God did not wish to create His angels perfect, that is, of such perfection that they were quite unable to sin or to do evil, for the Lord himself would have shown them no favor for their service, as has already been said.

They also say that God was not willing to create the angels of such nature that they could always do only evil and not good, because the aforesaid angels could reasonably excuse themselves, saying: We were unable to do anything but evil because of the character which you gave us from the beginning. So they say that God created His angels of such character from the beginning that they could do good and evil. As a result the Lord himself could reasonably judge His angels, in that they were able to sin and had not sinned, or they could refrain from sin and had sinned. And thus our opponents unwisely exult at our expense.

[12] *Refutation of the Thesis of Our Opponents.*—I shall now clarify what has just been said, namely, their declaration that if God had made His angels perfect from the beginning, in such perfection that they would have been unable to sin at all or to do evil, the Lord would have given them no thanks for their service because they would have been unable to do otherwise. I am convinced that their statement greatly strengthens my position. For if God shows favor to anyone for his service, this seems to me necessarily to follow: namely, that there is

something wanting to God and to His will, that He wishes for and desires something done which does not yet exist, or that He desires to have what He does not have. And so, pursuant to this, it seems that we can serve God by fulfilling what is wanting to His will or by rendering to Him something which He needs and desires, either for Himself or for others, as the Gospel text quoted above clearly implies, to wit: "For I was hungry and you gave me to eat, I was thirsty and you gave me to drink," and so on; and again, "As long as you did it to one of these my least brethren, you did it to me." [33] And again, Christ said to Jerusalem, "How often would I have gathered together thy children, as the hen doth gather her chickens under her wings, and thou wouldst not?" [34] And the Lord, speaking through Ezechiel to Samaria, says, "Thy uncleanness is execrable. Because I desired to cleanse thee and thou art not cleansed from thy filthiness." [35] From this it seems manifest that the will of God and of His Son, Jesus Christ, was not then wholly fulfilled. This would be impossible, were there only one First Principle, good, holy, just, and perfect.

Hence, this is the basis on which we can serve God and Christ, when we carry out their will with the aid of the true Father, namely, by alleviating hunger and other hurtful things among the creatures of the good Lord. Then the Lord himself may thank us for fulfilling that which He wishes for and desires to exist. And this seems to uphold my thesis, for neither God nor man can desire or wish anything unless first He have that which He does not desire and which troubles Him, either on His own account or on another's behalf. In particular, to declare that this Principle could be burdened with anything which He does not desire, and that there could be something which could trouble Him and make Him sorrowful on His own behalf or for others seems quite in contradiction to the position of those who say that there is only one First Principle, whole and perfect.

[This could not be] [36] unless He were divided against Himself, harmful to His very self and His Son, that is to say, by Himself alone without extraneous compulsion from anyone doing that which would be wholly contrary to Himself and to His own in the future, that which would make Him sad, sorrowful, and dolorous. For that Lord who, according to our opponents, created male and female and all other living things says in Genesis, "And being touched inwardly with sorrow of heart, he said, 'I will destroy man, whom I have created, from the face of the earth, from man even to beasts, from the creeping thing even to the fowls of the air, for it repenteth me that I have made them." [37] This the true God most certainly would not do in and of himself, were there but one First Principle, holy and perfect. However, the above text can be interpreted as though He said: There is another, a principle of evil, which makes my heart to sorrow by so acting against my creation that it compels me to destroy the created from the face of the earth because of their sins. This principle makes me repent that I made them, that is to say, [makes me] suffer on their account. On the other hand, following the doctrine of one Principle, the text is best understood thus: It repenteth me that I have made them; namely, I shall have to undergo suffering and pain in the future, through myself alone, because I made them. And so it seems manifest, according to the doctrine of those persons who believe that there is only one First Principle, that this God and His Son, Jesus Christ, who, according to them are one and the same, causes Himself sadness, sorrow, and suffering, bearing pain in Himself without any extraneous intervention by anyone. But it is impossible and wicked to believe this of the true God.

[13] *On the Principle of Evil.*—Therefore, it behooves us of necessity to confess that there is another principle, one of evil, who works most wickedly against the true God and His creation; and this principle seems to move God against His own creation and the creation against its God, and causes God himself to wish for and desire that which in and of himself He could never wish for at all. Thus it is that through the compulsion of the evil enemy God yearns and is wearied, relents, is burdened, and is served by His own creatures. Whence God says to His people through Isaiah: "But thou hast made me to serve with thy sins, thou hast wearied me with thy iniquities"; [38] and again, "I am weary of bearing them." [39] And Malachi says, "You have wearied the Lord with your words." [40] And David says, "And [he] repented according to the multitude of His mercies." [41] And the Apostle says in his first Epistle to the Corinthians, "For we are God's coadjutors." [42] Of the compulsion of God, however, the Lord himself says to Satan in the Book of Job, "But thou hast moved me against him, that I should afflict him without cause." [43] And through Ezechiel the same Lord says, "And when they caught the souls of my people, they gave life to their souls. And they violated me among my people, for a handful of barley and a piece of bread, to kill souls which should not die and to save souls alive which

should not live." [44] And the Lord, lamenting over His people, says through Isaiah: "Because I called and you did not answer; I spoke and you did not hear, and you did evil in my eyes, and you have chosen the things that displease me." [45]

And so it appears plainly that this concept of how one may serve God buttresses my argument. For if there were only one First Principle, holy, just, and good, as has been declared of the true Lord God in the foregoing, He would not make Himself sorrowful, sad, or dolorous; neither would He bear pain in himself, nor grow weary or repent, nor be aided by anyone, nor be burdened with the sins of anyone, nor yearn or wish for anything to be done which was delayed in coming to pass, since nothing at all could be done contrary to His will; nor could He be moved by anyone or injured, nor could there be anything which would trouble God, but all things would obey Him from overwhelming necessity. And most especially would this be true because all things would be by Him and in Him and of Him,[46] in all their dispositions, if there were only one First Principle, holy and just, as I have shown above in discussing the true God.

[14] *On Service to God.*—From this comes the basis for our service to God, in that we may fulfill His works, or rather, that God may consummate through us that which He proposes and wishes to be done. In this wise He achieved salvation of His people through the Lord Jesus, although Christ did nothing good through himself or even by free will. For He said of himself: "I cannot of myself do anything"; [47] and again, "But the Father, who abideth in me, he doth the works." [48] And so, we serve God when we fulfill His will with His help, not that we are able through free will to do anything good of which He himself is not the cause and principle. Thus, the Blessed James says in his Epistle, "Every best gift and every perfect gift is from above, coming down from the Father of Lights." [49] And in the Gospel of John, Christ says, "No man can come to me except the Father, who hath sent me, draw him." [50] And of himself, He said: "I cannot of myself do anything. As I hear, so I judge"; [51] and again, "But the Father, who abideth in me, he doth the works." [52] And the Apostle says to the Ephesians: "For by grace you are saved through faith, and that not of yourselves, for it is the gift of God; not of works, that no man may glory." [53] And the same Apostle says to the Romans, "So then it is not of him that willeth nor of him that runneth, but of God that showeth mercy." [54] And to the Philippians, he says:

"Being confident of this very thing, that He who hath begun a good work in you will perfect it unto the day of our Lord Christ Jesus"; [55] and again, "For it is God who worketh in you both to will and to accomplish, according to His good will." [56] And in his second Epistle to the Corinthians the same Apostle says: "And such confidence we have through Christ toward the Lord. Not that we are sufficient to think anything of ourselves as of ourselves; but our sufficiency is from God, who also hath made us fit ministers of the new testament, not in the letter but in the spirit. For the letter killeth, but the spirit quickeneth." [57] And John the Baptist said, "A man cannot receive anything unless it be given him from heaven." [58] And David says: "Unless the Lord build the house, they labor in vain that build it. Unless the Lord keep the city, he watcheth in vain that keepeth it." [59] And Jeremiah says, "I know, O Lord, that the way of a man is not his, neither is it in a man to walk and to direct his steps." [60] And Paul says to the Corinthians, "But by the grace of God I am what I am." [61] And in the parables of Solomon it is written: "Counsel and equity is mine, prudence is mine, strength is mine. By me kings reign, and lawgivers decree just things. By me princes rule and the mighty decree justice"; [62] and again, "The steps of a man are guided by the Lord; but who is the man that can understand his own way." [63] And in the Gospel of Matthew, Christ says: "All things are delivered to me by my Father; and no one knoweth the Son but the Father, neither doth anyone know the Father but the Son and he to whom it shall please the Son to reveal Him." [64] And in the Gospel of John, He says of himself: "I am the way, the truth, and the light. No man cometh to the Father, but by me"; [65] and again, "For without me you can do nothing." [66] And in the Gospel of the Blessed Luke, He says, "Strive to enter by the narrow gate; for many, I say to you, shall seek to enter and shall not be able." [67]

[15] *On Destroying the Concept of Free Will.*—From this it is quite evident that we cannot serve God by doing anything good by free will, as a result of which He would give thanks to us as if for our own individual strength and power—that is, a good of which He is not the cause and principle, as was plainly pointed out above. And most especially is this so because we have no powers at all of ourselves, as the Blessed Peter says in the Acts of the Apostles, in regard to the lame man made whole: "Ye men of Israel, why wonder you at this or why look you upon us, as if by our own strength or power we had made this man to walk?" [68]

This is as if he had said: Not we but "the God of Abraham, and the God of Isaac, and the God of Jacob"[69] did this.

And so it clearly seems that whatever of good is found in the creatures of God is directly from Him and of Him,[70] and He brings the good into being and is its cause, as was explained above. If evil, however, is found in the people of God,[71] it is not truly from God himself, nor of Him, nor does He bring it into being, nor was He nor is He its cause, as Jesus the son of Sirach says, "He hath commanded no man to do wickedly, and He hath given no man license to sin."[72] This is to be understood to mean that He did not of himself absolutely and directly do so. And also, no evil can come from a creature of God, itself good, unless there be a cause of evil. For through Ezechiel the Lord says: "The rod hath blossomed, pride hath budded. Iniquity is risen up into a rod of impiety; not of them nor of the people nor of the noise of them"[73]—therefore, from some other source! And Christ says in the Gospel of Matthew: "The kingdom of heaven is likened to a man that sowed good seed in his field; but while men were asleep, his enemy came by night and over-sowed cockle among the wheat, and went his way."[74] And David says: "O God, the heathens are come into thine inheritance; they have de-filed thy holy temple; they have made Jerusalem as a place to keep fruit."[75] And the Lord through the prophet Joel says: "For a nation is come up upon my land, strong and without number; his teeth are like the teeth of a lion, and his cheek teeth as of a lion's whelp. He hath laid my vineyard waste, and hath pilled off the bark of my fig tree; he hath stripped it bare and cast it away; the branches thereof are made white."[76] So one may clearly understand that pride and wickedness and impiety, the weeds and the pollution of the holy temple of God, and the wasting of His vineyard, cannot proceed exclusively and essentially from the good God or from a good creature of His which is wholly from Him in all its characteristics. It now follows, therefore, that there is another principle, one of evil, who is the source and cause of all pride and wickedness, of all defilement of the people, and of all other evils.

[16] *On the Contention of My Opponents That God Did Not Wish to Create His Angels Perfect.*—I now intend to discuss my opponents' contention that God did not wish to create His angels perfect, that is, of such perfection that they should forever be capable only of good actions, never of evil, nor, on the other hand, that they should be forever capable only of evil, never of good; but, in their words, that He created

them of such nature that they could do good or do evil according to their pleasure, as may be seen set forth above.[77]

Now, I say that if it did not please God to create His angels of such nature that they were capable only of always doing good, never evil, or capable of always doing evil, never good, but it pleased Him to create them of such nature that they were capable of doing both good and evil, the statement must be understood to mean "capable of so acting at different times." For it is impossible that angels could have been so created by God that simultaneously, at one and the same time, they were capable of doing both good and evil. From this, if we accept the doctrine stated, it follows of necessity that the aforesaid angels did good acts and evil acts, not merely good alone or evil alone, but in veyr truth both good and evil. And so it seems clear that these angels could in no way for all time escape evil, because of the character which they had from their Lord. And thus, according to this, God would be the cause and origin of that evil; which is an impossibility, and it is foolish to suggest it.

And yet perhaps at this point my opponents, speaking calmly at first and then shouting, would cry out, saying: Indeed these angels were always capable of doing both good and evil, had they so desired, because they had free will from God, that is, a free strength or power by which they were equally capable of good and evil at their pleasure. And thus, they would declare, God is not the First Cause of that evil, because the angels sinned by the free will given to them, by their own choice.

[17] *Proof That There Is No Free Will.*—If anyone should scrutinize minutely the arguments set forth above, he would see that my position is not weakened by the concept of free will, meaning a free strength or power which our opponents say was given by God, by which the angels were capable of good or evil at their pleasure. Yet, in the opinion of the wise, it will appear impossible for anyone to have a potency for two contraries simultaneously, at one and the same time; that is, for one to have a potency for doing good for all time and for doing evil for all time. And especially is this true in God, who has complete knowledge of the future, and according to whose wisdom all things are done of necessity from eternity.

And it is particularly puzzling how the good angels would have been capable of hating goodness like unto their own, which existed from eternity as did its cause, and of delighting in wickedness, which did not yet exist and which is the exact opposite of goodness; and this without cause if, as the unenlightened say, there was no cause of evil at all. And especially is this so because it is written in the Book of Jesus the son of Sirach: "Every beast loveth its like, so also every man him that is nearest to himself. All flesh shall consort with the like to itself and every man shall associate himself to his like." [78] And again, "Birds resort unto their like, so truth will return to them that practice her." [79] And so it seems clear that the good angels would have sought rather to choose the good like unto themselves, which existed from eternity, than to spurn good and cleave to evil, which was not in existence (nor indeed was its cause [Satan], if I follow the belief of my opponents); yet it does not seem possible that anything can come into being without a cause. For so it is written: "It is impossible that whatever has a beginning should have no cause"; and again, "Everything which changes from potency to effect needs a cause by which it can be brought into effect." And also, according to my opponents, that which existed, namely good, had less effect than that which did not exist, namely evil; [80] and this despite the fact that it is written, "A thing must have existence before it can have an effect." And also, one should clearly recognize that if a cause should wholly retain its original character, nothing would result from it other than that which it first produced. For every new effect is a result of a new factor of some sort, as is written: "For if something which was not an agent becomes an agent, this inevitably takes place because of a new factor of some sort." [81] From this, one must realize that if the dispositions of the agent were to continue just as they originally were, and if it were, up to that point, affected by nothing new either internally or externally, assuredly the agent would have less the function of causing-to-exist than that of nonexistence, and nonexistence would persist indefinitely. For just as from diversity something different may arise, so from uniformity sameness persists.[82]

And if, in fact, none of the angels could have sinned without free will, God would in no wise have given it, since He would have known that from this cause alone His kingdom would be corrupted. Moreover, the corruption of the angels would of necessity have come from the God who "is above all praise," [83] which is a wicked thing to suppose. It follows from this that there is another principle, one of evil, who is the source and cause of the corruption of the angels and of all evil.

[18] *On Free Will: That the Angels Had It Not.*—Whence, it is

obvious to the wise that the angels discussed above never had any such choice from God, that is, such power to desire, to know, and to do only good for all time, and not evil. If they had had, they would from overwhelming necessity have done and desired good for all time, never evil.

Therefore, by what reasoning, by what audacity, can the unenlightened say that the aforesaid angels could indeed always do only good if they chose? For from God, who knows the future completely, they had no potency, desire, knowledge, will, nor any other attribute (*causa*) whatsoever by which they could wholly avoid evil, as was made quite clear above. It may somehow be said, among men who are completely ignorant of the future and of all the causes which necessitate doing good or evil for all time or on different occasions, that the angels had such strength or power from God that they could do good and evil for all time. It seems, however, most clearly false in God, who has complete knowledge of the future, who knows from eternity all causes (the effect of which is to render it impossible for that which is future not to be in the future), according to whose wisdom all things are of necessity done from eternity.

So it happens that conflicting statements are many times heard among men who are entirely ignorant of the future or of the truth of things; to wit, when they declare that what never shall be may be, and what most certainly shall be cannot be. For instance, we sometimes say that Peter may live until tomorrow and that he may die today. Although it is impossible for Peter both to live until tomorrow and to die today, yet, because we are ignorant of the future, as of all the causes which control the life and death of Peter, we affirm that which is impossible to be possible, and that which is possible we say to be impossible. If, however, we knew the future completely and also all the causes which control the life or death of Peter, then we would not say that Peter may live until tomorrow and that he may die today. For if we knew that Peter would die today, then we would say that it is clearly necessary for Peter to die today, or that it is impossible for him to live until tomorrow. And if we knew that he would live until tomorrow, then we would say that it is clearly necessary for him to live until tomorrow, or that it is impossible for Peter to die today. However, because we do not know the future, we put forward the possible for the impossible and the impossible for the possible. But this cannot be true of Him who has complete knowledge of all the future.

I say further: Suppose a certain man was in a house with Peter and unquestionably saw him. And another man outside this house inquired of the one within, "Can it be that Peter is in the house?" If he who knows unquestionably that Peter is in the house because he sees him before his very eyes should answer the other, "It may be that Peter is in the house and it may be that he is not," there is no doubt that he would be speaking wrongly and contrary to his own knowledge in saying, "It may be that Peter is not in the house." For he knows without any doubt whatever that Peter was in the house because he saw him before his very eyes.

So I say of the free will said by my opponent to be given by God: As pertains to the God who knows wholly all the future, in whom are known from eternity all the causes which render it impossible for that which is future not to be in the future, in whose wisdom are all things of necessity done from eternity, the aforesaid angels never had from Him a free capacity for freedom to choose, to know or to do good for all time. This is so especially because God himself without doubt knew and saw the end of all His angels before they came into being, just as the man who saw Peter and knew him unquestionably to be in the house would be speaking wrongly if he had said, "It may be that Peter is not in the house." So I say in the matter of free will of the angels in God that it was never true to say that the angels could not sin; this is especially true in respect of a God who wholly knows the future. And to say that they did not wish to sin signifies nothing, because good angels do not, without a cause, wish to do evil. For the wise realize that it is impossible for the good, without a cause, to hate good and desire evil, since, as was stated above, nothing at all can exist without a cause. It was, therefore, necessary in God for those angels to become things of evil and demons in the future, because within His providence existed without exception all the causes by which they must be found wanting in the future. Without doubt, it was impossible in Him that they could remain good and holy for all time.

In the view of men who are ignorant of the future and of the whole truth it may, perhaps, somehow be said that the aforesaid angels could both do good and do evil for all time. But in the view of men who know the whole truth, be it of the future or of all causes which are requisite to doing good for all time or to so doing on different occasions, it is absolutely impossible that the angels could have freedom to do good for all time, together with freedom to do evil for all time; rather, in their view, it would be wholly necessary for these angels to be found wanting in the future. And in the opinion of such men it would also be an impossibility for these angels to remain good and holy for all time, for they also realize that all causes are not fitted for these angels to both do good for all time and yet act in a completely evil manner in the future. Whence, to the wise it is quite evident that the aforesaid angels never had from God—as the statement of the dullards asserts—a free capacity or the freedom to do good for all time, but from overwhelming necessity [must] act in a completely evil manner in the future, as was clearly explained in the preceding. To believe that they had [free will] is most evil and foolish.

[19] *On the Thesis of Master William.*—I have now no intention of overlooking the thesis of Master William,[84] albeit he may seem to be wise in many matters. For I have heard him discussing ideas such as the following: that the angels were not made perfect by God from the beginning, because their God could not make them perfect. The reason for this is that God could not and cannot make anyone like Himself or coequal with Himself in any way; and although God himself may be called almighty by many, yet this He cannot do at all. And thus, in so much as they were inferior to God in beauty and greatness—that is to say, as they were not like Him or coequal with Him—these angels could be found wanting to the extent that they could covet His beauty and greatness. So, one reads of Lucifer in Isaiah: "I will exalt my throne above the stars. I will be like the Most High." [85] And thus, such a one would perhaps say that on this account we cannot reasonably blame God for not making His angels so perfect that they could not have coveted His beauty and greatness at all, because their God could not do so, as is stated above.

I have decided to refute the doctrine just stated with the most cogent argument. For if we cannot reasonably blame God because He could not make his angels so perfect that they would not covet His beauty and greatness, for the reason that He could not make them like Himself or coequal with Himself, much less therefore can we blame those angels because they could by no means avoid coveting the beauty and greatness of God as a result of the character which they had from their maker; in other words, because He could not make them so perfect that they would not covet His beauty and greatness.

I say again: If God could not make His angels of such perfection that they would not so covet His beauty and greatness and thus would not, for this reason, become demons, neither could those angels avoid that evil in any way. And so, according to certain persons,[86] it necessarily follows that all angels and indeed men who now are saved are bound always to covet that beauty and greatness and always to sin against their God by this covetousness, and of necessity to become demons because of it, just as they say befell the other angels. And this is true particularly because God could not nor cannot nor ever will be able to make anyone like Himself or coequal with Himself in any way.

And if Master William should say: They who were saved could not covet any more or sin, because they were enlightened and subtly warned by the punishment of the other angels, who became demons through their covetousness, this may be answered as follows: God, who above was called good, holy, and just, would be the sole cause and principle of the punishment and ruin of all His angels. For He would have inflicted eternal punishment on His angels without reason or justice, in that He could not make them of such perfection that they would not covet His beauty and greatness, nor could those angels in any way avoid that evil, because they had been created at an earlier time than the other angels, who were enlightened by their punishment and fall. Indeed, those angels, who, as many say, became demons, could not be enlightened and warned by the punishment of other angels, because there were no other angels created before them. And so the aforesaid angels could with reason bring most very great complaint against their Lord for afflicting them with those countless punishments, the more so because He could not make them so perfect that they would not covet His beauty and greatness; therefore those angels could not by any means avoid that covetousness. Hence, it is utterly amazing that it can ever enter the mind of any wise man that God, who is good, holy, and just, should condemn His angels for all time, afflicting them with eternal torture, because He could not make them of such perfection that they would not envy His beauty and greatness, nor could they ever in any way receive that perfection from Him.

[20] *Concerning the Angels.*—And if it be objected: Although God cannot make His angels like Himself or coequal with Himself, yet He could indeed have perfected them, had He so wished, to such a degree that they would never have envied His beauty. But He did not choose to do this, because they had free will from God, that is, the free capacity or

the freedom to envy or not to envy His beauty and greatness, at their pleasure. Thus, there is no validity in what has been said above to the effect that God could not make His angels so perfect that they would not envy His beauty and greatness, because He could not make them like Himself or coequal with Himself in any way.

And thus it is obvious, if we accept the doctrine discussed above, that God did not choose to make His angels so perfect that they could not envy His beauty and greatness; but, knowingly and in full awareness, He made them of such imperfection that they could not in the least avoid covetousness, and He bestowed on them all the causes by which He knew those angels would fall in the future; and particularly [is it evident] in Him, who wholly knows all the future, in whom all causes by which those angels were to be covetous in the future were known from the beginning, by whom all things are done of necessity from eternity, as was made sufficiently clear above where free will was discussed. And so, to the wise, it is obvious, according to the above doctrine, that God cannot absolve Himself on rational grounds, because He did not choose to avert that evil in any way, but knowingly and in full awareness created His angels of such imperfection that it was from eternity impossible in Him for them not to covet His beauty and greatness.

From this one may know that those angels did not have from God a free will by which they could entirely avoid covetousness, and especially not from a God who knows directly all the future, in whom it is impossible that that which is future, with all the causes which determine it, can fail to be in the future. And this is so particularly because, if there is only one First Principle, He is directly the cause of all causes. It follows therefore of necessity, according to the said doctrine, that God would be the first cause of all envy and indeed of all evil, as is written, "He who provides the occasion for harm should be held to have done the harm." [87] One most certainly cannot believe this of the true God.

[*II. On Creation*]
[1] *The Contention of Our Opponents That God Is the Creator or Maker of All Things.*—Although our opponents have no argument based on truth, yet they may perchance still spurn the arguments set forth above and loudly assert: These words deserve no credence at all,

for they represent the opinions of men and the argumentations of philosophers, of which the Apostle says to the Colossians, "Beware lest any man cheat you by philosophy and vain deceit, according to the tradition of men, according to the elements of the world, and not according to Christ." [1] And so, perchance, they might say that one need give absolutely no credence to two principles, for the reasons advanced above because they were not at all confirmed by testimony of the Holy Scriptures [2] and, in particular, because one cannot discover through biblical texts that there is any god other than the true Lord God, creator or maker of all, omnipotent, eternal or everlasting, ancient, without beginning or end.

To prove that the true Lord God is the creator or maker of all, they may perhaps vigorously fortify their argument by the following texts and others like them. It is written in the Apocalypse: "Thou art worthy, O Lord our God, to receive glory and honor and power, because Thou hast created all things, and for Thy will they were and have been created"; [3] and again: "And the angel whom I saw standing upon the sea and upon the earth lifted up his hand to heaven, and he swore by Him that liveth forever and ever, who created heaven and the things which are therein, and the earth and the things which are in it, and the sea and the things which are therein, that time shall be no longer." [4] And the Apostle says to the Hebrews, "For every house is built by some man, but He that created all things is God." [5] And Jesus the son of Sirach says: "He that liveth forever created all things together"; [6] and [the Book of Wisdom says,] "For He created all things that they might be." [7] And the apostles in their Acts say, "Lord, thou art He that didst make heaven and earth, the sea, and all things that are in them." [8] And Paul, in the same book, says to the Athenians: "That I preach to you God, who made the world and all things therein, He, being Lord of heaven and earth, dwelleth not in temples made with hands; neither is He served with men's hands as though He needed anything, seeing it is He who giveth to all life and breath and all things." [9] And John in his Gospel says, "All things were made by Him, and without Him was made nothing that was made." [10]

[2] *That God Is Called Father of All.*—Not only is the Lord our God called the creator or the maker of all, but He is called the Father of all, as the Blessed Paul says to the Ephesians: "One Lord, one faith, one baptism, one God and Father of all, who is above all and through all

and in us all." [11] And again, "For this cause I bow my knees to the Father of our Lord Jesus Christ, of whom all paternity in heaven and earth is named." [12] And in the first Epistle to the Corinthians, the same Apostle says, "Yet to us there is but one God, the Father, of whom are all things and we unto Him, and one Lord Jesus Christ, by whom are all things and we by Him." [13] And he says to the Romans, "For of Him and by Him and in Him are all things." [14] Also, all things were created in the Lord Jesus Christ, and by Him and in Him all things were created, as Paul says to the Colossians of Christ, "who is the image of the invisible God, the first-born of every creature; for in Him were all things created, in heaven and on earth, visible and invisible, whether thrones, or dominations, or principalities, or powers; all things were created by Him and in Him. And He is before all, and in Him all things consist." [15]

Thus our opponents appear to confirm their doctrine many times over by these texts and others like them.

[3] *On the Omnipotence, the Eternity, and the Sempiternity of God.* —Our opponents may indeed advance certain passages from Holy Scriptures to show that the aforesaid Lord our God is omnipotent and eternal or everlasting and ancient, insisting that there is no other power or domination but His, as David says: "For I have known that the Lord is great, and our God is above all gods. Whatsoever the Lord pleased he hath done, in heaven, in earth, in the sea, and in all the deeps." [16] And the Apostle, in the first Epistle to Timothy, says, "I charge thee before God, who quickeneth all things and before Christ Jesus, who gave testimony under Pontius Pilate, a good confession, that thou keep the commandment without spot, blameless, unto the coming of our Lord Jesus Christ; which in His times He shall show, the King who is the Blessed and only Mighty, the King of kings, and the Lord of lords." [17] And in the Apocalypse is written, "I give Thee thanks, O Lord God Almighty." [18] And the Apostle says to the Romans, "For there is no power but from God, and those [powers] that are, are ordained of God." [19]

Moreover, that the true Lord God is eternal, or everlasting and ancient, is shown by the following texts: David says, ". . . that ye may relate it in another generation. For this is God, our God unto eternity, and forever and ever. He shall rule us forevermore." [20] And Isaiah says, "For thus saith the Lord High and Eminent that inhabiteth eternity." [21] And the Apostle says to the Romans, "According to the revelation of the mystery which was kept secret from eternity (which now is made manifest by the scriptures of the prophets, according to the precept of the eternal God)." [22]

Of the sempiternity of this true God Isaiah says, "The Lord is the everlasting God, who hath created the ends of the earth." [23] And Jeremiah says, "But the Lord is the true God, He is the living God and the everlasting king." [24]

Of the antiquity of the Lord, Daniel says: "I beheld therefore in the vision of the night, and lo, one like the son of man came with the clouds of heaven, and he came even to the Ancient of days"; [25] and again, "Till the Ancient of days came." [26]

Thus indeed they might say that, because of these texts quoted and others like them, one must firmly believe in one sole God, Lord and omnipotent Prince, who is eternal or everlasting, and ancient, as seems to be made manifest above.

[4] *A Reply to the Objections Raised Above.*—It is my intent, with the aid of Jesus Christ, to resolve their objections in accordance with my concept. Now, in the first place, I wish to clarify by scriptural references the precise meaning of "creating" and "making," in connection with which our Lord God is called "creator" and "maker" of all; and secondly, I wish to show what is meant by "all" and other terms of universality in the Holy Scriptures.[27]

I perceive the words "to create" or "to make" used throughout the Scriptures in three senses.[28] Now, I say: It is "to create" or "to make" when the true Lord God adds to the essences of those beings who were already exceedingly good something which ordains them to aid those who are to be saved. In this sense, our Lord Jesus Christ was ordained bishop by the true Lord God and "anointed with the Holy Spirit and with power," so that He could free all those "oppressed by the devil";[29] and in the same sense the angels and ministers of God the Father were made so that they might aid those who receive the inheritance of salvation. Sometimes the words "to create" or "to make" are used when God himself adds something to the essences of those who had become evil and disposes them to good works. I also call it "to create" or "to make" when something is permitted by God himself to him who is wholly evil, or to his minister, who cannot achieve what he desires unless the good Lord himself endures his deceit patiently for a time, to His own honor and to the shame of that most wicked enemy of His.

[5] *On the First Meaning of "Creating" or "Making."*—As for the

first meaning of "creating" or "making," I have sought to provide the clearest proof as it appears in passages from Holy Scripture: Thus the Blessed Paul, referring to the creation of our Lord Jesus Christ, says to the Colossians, "Lie not to one another; stripping [yourselves] of the old man with his deeds, and putting on the new, him who is renewed unto knowledge of God according to the image of Him that created him." [30] And the same Apostle says to the Ephesians, "And be renewed in the spirit of your mind, and put on the new man, who according to God is created in justice and holiness of truth." [31] And through Isaiah the Lord says: "Drop down dew, ye heavens, from above, and let the clouds rain the just; let the earth be opened and bud forth a savior, and let justice spring up together; I the Lord have created him." [32]

Of the "making" of the Lord Jesus Christ himself, moreover, the Blessed Peter says in the Acts of the Apostles, "Therefore let all the house of Israel know most certainly that God hath made both Lord and Christ, this same Jesus whom you have crucified." [33] And Paul says to the Hebrews: "Wherefore, holy brethren, partakers of the heavenly vocation, consider the apostle and high priest of our confession, Jesus, who is faithful to Him that made Him"; [34] and again, "For to which of the angels hath He said at any time, 'Thou art my Son, today have I begotten Thee'?" [35]

Moreover, in regard to the making of the good spirits and angels,[36] who were made by the true Lord God, the Blessed Apostle says to the Hebrews: "And to the angels indeed He saith, 'He that maketh his angels spirits and His ministers a flame of fire' "; [37] and again, "Are they not all ministering spirits, sent to minister for them who shall receive the inheritance of salvation?" [38] And the Lord says through Isaiah, "Go, ye swift angels," [39] and so on.

[6] *That "to Create" or "to Make" May Mean to Create or Make from Something, as from Some Pre-existent Matter.*—From the foregoing, one must firmly believe that our Lord Jesus Christ and the other good angels of the true Father are not said to be "created" or "made" by the true Lord God in the sense that their essence originated only with this creation or production, nor [is it said] that their essence was constituted out of nothingness in the sense apparently asserted by our opponents, who believe that for God "to create" is to make something exclusively and essentially from nothing. Their opinion is most clearly refuted by the testimony of Holy Scriptures. For the angel of the Lord

says to Joseph in the Gospel of Matthew, "Joseph, son of David, fear not to take unto thee Mary thy wife, for that which is conceived in her is of the Holy Spirit." [40] He did not say, "is created from nothing." And in the Book of Wisdom it is written, "For Thy almighty hand, which made the world of matter without form, was not unable," [41] and so on. And in Genesis it is written, "And God formed man of the slime of the earth, and breathed into his face the breath of life; and man became a living soul." [42] And Jesus the son of Sirach says: "The most High hath created medicines out of the earth"; [43] and again, "God created man of the earth and made him after his own image." [44]

And so it is clear that in the judgment of the wise, we may with most excellent reason reject the doctrine of our opponents by the testimony of the Scriptures.

[7] *On Creating and Making.*—Therefore my exposition given above is true; to wit, that "to create" or "to make" means to add something to the essences of those who already were exceedingly good, as has been demonstrated with sufficient clarity in the foregoing. This is the way I construe its meaning. The good are said to be created and made by the true Lord God, that is, formed by Him for the salvation of sinners. It is in this sense that the Apostle speaks of our Lord Jesus Christ to the Hebrews: " 'What is man that Thou art mindful of him, or the son of man, that Thou visiteth him?' " [45] and so on; and " 'Thou hast set him over the works of thy hands.' " [46] And David, in the character of Christ, as we believe, says, "But I am appointed king by Him over Zion His holy mountain." [47] And so, according to this concept, this creation or production of the good is a noble one, of which, for instance, Ecclesiastes says: "He hath made all things good in their time"; [48] and again, "I have learned that all the works which God hath made continue forever; we cannot add anything nor take away from those things which God hath made that He may be feared." [49] And Jesus the son of Sirach says, "All the works of the Lord are exceeding good." [50] And in Ecclesiasticus is written, "O how desirable are all His works; all these things live and remain forever, and for every use all things obey Him." [51] And David says: "How great are Thy works, O Lord? Thou hast made all things in wisdom"; [52] and again, "By Thy ordinance the day goeth on, for all things serve Thee"; [53] and again, "For He spoke and they were made, He commanded and they were created. He hath established them forever and for ages of ages." [54]

And so it clearly seems that this noble creation and production of the good is established forever and for ages of ages by the true Lord God. But if one follows the doctrine of our opponents as I interpret it, this cannot be so, most particularly if all the heavens which now are, and the earth, and all the elements are to be completely destroyed by the heat of fire as, in their opinion as I interpret it, the Blessed Peter testified.[55]

[8] *On the Second Meaning of "Creating" and "Making".*—I now intend to treat of the second meaning of "making" and "creating," of which I said above that "to create" and "to make" mean to add something to the essence of those who had been made evil which disposes them unto good works.[56] For the Apostle says to the Ephesians, "For we are His workmanship, created in Christ Jesus in good works, which God hath prepared that we should walk in them." [57] And David says: "All expect of Thee that Thou give them food in season. What Thou givest to them, they shall gather up; when Thou openest Thy hand, they shall all be filled with good. But if Thou turnest away Thy face, they shall be troubled; Thou shalt take away their breath, and they shall fail and shall return to their dust. Thou shalt send forth Thy spirit, and they shall be created; and Thou shalt renew the face of the earth." [58]

[9] *Explanation of the Text of Isaiah "I Am the Lord, and There Is None Else."*—The Lord says through Isaiah: "I am the Lord and there is none else. I form the light and create darkness; I make peace and create evil, I the Lord that do all these things." [59] This text can be interpreted as though its meaning were: There is no Lord but I who "form the light"—which is Christ, who is the "true light, which enlighteneth every man that cometh into this world," [60] as the Blessed John says in his Gospel. And I who "create darkness"—which means to ordain the Gentile people to good works, as was set forth above; they who were become part of darkness, walking in darkness, as one reads in the Gospel, "The people of the Gentiles that walked in darkness hath seen great light." [61] And the Apostle says to the Ephesians: "For you were heretofore darkness, but now light in the Lord. Walk then as children of the light." [62] "I make peace"—that is, Christ, who was our peace, as the Apostle says of Him to the Ephesians, "For He is our peace who hath made both one, and hath broken down the middle wall of partition"; [63] or [Christ], who made peace between the people of the Gentiles and the people of Israel, as is contained in the same Epistle: "[That He might make the two in himself] into one new man, making peace, and might

reconcile both to God in one body. And coming, He preached peace to you that were afar off and peace to them that were nigh; for by Him we have access both in one Spirit to the Father." [64] And I "create evil"— that is, I appoint the people of Israel, who had become evil, unto good works, as Christ says of them in the Gospel of Matthew, "If you then, being evil, know how to give good gifts to your children, how much more will your Father who is in heaven give good things to them that ask him?" [65] It is in this sense that the Lord is said to create darkness and evil. But this is not possible, according to the opinion of our opponents, who believe that "to create" is to make something from nothing. And their opinion is most clearly disproved. For surely, if the true Lord God exclusively and essentially created darkness and evil, undoubtedly He would be the cause and beginning of all evil, which is an utterly vain and wicked conclusion.

[10] *On the Making of Those Who Had Become Evil.*—Moreover, Paul says to the Corinthians in his second Epistle, in regard to the making of those who had become evil, "But our sufficiency is from God, who also hath made us fit ministers of the new testament, not in the letter but in the spirit; for the letter killeth, but the spirit quickeneth." [66] And again, the same Apostle says to the Colossians, "Giving thanks to God the Father, who hath made us worthy to be partakers of the lot of the saints in the light of truth." [67] And he says to the Corinthians, "If, then, any be in Christ a new creature, the old things are passed away; behold all things are made new." [68] Also, of this making, as is believed, the Blessed John says in the Apocalypse, "And He that sat on the throne said, 'Behold, I make all things new.' " [69] Now, according to this interpretation, our Lord God is called "creator" or "maker" for constituting sinners unto good works, as is clearly enough explained in the foregoing.

[11] *On the Third Meaning of "Creating" and "Making."*—In regard to the third meaning of "creating" and "making"—about which I remarked above that one says "to create" or "to make" when something is permitted by the true Lord God to the one who is wholly evil or to his minister, who cannot accomplish his desires unless the good Lord himself suffers the deceit patiently for a time, to His own honor and to the shame of His most wicked enemy—I intend to confirm my interpretation by biblical proofs.

For the prophet Ezechiel says of the Assyrian king, who represents the devil: [70] "The cedars in the paradise of God were not higher than he, the fir trees did not equal his top, neither were the plane trees to be compared with him for branches; no tree in the paradise of God was like him in his beauty. For He made him beautiful and thick set with many branches, and all the trees of pleasure that were in the paradise of God envied him." [71] And the Lord says through Isaiah: "I have created the smith that bloweth the coals in the fire and bringeth forth an instrument for his work. And I have created the killer to destroy"; [72] and again, "I am the Lord, and there is none else. I form the light and create darkness; I make peace and create evil, I the Lord that do all these things." [73] And David says, "This sea dragon which thou hast formed to play therein." [74] And in the Book of Job the Lord says to him, "Behold behemoth, whom I made with thee; he eateth grass like an ox." [75] Now, if the Assyrian, the smith, the killer, the darkness, the evil, the dragon, and the behemoth signify him who is the chief principle of all evil, one must necessarily interpret the words, "to create" darkness and evil and the killer, and so on, to mean that God endures from one who is His most wicked enemy deceit and malice against His people for a time, in order to permit them to be trampled underfoot for their sins. So our Lord God is said "to make" the evil which, for our sins, He does not forbid, just as Isaiah says, "But he that is the wise one hath brought evil, and hath not removed his words." [76] And through Jeremiah, the Lord again says, "For I bring evil from the north and great destruction." [77] And through Habakkuk the Lord also says, "For I will raise up the Chaldeans, a bitter and swift nation, marching upon the breadth of the earth to possess the dwelling places that are not their own." [78] And the Lord says through Amos: "Shall the trumpet sound in a city and the people not be afraid? Shall there be evil in a city which the Lord hath not done?" [79] And the Blessed Job says, 'The tabernacles of robbers abound, and they provoke God boldly, whereas it is He that hath given all into their hands." [80] And the prophet Daniel says of the king of Babylon: "Thou art a king of kings, and the God of heaven hath given thee a kingdom, and strength, and power, and glory, and all places wherein the children of men and the beasts of the field do dwell; He hath also given the birds of the air into thy hand and hath put all things under thy power." [81] All this must be understood as occurring by the sufferance of the Lord, because of the sins of the people, as Elihu says in the Book of Job: "And upon nations and over all men He maketh a man that is a hypocrite to reign for the sins of the people" [82]—that is, endures his reign because of the sins of the people. In this wise the Apostle says to the Romans, "What if God, willing to show His wrath and to make His power known, endured with much patience vessels of wrath fitted for destruction, that He might show the riches of His glory on the vessels of mercy." [83] This does not mean, however, that to do evil may be a function directly and essentially of the true Lord God, for were that the case—if there were no evil which the true Lord God had not directly and essentially done—the true Lord God would be fundamentally the cause and beginning of all evil, which is an utterly vain and foolish belief.

Whence, in accordance with our interpretation, we can most intelligibly conclude that God "created" darkness, evil, and murder; "made" the Assyrian; and "formed" the dragon and the many other baneful things noted in the Holy Scriptures; that is to say, He suffers them to prevail over His people for their sins, and in consonance with this, evils are said to be "done" by Him —that is, He gives sufferance for a time to malice directed against His own. And in this sense we can freely concede that Satan was 'created" or "made" by the true Lord God—that is, after he was given license to afflict Job—for by permission which he obtained from the true Lord God he did that which he was unable to achieve by himself. And so he can be said to be "made" by God—that is, he was acknowledged as ruler over the people, not absolutely but, so to speak, indirectly and nonessentially.[84]

And Satan is allowed not only to rule over sinners but also to tempt the just, as is written in the Gospel of the Blessed Matthew about our Lord Jesus Christ, "Then Jesus was led by the Spirit into the desert to be tempted by the devil." [85] And the Blessed Mary says: "And immediately the Spirit drove Him out into the desert. And He was in the desert forty days and forty nights and was tempted by Satan." [86] And the faithful Luke says: "And Jesus, being full of the Holy Spirit, returned from the Jordan and was led by the Spirit into the desert for the space of forty days, and was tempted by the devil"; [87] and again, "And the temptation being ended, the devil departed from Him for a time." [88] And the same thing may be noted in regard to the Blessed Job, as the Lord himself says to Satan, "Behold, all that he hath is in thy hand." [89] And in particular reference to Job the Lord again says, "Behold, he is in thy hand; but yet save his life." [90] And Job says of himself: "God hath shut me up with the unjust man and hath delivered me into the hands of the wicked"; [91] and again, "Doth it seem good to Thee that Thou shouldst calumniate me and oppress me, the work of Thy own hands, and help the counsel of the wicked?" [92] And in the Gospel of John, Christ says to Pilate, Satan's minister, "Thou shouldst not have any power against me unless it were given thee from above"; [93] which is to say, conceded to you, and this may be interpreted as meaning from God. And in this way our Lord God is said "to create" evil when for some reasonable cause He does not prohibit it. Of this one finds clear confirmation in the case of the Blessed Job where in the Book of Tobias one reads of Tobias: "Now this trial the Lord therefore permitted to happen to him, that an example might be given to posterity of his patience, as also of holy Job." [94] And the Blessed James says, "You have heard of the patience of Job, and you have seen the end of the Lord." [95]

That the aforesaid texts, moreover, properly should be so interpreted, even according to the concept of those who believe that "to create" means to make something from nothing, is proved as follows: The Apostle says to Timothy, "For every creature of God is good, and nothing to be rejected." [96] And Ecclesiastes says, "He hath made all things good in their time." [97] And it is written in the Book of Wisdom, "For so much then as Thou art just, Thou orderest all things justly." [98] Therefore, if God made and created and justly ordered all things good, He did not create the darkness or evil, nor did He form the dragon. Nor are even our opponents wont to believe that God had formed the devil as a dragon, but rather as a beautiful angel, nor that He had created angels as demons and things of darkness, but rather as angels shining and luminous.

[12] *That God Did Not Create Darkness or Evil.*—Whence, one should give no credence at all to the belief that the true Lord God absolutely and directly created darkness or evil, especially from nothing, which our opponents think is the proper meaning of "to create." And most particularly this is so because the Blessed John can say in the first Epistle: "That God is light and in him there is no darkness," [99] nor, consequently, [darkness] through Him. Therefore, darkness does not fall within that all-inclusive term which the Apostle employs in his Epistle to the Romans: "For of Him and by Him and in Him are all things," [100] nor yet within that used by the same Apostle with reference to Christ

in his Epistle to the Colossians, "For in Him were all things created, in heaven and on earth, visible and invisible, whether thrones, or dominations, or principalities, or powers: all things were created by Him and in Him. And He is before all, and in Him all things consist." [101] Wherefore Christ says of Himself, "I am the light of the world; he that followeth me walketh not in darkness, but shall have the light of life." [102] So, darkness is not created absolutely and directly by our Lord God and His Son Jesus Christ but only in an indirect and relative sense,[103] which was shown clearly enough above; albeit, in keeping with our thesis, the aforesaid texts can be otherwise interpreted, as is seen in some part to have been done in the foregoing.[104]

Hence, by using the three senses [of "creation"] discussed above and the various meanings which are assigned in Holy Scriptures to "all" and other terms of universality, the texts quoted above can be given their correct interpretation in accordance with our belief. That is, the Lord our God created and made all things, namely, heaven and earth, the sea, and all things which are therein; He made all things in heaven and earth through our Lord Jesus Christ; and all things were created by Him, in Him, and of Him, as has already been demonstrated by many texts.

[*III.   On the Terms of Universality*]

[1] *A Rebuttal: Good and Evil Are Not Denoted by "All" and Other Terms of Universality.*[1]—I have resolved to discuss a subject on which our opponents have often vaunted themselves over us, in that they frequently seek to confirm their doctrine by those terms of universality such as "all" (*omnia*), "all things whatsoever" (*universa*), and "all things" (*cuncta*), and other terms which in biblical texts denote the total number of things. They make no distinction at all among substances and insist, moreover, that all substances whatsoever, the evil as well as the good, the transitory as well as the permanent, have been made and created without exception by the just, true, and holy Lord God. With the aid of the true Father I have determined to rebut their doctrine by the testimony of the Scriptures and the soundest of arguments.

[2] *On the Terms of Universality.*—It should, then, be understood that the terms of universality mentioned above, although they may be so called by grammarians, cannot be categorically so designated by men of real wisdom, to wit, that under any term of universality all substances

and actions whatsoever may be neatly comprehended, and indeed even all accidents. Whence, it is obvious that, among the learned, these terms are called universals according to the construction placed upon them in the minds of those using them, but not at all because all things both good and evil may be absolutely and finally summed up under any given term of universality. And this is particularly true inasmuch as good and evil do not harmonize, nor can one come from the other, since they mutually destroy one another and battle in active and continuous opposition.

Because of this, one should realize that the aforesaid terms of universality are used in scriptural texts with several meanings. Now, there are some such terms which refer to those things which are good, clean, made in wisdom, and highly desirable, which persist forever and which obey our Lord God in every use, as is clearly revealed in the Holy Scriptures. On the other hand, there are other terms of universality, which designate those things that are evil, vain, and transitory, and that ought to be cast aside, to be counted but as dung by the faithful of Jesus Christ,[2] that they may gain our Lord Jesus Christ. There are still other terms of universality, which, as one reads, relate to those who, once established under the power of the king of Babylon, were to have been given into the hands of robbers, and were rather to have been laid waste by "a king of a shameless face." [3] These terms also, we believe, were "concluded under [i.e. confined under the power of] sin, that the promise, by the faith of Jesus Christ, might be given to them that believe." [4] They were also confined in unbelief by the true Lord God "that he may have mercy on all" [5] of them. Now, these terms of universality represent those who are to be reconciled, restored, renewed, re-established, fulfilled, and quickened by our Lord God, and by His Son Jesus Christ, as is manifestly dwelt upon by the Scriptures.

[3] *On the Terms of Universality Referring to the Good.*—I wish to expound the soundest interpretation of those terms of universality which I characterized above as referring to what is good, clean, made in wisdom, and the like, using the evidence of Holy Scriptures. For the Apostle says in the first Epistle to Timothy, "For every creature of God is good and nothing to be rejected." [6] And Ecclesiastes says, "He hath made all things good in their time"; [7] and again, "I have learned that all the works which God hath made, continue forever; we cannot add anything,

nor take away from those things which God hath made that He may be feared." [8] And it is written in Ecclesiasticus: "O how desirable are all His works! All these things live and remain forever, and for every use all things obey Him." [9] And David says: "How great are Thy works, O Lord? Thou hast made all things in wisdom"; [10] and again, "By Thy ordinance the day goeth on, for all things serve thee." [11] And the Apostle says to the Romans: "All things indeed are clean"; [12] and again, "All things are clean to the clean"; [13] and again, "And we know that to them that love God all things work together unto good," [14] and so on.

In this way it is clearly proved by scriptural evidence that the aforesaid terms of universality designate those things which are most excellent and clean, and which persist forever. Hence, among wise men, it seems impossible that the good and the evil, the transitory and the permanent, can be wholly summed up absolutely and directly under these terms of universality, as these wise men can very clearly discover.

[4] *On the Universal Symbols Which Refer to the Evil.*—The discussion now turns to the question of those terms of universality which I characterized above as designating those things which are evil, vain, transitory, and which are to be cast aside, and so on. For Ecclesiastes says: "Vanity of vanities and all is vanity"; [15] and again, "I have seen all things that are done under the sun and behold, all is vanity and vexation of spirit." [16] And again: "All things have their season and in their times all things pass under heaven. A time to be born and a time to die." [17] And again: "All things are subject to vanity. And all things go to one place; of earth they were made and into earth they return together." [18] And again, "And therefore I was weary of my life, when I saw that all things under the sun are evil; and all vanity and vexation of spirit." [19] And the Apostle says to the Colossians: "If then you be dead with Christ from the elements of this world, why do you yet decree as though living in the world? Touch not, taste not, handle not, which are all unto destruction by the very use." [20] And to the Philippians the same Apostle says: "If any other thinketh he may have confidence in the flesh, I more; being circumcised the eighth day, of the stock of Israel, of the tribe of Benjamin, an Hebrew of the Hebrews; according to the Law, a Pharisee; according to zeal, persecuting the church of God; according to the justice that is in the Law, conversing without blame. But the things that were gain to me, the same I have counted loss for Christ. Furthermore I count all things to be but loss for the excel-

lent knowledge of Jesus Christ my Lord, for whom I have suffered the loss of all things and count them but as dung, that I may gain Christ." [21] And in the Gospel of the Blessed Matthew, Christ says to the scribe, "If thou wilt be perfect, go, sell what thou hast"; [22] that is, put away all your material possessions in accordance with the Law. Thence there follows: "Then Peter answering, said to him: 'Behold, we have left all things and have followed Thee; what therefore shall we have?' " [23] In answer, He said, "You have left all things and followed me," [24] and so forth. And the Apostle says to the Colossians, "But now put you also all away: anger, detraction, indignation, malice, blasphemy." [25] And the Blessed John says in his first Epistle: "Love not the world nor the things which are in the world. If any man love the world, the charity of the Father is not in him. For all that is in the world is the concupiscence of the flesh and the concupiscence of the eyes and the pride of life, which is not of the Father but is of the world," [26] and so on.

Thus, it should be clearly realized that these universal symbols which refer to what is evil, vain, and transitory are not of the same sort as those other universal symbols already mentioned, which designate the good, clean, and highly desirable, and which persist forever. And this is particularly true because they cannot be in harmony nor exist together under any form of universality, because they mutually destroy and oppose one another. Nor is it possible that they can derive entirely from the same cause.

[5] *On Those Terms of Universality Designating Those Who for Their Sins Were Established in the Power of the King of Babylon.*—I now propose to clarify the matter of those terms of universality which were once established under the power of the king of Babylon, which were to have been given into the hands of robbers, and were rather to have been laid waste by "a king of a shameless face." [27] These terms, also, we believe, apply to all that are to be reconciled, re-established, fulfilled, and quickened by the true Lord God and by His Son Jesus Christ, as is clearly set forth in the Scriptures. [28] For the prophet Daniel says to Nebuchadnezzar, the Babylonian king: "Thou art a king of kings, and the God of heaven hath given thee a kingdom, and strength, and power, and glory, and all places wherein the children of men and the beasts of the field do dwell; He hath also given the birds of the air into thy hand and hath put all things under thy power." [29] And again: "And after their reign, when iniquities shall be grown up, there shall arise a

king of a shameless face and understanding dark sentences. And his power shall be strengthened but not by his own force, and he shall lay all things waste and shall prosper and do more than can be believed. And he shall destroy the mighty, and the people of the saints, according to his will. And craft shall be successful in his hand, and his heart shall be puffed up. And in the abundance of all things he shall kill many; and he shall rise up against the prince of princes." [30] And Job says, "The tabernacles of robbers abound, and they provoke God boldly, whereas it is he that hath given all into their hands." [31] All this you must interpret as caused by the sins of the people, as the already quoted Daniel, referring to the "little horn," [32] says, "And strength was given him against the continual sacrifice, because of sins; and truth shall be cast down on the ground." [33] And Elihu in the Book of Job says, "And upon nations and over all men He maketh a man that is a hypocrite to reign for the sins of the people." [34] And it was in this way that those who are represented by the aforesaid terms of universality, because of their sins, were once, we believe, put under the power of sin and also of unbelief, given into the hands of robbers, and established under the power of the king of Babylon, so that in the last times God may have mercy on all of those who forsake their wickedness. For the Apostle says to the Galatians, "But the scripture hath concluded all under sin, that the promise by the faith of Jesus Christ might be given unto them that believe." [35] And the same Apostle says to the Romans, "For God hath concluded all in unbelief, that He may have mercy on us all." [36]

[6] *On the Mercy of the Lord Our God.*—So the Lord our God "for His exceeding charity wherewith He loved us" [37] has had mercy upon us, as the Apostle writes to the Ephesians: "Even when we were dead in sins, [God] hath quickeneth us together in Christ"; [38] and as the same Apostle says to Titus: "Not by the works which we have done but according to His great mercy He saved us, by the laver of regeneration and renovation of the Holy Spirit, whom He hath poured forth upon us abundantly through Jesus Christ our Savior, that, being justified by His grace, we may be heirs according to hope of life everlasting." [39] Whence it is written in the Book of Wisdom: "But Thou, our God, art gracious and true, patient, and ordering all things in mercy." [40] And again: "But Thou hast mercy upon all because Thou canst do all things and overlookest the sins of men for the sake of repentance. For Thou lovest all things that are and hatest none of the things which Thou hast made, for

Thou didst not appoint or make anything hating it. And how could anything endure if Thou wouldst not? or be preserved if not called by Thee? But Thou sparest all because they are Thine, O Lord, who lovest souls." [41] And again: "For it was neither herb nor mollifying plaster that healed them, but Thy word, O Lord, which healeth all things." [42] And David says: "All expect of Thee that Thou give them food in season. What Thou givest to them they shall gather up, when Thou openest Thy hand they shall all be fulfilled with good." [43] And Christ says in the Gospel of John, "And I, if I be lifted up from the earth, will draw all things to myself." [44] Thus, it is clearly discovered through statements of the Scripture that God wishes to have mercy upon all His creatures.

[7] *On the Reconciliation of Those Represented by Terms of Universality.*—It can be clearly found through evidence of Scripture that those to whom the aforesaid terms of universality refer are to be reconciled, restored, re-established, fulfilled, and quickened [45] by the Lord our God and by His Son Jesus Christ. For the Apostle says of our Lord Jesus Christ in his Epistle to the Colossians: "Because in Him it hath well pleased the Father that all fullness of divinity should dwell, and through Him to reconcile all things unto himself, making peace through the blood of His cross, both as to the things that are on earth and the things that are in heaven." [46] And in the Gospel of Matthew, Christ says, "Elijah indeed shall come and restore all things." [47] And the Apostle says to the Ephesians: "That He might make known unto us the mystery of His will, according to His good pleasure which He hath purposed in Him in the dispensation of the fullness of times, to re-establish all things in Christ that are in heaven and on earth in Him." [48] And it is written in the Apocalypse, "And He that sat on the throne, said, 'Behold, I make all things new.' " [49] And it is of Christ, we believe, that the Apostle says to the Ephesians, "He that descended is the same also that ascended above all the heavens, that He might fill all things." [50] And in his first Epistle to Timothy, the same Apostle says, "I charge thee before God, who quickeneth all things." [51] It is revealed, moreover, [52] that what is represented by the term "all" has been subjected under the feet of Jesus Christ by the true Lord God, as David says and the Apostle points out to the Hebrews: " 'He has subjected all things under His feet.' For in that He hath subjected all things to Him, He left nothing not subject to Him. But now we see not as yet all things subject to Him." [53]

And again, the same Apostle says in the first Epistle to the Corinthians: " 'For He hath put all things under His feet.' And whereas he saith, 'All things are put under Him'; undoubtedly, He is excepted who put all things under Him. And when all things shall be subdued unto Him, then the Son also himself shall be subject unto Him that put all things under Him, that God may be all in all." [54]

[8] *That All Good and Evil Whatsoever Come Not from One and the Same Cause.*—To wise men, therefore, it is obvious that the good and the evil, the clean and the polluted, the transitory and the permanent, are not summed up under these terms of universality, to wit, "all," "all things whatsoever," and "all things," and others which are found in Holy Scriptures, most particularly because they are complete opposites and contraries. Nor could they all arise entirely from one cause alone. For Jesus son of Sirach says: "Good is set against evil, and life against death, so also is the sinner against a just man. And so look upon all the works of the Most High." [55] And Paul says in the second Epistle to the Corinthians: "For what participation hath justice with injustice? Or what fellowship hath light with darkness? And what concord hath Christ with Belial? Or what part hath the faithful with the unbeliever? And what agreement hath the temple of God with idols?" [56] It is as if he were saying: Justice has absolutely no harmony with injustice, nor light with darkness, nor is there concord between Christ and Belial; which should be understood to mean that these opposites and contraries may not arise from one and the same cause. If it were otherwise—if justice and injustice, light and darkness, Christ and Belial, the faithful and the unbeliever, came absolutely and directly from the Highest Cause of all good—they would be in partnership and in concord, and would not destroy one another in the way that good and evil obviously do every day. For it was clearly pointed out above that, "Good is set against evil, and life against death," [57] and so on.

Hence, it follows that there is another principle, one of evil, who is the source and cause of all wickedness, foulness, and unbelief, as also of all darkness. For otherwise, the true God himself, who is most faithful, and the height of justice, the essence of purity, would be entirely the cause and origin of all evil. All opposites and contraries would emanate entirely from the Lord himself. To suppose this is a most foolish fancy.

[*IV. A Compend for the Instruction of Beginners*]

[1] *On the Creation of Heaven, the Earth, and the Sea.*—I have resolved, further, to treat in brief form for the instruction of beginners [1] the subject of the creation of heaven, the earth, and the sea, of which something has already been said.[2] Now, I say that sometimes in the Holy Scriptures the terms "heavens" and "earth" refer not to the permutable and unreasoning elements of this world only, but to intelligent creatures of the true God, those which have comprehension and understanding.[3] For David says: "The heavens show forth the glory of God, and the firmament declareth the work of his hands." [4] And again, "Hear, O ye heavens, the things I speak; let the earth give ear to the words of my mouth." [5] And Isaiah says, "Hear, O ye heavens, and give ear, O earth, for the Lord hath spoken." [6] And Jeremiah [7] says: "O earth, earth, hear the word of the Lord." And David, "Thy way is in the sea and Thy paths in many waters." [8] It is to these paths, I believe, that David also refers in the passage "All the ways of the Lord are mercy and truth." [9]

Thus, by the terms "heaven," "earth," and "sea" a spiritual existence is implied, as the Blessed John says in the Apocalypse: "And every creature which is in heaven and on the earth and under the earth, and such as are in the sea, and all that are in them, I heard all saying, 'To Him that sitteth on the throne and to the Lamb, benediction and honor and glory and power, forever and ever.' " [10] Thus, David says: "I believe to see the good things of the Lord in the land of the living"; [11] and again, "Thy good spirit shall lead me into the right land." [12] And David [13] says, "But the just shall inherit the land and shall dwell therein forevermore." And Christ commanded "not to swear by heaven, for it is the throne of God," of which, indeed, David says, "Thy throne, O God, is forever and ever" [14]—"nor by earth, for it is His footstool," [15] the Lord added. It is of this footstool that David is believed to have written, "Fear ye the Lord our God, and adore His footstool, for it is holy." [16]

I grant that the Lord our God is the creator and maker of this creation, but not of the "weak and needy elements" of this world, to which the Apostle, for example, refers in saying to the Galatians, "How turn you again to the weak and needy elements, which you desire to serve again?" [17] And to the Colossians the same Apostle says: "If then you be dead with

Christ from the elements of this world, why do you yet decree as though living in the world? Touch not, taste not, handle not, which are all unto destruction by the very use." [18] Therefore, it can by no means be conceded that the Lord our God is creator or maker of death, or of those things which are wholly in death, as is written in the Book of Wisdom, "For God made not death, neither hath He pleasure in the destruction of the living." [19] So undoubtedly there is another creator or maker, who is the source and cause of death and perdition, as of all evil, just as we pointed out with sufficient clarity above.

[2] *On the Omnipotence of the True Lord God.*—Now it is my intention to discuss the omnipotence of the true Lord God, a subject on which our opponents have often vaunted themselves over us, saying that there is no power or potency other than His.

Although the true Lord God may be called almighty by the testimony of Holy Scriptures, it is, however, not to be believed that He ought to be called omnipotent in the sense that He can and does do all evils, since there are many evil things which the true God cannot and never will be able to do. For the Apostle says to the Hebrews, "It is impossible for God to lie." [20] And in the second Epistle to Timothy, the same Apostle says, "If we believe not, He continueth faithful, He cannot deny himself." [21] Nor should one believe that the good God can utterly destroy himself or, contrary to all reason and justice, do absolutely all evil things, this especially because He is not the absolute cause of that evil.

But our opponents may rejoin: On the contrary, we can indeed assert that the true Lord God is almighty, in that He can and does do all good things, and also in that He can do all evil things; he can even lie and destroy Himself if He wishes, but He does not choose to do so.

[3] *That God Cannot Be the Author of Evil.*—The reply is obvious. For if God does not desire all evil things, nor to lie, nor to destroy Himself, there is no doubt that He cannot do so, because that which God most certainly does not desire He cannot do, and what He absolutely cannot do He does not desire. From this it is clear that in the true Lord God there exists no potency for sinning or for doing all evil things. The argument for this is as follows: Since anything predicated of God is indeed God himself, especially because, in the view of wise men, He is not composite nor are there in Him any accidents; it thus follows that God himself and His will are one and the same thing.[22] Therefore,

the good God cannot lie or be the author of all evils unless He so desires, because what He himself does not desire the true God cannot do, for He and His will are one and the same, as was said above.

[4] *That God Cannot Make Another God.*—Now, with reason and without fear I can say further that the true God himself, with all His powers, could not, cannot, and never will be able in any manner, either intentionally or unintentionally, to make another god and lord and creator, like and coequal unto himself in all things. This I prove.

I say, indeed, that it is impossible for the good God to make another god like unto himself in all things, that is to say, eternal and ever-lasting, creator and maker of all things that are good, with neither beginning nor end, one who was never made, created, or born of anyone in the sense that the good God was not made, created, or born of any-one. Yet in Holy Scriptures the true Lord God is not called impotent, because of this. Hence it must firmly be believed that the reason the good God is called omnipotent is not that He can make, has made, or shall make all the evils which are, were, and shall be made hereafter, but because He is omnipotent over all things which were, are, and shall be good; and this particularly because He is wholly the cause and origin of all good, but is in no way, of himself exclusively and essentially, the cause of any evil. It follows, therefore, that among wise men the true God is called omnipotent in respect of all things that He has done, does, and shall do in the future; but among those who understand correctly He is not called omnipotent in the sense that He can do what He has not done, does not do, and never will do. And if our opponents say that He has no desire to do so, the argument carries no weight against me, be-cause He and His will are one and the same, as was demonstrated above.

[5] *That God Is Not Mighty in Evil, but That There Is Another and Evil Potency.*—Therefore, it is firmly to be believed that because there exists in God no potency for evil by which He might bring evil things into existence, there is another principle, one of evil, who is potent in evil. From that one flow all evils which were, are, and shall be.[23] It is evidently of him that David says: "Why doest thou glory in malice, thou that art mighty in iniquity? All the day long thy tongue hath devised injustice; as a sharp razor thou hast wrought deceit. Thou hast loved malice more than goodness, and iniquity rather than to speak righteous-ness."[24] And the Blessed John says in the Apocalypse, "And that great dragon was cast out, that old serpent who is called the devil and Satan,

who seduceth the whole world." [25] And Christ says in the Gospel of
Luke: "The seed is the word of God. And they by the wayside are they
that hear; then the devil cometh and taketh the word out of their heart,
lest believing they should be saved." [26] And the prophet Daniel says:
"I beheld, and lo, that horn made war against the saints and prevailed
over them, till the Ancient of Days came and gave judgment to the
saints of the Most High," [27] and so on. And again: "And another shall
rise up after them; and he shall be mightier than the former, and he shall
bring down three kings. And he shall speak words against the High One,
and shall crush the saints of the Most High, and he shall think himself
able to change times and laws." [28] And again: "And it [the little horn]
became great against the south, and against the east, and against the
strength. And it was magnified even unto the strength of heaven; and it
threw down of the strength, and of the stars, and trod upon them. And it
was magnified even to the prince of the strength; and it took away from
him the continual sacrifice, and cast down the place of his sanctuary." [29]
And the Blessed John says in the Apocalypse: "And there was seen
another sign in heaven; and behold a great red dragon, having seven
heads, and ten horns, and on his head seven diadems, and his tail drew
the third part of the stars of heaven, and cast them to the earth." [30] And
again: "And power was given to him to do two and forty months; and
he opened his mouth unto blasphemies against God, to blaspheme
his name and his tabernacle and them that dwell in heaven. And it was
given unto him to make war with the saints and to overcome them." [31]
So, in the view of wise men, it is deemed wholly impossible that from
the true Lord God derive absolutely and directly this mighty one and
his potency or power, he who daily works in the most evil fashion against
God and His creation, against whom the Lord our God seeks mightily
to contend. This the true God could not do if that one, in all his characteristics, were entirely from Him, as most of our opponents declare.

[6] *On the Destruction of the One Mighty in Iniquity.*—It is most
clearly found in the Holy Scriptures, moreover, that the true Lord God
is about to destroy, together with all his powers,[32] this mighty one who
daily strives against God and His creation. For David says of him who
is mighty in iniquity: "Therefore will God destroy thee forever; he will
pluck thee out and remove thee from thy dwelling place, and thy root
out of the land of the living." [33] And David, invoking his God against
this mighty one, as we believe, says: "Break thou the arm of the sinner

and of the malignant; his sin shall be sought and shall not be found. The Lord shall reign to eternity, yea, forever and ever." [34] And again, "For yet a little while, and the wicked shall not be; and thou shalt seek his place and shalt not find it." [35] And in the Proverbs of Solomon is written, "The wicked man shall be driven out in his wickedness." [36] And the Apostle, referring to the destruction of this mighty one by the coming of our Lord Jesus Christ, says in the Epistle to the Hebrews, "That, through death, he might destroy him who had the empire of death, that is to say, the devil." [37] And so, the Lord our God not only seeks to destroy this mighty one but also all the powers and dominations which sometimes seem through this mighty one to rule over the creatures of the good Lord when they are subjected to this evil dominion. So speaks the Blessed Virgin Mary in the Gospel according to Luke, "He hath put down the mighty from their seat, and hath exalted the humble." [38] And the Apostle says in the first Epistle to the Corinthians, "Afterward the end, when he shall have delivered up the kingdom to God and the Father, when he shall have brought to nought all principality, and power, and virtue, and domination and the enemy of all, death, shall be destroyed last." [39] And the same Apostle says to the Colossians: "Giving thanks to God the Father, who hath made us worthy to be partakers of the lot of the saints in light of truth, who hath delivered us from the power of darkness and hath translated us into the kingdom of the Son of His love." [40] And again: "And you, when you were dead in your sins and the uncircumcision of your flesh, He hath quickened together with Him, forgiving you all offenses, blotting out the handwriting of the decree that was against us, which was contrary to us. And he hath taken the same out of the way, fastening it to the Cross; and despoiling the principalities and powers, he hath exposed them confidently in open show, triumphing over them in himself." [41] Thus the Blessed Paul was sent by the Lord Jesus Christ to despoil the power referred to, as is written of him in the Acts of the Apostles: "For to this end have I appeared to thee, that I may make thee a minister and a witness of those things which thou hast seen and of those things wherein I will appear to thee, delivering thee from the people and from the nations, unto which now I send thee, to open their eyes that they may be converted from darkness to light and from the power of Satan to God, that they may receive forgiveness of sins and a lot among the saints by the faith that is in me." [42] And Christ, in the Gospel of the Blessed Matthew, says: "You are come out as it were to a robber, with swords and clubs to apprehend me. I sat daily with you, teaching in the temple, and you laid not hands on me.[43] But this is your hour, and the power of darkness." [44] Whence one must firmly believe that the power of Satan and of darkness cannot be absolutely and directly from the true Lord God. Otherwise, if, as the unlearned say, the power of Satan and of darkness in all its manifestations were absolutely and directly from the true Lord God, along with other powers, and all virtues and dominations, Paul and the other faithful of Jesus Christ could in no way have been snatched from the power of darkness. And also there would have been no way by which anyone could have been converted from the power of Satan to the true Lord God. This is particularly true because, if all powers, virtues, and dominations were derived exclusively and essentially from the good God, anyone who is extricated from the power of Satan and of darkness would be released from the exclusive and essential power of the true Lord God himself. Nor could the Lord himself despoil and bring to nought any power other than His own, if no other power whatsoever is to be found, as say all the opponents of those true Christians who are rightly known by the name of Albanenses.[45]

[7] *On the Evil Principle.*—For this reason, in the opinion of the wise it is firmly to be believed that there is another principle, one of evil, who is mighty in iniquity, from whom the power of Satan and of darkness and all other powers which are inimical to the true Lord God are exclusively and essentially derived, as was demonstrated above and will appear below, God willing. Otherwise, it would seem obvious to these same [wise] persons that this Divine Might struggles, destroys, and wars against itself. For the Apostle says to the Ephesians: "Finally, brethren, be strengthened in the Lord and in the might of His power. Put you on the armor of God, that you may be able to stand against the deceits of the devil. For our wrestling is not against flesh and blood, but against principalities and powers, against the rulers of the world of this darkness, against the spirits of wickedness in the high places. Therefore take unto you the armor of God, that you may be able to resist in the evil day, and to stand in all things perfect," [46] and so on; "in all things taking the shield of faith, wherewith you may be able to extinguish all the fiery darts of the most wicked one." [47] Thus, the virtues and the powers of the true Lord God by His will would daily be in opposition to one another, were there no other might but His. It is utter foolishness to

believe this of the true God. Therefore, it follows indubitably that there is a might or power other than the true one, which the true Lord God daily seeks to assail, as was most clearly demonstrated to the wise [48] in the foregoing.

[8] *On the Strange God and Many Gods.*—Now, if anyone should be so foolish as to spurn the most valid arguments set forth above, let him fully realize that through the evidence of the Holy Scriptures it may clearly be learned that there is another god, a lord and prince other than the true Lord God. For the Lord says through Jeremiah,[49] "As you have forsaken me and served a strange god in your own land, so shall you serve strange gods in a land that is not your own." And [through Isaiah], "Assemble yourselves and come, and draw near together, ye that are saved of the Gentiles! They have no knowledge that set up the wood of their graven work, and pray to a god that cannot save." [50] And again, "O Lord our God, other lords besides thee have had dominion over us, only in Thee let us remember Thy name." [51] And David says: "Hear, O my people, and I will testify to thee! O Israel, if thou wilt hearken to me! there shall be no new god in thee; neither shalt thou adore a strange god." [52] And again, "If we have forgotten the name of our God, and if we have spread forth our hands to a strange god, shall not God search out these things?" [53] And again: "The princes of the people are gathered together with the God of Abraham; for the strong gods of the earth are exceedingly exalted." [54] And again, "For all the gods of the Gentiles are devils." [55] And Zephaniah says, "The Lord shall be terrible upon them and shall consume all the gods of the earth." [56] And Jeremiah says: "A conspiracy is found among the men of Judah and among the inhabitants of Jerusalem so these likewise have gone after strange gods, to serve them and adore them." [57] And again: "Because your fathers forsook me and went after strange gods and served them and adored them, and they forsook me and kept not my law; and you also have done worse than your fathers, for behold, every one of you walketh after the perverseness of his evil heart, so as not to hearken to me. So I will cast you forth out of this land into a land which you know not, nor your fathers; and there you shall serve strange gods day and night, which shall not give you any rest." [58] And Malachi says: "Judah hath transgressed, and abomination hath been committed in Israel and in Jerusalem, for Judah hath profaned the holiness of the Lord, which He loved, and hath married the daughter of a strange god." [59] And Micah says: "For all people will

walk away every one in the name of his god, but we will walk in the name of the Lord our God forever and ever." [60] And the Apostle says in the second Epistle to the Corinthians: "And if our gospel be also hid, it is hid to them that are lost, in whom the god of this world hath blinded the minds of unbelievers, that the light of the gospel of the glory of Christ, who is the image of God, should not shine unto them." [61] And the same Apostle says in the first Epistle to the Corinthians: "For although there be that are called gods, either in heaven or on earth (for there be gods many, and lords many), yet to us there is but one God." [62] And Christ says in the Gospel of Matthew: "No man can serve two masters. For either he will hate the one and love the other, or he will sustain the one and despise the other. You cannot serve God and mammon." [63] And again, in the Gospel of John, Christ says: "For the prince of this world cometh and in me he hath not anything"; [64] and again, "Now is the judgment of the world, now shall the prince of this world be cast out"; [65] and again, "Because the prince of this world is already judged." [66] And the apostles say in their Acts: " 'Why did the Gentiles rage, and the people meditate vain things? The kings of the earth stood up, and the princes assembled together against the Lord and his Christ.' For of a truth there assembled together in this city against Thy holy child Jesus, whom Thou hast anointed, Herod, and Pontius Pilate, with the Gentiles and the people of Israel," [67] and so on. So it is clearly seen that through the evidence of the Holy Scriptures many gods, lords, and princes in enmity to the true Lord God and His son Jesus Christ can manifestly be discovered, as has just been plainly set forth.

[9] *That an Evil Eternity May Also Be Discerned.*—That for these gods an eternity, a sempiternity, and an antiquity may be discerned different and distinct from that of the true Lord God we can clearly prove through the Scriptures. Christ says in the Gospel of Matthew, "Then shall the king say to them that shall be on his left hand, 'Depart from me, you cursed, into everlasting fire which was prepared for the devil and his angels.' " [68] And the Blessed Jude [brother of] James: "And the angels who kept not their principality but forsook their own habitation He hath reserved under darkness in everlasting chains unto the judgment of the great day"; [69] and again, "As Sodom and Gomorrah and the neighboring cities in like manner, having given themselves to fornication and going after other flesh, were made an example, suffering the punishment of eternal fire." [70] And the Blessed Job says, "Where

the shadow of death, and no order, but everlasting horror dwelleth." [71] And through Ezechiel, the Lord says of Mount Seir: "I will make thee everlasting desolations"; [72] and again, "Behold, I come against thee, Mount Seir, and I will stretch forth my hand upon thee, and I will make thee desolate and waste. I will destroy thy cities, and thou shalt be desolate; and thou shalt know that I am the Lord. Because thou hast been an everlasting enemy, and hast shut up the children of Israel in the hands of the sword in the time of their affliction, in the time of their last iniquity." [73] This [Mount Seir] is a symbol for the devil, who is the enemy of the true God, as Christ pointed out in the Gospel of Matthew. [74] And the Apostle says in the second Epistle to the Thessalonians, "Who also shall suffer eternal punishment in destruction." [75] And Christ says in the Gospel of Matthew, "And these shall go into everlasting punishment." [76] And in the Gospel of the Blessed Mark, He says, "But he that shall blaspheme against the Holy Spirit shall never have forgiveness, but shall be guilty of an everlasting sin." [77]

Habakkuk the prophet, referring to the eternity of the devil, says: "God will come from the south, and the holy one from Mount Pharan. His glory covered the heavens, and the earth is full of his praise. His brightness shall be as the light, horns are in his hands; there is his strength hid. Death shall go before his face, and the devil shall go forth before his feet. He stood and measured the earth; he beheld and melted the nations; and the ancient mountains were crushed to pieces. The hills of the world were bowed down by the journeys of his eternity." [78]

Moreover, regarding the antiquity of the devil it is written in the Apocalypse, "And that great dragon was cast out, that old serpent, who is called the devil and Satan." [79] Whence, if it be fully understood that the essences of things have neither beginning nor end by reason of their eternity, sempiternity, or antiquity (just as, for example, it is evident to anyone is true in the case of the good God), it has, then, been clearly demonstrated in the foregoing that sin, penalties, desolations,[80] error, fire, punishment, chains, and the devil have neither beginning nor end. They are the names either of the chief principle of evil or of his effects.[81] They are evidences of one evil cause, eternal or everlasting or ancient, because if the effect has been eternal or everlasting, it necessarily follows that the cause was the same. There is, then, without doubt, a principle of evil from which this eternity or sempiternity and antiquity are exclusively and essentially derived.

[10] *That There Is Another Creator or Maker.*—That there is, in addition to the faithful Creator to whom they that suffer "commended their souls in good deeds," [82] another god and lord who is a creator and maker, I propose to prove clearly from the Scriptures, chiefly from the Old Testament, in accord with the trust which our opponents place in it.[83] For they openly assert the Lord to be the creator and maker who created and made the visible things of this world, namely heaven and earth, the sea, men and beasts, birds and all creeping things, as we read in Genesis: "In the beginning God created heaven and earth. And the earth was void and empty." [84] And again: "And God created the great whales, and every living and moving creature and every winged fowl according to its kind." [85] And again, "And God made the beasts of the earth according to their kinds, and cattle, and everything that creepeth after its kind." [86] And again, "And God created man to His own image; to the image of God he created him; male and female he made them." [87] And Christ says in the Gospel of the Blessed Mark, "But from the beginning of the creation, God made them male and female." [88]

Now it must be kept in mind that no one can point to the temporal and visible existence of the evil god in this world, nor, indeed, to that of the good God. But a cause is known by its effects. From this, it should be understood that no one can prove him to be an evil god or a creator, except by the fact of his evil works or his fickle words. But I say that he who created and made the visible things of this world is not the true Creator. This I intend to prove by the fact of his evil works and his fickle words, assuming to be true what our opponents most openly affirm, that the works and words which are recorded in the Old Testament were actually produced, visibly and materially, in this world.[89]

For heartily we detest these works, namely adultery, theft of another's property, murder, blasphemy, concurring in falsehood, giving one's word either with or without an oath and never keeping it. All these evil things enumerated were done by the god or creator discussed above, visibly and materially, in this temporal world, according to that interpretation which our opponents put on the Old Testament. They believe that these scriptures speak of the creation and production of this world and of the works which are openly and actually seen on this earth. This also those persons who believe there is only one First Principle are of necessity forced to admit. These things I propose clearly to prove by those scriptures to which our opponents give great credence.

[11] *That the Evil God Brought About Fornication.*—Now, this lord and creator commanded in Deuteronomy: "If a man shall lie with another man's wife, they shall both die, that is to say, the adulterer and the adulteress, and thou shalt take away the evil out of Israel"; [90] and again, "No man shall take [his] father's wife nor remove his covering." [91] And in Leviticus, the Lord again says: "Thou shalt not uncover the nakedness of thy father's wife, for it is the nakedness of thy father"; [92] and again, "If a man lie with his stepmother and discover the nakedness of his father, let them both be put to death." [93]

But contrary to the above-mentioned precept, it is obvious that this lord and creator caused this adultery to be committed openly and carnally in this temporal world, according to the belief and the interpretation of our opponents, as will be found most clearly expressed in the second Book of Kings, read according to their belief, for there this lord and creator says to David through the prophet Nathan: "Why therefore has thou despised the word of the Lord, to do evil in my sight? Thou hast killed Uriah the Hittite with the sword, and hast taken his wife to be thy wife, and hast slain him with the sword of the children of Ammon. Therefore the sword shall never depart from thy house, because thou hast despised me, and hast taken the wife of Uriah the Hittite to be thy wife. Thus saith the Lord, 'Behold, I will raise up evil against thee out of thy own house, and I will take thy wives before thy eyes and give them to thy neighbor, and he shall lie with thy wives in the sight of this sun. For thou didst it secretly; but I will do this thing in the sight of all Israel.' " [94] Thus, according to the belief of our opponents, either this lord and creator was a liar, or without doubt he actually brought about this adultery, as he is clearly found to have done, according to their interpretation, in the second Book of Kings: "And Ahithophel said to Absalom: 'Go in to the concubines of thy father, whom he hath left to keep the house; that when all Israel shall hear that thou hast disgraced thy father their hands may be strengthened with thee.' So they spread a tent for Absalom on the top of the house; and he went into his father's concubines before all Israel." [95] So, as he had threatened, this lord and creator, according to our opponents' interpretation, consummated that deed of adultery temporally and visibly in this world, and also contrary to his own commandment as cited above, "If a man shall lie with another man's wife," [96] and so on.

No wise man, therefore, assumes that the true Creator was he who actually gave a man's wives to his son or to any other man for purposes of fornication, as that creator who, according to the belief of the ignorant made the visible things of this world is believed to have done, as is clearly shown in the foregoing. Wherefore it should be realized that the Lord our God, the true Creator, never decreed that adultery or fornication should actually be committed in this world. For the Apostle says, in his first Epistle to the Corinthians, "Do not err; neither fornicators nor adulterers shall possess the kingdom of God." [97] And the same Apostle says to the Ephesians, "For know you this and understand, that no fornicator or unclean person hath inheritance in the kingdom of Christ and of God." [98] And he says to the Thessalonians, "For this is the will of God, your sanctification: that you should abstain from fornication." [99] Our true Creator, therefore, did not in this temporal world take the wives of David, nor give them to his neighbor to lie with in the sight of all Israel and in the sight of the sun, as was set forth above. But there is, without doubt, an evil creator, who is the source and cause of all the fornication and adultery of this world, as has been proven above and will appear below, God willing.

[12] *That the Evil God Caused the Goods of Others to Be Plundered by Force, and Murder to be Committed.*—We can, moreover, clearly prove through the Old Testament, if we accept the belief of our opponents, that the aforesaid lord and creator caused the goods of others to be plundered by force and caused the actual theft—under the guise of a loan—of the wealth of the Egyptians and even caused most bloody murders. For this very lord says to Moses in Exodus: "Therefore thou shalt tell all the people that every man ask of his friend, and every woman of her neighbor, vessels of silver, and of gold. And the Lord will give favor to his people in the sight of the Egyptians." [100] And again: "And the children of Israel did as Moses had commanded; and they asked of the Egyptians vessels of silver and gold, and very much raiment; and the Lord gave favor to the people in the sight of the Egyptians, so that they lent unto them; and they stripped the Egyptians." [101] And in Deuteronomy, Moses says to the people: "If at any time thou come to fight against a city, thou shalt first offer it peace. If they receive it and open the gates to thee, all the people that are therein shall be saved and shall serve thee paying tribute. But if they will not make peace, and shall begin war against thee, thou shalt besiege it. And when the Lord thy God shall deliver it into thy hands, thou shalt slay all that are therein of the male sex, with the edge of the sword, excepting women and

children, cattle, and other things that are in the city. And thou shalt divide all the prey to the army; and thou shalt eat the spoils of thy enemies, which the Lord thy God shall give thee. So shalt thou do to all cities that are at great distance from thee and are not of these cities which thou shalt receive in possession. But of those cities that shall be given thee, thou shalt suffer none at all to live, but shalt kill them with the edge of the sword, to wit, the Hittite, and the Amorite, and the Cana-anite, the Perizzite, and the Jebusite, and the Hivite as the Lord thy God hath commanded thee." [102] And again in the same book: "And Sihon came out to meet us with all his people to fight at Jahaz. And the Lord our God delivered him to us; and we slew him with his sons and all his people. And we took all his cities at that time, killing the inhabitants of them, men and women and children; we left nothing of them." [103] And again: "So the Lord our God delivered into our hands Og also, the king of Bashan, and all his people; and we utterly destroyed them, wasting all his cities at one time. There was not a town that escaped us; sixty cities, all the country of Argob the kingdom of Og in Bashan," and so on. "And we utterly destroyed them, as we had done to Sihon the king of Heshbon, destroying every city, men and women and children. But the cattle and the spoils of the cities we took for our prey." [104]

Regarding the man gathering sticks on the Sabbath it is written in the Book of Numbers: "And it came to pass, when the children of Israel were in the wilderness and had found a man gathering sticks on the Sabbath day, that they brought him to Moses and Aaron and the whole multitude. And they put him into prison, not knowing what they should do with him. And the Lord said to Moses, 'Let that man die; let all the multitude stone him without the camp.' " [105] And again this lord says in Exodus to the people of Israel: "I will fill the number of thy days. I will send my fear before thee, and will destroy all the people to whom thou shalt come, and will turn the backs of all thy enemies." [106] And in Leviticus the same lord says: "You shall pursue your enemies, and they shall fall before you. Five of yours shall pursue a hundred others, and a hundred of you ten thousand; your enemies shall fall before you by the sword." [107] And he says in the Book of Numbers: "But if you will not kill the inhabitants of the land, they that remain shall be as nails in your eyes and spears in your sides, and they shall be your adversaries in the land of your habitation. And whatsoever I had thought to do to them, I will do to you." [108]

[13] *On the Evil Creator.*—And so, in the opinion of the wise it is quite evident that he cannot be a true creator who, in the temporal world, caused the manifest and merciless destruction of so many men and women with all their children. For it does seem incredible that in the case of the children—since they had not the knowledge rightly to distinguish good from evil, nor the free will, according to the belief of our opponents—the true Creator could in this temporal world have destroyed them pitilessly by a most revolting death; especially when the Lord had said through Ezechiel, "The son shall not bear the iniquity of the father, but the soul that sinneth, the same shall die." [109] Nor does Jesus Christ, faithful Son of our Creator, enjoin his followers to visit utter destruction upon their enemies in this temporal world, but commands rather that they do good unto them. Thus, He says in the Gospel of the Blessed Matthew: "You have heard that it hath been said to them of old, 'Thou shalt love thy neighbor and hate thy enemy.' But I say to you, 'Love your enemies.' " [110] He did not say: In this temporal world, persecute your enemies as your Father did of old; but said, "Love your enemies; do good to them that hate you; and pray for them that persecute and calumniate you, that you may be the children of your Father who is in heaven." [111] It is as though He were saying: that you may be in the love of your Father who is in heaven, to whom belongs this work of mercy. Hence, the Son of God, Jesus Christ himself, was taught by His Father to do this work of mercy in the present, just as He says of himself in the Gospel of John, "The Son cannot do anything of himself, but what he seeth his Father doing; for what things soever he doth, these the Son also doth in like manner." [112] Therefore, it is evident that the Father of Jesus Christ did not cause the manifest destruction of so many men and women with all their children in this temporal world; particularly since this very God is the "Father of mercies, and the God of all comfort," [113] as the Apostle points out to the Corinthians.

[14] *That the Evil God Cursed Christ.*—Moreover, not only did the lord and creator whom we are discussing command that the aforesaid murder be committed in this temporal world, if we accept the belief of our opponents, but he cursed our Lord Jesus Christ, as is recorded in Deuteronomy: "When a man hath committed a crime and is to be punished with death and, being condemned to die, is hanged on a gibbet, his body shall not remain upon the tree, but shall be buried the same day, for he is accursed of God that hangeth on a tree." [114] And the

Apostle says to the Galatians: "Christ hath redeemed us from the curse of the Law, being made a curse for us, for it is written, 'Cursed is everyone that hangeth on a tree.' " [115] Whence, in the opinion of the wise, it is not at all to be believed that the Most Benevolent God, entirely of himself and not at all under the influence of His enemy, cursed His son Jesus Christ—or, rather, cursed himself, if it is true that the Father, the Son, and the Holy Spirit are one and the same, as the uninformed say. But there is indubitably an evil creator, who is the source and cause of the malediction on Jesus Christ as, indeed, he is of all evil.

[15] *How That [Evil] God Concurred in Falsehood.*—Now, according to our opponents, the same lord and creator is found to have concurred in falsehood by sending a very evil and lying spirit. Indeed, the spirit of this god is called an "evil spirit" and a "wicked spirit," as is recorded in the first Book of Kings: "But the spirit of the Lord departed from Saul, and an evil spirit from the Lord troubled him"; [116] and again, in the same book, "So whensoever the evil spirit of God was upon Saul, David took his harp and played with his hand, and Saul was refreshed and was better, for the evil spirit departed from him." [117] And in the Book of Judges it is written: "So Abimelech reigned over Israel for three years. And the Lord God sent a very evil spirit between Abimelech and the inhabitants of Shechem." [118] But the Lord our God sent the spirit of truth, as Christ declares in the Gospel. [119]

And in the third Book of Kings, [120] Micaiah the prophet says: "I saw the Lord sitting on his throne, and all the army of heaven standing by him on the right hand and on the left. And the Lord said, 'Who shall deceive Ahab, king of Israel, that he may go up and fall at Ramothgilead?' And one spoke words of this manner, and another otherwise. And there came forth a spirit and stood before the Lord and said, 'I will deceive him.' And the Lord said to him, 'By what means?' And he said, 'I will go forth and be a lying spirit in the mouth of all his prophets.' And the Lord said, 'Thou shalt deceive him, and shalt prevail; go forth and do so.' Now therefore behold the Lord hath given a lying spirit in the mouth of all thy prophets that are here; and the Lord hath spoken evil against thee." And so, once more it is clearly seen, if we follow our opponents, that he, lord and creator, sent a very evil and a lying spirit. This the true God absolutely could not do in any fashion.

[16] *That the Evil God Did Not Keep His Promise.*—This very lord and creator, moreover, promised to Abraham, and confirmed to his

seed, that he would give to him and to his seed after him all the land which Abraham saw to the north and to the south, to the east and to the west, as one reads in Genesis: "And the Lord said to Abraham, after Lot was separated from him, 'Lift up thy eyes, and look from the place wherein thou now art, to the north and to the south, to the east and to the west. All the land which thou seest I will give to thee and to thy seed forever.' " [121] And again: "Arise, walk hrough the land in the length, and in the breadth thereof, for I will give it to thee." [122] And in Deuteronomy it is written: "Go in and possess the land concerning which the Lord God swore to our fathers Abraham, Isaac, and Jacob, that he would give it to them and to their seed after them." [123]

But although this very lord made the promise aforesaid under oath to Abraham, yet it must be believed that in a temporal sense he never fulfilled it at all. This is what the Blessed Stephen says in the Acts of the Apostles: "For he, the Lord, said to Abraham, 'Go forth out of thy country and from thy kindred and come into the land which I shall show thee.' Then he went out of the land of the Chaldeans, and dwelt in Charan. And from thence, after his father was dead, he removed him into this land wherein you now dwell. And he gave him no inheritance in it, no, not the pace of a foot, but he promised to give it him in possession and to his seed after him." [124] And so, it is clearly seen that he, the lord and creator, failed to fulfill a promise made under oath; nor did he ever, even according to the views of our opponents, fulfill it in the temporal and visible world. Moreover, it does not appear that Abraham in a temporal sense possessed this land at any time, whatever the unlearned may stammer about it.

[17] *How This God Was Actually Seen in This Temporal World.*— It appears, also, in accordance with the belief of the dullards, that the aforesaid lord and creator was plainly seen in this world, by several persons face to face.[125] So we read in Genesis, "And Jacob called the name of the place Penuel, saying, 'I have seen the Lord face to face.' " [126] And in Exodus it is written: "Then Moses and Aaron, Nadab and Abiu, and seventy of the ancients of Israel went up, and they saw the God of Israel"; [127] and again, "And the Lord spoke to Moses face to face, as a man is wont to speak to his friend." [128] And in the Book of Numbers this lord says, "But it is not so with my servant Moses who is most faithful in all my house, for I speak to him mouth to mouth and plainly and not

by riddles and figures." [129] But our true Creator is never seen by anyone with the corporeal eyes of this world, as the Blessed John says in the Gospel, "No man hath seen God at any time; the only begotten Son who is in the bosom of the Father, he hath declared him." [130] And the Apostle says in the first Epistle to Timothy, "To the king of ages, immortal, invisible, the only God, be honor and glory." [131] And to the Colossians the same Apostle says, referring to Christ, "Who is the image of the invisible God." [132]

Therefore, the wise may read [the Scriptures] and believe without doubt that there is an evil god, lord and creator; he is the source and cause of all the evils referred to above. Otherwise, one would be led of necessity to confess that the true God himself, who is shining and good, holy, the living fountain and source of all sweetness, delight, and justice, was directly the cause and origin of all evil, wickedness, bitterness, and injustice. All opposites and contraries would flow forth entirely from the Lord himself. In the opinion of the wise, such a supposition is a most foolish fancy.

[*V. Against the Garatenses*]

[1] *Rebuttal of the Garatenses.*[1]—I have decided to write a further rebuttal of the Garatenses, who often have repeated a boasting challenge to us by saying: You Albanenses cannot prove by evidence from the Holy Scriptures that an evil god is the creator of heaven and earth and all other visible things, which repeatedly you proclaim him to be. I am led to reply briefly to them . . .[2] but it is known, however, that great hostility repeatedly appears between Saracens, the baptized,[3] Jews, Tatars, and other religiously minded persons of this world. Although all believe that there is only one Principle, holy, good, and merciful, they are nonetheless found in constant contention with each other with their harsh words and the cruelest of deeds—even though all undoubtedly believe that in creation all men are brothers. I have already refuted this most foolish belief of theirs with clarity sufficient for the wise.[4]

[2] *Exposure of the Foolish.*—Now, however, I wish to expose to those who do have understanding the folly of the Garatenses; they, like the others, believe in only one most benevolent Creator, and yet are wont repeatedly to assert that there is another lord, the evil prince of this world, who was a creature of the most excellent Creator. He, they

say, corrupted the four elements of the true Lord God. Out of these elements this evil lord in the beginning formed and made man and woman and all the other visible bodies of this world,[5] from which have sprung all other bodies whatsoever which today prevail on earth.

But since this opinion of theirs seems most foolish to the learned, I demand that they confirm their interpretation by evidence from Holy Scriptures, by stating where—in what book, in what text, or in what part of the Bible—one may find that which they believe and openly preach to men, namely, that an evil god or lord corrupted the four elements of the good Lord God and that an evil lord in the beginning made man and woman and all other bodies whatsoever, those of birds, of fishes, of creeping things, and of cattle of this world, as they preach and attest before men.

But perchance they may say: We can indeed prove that an evil god in the beginning made man and woman and all other beings whatsoever from which all carnal bodies are derived. For as one clearly finds in Genesis, he, the evil lord, says to man and woman, to the birds, cattle, and all the other carnal bodies: "Increase and multiply and fill the earth."[6] He says to the fishes: "Increase and multiply and fill the waters of the sea."[7] In that book also, one finds that this god, whom we believe to be evil, says: "Let us make man to our image and likeness";[8] and again, "And God made the beasts of the earth according to their kinds, and cattle and everything that creepeth after its kind";[9] and again, "And the Lord God built the rib which he took from Adam into a woman."[10] And again, He said: "Wherefore a man shall leave father and mother and shall cleave to his wife, and they shall be two in one flesh."[11] And Christ says in the Gospel of the Blessed Mark: "But from the beginning of the creation, God made them male and female." And he adds, "For this cause a man shall leave his father and mother and shall cleave to his wife, and they two shall be in one flesh. Therefore now they are not two, but one flesh,"[12] and so on. And it is in such wise, perhaps relying on the foregoing texts and others like them, that they may allege that an evil god in the beginning made the visible bodies of this world.

I will accept their allegation, so far as I am able, provided they believe the foregoing evidence to be completely true. But let them tell me whether or not they really believe and wish to accept the foregoing evidence and other words which are recorded in the Book of Genesis. If they say they do not, because the evil god is the author and no faith at all is to be put in his words, I answer that denial: Therefore, you have produced no proof from Scripture to substantiate doctrine such as you daily preach. Therefore, how, by what boldness, can you utter such words if you can provide no argument from Holy Scripture to buttress your opinion?

But suppose they say: Although we believe this god to be evil, none-theless we accept as true this evidence which we have advanced just as it is recorded in Genesis, to wit, that he, the evil god, made the visible bodies of this world, as was pointed out in the foregoing. To them I reply: If you seek to confirm from the Book of Genesis doctrine such as you preach daily—namely, that an evil god corrupted the four elements and in the beginning made man and woman and all fleshly bodies—then why do you daily contend with us, saying that we cannot prove to you one evil creator god? Can we not plainly prove to you, through the texts from Genesis with which you buttress your opinion, that this god, whom you believe to be evil, is the creator of heaven, earth, and all other things which are visible, just as he is their maker? For in Genesis, one reads: "In the beginning God created heaven, and earth. And the earth was void and empty";[13] and again, "And God created the great whales, and every living and moving creature"; and so on, "and every winged fowl according to its kind."[14] And again: "And God created man to his own image, to the image of God he created him, male and female he created them";[15] and again, "And he blessed the seventh day and sancti-fied it, because in it he had rested from all his work which God created and made."[16] And again, "But Melchizedek, the king of Salem, bringing forth bread and wine, for he was the priest of the most high God, blessed him and said, 'Blessed be Abram by the most high God, who created heaven and earth. And blessed be the most high God by whose protection the enemies are in thy hands.' "[17]

And so by testimony from Genesis, in accordance with the demon-stration which we have presented for the Garatenses, we can plainly prove the existence of an evil creator, who created heaven, earth, and all other visible bodies whatsoever, exactly as has already been pointed out with respect to the evil "maker" by evidence from Genesis.

[3] *On All Creation.*[18]—But perhaps some imprudent person among them will say: We do, indeed, believe in only one Creator and Maker of all, who created and made all visible and invisible things, just as is written in the Gospel of the Blessed John: "All things were made by

him, and without him was nothing made."[19] And Paul says in the Acts of the Apostles: "That I preach to you: God, who made the world, and all things therein," and so on, "and hath made of one all mankind to dwell upon the whole face of the earth."[20] In the same book the apostles said: "Lord, Thou art He that didst make heaven and earth, the sea, and all things that are in them."[21] And in the Apocalypse is written: "Fear the Lord and give Him honor, and adore ye Him that made heaven and earth, the sea, and the fountain of waters."[22] And the Apostle says to the Hebrews: "He that created all things is God."[23] And so, perhaps, by these passages and others like them might they attest one sole Creator and Maker of all.

Against this I object as follows: If, indeed, the true Lord God in the beginning made male and female, fowls and cattle, and all the other visible bodies, why then, do you daily censure the carnal union of man and woman, calling it the work of the devil? Why do you not produce sons and daughters for your Lord God? Why do you not eat the meat, the eggs, and the cheese which are from your Creator, most good? And wherefore do you utterly condemn eating them, if you believe that there is only one Creator and Maker of all visible things? It is not surprising that the Romans[24] constantly cite against you[25] the text of the Blessed Paul, who says to Timothy: "Now the Spirit manifestly saith, that in the last times some shall depart the faith, giving heed to spirits of error, and doctrines of devils, speaking lies in hypocrisy, and having their conscience seared, forbidding to marry, [enjoining] to abstain from meats, which God hath created to be received with thanksgiving by the faithful, and by them that have known the truth. For every creature of God is good, and nothing to be rejected."[26] Now if it be true that the most benevolent and merciful God created and made man and woman and the visible bodies of the world, you repeatedly scorn the creation of the true Lord God when you condemn His matrimony.

The Garatenses are thus ensnared by their own words.

[4] *A Declaration to the Faithful.*—Let it be spread abroad to all the faithful in Christ that, because of the slanderous statements of a certain member of the Garatenses who boasted excessively in the presence of our friends, I have been moved to write against him—as by Satan the Lord was moved when He said in the Book of Job: "Thou hast moved me against him,"[27] and so on—although I have not troubled myself to do this previously. But by the aid of Jesus Christ, I may say

with the prophet: "His sorrow shall be turned on his own head: and his iniquity shall come down upon his crown."[28] Now, however, I serve notice upon you Alb . . .[29] and the whole group of your Garatenses that if using the whole text of the Bible you wish to uphold and defend your faith, that which you hold and preach every day before your believers— which is that the devil corrupted the four elements of the true Lord God, to wit, heaven, earth, water, and fire; that he in the beginning made man and woman and the other visible bodies of this world—I intend to uphold and defend my faith, which I hold and openly preach before Christ's faithful, by testimony of the Law, the prophets, and the New Testament, which I believe to be true and to declare the truth, namely, that there is an evil god who created heaven and earth, the great whales, and every living and moving creature, and every winged fowl according to its kind, and made man and woman; who formed man of the slime of the earth, and breathed into him the breath of life— things which this god has done, as I have clearly read in the Book of Genesis.[30] If you desire to meet this challenge, choose any place which seems to you appropriate and convenient, in the full knowledge that I, as I have already made clear, am prepared with the aid of the true Father to sustain my position.

[5] *A Challenge.*—Again, I wish you to know, Al . . .,[31] that I have been informed by Peter of Ferrara[32] of your admission to him that you are unable to establish through the text of the New Testament this belief of yours to the effect that the devil corrupted the four elements of the good God and that he made male and female, or words to this effect. Whence I say this to you and to all your Garatenses: If you wish to confess this in the presence of our faithful followers and friends, to wit, that you cannot prove the truth of your faith by texts which you believe to be valid and to declare the truth; if, as is reported, you wish to confess this, know you that I elect to uphold my faith and to prove it by the Holy Scriptures and by texts which I believe to declare the truth. My position is that this god, whom I believe to be evil, created heaven and earth and the other things enumerated above. If you are unwilling to admit this, defend, then, your faith, which you so assiduously preach, by texts which you believe to be true and to declare the truth, just as I stand ready to defend my faith. If, indeed, you do not wish to do this, it is truly most astonishing that you ask men to accept your belief, which is that the devil corrupted the four elements of the true Lord God, out

of which in the beginning he made the visible bodies of this world. It is astonishing, moreover, that you cannot produce solid proof by texts which you believe to be valid and to declare the truth, yet you choose to reject my most benevolent faith, which I am prepared to buttress strongly by evidence from the Law, the prophets, and from the New Testament.

Now let the adversary of truth keep silent and never again dare to utter the words referred to above!

[6. *A Further Argument against the Garatenses.*][33]—A further argument against the Garatenses is this: that every day they preach and assert that in the beginning the devil corrupted the four elements of the true Lord God, namely, heaven, earth, water, and fire. If this is true, as they believe and repeatedly preach and affirm to their believers, let the Garatenses answer the following objection which I pose against them: Was this corruption of the holy elements of the true Lord God, which was accomplished by the devil, a good and holy thing, or was it evil and most vain? If they should answer that it was good and holy, the reply then would be: If that were true, they would falsely believe and preach. For they say the devil corrupted the four elements of the true God, which would be untrue, since a good and holy act would not corrupt the holy elements which were from the good Lord God. And, pursuing this argument, it would be necessary for them to believe that the formation of male and female, from which visible bodies were produced and which they hold to have been effected in the beginning by the devil, was good and holy. This is the exact opposite of their belief, since they preach and absolutely affirm that acts of union of male and female are wicked and not in accordance with the will of God. Why, then, do they reject meat, eggs, and cheese, made from the most holy elements, if that corruption or formation which was accomplished by the devil in the beginning was good and holy? Hence, whoever may say this is admirably refuted.

But assume them to reply: That corruption or formation of the most holy elements of the true Lord God which was accomplished by the devil was evil and most vain and contrary to God's will, as they indubitably believe and affirm. The rejoinder then would be: Now let the Garatenses answer whether the corruption of the most holy elements— which was evil and vain, which was accomplished by the devil, as was admitted above—was done by the will of the Most Holy Father or entirely against His will. If they should say that the corruption of the holy elements was done by the will of the Lord, for it is incredible that the devil could corrupt the most holy elements contrary to the will of God, the rejoinder would be: Thus it follows that the Lord had an evil will when He desired evil and most vain corruption to be accomplished in His most holy elements, as just stated. And if they should say that the will of God was good and holy when He wished His holy elements to be corrupted, for by that corruption or formation was established the kingdom of the most holy Creator, namely, the kingdom of new souls, who had been created from eternity and are now daily given form[34] through the union of man and woman, then it would follow of necessity that the union of man and woman is entirely good and holy, if thus and in no other way God seeks completely to renew His kingdom with new souls. Now this union ought not to be utterly repudiated, as the Garatenses repeatedly do, were it the true means by which new souls are given form. If, however, they should say: Indeed, we believe this corruption or formation was effected in the most holy elements contrary to the will of God, then it follows of necessity that there is another principle, one of evil, which can corrupt the four elements of the most holy Creator entirely against the latter's will. This would not be true if there were only one First Principle. Also, had the devil been a creature of the true Lord God, he could not have done any violence to the most holy elements against the latter's will. Therefore, it follows that there are two principles of things, to wit, one of good, the other of evil; and the latter is the source of the corruption of the holy elements and also the source of all evil. Therefore, the Garatenses are entangled in their own most foolish arguments.

But perhaps they would still protest by saying: The corruption of the holy elements was not accomplished by the will of the Lord nor against His will, but was done by His permission and acquiescence. But let the Garatenses answer whether this acquiescence and permission, by which the most holy elements were corrupted, was good and holy, or evil and most vain. If they should say: This acquiescence was good and holy, then it follows of necessity that the holy elements were not corrupted at all, since the most holy elements would not be corrupted by a good and holy acquiescence. And also, that formation of man and woman which, as they believe, was effected by the devil would be most good and holy; which is the direct opposite of what the Garatenses believe. If, however,

they should say: It was evil and vain (as is the truth of the matter)—
then God made a most foolish and wicked concession, and thus God
was the cause of this evil, as the Apostle says to the Romans: "Not only
they that do them are worthy of death, but they also that consent to
them."[35] It is absolutely impossible to believe this of the true Lord God.
It then follows of necessity that there is another principle, one of evil,
who forced the true God to permit and suffer the wicked and most vain
corruption in His most holy elements, quite against His will. This in no
wise would the true Lord God do entirely and directly of His own will.

And so, in all the ways recounted above, the Garatenses are ensnared
in their own words.

[*VI.   On Will*]

[1]   *On the Ignorance of Many Persons.*—Since many persons enveloped in the darkness of ignorance maintain that not only those who
will be saved but those who never will be saved have a potency for
salvation and can be saved, I have decided to demolish this absurd
opinion with most valid argument. Now, let the unlearned answer the
question whether a person can at any moment do that which he has not
done, does not do, never will do. If they reply in the negative, [they
admit that] there is no doubt of its impossibility, for that which cannot
be accomplished at any time is never possible of accomplishment.

At this point I state the issue:[1] Let us presume that there is a certain
person who never did good in order to merit salvation, is not doing so,
and never will do so. Therefore, in accordance with the above reply, it
was impossible for him at any moment to do good in order to merit
salvation; hence, the potency for salvation was never in him. Nor, if the
potency for salvation was never in him, did this individual ever have a
free will by which he might merit salvation. Why, then, will God judge
him, as the dullards opine, if in him there never was the potency for
salvation nor for doing good in order to merit salvation, as was admitted
above? Hence, by this reasoning, vain will be the belief of those who
declared that those persons who are to be saved as well as those who
never are to be saved have a potency for salvation and can be saved,
as was said above.

However, they may say: Indeed, this person could do good if he chose
—although he never has done, does not now, and never will do good—

but he does not wish to. This is the opinion of dullards. Now, I raise the question of will in the same way as above I raised the question of potency. For instance, there is a certain person who never had a good will by which to merit salvation; he does not now have and never will have it. Let them tell me whether this person can ever have the good will which merits salvation. If they say no, because he never had this desire and never will have it—as was said above in the matter of potency and as also is the truth of the matter—then, if he had not the good will which would merit salvation, he indubitably has not the potency to achieve salvation or to do good in order to merit it, since without good will no one can be saved. Therefore, there was never in him the capacity for desiring to do good or for doing good in order to be saved.

In the same way I raise the question of knowledge. Suppose there is a certain person who never was wise enough to tell good from evil or truth from falsehood in order to merit salvation, one who never was and never will be wise enough (undoubtedly many such are to be encountered in this world). If the reply to my question is in the negative, as it was in the matter of potency and of will, then never can this person have the wisdom to distinguish good from evil so as to merit salvation. Therefore, he can not be saved, because without discernment no one can be saved. Therefore, as was pointed out above, this man never had within himself the capacity for salvation or to desire or know the good in order to merit salvation; and by this reasoning will be destroyed the belief of those who say that God shall judge men on their ability (*arbitrium*) to distinguish good from evil and that in those who never will be saved there is the potency for salvation.

But if they reply rashly, saying that indeed this person was able to do what he did not, does not now, and never will do; and was able to have this desire which he had not, has not, and never will have; that he was able to have this knowledge which he had not, has not, and never will have, my answer is this: If that were absolutely true, we might say as well that one can make a goat pope of the Church of the Romans and do all things which are impossible! That one could wish to burn in eternal fire, to suffer all evils and the worst of misfortunes, and, indeed, could have perfect knowledge of the true Lord God, knowledge as whole and perfect as God has!—This is stupid to say and absurd to believe. In truth, if that which was not, is not, and never will be can come to pass, and if it wholly and directly exists in potency, it follows without a doubt that the angels and all the saints could become demons, demons could become glorious angels; Christ could become the devil, and the devil the glorious Christ; and all impossibilities could exist and do exist in potency! This is most false to say and most absurd to believe.

Now the right of the matter is this: A person is able to do whatever he has done, does now, and will do in the future; this existed or exists in him potentially. That which he has not done, does not now do, and never will do, a person cannot do. It did not and does not exist potentially in him in any way, for we cannot properly affirm that that which never eventuates in act in any way exists in potency.[2]

A second comment:[3] I say that in all things which were, are, and shall be the following two things were necessary before they came into existence: the necessity of being and the impossibility of not being. This is particularly true in respect of Him who has complete knowledge from eternity of all the past, the present, and the future. For if God knows that something will be before it exists, it is impossible for it not to come into existence, because God could not know that it would come to pass were there the possibility that it would not. For instance, if before Peter dies someone knows that he is to die today, it is necessary for him to die today, since it is impossible for him both to die and not to die today. Therefore, before his death there pre-existed the necessity of dying and the impossibility of not dying. In respect of him who knew that Peter would die today, then, it was necessary for Peter to die today and impossible for him not to die today.

Here is another argument [against free will]: God, as many believe, made His angels good and perfect. Did He, or did He not, know before they existed that they would become demons? If He did not know it, then He is imperfect, not absolutely all-knowing. In the minds of wise men this is impossible. Therefore, He indubitably knew that they would become demons before they did so, since the First Cause is intelligence, knowing perfectly that which shall come to pass in accordance with that which has the possibility of coming to pass, as Aristotle proves in the third book of *Physics*, where he says that to the First Cause all things are in the present.[4] Therefore, the necessity of their being demons and the impossibility of their not being demons preceded the existence of the angels. It was, then, utterly impossible for them not to be demons, and especially so in respect of God, in whom all things which were, are, and shall be, are in the present, as was said previously. How, by what audacity, can the ignorant say that the aforesaid angels could remain good and holy with their Lord for all time, since that was forever impossible in God, who knows all things before they come to pass, as Susanna says in the Book of Daniel, "O eternal God, who knowest hidden things, who knowest all things before they come to pass"?[5] And so it naturally follows that all things, of necessity, were created in the First Cause. Therefore, those things which are created have being and can exist; and, conversely, those things which are not created have no being and cannot exist in any way. So vanishes the opinion of those who said that the angels had the power both to sin and not to sin.

[2] *More on This Concept.*[6]—The concept presented above cannot, I maintain, be reconciled with the theories of those who believe that there is only one First Principle, who believe that new souls or spirits are daily being created, and that the Lord must judge the good and the wicked, adults and children (*magnos et parvos*), entirely on the basis of their free will or choice. Let these persons answer this question: According to their belief are all peoples to be gathered together before God? If this were true, there would be an untold multitude of children of all races, four years of age or less,[7] and an astonishing multitude of the dumb, the deaf, and the simple-minded, none of whom were ever able to do penance, none of whom had from God in any measure either the ability or the knowledge to do good. Why or how would the Lord Jesus be able to say to these: "Come, ye blessed of my Father, possess you the kingdom prepared for you from the foundation of the world. For I was hungry and you gave me to eat,"[8] and so on? Such a statement most certainly could not be true, since they never were in any way able to do so [of their free will], nor have they done so. But if, perchance, anyone should say that they are to be damned to eternity, I answer that this is wholly rejected in terms of free will. How would the Lord be able to say to these: "Depart from me, you cursed, into everlasting fire. For I was hungry and you gave me not to eat,"[9] and so on? For they could reasonably excuse themselves on the very grounds of free will, saying: We were never able in any way to do this because You never bestowed upon us the capacity for or the knowledge of how to do good. And so free will as it is conceived of by our opponents is entirely rejected.

Consider this most evil concept! There are, indeed, some who believe that children who are born and who die on the same day and whose souls have been newly created will be tortured in eternal punishment forever and ever, and that they can never escape therefrom. Indeed, how utterly astounding is their boldness in preaching that the Lord Jesus must judge all men in terms of free will, for that concept, as was shown above, is utterly untrue.

[*VII.   On Persecutions*]

[1]   *On Striking*[1] *the Shepherd.*—"For it is written, 'I will strike the shepherd, and the sheep of the flock shall be dispersed.'"[2] "The shepherd" means Christ; "the dispersed sheep of the flock" refers to the disciples. But the true Lord God did not by His own act absolutely and directly strike His Son Jesus Christ, for if He had committed this murder by His own act exclusively and essentially no one could incriminate Pilate or the Pharisees or Judah in any way, for they would have carried out the will of God fully; on the contrary, it would have been a sin to resist the will of God. Whence the explanation is this: God "struck" His Son by enduring His death, for they were powerless to carry out the deed unless the Lord himself had permitted it. And this is what Christ said to Pilate: "Thou shouldst not have any power against me unless it were given thee from above."[3] "Unless [permission] were given," He said—not "unless the power were given"—as though He were saying: Unless it were allowed you by God, you would have no power to do me any hurt.[4] For it was the evil principle through whom Pilate and the Pharisees and Judah and the others committed this murder. The true Lord God endured this wicked deed, being unable in a better way to deliver His people from the power of the enemy. He says through Isaiah: "For the wickedness of my people have I struck him."[5] For the disciples, too, have been dispersed, that is, put apart from Christ by the power of evil spirits, for a certain purpose, which was not a good one, as is subsequently recorded: "Then the disciples all leaving Him fled."[6]

[In the manuscript, the passage just translated is followed by miscellaneous items, chiefly excerpts from the Pauline epistles, which occupy one folio.[7] Thereafter appears the Catharist ritual in Latin (see No. 57, part A) and then the following passages on persecution.]

[2]   *On the Persecution of the Prophets, of Christ, of the Apostles, and of Others Who Followed Them.*—As I pondered when reading and rereading the Holy Scriptures, it seemed to me that many times in them

were attested the evils which the prophets and Christ and the apostles once bore in all forgiveness while doing good for the salvation of their souls; and as well, how in the last days the followers of Christ must bear many scandals, tribulations, persecutions, afflictions, sorrows, even death through false Christs and false prophets, and through evil men and seducers; and how they should forgive them that persecute and calumniate them, pray for them, do good unto them, likewise seeking not to resist them. In just that way now the true Christians are seen to act, fulfilling the Holy Scriptures to their own good and honor, and indeed the ungodly and the sinners are seen to act to their own hurt, so as to fill up their sins always to the measure of their fathers.

Whence Paul says in the second Epistle to Timothy: "Know also this, that in the last days shall come dangerous times. Men shall be lovers of themselves, covetous, haughty, proud, blasphemers, disobedient to parents, ungrateful, wicked, without affection, without peace, slanderers, incontinent, unmerciful, without kindness, stubborn, puffed up, and lovers of pleasures more than of God, having an appearance indeed of godliness, but denying the power thereof. Now these avoid."[8] And Christ says in the Gospel of Matthew: "There shall arise false Christs and false prophets, and shall show great signs and wonders, insomuch as to deceive, if possible, even the elect."[9] And to the Romans Paul says: "And as they liked not to have God in their knowledge, God delivered them up to a reprobate sense to do those things which are not convenient; being filled with all iniquity, malice, fornication, avarice, wickedness; full of envy, murder, contention, deceit, malignity; whisperers, detractors, hateful to God, contumelious, proud, pleasing to themselves, haughty, inventors of evil things, disobedient to parents, foolish, dissolute, without affection, without fidelity, without mercy."[10] And the Blessed Peter says in his second Epistle: "But there were also false prophets among the people, even as there shall be among you lying teachers, who shall bring in sects of perdition and deny the Lord who bought them, bringing upon themselves swift destruction. And many shall follow their riotousnesses, through whom the way of truth shall be evil spoken of. And through covetousness shall they with feigned words make merchandise of you, whose judgment now of a long time lingereth not, and their perdition slumbereth not."[11] And Paul says to Timothy in the second Epistle: "But evil men and seducers shall grow

worse and worse, erring and driving into error."[12] And in the Acts of
the Apostles Paul says: "Take heed to yourselves, and to the whole
flock, wherein the Holy Spirit hath placed you bishops, to rule the
Church of God which He hath purchased with His own blood. For I
know that after my departure ravening wolves will enter in among you,
not sparing the flock. And of them shall arise men speaking perverse
things, to draw away disciples after them. Therefore watch, keeping in
memory."[13]

[3] *On the Persecution of the Prophets.*—Moreover, one finds many
references to the persecution of the prophets and of Christ and of the
apostles. For Paul says to the Hebrews concerning the persecution of
the prophets: "And what shall I yet say? For the time would fail me to
tell of Gideon, Barak, Samson, Jephthah, David, Samuel, and the
prophets, who by faith conquered kingdoms, wrought justice, obtained
promises, stopped the mouths of lions, quenched the violence of fire,
escaped the edge of the sword, recovered strength from weakness, became valiant in battle, put to flight the armies of foreigners. Women
received their dead raised to life again. But others were racked, not
accepting deliverance, that they might find a better resurrection. And
others had trial of mockeries and stripes, moreover also of bands and
prisons. They were killed, they were cut asunder, they were tempted,
they were put to death by the sword; they wandered about in sheepskins,
in goatskins, being in want, distressed, afflicted, of whom the world was
not worthy; wandering in deserts, in mountains, and in dens, and in
caves of the earth. And all these, being approved by the testimony of
faith, received not the promise, God providing some better thing for us,
that they should not be perfected without us."[14] And Christ says in the
Gospel of the Blessed Matthew: "For so they persecuted the prophets
that were before you."[15] And in the Acts of the Apostles, the Blessed
Stephen says: "You stiffnecked and noncircumcised in heart and ears,
you always resist the Holy Spirit. As your fathers did, so do you also.
Which of the prophets have not your fathers persecuted? And they have
slain them who foretold of the coming of this just Christ, of whom you
have been now the betrayers and murderers who have received the Law
by the disposition of angels and have not kept it."[16] And in the Gospel
of Matthew, Christ says: "Woe to you, scribes and Pharisees, hypocrites!
that build the sepulchers of the prophets and adorn the monuments of
the just, and say, 'If we had been in the days of our fathers, we would

not have been partakers with them in the blood of the prophets.' Wherefore you are witnesses against yourselves, that you are the sons of them
that killed the prophets. Fill ye up, then, the measure of your fathers.
You serpents, generation of vipers, how will you flee from the judgment
of hell? Therefore behold, I send to you prophets and wise men and
scribes, and some of them you will put to death and crucify, and some
you will scourge in your synagogues and persecute from city to city, that
upon you may come all the just blood that has been shed upon the
earth, from the blood of Abel the just even unto the blood of Zechariah
the son of Berechiah, whom you killed between the temple and the
altar. Amen, I say to you, all these things shall come upon this generation. Jerusalem, Jerusalem, thou that killest the prophets and stonest
them that are sent unto thee! How often would I have gathered together
thy children as the hen doth gather her chickens under her wings, and
thou wouldst not! Behold, your house shall be left to you desolate. For
I say to you, you shall not see me further, till you say, 'Blessed is he
that cometh in the name of the Lord.'"[17] And the Blessed James says
in the Epistle: "Take, my brethren, for an example of suffering evil, of
labor and patience, of forbearance, the prophets, who spoke in the name
of the Lord. Behold, we account them blessed who have endured. You
have heard of the patience of Job, and you have seen the end of the
Lord, that the Lord is merciful and compassionate."[18]

[4] *On the Passion and Persecution of Christ.*—Moreover, the tribulation and persecution and passion and death of our Lord Jesus Christ,
occurring after the tribulation of the prophets of which we spoke above,
is manifestly displayed in Holy Scriptures. For it is found in the Gospel
of the Blessed Matthew that when Christ was a child it was announced
to Joseph by an angel: "'Arise, and take the child and His mother, and
fly into Egypt, and be there until I shall tell thee. For it will come to
pass that Herod will seek the child to destroy Him.' Who arose, and
took the child and His mother and retired into Egypt, and he was there
until the death of Herod."[19] And in the Gospel of the Blessed Luke it
is written of Christ: "And Joseph and His mother were wondering at
those things which were spoken concerning Him. And Simeon blessed
them and said to Mary his mother, 'Behold, this child is set for the fall
and for the resurrection of many in Israel, and for a sign which shall be
contradicted, and thy own soul a sword shall pierce, that out of many
hearts thoughts may be revealed.'"[20] And it is written in the Gospel of

the Blessed Matthew: "And Jesus, going up to Jerusalem, took the twelve disciples apart and said to them, 'Behold, we go up to Jerusalem, and the Son of man shall be betrayed to the chief priests and the scribes, and they shall condemn Him to death. And shall deliver Him to the Gentiles to be mocked, and scourged, and crucified, and the third day He shall rise again'"; and again, "You know that after two days shall be the pasch, and the Son of man shall be delivered up to be crucified."[21] And in the Gospel of John, Christ says: "'Amen, amen, I say unto you, before Abraham was made, I am.' They took up stones therefore to cast at Him; but Jesus hid himself, and went out of the temple";[22] and again, "The chief priests, therefore, and the Pharisees gathered a council and said, 'What shall we do, for this man doth many miracles? If we let him alone so, all will believe in him, and the Romans will come and take away our place and nation.' But one of them, named Caiaphas, being the high priest that year, said to them, 'You know nothing; neither do you consider that it is expedient for you that one man should die for the people, and that the whole nation perish not.' And this he spoke not of himself, but, being the high priest of that year, he prophesied that Jesus should die for the nation, and not only for the nation, but to gather together in one the children of God that were dispersed. From that day therefore they devised to put Him to death";[23] and again, "The world cannot hate you, but me it hateth because I give testimony of it that the works thereof are evil."[24] And again, "These things I command you, that you love one another. If the world hate you, know ye that it hath hated me before you. If you had been of the world, the world would love its own; but because you are not of the world, but I have chosen you out of the world, therefore the world hateth you. Remember my word that I said to you, 'The servant is not greater than his master.' If they have persecuted me, they will also persecute you; if they have kept my word, they will keep yours also. But all these things they will do to you for my name's sake, because they know not him that sent me."[25] And the Blessed John says in the Apocalypse: "And the dragon stood before the woman who was ready to be delivered, that when she should be delivered, he might devour her son."[26] And the Blessed James says: "You have feasted upon earth, and in riotousness you have nourished your hearts in the day of slaughter. You have condemned and put to death the Just One and he resisted you not."[27] And in the Acts of the Apostles, the Blessed Peter says: "Ye men of Israel, hear these words:

Jesus of Nazareth, approved of God among you by miracles and wonders and signs which God did by Him, in the midst of you, as you also know; this same being delivered up, by the determinate counsel and foreknowledge of God, you, by the hands of wicked men, have crucified and slain. Whom God hath raised up, having loosed the sorrows of hell, as it was impossible that He should be holden by it."[28] And again, "Therefore let all the house of Israel know most certainly that God hath made both Lord and Christ, this same Jesus, whom you have crucified."[29] And again: "Ye men of Israel, why wonder at this, or why look you upon us, as if by our strength or power we had made this man to walk? The God of Abraham and the God of Isaac and the God of Jacob, the God of our fathers, hath glorified His Son Jesus, whom you indeed delivered up and denied before the face of Pilate, when he judged He should be released. But you denied the Holy One and the Just, and desired a murderer to be granted unto you. But the author of life you killed, whom God hath raised from the dead, of which we are witnesses. And in the faith of His name, this man, whom you have seen and known, hath His name strengthened; and the faith which is by Him, hath given soundness in the sight of you all. And now, brethren, I know that you did it through ignorance, as did also your rulers. But those things which God before had showed by the mouth of all the prophets, that His Christ should suffer, He hath so fulfilled. Be penitent, therefore, and be converted, that your sins may be blotted out, that when the times of refreshment shall come from the presence of the Lord, and He shall send Him who hath been preached unto you, Jesus Christ, whom heaven indeed must receive until the times of the restitution of all things, which God hath spoken by the mouth of his holy prophets from the beginning of the world."[30] And again, the apostles with one accord said: "Lord, thou that didst make heaven and earth, the sea, and all things that are in them, who, by the Holy Spirit, by the mouth of our father David, thy servant, hast said, 'Why did the Gentiles rage, and the people meditate vain things? The kings of the earth stood up, and the princes assembled together against the Lord and his Christ. For of a truth there assembled together in this city against Thy holy child Jesus, whom Thou hast anointed, Herod and Pontius Pilate, with the Gentiles and the people of Israel, to do what thy hand and thy counsel decreed to be done."[31] And again, "But Peter and the apostles answering, said, 'We ought to obey God, rather than men. The God of our fathers hath raised up Jesus, whom you put to death, hanging Him upon a tree. Him hath God exalted with His right hand, to be Prince and Savior, to give repentance to Israel, and remission of sins. And we are witnesses of these things, and the Holy Spirit, whom God hath given to all that obey Him.' When they had heard these things, they were cut to the heart and they thought to put them to death."[32] And again, "God sent the word to the children of Israel, preaching peace by Jesus Christ (He is Lord of all). You know the word which hath been published through all Judea, for it began from Galilee after the baptism which John preached: Jesus of Nazareth, how God anointed Him with the Holy Spirit and with power, who went about doing good and healing all that were oppressed by the devil, for God was with Him. And we are witnesses of all things that He did in the land of the Jews and in Jerusalem, whom the Jews rejected and killed, hanging Him upon a tree. Him God raised up the third day, and gave Him to be made manifest; not to all the people but to witnesses preordained by God, even to us, who did eat and drink with Him after he arose again from the dead. And He commanded us to preach to the people, and to testify that it is He who was appointed by God to be judge of the living and the dead. To Him all the prophets give testimony that by His name all receive remission of sins who believe in him."[33] And again, "Men, brethren, children of the stock of Abraham, and whosoever among you fear God, to you the word of this salvation is sent. For they that inhabit Jerusalem, and the rulers thereof, not knowing Him nor the voices of the prophets which are read every Sabbath, judging Him have fulfilled them; and finding no cause of death in Him, they desired of Pilate that they might kill Him. And when they had fulfilled all things that were written of Him, taking Him down from the tree, they laid Him in a sepulcher. But God raised Him up from the dead the third day."[34] And the Blessed Peter says in the first Epistle: "Christ, therefore, having suffered in the flesh, be you also armed with the same thought, for he that hath suffered in the flesh hath ceased from sins, that now he may live the rest of his time in the flesh, not after the desires of men but according to the will of God."[35] And the Blessed Mark says in the Gospel: "And He taketh Peter and James and John with Him, and He began to fear and be sorrowful and be heavy. And He saith to them, 'My soul is sorrowful even unto death; stay you here and watch.'"[36] And again: "And when the sixth hour was come, there was darkness over the whole earth until the ninth hour. And at the ninth hour Jesus cried out with a loud voice, saying, 'Eloi, Eloi, lama sabacthani?' which is, being interpreted, My God, my God, why hast thou forsaken me?"[37] And again, "And Jesus, having cried out with a loud voice, gave up the ghost."[38] And the Blessed Matthew says: "Then they crucified with Him two thieves, one on the right hand and one on the left";[39] and again, "And Jesus, again crying with a loud voice, yielded up the ghost."[40] And the Blessed Luke says: "And Jesus, crying with a loud voice, said, 'Father, into thy hands I commend my spirit.' And saying this, He gave up the ghost."[41]

[5] *On the Tribulation of the Saints.*—The subject of our Lord Jesus Christ's tribulation and passion has been quite clearly attested, as was shown most abundantly in the foregoing. Now we must speak of the tribulation and persecution and death which the apostles and their heirs had to suffer in time to come, doing good and forgiving, and how they must also endure in their own time. In just that way true Christians now are seen to act, those called heretics now, as they were in the time of Paul, as he himself says in the Acts of the Apostles: "But this I confess to thee, that according to the way which they call a heresy, so do I serve God my father";[42] and again, "For as concerning this sect, you know that it is everywhere contradicted."[43] Whence our Lord Jesus Christ when describing the forthcoming persecution to His disciples says in the Gospel of the Blessed Matthew: "Blessed are they that suffer persecution for justice's sake, for theirs is the kingdom of heaven. Blessed are ye when they shall revile you and persecute you and speak all that is evil against you untruly for my sake; be glad in that day and rejoice, for your reward is very great in heaven, for so they persecuted the prophets that were before you."[44] And again: "Behold, I send you as sheep in the midst of wolves. Be ye, therefore, wise as serpents and simple as doves. But beware of men; for they will deliver you up in councils, and they will scourge you in their synagogues, and you shall be brought before governors and before kings for my sake, for a testimony to them and to the Gentiles. But when they shall deliver you up, take no thought how or what to speak, for it shall be given you in that hour what to speak. For it is not you that speak, but the Spirit of your Father that speaketh in you. The brother also shall deliver up the brother to death, and the father the son, and the children shall rise up against their parents and shall put them to death; and you shall be hated by all men for my name's sake. But he that shall persevere unto the end,

he shall be saved. And when they shall persecute you in this city, flee into another. Amen, I say to you, you shall not finish all the cities of Israel till the Son of man come. The disciple is not above his master, nor the servant above his lord; it is enough for the disciple that he be as his master, and the servant as his lord. If they have called the goodman of the house Beelzebub, how much more them of his household?"[45]

And in the Gospel, Christ says: "Amen, amen, I say to you, that you shall lament and weep, but the world shall rejoice; and you shall be made sorrowful, but your sorrow shall be turned into joy. A woman, when she is in labor, hath sorrow, because her hour is come; but when she hath brought forth the child, she remembereth no more the anguish, for joy that a man is born into the world. So also you now indeed have sorrow, but I will see you again and your heart shall rejoice; and your joy no man shall take from you."[46] And in the Gospel of the Blessed Matthew Christ says: "Take heed that no man seduce you. For many will come in my name saying, 'I am Christ,' and they will seduce many. And you shall hear of wars and rumors of wars; see that ye be not troubled; for these things must come to pass, but the end is not yet. For nation shall rise against nation, and kingdom against kingdom, and there shall be pestilences and famines and earthquakes in places; now all these are the beginnings of sorrows. Then shall they deliver you up to be afflicted, and you shall be hated by all nations for my name's sake. And then shall many be scandalized, and shall betray one another, and shall hate one another. And many false prophets shall rise and shall seduce many. And because iniquity hath abounded, the charity of many shall grow cold. But he that shall persevere to the end, he shall be saved."[47] And in the Apocalypse it is said: "Behold, the devil will cast you into prison, that you may be tried, and you shall have tribulation ten days. Be thou faithful until death, and I will give thee the crown of life."[48] And in the Gospel of John, Christ says to His disciples: "These things I command you, that you love one another. If the world hate you, know ye that it hath hated me before you. If you had been of the world, the world would love its own; but because you are not of the world, but I have chosen you out of the world, therefore the world hateth you. Remember my word that I said to you, 'The servant is not greater than his master.' If they have persecuted me, they will also persecute you; if they have kept my word, they will keep yours also. But all these things they will do to you for my name's sake, because they know not Him that sent me."[49]

[6] *How the Saints Have Suffered.*—It is made quite clear in Holy Scriptures, as we pointed out in the preceding, how our Lord Jesus Christ showed through His words that in His name His disciples would bear tribulations and persecutions and even death in days to come. But now we must describe how they in their time bore many evils and tribulations and persecutions and even death in the name of the Lord Jesus Christ, just as He himself foretold to them in the Holy Scriptures. For He says in the Gospel of John: "And now I come to thee; and these things I speak in the world, that they may have my joy filled in themselves. I have given them Thy word; and the world hath hated them because they are not of the world, as I also am not of the world. I pray not that Thou shouldst take them out of the world, but that Thou shouldst keep them from evil. They are not of the world, as I also am not of the world."[50] And the Blessed John in the first Epistle says: "Wonder not, brethren, if the world hate you. We know that we have passed from death to life, because we love the brethren."[51] And the Blessed Peter in the first Epistle says: "Dearly beloved, think not strange the burning heat which is to try you, as if some new thing happened to you. But if you partake of the sufferings of Christ, rejoice that when His glory shall be revealed you may also be glad with exceeding joy. If you be reproached for the name of Christ, you shall be blessed, for that which is of the honor, glory, and power of God, and that which is his Spirit shall rest upon you. But let none of you suffer as a murderer, or a thief, or a railer, or a coveter of other men's things; but if as a Christian, let him not be ashamed, but let him glorify God in that name. For the time is that judgment should begin at the house of God. And if first at us, what shall be the end of them that did not believe the gospel of God? And if the just man shall scarcely be saved, where shall the ungodly and the sinner appear? Wherefore let them also that suffer according to the will of God commend their souls in good deeds to the faithful Creator."[52] And Paul in the Acts of the Apostles says of himself: "And I, indeed, did formerly think that I ought to do many things contrary to the name of Jesus of Nazareth. Which also I did at Jerusalem, and many of the saints did I shut up in prison, having received authority of the chief priests, and when they were put to death, I brought the sentence. And oftentimes punishing them, in every synagogue, I compelled them to blaspheme, and being yet more mad against them, I persecuted them even unto foreign cities."[53] And the Blessed Peter in the first Epistle says: "For this is thankworthy, if for conscience toward

God, a man endure sorrow, suffering wrongfully. For what glory is it if committing sin and being buffeted for it, you endure? But if doing well you suffer patiently, this is thankworthy before God, for unto this are you called because Christ also suffered for us, leaving you an example that you should follow His steps. Who did no sin, neither was guile found in His mouth; who, when He was reviled, did not revile; when He suffered, He threatened not, but delivered himself to him that judged him unjustly. Who His own self bore our sins in His body upon the tree, that we, being dead to sins, should live to justice; by whose stripes you were healed. For you were as sheep going sometimes astray, but you are now converted to the shepherd and bishop of your souls."[54] And in the Acts of the Apostles it is written: "And at that time there was raised a great persecution against the church which was at Jerusalem, and they were all dispersed through the countries of Judaea and Samaria, except the apostles."[55] And Paul says to the Romans: "Who then shall separate us from the love of Christ? Shall tribulation, or distress, or famine, or nakedness, or danger, or persecution, or the sword? As it is written, 'For Thy sake we are put to death all the day long; we are accounted as sheep for the slaughter.' But in all these things we overcome because of Him that hath loved us. For I am sure that neither death, nor life, nor angels, nor principalities, nor powers, nor virtues, nor things present, nor things to come, nor might, nor height, nor depth, nor any other creature shall be able to separate us from the love of God, which is in Christ Jesus our Lord."[56] And the Blessed Peter in the first Epistle says: "If now you must be for a little time made sorrowful in divers temptations, that the trial of your faith, much more precious than gold which is tried by the fire, may be found unto praise and glory and honor at the appearing of Jesus Christ."[57] And Paul in the Acts of the Apostles says: "'Men, brethren, I have conversed with all good knowledge before God until this present day.' And the high priest Ananias commanded them that stood by him to strike him on the mouth."[58] And again Paul himself says to the Corinthians in the first Epistle: "Even unto this hour we both hunger and thirst and are naked and are buffeted and have no fixed abode; and we labor, working with our own hands. We are reviled and we bless; we are persecuted and we suffer it. We are blasphemed and we entreat; we are made as the refuse of this world, the offscouring of all even until now. I write not these things to confound you, but I admonish you as my dearest children."[59] And the

Blessed Peter in the first Epistle says: "And who is he that can hurt you, if you be zealous of good? But if also you suffer anything for justice' sake, blessed are ye. And be not afraid of their fear, so that you be not troubled." [60] And Paul in the first Epistle to the Corinthians says of himself: "For I am the least of the apostles, who am not worthy to be called an apostle, because I persecuted the Church of God." [61] And Paul in the second Epistle to the Corinthians: "In all things we suffer tribulation, but are not distressed; we are straitened, but are not destitute; we suffer persecution, but are not forsaken; we are cast down, but we perish not. Always bearing about in our body the mortification of Jesus, that the life also of Jesus may be made manifest in our bodies. For we who live are always delivered unto death for Jesus' sake; that the life also of Jesus may be made manifest in our mortal flesh." [62] And to the Ephesians, the same Apostle says: "Finally, brethren, be strengthened in the Lord and in the might of His power. Put you on the armor of God, that you may be able to stand against the deceits of the devil. For our wrestling is not against flesh and blood, but against the principalities and powers, against the rulers of the world of this darkness, against the spirits of wickedness in the high places. Therefore take unto you the armor of God, that you may be able to resist in the evil day, and to stand in all things perfect. Stand, therefore, having your loins girt about with truth, and having on the breastplate of justice, and your feet shod with the preparation of the gospel of peace; in all things taking the shield of faith, wherewith you may be able to extinguish all the fiery darts of the most wicked one. And take unto you the helmet of salvation, and the sword of the Spirit, which is the word of God. By all prayer and supplication praying at all times in the spirit, and in the same watching." [63] And in the second Epistle to the Corinthians, the same Apostle says: "Blessed be the God and Father of our Lord Jesus Christ, the Father of mercies and the God of all comfort. Who comforteth us in all our tribulation, that we also may be able to comfort them who are in all distress, by the exhortation wherewith we also are exhorted by God. For as the sufferings of Christ abound in us, so also by Christ doth our comfort abound. Now whether we be in tribulation, it is for your exhortation and salvation; or whether we be exhorted, it is for your exhortation and salvation, which worketh in us in the enduring of the same sufferings which we also suffer. That our hope for you may be steadfast, knowing that as you are partakers of the sufferings, so shall you be also of the consolation. For we would not have you ignorant, brethren, of one tribulation, which came to us in Asia, that we were pressed out of measure above our strength, so that we were weary even of life. But we had in ourselves the answer of death, that we should not be confident in ourselves but in God who raiseth the dead. Who hath delivered and doth deliver us out of so great dangers; in whom we trust that He will yet also deliver us. You helping withal in prayer for us." [64] And to the Galatians Paul said: "For you have heard of my conversation in times past in the Jews' religion: how that, beyond measure, I persecuted the Church of God and wasted it. And I made progress in the Jews' religion above many of my equals in my own nation, being more abundantly zealous for the traditions of my fathers." [65] And again, to the Corinthians in the second Epistle: "I speak according to dishonor, as if we had been weak in this part. Wherein if any man dare (I speak foolishly), I dare also. They are Hebrews? So am I. They are the seed of Abraham? So am I. [They are ministers of Christ?] [66] I speak as one less wise. I am more, in many more labors, in prisons more frequently, in stripes above measure, in deaths often. Of the Jews five times did I receive forty stripes save one. Thrice was I beaten with rods; once I was stoned. Thrice I suffered shipwreck; a night and a day I was in peril of the sea; in journeying often, in perils of waters, in perils of robbers, in perils from my own nation, in perils from the Gentiles, in perils in the city, in perils in the wilderness, in perils in the sea, in perils from false brethren; in labor and painfulness, in much watchings, in hunger and thirst, in fastings often, in cold and nakedness. Besides those things, which are without, my daily instance, the solicitude for all the churches. Who is weak, and I am not weak? Who is scandalized, and I am not on fire?" [67] And in the second Epistle to the Thessalonians, Paul says: "So that we ourselves also glory in you in the churches of God for your patience and faith, and in all your persecutions and retributions which you endure, for an example of the just judgment of God, that you may be counted worthy of the kingdom of God, for which also you suffer. Seeing it is a just thing with God to repay tribulation to them that trouble you, and to you who are troubled, rest with us when our Lord Jesus shall be revealed from heaven." [68] And in the first Epistle to Timothy, Paul says of himself: "I give Him thanks who hath strengthened me, even to Christ Jesus our Lord, for that He hath counted me faithful, putting me in the ministry who before was a blasphemer, and a persecutor, and contumelious. But I obtained the mercy of God, because I did it ignorantly in unbelief."[69] And to the Thessalonians, in the first Epistle, the Apostle himself says: "You, however, are become followers of the brethren of the churches of God which are in Judaea, in Christ Jesus. For you also have suffered the same things from your own countrymen, even as they have from the Jews, who both killed the Lord Jesus and the prophets, and have persecuted us, and please not God, and are adversaries to all men, prohibiting us to speak to the Gentiles that they may be saved, to fill up their sins always, for the wrath of God is come upon them to the end."[70] And again: "And we sent Timothy, our brother and the minister of God in the gospel of Christ, to confirm you and exhort you concerning your faith, that no man should be moved in these tribulations, for yourselves know, that we are appointed thereunto. For even when we were with you, we foretold you that we should suffer tribulations, as also it is come to pass and you know. For this cause also, I, forbearing no longer, sent to know your faith, lest perhaps he that tempteth should have tempted you, and our labor should be made vain."[71] And to the Corinthians, in the first Epistle, Paul says: "If in this life only we have hope in Christ, we are of all men most miserable."[72] And to the Philippians, Paul says: "And in nothing be ye terrified by the adversaries, which to them is a cause of perdition but to you of salvation, and this from God. For unto you it is given for Christ not only to believe in Him, but also to suffer for Him, having the same conflict as that which you have seen in me and now have heard of me."[73] Whence, the same Paul in that second Epistle to Timothy says: "But thou hast fully known my doctrine, manner of life, purpose, faith, long-suffering, love, patience, persecutions, afflictions, such as came upon me at Antioch, at Iconium, and at Lystra, what persecutions I endured, and out of them all the Lord delivered me. And all that will live godly in Christ Jesus, suffer persecution."[74]

And now the book is finished; let us give thanks to Christ.

60. The Catharist Church and Its Interpretation of the Lord's Prayer

The two documents translated here are among the most recent to be identified as Catharist works. Both are found in a small manuscript written in Provençal, which before 1635 came into the possession of James Ussher, the scholarly Anglican archbishop of Armagh (1625-1656).[1] In certain respects —their language,[2] their copious citation and paraphrase of Scripture, and their foundation in dualism—they are alike; but it was probably more by accident than because of a common origin that they were copied into the same manuscript, for they appear to present the views of two different factions of Cathars. The first document, for which we have supplied the title *A Vindication of the Church of God*, is an exposition of the character, powers, ethical standards, and practices of a Catharist church which taught mitigated dualism. The second document, a gloss on the Lord's Prayer comparable in form but not in substance to the gloss in the Catharist ritual in Latin (No. 57, part B), was composed by a believer in absolute dualism.

Chapters I and II of the *Vindication* are devoted to a discussion of the character and powers of the Church of God, or of Christ. The argument parallels the discourse on the same theme in the Catharist ritual in Provençal (see No. 57, part B), at the point when the power to say the Lord's Prayer is being transmitted to the initiate. The moral code described in chapters III-IX is essentially that outlined in the rituals in the injunctions to the believer—against murder, adultery, lying, oath-taking, and theft—but the *Vindication* makes no mention of the ascetic practices required of the perfected heretic. Chapter X, demonstrating that the persecution of true Christians is inevitable, is similar to, though briefer than, the passages on persecution in *The Book of the Two Principles* (No. 59, part VII). Chapter XI, which defends the spiritual baptism by imposition of hands as the true baptism taught by Christ, parallels the discussion of the same subject in the rituals and relies on many of the same biblical texts; but unlike them it includes a polemic against the Roman Church on the question of baptism in water.[3]

Venckeleer argues that the *Vindication*, or a text which was the model for it, was composed sometime between 1210 and 1240.[4] A later date is more probable, however, in view of the tenor of the treatise's remarks about John the Baptist, who in chapter XI is referred to as a forerunner of Christ who baptized with water "only to lead the people to believe in the baptism of Christ, and to give firm testimony of Christ, whose coming he preached" and "in order to show the people that it was Christ who would perform the other baptism." All early Cathars condemned John the Baptist as an emissary of the devil, who sent him to baptize in water in order to hinder Christ's mission;[5] but toward the middle of the thirteenth century some began to accept John's inspiration as divine, according to Moneta of Cremona, writing in 1241-1244.[6] Rainerius Sacconi in 1250 also noted that the Cathars of Concorezzo "only recently came to believe correctly about John the Baptist, whom they all formerly condemned." [7] The *Vindication* seems to reflect this changing attitude.[8]

There are two hints that the *Vindication* emanated from a group of mitigated dualists.[9] One is the attitude toward John the Baptist just referred to, which is comparable to the position taken by the church of Concorezzo. The other is that among more than one hundred scriptural texts cited, only two come from the Old Testament, both identified as from the Book of Wisdom, although one is actually from Proverbs. Mitigated dualists were more sweeping than radical dualists in rejecting the Old Testament as the work of the devil.[10] Otherwise, the exposition presents ideas which would have been acceptable to all factions among the Cathars, and states their ethical teaching and their view of themselves in terms that accord very well with other evidence from about the middle of the thirteenth century.[11]

The gloss on the Lord's Prayer (part B), commenting on each phrase of the Prayer, describes the relationship between God and his creation in symbolic terms derived from biblical texts and emphasizes the promise stated in its Prologue that God will redeem His people from captivity through His Son Jesus Christ, who taught the people of God how to pray and who, after the Last Judgment, will rule over the kingdom of the elect. It describes creation as a hierarchy of seven substances through which the divine will works. Three of these substances are celestial in nature: They are "lights" or "charities," "visitations" or "mercies," and "spirits." But the last named have fallen away to become the "people of God" in exile. In their terrestrial captivity the spirits are linked with two substances, "lives" and "souls"; two other substances, "hearts" and "bodies," [12] are mentioned as subordinate to souls. Each substance is also symbolized by other names of biblical origin, with the result that the Prayer can be interpreted in terms of many other scriptural passages.

God is the Father of all substances. He himself is charity and dwells in "heaven," which is the symbol of the first of His substances, the charities or lights. This is the seventh heaven which Isaiah saw in a vision.[14] There also Jesus Christ, the Son, is in the Father and the Father in Him, and the people of God are linked to the Father through Christ (chap. I). The third person of the Trinity is mentioned only incidentally, in connection with Christ's mission of redemption and as inspiring David and the prophets (chaps. III, V, VI, VIII).

We will return to the charities and the visitations after noting the situation of the third of the heavenly substances, the spirits. As already said, they had sinned in a manner not explicitly stated. They confess themselves now guilty of many offenses (chap. VI), for which Christ came to give penance (chap. I). The psalmist David is called the first father of the people, the spirit of their first form (chaps. IV, VI), and he is also designated as "Amen," [15] meaning one whose sin made it necessary for Christ to suffer and die (chap. XI). David's life is joined with the life of the people, his soul with theirs; his voice utters their lament in captivity.[16]

The bondage of the people is to evil, for side by side with the charities and visitations of the Father are found "strange charities" and their visitations, which represent night as the substances of the Father represent light (chap. I). These are also the cords and bonds of iniquity, which the Lord must break (chap. II). How the captivity occurred is depicted in the words of biblical texts. The enemy invaded the land of the living, entered the gates of Jerusalem, brought her children down to earth to dwell in darkness (chap. VIII), under the power of the four kingdoms of Babylon[17] (chap. III). There the spirits, joined with lives and souls (the three substances are symbolized by "the kingdom, the power, and the glory" of the doxology [chaps. IX, X, XI]), acknowledge that they belong to God the Father, although they are held captive by evil. "Evil" means the devil, he who in the Scriptures is called Satan, the enemy who sowed weeds in the Lord's field, the evil man of whom the psalmist spoke, the unjust man named by Job; but especially is he typified by the king of Assyria [18] (chap. VIII). Under his power, the people suffer hunger and thirst (chap. VI), for they have lost part of their substance in a far land, the earth of their captivity, and have not yet received from God another part, which is charity (chap. V). In their exile they are doubly tempted. God tempts them as a penalty for their having tempted Him, but even more as a trial, because by enduring it they will prove themselves worthy of the crown of life. Another temptation is by the devil, whose temptation is unto death. It is from the devil's temptation that the people pray to be delivered.[19] To help them, God has given them the examples of the prophets and Christ, who was himself tempted by the devil (chap. VII).

Hearing the prayer of His people in exile, the Father commanded Christ to go forth and dwell on earth. In that mission Christ was guilty of a sin of will when He desired something other than the will of the Father; [20] hence, He must sanctify himself and thereby sanctify the people for whom He was to suffer (chap. II) after He was made flesh of the lineage of David to redeem David and His children (chap. III). Christ endured without sin the temptation of the devil (chap. VII) and illumined the people by revealing the name of the Father (chap. III) and by teaching the commandments of the New Testament, which are the will of the Father (chap. IV). Thus, He was a "kingdom" which laid waste the four kingdoms of Babylon, a kingdom of all time, preached by the saints. But as a kingdom, Christ will come again, when He will render to all men their reward; vengeance will fall on unbelievers, while His elect will be gathered in to constitute the kingdom over which Christ will reign. That second coming will be swift and terrible (chap. III).

A further link between the Father and the people of God is through the celestial substances. The charities are the first in rank and their influence pervades all the others. Charity is the supersubstantial bread, that is, the part of their substance which David and his children were unable to receive from the Father before the coming of Christ. Christ taught the people to pray for the supersubstantial bread, which, when received, is a bond of perfection, nay rather, perfection itself, allowing the people to become perfect before God [21] (chap. V). Indeed, the debt of the people from the beginning was to practice mutual charity among themselves (chap. VI), for charity constitutes the supreme bond and the fundamental force in fulfilling God's will.

The visitations, the second of the celestial substances, are illumined by the charities and are inspired to spread grace and mercy on the spirits beneath them, for they are the children of the charities (chap. XI). The visitations are symbolized by clouds suffused with the dew of charity, which drops upon the spirits (chap. I). The name of God, invoked by the people in prayer, is a visitation which must be hallowed because the people profaned it when they were cast out among the nations; its equivalent is "Jacob," who sanctifies himself in order to sanctify "Israel," which connotes the spirits of whom Jacob is the head. The mountains through which peace and help come from God and on which His city is built are also visitations. Visitations are formed by the charities into ties of love which bind each substance to its superior, bonds which are called Adam [22] (chap. II).

In their captivity, the people pray for God's will to be done as it is expressed in the New Testament and was fulfilled by Christ. It must be done by the people because they are spirits, that is, heavenly; but it must also be done by their lives and souls, that is, on earth (chap. IV). They also pray that their debts be forgiven. Debts are sins, and the people acknowledge that in order to be forgiven their own sins they must forgive those of others. But "debts" also has a profounder meaning; the people from the first owed the debt of charity and mutual love to each other, and this too they pray to be able to discharge (chap. VI).

Of Catharist thought in this gloss on the Prayer there can be no doubt; the inclusion of the phrase "supersubstantial bread" and the doxology in the Lord's Prayer, the theme of two creations, the description of the captivity of "the people of God," the equating of Christ with the kingdom of God and evil with the devil, and the quotation from *The Vision of Isaiah* are proof. But among what faction of the Cathars did it have currency? When was it composed? Venckeleer feels certain that the doctrines of a radical dualist group underlie the exposition because it contains references to the devil's power and uses citations from the Old Testament. More specifically, he sees it as influenced by the ideas of John of Lugio.[23] The correctness of this interpretation is reinforced if references to "the first Moses" and to David as "the first father" can be read as referring to existence on that other earth where, as John of Lugio taught, the events of the Old Testament took place.[24] But there are some problems: The role of the Holy Spirit is only briefly mentioned and not in the terms characteristic of Catharist teaching as described in Catholic sources; the Catharist doctrine of the Fall, in which the bodies and spirits of angels remained in heaven while their souls came into the devil's power, is not reflected here; nor is there any mention of the

Church of Christ as an assemblage of redeemed souls on earth and a transmitter of the Prayer.[25] Thus, we feel that at the present stage of study, to assign an exact provenance or date for the tract is too speculative.

The translation is made from the text published by Theo Venckeleer in "Un Recueil cathare: Le manuscrit A.6.10 de la Collection vaudoise de Dublin, I: Une Apologie; II: Une glose sur le Pater," *Revue belge de philologie et d'histoire*, XXXVIII (1960), 820-31; XXXIX (1961), 762-85, by permission of the editor and the Librairie Falk Fils. We are deeply indebted to Miss Joan Ferrante, who made the initial translation.

A. A VINDICATION OF THE CHURCH OF GOD

circa 1250

[Chapter I]

In the name of the Father, and of the Son, and of the Holy Spirit.

We propose to recount some testimony from Holy Scriptures in order to give knowledge and understanding of the Church of God. This Church is not made of stones or wood, or of anything made by hand, for it is written in the Acts of the Apostles that "the Most High dwelleth not in houses made by hands."[1] But this Holy Church is the assembly of the faithful and of holy men in which Jesus Christ is and will be until the end of the world, as our Lord says in the Gospel of St. Matthew, "Behold, I am with you all days, even to the consummation of the world."[2] And in the Gospel of St. John He says, "If anyone love me, he will keep my word, and my Father will love him, and we will come to him and will make our abode with him."[3] And again He says: "If you love me, keep my commandments. And I will ask the Father and He will give you another Paraclete, that He may abide with you forever: the Spirit of Truth, whom the world cannot receive because it seeth Him not nor knoweth Him; but you shall know Him, because He shall abide with you and shall be in you. I will not leave you orphans; I will come to you."[4] St. Paul speaks further of this Church to the Corinthians: "Know you not that you are the temple of God and that the Spirit of God dwelleth in you? But if any man violate the temple of God, him shall God destroy. For the temple of God is holy, which you are."[5] And again he says, "Know you not that your members are the temple of the Holy Spirit who is in you, whom you have from God?"[6] And again he says: "You are the temple of the living God, as God saith: 'I will dwell in them, and walk among them; I will go and be their God and they shall be my people.' Wherefore, 'Go out from among them, and be ye separate, and touch not the unclean thing; and I will receive you and will be a Father to you, and you shall be my sons and daughters, saith the Lord Almighty.'"[7] And again St. Paul says to Timothy: "These things I write to thee hoping that I shall come to thee shortly. But if I tarry long, that thou mayest know how thou oughtest to behave thyself in the house of God, which is the Church of the living God, which is the pillar and mainstay of the truth."[8] And again he says to the Hebrews, "Christ is as the Son in His own house, which house are we."[9] But in the Gospel of St. Matthew Christ says of this Church to St. Peter, "Thou art Peter, and upon this rock I will build my church, and the gates of hell shall not prevail against it."[10] And St. Luke says in the Acts of the Apostles, "Now the Church had peace throughout all Judaea and Galilee and Samaria, and was edified, walking in the fear of the Lord, and was filled with the consolation of the Holy Spirit."[11] And our Lord Jesus Christ says in the Gospel of St. Matthew: "If thy brother shall offend against thee, go and rebuke him between thee and him alone. And if he shall hear thee, thou shalt gain thy brother. But if he will not hear thee, take with thee one or two more, that on the word of two or three witnesses every word may stand. And if he will not hear them, tell the Church. And if he will not hear the Church, let him be to thee as the heathen and the publican."[12] But the Church of Christ could not do all these things if it were a house of the sort men call a church, for such houses cannot walk, or hear, or speak. But St. Paul said to the Ephesians of this Holy Church of the living God, "Christ so loved the Church that He delivered himself up for it that He might sanctify it, cleansing it by the laver of water, by the word of life, that He might present it to himself a glorious Church, not having spot or wrinkle, or any such thing, but that it should be holy and without blemish."[13] And this holy and unblemished Church is the chamber of the Holy Spirit, as was shown above, of whom Christ says, "For it is not you that speak but the Spirit of your Father that speaketh in you."[14]

[*Chapter II*]

This Church of God of which we speak has received such power from our Lord Jesus Christ that sins are pardoned by its prayer, as Christ says in the Gospel of St. John, "Receive ye the Holy Spirit. Whose sins you shall forgive, they are forgiven them; and whose sins you shall retain, they are retained."[15] And St. Matthew says, "He gave them power that they might cast out unclean spirits."[16] And St. Mark says, "He gave them power to heal sicknesses and to cast out devils."[17] And St. Luke says, "He gave them power over all devils."[18] And Christ [says] in the Gospel of St. Matthew: "If your brother will not hear the Church, let him be to thee as the heathen and the publican. For I say to you truly, whatsoever you shall bind on earth shall be bound in heaven, and whatsoever you shall loose on earth shall be loosed in heaven. Again I say to you, that if two of you shall consent upon earth about anything whatsoever they shall ask, it shall be done to them by my Father who is in heaven. For where there are two or three gathered in my name, there am I in the midst of them."[19] And St. Peter says in the Epistle, "Because the eyes of the Lord are upon the just, and His ears unto their prayers."[20] And St. James says, "For the continuing prayer of a just man availeth much."[21] And Christ says in the Gospel of St. Mark, "Therefore I say unto you, all things whatsoever you ask when ye pray, believe that you shall receive, and they shall come unto you."[22] And again He says: "These signs shall follow them that believe: In my name they shall cast out devils; they shall speak with new tongues. And they shall take up serpents; and shall lay their hands upon the sick and they shall re-cover."[23] But for them who are sick with the sickness of sin, St. James reveals the manner in which the infirmity of the soul must be healed, saying: "If anyone among you is sick, let him bring in the priests of the Church, and let them pray over him, anointing him with oil in the name of the Lord. And the prayer of faith shall save the sick man, and the Lord shall raise him up; and if he be in sins, they shall be forgiven him."[24]

And for these reasons and many others, it is manifest that only through the prayers of the Holy Church of Christ are sins pardoned, as Christ says, "Whose sins you shall forgive, they are forgiven them; and whose sins you shall retain, they are retained."[25] But if any be so blind and mistaken as to think that He said that this power fell to and was given only to the apostles, let him examine the Gospel of St. John where Christ says, "O Father, not for them only do I pray, but for them also who through their word shall believe in me, that they all may be one."[26] And again, Christ says in the Gospel of St. Matthew, "Behold, I am with you all days, even to the consummation of the world."[27] And again

He says, "This generation shall not pass, till all things be done."²⁸ For these reasons, it is assured that the power which the Church of Christ had, it holds and will hold until the end.

[*Chapter III*]

This Church refrains from killing, nor does it consent that others may kill. For our Lord Jesus Christ says, "If thou wilt enter into life, thou shalt do no murder."²⁹ And again He says: "You have heard that it was said to them of old, 'Thou shalt not kill.' For whosoever shall kill shall be in danger of the judgment. But I say to you that whosoever is angry with his brother shall be in danger of the judgment."³⁰ And St. Paul says, "Thou shalt not kill."³¹ And St. John says in his Epistle, "And you know that no murderer hath eternal life abiding in himself."³² And he says in the Apocalypse that murderers are outside the holy city;³³ and again he says, "He that shall kill by the sword must be killed";³⁴ and again he says that the portion of murderers "shall be in the pool burning with fire and brimstone."³⁵ And St. Paul says to the Romans [about those who are] "full of envy, murder, contention, deceit, and malignity: Those who do such things are worthy of death; and not only they that do them, but they also that consent to them that do them."³⁶

[*Chapter IV*]

This Church refrains from adultery and all uncleanness, for our Lord Jesus Christ says, "Thou shalt not commit adultery."³⁷ And again He says in the Gospel of Matthew: "You have heard that it was said to them of old, 'Thou shalt not commit adultery.' But I say to you that whosoever shall look on a woman to lust after her hath already committed adultery with her in his heart."³⁸ And again He says: "From the heart come forth evil thoughts, adulteries, and fornications. And these are the things that defile a man."³⁹ And in the Book of Proverbs⁴⁰ it is written, "He that is an adulterer, for the folly of his heart shall destroy his own soul." And St. Paul says to the Ephesians,⁴¹ "Fornication and all uncleanness, let it not be named among you." And again he says, "And know this and understand, that no fornicator or unclean or covetous person hath inheritance in the kingdom of Christ."⁴² And to the Galatians he says, "The works of the flesh are manifest, which are fornication, uncleanness, unchastity, luxury,"⁴³ and so on. And again he says to the Corinthians:⁴⁴ "Do not err: neither fornicators, nor the covetous, nor adulterers shall possess the kingdom of God." And again he says to the Hebrews, "For the fornicators and adulterers God will judge."[45] And in the Apocalypse it is written that the unchaste will be outside the holy city;[46] and again St. John says that the portion of the adulterer shall be "in the pool burning with fire and brimstone, which is the [second] death."[47]

[Chapter V]

This Church refrains from theft or robbery, for our Lord Jesus Christ says in the Gospel of St. Matthew, "Thou shalt not steal."[48] And St. Paul says to the Ephesians, "He that stole, let him now steal no more, but rather let him labor, working with his hands the thing which is good, that he may have something to give."[49] And again he says to the Romans, "Thou shalt not steal nor covet anything of thy neighbor's."[50] And St. Peter says in his Epistle, "Let none of you suffer as a murderer, or a thief, or as a covetor of other men's things."[51]

[Chapter VI]

This Church refrains from lying and from bearing false witness, for our Lord Jesus Christ says, "Thou shalt not bear false witness."[52] And St. Peter says in the Epistle, "He that will love life and see good days, let him refrain his tongue from evil and his lips that they speak no guile."[53] And St. Paul says to the Romans, "Thou shalt not bear false witness."[54] And again he says to the Ephesians, "Wherefore, putting away lying, speak ye the truth, every man with his neighbor."[55] And in the Apocalypse Christ says that there shall not enter the holy city "anything defiled or that worketh abomination or maketh a lie."[56] And again He says, that outside the holy city will remain "everyone who loveth and maketh a lie."[57] And again He says that for all liars, their portion will be "in the pool burning with fire."[58] And therefore St. Paul says to the Colossians, "Lie not to one another."[59] And in the Book of Wisdom is written, "The mouth that belieth killeth the soul."[60]

[Chapter VII]

This Church refrains from oaths, for our Lord Jesus Christ says in the Gospel of St. Matthew: "Swear not at all, neither by heaven, for it is the throne of God; nor by earth, for it is His footstool; nor by Jerusalem, for it is the city of the great king. Neither shalt thou swear by thy head, because thou canst not make one hair white or black."[61]

Furthermore, after forbidding oaths, He teaches man how he should speak, saying, "Let your speech be yea, yea; no, no,"[62] as if He were saying: Let what you have in your heart sound in the mouth through the word alone, without an oath. For Christ says that "that which is over and above these is of evil,"[63] meaning of the devil, who is called evil, from whom we ask God in our prayers to set us free, saying, "But deliver us from evil."[64] But contrary to these precepts, the wicked Roman Church says and affirms that man should swear and it says that God swore and the angels swore.[65] But for all of that, if they did swear, we must not, for no law or commandment against oaths was given either to God or to the angels, and St. Paul says that "where there is no law, neither is there transgression."[66] And therefore, man should not swear, for he is commanded not to swear. For if a man swears, he will often perjure himself, and it is[67] manifest that more than a hundred thousand perjuries have been committed by the wicked church. And therefore, St. James the apostle, who had heard the truth from our Lord Jesus Christ, says in his Epistle: "But above all things, my brethren, swear not, neither by heaven, nor by the earth, nor by any other oath. But let your speech be yea, yea; no, no, that you fall not under judgment."[68] And therefore, the Church of Christ should not swear, for if it did, it would transgress the law of Christ which says, "Swear not."

[Chapter VIII]

This Church refrains from blasphemy and from cursing, for St. James says, "If any man thinks himself to be religious, not bridling his tongue from evil, but deceiving his own heart, this man's religion is vain."[69] And St. Paul says to the Ephesians, "Let no evil speech proceed from your mouth."[70] And again he says, "Let all bitterness and anger, and indignation, and clamor, and blasphemy be removed from you."[71] And to the Colossians he says, "Now put you all away anger, and indignation, and blasphemy, and filthy speech out of your mouth."[72] And St. Peter says in his Epistle: "Render not evil for evil, but contrariwise, blessing, for unto this are you called that you may inherit a blessing. For he that will love life and see good days, let him refrain his tongue from evil and his lips that they speak no guile."[73] Jesus Christ said further in the Gospel of St. Matthew: "But I say unto you truly that every idle word that men shall speak, they shall render an account for it in the Day of Judgment. For by thy words thou shalt be justified, and by

thy words thou shalt be condemned."[74] And because the righteous utter
blessings, when they are at the Day of Judgment they will be called
blessed. And the wicked ones who utter curses will be named the accursed, as the Gospel of St. Matthew reveals: When Christ shall sit upon
the seat of his majesty, he will separate the evil from the good.[75] And
Christ will say to the good, "Come, ye blessed of my Father, possess you
the kingdom prepared for you,"[76] and so on. And to the wicked He will
say, "Depart from me, you cursed, into everlasting fire."[77]

[*Chapter IX*]

This Church keeps and observes all the commandments of the law of
life, for St. James says in his Epistle: "Whosoever shall keep the whole
law but offend in one point, is become guilty of all. For He that said,
'Thou shalt not commit adultery,' said, 'Thou shalt not kill.' Now if
thou do not commit adultery, but shalt kill, thou art become a transgressor of the law."[78] And Christ says, "Either make the tree good and
its fruit good, or make the tree evil and its fruit evil."[79] And therefore
the Church of God desires all its fruit to be good, so that it may be like
its good teacher and pastor, Jesus Christ, for all that which He taught
to others He first did and fulfilled in His works, so that if anyone does
not wish to believe in Him through His words, he may believe through
His good works. Of this He says in the Gospel of St. John, "If you are
not willing to believe the words, believe the works."[80] Therefore St.
Peter says, "Christ suffered for us, leaving us an example that we may
follow in His steps, 'Who did not sin, neither was guile found in His
mouth.'"[81] Thus the Holy Church of God, which is called the body of
Christ, seeks to follow its head, who is Jesus Christ. Whence St. Paul
says: "All things are subjected under the feet of Christ, and Him He
gave as head over all the Church, which is His body";[82] and again, "You
are the body of Christ";[83] and again, "Your bodies are the members of
Christ,"[84] and so on. Thus, since righteous Christians are members of
Christ, it behooves them to be holy, pure, and chaste, and soiled with no
sin even as their head, Jesus Christ, for St. John says, "Whosoever
abideth in Him sinneth not, and whosoever sinneth, hath not seen Him
nor known Him."[85] And again he says, "He who says that he abides in
Him, ought himself also to walk just as He walked."[86] And again he
says: "If we say that we have fellowship with Him, and walk in darkness, we lie, and do not the truth. But if we walk in the light, as He also

is in the light, we have fellowship with Him."[87] Therefore, he says, "He that doth justice is just, even as He is just."[88]

[Chapter X]

This Church suffers persecutions and tribulations and martyrdom in the name of Christ, for He himself suffered them in the desire to redeem and save His Church and to show them by deed and word that until the end of the world they must suffer persecution and contumely and malediction,[89] just as He says in the Gospel of St. John, "If they have persecuted me, they will persecute you."[90] And in the Gospel of St. Matthew He says: "Blessed are they that suffer persecution for justice' sake, for theirs is the kingdom of heaven. Blessed are ye when they shall revile you, and persecute you, and speak all that is evil against you, untruly, for my sake. Be glad and rejoice, for your reward is very great in heaven. For so they persecuted the prophets who were before you."[91] And again He says: "Behold, I send you as sheep in the midst of wolves";[92] and again, "And you shall be hated by all men for my name's sake; he that shall persevere unto the end, he shall be saved. And when they shall persecute you in this city, flee into another."[93]

Note how all these words of Christ contradict the wicked Roman Church. For it is not persecuted for the goodness or justice which is in it, but on the contrary it persecutes and kills all who refuse to condone its sins and its actions. It flees not from city to city, but rules over cities and towns and provinces and is seated in grandeur in the pomp of this world; it is feared by kings and emperors and other men. Nor is it like sheep among wolves, but rather like wolves among sheep or goats, for it endeavors to rule over pagans and Jews and Gentiles. And above all does it persecute and kill the Holy Church of Christ, which bears all in patience like the sheep, making no defense against the wolf. Therefore St. Paul says: "For Thy sake we are put to death all the day long. We are accounted as sheep for the slaughter."[94] But in contrast to this, the shepherds of the Roman Church feel no shame in saying that they are the sheep and lambs of Christ, and they declare that the wolves are the Church of Christ, which is persecuted by them. But this is a contradiction, for in times past the wolves persecuted and killed the sheep; now all would be reversed, for the sheep are to be so enraged that they bite and persecute and kill the wolves. And the wolves are to be so patient that they let themselves be devoured by the sheep. But the Roman

Church says further, "We do not persecute heretics for their good works but for faith, because they refuse to accept our faith." Note how they seem to be the sons of those who killed Christ and the apostles, for they have killed and persecuted and will do so until the end, because the saints speak out against their sins, and preach to them the truth which they cannot understand. Whence Christ in the Gospel of St. John says to them: "Many good works have I showed you from my Father; for which of these works do you stone me?"[95] And they answered Him, "For a good work we stone thee not, but for blasphemy."[96] Thus it is manifest that from the beginning of the world the wolves killed and persecuted the sheep, and the wicked persecuted the good, and sinners persecuted the saints. And therefore St. Paul says, "All that will live godly in Christ Jesus shall suffer persecution."[97] Note that he did not say "shall persecute" but "shall suffer persecution." And Jesus Christ in the Gospel of St. John says to His Holy Church, "The hour cometh that whosoever killeth you will think that he doth a service to God."[98] Note that He did not say, "The hour cometh for you to persecute and kill men and offer worship to God." And again the good Jesus Christ says to persecutors, "Behold, I send you scribes and wise men, and you will put them to death and crucify them and scourge them and persecute them from city to city."[99] And in the Acts of the Apostles, the apostles said, "For through many tribulations and persecutions we must enter into the kingdom of heaven."[100] And therefore St. John the apostle says, "Wonder not, brethren, if the world hate you."[101]

[*Chapter XI*]

This Church performs a holy spiritual baptism, which is the imposition of hands through which is given the Holy Spirit,[102] of which John the Baptist says, "He that shall come after me shall baptize you in the Holy Spirit."[103] And therefore, when our Lord Jesus Christ came from the seat of His grandeur to save His people, He taught His Holy Church to baptize others with this holy baptism, just as He says in the Gospel of St. Matthew, "Go and teach ye all nations, baptizing them in the name of the Father, and of the Son, and of the Holy Spirit."[104] And in the Gospel of St. Mark He says to them: "Go ye into the whole world and preach the gospel to every creature. And he that believeth and is baptized shall be saved, but he that believeth not shall be condemned."[105]

But the wicked Roman Church, like the blind leading the blind, says that Christ referred to temporal water, which John the Baptist used before Christ preached. This can be refuted on many counts. For, if the baptism which the Roman Church performs were that which Christ ordained for His Church, then almost all of those who are baptized by them will be condemned. For Christ says, "He that believeth not will be condemned."[106] And they baptize little children who do not believe and who have no knowledge of good and evil; thus by their words do they condemn them. Furthermore, if people are saved by the baptism of temporal water, then in vain did Christ come to die, for they already had the baptism of water. But it is certain that the Church of Christ baptized with a baptism other than that of John the Baptist, as St. John the Evangelist reveals when he says, "But when Jesus understood that the Pharisees had heard that Jesus maketh more disciples and baptizeth more than John (although Jesus himself did not baptize, but His disciples),"[107] and so on. And John the Baptist himself clearly showed this, saying, "I have baptized you with water, but He shall baptize you with the Holy Spirit."[108] Now, John had come to baptize with water only to lead people to believe in the baptism of Christ, and to give firm testimony of Christ, whose coming he preached, for upon none of all those whom John baptized was the Holy Spirit to come except upon Jesus; whereby John knew that He was the Christ who would baptize with the Holy Spirit. For otherwise John knew not who Christ was, as he discloses in the Gospel of St. John, saying, "And I knew Him not, but that He may be made manifest in Israel; therefore am I come baptizing with water. For I saw the Spirit coming down, as a dove from heaven, and He remained upon Him. And I knew Him not; but He who sent me to baptize with water said to me, 'He upon whom thou shalt see the Spirit descending, and remaining upon Him, He it is that baptizeth with the Holy Spirit.' And I have seen and borne witness that this is the Son of God."[109] And therefore John baptized, for, baptizing in water, he must recognize Christ, in order to show the people that it was He who would perform the other baptism. But St. Paul showed that of these two baptisms only one was unto salvation, for he says, "One faith, one Lord, one baptism,"[110] and so on. And St. Luke declares in the Acts of the Apostles which baptism it is that the Church of God performs, and shows clearly that baptism of water was little valued, saying: "When Paul came to Ephesus, he found certain disciples and asked them if they had received the Holy Spirit when they became believers. And they said

to him, 'We have not so much as heard whether there be a Holy Spirit.'
And Paul said to them, 'In what then were you baptized?' And they
said, 'In John's baptism.' And Paul said to them, 'John baptized the
people with the baptism of penance, saying that they should believe in
Him who was to come after him, that is, in Jesus.' Having heard these
things, they were baptized in the name of the Lord Jesus. And when
Paul had imposed his hands on them, the Holy Spirit came upon
them."[111] Note that if these, who were men of mature age, having belief
in their hearts and knowing good from evil, did not receive the Holy
Spirit through the baptism of water, then it is not to be credited that
thereby little children, who do not have belief in their hearts nor knowledge of good and evil, can receive it. Furthermore, St. Luke proves this
argument again, saying: "When the apostles who were in Jerusalem had
heard that Samaria had received the word of God, they sent unto them
Peter and John. Who, when they were come, prayed for them that they
might receive the Holy Spirit. For He was not as yet come upon any of
them, but they were only baptized in the name of the Lord Jesus. Then
the apostles laid their hands upon them, and they received the Holy
Spirit."[112] And St. Paul says to Timothy, whom he had baptized with
this holy baptism, "I admonish thee, that thou stir up the grace of God
which is in thee by the imposition of my hands."[113] And thus did
Ananias baptize St. Paul.[114] And one finds that many others who were
not apostles performed this holy baptism just as they had received it
from the Holy Church, for the Church of Christ has kept it uninter-
ruptedly and will keep it until the end, as Christ says to them: "Baptize
them in the name of the Father, and of the Son, and of the Holy Spirit.
And behold, I am with you all days, even to the consummation of the
world."[115] And St. Peter shows clearly that one cannot be saved without
that baptism, saying, "As in the days of Noah a few, that is, eight souls,
were saved by the ark, the like form, baptism, saveth you,"[116] and so
on. Hence, no man is saved who is not baptized with this baptism, just
as all those who were outside the ark were drowned in the flood, for he
says, "Its like form, baptism, saveth you," and so on.

Let this be enough about baptism.[117]

Thirteenth or Fourteenth Century (?)

[*Prologue*]

   ... even as He revealed through the prophet Jeremiah, saying: "Behold, I will bring them from the north country, and will gather them from the ends of the earth.[1] They shall come with weeping and I will bring them back in prayer."[2] And again: "When the seventy years shall begin to be accomplished," He said, "I will visit you, and I will perform my good word in your favor, to bring you again to this place. And you shall call upon me, and you shall go and you shall pray to me and I will hear you. You shall seek me and shall find me. And I will bring back your captivity and I will gather you out of all nations and from all the places to which I have driven you out, saith the Lord."[3] And therefore our Lord Jesus Christ was sent by the Lord to seek that people which had been driven out and to save them, as Jesus Christ says in the Gospel: "The Son of man is come to seek and to save that which was lost."[4] And, therefore, our Lord Jesus Christ, when He had come from the seat of grandeur to seek and to save that people, to lead it forth from the land of the enemy, as was said above, spoke[5] to that people. Whence, He says in the Gospel: "Amen, amen, I say to you that you shall weep and lament, but the world shall rejoice; and you shall be made sorrowful";[6] and again, "They ought always to pray and not to faint";[7] and once more, "Watch ye and pray that ye enter not into temptation."[8] And therefore He teaches us to pray in this way.

[*Chapter I*]

   Our Father who art in heaven.[9]—[He is] the Holy Father in whose sight our prayer is addressed as incense, as the psalmist David says: "O Lord, let my prayer be directed as incense in Thy sight."[10] He is the Father of lights, that is, of charities, as St. James says in the Epistle: "Every best gift and every perfect gift is from above, coming down from the Father of lights."[11] This is the perfect [gift], of which the Apostle says to the Corinthians, "But when that which is perfect has come, that which is in part will be done away with."[12] And He is the Father of mercies, that is, of visitations, as the Apostle says to the Corinthians, "Blessed be the God, Father of our Lord Jesus Christ, the Father of mercies."[13] The Psalmist speaks further of these mercies,

saying, "They confess unto the Lord His mercies."[14] And He is also the
Father of spirits, as St. Paul says to the Hebrews, "When we shall much
more obey the Father of spirits and live."[15] Therefore was the Savior
first sent to give penance, for they had been seen,[16] and that very Spirit
who is a sign of the Lord himself [was sent] to keep the commandments
of the Gospel and to say this prayer.

And again, it should be known that the Lord who is the Father of
lights and of mercies—that is, of charities and visitations—and [the
Father] of spirits is also the Father of all other substances, to wit, lives,
souls, hearts, and bodies, for so St. Paul bore witness, saying, "All
paternity is named, which is one God and Father of all things."[17] And
He dwells in the heavens, as the psalmist says: "To Thee have I lifted
up my eyes, who dwellest in heaven."[18] But these heavens in which our
Father dwells are charities. And He is charity as well, as St. John says:
"God is charity."[19] And again, that same Father who dwells in the
heavens is He from whom our Lord Jesus Christ came forth and,
sustaining Himself in Him, dwelt on earth, as the psalmist says: "His
going out is from the end of heaven."[20] And He, the Lord, says in the
Gospel, "I came out from God [and] am come."[21] And again, "I came
forth from the Father and am come into the world."[22] Furthermore, our
Lord dwelt in that same heaven, as He says in the Gospel: "No man
hath ascended into heaven but He that descended from heaven, the Son
of man, who is in heaven";[23] and so is the Father from whom the Son
of God came forth and who dwells in the heavens. Therefore, He says
later, "Do you not believe that the Father is in me and I in the Father?"[24]
And again, He says, "That you may know that the Father is in me and
I in the Father."[25] It should be understood that just as the Holy Father
is in the heavens, so the Son is in all of us, as the Apostle tells the
Ephesians, "One God, Father of all things, who is above all, and
through all, and in us all."[26] So also the Son is not only in the Father
but in us too, and in all things that are in Him and of Him, as St. Paul
says to the Romans: "For of Him and by Him and in Him are all things.
To Him be glory forever."[27] And in the Acts of the Apostles he says,
"For in Him we live and move and are."[28] And the Lord says in the
Gospel, "And not for them only do I pray, but for them also who
through their word shall believe in me, that they all may be one, as
thou, Father, in me and I in Thee; that they also may be one in us."[29]

And again, it should be known that all the heavens in which our

Father dwells, to wit, the charities, are in the seventh heaven, as the angel teaches the prophet Isaiah and tells him in his vision: "Here there are neither thrones nor angels of the left, but they receive their direction from the virtue of the seventh heaven, where dwells the powerful Son of God; and all the heavens [and His angels hearken to Him]."[30] And further, the heavens, the charities, spread their grace thence over the clouds, that is, over the visitations; and they, thus moistened by the dew of love, spread their rain, meaning their benediction, over the earth, the spirits; and thus those spirits, moistened by the blessing of the visitations, bud forth the Savior in His substances, even as the prophet Isaiah says: "Drop down dew, ye heavens, from above, and let the clouds rain the just; let the earth be opened and bud forth the savior."[31] Thus the spirit of our first form,[32] when he speaks of the moistening of his head, that is, of his visitation, says in the Canticle of Canticles, "Open to me, my sister, my love, my dove, my undefiled, for my head is full of dew,"[33] meaning of mercy, for his visitation, which is his head, had received and found grace and mercy from his charity. But his hair was filled with droplets from the clouds—that is, with the ministering spirits serving their head, which is his visitation, were filled with filth, strange charities, which are called night, as our charities are called lights, even as St. James says: "Every best gift and every perfect gift is from above, coming down from the Father of lights,"[34] meaning the Father of the charities which are the lights of the visitations, for they illumine. But those visitations are the clouds which, when they had received the celestial dew raining the just, presented Him in the sight of the Ancient of Days, as the prophet Daniel tells, saying, "I beheld therefore in the vision of the night, and lo, one like the Son of man came with the clouds of heaven, and He came even to the Ancient of Days, and they presented Him before Him."[35] And St. John, referring to those clouds, says, "Behold, He cometh with the clouds of heaven,"[36] that is, with the visitations of the Father. And the psalmist, speaking of our Lord and of the aforesaid clouds, says, "And His power is in the clouds,"[37] and so on.

Chapter II

Hallowed be thy name.—This people in offering this prayer to the Lord profanes the name of its God amid the nations whither they went,[38] as the Lord says through the prophet Ezechiel: "It is not for your sake that I will make the house of Israel, but for my holy name's sake, which you have profaned among the nations whither you went."[39] And this holy name was blasphemed by this people among the nations, as the Apostle says to the Romans: "For the name of God is blasphemed through you among the Gentiles, as it is written."[40] Therefore, this people first asks of its God that He sanctify His name, which has been defiled among them, so that they may be sanctified. Thus the Lord heard their prayers before they cried to him, as He says through the prophet Isaiah: "Before they call, I will hear; as they are yet speaking, I will hear."[41] Of the sanctification of His name and also of His people, the Lord says through the prophet Ezechiel: "I will sanctify my great name, which was profaned among the Gentiles, which you have profaned in the midst of them, that the Gentiles may know that I am the Lord, when I shall be sanctified in you before them. I will take you from among the Gentiles,"[42] and so on. But this name which was profaned by the people is the visitation of the Father, which sinned in will and not by profanation; but the congregation of visitations is called the Son of God. Thus the first Moses says, "They have sinned against Him and are none of his children in their filth."[43] But these visitations had first to be sanctified, for they sinned only in will, even as the Son of God, who was a visitation, desired something other than did His Father, as He says in the Gospel: "My Father, if it be possible, let this chalice pass from me; nevertheless not as I will, but as Thou wilt";[44] and again, "Father, if Thou wilt, remove this chalice from me; but yet not my will but Thine be done."[45] Thus, that Son of God sanctified himself so that He might then sanctify the people of God, as He says in the Gospel, "For them do I sanctify myself, that they also may be sanctified in truth."[46] And one should know that our Lord Jesus Christ not only sanctified himself for the sanctification of the people, but suffered for it, as St. Paul says to the Hebrews: "Wherefore Jesus also, that He might sanctify the people, suffered outside the gate."[47]

But it should be known further that the name of the Father, that is, the visitation which is sanctified by the Father, is called Jacob, while the spirit subject to him is called Israel; therefore, the Lord, wishing to sanctify His name, the visitation which is the head of the other visitations which sinned in will, the one which is also called Jacob, sent His word first to him, not that he should do penance, for the gifts and the call of God are without repentance, and also sin was not imputed to him by the Lord, as the Apostle says to the Romans: "Blessed is the man to whom the Lord hath not imputed sin."[48] And again he says, "[For the gifts and the call of God] are without repentance,"[49] and so on. But the Lord, therefore, sent His word first to Jacob so that the word might fall in Israel, that from the visitation it might fall upon the spirit, Israel, which is the head of the other spirits which sinned. Thus, the prophet Isaiah says, "The Lord sent his word into Jacob, and it hath lighted upon Israel."[50] Thereby Jacob, the visitation, rejoiced when he received the grace and mercy of God; and Israel, the spirit, was glad in his joy, as the psalmist says: "Who shall give out of Zion the salvation of Israel? When the Lord shall have turned away the captivity of His people, Jacob shall rejoice and Israel shall be glad."[51] But this is the holy Jacob, who is the sanctifier of his sons by prayer to the God of Israel, as the Lord says through the prophet Isaiah: "Jacob shall not now be confounded, neither shall his countenance now be ashamed; but when he shall see his children, the work of my hands in the midst of him sanctifying my name, and they shall sanctify the Holy [One of] Jacob and shall glorify the God of Israel."[52] It should be known further that these visitations which are called by the name of Jacob are those mountains that must receive the sowing of the Lord in order to bear fruit to the people of Israel, that is, to the spirit, as the Lord says through the prophet Ezechiel: "But as for you, O mountains of Israel, shoot ye forth your branches that ye may yield your fruit to my people Israel. And you shall be plowed and sown. And I will multiply men upon you, and all the house of Israel."[53] And speaking of those mountains and praying for the peace of Israel, the psalmist says, "Let the mountains receive peace for the people."[54] Thus, the prophet raised his eyes to those mountains, for his helper was to come from them, even as he says: "I have lifted up my eyes to the mountains, from whence help shall come to me."[55] But the City of God is founded on these mountains, even as that prophet says: "The foundations thereof are in the holy mountains."[56]

And again, one should know that our Lord, wishing to draw His people to Him—for Truth says in the Gospel, "No man can come to me except the Father draw him"[57]—commanded Jacob, the visitation, to draw Israel, the spirit, to him. For Jacob is the cord by which Israel is bound and drawn, as the first Moses says. He says, "Jacob, the cord of his inheritance";[58] of which inheritance the Lord says through the prophet Isaiah, "But Israel is my inheritance." [59] Therefore, the Lord says through the prophet Osee, "I will draw them with the bonds of Adam, with the cords of love." [60] For charity is called Adam, and is "the bond of perfection," as St. Paul says. [61] And he [Jacob] has his own bonds, his cords, which are the charities, by which he binds and draws the spirit to himself. Even so, the visitation is the cord of charity, by which it draws the spirit to itself. And it is also the cord of the spirit, by which the spirit itself is bound and drawn up, as was said above. The Lord himself, through the prophet David, says further of those cords, the visitations which had fallen in the inheritance of the God of Israel, "The lines are fallen unto me in goodly places, for my inheritance is goodly to me." [62] Again, it should be known that the strange visitations are also called cords and bonds, as the psalmist, the spirit of the first form, says, "They have stretched my cords for a snare." [63] And again he says, "The cords of the wicked have encompassed me." [64] And that same prophet, giving thanks to his Lord that He hath broken those aforesaid cords, says: "O Lord, Thou hast broken my bonds. I will sacrifice to Thee the sacrifice of praise." [65] And speaking of these bonds, the Lord says through the prophet Isaiah, "Woe to you that draw iniquity with cords of vanity, and sin as the rope of the cart." [66] And again, it should be known that the spirit is the cord of life which draws and binds the life. It binds, as St. Paul, personifying his life, says in the Acts of the Apostles. He says, "And now behold, being bound in the spirit, I go to Jerusalem." [67] Moreover, the life is the cord of the soul which, aided by the visitation, draws and joins the soul to itself. Thus David, praising God for his joining and for his life, says, "Who hath set my soul to life." [68]

[Chapter III]

Thy kingdom come.—This kingdom, for whose coming this people prays to its Father, is the son of David, who is the Son of God, our Lord Jesus Christ, as St. Mark says in the Gospel: "And they that went before, and they that followed, cried, saying, 'Hosanna! Blessed is he that cometh in the name of the Lord! Blessed be the kingdom of our father David that cometh!'" [69] But this is the kingdom which the God of heaven must set up in order to lay waste the four kingdoms of Babylon, but which will not be laid waste but will stand forever. This kingdom will not be delivered up to another people, as Daniel the prophet shows, saying: "But in the days of those kingdoms the God of heaven will set up a kingdom that shall never be destroyed and His kingdom shall not be delivered up to another people, and it shall break in pieces and shall consume all these kingdoms, and itself shall stand forever."[70] This kingdom is the kingdom of all time, whose glory and grandeur the saints of God will preach and make known to the sons of men, as David says, speaking to his God: "Let all thy works, O Lord, praise Thee and let Thy saints bless Thee, and they shall speak of the glory of Thy kingdom and shall tell of Thy power, and the glory of the magnificence of Thy kingdom. Thy kingdom is a kingdom of all ages."[71] But this kingdom, which is the Son of God, made His brethren a kingdom and priests to His God, as St. John says in the Apocalypse, "John, to the seven churches that are in Asia: Grace be unto you and peace from Him that is and that was and that is to come; from Jesus Christ, who hath loved us, and hath made us a kingdom and priests to God His Father."[72] In the same way, the same St. John says of the four living creatures and the twenty-four elders, "And when he had opened the book, the four living creatures and the four and twenty elders fell down before the Lamb, saying, "Thou art worthy, O Lord, to take the book, for Thou hast made us to our God a kingdom and priests, and we shall reign on the earth."[73] And therefore David, calling those very created kingdoms to our God, says, "Sing ye to God, ye kingdoms of earth; rejoice in the Lord."[74] But it should be known that even if this kingdom came once to illumine those existing in darkness and in the shadow of death, and to teach [His] brethren and declare the name of His Father to them, even as He says, "I will declare Thy name to my brethren,"[75] it is necessary for Him to come here again with His angels and with His power, with the flame of fire, dispensing vengeance to those who did not know God and did not believe in the Gospel of our Lord Jesus Christ, in order that "He might be made great in His act and honorable in all those who believed,"[76] as St. Paul says to the Thessalonians, and in order to save and "gather His elect from the four winds, from the farthest parts of the heavens to the utmost bounds of them,"[77] as is written in the Gospel, and in order to render to each according to his works, even as He says in the Apocalypse: "Behold, I come quickly. And my reward is with me to render to every man according to his works."[78] And in the same way, He must come here so that when He comes and descends from heaven with commandment and with the power of the archangel and with the trumpet of God, His friends may be taken up toward him into the air, to be with Him always, as St. Paul tells the Thessalonians, saying: "And we will not have you ignorant, brethren, concerning them that are asleep, that you be not sorrowful, even as others who have no hope. For if we believe that Jesus died and rose again, even so them who have slept through Jesus will God bring with Him. For this we say unto you in the word of the Lord, that we who are alive, who remain unto the coming of the Lord, shall not precede those who have slept. For the Lord himself shall come down from heaven with commandment and with the voice of the archangel, and with the trumpet of God; and the dead who are in Christ shall rise first. Then we who are alive, who are left, shall be taken up together with them in the clouds to meet Christ, into the air, and so shall we be always with the Lord. Wherefore, comfort ye one another with these words." [79] Moreover, that the redemption of this people was at hand and the coming of this kingdom, the Lord shows in the Gospel, saying: "They will see the Son of man coming upon the clouds of heaven with much power and glory.[80] And he shall send His angels and they shall gather together His elect from the four winds, from the farthest parts of earth to the farthest parts of heaven." [81] Therefore, this people, most concerned about the coming of its Lord, asks Him secretly, as the evangelist discloses, "Tell us, when shall these things be, and what shall be the sign of Thy coming and of the consummation of the world?" [82] For this people hopes to receive its reward and its salvation from the Lord at His coming, as was said above and as St. Paul says to the Romans, that "He will render to every man according to his works. To them who, according to patience in good works, seek glory and honor and incorruption, eternal life; but to them that are contentious and who obey not the truth but iniquity, wrath and indignation and tribulation and anguish; but glory, honor, and peace to all who do good." [83] Therefore David, inspired by the Holy Spirit, praying for the coming of that Lord, says: "Give ear, O Thou that rulest Israel; Thou that leadest Joseph like a sheep. Stir up Thy might and come to save us." [84] And St. John, recalling this prayer in the Apocalypse, says, "And the bridegroom and bride say, 'Come!' and he that heareth, let him say, 'Come!'" [85] And the same St. John, uttering this prayer, says, "Come, O Lord." [86] Therefore, the Lord himself, speaking for the comfort of this people, says in the Apocalypse, "Behold, I come quickly; hold fast that which thou hast"; [87] and again,

"Behold, I come quickly. And my reward is with me, to render to every man according to his works."[88] And St. James says that "the coming of the Lord is at hand."[89] And St. Paul says to the Hebrews, "Yet a very little while and He that is to come will come, and will not delay."[90]

The kingdom mentioned above by our father David, that is, our Lord Jesus Christ, therefore came thus. And again He must come here in order that He, sitting upon the kingdom of His father David, may confirm it in judgment and in justice from henceforth and forever, as He says through the prophet Isaiah,[91] and so that, established by His Father over all principalities and powers and virtues and dominations that were made by Him and of which He is the chief, He might do away with every power and principality, virtue and domination, despoiling them; and at His coming they will praise God and the Father, as St. Paul tells the Ephesians, saying, "And setting Him at his right hand in the heavenly places, above all principality and power and virtue and domination."[92] And to the Colossians he says, "For in Him were all things created in heaven and visible on earth, whether thrones or dominations or principalities or powers."[93] And he says to the Colossians, "Despoiling the principalities and powers, He hath exposed them in open show, triumphing over them in himself."[94] But of this end, the Lord himself says in the Apocalypse, "I am Alpha and Omega, the beginning and the end."[95] Even so Malachi the prophet speaks of the coming of this Lord and of the work that He must accomplish at His coming, saying: "And presently the Lord whom you seek, and the angel of the testament whom you desire, shall come to His holy temple. Behold, He cometh, saith the Lord of hosts. And who shall be able to think of the day of His coming? And who shall stand to see Him? For He is like a refining fire and like the fuller's herb."[96] Moreover, it is said that our Lord Jesus Christ will come soon and will not delay, because some "scoffers, men walking according to their own lusts," as St. Peter says in the Epistle, doubting the coming of our Lord Jesus Christ and not knowing in what way or when He is to come, say, "Where is His promise or His coming? For since the time that the fathers slept, all things continue as they were from the beginning of creation."[97]

But the way in which this blessed kingdom of our father David, which is the Son of God, will come and what the sign of His coming will be He himself reveals in the Gospel, saying: "And immediately after the tribulation of those days, the sun shall be darkened and the moon shall not give her light, and the stars shall fall from heaven, and the powers of heaven shall be moved. And then shall appear the sign of the Son of man in heaven; and then shall all the tribes of earth mourn, and they shall see the Son of man coming in the clouds of heaven with much power and majesty. And as in the days of Noah, so shall also the coming of the Son of man be."[98] And again, "Thus will He sit on the seat of His majesty; and all nations shall be gathered together before Him,"[99] and so on. And St. John says in the Apocalypse, "Behold, He cometh with the clouds of heaven, and every eye shall see Him, and they also that pierced Him. And all the tribes of earth truly."[100] And St. Peter speaks of this Lord who says in the Apocalypse, "Behold, I come as a thief";[101] which Lord is the day of the Holy Father and we are of this day, as St. Paul says: "For you are all children of the light and children of the day; but let us who are of the day be sober."[102] St. Peter says in the Epistle that "the day of the Lord shall come as a thief";[103] and St. Paul says to the Thessalonians, "For you know that the day of the Lord shall so come as a thief in the night."[104] Therefore, the people of the Lord, hoping for His promise, pray the Holy Father that He come here to His kingdom in order to accomplish the things we have discussed.

[*Chapter IV*]

Thy will be done on earth as it is in heaven.—This people, having prayed to the Father for the sanctification of His name and for the coming of His kingdom, prays further to its Father for His will to be done on earth as in heaven. But St. Paul reveals to the Thessalonians what the will of God is which must be done on earth as it is in heaven, saying: "This is the will of God: that you should abstain from fornication; that every one of you should know how to possess his vessel in sanctification and honor and not in the passion of lust like the Gentiles that know not God; and that no man deceive and overreach his brother in business, because the Lord is the avenger of all these things. Rebuke the unquiet, comfort the fainthearted, receive the weak, be patient toward all men; and see that none render evil for evil to any man; but ever follow that which is good toward each other and toward all men. Rejoice now in the Lord, pray without ceasing. In all things give thanks; for this is the will of God in Christ regarding you all."[105] And because the Father "worketh all things according to the counsel of His will,"[106] as St. Paul says to the Ephesians, His Son descends from heaven to do

His will and to teach His brethren what the will of the Father is, as He reveals in the Gospel, saying: "Because I came down from heaven, not to do my own will, but the will of Him that sent me. Now this is the will of the Father who sent me, that of all that the Father hath given me I should lose nothing, but should raise it up on the Last Day. For this is the will of my Father that sent me, that everyone who seeth the Son, and believeth in Him, may have life everlasting, and I will raise him up in the Last Day." [107] And therefore the Apostle prays his brethren to understand and try what the will of God is, good, well-pleasing, and perfect, [108] and on their behalf he also prays God to fit them with all goodness so that they may do His will. And to the Hebrews he says, "God fit you in all goodness to do his will, doing in you that which is well-pleasing in His sight, through Jesus Christ." [109] And it should be known that the Holy Father to whom this people prays is the Father of heaven and of that earth in which His will must be done, as well of one as of the other, as our Lord reveals in the Gospel, saying, "I confess to thee, Lord of heaven and earth." [110] And that heaven is the spirit, for the spirit is called heaven. The visitation and the charity are also called heavens, as is written in the book of Jesus [the son of] Sirach, "Behold, the heaven and the heaven of heavens shall be moved in His sight, and when God shall look upon them, they shall be shaken with trembling." [111] But the earth in which the will of God must be done is the earth of the life which is under the power of heaven, that is, of the spirit. Therefore, this people, that is, the congregation of the spirits, prays that the merciful Lord may show mercy unto them as to their lives, and may sanctify them, so that the Lord may work in the life as He works in the spirit. Therefore, the psalmist, who is the spirit of the first form, forseeing in the spirit the mercy of the Lord which was to come upon the lives, promises and declares that he will praise and bless God in his life, saying, "For thy mercy is better than lives; Thee my lips shall praise, and thus will I bless Thee in my life." [112] But then that same prophet, praying for the salvation of his soul, says, "O Lord, be Thou merciful to me; heal my soul, for I have sinned against Thee." [113] And again he says, "O Lord, deliver my soul from wicked lips and a deceitful tongue." [114] But that same prophet knew that his prayer had been heard by God, that is, that the Lord had been good to his soul and had delivered it from death, as he shows, saying, "Turn, O my soul, into thy rest, for the Lord has been bountiful to thee." [115] And he invites that same soul to the praise of his Lord God; and he declares also that he will praise that Lord in his life, saying, "Praise the Lord, O my soul; in my life I will praise the Lord; I will rejoice to my God as long as I shall be."[116] That same prophet invites his soul to bless his Lord because He had redeemed its life from death, saying, "Bless the Lord, O my soul, who redeemeth thy life from death."[117] And thus these three substances, that is, the spirit and the life and the soul, when they have received grace and mercy from their Father, are led with one mouth to praise and bless and rejoice in the Lord.

[Chapter V]

Give us this day our supersubstantial bread.[118]—This afore-mentioned people, making this prayer to its Father, is a bread, as St. Paul reveals to the Corinthians, saying, "For we are all one bread and one body, and we all partake of the one bread and of one cup."[119] And since this people has long hungered and thirsted, as the prophet David says, "They were hungry and thirsty; their soul fainted in them,"[120] they sought bread for a long time and there was no one to make it for them, as says the prophet Jeremiah, "The little ones have asked for bread and there was none to break it unto them."[121] Therefore, the Lord "hath remembered his mercy toward the house of Israel," as the psalmist says,[122] and as the Blessed Mary says, "He has filled the hungry with good things and the rich He has sent empty away."[123] He gave them that bread of which the Lord speaks in the Gospel, "I am the living bread which came down from heaven,"[124] just as Isaiah, speaking of that Son of God who was given to this people, reveals when he says, "A child is given to us and a son is born to us."[125] But when this living bread, one bread and one body, descends from heaven and is given to this people aforesaid, He teaches them to seek still other bread from the Father, the supersubstantial bread, which is charity. For charity is called supersubstantial bread because it is above all other substances, that is, above visitation, spirit, life, soul, heart, body; and all these substances are sustained by that bread, as the Apostle tells the Corinthians, saying, "Charity is patient, kind; charity beareth all things, believeth all things, hopeth all things, and sustaineth all things."[126] But this charity which sustains all things, as St. Paul says, even so preserves and sustains the visitation, and the visitation, with the aid of charity, preserves and sustains the spirit, as the Blessed Job says, speaking of His God, "Thou hast granted me life and mercy, and Thy visitation has preserved my spirit." [127] And the spirit sustains and preserves the life, as is written in the parables of Solomon, "The spirit of a man upholdeth his infirmity." [128] And the Apostle, personifying the life, says to the Romans, "Likewise the Spirit also helpeth our infirmity." [129] And the life sustains and preserves the soul. And the soul, turned to its rest, preserves the heart, which heart sustains the body. Thus, each of these substances is preserved by its superior with the aid of charity.

But the psalmist, who by luxurious living in a far country had wasted not all his substance but that part belonging to him which he had received from his Father, addressing his Father in regard to his substance, that is, charity, which as yet he had not received from the Father, says, "My substance is with Thee"; [130] and again, referring to the substance which he had lost, meaning the life and the soul, he says, "My substance is in the lower parts of the earth." [131] And therefore that psalmist, who had lost one substance and was unable to have the other, cried to his God, saying, "Save me, O God, for the waters are come in even unto my soul. I stick fast in the mire of the earth and there is no substance." [132] Thus spoke that prophet who is our father and the servant of our God, as said the apostles, confessing to God in the Acts of the Apostles, "O Lord God, who didst make heaven and earth and the sea and all things that are in them, who, by the Holy Spirit, by the mouth of our father David, thy servant, hast said," [133] and so on. And he was found imperfect in the sight of his God, as he says, "Lord, Thy eyes did see my imperfect being"; [134] and again, "I am brought to nothing and I knew not." [135] Therefore, our Lord, who is made of his seed become flesh, descends to the lowest parts of the earth, as the Apostle tells the Ephesians: "Now that He ascended, what is it, but because He also descended first into the lower parts of the earth? He that descended is the same also that ascended above all the heavens, that He might fulfill all things." [136]

Thus, the God of all grace commanded His beloved Son [to bring] the gift of charity to David [137] and the people, to perfect, to strengthen, and to establish, as St. Peter reveals in his Epistle and says, "But the God of all grace, who hath called us after a little suffering into His eternal glory in Jesus Christ, He himself will perfect, confirm, and establish." [138] Therefore, that people asks its Father that He give it the supersubstantial bread, which is charity, this day, that is, in Him, Christ, who is that day of ours of which the psalmist speaks: "This is the day which the Lord hath made. Let us rejoice therein";[139] and says again, "Day to day uttereth speech"[140]—that is, the Father reveals the word to the Son, as our Lord himself shows in the Gospel when he says, "For I have not spoken of myself, but the Father who sent me, He gave me commandment what I should say, and what I should speak. And I know that His commandment is life everlasting. The things, therefore, that I speak, even as the Father hath said unto me, so do I speak."[141] And the Apostle, referring to that day, says to the Romans, "The night is passed and the day is at hand";[142] and again, to the Hebrews he discloses that the Holy Spirit sends this day in David—referring to His rest[143]—saying therefore, "Since it remaineth that some are to enter into the rest of God, and they to whom it was first preached did not enter into it because of unbelief; again he limiteth a certain day, saying in David after so long a time, as it is said above, 'Today if you shall hear His voice, harden not your hearts.'"[144] Therefore, this people prays its Father—for in this day, which is Christ, is suffered the appointed time of its salvation and the end of its travail—that in Him they may be given His supersubstantial bread, which is charity, in such wise that it be not delayed to another day, but that it be given them by the Father. For it is the bond of perfection; rather, it is perfection itself, as the Apostle says to the Corinthians, "But when that which is perfect has come, that which is in part will be done away."[145] It is perfection such that without it no man can be perfect, as St. Paul tells the Corinthians: "If I speak with the tongues of men and of angels, and have not charity, I am become as sounding brass or a tinkling cymbal. And if I should have prophecy and should know all mysteries and all knowledge, and if I should have all faith that I could remove mountains, and have not charity, I am nothing."[146] Therefore, this people prays that this supersubstantial bread, charity, be given them by the Father so that after receiving it, they may be found perfect in the sight of their God, as the Living Bread which descends from heaven reveals, when He teaches them in the Gospel, saying, "Be you therefore perfect, as also your heavenly Father is perfect."[147]

[Chapter VI]

And forgive us our debts, as we also forgive our debtors.—But the evangelist discloses what those debts are which this people prays its

Father to pardon when he says, "And forgive us our sins."[148] Therefore, we should know that the first father of this people sinned before his God, as the Lord reveals through the prophet Isaiah, saying to the people, Israel, "Thy first father sinned."[149] Therefore, that father, the spirit of the first form, confessing his sins to his God, says in the Gospel, "Father, I have sinned against heaven before thee."[150] And in the psalm he says, "To Thee only have I sinned and have done evil before Thee."[151] And in the same way, the people of that first father sinned before their God, as the spirit of the Lord speaking through the prophet Jeremiah, tells them, "For the sins that you have committed before God, you shall be carried away captive into Babylon by the king of Babylon."[152] And the prophet Daniel, praying for himself and for his people, says: "O my Lord God, great and terrible, we have sinned, we have committed iniquity, we have done wickedly. For by reason of our sins and the iniquities of our fathers, Israel, Thy people are a reproach."[153] And again, that same people hated one another and sinned one against the other, as the Apostle, speaking to his son Titus, says, "For we ourselves also were once unwise, incredulous, erring, slaves to divers desires and pleasures, living in malice and envy, hateful, and hating one another."[154] And the Lord, referring to that sinful people, says through the prophet Jeremiah: "Let every man take heed of his neighbor and let him not trust in any brother of his, for every supplanting brother will utterly supplant, and every friend will walk deceitfully with his brother. And a man shall mock his brother and shall not speak truth, for they have taught their tongue to speak lies; they have labored to commit iniquity."[155] And the Lord, speaking to His city Jerusalem of the same thing, says through the prophet Ezechiel: "Behold the princes of Israel, every one hath employed his arm in thee to shed blood. They have abused father and mother in thee, they have oppressed the stranger in the midst of thee, they have grieved the child and the widow in thee; and every one hath committed abomination,"[156] and so on. And in the Book of Wisdom it is written of the sins of this people: "For either they sacrifice their own children, or keep watches full of madness, so that now they neither keep life nor marriage undefiled, but one killeth another through envy, or grieveth him through adultery. And all things are mingled together: blood, murder, thefts, dissimulation and corruptions, unfaithfulness, tumults and perjury, mutilations, forgetfulness of the good things of God, defiling of souls, changing of births, disorder in marriage, the irregularity of adultery and uncleanness."[157] Therefore, through His Son the Holy Father commanded that the people who had sinned against one another must themselves forgive, saying, "Forgive and you shall be forgiven. But if you will not forgive men their offenses, neither will your heavenly Father forgive you your offenses."[158] And again, our Lord Jesus Christ says in the Gospel, when discussing the lord who was angry with the wicked servant who did not wish to forgive his fellow servant, commanding him to be delivered to the torturers until he paid all the debt, "So also shall my heavenly Father do to you, if you forgive not each the other from your hearts."[159] And the Apostle, to whom Christ spoke, says to the Ephesians, "Be ye kind one to another, and merciful, forgiving one another, even as God has forgiven you in Christ."[160] And to the Colossians he says, "Bear with one another, and yourselves forgive, if any have a complaint against another; even as the Lord hath forgiven you, so do you also."[161] Therefore, this people, wishing to forgive as the Lord commands, so that they may be forgiven, prays to their Father to forgive them their debts as they forgive all those owed to them.

And it should be known that they were debtors from the beginning, that is, one to the other, to love among themselves, as St. John discloses in the Epistle, saying, "And now I beseech thee, lady, not as writing a new commandment to thee, but that which we have had from the beginning, that we love one another."[162] In the same way that very people is in debt for that debt, which is mutual charity, at the fitting time and on the day of salvation, as the Apostle tells the Romans, saying, "We are debtors, not to the flesh, to live according to the flesh."[163] And again he says, "Owe no man anything but to love one another. For he that loveth hath fulfilled the Law."[164] Moreover, our Lord Jesus Christ recalling that debt, which is love, says in the Gospel, "These things I command you, that you love one another."[165] And St. John says in the Epistle, "O dearest, if God hath so loved us, we also ought to love one another. This is His commandment, that we should believe in the name of His Son Jesus Christ, and love one another."[166] Therefore, this people loves one another and forgives all its debtors, accepting what St. Luke says when he prays to his Father, saying, "Forgive us our sins, for we also forgive everyone that is indebted to us."[167]

[*Chapter VII*]

And lead us not into temptation.—Again, the holy people prays its Holy Father that He lead it not into temptation lest, caught up in that temptation, it should fall, as the Apostle says to the Corinthians, "He that thinketh himself to stand, let him take heed lest he fall. Let no temptation take hold on you but such as is human." [168] Therefore, our bishop, Jesus Christ, was tempted by the semblance of all things without sinning, so that He might aid His brethren in their temptations, as St. Paul tells the Hebrews, "For we have not a bishop who cannot have compassion on our infirmities, but one tempted by the semblance of all things, without sin"; [169] and, "In that, wherein he himself hath suffered and been tempted, He is able to succor them also that are tempted." [170] And we should know that our Lord sometimes tempts His people, as Wisdom says: "The souls of the just are in the hands of God, and the torment of death shall not touch them, because God hath tried them and found them worthy of himself, like gold in a furnace." [171] And the Apostle, referring to this temptation, says to the Hebrews, "By faith Abraham offered Isaac, when he was put to the test to offer up his only begotten son, he who should have received the promises." [172] Again, the Lord suffered His people to be tempted, as St. Peter says in the Epistle: "Dearly beloved, think not strange the burning heat which is taking place among you to try you, and do not be afraid, as if some new thing happened to you; but if you partake of the sufferings of Christ, rejoice." [173] And St. James says, "But every man is tempted by his own concupiscence, being drawn away and allured." [174] But this temptation is contrived by that tempter of whom St. Matthew says, "Then Jesus was led by the Spirit into the desert, to be tempted by the devil; and the tempter coming, said," [175] and so on. And St. Luke says, "And all the temptation being ended, the devil departed from Him for a time." [176] And the Apostle says to the Thessalonians, "For this cause also, I, forbearing no longer, sent to know your faith lest perhaps he that tempteth should have tempted you, and our labor should be made vain." [177]

And it should be known that our Lord sometimes suffered temptation so that an example of His patience might be given to those to come, as it is written in the Book of Tobit, the elderly man who feared God: "Now this trial the Lord therefore permitted to happen to him, that an example might be given to posterity of his patience, as also of holy Job." [178] And St. James says in the Epistle, "Take, my brethren, for an example of labor and patience, the prophets,"[179] and so on. And it should be known that the Lord causes this temptation for His people for two reasons. One is that in the days of old that people tempted the Lord and tried Him, according to what St. Paul tells the Hebrews.[180] And to the Corinthians, he says, "Neither let us tempt God, as some of them tempted, and perished by the serpents."[181] And, therefore, that same Lord, wishing to bring about what He had said of His vineyard, which is the house of Israel, says through the prophet Isaiah, "In measure against measure, when it shall be cast off, I shall judge it."[182] And, therefore, the Lord wishes to try and to tempt this people, for the people tempted Him. The other reason for the Lord's temptation is that when that people shall be tried with temptations, they may receive the crown of life, as is written in the Book of Wisdom, "Because God hath tried them, and found them worthy of himself; He hath proved them as gold in the furnace, and as a victim of a holocaust."[183] And St. James says, "Blessed is the man that endureth temptation; for when he hath been proved, he shall receive the crown of life which God hath promised to them that love Him."[184] Therefore, the Lord, speaking to those who with Him had suffered temptation, tells them: "But you are they who have continued with me in my temptations; and I dispose to you, as my Father hath disposed to me, a kingdom, that you may eat and drink at my table in my kingdom; and you may sit upon twelve thrones, judging the twelve tribes of Israel."[185]

And it should be known that the double temptation that is the lot of the people of God, the temptation of God and the temptation of the devil,[186] befalls them for two causes: the temptation of God to life and the temptation of the devil to death. The temptation to life is that of which Wisdom says, "Afflicted in few things, in many shall they be well rewarded, because God hath tried them, and found them worthy of himself,"[187] and so forth. And St. James says, "Blessed is the man that endureth temptation."[188] And it is written in the Book of Wisdom: "Wisdom inspireth life into her children, that they may remain secure. For she walketh with him [who is] in temptation. She will bring upon him fear and dread and trial, till she try him in his thought; and she will give him joy, and will disclose her secrets to him, and will heap upon him treasures of knowledge, understanding, and justice."[189] The temptation of the devil to death is that of which St. Paul, speaking to Timothy, says, "For they that will become rich, fall into temptation, and into the snare of the devil."[190] And St. John says in the Apocalypse, "Behold, the devil will cast some of you into prison that you may be tried, and you shall have tribulation ten days";[191] and again, he says to the angel of Philadelphia, "I too will keep thee from the hour of temptation, which shall come upon the whole world to try them that dwell upon the earth."[192]

It should be known that this people, like their father, the psalmist David, when praying to his Father, "Search me, O Lord, and try me,"[193] does not pray its Father not to tempt them, but prays the Holy Father not to lead them into the temptation of the devil and to death for their sins. Therefore, our Lord, knowing beforehand the temptation prepared for Simon and the other apostles, says in the Gospel: "Behold, Simon, Satan hath desired to have you, that he may sift you as wheat. But I have prayed for thee, that thy faith fail not: and thou, being once converted again, confirm thy brethren."[194] And then He says to them, "Watch ye, and pray that ye enter not into temptation."[195]

[Chapter VIII]

But deliver us from evil.—This people which prays to the Holy Father is the flock of the Lord which prays to Him to be delivered from evil, for it has been taken captive, as the prophet Jeremiah discloses when he says: "My soul shall weep for your pride; weeping it shall weep, and my eyes shall run down with tears, because the flock of the Lord is taken away captive and scattered."[196] Of this flock the Lord says in the Gospel, "Fear not, little flock, for it hath pleased your Father to give you the kingdom of life."[197] This flock, which is the people of the Lord, has been captured in such wise that those who took them would not let them go, as the prophet Jeremiah says: "The children of Israel and the children of Judah are oppressed; all that have taken them captives hold them fast, they will not let them go. Their redeemer is strong, the Lord of hosts is His name."[198] And when that people was thrust into that prison, they cried to the Lord, saying, "Deliver us from evil."[199] We understand this evil from which the people of God prays for deliverance to be the devil, for in the Holy Scriptures he is called evil, and Satan, and the devil. He is called evil as St. Matthew reveals in the Gospel in regard to the sowing, saying, "When anyone heareth the word of the kingdom, and understandeth it not, there cometh the wicked one, and catcheth away that which was sown in his heart."[200] He is also called

Satan, as St. Mark discloses in referring to the same thing, saying, "As soon as they have heard the word, Satan cometh and taketh away the word that was sown in their hearts."[201] And further, he is called the devil, as St. Luke says, "The devil taketh the word out of their heart."[202] And he is called the enemy, as St. Matthew reveals when speaking of the sowing of the weeds, saying, "Sir, didst thou not sow good seed in thy field? Whence then hath it cockle?"[203] And thereafter Christ says in exposition of that parable, "The enemy that oversowed is the devil."[204] Moreover, he is that evil man from whose malice the psalmist, crying to the Lord, prayed to be delivered,[205] saying, "Deliver me, O Lord, from the evil man, rescue me from the unjust man."[206] And again he says, "Have mercy on me, O Lord, for man hath trodden me under foot, all the day long he hath afflicted me, fighting against me."[207] In the same way, the people of God, crying the same plea, says, "Arise, O Lord, help us and deliver us for thy name's sake."[208] But this evil man reigned over them for their sins and yet reigns over many, as is written in the Book of Job, ". . . and over the nations and over all men who maketh a man that is a hypocrite to reign for the sins of the people."[209] Therefore, that same Job says, "God hath shut me up with the unjust man, and hath delivered me into the hands of the wicked."[210] This is the very same enemy of whom David complains to his God, saying: "Hear, O Lord, my prayer. For the enemy hath persecuted my soul; he hath brought down my life to the earth. He hath made me to dwell in darkness as those that have been dead of old."[211] And our mother, Jerusalem, complaining of that enemy, says through the prophet Jeremiah: "My children are lost because the enemy hath power. Those that I nourished, my enemy hath consumed them."[212] And again she says through the prophet Baruch: "The Lord hath brought upon me great mourning. For I have seen the captivity of my children. My children, suffer patiently, for through the wrath of God the enemy hath persecuted thee."[213] Because of this, the Apostle, speaking to the children of Jerusalem, says of that enemy, "And the God of peace crush Satan under your feet."[214] And the prophet Jeremiah, speaking of that same Jerusalem, which is our mother, says: "The enemy hath put out his hand to all her desirable things. The kings of the earth would not have believed that the enemy should enter in by the gates of Jerusalem. The Lord hath cast off his altar. He hath delivered the walls of the towers thereof into the hands of the enemy."[215]

And it should be known that this enemy, which has reigned over nations and over all men, as was said above, is called not only devil and Satan, but, in the interpretation of Holy Scriptures, he is also called the king of Assyria,[216] who devoured the people and cut off their seat on high, and he seized the princes of the people, and placed his terror on earth among the living, and the cedars were not higher in the paradise of God. Him all the trees that were in the paradise of God envied;[217] he was the ruler of the people of God, for they would not be converted. The Lord promised that He would deliver His people from him, and that the city would be taken from the powerful, and what had been made captive would be rescued from the mighty. And the Lord will deliver His people from the hand of the most powerful, even as the prophet Jeremiah says, "Israel [is a] scattered flock, the lions have driven him away; first Assyria devoured him."[218] And the Lord says through the prophet Isaiah: "I will visit the fruit of the proud heart of the king of Assyria, and the glory of his haughtiness. For he hath said: By the strength of my own hand I have done it, and by my own wisdom I have understood. And I have removed the bounds of the people, and have taken their princes and pulled down them that sat on high. And my hand hath found the strength of the people as a nest."[219] And the Lord says through the prophet Ezechiel: "Behold the Assyrian like a cedar in Lebanon. The waters nourished him, the deep set him up on high. The cedars in the paradise of God were not higher than he. All the trees of delight in the paradise envied him."[220] And again: "Ashur is there and all his multitude, all of them slain, and fallen by the sword, they that had heretofore spread terror in the land of the living."[221] And the Lord, speaking of His people, says through the prophet Osee: "But the Assyrian himself [shall be] their king, because they would not be converted."[222] And the prophet Micah says, "And the Lord shall deliver us from the Assyrian, when he shall come into our land, and when he shall tread in our borders."[223] And the Lord says through the prophet Isaiah: "Shall the prey be taken from the strong? Or can that which was taken by the mighty be delivered? Verily, the city[224] shall be taken away from the strong; and that which was taken by the mighty shall be delivered."[225] And the Holy Spirit, speaking through the prophet Jeremiah, says: "Hear the word of the Lord, O ye nations. The Lord will redeem Jacob, and the Lord will deliver him out of the hand of one mightier than he. And they shall come and give praise in Mount Zion. And they shall flow together to the good things of the Lord. And my people shall be filled with my good things, saith the Lord."[226]

Therefore, the people of God, trusting and hoping in these promises aforesaid and in others of the Lord, because many of them are still held in the snares of the devil, "captive at his will,"[227] as St. Paul explains, cry out to the Holy Father day and night, saying, "Deliver us from evil."

[*Chapter IX*]

For Thine is the kingdom.—As for this kingdom, we understand it to be the spirit of the first form and, likewise, the uniting of the spirits subject to him, of which kingdom the four beasts, that is, the four kingdoms that must rise from the earth, were receivers and holders forever and ever, as the prophet Daniel shows, when he says, "These four great beasts are four kingdoms, which shall arise out of the earth; and they shall receive the kingdom of the most high holy God forever and ever."[228] But the blessed kingdom of our father David, of whom we have spoken above, that is, our Lord Jesus Christ, "going into a far country to receive for Himself a kingdom and to return,"[229] as is written in the Gospel, has redeemed the aforesaid kingdom with His blood and has made that kingdom a kingdom for his God, even as this kingdom growing great declares in the Apocalypse, saying: "Thou art worthy, O Lord, to take the book and to open the seals thereof; because Thou wast slain and hast redeemed us in Thy blood, out of every tribe, and tongue, and people, and nation. And hast made us to our God a kingdom and priests, and we shall reign on the earth."[230] But over this kingdom the same Jesus Christ is to sit when He has delivered it to God and the Father, that He may confirm and strengthen it in judgment and justice, from henceforth unto eternity, as was said above. Therefore, those spirits make a kingdom for their God, as was said before, praying him to deliver them from evil, for they are His. Praying for this, the psalmist, who is their chief, praying to his God, says, "I am thine, save thou me; for I have sought thy justifications."[231] And again, "I am Thy servant. Give me understanding that I may know Thy commandments."[232] And the Apostle says to the Romans, "For none of you liveth to himself, and no man dieth to himself. For whether we live, we live unto the Lord; or whether we die, we are the Lord's."[233] And it is written in the Book of Wisdom: "But Thou, our God, art gracious and true, and ordering all things in mercy. For if we sin, we are Thine, knowing Thy greatness, and if we sin not, we know that we are counted with Thee." [234]

[*Chapter X*]

And the power.—As for this power, we understand it to be the life of the first form, which is from the Lord, and other lives are placed in him. It should be known further that the strength of the psalmist—whom we understand to be the spirit of the first form—which is his life, leaves him, as that psalmist reveals when he says, "My heart is troubled, my strength hath left me." [235] Therefore, that strength, which is life, weakens with the loosing of the spirit and wanes, as the psalmist shows, saying, "My strength is weakened through poverty." [236] Likewise, the strength of our mother [Jerusalem] weakens, as she herself reveals through the prophet Jeremiah, saying: "My strength is weakened. The Lord hath delivered me into a hand out of which I shall not be able to rise." [237]

[*Chapter XI*]

And the glory.—This glory is of our Father who is in heaven. We understand this glory to be the soul of our father David and the souls also of his sons. Therefore, the Lord says through the prophet Ezechiel, "Behold, all souls are mine; as the soul of the father, so also the soul of the son is mine." [238] The psalmist, speaking of this glory, which is his soul, says further, "I will sing and will rejoice in my glory." [239] And because he himself wished to sing and rejoice in his glory, he cried to it, saying, "Arise, O my glory, arise psaltery and harp." And that glory said in answer, "I will arise early." [240] For this reason that same prophet, being aided by God and rejoicing, cried to Him, saying, "Thou hast turned for me my mourning into joy; Thou hast cut my sackcloth and hast compassed me with gladness, to the end that my glory may sing to Thee." [241] Therefore, these three substances, that is, the kingdom and the power and the glory, which are the spirit and the life and the soul, are of the Holy Father in the ages, [242] that is, in the fathers, which means in the visitations. For visitations are called ages, that is, fathers, because they are fathers of the spirits. Of this the psalmist personifying the spirit, says, "We have heard, O God, with our ears; our fathers have declared to us the work Thou hast wrought in their days, and in the days of old." [243] And again, he says, "In Thee our fathers hoped, and Thou hast delivered them. They cried to Thee, and they were saved; they trusted in Thee and were not confounded." [244] In the same way, we understand that the charities are the ages of ages,[245] that is, fathers of the fathers, visitations. Therefore, St. John says in the Apocalypse, "Benediction, splendor, and wisdom; the making of grace, honor, and glory, and power to our Lord in ages of ages. Amen";[246] meaning in the charities which are the fathers of the visitations, which visitations are fathers of Amen,[247] in our understanding. It is the spirit of the first form which is called Amen, as St. John shows in the Apocalypse: "And all the tribes of the earth shall bewail themselves over him. Even so. Amen."[248] For this Amen will be bewailed by all the tribes of earth because our Lord Jesus Christ suffered and died for his sins so that through death He might overcome him who had command over death, that is, the devil, as the Apostle says to the Hebrews, "And that He might deliver them who through the fear of death were all their lifetime subject to servitude."[249]

Glory be from all the faithful who are in Jesus Christ.

AMEN.

Abbreviations

Used in the Appendix, Notes, and Bibliography

AA SS	*Acta sanctorum (q.v.* in the Bibliography).
AFP	*Archivum fratrum praedicatorum.*
AHDLMA	*Archives d'histoire doctrinale et littéraire du moyen âge.*
ALKG	*Archiv für Literatur- und Kirchengeschichte des Mittelalters.*
ASRSP	*Archivio della Società romana di storia patria.*
BEC	*Bibliothèque de l'École des chartes.*
BISIAM	*Bullettino dell'Istituto storico italiano per il medio evo e Archivio Muratoriano.*
Concilia	*Sacrorum conciliorum nova et amplissima collectio* (see the entry under Mansi in the Bibliography).
DNB	*The Dictionary of National Biography (q.v.* in the Bibliography).
DTC	*Dictionnaire de théologie catholique (q.v.* in the Bibliography).
MA	*Le Moyen âge: Revue d'histoire et de philologie.*
MGH SS	*Monumenta Germaniae historica, Scriptores (q.v.* in the Bibliography).
MS	*Mediaeval Studies.*
PL	*Patrologia latina* (see the entry under Migne in the Bibliography).
RBPH	*Revue belge de philologie et d'histoire.*
RHE	*Revue d'histoire ecclésiastique.*
RHLL	*Revue historique et littéraire de Languedoc.*
RHPR	*Revue d'histoire et de philosophie religieuse.*
RHR	*Revue de l'histoire des religions.*
Rolls Series	*Rerum britannicarum medii aevi Scriptores (q.v.* in the Bibliography).
RQH	*Revue des questions historiques.*
RSCI	*Rivista di storia della Chiesa in Italia.*
RSI	*Rivista storica italiana.*
RSPT	*Revue des sciences philosophiques et théologiques.*
RTAM	*Recherches de théologie ancienne et médiévale.*
ZKG	*Zeitschrift für Kirchengeschichte.*

Appendix

A List of Polemical Sources

The following list includes, in approximately chronological order, those works written in the twelfth, thirteenth, and early fourteenth centuries which had a polemical purpose, in that they were attacks on heresy or hostile descriptions of it. The dates of composition are given as they are now known, and mention is made of the sects against which each treatise is directed. An asterisk (*) denotes those which are translated in whole or in part in this volume, and in such cases the reader is referred to the introductions and notes accompanying the translations for bibliographical data. For other entries, the most recent or most available publication of the source is noted (or the manuscripts, if the source is still unpublished), with a reference to at least one scholarly discussion from which further information may be obtained. Occasionally other documents are mentioned which do not quite fit into the category of polemical literature, but which do contain substantial information about heresy; these are not given separate numbers but are placed where chronologically appropriate and are designated by letters. For the fourteenth- and fifteenth-century literature on heresy, see note 185 to the first part of the Introduction, and Vekené, *Bibliographie der Inquisition*. See page 631 for the book and periodical titles abbreviated here.

*i. Peter the Venerable. *Epistola sive tractatus adversus petrobrusianos*. 1131-1133. Against the heresy of Peter of Bruys, with brief mention of the heretic Henry. See Number 13.
*ii. William, a monk. *Contra Henricum schismaticum et hereticum*. 1133-1135. Against the heretic Henry. See Number 12.
iii. Hugh of Amiens, archbishop of Rouen (d. 1164). *Contra haereticos sui temporis sive de ecclesia et eius ministri libri tres*. 1145-1146. An essay on Christian dogma and discipline giving a little information about the heretics he attacked, who were probably found in Nantes. Discussed in Manselli, "Per la storia dell'eresia: Studi minori," *BISIAM*, LXVII (1955), 235-44.
iv. Eckbert of Schönau. *Sermones tredecim contra haereticos*. 1163-1167. In Migne, *PL*, CXCV, 11-98. An attack on dualist heretics discovered at Cologne in 1163. Eckbert was somewhat influenced by St. Augustine's description of Manichaeans. Brief comment in Borst, pp. 6-7. F. W. E. Roth, *Die Visionen und Briefe der hl. Elisabeths, sowie die Schriften der Abte Eckbert und Emecho von Schönau*, 2d ed. (Brünn, 1886), was not available to us.

*v. Bonacursus. *Manifestatio haeresis catharorum quam fecit Bonacursus*. 1176-1190. Statements about the Cathars by a convert, with appended scriptural texts for refutation of those and other heretics (Passagians and Arnoldists). See Number 25.

*vi. Vacarius. *Liber contra multiplices et varios errores*. 1177-1185. A treatise in the form of a letter refuting the errors of Hugo Speroni. See Number 21.

   (a) Abbot Joachim of Flora (*ca.* 1135-1202), the Calabrian mystic, attacked the Cathars in his *Apocalipsim*, written after 1183, and also denounced the Poor of Lyons in his *De articulis fidei* (1183-1184) and in his *Tractatus super quatuor evangelia* (*ca.* 1200). Pertinent passages from these sources are quoted in notes in Thouzellier, *Catharisme et valdéisme*, pp. 115-27.

*vii. Bernard of Fontcaude. *Adversus Waldensium sectam liber*. Ca. 1191. Arguments against the Waldenses with brief mention of other heretics. See Number 34.

   (a) Ralph the Ardent. *Homilia* xix. 1150-1200. In Migne, *PL*, CLV, 2010-13. A sermon denouncing the Cathars. See the second part of the Introduction, p. 58 and n. 23.

*viii. Alan of Lille. *De fide catholica contra haereticos sui temporis*. 1190-1202. The first full-scale polemic, widely copied in the Middle Ages. Books I and II are against the Cathars and Waldenses; Books III and IV are directed at Jews and Saracens. See Number 35.

*ix. Prevostin (Praepositinus) of Cremona (?). *Summa contra haereticos*. Ca. 1200. Against Cathars and Passagians with brief mention of other heretics, perhaps Waldenses. See Number 26.

*x. *De haeresi catharorum in Lombardia*. 1200-1215. Historical account of the rise of Catharism in twelfth-century Italy, with a description of the sect's beliefs and a list of the hierarchies of the several divisions. See Number 23.

*xi. *Manifestatio haeresis Albigensium et Lugdunensium*. 1200-1215. Description of the beliefs of Cathars and Waldenses in Languedoc. See Number 37.

xii. Durand of Huesca. *Liber antiheresis*. Before 1207. Prologue printed in Dondaine, "Aux Origines du Valdéisme," *AFP*, XVI (1946), 232-35. (English translation of the Prologue in Petry, *History of Christianity*, pp. 351-52.) Other excerpts printed in Thouzellier, "La Profession trinitaire," *RTAM*, XXVII (1960), 283-89, and "Controverses vaudoises-cathares à la fin du XIIᵉ siècle," *AHDLMA*, XXXV (1960), 206-7. A most important polemic against the Cathars by a follower of Waldes of Lyons, it reveals not only the hostility of Waldenses toward Cathars but also the doctrinal orthodoxy of the faction to which Durand belonged before his return to the Church in 1207. The *Liber antiheresis* provided also much of the material for other tracts by Durand (items xiii, xvii) and by his associate Ermengaud (item xiv). One manuscript preserved the profession of faith of Waldes translated in Number 32. See Thouzellier, *Catharisme et valdéisme*, pp. 60-81. Dondaine and Mlle Thouzellier agree that the treatise was composed before 1207; the latter believes it a decade or more earlier.

xiii. Durand of Huesca (?). "Opusculum contra hereticos et eorum errores." 1200-1210? In Madrid, Biblioteca nacionale, MS 6911, fols. 62r-122r. Table of chapters printed in Dondaine, "Durand de Huesca," *AFP*, XXIX (1959), 228-76. Against the Cathars, who are not named, this incorporates the earlier work of the monk William (item ii, above) and is related to one "edition" of the work of Ermengaud (item xiv, below).

xiv. Ermengaud of Béziers. *Contra haereticos*. 1200-1210. In Migne, *PL*, CCIV, 1235-72, and CLXXVIII, 1823-46. Written against the Cathars by a companion of Durand of Huesca, it is known only in incomplete form. Additions in one manuscript which refer to the Waldenses have been shown not to be part of the original work in its several versions. The additions are published in Gonnet, "Waldensia," *RHPR*, XXXIII (1953), 250-54. Discussion in Dondaine, "Durand de Huesca," *AFP*, XXIX (1959), 228-76; and Thouzellier, "Le 'Liber antiheresis' de Durand de Huesca et la 'Contra hereticos' d'Ermengaud de Béziers," *RHE*, LV (1960), 130-41.

xv. Guarnerius of Rochefort (?). *Contra Amaurianos*. Ca. 1210. Published and discussed in Clemens Bäumker, *Ein anonymer, wahrscheinlich dem Garnerius von Rochefort zugehöriger Traktat aus dem Anfang des XIII Jahrhunderts*. Against the short-lived sect of Amalricians of Paris.

xvi. Ebrard of Béthune. *Liber antiheresis*. Before 1212. In *Maxima bibliotheca veterum patrum*, XXIV, 1525-84. A work of little value; against dualists, with whom the author confuses the Waldenses; he also attacks Jews. Brief notice in Borst, p. 9.

*xvii. Durand of Huesca. *Liber contra manicheos*. Ca. 1222-1223. Ed. by Thouzellier in *Une Somme anti-cathare*. A treatise replying to a work by an Albigensian heretic, for which purpose Durand copied passages of the heretic's tract into his own. Only the first two books of the *Liber* have survived. The portions of the heretical exposition preserved in this way were earlier published by Thouzellier in *Un Traité cathare* and are translated in Number 58. Exhaustive commentary on the *Liber* is in Thouzellier, *Catharisme et valdéisme*, pp.303-424.

(a) William of Auvergne, bishop of Paris (1228-1249), in his theological works, particularly *De universo* (1231-1236), refuted some Catharist doctrines. His *Opera omnia* (2 vols.: Orleans, 1674; reprint, 1962) was not available to us. Borst (p. 16) considers William's work important, citing also N. Valois, *Guillaume d'Auvergne: Sa vie et ses ouvrages* (Paris, 1880).

(b) Luke, bishop of Tuy (d. 1249). *De altera vita fideique controversiis adversus Albigensium errores libri tres*. 1234. This is an excerpt from Luke's life of Isidore of Seville (*Maxima biblio-*

theca veterum patrum, XXV, 188-251). Made up largely of excerpts from the works of Gregory I and Isidore, it also contains passages intended to refute heretical errors about life after death and to warn against heretical perversities, and it gives a number of anecdotes about the Albigenses. Brief comment in Borst, p. 14, n. 4.

*xviii. Salvo Burci. *Liber supra Stella.* 1235. Attack on the Cathars, the Poor of Lyons, and the Poor Lombards by a layman of Piacenza. See Number 45, part B.

*xix. St. Peter Martyr of Verona (?). *Summa contra haereticos.* 1235-1238. Against the Cathars and various other sects: Predestinarians, Circumcisers, Speronists, Poor of Lyons, Rebaptizers. See Number 45, part C.

*xx. George. *Disputatio inter catholicum et paterinum hereticum.* 1240-1250. Composed in the form of a debate between a Catholic and a member of the sect of Bagnolenses in Lombardy. See Number 47.

*xxi. James Capelli (Jacopus de Capellis). *Summa contra hereticos.* 1240-1250. Against the Cathars. See Number 49.

*xxii. Moneta of Cremona. *Adversus Catharos et Valdenses libri quinque.* 1241-1244. A massive work, primarily against the Cathars but with some comment on the Waldenses and other heretics. See Number 50.

(a) A poem in Provençal, written after 1244, purports to be the discussion between Sicart of Figueiras, a heretic, and the inquisitor Izarn. It was, perhaps, issued as Catholic propaganda to show the heretics in a bad light after the capture of their stronghold, Montségur, and the massacre there. Published by Paul Meyer, as "Le Débat d'Izarn et de Sicart de Figueiras," *Annuaire-bulletin de la Société de l'histoire de France*, XVI (1879), 233-92; and separately (Nogent-le-Retrou, 1880). There is an abridged English translation in Oldenbourg, *Massacre at Montségur*, Appendix F.

*xxiii. Rainerius Sacconi. *Summa de Catharis et Pauperibus de Lugduno.* 1250. Probably the best-known tract against these heretics. See Number 51. A second and longer version was created when a German inquisitor, known only as the "Pseudo-Rainerius" or "Anonymous of Passau," added other materials, largely pertaining to the Waldenses. It was edited under the name of Rainerius by Jacob Gretser in 1614 and appeared in various editions of the *Bibliotheca veterum patrum*—for example, that of Lyons (1677), XXV, 262-77. On it, see Preger, "Beiträge zur Geschichte des Waldesier im Mittelalter," *Abhandlungen der historischen Classe der königlich bayerischen Akademie der Wissenschaften*, XIII (1877), 184-86; and Franz Unterkircher, "'Pseudo-Rainier' und 'Passauer Anonymus,'" *Mitteilungen des Instituts für österreichische Geschichtsforschung*, LXIII (1955), 41-46.

xxiv. *Summa contra hereticos.* After 1250. Unpublished, it is found in three manuscripts: Vatican, MS lat. 4255, fols. 54r-72r; Florence, Laurentian, Pluteus VIII, dext. 6, fols. 288r-296v; and in the same library, MS 404, fols. 174r-240v. A few lines from the Vatican manuscript were published in Döllinger, *Beiträge,* II, 326-27.

*(a) Stephen of Bourbon. *Tractatus de diversis materiis praedicabilis.* 1249-1261. Contains anecdotes about the Albigenses and Waldenses. See Numbers 33 and 52.

*xxv. "Summae contra haereticos." These are six compilations of scriptural texts considered pertinent to the defense of various points of Catholic doctrine which were denied by heretics. Their dates are uncertain, perhaps the second quarter of the thirteenth century and later, although they may be based on earlier models. Chapter headings from two of these compilations appear in Number 48; see note 2 there for the list of the summas published or still in manuscript.

xxvi. Benedict of Alignan. "Tractatus fidei contra diversos errores super titulum de summa trinitate et fide catholica in decretalibus." 1261. Benedict was abbot of Notre-Dame de la Grasse (1224), then bishop of Marseilles (1229-1268), and, probably in 1258, joined the Franciscan order. Seventeen manuscripts of his summa are enumerated in the study by Martin Grabmann, "Der Franziskanerbischof Benedictus de Alignano († 1268) und seine Summa zum Caput Firmiter des vierten Laterankonzils," in *Kirchengeschichtlichen Studien,* pp. 50-64, esp. pp. 51-53; the content of the summa is analyzed *ibid.,* pp. 55-59. Five pieces which are in the nature of appendices to the summa were printed by Douais, "Les Hérétiques du Midi au XIIIe siècle: Cinq pièces inédits," *Annales du Midi,* III (1891), 367-80. The commentary on the decree of the Fourth Lateran Council is an extensive discussion and refutation of heretical errors, ancient and contemporary, but is concerned chiefly with those of the Waldenses and Albigenses and, in Grabmann's opinion (*ibid.,* pp. 62-63), puts Benedict's summa in the tradition of the great polemical tracts of the thirteenth century.

xxvii. David of Augsburg (?). *De inquisitione haereticorum.* This, which was intended for the use of inquisitors, exists in two versions: The shorter, probably written in the second half of the twelfth century, was published in Martène and Durand, *Thesaurus novus anecdotorum,* V, 1777-94. A longer one was edited by Preger, "Der Traktat des David von Augsburg über die Waldesier," *Abhandlungen der historischen Classe der königlich bayerischen Akademie der Wissenschaften,* XIV (1878), 181-235; see esp. pp. 204-35. It is probable, though not certain, that the shorter version is the earlier; its attribution to the Franciscan inquisitor, David of Augsburg (d. 1271), is not certain. The heresy chiefly in view is that of the Waldenses. See the work of Preger just cited and a description of the tract with a review of the problems connected with it in Dondaine, "Le Manuel de l'inquisiteur," *AFP,* XVII (1947), 93, 104-5, 180-83.

*xxviii. *Brevis summula contra herrores notatos hereticorum.* 1250-1260?
A composite work; probably none of its parts were original with
the Franciscan friar whose copy survives. The heretics described
are the various groups of Cathars in Lombardy. See Number 53.

*xxix. Anselm of Alessandria. *Tractatus de haereticis.* 1260-1270. Various
components include a narrative of the origin of the Cathars in
Lombardy and paragraphs of information about the beliefs of
Cathars and Waldenses and the hierarchy of the Cathars. See Numbers 24 and 54.

Listed here although they originated in different times are four
relatively short statements about the Waldenses:

(a) *Litterae episcopi Placentini de Pauperibus de Lugduno.* In
Dondaine, "Durand de Huesca," *AFP*, XXIX (1959), 273-74.
The identification of the author as Ardicius, bishop of Piacenza
(1192-1199), is probable. The letter enumerates errors confessed by members of the sect of Poor of Lyons.

*(b) Three short statements often found together in manuals for
inquisitors, concerning (1) errors shared by the Poor of Lyons
and Poor Lombards; (2) the method by which the Waldenses
consecrated the Eucharist; and (3) a list of Waldensian errors.
All are from the second half of the thirteenth century. They
were printed in Martène and Durand, *Thesaurus novus anecdotorum*, V, 1754-56; and one version of them from Anselm
of Alessandria's copy, is translated in Number 54 (§ 15). See
Dondaine, "Le Manuel de l'inquisiteur," *AFP*, XVII (1947),
95, 150, 166; and the same author's "La Hiérarchie cathare,
II-III," *AFP*, XIX (1949), 250.

(c) *Hec sunt manifesta per conversos de secta Waldensium.* Date
uncertain. In Dondaine, "Durand de Huesca," *AFP*, XXIX
(1959), 274-75. The learned editor overlooked the fact that the
same statement from another manuscript (Paris, Bibliothèque
nationale, MS lat. 15179, fols. 354r-55v) had already been
published by Paul Guillaume in *Bulletin de la Société d'études
des Hautes-Alpes*, VII (1888), 220-22, and reprinted from
there by Jules Chevalier, *Mémoire historique sur les hérésies
en Dauphiné avant le XVIe siècle*, p. 8, n. 1.

(d) *De pauperibus de Lugduno.* Late thirteenth to early fourteenth
century. In Döllinger, *Beiträge*, II, 92-97, without the prologue
which is given in Dondaine, "Le Manuel de l'inquisiteur,"
AFP, XVII (1947), 184, cf. 93. Describes the ecclesiastical
organization and the practices of Waldenses.

*xxx. Bernard Gui. *Practica inquisitionis haeretica pravitatis.* 1323-1324.
An inquisitor's description of Cathars, Waldenses, "pseudo-Apostles,"
Beguins, Jews, and sorcerers; part of his manual on inquisitorial
practice. See Number 55.

Notes

A HISTORICAL SKETCH OF THE MEDIEVAL POPULAR HERESIES

For book and periodical titles abbreviated in the notes, see the list of abbreviations on page 631.

1. It should be noted at the outset that in this Introduction, when the literature in which various topics may be pursued is cited, studies in English whenever known to us, are preferred. The history of medieval heresies bristles with problems of interpretation, particularly of their origins, but also in the assessment of their character, their interrelationships with the whole spiritual and intellectual development of the Christian West and with the socioeconomic situation of the time, and their influence on the development of the doctrines and institutions of the Church. Most such problems are only mentioned in passing in these pages. One recent survey is by Luciano Sommariva: "La Compréhension historique de l'hérésie," in René Nelli, ed., *Spiritualité de l'hérésie*, pp. 63-89. Reference to many studies on various aspects and interpretations of heresy is made by Jeffrey B. Russell in "Interpretations of the Origins of Medieval Heresy," *MS*, XXV (1963), 25-53. A useful bibliography of works published before 1960 is Kulcsár's *Eretnekmozgalmak a XI-XIV században* [heretical movements from the eleventh to the fourteenth century]. Another comprehensive bibliography is being prepared by Professor Herbert Grundmann.

2. See, for example, the statements Gratian selected for his *Decretum* II, C. xxiv, Q. i, cc. 12 and 15 (Friedberg, I, 970). Gratian's treatment of heresy is analyzed in Henri Maisonneuve, *Etudes sur les origines de l'Inquisition*, rev. ed., pp. 65-79.

3. I Cor. 11:19. See Herbert Grundmann, *Ketzergeschichte des Mittelalters*, pp. 1-2, and references there cited.

4. Tit. 3:10 and Gal. 1:8.

5. See Ernest W. Nelson, "The Theory of Persecution," in *Persecution and Liberty*, pp. 3-20. M. Searle Bates (*Religious Liberty*) discusses the topic in broad historical perspective. On the imperial and ecclesiastical traditions of legislation about heresy, see Maisonneuve, chap. I.

6. *Decretum* II, C. xxiv, Q. iii, cc. 27-31 (Friedberg, I, 997-98).

7. *Summa theologica* II, part ii, q. 11, art. 2, r. o. 3. After quoting the *Decretum* as just cited (c. 27) Aquinas says that doctors of the Church might differ in matters undefined by the Church but if one were to deny

articles of faith after definition he would be a heretic.

8. James Capelli, *Summa contra hereticos*, ed. by Bazzocchi, in *La eresia catara*, Appendix, p. xvii. Cf. Aquinas *Summa theologica* II, part ii, q. 11, art. 1: "Heresy is so called from being a choosing"; and Gratian *Decretum* II, C. xxiv, Q. iii, c. 27 (Friedberg, I, 997-98), quoting St. Jerome.

9. This appears in a manuscript of Alan of Lille's *De fide catholica* (on which see No. 35), Bern, Stadt und Universitäts Bibliothek, Bongarsiana MS 335, fol. 65r, but is not in the printed edition of the work. Cf. Gratian *Decretum* II, C. xxiv, Q. iii, c. 28 (Friedberg, I, 998), quoting St. Augustine.

10. See No. 2, n. 1.

11. Albert C. Shannon, *The Popes and Heresy*, pp. 3-10.

12. See, for example, the actions described in Nos. 6, 9, and 10. C. H. Haskins (*Studies in Mediaeval Culture*, p. 200) cites others, remarking: "Indeed the preliminary question as to what constituted heresy might often puzzle anyone but a theological expert."

13. Robert Grosseteste is quoted as asserting that prelates who failed to protect their flocks from "wolves" were themselves guilty of heresy (Matthew Paris *Chronica majora*, V, 401).

14 Pagans, Moslems, and Jews were not regarded as heretics, but sometimes were suspected of making common cause with them against the Church.

15. An exception reported in this volume (No. 44) is the sect of Amalricians at Paris, who may be said to have been in the process of building a following outside the enclave of the university when they were detected.

16. *History of the Inquisition*, III, 550; cf. *ibid.*, I, 60-61.

17. Cf. Ilarino da Milano, "Le eresie popolari," in *Studi Gregoriani*, II, 43, where he uses the phrase "questo laicismo religioso." For a review of the concepts, practices, and emphases of the "popular piety" of the eleventh century, see Delaruelle, "La pietà popolare," in *Relazione del X Congresso*, III, 309-32. See also the essay by C. N. L. Brooke on the laity in the Middle Ages in *The Layman in Christian History*, pp. 111-34; and Georges de Lagarde, *La Naissance de l'ésprit laique*, I, 83-90.

18. Grundmann ("Eresie e nuovi ordini religiosi," in *Relazione del X Congresso*, III, 377-89) discusses the concept of the *vita apostolica* in the twelfth century, insisting on its origin as a religious, not a lay, movement, and (*Ketzergeschichte*, p. 9) warns against stressing the lay character of the popular heresies.

19. See Ilarino da Milano, "Le eresie popolari," in *Studi Gregoriani*, II, 88, and the same author's "Le eresie medioevali (sec. XI-XV)," in *Grande antologia filosofica*, IV, 1599-1601. Grundmann takes a similar position in his *Religiöse Bewegungen*, and other authors expressing comparable views are cited in Russell, "Interpretations of Medieval Heresy," *MS*, XXV (1963), 43-46, 51-52.

20. On the social circumstances of heretical movements, see Austin P. Evans, "Social Aspects of Medieval Heresy," in *Persecution and Liberty*, pp. 93-116; also the review of the problem by Grundmann, "Eresie e nuovi

ordini religiosi," in *Relazione del X Congresso*, III, 396-402. Ernst Werner (*Pauperes Christi*) discusses the relationship between social and religious unrest in the eleventh century. A number of other works emphasizing social motivations for heresy are cited in Russell, "Interpretations of Medieval Heresy," *MS*, XXV (1963), 32-34. See also n. 27, below.

21. See Grundmann, *Religiöse Bewegungen*, pp. 5-6, on the tendency of religious movements to coalesce into orders or sects; also his discussion of them in the twelfth century in "Eresie e nuovi ordini religiosi," in *Relazione del X Congresso*, III, 357-69. We are here using "sect" very broadly to designate groups sharing unorthodox ideas. Paul Alphandéry ("Remarques sur le type sectaire," in *Transactions of the Third International Congress*, II, 354-57) argues that one should distinguish between heresies like Catharism, which are potentially universal religions, those like the Waldenses, which were essentially Christian and reformist, and the messianic, apocalyptic sects, such as the Amalricians, limited to a chosen few.

22. Rainerius Sacconi (No. 51) gives an estimate of the number of "perfected heretics" among the Cathars. Salvo Burci (No. 45, part B) speaks of the comparative size of certain sects.

23. "On the one hand we have sectaries holding fast to all the essentials of Christianity with antisacerdotalism as their mainspring, and on the other we have Manichaeans" (Lea, *History of the Inquisition*, I, 61).

24. See, for example, Jean Guiraud, *Histoire de l'Inquisition au moyen âge*, I, 32; Ilarino da Milano, "Le eresie medioevali," in *Grande antol. filos.*, IV, 1601-18 (cf. the critical comments of Grundmann, "Eresie e nuovi ordini religiosi," in *Relazione del X Congresso*, III, 375); Alphandéry, "Le Gnosticisme dans les sectes médiévales latines," *RHPR*, VII (1927), 396; and Giovanni Gonnet, "Un decennio di studi sull'eterodossia medioevale," *Protestantesimo*, XVII (1962), 226-27, 230-31.

25. Russell ("Interpretations of Medieval Heresy," *MS*, XXV [1963], 27) cites examples—especially Cesare Cantù, writing in 1885, who "could attribute the rise of heresy to the wiles of '*l'antico serpente*.'" We are indebted to this article for several of the citations in the following notes.

26. Major examples in English are Lea's *History of the Inquisition* and G. G. Coulton's *Inquisition and Liberty*. See also Thomas de Cauzons, *Histoire de l'inquisition en France*, Vol. I. A moderate Catholic view is expressed in Elphège Vacandard, *The Inquisition*, trans. by B. L. Conway.

27. For example, Antonino de Stefano, *Riformatori ed eretici del medioevo*; and particularly in respect of the heresy of the Humiliati, Luigi Zanoni, *Gli Umiliati nei loro rapporti con l'eresia, l'industria della lana ed i comuni nei secoli XII e XIII*. Learned spokesmen for the Marxist interpretation are Ernst Werner, in such works as *Pauperes Christi* and (with Martin Erbstösser) *Ideologische Probleme des mittelalterlichen Plebejertums*, and Gottfried Koch, *Frauenfrage und Ketzertum im Mittelalter*.

28. Russell, "Interpretations of Medieval Heresy," *MS*, XXV (1963), 42-43.

29. See, in addition to the works cited in this note, others listed by Russell, "Interpretations of Medieval Heresy," *MS*, XXV (1963), 43ff. Studies of the relationships among religious movements include the following: For the Premonstratensians and contemporary sects, J. B. Valvekens, "Haereses ac sectae ineuntis medii aevi et Praemonstratenses," *Analecta Praemonstratensia*, XXXIII (1957), 143-47; for Arnold of Brescia and other reformers, Antonio Suraci, *Arnaldo da Brescia*; for the Waldenses and Franciscans, Antoine Dondaine, "Aux Origines du Valdéisme," *AFP*, XVI (1946), 191-235; and Bernard Marthaler, "Forerunners of the Franciscans," *Franciscan Studies*, new ser., XVIII (1958), 133-42; for apostolics, orthodox and heretical, Luchesius Spätling, *De Apostolicis, Pseudo-Apostolicis, Apostolinis*; for the narrow line between orthodoxy and heresy among Beguines and Beghards, Ernest W. McDonnell, *The Beguines and Beghards in Medieval Culture.*

30. See n. 146, below.

31. Certain members of the African Church of the fourth century for whom Donatus became a spokesman refused to accept the services of bishops and priests who had wavered even slightly under persecution, and claimed that such clerics had lost grace and the power to perform the sacraments. Under attack from Catholic polemicists and the emperors they became a schismatic faction. As a group they disappeared in the seventh century, although their fundamental ideas were to reappear repeatedly; see W. H. C. Frend, *The Donatist Church.*

32. See the opening words of No. 24.

33. Arno Borst, *Die Katharer*, p. 59. See also R. M. Wilson, *The Gnostic Problem.* There are short statements on dualism in Dmitri Obolensky, *The Bogomils*, pp. 1-4; and Steven Runciman, *The Medieval Manichee*, chap. VII and Appendix IV.

34. On Neo-Platonism see Thomas Whittaker, *The Neo-Platonists: A Study in the History of Hellenism* (Cambridge, 1918). M. H. H. Wendt *(Christentum und Dualismus)* argues that Judaism and Christianity were both influenced by dualism but excluded the absolute opposition of good and evil. See also the excellent study by Simone Pètrement, *Le Dualisme chez Platon, les gnostiques et les manichéens.*

35. A few excerpts from Gnostic texts are translated in Ray C. Petry, *A History of Christianity*, pp. 85-90. More are in Robert M. Grant, *Gnosticism: A Source Book.* See also Grant's *Gnosticism and Early Christianity*, and Hans Jonas, *The Gnostic Religion.*

36. Brief translations from sources illustrating Marcion's doctrines are in Petry, *History of Christianity*, p. 89. Short discussions are in Runciman, *Medieval Manichee*, pp. 8-10, and Jonas, *Gnostic Religion*, chap. VI; see also Robert S. Wilson, *Marcion*; and E. C. Blackman, *Marcion and His Influence.*

37. In a polemic against the Cathars in the early thirteenth century, Durand of Huesca called them, among other things, *"moderni Marchionite"* (Christine Thouzellier, *Une Somme anti-cathare*, pp. 34, 239, 303).

38. Translated excerpts illustrating Mani's teaching are in Petry, *History of Christianity*, pp. 90-94. Short accounts are in Runciman, *Medieval Manichee*, pp. 12-17; Obolensky, *The Bogomils*, chap. I; and Jonas, *Gnostic Religion*, chap. IX.

39. See No. 2, n. 1, and Runciman, *Medieval Manichee*, pp. 4, 17-18.

40. Short accounts are in Runciman, *Medieval Manichee*, pp. 21-25, and Obolensky, *The Bogomils*, pp. 48-52 and *passim*.

41. A short account is given in C. A. Scott, "Priscillianism," *Encyclopaedia of Religion and Ethics*, X, 336-38. See also E. C. Babut, *Priscillien et le Priscillienisme*.

42. A religious work used by Paulicians is translated in F. C. Conybeare, *The Key of Truth*. Short accounts are in Runciman, *Medieval Manichee*, chap. III, and Obolensky, *The Bogomils*, chap. II. See also n. 46, below.

43. Runciman, *Medieval Manichee*, pp. 27-31.

44. See No. 40, n. 3.

45. Runciman, *Medieval Manichee*, p. 46.

46. A recent study of the sources is Nina Garsoian's *The Paulician Heresy*. She concludes that there were two groupings of Paulicians—in Armenia and in the Byzantine Empire—representing the two doctrinal traditions, but she emphatically denies that Manichaean doctrines had a significant place in either. The traces of dualism among the Paulicians are interpreted either as a product of internal development or as a relatively late influence from extremists among the Byzantine iconoclasts.

47. On the Bogomils see Obolensky, *The Bogomils*; Runciman, *Medieval Manichee*, chaps. IV-V; and H. C. Puech and André Vaillant, *Le Traité contre les Bogomiles de Cosmas le Prêtre*. Borst, pp. 66-71, has a concise summary based on these and other studies, with independent judgment on certain critical points. See also n. 73, below. The Bogomils have been the subject of recent works published in Eastern European languages, some of which are reviewed in "Le Problème des Bogomiles," in [Yugoslav] National Committee for Historical Studies, *Ten Years of Yugoslav Historiography*, pp. 180-91; see also the comments on the Bogomil church in Bosnia in Christine Thouzellier, *Un Traité cathare inédit*, pp. 34-37. The valuable survey by Ivan Dujčev, "I Bogomili nei paesi slavi e la loro storia," in Accademia nazionale dei Lincei, *Problemi attuali di scienza e di cultura*, Quaderno LXII (1964): *L'Oriente cristiano nella storia della civiltà*, pp. 619-41, reached us too late to be utilized. It should be consulted on points mentioned here.

48. For the early history of Bulgaria, see Steven Runciman, *The First Bulgarian Empire*; see also his *Medieval Manichee*, pp. 63-66, and Obolensky, *The Bogomils*, chap. III.

49. Obolensky, *The Bogomils*, pp. 72-79, 84-93, 101-10.

50. Runciman, *Medieval Manichee*, pp. 87-91; Obolensky, *The Bogomils*, pp. 59-60, 68-70, 79-84.

51. Puech and Vaillant, *Le Traité contre les Bogomiles*, p. 310.

52. The first meaning is preferred by Obolensky, *The Bogomils*, p. 117, n. 4, and pp. 119-20. The others are given by Puech and Vaillant, *Le Traité contre les Bogomiles*, pp. 27, 282-83.

53. On date and place, see Obolensky, *The Bogomils*, pp. 117-20, 137-43, 151-56, 167. Borst (pp. 67-68) agrees with Obolensky on the date given here as against the earlier one proposed by Puech and Vaillant (*Le Traité contre les Bogomiles*, pp. 285-89).

54. This is the treatise published in French translation by Puech and Vaillant as *Le Traité contre les Bogomiles*. There is a short excerpt from it in English translation in Petry, *History of Christianity*, pp. 342-43. The work of Cosmas is summarized in Runciman, *Medieval Manichee*, pp. 73-74, and Obolensky, *The Bogomils*, pp. 117-38.

55. On the question of whether Christ or the devil was the older, see Obolensky, *The Bogomils*, p. 122, and Puech and Vaillant, *Le Traité contre les Bogomiles*, pp. 190-92; see also the Cathars' version of this relationship in Nos. 37, 38, and 50, n. 24.

56. On early Bogomil organization, see Obolensky, *The Bogomils*, pp. 133-36; for the division between "Perfect" and "believers," *ibid.*, pp. 214-17.

57. *Ibid.*, p. 138.

58. Runciman (*Medieval Manichee*, pp. 88-90) considers the Bogomils to be the product of Paulician ideas fused with Gnostic teachings transmitted through the Messalians. According to Obolensky (*The Bogomils*, pp. 111, 115, 118, 138-40), Bogomil himself developed a personal synthesis of Paulician and Messalian doctrines, influenced by orthodox Christianity. Puech and Vaillant (*Le Traité contre les Bogomiles*, pp. 310-25) say that preceding heresies do not suffice to explain Bogomilism and, although it owes something to the Paulicians, it was not influenced by the Messalians; there are new elements in Bogomilism (*ibid.*, p. 340). Borst (p. 68, n. 12, and p. 71) attributes it to a mixture of renewed Christian zeal with dualistic ideas, in which Bogomil's personal "crystallization" of experience was most important.

59. Runciman, *Medieval Manichee*, pp. 69-70; Obolensky, *The Bogomils*, pp. 174-88, 197-201, 219-29.

60. The chief twelfth-century source for Bogomilism, *The Dogmatic Panoply* of Euthymius Zigabenus, is summarized in Runciman, *Medieval Manichee*, pp. 74-79; and in Obolensky, *The Bogomils*, pp. 205-19. On the Bogomil hierarchy, see Puech and Vaillant, *Le Traité contre les Bogomiles*, pp. 237-43.

61. Obolensky, *The Bogomils*, p. 154, n. 2; Puech and Vaillant, *Le Traité contre les Bogomiles*, pp. 129-31. Two apocryphal pieces transmitted by the Bogomils to the Cathars are translated in No. 56, with citation of additional studies.

62. The problems posed by the evidence of both absolute and mitigated dualism in Balkan sects have been variously resolved. Runciman (*Medieval Manichee*, pp. 79, 88-89, 91) thinks that absolute dualism was Bogomil's original teaching, mitigated dualism a somewhat later innovation by a priest,

Jeremiah. Obolensky (*The Bogomils*, pp. 123-25; 162, n. 4; 202) sees absolute dualism as Paulician, mitigated dualism as the creed of Bogomil. Hans Söderberg (*La Religion des Cathares*, chaps. V and VI, and pp. 269-70) argues that absolute dualism among the Bogomils resulted from Paulician influence, while mitigated dualism was transmitted to them under Gnostic influences surviving from antiquity.

63. See Nos. 23 and 24.

64. Runciman, *Medieval Manichee*, chap. V; Obolensky, *The Bogomils*, p. 229, chap. VI, and Appendix IV.

65. Studies in point are cited by Russell, "Interpretations of Medieval Heresy," *MS*, XXV (1963), 35-41. See also Borislav Primov, "Medieval Bulgaria and the Dualistic Heresies in Western Europe," *Etudes historiques à l'occasion du XIe Congrès international des sciences historiques, Stockholm, août 1960* (Sofia, 1960), pp. 79-106, as cited in *RHE*, LV (1960), 1083-84.

66. On the problem posed by lack of evidence of the filiation of sects and the importance of comparison of doctrines, see Antoine Dondaine, "Nouvelles Sources de l'histoire doctrinale du néo-manichéisme au moyen âge," *RSPT*, XXVIII (1939), 465-88, esp. 465-69; and the same author's *Un Traité néo-manichéen du XIIIe siècle*, pp. 52-57.

67. *The Bogomils*, pp. 18, 19, 21.

68. *The Paulician Heresy*, chap. V and p. 233.

69. *La Religion des Cathares*, pp. 33, 267-68.

70. For example, Lucie Varga, "Les Cathares sont-ils des néo-manichéens ou des néo-gnostiques?" *RHR*, CXX (1939), 175-93, esp. 175-83; and the same author's "Un Problème de méthode en histoire religieuse," *Revue de synthèse*, XI (1936), 133-43 (a review of Guiraud, *Histoire de l'Inquisition*, Vol. I).

71. Paul Alphandéry, "Traces de manichéisme dans le moyen âge latin (VIe-XIIe siècle)," *RHPR*, IX (1929), 451-67; Renato Esnault, "Tracce ereticali nel medio evo francese," *Religio*, XIV (1938), 18-53; Eugenii Anichkof, "Les Survivances manichéennes en pays slave et en Occident," *Revue des études slaves*, VIII (1928), 203-26. Cf. *Romania*, LVI (1930), 526-57, and LVIII (1932), 274-86, for criticism of his work by Mme Myrra Lat-Borodine and his reply.

72. Varga, "Les Cathares sont-ils des néo-manichéens?" *RHR*, CXX (1939), 183-93.

73. "Catharisme médiéval et Bogomilisme," in *Convegno "Volta" di scienze morale, storiche e filologiche, 27 maggio-1 giugno 1956*, Accademia nazionale dei Lincei, *Atti*, 8th ser., XII (1957), 56-84. This article also contains useful bibliographical comments on Bogomilism.

74. *Ibid.*, pp. 56-62.

75. *Ibid.*, pp. 62-74.

76. *Ibid.*, pp. 77-82.

77. *Ibid.*, pp. 82-83, citing Leonard, "Remarques sur les 'Sectes,'" Ecole-

pratique des hautes études, Section des sciences religieuses, *Annuaire*, 1955-1956 (Paris, 1956).

78. *Die Katharer*, pp. 65-66.

79. *Ibid.*, p. 71.

80. *Dissent and Reform in the Early Middle Ages*, pp. 205-15.

81. *Medieval History*, pp. 456-57.

82. Russell, *Dissent and Reform*, pp. 5-17 and *passim*.

83. These are the areas mentioned in the sources translated in Nos. 1-6. In other sources there are references to heresy in Ratisbon (late tenth century), Mainz (1012), Verona (before 1048), and "in Greek lands." We have omitted mention of the supposed evidence of dualism in the profession of faith of Gerbert of Aurillac in 991 for reasons stated in the introduction to No. 32; and, as explained in the introduction to No. 17, we cannot accept the evidence for heresy at Liège in the eleventh century. The best discussion of eleventh-century heresies is Ilarino da Milano's "Le eresie popolari," in *Studi Gregoriani*, II, 43-89. See also Borst, pp. 73-80. Antoine Dondaine ("L'Origine de l'hérésie médiévale," RSCI, VI [1952], 47-48) confines his survey to evidence of alleged Bogomil influence. We have not seen Ernst Werner's *Die gesellschaftlichen Grundlagen der Klosterreform im 11. Jahrhundert*, cited by Grundmann, *Ketzergeschichte*, p. 9, n. 1. The latter discusses eleventh-century heresy on pp. 8-11.

84. Dondaine ("L'Origine de l'hérésie médiévale," RSCI, IV [1952], 53-54) argues that the diversity of social classes represented in these sects shows the spread of Bogomilism rather than spontaneous local development from social and economic conditions. Differentiation between heretical ideas as understood in aristocratic and clerical circles and the "unchristian and ascetic" tenets accepted among the peasantry is urged by Ernst Werner "Παταρηνοι–patarini: Ein Beitrag zur Kirchen- und Sektengeschichte des 11. Jahrhunderts," in *Von Mittelalter zur Neuzeit*, pp. 404-19, esp. 413-14).

85. The heresy of Vilgard (No. 1) does not belong in these categories, for its alleged origin in literary studies is almost unique. Anticlericalism is plain in some instances of heresy; in others clerics were the leaders in a search for a higher spirituality attained through knowledge (see No. 3).

86. See No. 2, n. 1, and No. 6, n. 9.

87. Works in which the trial and punishment of heretics in the Middle Ages are discussed are: Julien Havet, "L'Hérésie et le bras séculier au moyen âge jusqu'au treizième siècle," BEC, XLI (1880), 488-517, 570-607 (also in his *Œuvres complètes*, II [Paris, 1896], 117-80); Henri Maillet, *L'Eglise et la répression sanglante de l'hérésie*; Maisonneuve, *Etudes sur les origines de l'Inquisition*; Hermann Theloe, *Die Ketzerverfolgungen im 11. und 12. Jahrhundert*; and G. G. Coulton, *The Death Penalty for Heresy from 1184 to 1921*.

88. Pp. 212-86. He based this study on his "Osservazioni critiche su alcune questioni fondamentali riguardanti le origini e i caratteri delle eresie medioevali," in "Miscellanea di studi storica, pubblicata in memoria di

Pietro Fedele," *Archivio della deputazione Romana di storia patria*, new ser., LXVII (1944), 97-151.

89. "Nouvelles Sources," *RSPT*, XXVIII (1939), 466-67.

90. Dondaine, "La Hiérarchie cathare en Italie, II: Le 'Tractatus de hereticis' d'Anselme d'Alexandrie, O.P.; III: Catalogue de la hiércharchie cathare d'Italie," *AFP*, XX (1950), 267-68.

91. "L'Origine de l'hérésie médiévale," *RSCI*, VI (1952), 47-78.

92. See n. 54, above.

93. Morghen, "Movimenti religiosi popolari nel periodo della riforma della chiesa," in *Relazione del X Congresso*, pp. 333-56; and the same author's "Il cosidetto neo-manicheismo occidentale del secolo XI," in *Convegno "Volta" di scienze morale, storiche e filologiche, 27 maggio-1 giugno 1956*, Accademia nazionale dei Lincei, *Atti*, 8th ser., XII (1957), 84-104.

94. See n. 73, above.

95. "Catharisme médiévale et Bogomilisme" (as cited in n. 73, above) pp. 77-83. Cf. the conclusions stated in 1955 by Grundmann, "Eresie e nuovi ordini religiosi," in *Relazione del X Congresso*, pp. 367-68; and in 1953 by Borst, pp. 90-91.

96. On the Pataria, see S. M. Brown, "Movimenti politico-religiosi a Milano ai tempi della Pataria," *Archivio storico Lombardo*, 6th ser., LVIII (1931), 227-78; Cinzio Violante, *La Pataria milanese e la riforma ecclesiastica, I: Le premesse (1045-1057)*. Further bibliography in Borst, p. 82, n. 4; Grundmann, *Ketzergeschichte*, p. 14, n. 7.

97. Landulf's chronicle is cited in No. 5; see Bk. III, cc. xviii, xxv. On the name *Patarini*, used for members of the Pataria, see No. 27, n. 3. The term *falsi Cathari*, used by Landulf to refer to them, has led to speculation about but no proof of relationships between them and the twelfth-century dualists (Borst, p. 82, n. 5).

98. See No. 7.

99. Charles Molinier, "L'Hérésie et la persécution au XIe siècle," *Revue des Pyrénées*, VI (1894), 30-31.

100. Mentioned and denied by Morghen, "Movimenti religiosi popolari," in *Relazione del X Congresso*, pp. 355-56.

101. *Die Katharer*, pp. 80-81. Cf. Grundmann, *Religiöse Bewegungen*, p. 483; Ilarino da Milano, "Le eresi popolari," in *Studi Gregoriani*, II, p. 83-84.

102. Works in English on the history of the Inquisition (see n. 187, below) mention most of the incidents, but new discoveries sometimes make those works outdated. Russell, *Dissent and Reform*, offers the most complete survey. Norman Cohn, *The Pursuit of the Millennium*, selects some incidents to discuss in connection with his particular thesis. For the first half of the twelfth century see also the works of Valvekins and Suraci cited in n. 29, above; also Grundmann, "Eresie e nuovi ordini religiosi," in *Relazione del X Congresso*, pp. 357-402; Raoul Manselli's *Studi sulle eresie del secolo XII*, also his "Per la storia dell'eresia nel secolo XII," *BISIAM*, LXVII

(1955), 189-264; and Theloe, *Die Ketzerverfolgungen*, pp. 30-106. Studies of particular incidents are cited in notes and introductions to Nos. 8-19.

103. See No. 8.

104. See Nos. 11, 12, 14.

105. See No. 13. James Fearns, "Peter von Bruis und die religiöse Bewegungen des 12. Jahrhunderts," *Archiv für Kulturgeschichte*, XLVIII (1966), 311-35, was not available to us in time to be utilized.

106. See Nos. 9, 10.

107. See No. 18.

108. See No. 19.

109. See Nos. 15, 16, 17. Heretics were also reported in Italy at Florence and Orvieto in 1117 and 1125 (Borst, p. 85) and at Liège (1135), where they were said to reject marriage and infant baptism and deny the value of prayers for the dead (Paul Fredericq, *Corpus documentorum inquisitionis haereticae pravitatis Neerlandicae*, I, 30). Some heretics in Brittany about 1145 had unorthodox views about infant baptism, the resurrection of bodies, relationships with women, and the nature of the Church, but whether these derived from the teaching of Henry, or of Peter of Bruys, or of Eudo, or were independently formed, is not clear: see Manselli, "Per la storia dell'eresia," *BISIAM*, LXVII (1955), 235-44; Grundmann, "Eresie e nuovi ordini religiosi," in *Relazione del X Congresso*, p. 370; and Borst, p. 5, n. 10.

110. On the apostolic ideal, see Ernest W. McDonnell, "The *vita apostolica*," *Church History*, XXIV (1953), 15-31; Pierre Mandonnet, *Saint Dominic and His Work*, trans. by Sister Mary Benedicta Larkin, pp. 272-78; Ellen S. Davison, *Forerunners of St. Francis, and Other Studies*, pp. 220-28; Grundmann, *Religiöse Bewegungen*, pp. 11-21; M. H. Vicaire, *Saint Dominic and His Times*, trans. by Kathleen Pond, pp. 73-76.

111. See No. 15, part A.

112. See the introduction to No. 15.

113. See No. 20, n. 2. The literature on the Cathars is enormous. Some of it is cited in notes and bibliography in this volume, but we know of no survey in English of the Catharist movement as a whole which takes advantage of recent European studies. Borst's *Die Katharer*, is by far the best treatment of that heresy and has comments on the sources and literature, pp. 1-58. Luciano Sommariva, "Studi recenti sulle eresie medievali (1939-1952)," *RSI*, LXIV (1952), 237-68, has an excellent critical discussion. See also Daniel Walther, "A Survey of Recent Research on the Albigensian Cathari," *Church History*, XXXIV (1965), 146-77. Short surveys of Catharism will be found in Raoul Manselli, "Profilo dell'eresia medievale (Catari e Valdesi)," *Humanitas*, I (1950), 384-96; and Ilarino da Milano, "Le eresie medioevali (sec. XI-XV)," in *Grande antol. filos.*, IV, 1601-2, with extracts from sources in Italian translation, pp. 1625-46, and bibliography, pp. 1646-68; and Eugenio Dupré-Theseider, *Introduzione alle eresie medievali* (Bologna, 1953). Russell, "Interpretations of Medieval Heresy," *MS*, XXV (1963), 25-53, names many of the studies of the heresy in canvassing his

special topic. See also the discussion of the medieval sources, pp. 56-67.

114. The date (1144-1145) of this episode has been challenged; see the introduction to No. 17.

115. See No. 16.

116. See p. 16.

117. See No. 24.

118. "Hérésie et croisade au XIIᵉ siècle," *RHE*, XLIX (1954), 855-72. On the question of Catharist doctrine in the Rhineland at this time—whether absolute or mitigated dualism—see No. 39, n. 3. That returning crusaders brought to Germany ancient Gnostic practices from the East is suggested also by Karl Heisig, in "Ein gnostische Sekte im abendlandischen Mittel-alter," *Zeitschrift für Religions- und Geistesgeschichte*, XVI (1964), 271-74.

119. Eckbert (*Sermones* II.2, in Migne, *PL*, CXCV, 19) declared that he had heard of heretics concealing their full doctrines from converts for as long as fifteen years out of fear of betrayal.

120. On that term as a synonym for "heretic," see No. 28, n. 6.

121. Councils of the Church had little to say about heresy beyond con-demning it. The Council of Toulouse (1119) denounced certain doctrines, probably those of Henry of Le Mans. Its words were repeated in canon 23 of the Second Lateran Council (1139): Mansi, *Concilia*, XXI, 225-77. Records of the Council of Pisa (1135) do not mention heresy, although Henry was haled before it (see No. 11, part B). The general council at Rheims (1148) under Pope Eugene III sent Eudo to prison and some of his followers to the stake (see No. 18), and anathematized heretics in Gascony and Provence without specifying their doctrines (Mansi, *Concilia*, XXI, 718).

122. See the works cited in n. 87, above.

123. See No. 14.

124. A sketch of twelfth-century heresy in Italy will be found in Lea, *History of the Inquisition*, I, 114-17, and II, 191-96, but neither that sketch nor the discussion in Guiraud, *Histoire de l'Inquisition*, Vol. II, chaps. XIV-XV, had the advantage of recent discoveries such as those of Father Don-daine, cited in Nos. 23 and 24. Maisonneuve, pp. 146-49, 155-56, 169-73, is useful. Best of all is Borst, pp. 96-120, with a good bibliography. Ilarino da Milano, *L'Eresia di Ugo Speroni nella confutazione del Maestro Vacario*, chap. XVII, has an excellent account of Italian sects in the later twelfth century.

125. See No. 21, taken from the definitive study by Ilarino da Milano, *L'Eresia di Ugo Speroni*, and references cited there; also No. 45, part B.

126. Davison, *Forerunners of St. Francis*, chap. V, discusses the Humil-iati. See also the works cited in No. 22.

127. The Arnoldists are not represented in any of the translations in this volume. See Davison, *Forerunners of St. Francis*, chap. IV. The best discus-sion is in Ilarino da Milano, "La 'Manifestatio heresis catarorum quam fecit Bonacursus' secondo il cod. Ottob. lat. 136 della Biblioteca Vaticana," *Aevum*, XII (1938), 301-24; summarized in his *L'Eresia di Ugo Speroni*, pp. 444-53.

128. See Louis I. Newman, *Jewish Influence on Christian Reform Movements*, pp. 240-302. Further references are given in No. 26.

129. Albert Lecoy de la Marche, *Anecdotes historiques, légendes et apologues tirées du recueil inédit d'Etienne de Bourbon, dominicain du XIIIᵉ siècle*, pp. 280-81. The practice of an annual communion was later noted among the Waldenses, and "Tortolani" may refer to them. The "Rebaptizati" developed within the Waldensian movement; see No. 37. On the "Josephini," see Ilarino da Milano, *L'Eresia di Ugo Speroni*, pp. 457-60, and No. 23, n. 30.

130. On Waldes and the origin of the Poor of Lyons, or Waldenses, see pp. 34-35. The story of the schism is told in No. 45, parts B and C; of the movement of reconciliation in No. 36.

131. The rest of this paragraph is based on the narratives in Nos. 23 and 24, and the works there cited.

132. See No. 23.

133. These sects are enumerated in No. 51.

134. See No. 56.

135. Alberic of Trois-Fontaines *Chronica*, in *MGH SS*, XXIIII, 846.

136. See No. 20.

137. See, in addition to the works cited in n. 124, above, Luigi Fumi, "I Paterini in Orvieto," *Archivio storico italiano*, 3d ser., XXII (1875), 52-81; and G. R. Ristori, "I Paterini in Firenze nella prima metà del secolo XIII," *Rivista storica-critica delle scienze teologiche*, I (1905), 10-11.

138. See No. 25.

139. See, for example, Nos. 51 and 54.

140. Canon 27 of this council condemned heretics, who, under the names of Cathars, Patarines, Publicans, and others, were infecting Gascony and the regions of Albi and Toulouse, as well as the mercenary soldiers who were the scourge of the Midi. Spiritual rewards were offered to all persons who, under the leadership of bishops, would take up arms against the excommunicates (Mansi, *Concilia*, XXII, 209).

141. *Ibid.*, XXII, 476-78. The decretal is discussed in Maisonneuve, pp. 151-55.

142. References are collected in Borst, p. 104, n. 2.

143. Mansi, *Concilia*, XXII, 955ff. Charles Edward Smith's *Innocent III* deals with Innocent III as an advocate of reform but without reference to heresy. Three volumes of Achille Luchaire's *Innocent III* are most useful: *Rome et l'Italie; La Croisade des Albigeois* (3d ed., 1911); and *Le Concile de Latran et la réforme de l'Eglise.*

144. There is an extensive literature on heresy in southern France. All the histories of the Inquisition (see n. 185, below) discuss the situation there. See also the works cited in n. 149, below. Too late for us to utilize it fully or even refer to it in more than a few places in these notes appeared the work of Christine Thouzellier, *Catharisme et valdéisme en Languedoc à la fin du XIIᵉ et au début du XIIIᵉ siècle*. Let it be said here that this work

should be consulted in the investigation of almost any aspect of medieval heresy or its repression and particularly for the literature of controversy in the period from 1170 to 1225. The scholarship and insight of the author, as well as the abundant documentation, make this an indispensable study.

145. This paragraph rests chiefly on Nos. 30-35. On the name "Waldes" —instead of "Peter Waldo," which is common in English usage but is not supported by the sources—see No. 30, n. 2. There is a large literature on the Waldenses, catalogued in Augusto Armand Hugon and Giovanni Gonnet, *Bibliografia valdese*, which is supplemented by Gonnet, "Un decennio di studi," *Protestantesimo*, XVII (1962), 209-39. Older works in English include Emilio Comba's *History of the Waldenses of Italy from Their Origin to the Reformation*, trans. by T. E. Comba; and H. C. Vedder, "Origin and Early Teaching of the Waldenses," *American Journal of Theology*, IV (1900), 465-89. See also the works listed in the introduction to No. 30. Petry, *History of Christianity*, pp. 350-54, has excerpts in translation from several documents, including the one translated in our No. 32.

146. Only in the nineteenth century did the claim of a more ancient origin for the Waldenses yield to proof that they arose no earlier than the preaching of Waldes. Formerly, they themselves had traced their ancestry to St. Peter. It had also been asserted that they dated from the days of St. Claudius of Turin (d. 839); see Russell, "Interpretations of Medieval Heresy," *MS*, XXV (1963), 28-30.

147. See No. 46.

148. See No. 38, n. 1.

149. The literature on the Albigenses forms a substantial part of that on the whole Catharist heresy. Studies in English include H. J. Warner, *The Albigensian Heresy*, Vol. I; Edmond G. A. Holmes, *The Albigensian or Catharist Heresy: A Story and a Study* (London, 1925); and descriptions of the heresy in histories of the Inquisition (see n. 185, below). Zoé Oldenbourg, *Massacre at Montségur*, trans. by Peter Green, chap. II, has a sympathetic account of them. It is close in spirit to publications produced by participants in the "Neo-Catharist" movement now active in southern France under the leadership of Déodat Roché and René Nelli (the group is the subject of a story in *Time*, LXXVII, No. 18 [April 28, 1961]). They are responsible for many special studies; see Pierre de Berne-Lagarde, *Bibliographie du catharisme languedocien*, and Walther, "Recent Research," *Church History*, XXXIV (1965), 146-77. Sommariva, "Studi recenti," *RSI*, LXIV (1952), 237-68, lists other works produced in the Midi. The Albigenses have also been the subject of sympathetically written novels, for example: Humphrey Slater, *The Heretics* (New York, 1947); Hannah Closs, *High Are the Mountains* (New York, 1959) and *Deep Are the Valleys* (New York, 1963); Zoé Oldenbourg, *Destiny of Fire*, trans. by Peter Green (New York, 1961), and *Cities of the Plain*, trans. by Anne Carter (New York, 1963). See also the works on Catharism mentioned in n. 113, above.

150. See No. 23, n. 12.

151. See No. 29.

152. See No. 29, n. 28.

153. See Luchaire, *Innocent III: La Croisade des Albigeois*.

154. On this famous experience, out of which was to come the inspiration for the Dominican order, see the studies of Marie-Humbert Vicaire, in Larkin's translation of the work of Mandonnet, cited in n. 110, above; also his *Saint Dominic* and other works cited in No. 36, n. 1.

155. See No. 36.

156. See the discussion of polemical literature on pp. 59-62.

157. For the early years of these orders see the works cited in nn. 110 and 154, above, and Raphael M. Huber, *A Documented History of the Franciscan Order: From the Birth of St. Francis to the Division of the Order under Leo X (1182-1517)* (Washington, 1944).

158. The words are those of Bishop Fulk of Toulouse, on establishing Dominic and his associates in his diocese (Vicaire, *Saint Dominic*, p. 171; F. Balme, P. Lelaidier, and A. I. Collomb, *Cartulaire ou Histoire diplomatique de Saint Dominique*, I, 515).

159. A brief history of the Albigensian Crusade is Austin P. Evans's "The Albigensian Crusade," in Kenneth M. Setton *et al.*, *A History of the Crusades*, Vol. II, chap. VIII. See also Hoffman Nickerson, *The Inquisition*; Oldenbourg, *Massacre at Montségur*; Warner, *The Albigensian Heresy*, Vol. II. Full-scale studies are Luchaire's *Innocent III: La Croisade des Albigeois*, and Pierre Belperron's *La Croisade contre les Albigeois et l'union du Languedoc à la France (1209-1249)*.

160. In the title affixed to the canon the heretics are called *Piphli*, a name which became prevalent a few years later. In the text they are called only Manichaeans (Mansi, *Concilia*, XXI, 843).

161. Havet ("L'Hérésie et le bras séculier," *BEC*, XLI [1880], 509-10), questions the authenticity of this canon, at least in respect of the penalty of branding, but there are precedents for that punishment (see Maisonneuve, pp. 55, 111) and it was inflicted on heretics in England a few years later (see No. 40).

162. *Sermones tredecim contra Catharos*, in Migne, *PL*, CXCV, 11-98.

163. *Ibid.*, v.xi, col. 34.

164. Letters of Pope Alexander III and Louis VII, king of France and brother of the archbishop, are published in Fredericq, *Corpus*, I, 37-39.

165. Paul Bonenfant, "Un Clerc cathare on Lotharingie au milieu du XIIe siècle," *MA*, LXIX (1963), 271-80.

166. Fredericq, *Corpus*, I, 45.

167. See No. 40.

168. See No. 41.

169. See No. 42, also Caesarius of Heisterbach *Dialogus miraculorum* v.xviii; ix.xii (I, 296; II, 175-76). The dates of the events he speaks about are uncertain.

170. Emile Chenon, "L'Hérésie à la Charité-sur-Loire et les débuts de

l'inquisition monastique dans la France du Nord au XIIIe siècle," *Nouvelle revue historique du droit français et étranger*, XLI (1917), 299-345; Borst, p. 103.

171. See No. 43.

172. Only part of the teaching of Joachim of Flora is mentioned here. Excerpts from sources illustrating his doctrines are translated in Petry, *History of Christianity*, pp. 473-77. See also the works cited in No. 44, n. 10.

173. See No. 44.

174. Cohn, *Pursuit of the Millennium*, chaps. VII-VIII; Grundmann, *Ketzergeschichte*, pp. 45-47, 52-58.

175. See No. 58.

176. In addition to the large numbers put to death during the Albigensian Crusade, about two hundred Perfect and their stubborn adherents perished in one holocaust after the Catharist refuge of Montségur was captured in 1244, and there was a steady attrition of their numbers by the action of the inquisitorial courts. It may be noted that the death penalty was imposed by inquisitors in a relatively small number of cases, comprising those who were impenitent heretics or who had relapsed into heresy after once abjuring it. Imprisonment was more common, and for most believers who recanted the penalty was to make pilgrimages and to wear yellow crosses sewed on their clothing. Statistics on inquisitorial penalties are scarce but see the analysis of sentences between 1246 and 1257 in Yves Dossat, *Les Crises de l'Inquisition toulousaine au XIIIe siècle (1233-1273)*, pp. 247-68; see also No. 55, introduction, n. 3.

177. The last activities of Catharist teachers in Languedoc are studied in J. M. Vidal's "Les derniers ministres de l'albigéisme en Languedoc," *RQH*, LXXIX (1906), 57-107; and his "Doctrine et morale des derniers ministres albigeois," *RQH*, LXXXV (1909), 357-409; LXXXVI (1909), 5-48. See also Borst, pp. 135-42. Our statement refers to Catharism as a vital religious force. Traces of its influence were to be seen long afterward. Nelli ("Survivances du Catharisme," in *Spiritualité de l'hérésie*, pp. 207-24) finds that Catharism influenced the Spiritual Franciscans and that Protestants in the Midi were also affected many years later. He notes other bits of evidence for the survival of Catharist ideas down to the twentieth-century revival of the "Neo-Cathars" in France (see n. 149, above). The appearance of Catharist traits in central Europe during the Reformation is mentioned in Claus-Peter Clasen, "Medieval Heresies in the Reformation," *Church History*, XXXII (1963), 406-7.

178. There are many studies of heresy and the Inquisition in various localities in Italy in the thirteenth and fourteenth centuries but no comprehensive, over-all account. Guiraud, *Histoire de l'Inquisition*, Vol. II, chaps. XVI-XXII, gives a survey of the situation in Italy; see also Lea, *History of the Inquisition*, Vol. II, chap. IV.

179. See No. 27; also Guiraud, *Histoire de l'Inquisition*, Vol. II, chap. IX.

180. S. H. Thomson, "Pre-Hussite Heresy in Bohemia," *English Historical Review*, XLVIII (1933), 23-42; Giovanni Gonnet, "Il movimento valdese in Europa secondo le più recenti ricerche (sec. XII-XVI)," *Bolletino della Società di studi valdesi*, C (1956), 21-30; Gonnet, "Waldensia," *RHPR*, XXXIII (1953), 202-54, esp. 218ff., reviewing recent studies of Waldensian history to the sixteenth century.

181. They formed a union with the Hussites of Bohemia and at the Synod of Chanforans (1532) associated with Swiss Protestant groups. Although fiercely persecuted in several periods thereafter, they survive in Europe and the United States today.

182. McDonnell, *Beguines and Beghards*, pp. 430-55, 488-504.

183. See n. 174, above.

184. See No. 55, IV; also David S. Muzzey, *The Spiritual Franciscans*; and Huber, *Documented History of the Franciscan Order*, pp. 191ff.

185. See R. R. Betts, "Correnti religiose nazionali ed ereticali dalla fine del secolo XIV alla metà del XV," in *Relazione del X Congresso*, pp. 485-513. Surveys of medieval heresy such as those of Ilarino da Milano ("Le eresie medioevali," in *Grande antol. filos.* IV, 1599-1689) and Grundmann (*Ketzergeschichte*, pp. 49-66), carry their story into the fifteenth century, with valuable citations of the literature. See also works listed in Kulscár, *Eretnekmozgalmak*, esp. pp. 241ff. Excerpts from documents on Church reform in the later Middle Ages are translated in Petry, *History of Christianity*, pp. 503-43. Reformist writings are translated also in Matthew Spinka, *Advocates of Reform from Wyclif to Erasmus*. Older translations of works of Hus and Wyclif are listed in Clarissa P. Farrar and Austin P. Evans, *Bibliography of English Translations from Medieval Sources*. On Hus, see also Matthew Spinka, trans., *John Hus at the Council of Constance*; and Spinka's *John Hus' Concept of the Church*. The work of Gordon Leff, *Heresy in the Later Middle Ages*, appeared as this volume was going to press. It should be consulted on all heretical movements after the mid-thirteenth century; the Prologue (I, 1-47) has perceptive comment on the nature of heresy, its influence, and the Church's reaction to it.

186. Maisonneuve, pp. 236, 243-57, 275; Christine Thouzellier, "La Répression de l'hérésie et les débuts de l'Inquisition," in Augustin Fliche, V. Martin, *et al.*, *Histoire de l'Eglise*, X, 300-10.

187. Works in English on the Inquisition vary greatly in quality. Lea's *History of the Inquisition*, the pioneer work, is still most useful despite some bias against the Church; there is a one-volume abridgement by Margaret Nicolson. George G. Coulton, *The Inquisition*, and the same author's *Inquisition and Liberty*, are very critical of the Church. Vacandard, *The Inquisition*, presents a moderate Catholic viewpoint. Other works in English that may be cited are Arthur S. Turberville, *Mediaeval Heresy and the Inquisition*; Alan L. Maycock, *The Inquisition from Its Establishment to the Great Schism*; Warner, *The Albigensian Heresy*, Vol II; Nickerson, *The Inquisition*; and Guiraud, *The Mediaeval Inquisition*, trans. by E. C. Mes-

senger. Some of the methods of the Inquisition are illustrated in Austin P. Evans, "Hunting Subversion in the Middle Ages," *Speculum*, XXXIII (1958), 1-22.

188. See, for example, No. 54.

189. See the studies of this literature by Dondaine, "Le Manuel de l'inquisiteur," *AFP*, XVII (1947), 85-194.

190. See, for example, Nos. 51, 54, 55.

191. This ceases to be true, however, in tracts prepared in the fourteenth and fifteenth centuries by jurists, whose interest was in legal procedure rather than in the description of heresy.

192. See No. 20, n. 2. On this and other names, see also Borst, pp. 240-53.

193. See No. 57, *passim*; No. 28, n. 6; p. 130; and No. 38, § 14. The Perfect were also called *induti, vestiti*, from the practice of wearing special garb; see No. 38. § 19.

194. See, for example, *The* Summa contra haereticos *Ascribed to Praepositinus of Cremona*, p. 4 (full citation under "Prevostin" in bibliography).

195. See No. 45, part C, § 23, and n. 39.

196. See n. 37, above.

197. See No. 40, n. 3.

198. See No. 27, n. 3.

199. See No. 23, n. 10; No. 24, § 1; also Thouzellier, *Une Somme anticathare*, pp. 139, 175.

200. For this volume, the names of persons and places have been standardized. At the first appearance of a name in the translations, a note will comment on its occurrence in the sources.

201. See No. 23, nn. 10, 21, 55; No. 59, V, 1.

202. See No. 23, nn. 13, 23; No. 59, V, 1.

203. See No. 23, § 2(b), and nn. 26, 58.

204. See No. 51, §§ 14, 15.

205. See No. 45, n. 15.

206. See No. 60, part A.

207. Jean Guiraud, "Le consolamentum cathare," *RQH*, new ser., XXXI (1904), 74-112, and also his *Histoire de l'Inquisition*, Vol. I, chap. IV.

208. For those who had not received this power, it was useless to say the Lord's Prayer; see No. 60, part B, n. 38.

209. The rituals for the consolamentum are translated in No. 57.

210. Daily conduct was described to initiates during the consolamentum; fasts are described in No. 54, § 7, and No. 55, I, 2.

211. Guiraud, *Histoire de l'Inquisition*, I, 144-45.

212. See No. 49, n. 15.

213. See No. 23, n. 10, and No. 54, § 6.

214. See No. 49 and No. 51, §§ 8, 10.

215. See No. 38, n. 17, on the degrees of complicity in heresy thus established.

216. Borst, p. 198.

217. See No. 57, introduction and n. 18.

218. See No. 49, n. 27.

219. See No. 57, introduction; also No. 55, I, 2.

220. See No. 55, I, 2.

221. For example: Guiraud, *Histoire de l'Inquisition*, I, chap. VI; J. M. Vidal, "Doctrine et morale des derniers ministres albigeois, *RQH*, LXXXVI (1909), 47-48.

222. See No. 57 and No. 60, part A.

223. In defense of Catharist morality, see Paul Alphandéry, *Les Idées morales chez les hétérodoxes latins au début du XIIIᵉ siècle*; and Olden-bourg, *Massacre at Montségur*, pp. 62-70. There is an analysis of Catharist teaching on sexual relations and procreation in John T. Noonan, Jr., *Contraception*, pp. 179ff., esp. pp. 183-93.

224. The following paragraphs are based on the words of polemicists against the Cathars, esp. No. 23, 35, 37-38, 47-51, 53-55, in which many variations in detail will be found to qualify these general statements. Guiraud, *Histoire de l'Inquisition*, Vol. I, chaps. II-VII, has details drawn from inquisitorial records.

225. Our translations do not display all the variations in Catharist teaching. See, for example, the confession of heretics in Florence in 1229 printed in Guiraud, *Histoire de l'Inquisition*, II, 456-57, in which Lucifer is depicted as an angel deceived by the devil; he becomes the devil's collaborator, but being repentant, he wishes to allow men to be saved.

226. See No. 54, § 3, and n. 10.

227. See No. 51, §§ 11, 16, 18-23; and No. 59.

228. Many other conclusions have been expressed. The references in Borst (*passim*) and his own comments (pp. 223-30) on the place of the Cathars in the world of the Middle Ages are the best guide.

229. See p. 31.

230. See No. 46.

231. On these and other aspects of the early history of the Waldenses, see Thouzellier, *Catharisme et valdéisme*, pp. 170-81.

232. Condemnation of Pope Sylvester I (314-335) for diverting the Church from its proper course was not original with the Waldenses (Borst, p. 215, n. 9). The Cathars also adopted this view; see No. 51, § 29, and No. 25.

233. See No. 54, § 15 (c), and No. 55, II, 4.

234. See No. 54, §§ 10, 15 (a).

235. See Nos. 34, 35, 37, and 38, § 18.

236. See No. 52.

237. See pp. 63-64 on Waldensian literature.

238. See No. 46, §§ 4, 15.

239. The foregoing is based on No. 55, II, 4 and 6, and the confession cited in n. 10 there; also on the *De pauperibus de Lugduno*, in Döllinger, *Beiträge zur Sektengeschichte*, II, 92-97, and the treatise of David of Augs-

burg (?), item xxvi of the list of polemics in the Appendix.

240. A Waldensian deacon confessing before the Inquisition spoke of the reception of the Holy Spirit in ordination but compared the rite to that of the Catholic Church rather than to the imposition of hands among the Cathars (Döllinger, *Beiträge*, II, 112, 115).

241. See No. 40.

242. See No. 55, III.

243. On the name, see No. 27, n. 7. A distinction should be made between the Beguins who are the subject here and the communities, generally orthodox, which were called by the same name and had been forming in northern Europe since the middle of the twelfth century: see p. 41, and McDonnell, *Beguines and Beghards*.

244. See the works cited in n. 184, above, and in No. 55, IV, on the Fraticelli, as well as for the content of the preceding paragraph.

SOURCES FOR THE HISTORY OF THE HERESIES

1. The characteristics of medieval annals and chronicles are discussed in R. L. Poole, *Chronicles and Annals: A Brief Outline of Their Origin and Growth* (Oxford, 1926), and T. F. Tout, *The Study of Mediaeval Chronicles.* On medieval historical writing, see also Harry Elmer Barnes, *A History of Historical Writing* (Norman, Okla., 1937), and James Westfall Thompson, *A History of Historical Writing* (2 vols., New York, 1942).

2. For example, Peter of Bruys in southern France went unnoticed by the chroniclers. Italian municipal chronicles of the late twelfth century say very little of the heresies there; they give more information in connection with the Inquisition. Heresy in Languedoc was reported outside that region more often than in local annals.

3. Examples are the participation of the king of France in the investigation of heresy at Orléans (No. 3), and the condemnation of Eudo in 1148 by a council over which the pope presided (No. 18).

4. No. 19, part A.

5. John of Salisbury devotes much attention to the case of Gilbert de la Porrée at Rheims in 1148 but does not mention Eudo. For Otto, see his *The Two Cities* and *The Deeds of Frederick Barbarossa.*

6. See No. 38.

7. A few of their anecdotes were chosen here because they came from personal experience or for their intrinsic interest (see No. 31, part B; No. 39; No. 42, part B). Although Map and other English authors supply some of the narratives in this volume which connect magic, sorcery, or devilworship with heresy, it would be unjust to regard the English as emphasizing this relationship. They only shared a popular viewpoint discernible all through the Middle Ages, a viewpoint which was to be blown up into the great witchcraft epidemics of early modern times (see the introduction to No. 42).

8. See No. 9.

9. See No. 20.

10. See No. 14, part B.

11. See the biographies of the great mendicant preachers mentioned on p. 58. Luke, bishop of Tuy, is something of an exception. He included remarks on the Albigenses in his biography of Isidore of Seville; see item xvii (b) in the list of polemics in the Appendix.

12. See No. 6; No. 8, part A; No. 15, part A; No. 16; No. 17; No. 29.

13. One example is No. 14, part A.

14. See Nos. 12, 13, 21.

15. The only two papal letters translated here refer to the reconciliation of Durand of Huesca (No. 36).

16. See, for example, the list of sources assembled in Borst, p. 104, n. 22.

17. See No. 46.

18. This coincided with the development of the art of preaching; see Louis Bourgain, *La Chaire française au XIIe siècle, d'après les manuscrits* (Paris, 1879); A. Lecoy de la Marche, *La Chaire française au moyen âge, spécialement au XIIIe siècle, d'après les manuscrits contemporains* (Paris, 1886).

19. See n. 154 to the first part of this introduction.

20. See No. 36.

21. Numerous examples of this may be cited. See the *Vita sancti Petri martyris*, in *AA SS*, April 29, III, 697-704; Gerard of Fracheto, *Vitae fratrum ordinis praedicatorum*, ed. by B. M. Reichert, pp. 236-38; *Actus beati Francisci et sociorum eius*, ed. by Paul Sabatier, pp. 147-50; and *Sancti Antonii de Padua vitae duae*, ed. by L. de Kerval, pp. 40-42, 219-22. See also Mary Purcell, *Saint Anthony and His Times*, and Antoine Dondaine, "Saint Pierre Martyr," *AFP*, XXIII (1953), 66-162.

22. Exceptions which are special cases are the bishop's discourse at Arras, 1025 (see No. 4), and the sermons of Eckbert of Schönau (see item iv, Appendix), written as a polemical guide for preachers.

23. *Homilia* XIX, in Migne, *PL*, CLV, 2010-13. He attacks "Manichaeans" of the Midi, who refused to lie, take oaths, or eat meat, condemned matrimony, rejected the sacraments, denied the resurrection of the body, and would accept neither the Old Testament nor some books of the New Testament. They called themselves apostles and believed that there were two gods. Ralph accuses them of being secret worshipers of the devil. On Ralph, see Thouzellier, *Catharisme et valdéisme*, p. 128, and the works there cited.

24. One of these sermons is translated in No. 15, part B.

25. Haskins, *Studies in Mediaeval Culture*, pp. 246-47, 250-52. Philip's target was one Echard, probably an adherent of the German branch of the Poor Lombards.

26. A legend of the Cistercian preaching campaign helps to explain their fate. At Montréal, Dominic and the heretics each had written down their arguments for the judges to consider. Put to the test of fire, Dominic's pages

flew out of the flames unscathed while the heretics' writings were consumed. However, when William of Puylaurens searched for Dominic's work a few years later, he found no trace and concluded that the heretics had somehow destroyed it (*Cronica*, ed. by Bessyier, in "Guillaume de Puylaurens et sa chronique," in *Troisièmes Mélanges d'histoire du moyen âge*, ed. by A. Luchaire, p. 128).

27. See item xxv, Appendix.

28. For example, Toulouse (1119), canon 3 (Mansi, *Concilia*, XXI, 226); Rheims, 1148 and 1157 (*ibid.*, cols. 718, 843).

29. See the lists of sects in papal and imperial decrees cited in Ilarino da Milano, *L'Eresia di Ugo Speroni*, p. 38, n. 1.

30. See Nos. 4, 28, 32; and 44, part B.

31. "Rapport à M. le Ministre de l'instruction publique sur une mission executée en Italie de février à avril 1885: Etudes sur quelques manuscrits des bibliothèques d'Italie concernant l'Inquisition et les croyances hérétiques du XIIe et XIIIe siècle," *Archives des missions scientifiques et littéraires*, 3d ser., XIV (1888), 133-336; and *L'Inquisition dans le Midi de la France au XIIIe et au XIVe siècle*. See also the study of the archives of the Inquisition in southern France in Dossat, *Les Crises de l'Inquisition toulousaine*, chaps. I-II.

32. *Documents pour servir à l'histoire de l'Inquisition dans le Languedoc.*

33. *The Inquisition at Albi, 1299-1300.*

34. *Liber sententiarum inquisitionis Tholosanae ab anno Christi MCCCVII ad annum MCCCXXIII* (Part II of Limborch, *Historia inquisitionis*). Notice has been given by Editions Edouard Privat, Toulouse, of the publication in three volumes of the register of the Inquisition of Jacques Fournier, bishop of Pamiers, for the years 1318-1325—edited by Jean Duvernoy from Vatican MS lat. 4030.

35. *Beiträge*, Vol. II. That epochal work must always by used with caution, for there are many differences between the texts in Döllinger's pages and the manuscripts from which he worked.

36. For examples of the value of research in the inquisitorial records, see the works of J. M. Vidal cited in the first part of this Introduction, n. 177.

37. The crowning achievement in this regard is the work of Moneta of Cremona. See No. 50.

38. A number of witnesses before the Inquisition testified that they knew of heretical doctrines only from having heard the orthodox clergy describe them (Célestin Douais, "Les Hérétiques du comté de Toulouse dans la première moitié du XIIIe siècle, d'après l'enquête de 1245," *Bulletin théologique, scientifique et littéraire de l'Institut catholique de Toulouse*, new ser., III [1892], 167).

39. See, for example, the references to their numerous disputes published in Lea, *History of the Inquisition*, Vol. II, Appendix X.

40. See the polemics listed under the names of Durand of Huesca and

Ermengaud of Béziers, items xii, xiii, xiv, xvii in the Appendix; also Thouzellier, *Catharisme et valdéisme*, pp. 215ff.

41. Twenty-eight manuscripts of George's *Disputatio* are known; thirty-two of Alan of Lille's *Quadripartita.* The greatest number of manuscripts is of the work of Rainerius Sacconi.

42. Historians of heresy or of the Inquisition usually comment on the polemical literature. We may cite particularly: Charles Schmidt, *Histoire et doctrine de la secte des Cathares ou Albigeois,* II, 225-51; C. de Smedt, "Les Sources de l'histoire de la croisade contre les Albigeois," *RQH*, XVI (1874), 476-81; Molinier, *L'Inquisition, passim*; Edmond Broeckx, *Le Catharisme*; Félix Vernet, "Cathares," *DTC*, II, 1987-99; W. L. Wakefield, "The Treatise against Heretics of James Capelli," chap. II; and Borst, pp. 6-26. Polemical writings published since the most recent of these (Borst) appeared include the work of William, a monk (item ii, Appendix), the summa attributed to Prevostin (item ix), a manifesto against the Albigenses (item xi), and the *Liber contra manicheos* of Durand of Huesca (item xvii).

43. This has been stated most flatly by Jean Guiraud, *Cartulaire de Notre Dame de Prouille,* I, xxi-xxviii; and Pierre Belperron, *La Croisade contre les Albigeois*, pp. 65-66.

44. On the stereotype of heresy, see Herbert Grundmann, "Der Typus des Ketzers in mittelalterlicher Anschauung," in *Kultur- und Universalgeschichte: Festschrift für Walter Goetz,* pp. 91-107.

45. It is proposed to study the amount of interdependence among authors of the polemics in another place.

46. Lucie Varga, "Peire Cardinal était-il hérétique?" *RHR*, CXVII (1938), 205-31, esp. 212-15.

47. "The chances are that the whole positive side of Catharist teaching is lost to us" (Oldenbourg, *Massacre at Montségur,* p. 33).

48. See the discussion and conclusions of Dondaine, "Nouvelles sources," *RSPT*, XXVIII (1939), 478-81.

49. See No. 56.

50. Peter the Venerable saw a volume said "to have been written down from his [Henry's] very words" (see No. 12).

51. Otto of Freising, *The Deeds of Frederick Barbarossa,* trans. by Mierow, i.lvi (lv), p. 94; see also *Annales Magdeburgenses*, in *MGH SS*, XVI, 190.

52. See No. 21.

53. See No. 29.

54. See No. 31, part B.

55. "La Profession trinitaire du vaudois Durand de Huesca," *RTAM*, XXVII (1960), 268.

56. See No. 55, II, 6, where Bernard Gui is following the words of David of Augsburg, written a generation earlier.

57. Haskins, *Studies in Mediaeval Culture,* p. 255, lists references from the first half of the thirteenth century to vernacular Bibles. See Samuel

Berger, "Les Bibles provençales et vaudoises," *Romania*, XVIII (1889), 353-422; also his "Nouvelles recherches sur les Bibles provençales et catalanes," *Romania*, XIX (1890), 505-61.

58. See No. 43, n. 10.

59. See No. 55, II, 5. In the second half of the thirteenth century an inquisitor noted that the Waldenses "have also composed some verses called 'The Thirty Steps (*gradus*) of St. Augustine,' in which they teach virtues to be desired and vices to be detested and in these they have adroitly inserted their rites and heresies, the better to induce people to learn them and firmly commit them to memory . . . and they have composed other attractive verses for this reason" (David of Augsburg [?] *De inquisitione hereticorum* 17, ed. by Preger, p. 215 [item xxvii in the list of polemics, Appendix]).

60. *Adversus catharos et valdenses*, p. 403.

61. The most famous piece of Waldensian literature, *La Nobla Leicon* [the noble lesson] was probably written late in the fourteenth century. It preserves the original teaching of the sect but has a tone of pessimism about the misery of human life and the dread of the Last Judgment, together with a preoccupation with apocalyptic lore and the appearance of Antichrist. See Antonio de Stefano, *La Noble Leçon des Vaudois du Piémont*, pp. lxxii-lxxxi, on the date of the poem; pp. xiii-xvi, on other Waldensian literature. See also the edition and translations in *Six Vaudois Poems from the Waldensian Manuscripts in the University Libraries of Cambridge, Dublin, and Geneva*, ed. and trans. by H. J. Chaytor. A "rule of faith," also of the fourteenth century, defends the concept that the Waldensians preserved the original, apostolic Christianity, which the Roman Church had abandoned. On this and other literature of the sect, see Thomas Käppeli and A. Zaninović, "Traités anti-vaudois," *AFP*, XXIV (1954), 297-305.

62. See No. 44, esp. n. 18.

63. See No. 55, IV, 2, and also the *Liber sententiarum* of Bernard Gui, p. 309.

64. There are, for example, numerous references in inquisitorial sources to physicians and notaries among them. Guiraud, *Histoire de l'Inquisition*, Vol. I, chap. III, discusses social classes and heresy with reference to the Midi.

65. Borst, p. 107, n. 35. But Walther, "Recent Research," *Church History*, XXXIV (1965), 166-67, states that no form of education or training of "instructors" was known among the Albigensian Cathars.

66. See No. 27.

67. Charles Molinier argues that Catharist literature existed in considerable quantity but was almost completely destroyed ("Un Traité inédit du XIIIe siècle contre les hérétiques cathares," *Annales de la Faculté des lettres de Bordeaux*, V [1883], 226-35). Mlle Thouzellier agrees (*Un Traité cathare*, p. 18). But Dondaine held that their literature was meager ("Nouvelles sources," *RSPT*, XXVIII [1939], 469-71). It was also poor in quality in the opinion of Yves Dossat, "Cathares et Vaudois à la veille de la croisade

albigeoise," *RHLL*, II (1945), 394. Delaruelle agrees; see "Le Catharisme en Languedoc," *Annales du Midi*, LXXII (1960), 157, and his review of Mlle Thouzellier's work, in *RHE*, LX (1965), 526-27. Such Catharist works as were known in 1935 are discussed in Guiraud, *Histoire de l'Inquisition*, I, xi-xv; and a partial list of references to them in the sources is given by Ilarino da Milano, *L'Eresia di Ugo Speroni*, p. 462, n. 1. The translations in this volume comprise all that are known from the thirteenth century.

68. Dondaine, *Un Traité néo-manichéen*, pp. 49-50; Thouzellier, *Un Traité cathare*, chap. III, esp. pp. 48, 58, 63-64. But F. B. Badham and F. C. Conybeare ("Fragments of an Ancient [?Egyptian] Gospel Used by the Cathars of Albi," *The Hibbert Journal*, XI [1913], 805-18), thought that they detected the influence of a pre-Jerome translation of the Gospel among the Cathars; and Walther ("Recent Research," *Church History*, XXXIV [1965], 163) writes: "The Cathari used a heterodox Gospel prior to Marcion —of Egyptian origin."

69. Guiraud, *Histoire de l'Inquisition*, I, x, n. 1; Douais, *Documents*, II, 97, n. 1: Molinier, "Rapport . . . Etude sur quelques manuscrits," *Archives des missions scientifiques et littéraires*, 3d ser., XIV (1888), 290-91. See also No. 55, I, 4. Sommariva ("La Compréhension historique de l'hérésie," in *Spiritualité de l'hérésie*, p. 70) asserts that most references in orthodox sources to heretical books are to vernacular versions of the New Testament.

70. The Council of Toulouse (1229) forbade the Bible to laymen but allowed them the Psalms, breviaries, and books of hours in Latin. Translations of the Scriptures into the Gallic tongue were forbidden by another council, at Rheims in 1230. In 1234 James I of Aragon added the first royal prohibition on the possession of the Bible *in Romancio*. At Béziers in 1246, a council forbade all theological works, even in Latin, to laymen; see Molinier, "Un Traité inédit," *Annales de la Faculté des lettres de Bordeaux*, V (1883), 234, n. 2; Lea, *History of the Inquisition*, I, 324, and III, 612; Haskins, *Studies in Mediaeval Culture*, pp. 246-48.

71. See No. 57, part B, and No. 60, part B. Witnesses before the Inquisition who said that they could not understand the prayers of the Perfect during the consolamentum no doubt were referring to the Lord's Prayer in Latin, but there was a heretic's prayer in the vernacular, which is printed in Döllinger, *Beiträge*, II, 177-78. It is translated in Oldenbourg, *Massacre at Montségur*, Appendix C. See also the analysis of it in René Nelli, ed., *Spiritualité de l'hérésie*, pp. 162-66.

72. Dondaine, *Un Traité néo-manichéen*, p. 50; Delaruelle, "Le Catharisme en Languedoc vers 1200," *Annales du Midi*, LXXII (1960), 156-57.

73. *De altera vita* (see item xvii [b] Appendix), pp. 247-48. Another heretical trick, Luke wrote, was to give false titles to works of the Fathers in order to confuse Catholic readers (*ibid.*, p. 246, cf. p. 240), and sometimes they wrote out little statements of their belief and scattered them for peasants and shepherds to find. By scenting them with musk, they encouraged simple folk to believe these had dropped from heaven (*ibid.*, p. 248).

74. Duvernoy, "Un Traité cathare," *Cahiers d'études cathares*, 2d ser., XIII (1962), 31, n. 1; Molinier, "Un Traité inédit," *Annales de la Faculté des lettres de Bordeaux*, V (1883), 233.

75. Guiraud, *Histoire de l'Inquisition*, I, xi-xii.

76. Dondaine, *Un Traité néo-manichéen*, p. 19; Borst, pp. 269-75. Rainerius Sacconi possessed "a large volume of ten quires" written by John of Lugio; see No. 51, § 23.

77. Dondaine, *Un Traité néo-manichéen*, pp. 22, 24-25; Dossat, "Cathares et vaudois à la veille de la croisade albigeoise," *RHLL*, II, (1945), 394. The heretical work is exhaustively analyzed in Borst, pp. 254-79, 283-310.

78. Peter of Vaux-de-Cernay *Hystoria albigensis*, ed. by Pascal Guébin and Ernest Lyon, I, 28-29; William of Puylaurens *Cronica*, ed. by Bessyier, p. 128.

79. See No. 45, part B.

80. Thomas Käppeli, "Une Somme contre les hérétiques de S. Pierre Martyr?" *AFP*, XVII (1947), 307, 310-11.

81. *De altera vita*, p. 241.

82. *Adversus Catharos et Valdenses libri quinque*, ed. by T. A. Ricchini, pp. 61, 71, 79.

83. *Ibid.*, pp. 248, 347; see also No. 54, n. 10.

84. Döllinger, *Beiträge*, II, 33.

85. Joannes H. Sbaralea, *Bullarium Franciscanum romanorum pontificum constitutiones . . .*, I, 133.

86. *Anecdotes historiques*, ed. by A. Lecoy de la Marche, pp. 275-77.

87. In English may be cited Denis de Rougement, *Love in the Western World*, trans. by Montgomery Belgion (New York, 1953), which seeks to show that the inspiration of the troubadours came from the Albigensian heresy; also James Westfall Thompson, "Catharist Social Ideals in Medieval French Romances," *Romanic Review*, XXVII (1936), 99-104. Jeffrey B. Russell, "Courtly Love as Religious Dissent," *Catholic Historical Review*, LI (1965), 31-44, argues that the troubadours were dissenters but not Catharist heretics. Walther, "Recent Research," *Church History*, XXXIV (1965), 171, takes a somewhat similar view. For the abundant literature on the subject see the last-named article, also Borst, pp. 49-50 and 107, n. 37, and for the vigorous rejection of any significant connection between Catharism and the troubadours or between Catharism and the legend of the Grail see Paul Imbs, "A la Recherche d'une littérature cathare," *Revue du moyen âge latin*, V (1949), 289-302; and Robert H. Gere, *The Troubadours, Heresy, and the Albigensian Crusade*.

A NOTE ON THE TRANSLATIONS

1. A short passage on a Catharist theme in the manuscript which contains the text of No. 60 was not translated. Two other documents which may display heretical inspiration may also be mentioned. One is an inscription on

the tomb of Bishop Maur of Cracow (1110-1119); on it see Pierre David, "Un Credo cathare?" *RHE*, XXXV (1939), 756-61. The other is a little moralistic work in Provençal, praising chastity, poverty, and other virtues; see Clovis Brunel, "Fragment d'un abrégé de théologie en ancien Provençal," *BEC*, CXII (1954), 1-23, although it is we, not Brunel, who suggest that Catharist influence may be seen in it.

1. EARLY TRACES OF HERESY IN FRANCE,
ITALY, AND SPAIN

1. See the Introduction, pp. 21-22. Dondaine, "L'Origine de l'hérésie médiévale," *RSCI*, VI (1952), 47-78, brings all the incidents dealt with in our Nos. 1-6 into his discussion of Bogomil penetration of the West in the eleventh century.

2. Nothing more of Leutard is known than appears in this narrative. There is, however, reference to a synod convened in 1015 by Bishop Roger I of Châlons-sur-Marne (1008-1042) to deal with the vestiges of Leutard's heresy (Jeanne-Marie Noiroux, "Les Deux Premiers Documents concernant l'hérésie aux Pays-Bas," *RHE*, XLIX [1954], 853).

3. Though prophetic visions were not uncommon in the Middle Ages, visitations of this particular sort appear to be rare in accounts of heresy. Gregory of Tours (*History of the Frank* x.xxv) tells a story of a woodcutter who became a false prophet after the experience of being surrounded by a swarm of flies, and who was reputed to be insane. See also Paul Alphandéry, "De quelques faits de prophétisme dans les sectes latines antérieures au Joachimisme," *RHR*, LII (1905), 177-218, esp. 185, note; cf. Borst, p. 73, n. 4.

4. Almost certainly this was Gebuin II, bishop of Châlons-sur-Marne (991-1004), although Alphandéry, in the article cited in n. 2 points out that there may be some doubt of the correct identification, for Ralph mentions the bishop as "Gebuinus senex," which might imply Gebuin I (d. 991), whose death Ralph erroneously puts in 1007.

5. But heretics were to reappear (see No. 6), and throughout the twelfth and thirteenth centuries heresy was endemic in the region.

6. The date can be only approximate; see n. 8.

7. Ilarino da Milano ("Le eresie popolari," in *Studi Gregoriani*, II, 48-49) sees in this incident an early humanist challenge to Christian orthodoxy, a challenge arising from enthusiasm for pagan and classical learning.

8. Peter VI was archbishop of Ravenna (927-971). There was no other prelate of this name at Ravenna in the late tenth or early eleventh centuries. If Ralph is correct in specifying that the incident occurred under Peter, it must have been prior to 971. Borst (p. 74, n. 6) gives the date we have adopted.

9. On the death penalty for heresy in Italy, see Havet, "L'Hérésie et le

bras séculier," *BEC*, XLI (1880), 490-97, 570-71.

10. *Exterminati sunt:* This is an equivocal term which we shall meet on subsequent pages (e.g., in No. 6). It may mean to expel forcibly—that is, to banish—or to destroy. In reference to heretics, the latter meaning came to prevail by the thirteenth century, but is would be hazardous so to construe the expression in all or even most cases where it appears before that date. In this particular context, following so closely the statement that heretics in Italy died by fire and sword, the probability is that the author meant to imply death, but this is only a guess. For a discussion of this term, see Coulton, *The Death Penalty for Heresy from 1184 to 1921*, pp. 9-19; Havet, "L'Hérésie et le bras séculier," *BEC*, XLI (1880), 511-12, 573; Cauzons, *Histoire de l'Inquisition*, I, 295.

11. Apoc. 20:7. It is not safe to accept the conclusion that the heretics of Sardinia and Spain shared Vilgard's bookish delusions. His spirit did not die, however. In mid-century a teacher named Anselm the Peripatetic, of Milan, complained that he was regarded almost as a heretic and shunned as a demoniac for his learning. He, too, had a vision in which saints and muses struggled to possess him, while he himself was unable to choose between their attractions; see Reginald Lane Poole, *Illustrations of the History of Mediaeval Thought and Learning*, 2d ed., p. 71.

2. "MANICHAEANS" IN AQUITAINE

1. This name was very often applied to heresy in the Middle Ages. Perhaps churchmen turned to the pages of St. Augustine when confronted by doctrinal aberrations they did not fully understand; see, for example, the remarks of the bishop of Châlons in No. 6 (esp. n. 2), of Guibert of Nogent (No. 9, esp. n. 4), and the polemical sermons of Eckbert of Schönau in Migne, *PL*, CXCV, 16-18, 41, 97-102. When the "genealogy" of heresy was discussed, Mani was usually prominent among ancient heresiarchs mentioned (see No. 45, part C, § 23, and n. 39), and attributing heresy to Mani's influence was quite common in the thirteenth century. But inquisitors—who may be presumed to have been most familiar with the heretics—seldom used the term "Manichaean" before 1260. Opinions of modern historians on the relationship between ancient and medieval dualism have already been mentioned; see pp. 00-00, above.

2. Adémar also records the discovery of "Manichaeans" in Toulouse in 1022 (III.lix, p. 184) and the summoning of a conference of clergy and nobles at Carroux in Aquitaine in 1026 to consider action against "Manichaean" heretics (III.lxix, p. 194).

3. HERESY AT ORLÉANS

1. The chartulary is divided into three parts, of which Paul compiled only the first. The title *Vetus Aganon* (or *Agano*) came from Haganus, or Aganus,

bishop of Chartres (931-*ca.* 941), from whose episcopate date the first pieces in the collection.

2. Robert the Pious, king of France (996-1031).

3. "From Périgord" appears to be an interpolation made in the twelfth century (Borst, p. 75, n. 10), when heresy in Périgord was still attracting attention (see No. 16). Ralph the Bald (*Histoires* III.viii, p. 74) attributed the propagation of heresy in Orléans to a woman missionary from Italy.

4. Adémar's reticence does not characterize other chroniclers of heresy, for allegations of devil-worship accompanied by obscene behavior were to become almost commonplace; see, for example, part B; No. 9; and No. 42, part B.

5. Bishop of Orléans, 1021-1035.

6. The number of victims is given as thirteen by Ralph the Bald (*Histoires* III.viii, p. 80) and as fourteen by John, a monk of Fleury (*Epistola ad Olibam abbatem*, in Bouquet, *Recueil*, X, 498).

7. Lisoius was a canon of the Cathedral of the Holy Cross in Orléans.

8. Ralph the Bald (*Histoires* III.viii, p. 74) also comments on their readiness to undergo suffering. This is the first recorded case of the penalty of death by burning for heresy in France. See Havet, "L'Hérésie et le bras séculier," *BEC*, XLI (1880), 495-503; and Maisonneuve, pp. 98-99. Maisonneuve believes that the penalty was a popular reaction against "sorcerers."

9. Immediately preceding this passage is the record of a gift of holdings, rents, and services made to the monastery of Saint-Peter-in-the-Valley by this Norman noble.

10. These are the two individuals most frequently named in the sources. Stephen was a canon of the collegiate church of Saint-Peter, and confessor to Queen Constance; on Lisoius, see n. 7, above. Ralph the Bald (III.viii, p. 74) mentions one Heribert as a leader, but this is probably a confusion of identity with the cleric spoken of in our text. Elsewhere a Fulcher is also named (Ilarino da Milano, "Le eresie popolari," in *Studi Gregoriani*, II, 53).

11. Duke Richard II of Normandy (996-1027). The author writes "count" (*comes*) here and elsewhere in the narrative when referring to the duke of Normandy.

12. Bishop of Chartres (1007-1029).

13. Stories of orgiastic rites and the preparation of a horrid food from the blood and ashes of infants are of ancient vintage. Something of the sort had been told of suspect groups for centuries: by Romans of Christians, by Christians of Montanists, Messalians, and other heretics, and of Jews (see Herman Strack, *The Jew and Human Sacrifice*, trans. by Henry Blanchamp, pp. 35-37 and chap. 20). In the middle of the eleventh century Michael Psellus accused heretics in Thrace of the use of magical ashes made from murdered infants (Obolensky, *The Bogomils*, pp. 186-87). In later medieval versions, the shining man or black man or little beast became a toad or a cat appearing in the assemblies of heretics to baptize them or to receive a shameful kiss. Gossip at first, such reports were eventually vouched for by respectable authority; see No. 42, introduction and part B; No. 45, part A;

and the anecdotes of Stephen of Bourbon (ed. by Lecoy de la Marche, pp. 34-35, 322-23). The association of heresy and the cat was common; see No. 35, n. 4. Toad, black man, cat, obscene behavior, and indiscriminate sexual relations are all mentioned in a letter by Gregory IX repeating stories told to him: *Les Registres de Grégoire IX* (ed. by L. Auvray), No. 1391, I, 780-81. These tales became standard among witch-hunters of later centuries. In medieval reports of heresy, tales of sexual orgies unadorned by devil-worship are too numerous to list. Typical is one told by Caesarius of Heisterbach (*Dialogus miraculorum*, I, 308) of a young man visiting Verona who, when accused of frequenting nocturnal meetings of heretics, protested that he himself was no heretic, he went only to enjoy the girls. That indiscriminate sexual relationships were part of the ceremonies of an ancient Gnostic cult revived in Germany about 1160 is asserted in Karl Heisig, "Ein gnostische Sekte im abendlandischen Mittelalter," *Zeitschrift für Religions- und Geistesgeschichte*, XVI (1964), 271-74. The concomitance of sexual and religious enthusiasm is too well attested in all eras for one to doubt some connection in the Middle Ages, but whether or not Adémar's story was more than a folk tale of ancient lineage, conveniently recollected (as we think), the reader must judge for himself.

14. Other beliefs, sometimes contradictory, are attributed to them in other sources. They are charged with denying that sins can be forgiven; repudiating ecclesiastical ordination; spurning matrimony; and insisting that the world is eternal. They are said in one source to deny the Trinity and in another to believe in the trinity and the unity of God; their refusal to eat meat is stated and denied (see Ilarino da Milano, "Le eresie popolari," in *Studi Gregoriani*, II, 53-59).

15. Note also the relationship between Lisoius and the king, mentioned in part A, above. Other sources remark that the group included distinguished clergymen and noble laymen.

16. The execution took place on December 28, 1022. As the flames arose, according to Ralph the Bald (iii.viii, pp. 80-81), voices repenting the diabolic deception which had brought about this fate could be heard from the fire, whereupon some bystanders attempted a rescue, but in vain.

4. THE CONVERSION OF HERETICS BY THE BISHOP OF ARRAS-CAMBRAI

1. The diocese of Arras was joined to that of Cambrai in 580, with episcopal residence in Cambrai. The two were divided again in 1093.

2. Noiroux, "Les Deux Premiers Documents," *RHE*, XLIX (1954), 842-55, presents the arguments for identifying "R." as Bishop Roger I of Châlons-sur-Marne (1008-1042). Jeffrey B. Russell, "A propos du synode d'Arras," *RHE*, LVII (1962), 66-87, argues that "R." probably refers to Bishop Reginald of Liège (1024/25-1036) and that the heretics came from that area.

3. *Veterum aliquot scriptorum qui in Galliae bibliothecis maxime Bene-dictorum delituerant Spicilegium,* XIII (Paris, 1677), 1-63; new ed. by L. F. J. de la Barre, I (Paris, 1723), 607-24.

4. If 1025 is the actual year, the synod was held on January 10 or 17 (Russell, "A propos du synode d'Arras," *RHE,* LVII [1962], 70).

5. Ps. 67 (A.V. 68).

6. See No. 3, n. 3, for another report of missionary activity at Orléans.

7. John 3:5.

8. *Regenerationis nupterium:* In a subsequent passage of the bishop's refutation *regenerationis mysterium,* which we have adopted here, is used.

9. This passage of D'Achéry's text was not printed but only summarized by Fredericq.

5. HERETICS AT MONFORTE

1. Ilarino da Milano ("Le eresie popolari, in *Studi Gregoriani,* II, 68, n. 35), suggests that the spot is probably the present Monforte d'Alba in the diocese of Alba, but notes also the possibility that there might have been another Monforte in the diocese of Asti, as indicated by Ralph the Bald (see n. 2). Since, by Landulf's account, the heretics were brought to Turin, the presumption would be that Monforte was under the jurisdiction of the bishop of Turin.

2. The heretics are discussed also by Ralph the Bald (*Histoires* IV.ii, pp. 94-96), whose narrative differs in many respects.

3. Archbishop of Milan (1018-1045).

4. *Italiam:* In the context this probably means north Italy. See P. de Grazia, "L'uso del nome Italia nel Medio Evo (VI-XII secolo)," *Bolletino della Reale società geographica italiana,* 5th ser., VIII (1919), 327-60.

5. *Episcopum et clerum civitatis, populum totius urbis:* The distinction is between the episcopal "city" and the whole urban agglomeration or town as a unit of civil jurisdiction.

6. *In castello:* This term, as used by authors of the Middle Ages, may have various meanings, the more common being (1) the castle of a landed noble, or (2) a fortified town or village, as distinct from an open town. Johann Plesner (*L'Emigration de la campagne à la ville libre de Florence au XIIIᵉ siècle,* chap. I, esp. pp. 2-12) argues that in northern Italy the second is the only meaning of the term, the fortified home of the noble being designated by the terms *rocca* or *arq.* Any such categorical statement would not be true for other parts of Europe. The problem of the *castrum* is mentioned at this length because it will recur in subsequent sources in this volume. For further discussion of the terms and their various meanings, consult J. F. Verbruggen, "Note sur le sens des mots *castrum, castellum,* et quelques autres expressions qui désignent des fortifications," *RBPH,* XXVIII (1950), 147-55; and J. F. Niermeyer, *Mediae latinitatis lexicon minus* (Leiden: 1955-), fasc. 2, p. 155 *s.v.* "castrum" (six meanings of the word

as used by medieval authors are given). In the present passage the words *castellum* and *castrum* occur three times as synonymous terms. The exact intent of the author is further clouded by mention of the countess of "that stronghold" (*castri illius*), which might seem to imply the castle of a noble, and which receives support from the narrative of Ralph the Bald (see n. 2, above), who states that the heretics were nobles. Borst (pp. 77-78) accepts this characterization. But beyond mention of the countess, Landulf gives no such impression, for he regards them as intruders alien to Italy.

7. According to Ralph the Bald (see n. 2, above), Olderic, the bishop of Asti (1018-1034), together with the Marchese Manfred, the count of Turin, and other notables, led expeditions against Monforte, captured some heretics, and burned them when they refused to recant.

8. *Maiores:* Perhaps this may be taken as evidence of a hierarchy, although the group otherwise seems to have led a communal existence.

9. This is a confusing passage and we are not sure of either the translation or the interpretation. Whether it is difficult because of Gerard's conscious attempt to cloud his thought or by reason of the failure of Landulf to understand and report his testimony correctly cannot well be determined at this distance. Gerard's statement regarding God the Father seems clear and direct, but in his references to Jesus and the Holy Spirit he resorts to symbolism—as Ilarino da Milano points out—by which is destroyed the fundamental doctrine of the unity of the Godhead. In affirming Jesus to be the "soul of man beloved of God," Gerard appears to be close to the early Adoptionist position. But his further remark that Jesus is "born of Sacred Scripture" would seem to mean that the soul may achieve salvation through knowledge of the Scriptures as interpreted by the Holy Spirit; this reflects certain aspects of Gnostic thought. See Döllinger, *Beiträge*, I, 69-70; Ilarino da Milano, "Le eresie popolari," in *Studi Gregoriani*, II, 69; Grundmann, *Ketzergeschichte*, pp. 9, 10.

10. About medieval belief in the virgin birth of bees, see Isidore of Seville *Etymologiarum libri XX* xii.viii.2 (Migne, *PL*, LXXXII, 469-70); and H. Bächtold-Stäubli, *Handwörterbuch des deutschen Aberglaubens* (10 vols., Berlin, 1927-1942), I, 1227-28.

11. These references to a pontiff other than the Roman pope do not bespeak an organized hierarchy, for the pontiff to whom Gerard refers seems pretty clearly to mean the Holy Spirit; see Borst, p. 78, n. 19, and Violante, *La Società milanese*, p. 178; Döllinger dissents (*Beiträge*, I, 70). See also No. 15, n. 38.

6. HERETICS AT CHÂLONS-SUR-MARNE
AND BISHOP WAZO

1. On Wazo, see Rudolf Huysman, *Wazo van Luik in den ideeënstrijd zijner dagen* (Nijmegen, 1932).

2. Matt. 12:31-32. The reference here to Mani may be compared with a

passage from the *De haeresibus* of St. Augustine, which consists of brief sketches of all the heresies known to him. His treatment of the Manichaeans (chap. XLVI) is much the longest. In it he says: "They claim that the promise of the Lord Jesus Christ regarding the Paraclete, the Holy Spirit, was fulfilled in their heresiarch Manichaeus. For this reason in his writings he calls himself the apostle of Jesus Christ, in that Christ had promised to send him and had sent the Holy Spirit in him" (quoted from *The* De haeresibus *of Saint Augustine*, trans. by L. G. Müller, p. 95). The similarity is clear, but at this distance one can only speculate whether the group at Châlons were familiar with Manichaean doctrines, or whether the bishop, or indeed, Anselm, put the words into their mouths. See Ilarino da Milano, "Le eresie popolari," in *Studi Gregoriani*, II, 74-76; and Borst, p. 79, n. 21.

3. These tenets seem to show a closer similarity to the beliefs of the scholars at Orléans than to those of other contemporary groups, although the social circumstances of the heretics in the two places had little or nothing in common.

4. *Exterminentur:* In the present context the clear implication is the death penalty, despite reference to the leaven which, in the biblical passage (I Cor. 5:6-7), is to be "purged out." Otherwise it would be difficult to explain the spirited argument of Bishop Wazo against the penalty of death for heretics. Cf. No. 1, n. 10.

5. Exod. 20:13.

6. Ps. 77 (A.V. 78):47.

7. I Cor. 15:36.

8. John 12:24-25.

9. This is the first known use of "Arian" to characterize heretics of the eleventh and later centuries. It seems to be used here as a synonym for "heretics," of whom Arius was the archetype for many theologians. In the next century the term would be employed by several writers but never by heretics themselves. At that time it is probable not only that the vigorous criticism of the Church made heretics appear troublesome and dangerous but also that the dualist tendencies of some sects seemed to resemble the early Arians' denial of the divinity of Christ. It is supposed that "Manichaean" was used to designate absolute dualism, "Arian" referred to mitigated dualism; see Raoul Manselli, "Una designazione dell'eresia catara: 'Arriana heresis,'" *BISIAM*, LXVIII (1956), 233-46; Y. M. J. Congar, "'Arriana haeresis' comme désignation du néo-manichéisme au XIIe siècle," *RSPT*, XLIII (1959), 449-61; and Thouzellier, "La Profession trinitaire," *RTAM*, XXVII (1960), 279-82.

10. Pope Gregory I *Moralia* II.75.

11. Cf. Matt. 13:37-39.

12. Matt. 13:29-30.

13. Ecclus. 13:1.

14. The idea was that abstinence from meat, which was regarded as evidence of heresy, caused the pallid complexion.

15. *Irreprehensibiliter:* This was obviously a scribe's mistake.

16. At Christmas, 1051, Henry III (king, 1039; emperor, 1046-1056) ordered the execution of some heretics captured by Godfrey, duke of Lorraine, of whom it is reported that they refused to eat meat (*Hermanni Augiensis Chronicon*, ed. by G. H. Pertz, in *MGH SS*, V, 130). Other sources for the incident are cited in Borst, p. 79, n. 23. Borst believes the Goslar heretics to have derived from those of Châlons.

17. St. Martin, bishop of Tours (371-397?), refused Communion to bishops who had consented to the slaughter of Priscillianists condemned by the Emperor Maximin for allegedly practicing magic.

7. RAMIHRDUS: HERETIC OR REFORMER?

1. See Introduction, pp. 22-23.

2. He was Gerhard II, whose predecessor died September 28, 1076. By September 10, 1077, Gregory VII had accepted his explanation of the imperial investiture—Gerhard pleaded ignorance of the papal decree which he had violated (Cauchie, *La Querelle des investitures*, I, 2, 8-9).

3. In his account, Cauchie publishes (pp. 9-12) a summary of a long letter, written some months later than the incident here recounted, from the clergy of Cambrai to the clergy of Rheims. The letter, which bitterly complains of the reform program being imposed on the clergy and suggests that they establish a common front in defense of customs hallowed by long usage, is published in Bouquet, *Recueil*, XIV, 779-80.

4. The date falls after September 28, 1076 (see n. 2, above) and somewhat before March 25, 1077 (see n. 7, below).

5. Of two villages of that name, the one near Douai is identified as the one referred to here, by Paul Beuzart, *Les Hérésies pendant le moyen âge et la réforme jusqu'à la mort de Philippe II, 1598, dans la région de Douai, d'Arras, et au pays de l'Alleu*, p. 8, n. 2.

6. There is a difference of scholarly opinion over the spelling: Schere, Scherem, or Ferem (possibly the present-day Férin, south of Douai; see Beuzart, p. 8, n. 3). We adopt the choice of Ilarino da Milano, "Le eresie popolari," in *Studi Gregoriani*, II, 81.

7. On March 25, 1077, Gregory VII wrote to Bishop Josfred of Paris and directed an investigation of various complaints against Manasses, archbishop of Paris. Part of that letter reads: "It is also reported to us that the people of Cambrai have burned a certain man because he dared to say that priests guilty of simony or fornication have no right to celebrate Mass and that their services should not be accepted. This seems to us terrible in the extreme and if the report is true, it should be punished with canonical severity. We call upon you, therefore, to inquire carefully into the truth of the matter" (quoted from *The Correspondence of Pope Gregory VII*, trans. by Ephraim Emerton, p. 117). The sources are silent on the results of this investigation.

8. This is the earliest of many references to heresy among clothworkers. In some later sources the connection between weavers and heresy is explicitly stated without any explanation of why this should be so; most of the sources are cited by Grundmann, *Religiöse Bewegungen*, pp. 31-33. On the possible social implications of these references, see also Evans, "Social Aspects of Medieval Heresy," in *Persecution and Liberty*, pp. 93-116; and Borst, p. 248, in both of which other pertinent secondary literature is cited.

8. THE HERESY OF TANCHELM

1. Henri Pirenne ("Tanchelin et le projet de démembrement du diocèse d'Utrecht vers 1100," *Académie royale de Belgique, Bulletin de la classe des lettres et des sciences morales et politiques*, 5th ser., XIII [1927], 112-19) sought to explain this project in the following terms: He suggested that Tanchelm was a notary in the court of Robert II, count of Flanders, who had already been instrumental in detaching Arras from the imperial diocese of Cambrai in 1093. A few years later Robert was seeking also to gain for the diocese of Tournai (not Thérouanne as in the text, because, Pirenne argued, Tournai and Utrecht were contiguous, Thérouanne and Utrecht were not) the area of Quatre-Métiers and even Zeeland from the Germanic diocese of Utrecht. Tanchelm and Everwacher, a priest of Robert's entourage, were the count's emissaries to Rome on the unsuccessful mission. To support his theory, Pirenne postulated a scribe's mistake in writing Thérouanne (*Teruwanensi episcopio*) for Tournai (*Tornacensi episcopio*). Jozef M. de Smet ("De monnik Tanchelm en de Utrechtse Bisschopszetel in 1112-1114," in *Scrinium Lovaniense: Mélanges historiques Etienne van Cauwenburgh*, pp. 207-34) rejects Pirenne's theory of a scribe's mistake, denies that Count Robert sponsored the project, and insists that the intended beneficiary of the transfer was the bishop of Thérouanne. Russell (*Dissent and Reform*, pp. 56-59) depicts Tanchelm as a reformer who became a heretic, but gives a somewhat different sequence of the events in his career. See also the work of Walter Mohr cited in the following note.

2. Mohr ("Tanchelm von Antwerpen: Eine nochmalige Überprüfung der Quellenlage," *Annales universitatis Saraviensis*, III [1954], 234-47) agrees with the Pirenne theory and concludes that Tanchelm was also an advocate of the Gregorian reform program and that his propapal and anti-imperial stand made him the target of attacks by the clergy of Utrecht and the archbishop of Cologne. Mohr points out the parallels with the narrative of Gregory of Tours and agrees with Albert Hauck (*Kirchengeschichte Deutschlands*, 6th ed. [Berlin and Leipzig, 1953], IV, 95-97) that the reference to Tanchelm's sacrilegious marriage with Mary was an exaggerated report based on Tanchelm's encouragement of the veneration of the Virgin, which was widely practiced at that time.

3. Ps. 2:8. The phrase "like the Donatist heretics . . . in Africa" is not in the text printed by Fredericq, nor does it appear in numerous other editions,

all apparently copied from an early one by Sebastian Tengnagel, *Collectio veterum monumentorum contra schismaticos* (1612), and included also in the collected works of Jacob Gretser, *Opera omnia*, VI, 429-61. On the manuscripts and editions, see De Smet, "De monnik Tanchelm," in *Scrinium Lovaniense*, p. 208, n. 4.

4. *Ennaratio in Psalmos* x.6 (Migne, *PL*, XXXVI, 135).

5. *Ibid.* 5 (col. 134).

6. *Se non inferius nec dissimilius Deum.*

7. Abelard, in his *Introductio ad theologiam* ii.iv (Migne, *PL*, CLXXVIII, 1056), writes: "Tanchelm, a layman . . . had become puffed up with such madness that over and over again he had himself proclaimed the Son of God and, so it is said, caused a temple to be built in his honor by the people whom he had deluded."

8. II Tim. 2:17.

9. According to one of the biographers of St. Norbert, there was at this time only one priest in Antwerp and he was living in sin with his own niece (Fredericq, *Corpus*, I, 23).

10. The *Vita Norberti* (Fredericq, *Corpus*, I, 23) adds that there was "no duke or prince who could stand against or attack him." Paul Alphandéry (*Les Idées morales chez les hétérodoxes latins au début du XIIIᵉ siècle*, pp. 102, 107) supposes that Tanchelm was seeking by force of arms to establish a theocratic commune, free from the oversight of the Church.

11. Tanchelm had apparently escaped from the custody in which, at the command of Archbishop Frederick of Cologne, he was held at the time of his denunciation by the clergy of Utrecht. Nothing further is known of this intrepid priestly exponent of direct action. The date of Tanchelm's death is variously given; most probably it was 1115.

12. St. Norbert (*ca.* 1082-1134), founder of the Premonstratensian order (1119) and archbishop of Magdeburg (1126-1134), was invited by Bishop Burchard of Cambrai (1116-1131) to establish in St. Michael's Church at Antwerp a house of Premonstratensian canons. This he did in 1124 (Fredericq, *Corpus*, I, 24, note). So effective was the work of Norbert that he was acclaimed as the "apostle to Antwerp." A popular biography is by Elie Maire, *Saint Norbert*.

9. "MANICHAEANS" NEAR SOISSONS

1. See Bourguin's Introduction to his edition of the autobiography, pp. xlix-li.

2. John, count of Soissons. The author has been describing instances of John's wickedness and has accused him of favoring Jews and heretics and of indulging in various depraved practices.

3. Bucy-le-Long, a few miles north of Soissons.

4. C. D. Du Cange, *Glossarium mediae et infimae latinitatis*, ed. by G. A. L. Henschel (10 vols., Paris, 1840-1850), Vol. II, *s.v.* "dispensatio,

1," where the term is defined as meaning the assumption of flesh by Jesus. Guibert probably had in mind a passage from St. Augustine's *De haeresibus* wherein the author says that the Manichaeans held that Christ "did not come in real flesh, but presented the simulated appearance of flesh to deceive human perception, and therein He feigned not only death, but resurrection as well." See Müller's translation of the *De haeresibus*, pp. 94-95. Cf., also, Letters 136 and 137 of St. Augustine (Migne, *PL*, XXX, 514-25), in the first of which Marcellinus urges Augustine to correct the false teaching of some "who defame the dispensation of the Lord's incarnation." In the letter following, Augustine argues at some length that Christ was in very truth born of the Virgin Mary and lived and wrought in the world.

5. The Latin of this passage is difficult and the sense obscure. We are not at all sure of our translation, but, in conjunction with similar passages elsewhere, it seems a more plausible rendering than a literal translation would afford (cf. Monod, *Le Moine Guibert*, pp. 212-13). The whole paragraph appears to have been dragged in out of context, since it may be noted that the promiscuity here recounted is in flat contradiction to what the author said in the preceding paragraph about the heretics' prohibition of sexual intercourse.

6. This is probably a reference to the *De haeresibus* XLVI. See n. 4, above.

7. Bishop of Soissons (1108-1126).

8. Luke 6:22. "Blessed shall you be when men shall hate you."

9. Mark 16:16.

10. Augustine *De haeresibus* LXX (trans. by Müller, pp. 110-11). The quotation occurs also in Letter 237 of Augustine to Ceretius, concerning the Priscillianists (Migne, *PL*, XXXIII, 1035).

11. In the present department of the Marne, twenty-two miles southwest of Rheims.

12. A manuscript of Durham Cathedral (B.III.7, fols. 364ff.) has the rubric *De hereticis qui Gallica lingua dicuntur Telier vel Deimai*, under which is copied this chapter of Guibert's autobiography.

10. HERESY IN IVOY, NEAR TRIER

1. Guiraud, *Histoire de l'inquisition*, I, 3; Fredericq, *Corpus*, I, 20, note.

2. In the Annals of Trier (printed by Fredericq, *Corpus*, I, 20-22), which were compiled by C. Brouwer early in the seventeenth century, revised and published by J. Masenius under the title *Antiquitatum et annalium Treverensium libri XXVI*. One cannot be certain whether the reference to Berengar was in the source from which Brouwer drew or was his own interpolation.

3. Borst, p. 85, n. 14.

4. The reference is to Archbishop Bruno of Trier (1102-1124).

5. Ivoy, in the present department of Ardennes, France.

6. The exact location of the first quotation from St. Augustine has not been found, although there are in his works numerous similar passages.

The second quotation is from Fulgentius, bishop of Ruspa (468-533), *De fide ad Petrum, sive de regula verae fidei liber unus* xxx (*regula* 27 [Migne, PL, LXV, 671-706]). The work was frequently ascribed to St. Augustine but was shown by Erasmus to have been written by Fulgentius. See the prefatory note in Migne, *PL*, XL, 753, where the treatise is included with the works of St. Augustine (cols. 753-78).

7. Matt. 18:17.

8. There is in canon law, under the general title of contumacy, a whole series of enactments covering this point and beginning in the early fifth century. See R. Naz, *Dictionnaire de droit canonique* (Paris, 1955), IV, 506-41, *s.v.* "contumacia," and the references to the *Corpus juris canonici* there cited.

9. This refers to the Canon of the Mass, or Eucharistic prayer, which follows the offertory prayers and constitutes the most solemn moment in the mystery of the Mass. It was, and is, usually whispered; hence the name *Secreta*. The term *Actio* derives from the act of consecrating the bread and the wine. See Adrian Fortescue, "Canon of the Mass," *Catholic Encyclopedia*, III, 255-67; *idem, The Mass: A Study of the Roman Liturgy*, chap. VIII; and H. Moreau, "Canon de la Messe," *DTC*, II, 1540-50.

10. Apoc. 22:11.

11. HENRY OF LE MANS

1. Henry's birthplace is unknown. He is associated with Le Mans because of the incident described here, and with Lausanne because St. Bernard lists that city as the first scene of his activity (see No. 14, part A, § 3). Walter (*Die ersten Wanderprediger Frankreichs, Neue Folge*, pp. 130ff.) argues to good effect that Henry was from northern France or Brittany and made his first reputation as a wandering preacher in those parts. The date of his appearance at Le Mans has been set as early as 1101, but the work of Adolphe Dieudonné establishes it between 1115 and 1120, most probably in 1116; see "Hildebert de Lavardin, évêque du Mans, archevêque de Tours, 1056-1133," *Revue historique et archéologique du Maine*, XLI-XLII (1896-1897), esp. XLI, 185. Manselli corroborates Dieudonné's conclusion in the studies cited in the last paragraph of this introduction.

2. Mansi, *Concilia*, XXI, 226-27. The canon was re-enacted at the Lateran Council of 1139. Cf. Manselli, *Studi sulle eresie*, p. 56.

3. *Ibid.*, p. 67 and chap. IV.

4. See the Introduction to the *Actus pontificum Cenomannis*, pp. xxxvii-xxxviii; also *Histoire littéraire de la France*, XXIV, 410-12.

5. The allusion is to the prophet praying in an upper chamber (Dan. 6:10); the quotation is from Jer. 9:21.

6. Fulk V, count of Anjou and Maine (1109/10-1129).

7. *Hugo de Osello, Willelmus qui-non-bibit-aquam, et Paganus Aldricus.*

8. Paschal II (1099-1118).

9. Monasteries in Le Mans.

10. *Exactor:* cf. Luke 12:58. It is rendered as "officer" in the A. V. and the New Catholic Edition, and as "exacter" in the Douay; but see Du Cange, *s.v.* "exactor."

11. Perhaps this was one of the two youths who later sought forgiveness from Bishop Hildebert. In a letter of uncertain date, but between 1117 and 1125, Hildebert wrote to his fellow prelates: "The bearers of these presents, Cyprian and Peter, while they aspired in their hearts to ascend, descended into the lake of death, led astray by a certain pseudo-prophet whose followers brought punishment upon themselves. This man was Henry, a great snare of the devil and a notorious armor-bearer of Antichrist. The brothers named above long clung to him, who made a pretense of religion in his garb and of learning in his words, until the shame in his life and the error in his teaching became evident to them. When they learned how wrong were his ways, they first returned to their senses, then they came back to us, whose diocese this plague had so infected that in resisting it our clergy with difficulty maintained their liberty inside the walls of their churches." The bishop begs that the two youths not be made to suffer for their mistake (Migne, *PL*, CLXXI, 242).

12. Ps. 82 (A.V. 83):17.

13. Ps. 30:20 (A.V. 31:19).

14. Bernard of Clairvaux repeats these accusations (see No. 14, part A, § 3), whether of his own knowledge or on the basis of reports from Le Mans we do not know.

15. Cicero *De officiis* II.xii.43.

16. He may have gone southward through Poitiers and Bordeaux (see No. 14, part A, § 3).

17. Ps. 101:18 (A.V. 102:17).

18. Bernard Guarin (1129-1138).

19. Innocent II (1130-1143).

20. The date of this council has often been given as 1134, but 1135 has been established as the correct year (Joseph Kramp, "Chronologisches zu Peters des Ehrwürdigen epistola adversus Petrobrusianos," in *Miscellanea Francesco Ehrle*, I, 74, n. 3). In view of their activities against Henry, it is interesting to note that both Bernard of Clairvaux and Peter the Venerable attended the council. None of its extant canons deal with heresy.

21. Bernard of Clairvaux and Geoffrey of Auxerre later referred to Henry as an apostate monk (see No. 14, part A, § 3, and part B), an accusation which may be explained by Geoffrey's statement, in a letter written in 1145, that at Pisa Henry had "abjured all the heresies he is now teaching and, being handed over to the Lord Abbot Bernard, received from him letters for Clairvaux, so that he might become a monk there" (*Epistola ad Archenfredum*, in Migne, *PL*, CLXXXV, 412).

22. This reference to a "new sect" is puzzling. Perhaps it is best explained by the distance of the chronicler from the events he recorded, so that the

later development of Henry's ideas seemed to him to be in marked contrast to what was recalled of his actions in Le Mans.

23. Peter the Venerable in a letter, the foreword of which is translated in No. 13, and St. Bernard (see No. 14, part A, § 1) describe the situation in Languedoc in equally gloomy terms.

12. A MONK'S DESCRIPTION OF THE ERRORS OF HENRY

1. Manselli, "Il monaco Enrico," *BISIAM*, LXV (1953), 38-39.

2. "Sur quelques écrits concernant les hérésies et les hérétiques au XIIe et XIIIe siècles," *RHE*, XXXVI (1940), 143-44, publishing only the chapter headings of the work. William cannot be identified. A name that suggests itself is that of William of St. Thierry, friend of Bernard of Clairvaux and polemicist against Abelard and Gilbert de la Porrée. There is no evidence either for or against this suggestion.

3. Another manuscript of the tract was identified by Antoine Dondaine. It is Seville, Colombina 7-6-6, fols. 59r-64v, which follows the Paris copy ("Durand de Huesca," *AFP*, XXIX [1959], 257, n. 72).

4. *Ibid.*, pp. 256-57. See also No. 36 and the references there cited. The version thus copied was that of the Paris MS.

5. This preface, which indicates that the tract was first written for the attention of some ecclesiastical dignitary, does not appear in the Nice MS.

6. Acts 5:29.

7. Matt. 28:19.

8. Matt. 19:19.

9. The Catholic reply which follows is in three parts: On obedience, On mission, On the writings of Jerome, Augustine, and other doctors. Neither the words of Henry nor the reply given in this paragraph appear in the Nice MS.

10. This doctrine in different words is attributed to the heretic in the Nice MS, where, in the last and unnumbered chapter (fol. 141v), he is made to say that "children of Christians, Jews, and Saracens, if they die before the years of understanding, are saved." On Pelagius, see No. 40, n. 6.

11. Ezech. 18:20.

12. Ezech. 18:20 and Gal. 6:5.

13. This tenet is not found in the Nice MS.

14. This tenet is not found in the Nice MS.

15. Rom. 3:23.

16. See No. 14, n. 13.

17. The Nice MS, chap. IV (fols. 140v-141r), states only Henry's view that marriages may be dissolved only on grounds of adultery.

18. Jas. 5:16.

19. This and the following passages on the episcopal office and on church

buildings are not found in the Nice MS.

20. This is surely a reference to some work which presented Henry's teaching in written form.

21. This assertion and a Catholic response appear only in the Nice MS (fols. 141r-v). The first words ("What follows") are another indication that the author had some written version of Henry's teaching before him as he wrote.

13. THE TEACHINGS OF PETER OF BRUYS

1. If Bruys was his birthplace, it may well have been the little village now in the department of Hautes-Alpes (Manselli, *Studi sulle eresie*, p. 30). The heretic's career lasted about twenty years, according to Peter the Venerable; and Kramp ("Chronologisches zu Peters des Ehrwürdigen epistola," in *Miscellanea Francesco Ehrle*, I, 73) argues that he died after 1131 but before 1135. Manselli (*Studi sulle eresie*, pp. 28-29) would put it, more precisely, late in 1132 or in 1133. Borst (p. 83) gives the date of his death as "perhaps 1126," but does not cite the work of Kramp. His account of Henry and Peter (pp. 83-86), also differs in minor points from that which we have sketched in the introductions and notes to these translations.

2. There is a brief comment in Abelard *Introductio ad theologiam* II.iv (Migne, *PL*, CLXXVIII, 1056), which mentions Peter's rejection of the Cross and of the sacrament of the Eucharist.

3. This letter, although intended as a preface to the work rebutting the Petrobrusian errors, in itself is one of a number of the same type appearing toward the middle of the twelfth century. These "epistolary polemics" were usually written by monks and were intended to alert their readers to the dangers of the heresies which were described. Of a similar nature are the letters of Bernard of Clairvaux, Eberwin of Steinfeld, and the monk Heribert —translated in Nos. 14, part A; 15; and 16, respectively—as well as that of the monk William in No. 12.

4. The persons addressed were: Bernard Guarin, archbishop of Arles (1129-1138), who was to capture Henry and take him to the Council of Pisa in 1135; William I, archbishop of Embrun (*ca.* 1120-1134/35); Uldric, bishop of Die (*ca.* 1130-1144); and William, bishop of Gap (1130-1149).

5. The author's first and longer but uncirculated letter had been addressed to the prelates of Embrun, Die, and Gap, all situated east of the Rhone, and a sentence in the letter (Migne, *PL*, CLXXXIX, 770), indicates that Arles was not troubled by heresy at the time of writing. The inclusion of the archbishop of Arles among the recipients when the two letters were later forwarded shows the spread of Peter's activities westward to the area where he met his death.

6. In earlier times Septimania meant the region bounded by the Pyrenees, the Garonne, the southern Cévennes, and the Rhone. Here Peter the Venerable seems to refer particularly to the area just west of the Rhone.

7. Rom. 1:28.
8. Ps. 56:5 (A.V. 57:4).
9. Mark 16:16.
10. Perhaps this was a version of the work of the monk William which is translated in No. 12.

14. BERNARD OF CLAIRVAUX AGAINST HENRY

1. It presents in slightly abbreviated form the author's "Les Origines de l'hérésie albigeoise," *RQH*, LV (1894), 50-83. We shall cite the original article in subsequent notes.
2. Cf. Matt. 7:15,16.
3. Matt. 19:14.
4. Cf. Rom. 5:12.
5. *Universitatis gratia pervenisse.*
6. The trip was made in May-August, 1145 (Vacandard, "Les Origines de l'hérésie albigeoise," *RQH*, LV [1894], 51 ff.; Raoul Manselli, "Alberico, cardinale vescovo d'Ostià e la sua attività di legato pontificio," *ASRSP,* LXXVIII [1955], 56-61).
7. Cf. Prov. 26:11.
8. *Gyrovagus:* a term applied to monks or priests who left their monasteries or parishes for aimless wandering. They were denounced in the first chapter of the rule of St. Benedict and were the subject of reproaches by St. Bernard and his contemporaries.
9. Cf. Matt. 7:18.
10. This was Alberic, cardinal-bishop of Ostia, legate to France (1144-1145). Cf. II Mach. 10:38; there, however, the reference is to the Lord. Alberic and Bernard were on cordial terms, especially later in the affair of Gilbert de la Porrée (Manselli, "Alberico," *ASRSP*, LXXVIII [1955], 62-64).
11. Bernard and Alberic were accompanied on the mission by Raymond Bernard, bishop of Agen (1128-1149); Geoffrey II of Lèves, bishop of Chartres (1116-1149); and Gerald of Cher, bishop of Limoges (*ca.* 1142-1177).
12. I Tim. 4:2.
13. When Bernard was preparing to return to Clairvaux, soon after August 1, 1145 (see the discussion of the date in Manselli, "Alberico," *ASRSP*, LXXVIII [1955], 58, n. 1), Geoffrey wrote a letter to the community at Clairvaux, describing the events which had occurred up to that time (*Epistola ad Archenfredum*, in Migne, *PL*, CLXXXV, 410-16). Of the heretics in Toulouse, he said that some called *Arriani* were found among the clothworkers in the city (on the use of the term "Arians" as a name for medieval heretics, see No. 6, n. 9, above). There was religious disaffection among other classes also, particularly the nobility, but, in Geoffrey's opinion, more out of hatred for the clergy than from sympathy with heretics. Bernard had persuaded the townspeople to repudiate heretics and swear that they

would have no more to do with them, but Geoffrey at that time felt that much preaching was still necessary to redeem the land.

14. The actual details of Henry's fate escape us. Manselli ("Il monaco Enrico," *BISIAM*, LXV [1953], 32) assumes that "the bishop" here refers to the legate Alberic. If this is true, Henry was apprehended between late August and early November. The first of these dates is set by the fact that sometime after Bernard returned to Clairvaux in August, he wrote a letter to the people of Toulouse (Migne, *PL*, CLXXXII, 436-37) in which he remarks that the heretics had been "disclosed but not captured" (*deprehensae sed non comprehensae*) and urges the people to pursue and seize them. The second date is set by the fact that Alberic was in Rome by November 17 (Manselli, "Alberico," *ASRSP*, LXXVIII [1955], 61). It may be added that under the date 1152, Robert of Torigni (*Chronique*, ed. by L. Deslisle [2 vols., Rouen, 1872-1873], I, 266) records that a young girl was inspired to preach against the heresy of Henry; but there is no indication in that passage of whether Henry was then at large, a prisoner, or dead. See also the discussion in Theloe, *Die Ketzerverfolgungen*, pp. 167-71, of how Henry's fate was confused with the punishment of Eudo of Brittany.

15. AN APPEAL TO BERNARD OF CLAIRVAUX AND A SERMON IN REPLY

1. Under the year 1143, the annals of Brauweiler reported: "In Cologne, in the church of the Blessed Peter, charges were brought against heretics before Archbishop Arnold [1138-1151]. Several of these heretics were taken and bound for the ordeal of water but they cleared themselves; others, however, oppressed by their sense of guilt, took to flight. At Bonn, three were put to death by fire at the command of Count Otto of Rheineck, for they chose to die rather than to yield to the holy Catholic faith" (*Annales Brunwilarensis*, in *MGH SS*, XVI, 727). It seems likely, however, that this episode preceded that which Eberwin describes (Theloe, *Die Ketzerverfolgungen*, pp. 55-57).

2. The extension of Bogomil influence from the Balkans into Western Europe in the mid-twelfth century is discussed in Thouzellier, "Hérésie et croisade," *RHE*, XLIX (1954), 855-72, esp. 858.

3. The assistant mentioned here may be the "elder son" of the Catharist hierarchy (see No. 49, No. 51, §§ 8, 9).

4. On the apostolic tradition, for example, see No. 49, No. 55, I, 4; on the rejection of this world, the Lord's Prayer, baptism by imposition of hands, see esp. No. 57; on the blessing of bread, see No. 49, No. 54, § 8b; and on the heretical hierarchy, No. 49, No. 51, §§ 8-12.

5. The influence of Henry and Peter of Bruys on the heretics at Cologne has been suggested, but the differences in views make that a doubtful conclusion; see Manselli, *Studi sulle eresie*, pp. 96-97.

6. Vacandard, "Les Origines de l'hérésie," *RQH*, LV (1894), 51, n. 1; Jean Leclercq, "Recherches sur les Sermons sur les Cantiques de Saint Bernard, IV: Les Etapes de la rédaction," *Revue bénédictine*, LXV (1955), 246.

7. These are treated in Sermon 66 of the *Sermones super Cantica canticorum* (ed. by Leclerq *et al.*, II, 178-88), which we have not translated because it is concerned more with orthodox doctrine than with heretical tenets and repeats much which appears elsewhere in this volume.

8. See source citation for part B.

9. Our No. 14, part A, and the two items here translated are found in II, 707-10, and IV, 388-93, 393-98, respectively.

10. The letter of Eberwin is in II, 237-45; Sermon 65 is in II, 246-57.

11. We have not seen the work cited by Manselli: T. Paas, "Entstehung und Geschichte des Klosters Steinfeld als Propstei," *Annalen des historischen Vereins für den Niederrein*, XCIII (1912), 1-53.

12. Ps. 118 (A.V. 119):162.

13. Ps. 144 (A.V. 145):7.

14. That is, the Canticle of Canticles.

15. John 2:10.

16. The reference is to the six waterpots of the feast at Cana (John 2:6-10).

17. The text reads *hydria*, but the plural seems to be called for.

18. I Tim. 4:1-3.

19. Cf. II Thess. 2:3.

20. II Thess. 2:4,9-10.

21. Adapted from Ps. 35 (A.V. 36):8-9, where the Psalmist is addressing God.

22. That is, in Sermons 63 and 64 of this series.

23. Cf. Apoc. 20:7 and Isa. 13:6.

24. Cant. 2:15.

25. Matt. 7:16.

26. Matt. 3:11.

27. John 1:26.

28. Acts 9:17.

29. Reading with Mabillon (*Vetera analecta sive collectio veterum aliquot operum et opusculorum omnis generis*, p. 474) *et episcopi*, which is omitted by Migne.

30. Matt. 23:2-3. The last sentence is abbreviated in the text. We quote the verse from the Douay Bible.

31. Reading with Mabillon (cited in n. 29, above) *non*, which is omitted by Migne.

32. Reading *propter* for *praeter* of the text.

33. Mark 16:16.

34. See Matt. 19:3-9 for the quotations and the sense of the whole passage.

35. Heb. 13:4.

36. Eccles. 11:3.

37. Cant. 4:4.

38. Most of the other sources containing a reference to a "pope" among the Cathars are cited in Borst, p. 210, n. 28. The circumstances surrounding one such allegation in 1223 are discussed in Thouzellier, *Un Traité cathare,* pp. 30-40; see p. 37, n. 3, for a summary of the verdicts of various scholars on the question; cf. Runciman, *Medieval Manichee,* p. 162. There is no convincing evidence that any Catharist leader attained such religious supremacy, to say nothing of presiding over a centralized organization, which, in fact, did not exist.

39. *Apostoli, apostolici:* terms used by other twelfth-century writers to refer to persons or groups who claimed to follow the manner of life of the apostles (see also No. 16). Contemporaries may have seen in them some similarity to the *apostolici* described by St. Augustine (*De haeresibus,* trans. by Müller, pp. 78-81). These persons should not be confused with the "Apostolics" of the late thirteenth and early fourteenth centuries (see No. 55, III) despite the similar motivations. See the Introduction, pp. 25-26 and n. 110, and, in addition to the works cited there, see Spätling, *De Apostolicis, Pseudo-apostolicis, Apostolinis.*

40. Cant. 2:15: "Catch us the little foxes that destroy the vines, for our vineyard hath flourished." These are Sermons 63 and 64, in which Bernard discussed the mystical meaning of the foxes and the vine, applying it more particularly to the temptations which may assail the monk. In the present sermon he turns to the wider vineyard of the world. On "fox" as a synonym for "heretic," see G. M. Dubarle, "Les Renards de Samson," *Revue du moyen âge latin,* VII (1951), 174-76; and Y. M. Congar, "Henri de Marcy," *Studia Anselmiana,* XLIII; *Analecta monastica,* V (1958), p. 13, n. 37.

41. Cf. Osee 9:14.

42. II Thess. 2:7.

43. Ps. 63 (A.V. 64):6.

44. See No. 10, n. 10.

45. Matt. 5:34, 35.

46. Luke 24:25.

47. Matt. 23:24.

48. Prov. 25:2, but Bernard alters the Vulgate text, reading *revelare* for *celare.*

49. Cf. Matt. 7:6.

50. Cf. Rom. 12:3.

51. Bernard again reverses the thought of his biblical reference (Prov. 25:2), which reads: "It is the glory of God to conceal the word and the glory of kings to search out [*investigare* for *revelare* of Bernard] the speech." Cf. n. 48, above.

52. Matt. 10:27.

53. II Cor. 4:3.

54. Peter the Venerable mentions this point in discussing Peter of Bruys (Migne, *PL*, CLXXXIX, 730).

55. Ps. 18:5 (A.V. 19:4).

56. Cf. Isa. 60:8.

57. The references to apostolic practice are perhaps based on I Cor. 7:25-29; 9:5-6. On the charge of sexual immorality, frequently made against heretics, see No. 3, n. 13.

58. Ps. 72 (A.V. 73):6, with change from plural to singular.

59. Cant. 2:15.

60. Cf. Matt. 7:16.

61. The reference is perhaps to canon 3 of the Council of Nicea (A.D. 325): see Mansi, *Concilia*, II, 670.

62. Cf. Matt. 18:8-9; Mark 9:44-46.

63. Matt. 18:17.

64. Ps. 54:15 (A.V. 55:14).

65. Prov. 11:9.

66. Tit. 3:10,11.

67. Prov. 11:6.

16. A WARNING FROM PÉRIGUEUX

1. There is a shorter version, perhaps based on this letter, in the *Annales de Margan*, ed. by H. R. Luard, in *Annales monastici*, I, 15, under the year 1163. Scholars have proposed other dates, some as early as 1140. In putting the letter about the year 1147, we follow Borst (pp. 4, n. 8, and 92, n. 12).

2. Borst, p. 4, n. 8.

3. The *Annales de Margan* states that they prayed seven times by day and as many by night. Each prayer among Cathars usually involved at least eight genuflections (see No. 57); the total of genuflections is approximately the same in both accounts. A century later they were said to pray fifteen times a day, saying the Lord's Prayer fifteen times on each occasion; see No. 54, § 8a; cf. Borst, p. 191.

4. The doxology which in the Authorized Version is added to the Lord's Prayer in Matt. 6:13—"For thine is the kingdom, and the power, and the glory, forever. Amen."—is not found in the Vulgate. It was included, however, in Greek and Slavonic versions of the Bible (Runciman, *Medieval Manichee*, p. 166), and was known and commented on by medieval theologians (see Dondaine, *Un Traité néo-manichéen*, p. 48, and Borst, p. 191, n. 6). Cathars of the thirteenth century used the words in the Lord's Prayer, explaining that they came "from the Greek or Hebrew" (see No. 57, part A); and their practice was a matter of reproach laid against them by Moneta of Cremona (*Adversus Catharos et Valdenses*, p. 445). Dondaine ("L'Origine de l'hérésie médiévale," *RSCI*, VI [1952], 71-73) argues that their use of the phrase is clear indication of their derivation from the Bogomils.

5. The consecratory prayer in the Mass.

6. Ps. 113 (A.V. 115):4-8.

7. The *Annales de Margan* adds that Pons was accompanied by twelve associates (*magistri*).

17. AN APPEAL FROM LIÈGE TO THE POPE

1. The argument is that because the letter was written in the name of the clergy of Liège rather than of a bishop, the see must have been vacant. This was in fact the case between March 23, and May 13, 1145, from the death of Bishop Albéron II to the election of his successor. See n. 3, below.

2. "Les Cathares de 1048-1054 à Liège," *Bulletin de la Société d'art et d'histoire du diocèse de Liège*, XLII (1961), 1-8. Russell concludes that news of the death of Lucius II on February 15 would surely have reached Liège before the see became vacant on March 23, and thus the letter could not have been addressed to Lucius II. He discards the theory that the letter was written during an interregnum at Liège. For various reasons, including the fact that Wazo, bishop of Liège, was consulted about heresy (see No. 6), Russell dates the incident between 1048 and 1054, the years of the pontificate of Leo IX.

3. Russell's argument was rejected in a review note by H. Silvestre (*RHE*, LVIII [1963], 979-80), who points out that Bishop Albéron II had been forced by quarrels with his clergy to go to Rome to defend himself before the pope. He was thus absent from his see from at least the beginning of the year 1145, dying on the journey back from Rome. In his absence, the clergy might well have presumed to address the pope in the name of their church, rather than of their bishop. Bonenfant ("Un Clerc cathare," *MA*, LXIX [1963], 278-79) also challenges Russell, on the basis of rates of travel in the Middle Ages.

4. *Monte Guimari:* identified formerly as a village in the Dauphiné but now more correctly as Montwimers (also known as Mont-Aimé) in Champagne, diocese of Châlons-sur-Marne (Russell [as cited in n. 2, above], pp. 2-3, cf. Borst, pp. 91-92). On heresy there in later years, see Chénon, "L'Hérésie à La Charité-sur-Loire," *Nouvelle revue historique de droit français et étranger*, XLI (1917), 301 ff.; and Haskins, *Studies in Mediaeval Culture*, pp. 222-24.

5. The bishop of Liège was also temporal ruler in his diocese, and the clergy could thus write of "our own" realm.

18. EUDO OF BRITTANY

1. *Eudo, Eunus, Eons, Eum, Eys, Eus*, are various forms of the name as recorded in the sources. The surname *de Stella*, given only by William of Newburgh, is inexplicable. Russell (*Dissent and Reform*, p. 289, n. 24) discusses the problem of the name, opting for Eudo.

2. *Chronicon Britannicum*, in Bouquet, *Recueil*, XII, 558.

3. Most of the sources are listed in Borst, p. 87, n. 20.

4. He is called a "would-be clergyman" who "arrogated to himself the language of Scripture (*verbum predicationis*)" by Otto of Freising in *The Deeds of Frederick Barbarossa by Otto of Freising and His Continuator, Rahewin*, trans. by C. C. Mierow, p. 94. After Eudo's condemnation some of his followers wandered about as penitents; see part B.

5. Other judgments are diverse. Alphandéry (*Les Idées morales*, p. 102) depicts Eudo against a background of Breton folklore, Celtic mysticism, and contemporary belief in sorcery, and sees Gnostic influences at work on him (see n. 17, below). Norman P. Zacour ("The Children's Crusade," in Setton *et al., History of the Crusades, II: The Later Crusades*, pp. 328-29) denies Gnostic influence and puts Eudo's recruitment of followers down to "a touch of madness in the air"; Cohn (*Pursuit of the Millennium*, pp. 38-40) accounts for the formation of his band in part by the unusual hardships caused by famine and severe winters in those years.

6. Kate Norgate, "William of Newburgh," *DNB*, XXI, 360-63.

7. The statements in the *Annales Magdeburgenses* (*MGH SS*, XVI, 190) and by Otto of Freising (see n. 4, above) that Eudo's heresy also infected Gascony might have arisen from the condemnation of heresiarchs in Gascony by the council (n. 9, below) or from confusing Eudo with Henry.

8. *Eunus.*

9. Eugene III (1145-1153). In so far as heresy was involved in the deliberations of the council, Bernard of Clairvaux presented charges of error relative to the Trinity against Gilbert de la Porrée, bishop of Poitiers (1142-1154), but was unable to obtain his condemnation; and in canon 18 the council forbade all persons to give support or shelter to heresiarchs and their followers who frequented the regions of Gascony, Provence, or elsewhere—on pain of excommunication. There is no reference to Eudo by name in the decrees of the council that have come down to us (see Mansi, *Concilia*, XXI, 711-35; canon 18 is in col. 718).

10. Guiraud (*Histoire de l'Inquisition*, I, 16) supposes it to have been the bishop of Saint-Malo. Cf. part B.

11. Otto of Freising (cited in n. 4, above) identifies the jailer as Suger, abbot of Saint-Denis and regent for Louis VII. But all other sources which speak on this point say that Eudo was handed over to Samson, archbishop of Rheims; and the *Annales Parchenses* (*MGH SS*, XVI, 605) although very brief in this entry add, for what it may be worth, the confirmatory detail that Eudo was confined in the *porta Martis*, which was, in fact, one of the four principal gates to that city, and a strong fortress.

12. More probably by some Breton prelate, as related in part A.

13. He was born in Loudéac (about forty-five miles southwest of Saint-Malo) according to the *Chronicon Britannicum*, in Bouquet, *Recueil*, XII, 558.

14. See another story of magical repasts in No. 42, part B.

15. *Per communionem Christianae gratiae.*

16. Cf. Rom. 1:28.

17. *Sapientiam ... Scientiam ... Judicium:* names of three of the eons in the Gnostic pleroma. Paul Alphandéry ("Le Gnosticisme," *RHPR*, VII [1927], 394-411, esp. 398-99, 400-1) suggests that this is one of the indications of the continuance of Gnosticism in Western Europe throughout the Middle Ages.

18. The difference between the penalty imposed on Eudo and that for his followers may have been due to the council's recognizing Eudo as demented and remanding him to protective custody. Otto of Freising, who was not present at the council, implies this by saying he was "undeserving of the name of heretic."

19. The biblical reference to Dathan and Abiron is Deut. 11:6.

19. ARNOLD OF BRESCIA

1. A biography of Arnold in English is George W. Greenaway's *Arnold of Brescia*. For the sources, see Pietro Fedele, *Fonti per la storia di Arnaldo da Brescia*, and Arsenio Frugoni, *Arnaldo da Brescia nelle fonti del secolo XII*. Borst (p. 88, n. 23) gives references to the various judgments of scholars on Arnold's relationship to contemporary heresies. The Arnoldists are discussed in Ilarino da Milano, *L'Eresia di Ugo Speroni*, pp. 444-52. See also Francesco Cognasso, "Filii Arnaldi," *Aevum*, XXXI (1958), 183ff., and the rejoinder by Frugoni, "Filii Arnaldi (per l'interpretazione di un passo di Ottone Morena)," *BISIAM*, LXX (1959), 521-24.

2. There is a biography by C. C. J. Webb, *John of Salisbury*. Our paragraph is based primarily on the sketch of John of Salisbury in the Introduction to Miss Chibnall's translation (pp. xi-xlvi). John was not primarily a historian, but "the most exacting modern research has never found him guilty of worse errors of fact in historical writing than occasional slips in chronology or place names" (*ibid.*, p. xxxv).

3. For further details regarding Otto see the introductions to Professor Mierow's translations of *The Two Cities* (pp. 3-23) and *The Deeds of Frederick Barbarossa* (pp. 4-6).

4. Eugene III was at Tusculum in October, 1149, and at the Lateran over the following winter. He left the city again in June, 1150, the negotiations having failed.

5. For the relations of Arnold of Brescia with Eugene III, see Wilhelm von Giesebrecht, "Uber Arnold von Brescia," *Sitzungsberichte der königlichen bayerischen Akademie der Wissenschaften zu München: Philosophisch-philologische und historische Klasse*, III (1873), 122-54; R. L. Poole, ed., *Joannis Saresberiensis historia pontificalis* (Oxford, 1927), Preface, p. vi; and Helmut Gleber, *Papst Eugen III (1145-1153)*, pp. 27-33 [C].

6. Hyacinth Orsini, cardinal-deacon of Saint-Mary-in-Cosmedin and many years later Pope Celestine III (1191-1198).

7. Abelard had gone to the council convoked at Sens to defend himself

against the attacks of Bernard of Clairvaux, but hardly had the council opened than he appealed to the pope and departed. En route to Rome, he stopped to rest at Cluny and stayed. With the help of Peter the Venerable, he made peace with St. Bernard after the pope had affirmed the condemnation of his doctrines by the Sens assemblage; and at Châlons-sur-Marne on April 21, 1142, he died.

8. St. Bernard, abbot of Clairvaux [C].

9. Poole has dated this reconciliation in 1146, not 1145 as earlier writers believed (*Hist. pont.*, Preface, pp. lxiv-lxv); and his dating is supported by Gleber (*Papst Eugen III*, pp. 30-32). Arnold cannot, then, have become associated with the political movement in Rome before 1147 [C].

10. *Heresis Lumbardorum.*

11. John 2:16.

12. Mark 11:17.

13. Cf. Ps. 5:7 (A.V. 6); 25 (A.V. 26):9. Arnold may have been moved to the statement by the attack of Eugene on Rome in 1149 [C].

14. For the date 1147, see n. 9, above.

15. Hadrian IV, the Englishman Nicholas Breakspear (1154-1159). Frederick met the pope at Sutri, just southwest of Viterbo, June 8, 1155 [M].

16. Cf. Matt. 7:15.

17. *Post se duxit, immo seduxit* [M].

18. The Lateran Council in 1139, held under Innocent II (1130-1143) [M].

19. Otto makes no reference to Arnold's activity in France, 1139-1141.

20. Ecclus. 8:4.

21. It was this street fighting which led Hadrian IV to impose an interdict on Rome during Holy Week, to last until Arnold was expelled.

22. Celestine II (1143-1144) [M].

23. The date is uncertain; it was probably after the emperor left Rome in June, 1155. Arnold's execution was technically on the grounds of rebellion (Maisonneuve, p. 145).

20. CIVIL UNREST AS A BACKGROUND FOR HERESY

1. The major sources for the story of heresy in Italy in the twelfth and early thirteenth centuries are the polemical tracts (see Nos. 21 and 23-26), supplemented by the letters of the popes. There is a sketch of the development of the Cathars at this time in Borst, pp. 99-104, *passim*, with abundant citations to sources and literature.

2. The name *Cathari* for dualist heretics was first used in narratives of the examination of heretics at Cologne in 1163 (see No. 39). Its occurrence as *heresis Cattorum* in a document formerly thought to have been issued in 1152-1156 is probably better dated 1164-1167 (see Bonenfant, "Un Clerc cathare," *MA*, LXIX [1963], 272-74). Although their connection with the *Catharistae*, a branch of the Manichaeans known to St. Augustine, has been

suggested, the derivation of the name from the Greek Καθαρός is generally accepted: "Cathars, that is, pure" (Eckbert of Schönau, *Sermones tredecim contra catharos*, in Migne, *PL*, CXCV, 13, 31). The name caught on with Catholic writers after it was used by the Third Lateran Council in 1179 (canon 27: Mansi, *Concilia*, 231-33), and in the Middle Ages other etymologies were suggested: from "cat," for example, or from the root *catha*, meaning "purifying flow" (see No. 35, n. 4). A great many variations in spelling are found, and the word is said to have been transliterated into the German *Ketzer*, Polish *Kacerz*, and Czech *Kacyr* (Borst, 240-41, 253); although the derivation is contested by scholars who prefer to derive *Ketzer* from the Walloon *catier* (cat): Y. M. J. Congar, *"Arriana haeresis,"* *RSPT*, XLIII (1959), 457.

21. THE LETTER OF MASTER VACARIUS AGAINST THE ERRORS OF HUGO SPERONI

1. *Speronistae:* They were condemned in a statute promulgated against various sects by Frederick II in 1220. Thereafter the name is often found in the imperial and papal decrees against heresy (Ilarino da Milano, *L'Eresia di Ugo Speroni*, p. 38, n. 1). Two other tracts of Italian origin, one by a layman of Piacenza, the other probably written by a Dominican who had been a prior of the convent there, comment on the Speronists; see No. 45, parts B and C.

2. Ilarino da Milano, "Le eresie medioevali," in *Grande antol. filos.*, IV, 1603.

3. The writer referred to here is now generally called "the Pseudo-Dionysius." During the Middle Ages he was incorrectly identified as the Athenian converted to Christianity by St. Paul (Acts 17:34), and by tradition he was revered as a martyr and the first bishop of Athens. He was often confused with St. Denis, the martyred first bishop of Paris. The works assigned to the Pseudo-Dionysius were probably written in the fifth century and were widely read in the Middle Ages in the Latin translation made by John Scotus Erigena in the mid-ninth century. Ilarino da Milano (*L'Eresia di Ugo Speroni*, p. 485, n. 5) identifies this passage as a reference to Letter 8 and quotes the pertinent lines from that source which, in translation, read as follows: "How may they who know not His virtue make known to the people the divine virtues? Or how may they of darkened understanding give enlightenment? . . . . If, then, the function of the priesthood is enlightenment, he who offers no enlightenment—or, rather, is himself without light— wholly lapses from the sacerdotal office and power. . . . For such a one is not a priest—no, he is not!—but an enemy, crafty, deluding himself, a wolf clad in sheep's clothing amid the holy flock." There is an English translation of the works of the Pseudo-Dionysius by the Rev. John Parker, *The Works of Dionysius the Areopagite*. The passage in question is in II, 157-58 (Letter 8, § 2).

4. This theme is discussed in Hugo's treatise (*L'Eresia di Ugo Speroni*, pp. 506-10) under the heading, "That only to those who from eternity are inwardly purified is given external purity." The exposition reveals that Hugo Speroni conceived of true inner purity existing only in those predestined by God to be His elect; and external purity was truly acquired only by those to whom, before time began, was given inner purity. The citations of the apostle Paul on which he based his concept of predestined worth were Ephes. 1:3-5 and II Tim. 1:8-10, to which he also added Jas. 1:17.

5. See Job 15:15, also 4:18.

6. Num. 19:22.

7. This is the sense, but not the exact wording, of Hagg 2:13-14.

8. Ezech. 22:26.

9. Cf. Gen. 17:14.

10. I Pet. 3:18 and Rom. 6:9, respectively.

11. Cf. Matt. 14:15-21; Mark 8:1-9; and John 6:4-14.

12. I Cor. 11:23-24.

13. This part of the line is illegible in the manuscript.

14. Cf. I Cor. 11:20-22.

15. The sense, but not the exact wording, of Matt. 26:26-29; Mark 14:22-25; Luke 22:17-20.

16. I Tim. 2:1.

17. I Cor. 3:7, with a slight change in wording.

18. Ps. 49 (A.V. 50):16. *Justicias* is translated as "justices" in the Douay, "precepts" in the New Catholic edition, and "statutes" in the Authorized Version.

19. Cf. Matt. 23:3.

20. Cf. I Cor. 11:18.

21. I Cor. 11:21.

22. I Cor. 11:22.

23. I Cor. 11:29-30.

24. Gal. 5:14.

25. II Thess. 3-10.

26. Several letters in the manuscript are illegible. The words in brackets are our conjecture.

27. Cf. Exod. 20:8-11; Deut. 5:12-15.

28. Ephes. 5:19; Col. 3:16.

29. Cf. Matt. 19:16-18; Mark 10:17-19; Luke 18:20.

30. I Cor. 3:6, 8.

31. Horace *Ep.* i.xvi.48.

32. *Corp. iur. civ., Digest* l.17.202.

33. Some letters are illegible in the manuscript.

22. THE ORIGINS OF THE HUMILIATI

1. Probably at the Third Lateran Council (March, 1179). This passage

appears in the Laon chronicle under the year 1178, but the chronicler used the system of dating which begins the year with Easter. In 1179 Easter fell on April 1.

2. The Humiliati were among the sects condemned by Lucius III in the bull *Ad abolendam,* issued in 1184 at Verona, where Emperor Frederick Barbarossa also proscribed the sects. Davison (*Forerunners of St. Francis,* p. 193, n. 1) and Pouzet ("Les Origines lyonnaises de la secte des vaudois," *Revue d'histoire de l'église de France,* XXII [1936], 18) refer to a presumed earlier condemnation at Rome in 1181 which was "renewed" at Verona in 1184. We know of no such earlier action.

23. THE HERESY OF THE CATHARS IN LOMBARDY

1. The confession of the convert Bonacursus was recorded a few years earlier; see No. 25.

2. Dondaine ("La Hiérarchie cathare, I," *AFP,* XIX [1949], 287, 290-91) calls him a Lombard and puts the date of writing before 1214-1215, perhaps as early as 1203. Borst (pp. 10-11) gives the date "about 1200" and suggests that he might have been a Milanese and a converted heretic.

3. *Recueil de l'histoire de l'église,* p. 268; see Dondaine, "La Hiérarchie cathare, I," *AFP,* XIX (1949), 281-82.

4. Dondaine ([as cited in n. 3], pp. 282-83, 294-305) discusses the borrowed portions.

5. The title is that supplied by Dondaine.

6. See p. 32, above.

7. See pp. 41-43, above.

8. Savino Savini, *Il Catarismo italiano,* attempts to give further precision to the chronology and the sectarian divisions, but the conclusions are not always reliable.

9. For more detailed information on Mark, see No. 24.

10. *Habet ordinem suum de Bulgaria:* This designated, as we have said, a Bogomil sect which taught mitigated dualism and was probably located in the vicinity of present-day Skoplje in Yugoslavia (Borst, p. 244). Derivatives such as *Bulgari, Burgari, Bulgri,* and *Bougres* gained currency in northern Europe with the general meaning of "heretics" (*ibid.,* p. 250, n. 7, for pertinent sources). Our "consecrated in the sect" reveals the problem of rendering the Latin word, *ordo,* which here bespeaks a distinctive heretical concept. The consolamentum, the heretical baptism by imposition of hands, as we shall see in subsequent pieces, set its recipients apart; for, by receiving that consecration (*ordinamentum Christi*) handed down by authentic tradition from Christ and His disciples, their souls had found the way of return to heaven. Only they were capable of transmitting the same gift of salvation to others. But the consolamentum was also bestowed within a doctrinal tradition: the "sect" (*ordo*) of Bulgaria—mitigated dualists—was at sharp odds with that of Drugunthia—radical or absolute dualists. Thus the word

ordo merges two concepts: (1) the spiritual status of the Elect, which was attained only within (2) the sect which its members regarded as the true Church of Christ (cf. the phrase in No. 57, part A: "the Church and its holy order"). This usage was known to Catholic contemporaries after about 1160; see the references compiled in Borst, p. 206, n. 14. But in yet another context the word *ordo* denotes the episcopal status; see No. 51, § 8. The bishop, chosen by his church, was confirmed in office by repetition of the consolamentum. If there was a change in the ritual for such occasions, no record of it has been discovered.

11. The name and title (*papa*, meaning "priest") are the same in No. 24, but are spelled *Papasniquinta* in the report of a heretical council discussed in the following note. The date of Nicheta's mission, 1167 or a little later, is fixed by that assigned to the council.

12. This is reported to have occurred at a council of heretics held in Saint-Félix-de-Caraman, a village not far from Toulouse, where Nicheta and Mark met with Cathars of northern and southern France. Nicheta induced all of them to accept the cult of radical dualism and to receive the consolamentum at his hands. Administrative decisions were made, establishing three new bishoprics in Toulouse, Carcassonne, and Val d'Aran (or perhaps Agen) in addition to the existing dioceses in northern France and at Albi. The only record of the council was published in 1660 from a manuscript now lost which purported to be a copy, dated 1232, of the proceedings of the council. The authenticity of the record was upheld against various doubts by Dondaine ("Les Actes du concile albigeois de Saint-Félix-de-Caraman," in *Miscellanea Giovanni Mercati*, V, 324-55). Subsequently Dondaine has agreed that 1167, the date originally given for the council, might be altered to one somewhat later ("La Hiérarchie cathare, II-III," *AFP*, XX [1950], 268). Y. M. J. Congar ("Henry de Marcy, abbé de Clairvaux, cardinal-évêque d'Albano et légat pontifical," *Studia Anselmiana*, XLIII; *Analecta monastica*, V [1958], 9, n. 27) argues on other grounds that the later date is preferable. The earlier doubts about the actual occurrence of the council have recently been revived by Yves Dossat ("Remarques sur un prétendu évêque cathare du Val d'Aran en 1167," *Bulletin philologique et historique du Comité des travaux historiques et scientifiques*, Années 1955-1956, pp. 339-47). Dossat thinks that the report of the council may be a sixteenth-century forgery and particularly that there is no reason to credit the existence of a Catharist bishop of Val d'Aran. C. Thouzellier (*Catharisme et valdéisme*, p. 14, n. 7) agrees with Dossat's second point.

13. *Drugonthie:* The name is found in several sources in a wide variety of spellings (e.g., *Dugunthia, Drugontie, Drugutis, Dorgovetis*). The reference is to the sect of Bogomil absolute dualists in the region of Dragovitsa in Thrace; see Dondaine, *Un Traité néo-manichéen*, p. 63, and Borst, pp. 213, n. 2; and 244.

14. Nothing more of Petracius is known. He was presumably an emissary from the Bulgarian Bogomils and came to Italy about 1175 (Borst, p. 100).

15. Simon was evidently a bishop of the absolute dualist sect of Bogomils. His name has been preserved only in this source (Borst, pp. 100, 203, n. 2) unless, as Runciman (*Medieval Manichee*, p. 73) suggests, he might possibly be identified with Nipon, a Bogomil monk active in Constantinople in 1144-1147.

16. John Judeus is named in No. 24 as a weaver, one of the early companions in heresy of Mark, and he is one of the bishops who, in a summa attributed to St. Peter Martyr, were said to have lost their churches (Käppeli, "Une Somme contre les hérétiques," *AFP*, XVII [1947], 306). The connotation of *Judeus* (Jew? convert from Christianity to Judaism and thence to dualism? a former Passagian?) is uncertain (Borst, pp. 99, n. 6; and 235).

17. On Peter of Florence, see also No. 24.

18. The basis for this appeal may be explained by the statement in No. 24 that Italian Catharism arose from missionary activity from a center in France. Borst (p. 93) suggests that the first Catharist bishopric in the West may have been established at Montwimers (Mont-Aimé), on which see No. 17, n. 4.

19. *Sine omni condictione:* corrected by Borst (p. 101, n. 10) from the *sine condictione* of the text.

20. A village between Mantua and Cremona (Dondaine, "La Hiérarchie cathare, I," *AFP*, XIX [1949], 285, n. 10).

21. *Garattus:* His name, variously spelled (*Garratus, Garathus, Gazarus*), is mentioned by Salvo Burci about 1235 (Ilarino da Milano, "I 'Liber supra Stella' del piacentino Salvo Burci contra i Catari e altre correnti ereticali, *Aevum*, XIX [1945], 323); and in the tract attributed to Peter Martyr (see n. 16, above) he is called a bishop who lost his church. The sect name *Garatenses* (also in the sources as *Garacti*) was derived from him; see No. 54, § 2. See also Borst, pp. 236, 244, and the polemic against them in No. 59, part V.

22. John *de Judice:* He is one of the bishops who lost their churches, according to Peter Martyr (cited in n. 16), who perhaps refers to the lot-casting here described. See also n. 29, below.

23. *Desenzano:* The name is encountered in several sources in various spellings (*Descenzano, Diszennzano, Donnezacho*, etc.). The place is identified as Desenzano sul Lago, in the province of Brescia (Dondaine, "La Hiérarchie cathare, II-III," *AFP*, XX [1950], 281). The sect itself is discussed in § 2a of the present tract; they were called the Albanenses at least by 1235 (see No. 45, part B), a name which they themselves adopted (see No. 59, IV, 6). That term may derive either from a person (a bishop named Albanus is suggested by Dondaine, "La Hiérarchie cathare, II-III,' *AFP*, XX [1950], 284, 286) or a place. If the latter, Albano S. Alessandro, about six miles east of Brescia has been suggested as most likely (Ilarino da Milano, "Il 'Liber supra Stella,'" *Aevum*, XVI [1942], 310).

24. *Johannes Bellus:* Dondaine (La Hiérarchie cathare, II-III," *AFP*, XX [1950], 285) suggests that his name might be a latinization of the Greek

Kaloian, which is also the name of a bishop of the Mantuan faction mentioned below.

25. *Amezo* here but *Amizo* later in this treatise (§§ 1, 2a, 3), where he is spoken of as still an elder son.

26. *Coloiannes*, but *Caloiannes* in a later passage (2b). In No. 24 the name is *Caloianus*. Salvo Burci, in 1235, knew the name of his sect as the *Caloiani* (see No. 45, part B), and the spelling we adopt is preferred by Dondaine ("La Hiérarchie cathare, II-III," *AFP*, XX [1950], 295). Borst (p. 237) uses the Greek form *Kaloian*.

27. "Sclavonia . . . that is, Bosnia," in No. 24. See the discussion of its geographical location in Thouzellier, *Un Traité cathare*, pp. 33-35.

28. He is called Nicola of Vicenza is a later passage, and Nicola of the March of Treviso in No. 24, where he is depicted as the instigator of the schism. A church of Vicenza or of the March of Treviso is discussed in No. 51, §§ 14, 15, 27.

29. Their groups are called the church of Florence or of Tuscany, and the church of Spoleto or the Spoletan Valley in No. 51, §§ 14, 15. Peter of Florence was the first bishop of the first of these (see No. 24) and Dondaine ("La Hiérarchie cathare, II-III," *AFP*, XX [1950], 302) suggests that John *de Judice* was the first prelate of the church of Spoleto.

30. Joseph was one of Mark's early companions in heresy, a smith from the same village; see No. 24. A sect called the *Josephini* or *Josephistae*, whose doctrines are not precisely known, is linked with him by Dondaine ("La Hiérarchie cathare, II-III," *AFP*, XX [1950], 290, n. 1) but Borst (p. 112, n. 11) dissents. See also Ilarino da Milano, *L'Eresia di Ugo Speroni*, pp. 457-60.

31. Presumably in the ritual greetings between the Perfect, an example of which will be found in No. 54, § 9.

32. The events discussed in the preceding paragraph probably took place between 1175 and 1190; see the list of bishops in Dondaine, "La Hiérarchie cathare, II-III," *AFP*, XX (1950), 295 ff., and Borst, pp. 235-39. Savini, *Il catarismo, passim*, argues for putting the dates a little later.

33. The place is the modern Sojano del Lago, near Desenzano. Marchisius was probably the second bishop of Desenzano after the schism and presided about 1180 or 1185 (Dondaine, "La Hiérarchie cathare, II-III," *AFP*, XX [1950], 285; Borst, p. 236).

34. *Mundiali machina*: Durand of Huesca *Liber contra manicheos* uses these and similar words (*mundana machina, machina mundi*) often, saying that they refer to the present age or life, as opposed to the life of the future (pp. 113, 114), to the heavens, earth, seas, air, and all the things visible therein (p. 122), but that they do not, as heretics say, mean a world which has its own prince and hates Christ (pp. 118, 128). See Borst (pp. 153, 371) for the use of a similar phrase in other documents.

35. John 8:44, with changes in the concluding words.

36. Isa. 14:13.

37. The words in brackets were added by the editor, who took them from sources which probably depended on this treatise.

38. Luke 16:1.

39. Apoc. 12:9.

40. Apoc. 12:4.

41. Ezech. 37:4.

42. Luke 9:56.

43. Matt. 15:24.

44. Matt. 18:11.

45. Ps. 78 (A.V. 79):1.

46. II Tim. 4:8.

47. John 16:11.

48. Reading *animabus* for the *spiritibus animabus* of the text, which was perhaps a slip of the scribe's pen. A related version of the text has *animabus* only (Célestin Douais, *La Somme des autorités à l'usage des prédicateurs méridionaux au XIIIᵉ siècle*, p. 123).

49. I Thess. 5:23.

50. On Caloiannes and Sclavonia, see nn. 26, 27, above; on Garattus and Bulgaria, nn. 21, 10, above.

51. That is, within the matter first created by God, not yet differentiated into its elements.

52. Matt. 18:28. See this myth in more detail in No. 50, part C.

53. John 3:6.

54. Cf. John 11:49-51.

55. A village about twelve miles northeast of Milan; its location, long in doubt, is established in No. 24. From it came the sect name *Concorezzenses*.

56. Further details on Nazarius are given in No. 51, § 25, that he introduced the apocryphal *Secret Supper* (No. 56) to the West; and in No. 54, § 3, that he was a bishop for forty years. Henri Grégoire ("Cathares d'Asie Mineure, d'Italie et de France," in *Mémorial Louis Petit*, p. 145) says he was a Greek or a Greco-Slav. Borst (p. 236) places his episcopate in the years 1195-1235.

57. Neither Gerald nor the Aldricus and Prandus whose names appear a few lines later are otherwise known.

58. Mentioned also in No. 54, § 2, as the bishop from whom the sect-name *Bagnolenses* was derived. Bagnolo is probably the present Bagnolo San Vito, a few miles from Mantua (Dondaine, "La Hiérarchie cathare, II-III," *AFP*, XX [1950], 294).

59. Peter Gallus is also named in No. 27 as a bishop who got into difficulties with his church. For other references to him in the sources, see Dondaine, "La Hiérarchie cathare, II-III," AFP, XX (1950), 297-98.

24. THE ORIGINS OF THE CATHARS IN ITALY

1. Dondaine, "La Hiérarchie cathare, II-III," *AFP*, XX (1950), 250, 252-

53; see also Borst, p. 23, n. 6.

2. Dondaine (as cited in n. 1), pp. 259-62, on the author; pp. 263-65 on the similarities to and differences from the *De heresi catharorum* in regard to the events here discussed.

3. As earlier documents also have shown (see No. 2, n. 2), a direct relationship between Manichaeans and Cathars was generally assumed in the Middle Ages. On Mani, see the Introduction, p. 12.

4. The identification of Philadelphia (*Filadelfie*) is disputed. Dondaine (*Un Traité néo-manichéen,* p. 62) argues for the ancient Philadelphia in Lydia, near Laodicea, today called Alashehr.

5. It seems indisputable that the reference is to the crusade of 1147-1148, rather than to the First Crusade or the conquest of Constantinople in 1204; see Borst, p. 90, and Thouzellier, "Hérésie et croisade," *RHE,* XLIX (1954), 859-62.

6. Today Cologno-Monzeze, about four miles from Milan on the road to Monza (Dondaine, "La Hiérarchie cathare, II-III," *AFP,* XX [1950], 244).

7. Today the Porta Venezia. "Conrencia" derives from Concorezzo.

8. He is not otherwise known.

9. Today a village about seven miles from Cuneo (Dondaine, "La Hiérarchie cathare, II-III," *AFP,* XX [1950], 244).

10. This is probably a reference to the probationary period required before one could receive the consolamentum. See No. 57.

11. He is not otherwise known.

12. *Argentea:* Dondaine ("La Hiérarchie cathare, II-III," *AFP,* XX [1950], 242) suggests various possible identifications but the place referred to cannot now be precisely named.

13. He is not otherwise known.

14. The same belief was reported from Languedoc early in the thirteenth century (No. 38, § 17) and was also attributed to some heretics burned in Alsace in 1212. A thirteenth-century inquisitor, known as the "Pseudo-Rainerius" (see item xxiii in the Appendix) lists it as one of the beliefs of the Runcarii, a faction in the Waldensian movement (*Bibliotheca maxima veterum patrum* [Lyons, 1677], XXV, 266. The error had been attributed by St. Augustine to the ancient *Paterniani* or *Venustiani,* who held that the lower parts of the body were of the devil's making (*De haeresibus,* trans. by Müller, pp. 118-19). Whether the medieval mention of it shows the survival of an ancient error, or shows that heretics coined it anew or that Catholics familiar with St. Augustine decided it was an appropriate charge to make against those who saw the devil as master of men's bodies we have no way of knowing.

15. *Octo de Bagnolo* here but we follow the spelling of his name given in No. 23.

16. Anselm ignores the church of the Spoletan Valley alluded to indirectly in No. 23, § 1, and directly by Rainerius Sacconi (No. 51, §§ 14, 15).

25. BONACURSUS: A DESCRIPTION OF
THE CATHARIST HERESY

1. What is said in this tract about the Passagians is translated in No. 26, n. 86. The Arnoldists presumably derived from the influence of Arnold of Brescia (No. 19). On them, see esp. Ilarino da Milano, *L'Eresia di Ugo Speroni*, pp. 444-52; also p. 30, above.

2. For the somewhat tangled history of the manuscripts and their publication, see pp. 281-89 of this article, where are printed excerpts from a version found in a manuscript of the Vatican library (MS Ottob. lat. 136). From them we have in three instances drawn readings which for clarity or completeness seem preferable to the text printed in Migne.

3. *Episcopum doctorem* in Migne, *PL*, CCIV, 775; *ipsorum doctorem* in MS Ottob. lat. 136 (Ilarino da Milano, "La 'Manifestatio heresis catarorum,'" *Aevum*, XII [1938], 296), which we follow here. In noting variants hereafter we will refer to these two versions as Migne and Ilarino da Milano, respectively.

4. The passage from the words "not only terrifying" through the quotation from Luke 10:30 a few lines below, was copied into a collection of materials compiled to illustrate sectarian quarrels among heretics, in B.N. MS lat. 14927, fol. 11v. Later on in the same manuscript the scribe copied a version of the whole confession. See Manselli, "Per la storia dell'eresia," *BISIAM*, LXVII (1955), 192 ff.

5. Luke 10:30. This verse is not quoted in the version printed by Manselli ("Per la storia dell'eresia," *BISIAM*, LXVII [1955], 206-10). In noting variants hereafter we will refer to this version as Manselli.

6. This passage varies somewhat in all the versions we have been able to examine. We follow Ilarino da Milano (p. 296): *Evam dicunt [diabolum] fecisse cum qua cumcubuit et inde natus est Cayn; investigatione cuius Adam Evam cognovit, et peperit Abel quem occidit Cayn, de sanguine cuius dicunt natos esse canes....* A version from Lucca MS 2110 (printed by Manselli, p. 207) is close to this. That from B.N. MS lat. 14927, as printed by Manselli (p. 206), is: *... cum qua concubuit et inde natus est* [Manselli indicates a lacuna at this point but there is none in the MS] *Abel quem dicunt quod occidit Caym et sanguine eius nati sunt canes....* Migne (cols. 775-76) is shorter: *Evam dicunt fecisse cum qua concubuit et inde natus est Cain, de sanguine cuius dicunt natos esse canes....*

7. The two preceding sentences, from the words "The union of Adam" to "by the devil" are not found in the text printed by Manselli.

8. Cf. Gen. 6:2-4.

9. Cf. Gen. 6:7.

10. Cf. Gen. 7:1.

11. Cf. Ecclus. 44:16; Heb. 11:5.

12. The words "God's speaking to Moses" are not found in the text printed by Manselli.

13. I Thess. 5:21. This verse is not quoted in the text printed by Manselli.

14. Cf. IV Kings (A.V. II Kings) 2:11.

15. Luke 7:28.

16. Luke 7:19.

17. The preceding passage, from the words "than whom none is greater" to "not of man," is not found in the text printed by Manselli. For the phrase on the birth of Mary, we follow Ilarino da Milano (p. 297) because Migne has the indication of a lacuna in the text of this passage.

18. *Animatum corpus* in Migne (col. 777); *corpus humanum* in Manselli (p. 208).

19. In Manselli (p. 208), this sentence reads: "They damn the innocents [i.e., children massacred by Herod] and likewise each thief."

20. John 14:28.

21. Apoc. 13. Cf. Matt. 24:25: "The abomination of desolation . . . standing in the holy place."

22. Pope Sylvester I (314-335), supposed recipient of the Donation of Constantine.

23. II Thess. 2:3,4. These verses are not quoted in the text of Manselli.

24. This statement on baptism of water is deferred in Manselli to follow the one on oaths (p. 210).

25. Cf. Nos. 50, part C; 54, § 3.

26. The last sentence and "Amen" are not found in Manselli, but several other tenets are listed (p. 210); that passage, translated here by permission of the Istituto storico italiano per il medio evo, reads: "They say that to pray for the dead or to do any other good work avails naught. Also, they say that the saints who now are asleep with Christ do not pray for us or for any person living in the world. They say that the soul of every man, at the moment of leaving the body, shall enter either into eternal rest, if it so merits, or eternal burning; and never in any place other than this world alone is purgation undergone for offenses, that is, for their sins. They say also that in this eternal beatitude or in this eternal punishment, all shall be equal in glory and no one shall precede another in love, and all in hell will be equally tormented. They believe that no Jew can be saved. There are also many among them so stupid as not to believe that the substance of highest divinity is so incomprehensible or uncircumscribed that it cannot be comprehended or circumscribed in any place."

26. THE HERESY OF THE PASSAGIANS

1. On various Latin spellings of the name in the sources, see Garvin and Corbett, eds., *The* Summa contra haereticos *Ascribed to Praepositinus of Cremona*, p. xxxiii, n. 7. *Pasagini* is preferred in manuscripts of that treatise, but we have kept the double *s*, more familiar in modern orthography. On the origin of the name there is no generally accepted explanation (see the works cited in the introduction to this piece).

2. A sect of Circumcisers (*Circumcisi*) is sometimes named together with the Passagians in contemporary documents. About 1235 the Circumcisers were charged with insisting on circumcision and the sacraments of the Old Law (see No. 45, part C, § 24), and in other documents the names of the two groups appear both separately and together: in an imperial constitution of 1220, Circumcisers but not Passagians, are mentioned; in another of 1238-1239, both are named, as they are in an antiheretical tract dating from about the middle of the century; in the edict of 1184 and in a bull of 1229, Passagians only. These and other sources are listed by Ilarino da Milano, (*L'Eresia di Ugo Speroni*, pp. 38, n. 1; 437, n. 3; 438, n. 1), who there concluded (p. 438) that the references are to the same sect, but subsequently he remarked (in "Le eresie medioevali," in *Grande antol. filos.*, IV, 1618) that the Circumcisers were probably a separate party, who did not reject Christian sacraments but did require in addition to them the strict observance of Mosaic Law and especially circumcision.

3. Various judgments have been made by scholars: that the Passagians were an offshoot of the Cathars; that they were a reaction against Catharist attacks on the Old Testament; that they were somehow related to the Waldenses (see the references cited in Borst, p. 112, n. 11).

4. *The* Summa *Ascribed to Praepositinus*, pp. xiv-xv.

5. Charles Molinier, "Les Passagiens," *Mémoires de l'Académie des sciences, inscriptions, et belles-lettres de Toulouse*, 8th ser., X (1888), 448-49.

6. A portion of the treatise found under the name of Bonacursus (No. 25) also presents Passagian doctrines; the passage is translated in n. 86, below.

7. The name of Prevostin is coupled with the tract in one manuscript and his authorship was proposed by George Lacombe, who admitted that the proof was not decisive (*La Vie et les œuvres de Prévostin*, pp. 43, 131-52; cf. his "Prévostin," *DTC*, XIII, 165-66). One manuscript gives the author's name as *G. Pergamensis*; two name him as *Magister Gallus* (perhaps indicating only that he was French; see *The* Summa *Ascribed to Praepositinus*, p. xiii). Käppeli ("Une Somme contre les hérétiques," *AFP*, XVII [1947], 311, n. 36) speculates on the possibility that the heretic Peter Gallus might have written the tract after he was converted to Catholicism.

8. *The* Summa *Ascribed to Praepositinus*, p. xv, although a date as late as 1230 has been advanced elsewhere; see Borst, p. 14, n. 3.

9. Dondaine ("Nouvelles Sources," *RSPT*, XXVIII [1939], 482) suggested that the number of manuscripts and the variations in the tradition of the text might be explained if the treatise had been used for instruction and the manuscripts were copies produced by students.

10. They may have been Waldenses or some associated group, for, while they accepted the validity of the priestly orders and the Eucharist, their complaints against the Church are characteristic of the Waldenses and their "fellow travelers."

11. We adapt the phrase from Borst, who discussed this type of antiheretical literature (pp. 13-21).

12. Garvin and Corbett have traced the author's dependence on Peter Lombard and the glossators for the exposition of texts cited by both Catholic and heretic. We have only occasionally reproduced these references in our notes, although we have thankfully profited by their apparatus in general.

13. See their remarks on the problem in their Introduction, pp. l-lv, lvii-lviii.

14. Numerous other works which touch, for the most part quite briefly, on the author and the treatise are cited in Borst, p. 14, n. 3.

15. Isa. 44:24,26.

16. Isa. 42:1, but the last four words are from Matt. 12:18.

17. Isa. 45:8, a few words omitted.

18. *Creavit me:* In the Vulgate Prov. 8:22 reads *possedit me in initio viarum suarum*, which is translated in the Douay and King James versions as "possessed me in the beginning of his ways" (or "way"); in the Revised Standard Version as "created me at the beginning of his work." The reading "way(s)" is based on the Hebrew; "works" on the Greek of the Septuagint. The Hebrew *qānāh* can mean either "possessed" or "created." Cf. *Interpreter's Bible*, IV, 830.

19. Ecclus. 1:4.

20. Ecclus. 24:14.

21. Matt. 20:8.

22. Matt. 28:18.

23. Mark 13:32.

24. John 5:46.

25. Matt. 26:39

26. John 10:33-36, with some changes in wording.

27. Ps. 81 (A.V. 82):6.

28. John 17:22.

29. John 10:30.

30. John 14:28.

31. I Cor. 15:28.

32. Isa. 42:8.

33. Ecclus. 31:10.

34. Apoc. 1:4-5.

35. Matt. 5:17.

36. Matt. 5:18.

37. Matt. 5:19.

38. *Ibid.*

39. Matt. 5:20.

40. Matt. 8:4.

41. Matt. 23:2-3.

42. Matt. 7:12.

43. Cf. I Tim. 4:4.

44. Matt. 22:35-40.

45. Rom. 3:31.

46. Rom. 7:12.
47. Rom. 7:14.
48. Jas. 2:10.
49. Gen. 17:4,9-11,13-14.
50. Ezech. 44:9.
51. John 7:23.
52. The text reads: *Ergo secundum animam vel secundum corpus; secundum corpus; non ergo secundum animam. Ergo mundabat animam.* We amend the punctuation of the second phrase to *secundum corpus non; ergo secundum animam.* Note the parallel passage on the same page (p. 121): [*non*] *in carne enim ... ergo in anima.*
53. Rom. 2:25.
54. Gal. 2:7.
55. Rom. 15:8. Douay: "made unto the fathers."
56. Gen. 2:3.
57. Identified by the editors as Peter Comestor.
58. Exod. 20:8,10.
59. Exod. 35:3.
60. Exod. 31:15-17.
61. Deut. 5:13-14.
62. Jer. 17:21-22.
63. Gen. 9:3-4.
64. Lev. 17:14.
65. Acts 15:28.
66. Lev. 5:1.
67. The reference is to one of the medieval commentators who "glossed" the texts. See n. 12, above.
68. Lev. 13:18.
69. Exod. 30:13,15.
70. Lev. 10:1-2.
71. Lev. 19:35-36.
72. Deut. 4:2.
73. Deut. 12:32.
74. Isa. 29:13, quoted approximately as in the Septuagint, from which it passed into Mark 7:7 and Matt. 15:9.
75. Isa. 40:9.
76. Osee 5:10. The other version referred to is the Septuagint.
77. Jonas 2:9.
78. Ps. 103 (A.V. 104):12.
79. These words are taken from Peter Lombard's commentary on Ps. 103:13 (Migne, *PL*, CXCI, 933-34). An English translation of Augustine's *Expositions on the Book of Psalms* (ed. and condensed from the Oxford translation by A. C. Coxe) may be found in *A Select Library of the Nicene and Post-Nicene Fathers*, ed. by Philip Schaff, Vol. VIII. The passage here referred to is on p. 513.

80. Cf. Ps. 103 (A.V. 104):10.
81. Ps. 103 (A.V. 104):12.
82. Prov. 30:5-6.
83. Matt. 5:17.
84. Rom. 15:18-19.
85. Gal. 1:9.
86. Apoc. 22:18. Among the additions to the confession of Bonacursus (No. 25) was a statement on the Passagians (Migne, *PL*, CCIV, 784) which may be compared with the foregoing: "Therefore, observe, you who know it not, how wicked is the faith and teaching of such persons. First, they say that the law of Moses must be observed to the letter and that the Sabbath, circumcision, and other observances of the Law should still be in force. They also say that Christ, the Son of God, is not equal to the Father, and that the Father, the Son, and the Holy Spirit, these three persons, are not one God and one substance. Furthermore, to augment their error, they judge and condemn all the doctors of the Church and the whole Roman Church, all in all. But since they seek to defend this error of theirs by the testimony of the New Testament and of the prophets, we shall, aided by the grace of Christ, kill it with their own sword, as David did Goliath." What then follows is a list of scriptural texts which might be used in refutation of these errors.

27. AN ACCOUNT OF THE HOSPITALITY
OF HERETICS BY YVES OF NARBONNE

1. Robert of Curson (the place name is variously spelled in the sources) was of English birth, studied at Paris, and was canon at Noyon and Paris before he became cardinal-priest of San Stefano in Monte Celio in 1212. As papal legate in France from 1213, he was especially occupied with preaching the crusade to deliver Jerusalem, but shifted his attention to the Albigensian Crusade and heresy about the end of that year. He was in southern France with the crusading forces, but left before January, 1215, in which year he was instrumental in providing regulations for the University of Paris. In 1218, he was sent to accompany the crusaders who attacked Damietta, where he died sometime after August of that year. See *DNB*, V, 344; also Marcel and Christine Dickson, "Le Cardinal Robert de Courçon," *AHDLMA*, IX (1934), 53-142.

2. See, for example, Käppeli, "Une Somme contre les hérétiques," *AFP*, XVII (1947), 307-8, 310; Dondaine, "La Hiérarchie cathare, I," *AFP*, XIX (1949), 288, 290; and Borst, pp. 105, n. 28; 249, n. 6.

3. The sect name "Patarines" as equivalent to "Cathars" is first encountered in the sources in 1179 in canon 27 of the Third Lateran Council (Mansi, *Concilia*, XXII, 209). It is reminiscent of the reforming Pataria of eleventh-century Milan (see The Introduction, p. 23, above). By mid-thirteenth century, the terms *Cathari* and *Patarini* had become common and

interchangeable in Italy. The question of how and why this happened has produced a great deal of learned discussion which also draws in the problem of the origin of the eleventh-century word *Pataria*. St. Augustine had mentioned heretics known to him as *Paterniani* (see No. 24, n. 14), but they do not seem to enter the question here. Runciman (*Medieval Manichee*, p. 103) thinks *Patarini* (or *Paterini*) might come from *patera*, a Latin word designating a utensil used in religious services. Guiraud (*Histoire de l'Inquisition*, I, 142) suggests that it might derive from *Pater* [Father] in the Lord's Prayer, or be a corruption of *Cathari* through *Catherini*. Duvernoy ("Un Traité cathare," *Cahiers d'études cathares*, 2d ser., XIII [1962], 24, n. 3), on the other hand, thinks that *Patari* gave rise to *Cathari*. Morghen ("Movimenti religiosi popolari," in *Relazione del X Congresso*, III, 335) argues that *Patarini* became a general term meaning "heretics" and thus was applied to the Cathars, although the Patarine and dualistic heresies were quite different (*ibid.*, p. 347). Werner ("Παταρηνοι-Patarini," in *Von Mittelalter zur Neuzeit*, 404-19, esp. 404-6) believes the word must be traced to Greek origins because the agitation of the Pataria gave occasion and impetus to the spread of Bogomil heresy in the eleventh century. Dondaine has recently suggested ("Durand de Huesca," *AFP*, XXIX [1959], 276) that the word came from Πατεριτσα designating a staff in the form of a *T* which was the mark of pastoral dignity carried by Basilian monks and by "Good Christians" of Bosnia and was also the cross of the patriarch of Constantinople. One medieval derivation of *Patarini* from *pati* [suffer] will be found in No. 42, part B.

4. There are many reports of couriers moving between heretical groups in Languedoc and Italy; see Guiraud, *Histoire de l'Inquisition*, Vol. II, chap. IX.

5. *Rabiolas:* "Raisins" (*uvae crispae*) is suggested by Du Cange, but J. H. Baxter and C. Johnson, *Medieval Latin Word-list from British and Irish Sources* (London, 1934), translate it as "rissoles."

6. See No. 23, n. 59.

7. Wiener Neustadt, twenty-eight miles south of Vienna, a town founded in the twelfth century at the junction of trade routes which converge on Vienna from the south. The route Yves followed from Italy is approximately that of the present rail line from Gemona to Vienna.

8. *Beguini:* The name is of uncertain origin. Early in the thirteenth century it began to be applied, probably as a corruption of *Albigenses*, to communities of religious women who put themselves under the direction of the Cistercian order with the desire to pursue lives of penitence and poverty. Thereafter it designated various religious groups of unconventional character, both orthodox and heretical. Beguins and Beghards in northern Europe were, by and large, orthodox, although they displayed tendencies toward mysticism and were perhaps influenced to some degree by Cathars. Beguins of southern France in the fourteenth century shared the intensely held convictions of the Spiritual Franciscans and were prosecuted as heretics (see

No. 55, IV). On the name see Frédégand Callaey, "Lambert li Beges et les Béguines," *RHE*, XXIII (1927), 254-59; McDonnell, *Beguines and Beghards*, pp. 430-38; Borst, p. 249, n. 6. For a convenient summary of the whole religious movement of which the Beguins were a part, see Grundmann, *Ketzergeschichte*, pp. 47-58. Hostility between Beguins and Albigenses in the early fourteenth century is revealed by a witness before the Inquisition in 1308 or 1309 who told of the murder of *quendam beguinum*. The Beguin was kidnaped and killed, the witness said, because "the said Beguin betrayed Christians, that is, heretics, and ambushed them in order to take them captive and turn them over to inquisitors" (Döllinger, *Beiträge*, II, 18-19).

28. A DEBATE BETWEEN CATHOLICS AND HERETICS

1. On the date, see Claude Devic and Joseph Vaissete, *Histoire générale de Languedoc*, ed. by Auguste Molinier *et al.*, VII, 1-5.

2. Canon 4 (Mansi, *Concilia*, XXII, 1177-78).

3. See, for example, No. 29 and No. 34.

4. Not long afterward, Cathars of France and Italy are reported to have met in council near Toulouse to discuss various affairs, see No. 23, n. 12.

5. It was translated in part in Samuel R. Maitland, *Facts and Documents Illustrative of the History, Doctrine and Rites of the Ancient Albigenses and Waldenses*, pp. 140-45. There is also an abridged version under the year 1176 in the chronicle of Roger of Hoveden (as cited in the introduction to No. 29), Vol. II, pp. 105-17.

6. *Boni homines:* The Cathars thus referred to those who had received the consolamentum, never using the term "Perfect," which, however, became common usage among their Catholic contemporaries and has been perpetuated by historians. This is the earliest known appearance of the term "Good Men." Grundmann (*Religiöse Bewegungen*, p. 22, n. 17) and Borst (p. 242, n. 11) cite numerous other occurrences in the sources. "Good men" was also a collective term applied to magistrates, officials, and distinguished attendants in legal hearings during the Middle Ages, as the use in the next sentence of our text illustrates.

7. The town and castle were held from the bishop of Albi by a "consortium" of nobles, related to each other (Lacger, "L'Albigeois pendant la crise de l'albigéisme," *RHE*, XXIX [1933], 281).

8. Neither the text which was the basis for the editions in Bouquet, *Recueil*, and Mansi, *Concilia*, nor that given by Roger of Hoveden accurately preserved the names of the ecclesiastics which follow, but the editor of our text, Dom Brial, has in many cases supplied them in his notes; these are in accord with the names given in the *Histoire de Languedoc* (Vol. IV, *passim*; VI, 3; VII, 2-4) by the authors and editors. We have corrected our text by reference to these studies.

9. I Cor. 7:9 (?).

10. Jas. 5:16.

11. Matt. 5:34-37; Jas. 5:12.
12. I Tim. 3:2-7; Tit. 1:7-9.
13. Of him nothing further is known.
14. Matt. 7:15.
15. Alexander III (1159-1181).
16. Louis VII (1137-1180).
17. Raymond V (1148-1194).
18. Raymond Trencavel (1150-1167), who was viscount of Albi, Béziers, Carcassonne, and Razès.
19. Cf. Juvenal *Sat.* ii.79-81.
20. Cf. Jas. 5:12; Matt. 5:34-37.

29. ACTION AGAINST HERESY IN TOULOUSE

1. On the situation in Toulouse, one example of the views of a horrified contemporary may suffice. Henry, abbot of Clairvaux, who played an important part in the events described in this translation, wrote of Toulouse, which he called the mother of heresy and the source of error: "Verily, we had not been told the third part of all the evil abominations which that noble city nourished in the bosom of its unbelief. The place of abomination of desolation (Matt. 24:15) was fixed therein and the counterpart of the reptiles of the prophets (cf. Jer. 8:17; Eccles. 10:11) had secured a dwelling among its hiding places. There the heretics ruled the people and reigned among the clergy, so that like people, like priest (Osee 4:9), and the life of the pastor was itself shaped for the ruin of the flock. Heretics spoke and all applauded. A Catholic spoke and they said, 'What is this?' making it seem wondrous and miraculous if anyone was found among them who would even dare to whisper about the word of faith. So much had the pestilence prevailed upon the land that they had not only created priests and pontiffs for themselves but had evangelists who, spoiling and canceling out the true Gospel, forged a new gospel for them and from their hearts wickedly preached a fresh teaching to the deluded people. . . . Upon our arrival there, so great was the license of the heretics everywhere that as we pursued our proper course through the streets and squares they railed at us, pointed their fingers at us, shouted at us that we were imposters, hypocrites, heretics (Roger of Hoveden *Chronica*, II, 160-61). Complaints hardly less severe had been voiced in a letter of 1173 from the archbishop of Narbonne (Bouquet, *Recueil*, XVI, 159-60).

2. Gervase of Canterbury *Chronica*, ed. by William Stubbs, in *The Historical Works of Gervase of Canterbury*, I, 270-71.

3. The letters are printed in Migne, *PL*, CCIV, 235-42, CXCIX, 1120-24, as well as in the edition of Roger of Hoveden and in the chronicle cited in n. 4.

4. *Gesta regis Henrici secundi Benedicti abbatis*, ed. by William Stubbs, I, 198-200. The chronicle is no longer assigned to Benedict's authorship.

5. The author is referring to his report of the confrontation at Lombers, (No. 28), which he dates 1176. On the name "Arians," see No. 6, n. 9.

6. Claudian xv.384. The report in the *Gesta regis Henrici*, which Roger of Hoveden is here paraphrasing, strikes a more martial note, saying (pp. 198-99) that the kings decided to send "wise and bellicose" men to convert the heretics or to drive them away.

7. Peter of Pavia, subsequently cardinal-bishop of Tusculum and archbishop of Bourges (1180), although he never occupied the see of Bourges. Peter was twice papal legate to France (1174-1178 and 1180-1182); see Hippolyte Delehaye, "Pierre de Pavie," *RQH*, XLIX (1891), 5-61.

8. Guarin (1174-1180) and Pons of Arsac (1162-1181), respectively. The latter was deposed in 1181 by Henry of Marcy, acting as papal legate.

9. Reginald Fitz-Jocelin (1174-1191) and John of the Fair Hands (1162-1179). The latter, when he became archbishop of Lyons, was to have difficulties with Waldes of Lyons and his followers (see No. 33).

10. Henry of Marcy entered Clairvaux about 1156, became abbot of Hautecombe in 1160, and of Clairvaux in 1176. In 1179 he became cardinal-bishop of Albano; he died in 1188. He, too, was to have further experience with heretics, as the leader of a brief crusade (see n. 28, below) and when he received Waldes's profession of faith in Lyons (see No. 32); see Congar, "Henri de Marcy," *Studia Anselmiana*, XLIII; *Analecta Monastica*, V (1958), 1-38

11. Acts 8:15-16.

12. Raymond II (1143-1190).

13. This was Peter Mauran, one of the ten wealthiest men in the city, according to Henry of Marcy (as quoted in *Gesta regis Henrici*, p. 215). The Mauran family was important in the bourg, for it was rising in wealth and was much involved in the social disturbances consequent upon the shifting fortunes of the landlord and business classes of Toulouse. The Mauran clan also owned considerable real property outside the town. See Mundy, *Liberty and Political Power:* on the social situation at the time, pp. 59-66; on the mission of 1178, pp. 60-62.

14. The abbot of Clairvaux in his letter (Roger of Hoveden *Chronica*, II, 165) calls Peter's residence, in which Peter allegedly held heretical conventicles, a *castrum*. Roger of Hoveden and the *Gesta Henrici*, which he is here following, make mention of two *castella* and in a subsequent passage "towers" (*turres*) which were to be destroyed. The house in the bourg was fortified with a strong tower; the one outside the walls might have been the "little fortress" at Valsegur (see Mundy, *Liberty and Political Power,* p. 61). On the problem of the word *castrum*, see No. 5, n. 6.

15. The disclosure was no doubt the result of the legate's demand that the bishop and consuls of Toulouse in conjunction with certain clergy and lay citizens furnish him with the names of notorious heretics (Roger of Hoveden *Chronica*, II, 161 [letter of Henry of Clairvaux]).

16. Peter Mauran, probably relying on the influence of his family and

friends, had ignored a first summons but was persuaded by the count to appear. He denied any heresy, although informants had described him as "the prince" of the sect and reported that he referred to himself as John the Evangelist. After demurring at an oath to attest his innocence, he yielded and then, at the moment of swearing, broke down and confessed that he had denied the reality of the sacrifice in the Eucharist (*ibid.*, pp. 162-64). His recantation involves this error alone—information we owe to the kindness of Professor John Mundy, who discovered the text of the confession in the archives of St. Sernin.

17. Either this Peter Mauran or his son and namesake was elected consul in Toulouse in 1183-1184 (Mundy, *Liberty and Political Power*, p. 270, n. 8).

18. Raymond of Baimac may have been the second bishop of the Catharist church of Val d'Aran (Borst, p. 234), but see the denial that there was such a church, cited in No. 23, n. 12. Bernard Raymond is named as the bishop of the Catharist church of Toulouse, elected at the council of Saint-Félix-de-Caraman (Dondaine, "Les Actes du concile albigeois," in *Miscellanea Giovanni Mercati*, V, 326).

19. Cf. II Cor. 11:14.

20. The two men had taken refuge with Roger Trencavel II (1167-1194), viscount of Béziers. Abbot Henry and the bishop of Bath had gone on a side trip to persuade Roger to release the bishop of Albi, whom he was holding prisoner. In that mission they were not successful, but they did encounter the two heretics here named, who apparently accepted an opportunity to defend themselves publicly (Roger of Hoveden *Chronica*, II, 165-66 [letter of Henry of Clairvaux], and p. 156 [letter of Peter of Pavia]).

21. Matt. 5:34,37.

22. Ps. 109 (A.V. 110):4.

23. Gen. 22:16.

24. Cf. Heb. 6:16.

25. I Thess. 4:14 (A.V. 15).

26. Rom. 1:9.

27. Cf. Ps. 77 (A.V. 78):57.

28. This was not the last encounter of the chief actors in these events. In 1181, Henry of Marcy, then cardinal and legate to France, led a crusade (the first within Christian lands) against heretics and their protectors in the lands of the viscount of Béziers. The fortress of Lavaur yielded to siege, and among the prisoners were Raymond of Baimac and Bernard Raymond. They were converted and became canons in churches in Toulouse (see Maisonneuve, p. 135; Lea, *History of the Inquisition*, I, 124; and Congar, "Henri de Marcy" [as cited in n. 10], pp. 36-38).

30. THE ORIGINS OF THE WALDENSIAN HERESY

1. These names are used interchangeably in the sources of the thirteenth century; but see Walter Mohr, "Waldes und das frühe Waldensertum," *Zeit-*

schrift für Religions- und Geistesgeschichte, IX (1957), 337-63, esp. 347-54, for the theory that the different names used in the earliest documents are significant evidence of a split among Waldes's followers (cf. No. 33, n. 7).

2. His name appears in documents of the late twelfth century and the thirteenth as *Valdesius* or some variant thereof (*Wandesius, Valdexius, Gualdesius,* etc.). There seems no good reason not to use the form "Waldes" in English. Although "Peter Waldo" has become the usual way of referring to him in English, it is not justified from contemporary sources, for the name Peter does not appear in documents until the second half of the fourteenth century (Gonnot, "Waldensia," *RHPR,* XXXIII [1953], 243-48). Gonnet suggests that Waldensian apologists were then seeking to trace the origins of their faith back to the earliest days of Christianity, for which "Peter" would have important connotations.

3. This interpretation has been frequently advanced in recent years; see Davison, *Forerunners of St. Francis,* chap. VII; Pouzet, "Les Origines lyonnaises," *Revue d'histoire de l'église de France,* XXII (1936), 6 and n. 3; Dondaine, "Aux Origines du Valdéisme," *AFP,* XVI (1946), 230; Gonnet, "Waldensia", *RHPR,* XXXIII (1953), 220-22; and Marthaler, "Forerunners of the Franciscans," *Franciscan Studies,* new ser., XVIII (1958), 133-42.

4. See also n. 145 to the Introduction. One may consult the studies of the sources and the comprehensive bibliographies in the works of Giovanni Gonnet, especially *Il Valdismo medioevale,* and "Il movimento valdese in Europà secondo le piu recenti ricerche (sec. XII-XVI)," *Bollettino della Società di studi Valdesi,* C (1956), 21-30; and the collection of sources in his *Enchiridion fontium Valdensium.* See also Gottfried Koch, "Neue Quellen und Forschungen über die Anfänge der Waldenser," *Forschungen und Fortschritten,* XXXII (1958), 141-49; and Manselli, *Studi sulle eresie,* chap. IV.

5. *Gallie:* the term our author uses for this region of France. Actually, the city of Lyons, along with the kingdom of Arles, had in 1032 been ceded to the Holy Roman Empire by the will of Rudolph III and was still technically under imperial authority.

6. St. Alexis was a fourth-century ascetic whose story was the subject of a poem in French, written about 1040. Son of a wealthy member of the equestrian order in Rome, Alexis married but immediately left home and wife for a mendicant life as a Christian in Syria. After many years he returned to Rome and, unrecognized, begged shelter in his old home. Only on his deathbed was his true identity revealed. The poem seems to have enjoyed great popularity in the eleventh and twelfth centuries and was frequently recited in castle and town. See Joseph Bédier and Paul Hazard, *Littérature française,* new ed. by Pierre Martino, I, 8-9. There is an English translation in *The Oldest Monuments of the French Language* (Oxford and London, 1912), pp. 28-56, and a prose version of the poem in Davison, *Forerunners of St. Francis,* pp. 239-43.

7. Matt. 19:21.
8. In 1173 from May 27 to August 1.
9. August 15.
10. Matt. 6:24.
11. Guichard (1165-1180/81). On the date of his death, see No. 32, n. 1.
12. Cf. Matt. 10:9; 6:34.

31. THE WALDENSES AT THE THIRD LATERAN COUNCIL

1. On this council see the first part of the Introduction, n. 140.

2. Mohr ("Waldes," *Zeitschrift für Religions- und Geistesgeschichte*, IX [1957], 345) argues that this statement cannot be taken literally, since Walter Map, who was present at the council, did not record the participation of Waldes.

3. Probably the archbishop of Lyons had already sought to restrain Waldes and his friends from preaching in public and thus prompted their appeal to the pope (Pouzet, "Les Origines lyonnaises," *Revue d'histoire de l'église de France*, XXII [1936], 14). Moneta of Cremona, writing sixty years later (*Adversus Catharos et Valdenses*, pp. 402-3), says that the pope insisted that their preaching conform to the teaching of four Church Fathers: Ambrose, Augustine, Gregory, and Jerome. It was the works of these fathers which the Waldenses of the early fourteenth century were said to cherish (see No. 55, II, 1), although some sources state that they used them only selectively; see Dondaine, "Durand de Huesca," *AFP*, XXIX (1959), 274.

4. We here follow James, who in his translation (p. 65) prefers *in quo* (which was the reading of the manuscript) to the *cifo* of his printed text.

5. Cf. Matt. 7:6.

6. Cf. Ps. 132 (A.V. 133):2.

7. Cf. Prov. 5:16.

8. Cf. Ps. 10:3 (A.V. 11:2).

9. Cf. Ps. 62:12 (A.V. 63:11).

10. *Qui respondere parabam.* Cf. Vergil *Eclogues* VII.5: *et respondere parati.*

11. This echoes a very old joke that may be traced back at least to republican Rome (see *Thesaurus linguae latinae*, III, 448, *s.v.* "carduus").

12. That is, by their answer the Waldenses seemed to put the Virgin on an equality with the Trinity and aroused derision at their ignorance of so fundamental a point of theology.

13. Ovid *Met.* II.192.

14. Cf. Acts 2:44.

32. A PROFESSION OF FAITH BY WALDES OF LYONS

1. The date is fixed by that of Guichard's death: probably July, 1180, according to Jean Leclercq ("Le Témoignage de Geoffroy d'Auxerre sur la vie Cistercienne," *Studia Anselmiana*, XXXI; *Analecta monastica*, II [1953], 195, n. 4); but more correctly on or before September 27, 1181, according to Ph. Pouzet ("La Vie de Guichard, abbé de Pontigny [1136-1165] et archevêque de Lyon [1165-1181]," *Bulletin de la Société littéraire, historique et archéologique de Lyon*, X [1929], 117-50). Christine Thouzellier ("La Profession trinitaire," *RTAM*, XXVII [1960], 267) prefers the date 1180.

2. Leclercq, "Le Témoignage de Geoffroy d'Auxerre" (as cited in n. 1), p. 195. Geoffrey made this statement in a sermon prepared some years later, in which he calls Waldes *Wandesius*.

3. The profession stands at the head of one of the two manuscript copies of a tract against the Cathars, the *Liber antiheresis*, written by Durand of Huesca (see item xii in the list of polemics in the Appendix; and No. 36 for Durand's career).

4. In the *Statuta ecclesiae antiqua*, attributed to Caesarius of Arles (502-542), in Migne, *PL*, LVI, 879-80; another version ascribed to a supposed council of Carthage in A.D. 398 passed into the pseudo-Isidorian *Collectio canonum* (Migne, *PL*, LXXXIV, 199-200). See also Dondaine, "Aux Origines du Valdéisme," *AFP*, XVI (1946), 202. See also n. 11, below.

5. As a *professio fidei* it also appears in an *Ordo Romanus antiquus* (tenth century?) published in *Maxima bibliotheca veterum patrum*, XIII, 708. It is also similar to one found in the *Liber diurnus*, a collection of documents and formulas useful to papal notaries (see the *Liber diurnus Romanorum pontificum*, ed by E. Rozière, No. 73).

6. Julien Havet, *Lettres de Gerbert (983-997)*, Letter 180, pp. 161 f. There is an English translation in *The Letters of Gerbert with His Papal Privileges as Sylvester II*, trans. by Harriet Pratt Lattin, Letter 192, pp. 224-25.

7. Ilarino da Milano, "Le eresie popolari," in *Studi Gregoriani*, II, 44-46; see also Borst, p. 73, n. 3.

8. Paul Ewald, "Vita Gauzlini abbatis Floriacensis von Andreas von Fleury (ca. 1041)," *Neues Archiv der Gesellschaft für ältere deutsche Geschichtskunde*, III (1878), 351-83. The episode at Orléans is recounted in chap. XLIV, the profession is given in chap. XLV. There is another comparable tradition of a profession of faith, which apparently derives from the form used in the Roman rite of ordination of bishops. The Roman version is printed in L. A. Muratori, *Liturgia Romana vetus*, II, 436-38. Pope Leo IX (1048-1054) used this as a statement of faith in a letter (April 13, 1053) to Peter, bishop of Antioch (Migne, *PL*, CXLIII, 769-73; English translation in Denzinger, *Sources of Catholic Dogma*, trans. by Deferrari, pp. 140-42). The differences—comparing the profession of Gerbert with that of Leo IX—are Leo's omission of the statements denying opposition to marriage or to eating meat, and denying that the devil was evil by nature.

This form of the profession of faith was to be useful in later years. It was sent to the Eastern emperor Michael Palaeologus in 1267 and was returned by him to Gregory X and the Council of Lyons in 1274 (Mansi, *Concilia,* XXIV, 70; English translation in Denzinger, *Sources of Catholic Dogma,* pp. 183-85). See also Dondaine, "Aux Origines du Valdéisme," *AFP,* XVI (1946), 201.

9. Waldes's profession was developed into a basic formula for reconciliation of heretics to which Innocent III perhaps refers when he mentions an oath for converts "in the form of the Church which is customarily offered by such persons" (letter to the bishop of Verona, December 6, 1199 [*Regesta* II.228, in Migne, *PL,* CCXIV, 789]). For its use by some converts from the Waldenses in 1208 and 1210, see No. 36. Together with the profession in the Roman tradition, mentioned in the preceding note, it influenced the phrasing of the first canon of the Fourth Lateran Council (Mansi, *Concilia,* XXII, 982; English translation in Petry, *History of Christianity,* pp. 322-23), which became the decretal *Firmiter credimus* of Gregory IX (*Corpus iuris canonici, Decretales Gregorii IX.* Lib. I. Tit. 1. cap. 1 [Friedberg, II, 5-6]). With a few further amendments it appears under the title *Qualiter debeant heresim abiurare et fidem catholicam confiteri, si ab heresi convertuntur,* in the commentary of Benedict of Alignan on that decretal in the mid-thirteenth century (see item xxvi in the list of polemics in the Appendix). The oath is one of the pieces printed by Douais, as noted there.

10. Jas. 2:17.

11. Since the preceding introduction and these notes were written, Christine Thouzellier has published a detailed analysis of Waldes's profession of faith in her *Catharisme et Valdéisme,* pp. 27-36. There the text of the profession is collated with the *Statuta ecclesiae antiqua* (which is assigned to the fifth century), as it is published in the edition of Ch. Munier (Paris, 1960). Mlle Thouzellier ascribes the preparation of the profession on that ancient base to the cardinal-legate (or perhaps to the Roman chancery), who added the new elements necessitated by experiences in Languedoc. To Waldes are attributed the phrases specifying the creeds, affirming his orthodoxy in respect of the sacraments and marriage, and stating his respect for the hierarchy. It is supposed that in return for his disavowal of heresy, the appended statement of his apostolic program was accepted.

33. STEPHEN OF BOURBON ON THE EARLY WALDENSES

1. Matt. 5:3. The term "Poor in Spirit" is one that the Waldenses applied to themselves; see No. 46, § 1.

2. Cant. 3:2.

3. John was archbishop from 1181 to 1193. Stephen of Bourbon has confused the earlier ban on preaching by Archbishop Guichard with the

expulsion of Waldes and his group by Archbishop John after 1181.

4. Acts 5:29.

5. Mark 16:15.

6. The reference to a condemnation in Rome at a council held "before the Lateran Council" (by which Stephen means that of 1215) is puzzling. The Waldenses were not condemned at the Third Lateran Council of 1179. Possibly Stephen confused it with the Council of Verona, 1184, at which they were excommunicated. A. W. Dieckhoff (*Die Waldenser im Mittelalter,* pp. 182, 343 f.) suggested that the Waldenses were condemned in a council under Innocent III; his argument is not convincing.

7. A thesis is advanced by Walter Mohr ("Waldes," *Zeiltschrift für Religions- und Geistesgeschichte,* IX [1957], pp. 337-63) that Waldes died before 1184 and that he had remained true to his vow, but that certain of his companions had refused to follow him in submission to the Church or to admit, as Waldes had done, that anyone who refused to practice holy poverty might be saved. Mohr holds that it was this recalcitrant faction that was subject to condemnation. See also No. 36, n. 31. Mohr does not seem to have noted the comment by Geoffrey of Auxerre (Leclercq, "Le Témoignage de Geoffroy d'Auxerre," *Studia Anselmiana,* XXXI; *Analecta monastica,* II [1953], 195) that after his appearance before the cardinal and council at Lyons Waldes returned to his former ways and continued to gather and commission disciples to preach (*sed reversus ad vomitum colligere et disseminare discipulos non desistit*). Such a statement is not easily explained away.

8. *Baculum penitenciarii et ferramenta.*

34. A DEBATE BETWEEN CATHOLICS AND WALDENSES

1. Probably not long before the death of the bishop in 1191. Libert Verrees, "Le Traité de l'abbé Bernard de Fontcaude contre les Vaudois et les Ariens," *Analecta Praemonstratensia,* XXXI (1955), 30, suggests a date somewhat before 1191.

2. In the manuscripts and in the earlier edition of Jacob Gretser, in *Trias scriptorum adversus Waldensiam sectam* (Ingolstadt, 1614), pp. 3-86, the title adds, "and against the Arians."

3. Lucius III (1181-1185).

4. *Daventria:* Of him nothing more is known.

5. I Pet. 5:4.

6. Acts 5:29.

7. Although rejection of good works on behalf of the deceased and denial of purgatory is later reported of the Waldenses (see No. 52 and No. 54, § 12), this chapter and the following one probably reflect the survival of the heretic Henry's teaching (see No. 13) or the doctrine of the Cathars. Verrees ("Le Traité de l'abbé Bernard," *Analecta Praemonstratensia,* XXXI

[1955], 29-30) doubts that the last four chapters are concerned with the Waldenses, in part because of a change in the style, which no longer seems to reflect a debate.

8. This is a Catharist tenet: see No. 25, n. 26.

9. Possibly this reflects the views of Cathars reported not long after Bernard wrote (see No. 37) which spoke of a "new earth" they would possess after death, before the Last Judgment. See also the later ideas of the Italian, Desiderius (No. 54, § 3).

10. Acts 7:48.

11. This attitude was shared by various sects; but that Bernard had Cathars particularly in mind is indicated by a sentence in the text of chapter XII. "They blaspheme the name of God when they say that He did not create and does not rule the world" (col. 836).

35. ALAN OF LILLE:
A SCHOLAR'S ATTACK ON HERETICS

1. See the works cited in the introductions to Nos. 28 and 37.

2. They have been translated into English: *The Complaint of Nature by Alain de Lille*, trans. by Douglas M. Moffat (New York, 1908); and *The Anticlaudian of Alain de Lille: Prologue, Argument and Nine Books*, trans. by William H. Cornog (Philadelphia, 1935).

3. Twenty-nine manuscripts are enumerated by Guy Raynaud de Lage, *Alain de Lille, poète du XIIᵉ siècle*, p. 42. Three others are Barcelona, Archivo General de la Corona de Aragon, Ripoll, MS 204, fols. 13r-52v; Breslau, Staats und Universitäts Bibliothek, MS I, F. 35; Munich, Bayerische Stadtbibliothek, MS 544, fols. 206-23. This is a larger number of manuscripts than has been discovered for any polemic except that of Rainerius Sacconi (No. 51). Alan's work was also subject to abridgment or distortion. The Munich MS 544, to judge from its partial printing in Döllinger, *Beiträge,* II, 279-85, gives portions of Book I out of their proper order. Another less extensive abridgment is found in Florence, Laurentian Library, Bibliotheca Aedilium, MS 37, fols. 70r-75v, published but not identified by Frederick C. Conybeare ("A Hitherto Unpublished Treatise against the Italian Manichaeans," *American Journal of Theology*, III [1899] 704-28). It distorts Alan's work by bringing chapters on the Cathars and the Waldenses together without differentiating between the sects. Such examples of careless copying are studied in Walter L. Wakefield, "Notes on Some Antiheretical Writings of the Thirteenth Century," *Franciscan Studies*, XXVII (1967), 285-321.

4. Alan uses only the term "heretics" throughout his first book, except in one place (chap. LXIII, Migne, *PL*, CCX, 366), where he writes: "They condemn marriages which restrain the flow of excesses whence, it is reported, they behave in the filthiest of ways in their assemblies. These persons are called Cathars, meaning those who are dissolved through vice, from

catha, that is, a purifying flow. Or [they are called] Cathars, with the meaning 'chaste,' because they make themselves out to be chaste or righteous; or Cathars, from 'cat,' because, it is said, they kiss the hinder parts of a cat, in whose likeness, so they say, Lucifer appears to them."

5. De Lage, *Alain de Lille*, p. 42.

6. Alan left Montpellier for Paris in 1194 (*ibid.*). The treatise is dedicated to Count William VIII of Montpellier (1172-1202), with praise for his action in resisting heresy; if it was written at Montpellier, it was probably composed between 1190 and 1194. However, it is from 1195 on that we have other evidence of antiheretical activity in that city. In that year a council ordered enforcement of the decree of the Third Lateran Council against heretics and mercenaries (Mansi, *Concilia*, XXII, 667-72). In 1199 Innocent III took Count William under apostolic protection and announced to him the appointment of a legate to assist with the work against heresy, as the count had requested (*Regesta* II.298,299, in Migne, *PL*, 860-61). See also the reference to the Waldenses driven from Montpellier in No. 43, part B.

7. Of first importance for the study of Alan's life and work is the earlier investigation by M. B. Hauréau, "Mémoire sur la vie et quelques œuvres d'Alain de Lille," *Mémoires de l'Académie des inscriptions et belles-lettres de l'Institut national de France*, Vol. XXXII, pt. 1 (1886), 1-27; see also Clemens Bäumker, "Handschriftliches zu den Werken des Alanus," *Philosophisches Jahrbuch der Görres-gesellschaft*, VI (1893), 163-75, 417-29. The *De fide catholica* is studied in Cesare Vasoli, "Il 'Contra haereticos' di Alano di Lilla," *BISIAM*, LXXV (1963), 123-72; and in Thouzellier, *Catharisme et valdéisme*, pp. 83-106; its author is discussed in most histories of scholastic philosophy and of the literature of the Middle Ages (references in Borst, pp. 9, n. 17; 10, nn. 18, 19).

8. Matt. 7:18.

9. Gen. 1:2.

10. John 14:30.

11. Matt. 6:24.

12. John 8:44

13. Cf. Rom. 7:20.

14. Rom. 7:23.

15. Cf. Gal. 5:17.

16. *Rationi:* In the text which is paraphrased (Rom. 7:23), the conflict is against mind (*mens*).

17. Matt. 15:24.

18. John 3:13.

19. Matt. 7:15.

20. Cf. the remarks of Walter Map (No. 31, part B).

21. There is a play on words in the Latin: *discipuli, imo muscipuli* [mouse-catchers].

22. Cf. II Thess. 3:10.

23. John 1:6.

24. Jer. 1:5.
25. Amos 1:1.
26. Mal. 3:1, as quoted in Matt. 11:10, Mark 1:2, Luke 7:27.
27. Isa. 1:1-2.
28. Chap. 16.
29. II Par. [II Chron.] 26:16.
30. Rom. 10:15.
31. Chap. 11.
32. Rom. 1:5.
33. Manuals on the "art of preaching" often discussed preaching under divisions such as these. Alan was the author of such a manual: *Summa de arte praedicatoria* (Migne, *PL*, CCX, 109-98). A brief analysis of it will be found in Harry Caplan, "Rhetorical Invention in Some Medieval Tractates on Preaching," *Speculum*, II (1927), 291-92.
34. I Cor. 14:34-35.
35. I Tim. 2:11-12.
36. II Tim. 3:1-7.
37. For comparison with the nearly contemporary work of Bernard of Fontcaude (No. 34) we may note the other errors with which the Waldenses are charged in Alan's other chapters: Some say that they need obey no one but God, yet others would also obey good prelates; some assert that the power to bind and loose belongs only to persons who follow the apostolic life. Believing merit worth more than ordination, they assume the power to bestow blessings, to bind and to loose. They say there is no need to confess to a priest if a layman is available; that absolution given by prelates has no validity; that the prayers of mortal sinners are of no value to the dead; that every lie is a mortal sin and no oath may be taken in any circumstances. No man should be put to death. Preachers ought not to work with their own hands for their livelihood but receive it from their auditors.

36. THE RECONCILIATION OF A GROUP OF WALDENSES TO THE CHURCH

1. See pp. 36-37, above. About the missionary campaigns of 1204-1208 see Mandonnet, *Saint Dominique*, esp. the studies of Vicaire, I, 83-156 (the English translation by Larkin omits some of these); Marie-Humbert Vicaire, *Saint Dominique de Caleruega d'après les documents du XIIIe siècle;* and the same author's *Histoire de Saint Dominique* (English translation as *Saint Dominic and His Times*) esp. Vol. I, chaps. V-VII. For the concept "preaching and example," see Christine Thouzellier, "La Pauvreté, arme contre l'Albigéisme en 1206," *RHR*, CLI (1957), 79-92.
2. Among the significant products of research on heresy in recent years has been the revelation of the polemical activity of Durand of Huesca and his associates; see the Introduction, p. 61, and also the list of polemical

tracts in the Appendix. A conference on the religious history of the Midi of France, held at Fanjeaux, France, in July, 1966, was devoted to the Waldenses of Languedoc. A brief report is given in *RHE*, LXI (1966), 1003; the record of the session is printed in *Cahiers de Fanjeaux*, Vol. II (Toulouse, 1966). Contributors to the discussion called attention to Durand's importance in bringing back to the Church Waldenses in the vicinity of Narbonne; the antipathy of the Waldenses for the Cathars; and the probability that Durand should be known as Durand of Osca (from Osques in Rouergue, France) rather than of Huesca (in Spain).

3. *Cronica*, ed. by J. Bessyier, in *Troisièmes Mélanges d'histoire du moyen âge*, p. 127 (translation ours). William of Puylaurens's narrative and Peter of Vaux-de Cernay's *Historia albigensis* are the chief sources for the debates of 1207-1208. Passages from them describing the disputation at Pamiers are reprinted in Gonnet, *Enchiridion*, I, 126-28.

4. Johann B. Pierron, *Die katholischen Armen*, pp. 53-67.

5. *Regesta* XII.17 (April 3, 1209), in Migne, *PL*, CCXVI, 29-30; Potthast 3694. Cf. Luigi Zanoni, "Valdesi a Milano nel secolo XIII," *Archivio storico lombardo*, 4th ser., XVII (1912), 5-22; and Pierron, *Die katholischen Armen*, pp. 31-32.

6. See No. 45, parts B and C.

7. The connection between Durand's potential converts and the Poor *lombardo*, 4th ser., XVII (1912), 5-22; and Pierron, *Die katholischen Armen*, following facts: After the Poor Lombards broke with the Poor of Lyons in 1205, they quarreled among themselves at a gathering near Milan. Some who split off at that time were called "those of the meadow" (*illi de prato*); see No. 45, part C, § 26. In his letter of April 3, 1209 (cited in n. 5, above), instructing the archbishop of Milan to investigate Durand's request, Innocent wrote: "Almost a hundred other persons have sought to be reconciled, with the proviso that you see fit to grant them . . . a certain meadow, which had once been turned over to them by the commune of Milan, where a school was built (*quoddam pratum quod commune Mediolanense ipsis olim concesserat in quo schola constructa*) . . . Your predecessor of good memory caused it to be destroyed at the time when they were under excommunication but it is now rebuilt," The identity of the disgruntled Poor Lombards, who were associated with a certain *pratum*, and the potential converts, also associated with a certain *pratum*, which had been the site of heretical meetings, seems undeniable. It may be added that Mlle Thouzellier has come to the same conclusion in her detailed study of the Poor Catholics; see *Catharisme et Valdéisme*, p. 226.

8. In 1245 a witness before the Inquisition recalled having seen Bernard Prim, "a Waldensian heretic," disputing with a Cathar in the year 1208 or thereabouts (Douais, "Les Hérétiques du comté de Toulouse," *Bulletin théologique, scientifique et littéraire de l'Institut catholique de Toulouse*, new ser., III [1892], 164). For another reference to Bernard, see also No. 45, part C, § 26.

9. *Regesta* xiii.94 (June 14, 1210), in Migne, *PL,* CCXVI, 289-93; Potthast 4014. Their statement of faith and proposal for a society is also printed in Gonnet, *Enchiridion*, I, 136-40. It belongs to the long tradition of professions of faith, though it differs from the statements of Durand and Waldes in various phrases. The proposed way of life also differs from that of the Poor Catholics by more emphasis on community life and labor, less on preaching and disputation. This rule was revised and reissued on July 23, 1212 (*Regesta* xv.137, in Migne, *PL,* CCVI, 648-50; Potthast 4567). There is only one other reference to the Reconciled Poor in the letters of Innocent III: August 1, 1212 (*Regesta* xv.146, in Migne, *PL,* CCXVI, 668; Potthast 4569).

10. *Regesta* xiii.78 (May 12, 1210), in Migne, *PL,* CCXVI, 274-75; Potthast 3998. The passages to which we refer were actually placed in the printed text of the letter of December 18, 1208, by the editor, with a note indicating that he transposed them there from the later letter (Migne, *PL,* CCXV, 1512-13). The profession of faith of May 12, 1210, appears in English in Denzinger, *Sources of Catholic Dogma*, pp. 166-68.

11. *Regesta* xv.82 (May 26, 1212), in Migne, *PL,* CCXVI, 602-3; Potthast 4504. See also Thouzellier, *Catharisme et Valdéisme*, pp. 255-59.

12. The pope wrote repeatedly to various prelates urging them to protect the converts from molestation and in 1212 formally placed the society under papal protection (*Regesta* xv.96 [May 29, 1212], in Migne, *PL,* CCXVI, 609; Potthast 4510).

13. Pierron, *Die katholischen Armen*, pp. 47-50; see also No. 45, part C, § 26.

14. On Burchard and his work, see the Introduction to the edition of his chronicle, written by Bernard von Simson, esp. pp. vii-xi, xxvii-xxx; and Wilhelm Wattenbach, *Deutschlands Geschichtsquellen im Mittelalter*, II, 448-50.

15. Under the same date, a copy of this letter was prepared for Durand and also a second one in which exemption from military service and from the need to take oaths in secular affairs was granted to laymen who might accept the supervision of the Poor Catholics (*Regesta* xi.197,198, in Migne, *PL,* CCXV, 1514; Potthast, 3572, 3573).

16. In later letters, full names are given. These initials refer to Bernard of Béziers, John of Narbonne, and either Ermengaud or Ebrinus, all of whom are named in a letter of May 12, 1210 (see n. 10, above). Ermengaud and Ebrinus are not mentioned again; the others were still with Durand of Huesca in 1212, along with William of St. Antonin and Durand of Naiac, whose names had first appeared in 1210 and 1212, respectively. Raymond of St. Paul appears only in the letter of May 12, 1210.

17. The italicized words here and in subsequent places are those which are not found exactly or in substance in the 1180 or 1181 profession of faith of Waldes.

18. Cf. Jas. 2:17.

19. The passage from "We have renounced the world" to this point is taken from the profession of Waldes.

20. Preachers among the Waldenses had adopted sandals with a special design as a mark of their vocation. See No. 37, n. 33.

21. Lev., chaps. 13-14.

22. We omit here and in later passages the scriptural verses cited by the pope to bolster his admonitions.

23. Gal. 5:18.

24. II Cor. 3:17.

25. Luke 17:21.

26. Rom. 14:15.

27. Cant. 2:15.

28. Matt. 11:29.

29. On the same date letters were written to the archbishops of Tarragona and Narbonne, urging them to lenient treatment and careful guidance of the Poor Catholics (*Regesta* XII.67,68, in Migne, *PL*, CCXVI, 73-74; Potthast 3767, 3768).

30. Cf. Ps. 102 (A.V. 103):5.

31. See No. 22.

32. This passage has given rise to some problems of interpretation. Its references to *Pauperes minores* have usually been taken to mean the Franciscan order, which was given verbal approval by Innocent III in 1209 but formal confirmation and approval of its rule only in 1223 by Honorius III. (The Dominican order, which Burchard discusses in the next paragraph, did not receive formal confirmation and approval by Honorius III until 1216.) Burchard's reference to the Poor of Lyons and their leader has also been thought to designate the Reconciled Poor under Bernard Prim. However, Walter Mohr ("Waldes," *Zeitschrift für Religions- und Geistesgeschichte,* IX [1957], 348-54) sees it differently. Pursuing his thesis that the reconciliation of Waldes in 1180/81 and his death soon afterward had split his followers, Mohr argues that Burchard here is recalling the events of his first trip to Rome about 1198, that the group called the Poor of Lyons here were unreconciled followers of Waldes, and that the *Pauperes minores* of this narrative were those who had followed Waldes in his return to the Church and were recognized as orthodox. We cannot accept Mohr's interpretation.

33. Cf. Deut. 23:25.

34. Cant. 4:4.

35. Cf. Ezech. 13:5.

37. AN EXPOSURE OF THE ALBIGENSIAN AND WALDENSIAN HERESIES

1. See item xiv in the list of polemics in the Appendix.

2. Dondaine, "Durand de Huesca," *AFP*, XXIX (1959), 260-61.

3. Jer. 5:19.

4. Cf. I John 5:19.

5. Matt. 7:18.

6. Cf. Rom. 7:5-6 and 4:15.

7. Matt. 26:26; Mark 14:22; Luke 22:19.

8. Matt. 5:28.

9. Mark 16:16.

10. I Cor. 15:50.

11. *Serenam:* This is the name given in Provençal to a bee-eating bird (*merops apiaster*); see Du Cange, *s.v.* "serena." The significance of these four created forms (if *serena*, indeed, is here properly translated) is not clear.

12. We have not encountered elsewhere this myth of creation in which the evil god is the first to act.

13. Cf. the names given to the evil one in No. 51, § 20, and No. 59, II, § 11.

14. *Testimonium:* We amend it to *testamentum* in accordance with the phrase in the second sentence following.

15. Reading *in terra sua* for *in ira sua* of the text.

16. Cf. Apoc. 12:9,4.

17. Matt. 15:24.

18. Luke 19:10.

19. Luke 9:56.

20. Deut. 33:2.

21. Ezech. 35:2-5, with omissions.

22. With the following tenets of absolute dualism among the Albigenses, cf. those revealed in the heretical tract written a few years later, No. 58.

23. II Cor. 13:3.

24. Rom. 7:14.

25. Cf. Ps. 26 (A.V. 27):13; 141:6 (A.V. 143:5).

26. Ps. 149:3,5,6-7,9.

27. Cf. Ezech. 23:4. This myth is found also in the passage translated in n. 35, below, and in No. 38, § 11. Runciman (*Medieval Manichee*, p. 166, n. 4) suggests that it reached the Cathars through a Greek or Slavonic source which in turn derived from the Hebrew. See also Newman, *Jewish Influence*, p. 67.

28. John 4:16.

29. Cf. John 8:3-11.

30. The words "recently sprung up" might be regarded as evidence of a revival at this time of mitigated dualism among the Albigenses, who had been persuaded to accept absolute dualism some forty years before at the Council of Saint-Félix-de-Caraman (see No. 23, n. 12). However, evidence that mitigated dualism had not, in fact, died out is found in a confession made by a converted heretic in 1181, who testified that he had once believed

that Lucifer in his pride had dared to rebel against the true God. The heretic was one of the two men who had appeared publicly in Toulouse in 1179 and been captured in 1181—see No. 29 and Leclercq, "Le Témoignage de Geoffroy d'Auxerre," *Studia Anselmiana*, XXXI; *Analecta monastica*, II (1953), 196. On Albigensian doctrine in the twelfth and thirteenth centuries, see Borst, pp. 92-98; Thouzellier, "Hérésie et croisade," *RHE*, XLIX (1954), 869-72; and *idem, Un traité cathare*, chap. III.

31. Matt. 21:28.

32. On Bogomil views of the relationship between God, Christ, and the devil, see p. 15, above, and n. 55. In a gloss on the Gospel used in the Bogomil church of Bosnia, the man with two sons is said to be the Father invisible, the younger son the fallen angels, the elder son the angels who remained faithful (A. V. Solovjev, "La Doctrine de l'église de Bosnie," in *Académie royale de Belgique, Bulletin de la classe des lettres et des sciences morales et politiques*, 5th ser., XXXIV [1948], 502). About 1240, Moneta of Cremona wrote that the Cathars believed that the devil and the angelic spirit in Adam were brothers, the devil being the elder of the two; see No. 50, n. 24.

33. *Dessotulati quia pertusos sotulares ferunt:* Waldensian evangelists adopted special sandals and were accordingly referred to in other sources as *sandaliati, insabatati*, etc. See No. 38, § 18; No. 54, § 10; No. 55, II, 2; also Du Cange, *s.v.* "insabatati."

34. On them, see also No. 45, part C, § 27.

35. A short sketch of Catharist doctrine is found standing alone and untitled in one manuscript. It seems to be related to this proclamation and to the related passage in No. 38, but has some interesting variations. It was published in Garvin and Corbett, eds., *The* Summa contra haereticos *Ascribed to Praepositinus*, Appendix B, p. 292, and reads as follows: "The Manichaeans say there are two gods and two beginnings: a good God and a malign god. The malign they hold to be the creator of this world, author of the Mosaic law. John the Baptist, they say, is damned. The Christ who appeared in this world was a pseudo-Christ and had pseudoapostles. They aver, also, that the Christ through whom we hope for salvation was born in a celestial Jerusalem. Christ [born of] Joseph and Mary, suffered in a celestial Jerusalem, betrayed by His brothers. They say that the good God had two wives, Collam and Hoolibam [*sic*], from whom He engendered sons and daughters in human fashion. They say that He had to do with the wife of the malign god, and the malign god, enraged thereby, sent his son into the court of the good God, whom he deceived, and took from thence gold and silver, human and animal souls, and sent them forth and dispersed them among his seven realms, those, indeed, to which Christ was sent. Hence, they say, Christ suffered seven times. They also declare that Christ was the husband of Mary Magdalen. To show this, they explain that he was alone with her three times: in the temple, in the garden, and at the well. They say that each one shall regain his wife, his sons, and his property in the kingdom of God. Certain

of them believe that when the soul leaves the human body, unless one shall die in their sect, it goes into another body, either human or animal; others say only into a human body."

38. A DESCRIPTION OF CATHARS AND WALDENSES BY PETER OF VAUX-DE-CERNAY

1. In a letter to Innocent III which serves as a preface (§§ 1-4), the author states his purpose, to show how the Church in Languedoc was saved, and explains his plan of work. He uses the word *Albigenses* to refer to anything connected with the heretics of southern France (see § 3 and the editor's notes, p. 3). The term "Albigensian heretics" was probably coined by a chronicler in 1181; it is in the title of canon 4 of the Council of Tours (1163), but that is probably a later addition, for the term is not in the text of the canon (Mansi, *Concilia*, XXI, 1177). As an adjective, "Albigensian" did not imply that the heretics were confined to the city or the diocese of Albi. In Peter's text, references to the orthodox diocese of Albi use the form *Albiensis* instead of *Albigensis*, and in the years before 1200 writers were also speaking of the Languedocian heretics as "heretics of Agen," or "heretics of Toulouse." At the time of the Albigensian Crusade (1209-1229), the substantive *Albigenses* came into general use for heretics throughout Languedoc. See the discussion of these words in Devic and Vaissete, *Histoire de Languedoc*, VII, 33-37; Borst, p. 249, n. 5; Thouzellier, "Hérésie et croisade," *RHE*, XLIX (1954), 867, n. 3; and Lacger, "L'Albigeois pendant la crise de l'albigéisme," *RHE*, XXIX (1933), 276-83.

2. Cf. Matt. 13:25.

3. Ps. 106. (A.V. 107):40.

4. From the Cistercian abbey of Fontfroide, near Narbonne. They were commissioned as legates by Innocent III in 1204. Ralph died in 1207; Peter was murdered in January of the following year, by an unknown hand. The culprit was generally supposed to be a retainer of Raymond VI, count of Toulouse. Peter's death was the immediate occasion for preaching the crusade against the heretics. See the works cited in No. 36, n. 1, and also H. Zimmerman, *Die päpstliche Legation in der ersten Hälfte des 13. Jahrhunderts vom Regierungsautritt Innocenz' III bis zum Tode Gregors IX (1198-1241)* (Veröffentlichungen der Sektion für Rechts- und Sozialwissenschaft der Gorresgesellschaft, XVII [Paderborn, 1913]), esp. p. 58.

5. Cf. II Cor. 4:6.

6. Heb. 12:15.

7. As the editors of the text point out, the reference appears to be to several attempts during the twelfth century to combat heresy in Toulouse, notably those by Bernard of Clairvaux (see No. 14) and by the mission of 1178 (see No. 29).

8. Cf. Jas. 3:15,17.

9. Cf. Apoc. 11:4.

10. Horace *Ep.* i.xvi.52-53.

11. *Hec Tolosa, tota dolosa:* The author is fond of alliterative phrases and plays upon words. Some of these we were able to approximate in English; for others, the alliteration is lost. Note, for example, in § 6, *ingressi et agressi* [entered and assailed] and *affecti et infecti* [weakened and poisoned]; and in § 9, *naturam hereticam et heresim naturalem* [heretical nature and natural heresy] and *mirabiliter et miserabiliter* [wonderfully and woefully].

12. The editors of the text (I, 8, n. 2) here point out that the allusion is probably based upon an incorrect reading of Jordanes *Roma et Getica.* (*MGH, Auctores antiquissimi,* V, 41). The reference goes back to Merovingian times.

13. Matt. 23:33.

14. Cf. Horace *Ep.* i.x.24.

15. Juvenal *Sat.* ii.79-81.

16. *Terre Provincialis:* i.e., the area later to be called Languedoc.

17. *Defensores et receptatores:* These terms rapidly assumed technical meaning as to the degree of implication in heresy. In a "consultation," presumably written about 1242 by Raymond of Pennafort (d. 1275) as a guide to inquisitorial practice in the see of Tarragona, "defenders" were defined as those who knowingly defended heretics in word or deed, hindering the Church's prosecution. "Receivers" were those who knowingly welcomed heretics to their houses several times. Lesser weight of guilt attached to "concealers" (*celatores*), who did not report heretics when they saw them, and "secreters" (*occultores*), who conspired to prevent such reports. All such persons were to some degree "fautors" (*fautores*), suspect of heresy, who must purge themselves. The consultation is published in F. Valls Taberner, ed., "El diplomatari de Sant Ramon de Penyafort," *Analecta sacra Tarraconensia: Anuari de la Biblioteca Balmes,* V (1929), 254-61.

18. It may be worth noting that this whole discussion of the heretics, §§ 10-18, inclusive, is written in the past tense. Did the author presume that when he wrote heresy had been eradicated by the crusade? Or is this due to his reliance on some source? In § 19 he again writes in the present tense.

19. Gen. 2:17, with changes.

20. John 8:3-11.

21. Cf. Apoc. 15:7; 16:1.

22. Isa. 1:4; I Tim. 4:2; and Rom. 16:18, respectively.

23. Matt. 21:13; Apoc. chap. 17.

24. A not uncommon argument of the heretics, mentioned, perhaps for the first time, by Eckbert of Schönau (*Sermones* xi.14, in Migne, *PL,* CXCV, 92) and often repeated. See Döllinger, *Beiträge,* II, 5 and note; Moneta of Cremona *Adversus catharos et valdenses,* p. 300; No. 55, I, § 4; Vidal, "Doctrine et morale," *RQH,* LXXXV (1909), 401; and Haskins, *Studies in Mediaeval Culture,* p. 252, where it is attributed to the Waldenses.

25. On these officials and their functions, see No. 49 and No. 51, §§ 8-10.

26. See Introduction, pp. 43-44, above.

27. Bertrand de Saissac was a prominent member of the nobility in the viscounty of Béziers. He seems to have had some reputation as an arbiter (Devic and Vaissete, *Histoire de Languedoc*, VIII, 412-14) and in 1194 was appointed guardian of the son and heir to Roger, viscount of Béziers. He got into trouble with the clergy and was, as our author indicates, favorable to heretics.

28. See No. 24, n. 14.

29. Cf. John 20:22.

39. AN INCIDENT AT COLOGNE IN 1163

1. The date is given in *Annales Coloniensis maximi*, in Fredericq, *Corpus*, I, 42-43, which says that the heretics came from Flanders. The number of victims stated in that source was four men and a girl, but the *Chronicon breve Coloniensis* puts it at six men and two women (*ibid.*, p. 40), and an account by Trithemius, written much later, raises the number to eight men and three women (*ibid.*, p. 41). Probably prosecutions were continued in the vicinity in following months (see Eckbert of Schönau *Sermones* VIII.iii; IX.viii, in Migne, *PL*, CXCV, 52, 84, 88).

2. Ep. 48, in Migne, *PL*, CXCVII, 224-53, esp. 249 ff.

3. Thouzellier ("Hérésie et croisade," *RHE*, XLIX [1954], 864-65), on the basis of Eckbert's remarks, believes that the heretics of Cologne in 1163 were absolute dualists, but her interpretation of this source is challenged by other historians, who insist that absolute dualism was not known in Western Europe before about 1167, at the earliest, when it was first introduced in Italy and southern France; see Manselli, "Per la storia dell'eresia," *BISIAM*, LXVII (1955), 219-23; and his "Il manicheismo medievale," *Ricerche religiosi*, XX (1949), 88-94, as cited by Russell, "Interpretations of Medieval Heresy," *MS*, XXV (1963), 48. Cf. Borst, pp. 94-96.

4. *Sermones* v.xi; XIII.i, in Migne, *PL*, CXCV, 34, 96.

5. Rainald of Dassel, archbishop (1159-1167) and imperial chancellor (1156-1167). He was in Italy from 1161 to 1164. The examining body may have been his regular court or a specially convened synod (Theloe, *Die Ketzerverfolgungen*, p. 58, n. 220).

6. Eckbert (*Sermones* VIII.iii, in Migne, *PL*, CXCV, 52) calls him an arch-Cathar (perhaps bishop?). Two other heretics, Marsilius and Theoderic, are named in the *Chronicon breve Coloniensis* (see n. 1, above); the second of these, according to Eckbert (*ibid.*), was burned at Bonn.

7. The date of the incident in Spain was probably about 1219. The attitude toward the Eucharist is characteristic of the Waldenses, who were the subject of an edict banning heretics, issued by Alfonso II of Aragon in 1194 (Theloe, *Die Ketzerverfolgungen*, pp. 143-46).

8. St. Lawrence, martyred August 10, 258, was burned on a gridiron.

9. This is not Caesarius's fancy. Several of the chronicles narrate the voluntary death of one or more of the group; see, for example, *Annales Coloniensis maximi*, in Fredericq, *Corpus*, I, 43.

40. THE FATE OF HERETICS IN ENGLAND

1. Heretics who worked as weavers were reported in the diocese of Worcester in the time of Bishop Roger (1164-1179), who asked the advice of Gilbert Foliot, bishop of London (1163-1188), on how to proceed against them and was told to use preaching and force. The result is unknown; see Gilbert Foliot *Epistolae* 249,250, in Migne, *PL*, CXC, 935-36. Other sources for the incident described here are listed in Russell, *Dissent and Reform*, p. 310, n. 80.

2. R. W. Eyton (*Court, Household, and Itinerary of Henry II* [London, 1878], pp. 41-88, esp. 82) puts the king at Oxford in December, 1163, and again for the last three months of 1165, and (p. 88) dates the assembly which condemned the heretics about Christmas, 1165. Borst (p. 94) suggests the date 1162. Russell (*Dissent and Reform*, p. 309, n. 79) argues for 1165/66.

3. *Publicani* (in other sources found as *popelicani, popelicant*, etc.): This was one of the earliest of specific sect names used in Western Europe. Crusaders had probably brought it back from the East, where they had heard the Greek *pavlikianoi* applied to contingents in the Moslem army, to ethnic groups in the Balkans, and to heretics (Runciman, *Medieval Manichee*, p. 122); references to the word in narratives of the crusades are collected in Garsoian, *The Paulician Heresy*, pp. 14-17. It seems to have carried implications from the biblical "publicans" (Matt. 21:31; see also No. 41, n. 3). As a name for heretics it first appears in a letter of Louis VII of France in 1162 (Bouquet, *Recueil*, XV, 790), after which it is not uncommon in sources written in northern Europe. References are collected in Borst, p. 247, n. 1; see also Puech, "Catharisme médiéval et Bogomilisme," in *Convegno "Volta,"* Accademia nazionale dei Lincei, *Atti,* 8th ser., XII (1957), 59-62.

4. Cf. Ps. 3:1.

5. Cf. Cant. 2:15.

6. Pelagius (d. *ca.* 425), monk and theologian who challenged the concept of original sin, the practice of infant baptism, and the essential functions of the Church in human salvation. His doctrines were condemned at the Council of Ephesus in 431, but traces of them remained until the end of the sixth century and perhaps later in France and the British Isles.

7. St. Germanus of Auxerre (d. 448) visited Britain in 429 or 430 and again in 447 to combat Pelagianism.

8. Of him nothing further is known.

9. They were weavers, according to a brief entry in the annals of Tewkesbury (*Annales monastici*, ed. by H. R. Luard, I, 49).

10. Matt. 5:10.

11. Cf. Matt. 5:11.

12. In the Assizes of Clarendon, 1166, Henry II forbade any communication with the heretics who had been punished at Oxford (William Stubbs, *Select Charters and Other Illustrations of English Constitutional History,* pp. 145-46). This is the first secular law promulgated against heretics in the Middle Ages; see Theloe, *Die Ketzerverfolgungen,* p. 136. There is no record of further appearance of heresy in England until 1191 in York (*ibid.,* p. 54), or thereafter, except 1211, when an Albigensian heretic was burned at London (*De antiquis legibus liber,* ed. by Thomas Stapleton, p. 3).

41. "PUBLICANS" AT VÉZELAY

1. Pons of Montboissier (1138-1161), brother of Peter the Venerable of Cluny.

2. This was the culmination of a series of conflicts during the first half of the twelfth century, the first of which ended with the murder of the abbot at the time and the burning of the monastery. The revolt of 1152 led to the establishment of a short-lived commune, which was put down in 1155. There has been some dispute about this; but Charles Petit-Dutaillis in *Les Communes françaises: Caractères et évolution des origines au XVIIIᵉ siècle* (L'Evolution de l'humanité, XLIV [Paris, 1947], p. 127 and n. 2, accepts the commune as a fact. It is a matter of some interest in that Vézelay is one of the towns in which a charge of heresy coincided with civilian opposition to temporal control by the clergy (for others, see Nos. 8, 20). The town of Vézelay, in the department of Yonne, is situated on the Cure River, a few miles east of the Yonne and about thirty miles northeast of Nevers. Now a picturesque village, it was in the twelfth century a place of some importance. The history of Vézelay by Aimé Chérest, *Vézelay: Etude historique,* makes some useful corrections and additions to the history by Hugh of Poitiers. The story of the insurrections in the town is told by Léon de Bastard ("Recherches sur l'insurrection communale de Vézelay au XIIᵉ siècle," *BEC,* 3d ser., II [1851], 339-65), who doubts a true communal uprising in 1152; his argument is rebutted by F. Bourquelot, "Observations sur l'établissement de la commune de Vézelay," *BEC,* III (1852), 447-63.

3. *Deonarii seu Poplicani:* This is the only known occurrence of the first of these names. De la Barre's suggestion that it is the scribe's error for *telonarii* [tax collectors], is accepted in Migne, *PL,* CXCIV, 1681; by Runciman (*Medieval Manichee,* p. 185), and by Borst (p. 247, n. 1). This would imply that the heretics were equated in popular opinion with the publicans of the Bible.

4. The verb is *circumvenientibus,* which should perhaps be translated as "passing by," but the context implies that they were called together to deal with the problem.

5. Guichard (1165-1180 or 1181). It was during his prelacy that Waldes

began to preach at Lyons.

6. Pons of Arsac (1162-1181). He had been present at the debate at Lombers in 1165 (see No. 28) and would be a member of the mission to Toulouse in 1178 (see No. 29).

7. Bernard of Saint-Saulge (1160-1177).

8. Walter II of Mortagne (1155-1174).

9. From this narrative the responsibility for pronouncing the death sentence is not clear, although the implication is that the decision, in one case modified by the abbot on his own authority, was given by the clergy and people and executed by the abbot; see Maisonneuve, p. 116, and Theloe, *Die Ketzerverfolgungen*, pp. 43-46. Abbot William had, in fact, sought advice on the correct judicial procedure from Herbert of Boscham, a member of the official family of Thomas Becket who was sharing Thomas's exile in France. Herbert replied at length, concluding that the abbot and associates should fix the guilt of the suspects but that any death penalty should be pronounced and executed by the king (*Ep.* 29, in Migne, *PL*, CXC, 1462-63). Runciman (*Medieval Manichee*, p. 122, n. 4) thinks that it was the lay authorities who carried out the execution of the seven who were burned.

42. FROM HERESY TO WITCHCRAFT

1. On the general subject of belief in demons, see Henry C. Lea, *Materials toward a History of Witchcraft*, ed. by Arthur C. Howland, I, 143-98. For some examples in sources readily available in translation, see Caesarius of Heisterbach *Dialogus miraculorum*, Vol. I, Bk. V, *passim* (trans. by Scott and Bland, I, 313-90).

2. For examples of penances to be laid on those who invoked demons by charms and incantations, see John T. McNeill and Helena M. Gamer, *Medieval Handbooks of Penance*, esp. pp. 330-31. The canon *Episcopi* has been erroneously attributed to the Council of Ancyra in the third century, but the earliest unmistakable reference to it is its inclusion in a collection of canon law compiled by Regino of Prüm about 900. Thence it found its way into the *Decreta* of Burchard of Worms (d. 1095), where it is the first entry in Book X, devoted to magicians and soothsayers (Migne, *PL*, CXL, 831-54).

3. See Nos. 3, 9, and 18.

4. On Conrad, see No. 45, part A.

5. The best introduction to the interest of inquisitorial courts in sorcery and witchcraft is through the fourteenth-century treatises on the institution; for one example see No. 55, VI, esp. n. 1. The development of papal policy from Boniface VIII to Innocent VIII may be traced in Joseph Hansen, *Quellen und Untersuchungen zur Geschichte des Hexenwahns und der Hexenverfolgung im Mittelalter* (Bonn, 1901), pp. 2-27. The bull of Innocent VIII has been many times published; see *ibid.*, pp. 25-27.

6. The subject of witchcraft in Europe from the fourteenth to the seventeenth century has an extensive bibliography; we mention here only a few works, principally those written in English, to illustrate the relationship between witchcraft and heresy. The best introduction in English is an essay by George Lincoln Burr, "The Literature of Witchcraft," in *Papers of the American Historical Association*, IV (1889-1890), 237-66, reprinted in *George Lincoln Burr: His Life by Roland H. Bainton and Selections from His Writings by Lois O. Gibbon* (Ithaca, N.Y., 1943), pp. 166-89. See also the introduction by Professor Burr to Lea's *Materials toward a History of Witchcraft*. Still of much value are the chapters on sorcery, the occult arts, and witchcraft in Lea, *History of the Inquisition*, Vol. III, chaps. VI and VII. Fundamental for a study of the subject are two works by Joseph Hansen: *Zauberwahn, Inquisition and Hexenprozess in Mittelalter und die Entstehung der grossen Hexenverfolgung* (Munich and Leipzig, 1900) and his already cited *Quellen und Untersuchungen*. A convenient summary is Antoinette C. Pratt, *The Attitude of the Catholic Church towards Witchcraft and the Allied Practices of Sorcery and Magic;* and a useful guide to the literature is by Rossell H. Robbins, *The Encyclopedia of Witchcraft and Demonology*, which on pp. 558-71 includes a bibliography of some twelve hundred titles.

The works listed above all treat of witchcraft in Western Europe during the later Middle Ages as a Christian heresy not to be identified with sorcery and demonology in general, which are world-wide phenomena. Anthropologists have challenged this view as too narrow, insisting that witchcraft lies in the realm of folklore rather than Christian theology. A spirited presentation of this point is by Margaret Murray in two books: *The Witch-cult of Western Europe,* and *The God of the Witches*. A later, more cautious development of the same general thesis is by Arne Runeberg, *Witches, Demons, and Fertility Magic*. Some lively reading in the newspapers of 1964 was provided by self-styled witches in England who accepted the Murray school of thought in explaining themselves.

A volume which fits neither of the categories mentioned above and which diffuses rather more heat than light is by Montague Summers, *The History of Witchcraft and Demonology*. For the author, witchcraft was no delusion, but a living reality, the god of the witches being in truth the devil. There is an urbane summing-up of various interpretations of witchcraft in Elliot Rose, *A Razor for a Goat*. See also Julio Caro Baroja, *The World of the Witches*, trans. by O. N. V. Glendinning.

7. William of Champagne, "of the White Hands," son of Count Thierry II of Champagne, uncle of Philip II of France, archbishop of Rheims (1176-1202), and cardinal.

8. Gervais was a widely traveled courtier of English birth who had been reared in Rome, studied law in Bologna, and was successively attached to the households of Archbishop William, Prince Henry of England, and William II of Sicily. In the service of Otto IV of Germany, to whom he

dedicated a book (about 1211), he became marshal of the kingdom of Arles. As this story indicates, he probably ended his days as a canon in England; see *DNB*, VII, 1120-21.

9. See No. 43.

10. See No. 40.

11. The reference is to a tale in the apocryphal *Acts of the Apostles Peter and Paul*, in which Simon Magus was an opponent of Peter in Rome. Simon regarded himself as a messiah who had descended through a series of heavens to travel on earth as a prophet and miracle worker, and claimed he would ascend again to heaven. On a certain day he did rise in flight, until St. Peter overcame his magic, whereupon he fell to his death. The legend may be read in translation in *The Ante-Nicene Fathers*, ed. by A. C. Coxe, VIII, 480-84; and in *The Golden Legend of Jacobus de Voragine*, trans. by Granger Ryan and Helmut Ripperger, I, 332-36 and *passim*. See also Jonas, *The Gnostic Religion*, pp. 103-11.

12. Witnesses before the Inquisition in the early fourteenth century described Luzabel (more commonly spelled Lucibel) as an angelic creature who became Lucifer after his rebellion against God or as the son of "the great devil" who had the name Lucibel while he was in heaven to seduce the angels (Döllinger, *Beiträge*, II, 33, and 32, 189, respectively). The name appears also in William of Nangis *La Chronique latine de 1113 à 1300*, ed. by H. Géraud, I, 76, in connection with an outbreak of heresy in Arras in 1183. See also Borst, p. 152, n. 5.

13. In the paragraph immediately preceding (xxix), Map describes mercenary troops, whose depredations were fearful both when they were employed in feudal war and, in intervals of peace, when they were left to pillage for themselves. Henry II employed them in the war with his sons in 1173, bringing some to England only once, in 1174. To Map they were heretics, no doubt, because no place or person, however sacred, was safe from them and because runaway clerics, monks, and other fugitives found shelter among them; moreover, the Third Lateran Council of 1179 had laid the same ban on mercenaries as on heretics and, with special reference to Languedoc, urged a crusade against them (see p. 650, n. 140). See also H. Géraud, "Les Routiers au XIIe siècle," *BEC*, III (1841-1842), 125-47; and J. Boussard, "Henry II Plantagenêt et les origines de l'armée de métier," *BEC*, CVI (1945-1946), 189-224.

14. John 6:61 (A.V. 60); cf. John 6:67 (A.V. 66).

15. See p. 42, above.

16. The MS is defective at this point. The printed text reads *erantque* but in a note the editor suggests that *errantes* would be preferable and that there is possibly a short lacuna thereafter. We have followed this suggestion. A faithful rendering of the printed text would yield "and they were . . ."— which is the solution adopted by James in his translation. Tupper and Ogle read "and they continue to wander from the truth."

17. Perhaps this is a reference to the hospices which the Cathars main-

tained as centers of instruction and places of shelter (see No. 49).

18. This is probably an error by Map, for the Cathars used the first seventeen verses of the Gospel of John as an essential part of their ritual of spiritual baptism.

19. The word "synagogue" was sometimes used in the Middle Ages with reference to heretical assemblies and schismatic groups and should not here be interpreted as linking heresy and Judaism. See Puech and Vaillant, *Le Traité contre les Bogomiles*, p. 238 and n. 16; also *Sathanas synagogam* in reference to a heretical refuge at Lavaur (William of Puylaurens *Cronica*, ed. by Bessyier, in *Troisièmes mélanges d'histoire du moyen âge*, p. 121). In 1387, in a document which seems to confuse Waldenses and Cathars, the former are said to meet in a *synagoga* to hear preaching, share blessed bread, and engage in sexual orgies (Döllinger, *Beiträge*, II, 251-57). *Facere synagogam* in that document (p. 255) seems to refer specifically to the distribution of the bread. By the fifteenth century, the words *synagoga diabolica* were used to refer to the witches' Sabbat (Runeberg, *Witches, Demons, and Fertility Magic*, pp. 24, 29; cf. p. 162). Here Map may be no more than recalling the biblical "synagogues of Satan" (Apoc. 2:9; 3:9).

20. The Latin makes a play on words: *pati quod desideravit . . . et a paciendo Paterini dicuntur.*

21. See No. 40. Cf. the decree of Frederick II which was copied by Bernard Gui (*Practica*, ed. by Douais, p. 307): *Set in exemplum martirum . . . Patherennos se nominant, velut expositos passioni.*

22. Whether an actual incident gave rise to the story Map tells here we have no way of knowing. He may have heard the tale at the time of his trip to Rome for the Lateran Council of 1179. Borst (p. 103, n. 19) cites this passage as evidence for heresy at Vézelay, on which see No. 41.

23. Gen. 3:6.

24. Cf. the similar tale involving Eudo (No. 18, part B). Another story of magical foods is encountered in the *Cronica* of Alberic of Trois-Fontaines (*MGH SS*, XXIII, 845).

25. *Virtutibus:* See Du Cange, *s.v.* "virtus," 2, and the references there cited.

26. Without knowledge of the date, we have no basis for precise identification. Possibly it was Robert of La Tour du Pin (1173-1195).

43. THE SPREAD OF HERESY IN NORTHERN EUROPE

1. See the list of incidents and sources in Borst, p. 103, n. 19.

2. 1174-1183. He died on April 19.

3. On him, see No. 42, n. 7.

4. *Catafrigias:* A synonym for *Cathari*, it had been applied to heretics in Cologne in 1163; see Borst, p. 241, n. 6.

5. In canon 27 of the Third Lateran Council (1179).

6. By the canon referred to in the preceding note (Mansi, *Concilia*,

XXII, 231-33), the property of condemned heretics was awarded to the secular power which aided the Church in the prosecution. Here the archbishop seems to have claimed the right to share. On the procedure used in these trials, see Maisonneuve, pp. 119-20.

7. Bishop of Metz (1180-1212). The episode is otherwise undated in our source. Havet ("L'Hérésie et le bras séculier," *BEC*, XLI [1880], 515, n. 2) places it between 1209 and 1212. We suggest the date 1199-1200 on the basis of Innocent III's letters, referred to in n. 10, below.

8. The reference may be to the provincial council held at Montpellier in December of 1195, at which canon 27 of the Third Lateran Council (1179), anathematizing heretics and mercenary soldiers, was renewed. But there is no record of the presence of the bishop of Metz at that council. See Mansi, *Concilia*, XXII, 668.

9. Rom. 10:15.

10. The bishop of Metz appealed to the pope in 1199 against certain persons who insisted on reading and discussing among themselves the Gospels, the Pauline letters, Psalms, Job, the *Moralia* of St. Gregory (an exegesis of the Book of Job), and other works in vernacular translation; when the clergy sought to deter them they turned on them in wrath. Innocent III in reply praised the zeal of the people for the Scriptures but not their private meetings and ordered the bishop to investigate carefully the nature of the translations. When the people grew more recalcitrant, the pope entrusted another investigation to three Cistercian abbots (*Regesta* II.141, 142,235, in Migne, *PL*, CCXIV, 695 ff., 793; Potthast 780, 781, 893). We are told in a later report by a chronicler that some of the translations were burned by the abbots (*Chronica Albrici monachi Trium Fontium*, in *MGH SS*, XXIII, 878). Maisonneuve (pp. 164-65) discusses the incident as one which set precedents for the Inquisition. On the use of vernacular translations of the Bible and devotional works, see the Introuction, pp. 63, 64-65, above.

44. THE AMALRICIANS

1. Borst, p. 114, n. 119; Cohn, *Pursuit of the Millennium*, chaps. VII-VIII; Claus-Peter Clasen, "Medieval Heresies in the Reformation," *Church History*, XXXII (1963), 392-413.

2. Many of the sources are printed in the study by Germaine C. Capelle, *Autour du décret de 1210, III: Amaury da Bène.* D'Alverny, "Un Fragment du procès des Amauriciens," *AHDLMA*, XXVI (1951), 325-26, sums up the views of various scholars and prints a document describing in part the preliminary examination of some of the sect after their arrest.

3. The names are listed by Caesarius more fully than in other sources but a few details may be added. A Master Bernard is named in the *Chronicon anonymi Laudunensis* (*MGH SS*, XXVI, 454) and is called the heresiarch of the group in the *Annales Coloniensis maximi* (*MGH SS*, XVII, 825). William

the Goldsmith is called "William of *Arria*, the goldsmith," in the decree condemning the group (*Chartularium universitatis parisiensis*, I, 70; trans. in Lynn Thorndike, *University Records and Life in the Middle Ages*, p. 26). Borst (p. 114, n. 19) denies that this denotes an occupation, for William was a theologian and is listed among those degraded from clerical office. According to the decree of condemnation, Dudo also was a priest; Odo and Elinand were attached to the church of Saint-Cloud; and Guarin was a priest of Corbeil. Two others, not mentioned by Caesarius, are reported also to have suffered for their association with the group. Dominic of Triangulo was burned with the others at Paris (*Chartularium*, I, 70, in Thorndike, *University Records*, p. 26), and a man named Godin was executed in the region of Amiens, probably soon afterward (*Chronicon anonymi Laudunensis*, in *MGH SS*, XXVI, 454).

4. This would have been prior to Stephen's consecration as archbishop of Canterbury. He had lectured in theology at Paris for over twenty years until his move to Rome, where he was created cardinal, in June, 1206, and was elevated to the see of Canterbury in 1207. From that date until 1213 he was in exile at the monastery of Potigny, northeast of Auxerre. Caesarius a few paragraphs later mentions a Master Stephen, to whom, along with the bishop of Paris and two other masters, an informer in 1210 reported the activities of the Amalricians. This raises the question of whether "Master Stephen" was Stephen of Rheims, who lectured in theology at Paris in the early thirteenth century and became chancellor of Notre Dame, probably in 1214; he was sometimes confused with Stephen Langton. For the two Stephens, see Palémon Glorieux, *Répertoire des maîtres en théologie de Paris au XIIIe siècle*, I, 238-60, 271.

5. I Cor. 12:6.

6. Matt. 24:24.

7. Ralph later became cantor in the church of Cambrai (D'Alverny, "Un Fragment," *AHDLMA*, XXVI [1951], 328, n. 2).

8. Philip II (1180-1223).

9. The future Louis VIII (1223-1226).

10. This and the preceding paragraph are reminiscent of the prophecy of Joachim of Flora, the Italian mystic, and his theory of the three ages—of the Father, of the Son, and of the Holy Spirit. In his thought the world was moving toward the end of the second age, which would occur in 1260. See Henry Bett, *Joachim of Flora*; Herbert Grundmann, *Neue Forschungen über Joachim von Fiore*; and M. W. Bloomfield, "Joachim of Flora," *Traditio*, XIII (1957), 249-309; also M. W. Bloomfield and Marjorie E. Reeves, "The Penetration of Joachism into Northern Europe," *Speculum*, XXIX (1954), 772-93.

11. John I (1204-1229).

12. Peter of Nemours (1208-1219).

13. On Robert of Curson, see No. 27, n. 1. We are unable to identify the dean of Salzburg or Brother Thomas.

14. How far the leaders had won adherents among laymen is conjectural. John, a priest of Orsigny, had no doubt instructed his parishioners in some particulars, for he testified that "when he was arrested and was leaving his parish, he told his parishioners that they should not put their trust in anyone who contradicted his words, if any should teach them things other than what he, himself, had taught" (Maria-Thérèse d'Alverny, " Un Fragment," *AHDLMA*, XXVI [1951], 332; see also her remarks, pp. 333-34). William of Nangis *Chronique*, I, 137, mentions women with whom they had sinned and simple folk whom they had deluded.

15. Part of the record of a preliminary examination in the court of the official of the bishop of Paris survives and has been printed by Mlle D'Alverny ("Un Fragment," *AHDLMA*, XXVI [1951], 330-33). Before the bishop himself as presiding officer, John, priest of Orsigny, and Odo, Elinand, and Stephen—deacon, acolyte, and priest, respectively, of La Celle-Saint-Cloud—were arraigned. Statements of the charges were read to them. John admitted certain errors but said there were other things in the statement he did not understand. Odo and Elinand admitted and repented of their errors. Stephen admitted some errors, but the record breaks off in the middle of his response.

16. They were degraded on November 14, 1210; the execution took place at Les Champeaux in the marketplace on November 20: see part B; also Thorndike, *University Records*, p. 27; and D'Alverny ("Un Fragment," *AHDLMA*, XXVI [1951], 328, nn. 3, 4, 5).

17. He had entered the monastery of Saint-Denis but he too was included in the group sentenced to life imprisonment (*Chartularium*, I, 70, in Thorndike, *University Records*, p. 26).

18. The works thus banned were probably Aristotle's *Physics*, his *De anima*, and part of his *Metaphysics* (Hastings Rashdall, *The Universities of Europe in the Middle Ages*, ed by F. M. Powicke and A. B. Emden, I, 356).

19. The first reference is to David of Dinant, on whom see Gabriel Théry, *Autour du décret de 1210, I: David de Dinant*. In the decree of condemnation (*Chartularium*, I, 70, in Thorndike, *University Records*, p. 27) the vernacular works are specified as the Apostle's Creed and the Lord's Prayer. A version of the latter, no doubt the one used by the accused, precedes the record of the investigation published by Mlle D'Alverny ("Un Fragment," *AHDLMA*, XXVI [1951], 330). In English it reads as follows: "Good Father who art in the heavens and on earth; confirm Thy name in our persons. Grant us Thy kingdom. Thy will be done on earth as it is in heaven. Give us that which is needful to us each and every day for our souls. Forgive us our wrongdoings as we forgive others. Keep us from the de[vil's] wiles (*des enginz du de. . .*). Deliver us from all evils."

20. Cf. Eccles. 1:2.

45. THE VARIETIES OF HERESY

1. He seems to have used one document which led him into an error about the doctrine of the Concorezzenses (Dondaine, "La Hiérarchie cathare, I," *AFP*, XIX [1949], 303).

2. *Beiträge zur Sektengeschichte*, II, 52-84.

3. On Conrad see Balthasar Kaltner, *Konrad von Marburg und die Inquisition in Deutschland*. A brief treatment in English will be found in Lea, *History of the Inquisition*, II, 325-46.

4. Conrad Tors was a Dominican, John a layman. After the murder of Conrad of Marburg and the revulsion of feeling induced by his overzealous prosecutions, both of these men also died violently (Kaltner, *Konrad von Marburg*, pp. 138-40, 172-73; Lea, *History of the Inquisition*, II, 333-34, 345).

5. On the policy of Gregory IX, see Ludwig Förg, *Die Ketzerverfolgung in Deutschland unter Gregor IX*. There is a brief treatment in Maisonneuve, pp. 257-64.

6. From this point, the narrative parallels closely that in Mansi, *Concilia*, XXIII, 241.

7. Lea (*History of the Inquisition*, II, 331) presumes from this that they belonged to a group called Luciferians, but it is a hazardous assumption. It may be noted that Gregory IX does not mention them by name in a letter of February, 1231, in which he catalogues and excommunicates seven groups (*Les Registres de Grégoire IX*, ed. by Auvray, Vol. I, No. 539).

8. A letter of June 25, 1231, to the archbishop of Trier, enclosing a decree of the senator of Rome against heretics (Johann Friedrich Böhmer, *Acta imperii selecta*, pp. 665-67).

9. See No. 15, n. 38.

10. Alberic of Trois-Fontaines (*Chronica*, in *MGH SS*, XXIII, 878, 945), twice tells a similar tale, in which heretics were said to name individuals "St. Mary," "Holy Church," etc.

11. Mansi, *Concilia*, XXIIII, 241, says that three men and the woman Leuchard were burned.

12. The date was copied into the Prologue from a passage in the tract where Salvo Burci had recorded it exactly because he wished to show how recently formed were the sects he discusses. Nothing more is known of Monachus. The family name (*del Cario* or *del Cairo*) was well known in medieval Piacenza, and Monachus was not an unusual given name (Ilarino da Milano, "Il 'Liber supra Stella,'" *Aevum*, XVI [1942], 288-92).

13. This is an adaptation of the first sentence of the Gospel of Luke.

14. See Apoc. 8:11.

15. The text seems not to be entirely clear: *et quidem dicunt id est Catheri, qui Caloianni et eciam Francigene nuncupantur....* The name *Francigene* was applied to Cathars who, according to Anselm of Alessandria, had established a bishopric in northern France after the Second Crusade (see

No. 24). Their bishop, Robert of Epernon, participated in the council of heretics at Saint-Félix-de-Caraman (No. 23, n. 12). Before 1250, perhaps as early as 1233-1239, Cathars of northern France migrated to Italy (Borst, p. 231; Ilarino da Milano, "Le eresie medioevali," in *Grande antol. filos.,* IV, 1602), where they formed the "church of France," located at Verona and in Lombardy (see No. 51, § 15).

16. Luke 11:17; Matt. 12:25.

17. *Pauperes Leoniste et Pauperes Lombardi et vos Speroniste:* The first of these terms is the form often used for the Poor of Lyons in contemporary Italian sources (see, for example, part C, and No. 51, § 28). *Pauperes Lombardi* is the term applied to Italians who broke away from the Poor of Lyons in 1205; *Speroniste* is likewise the most common name for the followers of Hugo Speroni (see No. 21).

18. The editor omitted a portion of the text at this point.

19. The author is referring to words of Paul which, in the passage immediately preceding, had been quoted from I Tim. 4:1: "In the last times *some* shall depart from the faith" [italics ours].

20. The editor omitted a portion of the text at this point.

21. *Roncho:* a place in the vicinity of Piacenza, also called *Runcharola* or *Roncarolo* in other contemporary sources (see part C, below, and No. 54, § 10). From John of Ronco came the name *Runcarii* and its variants, often used in later years and particularly in Germany to designate heretics who, presumably, had adopted the doctrines of the Poor Lombards (Ilarino da Milano, "Il 'Liber supra Stella,'" *Aevum,* XVII [1943], 98-105). According to Duvernoy ("Un Traité cathare," *Cahiers d'études cathares,* 2d ser., XIII [1962], 25), the form *Runcharolorum,* found in the *Liber contra Manicheos* of Durand of Huesca (ed. by Thouzellier, p. 80), is a variant of *Ranchayrol,* a typical Languedocian name, and therefore shows that the heretics referred to by this name must be differentiated from the *Runcarii;* but this seems too heavy a conclusion to be supported by the slender evidence of a variation in spelling.

22. The editor omitted a portion of the text at this point.

23. *Sub regimine Gualdensis:* The Italian form of Waldes's name is also used in part C.

24. This doctrine, which was shared with and perhaps adopted from certain of the mitigated dualists (see No. 23, § 2b), differs sharply from the view of the Poor of Lyons (see No. 52). Salvo Burci's statement is confirmed by other sources (Ilarino da Milano, "Il 'Liber supra Stella,'" *Aevum,* XVII [1943], 113; also, No. 54, § 15). Yet this had not been one of the points at issue when a reconciliation between Italian and French factions had been attempted in 1218 (see No. 46).

25. In the conference held in 1218, referred to in the preceding note, the Poor Lombards had supported matrimonial life against the arguments for separation and celibacy advanced by the Poor of Lyons. Salvo Burci's testimony, confirmed by that in part C, below, seems to show their doctrine

in transition toward the celibacy reported in later sources (Ilarino da Milano, "Il 'Liber supra Stella,'" *Aevum*, XVII [1943], 110-12).

26. Matt. 19:29.

27. The author uses the same term, *impositio manuum*, for the Catholic sacrament of ordination and for the heretical baptism by imposition of hands.

28. Matt. 26:26; Mark 14:22; Luke 22:17.

29. Luke 22:19; I Cor. 11:24.

30. On these officials, see Nos. 49 and 54, §§ 8-10.

31. Matt. 26:75; Luke 22:62.

32. Matt. 5:5.

35. Cf. Luke 7:38.

34. Cf. Luke 7:39.

35. According to St. Augustine (*De haeresibus*, ed. by Müller, pp. 64-65), Simon Magus taught that God had not created the world and also denied the resurrection of the body. See also No. 42, n. 11.

36. Moneta of Cremona *Adversus Catharos et Valdenses* discusses certain errors in respect of predestination (pp. 549-59) and the Aristotelian theory of infinity of the world (pp. 478-88, 496-500) but does not attribute them to specific sects. There are passages on predestination in other polemical tracts, for example, that of Benedict of Alignan (Grabmann, "Der Franziskanerbischof Benedictus de Alignano," in *Kirchengeschichtliche Studien P. Michael Bihl*, pp. 57-58) and in the *Liber contra manicheos* of Durand of Huesca (ed. by Thouzellier, chap. XXI).

37. Cf. Acts 23:8.

38. St. Augustine (*De haeresibus*, ed. by Müller, pp. 116-19) says that he learned from Eusebius of a sect in Arabia called *Arabici* who believed that souls dissolve when bodies die but will be resurrected at the end of time. An anonymous inquisitor of Passau in the thirteenth century repeats the sect name and Augustine's comment (*Maxima bibliotheca veterum patrum*, XXV, 264). Our author apparently has a garbled version of this in mind.

39. We cannot identify "Zeno" unless it is a scribe's mistake for "Zarohen," the name of an oriental sage accused in apocryphal legends of disputing the teaching of the apostles. He, with Arphaxat, is accused of holding this error on the nature of the soul. Moneta of Cremona (*Adversus Catharos et Valdenses*, pp. 416-29) refutes heretics who say the soul dies with the body, but remarks that this is not a tenet of either the Cathars or the Waldenses. It may be noted that the "genealogy" of error in respect of predestination given here somewhat resembles the more detailed statements of the antecedents of the Cathars by Durand of Huesca in his *Liber antiheresis* (Dondaine, "Aux Origines du valdéisme," *AFP*, XVI [1946], 234) and his *Liber contra manicheos* (Thouzellier, *Une Somme anti-cathare*, p. 237, n. 14), and by Moneta of Cremona (*Adversus Catharos et Valdenses*, p. 411).

40. *Predestinati . . . disperati.*

41. We cannot throw any light on the references to the "Great Year" or

the city of Sodom. Father Dondaine discovered a different, shorter version of this passage in another manuscript (see "Durand de Huesca," *AFP*, XXIX [1959], 266). Referring to the first type of Predestinarian described here it reads, "These are the Patarines"; of the second, "These are false astrologers"; of the third, "This is the opinion of the rabble." Of the fourth group, the comment is that they believe all things arise by chance from eternity.

42. See No. 26, esp. n. 2.

43. Cf. No. 21, where the first two errors stated here are touched on in the Prologue and are treated in detail in the body of Vacarius's work. The error on the Eucharist is not mentioned there, however. Among the "common errors" which the Speronists shared with others, the following may have been included, according to the chapter titles of Book III (Käppeli, "Une Somme contre les hérétiques," *AFP*, XVII [1947], 300): (1) that the Roman Church does not possess the true faith, which exists only in the heretics' church and comes from God and the apostles; (2) that a wicked priest cannot fulfill his office; (3) that oaths are forbidden; (4) that temporal justice is against God's will; and (5) that purgatory does not exist.

44. *Illi de Prato:* This is the only direct reference we have to the schism among the Poor Lombards. The disappearance of "those of the meadow" was due to the activities of Durand of Huesca, who sought to reconcile them to the Church; see the introduction to No. 36, esp. n. 7.

45. On Bernard Prim, see the introduction to No. 36.

46. Cf. the statement in No. 37 that the Rebaptizers were an offshoot of the Poor of Lyons. They were among the many sects found in Milan in the mid-thirteenth century according to Stephen of Bourbon; see p. 31, above.

47. The author's reticence prevents identifying any but the Arnoldists (*Arnaldones*), unless *Cappelleti* is another name for the associations of peasants around Le Puy in France who were there called *Capuciati*. Originally formed to keep the peace and destroy marauding bands of brigands, the *Capuciati* were denounced as heretics about 1184 (*Historia episcoporum Autissiodorensium*, in Bouquet, *Recueil*, XVIII, 730). Käppeli ("Une Somme contre les hérétiques," *AFP*, XVII [1947], 335, nn. 94-95) suggests that *Corrucani* may be a corruption of *Runcarii* and that *Milui* resembles *Pomilui*, a Slavic term for heretics.

46. DISSENT BETWEEN THE POOR LOMBARDS AND THE POOR OF LYONS

1. Preger suggested dating the letter *ca.* 1230, but Karl Müller (*Die Waldenser und ihre einzelnen Gruppen bis zum Anfang des 14 Jahrhunderts*, p. 27) argues effectively that it was written soon after the conference.

2. The title in the manuscripts, *Rescriptum heresiarchum Lombardie ad pauperes de Lugduno qui sunt in Alamania* [a letter from the heresiarchs of

Lombardy to the Poor of Lyons who are in Germany], was supplied by the anonymous inquisitor who copied the letter into his treatise against heretics (Preger, *Beiträge*, pp. 184-86).

3. The question of whether Waldensian societies were composed only of fully ordained, preaching members—who later, by analogy with the Cathars, would be called "the Perfect" by Catholic writers (see No. 53)—or also included their followers, the "believers and friends," is discussed by Müller (*Die Waldenser*, pp. 12-16), who concludes that the first definition is correct.

4. Probably the influence of the Humiliati (see No. 22) was a factor here.

5. To judge from the comments of Salvo Burci (No. 45, part B) and of an inquisitor writing about 1266 (see No. 54, § 12), the Poor Lombards were much less numerous than the Poor of Lyons.

6. The meaning of the term "confrater" here is not entirely clear to us; it may designate the provost elected for a life term who is mentioned in § 4, of the letter. By the middle of the century the Poor Lombards were described as having a bishop (see No. 54, §§ 10, 12). On the Waldensian hierarchy in later years, see pp. 52-53, above.

7. Five of these persons (or six, if the Marinus here is the Maifredus of § 15) were respresentatives of the Italian party in the negotiations of 1218, and from § 15 we are able to expand the initial *J* to John in two cases. Preger's text reads *Thaddeus Marinus*, as though this were the name of one person (cf. Gonnet, *Enchiridion*, p. 171), but in § 15 Thaddeus is named separately. Ilarino da Milano ("Il 'Liber supra Stella,'" *Aevum*, XVII [1943], 107, n. 2) punctuates as we do. John Franceschus is perhaps the John Francigenas named in § 13.

8. Since the letter was preserved in the work of an inquisitor in the diocese of Passau, which at that time included Bavaria and much of Austria, it is presumably directed to the Waldenses in that area. The influence of the Poor of Lyons had spread into Germanic lands along two routes: north and east from Lyons and by a detour southward into Lombardy, then north across the Alps (see Pouzet, "Les Origines lyonnaises," *Revue d'histoire de l'église de France*, XXII [1936], 26; and S. H. Thomson, "Pre-Hussite Heresy in Bohemia," *English Historical Review*, XLVIII [1933], 24).

9. Cf. Phil. 1:3-11.

10. Preger reads: *carte, mendacis a fine, quodam Massario . . . fraudulenter tradite*. We follow Gonnet (*Enchiridion*, p. 172) and Döllinger in reading *carte mendacis a fratre quodam Massario*. Of Massarius nothing more is known.

11. Preger reads: *in fine cuiusdam cedule, quam nobis tradiderunt, legitur ad effectum perducerent quod eciam [promiserunt] et hec tria supradicta*. We follow Gonnet (*Enchiridion*, p. 174), who cites Döllinger and Müller, in reading *perducerent quod est: et hec tria*.

12. That is, when a married man or woman wished to adopt the ascetic life of the preacher, the Lombards insisted that the wife or husband consent. The Poor of Lyons agreed (see § 12), with reservations about the right

of the community to intervene. It may be noted that Waldes, in his profession (No. 32), had disavowed the intent to cause married couples to separate.

13. The controversy referred to here arose over questions of organization. Waldes had taken a stand against any established hierarchy but the Italians did not agree. The position taken by Thomas is described by Moneta of Cremona (*Adversus Catharos et Valdenses*, ed by Ricchini, p. 403) thus: Thomas maintained that each individual could transfer to Waldes the right (*ius*) to rule as pontiff over him. Therefore the whole congregation could do so and give him control over all. "Thus the whole society made him pontiff and prelate over all." Such an argument, of course, offended the Poor of Lyons, who preferred annually elected officials to a lifetime hierarchical leader.

14. See n. 7, above.

15. He is not otherwise known but must have been an important figure in the early days of the Poor of Lyons.

16. *G. de Cremano* in Preger's text, but we follow Müller and Gonnet (*Enchiridion*, p. 176). Nothing further is known of him or the other spokesmen for the Poor of Lyons.

17. I Tim. 4:5.

18. Preger reads: *contra confessionem eorum est, quod.* Müller (*Die Waldenser*, p. 23) tentatively suggests *quando* instead of *quod.* We follow Döllinger and Gonnet (*Enchiridion*, p. 177) in reading *qui.*

19. Matt. 5:13.

20. Luke 14:34-35.

21. John 9:31.

22. John 15:4,5.

23. John 15:7.

24. II Cor. 6:14-16.

25. Tit. 1:15-16.

26. II Cor. 5:17.

27. Heb. 2:2-3.

28. Cf. Heb. 10:28-29.

29. Rom. 3:19.

30. Rom. 15:4.

31. *Si minister ad hoc conficiendum accesserit ... credimus panis et vini substanciam post benediccionem esse Christi corpus et sanguinem, alioquin minime quod ad se et per se.*

32. Ps. 102 (A.V. 103):5.

33. Ps. 144 (A.V. 145):19.

34. Ps. 9 [pt. 2]:17 (A.V. 9:18).

35. I Cor. 10:17.

36. See Gal. 2:6.

37. We have not found the passage in Cyprian.

38. See Jerome's commentary on Zephaniah (Migne, *PL*, XXV, 1440); the passage is also in Gratian *Decretum* II, C. i, Q. i, c. 90 (Friedberg, I,

391). The scriptural quotation paraphrases Lev. 21:21.

39. See Jerome's commentary on Haggai in Migne, *PL*, XXV, 1477.

40. This and the following passage were included by Gratian in his *Decretum* (II, C. i, Q. i, cc. 12 and 5, respectively [Friedberg, I, 361, 358]) as from Pope Gregory I. But Friedberg remarks in a note that the exact words are not found in the letters of Pope Gregory and that he is inclined to ascribe them to Pope Pascal I (817-824). Similar passages however, do appear in the letters of Gregory I; see Paul Ewald, *Gregorii I papae registrum epistolarum* (2 vols., Berlin, 1887, 1890), index, *s.v.* "heresis simoniaca."

41. We have not identified the passage in the letters of Innocent I. The scriptural passages are Prov. 28:9 and Mal. 2:2, respectively.

42. I Cor. 13:11.

43. Cf. Acts 5:29.

44. Cf. Gal. 2:5.

45. Cf. Acts 10: esp. vv. 45-48.

46. Acts 11:18.

47. Of them nothing further is known.

48. Ps. 118 (A.V. 119):105.

49. Ps. 18:9 (A.V. 19:8).

50. John 7:38.

51. II Cor. 13:13.

47. A DEBATE BETWEEN A CATHOLIC
AND A PATARINE

1. Cf. the record of the session at Lombers (No. 28), that at Toulouse (No. 29), the remarks of Bernard of Fontcaude (No. 34), and the debates during the Cistercian mission in Languedoc, referred to in No. 36, n. 1. Biographies of the great mendicant preachers also reveal the interest in such disputations (see the second part of the Introduction, n. 21).

2. The former attribution to Gregory of Florence, bishop of Fano, was corrected in favor of the layman, George, by Dondaine, "Le Manuel de l'inquisiteur," *AFP*, XVII (1947), 174-80.

3. See No. 51, § 15.

4. The passage on predestination is the same as one in Moneta of Cremona *Adversus Catharos et Valdenses*, p. 549, but scholars have not agreed on the significance of this. Schmidt (*Histoire et doctrine*, II, 230) believed that the copyist of the *Disputatio* was the borrower. Charles Molinier ("Un Traité inédit," *Annales de la faculté des lettres de Bordeaux*, V [1883], 246, n. 3) thought the reverse might be true. Dondaine "Le Manuel de l'inquisiteur," *AFP*, XVII [1947], 179) was not ready to admit that there was any dependence of one on the other. The passage is, indeed, found in another manuscript, independent of these (Prague, Metropolitan Chapter, MS 1561 [N. XXXVII], fols. 122v-123r). Another link between the *Disputatio* and

Moneta's work does not seem to have been noticed previously. It is that the chapter on the Eucharist in the *Disputatio* is virtually identical with Moneta's treatment of the subject, except for the sequence of sentences (cf. the edition of Martène and Durand, cols. 1728-31, with the text of Moneta, p. 300, line 6, p. 302). Of nine heretical statements rebutted by Moneta all but one are in the *Disputatio* in the same words; as for the exception, the words of the *Disputatio* are found in another place in Moneta's tract (p. 296, col. 2). The only difference between the two passages is that the first two items given by Moneta are placed last in the *Disputatio*.

5. Cf. II Tim. 3:1; I Tim. 4:1.

6. Cf. II Tim. 4:3.

7. Cf. Rom. 12:3.

8. Jas. 1:17.

9. Cf. Ezech. 13:5.

10. We omit the table of chapters which occurs at this place in the text.

11. Martène and Durand omit these three words; we follow Ilarino da Milano.

12. John 1:3.

13. John 1:10; cf. v. 11.

14. Ephes. 3:9.

15. Ephes. 2:10.

16. Heb. 3:4.

17. Rom. 11:33.

18. Rom. 11:36.

19. I Tim. 4:3.

20. Apoc. 10:6.

21. Acts 4:24.

22. Acts 17:24. On variant readings (the world/this world) in this verse, see Thouzellier, *Une Somme anti-cathare*, p. 9, note.

23. John 1:3.

24. John 1:10.

25. We follow Ilarino da Milano: *corpora nostra et omnia alia visibilia.* Martène and Durand have *corruptibilia ista visibilia.*

26. Col. 1:15-16.

27. Heb. 1:10.

28. Heb. 1:11.

29. II Pet. 3:7.

30. *Ibid.*

31. I Cor. 11:12. The author alters the biblical text, which reads: "For as the woman is of the man, so also is the man by the woman."

32. Ilarino da Milano here adds the phrases: "The other world is, indeed, from God."

33. John 8:44.

34. Ephes. 2:3.

35. Rom. 9:22.

36. John 14:30.
37. Matt. 4:8-9.
38. I John 5:19.
39. Matt. 20:25; Luke 22:25.
40. II Cor. 4:4.
41. Rom. 9:18.
42. Phil. 3:19.

43. John 1:3-4. The heretic is using a punctuation which differs from that used in the Vulgate and followed in the Douay and Authorized translations, but it corresponds to that in J. Wordsworth and H. J. White, *Novum Testamentum Latine, editio minor* (Oxford, 1911). *The Interpreter's Bible,* VIII, 465, suggests that it is preferable on linguistic and interpretative grounds, noting that it was so taken by commentators in the first four centuries of the Christian era. The verses would thus read: "Without Him was made nothing. That which was made in Him was life." This rendering is also found in a ritual used by the Albigenses (see No. 57, part B) and also in the tract of an Albigensian heretic (see No. 58, chaps. XII, n. 125; XIII, n. 138; XIV, n. 146), where other questions of interpretation arise from the punctuation.

44. I Kings (A.V. I Sam.) 2:6.
45. John 1:4.
46. Matt. 6:24.
47. I Cor. 8:5.
48. I Cor. 8:5-6.
49. Cf. Luke 8:2.
50. Luke 13:16.
51. Eccles. 1:2.
52. Ps. 38:6 (A.V. 39:5).
53. II Cor. 4:18.
54. John 18:36.

55. The correct reference is Ephes. 3:14-15. The words "in the beginning" were added to the verse by the author.

56. I Tim. 1:17.
57. Heb. 1:2.
58. Heb. 11:3.
59. Rom. 9:21, with changes in the word order.
60. Jude 1:4.
61. *Ibid.*
62. Jas. 1:15.
63. Gen. 2:17.
64. Gen. 6:2.
65. Gen. 2:8.

48. SUBJECTS AND TEXTS FOR PREACHING
AGAINST HERESY

1. Douais, *La Somme des autorités*, pp. 7-22. See also the remarks on the techniques of preaching and disputation in Ilarino da Milano, "Fr. Gregorio," *Aevum*, XIV (1940), 108.

2. See the introduction to No. 49.

3. Douais's No. I (*La Somme des autorités*, pp. 34-41) comes from Paris, B.N., MS lat. 174, fol. 181v. His Nos. II and III (pp. 42-66) are from the same library, MS lat. 13152, fols 1-3. His No. IV (pp. 67-143) is from Toulouse, MS 379, fols. 76v-82b. A better copy of it, unnoticed by Douais, is in *Collection Doat*, XXXVI, fols, 129r-203r. Two more compilations of texts, in format exactly like those discussed here, but differing in the range of topics, are in Paris, B.N., MS lat. 14927, fols. 2r-7r, and still another is mentioned in Dondaine, "Durand de Huesca," *AFP*, XXIX (1959), 262-63.

4. We follow for chaps. XI-XIII the titles printed by Douais in his No. II, the text of which corresponds to Leipzig MS 894.

5. *Deus omnipotens* in Douais. Leipzig MS 894 has *David*, and all the texts cited refer to him.

6. *Secundum humanitatem* in Douais. Leipzig MS 894 has *divinitatem*. Cf. chap. XXVII.

7. That is, the angels who fell from heaven. Cf. Alan of Lille *Quadripartita*, in Migne, *PL*, CCX, 317, and Moneta of Cremona (No. 50, part A).

8. In this chapter the scriptural citations are interrupted by a harangue and challenge to heretics on the subject of Christ's body. This passage appears also in the summa of James Capelli (see No. 49) on pp. CXVI-CXX of Bazzochi's edition, where the same scriptural texts cited as proofs appear in the same order as in this chapter.

9. Douais adds: "and the attributes of a soul" (*et anime qualitates*), which we omit, following Leipzig MS 894, because of the wording of the next chapter title.

10. Chap. XI, part B, of the *Summa contra haereticos* attributed to Prevostin of Cremona (see No. 26) deals with the same subjects. All the citations from the New Testament used there are the same as those used in this chapter (including two from Ephesians which appear only in the Leipzig MS), and are given in almost the same order.

11. We follow Leipzig Ms 894: *Quod quilibet tenetur baptizari et quod prodest ante discretam etatem*. Douais reads: *De quibus iure baptizati[s] et quid prodest illis qui discretionem et etatem non habent*.

12. The content of this chapter much resembles chap. X, part B, § 2 (pp. 155-57) of the work of Prevostin cited in n. 10. All but two of the citations are the same in both works.

13. The content of this chapter is close to that of chap. X, part B, § 1, of the work of Prevostin (pp. 150-55). Most of scriptural citations are in both and in the same order.

14. The content of this chapter is comparable to chap. VI, part B, of the work of Prevostin, having nineteen citations of the same verses in much the same order, although the summa of Prevostin has many additional comments.

15. The content of this chapter is comparable to chap. VIII, part C, of the work of Prevostin (pp. 135-38), the citations being largely the same and appearing in almost the same order.

16. II Pet. 2:3.

49. JAMES CAPELLI ON THE CATHARS

1. Ilarino da Milano, "La 'Summa contra haereticos'" (full citation later in this Introduction), pp. 66-82. He also suggests (p. 78) that James Capelli might have been an inquisitor.

2. Demonstration of these relationships is not feasible here but a discussion of them may be found in an unpublished study: Walter L. Wakefield, "The Treatise against Heretics of James Capelli" (Ph.D. dissertation, Columbia University). The article in *Franciscan Studies* cited in No. 35, n. 3, also deals with this subject.

3. "Rapport . . . Etude sur quelques manuscrits des bibliothèques d'Italie," *Archives des missions scientifiques et littèraires*, 3d ser., XIV (1888), 150-53. The manuscript Molinier examined is Milan, Bibliotheca Ambrosiana, J.5. Inf. Molinier prints its table of chapter on pp. 280-82, and on pp. 289-90 a passage which constitutes part of our third excerpt.

4. *Beiträge*, II, 273-79. The manuscript is Cesena, Biblioteca Malatestiana, Pluteus I, viii. Döllinger selected passages at random.

5. There is another copy of the treatise in MS 527 of the library of the Metropolitan Chapter, Prague, fols. 111r-131v; and Dondaine ("Durand de Huesca," *AFP*, XXIX [1959], 266) mentions one in the library of the chapter at Seville: Cabildo, Colombina, MS 5-1-26, fols, 25r-87r.

6. Molinier (as cited in n. 3), p. 151; Ilarino da Milano, "La 'Summa contra haereticos,'" *Collectanea franciscana*, X (1940), 68.

7. This passage is found in the Cesena manuscript (hereafter referred to as C), fols. 27v-28r.

8. Mark 16:16.

9. The author has in mind friars delegated by their provincial chapters to investigate affairs in individual houses of an order.

10. *Arbitrium suum*. Bazzocchi (hereafter cited as B) omits *suum*.

11. *Protrahit*. B: *perthrait*.

12. *Docet*. B: *nocet*.

13. John 1:1 ff.

14. All the foregoing passage from the heading "On the Customs of Heretics" to this point is found in virtually the same words in Moneta of Cremona *Adversus Catharos et Valdenses*, pp. 277-78. This is only one of a number of such parallel passages.

15. Such oft-repeated charges are not supported by evidence from the sources of this period. It may be, however, that suicide to avoid falling into the hands of the Inquisition or while in its custody, or deaths which resulted from the refusal of invalid Cathars to eat when they were too ill first to say the Lord's Prayer (see No. 51, § 7) account for the considerable emphasis which later writers placed on suicide among the Cathars. In the last quarter of the thirteenth century in Italy and early in the fourteenth century in France, the practice of "endura" did appear. It was described as the with-holding of food and drink after baptism, from the moribund or from children, for in such cases the consolamentum had been administered with-out the preliminary demonstration of the recipients' ability to endure the abstinence imposed on the Perfect and they might have been unable to maintain their purity. It seems to have been rarely practiced by those who had been perfected in the usual way. See Charles Molinier "L'Endura," *Annales de la Faculté des lettres de Bordeaux*, 1st ser., III (1881) 282-99; and Yves Dossat, "L'Evolution des rituels cathares," *Revue de synthèse*, XXIII (1948), 29-30. However, Manselli ("Per la storia dell'eresia," *BISIAM*, LXVII [1955], 225-31) argues, from a reference to martyrdom in the recan-tation of a heretic in the twelfth century, that the endura was practiced then.

16. *Se bone operari.* B: *se bona opera.*

17. II Cor. 11:13-15 and Rom. 10:2-3.

18. *Per dulces sermones.* B: *perducentes sermones.*

19. The following passage is found in C, fol. 30v.

20. *Perfidie.* B: *per fidem.*

21. *Quomodo.* B: *quando.*

22. Matt. 26:26; Mark 14:22; Luke 22:19.

23. I Cor. 10:4.

24. Cf. Luke 22:19.

25. *Quandocumque.* B: *quaecumque.*

26. *Unicuique portiunculam.* B: *unicuicumque particulam.*

27. This ceremony, on which see also Nos. 51, § 5; 54, § 8; and 55, I, 2, has been likened to the agape, the love-feast of early Christianity but, as pointed out by Borst (p. 201, n. 31), it is more properly compared with the Eulogia, a distribution of blessed but not consecrated bread to those who were not present at Communion. References to it abound in testimony be-fore the Inquisition; see, for example, Douais, *Documents*, II, 27, 34, 39, 43, 45, 50, and on many other pages.

28. The following passage is in C, fol. 32r-v.

29. *Tamem.* B: *tantum.*

30. See No. 54, § 6.

31. John 15:20.

32. Mark 13:13.

33. Matt. 5:11, with a slight change in wording.

34. Apoc. 22:2.

35. This is the Service, also described in No. 51, § 7. A ritual for this

monthly penitential gathering is translated in No. 57, part B. Catholic
sources, especially the inquisitorial records, usually refer to it as *apparellamentum*; see the citations listed in Borst, p. 200, n. 28.

36. The following passage is found in C, fol. 39r.

37. Cf. Gal. 5:24.

50. MONETA OF CREMONA: EXCERPTS FROM
A SUMMA AGAINST THE CATHARS

1. A passage in the printed edition (p. 245) indicates that Moneta was
writing in 1244 but there are two manuscripts in which, in the same passage,
the date 1241 is indicated; see *DTC*, X, 2211; and Dondaine, "Le Manuel
de l'inquisiteur," *AFP*, XVII (1947), 179, n. 26. Moneta also writes (p. 402)
that it had been eighty years since Waldes began to preach in Lyons. If he
were writing in 1241 this estimate would be too great by at least a decade;
but the terms of the reference are not exact enough to contradict the earlier
statement seriously.

2. Tetricus is named on pp. 61, 71, 79. It has been suggested that he
should be identified with the canon of Nevers who fled to southern France,
to escape prosecution, changed his name from William to Theodoric, and
won great fame among the Cathars. See No. 59, I, 19, and n. 84; and also
Peter of Vaux-de-Cernay, *Hystoria albigensis*, ed. by Guébin and Lyon, I,
24; and Molinier, "Un Traité inédit," *Annales de la Faculté des lettres de
Bordeaux*, V (1883), 228.

3. Desiderius is named on pp. 248, 347, 357. On him, see No. 54, § 3.

4. Moneta refers to heretical works, which he does not identify, on pp.
2, 42, 94, 398. Duvernoy ("Un Traité cathare," *Cahiers d'études cathares*,
2d ser., XIII [1962], 29-30) believes that Moneta knew the treatise translated
in our No. 58. Venckeleer ("Un Recueil cathare," *RBPH*, XXXVIII [1960],
833) thinks that Moneta knew the one translated in our No. 60, part A.
Moneta also knew the theories of leadership discussed among the Poor
Lombards; see No. 46, n. 13.

5. See nn. 27, 28, below; also the introduction to No. 49. Another case
in point is that the passage on absolute dualism in part A here is very close
to one in the *Brevis summula* (see No. 53; ed. by Douais, pp. 115-21; ed. by
Molinier, pp. 199-206). If one comes directly from the other, Moneta may
be thought to be the borrower; however, it is more likely that both tracts
derive from a third source.

6. It is well attested that St. Dominic died in Moneta's cell at Bologna in
1221 and that Moneta shared in activities connected with church building
in Cremona in 1228 and 1233. His name is also found affixed to a *socida*,
an agricultural investment in which risk and profit were jointly shared
(Mauri Sarti and Mauri Fattorini, *De claris archigymnasii bononiensis pro-
fessoribus a saecula XI usque ad saeculum XIV*, new ed. [2 vols., Bologna,

1888-1896], II, 243). Legends of his courage in the face of heretical threats, and of his becoming blind from study appeared in the sixteenth century; see Ricchini's Introduction to the treatise, pp. viii-ix.

7. A volume of 560 folio pages with double columns.

8. II Cor. 4:4.

9. Cf. Ps. 50:14 (A.V. 51:12).

10. The phrase is repeatedly used in the heretical rituals in No. 57.

11. I Pet. 1:12.

12. The word is used frequently with reference to the two gods and their creations in No. 59, II, § 3; IV, § 9.

13. That is, angelic creatures.

14. A.V. Ps. 102:26-27.

15. A.V. Ps. 36:3.

16. A.V. Ps. 127:1.

17. A.V. Ps. 62:10.

18. Reading *eos* for *eam* of the text.

19. Matt. 18:28,29.

20. John 21:17.

21. Matt. 10:10.

22. Several glosses on the Gospel which were used in the Bogomil church of Bosnia are described in A. V. Solovjev, "La Doctrine de l'église de Bosnie," Académie royale de Belgique, *Bulletin de la Classe des lettres et des sciences morales et politiques*, 5th ser., XXXIV (1948), 501-11. Glossing Luke 10:30-35 less thoroughly than does this passage, two of them make several of the same interpretations—of the traveler, Jerusalem and Jericho, and the Samaritan. But the priest and the Levite are Moses and John the Baptist. In one gloss the oil and the wine are God's mercy; the innkeeper is either Peter or Paul. In one gloss the two pence are the Jewish faith, in another the Old and New Testaments. Thus if the Cathars derived this interpretation of the parable from the Bogomils and if it is accurately described by Moneta, there were significant changes in details.

23. Cf. Luke 16:8-9.

24. In a later passage (p. 115) Moneta says that the Cathars believed the devil to be the elder son. Cf. No. 37, n. 32.

25. Reading *serpens* for *semper* of the text.

26. Rom. 7:16.

27. It may be noted that the wording and order of this and the following four paragraphs correspond quite closely with the titles of chaps. VII-XIV of No. 48.

28. The reference is to a passage on p. 248. It was borrowed directly or indirectly from *De heresi catharorum in Lombardia* (see No. 23, § 2b), beginning with the words, "Some of the heretics of Bulgaria," and ending "at His ascension"; see Dondaine, "La Hiérarchie cathare, I," *AFP*, XIX (1949), 298-99.

29. A.V. Ps. 26:5.

30. We omit here and in the following paragraphs Moneta's rebuttal.

31. The biblical text concerns requirements in the early Church for membership in the "order of widows," which was eventually absorbed in the regular orders for women; see *Interpreter's Bible*, XI, 436-37. The heretical complaint, however, seems to be based on the contrast between orthodox exclusion of women from the priesthood and their own practice of admitting women to the consolamentum and full membership in their church.

32. A chariot drawn by oxen, used in warfare in the Italian cities. It bore an altar and the standards of the city and served as a rallying point for the warriors.

51. THE SUMMA OF RAINERIUS SACCONI

1. More than fifty manuscripts of the tract survive. To those listed by Dondaine ("Le Manuel de l'inquisiteur," *AFP*, XVII [1947], 173) should be added Rada Jugoslav Academya 240 (Thouzellier, *Un Traité cathare*, p. 35).

2. See the introduction to No. 45.

3. Rainerius was apparently less well informed about the Waldenses; he gives them only cursory treatment.

4. Dondaine's edition is a reprinting of the edition of Martène and Durand, *Thesaurus novus anecdotorum*, V, 1761-76, collated with two additional manuscripts. Dondaine defends it as an adequate, if not scientifically established, text in "Le Manual de l'inquisiteur," *AFP*, XVII (1947), 173-74.

5. *Ibid.*, pp. 57-58.

6. At this point in one manuscript (Dublin, Trinity College, MS C.5.19) appears a variant reading, perhaps a later addition, but one which rounds out the list of common beliefs: "The Albanenses disagree, saying that no creature of the good God shall perish. Also they all deny purgatory. It is the common opinion of all Cathars that one of them would sin very gravely by deliberately killing any bird, from the smallest to the largest, or any quadruped, from a weasel to an elephant in size; but they make no reference to other living things (*animalibus*). The passage is printed *ibid.*, p. 174, n. 9.

7. *Ordo*: See No. 23, n. 10.

8. On the practical importance to an inquisitor of this distinction, see No. 54, § 5.

9. *Professione vel ordine.*

10. Cf. No. 54, § 6.

11. See No. 54, § 6, which seems to qualify this assertion.

12. That is, in Western Europe, as opposed to the Balkans.

13. *Donnezacho:* Printed versions of the *Summa* use this for *Desenzano*, but one reliable manuscript has the latter form (Dondaine, "La Hiérarchie cathare, II-III," *AFP*, XX [1950], 253).

14. The words "persists at Vicenza" are supplied at the editor's suggestion.

15. The numbers refer only to perfected heretics. One manuscript (Munich MS Clm, 311, fol. 96) adds "but they have countless believers" (*sed credentes innumeri*).

16. His name is variously spelled in this and other sources. The form we adopt is that used in No. 54. Borst (p. 236) suggests the dates *ca.* 1210-1250 for Belesmanza's episcopate. It is elsewhere suggested that he should be identified with a heresiarch Belizmen'č, who was condemned by a Serbian synod in 1221; see Thouzellier, *Un Traité cathare*, pp. 35-36; Puech, "Catharisme et Bogomilisme" (see Bibliography for full citation), pp. 70-71.

17. Rainerius gives the only explicit information we have on this important person. *The Book of the Two Principles* (No. 59) expounds some of his ideas, and part of the polemic *Brevis summula* (see No. 53, n. 4) is said to have been based on information he provided. Dondaine at one time suggested the form *de Luglio* for his name ("La Hiérarchie cathare, II-III," *AFP*, XX [1950], 256, 286), while Savini (*Il catarismo*, p. 145, n. 1) asserts that *Lugio* is derived from the name of l'Osio, a locality near Bergamo. Other suggestions about him are that he may once have been a Cistercian monk, and that he had some education in law as well as theology; see Dondaine, *Un Traité néo-manichéen*, pp. 18-20; and Borst, pp. 270-71.

18. Luke 3:23.

19. See No. 59, II, § 11, for other names applied to the evil god in accordance with John of Lugio's ideas.

20. Jas. 3:8.

21. Matt. 6:34.

22. II Cor. 1:17-20.

23. Cf. Ezech. 35:5.

24. Phil. 3:19.

25. With the following passage on creation, cf. No. 59, II, §§ 4 ff.

26. Isa. 45:8.

27. Heb. 6:20.

28. Ephes. 2:10.

29. Gen. 1:1.

30. John 8:25.

31. Ephes. 2:10.

32. *Codex Justinianus, Digesta: De haereticis et Manicheis* I.5.2; in *Corpus iuris civilis*, Vol. II (Berlin, 1892), p. 50, as cited by Dondaine, *Un Traité néo-manichéen*, p. 73, note.

33. Gen. 6:4.

34. Job 2:3.

35. Job 30:21.

36. Ecclus. 31:10.

37. Job 4:18.

38. Job 25:5.

39. Gen. 3:1.

40. The text has "in the Book of Wisdom," but the quotation is actually from Ecclus. 31:9.

41. Rom. 8:20.

42. Rom. 8:22.

43. Isa. 45:22.

44. Cf. Deut. 32:39.

45. Cf. Job 33:14.

46. See the introduction to No. 59.

47. But *The Book of the Two Principles* is a work of exposition of these doctrines in part addressed to "beginners"; see the introduction to No. 59.

48. Matt. 1:23, quoting Isa. 7:14.

49. See I Tim. 4:1-3.

50. Pope Sylvester I (314-335), alleged recipient of the Donation of Constantine.

51. This was not true of the group in 1218; see No. 46.

52. WALDENSES IN THE THIRTEENTH CENTURY

1. That is, the sandal-wearers, wandering teachers; see p. 52, above.

2. Gen. 2:7.

3. See Luke 22:3.

4. Matt. 10:20.

5. Matt. 1:20. The words "and is begotten" are additions to the scriptural verse.

6. John 14:26.

7. See the description of the sacrament in No. 54, § 15c.

8. We cannot explain the distinction between the ordinary and the "infernal" Saracens and Albigenses.

9. Apoc., chap. 17.

53. TENETS OF THE ITALIAN CATHARS

1. The manuscript is Paris, B.N., MS lat. 13151, fols. 347c-350d, described by Douais (*La Somme des autorités*, pp. 22-28), who suggests the identification of the compiler as an Italian Franciscan, perhaps from Milan or its vicinity (pp. 25, 27). See also Dondaine, "La Hiérarchie cathare, I," *AFP*, XIX (1949), 294-305.

2. See the evaluations by Douais (*La Somme des autorités*, p. 27) and Molinier, "Une Texte de Muratori," *Annales du Midi*, XXII (1910), 195-96.

3. See No. 50, n. 6. In the present tract the information is said to have been given by two heretics: "That they believe and understand all this I have gathered and learned from the words of John of Bergamo, one of their preachers and teachers, who told me he had been a Cathar for forty years, and from the words of John *de Cucullio*, who, as he told me, was likewise a preacher and teacher among them for twenty-five years" (Douais, *La Somme*

des autorités, p. 121; Molinier, "Une Texte de Muratori," *Annales du Midi*, XXII [1910], 206; we will hereafter cite these as D and M respectively). It has been assumed by all commentators that the first of these persons was John of Lugio, of the Albanenses (see No. 51), but if he revealed these doctrines after he had been forty years a heretic, the date at which he did so could hardly have been before 1250; see Dondaine, "La Hiérarchie cathare, I," *AFP*, XIX (1949), 297. This is not easy to reconcile with the fact that Moneta of Cremona seems to have known the basic content of this passage in 1241; furthermore, while the tenets are those of absolute dualism, they are not those most characteristic of John of Lugio's teaching. Was the informant another heretic of Bergamo named John? Or could the statement have been made before the schism appeared among the Albanenses in 1230 and could the "forty years" refer to John's age at the time?

4. Dondaine ("La Hiérarchie cathare, I," *AFP*, XIX [1949], 294-96) discusses the relationship.

5. The substitution of *Albigenses for Albanenses* appears throughout the composite treatise, even in a passage copied from the *De heresi catharorum in Lombardia*, except that in one place in the chapters of refutation the words *Set Albanenses dicunt* appears (D, p. 134). In every known copy of the catalogue of tenets also (see n. 6, below) *Albigenses* is substituted for *Albanenses*. This may be put down either to the similarity of spelling, which could confuse an uninformed scribe, or to the notoriety of the Albigenses, or to the similarity in doctrine of the two sects. See the discussion of this point in M, p. 180, n. 2; Ilarino da Milano, "Il 'Liber supra Stella,'" *Aevum*, XVI (1942), 304-6; and Delaruelle, "Le Catharisme en Languedoc," *Annales du Midi*, LXII (1960), 152.

6. This catalogue of tenets in itself was thought valuable enough to be reproduced separately by contemporaries, notably in manuals of procedure for inquisitors. Its appearance in the manuscripts are enumerated in Dondaine, "La Hiérarchie cathare, I," *AFP*, XIX (1949), n. 32. It was published in Muratori, *Antiquitates italicae*, V, 93-96, and reprinted by Ricchini in his Preface to the work of Moneta of Cremona, pp. xxi-xxiii.

7. Their format is much like that of the manuals for preachers which were the basis for our No. 40.

8. This analysis of the tract differs somewhat from that offered by D, p. 26; and Dondaine, "La Hiérarchie cathare, I," *AFP*, XIX (1949), 294 ff.

9. Neither of the editors attempted to fix the date precisely. Among other entries in the manuscript is a calendar written in a hand comparable to that of the *Brevis summula*. A later addition to it is the feast-day of St. Peter Martyr, canonized in 1253 (D, pp. 22, n. 1; 24); thus some portions of the manuscript were written before that date. Dondaine ("La Hiérarchie cathare, I," *AFP*, XIX [1949], 297) dates the treatise after 1250. Thouzellier (*Un Traité cathare*, p. 53) calls it the work of a Franciscan inquisitor and dates it about 1270-1285.

10. Cant. 2:15.

11. *Instinctu* D; *instituto* M.

12. *Leo* D; *Boetius?* M. We have not identified the source of the following quotation.

13. *Revertantur* M; *evertantur* D.

14. Acts 27:31.

15. II Pet. 2:5.

16. Luke 5:3.

17. James 5:20.

18. Quoted in *Corpus iuris canonici, Decretales Gregorii IX,* Lib. V. Tit. 7. cap. 3, ed. by Friedberg, II, 778, where the editor identifies the words not as Augustine's but as a passage from the *De fide ad Petrum diaconum* of Fulgentius (468-533), bishop of Ruspa.

19. *Decretales Gregorii IX,* as cited in the preceding note.

20. *Ibid.,* cap. 1, quoting Pope Stephen. *Extravagantes* is a name given to the compilation of decretals published by Gregory IX in 1234.

21. *Ibid.,* cap. 2, quoting Pope Leo I.

22. See the introduction and n. 5, above.

23. Douais's difficulty with the following two or three sentences in the manuscript left several lacunae in his edition. We have supplied this passage from Döllinger's publication of another manuscript which contains what seems to be the same myth (*Beiträge,* II, 612-13); on it see Dondaine, "La Hiérarchie cathare, I," *AFP,* XIX (1949), 299, n. 38.

24. Apoc. 11:15.

25. At this point we resume translation from Douais's text.

26. Matt. 15:24.

27. This theory of triple inspiration of the prophets is put rather more clearly in other contemporary sources; see, for example, No. 54, § 3.

28. Matt. 15:24.

29. There is a lacuna of several lines in the published text because the manuscript is illegible.

30. Reading *erit* for *citra* of the printed text here and in the next paragraph.

31. The words in brackets were supplied by Douais.

32. *Decime* here but in comparable passage in the following catalogue of errors *elemosine* (alms).

33. Reading *ablata* for *oblata* of the text, as does Molinier in a comparable passage in the following catalogue of tenets.

34. *Peccatum non est abbutere arbitrio,* but in the following catalogue of tenets the comparable phrase is *a libero arbitrio* and we have so construed it here.

35. In one manuscript of the *Contra haereticos* of Ermengaud of Béziers (see item xiv in the Appendix), the author, citing I John 4:20, reproaches the Cathars for teaching their followers to love only their brothers in heresy, which doctrine, he declares, is reprehensible, because every man is a brother and a neighbor in the Catholic faith; see Thouzellier, *Catharisme et valdéisme,* p. 281.

36. Perhaps a reference to II Cor. 4:16, "Though our outward man is corrupted, yet the inward man is renewed day by day."

37. The translation of the sentence is conjectural. The text reads: *Contra hereticos qui dicunt quod non est iustitia; credentes vero dicunt quod occidendo potest fieri iustitia.*

38. The text reads "of Solomon"; the reference is to Ecclus. 42:25.

39. Reading *praeter hoc* for the *propter hoc* of the text. Cf. the diversity of views among the Bagnolenses on the following point, as explained in No. 23, § 2b.

40. Molinier resumed transcription of the manuscript with this heading. When Molinier and Douais do not agree and internal evidence throws no light on the correct reading, we have consulted the version published by Ricchini (see n. 6, above).

41. *Vetus testamentum* D; *veritatem* M.

42. Molinier has *A et pars illorum de B*, with which Ricchini agrees (p. xxii); Douais gives only *B*.

43. Douais omits *C*, but it is given in Molinier and Ricchini.

44. Douais reads *Quod aliud est opus*; Molinier supplies *non*, as does Ricchini.

45. Molinier omits this tenet. It is given by Ricchini.

46. Douais omits *B*, but is is given by Molinier and Ricchini.

54. AN INQUISITOR'S NOTEBOOK,
BY ANSELM OF ALESSANDRIA

1. Dondaine, "La Hiérarchie cathare, II-III," *AFP*, XX (1950), 238-49, 262.

2. Those omitted deal with the interrogation of heretics and the formal processes and powers of the inquisition, and include a slightly revised copy of Isidore of Seville's list of ancient heresies.

3. Cf. § 19, below, where he is called Hubert Manderius.

4. He is not otherwise known.

5. Dondaine ("La Hiérarchie cathare, II-III," *AFP*, XX [1950], 243, 286-87) identifies him as John of Lugio. Borst (p. 237, n. 17) disagrees.

6. *De Gona* here, but he is named as Bonaventura of Verona in § 19, below, and as Bonaventura della Torre of Verona in records of the Inquisition (Dondaine, "La Hiérarchie cathare, II-III," *AFP*, XX [1950], 287).

7. *Andrea:* He is not otherwise known.

8. His name is given in inquisitorial records as *Johannes de Casalolto* (Dondaine, "La Hiérarchie cathare, II-III," *AFP*, XX [1950], 296; Borst, p. 237, n. 24).

9. Dondaine ("La Hiérarchie cathare, II-III," *AFP*, XX [1950], 258) identifies him as a heretical bishop of Toulouse who fled to Italy in 1250. See also Borst, p. 233. This sentence appears in the text as the first of the

following paragraph but seems clearly to belong with the list of bishops.

10. The schism promoted by Desiderius should be dated about 1230 or a little later (Borst, pp. 12, 122, 162, 165). Moneta of Cremona, who wrote about 1241-1244 (see No. 50), also mentions Desiderius. In enumerating the ideas of mitigated dualists, Moneta says (*Summa*, ed. by Ricchini, pp. 247-48) that they insisted that Christ had a spiritual body and suffered no ailments or weaknesses of the flesh, although He pretended to do so. Desiderius is cited as agreeing with this although he had sometimes preached and written to the contrary (*ibid.*, p. 248). This would imply that the schism had been healed by 1241. Moneta elsewhere (*ibid.*, p. 347) quotes Desiderius as denying the resurrection of the body. Thomas Aquinas also knew the work of Desiderius. Desiderius was buried with Nazarius, but the bones of both were exhumed and burned by inquisitors (Dondaine, "La Hiérarchie cathare, II-III," *AFP*, XX [1950], 292).

11. We follow the tenses of the text, although at the time that Anselm was writing, Nazarius had been dead for thirty years.

12. This is the apocryphal work translated under the title *The Secret Supper* in No. 56, part B. It is also known as *Secretum hereticorum* [the secret of the heretics] and *Interrogatio Johannis* [the questions of John]. See also § 13.

13. Matt. 24:28.

14. Isa. 7:14, Matt. 1:23.

15. Matt. 27:52.

16. These views of Nazarius reflect the influence of the apocryphal *Secret Supper*.

17. Cf. the belief reported in No. 55, III, 1, that there is a spiritual marriage of the soul to God when one is perfected as a heretic.

18. *Lanfrancinus de Vaure:* He is not otherwise known.

19. John 10:16.

20. Cf. Matt. 18:26.

21. This is the most complete description of the consolamentum known from a Catholic source. For a discussion of acts and phrases see the introduction to No. 57.

22. John 1:1 ff.

23. Matt. 11:29. This verse is not mentioned in other descriptions of the ceremony or in the rituals themselves.

24. Sixteen repetitions of the Lord's Prayer, with genuflections; see the introduction to No. 57.

25. Although the need to be reconsoled after such sin is not stated here, it is implied by mention in the two following contingencies; cf. Dondaine, "La Hiérarchie cathare, II-III," *AFP*, XX (1950), 247, n. 25.

26. Cf. No. 55, I, 2, and n. 4. See also Borst, p. 184, n. 18, on comparable orthodox usages. It will be recalled that meat, milk, eggs, and cheese were forbidden to the Cathars at all times.

27. June 29.

28. November 24.

29. The text has *De tempore*, to which Dondaine adds *manducationis*. We have added further words because the prayers described here were repeated not only at meals but at many other times.

30. *Ancianus:* The word designates the chief person in a group of heretics living together or one who presides at ceremonies (see the rituals in No. 57). In Italian civic life, *ancianus* was applied to a leading citizen (Du Cange, *s.v.* "ancianus," 1). The status of the elder was determined by seniority as a heretic, as is shown by a phrase in Döllinger, *Beiträge*, II, 39: *antiquior in haeresi sive qui primus fuit haereticatus.*

31. What follows is a description of the act of melioramentum, on which see the introduction to No. 57.

32. *Faciamus aliud.*

33. *Bessea trona! Possumus facere de nostro melioramento?* We are unable to cast any light on the significance of the first two words; even the reading of the first word as *trona* (according to the editor) is uncertain.

34. In the work of an anonymous German inquisitor of the thirteenth century, who copied with considerable additions the work of Rainerius Sacconi, heretics are said to have met secretly, "and when they have come together, first they say, 'Beware lest there be a curved stick (*curvum lignum*) among us,' meaning any stranger" (*Maxima bibliotheca veterum patrum,* XXV, 264).

35. *Scampet te.*

36. Cf. No. 55, I, 5

37. At this point the summa of Rainerius Sacconi was copied into the text of the manuscript, interrupting this paragraph. Dondaine's explanation of this oddity is that Rainerius's summa was a separate manuscript thrust between the folios of Anselm's work. A methodical, if not very alert scribe, on copying the latter, copied the summa in just the place he found it (Dondaine, "La Hiérarchie cathare, II-III," *AFP*, XX [1950], 229).

38. Ps. 113² (A.V. 115):4.

39. *Est sandaliatus et portat clericatam super subtellaribus.* The editor (p. 318, n. 2) cites the comparable statement of Evrard of Bethune: "They tonsure their shoes but not their heads."

40. The supposed Donation of Constantine.

41. *Villelmus albigensis:* he is not otherwise known.

42. Cf. No. 45, part B. The epithet "the Good" does not appear in other sources which give his name.

43. This phrase perhaps applies only to the immediately preceding item. It seems to indicate that at the moment the author regarded his tract as finished.

44. Section 11, which we omit, is the summa of Rainerius Sacconi; see n. 37, above.

45. Neither of the persons mentioned is otherwise known.

46. A pilgrimage or crusade to the Holy Land.

47. The quoted words are the opening and closing phrases of the work; see No. 56, part B.

48. Section 14, which we omit, is a fragment of the interrogation of a heretic. It is dated 1266.

49. The three paragraphs which make up this passage are known from other sources; see item xxix (b) in the Appendix. The third of them is also in No. 55, II, 4. Anselm's change in terminology ("Poor of Lyons" and "Poor Lombards" here; "Ultramontanes" and "Lombards" in other passages) indicates that he copied this section from another source.

50. Pope Linus (67?-76?); Pope Clement I (88?-97?).

51 Sections 16 and 17, which are omitted, deal with inquisitorial processes and the powers of the inquisitor, respectively. Section 17 is of some interest because of the possibility that Bernard Gui, who included it in the fourth book of his manual, drew it from Anselm. Section 18, also omitted, is a list of heresies. The only sects named in it which fall within our area of interest are Cathars, Waldenses, Speronists, Circumcisers, and Arnoldists.

52. In the following list, the only individual surely known from other sources is Bonaventura of Verona (see n. 6, above). Henry of Arezzo may be the bishop named in a cryptic record of consolamentum which was written in the margin of the manuscript containing *The Book of the Two Principles* (see the introduction to No. 59). Borst (pp. 236-37) estimates that this list was drawn up about 1275.

55. BERNARD GUI'S DESCRIPTION OF HERESIES

1. This biographical sketch is based on the remarks of Mollat in his Introduction (I, vi-vii). His work will hereafter be cited as M. On Gui's literary activity, see Antoine Thomas, "Bernard Gui, frère prêcheur," *Histoire littéraire de la France*, XXXV (1921), 139-232. Thomas groups Gui's works under ten categories: theology, liturgy, hagiography, history of the Church councils, history of the popes, history of the emperors, history of the French kings and the geography of Gaul, history of the Dominicans, history of the Inquisition, and local history.

2. These are the solemn ceremonies, the "acts of faith," in which those adjudged guilty of heresy received sentence or, in the case of the ultimate penalty, were relaxed to the secular authorities for sentence and execution.

3. It may come as a surprise to some to learn that of the total number only forty-two were turned over to the secular arm to be executed. Three others, who had fled, were to be executed if apprehended. Douais (*Documents*, I, ccv) publishes a table indicating the penalties assigned. The largest group of sentences, numbering 307, were to imprisonment.

4. M, I, xi-xv. It was intended for the guidance of inquisitors in the general area around Toulouse, Carcassonne, and Albi (M, I, vii-viii).

5. M, I, xvi-xvii.

6. Dondaine, "Le Manuel de l'inquisiteur," *AFP*, XVII (1947), 114-15;

correcting the date given by M (I, xviii) as 1267-1273. Dondaine analyzes the source briefly, pp. 113-14.

7. M, I, xviii; Dondaine, "Le Manuel de l'inquisiteur," *AFP*, XVII (1947), 116-17. See also Dondaine, "La Hiérarchie cathare, II-III," *AFP*, XX (1950), 250-52, on the theory that Gui knew and used the work of Anselm of Alessandria (No. 54).

8. This is the name Bernard Gui used to refer to a group which called themselves "Apostles" (*apostoli, apostolici*).

9. M, I, xix.

10. M, I, xxii-xxiii. On the *De inquisitione hereticorum*, the two forms in which it appears in the manuscripts and printed editions, and the validity of the ascription to David of Augsburg, see Dondaine, "Le Manuel de l'inquisiteur," *AFP*, XVII (1947), 104-5, 180-83.

11. M, I, xxiii. Karl Müller, *Die Waldenser*, pp. 157-59.

12. Gui's separate report on the pseudo-Apostles is published (with French translation) in M, II, Appendix I.

13. See chap. V, nn. 2, 3.

14. "Le Manuel de l'inquisiteur," *AFP*, XVII (1947), 117.

15. There is a difference in the two editions. Some of the extant manuscripts of the *Practica* include in a section at the end additional formulas, important papal bulls, and the work on the pseudo-Apostles referred to in n. 12, above. Douais adds this material as chap. VIII of the fifth part of the *Practica*. Mollat places it in two appendices (II, 66-153). See his Introduction, I, ix-xi.

16. We omit §§ 9 and 10 of chap. IV, containing formulas for excommunication; the formulas for abjuration of various sects (chap. VII); and the material printed by M as appendices.

PREFACE AND CHAPTER I

1. In the manuscripts and in the edition of the work by Douais, this preceding paragraph constitutes the full title of Part V. It appears in M only as a footnote, but it seems of sufficient interest here to include it in the translation as part of the prefatory remarks.

2. Various degrees of complicity in heresy were recognized by the Inquisition. In the consultation of Raymond of Pennafort alluded to in an earlier place (No. 38, n. 17), "heretics" (*haeretici*) are those who persist in their error, and "believers" (*credentes*) are held to be the same as heretics in judicial proceedings. One might be "suspect" of heresy in varying degrees: "merely" (*simpliciter*), "seriously" (*vehementer*), or "most seriously" (*vehementissime*). Those who assist heretics are also differentiated according to the seriousness of their involvement with them. Bernard Gui also discussed such distinctions in the fourth part of his *Practica* (ed. by Douais, pp. 218-32).

3. Death did not end the possibility of prosecution as a heretic. See an early instance of this in No. 3 (p. 75); another is referred to in No. 54, n. 10.

4. Cf. the testimony before the Inquisition in the fourteenth century printed in Döllinger, *Beiträge*, II, 246, which gives slightly different dates for the fasts and suggests that dispensations were allowed for those who were working. See also No. 54, § 7.

5. See No. 38, § 15, for the case a century earlier, of a heretic who was consoled although he was too ill to repeat the Lord's Prayer. A striking illustration of the *covenensa* and perhaps among the earliest occasions for its use was the agreement between heretical partisans besieged et Montségur in 1243-1244 and the heretical bishop, Bernard Marty, by which agreement he promised to console them even if they were beyond the power of speech (Guiraud, *Histoire de l'Inquisition*, I, 137; Dossat, "L'Evolution des rituels cathares," *Revue de synthèse*, XXIII [1948], 28-29).

6. John 1:1-14.

7. Cf. Matt. 23:3.

8. See the works cited in nn. 49, 50, 52 of the Introduction.

CHAPTER II

1. Cant. 3:2.

2. Acts 5:29.

3. Mark 16:15.

4. Gui has here followed Stephen of Bourbon (No. 33) very closely.

5. *Insabbatati.*

6. Matt. 5:34 and Jas. 5:12.

7. *Corpus iuris canonici* Lib. V. Tit. 7 (*De haereticis*). Cap. 13, § 7: Friedberg, II, 788-89. For *superstitione* [superstition] Friedberg and Mansi (*Concilia*, XXII, cols. 989-90) read *obstinatione*, Friedberg giving *superstitione* as a variant reading in two manuscripts.

8. Matt. 7:1 and 5:21, respectively.

9. Cf. the discussion of a century earlier on these points in No. 46.

10. In his third book, Bernard Gui had entered a passage on the orders among the Waldenses which was based on a confession before the Inquisition at Pamiers (*Practica*, ed. by Douais, pp. 136-38). It is printed in Appendix II of M, II, 148-52. According to it, all three orders were elective and were ordained by the imposition of hands and the Lord's Prayer. Bishops and priests could hear confessions, but only the former had the power, rarely used, to remit some or all of the penalty for sin. Bishops consecrated the Eucharist, granted the power to priests to preach. Deacons provided for the material wants of priests and bishops but could not hear confessions. Only those ordained as deacons or in the higher ranks were called "the Perfect"; the term for all others was "believers," or "friends." See also the confession published in Döllinger, *Beiträge*, II, 97-143.

11. This accusation of obscene and lascivious behavior by the heretics is quite uncharacteristic of Bernard Gui. In the work attributed to David of Augsburg (*De inquisitione hereticorum*, ed. by Preger, in "Der Traktat des David von Augsburg," *Abhandlungen der historischen Classe der königlich*

bayerischen Akademie der Wissenschaften, XIV [1878], 210-11), which Bernard Gui had before him as he wrote, doubt of the truth of such stories is expressed.

12. *Majoralis*: The highest office among the Waldenses. The Waldensian hierarchy was discussed before Bernard Gui and others by two witnesses who testified that they had learned their doctrines from one John of Lorraine, *majoralis* of their sect, who, although not an ordained priest, could celebrate Mass, and to whom they owed "greater obedience than to the lord pope" (*Liber sententiarum*, pp. 289-92). Further details on the Waldensian hierarchy are found in other confessions printed in Döllinger, *Beiträge*, II, 97-144, and in a little tract (*De pauperibus de Lugduno* [on the Poor of Lyons], *ibid.*, II, 92-97). In the passage in Book III of the *Practica* cited in n. 10, above, *major* is used with reference to a bishop (*episcopus autem eorum major omnium appellatur*). Cf. § 5 below.

13. I Cor. 7:9.

14. *Benedicite, Kyrie eleison, Christe eleison, Kyrie eleison, Pater noster.*

15. See Matt. 14:17-21.

16. Apoc. 7:12.

17. Cf. Matt. 10:23.

18. See n. 10, above. Although Bernard Gui does not make it clear here, the other "rank" comprises the believers and friends.

19. Wisd. 1:11.

20. Cf. Matt. 7:12 and 19:17, respectively.

21. Matt. 5:34-37; vv. 35 and 36 are somewhat modified by the author.

22. An anonymous inquisitor in the diocese of Passau remarked: "I saw and heard an illiterate countryman who recited Job word for word, and I saw and heard several others who knew the whole of the New Testament perfectly" (W. Preger, "Beiträge zur Geschichte der Waldesier," in *Abhandlungen der historischen Classe der königlich bayerischen Akademie der Wissenschaften*, XIII [1875], 226n). Stephen of Bourbon also encountered a Waldensian preacher who knew the whole of the New Testament and most of the Old by heart (Lecoy de la Marche, *Anecdotes historiques*, p. 280).

23. The text reads: *et propter hoc non evades*. Gui is here following David of Augsburg, whose words are more explicit: *non evades sententiam mortis* (M, I, xxiii).

24. Here the author is copying the words of his source and not recounting his own experience (M, I, 70n).
I, 70n).

25. Cf. I Kings (A.V. I Sam.) 21:12-15.

26. Here Bernard Gui seems to be independent of his sources, remarking on his own observations.

27. This and the reference to the Eucharist in the following paragraph are in accord with the prescription in canon 22 of the decrees of the Fourth Lateran Council (1215), to the effect that confession and Communion must

be observed at least once a year, at Easter, in one's own church and under the ministration of one's own priest (Mansi, *Concilia*, XXII, 1007). That such a rule would be helpful in hunting down heretics can easily be understood.

28. *Inter perfectos credentes suos.* Cf. M, I, 81.

1. On the pseudo-Apostles, the best short treatment is by J. M. Vidal in "Apostoliques," *Dictionnaire d'histoire et de géographie ecclésiastique*, III, 1038-48; an adequate discussion in English may be found in Lea, *History of the Inquisition*, III, 103-24. Somewhat longer accounts are Felice Tocco, "Gli apostolici e fra Dolcino," *Archivio storico Italiano*, 5th ser., XIX (1897), 241-75; Gioacchino Volpe, *Movimenti religiosi e sette ereticali nella società medievale italiana*, 2d ed.; Arnaldo Segarizzi, in the Preface (pp. vii-l) to his edition of works on the pseudo-Apostles published in Muratori, *Rerum Italicarum scriptores*, new ed., Vol. IX, pt. 5 (1907); and Cesare Violini, *Fra Dolcino e la setta degli apostolici*. A recent detailed study on Dolcino and the pseudo-Apostles is E. Anagnine, *Dolcino e il movimento ereticale all'inizio del trecento* (Florence, 1964). The principal sources include the *Chronicle* of Salimbene, ed. by Oswald Holder-Egger in *MGH SS*, Vol. XXXII, pt. 1, pp. 255-94, 489, 563, 619-20, and more recently by Ferdinando Bernini in two volumes (Bari, 1942). An English paraphrase of Salimbene's work is in G. G. Coulton, *From St. Francis to Dante*. Other sources are printed in the work of Segarizzi just cited; for criticism of that edition, see Dondaine, "Le Manuel de l'inquisiteur," *AFP*, XVII (1947), 94, n. 27.

2. Segarelli, an unlettered peasant with little gift for leadership, was at first tolerated by Church leaders but was finally recognized as dangerous, haled before the Inquisition, and burned by the secular arm on July 18, 1300. Dolcino was a man of a different stripe. He had some education, a certain magnetism, and much determination. After the execution of Segarelli, he assumed direction of the group in northern Italy and offered armed resistance to ecclesiastical and secular authority, which declared a crusade against him. He met a fearful death on July 1, 1307. A fourteenth-century inquisitorial manual maligns him by saying that he confessed that he taught, not because he believed what he said but out of vainglory and because he thus won many advantages, temporal delights, and prestige; see Dondaine, "Le Manuel de l'inquisiteur," *AFP*, XVII (1947), 118, n. 6. Margarita is pictured as a woman of singular beauty, noble blood, and much wealth. We are told that she was offered freedom and a suitable husband if she would abjure heresy. She chose death at the stake. The treatise here referred to by Gui was included by him at the end of his work (Douais, pp. 327-55; Mollat, II, 66-120) and is also published, as noted above in n. 1, by Segarizzi. For the present discussion our author borrows freely from this work, but it has not seemed necessary here to indicate specific passages.

3. Apoc. 17:5.

4. As pointed out in M, p. 89, n. 1, the beliefs to which Gui here refers are those of Dolcino, not Segarelli. The latter seems to have had no system.

5. Pope Celestine V (July 5-December 13, 1294), a saintly recluse who was chosen by acclaim by the cardinals after a two-year vacancy in the See. He accepted the election with great hesitation, showed himself quite incapable of meeting the demands of the office, and resigned after five months. As here indicated, he won the warm approval of those who emphasized the strict rule of absolute poverty.

6. Matt. 4:17.

7. Matt. 10:16.

8. John 14:27.

9. Since the heresy of the pseudo-Apostles was found chiefly in northern Italy, Gui would have a natural interest in learning why any of them came to southern France. The register of his sentences lists only one of the sect who appeared before him (pp. 338-39, 360-63), and he had come from the Spanish province of Galicia, south of the Pyrenees; see M, I, 99n.

10. Cf. Matt. 16:18-19.

11. See chap. I, n. 2, above. A good illustration of the treatment of such a suspect is the case of Peter of Lugo, the individual alluded to in n. 9 above and in Bernard Gui's concluding paragraph in this section. He was held in prison for some two years, until finally a confession was drawn from him and he abjured his heresy.

12. The allusion is probably to the execution of Dolcino and some few of his followers after their overthrow and capture on Monte Rebello, and to the active pursuit of fugitives immediately thereafter (cf. M, I, 105, n. 1). Most of those who remained faithful to him to the end seem to have been killed either by cold and famine or by the crusaders who were sent out to destroy them.

13. See n. 9, above.

CHAPTER IV

1. The diocese of Toulouse was in 1317 raised by Pope John XXII to a province, with Raymond of Comminges as its first archbishop.

2. In 1317 Pope John XXII issued two bulls affecting the dissident groups in the Franciscan order: *Quorundam exigit* on October 7 and *Sancta romana* on December 30. The first ordered the abandonment of the short, skimpy habits the Spirituals affected, and held it to be lawful, under the rule of St. Francis, for the brothers to store up food for future use. The second ordered the Fraticelli and the Beguins to conform or to suffer excommunication. On the basis of these pronouncements there began a vigorous persecution of these factions. See J. M. Vidal, *Bullaire de l'Inquisition française* (Paris, 1913), pp. lii-liv; Lea, *History of the Inquisition*, III, 75-79; and Decima L. Douie, *The Nature and Effect of the Heresy of the Fraticelli*, pp. 16-21.

3. They were Peter *Dominici* from Narbonne, Peter *Hospitalis* from Montpellier, and Peter *Giraudi* from Béziers. The *Liber sententiarum*, pp. 383-95, records that they were sentenced as relapsed heretics. They were foreigners (*alienigene*) only in having come from outside the province of Toulouse. They were burned September 22, 1322.

4. Peter John Olivi was a leader of the Spiritual Franciscans; he spent most of his life in Languedoc. Trained at the University of Paris, he was active in teaching and writing. Early in his career he fell into disfavor with the Conventuals, the dominant faction in his order, for advocating the principle of absolute poverty. During the last fifteen years of his life (he died in 1298), he was under the necessity of defending himself against their criticism, but it was not until 1319 that the reading of his works was officially forbidden to the friars by the minister-general, Michael of Cesena. Peter's commentary on the Apocalypse was specifically condemned by Pope John XXII in 1326. Though himself loyal to the Church and greatly wounded by the charge of heresy brought against him by his critics, Peter was much revered by the heretical faction of the Beguins. Accounts in English of his life and works may be found in Huber, *Documentary History of the Franciscan Order* (Milwaukee and Washington, 1944), pp. 191-213; Douie, *Fraticelli*, pp. 81-119; and Carter Partee, "Peter John Olivi," *Franciscan Studies*, XX (1960), 215-60. The basic study is Franz Ehrle, "Petrus Johannes Olivi," *ALKG*, III (1887), 409-552. See also Raoul Manselli, *La "Lectura super Apocalipsim" di Pietro di Giovanni Olivi*, and the same author's *Spirituali e Beghini in Provenza*.

5. *Postilla:* a term employed since the early thirteenth century to refer to commentaries written as a continuous gloss on the sacred text. See Beryl Smalley, *The Study of the Bible in the Middle Ages*, pp. 270-71.

6. In a "letter of seven seals" this commission condemned articles drawn from the commentary of Peter John Olivi. The condemnation is published in Stephen Baluze, *Miscellanea*, ed. by Mansi, II, 258-70. Subsequent studies have done much to modify the adverse contemporary judgment of Olivi and his work; see Douie, *Fraticelli*, p. 94; and Partee, "Peter John Olivi," *Franciscan Studies*, XX (1960), 215-60, *passim*.

7. Probably the work cited by Ehrle in "Petrus Johannes Olivi," *ALKG*, III (1887), 476; see also *Histoire littéraire de la France*, XIX, 307-16.

8. *Contra Faustum* XIX.xi (Migne, *PL*, XLII, 355).

9. This is the point upon which they came into most serious dispute with authority, and it was the chief ground upon which John XXII condemned them. See Douie, *Fraticelli*, pp. 8-10, 96-102, 153-208, for a brief discussion of the problem. See also Felice Tocco, *La questione della povertà nel secolo XIV*; Noel Valois's article on Pope John XXII in *Histoire littéraire de la France*, XXXIV, 426-72; and M, I, 118n.

10. The *usus pauper*, or frugal consumption of goods, represented the extreme position of the Spiritual Franciscans in opposition to the Conventuals. In this the Spirituals received support from St. Bonaventure,

general of the order (1257-1274), and from Pope Nicholas III in the bull *Exiit qui seminat,* promulgated in 1279. But in raising evangelical poverty to a dogma, belief in which was necessary to salvation, the Spirituals and those Beguins who agreed with them went further than the Church was willing to go. Peter John Olivi wrote two influential tracts on the subject, discussed and published in part by Ehrle in *ALKG,* III (1887), 506-17. See also the references in the preceding note.

11. The notion of the "sixth era" is from the apocalyptic teaching of Peter John Olivi, who drew many of his ideas from Abbot Joachim of Flora (on whom see No. 44, n. 10). Olivi divided the history of the world into three ages: (1) the age of the Father, or of the Old Testament; (2) that of the Son, from the birth of Christ until about 1300; (3) that of the Holy Spirit, which was to be ushered in by the return of Christ, the overthrow of the mystical Antichrist (whom the Beguins identified with the pope) and the real Antichrist (possibly a descendant of Emperor Frederick II), and the completion of the work of the apostles by the Spiritual Franciscans. The second age, that of the Son, Olivi believed was divided into seven eras, the sixth of which commenced with the founding of the Franciscan order. The seventh he prophesied would be the time of cataclysm in preparation for the coming of the third age, that of the Holy Spirit. See Douie, *Fraticelli,* pp. 6-10, 251-57, for a brief discussion; J. M. Vidal, "Procès d'inquisition contre Adhémar de Masset," *Revue d'histoire de l'Eglise de France,* I (1910), 561-66; and Manselli, *La "Lectura super Apocalipsim."* For an illustration of how the ideas of Olivi were distorted by some of his followers, see the record of the trial of Na Prous Boneta, published with a brief introduction by William H. May, "The Confession of Prous Boneta, Heretic and Heresiarch," *Essays in Medieval Life and Thought* (New York, 1955), pp. 3-30.

12. "A vow is solemn if it is acknowledged as such by the Church; otherwise it is simple" (John A. Abbo and Jerome D. Hannan, *The Sacred Canons: A Concise Presentation of the Current Disciplinary Norms of the Church* [2 vols., St. Louis and London, 1952], II, 550 [col. 1308, art. 2]).

13. Issued October 7, 1317; see n. 2, above. The bull may be found in *Corpus iuris canonici. Extravagantes Joannis.* Tit. XIV. cap. 1 (*Quorundam exigit*): Friedberg, II, 1220-24.

14. This statement, together with much else that appears in the description of beliefs and practices of the Beguins, finds corroboration in the few pages of Gui's sentences devoted to them (*Liber sententiarum,* pp. 381-94). See especially the testimony of Peter *Giraudi* (p. 390), concerning the veneration of the bones and ashes of executed Spirituals and Beguins, who were looked upon as saints and martyrs.

15. Peter *Dominici,* in his testimony before the Inquisition, asserted that if John the Evangelist is in paradise, Peter John Olivi is also; though he did accord to the Evangelist the greater glory. And he went on to affirm that the beliefs and writings of Olivi were true no matter if the pope condemned

them "under a thousand bulls" or if they were condemned by a council of cardinals and all the prelates (*Liber sententiarum*, p. 384). The Council of Vienne had in 1312 condemned three of Olivi's propositions, notably his assertion that Christ was alive when His side was pierced by the lance (M, I, 139n).

16. John 19:33-34.

17. Apoc. 10:1-2. The assertion that such a belief was held by some persons was made by the Franciscan community in its efforts to discredit the Spirituals and to curb Olivi's influence (Partee, "Peter John Olivi," *Franciscan Studies*, XX [1960], 231).

18. Presumably this is a reference to the condemnation of Olivi's writings by the chapter-general of the order, held at Marseilles in the spring of 1319 (M, I, 141, n. 1).

19. For a description of Olivi's writings see Douie, *Fraticelli*, pp. 94-119; Partee, "Peter John Olivi," *Franciscan Studies*, XX (1960), 256-59; Ehrle, "Petrus Johannes Olivi," *ALKG*, III (1887), 459-533; and Manselli, *La "Lectura super Apocalipsim,"* chaps. IV and V. For a brief discussion of their influence on the Beguins of southern France, see Douie, *Fraticelli*, pp. 252-53. In testimony before Bernard Gui, Bernard de na Jacma reported that he possessed many books of the Beguins written in the vernacular (*Liber sententiarum*, p. 309).

20. Apoc. 17:1-6.

21. The reference is to Frederick II of Sicily, by the treaty of Caltabellatta (1302) titled "king of Trinacria." He was the third son of Peter III of Aragon and Sicily and became regent of the island in 1291 at the age of nineteen. His rule was a troubled one; he had to cope with the opposition of the Angevin claimants to the throne, first Charles II, then his son, Robert, who were aided by the king of France and the pope. But he managed to keep his throne and consolidate his power, so that his son Peter succeeded him upon his death in 1337. He is of interest in the present context because he gave asylum for a time to Spiritual Franciscans who fled from Italy, and also because his name was linked with the apocalyptic beliefs of the extremists. They presumed that one hundred years after the death of St. Francis, Robert and his allies, the ten kings of the Saracens, would overthrow the existing "carnal" Church and thus usher in the new era of the Holy Spirit, fulfilling the prophecy in Apoc. 17:12; see Douie, *Fraticelli*, pp. 16, 250, 256; and M, I, 145, nn. 1-3.

22. A branch of the Spiritual Franciscans found mostly in southern Italy. In their tenets they resembled the Beguins of southern France, and they were, like them, condemned specifically in the bull of John XXII, promulgated December 30, 1317. It is interesting to note, however, that they were one of the Franciscan groups marked by the Beguins for destruction; see Douie, *Fraticelli*, pp. 209-47 and *passim*; Félix Vernet, "Fraticelli," *DTC*, VI, 770-84; and M, I, 147n.

23. I.e., the Beguins.

24. I.e., John XXII; see M, I, 149, n. 1.

25. This is an obscure paragraph, upon which some light is thrown by the eleventh chapter of Olivi's commentary on the Apocalypse. There, as one may gather from the report of a commission appointed to examine the commentary and decide upon passages which might be "heretical, erroneous, or audacious," Olivi taught that between the time of the mystical Antichrist and the real Antichrist, the Spiritual Franciscans would preach actively to all peoples. When they had finished this mission, the beast which "rose up out of the bottomless pit" (Apoc. 17:8) would make war upon them, would conquer and slaughter them. These are the saints referred to in Apoc 7:3-9, in which their number is given as one hundred and forty-four thousand "marked by the sign of the living God." Thus it was given to Antichrist to triumph for a time (Apoc. 13:7-8). But he will finally be overthrown through the teaching of a small band of Spirituals, as recounted later, and thus the way will be prepared for the second coming of Christ and the Last Judgment. In our text, therefore, the first reference to Antichrist would seem to be to the mystical Antichrist, the second reference to the real. The reference to Elijah and Enoch is merely the Beguin version of a tradition which ran through the Middle Ages in various forms; they are the two Old Testament figures, the prophet and the patriarch who escaped death by being caught up into the terrestrial paradise, there to await the second coming of Christ. Some of Olivi's followers seem to have believed that "Enoch" and "Elijah" referred to St. Francis and Olivi. For a brief discussion of the tradition, though without reference to the Spirituals, see Arturo Graf, *Miti, leggende e superstizioni del medio evo*, I, 64-66; see also Manselli, *La "Lectura super Apocalipsim,"* pp. 98-99, 154-59, 180-86. For the report of the commission which examined the commentary, see Baluze, *Miscellanea*, II, 266.

26. For a graphic description of this carnage, see the testimony of Bernard de na Jacma, in the *Liber sententiarum*, p. 39.

27. Cf. Ps. 79:14 (A.V. 78:13); see the testimony of Peter Moresii in the *Liber sententiarum*, pp. 303-7: "Lord Pope John XXII . . . whom he calls a wild boar of the forest" (p. 306).

28. See n. 2 above.

29. Rather, in 1322, when the pope commissioned the bishop of Pamiers, Jacques Fournier, to proceed against them. The register of the Inquisition of Jacques Fournier is extant in manuscript (Vatican lat. 4030; published in part, though defectively, in Döllinger, *Beiträge*, II, 97-251) and is discussed by J. M. Vidal, *Le Tribunal d'Inquisition de Pamiers*. We have not seen the edition of this inquisitorial register by Jean Duvernoy, announced in 1965.

30. In these suggestions for specific questioning of the Beguins, Gui is drawing upon his own experience, as appears from pp. 298-333 of the *Liber sententiarum*.

31. See n. 25, above. The reference to the sixth and seventh heads of the

dragon apparently is an allusion to Apoc. 13:1, which describes a beast with seven heads. The heads were interpreted as the seven great empires which successively ruled the world: the first five being the Egyptian, Assyrian, Chaldean, Persian, and Greek (or Macedonian); the sixth, the Roman, or as the Beguin would say, the era of papal rule; and the seventh, that of Antichrist. With the overthrow of Antichrist will end the second era of the world; and the third era, that of the Holy Spirit, will be inaugurated by the Last Judgment.

32. Cf. Luke 6:39.

33. *Peremptorie*: This is a technical term designating procedure designed to expedite action of the court; see M, I, 181, n. 1.

34. *Questionari*: This is one of the very few references to the use of torture in Gui's work. For another, see the *Practica*, ed. by Douais, pp. 138-39.

35. Sections 9 and 10 (M, pp. 182-88) have not been translated. They contain, respectively, a formula for a first sentence and a sentence of excommunication against one who is contumacious.

36. See § 5.

37. On which, see Ehrle, "Petrus Johannes Olivi," *ALKG*, III (1887), 411.

38. The text has 1297 because Bernard Gui used the calendar beginning the year with the Feast of the Annunciation (March 25).

39. For some years after his death Peter John Olivi was venerated as a saint by the people and many clergy, but in 1318 the Conventual community destroyed the tomb and did away with his remains (Partee, "Peter John Olivi," *Franciscan Studies*, XX [1960], 233-34, 239).

CHAPTER V

1. Unless the Jew actively resisted and protested during the ceremony, the compulsion was not held to be absolute; see Yosef H. Yerushalmi, "The Inquisition and the Jews of France in the Time of Bernard Gui," *Rutgers Hebraic Studies*, I (1965), 24-25.

2. This paragraph is quoted from the *Sixtus* of Boniface VIII, Lib. v. Tit. 2. cap. 13: *Contra Christianos* (Friedberg, II, 1075). The Inquisition had been given competence to deal with proselytes and the re-judaized (converts to Christianity who returned to Judaism) by Clement IV in 1267, in the bull *Turbato corde*. That bull was several times reissued before the end of the century. On the Inquisition and the Jews, see Newman, *Jewish Influence on Christian Reform Movements*, which should be used with some caution, however. We have profited by the friendly advice of Professor Yerushalmi, and on his "The Inquisition and the Jews," *Rutgers Hebraic Studies*, I (1965), 1-60, depends the content of several of the following notes.

3. Many of the details in the ceremony described here appear in the case of a relapsed Jew tried by Bernard Gui in Toulouse in 1317 and sentenced

to life imprisonment; see *Liber sententiarum*, p. 230. Newman (pp. 385-86) is skeptical of most of the practices enumerated here; but Yerushalmi (pp. 47-58) concludes that most of them, although not required in Jewish law, have parallels in other prescriptions and practices, such as those for proselytes, and that the use of a rite substantially like the one described here is not improbable.

4. *Tymla*: for the Hebrew *tebilah*.

5. *Baaltussuna*: for the Hebrew *baal-seshuba*.

6. As noted in M, II, 10, n. 1, this interrogatory is heavily dependent on one in a thirteenth-century manual of the Inquisition (Paris, Bibl. Mazarine, MS 2015). Another manual, dated about 1265, with similar interrogatories is described from Vatican MS lat. 3987 in Dondaine, "Le Manuel de l'inquisiteur," *AFP*, XVII (1947), 141-54, esp. 149. Gui's list of questions is also very like one from the archives of the Inquisition at Carcassonne (*Collection Doat*, XXXVII, fols. 262r-263v; printed in Devic and Vaissete, *Histoire de Languedoc*, VIII, 987-88). The record of a trial in Pamiers in 1320 of a relapsed Jew whose conversion to Christianity had occurred under duress has been published by J. M. Vidal, "L'Emeute des Pastoreaux en 1320," *Annales de St. Louis-des-Français*, III (1898-1899), 154-74; English translation by Solomon Grayzel, "The Confession of a Medieval Jewish Convert," *Historia Judaica*, XVII (1955), 89-120. Yerushalmi ("The Inquisition and the Jews," *Rutgers Hebraic Studies*, I [1965], 12-17) analyzes the proceedings.

7. The text reads *per quos*, which we interpret as repeating the sense of the previous question as to a godfather.

8. The paragraph on circumcision appears in the short version of the *De inquisitione hereticorum* attributed to David of Augsburg (see item xxvii in the Appendix) and in the Mazarine MS referred to in n. 3, above. The practice here described is doubtless that alluded to in the interrogatory published in Devic and Vaissete, *Histoire de Languedoc*, VIII, 987-88, by the question *Quomodo circumcidunt Christianos aliter quam suos?* Newman (pp. 263-64, 305) and Yerushalmi (pp. 58-60) are in general agreement that partial circumcision is otherwise unknown, that it would have been quite unlikely among medieval Jews, and that this alleged practice may have been a figment of Christian imagination.

9. This is one of the blessings in the morning service; today, in the Ashkenazic rite, it is rendered as "hast not made me a heathen." See Joseph P. Hertz, *The Authorized Daily Prayer Book*, rev. ed. (New York, 1955), p. 19 and note.

10. This is, with certain interpolations, the *birkath ha-minim* (originally a prayer against heretics and schismatics), the twelfth of the eighteen blessings which are recited three times daily. The text was many times revised over the years. For the modern English text, see Hertz, *Daily Prayer Book*, pp. 143-45. See also Yerushalmi, "The Inquisition and the Jews," *Rutgers Hebraic Studies*, I (1965), 41-43.

11. A version of the Oleynu Prayer, which today closes congregational services. The sentences referring to those who bow down before vanity, invoke a powerless God, etc., which Bernard Gui and his fellow Christians found so offensive, are from a passage deleted in the eighteenth century from the prayer in the Ashkenazic rite; see Hertz, *Daily Prayer Book*, pp. 208-9 and note; Yerushalmi, p. 43. For an English translation of the prayer in the Sephardic rite, see David de Sola Pool, ed. and trans., *Prayers for the Day of Atonement: According to the Custom of the Spanish and Portuguese Jews*, p. 17. The scriptural verse is Exod. 15:18.

12. The word is usually applied to a prayer book which contains the holiday liturgy.

13. *Cematha*: A transliteration of *shamta*, which M, II, 17, incorrectly identifies as *shema*, a confession of faith. *Shamta* is an Aramaic word used in Jewish legal literature in the sense of curse, ban, or excommunication. Yerushalmi (pp. 44-47) shows that in twelfth-century France a malediction in poetic form was sometimes recited in synagogues in the afternoon service on the Day of Atonement and that anti-Christian prayers were in existence. He concludes that Bernard Gui's testimony here is correct.

14. Solomon son of Isaac, that is, Rashi (1040-1105). On him, see *Jewish Encyclopedia*, X, 324-28, and particularly with respect to his influence, Herman Hailperin, *Rashi and the Christian Scholars* (Pittsburgh, c1965).

15. At the instigation of an apostate Jew who had become a Dominican, Gregory IX ordered an inquistition of the Talmud and other Jewish books suspected of containing blasphemous passages. At Paris, in proceedings begun in 1239, several rabbis defended their books, but unsuccessfully, and the offending works were condemned and burned in large numbers in 1244. Similar burnings took place elsewhere in subsequent years. On Jewish-Christian controversies in the Middle Ages, see Isidore Loeb, "La controverse religieuse entre les Chrétiens et les Juifs au moyen âge en France et en Espagne," *Revue de l'histoire des religions*, XVII (1888), 311-37; XVIII (1888), 133-56; Newman, *Jewish Influence*, pp. 318-21; and Solomon Grayzel, *The Church and the Jews in the Thirteenth Century* (Philadelphia, 1933), 94-98, 239 ff. Bernard Gui himself was active in searching out and condemning Jewish books in 1310, using formulas under that date which may in fact have originated much earlier. Again, in 1319, he supervised the burning of two wagonloads of copies of the Talmud. The sentence condemning the books in 1319 is in *Liber sententiarum*, pp. 273-74. See also Grayzel, *The Church and the Jews*, pp. 341-43; and Yerushalmi, pp. 7-10.

16. Moses son of Maimon, better known as Maimonides (1135-1204), author of commentaries on Jewish law and on the Torah and of other theological works, notably *The Guide of the Perplexed* (trans. by Shlomo Pines [Chicago, 1963]), all of which attained international renown. The work to which Bernard Gui here refers is his *Mishnah Torah*, the code of Jewish law, of which an English translation is in progress in the Yale Judaica series. There is a recent short biography: Solomon Zeitlin, *Maimonides: A Biography*, 2d ed. (New York, 1955).

17. This was Rabbi David Kimhi, also known as RaDaK (1160-1235), a Provençal grammarian and exegete, whose commentaries, such as that on the Psalms, contain sharp polemical passages. See Yerushalmi, "The Inquisition and the Jews," *Rutgers Hebraic Studies*, I (1965), 37, and n. 85; and Newman, *Jewish Influence*, pp. 326-39.

CHAPTER VI

1. On witchcraft and sorcery, see the works cited in No. 42. Neither the distinction between mere practice of occult arts and actual worship of the devil nor the competence of inquisitorial courts in cases involving the former had been clearly established when Bernard Gui wrote. In 1320 Pope John XXII conferred upon the Inquisition jurisdiction over cases of sorcery, although he rescinded that grant of power in 1330. The *Liber sententiarum* does not disclose any sentences by Bernard Gui for sorcery, but he did include in the *Practica* (part III, ed. by Douais, pp. 150-55, 156-59) three formulas for degrading and sentencing clerics who were guilty of dabbling in magic; and six cases involving sorcery were tried at Pamiers in 1321, shortly before he completed his work. Such cases became more numerous thereafter; see Lea, *History of the Inquisition*, III, 452-54; *idem, Materials toward a History of Witchcraft*, I, 230 ff. About forty years after Bernard Gui wrote, another inquisitor, Eymeric, went into more detail in his *Directorium inquisitorum* (ed. with commentary by Francis Pegna [Venice, 1609]). He distinguishes between sorcerers and diviners who were mere soothsayers and those whose practices "smell' of heresy (part II, q. lxii, pp. 335-38). In the following chapter (q. lxiii, pp. 338-51) Eymeric discusses invocations of the devil, stating that if invocation involves adoration (*latria*) or coupling the names of demons with those of saints in prayer (*dulia*), it is clearly heretical. See Lea, *Materials toward a History of Witchcraft*, I, 205-20, for other instances of fourteenth-century opinion.

2. The interrogatory which follows is not entirely original with our author (M, II, 10, n. 1); see also the interrogatory published by Vaissete and cited in chap. V, n. 6, above.

3. Consecrated materials wrongfully taken from the altar were considered especially valuable for divination.

4. Using figurines to cast spells on individuals for various purposes is an ancient practice. In one of the model sentences given earlier by Bernard Gui, the figurine referred to had been baptized; in another it had not (*Practica*, ed. by Douais, pp. 156, 153, respectively).

56. BOGOMIL LITERATURE ADOPTED
BY THE CATHARS

1. *The Ascension of Isaiah* survives in three Ethiopian manuscripts and in fragments of Greek and Latin copies. On the origin and date of its component parts, see R. H. Charles, *The Ascension of Isaiah*, pp. xi-xiv, and

René Nelli and Déodat Roché, "La Vision d'Isaïe," *Cahiers d'études catha-res*, XXXIII (1958), 19-51, esp. 19-20. We have not seen E. Tisserant, *Ascension d'Isaïe: Traduction de la version éthiopienne* . . . (Paris, 1909); nor Jordon Ivanov, *Bogomilski knigi i legendi* [Bogomil books and legends] (Sofia, 1925). Their studies were utilized by Nelli and Roché and also by Turdeneau in the work cited in the following note.

2. Six known manuscripts of *The Vision* in various European languages (the earliest is from the twelfth century) reflect a common Slavonic text prepared in Bulgaria (Slavonic was the official language of Bulgaria after A.D. 893; thus the manuscripts are called either Slavonic or Bulgarian). The Latin translation from the Slavonic, first printed in Venice in 1522, came from a manuscript now lost. Emile Turdeneau ("Apocryphes bogomiles et apocryphes pseudo-bogomiles," *RHR*, CXXXVIII [1950], 216-18) shows how the Bogomils edited *The Vision* to suit their doctrine. They omitted passages which put personages of the Old Testament in heaven, those which referred to the Son of God as Jesus or the Christ, and those which men-tioned the Cross as an object of veneration, as well as words which might be construed as supporting the divine motherhood of Mary.

3. Its influence may have been felt even earlier. A letter of St. Boniface tells of the vision of a woman in the eighth century who saw a plurality of heavens (Paul Alphandéry, "Traces de manichéisme dans le moyen âge latin [VIe-XIIe siècle]," *RHPR*, IX [1929], 452-53).

4. Thouzellier, *Une Somme anti-cathare*, pp. 256-57, 288.

5. *Summa contra hereticos*, ed. by Bazzocchi, p. XCIII; and *Adversus catharos et valdenses*, ed. by Ricchini, p. 218, respectively.

6. Döllinger, *Beiträge*, II, 166-67, 208-10. These are passages of testi-mony before the Inquisition in 1321.

7. The Charles edition of *The Ascension of Isaiah* contains an English translation of the Ethiopic text on pp. 1-82 and a parallel edition of the Ethiopic, Greek, and Latin texts on pp. 83-139. The Latin text from which our translation is made is on pp. 98-139. Another publication of Charles's translation appeared in 1917: Society for Promoting Christian Knowledge, *Translations of Early Documents*, 1st ser., No. 7: *Palestinian and Jewish Texts (pre-rabbinic)*.

8. See Turdeneau, "Apocryphes bogomiles," *RHR*, CXXXVIII (1950), 207-12; and Borst, pp. 8, 161, for discussion of its origin and citation of pertinent literature.

9. Nazarius probably went to the Balkans for ordination about 1190 (Borst, pp. 8, 101-2). A note appended to copies of the tract known to inquisitors recorded his role in obtaining the work and commented that the tract is "full of errors"—and "full of bad Latin," Anselm of Alessandria added on a copy in his possession (see No. 54, § 13). The latter is a com-ment we echo after our difficulties with the translation. The influence of *The Secret Supper* is discernible among the Albigenses soon after 1220

according to Thouzellier, *Un Traité cathare*, pp. 65-66 and 90-112, *passim*.

10. See No. 54, § 3.

11. F. Benoist, *Histoire des Albigeois et des Vaudois ou Barbets*, I (Paris, 1691), 283-96.

12. Vol. XXXVI, fols. 26v-35r. A copy, apparently of the fifteenth century, also survives in MS 109 of the public library of Dôle, fols. 44r-46r (Dondaine, "Le Manuel de l'inquisiteur," *AFP*, XVII [1947], 94-95, 134-35).

13. Editions are listed in Turdeneau, "Apocryphes bogomiles," *RHR*, CXXXVIII (1950), 204, n. 1; and Dondaine, "Le Manuel de l'inquisiteur," *AFP*, XVII (1947), 134, n. 9.

14. *Die Vorgeschichte der christlichen Taufe*. The text, pp. 297-311, comprises editions of both the Vienna and the Doat version (here designated as V and D, respectively), together with scholia to V.

15. In *Ecritures cathares*, pp. 34-66.

A. THE VISION OF ISAIAH

1. The chapters are numbered I-VI here because *The Vision* as the Cathars knew it was an independent work. Our chapters are VI-XI of the composite *Ascension of Isaiah*.

2. Charles (*Ascension*, p. 98) prefers to treat these words as a title and begins v. 1 with "In the twentieth year."

3. This expectation of prophecy from them, rather than from Isaiah, is explained in the Ethiopic version (Charles, *Ascension*, pp. 43-44) as a consequence of Isaiah's placing his hands on them. Hereafter, the Ethiopic version will be referred to as E, with page reference to Charles's translation. A Latin translation of a Slavonic version, also published by Charles, will be referred to as S.

4. Perhaps the angel who conducted Isaiah through the heavens; see chap. II, v. 2. The Latin is less clear than the different reading of E, p. 45: "and he saw not the men that stood before him."

5. V. 13 is lacking from the Latin text. It identifies the angel as the one who was sent to conduct Isaiah.

6. *Elevatio accepisset*.

7. *Quando prophetavi auditum, quem vos vidistis*.

8. *Post illos cum eis*. We amend the last two words, with Charles (*Ascension*, p. 107, n. 11), to *cantabant*.

9. I.e., the angel mentioned by the guiding angel in the next phrase.

10. I.e., at the resurrection.

11. *Parvum thronum*: probably a defect in the translation of the Latin from the Slavonic or of the Slavonic from the Greek, and should be read "a throne in the midst," as in E, p. 52. Cf. S, p. 110.

12. *Memoria ... non nominabitur*: that is, was not worthy of memorial, even in a name. Cf. Charles, *Ascension*, p. 52, note; and see also v. 26.

13. The explanation seems to be that Isaiah was successively transformed

into the likeness of the angels of each heaven, just as Christ would be transformed when He descended through them to earth; see x.9. Nelli ("La Vision d'Isaïe," *Cahiers d'études cathares*, XXXIII [1958], 27, n. 18), gives this explanation, following Tisserant.

14. I.e., the angel of the second heaven.

15. Greater, that is, than the distance from the first to the second heaven (see v. 18) or the distance from the earth to the firmament, as explained in E, p. 53.

16. V. 30 is lacking from the Latin. In E (p. 53) and S (p. 111) it is said that the glory and the song of the angels on the right were greater than of those on the left.

17. V. 35 is lacking in the Latin text. In E (pp. 53-54) vv. 34 and 35 repeat the sense of v. 31 as to the greater glory of the angels compared to their inferiors.

18. *Angelum.* We correct to *angelos* with E (p. 54) and S (p. 113).

19. *Consiliator.* Translated as "companion" in E (p. 54, note), which Charles explains as the equivalent of "fellow servant" (*conservus*) of Matt. 18:28,31. Nelli ("La Vision d'Isaïe," p. 28, n. 23), following Tisserant, finds the analogy to be with *conservus* as applied to the angel in Apoc. 19:10; 22:9.

20. V. 6 is lacking from the Latin text. In E (p. 55) it poses the question about the absence of angels on the left which is answered here.

21. We change the punctuation of the Latin text: *Dixit mihi: De sexto coelo, et hic jam thronus non est.* Nelli ("La Vision d'Isaïe," p. 28) translates: *A partir du sixième ciel et au-dessus, il n'y a plus de trône* .... For the distinction of the sixth and seventh heavens from the first five, see also part B, § 2, in which Satan is able to seduce only angels of the first five heavens.

22. *Dives:* Nelli ("La Vision d'Isaïe," p. 28, n. 25) compares this in meaning with the Provençal *ric* [powerful], which is in fact the very word used in a Provençal translation of this verse, in a work discovered after Nelli wrote; see No. 60, chap. I, n. 30.

23. V. 10, lacking in the Latin text, in E (p. 56) concerns the successive transformations of the Lord into the likenesses of angels and men—the substance of chap. IX, vv. 17 ff.

24. *Ego magnificavi me ... domino,* corrected to *ego magnificavi meum dominum,* as in S (p. 115).

25. *Sexto,* corrected to *septimo,* as in S (p. 115); cf. E (p. 57, n. 14).

26. See Charles, *Ascension,* p. 57, note, referring to testimony in another apocryphal treatise that all angels of the sixth heaven were alike in appearance.

27. In E (p. 58) these words are addressed by Isaiah to Hezekiah, Jozabad, and Micah.

28. *Exercitus,* corrected to *vestes* with Charles (*Ascension,* p. 117, n. 12), who supposes a corruption in the translation from the Greek.

29. V. 8 is lacking in the Latin text. In E (p. 60) vv. 7-9 are quite different, for they describe Adam, "the holy" Abel, and Enoch among the righteous. The Bogomils held the Old Testament patriarchs to be the devil's servants, and this change in the text is one example of their editing *The Vision* to suit their doctrines; see Turdeneau, "Apocryphes bogomiles," *RHR*, CXXXVIII (1950), 216-18.

30. Again, this alters the text as found in E (pp. 61-62), by omitting the words "the Lord, who will be called Christ"; it is another hint of Bogomil editing, according to Turdeneau (as cited in n. 29).

31. One interested in the fine points of the eschatology of the Ethiopic version may consult Charles, *Ascension*, p. 63, notes; and Nelli, "La Vision d'Isaïe," p. 32, n. 40. Both of them argue the question of which among the righteous will not receive even their vestments until the day of Christ's ascension; this does not seem entirely relevant to Catharist thought, however, since the Latin text does not pose such a problem.

32. The reference is to a request Isaiah made in the third heaven: He asked to be told how events of the world were known in heaven (E, p. 52). The verse with this request is lacking in the Latin text.

33. *Pro humanitate et humilitate*: Nelli ("La Vision d'Isaïe," p. 33) translates this as *pour l'humanité et pour la bonté (pour la triomphe de la bonté)*, with a note that Michael is the protector of humanity.

34. The Latin text omits the phrase "That One who shall be named" and a reference to those who "believe in His cross," which are found in E, p. 65—more evidence of Bogomil editing.

35. *Et ille cantabat*, corrected to *ego cantabam*, with Charles, *Ascension*, p. 125, n. 12.

36. *Et non transfiguravit se in visu illorum*. We follow Charles (*Ascension*, p. 125, n. 13) in correcting to *transfiguravi me*. Charles (*Ascension*, p. 67, note) explains: "Isaiah was transformed into the likeness of the *angels* and could thereby enjoy certain visions, but he was not transformeu into the likeness of the *righteous*, and was on that account excluded from steadfastly beholding the ineffable vision in verse 37, which angels could not behold but only the righteous, verse 38." Nelli ("La Vision d'Isaïe," p. 33) rejects Charles's correction.

37. *Secundo insimul*, corrected with Charles (*Ascension*, p. 127, n. 11) to *duo insimul*. The Son and the Holy Spirit are here adoring the Father.

38. *In sexto caelo*. Charles (*Ascension*, p. 127, n. 13; p. 128, n. 9) would correct this to *in singulis sex caelis* [in each of the six heavens] to correspond to the Ethiopic version.

39. Vv. 3-4 are lacking in the Latin text. In E (p. 69) they repeat that Isaiah heard and saw the praise and song, as did the Lord and the Holy Spirit.

40. The Latin text omits this phrase of E (pp. 69-70): "my Lord Christ, who will be called Jesus." See n. 30, above.

41. The Latin text lacks v. 10. In E (p. 70) it repeats the injunction to

the Son to take on the form of the angels of the firmament and hell.

42. *Initia.* See Charles, *Ascension*, p. 130, n. 19 ("*initium* = ἀεχή = 'principality' "); and Nelli ("La Vision d'Isaïe," p. 35, n. 51), who suggests that the Cathars would interpret these to be the spirits of the elements created by the good God.

43. The six and seventh heavens being of different quality from the first five, the Lord did not transfigure himself there.

44. V. 24 is lacking in the Latin text. In E (p. 73) it recounts that the angels guarding the gate of the third heaven demanded the "password," which the Lord gave in order not to be recognized.

45. In E (p. 73) Charles translates the Ethiopic equivalent as "password."

46. Nelli ("La Vision d'Isaïe," p. 36, n. 55), following Tisserant, notes that because the angels of the air were engaged in constant strife (E, p. 74: "one was plundering and doing violence to the other"), the Son of God could pass without their noticing.

47. The Latin text lacks vv. 2-18. In E (pp. 75-78) they recount the story of Mary and Joseph, both of the family of David. The angel of the Spirit persuaded Joseph not to abandon Mary when she seemed to be with child before their marriage. After two months, Mary was stunned ("astonied" in Charles's translation) to see a small babe. Joseph, when his eyes were opened, saw the infant and praised God. There was much puzzled discussion of the event by the people in Bethlehem, who were blinded about the babe. Jesus pretended to be a child to avoid recognition of his true nature, but later he worked wonders. This passage and vv. 20-22, which were also omitted from the Latin text, are regarded by Turdeneau ("Apocryphes bogomiles," *RHR*, CXXXVIII [1950], 216-18) as important evidence of Bogomil revision.

48. The Latin text omits vv. 20-22. In E (p. 78) they relate that the adversary, envying Jesus without knowing who He was, caused His crucifixion. Jesus descended into hell, rose again after three days, and remained on earth for some time, sending out His apostles.

49. *Ascendisti*, corrected to *descendisti*, following Charles, *Ascension*, p. 135, n. 12, Nelli ("La Vision d'Isaïe," p. 37) makes the same correction.

50. *Gloriae suae conjungebat se.* E (p. 80) has "the praise increased," which Nelli ("La Vision d'Isaïe," p. 37) also adopts.

51. Cf. I Cor. 2:9.

52. The passage seems corrupt. It probably means: "How many things will be understood after this book has been read!"

53. E, vv. 41-43 (pp. 81-82), adds that because of these prophecies, Satan caused Isaiah to be sawn asunder. Hezekiah delivered these things to Manasseh; but Manasseh did not remember them, and as Satan's servant he was destroyed.

54. Another witness told a variant of the same story (Döllinger, *Beiträge*, II, 208-10). He said it was found in a prophecy of Isaiah that when a heretic was searching in books for answers to his doubts he was visited by

an angel and carried to the heavens. The "people" of the first five heavens, he was told, were spirits, neither good nor evil, waiting the Day of Judgment. In the seventh heaven he beheld the righteous (heretical) men and women, who there were all alike. It was explained that differences in their earthly bodies had been the work of the devil. He adored the Holy Father, who was Father of the people of Israel, that is, the heretics. God, however, would not let the heretic address Him as "Father," because he had doubted. However, he was assured that subsequently, when he had put off the tunic of the world, which is the body conceived in uncleanliness, his soul could return.

B. THE SECRET SUPPER

1. That is, the heavenly archetype of the Last Supper instituted by Christ in this world; cf. John 13:23-31; also Matt. 26:26-29; Mark 14:18-21.

2. Cf. Apoc. 1:9.

3. Cf. John 13:25-27; Matt. 26:21-23.

4. One of the orders of the celestial hierarchy. See Ephes. 1:21; the Pseudo-Dionysius, *The Celestial Hierarchy* x (see No. 21, n. 3).

5. Our text reads *et sedebat ego apud patrem meum*. Reitzenstein (whom we follow) deletes *ego*. D reads *Ego autem sedebam*, which Reitzenstein thinks should be amended to *ego autem nondum sedebam*. Note that in *The Vision of Isaiah* (chap. V, v. 14) Christ does not sit at the right hand of God until after His mission to earth.

6. Cf. Isa. 14:13-14.

7. Cf. Ephes. 2:2: "prince of this air." *The Vision of Isaiah* (chap. V, v. 30) speaks of angels of the air. Nelli (*Ecritures cathares*, p. 53, n. 3) defines the air as "distinct from the firmament."

8. Cf. Apoc. 16:5.

9. D reads (translation ours): "They were like oxen yoked to the plow." A marginal gloss (no. 2) to this passage says: "It is true that these were none other than fish; but they represent the Gospels and the Epistles, which support the Church, just as the fish support the earth . . . ."

10. Cf. Isa. 14:13-14.

11. Cf. Gen. 1:9.

12. Cf. Apoc. 11:15.

13. Cf. Luke 16:5-7.

14. Cf. John 13:27.

15. Cf. Apoc. 4:4.

16. *Praecepit pater meus et transfiguravit se propter elationem suam.* D reads *transfiguravit eum*.

17. There is here a lacuna in the text, which may be partially explained by a marginal gloss (no. 4), likewise mutilated, which seems to state: ". . . his face changed color [like that of a man caught?] by his lord in some evil deed. His countenance was altered, like that of a man who had lost the light that was in him, and was darkened because of the evil which he was planning." D gives no help at this point.

18. Cf. Apoc. 12:4. Marginal gloss no. 5 reads: "The seven tails are the seven sins or vices by which he has, until the present, seduced men, to wit: lying, adultery, greed, theft, blasphemy, envy, and discord." Cf. the list of the works of the Evil One, author of the Old Testament, as given in No. 59, IV, 10.

19. Cf. Matt. 18:26.

20. That is, the seventh age of the world.

21. A lacuna in the text.

22. We follow the text as edited, omitting the phrase *et medium lumen solis* [and from half the light of the sun], which Reitzenstein deletes, probably because of "the light of day" in the following phrase.

23. *Omnem militiam et stellas.* D has *omnem militias stellarum.*

24. *Omne vivens.* Cf. Gen. 1:24. A marginal gloss (no. 6) to this passage reads: "Birds and fishes have no spirit, nor do beasts have the spirit of man; but birds and fishes receive all their attributes from the air and the water, beasts from the earth."

25. Cf. Gen. 2:7.

26. Cf. Gen. 2:21-22.

27. D names these as angels of the third and second heavens, repectively.

28. Cf. Gen. 2:8. At this point there is a long marginal gloss (no. 7) which describes Paradise. According to the gloss, the first man thought Paradise was good, even as men continued to do after him, but it was actually evil. Death came to man not because of his disobedience, but because of the wiles of the devil. Man, the glossator remarks, would not have escaped death even had he refused to eat of the fruit.

29. *Aequitatis et iniquitatis.* D reads *scientiae boni et mali*, which is closer to the biblical text, Gen. 2:16-17.

30. Marginal gloss no. 8 here remarks that the serpent who deceived Eve had the form of an attractive youth.

31. Cf. II Cor. 11:3.

32. Cf. Gen. 6:2.

33. Cf. John 8:44; Matt. 3:7.

34. Cf. Rom. 4:15.

35. There is a lacuna in the text which the editor has partially supplied by the words *simul spiritum.*

36. Cf. John 3:6.

37. *Et ita [non] finitur regnum sathanae in hoc mundo*, i.e., Satan's reign is perpetuated by the propagation of souls as well as bodies until the consummation of the world; see § 12.

38. There is a lacuna in our text. D reads: "From the time that the devil fell from the glory of the Father and desired his own glory, he was seated above the clouds and sent his ministers, the angels of searing fire, to men below from Adam to Enoch, his minister."

39. D reads "sixty-six."

40. Matt. 23:13.

41. Cf. Deut. 4:35; Judith 9:19; Mark 12:32.

42. *Nomen meum*, but "His" seems called for, as the editor observes.

43. A marginal gloss (no. 10) comments that this was the wood with which Moses divided the waters of the Red Sea to allow the children of Israel to pass.

44. Cf. Exod. 14:16.

45. Matt. 18:11; Luke 19:10.

46. Cf. Matt. 17:12-13.

47. The text reads *eum* where *me* would be expected in obvious reference to Jesus. From here to the end of the paragraph, the text offers some difficulty. It follows biblical passages in which John is speaking (it is a combination of John 1:26,33; Matt. 3:11; Mark 1:4; and Luke 3:16 and 9:56); but here the words are given either to the devil or to Jesus, with consequent confusion of pronouns. Nelli (*Ecritures cathares*, pp. 61-62, and nn. 27-30) wrestled with the problem, and we have borrowed some of the fruits of his efforts, for which we render due thanks. D is of no help in construing the text at this point.

48. The manuscript was illegible; the words in brackets accord with the passage in D.

49. Cf. John 6:33,41,51,54-55.

50. Cf. Mark 12:25; Luke 20:35-36.

51. Matt. 19:11-12.

52. Matt. 24:3.

53. Cf. Apoc. 6:9-11.

54. Apoc. 20:7.

55. Matt. 24:29. At this point, there is a marginal gloss (no. 12) explaining that the sun is the prince (Satan) and his throne; the moon is the law of Moses; and the stars are the spirits of the prince's ministry. These will have no more place over which to rule, "but Christ, the Son of God, who is a sun of sevenfold light, shall reign."

56. Apoc. 7:1. A marginal gloss (no. 11) states: ... "The four winds are the kings who will persecute the existing Church and in war will pitilessly kill other men."

57. Cf. Matt. 24:30.

58. "The fourth hour" in D.

59. Cf. Matt. 25:31 and 19:28.

60. Cf. Apoc. 20:12.

61. The Latin of this passage is obscure and probably corrupt. It reads *et adducent eos [se]cum sua in ovi[li]a mihi super nubem in aerem*. The author seems to have had in mind I Thess. 4:16: "We ... shall be taken up together with them in the clouds to meet Christ, into the air" (*simul rapiemur cum illis in nubibus obviam Christo in aera*).

62. The text is defective and our translation conjectural.

63. Cf. Isa. 22:13.

64. Matt. 25:34.

65. Matt. 25:41.

66. Ps. 9:18 (A.V. 17).

67. John 10:16.

68. V ends here, in the middle of this sentence. From this point to the end we follow D.

69. *Et erit dominus.*

70. Nelli (*Ecritures cathares*, p. 50, n. 138), calls attention to similar passages in two other apocryphal writings, one of Bogomil origin, suggesting that the man thirty years of age may symbolize Christ. See also Turdeneau, "Apocryphes bogomiles," *RHR*, CXXXVIII (1950), 209.

71. Cf. Apoc. 20:14,15.

72. Reitzenstein (p. 308) prints *operi nos, mare.* The reading in Doat (*operi nos in te*) is clear. Cf. Num. 16:30.

73. Heb. 2:13.

74. Cf. John 17:25.

75. Matt. 22:44; Mark 12:36; Luke 20:43 (from Ps. 109 [A.V. 110]:1).

76. Cf. Deut. 4:35.

77. Cf. Matt. 8:12, 13:42.

78. Apoc. 7:16,17.

79. This notation was probably made by an inquisitor or a scribe of an inquisitorial court.

57. THE CATHARIST RITUALS

1. The word was known to orthodox writers in the early thirteenth century, its first known appearances being in the treatise against heretics of Ermengaud (Migne, *PL*, CCIV, 1262; see item xiv in the Appendix) and in the work of Peter of Vaux-de-Cernay (No. 38, § 15). It perhaps developed from scriptural phrases such as *consolari in vos* (Rom. 1:2) and *ut consolentur* (Col. 2:2). The term appeared first in Provençal speech and from that was taken over into Latin (Borst, p. 193, n. 10).

2. Cf. No. 23, § 2a,b; No. 38, §§ 13-15; and No. 50, part A.

3. Jean Guiraud, "Le Consolamentum cathare," *RQH*, new ser., XXXI (1904), 74-112, compares the consolamentum with early Christian practice. The substance of this article is repeated in his *Histoire de l'Inquisition*, Vol. I, chap. IV. See also the remarks of Dondaine (*Un Traité néo-manichéen*, pp. 45-46) and Borst (pp. 193-96).

4. References in some sources to a distinction between the newly converted and the fully professed heretics perhaps arise from the distinction between one who has received the right to say the Prayer but on whom the consolamentum had not yet been conferred.

5. Cf. No. 28, n. 6. In the language of the Latin ritual, the initiate, who is a "believer" (*credens*) at the beginning, becomes a "Christian" (*christianus*) at the end.

6. Cf. the ethical standards set forth in No. 60, part A, and the discourses on persecution there and in No. 59, VII.

7. Dondaine, *Un Traité néo-manichéen*, pp. 34-39; Borst, pp. 279-83.

8. Dondaine (*Un Traité néo-manichéen*, p. 49) says that the words about baptism were intended to veil the true attitude of the heretics from the new convert. Borst (p. 282, n. 16) disagrees. See part A, n. 75, below.

9. Schmidt (*Histoire et doctrine*, II, 115-19), writing before the texts of the rituals had been discovered and basing his interpretation on inquisitorial records, used the term "Benediction." Alexander Solovjev ("La Messe cathare," *Cahiers d'études cathares*, XII [1951-1952], 199-206) compares the phrases with those used by the Bogomils (see part B, n. 1, below) and uses the term "Mass."

10. Guiraud (*Histoire de l'Inquisition*, I, 185-90), describes this ceremony as a confession by believers to a Perfect. But the wording of the Service belies this. It refers to eliminating the desires of the flesh, keeping the fasts, and reciting the Prayer, all of which were obligations of the Perfect. Moreover, the participants in the Service are in other sources called either "heretics" or "Cathars" (see No. 49 and No. 51, § 7), both of which terms are normally restricted to the Perfect. It does not seem likely, therefore, that believers took part in the Service, although they may have been present. If the believers did confess in the Service, we have proof that high moral standards were demanded of them—a contradiction of the charge, not infrequently made, that Catharist believers were prone to immorality, even encouraged in it.

11. Borst (p. 200, n. 28) notes similarities to Catholic practice.

12. Ermengaud, *Tractatus*, in Migne, *PL*, CCIV, 1262: *ille qui major est et ordinatus dicitur*. On the title *l'ancia*, or *ancianus*, see No. 54, n. 30.

13. Cf. No. 49; No. 54, §§ 8,9, and n. 30. Borst (p. 212) points out that in southern France by 1300 Catharist leaders are regularly called "elders," rather than "bishops."

14. See No. 54, § 9. Catholic sources often refer to this form of greeting as *reverentia* or *adoratio*; see No. 55, I, 2; also Dondaine, *Un Traité néo-manichéen*, p. 44, and Borst, pp. 198-99, who cite many appearances of the different terms for the practice in the sources.

15. The embrace is called *caron* in No. 54, § 9. Numerous references in the sources are cited in Borst, p. 199, n. 27.

16. See the Provençal ritual, under "Rules of Conduct"; cf. No. 54, § 5. That genuflections as well as prayer were involved is shown by a phrase in another reference: "They perform ... their genuflections in the heretical fashion *vel in duplo vel in simplici*" (Döllinger, *Beiträge*, II, 39).

17. *Un Traité néo-manichéen*, pp. 34-39.

18. *Die Katharer*, pp. 280-83.

A. THE RITUAL TRANSLATED FROM THE LATIN TEXT

1. The manuscript being mutilated, the first part of the ritual is lost. The

extant text begins in the midst of a discourse to the initiate, with this passage from Isaiah (29:19-21).

2. That is, the "people of God," the fallen angels. See the definition of the kingdom of God in the following commentary; cf. also No. 60, part B, introduction and *passim*.

3. Ps. 140 (A.V. 141):2.

4. With all of the following commentary on the Lord's Prayer cf. that in No. 60, part B.

5. Luke 17:21.

6. Joel 2:17.

7. John 6:38, with minor changes.

8. *Panem nostrum supersubstancialem*: In many manuscripts of the Vulgate these words appear in Mark 6:11, but are replaced by *panem quotidianum* [daily bread] in the Lord's Prayer in Luke 11:2, and the use of the latter has generally prevailed. Although *panem supersubstancialem* was quite familiar to orthodox commentators (see Dondaine, *Un Traité néo-manichéen*, p. 48; Borst, p. 311) the use of these words in the Lord's Prayer was considered evidence of heresy in the Middle Ages; see Giuseppe Boffito, "Gli eretici di Cuneo," *Bolletino storico-bibliografico subalpino*, I (1896), 324-33, esp. 329. The editor of our text notes that just after the word "people" in the sentence which follows, some lines are marked for deletion from the text. They read: " 'Give us this day,' as if one were to say: Holy Father, bestow Thy strength on us, so that in the time of grace we may be worthy to fulfill the law and commandments of Thy Son, who is the living bread." The deletion seems to have been made in order to substitute the long exposition of *panem supersubstancialem*, which is to be regarded as an interpolation in the original commentary; the original passage reappears in substance at the end of the interpolation (Dondaine, *Un Traité néo-manichéen*, p. 47). See also the definition of *panem supersubstancialem* in No. 60, part B, chap. V.

9. Isa. 4:1.

10. Ps. 101:5 (A.V. 102:4).

11. Wisd. 16:20-21.

12. Isa. 58:7.

13. Lam. 4:4.

14. John 6:32-33.

15. John 6:35.

16. John 6:47-48,50-55.

17. John 4:34.

18. John 6:56.

19. I John 2:5-6.

20. The following quotation, in which the author's commentary and other biblical texts are interpolated, is Matt. 26:26.

21. Apoc. 10:9,11.

22. John 6:52 (A.V. 51).

23. I Cor. 10:16-17.

24. I Cor. 11:23-25.

25. I Cor. 10:13. Cf. the two kinds of temptation described in No. 60, part B, chap. VII. We have not seen René Nelli, "Les Deux Tentations chez les Cathares du XIIIᵉ siècle," *Cahiers d'études cathares*, IV (1949), 7-12.

26. Cf. the text of the Lord's Prayer in Latin in the first portion of the Provençal ritual, which also includes this doxology; and No. 60, part B, chaps. IX-XI, which has an explanation of its significance. Also see No. 16, n. 4.

27. That is, over the suprasensible world, the dominion of the good God, as opposed to this material world, the realm of the devil.

28. Matt. 6:15.

29. Elsewhere in this ritual and in the Provençal version as well, comparable phrases omit the pledge of obedience.

30. A copy of the Gospel of John or of the New Testament, whole or in part.

31. In the ritual for the consolamentum which follows in our text, this individual is identified as an elder (*ancianus*).

32. On the concept of "order," see No. 23, n. 8.

33. On the Service and the Act of Peace, see the introduction, and for the Act of Peace, part B, n. 51.

34. *De bono*. The boon requested here is salvation through the consolamentum, as shown by the subsequent ritual responses: "Receive it to His honor and your salvation" and "Receive it to His honor and your good."

35. Matt. 3:11.

36. John 3:5.

37. *Supertinctio*: see Du Cange, *s.v.* "tingere."

38. Bar. 3:9-13.

39. Ps. 78 (A.V. 79):1.

40. Ephes. 5:25-27.

41. John 20:21-23.

42. Matt. 18:18-19.

43. Matt. 16:13-19.

44. Mark 16:15-18.

45. Matt. 28:16-20.

46. Acts 8:14-17.

47. Acts 19:1-7.

48. Acts 9:11-12,17-19.

49. Acts 28:8.

50. II Tim. 1:6.

51. I Tim. 5:22.

52. Heb. 6:2.

53. I Pet. 3:20-21.

54. Gen. 9:25.

55. Heb. 11:7.

56. Ecclus. 44:17-19.

57. II Pet. 2:5.

58. I Pet. 3:21. The printed text has *facit nos* but Borst (p. 285) corrects to *facit vos* from the manuscript.

59. Ps. 73 (A.V. 74):12.

60. The scribe wrote, "Isaiah says," but the quotation is actually from Jer. 8:20.

61. Heb. 2:10.

62. I Pet. 3:21.

63. I Cor. 12:31-13:3.

64. Luke 10:27. With this and the following precepts, cf. the similar passages in the discourse in part B and also the moral and ethical code set forth in No. 60, part A.

65. The source of these quotations is not known, but similar phrases are cited by the editor (p. 162, note) from the works of Irenaeus, Augustine, and Bernard of Clairvaux.

66. Wisd. 6:20.

67. Meaning, no doubt, faithful discharge of obligations in respect of personal property and the common possessions of the group. Cf. in the consolamentum for invalids in the Provençal ritual, the injunction to inquire as to the lawful behavior of the one who is to be baptized.

68. I Cor. 6:10, omitting a substantial portion of the verse.

69. Ps. 115 (A.V. 116):14-15.

70. Heb. 10:39.

71. II Tim. 2:4.

72. Luke 9:62.

73 Ecclus. 34:30-31.

74. II Pet. 2:20-22.

75. Moneta of Cremona (*Adversus Catharos et Valdenses*, ed. by Ricchini, p. 292) states that some heretics taught that they would receive and perform baptism in water in order by that sign to draw men on to the baptism of the Holy Spirit. In other orthodox sources, the Cathars are represented as entirely repudiating the baptism of water. It is emphatically rejected in another heretical work; see No. 60, part A, chap. XI.

76. This Scripture lesson was usually John 1:1-17.

77. *Levet gratiam.*

B. THE RITUAL TRANSLATED FROM THE PROVENÇAL TEXT

1. All of this section is written in Latin, with the exception of the thrice-repeated directions "Three times." Solovjev ("La Messe Cathare," *Cahiers d'études cathares*, XII [1951-1952], 199-206) analyzes this as a four-part service (each part represented by one paragraph here), consisting of a litany, the Lord's Prayer, another litany, and the Gospel of John, and supposes that preaching from a Gospel text would also be part of this worship. Solovjev finds a close parallel between this and the usage of Bogomils of Bulgaria

and Bosnia, the only exception being the absence here of a phrase found in the Eastern texts: *Dignum et justum est* [he is worthy and just]. Solovjev had not noticed that in the description of the consolamentum by Anselm of Alessandria (No. 54, § 5) that phrase does occur. Slight variations in phraseology are to be expected over wide areas and many years, but the similarity which Solovjev pointed out is, in fact, closer than he supposed.

2. Matt. 6:9-13.

3. See part A, n. 26, above.

4. John 1:1-17. On the punctuation of vv. 3-4, see No. 47, n. 43.

5. The words in italics here and subsequently in this translation were inscribed in Latin in the manuscript.

6. This probably means failure to say the Lord's Prayer at the usual times with the requisite number of repetitions.

7. *Venias*: genuflections or prostrations as an accompaniment to prayer, presumably similar to those common in orthodox practice.

8. Matt. 18:20.

9. John 14:23.

10. II Cor. 6:16-18.

11. II Cor. 13:3.

12. I Tim. 3:14-15.

13. Heb. 3:6.

14. John 14:15-18.

15. Matt. 28:20.

16. I Cor. 3:16-17.

17. Matt. 10:20.

18. I John 4:13.

19. Gal. 4:6.

20. We alter the punctuation used by Clédat (*per l'avenement del seu fil Jesu Christ, don es aquesta l'ocais. Quar esz aici devant los decipols ....*) and follow the lead given by the Latin ritual in the corresponding place. This emendation is also adopted by Dondaine (*Un Traité néo-manichéen,* p. 37) and Nelli (*Ecritures cathares*, p. 217).

21. Matt. 6:15.

22. Matt. 28:19-20.

23. Mark 16:15-16.

24. John 3:5.

25. John 1:26-27; Matt. 3:11. The author combines elements of both texts.

26. Acts 1:5.

27. Mark 16:18.

28. Acts 8:14-17, omitting part of v. 16.

29. John 20:21-23.

30. Matt. 16:18-19.

31. Matt. 18:19-20.

32. Matt. 10:8.

33. John 14:12.
34. Mark 16:17-18.
35. Luke 10:19.
36. Cf. Matt. 5:21-48.
37. I John 2:15-17.
38. John 7:7.
39. Eccles. 1:14.
40. Jude 1:23.
41. *Las parcias*: On this and the terms in nn. 42-45 and 47, see our introduction to the rituals.
42. *Adoremus*.
43. *Sezena*.
44. *Far patz*.
45. *Dobla*.
46. *Et auran liurat*: The editor (p. xxi) translates this as "et ils [lui] auront [ainsi] livré [l'oraison]. But the ministration of the Prayer is not involved here. Nelli (*Ecritures cathares*, p. 233) translates it as "la cérémonie est terminée."
47. *Sembla*.
48. Apoc. 21:8.
49. *Si pod lavar* (corrected by Clédat to *levar*) *las mas*. Clédat (p. xxiii, n. 6) suggests the possibility of correcting the reading further to "sit up if he can and wash his hands."
50. That is, proffer the Gospels to be kissed; see the following note.
51. The difference between this and the earlier salutation "used for women" is made clear by the description of a heretication about 1231 (Vaissete, *Histoire du Languedoc*, VIII, 1017) in which, after the believer had declared his wish to be consoled and his obligations had been explained, he performed his melioramentum and "afterward kissed the Book of the heretics; this done, they placed the Book and their hands on his head and read the Gospel. Thereafter these heretics made their confession (*fecerunt apparellamentum*) and performed the Act of Peace, at that time kissing each other once on each cheek."
52. This sentence indicates that the consolamentum bestowed on the deathbed was of a provisional nature. If the initiate recovered he had to receive baptism again to be assured of its full effect; see Nelli, *Ecritures cathares*, p. 209.

58. A "MANICHAEAN" TREATISE

1. On Durand of Huesca, see No. 36, and on his polemical writings, see items xii, xiii, and xvii in the Appendix.
2. Only one half of Durand's treatise (Book I) is now known. Book II contained other excerpts from the heretical work; see n. 16, below, and Thouzellier, *Un Traité cathare*, pp. 85-86.

3. *Ibid.*, pp. 28, 33, 40. Elsewhere he speaks of the heretics inhabiting Gothia and Aquitaine. "Gothia" is a name which was passing out of use at the time Durand wrote. It specifies the region which later became known as Lower Languedoc (Thouzellier, *Une Somme anti-cathare*, pp. 35; 119, note to l. 15; and 210, note to l. 31).

4. He knew of the division of the Cathars into followers of the Greek, Bulgarian, and Dragovitsan churches, and also calls his opponents "Bulgars," "Marcionites," and "Marcionite Cathars," accusing them of drawing freely from other ancient heresies as well (*ibid.*, pp. 115, 138-39, 175, 237-39, and 303).

5. *Tractatus manicheorum* (Thouzellier, *Un Traité cathare*, p. 87).

6. *Ibid.*, p. 29; Dondaine, "Durand de Huesca," *AFP*, XXIX (1959), 246-47.

7. He writes "we believe" and "we say" and uses the first person singular only in a passage of invective against his opponents (chap. XIV).

8. Duvernoy ("Un Traité cathare," *Cahiers d'études cathares*, 2d ser., XIII [1962], 27), opposes both of the following suggestions on the ground that Durand of Huesca or Moneta of Cremona (whom Duvernoy supposes also knew the heretical treatise) would have known and stated the names of the men here suggested as the author.

9. His story is told by Peter of Vaux-de-Cernay *Hystoria albigensis* I.xxii-xxiii, ed. by Guébin and Lyon, I, 24-26. See also No. 59, I, 19.

10. Thouzellier, *Un Traité cathare*, pp. 29-33. In the discussion of the possibility of his authorship, there is a valuable review (pp. 33-40) of the question of dualism in the Bosnian church in the twelfth and thirteenth centuries and the relationships between that church and the Cathars.

11. On the date of the *Liber*, see Thouzellier, *Une Somme anti-cathare*, p. 38; on the date of the heretical work, see *idem, Un Traité cathare*, p. 28. Cf. Dondaine, "Durand de Huesca," *AFP*, XXIX (1959), 243. Duvernoy ("Un Traité cathare," *Cahiers d'études cathares*, 2d ser., XIII [1962], 25) would assign the heretical tract to a date nearer the beginning of the century.

12. The heretic quotes the Bible in the Vulgate. The Psalter follows the Gallican tradition and the whole is in the "French" tradition whose use was stimulated by Alcuin and his successors: Thouzellier, *Un Traité cathare*, pp. 56-64, 84. Cf. n. 25, below.

13. *Ibid.*, p. 67.

14. Reliance on the Old Testament as well as the New and the exposition of the meaning of the words "create" and "make" are two of the points of likeness: *ibid.*, pp. 50-56, 71-72.

15. The exposition of the heretic's teaching in chap. III of Thouzellier's introduction is made with insight and mastery of detail and is drawn on heavily in the following paragraphs. It should be consulted directly for fullest appreciation of the doctrines.

16. From a statement in chap. IV and from a table of contents for a

missing Book II of Durand's work *(ibid.,* p. 86), it appears that in that lost book was a discussion of food and drink, the nature of the carnal world, Christ, human procreation, the "new man" and his regeneration and spiritual food, the analogy of the good and evil sheep, the prince of this world, and good and evil angels who served God and the devil.

17. Cf. similar monotheistic professions by heretics in No. 28 and No. 29.

18. Cf. Duvernoy, "Un Traité cathare," *Cahiers d'études cathares,* 2d ser., XIII (1962), 27-29. See also nn. 138 and 146, below.

19. Thouzellier, *Un Traité cathare,* pp. 77-78.

20. This probably does not mean that the wicked world will cease entirely to be, but that the incarceration of the heavenly spirits therein will end. See n. 210, below.

21. The chapter titles are those of Durand's treatise of refutation, with minor changes.

22. Ps. 145 (A.V. 146):6.

23. Isa. 48:12-13.

24. Isa. 65:17.

25. Apoc. 14:7. The reading of this verse offers one example of the variants in biblical texts, by close study of which Mlle Thouzellier was able to demonstrate that the Catharist author used the Bible in the Vulgate, rather than in a version of Eastern origin or one derived from pre-Vulgate texts, as has sometimes been asserted of the Cathars' Bibles; see *Un Traité cathare,* pp. 54-64. Variants will not be noted here except when they seem to have significance for the author's argument.

26. Apoc. 4:11.

27. Acts 14:14.

28. Acts 4:24.

29. Acts 17:24. Cf. this and the preceding citations with No. 59, V, where they are listed as authorities used by the Garatenses, mitigated dualists, to demonstrate the existence of one supreme creator. See also the demonstration of their frequent use in Catholic polemics: Thouzellier, *Un Traité cathare,* pp. 87-88.

30. Ps. 113 ² (A.V. 115):15.

31. Apoc. 3:14.

32. *Fecisse pariter et creasse.* The significance of these words is related to the controversy between Catharist groups and between some of them and Catholics as to whether creation is from pre-existent matter or from nothing. The distinction is important to the author of *The Book of the Two Principles* (see No. 59, *passim,* esp. I, n. 28).

33. *Etc.* appears at the end of each excerpt from the heretical work, showing that only portions of it were copied by Durand.

34. For the two created realms the author uses the words *seculum, mundus,* and *orbis.* All may be rendered as "world," as they are in standard translations of the Bible. A consistent distinction in the use of *seculum* and

mundus appears in this treatise, however: In chap. III all the selected scriptural texts use *seculum* for "world"; in chap. IV all use *mundus*; and the chapter titles devised by Durand of Huesca respect this difference. Since we have not been able to make a satisfactory distinction in English, we show the Latin term, in parentheses.

35. See Thouzellier, *Un Traité cathare*, pp. 73-74, on the twelfth-century theological argument for the rationality of Christian belief based on the juxtaposition of "faith" and "hope." Mlle Thouzellier regards our author's use of the phrase as evidence of his theological erudition.

36. Heb. 11:1.
37. Luke 20:34-35.
38. Gal. 1:3-4.
39. Ephes. 2:1-2.
40. Rom. 12:2.
41. I Cor. 2:6-8.
42. Cf. I John 5:19.
43. Jas. 4:4.
44. I Cor. 7:31.
45. I John 2:15-16.
46. John 14:30.
47. John 18:36.
48. John 17:9.
49. John 17:25.
50. John 17:16.
51. John 16:33.
52. John 15:19.
53. John 17:14.
54. I John 3:13-14.
55. I John 3:1.
56. John 17:10.
57. John 18:36.
58. Dan. 7:14.
59. Luke 1:33,32.
60. Ps. 144 (A.V. 145):13.
61. I Cor. 15:50.
62. Ephes. 5:5.
63. Apoc. 11:15.
64. A reference to the words preceding the foregoing quotation (Apoc. 11:15): "There were great voices in heaven saying, The kingdom . . . ."
65. Matt. 12:26.
66. Matt. 8:12.
67. Isa. 66:22.
68. II Pet. 3:13.
69. Apoc. 21:1.
70. Isa. 60:20.

71. Wisd. 5:6.
72. Apoc. 21:2.
73. Apoc. 21:18.
74. Gal. 4:26.
75. Apoc. 2:7.
76. Apoc. 22:1-2.
77. Dan. 7:10.
78. I Cor. 2:9.
79. John 1:11.
80. I John 2:15.
81. I John 5:19.
82. Luke 1:38.
83. Cf. John 1:13.
84. Matt. 13:24.
85. Matt. 13:37-39.
86. I John 3:10.
87. Luke 11:39, with changes based on Matt. 23:25,26.
88. Matt. 15:19. The thought of the paragraph is obscure. Mlle Thouzellier (*Un Traité cathare*, p. 79), finds in it an allusion to the heretical doctrine of fallen angels, souls imprisoned in bodies made by the devil while their spirits, not under demonic power, remained in the heavenly world (cf. No. 23, § 2; No. 50, part A). While "less capable interpreters" assert that Christ's words are evidence that both body and spirit are of the Father, the heretic declares that there is no reference to the spirit here, but only to the heart, from which flow the vices enumerated. The body (that which is without) and the heart (that which is within) are the work of Satan and the soul is their prisoner.
89. Ephes. 5:15-16.
90. Ephes. 6:13.
91. Matt. 6:34.
92. Ps. 101 (A.V. 102):12.
93. Job 7:6.
94. Job 29:2.
95. I Pet. 3:10.
96. II Pet. 3:8.
97. John 7:7.
98. John 3:19-20.
99. John 1:9; 3:20.
100. John 8:34.
101. Cf. No. 51, § 20; No. 59, II, 11, for names, including "sin," applied to the principle of evil.
102. I John 3:8.
103. Ecclus. 14:20.
104. Ephes. 2:2.
105. Cf. II Cor. 11:13.

106. Eccles. 1:14.
107. Eccles. 3:19-20.
108. Ecclus. 39:21.
109. Wisd. 11:25.
110. Eccles. 3:11.
111. Eccles. 3:14.
112. Ecclus. 14:21.
113. Phil. 2:13.
114. *Ponitur pro operatione.*
115. Heb. 9:11-12.
116. Wisd. 3:12-13.
117. Cf. Matt. 24:35.
118. II Pet. 3:5-10.
119. Heb. 6:8.
120. Ecclus. 17:30.
121. Cf. the more extensive treatment of this subject in No. 59, III.
122. Col. 1:19-20; cf. *ibid.* 2:9.
123. John 12:32.
124. Matt. 11:27.
125. John 1:3-4. On the phrasing of this verse see nn. 138, 146, below.
126. Phil. 3:8.
127. Eccles. 1:2.
128. Eccles. 1:14.
129. Eccles. 3:19-20.
130. Ecclus. 42:25.
131. I Cor. 8:4.
132. I Cor. 13:2. Cf. the treatment of "charity" in No. 60. chap. V.
133. Isa. 40:17.
134. Ps. 58 (A.V. 59):9.
135. Ps. 14 (A.V. 15):4.
136. Ezech. 28:19.
137. Isa. 41:24.
138. The heretic is using an interpretation found in several other of the controversial works (see Thouzellier, *Un Traité cathare*, p. 103, nn. *a,b*): That which is called "nothing" was made without Christ, while that which is made by Him is "life." In his reply, Durand said that the Cathars believed *nihil* [nothing] to mean visible creatures (Thouzellier, *Une Somme anti-cathare*, p. 217; cf. a similar statement by a heretic of the early fourteenth century in Döllinger, *Beiträge*, II, 40). This and other interpretations Durand rejected, arguing that the verse means that no substance at all can exist without God. Moneta of Cremona *Adversus Catharos et Valdenses*, p. 89, also rebutted heretics on this point. Cf. Duvernoy, "Un Traité cathare," *Cahiers d'études cathares*, 2d ser., XIII (1962), 27-28; and n. 146, below.
139. I Cor. 13:2.
140. Heb. 3:4.

141. Ecclus. 18:1.
142. Col. 1:16-17.
143. The reference is to thrones, dominations, etc., as ranks in the angelic hierarchy. See No. 56, part B, n. 4.
144. Rom. 1:20.
145. John 1:3.
146. John 1:3-4. The proper punctuation of this passage has long been a subject of controversy. Augustine accused the Manichaeans of placing a comma after *in ipso* [in him], and Durand berates the Cathars for the same punctuation, which allows the interpretation that life existed before it was "made' 'in God, rather than the orthodox reading: Whatever was made had life in God, who made all things; the world pre-existed in Him as the Logos. See the discussion in Thouzellier, *Une Somme anti-cathare*, p. 233, note at line 34; cf. No. 47, n. 43.
147. I Tim. 4:4.
148. Cf. I John 2:16.
149. Cf. Gal. 3:1.
150. Cf. Acts 13:10; Phil. 3:18.
151. Cf. Matt. 15:14.
152. Cf. Matt. 13:13; Acts 28:6.
153. Cf. Gal. 3:22.
154. Cf. Rom. 11:8.
155. Ps. 92 (A.V. 93):1.
156. Heb. 1:2.
157. Heb. 1:10; Ps. 101 (A.V. 102):26.
158. Ps. 26 (A.V. 27):13.
159. Ps. 141:6 (A.V. 142:5).
160. Ps. 142 (A.V. 143):10.
161. Ps. 23 (A.V. 24):1.
162. Ps. 136 (A.V. 137):4.
163. Cf. Ps. 2:2.
164. Luke 11:23.
165. John 8:47.
166. Matt. 5:4.
167. Job 28:6.
168. Ezech. 36:24.
169. Job 28:6.
170. Ashur commonly symbolizes the devil in heretical thought; see No. 59, II, 11.
171. Ezech. 32:22-24.
172. *Nunc dormient.* Vulgate *non dormient.*
173. Ezech. 32:26-27.
174. Ezech. 32:30-32.
175. Jer. 5:19. The preceding verses describing the evil world may also be taken to reflect the heretical myth of the invasion of heaven, "the land

of the living," by the hosts of Satan, who, having been defeated, now lie here in their original home, although a third of the creatures of God were swept away "to serve strange gods" (Thouzellier, *Un Traité cathare*, p. 78; cf. n. 88, above).

176. Ezech. 34:12-13.
177. Isa. 66:1.
178. Isa. 45:12.
179. Cf. Isa. 65:17.
180. Isa. 45:8.
181. Jer. 27:5.
182. Acts 7:49; Isa. 66:1.
183. Matt. 6:9.
184. Isa. 66:22.
185. II Pet. 3:13.
186. Isa. 45:12.
187. Isa. 65:17.
188. Isa. 1:2.
189. Ps. 101:26 (A.V. 102:25).
190. Ps. 101:27 (A.V. 102:26).
191. Cf. Matt. 12:35.
192. II Pet. 3:7.
193. II Pet. 3:10-12.
194. Isa. 51:6.
195. Matt. 15:13.
196. Ps. 101:26 (A.V. 102:25).
197. See n. 190.
198. Isa. 1:2.
199. I Cor. 10:10.
200. Ezech. 34:16.
201. Luke 19:10.
202. Matt. 10:5-6.
203. Matt. 15:24.
204. Ps. 18:2 (A.V. 19:1).
205. Ps. 113 ² (A.V. 115):16; Ps. 148:4.
206. Cf. Bar. 3:11.
207. Ps. 6:8.
208. I Cor. 15:51.
209. I Cor. 15:52.
210. Ps. 76 (A.V. 77):11. With the preceding description of the Last Judgment, cf. chap. XI. Should the passage be taken to mean that the present evil world will be destroyed in an absolute sense? This would seriously modify the doctrine of radical dualism, of two coeternal creations, which is manifested elsewhere in the treatise. Mlle Thouzellier (*Un Traité cathare*, pp. 81-82) suggests that in the light of chap. XI, especially the paraphrase of Matt. 24:35 therein, the interpretation is not that the diabolic

creation will be utterly dissolved but that the state of imprisonment of souls in terrestrial life will end; that is, in so far as God's creatures are concerned, the domination of evil over them will be destroyed. The good and imperishable heavens spoken of in this chapter symbolize the fallen souls whom Christ redeemed.

211. Matt. 15:24.
212. Matt. 10:6.
213. Ezech. 34:11-12.
214. Ezech. 34:16.
215. Luke 19:10.
216. Luke 9:56.
217. Matt. 23:37.
218. Ezech. 36:24.
219. II Tim. 4:8.
220. Ps. 50:14 (A.V. 51:12).
221. Lam. 5:16.

222. Durand refers here to his chap. XX, "On the Creation or the Origin of Souls, against the Cathars As Well As against All Other Adversaries of the Orthodox Faith"; and chap. XXI, "On Predestination, against the Modern Manichaeans and against All Others Who Dissent from the Catholic Truth." They contain no excerpts from the heretical work, and only the titles are given in the edition by Thouzellier.

223. *Antifrasice calamum.* See Thouzellier, *Une Somme anti-cathare,* p. 124, note to line 23.

59. THE BOOK OF THE TWO PRINCIPLES

1. See the comment by Dondaine in his Introduction (p. 24) and the harsher judgment by Borst (pp. 264-65, 268-69) on the style and the intellectual quality of the treatise.

2. Borst, pp. 261-62, 270.

3. Dondaine, *Un Traité néo-manichéen,* pp. 18, 19. Runciman (*Medieval Manichee,* p. 127, n. 1) and Thouzellier (*Un Traité cathare,* pp. 19, 20) accept John of Lugio's authorship; Borst (p. 261) flatly rejects it. Most other commentators hesitate to make judgments so positive.

4. On the manuscript, see the Introduction by Dondaine (pp. 9-14), and Borst, pp. 254-61. The date *post quem,* 1254 or 1258, depends on the interpretation of a cryptogram written in the margin at the end of the last section of the treatise in the manuscript. A photograph of that folio is reproduced on p. 147 of Dondaine's edition and the cryptogram is transcribed on p. 13. It records that one *Sagimbenus,* at the age of fifty-one and a half years, received the consolamentum from Henry *in Salmignono.* Dondaine read the coded numerals denoting the date as 1258, Borst (p. 259) as 1254, but both admit that the transcription is not entirely assured. Savini (*Il catarismo,* p. 120, n. 11) suggests that it could be 1238.

5. Dondaine, *Un Traité néo-manichéen*, pp. 18-21. Nelli devotes most of the Introduction to his French translation of the work (*Ecritures cathares*, pp. 71-82) to an exposition of John of Lugio's teaching.

6. The preceding paragraph is based primarily on Borst, pp. 269-75.

7. On acceptance of the Old Testament among the Cathars, see part IV, n. 83.

8. Borst, pp. 265-66.

9. For commentaries on the system of John of Lugio, one may also consult Dondaine's Introduction, pp. 18-20, 31-33; Borst, pp. 270-71; and Nelli, *Ecritures cathares*, pp. 71-82.

10. The unity of knowledge and will in God is a point made explicitly in IV.3.

11. This portion of the treatise is in two parts in the manuscript, being interrupted after the first paragraph by other material, chiefly the text of the Catharist ritual in Latin.

12. With this, cf. the passage on persecution in No. 60, chap. X.

[I. ON FREE WILL]

1. *Pater sanctissimus*, a term also employed in the ritual in Latin (No. 57, part A).

2. Borst (p. 287) notes the similarity of this passage to Aristotle *Physica* I.2: "The principles in question must be (a) one or (b) more than one" (the translation is from *The Works of Aristotle Translated into English*, ed. by J. A. Smith and W. D. Ross [Oxford, 1910-1952], II, 184^{b}15). Borst (pp. 274-75) is of the opinion that our author found this and other such passages in the work of some orthodox contemporary, perhaps William of Auvergne, bishop of Paris (d. 1249).

3. Matt. 7:17-18.

4. Jas. 3:11-12.

5. The author seems to have in mind here not only the Garatenses, his "opponents" in a later passage (part V; see also n. 28, below), but also Catholic Christians, for it may be noted that he attributes to them citations from the Old Testament, to which the Garatenses gave no credence.

6. *Istis rationibus*. The author uses *ratio* in various meanings, and it is not always easy to find a phrase acceptable in English and faithful to the Latin. *Rationes* may designate, as noted by Borst (p. 267, n. 7), lists of scriptural verses cited to support a point, and in such cases is synonymous with *auctoritates* [texts] or *divina testimonia* [testimony of the Scriptures]. Elsewhere the word may imply something more, the proper exegesis of such texts; for example, in IV, 4: *per divina testimonia verissimam rationem demonstrare* [to clarify the precise meaning by scriptural references]. *Rationes* may also refer to logical arguments or "philosophical" conclusions; for example, the arguments in §§ 16-20 are subsequently (II, 1) referred to as "the argumentations of philosophers." In the singular, *ratio* usually means simply "argument" in the sense of a valid conclusion; for example, II, 1:

nostri adversarii . . . nullam habeant rationem [our adversaries . . . have no argument]. Other shades of meaning may also be found: *Qua ratione* [How] in § 8; and *rationabiliter* [reasonably] juxtaposed with *ratione et merito* [in reason and justice] in § 11.

7. Ecclus. 43:32-33.

8. Ps. 144 (A.V. 145):3.

9. Ps. 146 (A.V. 147):5.

10. Rom. 11:33.

11. The text reads: *in libro De causa causarum*. This pseudo-Aristotelian work was known and used by such polemicists against the Cathars as Alan of Lille, Peter Martyr(?), and Moneta of Cremona, as well as by St. Thomas Aquinas. It has been edited by Otto Bardenhewer, *Die pseudo-aristotelische Schrift . . . Liber de causis* (Freiburg im Breisgau, 1882); see esp. p. 168. See also the remarks of Dondaine, *Un Traité néo-manichéen*, p. 182, n. 6; and Borst, p. 273, n. 14.

12. Dan. 13:42.

13. Ecclus. 23:29.

14. Heb. 4:13.

15. Ps. 72 (A.V. 73):1.

16. Ps. 144:13 (not in A.V.).

17. Ps. 24 (A.V. 25):8.

18. Ps. 7:12 (A.V. 11).

19. Wisd. 12:15.

20. Cf. II Par. 20:6.

21. Eccles. 8:3-4.

22. Ps. 113 ² (A.V. 115):3.

23. Apoc. 1:8.

24. Apoc. 15:3-4.

25. Ps. 144:13 (not in A.V.).

26. Cf. the Catharist ritual translated from Latin (No. 57, part A), where evil is described as the work of the devil. According to Rainerius Sacconi (No. 51, § 22), John of Lugio attributed the potentiality for sin to the evil adversary's influence upon the creatures of the good God.

27. Perhaps the example is influenced by the words of Gen. 28:20 or Judg. 18:6.

28. *Facturam sive creationem*. The author almost invariably links the words *creare* [create] and *facere* [make] and their derivatives, such as *creatio* and *factura*. Such coupling of words or phrases is characteristic of his style. The linking of "create" and "make," however, may also reflect his basic disagreement with other Catharist groups, the mitigated dualists. They saw in God the only true "creator" but they attributed to the evil one the construction, or the making, of this world and its inhabitants out of the pre-existent matter brought into being by God; that is, for them God "created," the devil "made," the world of matter (see V, 2). This doctrine the author of *The Book of the Two Principles* firmly opposes, for he and

his fellow Albanenses conceived of two creations, good and evil, existing eternally with their creators; "to create and make" he understands as producing changes in the mode of existence, in one of the three ways expounded by John of Lugio (see II, 4-11). Cf. the opinion of the Albigensian author of the *"Manichaean" Treatise* (No. 58), chap. I.

29. Cf. Jer. 13:23.
30. Luke 12:47.
31. Matt. 25:34-35.
32. Matt. 25:41-42.
33. Matt. 25:40.
34. Matt. 23:37.
35. Ezech. 24:13.
36. Words in brackets supplied by the editor.
37. Gen. 6:6-7.
38. Isa. 43:24.
39. Isa. 1:14.
40. Mal. 2:17.
41. Ps. 105 (A.V. 106):45.
42. I Cor. 3:9.
43. Job 2:3.
44. Ezech. 13:18-19.
45. Isa. 65:12.
46. Cf. Rom. 11:36.
47. John 5:30.
48. John 14:10.
49. Jas. 1:17.
50. John 6:44.
51. John 5:30.
52. John 14:10.
53. Ephes. 2:8-9.
54. Rom. 9:16.
55. Phil. 1:6.
56. Phil. 2:13.
57. II Cor. 3:4-6.
58. John 3:27.
59. Ps. 126 (A.V. 127):1.
60. Jer. 10:23.
61. I Cor. 15:10.
62. Prov. 8:14-16.
63. Prov. 20:24.
64. Matt. 11:27.
65. John 14:6.
66. John 15:5.
67. Luke 13:24.
68. Acts 3:12.

69. Cf. Acts 3:13.

70. For references to the same conclusion in contemporary orthodox sources, see Borst, p. 290.

71. *Populus dei*: the souls who were to be redeemed (see No. 51, § 17).

72. Ecclus. 15:21.

73. Ezech. 7:10-11. The author seems to take this passage in the literal, although not entirely intelligible, sense that iniquity does not arise from "the people." Translators of the Bible have interpolated various phrases in an attempt to give meaning to the verse (see *Interpreter's Bible*, VI, 102).

74. Matt. 13:24-25.

75. Ps. 78 (A.V. 79):1.

76. Joel 1:6-7.

77. See § 10.

78. Ecclus. 13:19-20.

79. Ecclus. 27:10.

80. *Id quod erat secundum illos eius causa scilicet bonum, minus eget quam id quod non erat, id est malum.* In translating, we have omitted *eius causa*, because Borst (p. 284) points out that these words were marked for deletion in the manuscript, and we have read *egit* instead of *eget*, to conform with *agat* [have effect] in the next sentence. Cf. Nelli (*Ecritures cathares*, p. 105, n. 15), where other textual changes are also suggested for reasons of clarity.

81. The sources of this and the preceding quotations and the other ideas expressed in this section have not been precisely identified. Dondaine (*Un Traité néo-manichéen*, p. 93, note) and Borst (p. 291) quote passages of similar import, chiefly from Aristotle, Al-Kindi, Ibn Gabirol, and William of Auvergne.

82. We take this jumble of words to mean approximately the following: A cause (God) which remains unchanged produces always the same result (good). A new result (the sin of the angels) can be explained only by supposing that a new cause (evil) has come into effect, for authority declares that whenever a new result is produced, it is because of the introduction of some new agent. If the "dispositions of the agent" (whatever was the cause of the angels' acts) remained unaffected by internal change or external influence, the result could not have been to bring evil into existence, but rather evil would have remained nonexistent. A change from good to evil could arise only from diversity of cause.

83. Ecclus. 43:33.

84. Dondaine (*Un Traité néo-manichéen*, p. 23) supposes him to be a Cathar and suggests that he might be the canon of Nevers who fled to the Albigenses in 1201 and whose story is told by Peter of Vaux-de-Cernay (*Hystoria albigensis*, ed. by Guébin and Lyon, I, 24). Borst (pp. 274-75) rejects this on the ground that an Albigensian would have been in close doctrinal agreement with the Albanenses and hence with the author of *The Book of the Two Principles*. His suggestion is that the latter had read and

misunderstood the views of William of Auvergne, bishop of Paris (d. 1249), whose words seem to be reflected in other places in this tract. It may be noted, however, that of Master William the Cathar says "I have heard (*audivi*) him." Nelli (*Ecritures cathares*, p. 110, n. 19) supposes Master William to have been a mitigated dualist.

85. Cf. Isa. 14:13-14.

86. This may be an allusion to the followers of Master William.

87. Cf. *Corpus iuris civilis. Digest* IX.2.30: *Ad legem Aquilam. Qui occidit*, cited by Dondaine (*Un Traité néo-manichéen*, p. 98, note) from the edition of Berlin (1893), I, 129.

[II. ON CREATION]

1. Col. 2:8.

2. It will be recalled that the arguments in the last paragraphs of part I were not supported by scriptural citations.

3. Apoc. 4:11.

4. Apoc. 10:5-6.

5. Heb. 3:4.

6. Ecclus. 18:1.

7. Wisd. 1:14.

8. Acts 4:24.

9. Acts 17:23-25.

10. John 1:3.

11. Ephes. 4:5-6.

12. Ephes. 3:14-15.

13. I Cor. 8:6.

14. Rom. 11:36.

15. Col. 1:15-17.

16. Ps. 134 (A.V. 135):5-6.

17. I Tim. 6:13-15.

18. Apoc. 11:17.

19. Rom. 13:1.

20. Ps. 47:14-15 (A.V. 48:13-14).

21. Isa. 57:15.

22. Rom. 16:25-26.

23. Isa. 40:28.

24. Jer. 10:10.

25. Dan. 7:13.

26. Dan. 7:22.

27. The second of these explanations is the subject of part III.

28. Cf. the following paragraph with the description of the teaching of John of Lugio given by Rainerius Sacconi in No. 51, § 21.

29. Acts 10:38. Cf. I Pet. 2:25, where Christ is referred to as a bishop.

30. Col. 3:9-10.

31. Ephes. 4:23-24.

32. Isa. 45:8.
33. Acts 2:36.
34. Heb. 3:1-2.
35. Heb. 1:5.
36. For heretical doctrine on the "spirits and angels" of the good creation, see No. 23, § 2a; and No. 50, part A.
37. Heb. 1:7.
38. Heb. 1:14.
39. Isa. 18:2.
40. Matt. 1:20.
41. Wisd. 11:18.
42. Gen. 2:7.
43. Ecclus. 38:4.
44. Ecclus. 17:1.
45. Heb. 2:6.
46. Heb. 2:7.
47. Ps. 2:6.
48. Eccles. 3:11.
49. Eccles. 3:14.
50. Ecclus. 39:21.
51. Ecclus. 42:23-24, with omissions.
52. Ps. 103 (A.V. 104):24.
53. Ps. 118 (A.V. 119):91.
54. Ps. 148:5-6.
55. Cf. II Pet. 3:10: "The heavens shall pass away with great violence, and the elements shall be melted with heat, and the earth and the works which are in it shall be burnt up."
56. "Those who had been made evil" are the fallen angels, the "people of Israel" (see the following section), who are to be redeemed by being turned again to good, disposed unto good works, and in that sense "created."
57. Ephes. 2:10.
58. Ps. 103 (A.V. 104):27-30.
59. Isa. 45:6-7.
60. John 1:9.
61. Isa. 9:2 and Matt. 4:16. The words "of the Gentiles" are added to the biblical text by the author.
62. Ephes. 5:8.
63. Ephes. 2:14.
64. Ephes. 2:15-18, omitting part of v. 16.
65. Matt. 7:11.
66. II Cor. 3:5-6.
67. Col. 1:12.
68. II Cor. 5:17.
69. Apoc. 21:5.
70. In this paragraph and in certain other passages which may be summed

up here, the author presents numerous texts, chosen chiefly from the Old Testament, which, symbolically interpreted, are meant to establish the existence, power, and influence of the evil principle. That evil god has already been described as the source and cause of all angelic imperfections (I, 8, 17), as he is also of pride, iniquity, the defilement of the people, and infidelity (I, 15; III, 8). In addition to the figures listed here—Ashur, the smith and killer in Isaiah, the dragon, the behemoth, darkness, evil, the Chaldeans, the king of Babylon, the hypocrite in the Book of Job—the principle of evil is also identified elsewhere with "a king of shameless face," Nebuchadnezzar, and the "little horn" in Daniel (III, 5). He is the enemy of David in Ps. 51 (A.V. 52), the dragon of the Apocalypse, and the one who wars on the saints (IV, 5); he is one mighty in iniquity and the chief of principalities and powers (IV, 6). He is a strange god and mammon (IV, 8); he is represented by Mount Seir, the enemy of the people (IV, 9), and is not only eternal (IV, 9) but a creator and maker (IV, 10) and the source of inspiration for all works of adultery, theft, murder, blasphemy, and falsehood (IV, 11). Cf. the list of names which John of Lugio, according to Rainerius Sacconi, assigned to the evil principle (No. 51, § 19).

71. Ezech. 31:8-9.
72. Isa. 54:16.
73. Isa. 45:6-7.
74. Ps. 103 (A.V. 104):26.
75. Job 40:10.
76. Isa. 31:2.
77. Jer. 4:6.
78. Hab. 1:6.
79. Amos 3:6.
80. Job 12:6.
81. Dan. 2:37-38.
82. Job 34:29-30.
83. Rom. 9:22-23.

84. *Et sic potest dici [Satan] factum a deo esse, id est concessum principem populi, non simpliciter, sed secundum quid improprie et per accidens.* In the author's thought, each god may affect the other's realm but not by his own right as creator. The good God, who for His own purposes permitted evil, which already existed in another creation, to affect His people, is the creator of evil in only a superficial sense. Cf. the passage in § 12, where the author reiterates his concept that evil (darkness), although a reality, is not part of God's creation.

85. Matt. 4:1.
86. Mark 1:12-13.
87. Luke 4:1-2.
88. Luke 4:13.
89. Job 1:12.
90. Job 2:6.

91. Job 16:12.
92. Job 10:3.
93. John 19:11.
94. Tob. 2:12.
95. Jas. 5:11.
96. I Tim. 4:4.
97. Eccles. 3:11.
98. Wisd. 12:15.
99. I John 1:5.
100. Rom. 11:36.
101. Col. 1:16-17.
102. John 8:12.
103. See n. 84.
104. As in § 9.

[III. ON THE TERMS OF UNIVERSALITY]

1. *Signa universalia.* As he has already said (II, 4), the author proposes to support his concept of two creations and the threefold meaning of "create" by showing the proper meaning of such inclusive terms as "all" in the Scriptures. He must show that they, like "create," have a threefold interpretation. Cf. the discussion of the meaning of "all" in No. 58, chap. XII.

2. Cf. Phil. 3:8.
3. Dan. 8:23.
4. Gal. 3:22.
5. Rom. 11:32.
6. I Tim. 4:4.
7. Eccles. 3:11.
8. The text reads "Jesus son of Sirach says," but the passage is actually from Eccles. 3:14.
9. The text reads "In the Book of Wisdom," but the passage is actually from Ecclus. 42:23-24.
10. Ps. 103 (A.V. 104):24.
11. Ps. 118 (A.V. 119):91.
12. Rom. 14:20.
13. Tit. 1:15.
14. Rom. 8:28.
15. Eccles. 1:2, with omissions.
16. Eccles. 1:14.
17. Eccles. 3:1-2.
18. Eccles. 3:19-20.
19. Eccles. 2:17.
20. Col. 2:20-22.
21. Phil. 3:4-8.
22. Matt. 19:21.

23. Matt. 19:27.

24. Cf. Matt. 19:28.

25. Col. 3:8. "Detraction" is added to the verse, perhaps in recollection of I Pet. 2:1.

26. I John 2:15-16.

27. Dan. 8:23.

28. The scriptural basis for much of the following passage is found in the apocalyptic visions of Daniel. In orthodox as well as heretical thought, the king of Babylon, Nebuchadnezzar, was not uncommonly taken to personify the devil (see references in Borst, p. 298), and the "king of a shameless face," now identified as Antiochus IV Epiphanes, the Seleucid successor to Alexander in Syria, was often taken to be a figure of Antichrist. The "little horn" of Dan. 8:9 is a reference to the same ruler. For a sketch of various interpretations which have been made of Daniel's words, see S. R. Driver, *An Introduction to the Literature of the Old Testament* (New York, 1956), chap. XI, esp. pp. 491-94; and *Interpreter's Bible*, VI, 341-54.

29. Dan. 2:37-38.

30. Dan. 8:23-25.

31. Job 12:6.

32. Cf. Dan. 8:9.

33. Dan. 8:12.

34. Job 34:29-30.

35. Gal. 3:22.

36. Rom. 11:32.

37. Ephes. 2:4.

38. Ephes. 2:5.

39. Tit. 3:5-7.

40. Wisd. 15:1.

41. Wisd. 11:24-27.

42. Wisd. 16:12.

43. Ps. 103 (A.V. 104):27-28.

44. John 12:32.

45. Reading *vivificanda* for *iustificanda* of the text because of the parallel with the second sentence in § 5 and the quotation from I Tim. 6:13 later in § 7.

46. Col. 1:19-20. In this and the following five citations it is even more evident than elsewhere that the scriptural quotations were chosen not so much with an eye to the meaning of the verses in context as because they included words such as "reconcile," "restore," etc., which the author wished to emphasize.

47. Matt. 17:11.

48. Ephes. 1:9-10.

49. Apoc. 21:5.

50. Ephes. 4:10.

51. I Tim. 6:13.

52. Reading *tamen* for *tantum* of the text.
53. Heb. 2:8, quoting Ps. 8:8 (A.V. 6).
54. I Cor. 15:26-28.
55. Ecclus. 33:15.
56. II Cor. 6:14-16.
57. Ecclus. 33:15.

[IV. A COMPEND FOR THE INSTRUCTION OF BEGINNERS]

1. *Rudium*: literally, "the ignorant" or "the inexperienced." They, for whom the author writes, are to be distinguished from his critics and opponents, who are characterized as "unlearned" and "dullards"; see Borst, p. 279, n. 21.

2. Cf. the last paragraph in II, 11.

3. In a Catharist exposition of the Lord's Prayer (No. 60, part B), the heavens are considered one of the substances of God's creation, one of the means by which He brings other substances, such as spirit, life, and soul, under His will. Cf. also No. 58, chap. XVII, and the commentary there on Isa. 1:2 ("Hear, O ye heavens . . ."): "Those heavens have ears for hearing, for unless they could hear, the Lord would not say to them 'Hear!' "

4. Ps. 18 (A.V. 19):1.

5. Deut. 32:1.

6. Isa. 1:2.

7. The text reads "David," but the quotation is actually from Jer. 22:29.

8. Ps. 76:20 (A.V. 77:19).

9. Ps. 24 (A.V. 25):10.

10. Apoc. 5:13.

11. Ps. 26 (A.V. 27):13.

12. Ps. 142 (A.V. 143):10.

13. The text reads "Solomon," but the quotation is actually from Ps. 36 (A.V. 37):29.

14. Ps. 44:7 (A.V. 45:6).

15. Matt. 5:34-35.

16. Ps. 98 (A.V. 99):5.

17. Gal. 4:9.

18. Col. 2:20-22.

19. Wisd. 1:13.

20. Heb. 6:18.

21. II Tim. 2:13.

22. Borst (p. 300) cites various contemporary authorities substantiating the doctrine that God is not composite; see also Thomas Aquinas *Summa Theologica* I, q. 3, art. 6,7: Anton C. Pegis, *Basic Writings of Saint Thomas Aquinas* (2 vols., New York, 1945), I, 32-34. But Borst also remarks (p. 278, n. 14) that the doctrine that God and His will were one had already been repudiated by orthodox theologians in the twelfth century.

23. See above, part II, n. 70.

24. Ps. 51:3-5 (A.V. 52:1-3). Historically, David's reference is to Doeg, the Edomite who at Saul's command slew priests who supported David. But for our author the comments are entirely directed at the evil one; see the remarks of Borst (pp. 267, 271) on the author's use of Old Testament citations.

25. Apoc. 12:9. Cf. the beliefs of the heretics of Desenzano, later known as Albanenses, as described in No. 23, § 2a, where this verse is cited in support of the narrative of the devil's repulse from heaven.

26. Luke 8:11-12.

27. Dan. 7:21-22. "The horn" is now generally taken as Daniel's reference to Antiochus IV Epiphanes, Seleucid ruler of Syria and persecutor of the Jews, but for the author of the *Liber* it is another symbol of the devil; cf. part III, n. 28, above.

28. Dan. 7:24-25. Historically, the reference is still to Antiochus IV Epiphanes, who waged campaigns against Antioch, Egypt, and Macedonia before suppressing the Jewish religion, defiling the holy places of Jerusalem (168 B.C.), and savagely punishing the Jews who resisted; see I Macc. 1:41-63. Used symbolically by the author of the *Liber*, the verse recalls Lucifer in Isa. 14:13-14, quoted above in II, 19.

29. Dan. 8:9-11.

30. Apoc. 12:3-4. Cf. No. 23, § 2a, where "the third part of the stars of heaven" is taken as a reference to the angels seduced by Lucifer and embodied in his realm.

31. Apoc. 13:5-7.

32. Evidently the author had in mind the words of Paul in Ephes. 6:12, quoted in § 7 (n. 46).

33. Ps. 51:7 (A.V. 52:5).

34. Ps. 9² (A.V. 10):15-16.

35. Ps. 36 (A.V. 37):10.

36. Prov. 14:32.

37. Heb. 2:14.

38. Luke 1:52.

39. I Cor. 15:24,26, the words "and domination" and "of all" being added to the biblical verses.

40. Col. 1:12,13, the words "of truth" being added to the biblical verse.

41. Col. 2:13-15.

42. Acts 26:16-18.

43. Matt. 26:55.

44. Luke 22:53.

45. On the sect name, see the introduction to No. 23 and also No. 51.

46. Ephes. 6:10-13.

47. Ephes. 6:16.

48. Following Borst (p. 284), we read *coram sapientibus* for the *contra sapientibus* of the text.

49. The text reads "through Isaiah," but the passage is actually from

Jer. 5:19 and the biblical verse reads "shall serve strangers."

50. Isa. 45:20.

51. Isa. 26:13.

52. Ps. 80:9-10 (A.V. 81:8-9).

53. Ps. 43:21-22 (A.V. 44:20-21).

54. Ps. 46:10 (A.V. 47:9).

55. Ps. 95 (A.V. 96):5.

56. Zeph. (Soph.) 2:11.

57. Jer. 11:9-10, omitting part of v. 10, but adding the words "and adore them."

58. Jer. 16:11-13.

59. Mal. 2:11.

60. Mic. 4:5.

61. II Cor. 4:3-4.

62. I Cor. 8:5-6.

63. Matt. 6:24.

64. John 14:30.

65. John 12:31.

66. John 16:11.

67. Acts 4:25-27. The quotation is from Ps. 2:1-2.

68. Matt. 25:41.

69. Jude 1:6.

70. Jude 1:7.

71. Job 10:22.

72. Ezech. 35:9.

73. Ezech. 35:3-5.

74. Cf. Matt. 13:25,37,39.

75. II Thess. 1:9.

76. Matt. 25:46.

77. Mark 3:29.

78. Hab. 3:3-6.

79. Apoc. 12:9.

80. *Solicitudines* in the text seems clearly a mistake for *solitudines* [desolations], as in the quotation from Ezech. 35:9 (n. 72, above).

81. Cf. No. 51, § 19, where Rainerius Sacconi lists the names applied to the devil by John of Lugio.

82. I Pet. 4:19.

83. From this passage it appears that the author considered his chief opponents at this point to be orthodox Christians. It may be recalled that of all the Cathars, only the faction of Albanenses led by John of Lugio accepted the entire Old Testament. Other radical dualists among the Albanenses and Albigenses accepted parts of the Old Testament as having been written in the celestial world before the destruction of the heavenly Jerusalem. Mitigated dualists of various sects regarded the Old Testament as of the devil's authorship, but some of them admitted that he had put good pas-

sages therein, in order to deceive, and that sometimes the prophets were inspired, without their knowledge, by the Holy Spirit; others accepted whatever passages of the Old Testament were repeated in the New. Contemporary testimony on this subject will be found in Nos. 25; 38, § 10; 50; 51, §§ 16, 20; 53; and 54, § 3. The question is discussed in Borst, pp. 156-62, and Thouzellier, *Un Traité cathare*, pp. 49-54.

84. Gen. 1:1-2.

85. Gen. 1:21, with omissions.

86. Gen. 1:25.

87. Gen. 1:27.

88. Mark 10:6.

89. The difference between his opponents' interpretation of the Old Testament, which the author now proposes to give, and the spiritual interpretation adopted by John of Lugio and his followers may be illustrated by comparing § 11 (nn. 90, 91), where Deuteronomy is cited as setting forth the commands of an evil god, with § 1 (n. 5), where passages from Deuteronomy are used to prove the existence of an intelligent spiritual creation.

90. Deut. 22:22.

91. Deut. 22:30.

92. Lev. 18:8.

93. Lev. 20:11.

94. II Kings (A.V. II Sam.) 12:9-12.

95. II Kings (A.V. II Sam.) 16:21-22.

96. Deut. 22:22.

97. I Cor. 6:9-10, omitting several phrases.

98. Ephes. 5:5, omitting a few words.

99. I Thess. 4:3.

100. Exod. 11:2-3.

101. Exod. 12:35-36.

102. Deut. 20:10-17.

103. Deut. 2:32-34.

104. Deut. 3:3-4,6-7.

105. Num. 15:32-35.

106. Exod. 23:26-27.

107. Lev. 26:7-8.

108. Num. 33:55-56.

109. Ezech. 18:20, reversing the order of phrases in the biblical verse.

110. Matt. 5:43-44; the words "to them of old," added to the biblical verse, recall Matt. 5:33.

111. Matt. 5:44-45.

112. John 5:19.

113. II Cor. 1:3.

114. Deut. 21:22-23; the author alters the wording but not the sense of v. 22.

115. Gal. 3:13.

116. I Kings (A.V. I Sam.) 16:14.
117. *Idem*, 16:23.
118. Judg. 9:22-23.
119. Cf. John 14:17.
120. The text reads "fourth book," but the quotation is actually from III Kings (A.V. I Kings) 22:19-23.
121. Gen. 13:14-15.
122. Gen. 13:17.
123. Deut. 1:8.
124. Acts 7:3-5, quoting Gen. 12:1.
125. Note the contradiction between this passage and that in § 10, which declares that the evil god is discerned only through his works.
126. Gen. 32:30.
127. Exod. 24:9-10.
128. Exod. 33:11.
129. Num. 12:7-8.
130. John 1:18.
131. The text reads "second Epistle," but the quotation is actually from I Tim. 1:17.
132. Col. 1:15.

[V. AGAINST THE GARATENSES]
1. On the name, see p. 42, above. The form "Garatenses" is found only here and in certain papal bulls.
2. The editor notes at this point a lacuna in the manuscript. There is a distinct break in the thought, and what follows does not constitute a sentence.
3. *Baptizatos*, meaning "all Christians," although the word usually refers to converts.
4. Dondaine (*Un Traité néo-manichéen*, p. 28) and Borst (p. 305) agree that the mention in the first sentence of a further rebuttal and this reference to an earlier discussion point to a part of the author's work which is now missing.
5. Note the language here applied to the action of the devil: "forming" or "making," not "creating." See part I, n. 28.
6. Gen. 1:28.
7. Gen. 1:22.
8. Gen. 1:26.
9. Gen. 1:25, omitting a few words.
10. Gen. 2:22.
11. Gen. 2:24.
12. Mark 10:6-8.
13. Gen. 1:1-2.
14. Gen. 1:21.
15. Gen. 1:27.

16. Gen. 2:3.

17. Gen. 14:18-20.

18. *De omni creatione*, but the author is less interested in discussing creation than in ridiculing the Garatenses.

19. John 1:3.

20. Acts 17:23-24,26.

21. Acts 4:24.

22. Apoc. 14:7.

23. Heb. 3:4.

24. That is, orthodox Christians.

25. Reading *vos* (as corrected by Borst, p. 285) for *nos* of the text.

26. I Tim. 4:1-4.

27. Job 2:3.

28. Ps. 7:17 (A.V. 16).

29. Only three letters of the name appear in the manuscript, and the individual has not been identified. Borst (pp. 236, n. 8; 262) suggests that he might have succeeded Nazarius as bishop of the Concorezzenses after 1235.

30. Cf. Gen. 1:1,21,27; 2:7.

31. See n. 29.

32. He is not otherwise known.

33. The heading was supplied by Dondaine.

34. The passage beginning with the words "of the Most Holy Creator" and ending with "given form" is in the margin of the manuscript in a hand different from that which wrote the text and was omitted from the body of the treatise by the editor. We include it, however, for the "new souls" in the following phrase seems to require this explanation. Cf. Borst, p. 285.

35. Cf. Rom. 1:32.

[VI. ON WILL]

1. In the following paragraphs the author returns to a theme he had discussed in I, 18: the necessity of potency, knowledge, and desire on the part of those who are to achieve salvation.

2. Borst (p. 307) cites Aristotle *Metaphysica* III.iv: "For it is that which exists potentially and not in complete reality that is indeterminate" (*Works of Aristotle*, ed. by Smith and Ross, VIII, 1007ᵇ28), as well as comparable passages from Richard of St. Victor and Ibn Gabirol.

3. *Secunda notula hec est.* Under this heading, the author touches again on points discussed in I, 18 (the example of Peter's death), and § 4 (God's foreknowledge).

4. The editor (*Un Traité néo-manichéen*, p. 141, n. 19) remarks that this seems not to be from Aristotle and suggests a passage from Ibn Gabirol *Fons vitae* III.57, as a possible source. Borst (p. 308) lists a number of comparable passages from Aristotle, St. Augustine, William of Auvergne, and Ibn Gabirol.

5. Dan. 13:42.

6. *De sententia*, that is, the concept of free will. The author now seeks to show, in language reminiscent of I, 11, that free will is incompatible with the theories of daily creation of new souls and the Last Judgment held by its advocates.

7. Three, seven, or twelve years were more commonly given as the ages at which a child progressed from one stage of growth to another. See Du Cange, *s.v.* "ablactatio," and Borst, p. 308.

8. Matt. 25:34-35.

9. Matt. 25:41-42, omitting part of v. 41.

[VII. ON PERSECUTIONS]

1. *De persecutione*, corrected by Borst (p. 285) to *de percutione*.

2. Matt. 26:31; Zach. 13:7.

3. John 19:11.

4. *Datum dixit et non datam quasi dicat: nisi hoc esset tibi concessum.*

5. Isa. 53:8.

6. Matt. 26:56.

7. See Dondaine, *Un Traité néo-manichéen*, pp. 11, 12-13.

8. II Tim. 3:1-5.

9. Matt. 24:24. Beginning with this verse, the edited text gives only the first and last words of each scriptural quotation. However, the notes in Borst, pp. 308-10, make it possible to quote them in full.

10. Rom. 1:28-31.

11. II Pet. 2:1-3.

12. II Tim. 3:13.

13. Acts 20:28-31.

14. Heb. 11:32-40.

15. Matt. 5:12.

16. Acts 7:51-53. The text changes the wording from "the Just One" in v. 52.

17. Matt. 23:29-39.

18. Jas. 5:10-11.

19. Matt. 2:13-15.

20. Luke 2:33-35.

21. Matt. 20:17-19 and 26:2, respectively.

22. John 8:58-59.

23. John 11:47-53.

24. John 7:7.

25. John 15:17-21.

26. Apoc. 12:4.

27. Jas. 5:5-6.

28. Acts 2:22-24.

29. Acts 2:36.

30. Acts 3:12-21.

31. Acts 4:24-28.

32. Acts 5:29-33.
33. Acts 10:36-43.
34. Acts 13:26-30.
35. I Pet. 4:1-2.
36. Mark 14:33-34.
37. Mark 15:33-34.
38. Mark 15:37.
39. Matt. 27:38.
40. Matt. 27:50.
41. Luke 23:46.
42. Acts 24:14.
43. Acts 28:22.
44. Matt. 5:10-12.
45. Matt. 10:16-25.
46. John 16:20-22.
47. Matt. 24:4-13.
48. Apoc. 2:10.
49. John 15:17-21.
50. John 17:13-16.
51. I John 3:13-14.
52. I Pet. 4:12-19.
53. Acts 26:9-11.
54. I Pet. 2:19-25.
55. Acts 8:1.
56. Rom. 8:35-39, adding "virtues" to v. 38.
57. I Pet. 1:6-7.
58. Acts 23:1-2.
59. I Cor. 4:11-14.
60. I Pet. 3:13-14.
61. I Cor. 15:9.
62. II Cor. 4:8-11. The text in vv. 10 and 11 does not accord exactly with the Vulgate (cf. Borst, p. 310). We follow the wording of the Douay translation.
63. Ephes. 6:10-18.
64. II Cor. 1:3-11, omitting part of v. 6.
65. Gal. 1:13-14.
66. The author omits from the biblical text the phrase in brackets, which we supply to preserve the sense of the passage. That Paul is satirizing the claims of false apostles is clear in the context of II Cor. 11:12. Perhaps the author was reluctant to designate Paul's detractors as "ministers of Christ."
67. II Cor. 11:21-29.
68. II Thess. 1:4-7.
69. I Tim. 1:12-13.
70. I Thess. 2:14-16.
71. I Thess. 3:2-5.

72. I Cor. 15:19.
73. Phil. 1:28-30.
74. II Tim. 3:10-12.

60. THE CATHARIST CHURCH AND ITS
INTERPRETATION OF THE LORD'S PRAYER

1. In Ussher's library were eight other volumes in the same language; they contained Waldensian literature and were also collected in the early seventeenth century. Before Venckeleer's study the manuscript with which we are concerned, like the others, was regarded as Waldensian in origin. (See, for example, Mario Esposito, "Sur quelques manuscrits de l'ancienne littérature religieuse des Vaudois du Piémont," *RHE*, XLVI [1951], 127-59, esp. 131-43.) The last folios in that manuscript contain a short passage which we have not translated because it repeats a theme more fully developed in part B and seems to have been composed primarily to fill up the blank pages in the manuscript volume (see Venckeleer, "Un Recueil cathare, I: Une apologie," *RBPH*, XXXVIII [1960], 818).

2. Venckeleer judges both to be written in the same dialect, that characteristic of the Dauphiné (*ibid.*, p. 820).

3. This is in contradiction to the statement in the ritual in Latin (No. 57, part A) that the believer should not scorn his earlier baptism, even though it was insufficient for his salvation. The present treatise has another polemical passage, in chapter X, against the Roman Church for its persecution of true Christians.

4. Venckeleer, "Un Recueil cathare, I: Une apologie," *RBPH*, XXXVIII (1960), 832-33. Ussher's manuscript was copied before 1375/76 (*ibid.*, p. 819).

5. See Borst, pp. 159-60, and the sources there cited.

6. *Adversus Catharos et Valdenses*, ed. by Ricchini, p. 231. Moneta adds that these heretics erroneously supposed that John was not born of a mortal male parent but of the Holy Spirit.

7. See No. 51, §§ 24 and 17. The doctrine of John of Lugio that the career of John the Baptist occurred in a world superior to this earth is not in point, for the present treatise clearly refers to affairs in this world. By the early fourteenth century even some radical dualists in southern France had come to accept John the Baptist as good and divinely inspired (Borst, p. 160, n. 17).

8. Venckeleer's date *ante quem*, 1240 ("Un Recueil cathare, I: Une apologie," *RBPH*, XXXVIII [1960], 833-34), is based on his conclusion that Moneta of Cremona knew and used a prototype of this treatise. However, the evidence Venckeleer cites—passages in Moneta's work which resemble those on persecution here—is not conclusive, for the necessity of enduring suffering was a common doctrine among the Cathars and their

analogy of themselves as sheep among wolves was not at all unusual (see, for example, No. 5; No. 15, part A; and No. 59, part VII). Also, the further assertion by Venckeleer (p. 834) that Moneta was the first "inquisitor" to notice a heretical argument for spiritual baptism which was based on Acts 8:14-17 (see the *Vindication*, chap. XI) ignores the reference to that argument in the works of Alan of Lille (Migne, *PL*, CCX, 351) and James Capelli (ed. by Bazzocchi, p. CXL). It was probably a point often made and Moneta could have found the argument elsewhere than in the *Vindication*.

9. Venckeleer ("Un Recueil cathare, II: Une glose," *RBPH*, XXXIX [1961], 792, n. 3) suggests this also, for reasons not stated.

10. For heretical attitudes toward the Old Testament, see No. 59, part IV, n. 83.

11. See n. 7, above. Is it possible that this treatise originated among the Concorezzenses of Lombardy and that the present Provençal text is a translation of a Latin original? Perhaps expert examination of the quotations from the Bible would show whether they belong to a recognizable tradition of vernacular Bibles or were a translator's own rendering from a Latin text of the Bible.

12. Both singular and plural forms of these terms are used: "The charities" are said to influence other substances, and "charity" is the supersubstantial bread; "lives" are associated with spirits, but the Psalmist speaks of his "life," etc.

13. Venckeleer, "Un Recueil cathare, II: Une glose," *RBPH*, XXXIX (1961), 785-89, describes the treatise chapter by chapter.

14. See part B, chap. I, esp. n. 30.

15. On the significance of "Amen," see also part B, n. 247.

16. Of a total of approximately two hundred and thirty biblical verses cited in the gloss, one fifth are from Psalms.

17. Quoting Isa. 10:12-14; Mic. 5:6; Ps. 142:1,3; Lam. 1:10; 4:12; 2:7. Cf. the style of No. 58, chap. XVI, although there is no similarity in the scriptural citations.

18. On other terms for the evil one, see part B, n. 216.

19. See part B, n. 186.

20. See Matt. 26:39—"Let this chalice pass from me; nevertheless not as I will, but as Thou wilt."

21. Cf. the gloss in the Latin ritual (No. 57, part A), in which "supersubstantial bread" is the law of Christ, the spiritual meaning of the New Testament. The scriptural basis for that exposition is of course quite different from the one employed here.

22. See Osee 11:4—"Draw them with the cords of Adam, with the bands of love."

23. "Un Recueil cathare, II: Une glose," *RBPH*, XXXIX (1961), 790-92.

24. Cf. No. 51, §§ 21, 22.

25. Is it possible that this gloss was composed by someone influenced by Catharist thought but not a member of an active group, perhaps such a

person as would have been attracted by the strong current of mysticism in the later Middle Ages, who may have been influenced by the surviving traces of Catharism? We have no evidence to support such a suggestion except the general impression given by the work.

A. A VINDICATION OF THE CHURCH OF GOD

1. Acts 7:48.
2. Matt. 28:20.
3. John 14:23.
4. John 14:15-18.
5. I Cor. 3:16-17.
6. I Cor. 6:19.
7. II Cor. 6:16-18.
8. I Tim. 3:14-15.
9. Heb. 3:6.
10. Matt. 16:18.
11. Acts 9:31.
12. Matt. 18:15-17.
13. Ephes. 5:25-27.
14. Matt. 10:20.
15. John 20:22-23.
16. Cf. Matt. 10:1.
17. Mark 3:15.
18. Luke 9:1.
19. Matt. 18:17-20.
20. I Pet. 3:12.
21. Jas. 5:16.
22. Mark 11:24.
23. Mark 16:17-18.
24. Jas. 5:14-15.
25. John 20:23.
26. John 17:20-21.
27. Matt. 28:20.
28. Matt. 24:34.
29. Matt. 19:17,18.
30. Matt. 5:21-22.
31. Rom. 13:9.
32. I John 3:15.
33. Apoc. 22:15.
34. Apoc. 13:10.
35. Apoc. 21:8.
36. Rom. 1:29,32.
37. Matt. 19:18.
38. Matt. 5:27-28.
39. Matt. 15:19-20.

40. The text reads "Book of Wisdom," but the correct citation is Prov. 6:32.
41. The text reads "Philippians," but the correct citation is Ephes. 5:3.
42. Ephes. 5:5.
43. Gal. 5:19,21.
44. The text reads "Ephesians," but the correct citation is I Cor. 6:9-10.
45. Heb. 13:4.
46. Apoc. 22:15.
47. Apoc. 21:8. The last words in the heretical text read *la sa mort*.
48. Matt. 19:18.
49. Ephes. 4:28.
50. Cf. Rom. 13:9 and Exod. 20:17.
51. I Pet. 4:15.
52. Matt. 19:18.
53. I Pet. 3:10.
54. Rom. 13:9.
55. Ephes. 4:25.
56. Apoc. 21:27.
57. Apoc. 22:15.
58. Apoc. 21:8.
59. Col. 3:9.
60. Wisd. 1:11.
61. Matt. 5:34-36.
62. Matt. 5:37.
63. *Ibid.*
64. Matt. 6:10. On the devil identified as evil, see chap. VIII of part B, and also No. 59, II, 11. The phrase "Deliver us from evil," is here written in Latin, the language in which the Cathars said the Lord's Prayer.
65. This argument is often found in the discussion of oaths by Catholic polemicists. See these examples: the treatise under the name of Bonacursus, chap. X (Migne, *PL*, CCIV, 783-84); Alan of Lille *Quadripartita* II.xix (Migne, *PL*, CCX, 394); Prevostin of Cremona (?) *Summa contra hereticos*, chap. XVIII [B] (ed. by Garvin and Corbett, pp. 214, 216); all earlier than Ermengaud *Contra hereticos*, chap. XVIII (Migne, *PL*, CCIV, 1271; cited by Venckeleer, "Un Recueil cathare, I: Une apologie," *RBPH*, XXXVIII [1960], 832); Georgius *Disputatio*, chap. XI (Martène and Durand, *Thesaurus novus anecdotorum*, V, 1737-40; James Capelli *Summa contra hereticos* (ed. by Bazzocchi, p. CLXXXI); and Moneta of Cremona *Adversus Catharos et Valdenses* (ed. by Ricchini, p. 463).
66. Rom. 4:15.
67. *Aisicom es.*
68. Jas. 5:12.
69. Jas. 1:26.
70. Ephes. 4:29.
71. Ephes. 4:31.

72. Col. 3:8.
73. I Pet. 3:9-10.
74. Matt. 12:36-37.
75. Matt. 25:31,32.
76. Matt. 25:34.
77. Matt. 25:41.
78. Jas. 2:10-11.
79. Matt. 12:33.
80. Cf. John 10:38.
81. I Pet. 2:21-22. The heretical text substitutes the pronouns "us" and "we" for the biblical "you."
82. Cf. Ephes. 1:22-23.
83. I Cor. 12:27.
84. I Cor. 6:15.
85. I John 3:6.
86. I John 2:6.
87. I John 1:6-7.
88. I John 3:7.
89. Cf. with the following, No. 59, VII, and the much earlier comments in Nos. 5 and 16 on the desire of heretics to die in torment or to be persecuted; also their words, quoted by Eberwin to St. Bernard (No. 15, part A): "We, the poor of Christ ... flee from city to city like sheep amidst wolves and are persecuted as were the apostles and martyrs ... because we are not of this world." In discussing this subject Moneta of Cremona (*Adversus Catharos et Valdenses*, ed. by Ricchini, pp. 393, 514) uses some phrases which resemble those of the present tract (see Venckeleer, "Un Recueil cathare, I: Une apologie," *RBPH*, XXXVIII [1960], 833).
90. John 15:20.
91. Matt. 5:10-12.
92. Matt. 10:16.
93. Matt. 10:22-23.
94. Rom. 8:36.
95. John 10:32.
96. John 10:33.
97. II Tim. 3:12.
98. John 16:2.
99. Matt. 23:34.
100. Acts 14:21.
101. I John 3:13.
102. With the following comments, cf. the discourses in the rituals in Latin and in Provençal (No. 57, parts A and B).
103. Matt. 3:11.
104. Matt. 28:19.
105. Mark 15:15-16.
106. Mark 16:16.

107. John 4:1-2.
108. Mark 1:8.
109. John 1:31-34.
110. Ephes. 4:5.
111. Acts 19:1-6.
112. Acts 8:14-17.
113. II Tim. 1:6.
114. Cf. Acts 19:11-19.
115. Matt. 28:19-20.
116. Cf. I Pet. 3:20-21.
117. This final phrase is in Latin.

B. A GLOSS ON THE LORD'S PRAYER

1. The beginning of the treatise is missing from the manuscript.
2. Jer. 31:8-9. "In prayer" is substituted for the biblical "in mercy." There are numerous small differences between the wording of the biblical passages in the text and the wording of the Vulgate. Only those which significantly affect the meaning will be noted.
3. Jer. 29:10,12-14.
4. Luke 19:10.
5. *Parlant.* This is one of a few places in which it has been necessary to alter a verb form to allow a grammatical sentence in English.
6. John 16:20.
7. Luke 18:1.
8. Matt. 26:41.
9. This, like all the phrases of the Lord's Prayer which begin the chapters, is written in Latin in the manuscript.
10. Ps. 140 (A.V. 141):2.
11. Jas. 1:17.
12. I Cor. 13:10.
13. II Cor. 1:3.
14. Perhaps Ps. 106 (A.V. 107):8.
15. Cf. Heb. 12:9.
16. *Car vistas eran.* The meaning of this phrase escapes us.
17. Ephes. 3:15; 4:6.
18. Ps. 122 (A.V. 123):1.
19. I John 4:8,16.
20. Ps. 18 (A.V. 19):7.
21. Cf. John 16:27.
22. John 16:28.
23. John 3:13.
24. Cf. John 14:10.
25. John 10:38.
26. Ephes. 4:6.
27. Rom. 11:36.

28. Acts 17:28.
29. John 17:20-21.
30. From *The Vision of Isaiah* (No. 56, part A), chap. III, vv. 7-8. We supply the words in brackets to give proper meaning to the passage.
31. Isa. 45:8.
32. *Lo sperit del noster primer format,* i.e., the spirit of the psalmist David. See chap. IV.
33. Cant. 5:2.
34. Jas. 1:17.
35. Dan. 7:13.
36. Apoc. 1:7.
37. Ps. 67 (A.V. 68):35.
38. This reflects a doctrine revealed in the Bogomil *Secret Supper* (No. 56, part B, § 9) and attested by witnesses before the Inquisition: The fallen angels had lost the right to say the Lord's Prayer, and no one on earth had the power to say the Prayer except those who were "in the way of truth." Others who did so committed a mortal sin. God was Father only of the Good Men (perfected heretics), for He was God only of truth and justice. For other men to address him as "our Father" was to sin by telling a lie (Döllinger, *Beiträge,* II, 159, 199, 212, 239). In another document a heretic paraphrasing *The Vision of Isaiah* revealed that because he had doubted, God refused to let him use the phrase "our Father" (*ibid.,* p. 210).
39. Ezech. 36:22.
40. Rom. 2:24.
41. Isa. 65:24.
42. Ezech. 36:23-24.
43. Deut. 32:5.
44. Matt. 26:39.
45. Luke 22:42.
46. John 17:19.
47. Heb. 13:12.
48. Rom. 4:8.
49. Rom. 11:29.
50. Isa. 9:8.
51. Ps. 13 (A.V. 14):7.
52. Isa. 29:22-23.
53. Ezech. 36:8-10.
54. Ps. 71 (A.V. 72):3.
55. Ps. 120 (A.V. 121):1.
56. Ps. 86 (A.V. 87):1.
57. John 6:44.
58. Cf. Deut. 32:9.
59. Isa. 19:25.
60. Osee 11:4.
61. Col. 3:14.

62. Ps. 15 (A.V. 16):6.
63. Ps. 139:6 (A.V. 140:5).
64. Ps. 118 (A.V. 119):61.
65. Ps. 115 (A.V. 116):16.
66. Isa. 5:18.
67. Acts 20:22.
68. Ps. 65 (A.V. 66):9.
69. Mark 11:9-10.
70. Dan. 2:44.
71. Ps. 144 (A.V. 145):10-13.
72. Apoc. 1:4-6.
73. Apoc. 5:8-10. We use "elders" in place of the "ancients" of the Douay translation.
74. Ps. 67:33 (A.V. 68:32).
75. Ps. 21 (A.V. 22):23.
76. Cf. II Thess. 1:10.
77. Matt. 24:31.
78. Apoc. 22:12.
79. I Thess. 4:12-17.
80. *Gloria* here, but in a subsequent quotation of this verse (see n. 98), the biblical reading (*majestat*) is followed.
81. Matt. 24:30-31.
82. Matt. 24:3.
83. Cf. Rom. 2:6-10.
84. Ps. 79:2-3 (A.V. 80:1-2).
85. Apoc. 22:17.
86. Apoc. 22:20.
87. Apoc. 3:11.
88. Apoc. 22:12.
89. Jas. 5:8.
90. Heb. 10:37.
91. Cf. Isa. 9:7.
92. Ephes. 1:20-21. We use "dominations" in place of the "dominions" of the Douay translation.
93. Col. 1:16.
94. Col. 2:15.
95. Apoc. 1:8; 21:6.
96. Mal. 3:1-2.
97. II Pet. 3:4.
98. Matt. 24:29-30,37.
99. Matt. 25:31-32.
100. Apoc. 1:7.
101. Apoc. 16:15.
102. I Thess. 5:5,8.
103. II Pet. 3:10.

104. I Thess. 5:2.
105. I Thess. 4:3-6; 5:14-18.
106. Ephes. 1:11.
107. John 6:38-40.
108. Cf. Rom. 12:2; Ephes. 5:17.
109. Heb. 13:21.
110. Matt. 11:25.
111. Ecclus. 16:18-19.
112. Ps. 62 (A.V. 63):4-5.
113. Ps. 40:5 (A.V. 41:4).
114. Ps. 119 (A.V. 120):2.
115. Ps. 114 (A.V. 116):7.
116. Ps. 145 (A.V. 146):1.
117. Ps. 102 (A.V. 103):1,4.
118. On the phrase "supersubstantial bread" in the Lord's Prayer, see also No. 57, part A, esp. n. 8.
119. Cf. I Cor. 10:17.
120. Ps. 106 (A.V. 107):5.
121. Lam. 4:4.
122. Ps. 97 (A.V. 98):3.
123. Luke 1:53.
124. John 6:51.
125. Isa. 9:6.
126. Cf. I Cor. 13:4,7.
127. Job 10:12.
128. Prov. 18:14.
129. Rom. 8:26.
130. Ps. 38:8 (A.V. 39:7).
131. Ps. 138 (A.V. 139):15.
132. Ps. 68:2-3 (A.V. 69:1-2).
133. Acts 4:24-25.
134. Ps. 138 (A.V. 139):16.
135. Ps. 72:22.
136. Ephes. 4:9-10.
137. *Ordene lo sio Fill ama e lo don de la carita a quel David.*
138. I Pet. 5:10.
139. Ps. 117 (A.V. 118):24.
140. Ps. 18 (A.V. 19):3.
141. John 12:49-50.
142. Rom. 13:12.
143. Cf. Heb. 4:1-5 and Ps. 94 (A.V. 95):11.
144. Heb. 4:6-7.
145. I Cor. 13:10.
146. I Cor. 13:1-2.
147. Matt. 5:48.

148. Luke 11:4.
149. Isa. 43:27.
150. Luke 15:18,21.
151. Ps. 50 (A.V. 51):6.
152. Bar. 6:1.
153. Dan. 9:4,5,16. The biblical text reads: "our fathers, Jerusalem."
154. Tit. 3:3.
155. Cf. Jer. 9:4-5.
156. Ezech. 22:6-7,11.
157. Wisd. 14:23-26.
158. Luke 6:37; Matt. 6:15.
159. Matt. 18:35.
160. Ephes. 4:32.
161. Col. 3:13.
162. II John 1:5.
163. Rom. 8:12.
164. Rom. 13:8.
165. John 15:17.
166. I John 4:11; 3:23.
167. Luke 11:4.
168. I Cor. 10:12-13.
169. Heb. 4:15. The heretical text has *evesque* [bishop] for the *pontificem* of the Vulgate, translated in Douay and A.V. as "high priest."
170. Heb. 2:18.
171. Wisd. 3:1,5-6.
172. Cf. Heb. 11:17.
173. I Pet. 4:12-13.
174. Jas. 1:14.
175. Matt. 4:1,3.
176. Luke 4:13.
177. I Thess. 3:5.
178. Tob. 2:12.
179. Jas. 5:10.
180. Cf. Heb. 3:9.
181. I Cor. 10:9.
182. Isa. 27:8.
183. Wisd. 3:5-6.
184. Jas. 1:12.
185. Luke 22:28-30.
186. Cf. the ritual in Latin (No. 57, part A), which also speaks of two temptations, but in different terms.
187. Wisd. 3:5.
188. Jas. 1:12.
189. Cf. Ecclus. 4:12,16,18-21.
190. I Tim. 6:9.

191. Apoc. 2:10.
192. Apoc. 3:10.
193. Ps. 25 (A.V. 26):2.
194. Luke 22:31-32.
195. Matt. 26:41.
196. Cf. Jer. 13:17.
197. Luke 12:32.
198. Jer. 50:33-34.
199. Matt. 6:13. Here and in the last words of this chapter, the phrase is written in Provençal, although all other quotations of the Lord's Prayer are in Latin.
200. Matt. 13:19.
201. Mark 4:15.
202. Luke 8:12.
203. Matt. 13:27.
204. Matt. 13:39.
205. Omitting the redundant *d'aquel mal home* which occurs in the text at this point.
206. Ps. 139:2 (A.V. 140:1).
207. Ps. 55:2 (A.V. 56:1).
208. Ps. 43 (A.V. 44):26.
209. Job 34:29-30.
210. Job 16:12.
211. Ps. 142 (A.V. 143):1,3.
212. Lam. 1:16; 2:22.
213. Bar. 4:9-10,21,25.
214. Rom. 16:20.
215. Lam. 1:10; 4:12; 2:7.
216. See No. 51, § 20, for various designations of the devil according to John of Lugio. The king of Assyria is not there mentioned; but in *The Book of the Two Principles* (No. 59, II, 11), the evil creator is equated with the Assyrian and is also identified with other biblical figures.
217. Cf. Ezech. 32:33; 31:8.
218. Jer. 50:17.
219. Cf. Isa. 10:12-14.
220. Ezech. 31:3-4,8-9.
221. Ezech. 32:22-23.
222. Osee 11:5.
223. Mic. 5:6.
224. *La cita.* The biblical text has "captivity."
225. Isa. 49:24-25.
226. Jer. 31:10-12,14.
227. II Tim. 2:26.
228. Dan. 7:17-18.
229. Luke 19:12.

230. Apoc. 5:9-10.

231. Ps. 118 (A.V. 119):94.

232. Ps. 118 (A.V. 119):125. "Commandments" (*comandamentz*) is substituted in the heretical text for the biblical "testimonies."

233. Rom. 14:7-8.

234. Wisd. 15:1-2.

235. Ps. 37:11 (A.V. 38:10).

236. Ps. 30:11 (A.V. 31:10).

237. Lam. 1:14.

238. Ezech. 18:4.

239. Ps. 107:2 (A.V. 108:1).

240. Ps. 56:9 (A.V. 57:8).

241. Ps. 29:12-13 (A.V. 30:11-12).

242. *Als segles*, literally "forever"; see n. 245.

243. Ps. 43:2 (A.V. 44:1).

244. Ps. 21:5-6 (A.V. 22:4-5).

245. *Segles dels segles* for the *saecula saeculorum* of the Vulgate, usually rendered in English as "forever and ever."

246. Cf. Apoc. 5:12-13.

247. Henri Grégoire, "Cathares d'Asie Mineure, d'Italie, et de France," in *Memorial Louis Petit*, pp. 144-55, cites a fourth-century Greek epitaph (of a priest of the ancient sect of Cathari), in which the Greek words for "ninety-nine" refer to Christ; the numeral "99" in many ancient inscriptions has been found to mean "Amen." Grégoire concludes that the use of "Amen" in the epitaph constitutes a reference to Christ as the first angel, a personage second only to God, as in John 3:14, "saith the Amen . . . who is the beginning of the creation of God." In a manuscript probably of the twelfth century Grégoire found the same term used in an anathema against the Bogomils and argues that this is evidence for a continuity of the Catharist name and tradition from the fourth century to the twelfth. In the present treatise, "Amen" designates the "spirit of the first form," which in turn is equated with the psalmist David. If this symbolism was derived from the ancient tradition cited by Grégoire, it had evidently undergone considerable alteration. See also the disparaging remarks of Borst (p. 241, n. 5) on Grégoire's thesis.

248. Apoc. 1:7.

249. Heb. 2:15.

Bibliography

This bibliography is not a complete list of works cited in the notes but includes those works which have been most referred to or which are especially valuable in connection with the contents of this volume. Publications which contain texts translated in this volume are preceded by *.

Abelard, Peter. *Introductio ad theologiam.* In Migne, *PL*, CLXXVIII, 979-1112.

Achéry, Luc d', ed. *Veterum aliquot scriptorum qui in Galliae bibliothecis delituerant Spicilegium.* 13 vols. Paris, 1657-1677. New ed. by L. F. J. de la Barre. *Spicilegium sive collectio veterum aliquot scriptorum . . . .* 3 vols. Paris, 1723.

*Acta concilii Lumbariensis. In Bouquet, *Recueil*, XIV, 430-34.

*Acta sanctorum quotquot toto orbe coluntur vel a catholicis scriptoribus celebrantur . . . . New ed. by Joannes Carnandet. 65 vols. in 67. Paris, 1863-1931.

*Acta synodi Atrebatensi a Gerardo Cameracensi et Atrebatensi episcopo celebrata anno 1025. In Fredericq, *Corpus*, I, 1-5.

Actus beati Francisci et sociorum eius. Ed. by Paul Sabatier. (Collection d'études et de documents sur l'histoire religieuse et littéraire du moyen âge, IV.) Paris, 1902.

*Actus pontificum Cenomannis in urbe degentium. Ed. by G. Busson and A. Ledru. (Archives historiques du Maine, II.) Le Mans, 1901.

**Adémar of Chabannes. *Chronique.* Ed. by Jules Chavanon. (Collection de textes pour servir a l'étude et à l'enseignement de l'histoire, XX.) Paris, 1897.

**Alan of Lille. *De fide catholica contra haereticos sui temporis.* In Migne, *PL*, CCX, 305-430.

────── *Summa de arte praedicatoria.* In Migne, *PL*, CCX, 109-98.

Albe, Ed. "L'Hérésie albigeoise et l'Inquisition en Quercy," *Revue d'histoire de l'église de France*, I (1910), 271-93, 412-28.

Alberic of Trois-Fontaines. *Chronica Albrici monachi Trium Fontium a monachi novi monasterii Hoiensis interpolata.* Ed. by Paul Scheffer-Boichorst, in *MGH SS*, XXIII, 631-950.

Alphandéry, Paul. "Le Gnosticisme dans les sectes médiévales latines," *RHPR*, VII (1927), 394-411.

────── *Les Idées morales chez les hétérodoxes latins au début du XIIIe siècle*. (Bibliothèque de l'Ecole des hautes études, Sciences religieuses, XVI, fasc. 1.) Paris, 1903.

—— "Sur les Passagiens," *Revue des études juives*, LXXXII (1926), 353-61.

—— "De quelques faits de prophétisme dans les sectes latins antérieures au Joachimisme," *RHR*, LII (1905), 177-218.

—— "Remarques sur le type sectaire dans l'hérésiologie médiévale latine," in *Transactions of the Third International Congress for the History of Religions*, II, 354-57. Oxford, 1908.

—— "Traces de manichéisme dans le moyen âge latin (VIᵉ-XIIᵉ siècle)," *RHPR*, IX (1929), 451-67.

Alverny, Maria-Thérèse d'. "Un Fragment du procès des Amauriciens," *AHDLMA*, XXVI (1951), 325-36.

American Waldensian Aid Association. *An Annotated Reading List on the Waldenses: Selected Books and Articles in English*. New York, 1933.

Anagnine, Eugenio. *Dolcino e il movimento ereticale all'inizio del trecento*. Florence, 1964.

Andreas of Fleury. *Vita Gauzlini abbatis Floriacensis*. Ed. by P. Ewald, in *Neues Archiv der Gesellschaft für ältere deutsche Geschichtskunde*, III (1878), 351-83.

Anichkof, Eugeniĭ. "Les Survivances manichéennes en pays slave et en Occident," *Revue des études slaves*, VIII (1928), 203-26.

Annales Brunwilarensis. Ed. by Wilhelm Pertz, in *MGH SS*, XVI, 724-28.

Annales Magedeburgenses. Ed. by Wilhelm Pertz, in *MGH SS*, XVI, 107-96.

Annales de Margan. Ed. by H. R. Luard, in *Annales monastici*, I, 3-40.

Annales monasterii de Theokesberia. Ed. by H. R. Luard, in *Annales monastici*, I, 43-180.

Annales monastici. Ed. by H. R. Luard. (Rolls Series, XXXVI.) 5 vols. London, 1864-1869.

Annales Parchenses. Ed. by Wilhelm Pertz, in *MGH SS*, XVI, 598-608.

*Anselm of Alessandria. *Tractatus de haereticis*. Ed. by Dondaine, in "La Hiérarchie cathare, II," *AFP*, XX (1950), 308-24.

Anselm of Liège. *See* Heriger and Anselm.

The Ante-Nicene Fathers: Translations of the Writings of the Fathers down to A.D. 325. American ed. by A. C. Coxe. 8 vols. Buffalo, 1885-1886.

De antiquis legibus liber. Ed. by Thomas Stapleton. (Camden Society, XXXIV.) London, 1846.

Aquinas, Thomas. *See* Thomas Aquinas.

Ascension of Isaiah. *See* Vision of Isaiah.

Augustine, Saint. *Epistolae*. In Migne, *PL*, XXXIII, 61-1094.

—— *The De haeresibus of Saint Augustine*. Trans., with introduction and commentary, by Rev. Liguori C. Müller. (Catholic University of America, Patristic Studies, XC.) Washington, 1956.

—— *De utilitate credendi ad Honoratum*. In Migne, *PL*, XLII, 63-92.

Babut, E. C. *Priscillien et le Priscillienisme*. (Bibliothèque de l'Ecole des hautes études, Sciences historiques et philologiques, XLIX.) Paris, 1909.

Badham, Francis Pritchett, and F. C. Conybeare. "Fragments of an Ancient (?Egyptian) Gospel Used by the Cathars of Albi," *The Hibbert Journal*, XI (1913), 805-18.

Balme, François, P. Lelaidier, and A. I. Collomb. *Cartulaire ou histoire diplomatique de Saint Dominique, avec illustrations documentaires* .... 3 vols. Paris, 1893-1901.

Baluze, Stephen, ed. *Miscellanea novo ordine digesta et non paucis ineditis monumentis ... aucta*. New ed. by Joannes Dominicus Mansi. 4 vols. Lucca, 1761-1764.

Baron, Salo W. *A Social and Religious History of the Jews*. 2d ed. rev. enl. Vol. I– . New York, 1952– .

Bastard, Léon de. "Recherches sur l'insurrection communale de Vézelay au XIIᵉ siècle," *BEC*, 3d ser., II (1851), 339-65.

Bates, M. Searle. *Religious Liberty: An Inquiry*. New York, 1935.

Bäumker, Clemens. *Ein anonymer, wahrscheinlich dem Garnerius von Rochefort zugehöriger Traktat aus dem Anfang des XIII Jahrhunderts*. (Beiträge zur Geschichte des Philosophie des Mittelalters, XXIV, fasc. 5-6.) Münster, 1926.

—— "Handschriftliches zu den Werken des Alanus," in *Philosophisches Jahrbuch der Görres-Gesellschaft*, VI (1893), 163-75, 417-29; VII (1894), 169-85.

*Bazzocchi, Dino. *La Eresia catara: Saggio storico filosofico con in appendice* Disputationes nonnullae adversus haereticos. Essay and appendix published separately. Bologna, 1919, 1920.

Bédier, Joseph, and Paul Hazard. *Littérature française*. New ed. by Pierre Martino. 2 vols. Paris, 1948-1949.

Belperron, Pierre. *La Croisade contre les Albigeois et l'union du Languedoc à la France (1209-1249)*. Paris, 1942.

Berger, Samuel. "Les Bibles provençales et vaudoises," *Romania*, XVIII (1889), 353-422.

—— "Nouvelles Recherches sur les Bibles provençales et catalanes," *Romania*, XIX (1890), 505-61.

Bernard Gui. *Liber sententiarum inquisitionis Tholosanae ab anno Christi MCCCVII ad annum MCCCXXIII*. In Limborch, *Historia inquisitionis*.

*—— *Practica inquisitionis haereticae pravitatis*. Ed. by Célestin Douais. Paris, 1886. Part V ed. by Guillaume Mollat as *Manuel de l'inquisiteur*. (Les Classiques de l'histoire de France au moyen âge, VIII, IX.) 2 vols. Paris, 1926-1927.

*Bernard of Clairvaux, Saint. *Epistolae* 241, 242. In Migne, *PL*, CLXXXII, 434-37.

*—— *Sermones super Cantica canticorum*. Ed. by Jean Leclercq, C. H. Talbot, and H. M. Rochais. (Sancti Bernardi Opera, I-II.) 2 vols. Rome, 1957-1958.

—— *Saint Bernard's Sermons on the Canticle of Canticles*. Trans. by a priest [Ailbe J. Luddy] of Mt. Melleray. 2 vols. Dublin, *ca.* 1920.

*Bernard of Fontcaude. *Adversus Waldensium sectam liber.* In Migne, *PL*, CCIV, 793-840.

Bernard, Paul P. "Heresy in 14th Century Austria," *Medievalia et Humanistica*, X (1956), 50-63.

Berne-Lagarde, Pierre de. *Bibliographie du catharisme languedocien.* (Institut des études cathares, Collection de textes et documents, I.) Toulouse, 1957.

Bett, Henry. *Joachim of Flora.* London, 1931.

Betts, Reginald R. "Correnti religiose nazionali ed ereticali dalla fine del secolo XIV alla metà del XV," in *Relazione del X Congresso*, III, 485-513.

Beuzart, Paul. *Les Hérésies pendant le moyen âge et la réforme jusqu'à la mort de Philippe II, 1598, dans la région de Douai, d'Arras, et au pays de l'Alleu.* Paris and LePuy, 1912.

Blackman, Edwin C. *Marcion and His Influence.* London, 1948.

Bloomfield, Morton W. "Joachim of Flora: A Critical Survey of His Canon, Teachings, Sources, Biography and Influence," *Traditio*, XIII (1957), 259-311.

―――― and Marjorie E. Reeves. "The Penetration of Joachism into Northern Europe," *Speculum*, XXIX (1954), 772-93.

Böhmer, Johann Friedrich. *Acta imperii selecta: Urkunden deutscher Könige und Kaiser, mit einem Anhange von Reichssachen.* Innsbruck, 1870.

*Bonacursus. *Manifestatio haeresis catharorum quam fecit Bonacursus.* In Migne, *PL*, CCIV, 775-92.

Bonenfant, Paul. "Un Clerc cathare en Lotharingie au milieu du XIIe siècle," *MA*, LXIX (1963), 271-80.

Borst, Arno. *Die Katharer.* (Schriften der Monumenta Germaniae historica, XII.) Stuttgart, 1953.

*Bouquet, Martin, *et al.*, eds. *Recueil des historiens des Gaules et de la France.* 24 vols. Paris, 1739-1904.

Bourquelot, F. "Observations sur l'établissement de la commune de Vézelay," *BEC*, III (1852), 447-63.

Boussard, J. "Henri II Plantagenêt et les origines de l'armée de métier," *BEC*, CVI (1945-1946), 189-224.

Breillat, Pierre. "Le Graal et les Albigeois," *Revue de Tarn*, X (1944), 458-67; XI (1945), 99-109, 161-71.

Brevis summula contra herrores notatos hereticorum. Ed. by C. Douais, in *La Somme des autorités*, pp. 114-33. Ed. by C. Molinier, in "Une Texte de Muratori," *Annales du Midi*, XXII (1910), 212-16.

Broeckx, Edmund. *Le Catharisme: Etude sur les doctrines, la vie religieuse et morale, l'activité littéraire et les vicissitudes de la secte cathare avant la croisade.* (Universitatis Catholicae Lovaniensis Dissertationes, 2d ser., VIII.) Hoogstraten, 1916.

Brooke, Christopher N. L. "The Church of the Middle Ages, 1000-1500," in *The Layman in Christian History*, pp. 111-34.

Brown, Sydney McGillvary. "Movimenti politico-religiosi a Milano ai tempi della Pataria," *Archivio storico Lombardo*, 6th ser., LVIII (1931), 227-78.

Bru, Charles P. "Elements pour une interprétation sociologique du Catharisme occitan," in Nelli, *Spiritualité de l'hérésie*, pp. 23-59.

Brunel, Clovis. "Fragment d'un abrégé de théologie en ancien Provençal," *BEC*, CXII (1954), 1-23.

*Burchard of Ursberg. *Chronicon.* Ed. by Oswald Holder-Egger and Bernard von Simson, in *Die Chronik des Propstes Burchard von Ursberg.* (Scriptores rerum Germanicarum in usum scholarum.) Hanover and Leipzig, 1916.

Burr, George Lincoln. "The Literature of Witchcraft," in *Papers of the American Historical Association*, IV (1889-1890), 237-66.

Butler, Alban. *The Lives of the Saints.* Ed. by Herbert Thurston and Donald Attwater. Rev. ed. 4 vols. New York, 1956.

*Caesarius of Heisterbach. *Dialogus miraculorum.* Ed. by Joseph Strange. 2 vols. Cologne, 1851. Trans. by Henry von Essen Scott and C. C. Swinton Bland as *The Dialogue on Miracles.* 2 vols. London, 1929.

Callaey, Frédégand. "Lambert li Beges et les Béguines," *RHE*, XXIII (1927), 254-59.

—— "Olieu ou Olivi (Pierre de Jean)," *DTC*, XI, 982-91.

Cantor, Norman. *Medieval History: The Life and Death of a Civilization.* New York and London, c1963.

Capelle, Germaine C. *Autour du décret de 1210, III: Amaury da Bène— Etude sur son panthéisme formel.* (Bibliothèque Thomiste, XVI.) Paris, 1932.

Caro Baroja, Julio. *The World of the Witches.* Trans. by O. N. V. Glendinning. Chicago and London, c1964.

Catholic Encyclopedia: An International Work of Reference on the Constitution, Doctrine, Discipline, and History of the Catholic Church. Ed. by Charles G. Hebermann, *et al.* 16 vols. New York, c1907-1914.

Cauchie, Alfred H. J. *La Querelle des investitures dans les diocèses de Liège et de Cambrai, I: Les réformes grégoriennes et les agitations réactionnaires (1075-1092).* (Université catholique, Recueil des travaux, II.) Louvain, 1891.

Cauzons, Thomas de. *Histoire de l'Inquisition en France.* 2 vols. Paris, 1909-1912.

Charles, R. H. See *The Vision of Isaiah.*

Chénon, Emile. "L'Hérésie à La Charité-sur-Loire et les débuts de l'Inquisition monastique dans la France du nord au XIIIe siècle," *Nouvelle revue historique de droit français et étranger*, XLI (1917), 299-345.

Chérest, Aimé. *Vézelay: Etude historique.* 3 vols. Auxerre, 1868.

Chevalier, Jules. *Mémoire historique sur les hérésies en Dauphiné avant le XVIe siècle, accompagné de documents inédits sur les sorciers et les vaudois.* Valence, 1890.

Chronicon Britannicum. In Bouquet, *Recueil,* XII, 557-58.

*Chronicon S. Andreae castri-Cameracesii. Ed. by L. C. Bethmann, in *MGH SS,* VII, 526-50.

*Chronicon universale anonymi Laudunensis. Ed. by Georg Waitz, in *MGH SS,* XXVI, 442-57.

Clasen, Claus-Peter. "Medieval Heresies in the Reformation," *Church History,* XXXII (1963), 392-414.

**Clédat, Léon. *Le Nouveau Testament traduit au XIIIe siècle en langue provençale, suivi d'un rituel cathare.* (Université de Lyon, Bibliothèque de la Faculté des lettres, IV.) Paris, 1887.

Cohn, Norman. *The Pursuit of the Millennium.* Fairlawn, N. J., 1957.

Comba, Emilio. *Storia dei Valdesi.* 4th ed. Torre Pellice, 1950. Trans. by Teofilio E. Comba from the 2d ed. as *History of the Waldenses of Italy from Their Origin to the Reformation.* London, 1889.

*Compilatio auctoritatum de sacramentis ecclesiae. Ed. by Douais, in *La Somme des autorités,* pp. 56-66. Also in Leipzig, Universitäts Bibliothek, MS 894, fols. 77v-79r.

Congar, Yves M. J. "*Arriana haeresis* comme désignation du néo-manichéisme au XIIe siècle," *RSPT,* XLIII (1959), 449-61.

—— "Henri de Marcy, abbé de Clairvaux, cardinal-évêque d'Albano et légat pontifical," *Studia Anselmiana,* XLIII; *Analecta monastica,* V (1958), 1-90.

Conybeare, Fred[erick] C. "A Hitherto Unpublished Treatise against the Italian Manichaeans," *American Journal of Theology,* III (1899), 704-28.

—— trans. *The Key of Truth: A Manual of the Paulician Church of Armenia.* Oxford, 1898.

Coulton, George Gordon. *The Death Penalty for Heresy from 1184 to 1921.* (Medieval Studies, XVIII.) London, 1924.

—— *The Inquisition.* New York, 1929.

—— *Inquisition and Liberty.* London, Toronto, and New York, 1938; reprint, Gloucester, Mass., 1960.

—— *From St. Francis to Dante: Translations from the Chronicle of the Franciscan Salimbene (1221-1288) with Notes and Illustrations from Other Medieval Sources.* 2d ed. London, 1927.

David of Augsburg. *De inquisitione haereticorum.* In Martène and Durand, *Thesaurus novus anecdotorum,* V, 1777-94. Another version ed. by Wilhelm Preger in "Der Traktat des David von Augsburg über die Waldesier," *Abhandlungen der historischen Classe der königlich bayerischen Akademie der Wissenschaften,* XIII (1878), 204-35.

David, Pierre. "Un Credo cathare?" *RHE,* XXXV (1939), 756-61.

Davis, Georgene W. *The Inquisition at Albi, 1299-1300: Text of Register and Analysis.* (Studies in History, Economics, and Public Law, DXXXVIII.) New York, 1948.

Davison, Ellen Scott. *Forerunners of St. Francis, and Other Studies.* Ed. by Gertrude R. B. Richards. New York, 1927.

Delaruelle, Etienne. "Le Catharisme en Languedoc vers 1200: Une enquête," *Annales du Midi*, LXXII (1960), 149-67.

—— "La pietà popolare nel secolo XI," in *Relazione del X Congresso*, III, 309-25.

Delehaye, Hippolyte. "Pierre de Pavie: Légat du pape Alexandre III en France," *RQH*, XLIX (1891), 5-61.

Delisle, Léopold. "Notice sur les manuscrits de Bernard Gui," *Notices et extraits des manuscrits de la Bibliothèque nationale publiés par l'Institut national de France*, Vol. XXVII, part 2 (1879), pp. 169-455.

*Denifle, Heinrich, and Emile Chatelain, eds. *Chartularium universitatis Parisiensis*. 4 vols. Paris, 1889-1897.

Denzinger, Heinrich. *Enchiridion symbolorum: Definitionum et declarationum de rebus fidei et morum*. 31st ed. Freiburg im Breisgau, 1957. Trans. by Roy J. Deferrari, from the 30th ed., as *The Sources of Catholic Dogma*. St. Louis and London, 1954.

Devic, Claude, and Joseph Vaissete. *Histoire générale de Languedoc*. Ed. by Auguste Molinier *et al.* 16 vols. Toulouse, 1872-1904.

Dickson, Marcel, and Christine Dickson. "Le Cardinal Robert de Courçon: Sa vie," *AHDLMA*, IX (1934), 53-142.

The Dictionary of National Biography. Ed. by Leslie Stephen and Sydney Lee. 22 vols. Oxford, 1885-1901; reprints, 1921-1922, 1937-1938.

Dictionnaire de théologie catholique contenant l'exposé des doctrines de la théologie catholique, leurs preuves et leur histoire. Ed. by A. Vacant and E. Mangenot. Vols. I– . Paris, 1903– .

Dieckhoff, August Wilhelm. *Die Waldenser im Mittelalter: Zwei historische Untersuchungen*. Göttingen, 1851.

Dieudonné, Adolphe. "Hildebert de Lavardin, évêque du Mans, archevêque de Tours (1056-1133): Sa vie, ses lettres," *Revue historique et archéologique du Maine*, XLI (1896), 51-85, 179-224, 379-421; XLII (1897), 1-44, 165-205, 236-83.

Dionysius the Areopagite. *The Works of Dionysius the Areopagite*. Trans. by Rev. John Parker. 2 vols. London and Oxford, 1887, 1889.

Döllinger, Johann J. I. von. *Beiträge zur Sektengeschichte des Mittelalters*. 2 vols. Munich, 1890. Reprint, New York, 1960.

Dondaine, Antoine. "Les Actes du concile albigeois de Saint-Félix-de-Caraman," in *Miscellanea Giovanni Mercati*, Vol. V. (Studi e testi, CXXV.) Vatican City, 1946.

*—— "Durand de Huesca et la polémique anti-cathare," *AFP*, XXIX (1959), 228-76.

*—— "La Hiérarchie cathare en Italie, I: Le 'De heresi catharorum in Lombardia'; II: Le 'Tractatus de hereticis' d'Anselme d'Alexandrie, O.P.; III: Catalogue de la hiérarchie cathare d'Italie," *AFP*, XIX (1949), 280-312; XX (1950), 234-324.

—— "Le Manuel de l'inquisiteur (1230-1330)," AFP, XVII (1947), 85-194.

—— "Nouvelles Sources de l'histoire doctrinale du néo-manichéisme au moyen âge," *RSPT*, XXVIII (1939), 465-88.

—— "L'Origine de l'hérésie médiévale: A propos d'un livre récent," *RSCI*, VI (1952), 47-78.

*—— "Aux Origines du Valdéisme: Une profession de foi de Valdès," *AFP*, XVI (1946), 191-235.

—— "Saint Pierre Martyr: Etudes," *AFP*, XXIII (1953), 66-162.

*—— *Un Traité néo-manichéen du XIIIᵉ siècle: Le* Liber *de duobus principiis, suivi d'un fragment de rituel cathare.* Rome, 1939.

Dossat, Yves. "Cathares et Vaudois à la veille de la croisade albigeoise," *RHLL*, II (1945), 390-97; III (1946), 70-83.

—— "Le Clergé méridional à la veille de la croisade albigeoise," *RHLL*, I (1944), 263-78.

—— "Le Comté de Toulouse et la féodalité languedocienne à la veille de la croisade albigeoise," *Revue de Tarn*, IX (1943), 75-90.

—— *Les Crises de l'Inquisition toulousaine au XIIIᵉ siècle (1233-1273).* Bourdeaux, 1959.

—— "L'Evolution des rituels cathares," *Revue de synthèse*, XXIII (1948), 27-30.

—— "Remarques sur un prétendu évêque cathare du Val d'Aran en 1167," *Bulletin philologique et historique du Comité des travaux historiques et scientifiques*, Années 1955-1956, pp. 339-47.

—— "La Société méridionale à la veille de la croisade albigeoise," *RHLL*, I (1944), 66-87.

Douais, Célestin. *Documents pour servir à l'histoire de l'Inquisition dans le Languedoc.* 2 vols. (Société de l'histoire de France, Publications, CCXCIX, CCC.) Paris, 1900.

—— "Les Hérétiques du comté de Toulouse dans la première moitié du XIIIᵉ siècle, d'après l'enquête de 1245," *Bulletin théologique, scientifique et littéraire de l'Institut catholique de Toulouse*, new ser., III (1892), 160-73, 206-9.

—— "Les Hérétiques du Midi au XIIIᵉ siècle: Cinq pièces inédits," *Annales du Midi*, III (1891), 367-80.

*—— *La Somme des autorités à l'usage des prédicateurs méridionaux au XIIIᵉ siècle.* Paris, 1896.

Douie, Decima L. *The Nature and Effect of the Heresy of the Fraticelli.* (Publications of the University of Manchester, CCXX; Historical Series, LXI.) Manchester, 1932.

Dubarle, G. M. "Les Renards de Samson," *Revue du moyen âge latin*, VII (1951), 174-76.

Dujčev, Ivan. "I Bogomili nei paesi slavi e la loro storia," in Accademia nazionale dei Lincei, *Problemi attuali di scienza e di cultura*, Quaderno LXII (1964): *L'Oriente cristiano nella storia della civiltà*, pp. 619-41.

*Durand of Huesca. *Liber contra manicheos.* In Thouzellier, *Un Traité cathare*, pp. 87-113.

Duvernoy, Jean. *Le Registre de l'Inquisition de Jacques Fournier, évêque de Pamiers.* Vols. I-II. Toulouse, 1965.

—— "Un Traité cathare du début du XIIIᵉ siècle," *Cahiers d'études cathares.* 2d ser., XIII (1962), 22-54.

*Eberwin of Steinfeld. *Epistola ad S. Bernardum* (Ep. 472). In Migne, *PL*, CLXXXII, 676-80.

Eckbert of Schönau. *Sermones tredecim contra haereticos.* In Migne, *PL*, CXCV, 11-102.

Ehrle, Franz. "Petrus Johannis Olivi: Sein Leben und seine Schriften," *ALKG*, III (1887), 409-552.

Encyclopaedia of Religion and Ethics. Ed. by James Hastings *et al.* 12 vols. Edinburgh and New York, 1908-1927; reprint, 1955.

English Historical Documents, Vol. II (1042-1189). Ed. by D. C. Douglas and G. W. Greenaway. New York and Oxford, 1953.

Epistola ecclesiae Leodiensis ad Lucum papam II. In Martène and Durand, *Veterum scriptorum*, I, 776-78.

Ermengaud of Béziers. *Contra haereticos.* In Migne, *PL*, CCIV, 1235-72; also CLXXVIII, 1823-46.

Esnault, Renato. "Tracce ereticali nel medio evo francese," *Religio*, XIV (1938), 18-53.

Esposito, Mario. "Sur quelques écrits concernant les hérésies et les hérétiques au XIIᵉ et XIIIᵉ siècles," *RHE*, XXXVI (1940), 143-62.

Evans, Austin P. "The Albigensian Crusade," in Setton, Wolff, and Hazard, *A History of the Crusades*, II, 277-324. Philadelphia, 1962.

—— "Hunting Subversion in the Middle Ages," *Speculum*, XXXIII (1958), 1-22.

—— "Social Aspects of Medieval Heresy," in *Persecution and Liberty*, pp. 93-116.

Eymeric, Nicholas. *Directorium inquisitorum.* Ed. by Francis Pegna. Venice, 1609.

Farrar, Clarissa P., and Austin P. Evans. *Bibliography of English Translations from Medieval Sources.* (Records of Civilization, XXXIX.) New York, 1946.

Fedele, Pietro. *Fonti per la storia di Arnaldo da Brescia.* (Testi medievali per uso delle scuole universitarie, I.) Rome, 1938.

Fliche, Augustin, Victor Martin, *et al. Histoire de l'Eglise depuis les origines jusqu'à nos jours. Vol. IX: Du premier concile de Latran à l'avènement d'Innocent III.* Paris, 1944; new ed., 1953. *Vol. X: La Chrétienté romaine.* Paris, 1950.

Foreville, Raymonde. "Les Grands Courants hérétiques et les premières mesures générales de répression," in Fliche and Martin, *Histoire de l'Eglise*, Vol. IX, chap. 3.

Förg, Ludwig. *Die Ketzerverfolgung in Deutschland unter Gregor IX: Ihre Herkunft, ihre Bedeutung und ihre rechtlichen Grundlagen.* (Historische Studien, CCXVIII.) Berlin, 1932.

Fortescue, Adrian. "Canon of the Mass," *Catholic Encyclopedia*, III, 255-67.

—— *The Mass: A Study of the Roman Liturgy.* New York, 1922.

*Fredericq, Paul. *Corpus documentorum inquisitionis haereticae pravitatis Neerlandicae.* 5 vols. Ghent, 1889-1906.

Frend, W. H. C. *The Donatist Church: A Movement of Protest in Roman North Africa.* Oxford, 1952.

Friedberg, Emil A., ed. *Corpus iuris canonici.* 2 vols. Leipzig, 1879-1881; reprint, 1922.

Frugoni, Arsenio. *Arnaldo da Brescia nelle fonti del secolo XII.* (Istituto storico Italiano per il medio evo, Studi storici, VIII-IX.) Rome, 1954.

—— "Filii Arnaldi (per l'interpretazione di un passo di Ottone Morena)," *BISIAM*, LXX (1959), 521-24.

Fulgentius. *De fide ad Petrum, sive de regula verae fidei liber unus.* In Migne, *PL*, LXV, 671-706.

Fumi, Luigi. "I Paterini in Orvieto," *Archivio storico Italiano*, 3d ser., XXII (1875), 52-81.

Garsoian, Nina G. *The Paulician Heresy: A Study of the Origin and Development of Paulicianism in Armenia and the Eastern Provinces of the Byzantine Empire.* The Hague and Paris, 1967.

*Geoffrey of Auxerre. *Epistola ad Archenfredum.* In Migne, *PL*, CLXXXV, 410-16.

—— *Sancti Bernardi . . . vita et res gestae . . . Liber tertius.* In Migne, *PL*, CLXXXV, 301-22. Trans. by Geoffrey Webb and Adrian Walker as *The* Vita prima Bernardi. London, 1960.

*George. *Disputatio inter catholicum et paterinum hereticum.* In Martène and Durand, *Thesaurus novus anecdotorum*, V, 1705-54.

Gerard of Fracheto. *Vitae fratrum ordinis praedicatorum necnon chronica ordinis anno MCCIII usque ad MCCLIV.* Ed. by B. M. Reichert. (Monumenta ordinis fratrum praedicatorum historica, I.) Rome, 1897.

Géraud, H. "Les Routiers au XIIe siècle," *BEC*, III (1841-1842), 125-47.

Gerbert of Aurillac (Pope Sylvester II). *Lettres de Gerbert (983-997).* Ed. by Julien Havet. (Collection de textes pour servir à l'étude et à l'enseignement de l'histoire, VI.) Paris, 1889. Trans. by Harriet Pratt Lattin as *The Letters of Gerbert, with His Papal Privileges as Sylvester II.* (Records of Civilization, LX.) New York, 1961.

Gere, Robert H. *The Troubadours, Heresy, and the Albigensian Crusade.* Ph.D. dissertation, Columbia University, 1956. Ann Arbor, Mich., University Microfilms (Publ. No. 15628, Microfilm AC-1), 1956.

Gervase of Canterbury. *Chronica.* Ed. by William Stubbs, in *The Historical Works of Gervase of Canterbury*, Vol. I. (Rolls Series, LXXIII.) London, 1880.

Gesta regis Henrici secundi Benedicti abbatis. Ed. by William Stubbs, in *The Chronicle of the Reigns of Henry II and Richard I, A. D. 1169-1192, Known Commonly under the Name of Benedict of Peterborough.* (Rolls Series, XLIX.) 2 vols. London, 1867.

Gesta Treverorum: Additamentum et continuatio prima; Continuatio quarta. Ed. by Georg Waitz, in *MGH SS*, VIII, 175-200; XXIV, 400-2.

Giesebrecht, Wilhelm von. "Uber Arnold von Brescia," *Sitzungsberichte der königlichen bayerischen Akademie der Wissenschaften zu München: Philosophisch-philologische und historische Klasse,* III (1873), 122-54.

Gleber, Helmut. *Papst Eugen III (1145-1153).* Arstadt, 1936.

Glorieux, Palémon. *Répertoire des maîtres en théologie de Paris au XIIIe siècle.* (Etudes de philosophie médiévale, XVII-XVIII.) 2 vols. Paris, 1933-1934.

Gonnet, Giovanni. "Un decennio di studi sull'eterodossia medioevale," *Protestantesimo,* XVII (1962), 203-39.

—— *Enchiridion fontium Valdensium. (Recueil critique des sources concernant les Vaudois au moyen âge: Du IIIe Concile de Latran au Synode de Chanforan [1179-1532].)* Vol. I. Torre Pellice, 1958.

—— "Il movimento valdese in Europa secondo le più recenti ricerche (sec. XII-XVI)," *Bollettino della Società di studi Valdesi,* C (1956), 21-30.

—— *Il Valdismo medioevale: Prolegomeni.* Torre Pellice, 1942.

—— "Waldensia," *RHPR,* XXXIII (1953), 202-54.

Gorce, M. M. "Moneta de Crémone, ou Simoneta," *DTC,* Vol. X, part 2, pp. 2211-15.

Grabmann, Martin. "Der Franziskanerbischof Benedictus de Alignano (†1268) und seine Summa zum Caput Firmiter des vierten Lateran-konzils," in *Kirchengeschichtliche Studien P. Michael Bihl, O.F.M., als Ehrengabe dargeboten.* Kolmar, 1944.

Graf, Arturo. *Miti, leggende e superstizioni del medio evo.* 2 vols. Turin, 1892-1893.

—— *The Story of the Devil.* Trans. by Edward Noble Stone. New York, 1931.

Grant, Robert M. *Gnosticism and Early Christianity.* (Lectures on the History of Religions, new ser., V.) New York, 1960.

—— *Gnosticism: A Source Book of Heretical Writings from the Early Christian Period.* New York, 1961.

Gratian. *Decretum.* In Friedberg, *Corpus iuris canonici,* Vol. I.

Grayzel, Solomon. *The Church and the Jews in the Thirteenth Century: A Study of Their Relations during the Years 1198-1254, Based on the Papal Letters and the Conciliar Decrees of the Period.* Philadelphia, 1933.

—— "The Confession of a Medieval Jewish Convert," *Historia Judaica,* XVII (1955), 89-120.

Greenaway, George W. *Arnold of Brescia.* Cambridge, 1931.

Grégoire, Henri. "Cathares d'Asie Mineur, d'Italie et de France," in *Memorial Louis Petit.* (Archives de l'orient chrétien, I.) Bucharest, 1948.

Gregory VII, Pope. *The Correspondence of Pope Gregory VII: Selected Letters from the Registrum.* Trans. by Ephraim Emerton. (Records of Civilization, XIV.) New York, 1932.

Gregory IX, Pope. *Les Registres de Grégoire IX: Recueil de bulles de ce pape.* Ed. by Lucien Auvray. (Bibliothèque de l'Ecole française d'Athènes et de Rome, 2d ser., IX.) 4 vols. Paris, 1896-1955.

Gregory, Bishop of Tours. *History of the Franks: Selections.* Trans. by Ernest Brehaut. (Records of Civilization, II.) New York, 1916.

Gretser, Jacob. *Opera omnia* .... 17 vols. Ratisbon, 1734-1741.

Grundmann, Herbert. "Eresie e nuovi ordini religiosi nel secolo XII," in *Relazione del X Congresso,* III, 357-402.

—— *Ketzergeschichte des Mittelalters.* Vol. II, Lieferung G (Part 1), of *Die Kirche in ihrer Geschichte: Ein Handbuch,* ed. by Kurt Dietrich Schmidt and Ernest Wolf. Göttingen, 1963.

—— *Neue Forschungen über Joachim von Fiore.* (Munstersche Forschungen, I.) Marburg, 1950.

—— *Religiöse Bewegungen im Mittelalter: Untersuchungen über die geschichtlichen Zusammenhänge zwischen der Ketzerei, den Bettelorden und der religiösen Frauenbewegungen im 12. und 13. Jahrhundert und über die geschichtlichen Grundlagen der deutschen Mystik.* (Historische Studien, 267.) Berlin, 1935; reprint with additions, 1961.

—— "Der Typus des Ketzers in mittelalterlicher Anschauung," in *Kultur- und Universalgeschichte: Festschrift für Walter Goetz,* pp. 91-107. Leipzig, 1927.

Gui, Bernard. *See* Bernard Gui.

*Guibert de Nogent: Histoire de sa vie (1053-1124). Ed. by Georges Bourgin. (Collection de textes pour servir à l'étude et à l'enseignement de l'histoire, XL.) Paris, 1907. Trans. by C. C. Swinton Bland as *The Autobiography of Guibert, abbot of Nogent-sous-Coucy.* London and New York, 1926.

Guillaume. *See* William.

Guillaume, Paul. "Doctrine du Vaudois au XIVᵉ siècle, d'après le manuscrit 15179 du fonds latin de la Bibliothèque nationale," *Bulletin de la Société d'études des Hautes Alpes,* VII (1888), 220-22.

Guiraud, Jean. *Cartulaire de Notre Dame de Prouille, précédé d'une étude sur l'albigéisme languedocien au XIIᵉ et XIIIᵉ siècles.* 2 vols. Paris, 1907.

—— "Le Consolamentum cathare," *RQH,* new ser., XXXI (1904), 74-112.

—— *Histoire de l'Inquisition au moyen âge.* 2 vols. Paris, 1935-1938.

—— *L'Inquisition médiévale.* Paris, 1928. Trans. by E. C. Messenger as *The Mediaeval Inquisition.* London, 1929.

*De haeresi catharorum in Lombardia. Ed. by Antoine Dondaine, in "La Hiérarchie cathare, I," *AFP,* XIX (1949), 306-12.

Haskins, Charles H. *Studies in Mediaeval Culture.* Oxford, 1929.

Hauréau, M. B. "Mémoire sur la vie et quelques œuvres d'Alain de Lille," *Mémoires de l'Académie des inscriptions et belles-lettres de l'Institut national de France,* Vol. XXXII, part 1 (1886), pp. 1-27.

Havet, Julien. "L'hérésie et le bras séculier au moyen âge jusqu'au treizième siècle," *BEC,* XLI (1880), 488-517, 570-607.

Heisig, Karl. "Ein gnostische Sekte im abendlandischen Mittelalter," *Zeitschrift für Religions- und Geistesgeschichte,* XVI (1964), 271-74.

*Heribert, a monk. *Epistola de haereticis Petragoricis.* In Migne, *PL*, CLXXXI, 1721-22.

*Heriger and Anselm of Liège. *Gesta episcoporum Leodiensium.* Ed. by Rudolph Koepke, in *MGH SS*, VII, 161-234.

Histoire littéraire de la France. 38 vols. Paris, 1733-1949.

*Hugh of Poitiers. *Historia Vizeliacensis monasterii.* In Bouquet, *Recueil*, XII, 317-44.

Hugon, Augusto Armand, and Giovanni Gonnet. *Bibliografia valdese.* (Società di studi valdesi.) Torre Pellice, 1953.

*Ilarino da Milano. *L'Eresia di Ugo Speroni nella confutazione del Maestro Vacario: Testo inedito del secolo XII con studio storico e dottrinale.* (Studi e Testi, CXV.) Vatican City, 1945.

—— "Le eresie medioevali (sec. XI-XV)," in *Grande antologia filosofica*, IV, 1599-1689. Milan, 1954.

—— "Le eresie popolari del secolo XI nell'Europa occidentale," in *Studi Gregoriani per la storia di Gregorio VII e della riforma Gregoriana*, ed. by G. B. Borino, II, 43-89. Rome, 1947.

—— "Fr. Gregorio, O.P., vescovo di Fano, e la 'Disputatio inter catholicum et paterinum hereticum,' " *Aevum*, XIV (1940), 85-140.

*—— "Il 'Liber supra Stella' del piacentino Salvo Burci contro i Catari e altre correnti ereticali," *Aevum*, XVI (1942), 272-319; XVII (1943), 90-146; XIX (1945), 281-341.

—— "La 'Manifestatio heresis catarorum quam fecit Bonacursus' secondo il cod. Ottob. lat. 136 della Biblioteca Vaticana," *Aevum*, XII (1938), 281-333.

—— "La 'Summa contra haereticos' di Giacomo Capelli, O.F.M., e un suo 'Quaresimale' inedito (secolo XIII)," *Collectanea franciscana*, X (1940), 66-82.

Imbs, Paul. "A la Recherche d'une littérature cathare," *Revue de moyen âge latin*, V (1949), 289-302.

*Innocent III, Pope. *Regestorum sive epistolarum libri XV.* In Migne, *PL*, Vols. CCXIV-CCXVI.

The Interpreter's Bible: The Holy Scriptures in the King James and Revised Standard Versions with General Articles and Introduction, Exegesis, Exposition for Each Book of the Bible. 12 vols. New York, 1951-1957.

Interrogatio Johannis. Ed. by Richard Reitzenstein, in *Die Vorgeschichte der christlichen Taufe*, pp. 293-311.

*Jaffé, Phillip, ed. *Monumenta Bambergensia.* (Bibliotheca rerum Germanicarum, V.) Berlin, 1869.

*James Capelli (Jacobus de Capellis). *Summa contra hereticos.* Ed. by Dino Bazzocchi, in *La Eresia catara*, appendix. Also in Cesena, Biblioteca Malatestiana, MS Pluteus I, viii.

James of Voraggio (Jacobus de Voragine), Saint. *The Golden Legend of Jacobus de Voragine.* Trans. by Granger Ryan and Helmut Ripperger. 2 vols. London and New York, 1941.

Janssen, H. Q. "Tanchelijn," *Annales de l'Académie royale d'archéologie de Belgique*, 2d ser., III (1867), 374-450.

The Jewish Encyclopedia: A Descriptive Record of the History, Literature, and Customs of the Jewish People from the Earliest Times . . . . Ed. by Cyrus Adler, Isidore Singer, *et al.* 12 vols. New York, 1961-; reprint, 1964.

*John of Salisbury. *John of Salisbury's Memoirs of the Papal Court* (Historia pontificalis). Trans. by Marjorie Chibnall. London, 1956.

Jonas, Hans. *The Gnostic Religion: The Message of the Alien God and the Beginnings of Christianity*. Boston, c1958.

Kaltner, Balthasar. *Konrad von Marburg und die Inquisition in Deutschland*. Prague, 1882.

*Käppeli, Thomas. "Une Somme contre les hérétiques de S. Pierre Martyr?" *AFP*, XVII (1947), 295-355.

—— and A. Zaninović, "Traités anti-vaudois dans le manuscrit 30 de la bibliothèque des Dominicains de Dubrovnik (Raguse)," *AFP*, XXIV (1954), 297-305.

The Key of Truth: A Manual of the Paulician Church of Armenia. Ed. and trans. by Fred. C. Conybeare. Oxford, 1898.

Knowles, David. "Peter the Venerable," *Bulletin of the John Rowlands Library*, XXXIX (1956), 132-45.

Koch, Gottfried. *Frauenfrage und Ketzertum im Mittelalter: Die Frauenbewegung im Rahmen des Katharismus und des Waldensertums und ihre sozialen Wurzeln (XII-XIV Jahrhundert)*. (Forschungen zur mittelalterlichen Geschichte, IX.) Berlin, 1962.

—— "Neue Quellen und Forschungen über die Anfänge der Waldenser," *Forschungen und Fortschritten*, XXXII (1958), 141-49.

Kramp, Joseph. "Chronologisches zu Peters des Ehrwürdigen epistola adversus Petrobrusianos," in *Miscellanea Francesco Ehrle*, I, 71-79. (Studi e Testi, XXXVII.) Rome, 1924.

Kulcsár, Zsuzsánna. *Eretnekmozgalmak a XI-XIV században*. (A Budapesti Egyetemi Könyvtár Kiadványai, XXII.) Budapest, 1964.

Kurth, O. *Landulf der Aeltere von Mailand*. Halle, 1885.

Lacger, Louis de. "L'Albigeois pendant la crise de l'albigéisme: L'episcopat de Guilhem Peire (1185-1227)," *RHE*, XXIX (1933), 272-315, 586-633, 849-904.

Lacombe, George. "Prévostin de Crémone," *DTC*, XIII, 162-69.

—— *La Vie et les œuvres de Prévostin*. (Bibliothèque Thomiste, XI.) Kain, 1927.

Lagarde, Georges de. *La Naissance de l'esprit laïque au déclin du moyen rum inquisitionis Tholosanae ab anno Christi MCCVII ad annum âge*. Rev. ed. 5 vols. Louvain and Paris, 1956-1963.

*Landulf the Elder. *Landulphi senioris Mediolanensis historiae libri quatuor*. Ed. by Alessandro Cutolo, in L. A. Muratori, *Rerum italicarum scriptores*, new ed., Vol. IV, part 2, pp. 5-128. Trans. by A. Visconti as

La Cronica milanese di Landolfo seniore, sec. XI. Milan, 1928.

The Layman in Christian History: A Project of the Department on the Laity of the World Council of Churches. Ed. by Stephen Charles Neill and Hans-Reudi Weber. Philadelphia, c1963.

Lea, Henry Charles. *A History of the Inquisition of the Middle Ages.* 3 vols. New York and London, 1888; reprint, 1955. Abridged ed. by Margaret Nicolson; New York, 1961.

——— *Materials toward a History of Witchcraft.* Ed. by Arthur C. Howland. 3 vols. New York, 1957.

Leclercq, Jean. "Les Ecrits de Geoffroy d'Auxerre," *Revue bénédictine,* LXII (1952), 274-91.

——— *Pierre le Vénérable.* Paris, 1946.

——— "Le Témoignage de Geoffroy d'Auxerre sur la vie Cistercienne," *Studia Anselmiana,* XXXI; *Analecta monastica,* II (1953), 174-201.

*Lecoy de la Marche, Albert, ed. *Anecdotes historiques, légendes et apologues, tirées du recueil inédit d'Etienne de Bourbon, dominicain du XIIIe siècle.* (Société de l'histoire de France, Publications, CLXXXV.) Paris, 1877.

Leff, Gordon. *Heresy in the Later Middle Ages: The Relation of Heterodoxy to Dissent c. 1250-c. 1450.* 2 vols. Manchester and New York, 1967.

Liber diurnus Romanorum pontificum. Ed. by E. Rozière. Paris, 1869.

Liber de duobus principiis. Ed. by Antoine Dondaine, in *Un Traité néomanichéen,* pp. 81-147.

The Life of St. Alexius. Trans. in *The Oldest Monuments of the French Language,* pp. 28-56. Oxford, 1912.

Limborch, Philip van. *Historia inquisitionis cui subiungitur Liber sententiarum inquisitionis Tholosanae ab anno Christi MCCCVII ad annum MCCCXXIII.* Amsterdam, 1692.

Loeb, Isidore. "La Controverse religieuse entre les Chrétiens et les Juifs au moyen âge en France et en Espagne," *RHR,* XVII (1888), 311-37; XVIII (1888), 133-56.

Luchaire, Achille. *Innocent III.* 6 vols. Paris, 1905-1908.

Mabillon, Jean. *Life and Works of Saint Bernard, Abbot of Clairvaux.* Trans. by Samuel J. Eales. 4 vols. London, 1889-1896.

——— ed. *Vetera analecta sive collectio veterum aliquot operum et opusculorum omnis generis.* Paris, 1723.

McDonnell, Ernest W. *The Beguines and Beghards in Medieval Culture, with Special Emphasis on the Belgian Scene.* New Brunswick, 1954.

——— "The *vita apostolica*: Diversity or Dissent?" *Church History,* XXIV (1955), 15-31.

McNeill, John T., and Helena M. Gamer. *Medieval Handbooks of Penance: A Translation of the Principal* libri *poenitentiales and selections from Related Documents.* (Records of Civilization, XXIX.) New York, 1938.

Maillet, Henri. *L'Eglise et la répression sanglante de l'hérésie.* Ed. by

K. Hanquet. (Bibliothèque de la Faculté de philosophie et lettres de l'Université de Liège, XVI.) Liège, 1909.

Maire, Elie. *Saint Norbert (1082-1134)*. Paris, 1922.

Maisonneuve, Henri. *Etudes sur les origines de l'Inquisition*. (L'église et l'état au moyen âge, VII.) 2d ed. Paris, 1960.

Maitland, Samuel R. *Facts and Documents Illustrative of the History, Doctrine and Rites of the Ancient Albigenses and Waldenses*. London, 1832.

Mandonnet, Pierre. *Saint Dominique, l'idée, l'homme et les œuvres* . . . . With additions by M. H. Vicaire. 2 vols. Paris, 1938. Trans. by Sister Mary Benedicta Larkin as *Saint Dominic and His Work*. St. Louis and London, 1944.

*Manifestatio haeresis Albigensium et Lugdunensium. Ed. by Antoine Dondaine, in "Durand de Huesca," *AFP*, XXIX (1959), 268-71.

Manselli, Raoul. "Alberico, cardinale vescovo d'Ostià e la sua attività di legato pontificio," *ASRSP*, LXXVIII (1955), 23-68.

—— "Una designazione dell'eresia catara: 'Arriana heresis,'" *BISIAM*, LXVIII (1956), 233-46.

—— *La "Lectura super Apocalipsim" di Pietro di Giovanni Olivi: Studi sull'escatologismo medioevale*. (Istituto storico Italiano per il medio evo, Studi storici, XIX-XXI.) Rome, 1955.

—— "Il manicheismo medievale," *Ricerche religiose*, XX (1949), 65-94.

—— "Il monaco Enrico e la sua eresia," *BISIAM*, LXV (1953), 1-63.

—— "I Passagini," *BISIAM*, LXXV (1963), 189-210.

—— "Profilo dell'eresia medievale (Catari e Valdesi)," *Humanitas*, I (1950), 384-96.

—— *Spirituali e Beghini in Provenza*. (Istituto storico Italiano per il medio evo, Studi storici, XXXI-XXXIV.) Rome, 1959.

—— "Per la storia dell'eresia nel secolo XII: Studi minori," *BISIAM*, LXVII (1955), 189-264.

—— *Studi sulle eresie del secolo XII*. (Istituto storico Italiano per il medio evo, Studi storici, V.) Rome, 1953.

Mansi, Giovanni Domenico, ed. *Sacrorum conciliorum nova et amplissima collectio* . . . . 53 vols. Florence, Venice, and Paris, 1759-1927.

**Map, Walter. *De nugis curialium*. Ed. by Montague R. James. (Anecdota oxoniensa . . . , medieval and modern series, XIV.) Oxford, 1914. Trans. by the editor as *Walter Map's "De nugis curialium."* London, 1923. Also trans. by Frederick Tupper and Marbury B. Ogle as *Master Walter Map's Book*, De nugis curialium (*Courtiers' Trifles*). London and New York, 1924.

**Martène, Edmond, and Ursin Durand, eds. *Thesaurus novus anecdotorum*. 5 vols. Paris, 1717.

**—— *Veterum scriptorum et monumentorum historicum, dogmaticarum, moralium amplissima collectio*. 9 vols. Paris, 1724-1733.

Marthaler, Bernard. "Forerunners of the Franciscans: The Waldenses," *Franciscan Studies*, new ser., XVIII (1958), 133-42.

Masenius, J. *Antiquitatum et annalium Treverensium libri XXVI.* 2 vols. Liège, 1670.

*Matthew Paris. *See* Paris, Matthew.

Maxima bibliotheca veterum patrum et antiquorum scriptorum ecclesiastcorum .... Ed. by Marguerin de la Bigne *et al.* 27 vols. Lyons, 1677.

Maycock, Alan L. *The Inquisition from Its Establishment to the Great Schism.* London, 1926.

Meyer, Paul. "Le Débat d'Izarn et de Sicart de Figueiras," *Annuaire-bulletin de la Société de l'histoire de France,* XVI (1879), 233-92. Separately published, Nogent-le-Retrou, 1880.

*Migne, Jacques Paul, ed. *Patrologiae cursus completus* ... *ab aevo apostolico ad tempora Innocentii III, anno 1216* ... *series latina.* 221 vols. Paris, 1844-1864.

Mohr, Walter. "Tanchelm von Antwerpen: Eine nochmalige Überprüfung der Quellenlage," *Annales universitatis Saraviensis,* III (1954), 234-47.

—— "Waldes und das frühe Waldensertum," *Zeitschrift für Religions- und Geistesgeschichte,* IX (1957), 337-63.

Molinier, Charles. "L'Endura: Coûtume religieuse des derniers sectaires albigeois," *Annales de la Faculté des lettres de Bordeaux,* 1st ser., III (1881), 282-99.

—— "L'Hérésie et la persécution au XIe siècle," *Revue des Pyrénées,* VI (1894), 26-38.

—— *L'Inquisition dans le Midi de la France au XIIIe et au XIVe siècle: Etude sur les sources de son histoire.* Paris, 1880.

—— "Les Passagiens: Etude sur une secte contemporaine des Cathares et des Vaudois," *Mémoires de l'Académie des sciences, inscriptions et belles-lettres de Toulouse,* 8th ser., X (1888), 428-58.

—— "Rapport à M. le Ministre de l'instruction publique sur une mission exécutée en Italie de février à avril 1885: Etudes sur quelques manuscrits des bibliothèques d'Italie concernant l'Inquisition et les croyances hérétiques du XIIe et XIIIe siècle," *Archives des missions scientifiques et littéraires,* 3d ser., XIV (1888), 133-336.

*—— "Une Texte de Muratori concernant les sectes cathares: Sa provenance réelle et sa valeur," *Annales du Midi,* XXII (1910), 180-220.

—— "Un Traité inédit du XIIIe siècle contre les hérétiques cathares," *Annales de la Faculté des lettres de Bordeaux,* V (1883), 225-55. Separately printed, Bordeaux, 1883.

*Moneta of Cremona. *Adversus Catharos et Valdenses libri quinque.* Ed. by Thomas A. Ricchini. Rome, 1743.

Monod, Bernard. *Le Moine Guibert et son temps.* Paris, 1905.

Monumenta Germaniae historica inde ab anno Christi quingentesimo usque ad annum millesimum et quingentesimum ... *Scriptores.* 32 vols. Stuttgart and Hanover, 1823-1896.

Moreau, Edouard de. *Histoire de l'église en Belgique.* 5 vols. Brussels, 1945-1952.

Moreau, H. "Canon de la Messe," *DTC*, II, 1540-50.

Morghen, Raffaelo. "Il cosidetto neo-manicheismo occidentale del secolo XI," in *Convegno "Volta" di scienze morale, storiche e filologiche, 27 maggio-1 giugno, 1956*. Accademia nazionale dei Lincei, *Atti*, 8th ser., XII (1957), 84-104.

—— *Medioevo cristiano*. (Biblioteca di cultura moderna, CDXCI.) 2d ed. Bari, 1958.

—— "Movimenti religiosi popolari nel periodo della riforma della Chiesa," in *Relazione del X Congresso*, III, 333-56.

—— "Osservazioni critiche su alcune questioni fondamentali riguardanti le origini e i caratteri delle eresie medioevali," in "Miscellanea di studi storica pubblicata in memoria di Pietro Fedele," *Archivio della deputazione Romana di storia patria*, new ser., LXVII (1944), 97-151.

Müller, Karl. *Die Waldenser und ihre einzelnen Gruppen bis zum Anfang des 14 Jahrhunderts*. Gotha, 1886.

Mundy, John H. *Liberty and Political Power in Toulouse, 1050-1230*. New York, 1954.

Muratori, Ludovico Antonio. *Liturgia Romana vetus*. 2 vols. Venice, 1748.

—— ed. *Rerum italicarum scriptores ab anno aerae christianae quingentesimo ad millesimum quingentesimum* . . . . New ed. by Giosue Carducci. Vol. I– . Città di Castello, 1900– .

Murray, Margaret Alice. *The God of the Witches*. London, 1933. Reprint, New York, 1952.

—— *The Witch-cult of Western Europe: A Study in Anthropology*. Oxford, 1921.

Muzzey, David S. *The Spiritual Franciscans*. New York, 1907.

Nelli, René. *Ecritures cathares: La Cène secrète, le livre de deux principes, le rituel latin, le rituel occitan, Textes précathares et cathares présentés, traduits et commentés avec une introduction sur les origines et l'esprit du Catharisme*. Paris, 1959.

—— and Déodat Roché. "La Vision d'Isaïe," *Cahiers d'études cathares*, XXXIII (1958), 19-51.

—— *et al. Les Cathares*. Paris, 1965.

—— ed. *Spiritualité de l'hérésie: Le Catharisme*. Toulouse, 1953.

Nelson, Ernest W. "The Theory of Persecution," in *Persecution and Liberty*, pp. 3-20.

Newman, Louis I. *Jewish Influence on Christian Reform Movements*. (Columbia University Oriental Series, XXIII.) New York, 1925.

Nickerson, Hoffman. *The Inquisition: A Political and Military Study of Its Establishment*. New ed. Boston and New York, 1932.

La Nobla Leycon. Ed. by Antonino de Stefano, in *La Noble Leçon*, pp. 5-37.

Noiroux, Jeanne-Marie. "Les Deux Premiers Documents concernant l'hérésie aux Pays Bas," *RHE*, XLIX (1954), 842-55.

Noonan, John T., Jr. *Contraception: A History of Its Treatment by the Catholic Theologians and Canonists.* Cambridge, Mass., 1965.

Norgate, Kate. "William of Newburgh," *DNB*, XXI, 360-63.

Obolensky, Dmitri. *The Bogomils: A Study in Balkan Neo-Manichaeism.* Cambridge, 1955.

Oldenbourg, Zoé. *Massacre at Montségur: A History of the Albigensian Crusade.* Trans. by Peter Green. New York, c1961.

Ordo romanus antiquus. In *Maxima bibliotheca*, XIII, 708.

*Otto of Freising. *The Deeds of Frederick Barbarossa by Otto of Freising and His Continuator, Rahewin.* Trans. by Charles C. Mierow with the collaboration of Richard Emery. (Records of Civilization, XLIX.) New York, 1953.

—— *The Two Cities: A Chronicle of Universal History to the Year 1146 A.D. by Otto, Bishop of Freising.* Trans. by Charles C. Mierow. (Records of Civilization, IX.) New York, 1928.

*Paris, Matthew. *Chronica majora.* Ed. by H. R. Luard. (Rolls Series, LVII.) 7 vols. London, 1872-1883. Trans. in part by John A. Giles as *Matthew Paris's English History from the Year 1235 to 1273.* 3 vols. London, 1852-1854.

Partee, Carter. "Peter John Olivi: Historical and Doctrinal Study," *Franciscan Studies*, XX (1960), 215-60.

*Paul, monk of St. Peter of Chartres. *Vetus Aganon.* Ed. by Benjamin-Edmé-Charles Guérard, in *Cartulaire de l'abbaye de Saint-Père de Chartres.* (Collection des cartulaires de France, Vol. I; in Collection de documents inédits sur l'histoire de France, ser. 1: Histoire politique.) 2 vols. Paris, 1840.

De pauperibus de Lugduno. In Döllinger, *Beiträge zur Sektengeschichte*, II, 92-97.

Persecution and Liberty: Essays in Honor of George Lincoln Burr. New York, 1931.

*Peter Martyr, Saint (?). *Summa contra hereticos.* Ed. by Thomas Käppeli, in "Une Somme contre les hérétiques," *AFP*, XVII (1947), 320-25.

*Peter of Vaux-de-Cernay. *Hystoria albigensis.* Ed. by Pascal Guébin and Ernest Lyon. 3 vols. Paris, 1926-1939.

*Peter the Venerable. *Epistola sive tractatus adversus petrobrusianos haereticos.* In Migne, *PL*, CLXXXIX, 719-850.

Pètrement, Simone. *Le dualisme chez Platon, les gnostiques et les manichéens.* Paris, 1947.

Petry, Ray C. *A History of Christianity: Readings in the History of the Early and Medieval Church.* Englewood Cliffs, N. J., 1962.

Philippen, L. J. M. "De Hl. Norbertus en de strijd tegen het Tanchelmisme te Antwerpen," *Bijdragen tot de geschiedenis*, XXV (1934), 251-88.

Pierron, Johann B. *Die katholischen Armen: Ein Beitrag zur Entstehungsgeschichte der Bettelorden mit Berücksichtigung der Humiliaten und der Wiedervereinigten Lombarden.* Freiburg im Breisgau, 1911.

—— "Poor Catholics," *Catholic Encyclopedia*, XII, 249-51.

Pirenne, Henri. "Tanchelin et le projet de démembrement du diocèse d'Utrecht vers 1100," *Académie royale de Belgique, Bulletin de la classe des lettres et des sciences morales et politiques*, 5th ser., XIII (1927), 112-19.

Plesner, Johann. *L'Emigration de la campagne à la ville libre de Florence au XIIIᵉ siècle*. Trans. from Danish by the author and F. Bleizal. Copenhagen, 1934.

Pool, David de Sola, ed. and trans. *Prayers for the Day of Atonement: According to the Custom of the Spanish and Portuguese Jews*. 3d ed. New York, 1949.

Poole, Reginald Lane. *Illustrations of the History of Mediaeval Thought and Learning*. 2d ed. London and New York, 1920.

Potthast, Augustus. *Regesta pontificum Romanorum inde ab anno post Christum natum MCXCVIII ad annum MCCCIV*. 2 vols. Berlin, 1874-1875.

Pouzet, Ph. "Les Origines lyonnaises de la secte des vaudois," *Revue d'histoire de l'église de France*, XXII (1936), 5-37.

—— "La Vie de Guichard, abbé de Pontigny (1136-1165) et archevêque de Lyon (1165-1181)," *Bulletin de la Société littéraire, historique et archéologique de Lyon*, X (1926-1928), 117-50.

Praepositinus. *See* Prevostin.

Pratt, Antoinette Marie. *The Attitude of the Catholic Church towards Witchcraft and the Allied Practices of Sorcery and Magic*. Washington, 1915.

*Preger, Wilhelm. "Beiträge zur Geschichte der Waldesier im Mittelalter," in *Abhandlungen der historischen Classe der königlich bayerischen Akademie der Wissenschaften*, XIII (1877), 181-250.

—— "Der Traktat des David von Augsburg über die Waldesier," *Abhandlungen der historischen Classe der königlich bayerischen Akademie der Wissenschaften*, XIV (1878), 181-35.

*Prevostin of Cremona (?). *The Summa contra haereticos Ascribed to Praepositinus of Cremona*. Ed. by Joseph N. Garvin and James A. Corbett. (Publications in Mediaeval Studies, XV.) Notre Dame, 1958.

"Le Problème des Bogomiles," in [Yugoslav] National Committee of Historical Studies, *Ten Years of Yugoslav Historiography, 1945-1955*. Ed. by Jorgo Tardić *et al.* Belgrade, 1955.

Puech, Henri C. "Catharisme médiéval et Bogomilisme," in *Convegno "Volta" di scienze morale, storiche e filologiche, 27 maggio-1 giugno, 1956*. Accademia nazionale dei Lincei, *Atti*, 8th ser., XII (1957), 56-84.

—— and André Vaillant. *Le Traité contre les Bogomiles de Cosmas le Prêtre: Traduction et étude*. (Travaux publiés par l'Institut d'études slaves, XXI.) Paris, 1945.

Purcell, Mary. *Saint Anthony and His Times*. Dublin, 1960.

*Rainerius Sacconi. *Summa de Catharis et Pauberibus de Lugduno*. Ed. by

Antoine Dondaine, in *Un Traité néo-manichéen*, pp. 64-78.

*Ralph of Coggeshall. *Chronicon anglicanum*. Ed. by Joseph Stevenson. (Rolls Series, LXVI.) London, 1875.

Ralph the Ardent. *Homilia* XIX. In Migne, *PL*, CLV, 2010-13.

*Ralph the Bald. *Raoul Glaber: Les cinq livres de ses histoires (900-1044)*. Ed. by Maurice Prou. (Collection de textes pour servir à l'étude et à l'enseignement de l'histoire, I.) Paris, 1886.

Rashdall, Hastings. *The Universities of Europe in the Middle Ages*. Ed. by F. M. Powicke and A. B. Emden. 3 vols. London, 1936.

Raynaud de Lage, Guy. *Alain de Lille: Poète du XIIe siècle*. (Institut d'études mediévales, Publications, XII.) Montreal and Paris, 1951.

Reagan, Joseph C. "Did the Petrobrusians Teach Salvation by Faith Alone?" *Journal of Religion*, VII (1927), 81-91.

Reinecke, Wilhelm. *Geschichte der Stadt Cambrai bis zur Erteilung der "Lex Godefridi," 1227*. Marburg, 1896.

*Reitzenstein, Richard. *Die Vorgeschichte der christlichen Taufe*. Leipzig and Berlin, 1929.

Relazione del X Congresso Internazionale di scienze storiche, Vol. III: Movimenti religiosi popolari ed eresie del medioevo. Florence, 1955.

Rerum britannicarum medii aevi Scriptores, or Chronicles and Memorials of Great Britain and Ireland during the Middle Ages. 99 works in 251 vols. London, 1858-1896.

Riol, J. L. "Dernières connaissances textuaires et folkloriques sur des questions cathares: Le salut spirituel et l'abrègement mystique de la vie," *Bulletin de la Société des sciences, arts, et belles-lettres du Tarn*, new ser., XXI (1961), 193-213.

Ristori, Giovanni B. "I Paterini in Firenze nella prima metà del secolo XIII," *Rivista storico-critica delle scienze teologiche*, I (1905), 10-23, 328-41, 754-60.

Robbins, Russell Hope. *The Encyclopedia of Witchcraft and Demonology*. New York, c1959.

*Roger of Hoveden. *Chronica magistri Rogeri de Houedene*. Ed. by William Stubbs. (Rolls Series, LI.) 4 vols. London, 1868-1871. Trans. by H. T. Riley as *The Annals of Roger de Hoveden*. 2 vols. London, 1853.

Rose, Elliot. *A Razor for a Goat: A Discussion of Certain Problems in the History of Witchcraft and Diabolism*. Toronto, 1962.

Rougement, Denis de. *Love in the Western World*. Trans. by Montgomery Belgion. Rev. ed. New York, 1956.

Rousset, Paul. "Raoul Glaber, interprète de la pensée commune au XIe siècle," *Revue d'histoire de l'église de France*, XXXVI (1950), 5-24.

Runciman, Steven. *The First Bulgarian Empire*. London, 1930.

—— *The Medieval Manichee: A Study of the Christian Dualist Heresy*. Cambridge, 1955.

Runeberg, Arne. *Witches, Demons, and Fertility Magic: Analysis of Their Significance and Mutual Relations in West-European Folk Religion*.

(Societas scientiarum Fernica: Commentationes humanarum litterarum, Vol. XIV, fasc. 4.) Helsinki, 1947.

Russell, Jeffrey B. "Les Cathares de 1048-1054 à Liège," *Bulletin de la Société d'art et d'histoire du diocèse de Liège*, XLII (1961), 1-8.

—— "Courtly Love as Religious Dissent," *Catholic Historical Review*, LI (1965), 31-44.

—— *Dissent and Reform in the Early Middle Ages*. (Publications of the Center for Medieval and Renaissance Studies, I.) Berkeley and Los Angeles, 1965.

—— "Interpretations of the Origins of Medieval Heresy," *MS*, XXV (1963), 25-53.

—— "A propos du synode d'Arras en 1025," *RHE*, LVII (1962), 66-87.

*Salvo Burci. *Liber supra Stella*. Ed. by Ilarino da Milano, in "Il 'Liber supra Stella,'" *Aevum*, XIX (1945), 309-41.

Sancti Antonii de Padua vitae duae. Ed. by Leon de Kerval. Paris, 1904.

Savini, Savino. *Il Catarismo italiano ed i suoi vescovi nei secoli XIII e XIV: Ipotesi sulla cronologia del Catarismo en Italia*. Florence, 1958.

Sbaralea, Joannes H. *Bullarium Franciscanum romanorum pontificum constitutiones, epistolas ac diplomata continens . . . .* 4 vols. Rome, 1759-1768.

Schmidt, Charles. *Histoire et doctrine de la secte des Cathares ou Albigeois*. 2 vols. Paris, 1849.

Scott, C. A. "Priscillianism," in *Encyclopaedia of Religion and Ethics*, X, 336-38.

Secret Supper. See Interrogatio Johannis.

A Select Library of the Nicene and Post-Nicene Fathers of the Christian Church. Ed. by Philip Schaff *et al.* 14 vols. New York, 1887-1894; reprint, Grand Rapids, Mich., 1956.

Setton, Kenneth, *et al. A History of the Crusades*. Vols. I-II. Philadelphia, 1962, 1965.

Shannon, Albert C. *The Popes and Heresy in the Thirteenth Century*. Villanova, Pa., 1949.

*Sigibert of Gembloux. *Chronographia*. Ed. by L. C. Bethmann. *Continuatio Acquinctina*, in *MGH SS*, VI, 405-38; *Continuatio Gemblacensis*, in *MGH SS*, VI, 385-90; *Continuatio Praemonstratensis*, in *MGH SS*, VI, 447-56.

Six Vaudois Poems from the Waldensian Manuscripts in the University Libraries of Cambridge, Dublin, and Geneva. Ed. and trans. by H. J. Chaytor. Cambridge, 1930.

Smalley, Beryl. *The Study of the Bible in the Middle Ages*. 2d ed. New York, 1952.

Smedt, Charles de. "Les Sources de l'histoire de la croisade contre les Albigeois," *RQH*, XVI (1874), 433-81.

Smet, Jozef M. de. "De monnik Tanchelm en de Utrechtse bisschopszetel in 1112-1114," in *Scrinium Lovaniense: Mélanges historiques Etienne van Cauwenbergh*, pp. 207-34. Gembloux and Louvain, 1961.

Smith, Charles Edward. *Innocent III: Church Defender*. Baton Rouge, 1951.

Söderberg, Hans. *La Religion des Cathares: Etude sur le gnosticisme de la basse antiquité et du moyen âge*. Uppsala, 1949.

Solovjev, Alexandre V. "La Doctrine de l'église de Bosnie" (trans. by Henri Grégoire), *Académie royale de Belgique, Bulletin de la classe des lettres et des sciences morales et politiques*, 5th ser., XXXIV (1948), 481-533.

—— "La Messe cathare," *Cahiers d'études cathares*, XII (1951-1952), 199-206.

Sommariva, Luciano. "La Compréhension historique de l'hérésie," in Nelli, *Spiritualité de l'hérésie*, pp. 63-89.

—— "Studi recenti sulle eresie medievali (1939-1952)," *Rivista storica italiana*, LXIV (1952), 237-68.

Spätling, Luchesius. *De Apostolicis, Pseudo-apostolicis, Apostolinis*. Munich, 1947.

Spinka, Matthew. *John Hus' Concept of the Church*. Princeton, 1966.

—— ed. *Advocates of Reform from Wyclif to Erasmus*. (Library of Christian Classics, XIV.) Philadelphia, 1953.

—— trans. *John Hus at the Council of Constance*. (Records of Civilization, LXXIII.) New York, 1965.

Statuta ecclesiae antiqua. In Migne, *PL*, LVI, 879-80.

Stefano, Antonino de. *La Noble Leçon des Vaudois du Piémont: Texte critique, introduction, et glossaire*. Paris, 1909.

—— *Riformatori ed eretici del medioevo*. Palermo, 1938.

*Stephen of Bourbon. *Tractatus de diversis materiis praedicabilis*. Ed. by A. Lecoy de la Marche, as *Anecdotes historiques*.

Strack, Hermann L. *The Jew and Human Sacrifice*. Trans. by Henry Blanchamp. New York and London, 1909.

Stubbs, William. *Select Charters and Other Illustrations of English Constitutional History*. 9th rev. ed. by H. W. C. Davis. Oxford, 1913.

Summa contra haereticos et Manicheos. Ed. by Célestin Douais, in *La Somme des autorités*, pp. 34-55. Also in Leipzig, Universitäts Bibliothek, MS 894, fols. 74v-77v.

Summers, Montague. *The History of Witchcraft and Demonology*. 2d ed. New York, 1956.

Suraci, Antonio. *Arnaldo da Brescia: Un agitatore del secolo XII (1095-1155)*. Asti, 1952.

Taberner, F. Valls, ed. "El diplomatari de Sant Ramon de Penyafort," *Analecta sacra Tarraconensia: Annuari de la Biblioteca Balmes*, V (1929), 254-61.

Tengnagel, Sebastian. *Collectio veterum monumentorum contra schismaticos*. Ingolstadt, 1612.

Theloe, Hermann. *Die Ketzerverfolgungen im 11. und 12. Jahrhundert: Ein*

Beitrag zur Geschichte der Entstehung des päpstlichen Ketzerinquisitions-gericht. (Abhandlungen zur mittleren und neueren Geschichte, XLVIII.) Berlin and Leipzig, 1913.

Théry, Gabriel. *Autour du décret de 1210, I: David de Dinant—Etude sur son panthéisme matérialiste.* (Bibliothèque Thomiste, VI.) Paris, 1925.

Theseider, Eugenio Dupré. *Introduzione alle eresie medievali.* Bologna, 1953.

Thomas, Antoine. "Bernard Gui, frère prêcheur," in *Histoire littéraire de la France,* XXXV, 139-232.

Thomas Aquinas, Saint. *The* Summa theologica. Trans. by fathers of the English Dominican Province, rev. by Daniel J. Sullivan. (Great Books of the Western World, XIX-XX.) 2 vols. Chicago, 1955.

Thompson, James Westfall. "Catharist Social Ideals in Medieval French Romances," *Romanic Review,* XXVII (1936), 99-104.

Thomson, S. Harrison. "Pre-Hussite Heresy in Bohemia," *English Historical Review,* XLVIII (1933), 23-42.

Thorndike, Lynn. *University Records and Life in the Middle Ages.* (Records of Civilization, XXXVIII.) New York, 1944.

Thouzellier, Christine. *Catharisme et valdéisme en Languedoc à la fin du XIIe et au début du XIIIe siècle: Politique pontificale-controverses.* (Publications de la Faculté des lettres et sciences humaines de Paris, Série 'Recherches,' XXVII.) Paris, 1966.

—— "Controverses vaudoises-cathares à la fin du XIIe siècle (d'après le livre II du *Liber antiheresis* Ms Madrid 1114 et les sections correspondants du Ms B.N. lat. 13346)," *AHDLMA,* XXXV (1960), 137-227.

—— "Hérésie et croisade au XIIe siècle," *RHE,* XLIX (1954), 855-72.

—— "Le 'Liber antiheresis' de Durand de Huesca et le 'Contra hereticos' d'Ermengaud de Béziers," *RHE,* LV (1960), 130-41.

—— "La Pauvreté, arme contre l'Albigéisme en 1206," *RHR,* CLI (1957), 79-92.

—— "La Profession trinitaire du vaudois Durand de Huesca," *RTAM,* XXVII (1960), 267-89.

—— "La Répression de l'hérésie et les débuts de l'Inquisition," in Fliche and Martin, *Histoire de l'Eglise,* Vol. X, chap. 3.

—— *Une Somme anti-cathare: Le* Liber contra manicheos *de Durand de Huesca.* (Spicilegium sacrum Lovaniense, Etudes et documents, XXXII.) Louvain, 1964.

—— Un Traité cathare inédit du début du XIIIe siècle d'après le Liber contra manicheos *de Durand de Huesca.* (Bibliothèque de la Revue d'histoire ecclésiastique, XXXVII.) Louvain, 1961.

—— "Les Versions bibliques utilisées par Durand de Huesca au début du XIIIe siècle," in *Mélanges Eugène Tisserant,* I, 419-35. (Studi e testi, CCXXI.) Vatican City, 1964.

Tiraboschi, Girolamo. *Vetera humiliatorum monumenta.* 3 vols. Milan, 1766-1768.

Tocco, Felice. "Gli apostolici e fra Dolcino," *Archivio storico italiano,* 5th ser., XIX (1897), 241-75.

—— *La questione della povertà nel secolo XIV secondo nuovi documenti.* Naples, 1911.

Tout, T. F. *The Study of Mediaeval Chronicles.* London, 1922.

Tractatus manicheorum. Ed. by C. Thouzellier, in *Un Traité cathare,* pp. 87-113.

Turberville, Arthur S. *Mediaeval Heresy and the Inquisition.* London, 1920; reprint, 1964.

Turdeneau, Emile. "Apocryphes bogomiles et apocryphes pseudo-bogomiles," *RHR,* CXXXVIII (1950), 22-52, 176-218.

Unterkircher, Franz. " 'Pseudo-Rainier' und 'Passauer Anonymus,' " *Mitteilungen des Instituts für österreichische Geschichtsforschung,* LXIII (1955), 41-46.

Vacandard, Elphège. *L'Inquisition: Etude historique et critique sur le pouvoir coercitif de l'église.* Paris, 1906; 5th ed., 1909. Trans. by B. L. Conway, from the 2d ed. as *The Inquisition: A Critical and Historical Study of the Coercive Power of the Church.* New York, 1921.

—— "Les Origines de l'hérésie albigeoise," *RQH,* LV (1894), 50-83.

—— *Vie de Saint Bernard, abbé de Clairvaux.* 2 vols. Paris, 1920.

Vacarius. Liber contra multiplices et varios errores. Ed. by Ilarino da Milano, in *L'Eresia di Ugo Speroni,* pp. 483-583.

Vaissete, Joseph. *See* Devic, Claude, and Joseph Vaissete.

Valvekens, J. B. "Haereses ac sectae ineuntis medii aevi et Praemonstratenses," *Analecta Praemonstratensia,* XXXIII (1957), 141-47.

Varga, Lucie. "Les Cathares sont-ils des néo-manichéens ou des néognostiques?" *RHR,* CXX (1939), 175-93.

—— "Peire Cardinale était-il hérétique?" *RHR,* CXVII (1938), 205-31.

—— "Un Problème de méthode en histoire religieuse: Le Catharisme," *Revue de synthèse,* XI (1936), 133-43.

Vasoli, Cesare. "Il 'Contra haereticos' di Alano di Lilla," *BISIAM,* LXXV (1963), 123-72.

Vaughan, Richard. *Matthew Paris.* (Cambridge Studies in Medieval Life and Thought, new ser., VI.) Cambridge, 1958.

Vedder, Henry C. "Origin and Early Teaching of the Waldenses, according to Roman Catholic Writers of the Thirteenth Century," *American Journal of Theology,* IV (1900), 465-89.

Vekené, E[mil] van der. *Bibliographie der Inquisition: Ein Versuch.* Hildesheim, 1963.

*Venckeleer, Theo. "Un Recueil cathare: Le manuscrit A.6.10 de la Collection vaudoise de Dublin, I: Une Apologie; II: Une glose sur le Pater," *RBPH,* XXXVIII (1960), 815-34; XXXIX (1961), 758-93.

Vernet, Félix, "Cathares," *DTC,* II, 1987-99.

—— "Fraticelli," *DTC,* VI, 770-84.

—— "Humiliés," *DTC,* VII, 311-21.

Verrees, Libert. "Le Traité de l'abbé Bernard de Fontcaude contre les Vaudois et les Ariens," *Analecta Praemonstratensia*, XXXI (1955), 5-35.

Vicaire, Marie-Humbert. *Histoire de Saint Dominique.* 2 vols. Paris, 1957. Trans. by Kathleen Pond as *Saint Dominic and His Times.* New York, 1965.

—— *Saint Dominique de Caleruega d'après les documents du XIIIᵉ siècle.* Paris, 1955.

Vidal, J. M. "Apostoliques," *Dictionnaire d'histoire et de géographie ecclésiastique*, Vol. III, cols. 1038-48. Paris, 1924.

—— "Les derniers ministres de l'albigéisme en Languedoc: Leurs doctrines," *RQH*, LXXIX (1906), 57-107.

—— "Doctrine et morale des derniers ministres albigeois," *RQH*, LXXXV (1909), 357-409; LXXXVI (1909), 5-48.

—— "L'Emeute des Pastoreaux en 1320: Déposition du Juif Baruc devant l'Inquisition de Pamiers," *Annales de St. Louis-des-Français*, III (1898-1899), 154-74.

—— "Procès d'inquisition contre Adhémar de Masset, noble rousillonnais inculpé de béguinisme (1332-1334)," *Revue d'histoire de l'Eglise de France*, I (1910), 555-89, 682-89, 711-24.

—— *Le Tribunal de l'Inquisition de Pamiers: Notice sur le registre de l'évêque Jacques Fournier.* Toulouse, 1909.

Vignier, Nicholas. *Recueil de l'histoire de l'église.* Leiden, 1601.

Violante, Cinzio. *La Pataria milanese e la riforma ecclesiastica, I: Le premesse (1045-1057).* (Istituto storico Italiano, Studi storici, XI-XIII.) Rome, 1955.

—— *La Società milanese nell'età precomunale.* Bari, 1953,

Violini, Cesare. *Fra Dolcino e la setta degli apostolici.* Turin, 1942.

The Vision of Isaiah. Trans. by R. H. Charles, in *The Ascension of Isaiah, Translated from the Ethiopic Version, Which together with the New Greek Fragment, the Latin Versions and the Latin Translation of the Slavonic, Is Here Published in Full.* London, 1900.

Vita sancti Galdini. In *AA SS*, 18 April, II, 590-95.

Vita sancti Petri martyris. In *AA SS*, 29 April, III, 697-704.

Volpe, Gioacchino. *Movimenti religiosi e sette ereticali nella società medievale italiana (secoli XI-XIV).* (Collana storica, VI.) 2d ed. Florence, 1926.

Wakefield, Walter L. "The Treatise against Heretics of James Capelli: A Study of Medieval Preaching and Writing against Heresy." Unpublished Ph.D. dissertation, Columbia University, 1951.

Walter, Johannes Wilhelm von. *Die ersten Wanderprediger Frankreichs: Studien zur Geschichte des Mönchtums*: Part I, *Robert von Arbrissel*; Part II, *Neue Folge.* Leipzig, 1903, 1906.

Walther, Daniel. "A Survey of Recent Research on the Albigensian Cathari," *Church History*, XXXIV (1965), 146-77.

Warner, Henry James. *The Albigensian Heresy.* 2 vols. London, 1922, 1928.

Wattenbach, Wilhelm. *Deutschlands Geschichtsquellen im Mittelalter bis zur Mitte des dreizehnten Jahrhunderts.* 6th ed. 2 vols. Berlin, 1893.

Webb, C. C. J. *John of Salisbury.* London, 1932.

Wendt, M. H. H. *Christentum und Dualismus,* Jena, 1909.

Werner, Ernst. "Παταρηνοι-patarini: Ein Beitrag zur Kirchen- und Sektengeschichte des 11. Jahrhunderts," in *Von Mittelalter zur Neuzeit: Zum 65 Geburtstag von Heinrich Sproemberg,* pp. 404-19. Berlin, 1956.

—— *Pauperes Christi: Studien zu sozial-religiösen Bewegungen im Zeitalter des Reformspapsttums.* Leipzig, 1956.

—— and Martin Erbströsser. *Ideologische Probleme des mittelalterlichen Plebejertums: Die freigeistige Haeresie und ihre sozialen Wurzeln.* (Forschungen zur mittelalterlichen Geschichte, VII.) Berlin, 1960.

*William, a monk. *Contra Henricum schismaticum et hereticum.* Ed. by Raoul Manselli, in "Il monaco Enrico," *BISIAM,* LXV (1953), 44-63. Also in Nice, Bibliothèque publique, MS 3 (R.18), fols. 136-43.

William of Nangis. *La Chronique latine de Guillaume de Nangis de 1113 à 1300.* Ed. by H. Géraud. 2 vols. Paris, 1843.

*William of Newburgh. *Historia rerum anglicarum.* Ed. by Richard Howlett, in *Chronicles of the Reigns of Stephen, Henry II and Richard I.* (Rolls Series, LXXXII.) 2 vols. London, 1884-1885. Trans. by Joseph Stevenson as *The History of William of Newburgh* (Church Historians of England, IV, part 2.) London, 1856.

William of Puylaurens. *Cronica.* Ed. by Bessyier, in "Guillaume de Puylaurens et sa chronique," in *Troisièmes mélanges d'histoire du moyen âge,* ed. by A. Luchaire, pp. 119-75. (Bibliothèque de la Faculté des lettres de Paris, XVIII.) Paris, 1904.

Williams, Watkin. *Saint Bernard of Clairvaux.* (Publications of the University of Manchester, CCXXXVII; Historical series, LXIX.) Manchester, 1935.

Wilson, Robert M. *The Gnostic Problem: A Study of the Relations between Hellenistic Judaism and the Gnostic Heresy.* London, 1958.

Wilson, Robert S. *Marcion: A Study of a Second Century Heretic.* London, 1933.

Yerushalmi, Yosef H. "The Inquisition and the Jews of France in the Time of Bernard Gui," *Rutgers Hebraic Studies,* I (1965), 1-60.

Zacour, Norman P. "The Children's Crusade," in Setton, *A History of the Crusades,* Vol. II, chap. 9.

Zanoni, Luigi. *Gli Umiliati nei loro rapporti con l'eresia, l'industria della lana ed i comuni nei secoli XII e XIII.* (Bibliotheca historica italica, 2d ser., II.) Milan, 1911.

—— "Valdesi a Milano nel secolo XIII," *Archivio storico lombardo,* 4th ser., XVII (1912), 5-22.

Index

Abelard, Peter, 121, 147, 148; quoted, 673n7

Act of Peace, *see* Peace

Ad abolendam (bull), 33, 690n2

Adam (heretic of Arras), 257

Adam, biblical, teaching of Cathars on: that his soul was an angel, 47, 165, 171, 313, 318, 319-20, 344, 364, 460, 461; that his body was created by the devil, 47, 165, 171, 344, 355, 460; as identified with St. Joseph, 233; that his soul was younger son of God, 321; that he inhabited another world, 342; as a symbol of charity, 612

Adelbert, bishop of Nîmes, 190

Adémar of Chabannes, chronicle of, 73-74, 74-76

Adoration (heretical ceremony), *see* Melioramentum

Adultery, forbidden by Cathars, 480, 489, 599-600

Agen, heretical church of, 169, 337

Aimery (heretic of Liège), 141

Alan of Lille (*Alanus de Insulis*), *De fide catholica*, 214-20, 634

Albanenses: Catharist church of, 42, 270, 272, 273, 274, 336, 337, 345, 362; doctrines of, 337-43, 353-57, 358-60 *passim*; hierarchy of, 362, 373; origin of the name, 629n23; confused with Albigenses, 749n5; *see also* Desenzano, Catharist church of; Drugunthia, Catharist church of

Alberic, cardinal of Ostia, 124, 125

Albertinus of Reggio (Cathar), 373

Albi, Catharist church of, 35, 169, 330, 336, 337

Albigenses, 35, 42; doctrines of, 231-34, 237-40, 469-510; origin of the name, 720n1; confused with Albanenses, 749n5; *see also* Cathars

Albigensian Crusade, 37

Aldricus *de Gilinguellis* (Cathar), 167

Aldricus of Bando (Cathar), 169, 371

Alexander III, pope: and Humiliati, 30, 159; and Waldes, 203; and Patarines, 257

Alexander IV, pope, 250-51

Alexis, Saint, 201

Algossus (Poor Lombard), 288

All (heretical concept), 503-4, 514, 544-50

Amalric (heretic of Ivoy), 105

Amalricians, 39-40, 64; doctrines of, 54, 258-63

Amalric of Bena, 39, 64, 258, 259, 262

Ambrose, Saint, condemned by Cathars, 173

Amen, heretical interpretation of, 629-30

Amizo (Cathar), 163, 167

Ancianus, see Elder

Andrew (Cathar), 362

Andrew of Gruara (Poor Lombard), 371

Angels, heretical doctrines on: that they became human souls, 47, 48, 164, 165, 217, 232, 239, 299, 309-10, 318, 338, 364, 368; that they had bodies, souls, and spirits, 48, 164-65, 309; that they had no free will, 517-33, 574-78

Anonymous of Passau, 636

Anselm, canon of Liège, 89

Anselm of Alessandria, *Tractatus*, 167-70, 361-73, 638

Anselm the Peripatetic, of Milan, 665n11

John Judeus (Cathar), 161-64 *passim*, 361, 371

John of Bergamo, *see* John of Lugio

John of Lorraine (Waldensian), 757 *n*12

John of Lugio, 66, 337, 748*n*3; doctrines of, 48-49, 339-43; treatise of, 343

John of Luzano (Cathar), 362

John of Narbonne (Poor Catholic), 222

John of Roncarolo, *see* John of Ronco

John of Ronco (Poor Lombard), 50, 272, 273, 277, 278, 370

John of Salisbury, *Historia pontificalis*, 146-48

John Scotus Erigena, 258

John the Baptist, Saint: sanctity of, denied, 172, 344, 358; as evil spirit, emissary of the devil, 167, 234, 238, 354, 362, 462, 592-93; accepted as a saint, 344, 592-93; identified with Elijah, 362, 462

John the Evangelist, Saint: as an angel, 48, 167; Gospel of, rejected, 254; awaits the Day of Judgment in another place, 362-63

John the Good (Cathar), 163

John Vulnerus (Cathar), 373

Jonas (heretic in Lorraine), 39

Jordan *de Dogno* (Poor Catholic), 279, 283

Joseph (Cathar), 163, 169, 371

Josephini (sect), 31, 33

Josfred, bishop of Paris, 671*n*7

Judgment: that it has already been made, 165, 234, 338, 356, 360; Day of, described, 463-65, 508-10

Julian (Waldensian), 283

Justice, of human agents, denied by heretics, 313, 323, 330, 345, 348, 357, 361, 371, 372, 389

Juvenal, 73

Killing, forbidden by heretics, 93, 361, 382, 383, 480, 489, 599, 746*n*6

Kimhi, Rabbi David, *see* RaDaK

Kingdom, heretical concept of, 612-16, 628, 629

Kiss of peace, *see* Peace

L. *de Leganio* (Poor Lombard), 279

Labor: refused by Waldensian preachers, 370, 371, 393

Laity, right to preach: affirmed, 30, 31, 35, 202, 209-10, 213, 258; denied, 159, 204, 217-20

Lambres, 95

Landulf the Elder, 23; *Historia,* 86-89

Lanfranc *de Vaure* (Cathar), 364

Lanfranc of Brescia (Cathar), 373

Last Judgment, *see* Judgment, Day of

Lateran Councils: Third (1179), 33, 203-4, 689*n*1; Fourth (1215), 33-34; Second (1139), 150, 649*n*121

Laurence *de Gradi* (Cathar), 373

Lauterius (Cathar), 373

Law of Moses: rejected by Bogomils, 15; accepted fully by Passagians, 175, 177-82, 276; rejected by Cathars, 172, 190, 231, 298, 322, 355, 358, 359; *see also* Old Testament

Lawrence, Saint; invoked by heretic, 344; sanctity of, denied, 372

Lea, Henry C., quoted, 3, 641*n*23

Lecoy de la Marche, A., 658*n*18

Legislation against heresy, 33-34, 36, 41

Le Mans, 24, 25, 108-14

Leonard, Emile G., 18

Leonists, *see* Poor of Lyons, Waldenses

Leuchard (heretic at Trier), 268

Leutard (heretic at Châlons), 72-73

Levantes (sect), 278

Liber de duobus principiis, see Book of the Two Principles, The

Liber sententiarum of Bernard Gui, 374

Liège, 24, 26, 27, 139-41, 648*n*109

Life (lives), heretical concept of, 618, 629

Limborch, Philip van, 59

Linus, Saint, pope, 372

Lion, created by the evil god, 231

Lisiard, bishop of Soissons, 103, 104

Lisoius (heretic at Orléans), 75, 76, 80

Literature of heretics, 62-67 *passim*, 269, 278-89, 343, 447-630 *passim*

Little Brothers (sect), 55

Lombards (sect), 30, 146, 148